D0116535

Lifespan Development

Lifespan Development

Infancy Through Adulthood

Laurence Steinberg
Temple University

Marc H. Bornstein
Editor, *Parenting: Science and Practice*
Eunice Kennedy Shriver National Institute of Child Health and Human Development

Deborah Lowe Vandell
University of California, Irvine

Karen S. Rook
University of California, Irvine

Australia • Brazil • Japan • Korea • Mexico • Singapore • Spain • United Kingdom • United States

Lifespan Development: Infancy Through Adulthood
Laurence Steinberg, Marc H. Bornstein, Deborah Lowe Vandell, and Karen S. Rook

Senior Publisher: Linda Schreiber-Ganster
Executive Editor: Jon-David Hague
Senior Acquiring Sponsoring Editor: Jaime Perkins
Managing Development Editor: Jeremy Judson
Development Editors: Shannon K. LeMay-Finn and Angela Kao
Assistant Editor: Rebecca Rosenberg
Editorial Assistant: Kelly Miller
Media Editor: Mary Noel
Marketing Director: Kimberly Russell
Marketing Manager: Jessica Egbert
Executive Marketing Communications Manager: Talia Wise
Senior Content Project Manager: Pat Waldo
Creative Director: Rob Hugel
Art Director: Vernon Boes
Print Buyer: Karen Hunt
Rights Acquisitions Account Manager, Text: Katie Huha
Rights Acquisitions Account Manager, Image: Jennifer Meyer Dare
Production Service: Graphic World Inc.
Text Designers: Susan Gilday, Jeanne Calabrese
Photo Researcher: Lisa Jelly Smith
Copy Editor: Graphic World Inc.
Illustrator: Graphic World Inc.
Cover Designer: Jim Scherer
Cover Image: Roycroft Design
Compositor: Graphic World Inc.

Library of Congress Control Number: 2010923142

Student Edition:
ISBN-13: 978-0-618-72156-6
ISBN-10: 0-618-72156-8

Loose-leaf Edition:
ISBN-13: 978-0-495-91161-6
ISBN-10: 0-495-91161-5

Wadsworth
20 Davis Drive
Belmont, CA 94002-3098
USA

Cengage Learning is a leading provider of customized learning solutions with office locations around the globe, including Singapore, the United Kingdom, Australia, Mexico, Brazil, and Japan. Locate your local office at **www.cengage.com/global**

Cengage Learning products are represented in Canada by Nelson Education, Ltd.

To learn more about Wadsworth, visit **www.cengage.com/Wadsworth**

Purchase any of our products at your local college store or at our preferred online store **www.CengageBrain.com**

Printed in the United States of America
1 2 3 4 5 6 7 14 13 12 11 10

To our families

About the Authors

Laurence Steinberg is the Distinguished University Professor and Laura H. Carnell Professor of Psychology at Temple University. Dr. Steinberg has focused his research on a range of topics in the study of contemporary adolescence, including parent-adolescent relationships, adolescent employment, high school reform, and juvenile justice. Dr. Steinberg is a former President of the Division of Developmental Psychology of the American Psychological Association as well as the Society for Research on Adolescence. The recipient of numerous honors recognizing his contributions to the field of human development, Dr. Steinberg has also been recognized for excellence in research and teaching by the University of California, the University of Wisconsin, and Temple University. He is the author or co-author of several hundred articles on growth and development during the teenage years, as well as several successful books, including the textbook *Adolescence* (now in its 9th edition).

Marc H. Bornstein serves as Senior Investigator and Head of Child and Family Research at the Eunice Kennedy Shriver National Institute of Child Health and Human Development and as Editor of *Parenting: Science and Practice*. He received his Ph.D. from Yale University and has since focused on studying aspects of cognitive, emotional, and language development across the lifespan and on parent-child relationships in cross-cultural contexts. He has held academic appointments at several prestigious universities around the world, including Princeton University, New York University, University College London, and the Sorbonne. Dr. Bornstein is the author of several hundred articles on infant development and parent-child relationships as well as the textbooks *Development in Infancy* and *Developmental Science: An Advanced Textbook*.

Deborah Lowe Vandell is the Chair of the Department of Education at the University of California, Irvine. After receiving her Ph.D. in psychology from Boston University, Dr. Vandell began conducting extensive research on the effects of early child care on children's development, as well as the effects of afterschool programs, extracurricular activities, and self-care during middle childhood and adolescence. Dr. Vandell has been recognized for excellence in teaching and research by the University of Texas and the University of Wisconsin. She has served on advisory boards and panels for the National Academy of Sciences, the National Institutes of Health, the U.S. Department of Education, the Charles Stewart Mott Foundation, and the National Institute for Early Education Research. She works with national, state, and local officials to translate research into effective policies to support children's development.

Karen S. Rook is Professor of Psychology and Social Behavior and Associate Dean for Research in the School of Social Ecology at the University of California, Irvine. Since receiving her Ph.D. in psychology from the University of California, Los Angeles, Dr. Rook has conducted extensive research on older adults' health, emotional well-being, and social relationships. Other research has examined loneliness, social support, and social networks in young and later adulthood. Dr. Rook has served on the advisory boards and panels of numerous professional societies, federal agencies, and private foundations. She has received awards for teaching and mentoring and for her scientific contributions to the study of health and aging.

Brief Contents

Part Seven: Middle Adulthood

Part Eight: Later Adulthood

Contents

CHAPTER 5

Cognitive Development in Infancy 122

CHAPTER 6

Socioemotional Development in Infancy 151

Part 3: Early Childhood 183

Part 4: Middle Childhood 255

CHAPTER 9 Physical and Cognitive Development in Middle Childhood 256

CHAPTER 10 Socioemotional Development in Middle Childhood 296

Part 5: Adolescence 329

CHAPTER 11 Physical and Cognitive Development in Adolescence 330

CHAPTER 12

Socioemotional Development in Adolescence 371

Part 6: Young Adulthood 403

CHAPTER 13

Physical and Cognitive Development in Young Adulthood 404

CHAPTER 14
Socioemotional Development in Young Adulthood 435

Part 7: Middle Adulthood 469

CHAPTER 15
Physical and Cognitive Development in Middle Adulthood 470

EPILOGUE

Death and Dying 605

Preface

This book grew out of our shared belief that a change in the way we teach students about the study of human development was long overdue. What distinguishes this text from other titles can be summarized with an acronym: **CARE**.

Cutting edge research
Applied developmental science
Readability
Essential knowledge

Some books share one, maybe two, of these features. But none has all four. And it is our view that students need the full combination to really understand and appreciate both how individuals develop and how scientists study this process.

Simply put, students should know what today's scientists are discovering about human development and how this knowledge can be applied in the real world. This information also needs to be presented in a style that is contemporary and engaging and that is free from the distractions of fluff and filler. These have been our overarching aims.

CUTTING-EDGE RESEARCH

There is no better way for a textbook author to keep up with the latest developments in the field than to be an actively engaged specialist in his or her own research. **Specialists are often the most knowledgeable about the science that is defining, and redefining, the field.** This book is the product of a collaboration among four active scientists who study different periods of development: Marc H. Bornstein specializes in infancy, Deborah Lowe Vandell in childhood, Larry Steinberg in adolescence, and Karen Rook in adulthood. All of us have been teaching and doing research on human development for more than 30 years, and all of us have occupied prominent positions in the fields' major organizations and on the fields' most important editorial boards.

APPLICATION THROUGH LUCID EXAMPLES

The authors of this book come at the study of development from different disciplinary perspectives: Marc was trained in developmental science, Deborah in education, Larry in human development and family studies, and Karen in social and clinical psychology with an emphasis on aging. One of us has taught elementary school (Deborah), another has done clinical work with children and families (Larry), another has conducted research all over the world (Marc), and another has conducted research and interventions with older adults and their families (Karen). **Our combined expertise allows us to raise examples that resonate with students from different backgrounds and fields of study and with different occupational goals in mind.** All four of us have made strong commitments in our professional careers to the application of developmental science in the real world, whether through the design of legal and social policy; the dissemination of information about children through television and film; the development of educational and afterschool programs; the authoring of books and articles written explicitly for parents, teachers, and health care practitioners; or the development of intervention strategies to promote adults' health and well-being. **Our commitment to the profession has enabled us to write a textbook that is full of examples and illustrations that permit students not simply to understand and appreciate the scientific study of human development, but to see how this knowledge can be used to improve the lives of individuals around the world.**

READABILITY WITH A GOAL TOWARD COMPREHENSION

We also strongly believe that there is no reason that a textbook has to be boring. We find the study of human development exciting, and we've tried to communicate this excitement to students in the way this text is written. Although each of us is an accomplished and well-published author, we worked closely with Ann Levine, a professional writer who has written several successful textbooks and trade books, to keep the writing lively and engaging, and to ensure that the book has a strong and common voice that cuts across chapters. And we worked closely with the design team to create an interior look that is coherent, contemporary, and attractive.

As soon as you start to read, you will see that the writing is more conversational than is usually the case. **The combination of cutting edge research coverage and conversational writing gives students comfortable access to core concepts through good explanations. In this way, each chapter tells a story.** We think that students are more likely to retain information that they have really read—not just scanned and memorized.

ESSENTIAL KNOWLEDGE THAT PROVIDES FOCUS ON CORE CONCEPTS

As we set out to write this book, we asked ourselves, "What do students *really* need to know?" And, "What content can students probably do without?" We know that there are topics that are mainstays in developmental textbooks not because they remain useful or important, but because they just have always been there.

We began our work by listing, for ourselves, every conceivable topic that might be covered in an introductory developmental textbook. Just as the brain overproduces synapses during infancy, we deliberately overproduced when formulating our list. And then, as is the case with brain development during childhood and beyond, we pruned. If a topic was essential, we kept it on the list. If it wasn't, we said goodbye. We elected to cover fewer, more important topics in depth than to create an encyclopedia that was shallow and superficial. **The result is a book that focuses more on core concepts and good explanations of those concepts.**

We also decided to eliminate the fluff—the boxed inserts that students never read because they know they won't be covered on the exam, the cartoons and comics that take up valuable real estate in a book, and the imaginary people invented to tell charming stories about development. We knew that we could illustrate our points with real-world examples, so why make them up? Our rule, which we adhered to fervently, was that if a topic wasn't important enough to have in the main body of the text, it wasn't important enough to include in the book. Every photo, figure, and table was selected to illustrate a very specific, substantive point. Our decision to eschew boxes had the added benefit of giving the interior design a clean, crisp feel.

Organization and Learning Aids

As we noted earlier, this book is organized in a way that will be familiar to most instructors who have taught lifespan development before and have followed a chronological (rather than topical) organization. The book is divided into eight parts. The first part introduces the scientific study of development with a chapter on theory and research design, a chapter on nature and nurture, and a chapter on prenatal conception, development, and birth.

- The coverage of theory in Chapter 1 departs from the usual in that we place less emphasis on classical theorists—Freud, Erikson, and Piaget—and give more attention to more contemporary views, including sociocultural, ecological, behavioral-genetic, evolutionary, and dynamic systems perspectives.

- Chapter 2 (Nature with Nurture) is a bit unconventional in its organization, in that we combine our discussion of genetics and our discussion of the context of development, culminating in a contemporary view of how nature and nurture work together.
- Chapter 3 begins at conception, covers prenatal development, and concludes with the birth of the baby.

Each of the next parts of the book focuses on a specific developmental period—Infancy, Early Childhood, Middle Childhood, Adolescence, Young Adulthood, Middle Adulthood, and Later Adulthood—and contains one chapter on Physical and Cognitive Development and one on Socioemotional Development. (Part Two—Infancy—divides the material on physical and cognitive development into two separate chapters, and Part Eight—Later Adulthood—is followed by an Epilogue on Death and Dying.)

Within each chapter we have included a series of interim summaries (one that follows the conclusion of each major subsection) and a running glossary in the margin, as well as three concluding pedagogical devices that we hope students will find helpful: a brief section called "Summing Up and Looking Ahead," which reviews the main themes covered in the chapter and foreshadows the next chapter; a section called "Did You Get It?," which tells students what they should have come away with after reading the chapter; and a list of "Important Terms and Concepts," which provides page numbers for each of the glossary terms so that students can quiz themselves on them.

Supplements

Instructor's Resource Manual: Save time, streamline your course preparation and get the most from the text by preparing for class more quickly and effectively. The *Instructor's Resource Manual* contains learning objectives, chapter outlines, lecture and discussion topics, and student activities and handouts.

Test Bank: Containing over 1,500 questions, the test bank contains both multiple-choice and essay questions. Each question is tied to a learning objective and marked with the main-text page reference to help instructors efficiently create quizzes and tests.

PowerLecture® with ExamView® and JoinIn™: This one-stop lecture and class preparation tool contains ready-to-use PowerPoint® slides and allows you to assemble, edit, publish, and present custom lectures for your course. PowerLecture lets you bring together text-specific lecture outlines and art from the text along with videos or your own materials, culminating in a powerful, personalized media-enhanced presentation. The CD-ROM also includes the JoinIn Student Response System that lets you pose book-specific questions and display students' answers seamlessly within the PowerPoint slides of your own lecture in conjunction with the "clicker" hardware of your choice, as well as the ExamView assessment and tutorial system, which guides you step by step through the process of creating tests.

Book Companion Website: Full of resources for both instructors and students, the website contains learning objectives, chapter quizzes, a glossary, flashcards, and more! To access the website, go to www.cengage.com/psychology/steinberg.

Study Guide: The study guide contains learning objectives, chapter outlines, key terms with fill-in-the-blank exercises, applied learning and critical thinking exercises, multiple-choice quizzes, and a quiz review.

CengageNOW with eBook, InfoTrac, and Psych Resource Center: CengageNOW is an easy-to-use online resource that helps you study in less time to get the grade you want—NOW.

ACKNOWLEDGMENTS

We deeply appreciate the contributions of all those who have supported this text's evolution, including the following colleagues:

Heather Alvarez, Ohio University Main Campus
Melissa Atkins, Marshall University
Elmida Baghdaserians, Los Angeles Valley College
Byran Bolea, Grand Valley State University
Eric Bridges, Clayton State University
Stacie Bunning, Maryville University
Melinda C. R. Burgess, Southwestern Oklahoma State University
Krista Carter, Colby Community College
Claudia Cochran, El Paso Community College
Melanie A. Conti, College of Saint Elizabeth
Caroline Cooke Carney, Monterey Peninsula College
Sheridan DeWolf, Grossmont College
Dan Dickman, Ivy Tech Community College of Indiana
William Fisk, Clemson University
Ross Flom, Brigham Young University
Pamela Flores, Nassau Community College
Eugene Geist, Ohio University
Belinda Hammond, Los Angeles Valley College
Sam Hardy, Brigham Young University
Amy Himsel, El Camino College
Suzy Horton, Mesa Community College
Maria Ippolito, University of Alaska–Anchorage
Lauri A. Jensen-Campbell, University of Texas–Arlington
Marygrace Kaiser, University of Miami
Bonnie G. Kanner, Worcester State College
Karen Kwan, Salt Lake Community College
Deborah J. Laible, Lehigh University
Judy Levine, Farmingdale State College
John Lindstrom, Virginia Commonwealth University
Kevin MacDonald, California State University–Long Beach
Ashley Maynard, University of Hawaii
Camille Odell, Utah State University
Wendy Orcajo, Menifee Valley Campus, Mt. San Jacinto College
Randall E. Osborne, Texas State University–San Marcos
Margaret Racek, Minnesota State University–Moorhead
Judith (Lyn) Rhoden, University of North Carolina–Charlotte
Sarita Santos, Santa Monica College
Pamela Schuetze, Buffalo State
Jack J. Shilkret, Anne Arundel Community College
David Shwalb, Southern Utah University
Elizabeth Soliday, Washington State University
Lisa Stein, Atlantic Community College
Kaveri Subrahmanyam, California State University, Los Angeles
Ada Wainwright, College of DuPage
Lois Willoughby, Miami Dade Community College

Producing *Lifespan Development: Infancy Through Adulthood* and its supplements was a formidable task. We are especially indebted to each of the following individuals for their contributions to this project:

Vernon Boes	Mary Noel
Jeremy Judson	Rebecca Rosenberg
Michelle Julet	Kim Russell
Shannon LeMay-Finn	Sean Wakely
Aileen Mason	Pat Waldo
Kelly Miller	

It has been a pleasure to work with such a gifted group of professionals and many others at Cengage and at Houghton-Mifflin. We would especially like to express our deepest gratitude to our publisher, Linda Schreiber-Ganster; editors Jon-David Hague and Jane Potter; and developmental editor, Rita Lombard.

Finally, we are indebted to Ann Levine, whose writing and editing helped produce a book that is not only informative, but also a pleasure to read.

Laurence Steinberg
Marc H. Bornstein
Deborah Lowe Vandell
Karen S. Rook

part one

Foundations

© Walter B. McKenzie/Getty Images

CHAPTER 1

The Study of Human Development

© Christina Renee/Getty Images

The study of human development begins with observation. You can do this yourself almost anytime, anywhere. While you are taking this class, why not make "people watching" a habit?

The next time you walk by a school playground, stop and watch the action. What age(s) do you think the children are? What games are they playing? Do some children seem to be at the center of the action, while others remain on the outskirts? If the children are from different ethnic groups, are they playing together or with "their own kind"? Try to figure out which children are popular and which less so, which are at the top of their class and which near the bottom, and which are "model" students and which are troublemakers.

What were you like at their age—say, 9 years old (about the fourth grade)? How would you describe yourself then—for example, as easygoing or high-strung, mostly quiet and subdued, or energetic, even a little wild? What were you interested in? How did you do in school? Did you have a lot of friends, or were you more of a loner? Are you similar now? If you had to name three of your current characteristic that have *not* changed, what would they be?

A central question for scientists who study human development is, "What traits are relatively stable over the course of human development?" For example, shy children tend to remain shy as adolescents, and shy adolescents tend to be shy adults. Notice that we said *tend* to: Many shy children overcome their fear of being noticed. Likewise, outgoing children *tend* to remain sociable and uninhibited as they grow up. Developmentalists are also interested in what traits tend to go together. For example, children who are above average in intelligence usually are outgoing and well liked. Contrary to the stereotype of "geeks" or "nerds," research shows that children who are above average in intelligence are popular. They have social as well as scholastic smarts (Hartup, 1983; Jarvinen & Nicholls, 1996).

Here's another informal assignment. When you are in a shopping mall, sit down for a while and watch parents with babies and small children. If you catch a child's eye and smile, does the child smile back? Do some small children seem curious and excited, whereas others appear bored or irritable? Take note of the parents, too. Are they paying attention to their child(ren)? If a child acts up, how do they respond? The impact of different styles of parenting is another central issue for developmentalists.

Last, think about what you were like at age 16. (Some of you may be only a few years older than age 16; others, twice that age or more. Regardless, most of you remember being 16.) Are you the same person as you were then? What experiences kept you on the same track or influenced you to change? Could people who knew you at age 16 (or age nine or in infancy)—including your family and close friends—have predicted what you are like now? Would *you* have predicted what you are like now?

Everyone has ideas about what makes individuals turn out the way they do. Some think it's all in the person's genes, that who we are is more or less biologically determined. (As the old saying goes, "The acorn doesn't fall far from the tree.") Others think

© Laura Dwight

© Laura Dwight

Some traits, such as the ability to focus sustained attention on a task, are highly stable over time.

what matters most is how someone was treated at home, by parents or other caregivers. ("Her parents were so busy with their own lives, they didn't have time to be parents.") Some place a lot of weight on experiences outside the family—with friends, in school, or around the neighborhood. ("She grew up in Beverly Hills. Of course she's 'stuck up'.") Others think that what's most important is the culture in which someone has been raised. ("That's the way Americans are; we Asians are different.") Commonsense explanations are not necessarily "wrong," but they are simplistic—based on stereotypes and isolated observations.

empirical evidence Information obtained through systematic observations and experiments.

The science of human development is more reliable, more informative, and—we believe—far more interesting than everyday "theories." Common sense is largely speculation. Science is based on **empirical evidence**—information obtained through systematic observations and experiments. Scientific theories about how and why people develop as they do are accepted, modified, or rejected on the basis of research.

developmental scientists Experts who study development—regardless of their disciplinary training.

The study of human development uses scientific methods to describe and explain the ways in which people grow and change over time—from birth through later adulthood. Although much of the research on human development has been conducted by psychologists, the study of development is an interdisciplinary enterprise, one that draws not only from psychology, but also from education, sociology, anthropology, biology, and medicine, to name just a few. Experts who study development—regardless of their training—are referred to as **developmental scientists**.

This chapter focuses on three main questions:

- What distinguishes developmental science from popular, commonsense ideas about people?
- How do developmental scientists think?
- How do developmental scientists work?

Before we get to these questions, here's an overview of this book.

WHAT LIES AHEAD?

This book is organized chronologically and divided into eight age periods: the **prenatal period**, from conception to birth; **infancy**, from birth to about age 2; **early childhood**, from about 2 to 6; **middle childhood**, from about ages 6 through 11; **adolescence**, from about ages 11 through 20; **young adulthood**, from about 20 to 40; **middle adulthood**, from about 40 to 65; and **later adulthood**, from age 65 on.

These time periods reflect major developments. The term *infancy* comes from the Latin for "unable to speak." Early childhood used to be called "the preschool years." However, today so many "preschoolers" go to daycare, nursery school, and kindergarten ("children's garden" in German) that this term no longer applies. Puberty, the period in which young people reach sexual maturity and are capable of reproduction, marks the end of childhood and beginning of adolescence. The stages of adult life are defined mainly by transitions into and out of different roles. Young adulthood is the period during which most individuals complete their education, begin their careers, and establish their own household. Later adulthood begins as individuals begin to transition into retirement. Middle adulthood—the murky period between the two—is probably the hardest stage to draw boundaries around, since how long it takes to settle into adult roles, as well as the age at which individuals retire, vary around the world and in different historical eras. There was a time, for example, when being 55 or 60 was considered "old." In contemporary America, however, individuals at this age are usually considered to be middle aged.

The age boundaries for each period are only approximate. Some children begin speaking at 11 months, others after 14 months. (Reportedly, Einstein did not start speaking until he was 2 years old—proving that it's all relative!) Not only does the age at which individuals enter puberty vary (from as early as 8 to as late as 16), but also, for more than a century, the average age of puberty in Europe and North America has been declining (Steinberg, 2008). The age at which young people see themselves, and are recognized by others, as adults varies widely around the world. In some cultures, boys and girls are expected to marry and assume adult responsibilities a few months after puberty. In the United States and other Western societies, teenagers are thought to be emotionally immature, though they may physically tower over their parents and act as their parents' "computer tutor." Some adults retire from work before they turn 60, but others work well into their 70s.

Within age periods, we've divided our discussion into three broad categories or *domains*: physical, cognitive, and socioemotional development.

- **Physical development** entails changes in size, shape, outward appearance, and inner physical functioning; changes in physical capabilities (locomotion, perception, and sensation); and changes in the structure and function of the brain.
- **Cognitive development** involves changes in intellectual abilities, including memory, thinking, reasoning, language, problem solving, and decision making.
- **Socioemotional development** covers changes in feelings and motivation, temperament and personality, and relationships with others.

Separating these domains is also somewhat arbitrary. The borders between them are not hard and fast. Indeed, it can be difficult to decide what goes where. Is brain

prenatal period The period of development from conception to birth.

infancy The period of development from birth to about age 2.

early childhood The period of development from about ages 2 to 6.

middle childhood The period of development from about ages 6 to 11.

adolescence The period of development from about ages 11 to 20.

young adulthood The period of development from about ages 20 to 40.

middle adulthood The period of development from about ages 40 to 65.

later adulthood The period of development from about age 65 on.

physical development The domain of development that includes changes in size, shape, outward appearance, and inner physical functioning; changes in physical capabilities; and changes in the structure and function of the brain.

cognitive development The domain of development that involves changes in intellectual abilities, including memory, thinking, reasoning, language, problem solving, and decision making.

socioemotional development The domain of development that includes changes in feelings and motivation, temperament and personality, and relationships with others. Sometimes referred to as *psychosocial development.*

development "physical" or "cognitive"? That is, does physical maturation lead to more advanced thinking, or the reverse; that is, does the more mature thinking that comes with experience cause physiological changes in the brain? The answer is, both. Is temperament "physical" or "social and emotional"? Are some individuals sensitive and others calm by nature (as a result of heredity) or is temperament acquired (as a result of early interactions)? Again, the answer is both (see Chapter 6). Are the psychological changes of midlife due to the physical changes individuals go through as they age, or to changes in the way people see themselves? Once again, the correct answer is both (see Chapters 15 and 16).

Ultimately, however, developmentalists are concerned with the "whole person," with how physical, cognitive, and socioemotional development work together as individuals move along the path from conception and birth to adolescence and beyond.

WHY STUDY DEVELOPMENT?

Why study development? Every individual developmentalist has his or her own answer. (So, no doubt, do you.) Some developmentalists are drawn to the field by the opportunity to study change, whether on a neurobiological or microgenetic level, or on the much wider evolutionary scale. Developmental science covers the entire spectrum of human thinking, feeling, and behavior; a scientist whose main interest is the brain, perception, or nonverbal communication, to pick just a few examples, might find a perfect niche. Others are more interested in the cultural aspects of development—how ideas about development vary from one culture to another, how the experience of development varies in relation to the context, and what impact globalization and other 21st-century trends might have on development. Still others are concerned about children's futures—in our own society and around the globe. The mass media have brought home pictures and stories of child soldiers, child prostitutes, child laborers, even child slaves—conditions we once believed we had left behind more than a century ago—as well as tell stories about and show pictures of children who live in substandard conditions in our own society. And some developmentalists, of course, are simply fascinated by how people develop.

The Goals of Developmental Research

Whatever their personal motivations, experts who study human development have four related goals:

1. *To describe* what people are like at different ages and how they change as a result of age (or in some cases as a result of specific experience—entering daycare, starting school, or going through puberty, or retiring from work).

2. *To explain* what causes developmental change. Some explanations deal with universal developments, such as language. All healthy children begin to talk at about the same age, and in the same sequence, whether they are growing up in a wealthy family in Boston, the *favelas* or slums of Rio De Janeiro, or a hill tribe in the Himalayas. We also seek to explain the origins of individual differences. Why does one baby develop into an introverted child whereas another develops into an extravert?

3. To *predict* or forecast what an individual will be like at a later point in development based on past and present characteristics. Is an infant who begins to walk at an early age likely to be athletic in childhood? Is an aggressive toddler destined to become an aggressive teenager? Is an intellectually curious teenager likely to be hungry for knowledge as an adult?

4. To *intervene,* that is, to use this knowledge to enhance the quality of people's lives by giving parents, teachers, public policy makers, and others who influence children, youth, and adults advice. How can we facilitate positive development, prevent problems, or correct problems that already exist? Does an intensive early education program, like Head Start, help prevent disadvantaged children from falling behind their peers when they start elementary school? Does incarcerating juvenile offenders make it less likely that they will commit crimes in the future, or does it have the unintended consequence of increasing their chances for criminal activity after they are released?

Defining Development

Development is a word we frequently use but rarely stop to define. The meaning is obvious . . . or is it?

On the simplest level, development is growth and change over time. In infancy, a baby grows bigger and stronger. His proportions change as his body begins to "catch up" with his head. We would describe this as physical development. As preschoolers become elementary school children, they become capable of using logic. Certainly we would describe this as cognitive development. As children become teenagers, they often begin to develop an interest in romantic relationships. Undoubtedly, we would describe this as social development.

But development is more than growth and change. When an adult gains weight, his or her body *grows* bigger, but this is not development. Likewise, becoming a vegetarian, moving across the country, or learning how to throw a fastball may be significant *changes*, but they are not development. Development differs from simple growth and change in three main ways (Overton, 2006; Valsiner, 2006):

1. *Development makes an individual better adapted to the environment*. Consider language. A baby has no way to tell his mother what he wants; all he can do is cry and hope that she knows why. By age 3½ or 4, a child can *say* what he wants and how he feels, *describe* something that happened to someone who wasn't there, and *ask* questions. Thus the development of language enables a child to become a more active participant in his or her world.

2. *Development proceeds from the relatively simple and global to the more complex and specific*. Language development begins one word at a time, with "Mama, "Bye," "Aw'gone," and the like. Between ages 2 and 3, children begin putting two words together, as in "Baby cry," "My ball," and "Bad doggie." To understand, the listener depends on the context and the infant's inflection (a rising tone is a question, "My ball?"; a descending tone, a command: "*My ball!*"). By age 5, children's conversation is more detailed and specific, as they fill in sentences ("Billy school" becomes "Billy goes to school"), learn verb tenses and concepts (or mental categories), and expand their vocabulary.

3. *Development is relatively enduring.* Change can be permanent, but it can also be fleeting. Once a child begins to talk there is virtually no stopping her (which may drive her parents crazy). Without formal instruction, she becomes increasingly fluent in her native tongue. Barring a severe brain injury, she will never forget or "unlearn" language, nor will she revert to "baby talk."

Thus, **development** is relatively enduring growth and change that makes an individual better *adapted* to the environment, by enhancing the individual's ability to engage in, understand, and experience more *complex* behavior, thinking, and emotions.

development Relatively enduring growth and change that makes an individual better adapted to the environment, by enhancing the individual's ability to engage in, understand, and experience more complex behavior, thinking, and emotions.

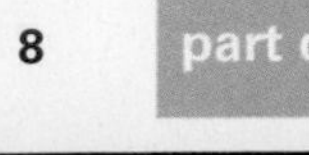

© Charles Gulling/Getty Images

Is there a link between the quality of individuals' early relationships and the quality of their later ones? One question asked by developmental scientists is whether different aspects of development are continuous or discontinuous.

Basic Questions

Much as developmentalists share a precise definition of development, so they are united by four basic questions about the *nature* of development.

1. *Which aspects of development are universal, and which vary from one individual or group to the next?* To what can we attribute differences between individuals in their interests, skills, and abilities? Do infants in China develop language along the same timetable as infants in the United States? Are the factors that contribute to high self-esteem in one ethnic group (Hispanic Americans) the same as those that boost self-esteem in another (Russian Americans)? For boys and girls? Does transitioning into the "empty nest" affect poor and affluent parents in the same way?

2. *Which aspects of development are continuous and which are not?* This question looks forward and backward. How much can we predict about a child's future development from information about his or her present state? Are aggressive toddlers likely to grow up to be aggressive children? Can we link a child's present state to his or her previous patterns of development? Did an adolescent who achieves high scores on intelligence tests demonstrate above-average intelligence as a young child? Will he or she continue to be above-average as a young adult?

3. *Which aspects of development are more or less fixed (like marble) and difficult to change, and which are relatively malleable (like clay) and easy to change?* For example, research shows that, across cultures, children who have authoritative (firm but responsive) parents are more cooperative than are children whose parents are authoritarian (dictatorial) or permissive (Bugental & Grusec, 2006). Can parent training improve children's behavior? (The answer is yes; see Collins et al., 2000). As early as age 3, children "know" that trucks, guns and hammers, and rough-and-tumble play are for boys; dolls, pots and pans, and playing house are for girls. They expect males in storybooks and on TV to be strong and brave and females to be soft and gentle. Can these early gender stereotypes be changed? (The answer here is more complex, a maybe; Ruble, Martin, & Berenbaum, 2006).

4. *What makes development happen?* What factors influence the course of development, and how do they do so? Is the development of language due solely to the maturation of the brain, or does it depend on input from the environment, or is it a product of the two? To what extent is the development of interest in romantic relationships in adolescence an inevitable outgrowth of the physical changes of puberty, and to what extent is it culturally determined?

Whether stated explicitly or not, most scientific research attempts to discover the following: whether the aspect of development studied is universal or variable; whether development is continuous or not; whether development is fixed or pliable; and what factors influence patterns of development over time.

Guiding Principles

Last, the study of human development, like all sciences, rests on the following set of shared principles about which all developmentalists (or almost all) agree:

1. *Development results from the constant interplay of biology and the environment.* All children come into the world with the set of genes they inherit from their parents, but only a few traits (such as eye color and blood type) are genetically "determined." The characteristics an individual develops are the result of interaction between

genetic and environmental influences over time (Gottlieb, Wahlstein, & Lickliter, 2006). A child may inherit a genetic tendency to be inhibited, for instance, but whether this leads to painful shyness or quiet confidence depends on the child's experiences.

2. *Development occurs in a multilayered context.* Children are profoundly affected by their *interpersonal* relationships, the *social* institutions that touch their lives, their *culture*, and the *historical* period in which they are developing (Bronfenbrenner & Morris, 2006).

3. *Development is a dynamic, reciprocal process.* People are not passive recipients of environmental influence. They actively shape their own development: by selecting the contexts in which they participate (for example, choosing their friends); by imposing their subjective appraisal on the context (children who believe that their parents love them have fewer mental health problems than those who feel unloved, even if their parents' behavior is the same); and most of all by affecting what takes place in the context (the way parents or peers behave toward a child is affected by that child's behavior toward them) (Lerner, 2006; Magnusson & Stattin, 2006).

© John Barry/Syracuse Newspapers/The Image Works

Development occurs over the entire lifespan. This father and son are both influenced by their interactions with each other.

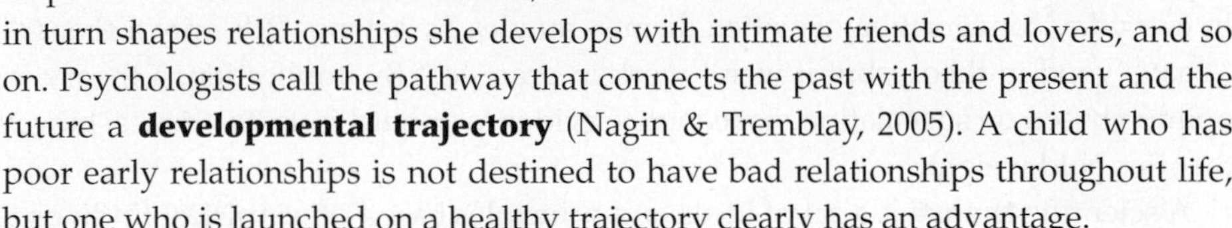

4. *Development is cumulative.* Development builds on itself. To understand an individual at one point in the lifespan, we need to look at earlier periods (Baltes, Lindenberger, & Staudinger, 2006). The quality of the infant's relationships at home lays the groundwork for the relationships she forms with school friends, which in turn shapes relationships she develops with intimate friends and lovers, and so on. Psychologists call the pathway that connects the past with the present and the future a **developmental trajectory** (Nagin & Tremblay, 2005). A child who has poor early relationships is not destined to have bad relationships throughout life, but one who is launched on a healthy trajectory clearly has an advantage.

developmental trajectory A pathway of developmental change that connects the past, present, and future.

5. *Development occurs throughout the lifespan.* The belief that the first years of life are a critical period in development has become part of our popular culture, or what "everyone knows." In reality, no one period of development overrides all others. Development continues from birth to death, and change is almost always possible, in infancy, childhood, adolescence, adulthood, and old age (Baltes et al., 2006; Elder & Shanahan, 2006).

In brief, virtually all developmentalists agree that development involves constant interplay between biology and the environment, occurs in a multilayered context, is cumulative, and continues throughout life. As the next section illustrates, however, developmental scientists are not "of a single mind." Some find one theory or approach more useful than others, sometimes to the exclusion of different points of view. (For a summary of the reasons to study development, see "Interim Summary 1.1: Why Study Development?")

INTERIM SUMMARY 1.1

Why Study Development?

The Goals of Developmental Research	■ To *describe* what people are like at different ages and how they change over time. ■ To *explain* what causes developmental change. ■ To *predict* what an individual will be like at a later point in development based on past and present characteristics. ■ To *intervene;* that is, to use this knowledge to enhance the quality of individuals' lives.
Defining Development	**Development** is relatively *enduring* growth and change that makes an individual better *adapted* to the environment, by enhancing the individual's ability to engage in, understand, and experience more *complex* behavior, thinking, and emotions.
Basic Questions	1 Which aspects of development are universal, and which vary from one individual or group to the next? 2. Which aspects of development are continuous and which are not? 3. Which aspects of development are more or less fixed and difficult to change, and which are relatively malleable and easy to change? 4. What makes development happen?
Guiding Principles	1. Development results from the constant interplay of biology and the environment. 2. Development occurs in a multilayered context. 3. Development is a dynamic, reciprocal process. 4. Development is cumulative. 5. Development occurs throughout the lifespan.

THEORIES OF DEVELOPMENT

In everyday conversation, we often dismiss an idea by saying, "It's only a theory" or "That's good in theory, but it won't work in practice." By implication, a theory is an opinion based on speculation, not concrete evidence or hard facts. In science, however, theories hold weight.

theory A set of ideas and principles based on empirical findings that explain related natural phenomena.

A scientific **theory** is a set of ideas and principles based on empirical findings that explain related natural phenomena. Members of the scientific community accept a theory because it stands up under testing, fits the known facts, and continues to be refined in response to new scientific discoveries.

A theory is a scientist's map. Theories help scientists to organize their thinking, to decide which phenomena are significant, and to generate new questions and ideas. Developmental science covers a vast array of topics. Without theories, scientists would be lost. Imagine trying to put together an 800-piece jigsaw puzzle without the image on the box lid for guidance. But theories are not engraved in stone. The history of science is one of widely accepted theories being replaced by new approaches.

Classical Theories

Through most of the 20th century, the study of development was guided by what we might call "classical theories": overarching visions that sought to explain every aspect of development from birth to adolescence, and in some cases, adulthood. Although less influential now than they were 50 years ago, classical theories laid the foundation for today's science of development.

Psychoanalytic Theory **Psychoanalytic theory** focuses on the inner self and how emotions determine the way we interpret our experiences and therefore how we act. Many emotions are irrational. A popular child lives in fear of being rejected by his peers. A student with a 3.8 grade point average panics before every exam, certain she will fail. After rave reviews of his latest film, an actor slips into depression. Where do these emotions come from? Why are they so persistent? According to psychoanalytic theory, they come from our early experiences, mainly in the family.

psychoanalytic theory The theory of human behavior and development, first articulated by Sigmund Freud, that focuses on the inner self and how emotions determine the way we interpret our experiences and thus how we act.

Sigmund Freud (1856–1939), the founder of psychoanalytic theory, is one of the best-known but most controversial figures in the history of psychology. Freud, who began his career as a physician specializing in nervous disorders, came to believe that his patients' symptoms were psychological, not neurological (or physiological) in origin. This led him to a revolutionary image of human nature. In Freud's view, we are not as rational as we think; indeed, often we do not understand the reasons for our own behavior (Freud, 1910).

Freud believed that infants are born with powerful sexual and aggressive urges—to suck, to defecate, to experience pleasure, and to avoid discomfort or pain. Babies want what they want now, not later! But the infant's insistence on immediate gratification collides with reality. The nipple is not always available; parents do not "give in" to the infant's every wish (at least in modern Western societies). As the infant matures, parents expect increasing self-control. The child's desires and wishes inevitably clash with his or her parents' rules and restrictions. How these conflicts are resolved—or *not* resolved—leaves a lasting imprint. According to Freud, a child's basic emotional outlook is set by age five or six.

Freud's theory of psychosexual development Freud divided psychosexual development into stages, named for the zone of the body a child finds most arousing at a given age: the *oral*, *anal*, *phallic*, and (after a period of latency) *genital* stages. In each stage, the child must learn to gratify his desires in socially approved ways. Parents declare, "Thou shall not." Initially the child protests; later he complies out of fear of being punished or (worse) losing his parents' love. Over time, his parents' commands are internalized as a conscience: The child forbids himself to do what his parents and culture condemn.

According to Freud, the key to healthy development is the emergence of the *ego*—the rational, adaptive part of the self—in middle childhood. The ego's job is to mediate between persistent sexual and aggressive urges, which originate in what Freud called the *id;* the demands of the *superego* (or conscience); and the demands of reality. Ideally, the ego becomes increasingly skilled at balancing the id, the superego, and reality during childhood and adolescence. But even with the development of the ego, childhood conflicts are never fully resolved, once and for all. They remain active in the *unconscious*, a reservoir of secret cravings, unspeakable memories, and suppressed rage too dangerous to admit even to oneself. Although hidden from waking awareness, unconscious wishes often overpower conscious intentions.

Erikson's theory of psychosocial development The developmental emphasis in Freud's theory was on the child's progression through psychosexual stages. In contrast, Erik Erikson, a follower of Freud, described a different sort of progression—a progression of social and emotional stages that went from infancy to later adulthood. Erikson's ideas about development would come to have a far greater impact on the field than Freud's.

Erikson (1902–1994) studied *psychoanalysis* (the term for the application of psychoanalytic theory to the treatment of psychological problems) before moving to the United States when he was in his 30s. Erikson's own ethnic identity was ambiguous. His Danish parents divorced soon after he was born, his mother remarried, and he was raised as a German Jew. He changed his last name from Homburger back to Erikson when he became an American citizen. This multicultural background and personal identity confusion clearly influenced his thinking.

psychosocial development See *socioemotional development.*

Erikson used psychoanalytic theory as a scaffold, but his theory of **psychosocial development** differs from Freud's in two important ways. Erikson disagreed with the idea that personality is fixed in early childhood. To the contrary, he held that development continues over the entire lifespan, from infancy to old age, "cradle to grave" (Erikson, 1959). He believed that just as children go through stages, so do adults. An individual's emotional disposition is not fixed at any one stage, but always subject to revision. Each of our lives, at every age, is "a work in progress."

Like Freud, Erikson believed that development takes the form of a series of predictable stages, each centered on a different challenge or crisis. But Erikson saw these problems as psycho*social*, not psychosexual; the result of social interaction, not inner conflict. As the individual develops new abilities and interests, society imposes new codes of conduct and offers new opportunities. What matters is that individuals find a niche—a position or activity that fits their talents and inclinations—in society.

Erikson emphasized that the transition from one stage to another depends on the society and culture in which the person lives. For example, many traditional societies have *initiation rites* to mark the transition from childhood to adulthood (Cohen, 1964; Schlegel & Barry, 1991). These rites may be physically brutal or psychologically terrifying, but the child emerges as a "certified" adult. In these societies, the young adult's future is often predetermined; for example, all men herd cattle and all women tend sheep and goats, as their parents and grandparents did before them. The rights and responsibilities of adulthood are clearly defined. In Western societies, the transition to adulthood is gradual and the point at which a child becomes a full-fledged adult is ambiguous. Faced with a wide array of possible occupations and lifestyles, each adolescent must create his or her own identity. According to Erikson, these conditions contribute to the "identity crisis" of adolescence (Erikson, 1959), which we discuss in Chapter 12.

Psychoanalytic theory's most important contribution to how we think about development today is the idea that childhood experiences can affect adult emotions, thoughts, and behavior, sometimes in ways of which we are not consciously aware. Freud was the first influential theorist to propose that individuals move through qualitatively different stages of development in a predictable sequence, and to emphasize that an individual's current psychological functioning builds on development in previous stages. Erikson pioneered the study of development throughout the lifespan, and he mapped out a sequence of psychosocial "crises" that individuals must resolve successfully in order to develop in healthy ways. Erikson's ideas about what issues are important at different periods of life remain highly influential.

learning theory The theory of human behavior, based on principles of classical and/or operant conditioning, as well as observational learning, that stresses the role of external influences on behavior.

Learning Theory In psychoanalytic theory, emotions are central to development. In contrast, **learning theory** stresses the role of external influences on behavior. Learning theorists argue that it isn't necessary to speculate about what is going on inside the person's head to explain development. Nor is it necessary to consider the individual's wider social and cultural environment. Rather, the way individuals behave is a consequence of their experiences in the *immediate* environment. All behavior is learned—including love, fear, laughter, generosity, shyness, and confidence, as well as knowledge and skills. Moreover, the basic principles of learning are the same, regardless of who is learning and what they are learning—whether a dog learning to obey a command to "Sit!" or a student learning to program computers.

classical conditioning A process of associative learning by which a subject comes to respond in a desired manner to a previously neutral stimulus (e.g., the sound of a steel bar being hit with a hammer) that has been repeatedly presented along with an unconditioned stimulus (e.g., a white furry object) that elicits the desired response (e.g., fear).

Behaviorism Pioneered by the Russian scientist Ivan Pavlov, the behaviorist approach found its widest audience in America and a champion in psychologist J. B. Watson (1924), who led an academic rebellion against "introspective psychology."

Watson was primarily interested in the simplest form of learning, **classical conditioning**, which is based on associations. In a famous experiment, "Little Albert" was introduced to a white laboratory rat, which he liked. On their next encounter, as Albert reached out to touch the rat, the experimenter hit a steel bar with a hammer. Frightened by the sound, the little boy cried and buried his face in his blanket. Watson repeated this procedure several times. Soon the sight of the rat alone made Albert cry—a conditioned or learned response. He developed a *generalized* fear of anything white and furry: a rabbit, a coat, even Santa Claus's beard.

Operant conditioning, studied extensively by B. F. Skinner (1953), refers to behavior that is acquired as a result of its prior consequences, rather than its associations with specific stimuli (as is the case in classical conditioning). Simply put, people are likely to repeat behavior that has positive consequences (the behavior is *reinforced*) and unlikely to repeat behavior that has negative consequences (the behavior is *punished*). A girl hits a winning home run; her teammates jump up cheering and carry her off the field. She begins to practice batting every day, striving to be a hero again. A boy rides his bike down a hill, falls, and badly scrapes his knee; he doesn't ride down that hill again.

Operant conditioning can be intentional—parents reward a toddler for using the "potty" with candy or punish a child for hitting her brother—or *unintentional*. A seventh-grader acts up in class, not for the first time. The teacher warns, "One more time, Tony!" When she turns to the blackboard, he gets up and imitates her, to the class's giggling amusement. "Out!" she shouts, marching him to the door and ordering the hall monitor to take him directly to the principal. Does Tony learn to behave in class? No, he learns that misbehaving wins attention. A better way to change Tony's behavior would be to quietly walk him into the hall and talk there. Without his audience, Tony will not be rewarded for showing off. Over time, behavior that is not reinforced fades away; in behaviorist terminology, it is *extinguished*. **Behavioral therapy** (an attempt to change behavior through the deliberate use of rewards and punishments) has proven successful in programs and therapy for troubled children (and their families), as well as a means of changing undesirable habits (smoking) and overcoming phobias (such as fear of flying).

operant conditioning A process of learning in which the likelihood of a specific behavior is increased or decreased as a result of reward or punishment that follows.

behavioral therapy An attempt to change behavior through the deliberate use of rewards and punishments.

social learning theory A theory of human behavior that emphasizes the ways in which individuals learn by observing others and through the application of social rewards (e.g., praise) and punishments (e.g., disapproval).

observational learning A process of learning based on the observation of others.

Social Learning Theory A more contemporary version of learning theory, developed by Albert Bandura (Bandura & Walters, 1959) and others, fills in the gaps left by behaviorism. One problem with behaviorism is that it doesn't explain the sudden appearance of complex behavior. Out of nowhere, a 4-year-old marches around the room, singing the jingle from a television commercial. How did she learn this? If children had to learn everything through conditioning, parents and teachers would have to spend every waking hour shaping children's behavior. Learning everything through trial and error would be time-consuming, dangerous—and probably ineffective. According to **social learning theory,** we also learn by watching what other people (*models*) do and imitating their behavior. **Observational learning** is most likely when the model is someone powerful or admired, like a parent, an especially popular peer, or a celebrity; when we perceive the model as similar to ourself; and especially, when the child sees the model rewarded for the behavior he or she is watching. Social learning theory is the basis for numerous preventive programs, such as workshops on peer pressure in which young people watch models refuse cigarettes, alcohol, or sex, then practice or role-play saying "No!" themselves.

Learning theory called attention to how much individual's development is shaped by the people around them. Whether studying the impact of parents, teachers, peers, or the mass media, contemporary developmentalists frequently invoke the concepts of reinforcement, punishment, and modeling. In particular, social learning theory led to research about what children see—on television, for example—and whether they imitate what they see.

© Laura Dwight

According to social learning theory, children learn by watching what other people do and imitating their behavior.

Cognitive-Developmental Theory Cognitive-developmental theory is concerned with what goes on in people's minds: how we learn, reason, solve problems, understand language, explain ourselves and our experiences, and form beliefs. (*Cognition* comes from the Latin for "getting to know.") The **cognitive-developmental perspective** emphasizes changes in the way individuals think about their physical and social world as they move from infancy through adolescence; although a few theorists from this school of thought have also examined adulthood, most have focused on infants, children, and adolescents. Behaviorism is essentially *non*developmental. Behaviorists explain complex adult behavior as an accumulation of simple behaviors, or changes in the *quantity* of associations. Cognitive-developmental theorists see development as the result of new levels in the organization or structure of thought, or *qualitative* changes.

cognitive-developmental perspective A perspective on human development that emphasizes qualitative changes in the ways that individuals think as they mature, mainly associated with the work of Jean Piaget.

sensorimotor stage In Piaget's theory, the stage of cognitive development from birth to about age 2, during which infants learn by relating sensations to motor action.

preoperational stage In Piaget's theory, the stage of cognitive development from approximately ages 2 to 7, during which children acquire a mental storehouse of images and symbols, especially spoken and written words.

concrete operational stage In Piaget's theory, the stage of cognitive development from approximately ages 7 to 11, during which children make giant strides in their ability to organize ideas and think logically, but where their logical reasoning is limited to real objects and actual experiences and events.

The Swiss scientist Jean Piaget (1896–1980) was a pioneer in the field of cognitive development. An amateur naturalist (whose first article was published when he was age 10!), Piaget earned a degree in natural science, worked at a psychiatric clinic in Zurich, and then became an instructor at the Sorbonne. There he met Alfred Binet and Theodore Simon, the inventors of the IQ test. Dissatisfied with the "right-or-wrong" format of intelligence tests, he used psychiatric techniques from his clinical experience to interview test subjects. He came to believe that children's mistakes revealed distinct changes in how children reason at different ages. Ultimately he concluded that the best way to understand development in general was to learn how children think at different ages (Piaget, 1952).

Piaget identified four stages of cognitive growth. In the **sensorimotor stage** (birth to age 2), infants learn by relating sensations to motor action. In the **preoperational stage** (ages 2 to 7), children acquire a mental storehouse of images and symbols, especially spoken and written words. As a result, they can think about things that are not physically present. But they cannot retrace their thoughts, imagine how an object looks from different angles, try out different ways of solving a problem, or perform other *operations* in their head. In the **concrete operational stage** (ages 7 to 11), youngsters make giant strides in their ability to organize ideas and think

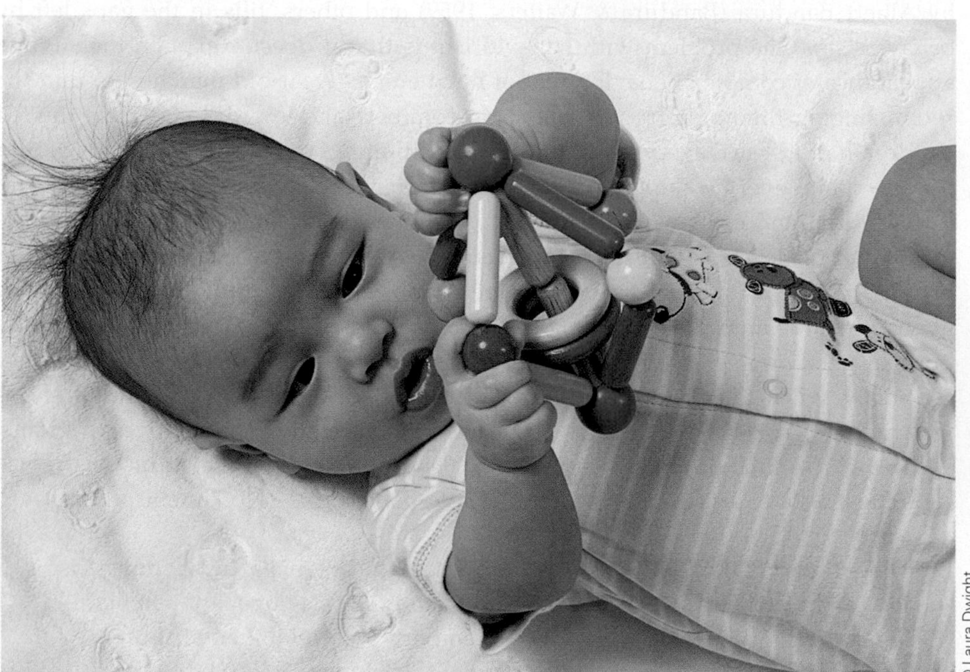

© Laura Dwight

During the sensorimotor stage, infants learn about the world by manipulating objects and experiencing them with their senses.

logically, but their thinking is limited to the concrete, physical world; that is, to real objects and people and actual experiences and events. In the **formal operational stage** (age 11 and beyond), children break free from the here-and-now of concrete experience and are able to think about the world in hypothetical, symbolic, abstract terms, transcending space and time.

formal operational stage In Piaget's theory, the stage of cognitive development that emerges approximately at age 11, during which individuals develop the ability to apply logical reasoning to abstract phenomena.

Piaget's theory is not limited to the kind of intellectual achievements we associate with school. Just as the ability to understand mathematics develops over time, so does the ability to understand what other people are thinking or feeling. Small children do not even realize that other people *have* different thoughts and emotions than they do. When her father is injured on the job and stays in bed the next day, a 4-year-old brings him her favorite toy for comfort. The cognitive capacity to see different points of view also affects the way children play with one another. One reason that toddlers often quarrel over toys is that they don't yet have the ability to understand what another child may be thinking or feeling when they try to grab *his* favorite toy.

Piaget saw cognitive development as a form of adaptation. When children encounter new information, they attempt to fit the information into their existing way of thinking, a process called **assimilation**. Thus a child may call all four-legged, furry animals "doggie." When this way of thinking is challenged—her mother tells her that this "doggie" is really a cat—a child adapts by developing a new understanding, a process called **accommodation**. She creates a new mental category for cats, and in time a general category for "animals," which includes cats, dogs, and perhaps horses and cows. Through the reciprocal processes of assimilation and accommodation, children develop a more advanced understanding of the world.

assimilation In Piaget's theory, the child's attempt to fit new information into his or her existing way of thinking.

accommodation In Piaget's theory, the child's adaptation of an existing way of thinking in response to new information.

Piaget's chief contribution to the study of development was to envision the child as an active organism who strives to make sense out of his or her world. In other words, development is self-motivated. Contemporary researchers have found that Piaget overemphasized the existence of clear-cut stages; cognitive development does not take the form of sudden leaps forward, but consists of many small and uneven steps in that direction. Still, Piaget is widely credited for changing the ways in which developmental scientists think about cognition, as well as for describing patterns of thinking at different ages.

Contemporary Theories

Ideas from the classical theories remain in contemporary scientists' library, like reference books, available for use as needed. The guiding principles, introduced earlier, still apply. But new approaches have expanded the range of developmental science. Here are some of the most influential.

The Ecological Perspective Ordinarily, we think of "ecology" as a branch of biology that deals with the complex interactions between living organisms and their natural environment, whether in a drop of pond water or on the African savannah. But the term applies equally well to the multilayered relationships between human beings and their social environment. In this perspective, the word *ecology* refers to the interconnected network of immediate and broader social and cultural settings in which individuals develop, as well as the physical environment.

The **ecological perspective** on development holds that we can never fully understand development without taking into account the *context* in which it occurs (Bronfenbrenner, 1979). This means studying not only the individual's immediate environments (like the home or school), but also the network of different relationships and settings individuals encounter as they grow older; the institutions that influence individuals, directly or indirectly (such as the world of work, the education system,

ecological perspective A perspective on human development that emphasizes the contexts, both proximal and distant, in which development occurs, often associated with the work of Urie Bronfenbrenner.

and the mass media); and the cultural values, economic conditions, and other forces that shape a society. Figure 1.1 illustrates this ecological model of development.

The ecological perspective broke barriers between academic disciplines. "Before Bronfenbrenner, [developmental psychologists] studied the child, sociologists examined the family, anthropologists the society, economists the economic framework of the times and political scientists the structure. . . . The concept of the ecology of human development [brought together] these environments. In this perspective all of these—from the family to economic and political structures—were viewed as part of the life course, embracing both childhood and adulthood" (*American Psychological Society*, 2005, p. 28). We look more closely at this influential viewpoint in the chapter on nature and nurture.

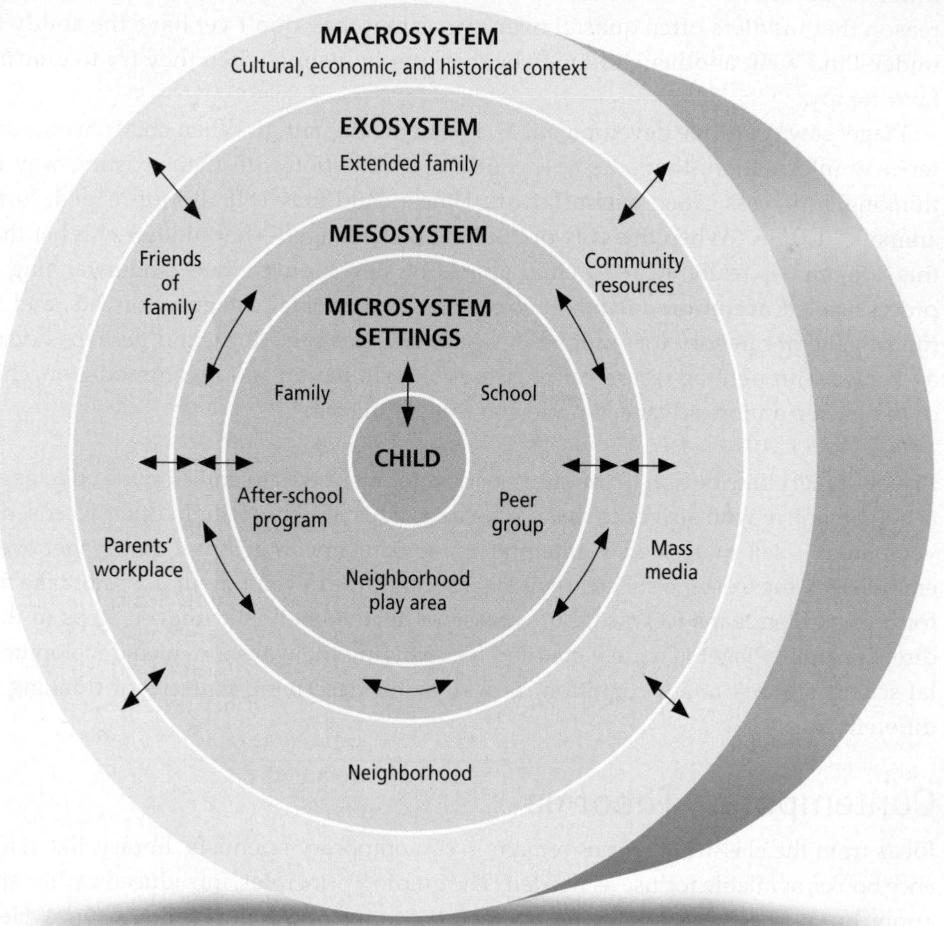

FIGURE 1.1

An Ecological Model of Human Development

To fully understand human development, the contexts in which it occurs must be taken into account. As depicted in this figure, children both influence and are influenced by their immediate "microsystems," environments like school, family, and peer groups. In addition to the bidirectional influences between a child and his or her immediate contexts, the "mesosystem," or network of connections *between* the environments, is also important. At a broader level, the "exosystem," which is composed of contexts in which a child does not directly participate—like a parent's place of employment or community resources—can still be influential, as is the "macrosystem," which refers to the overarching cultural context in which development takes place.

Source: Kopp, C. & Krakow, J., *Child development in a social context*, © 1982. Reprinted by permission of Pearson Education, Inc., Upper Saddle River, New Jersey.

© Don Hammond/Design Pics/Corbis

Development is influenced by the cultural context in which it takes place.

The Sociocultural Perspective Culture is a pervasive presence in all of our lives, so much so that we take it for granted. Yet everything we do—and many things we don't—is based in culture: where we sleep, what we eat, whom we admire, how we see ourselves, and, of course, what we think of as "normal" development.

In the past, developmentalists used cross-cultural studies mainly to identify universal patterns of development. Today, we see culture itself as a key contributor to development: There is much to learn from studying development in different cultures in their own right. The study of cultural influences provides a window on how development takes place.

The **sociocultural perspective** on development is similar to the ecological approach, in that both insist that we examine development within the specific context in which it occurs. But the ecological perspective gives equal weight to all aspects, all levels, of the individual's environment, whereas the sociocultural perspective stresses that development must be seen as adaptation to specific *cultural* demands (Shweder et al., 2006). For example, children in societies with little formal education tend to do poorly on standardized tests of math. But they perform complicated mathematical computations in the marketplace—transactions that children with book learning alone would find extremely difficult (Saxe, 1991). As this example shows, concepts of "healthy" or "successful" development cannot be separated from the requirements of a particular cultural setting.

sociocultural perspective A perspective on human development that stresses the ways in which development involves adaptation to specific cultural demands.

Behavioral Genetics Obviously, people inherit physical traits from their parents: the color of their eyes, the shape of their face, and perhaps certain gestures. But do we also inherit *behavioral* traits? Is intelligence hereditary? Generosity? Aggressiveness? Homosexuality? (Of course, everyone has intelligence; the question is whether some individuals inherit high intelligence and others, average or below-average intelligence.) The fact that we even ask these questions is due in part to the influence of **behavioral genetics**, the study of the inherited bases of behavior. We will say more about this field in Chapter 2. Here, let's focus on what it is *not*.

behavioral genetics The study of the inherited bases of behavior.

Contemporary behavioral geneticists do *not* study which behavior is "genetically determined" and which is not. Virtually all scientists today agree that development is a result of *reciprocal* influences between biology and experience, genes and environment (Gottlieb et al., 2006). And although it was once common in developmental science to try to estimate how much of a behavioral trait is genetic and how much is environmental, this question is rarely asked today. Human behavior is not a cocktail, "Mix two parts heredity with one part context and shake."

Neither is behavioral genetics abstract or speculative. Thanks to remarkable advances in the study of genetics over the past two decades, culminating in the map of the human genome (i.e., a map of all the human chromosomes), scientists are beginning to study inheritance directly. As we will explain in Chapter 2, scientists can now look at the actual processes through which the chemicals that code genetic information influence patterns of development and behavior.

© Gerald Hinde/Getty Images

Developmental scientists do not restrict their research to studies of humans. Much has been learned about human development from studies of other species.

One of the main contributions of behavioral genetics is that scientists who study development today—whether they are interested in personality traits, social relationships, family contexts, or cultural dynamics—cannot ignore possible genetic influences.

The Evolutionary Perspective Behavioral geneticists are primarily interested in the origin of individual differences; evolutionary psychologists are mainly interested in the universals in human development. Psychologists who take an **evolutionary perspective** on development look at changes in the individual's behavior over the course of development in light of the evolution of the human species (Bjorklund & Pellegrini, 2001). How was the appearance of a certain pattern of behavior at a certain point in development *adaptive* for the human species during the course of our evolution? What advantage did it give our ancestors over their competitors?

To answer these questions, evolutionary psychologists sometimes study behavior patterns in other animals, especially our nearest kin, the great apes (chimpanzees, gorillas, and orangutans). The reason is not that human beings are descended from monkeys and apes (a common misperception), but rather that we are all descended from a common ancestor. We humans became a distinct species "only" about 5 million years ago, a mere blip on an evolutionary time scale. Today, we share more than 95 percent of our genes with apes (and almost 99% with chimpanzees). What does their behavior tell us about the evolutionary origins of, say, attachment, the close bond that infants form with their caregivers (usually mothers) during the first year of life (see Chapter 6)?

The existence of similar patterns of behavior and development in species who share our ancestry indicates that these patterns were probably a part of the human developmental repertoire before we became a distinct species. The evolutionary perspective has been applied to a wide range of developmental patterns, from the infant's early preference for looking at faces, to parents and children bickering during early adolescence (Collins & Steinberg, 2006).

evolutionary perspective
A perspective on human development that emphasizes the evolved basis of human behavior.

The Dynamic Systems Perspective By tradition, scientists have divided the study of development into separate age periods or stages, different domains of development, and different social contexts. In fact, most developmental scientists have become so specialized that they study one aspect of development, during one developmental period, in one specific setting (e.g., the influence of the peer group on the development of self-esteem in elementary school students, or the contribution of daycare to language acquisition during late infancy, or the impact of marital conflict on stress reactivity during midlife). In short, the study of development has become fragmented and specialized. Some developmental scientists have declared, "Enough!"

Dynamic systems theory looks at the many facets of development as part of a single, dynamic, constantly changing system—including multiple levels of human functioning (e.g., genes, cells, organs, systems, whole persons), multiple domains of development (e.g., physical, cognitive, social and emotional), and multiple levels of context (e.g., interpersonal, institutional, social, cultural) (Thelen & Smith, 2006).

dynamic systems theory
A perspective on human development that views the many facets of development as part of a single, dynamic, constantly changing system.

Central to dynamic systems theory is the idea that any change in one context or domain of development can disrupt the entire system, prompting a reorganization that leads to more adaptive functioning. Thus, changes in a specific context (e.g., the classroom) that stimulate changes in a young adolescent's cognitive development do not merely affect academic achievement, but may provoke a change in the child's social behavior (e.g., extra attention from a teacher following a dramatic improvement in the child's school performance boosts her confidence), which may provoke a change in the child's relationships in an entirely different context (e.g., she is in a much better mood at home, which leads to her parents spending more time conversing with her), which may provoke a further change in the child's thinking (e.g., the extra time with her parents stimulates further cognitive development), and so on.

What's important is that from a dynamic systems perspective, it is impossible to understand one domain of development in isolation from any other, impossible to study one level of context in isolation from any other, and, of course, impossible to study the individual in isolation from the context in which he or she lives.

In sum, new theoretical approaches have expanded the scope of developmental science. Ecological and sociocultural theories require developmentalists to look more closely at the developing person's social and cultural surroundings. In different ways, behavioral genetics and evolutionary psychology direct attention to the impact of genes on behavior. Dynamic systems theory calls for a more integrated approach to studying development.

The different theories we have introduced draw different conclusions about the nature of human development. Some place more weight on biology and others on the environment. Among the environmental approaches, some emphasize one context (early family experiences) more than another (the broader culture). How do scientists decide which features of what theories are correct, and which aspects are not? How do we decide whether early experience in the family truly is especially important, or whether children actually do model what they see on television, or whether what happens in the classroom really does spill over into the home environment? The answer is research. (For a summary of developmental theories, see "Interim Summary 1.2: Theories of Development.")

THE SCIENTIFIC STUDY OF DEVELOPMENT

"Trust yourself. You know more than you think you do."

This is the opening of Dr. Spock's *Common Sense Book of Baby and Child Care*, first published in 1946. For decades, Dr. Spock's advice was "the gospel" on child rearing for middle-class American parents. Indeed, his book sold nearly 50 million copies, second only to the Bible on all time bestseller lists (Garner, 1998). But common sense—that mixture of folk wisdom, gut feelings, counsel by relatives and strangers, advice gleaned from books and magazines, and vague memories of one's own upbringing—is often wrong, and certainly not a sound basis for making decisions that will affect children's lives. To be fair, when Dr. Spock wrote "Trust yourself," the study of human development was in its infancy. Neither pediatricians like Dr. Spock nor parents had a body of concrete, reliable research on why children develop in certain ways.

Today, the study of human development (including the impact of different styles of parenting) is a science. Systematic research allows developmentalists to test elements of the different theories, to put their own ideas to the test, and to gather information that can be used to guide public policy and practice.

INTERIM SUMMARY 1.2

Theories of Development

Theory	Major Concept
Classical Theories	
■ Psychoanalytic theory	Focuses on the inner self and how emotions determine the way we interpret our experiences and therefore how we act. Key theorists: Freud, who emphasized psychosexual stages of development and the dynamic struggle among the id, the ego, and the superego; and Erikson, who stressed the psychosocial crises we face over the entire lifespan.
■ Learning theory	Stresses the role of external influences on behavior. Key theorists: Behaviorists, such as Pavlov, Watson, and Skinner, who emphasized the role of classical and operant conditioning in learning; and social learning theorists, such as Bandura, who emphasized the importance of learning through observation and imitation of the behaviors displayed by others.
■ Cognitive-developmental theory	Concerned with development of thinking. Key theorist: Piaget, who described the child as an active organism striving to make sense out of his or her world; Piaget proposed four stages of cognitive development: sensorimotor, preoperational, concrete operational, and formal operational.
Contemporary Theories	
■ Ecological perspective	Context is key to understanding development.
■ Sociocultural perspective	Stresses that development must be seen as adaptation to specific *cultural* demands.
■ Behavioral genetics	Studies the inherited bases of behavior.
■ Evolutionary perspective	Looks at changes in the individual's behavior over the course of development in light of the evolution of the human species.
■ Dynamic systems theory	Looks at the many facets of development as part of a single, dynamic, constantly changing system.

The Scientific Method

scientific method A systematic, step-by-step procedure for testing ideas.

hypothesis A prediction that can be tested empirically and supported or rejected on the basis of scientific evidence.

The scientific study of human development follows the same principles that govern other sciences. The **scientific method** is a systematic, step-by-step procedure for testing ideas (see Figure 1.2). The main steps are:

1. Formulate a question based on theory, past research, or an applied issue. For example, Are mothers more likely to discipline boys than girls for disobedience?
2. Develop a **hypothesis**—a prediction that can be tested empirically and supported or rejected. For example, mothers are more likely to discipline boys than girls.
3. Conduct a study that tests the hypothesis. A researcher might give mothers of boys and mothers of girls a questionnaire on how they handle disobedience.

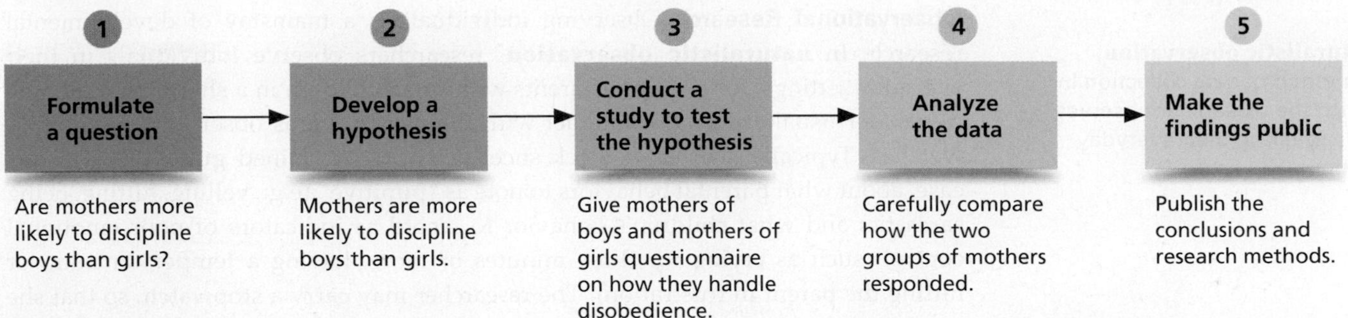

FIGURE 1.2

The Scientific Method

When investigating new questions, psychologists and other researchers use the scientific method to systematically test their ideas. In many cases, the findings from one investigation lead to new questions and hypotheses about human development, and so the process of scientific inquiry continues.

4. Analyze the data, carefully comparing how the two groups of mothers responded, and decide whether to accept or reject the hypothesis.
5. Make the findings public. Scientists publish their conclusions *and* their research methods so that other scientists can evaluate their findings or replicate the study. **Replication**—a repetition of the study using the same methods, but by another researcher and with different subjects—may verify or challenge the original.

replication The repetition of a study using the same methods.

Obviously scientists cannot question *every* mother of girls or boys. Rather, they study a **representative sample**, a group of participants who represent the larger population the scientists want to describe. If all of the participants were mothers whose children attended the same school, or lived in the same city or state, the results might not apply to the entire country. Social scientists often use census data to determine the proportions of individuals from different socioeconomic and ethnic groups who are members in the population of interest and select participants for their research accordingly. Note that the goal of sampling isn't always to identify a group that represents an entire country—just one that accurately reflects the particular population of interest for that study (e.g., 8-year-old girls attending public school in Toronto; infants born to teenage mothers in rural Alabama; junior high school students in New York State; newlyweds in Japan).

representative sample A group of participants in a research study who represent the larger population the scientist wants to draw conclusions about.

To illustrate how developmental researchers conduct research, we will focus on one main example. Suppose we are interested in how different styles of parenting affect child development—a broad topic. To narrow the subject, we decide to study the impact of "punitive parenting": parents using threats, punishment, and physical force (grabbing, pushing, or hitting) when a child does not obey them. Then we generate a hypothesis: Children of punitive parents have difficulty regulating their emotions; they are easily upset and slow to calm down.

We begin this section by describing the research methods or "tools" developmentalists use to collect data, using our study of punitive parenting and children's emotional development as a recurring example. Then we will explain why different types of questions call for different research designs.

Research Methods

The first step in all scientific research is to collect empirical data (i.e., evidence from an observation or experiment). Researchers use basically three ways to gather information about people: observe them, ask them, or test them.

naturalistic observation
A method of data collection in which the researcher observes individuals in their everyday settings.

Observational Research Observing individuals is a mainstay of developmental research. In **naturalistic observation**, researchers observe individuals in their everyday settings; for example, parents with small children in a shopping mall. The researcher usually does not interact with the people she is observing, but simply watches. Typically she has a check sheet with predetermined guidelines—in this case, about what parental behaviors to note as "punitive" (e.g., yelling, hitting, being sarcastic) and what children's behavior to record as indicators of poor emotional control (such as crying for three minutes or more, having a temper tantrum, or hitting the parent in frustration). The researcher may carry a stopwatch, so that she can record not just what she sees, but also how long it lasts.

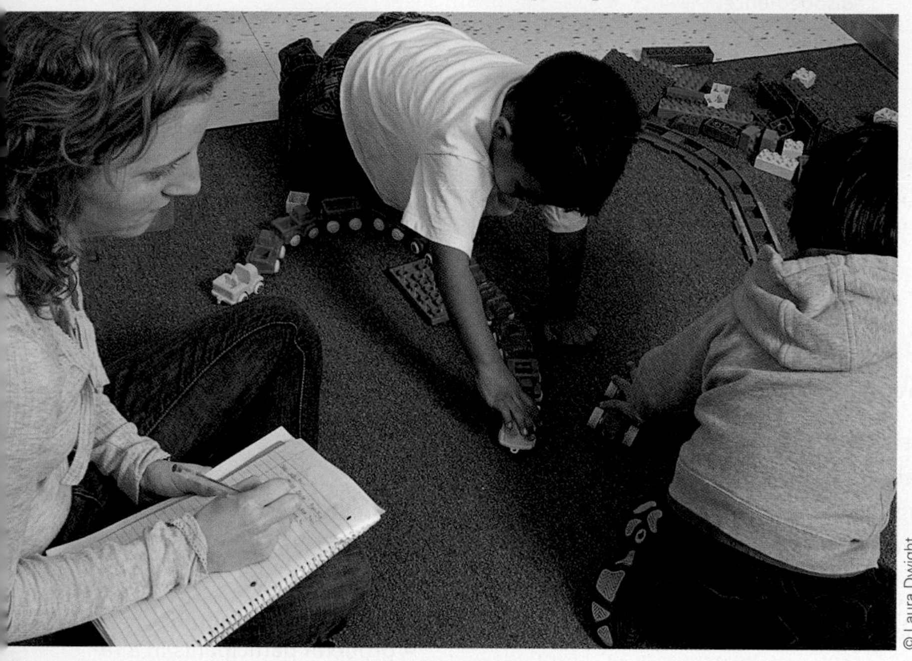
© Laura Dwight

Observation is one of the developmental scientist's most important tools.

In some cases, the observer *does* interact with the people she is watching, a method called **participant observation**. For example, one of the authors had a student who was interested in the way that adolescent girls talked about food, and the implications of this for understanding why so many girls dieted (Sugarman, 2001). To study this, she sat at the same junior high school girls' cafeteria table, every day, for an entire semester. She ate with the girls; took notes on their conversation, behavior, and what they ate; and interviewed them.

An obvious advantage of naturalistic observation is that it allows researchers to see behavior in the actual contexts where people live. The major disadvantage is time, especially if what the researcher is hoping to observe does not occur very often: An observer interested in the impact of harsh parenting on children's development might sit for hours and see only one example of punitive parenting, if that.

participant observation
A method of data collection in which the researcher observes and interacts with individuals in their everyday settings.

structured observation
A method of data collection in which the researcher creates a setting and tasks that are likely to evoke a behavior of interest.

In **structured observation**, researchers create a setting and tasks that are likely to evoke the behavior they want to observe. For our example, we might ask mothers to bring their 4- to 5-year-old child to an observation room equipped with a number of toys and interesting objects and a one-way mirror that allows us to watch the child and parent without their seeing us. We then chat with the pair for a short time to put them at ease, tell the child that everyone gets a prize when the experiment is over, and leave the room. We have assigned the mother-child pair various tasks. For example, we asked the mother to encourage the child to play with some building blocks, and then to ask the child to clean up (which will allow us to see whether the mother uses punitive or other strategies to get her child to cooperate).

To measure emotion regulation, we need to devise a situation that will allow us to see how well children manage their feelings. Here's our plan: At some point while the mother and child are playing, the researcher reenters the room with a tray holding ten items, some of which children this age like (whistles, bubbles, and stickers) and some they do not like (such as socks, a baby rattle, and a broken pair of sunglasses). We then ask the child to rank these objects from best to worst by placing them in slots marked one through ten on the tray.

Near the end of the session, we use a "disappointment task," designed to study how children control negative emotions (Cole, Zahn-Waxler, & Smith, 1994). We bring in a large, brightly wrapped gift box, give it to the child, and leave the room. However, the package contains the item the child had ranked tenth, or worst. We observe the child's reaction to the "prize" through the mirror, recording how upset the child becomes, how long the child takes to recover, and what role the mother plays in this scenario. After a short time we come back into the room with another gift box for the child and explain there had been a "terrible mistake." This box holds the child's first choice. Note that the disappointment task is mildly upsetting to some children; giving the child his or her favorite gift is intended to relieve whatever distress this test might have caused. A research review committee, which is responsible for ensuring that scientists use ethical procedures and do not cause participants in a study harm or distress, must approve the procedure before the experiment begins. (We'll say more about ethics and research later in the chapter.)

Structured observations like this enable researchers to make sure that the behavior they want to study actually occurs. This method also allows researchers to eliminate factors that might interfere with a naturalistic study, such as whether a mother is directing the way her child ranks the objects on the tray during the disappointment task, or whether the child is hungry (which might make the child more easily frustrated than usual). The main drawback is that participants may not behave naturally in an unfamiliar setting. Knowing that they are being watched, the mother may be on her "best behavior" and instruct her child to "be good," with a promise of ice cream after the session.

Self-Reports Another way to gather information is to ask individuals about themselves, or collect **self-reports**. This can be done by giving research participants questionnaires or by interviewing them face-to-face. Both interviews and questionnaires can be open-ended ("Tell me how you usually discipline your child") or structured ("Which of the following methods of discipline did you use in the previous week: [a] time-outs; [b] spanking; [c] taking away something my child enjoys; [d] yelling").

self-report A method of data collection in which the researcher asks individuals about themselves, either through questionnaires or interviews.

Well-constructed self-report measures are an important and widely used tool for developmental researchers. For our study, researchers might combine questions about routine discipline ("What do you do when your child ignores you?" and "When do you think it is necessary to hit a child who is misbehaving?") with questions about the parent's child ("When your child is upset, does it take him/her a long time to calm down?").

As in this case, surveys or interviews include questions about different aspects of the topic researchers are studying, and they often combine answers to a series of questions to make a measure or "score." For instance, at the end of a semester, most colleges and universities ask students to complete an evaluation form that has many different items to measure the quality of an instructor (e.g., how well organized he or she was, how engaging, how responsive to questions). The instructor's ratings on these different measures are combined to create an overall rating of the instructor's performance.

Self-report measures allow researchers to collect a large amount of data in a much shorter time and at a lower cost than is possible when conducting observations. But relying on self-reports has several drawbacks. First, we are dependent on respondents answering our questions accurately. Sometimes people simply do not tell the truth, although this is not as common as you might think. More frequent sources of inaccuracy are misremembering or misinterpreting the question. Promising that responses will remain anonymous, careful wording of questions, and, in interview situations, establishing rapport with the individual can help minimize these problems. Asking mothers, "When do you think it's necessary to punish a child?" is more likely to elicit honest answers than asking, "Do you beat your child?" Asking the same questions in different ways—"Have you ever smacked your child?" and, 20 questions later, "Do you agree with the saying, 'Spare the rod and spoil the child'?"—can reveal patterns or inconsistencies.

standardized tests Measures that are generally accepted by other scientists as reliable and valid, often with norms derived from their prior administration to large and representative samples.

Standardized Tests Developmental researchers also use a variety of **standardized tests** to measure intellectual level (whether general intelligence or a specific ability, such as memory), psychological characteristics (such as temperament or self-esteem), or an individual's physiological state (heart rate, patterns of brain activity, or hormone levels). In our example, we might want to measure the child's level of stress hormones before, during, and after a disappointment task to see how much the child's hormone levels fluctuate and how quickly he or she becomes stressed (e.g., Boyce, 2006).

Standardized tests have norms—average scores based on previous studies of large groups of individuals—so it is possible to compare a child with other children who have been studied by other researchers. In addition, the tests have been carefully developed and they are generally accepted by other scientists as having **reliability** (i.e., the test provides measurement that is consistent, like a ruler that yields the same result when used to measure the same object over and over again) and **validity** (i.e., the test measures what it is supposed to measure rather than something else). A measure of self-esteem that yielded markedly different scores from one day to the next or that was uncorrelated with other measures of how highly people thought of themselves wouldn't be very useful.

reliability The extent to which a measure yields assessments that are consistent, or the degree to which an instrument measures something the same way each time it is used under the same condition with the same subjects.

validity The extent to which a measure assesses what it is supposed to measure rather than something else; also can be used to refer to the truth or accuracy of a conclusion drawn from a scientific study.

However, in many cases there is no standardized test that measures exactly what the scientist is interested in. Many tests are long and many are expensive to administer, because the researcher has to purchase the test or equipment (rather than writing his or her own questions).

This, then, is the developmental scientist's basic tool kit: naturalistic and structured observations; interviews and questionnaires; plus standardized and newly developed tests. Which tools a researcher uses depends on what questions he or she wants to answer.

Research Design

Another decision researchers must make concerns how the study is going to be designed. Most developmental research uses one of three research designs: a case study, a correlational study, or an experiment.

case study An intensive study of one or a small number of individuals or families.

Case Studies A **case study** is an intensive study of one or a small number of individuals or families. In contrast to the other methods we have described, case studies allow a researcher to improvise. He or she is not limited to a particular set of observations or predetermined questions, but can follow up on an ambiguous answer, let the participant "ramble," conduct unobtrusive, naturalistic observations one day and structure situations the next, and interview neighbors, relatives, and others connected to the family. In short, case studies are open-ended. Typically, the researcher sees the individual or visits the family many, many times and records all observations and conversations in a journal. Some case studies last several years (e.g., a case study of an adolescent making the transition to young adulthood); others last several months (e.g., a case study of classroom dynamics over the course of a semester); others may be even briefer (e.g., a case study of a hyperactive child's initial response to a new medication).

For example, Alex Kotlowitz (1991) devoted two years to a case study of Lafeyette and Pharaoh Rivers, two young boys growing up in Chicago's Henry Horner Housing Project. The project was an isolated enclave where children lived in hand-to-mouth poverty and witnessed crime and violence daily. Staying alive—something better-off children rarely think about—was a priority. The boys talked about what they wanted to be *if* (not *when*) they grew up. When Kotlowitz told the boys' mother that he wanted to write a book about her sons and other kids in the neighborhood, she liked the idea but paused and then said, "But you know, there are no children here. They've seen too much to be children." Kotlowitz used *There Are No Children Here* as the title of his book.

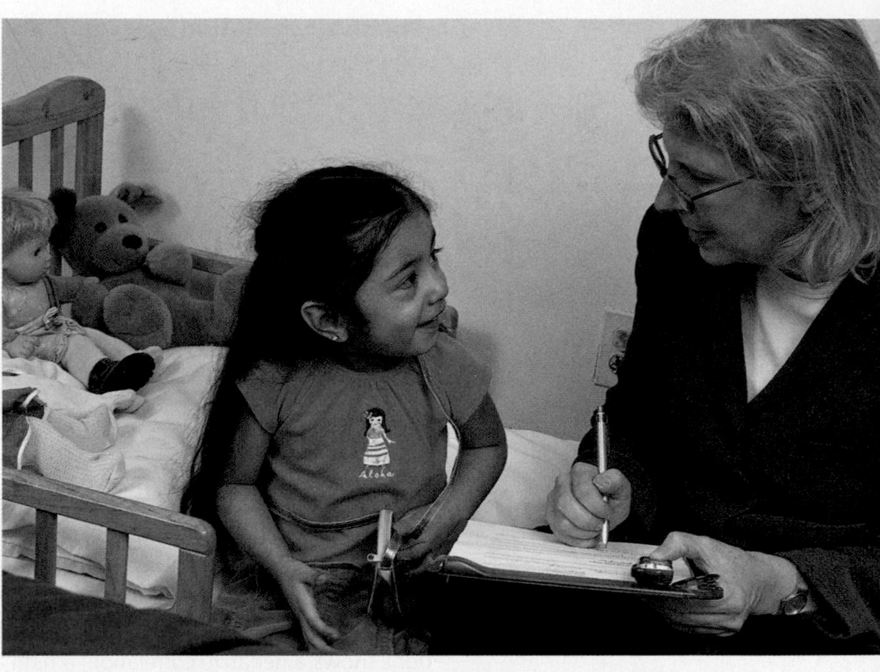

© Laura Dwight

In addition to observation, developmental scientists often gather information by interviewing research participants.

An important role of case studies in developmental psychology is inspiration. Freud's theory of psychosexual development was based on case studies of his patients. Likewise, Piaget's theory of cognitive development was based on intensive interviews and observations of a small number of children, including his own. No other research method provides as rich detail, intimate revelations, or complete pictures. Often, case studies generate hypotheses that can be systematically tested in a larger sample. But case studies have built-in limitations.

Because a case study is unique, the findings cannot be *generalized* or applied to others. (In evaluating all research, not just case studies, you should always ask how far the findings can be generalized beyond the specifics of the study.) Because a case study is intensive and long term, it is difficult for the researcher *not* to become personally involved with the subjects. He or she may ask leading questions, "fill in" gaps in participants' self-descriptions, or interpret what individuals do and say as upholding a favored theory. Because a case study is freeform, it's difficult to compare with other case studies or to verify results with other types of research.

Correlational Studies Often, developmentalists want to "connect the dots." In a **correlational study**, researchers examine two or more variables to see if they are linked in any way. A *correlation* is a relationship or connection between two things. The "things" might be age, income, grade-point average, or marital status—anything that (a) varies or changes and (b) can be counted, scored, rated, or measured in some way. Two variables are correlated if they change together.

correlational study A study in which the researcher examines two or more variables to see if they are linked in any way.

Correlations can be positive or negative. In a **positive correlation**, two variables change in the *same* direction: High levels of one variable are associated with high levels of the other, and low levels of one are associated with low levels of the other. For example, parents' and children's IQ scores are positively correlated (Scarr & Weinberg, 1983). If parents score above average (or below average) on IQ tests, their children usually score above (or below) average on IQ tests. Note that we said "usually": Correlations are rarely perfect; some parent-child scores differ widely. In a **negative correlation**, two variables are linked in the *opposite* direction; the higher the level of one variable, the lower the level of the other. For example, a high level of watching television is correlated with low school grades (Roberts, Henriksen, & Foehr, 2004) as shown in Figure 1.3. Correlations range from –1.0 (reflecting a very strong negative correlation) to +1.0 (reflecting a very strong positive correlation). In developmental science, a correlation of .2 (or –.2) is considered mild; of .5 (or –.5) moderate; and of .8 (or –.8) strong.

positive correlation When two variables are correlated such that high levels of one variable are associated with high levels of the other, and low levels of one are associated with low levels of the other.

negative correlation When two variables are correlated such that high levels of one variable are associated with low levels of the other, and low levels of one are associated with high levels of the other.

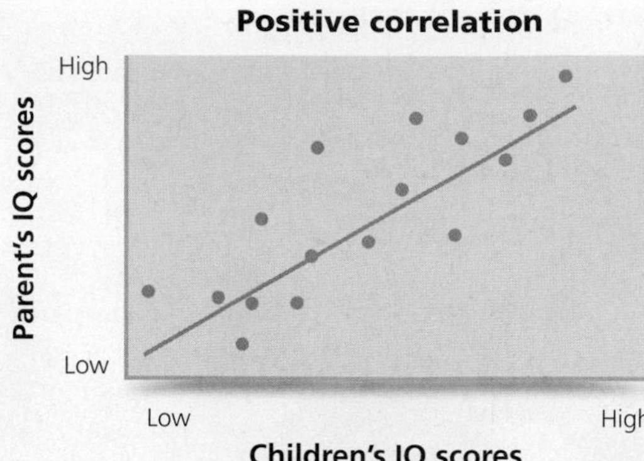

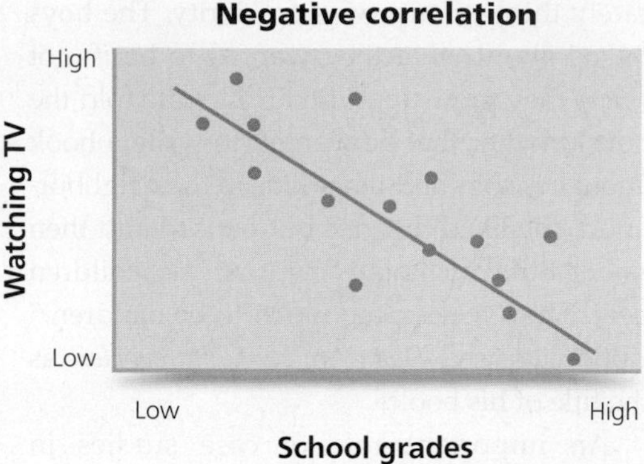

FIGURE 1.3

Positive and Negative Correlations

These scatterplots represent correlations between two variables. Each point on the graph represents an individual pair of scores, one for each of the variables. The scatterplot on the left shows a positive correlation; parents with high IQ scores tend to have children with high IQ scores, whereas lower parental IQ is associated with lower child IQ. The scatterplot on the right shows a negative correlation; a high amount of TV-watching time is associated with *lower* grades in school, whereas children who watch less TV have higher grades. Keep in mind, however, that just because two variables are correlated, we still cannot determine if there is a cause-and-effect relation between them.

Developmentalists might look at the correlation between popularity and self-esteem in middle school, or between watching television and IQ scores. They frequently examine correlations between some aspect of development and chronological age (e.g., the number of words in a child's vocabulary and his/her age). Findings from correlational studies are useful in establishing whether phenomena are related to one another, but limited by the fact they cannot establish cause and effect. Nevertheless, correlational research is by far the most commonly used research design in the study of human development.

The difference between correlation and causation is important to understand. Popularity and self-esteem in middle school are correlated: If one is high, the other is usually high, too (Hartup, 1983). But this could be because the first causes the second (being popular causes children to feel better about themselves), because the second causes the first (feeling good about oneself leads to popularity), or the result of a third, unmeasured factor (coming from a wealthy family causes both popularity and high self-esteem). One of the more common mistakes in interpreting and reporting research in the mass media is confusing correlation with causation. A study finding that children who play violent video games are more aggressive does not prove that watching violent games *causes* aggression (as many may interpret the finding), because it is probably the case that aggressive children are more likely than nonaggressive ones to choose to play violent games.

Despite the fact that correlational studies cannot by themselves demonstrate cause and effect, an important step in proving cause and effect is showing that, at a minimum, the presumed "cause" and the presumed "effect" are related. If we did a study on parental punitiveness and children's emotional regulation and found that they weren't even correlated, further investigation of whether one caused the other would be a waste of time.

Experiments Experiments are the only reliable way to establish cause and effect. In an **experiment**, researchers are in control. Instead of simply observing behavior or collecting data, they do something that might change the participants' behavior and study the consequences. The researchers' hypothesis is, "If we do *X* (feed children sugary soft drinks for a year), the subjects in the study will do *Y* (become obese)." *X*, the element the researchers introduce or manipulate, is called the **independent variable** (in this case, whether the child did or did not receive the soft drinks). *Y*, the consequence the researchers want to measure (here, the child's weight), is called the **dependent variable** (it *depends* on the researchers' actions). Ideally, every aspect of the experiment is the same for all participants except for the independent variable.

experiment A research design in which the researcher controls conditions in the hopes of drawing conclusions about cause and effect.

independent variable In an experiment, the element the researcher introduces or manipulates in order to examine its effects on one or more outcomes of interest; in nonexperimental research, this can refer to variables that are used to predict outcomes of interest.

dependent variable In an experiment, the outcome of interest; in nonexperimental research, this can refer to variables that are predicted by other factors.

One way of testing the hypothesis that parental punitiveness leads to problems in emotion regulation is to manipulate the former and see what happens to the latter. But it would be unethical to try to *make* parents behave in a way that we think is bad for children. What do we do? Suppose we try to teach parents *non*punitive ways of handling their children, such as reasoning and distraction, by enrolling them in a program designed to educate parents, and then see if children's emotion regulation *improves* as a result. The hypothesis is, if punitive mothers take part in this program (*X*, the independent variable), they will be less dictatorial and severe with their child, and the child's ability to control his or her emotions will improve (*Y*, the dependent variable).

The first step is to identify a sample of punitive mothers, perhaps from a structured observation, and ask them to participate in the educational program. A month after the program ends, we ask the mothers to participate in another round of structured observations with new tasks. If the mothers act differently than they did during the first observation, and their children are calmer, the researchers can conclude that the program *caused* the change. Their hypothesis was supported and the program was successful. (And if the mothers and/or children do not behave differently, we know the program did not work as hoped.)

There's one hitch, though: We need to make certain that the experience of participating in the experiment, by itself (e.g., just the mere fact that one is being observed by researchers could affect a person's behavior), or some other influence we did not anticipate—not the educational program—wasn't the cause of this change. The most common way to guard against this is to divide the participants into two groups: the **treatment** (or **experimental**) **group**, who participate in the education program, and the **control group**, who go through the two structured observations but do not participate in the education program. To select these groups, we use **random assignment**: Mothers are assigned to one group or the other by a flip of a coin (or another method that depends on chance). Only if we find a significant difference between mothers in the treatment and control groups (and their children) can we conclude that the education program caused a change. By the way, you might be interested to know that research has shown that such programs can teach parents to change their parenting style (Collins et al., 2000).

treatment (or **experimental**) **group** In an experiment, a group of participants who receive a predetermined program, intervention, or treatment and who then are compared with a control group and/or other treatment groups.

control group In an experiment, a comparison group of participants who do not receive the predetermined program, intervention, or treatment received by the treatment group.

random assignment In an experiment, the practice of assigning participants to treatment or control groups on a random basis, to attempt to limit any observed differences between them to the presence or absence of the treatment.

The obvious advantage of experiments is control. But like other research methods, experiments have drawbacks. Because researchers design and control all phases of an experiment, the situation in which data are collected may be artificial and unfamiliar, and the results may not apply to real-life situations. Suppose you were asked to participate in a study on dating with people you had not met before; would you behave the same way you would at a party or in a local hangout? Some participants might be intimidated by a university setting and a scientist ("Dr. Jackson") in a lab coat, both symbols of authority. In our example, mothers may use techniques they learned in the parenting program when they know that they are being observed, but not in their everyday settings. In addition, many questions simply cannot be studied experimentally because it would be unethical to deliberately try to do something that might be harmful to a participant. We can't do experiments to learn how infants' brain development is affected by not having adequate social stimulation, how children are influenced by peer rejection, or how poverty affects adolescent substance abuse. These are all important questions, but ones where a traditional experimental design would be unethical.

natural experiment A research design that takes advantage of naturally occurring events that affect some individuals but not others, or that makes use of an opportunity to measure development before and after a naturally occurring event has occurred.

Natural experiments are one way of overcoming some of the limitations of laboratory experiments. Instead of calling for volunteers, researchers study groups that already exist in the real world. For example, we could identify a parent education program in the community that teaches nonpunitive parenting and compare the children of parents who were in the program with the children of parents from the same community who were not. In this case, we have our "treatment" group (program participants) and our "control" group (nonparticipants), but we also have a big problem: We don't know if the parents who choose to enroll in parenting programs are different from those who do not in ways that might affect their child's development. Perhaps the program participants were more motivated to raise their children in positive ways and treated their children differently because of that, even before they started the parenting program. Perhaps some parents enrolled in the program because they had a child who was difficult to discipline. Because this would be a natural experiment, it is impossible to conclude that any differences between the groups were *caused* by the parenting program.

Studying Change over Time

Developmental researchers face a special challenge in research design: assessing consistency and change over time. The three basic strategies for studying development over time are longitudinal research, cross-sectional research, and accelerated longitudinal (or cross-sequential) research (see Figure 1.4).

longitudinal study A study in which researchers follow the same individuals over time and assess them more than once.

Longitudinal Studies In a **longitudinal study**, researchers follow the same individuals and assess them at regular intervals. This type of study can be done with one group (to see how emotional control develops over a period for children in general) or with several groups (to see how children from punitive versus nonpunitive homes compare emotionally over this age span). Researchers may use these findings to chart *developmental trajectories*, which show the pattern of development over time for one or more groups (Nagin & Tremblay, 2005). The longitudinal approach can also be used to assess stability in characteristics like temperament, extraversion, or memory.

The advantage of longitudinal studies is that they allow researchers to study change or stability *directly*. Because they study the same people, usually in the same setting (a laboratory or the participants' homes) and with the same tools (observation, interviews, tests, or some combination of these), researchers can be reasonably sure that changes in what they are studying are the result of the passage of time.

On the downside, longitudinal studies are time-consuming and costly. In long-term longitudinal research, researchers may be required to commit 10 years or more to a study—and therefore wait 10 years or more for results. Individuals may decide to quit the study or simply drift away. Furthermore, participating in a long-term study may alter behavior. Being tested and retested might make people feel "special" or "different," self-conscious or bored, which will be reflected in their behavior and answers. Knowing that they will see the researchers again (and again) may make participants especially eager to cooperate or present themselves in a positive light. And, of course, there is always the possibility that some event that occurs during the course of the study could change the outcome. Suppose that you tracked the emotional development of children in New York City in a study that started in 1999 and ended in 2002. It is quite possible that any change you observed in children's emotional functioning was due to the events of September 11, 2001, and not the fact that they grew older.

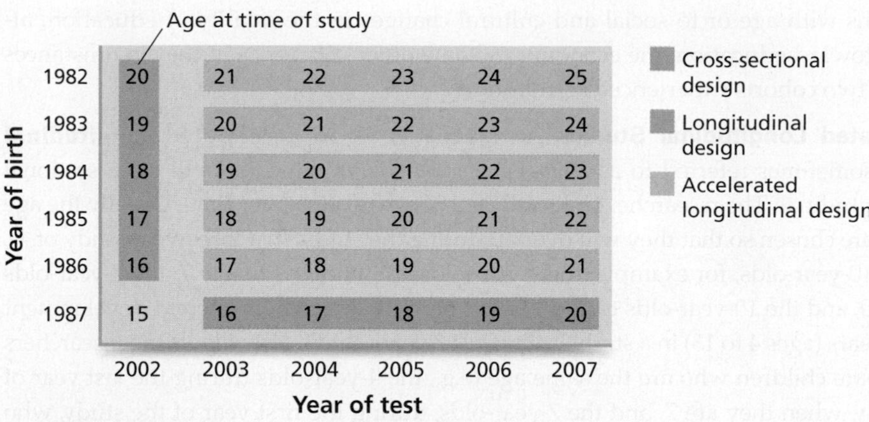

FIGURE 1.4

Research Designs for Studies of Development

Developmental scientists often have to make decisions about how to study whether some aspect of development changes with age. This figure illustrates three common approaches. In *longitudinal* studies, the same group of individuals is followed over a period of time. The purple shaded area shows a group of individuals who were originally tested in 2003 when they were 16 years old and then again every year until 2007 when they were 20. In *cross-sectional* studies, individuals of different ages are studied at one point in time. For example, the area shaded in blue shows a study conducted in 2002 that tested individuals who ranged in age from 16 to 20. Finally, in *accelerated longitudinal* (also called *cross-sequential*) studies, individuals from multiple age groups are selected and studied over time simultaneously. The orange shaded areas show that groups of participants who were 17, 18, 19, 20, or 21 in 2003 were all studied for 5 years.

Cross-Sectional Studies In a **cross-sectional study**, researchers study individuals of different ages at the same time. For example, they might place mothers with a child who is 2, 4, or 6 years old (one age group at a time) in an observation room where there are more toys than children, and record the consequences. Instead of showing development over time (a developmental trajectory), a cross-sectional study measures average behavior at different ages.

cross-sectional study A study in which researchers compare individuals of different ages at the same time.

The advantages of cross-sectional studies are that they are less expensive than longitudinal studies, yield immediate results, eliminate the effects of repeated testing, and, if well controlled, rule out alternative explanations of what seem to be age differences. But there are disadvantages as well. Unless the age groups are carefully matched on characteristics that might affect the outcome (e.g., their family circumstances, gender, intelligence, etc.), any differences between them may reflect personal and social differences, as well as age. Usually, a researcher makes sure that the age groups are comparable on these and other relevant characteristics.

The results of a cross-sectional study may also be skewed by the **cohort effect**: People of different ages grew up in different eras and had different experiences. Barring an event like 9/11, this is not a problem when the groups are very close in age (e.g., if we are comparing 3-, 4-, and 5-year-olds) but could be a substantial factor in a study comparing 10-year-olds and 20-year-olds. People born 10 years apart belong to different generations, which may have a significant effect on their personalities, values, skills, and beliefs. If we found, for example, that a sample of 10-year-olds born in 1998 scored higher on a measure of educational ambition than a sample of 20-year-olds born in 1988, we could not tell whether this was due to an increase in educational

cohort effect The influence of the fact that people of different ages grew up in different eras and had different experiences, which complicates drawing conclusions about age differences found in cross-sectional studies.

ambitions with age or to social and cultural changes in the quality of education, attitudes toward education, the economy, or some other difference in the circumstances that the two cohorts experienced as children.

accelerated longitudinal study (sometimes referred to as a *cross-sequential study*) A study that is both cross-sectional and longitudinal, in which the researcher follows different age groups over time and assesses them more than once.

Accelerated Longitudinal Studies An alternative is an **accelerated longitudinal study** (sometimes referred to as a *cross-sequential study*), which is both cross-sectional *and* longitudinal: The researchers follow different age groups over time. Usually the age groups are chosen so that they will overlap during the study. In a three-year study of 4-, 7-, and 10-year-olds, for example, the 4-year-olds are followed to age 7, the 7-year-olds to age 10, and the 10-year-olds to age 13. This permits researchers to chart development over 9 years (ages 4 to 13) in a study lasting just 3 years, and it also allows the researchers to compare children who are the same age (e.g., the 4-year-olds during the last year of the study, when they are 7, and the 7-year-olds, during the first year of the study, who also are 7) but who are from different cohorts. But as in cross-sectional studies, matching study participants on socioeconomic level, family situation, and other variables may be difficult. An accelerated longitudinal study also takes more time than a cross-sectional one, but depending on the age range studied, it is much faster than a longitudinal study.

Research Ethics

Remember Little Albert, the boy we discussed earlier in the chapter who was conditioned to fear white, furry things in an experiment? Watson and his colleague (Watson & Rayner, 1920) could have used behavior modification to extinguish his fears, but they lost track of the child. For all we know he lived in terror of white dogs, shaggy white rugs, and who knows what else for the rest of his life, never knowing why—or that he was a famous figure in the history of psychology! But that experiment was conducted nearly 100 years ago, before scientists uniformly adhered to a common code of ethics.

Today developmental scientists judge themselves—and one another—by a strict ethical code. The following is a summary of the ethical standards published by the Society for Research in Child Development (1993).

Rule 1: Nonharmful Procedures. Researchers should not use any procedure that might harm a child, physically or psychologically. For this and other reasons, all colleges, universities, and other research organizations have review committees that must approve scientists' research plans.

Rule 2: Informed Consent. First and foremost, researchers must obtain the individual's voluntary willingness to participate in the study by describing the study in terms the individual can understand or, with infants, paying attention to any signs of distress. Under virtually all circumstances, researchers studying individuals under 18 also must obtain the parents' written consent (one exception is if the research is part of a school's normal educational program). In addition, researchers must inform parents, teachers, and others who might be affected by a study about any feature of the research that might affect their willingness to participate. When researchers feel that a degree of deception is necessary, they must justify this to ethics committees. If, at any point, they suspect that a study may jeopardize the child's well-being or have unanticipated consequences, they must inform the participant or, if a minor, the child's parents or guardians and attempt to correct the situation.

Rule 3: Confidentiality. Researchers must conceal the identity of participants, in their records and informal discussions as well as in published reports.

Rule 4: Debriefing. Immediately after the study, researchers should inform participants of any deceptions they employed and of the study's purpose. In addition, researchers must keep in mind that because their conclusions might have a powerful impact on participants, they must exercise caution in their public statements or private advice.

Rule 5: Implications. In publishing research and making public statements, researchers must consider the social and human implications of their findings. This does not mean that they should hesitate to publish controversial results, but rather that they should make every effort to ensure that their results are not misinterpreted or their statements misquoted in the media.

Rule 6: Misconduct. Universities and other institutions that employ researchers are required by law to have review boards that monitor the practices of their scientists to make sure they are in compliance with the rules of ethical conduct. These boards review proposed research before it is conducted and investigate any allegations of misconduct in research that is under way or that has been completed.

Researchers who do not comply with review boards or who engage in professional misconduct (fabrication of data, plagiarism, and the like) or personal misconduct (violation of university codes or criminal law) face severe consequences, which may include losing their job or their ability to receive public funding for their work, or in some cases, criminal penalties. (For a summary of this section, see "Interim Summary 1.3: The Scientific Study of Development.")

DEVELOPMENTAL SCIENCE IN THE REAL WORLD

Developmental science can have a powerful impact on how we view people of different ages—as parents, as professionals, and as a society. The study of people of different ages provides advice to the following:

- *Parents:* First-time parents, especially, may feel frustrated, angry, and depressed because they do not know what to expect from a child at a given age and see the child's behavior as reflecting on their skill as parents (or lack thereof). Indeed, unrealistic expectations sometimes contribute to child abuse. Developmental science provides parents with information on what behavior is normal at a given age, what behavior is not normal and suggests that they should consult a professional, and what effects different approaches to parenting have on childen. For example, a punitive approach might be effective in dangerous situations (the child runs into the street), but it creates problems when it is the only form of discipline parents use.
- *Teachers:* Knowing what children at a given age can understand and what they cannot helps teachers to develop age-appropriate lesson plans and the most effective ways of dealing with misbehavior. If a teacher recognizes a gifted child in his class, how can he stimulate that child intellectually without isolating the child socially? Should he recommend the child be moved to a special program?
- *Health care practitioners:* Similarly, knowing what is normal and what is atypical for children at different ages helps in diagnosis of problems and the design and delivery of treatment. For example, understanding how children of different ages think about illness helps pediatricians better explain to their patients why they need to treat their problem in a particular way.
- *Program developers:* Professionals who design programs for "special children," or afterschool programs for toddlers, children, and adolescents, need to know what their young clients need. Today we take for granted Head Start, a program designed to bring poor children up to the level of their better-off peers before they start first grade. When initiated in 1965, however, it was considered a radical departure from standard schooling.
- *Policymakers:* Elected and appointed government officials write and enforce laws regarding children and youth and decide which programs should be funded

INTERIM SUMMARY 1.3

The Scientific Study of Development

The Scientific Method	1. Formulate a question. 2. Develop a **hypothesis**. 3. Conduct a study that tests the hypothesis. 4. Analyze the data. 5. Make the findings public.
Research Methods	
■ Observational research	Conduct naturalistic, participant, or structured observation.
■ Self-reports	Ask individuals about themselves using questionnaires or interviews.
■ Standardized tests	Administer an established test that has norms.
Research Design	
■ Case studies	Intensive study of one or a small number of individuals or families.
■ Correlational studies	Examination of two or more variables to see if they are linked in any way.
■ Experiments	Manipulations of one variable and observation of the effect of that manipulation on another variable, while holding all other factors constant.
Studying Change over Time	
■ Longitudinal studies	Researchers follow the same individuals and assess them at regular intervals.
■ Cross-sectional studies	Researchers study individuals of different ages at the same time.
■ Accelerated longitudinal studies	Both cross-sectional *and* longitudinal: Researchers follow different age groups over time.
Research Ethics	■ Rule 1: Nonharmful Procedures ■ Rule 2: Informed Consent ■ Rule 3: Confidentiality ■ Rule 4: Debriefing ■ Rule 5: Consider Implications ■ Rule 6: Monitor Misconduct

and which should not. Although policymakers may not interact directly with children outside their family and social circle, their impact on children is powerful. Here's one example: In recent decades, public concern—and political debate—about juvenile crime has escalated. Should the courts treat juveniles who commit serious crimes as adults, subject to adult penalties? Science cannot decide what is "right" or "wrong." But developmental scientists can provide decision makers with advice based on research, not on political considerations or popular opinion. In our legal system, individuals accused of a crime must be "competent to stand trial"—that is, capable of understanding the trial process and contributing to their own defense. A recent study found that 16- and 17-year-olds are just as competent to stand trial as adults, but that this is not the case for juveniles 15 and younger (Grisso et al., 2003).

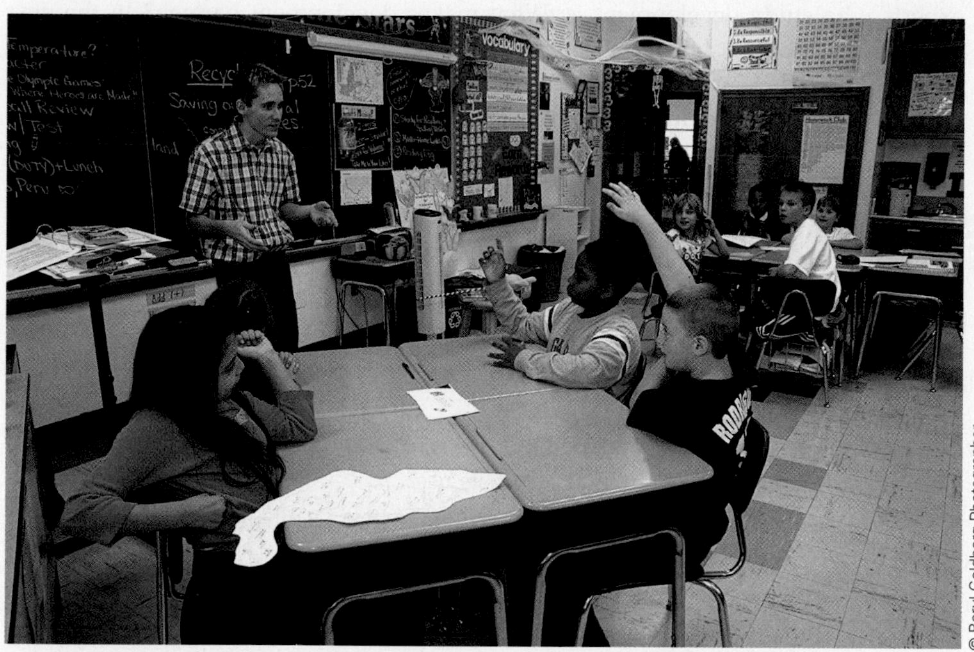

© Beryl Goldberg Photographer

Findings from scientific studies of development often have practical implications for teachers and other individuals who work with children.

- *Business and industry leaders:* Children, teenagers, and young adults are among the most influential consumers in our society. Although they may not pay for items themselves, they influence decisions on purchases of everything from breakfast cereals, to athletic shoes and jeans, to video games, iPods, and other high-tech goods. From a marketing point of view, it's important to understand how individuals think and what motivates them. (For a summary of this section, see "Interim Summary 1.4: Developmental Science in the Real World.")

SUMMING UP AND LOOKING AHEAD

In this chapter, we've introduced you to the study of human development, including the sort of questions that developmentalists ask, their theoretical approaches, how they investigate questions scientifically, and how the knowledge gained from this research might be used. As noted earlier, one of the questions that has long fascinated

INTERIM SUMMARY 1.4

Developmental Science in the Real World

Developmental Science Has Practical Implications for

- Parents
- Teachers
- Health care practitioners
- Program developers
- Policymakers
- Business and industry leaders

For further information go to http://www.apa.org/topics/psychologycareer.html

experts who study development is: What makes development happen? In the next chapter, we'll look at what probably is the longest-running controversy in the history of human development: whether development is mostly a product of nature (our genes) or mostly due to nurture (the environment).

The answer may surprise you.

HERE'S WHAT YOU SHOULD KNOW

Did You Get It?

After reading this chapter, you should understand the following:

- The main reasons scientists study development, and the types of questions they ask
- How development is defined
- The five basic principles of development
- The main theories of development, and the people and ideas associated with them
- The methods, designs, and types of studies that developmental scientists use
- The ethical guidelines that scientists who study children must follow
- Some ways in which the results of developmental research are applied in the real world

Important Terms and Concepts

accelerated longitudinal study (p. 30)
accommodation (p. 15)
adolescence (p. 5)
assimilation (p. 15)
behavioral genetics (p. 17)
behavioral therapy (p. 13)
case study (p. 24)
classical conditioning (p. 12)
cognitive development (p. 5)
cognitive-developmental perspective (p. 14)
cohort effect (p. 29)
concrete operational stage (p. 14)
control group (p. 27)
correlational study (p. 25)
cross-sectional study (p. 29)
dependent variable (p. 27)
development (p. 7)
developmental scientists (p. 4)
developmental trajectory (p. 9)
dynamic systems theory (p. 18)
early childhood (p. 5)
ecological perspective (p. 15)
empirical evidence (p. 4)
evolutionary perspective (p. 18)
experiment (p. 27)
formal operational stage (p. 15)
hypothesis (p. 20)
independent variable (p. 27)
infancy (p. 5)
later adulthood (p. 5)
learning theory (p. 12)
longitudinal study (p. 28)
middle adulthood (p. 5)
middle childhood (p. 5)
natural experiment (p. 28)
naturalistic observation (p. 22)
negative correlation (p. 25)
observational learning (p. 13)
operant conditioning (p. 13)
participant observation (p. 22)
physical development (p. 5)
positive correlation (p. 25)
prenatal period (p. 5)
preoperational stage (p. 14)
psychoanalytic theory (p. 11)
psychosocial development (p. 12)
random assignment (p. 27)
reliability (p. 24)
replication (p. 21)
representative sample (p. 21)
scientific method (p. 20)
self-report (p. 23)
sensorimotor stage (p. 14)
social learning theory (p. 13)
sociocultural perspective (p. 17)
socioemotional development (p. 5)
standardized tests (p. 24)
structured observation (p. 22)
theory (p. 10)
treatment (or experimental) group (p. 27)
validity (p. 24)
young adulthood (p. 5)

CHAPTER 2

Nature with Nurture

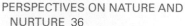

© Mascarucci/Corbis

human genome The complete set of genes for the creation and development of the human organism.

In February 2001—to much acclaim—scientists published a map of the **human genome**, the complete set of genes for building and operating a human body (IHGSC, 2001; Venter et al., 2001). For the first time ever, a species could read its own instruction manual (Ridley, 2003)! The goal now is to determine which genes influence which characteristics. The hope is that the genome will provide insights into even complex behavior and enable us to prevent or reverse diseases with a genetic component. Since 2001, discoveries about human genes have escalated. New findings are published almost every month. But the headlines that accompany popular articles about this research are often misleading.

Nothing as complex as human intelligence is "determined" by a single gene, or even multiple genes. The same is true of mental health, the aging process, and even many aspects of physical appearance. Scientists used to think that genes were stable, fixed units of heredity, passed from generation to generation. New research has revealed that genes are more variable and complex than anyone imagined 25 years ago. Almost inevitably, and ironically, these revelations led scientists to "rediscover" the environment. Genes do not act in a vacuum (Plomin, 2004). One cannot understand genes without considering their surroundings—at the cellular level, in a living organism, and from a broader sociocultural perspective.

The early part of the twenty-first century has been a remarkable "age of discovery" for developmental scientists. New lines of research and new insights have led us to reexamine not only our explanations of development but also the questions we ask. This chapter introduces current thinking about "what makes development happen." We focus on four main questions:

- How have ideas about nature and nurture changed?
- What are genes? What exactly do they do?
- What is the "environment"?
- How do the genetic code and environmental contexts interact in development?

PERSPECTIVES ON NATURE AND NURTURE

For centuries, scientists and philosophers have debated how and why people turn out the way they do. How can it be that each person is like all other humans in some ways and yet unique? What roles do nature and nurture, heredity and experience, play in who we become? Over time, four main views have been put forward:

1. Development is driven by nature.
2. Development is driven by nurture.
3. Development is part nature, part nurture.
4. Development results from the interaction of nature with nurture.

All of these views are still alive in popular culture—for example, in how we think about intelligence. Ask yourself this: Why are some individuals exceptionally quick, other individuals slow, and most individuals bright but not brilliant? Many people believe intelligence is innate; thus, some children are simply born smart (the nature view). Some people hold that intelligence is more a result of experience, of having well-educated parents, going to good schools, being encouraged to ask questions and find answers, and making friends whose families hold similar values (the nurture view). Others feel that intelligence is a little bit of both; that is, brains plus upbringing contribute (the nature + nurture position). We'll look at these perspectives, and then introduce the fourth—and newest—view, that genes and environment are in constant interplay.

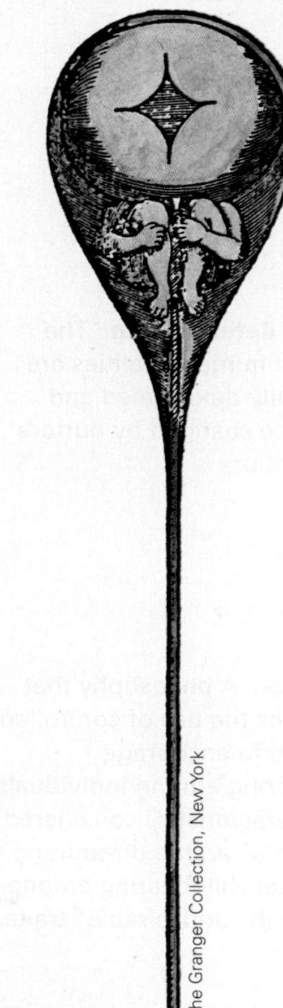
The Granger Collection, New York

FIGURE 2.1

Preformationism

Preformationists believed that the adult who would ultimately emerge was already present at the time of conception—or perhaps even before.

Development Is Driven by Nature

The idea that intelligence and other characteristics are innate or inborn, not acquired or learned, called **nativism**, has a long history (Spelke & Newport, 1998).

Preformationism In the seventeenth century, biologists and others took the concept of inborn traits quite literally. The prevailing view was that the embryo was *preformed*, a miniature adult whose future anatomy and behavior were already determined (Ariès, 1962). Some held that the "little person" was in the father's sperm; others, that he or she was in the mother's egg (see Figure 2.1). But preformation was assumed; the man or woman who eventually emerged was already present at the time of conception—or perhaps even before—just bottled up and miniaturized, waiting to grow into a full-sized adult. Well into the seventeenth century, paintings portrayed young children as miniature adults—with adult-like features, in adult clothes and adult poses.

The belief in **preformationism** was accompanied by beliefs about human nature. In general, Western culture has viewed children as innately bad (Clarke-Stewart, 1998). This outlook comes from the biblical concept of "original sin," the belief that all human beings are descended from Adam and Eve and inherit the weakness that led them to disobey God and eat fruit from the Tree of Knowledge. As a result, they and their descendants were expelled from the Garden of Eden. All humans inherit this original sin.

The Puritans, for example, believed that children were, by nature, evil and vulnerable to temptation. Parents had an obligation to teach children morality, by whatever means necessary. This meant keeping a constant, watchful eye on the child and punishing transgressions, for the child's own good. A parent's main role in development was "beating the devil" out of his or her children, sometimes literally. The idea that children are trouble waiting to happen—in adolescence if not before—remains part of Western folk wisdom.

nativism The idea that human characteristics are innate or inborn, not acquired or learned.

preformationism The seventeenth-century theory of inheritance that hypothesized that all the characteristics of an adult were prefigured in miniature within either the sperm or the ovum.

Rousseau's Innocent Babes The French philosopher Jean Jacques Rousseau (1762/1911) was an exception. He rejected both preformationism and the idea that children, like wild horses, needed to be broken. Rather, he believed that children are innocent at birth and develop according to nature's plan, much as a flower develops. A tulip bulb is not a little flower, nor does it have a tiny little tulip inside of it—it is something entirely different. But the development of a tulip from a bulb is predetermined, in the sense that it is directed by nature and influenced only slightly by the environment. Depending on the weather and soil—and the gardener—the flower may be strong and sturdy or weak and short-lived. Thus the environment matters, but nature plays the leading role. Under no circumstances will a tulip bulb develop into a crocodile or even a rose bush.

Rousseau saw child development in much the same way. Infants are not miniature adults; neither are they rife with temptation. Children are innocent at birth, and development follows nature's plan. Like flowers, with proper nurturing children grow up into beautiful beings. A parent's job is to protect the child from harmful interference and let the child's development unfold. The expression "innocent as a baby" comes from Rousseau. So did the open school movement, carried forward today by Montessori schools, which hold that children should follow their own interests and not be bound by rigid curricula.

Genetic Determinism and Eugenics Genetics was the cutting edge of science at the beginning of the twentieth century, much as it is today. Unlike today, however, early genetics was largely speculative. Scientists could study patterns of heredity only indirectly, and they did not know how or why they occurred.

genetic determinism The idea that human qualities are genetically determined and cannot be changed by nurture or education.

A number of scientists (and nonscientists) came to believe in **genetic determinism**: the idea that human qualities are genetically determined and cannot be changed by nurture or education. Preformationism and genetic determinism share a central assumption. Internal (natural, genetic) factors control development, and external (nurturing, environmental) factors have little impact. Thus, the complete individual is already present in the fertilized egg—literally, according to preformationism—or locked in genes, and development is merely a process of growing.

Carried to an extreme, genetic determinism led to one of the most disturbing chapters in early twentieth-century science, the eugenics movement (Rutter, 2006). ("Eu-" comes from the Greek word for "good," so **eugenics** means "good genes.") Eugenicists advocated the use of controlled breeding to encourage childbearing among people with characteristics considered "desirable" and to discourage (or eliminate) childbearing among those with "undesirable" traits, often members of ethnic minority groups.

eugenics A philosophy that advocates the use of controlled breeding to encourage childbearing among individuals with characteristics considered "desirable" and to discourage (or eliminate) childbearing among those with "undesirable" traits.

Farmers practice selective breeding all the time, to improve the quality of their livestock. Eugenicists sought to apply this idea to *human* populations. The best-known example was Hitler's effort to "purify" the Aryan race by exterminating Jews, gypsies [or Romany], Poles, homosexuals, and other "undesirables" in Nazi Germany during World War II. But there were advocates of forced sterilization of people who were mentally challenged and other groups in the United States as well.

Perhaps because of this shameful history, the study of genetic influences on *normal* human development fell into disrepute among developmental scientists and was not revisited until the latter part of the twentieth century (Rutter, 2006). Even today the idea that some characteristics are genetically determined remains strong. Think how often we say someone is a "born musician" or a "born athlete." Likewise, Americans, especially, tend to hold that some people are "born smart" and others, not so smart (Holloway, 1988).

Development Is Driven by Nurture

At the opposite extreme were those who believed that external forces are entirely responsible for development. *Environmentalists* hold that the newborn is unformed, like a lump of clay, and the individual's characteristics are entirely the product of experience, upbringing, and learning.

The Blank Slate The English philosopher John Locke (1690) introduced the environmentalist view in a highly influential essay, "Concerning Human Understanding." At the time, it was assumed that human nature was predetermined. Philosophers and religious thinkers may have disagreed about whether human nature was good or evil, but they agreed that it was fixed by the time the child was born, and impossible to alter. Locke had a radically different idea.

tabula rasa ("blank slate") The notion, usually associated with the philosopher John Locke, that nothing about development is predetermined, and that the child is entirely a product of his or her environment and experience.

Locke argued that the infant's mind is a **tabula rasa**, or "blank slate." In his view, *nothing* about development was predetermined; *everything* the child becomes is a product of his or her environment and experience. Childhood is a formative period, and parents have responsibility for teaching children reason, self-restraint, and respect for authority. Whatever successes—or failings—children exhibit are the result of their experiences.

The idea that nurture was the driving force behind development dominated nineteenth-century thinking and spilled over into the twentieth century. One social consequence was the mental hygiene movement (Rutter, 2006). Until this time, the "insane" were believed to be possessed by demons, and they were locked up in asylums, chained, beaten, and generally treated no better than animals. Their psychological condition was considered irreversible—and threatening. Advocates of mental hygiene, in contrast, took an environmentalist view. They held that insanity was an illness that, like other illnesses, could be treated and cured. The first step was "cleaning up" the environment in which disturbed people were housed.

Watson's Behaviorism In academic circles, the two dominant views of development during the first half of the twentieth century—learning theory and psychoanalytic theory—saw development primarily as the product of experience, not nature (see Chapter 1). Watson's theory of behaviorism was, in effect, a revival of Locke's *tabula rasa,* a strict, "fundamentalist" version of environmentalism. In an often quoted statement, Watson (1930) declared:

> Give me a dozen healthy infants, well-formed, and my own specified world to bring them up in and I'll guarantee to take any one at random and train him to become any type of specialist I might select—doctor, lawyer, artist, merchant-chief, and, yes, even beggarman and thief, regardless of his talents, penchants, tendencies, abilities, vocations, and race of his ancestors (p. 104).

By extension, anyone can become intelligent if he or she is rewarded (reinforced) for studying and learning and for solving problems with intellect rather than emotions. Nurture is everything.

Development Is Part Nature, Part Nurture

By the mid-twentieth century, many developmental scientists were dissatisfied with both the nativist and environmentalist views. Evidence collected in many fields convinced them that both nature *and* nurture were critical to development. The central question changed from whether nature or nurture drove development, to *how much* each contributed to different traits. This in turn led to attempts to measure their relative contributions.

Heritability Developmentalists began attempting to calculate the degree to which different traits were influenced by genetic factors, or the **heritability** of the trait. This measurement was called the *heritability quotient.* For example, right- or left-handedness has a very high heritability quotient. People do not learn to be right- or left-handed; indeed attempting to override natural handedness is exceedingly difficult. In contrast, speaking fluent Spanish has a very low heritability quotient. It depends on being exposed to Spanish as a young child, usually by growing up in a Spanish-speaking family and society, or by making a determined effort to study and learn Spanish as an adult.

Studies of heritability employed one of several research designs. The most common, **twin studies**, took advantage of a "natural experiment" (see Chapter 1). **Identical twins** are born when a single fertilized egg divides, resulting in the birth of two individuals whose genetic makeup is identical. **Fraternal twins** are born when two separate egg cells are fertilized, and so they are no more alike genetically than other brothers and sisters. If identical twins are more alike than fraternal twins on a trait such as intelligence, this trait is likely to be genetic in origin and have a high heritability quotient (Elkins, McGue, & Iacono, 1997). (See Figure 2.2.) Additional evidence comes from studies of identical twins who were separated at birth and raised in different families. Presumably their similarities are genetic and their differences reflect the environment.

In **adoption studies**, researchers looked at children who were adopted soon after birth and raised by parents to whom they were not genetically related (e.g.,

heritability The extent to which a phenotypic trait is genetically determined.

twin studies A method for estimating heritability in which the degree of similarity in a trait that is observed among identical twins is compared with that observed among fraternal twins.

identical twins Twins born when a single fertilized egg divides, resulting in the birth of two individuals whose genetic makeup is identical.

fraternal twins Twins born when two separate eggs are fertilized, who are therefore no more alike genetically than other brothers and sisters.

adoption studies A method for estimating heritability in which similarities between children and their adoptive parents are compared with similarities between children and their biological parents.

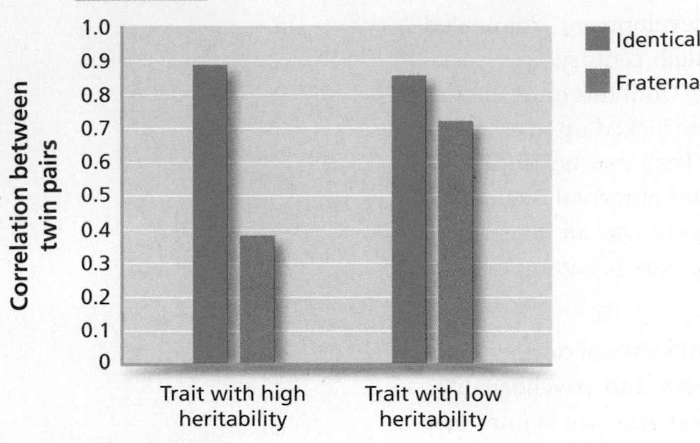

FIGURE 2.2

Heritability of Traits in Twins

In twin studies, the difference in magnitude between the resemblance of identical twins (who share all the same genes) versus fraternal twins (who only share, on average, half their genes) is used to measure heritability. The trait displayed on the left has a high heritability coefficient, which means that variation in that trait is largely influenced by genetic factors. As you can see, the correlation is much stronger between identical twins than between fraternal twins. The trait on the right of the figure has a low heritability coefficient, which means that less variation is due to genetic differences and relatively more variation is due to aspects of the shared and nonshared environments. Therefore, the correlation of scores on that trait between identical twins will be more similar to that between fraternal twins.

Abrahamson, Baker, & Caspi, 2002; Deater-Deckard & Plomin, 1999). Were they more like their birth parents or their adoptive parents? Several studies found that, at least with respect to intelligence, adopted children resemble their biological parents more than their adoptive ones, but that the quality of the adoptive family environment also matters—children who are adopted into more affluent families show more advanced intellectual development than children from similar origins but who are adopted into less advantaged homes (Scarr & Weinberg, 1983).

In **family relatedness studies**, developmentalists also studied families that combined children from prior marriages and remarriage, sometimes referred to as *blended families.* A blended family might include stepsiblings (from the mother or father's previous marriage), half-siblings (a child born to the new couple and thus half related to stepsiblings, on the mother or father's side), and full siblings (two or more children born after the new marriage). What's interesting here is that children with different degrees of relatedness live in the same family and thus grow up in the same general environment. Studies of blended families thus provide another means to examine the relative contributions of nature and nurture to different aspects of child development. Generally speaking, studies of individuals growing up in blended families have shown that children who are more closely related biologically (i.e., who share more genes in common) are more similar in personality, attitudes, abilities, and behavior than children who grow up in the same family but whose genetic backgrounds are dissimilar (e.g., Hetherington, Henderson, & Reiss, 1999).

family relatedness studies A method for estimating heritability by comparing the similarity of children who vary in their genetic relatedness (e.g., siblings, half-siblings, and stepsiblings).

Research on heritability produced some tantalizing results about both nature and nurture. On the one hand, twin, adoption, and family relatedness studies have shown conclusively that virtually all human traits—whether physical (e.g., handedness, athletic ability), intellectual (e.g., verbal ability, intelligence), social (e.g., shyness, aggressiveness), or emotional (e.g., self-esteem, anxiety)—have substantial heritability quotients (Plomin, 2004).

At the same time, however, studies of twins, adopted children, and siblings of different degrees of relatedness have also revealed that these very same traits are also influenced by the environment. Ironically, then, behavioral genetics studies have taught us just as much—some might say even more—about nurture as they have about nature. In some cases, for instance, the aspect of nurture that matters most is the environment that children growing up in the same household have in common—what developmentalists call the **shared environment**. If two siblings are similar not because they share genes in common, but because they have been both exposed to the same sort of parenting, that would point to a shared environmental influence. In other cases, however, the aspect of nurture that matters most is the environment that children growing up together do not share—the **nonshared environment** (Plomin & Daniels, 1987). For example, siblings are often different from each other not just because they have different genes, but because they have different experiences either inside the home (e.g., siblings are treated differently by their parents) or outside the home (e.g., siblings run with very different types of crowds). What heritability studies made clear is that, for virtually all human characteristics, nature and nurture both matter.

shared environment In behavioral genetics, the environment that siblings have in common.

nonshared environment In behavioral genetics, the environment that siblings do not have in common, such as the peers with whom they are friends.

Heritability studies—and the idea that it is possible to accurately estimate how much of a trait is due to genes and how much is due to the environment—have been criticized, however, on three main counts (e.g., Collins et al., 2000). First, genetic and environmental influences often work hand in hand. Bright children ask bright questions and usually get adult-level answers. Slow children ask more basic questions and usually get simpler answers. Thus their genetic potential and experiences are matched.

Second, as we discuss later in this chapter, the idea that genes have the same impact in all environments is questionable. For example, the impact of genes on intelligence is stronger in high-quality environments (which let genes "shine through") than in low-quality environments, where children do not receive much stimulation and curiosity is discouraged. Their innate intelligence remains dormant.

Finally, heritability estimates do not consider malleability. Even a trait that is largely inherited can change. Your hair color, which is almost entirely determined by your genes, can become lighter if you spend a lot of time in the sun. We know that intelligence has a large genetic component. (Scientists may argue about the *extent* to which intelligence is genetically determined, but no one debates the fact that genes play *some* role.) But we also know that an adopted child reared in an enriched environment usually becomes "smarter" than his or her biological parents. Moreover, even genes are flexible, as described later.

In a nutshell, both nature and nurture count (Gottlieb, Wahlstein, & Lickliter, 2006; Rutter, 2006; Turkheimer, 1998). Think about it. Knowing that intelligence or another trait is 75 percent inherited, as opposed to 50 percent inherited, or 20 percent inherited, or even 5 percent inherited, is not terribly useful. Why? Because this also means the trait is 25 percent environmental (or 50% . . . and so on), and that therefore the context in which the individual develops matters.

Although heritability studies have been criticized, they contributed to a major shift in how scientists view development. Most scientists were convinced by heritability research that studying genetics was a necessary part of understanding human development. We no longer debate whether development is mostly (or entirely) the result of nature or mostly (or entirely) nurture. Instead, contemporary developmental scientists accept the idea that every aspect of development—that's right, every aspect—is the product of *both* biological and environmental factors. Today the question has become, How do genes and environments affect each other and, together, guide development?

Development Results from the Interplay of Nature and Nurture

The contemporary view of nature and nurture emphasizes interaction, an important concept. Interaction is more than combination. For example, a teaspoon of vinegar and a teaspoon of baking soda are, by themselves, motionless. But if you mix them together, you produce a fizzing, bubbling volcano (try it and see for yourself). Thus the result of the interaction between them is something quite different from the initial ingredients.

So it is with development. Measuring genetic and environmental influences doesn't tell the full story. The key to development is how genes and their environments *interact.* This idea is not a new one but rather one that has been revived in light of new discoveries in genetics and studies of the environment. It began with Darwin's theory of evolution.

Darwin's Influence Charles Darwin (1809–1882) is surely the most famous interactionist in Western history. Darwin was not primarily interested in individual development, although he kept detailed diaries of his own children's development. Rather, he was a naturalist who devoted his life to understanding the complexity of nature. Yet his ideas have had a profound effect on how we view development today.

Like others before him, Darwin believed that living plants and animals, including humans, were descended from earlier, simpler forms. But what caused these changes?

theory of evolution Typically refers to the variant of the model of evolution formalized by Charles Darwin, which asserts that organisms evolve and change through the process of natural selection.

survival of the fittest Within Darwin's theory of evolution, the notion that organisms that are best equipped to survive in a given context are more likely to reproduce and pass their genetic material on to future generations.

natural selection Within Darwin's theory of evolution, the process through which adaptive traits that are heritable become more common while maladaptive traits that are heritable become less so.

epigenesis The gradual process through which organisms develop over time in an increasingly differentiated and complex fashion as a consequence of the interaction between genes and the environment.

Darwin's **theory of evolution** rests on two main ideas: **survival of the fittest** and **natural selection**. In nature, most organisms do not survive long enough to reproduce. Few seedlings become trees, for example, and a small percentage of tadpoles become frogs. Individual variations—found in every species and every generation—provide the raw material for natural selection. Only the "fittest"—those best adapted to their environment—survive. Through reproduction, these individuals pass their adaptive traits to their offspring, who in turn survive to reproduce. And so, over time, adaptive traits become more common in the species and maladaptive traits die out.

Environments are not stable. When the climate changes, the number of predators increases, or the availability of reliable food sources declines, some traits become more or less adaptive than before. This accounts for the emergence of new traits in a species and for the survival of some species and extinction of others (such as dinosaurs). Natural selection is nothing more or less than the outcome of interaction between members of a species and their environment.

Epigenesis Today most developmental scientists view development as **epigenesis**: a gradual process of increasing complexity due to interaction between heredity (genes) and the environment (Gottlieb et al., 2006). In this view, nothing—or very little—is *pre*determined, just as in evolution no species' survival is guaranteed. Even identical twins—who share the same genes—differ in size, weight, hardiness, and brain patterns at birth, because of slight variations in the prenatal environment they shared (Finch & Kirkwood, 2000).

Epigenesis is rooted in embryology on the one hand, and in the theory of evolution, on the other. By the beginning of the nineteenth century, embryologists had charted the progress of the human embryo and fetus, month by month, stage by stage, in a timed sequence of changes in structure and function. In four days a single cell, the fertilized egg, becomes a cluster of dozens of cells; at four weeks the embryo has a distinct heart, digestive tract, and tail (which disappears); at four months the fetus can kick, turn its head, make a fist, squint, and swallow (see Chapter 3). Biologists could *see* that the embryo was not a miniature adult. Molecular genetics lay far in the future. But it was clear that prenatal development was a form of biological self-assembly.

Soon after Darwin published *The Origin of Species* (1872/2003), some scientists began to apply the theory of evolution to development—including G. Stanley Hall (1844–1924), the first president of the American Psychological Association. Hall held that the early life of an individual resembled the evolutionary history of the species—in other words, that the development of the individual repeats the evolution of a species over time. This specific theory was later rejected, though. The human embryo does not go through a "fish stage," "a reptilian phase," and so on. From the beginning, the embryo is distinctively human. But Darwin's central concept—change through interaction with the environment—remains a powerful principle in the contemporary study of development.

stem cells Primitive, undifferentiated cells or "precells," found in large numbers in the embryo.

Stem cells illustrate epigenesis. **Stem cells** are primitive, undifferentiated cells or "precells," found in large numbers in the embryo (and small numbers in adults) (see Figure 2.3). These cells are the raw material of prenatal development. Each stem cell has a full set of chromosomes and the potential to become anything the body needs. During embryonic development, they become increasingly specialized, eventually developing into blood cells, nerve cells, muscle cells, and so on, and assembling themselves into functioning organs and tissues. We do not yet know exactly why this happens, just that it does. This biological process gives us a model for looking at other levels of development.

At birth, many traits are—by analogy, not literally—like stem cells. Intelligence, for example, is almost entirely a potential (inherited from the baby's parents, as modified by the prenatal environment). As the baby matures, her brain develops, her senses become more finely tuned, her actions (or motor skills) turn more coordinated, and her intelligence begins to take shape. Her experiences in the world and her relationships with others are part of this process. So are nutrition, health, and her physical setting. This process continues through childhood and adolescence, indeed throughout life.

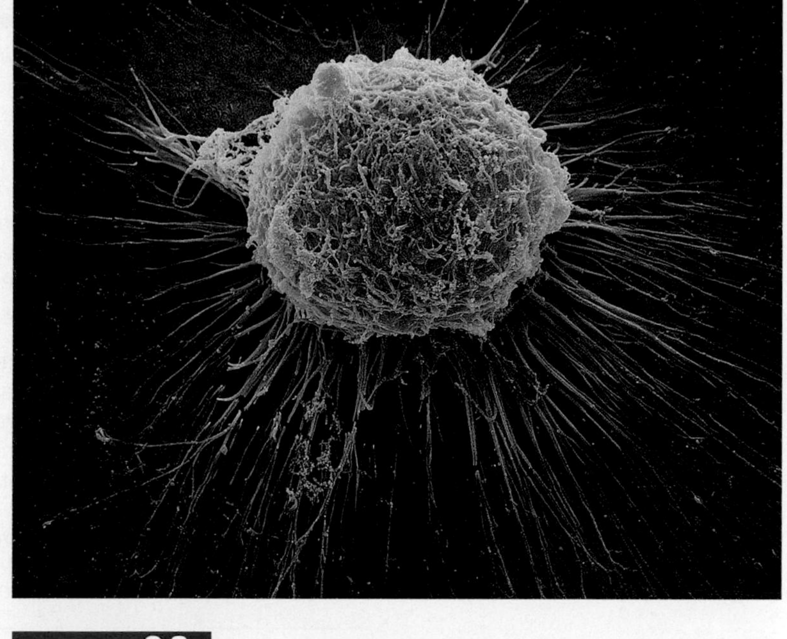

FIGURE 2.3

A Human Embryonic Stem Cell

Stem cells are the raw material of prenatal development. Each stem cell has a full set of chromosomes and the potential to become any kind of cell that the body needs.

We started this section with the old idea that development is predetermined (preformed), which later resurfaced as genetic determinism—the belief that genes are destiny. Then we looked in the opposite direction—to the environmentalist view that children come into this world unformed, and that experience is everything. We saw the first attempts to restore genetics to the study of development, by calculating what proportions of different traits were innate or acquired. And, finally, we arrived at epigenesis, which puts nature and nurture back together again as active copartners in development. (See "Interim Summary 2.1: Perspectives on Nature and Nuture.") We'll return to the subject of gene-environment interactions at the end of this chapter. First, though, we need to explain what genes are and how they work.

WHAT ARE GENES, AND WHAT DO THEY DO?

Genes provide the continuity that makes us human, generation after generation. They direct the cells of an embryo to become a human being, not an armadillo or an apple tree. They help to establish our common modes of thinking, feeling, acting, and communicating. At the same time, genes contribute to the wide diversity within the human species—in appearance, abilities, health, and even happiness.

Thus the study of human genetics deals with two different, related questions. First, how do genes make us human and distinct from other species? Second, within this human pattern, how do genes influence individual differences?

Becoming Human

All human beings have some traits in common: for example, walking upright on two feet, or **bipedalism**. Our upright posture and gait are the result of natural selection; these characteristics made our ancestors better adapted to their environment than their competitors. Our closest cousins, the great apes, are capable of bipedalism and sometimes walk upright, but only humans are routinely, habitually bipedal. Walking upright on two feet freed our ancestors' hands to make and use tools and weapons and to carry food and other goods back to a home base. Bipedalism is one of the defining

bipedalism Being able to stand and walk on two feet.

INTERIM SUMMARY **2.1**

Perspectives on Nature and Nurture

Development Is Driven by Nature	The view that genes alone determine the course of development is referred to as **nativism**. An extreme early version of this view, **preformationism**, held that the individual's adult characteristics were present from conception, or even before.
Development Is Driven by Nurture	In contrast to nativists, extreme environmentalists believed that external forces were entirely responsible for development. Locke's notion that the infant is a "blank slate" reflects this view.
Development Is Part Nature, Part Nurture	By the middle of the twentieth century, the central question in the study of nature and nurture changed from whether nature *or* nurture drove development, to *how much* each contributed to different traits. The extent to which a trait is genetically determined is known as **heritability**.
Development Results from the Interplay of Nature and Nurture	Today, developmental scientists view development as the product of a dynamic interaction between genes and environment, a process called **epigenesis**.

characteristics of our species. Other defining human traits include handiness (opposable thumbs, the better to grasp things), language, the ability to alter our surroundings, a knack for calculations, and self-awareness.

In recent decades, scientists have learned that none of these traits, by itself, is unique to humans. Great apes demonstrate self-awareness (though monkeys don't). Birds and whales communicate through sound and even have local "dialects." Apes use tools; so do some birds. Birds build intricate nests, sometimes in "colonies," and even ants alter their environment. Moreover, raccoons as well as primates (apes, monkeys, and prosimians, such as lemurs and bush babies) have opposable thumbs; orangutans have grasping hands *and* feet. In experiments, parrots and great apes have demonstrated basic comprehension of words, grammar, and number. But no other animal develops this combination of abilities so easily or naturally.

canalization The degree to which an element of development is dictated by the common genetic program that all humans inherit.

"Like a Rolling Stone" These universal aspects of human development are under tighter genetic control than are other traits, a phenomenon known as canalization. **Canalization** is the degree to which an element of development is dictated by the genetic program that all humans inherit. Think of development as a stone rolling down a hill inside a canal (Waddington, 1940). Gravity (maturation) pulls the stone down the hill, but where each stone ends up depends on the terrain, or environment. In some places the canal is deep and narrow, so every stone follows that route. For example, all normal children learn to walk, regardless of the environment in which they grow up; locomotion is highly canalized. But in other places the canal is shallow and bumpy, so the stone may roll around and even bounce out of the canal. The development of morality is less highly canalized than the development of walking—which is why the world is made up of people who are as moral as Mother Teresa; those who are mass murderers, serial killers, and others who show no concern for others; and most of the rest of us, who fall somewhere between these two extremes.

In general, early development is more highly canalized than later development. Thus there are more universals in early development (walking, talking, wondering why) than in later development (dancing, writing poetry or rap, or becoming a scientist or philosopher, a poet or criminal investigator).

The Importance of Being Cute One distinctive feature of human development is that we are born "prematurely." The great evolutionary biologist Stephen Jay Gould (1977) wrote that human babies are essentially "embryos" at birth and remain so for their first year. Horses are able to stand, walk, run, and whinny within hours of birth. Kittens and puppies need care for their first month or two but thereafter can survive independently. Humans can't even get from one place to another by themselves until age 9 or 10 months, when they first begin crawling.

Babies of many species are cute, which draws caregivers to them, thereby increasing their chances of survival.

One reason for this is that humans have evolved to be highly social animals. A prolonged period of juvenile appearance and behavior promotes the development of social bonds by attracting caregivers to infants, and vice versa. Quite simply, babies of many species are "cute"—think kittens, puppies, and bunnies. Complete strangers go "gaga" when they see an infant and will do almost anything to get a baby to smile. (Borrow an infant and see for yourself!) This is why advertisers so often use babies to sell everything from automobile tires to paper towels. An adult smiles at a baby, the baby smiles back, the adult responds, and so on, in a natural cycle of attraction. Both the baby and the adult are "programmed" to form a bond.

From an evolutionary perspective, babies who smiled a lot (even reflexively as newborns do, usually while sleeping) probably got more attention than somber babies, so the trait became common. Likewise, parents who were drawn to their babies probably reared more offspring who survived (and later had children of their own) than parents who were unresponsive, so this trait became widespread.

A second reason for the prolonged immaturity of human infants is that humans depend on learning more than other species do. Like newborn horses, most mammals are capable of getting around on their own soon after they are born; human babies aren't. Our evolutionary cousins, the great apes, also stay with their mother for a long time. Only elephants have as long a period of dependency. Our "immaturity" at birth makes us more receptive to environmental influence. At the same time, we are predisposed to learning and thus better able than most other species to change our behavior in response to environmental conditions. We are adaptable in part because much of our early development takes place in the world, not the womb.

We are not as unique as we might think, however. The Human Genome Project has shown that we share some of our genes with even the simplest organisms, such as bacteria and molds; many of our genes with all other mammals; and most of our genes with our closest evolutionary kin, the great apes. Humans' and chimpanzees' DNA is 98–99 percent identical. If blood types are matched, a human can receive a transfusion from a chimpanzee and vice versa (McGrew, 2004). Within the human species, 99.9 percent of genetic material is identical—that's right, you and the person sitting next to you in class have 99.9 percent of your genes in common. Yet we have so many genes that even the small amount we don't share with others leaves much room for variation (Plomin et al., 2001).

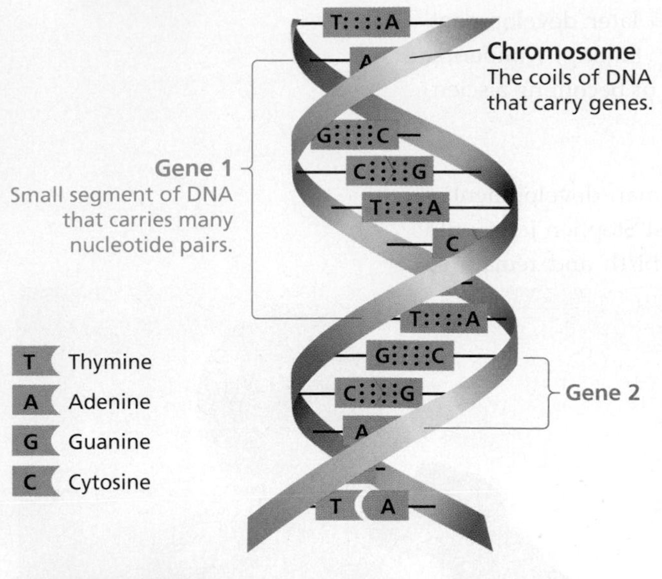

FIGURE 2.4

Chromosomes and Genes

Chromosomes are made up of two long strands of DNA twisted into a ladder-like structure called a *double helix*; each cell nucleus contains 23 identical pairs of chromosomes. The rungs of the DNA ladder are composed of pairs of chemical bases (adenine pairs with thymine, and guanine pairs with cytosine), and the chromosomes have millions of base pairs. Short segments of DNA are called *genes*, which contain about 3,000 base pairs on average but can be as long as 2 million base pairs.

Human Diversity

That we are related to all living things makes diversity within our species even more remarkable. No two human beings have the exact same genes, except (as you know) identical twins. Here we will explain why—and why this is important.

The Genetic Code

The human body is made up of trillions of cells. The nucleus of almost every human cell contains 23 pairs of chromosomes, one set from the individual's mother, one from his or her father. (The exceptions are reproductive cells, or sperm and ova, described later.) **Chromosomes** are long strands of DNA (deoxyribonucleic acid). These chromosomes, present in every cell, contain a complete set of instructions for the development of a unique human being.

The rungs of the DNA ladder consist of pairs of four chemical bases: adenine (A), thymine (T), guanine (G), and cytosine (C). (See Figure 2.4.) Adenine always connects with thymine (as A-T or T-A), and guanine with cytosine (as C-G or G-C). The order of **base pairs** determines genetic instructions, much as the order of letters determines the meaning of a word (as in "dog" versus "God").

Chromosomes direct activities in the cell by attracting molecules of RNA (ribonucleic acid). RNA functions as a messenger, carrying genetic instructions out of the cell's nucleus into the cytoplasm, which contains the raw materials for synthesizing enzymes, hormones, and other proteins. Different proteins are created by combining different amino acids (and different numbers of amino acids) in different ways. Proteins, in turn, cause chemical reactions in the body that lead to the production and reproduction of cells.

Genes are the units of heredity that pass characteristics from one generation to the next, and the next. In biochemical terms, a **gene** is a segment of the chromosome that controls a particular aspect of the production of a specific protein; a gene is about 3,000 base pairs long (though length is highly variable). The key to heredity is DNA. DNA has the unique ability to reproduce itself, which permits a single cell, the fertilized egg, to develop into an adult human being, in all his or her complexity. Of course, the genetic code does not apply to humans only. It explains how *every living thing* comes into being, from elephants and snails to roses; from mice to men and women, including you and us, the authors of this book.

chromosomes Strands of DNA that carry genes and associated proteins.

base pairs Pairs of adenine and thymine and of guanine and cytosine that make up the "rungs" of the DNA molecule.

gene A segment of DNA, occupying a specific place on a chromosome.

genotype The underlying genetic makeup of an individual organism (contrast with *phenotype*).

phenotype The observable traits and characteristics of an individual organism (contrast with *genotype*).

Genotypes and Phenotypes

The 23 pairs of chromosomes you inherit from your parents make up your **genotype**, a package of biochemical information that is yours and yours alone (unless you have an identical twin). Your genotype is contained in almost every cell in your body, throughout life. (This is why criminal investigators can identify a person from a single strand of hair or a few skin cells.) But—an extremely important qualification—your genotype does not *determine* who you become.

Your observable characteristics and behavior, or **phenotype**, depends on your environment and experiences, from the moment of conception. In other words, your genotype is not a tiny edition of you, a modern version of the seventeenth-century homunculus. When talking about genes, we are talking about potentials, not predetermination. What each of us becomes is only one of many possible outcomes.

To explain why (almost) everyone's genotype is unique, we look first at sexual reproduction.

Sexual Reproduction Bacteria, many plants, and some fish and reptiles reproduce asexually. The offspring are a genetically identical clone of the parent. Sexual reproduction creates more variety, and thus makes it more likely that some members of a population will be able to adapt to changes in the environment.

Mitosis and meiosis As we said, the nucleus of every human cell contains 23 pairs of chromosomes. During ordinary cell reproduction (called **mitosis**), a cell divides and each daughter cell receives a full copy of all 46 chromosomes. Reproductive cells (or **gametes**) are different. They are produced through a different process, called **meiosis** (see Figure 2.5).

mitosis The process through which all cells other than gametes reproduce, in which a cell divides and each resulting cell receives a full copy of all 46 chromosomes.

gametes Reproductive cells; sperm in males and ova (eggs) in females.

meiosis The process through which gametes (sperm and ova) are produced, in which each resulting gamete has half of the genetic material of the parent cell.

Meiosis—the production of sperm and ova—produces cells with only half a set of chromosomes. The first phase of meiosis is known as "crossing over." Each of the 23 pairs of chromosomes line up, wrap around each other, and exchange bits of genetic material. For example, one chromosome may contain a gene for red hair and one for green eyes; the other a gene for brown hair and one for blue eyes. The gene for brown hair may cross over and link to the gene for green eyes, and the gene for red hair may cross over and link to the gene for blue eyes. (This is somewhat simplified, to give you the general idea.) These "new" chromosomes separate and migrate to opposite sides of the cell nucleus.

In the second phase of meiosis, some of the mother's chromosomes align with the father's chromosomes and vice versa. In effect, the chromosome deck is reshuffled (Krogh, 2005). The cell then divides in two, and the "new" chromosomes produce duplicates of themselves. Last, these daughter cells divide, producing four cells with only 23 chromosomes each. Because of crossing over and reshuffling, no two ovum or sperm are exactly alike. (If this weren't the case, every time a couple produced a child, he or she would have the exact same genotype as every other one of the couple's children.)

At fertilization, two reproductive cells merge, and the chromosomes from the mother's ovum link to the chromosomes from the father's sperm. Note that each individual has two sets of chromosomes and thus two copies of every gene, called **alleles**. The outcome of this merger depends primarily on which genes from each parent are matched with the other's genes, or gene-gene interaction.

alleles Different forms of the same gene occupying the same location on each of the chromosomes that make up a chromosomal pair.

Gene-Gene Interaction Twenty-two of our 23 pairs of chromosomes are "homologous"; they contain two versions of the gene for each trait (one allele from each parent). But the 23rd pair, which determines the sex of the individual, is different. Every female has two X chromosomes; every male has one X and one Y chromosome. (There are some unusual exceptions to this that are caused by errors during fertilization, but these are very rare.) We'll say more about sex chromosomes and how they may affect development in Chapter 3. Here, we focus on what takes place when the other 22 pairs are formed. What happens when the mother's genes link to the father's genes in a new individual? As you'll see, it all depends on the specific genes in question and the way they interact.

Additive heredity In the case of **additive heredity**, a number of the mother's and the father's genes affect a trait, and the child's phenotype, or visible traits, is a mix of the two. For example, the child of a Caucasian father and an African American mother has tan skin. Hair texture or curliness and height are also additive. If a tall man and a short woman have children, the children will probably be of medium height (assuming adequate nutrition and good physical health). Additive traits are a blend of all of both parents' genes. But because the genotype of the medium-height children includes genes for being short and tall, some of their own children may be taller or shorter than they are.

additive heredity The process of genetic transmission that results in a phenotype that is a mixture of the mother's and father's traits.

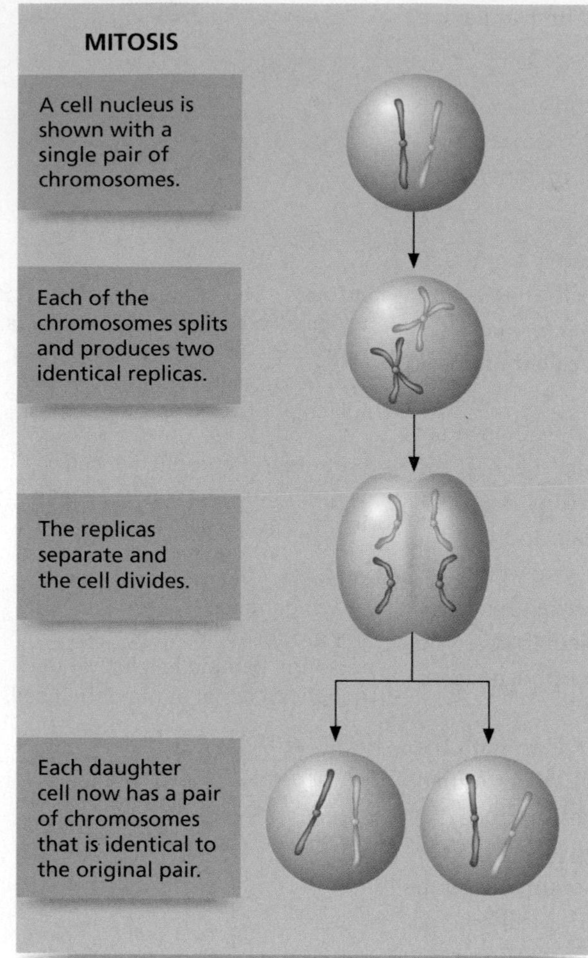

MITOSIS
A cell nucleus is shown with a single pair of chromosomes.
Each of the chromosomes splits and produces two identical replicas.
The replicas separate and the cell divides.
Each daughter cell now has a pair of chromosomes that is identical to the original pair.

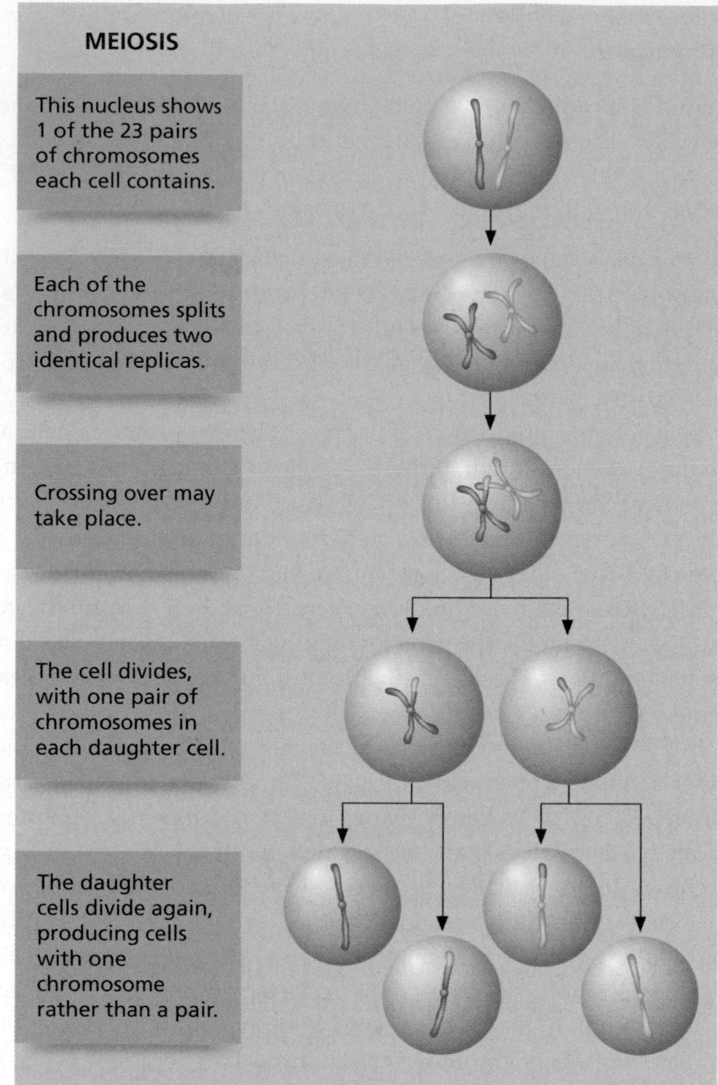

MEIOSIS
This nucleus shows 1 of the 23 pairs of chromosomes each cell contains.
Each of the chromosomes splits and produces two identical replicas.
Crossing over may take place.
The cell divides, with one pair of chromosomes in each daughter cell.
The daughter cells divide again, producing cells with one chromosome rather than a pair.

FIGURE 2.5

Mitosis and Meiosis

Mitosis is the process of cell reproduction. First, every chromosome gets duplicated and then the cell divides, resulting in two "daughter" cells that each has a full copy of all 46 chromosomes (in 23 pairs). In *meiosis,* or the production of reproductive cells (sperm and ova), the 23 pairs of chromosomes first undergo a "crossing-over" process in which some of their genetic material gets exchanged. Like in mitosis, the chromosome pairs duplicate and then divide into two daughter cells, each with 46 chromosomes. But unlike mitosis, the daughter cells divide again, resulting in four cells with only 23 chromosomes each.

dominant/recessive heredity The process of genetic transmission where one version (allele) of a gene is dominant over another, resulting in the phenotypic expression of only the dominant allele.

Dominant/recessive heredity In the case of **dominant/recessive heredity**, one version of a gene is dominant over another. The gene for brown eyes, for example, is dominant over the gene for blue eyes, which is recessive. A child who inherits the gene for brown eyes from both parents will have brown eyes. So will a child who inherits the dominant gene for brown eyes from one parent and the recessive gene for blue eyes from the other. Only a child who inherits the recessive gene for blue eyes from both parents will have blue eyes. A gene may be dominant in one combination but not another. Hazel eyes result from a combination of green-eye and brown-eye genes, for example. In other words, the genotype brown-eye gene + green-eye gene produces the phenotype hazel eyes.

"Regulator" genes One of the most surprising findings from the Human Genome Project is that some genes are not tied to a particular phenotypic trait; rather, their function is to turn other genes on or off at different points in the life cycle or in response to events in the environment. In effect, they act as moderators at a convention of genes, some of which are involved in debates about whether development should take one path or another. In turning genes on or off, **regulator genes** exercise considerable power over phenotypes. For example, chimpanzees have larger jaws than humans do—not because they have different "jaw-growing" genes, because the *same* jaw-growing gene is turned on longer while the jaw is developing in a chimpanzee fetus than in a human fetus (Ridley, 2003). In other words, chimps and humans share the same jaw-growing genotype, but their phenotype is quite different.

regulator genes Genes whose function is to turn other genes on or off at different points in the life cycle or in response to events in the environment.

Environmental influences The gene actions and interactions we have been describing do not take place in a vacuum. The environment is an active partner, often the most influential partner, in the translation of a genotype into a phenotype.

mutations Copying errors in the replication of DNA that alter the proteins a gene or chromosome produces.

One example (among many identified with the help of the Human Genome Project) provides a concrete illustration of environmental influence. Researchers have identified a gene labeled 5-HTT, which influences levels of serotonin, a brain chemical known to affect depression. The alleles for this gene vary in length. Individuals with short versions of the gene are much more likely to respond to stress by becoming depressed than individuals with longer versions (Caspi et al., 2003). Note that the gene does not "cause" depression, but rather affects individual vulnerability to depression in the face of stress. In a chain reaction, stress hormones affect how the 5-HTT gene acts, which affects the proteins it instructs the body to make, which affects serotonin levels, which affects vulnerability to depression (see Figure 2.6).

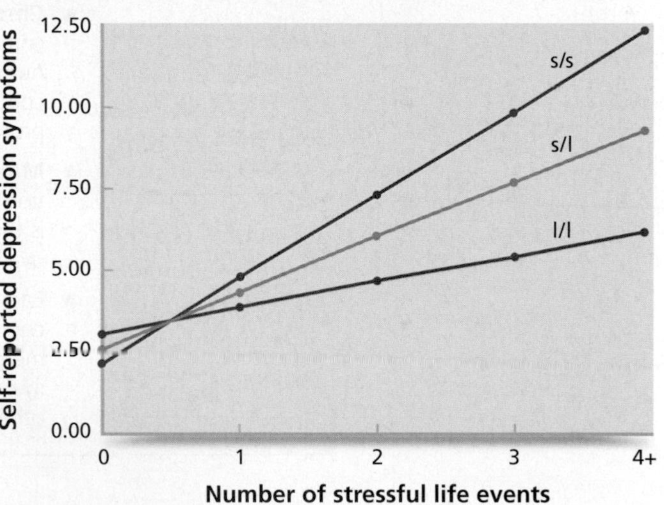

FIGURE 2.6

Environmental Influences on Gene Expression

This figure demonstrates how experience can influence the phenotypic expression of our genes. The 5-HTT gene plays a role in producing brain chemicals associated with depression, and there are three different versions of the gene whose allele pairs vary in length (short/short, short/long, and long/long). A group of researchers found that individuals who had experienced very few stressful life events all reported low levels of depressive symptoms. But among people who experienced multiple stressful life events, the level of depressive symptoms varied based on the type of 5-HTT gene they carried. Individuals with the short/short 5-HTT genotype were most affected by stressful life events and reported higher levels of depressive symptoms than individuals with the short/long or long/long genotype who were exposed to comparable levels of stress.

Source: From Avshalom Caspi et al. (2003). "Influence of life stress on depression: Moderation by a polymorphism in the 5-HTT gene," *Science, 301*:386 (2003). Reprinted with permission from AAAS.

Thus, the short 5-HTT gene may or may not have an impact on serotonin (and, hence, depression) depending on other aspects of the person's biology and on context. A child whose mother dies when she is young, who moves to an unfamiliar place where she has no friends at age 12, or who faces other stressful situations might sink into depression. Another child, with the same 5-HTT gene, who grows up in a stable environment, whose family members accept (but do not fuss about) his moods, and who has supportive friends and discovers rewarding activities might never experience clinical depression. If, at age 45, as a husband and father of three, he is laid off and cannot find employment, the 5-HTT gene might kick in. Perhaps the best description of the translation of a genotype into a phenotype is, "It all depends. . . ."

Luck also plays a role. Occasional copying errors, or **mutations**, alter the proteins a gene or chromosome produces. The impact of mutations is usually neutral or slight, but in some cases can cause adaptive or maladaptive change.

INTERIM SUMMARY 2.2

What Are Genes, and What Do They Do?

Becoming Human

- Humans possess a unique combination of genes that distinguish our species from others.
- Many universal aspects of human development are under tight genetic control, a phenomenon known as **canalization**.
- One distinctive aspect of human infancy is a prolonged period of immature appearance and behavior, which promotes the development of social bonds by attracting caregivers to infants, and vice versa.
- Even though virtually all of our genes are common to all humans, we have so many genes that even the small amount we don't share with others leaves much room for variation, which accounts for diversity in human characteristics.

Human Diversity

- The nucleus of almost every human cell contains 23 pairs of chromosomes—one set from the individual's mother, one from his or her father. This is referred to as the individual's **genotype**.
- An individual's observable characteristics and behavior, or **phenotype**, depend on both the genotype and the environment.
- **Chromosomes** are long strands of DNA, which contain a complete set of instructions for the development of a unique human being. A **gene** is a segment of the chromosome that controls a particular aspect of the production of a specific protein.
- **Mitosis** is the process through which all cells, with the exception of reproductive cells, are produced, whereas **meiosis** is the process through which reproductive cells—sperm and ova—are produced.
- Each individual has two sets of chromosomes and thus two copies of every gene, called **alleles**. The outcome of the merger of the mother's and father's genes depends primarily on which genes from each parent are matched with the other's, referred to as gene-gene interaction.

A key point here is that genes produce proteins, not human traits, and the ultimate impact of these proteins varies as a function of many other factors. To suggest that people inherit a gene for intelligence, sociability, aggression, acrophobia (fear of heights), or any other characteristic is quite simply wrong. The reality is far more complex. (For a summary of this section, see "Interim Summary 2.2: What Are Genes and What Do They Do?")

Likewise, to speak of the environment (singular) as "everything out there" is also wrong. As we will see, the reality is far more complex.

THE IMPORTANCE OF CONTEXT

Just as our current understanding of genetic influences is more complex than earlier views, so is our understanding of the environment, or context, and its role in development. From birth (and even before), a developing child is exposed to countless overlapping, interacting relationships and experiences that change as he or she grows older and the world itself changes (Bronfenbrenner & Morris, 2006).

The Ecological Perspective on Development

The ecological perspective (introduced in Chapter 1) focuses on these external influences. Urie Bronfenbrenner, a pioneer in this field, compared the context of development to a set of Russian dolls (hollow wooden dolls of increasing size, designed to fit inside one another). As he explained, "The inner doll is the developing human being. The next doll is the immediate setting; the physical setting and the people the child is interacting with now. The next doll is the community as it influences activities and relationships; and so on" (Scarr, Weinberg, & Levine, 1986, p. 48). Thus an individual lives in a family, which lives in a neighborhood, which exists within a society, which exists within a culture at a particular point in history.

One of Bronfenbrenner's important contributions was to provide a framework to organize the way we think about contexts: the micro-, meso-, exo-, and macrosystems. His view challenged developmental scientists to think about the way that individuals are influenced not only by the immediate settings in which they spend time (like their home or classroom) but also by more distant contexts—their neighborhood, society, and culture. Bronfenbrenner even encouraged developmentalists to study the ways in which events in settings in which individuals never even set foot—like their parents' workplaces—could nonetheless influence how they developed.

Scientists who use an ecological perspective to study human development start by identifying a question and then thinking through how to look at that question at different levels of analysis. To illustrate how this might be done, let's try applying Bronfenbrenner's framework to a specific question and see where it leads us.

The question we ask is grounded in an unfortunate social fact: Hispanic American teenagers are less likely to graduate from high school than individuals from other ethnic groups (U.S. Census Bureau, 2006). Although the problem is most concentrated among foreign-born individuals who never attended high school in the United States, the dropout rate among Hispanic Americans who enrolled in U.S. high schools is about twice that for non-Hispanic white youth. This is an important social problem, because dropping out of high school often has dire consequences for the future. Individuals who don't complete high school are far more likely than graduates to live at or near the poverty level, to experience unemployment, to depend on public assistance, to become a parent while still a teenager, and to be involved in delinquent and criminal activity (Manlove, 1998). If we better understood the causes of the high dropout rate among Hispanic American youth, perhaps we could do something about it.

OK, then. Why do *you* think Hispanic American teenagers are less likely to finish high school than other adolescents? Let's see how employing an ecological perspective might help us design a research study to answer this question. We begin by looking at the immediate environment in which the child develops.

Microsystems

In Bronfenbrenner's framework, a **microsystem** is a setting in which the individual interacts with others face-to-face every day. The most important microsystems in individual's lives are the family, the school or work setting, and—especially in middle childhood and adolescence—the peer group. When researchers ask questions about the way children are affected by different forms of discipline, by variations in class size, or by being popular with peers, they are asking questions about the microsystem. But keep in mind that influences within a microsystem are *bidirectional.* Not only do parents, teachers, and peers influence the child, the child influences them. Adults are influenced by their romantic partners, children, and co-workers, but adults influence these other individuals as well. Relationships within microsystems are also *multifaceted* (or many-sided). Many settings—the family living room,

microsystem In Bronfenbrenner's ecological perspective on development, a setting in which the child interacts with others face-to-face, such as a family or classroom.

a cafeteria table at school—include more than two people. When a mother is dressing a toddler, for example, the presence of the father, a second child, a grandparent, or a neighbor affect how she and the toddler act toward each other. Thus microsystems are more dynamic and complex than the term "micro" might suggest.

Is it possible that features of these microsystems in the lives of Hispanic American children might account for their lower graduation rate? Absolutely. Consider the family setting, for instance. Researchers have consistently found that the ways in which parents interact with their children influences how well they do in school. In particular, children whose parents are more involved in their education and who parent in a way that is simultaneously warm and strict—a style of parenting called "authoritative parenting" (see Chapter 8)—do better in school than children whose parents rarely attend school programs or monitor their children's schoolwork, and who are more aloof, more lenient, or both. So one thing we would surely want to study is whether Hispanic American children are raised in ways that hinder their success in American schools. For example, are their parents less likely to practice authoritative parenting? Several studies say that this may be the case (Steinberg, Dornbusch, & Brown, 1992).

The family isn't the only microsystem that influences student achievement, however. And, in fact, rarely is it the case that something as complicated as dropping out of school can be explained by looking at one microsystem alone. Perhaps there are additional factors operating in the classroom or peer group that contribute as well. We know, for example, that dropping out is less likely from schools where the environment is orderly, where academic pursuits are emphasized, and where the faculty is supportive and committed (Connell et al., 1995). So, to continue our exploration of the microsystem, we would want to ask if the quality of schools attended by Hispanic American students is lower on average than that attended by students from other ethnic groups.

The third major microsystem in children's lives is the peer group. Is it possible that something in the peer groups of Hispanic American children affects their engagement in school? One factor that has been shown to have an especially strong influence on school achievement during adolescence is the extent to which doing well in school is valued by the adolescents' friends. Although it is true that adolescents who do well in school usually choose friends who also are high achievers, research has shown that teenagers are also influenced by the peers they hang around with. A "C" student who has relatively more "B" students as friends is more likely to do well over time than a "C" student whose friends themselves aren't making high grades, either (Epstein, 1983). Another interesting microsystem question to study, then, is whether Hispanic American students are less likely than other students to have friends who are high achievers.

The Mesosystem

mesosystem In Bronfenbrenner's ecological perspective on development, the system of interconnected microsystems.

According to Bronfenbrenner's model, the next level of context is the mesosystem. The **mesosystem** refers to the ways in which microsystems are connected. Although it is convenient for researchers to divide individuals' worlds into separate microsystems, in reality, they rarely are separate. Two types of interconnections among microsystems are important. The first is that what takes place in one setting often reverberates in others. How children are reared at home affects how they behave in preschool, the values and attitudes adolescents pick up from their friends influence how they interact with their parents, and the experiences that adults have at work influences how they behave when they return home at the end of the day. One set of questions about the influence of the mesosystem on child development therefore asks how events in one microsystem affect events in another. Some questions of this sort concern simultaneous experiences in two or more settings (e.g., how experience in daycare affects children's attachments to their parents; NICHD ECCN, 1997); others concern the ways in which events in one setting affect events in another in the future (e.g., how children are raised affects their subsequent choice of peer groups; Brown et al., 1993).

A second type of interconnection among microsystems has to do with whether characteristics of one microsystem reinforce or conflict with characteristics of another. In some instances, conflict between microsystems isn't a problem—your parents expect you to be quiet and reserved around the house, but your friends expect you to be loud and boisterous, so you just shift gears when you move back and forth between these settings. But very often, experiences and expectations in different microsystems—for example, a permissive family and a disciplined classroom—conflict, which require adjustments.

According to the ecological perspective, the mesosystem—the interconnections among microsystems—is an important influence on development. A child whose mother and daycare provider treat her similarly may find it easier to transition from home to daycare each day than one whose mother and daycare provider behave differently.

How might the mesosystem in which Hispanic American children live affect their success in school? One fascinating question concerns the degrees to which cooperation and competition are valued in the home and school environments of Hispanic American children.

If you attended elementary and secondary school in the United States, you know how much emphasis is placed on individual achievement and competition. Individuals are judged by how well they perform as *individuals*. Teachers go out of their way to make sure that each student's work is his or her own—and violations of this are usually seen as cheating. Teachers may note on students' report cards how well they play with others, but in the end, it is every student for him- or herself. Unless it is explicitly encouraged by the teacher, students who help each other on tests, do homework together, or collaborate on projects are penalized—or sometimes even failed—for doing so.

In many cultures, however, and in Mexican culture especially, cooperation is valued much more than competition (Kagan & Knight, 1979). Individuals are expected to place their own needs behind those of others, and they are often judged by how well the group to which they belong performs, rather than on the basis of individual achievement. Imagine how these worlds might collide in influencing Hispanic American students' school performance. They are reared in a home environment in which cooperation, not competition, is valued, but they face a classroom setting in which just the opposite is true. One question we might ask, therefore, is how discrepant a child's home and school expectations are, and whether this contributes to academic difficulties.

When researchers look at the mesosystem, it is the connection between settings, and not any one setting considered alone, that's important. In the example we've just considered, it's not the fact that the school environment is competitive or that the home environment is cooperative that is of interest. It is the relation between them—and in this specific instance, the mismatch between them—that matters.

The Exosystem

The **exosystem** is made up of contexts outside the child's immediate, everyday experience. The exosystem includes larger settings that children know only in part, such as the neighborhood, and settings in which children themselves do not participate,

exosystem In Bronfenbrenner's ecological perspective on development, the layer of the context that includes the larger settings that children know only in part, such as the neighborhood and settings in which children themselves do not participate, such as parents' workplaces.

© Jeff Greenburg/The Image Works

The ecological perspective emphasizes the importance both of immediate settings, such as the home or classroom, as well as aspects of the broader environment, such as the neighborhood, on development.

such as parents' workplaces. The exosystem influences a child indirectly, by shaping the behavior of people with whom the child does interact directly and by defining a larger context that affects what takes place inside the institutions that touch the child's life.

For example, living in an impoverished, high-crime Hispanic neighborhood such as South Central Los Angeles or the South Bronx puts chronic stress on the family, which may cause parents to be bad-tempered and punitive with a child (McLoyd, 1990). A working- to middle-class neighborhood in Los Angeles or New York City is a safer atmosphere, which allows parents to be more secure about their own roles and more responsive to a child. We noted earlier that children do better in school when their parents are "authoritative." And research shows that it is much easier to be this type of parent in a well-to-do neighborhood than in a disadvantaged one. As part of the child's exosystem, therefore, the neighborhood can have a profound impact on his or her performance in school through its influence on what takes place at home. One question we might want to study is whether Hispanic American children are more likely to grow up in families that live under the sorts of stressful circumstances that undermine effective parenting.

Neighborhoods influence student achievement in other ways, too, though. In some parts of the inner city, children can grow up without having contact with adults who have regular, paying jobs—where they almost never see individuals engaged in the daily routine of going to work. In contrast, they may be exposed to individuals who earn money illegally, through activities like drug dealing. As a consequence, many young people in impoverished neighborhoods may come to believe that succeeding in school in order to develop the skills and knowledge necessary to secure a good job is not an effective route toward earning a living as an adult (Little & Steinberg, 2006). Some may even believe that there are so few job opportunities in their neighborhood that even going to school—much less trying to do well there—is a waste of time. In this regard, conditions in the neighborhood—part of the child's exosystem—can affect a student's achievement without its influence operating through the family. One way to study this might be to ask whether Hispanic American children are more likely, as a group, to live in neighborhoods with unusually high unemployment rates.

The Macrosystem

macrosystem In Bronfenbrenner's ecological perspective on development, the layer of the context that includes the larger forces that define a society at a particular point in time, including culture, politics, economics, the mass media, and historical events.

The **macrosystem** is the outermost layer of the context in Bronfenbrenner's model. It includes the larger forces that define a society at a particular point in time. Among the most important of these forces are overarching cultural and religious values, the society's economic and political systems, the mass media, and major historical events that have a lasting and pervasive influence, such as wars, economic depressions, and natural disasters. It is not hard to imagine how development is influenced by the macrosystem. Think about what it might be like growing up in a developing country where farming is still the way of life for most people, opportunities for schooling beyond elementary school are limited, high technology has not yet defined daily life, and almost everyone shares the same cultural heritage. Now compare that with the

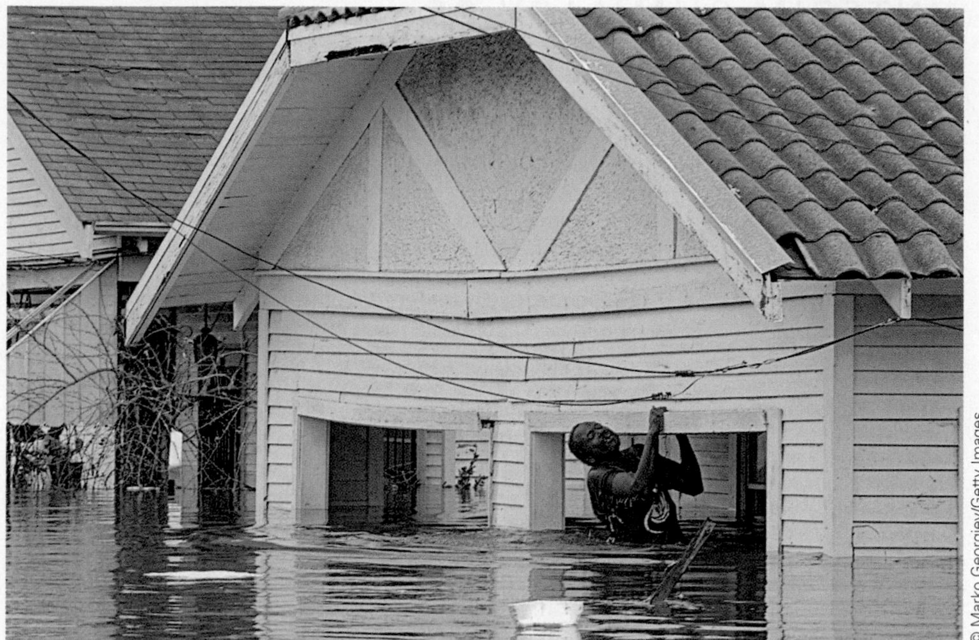

Within the ecological perspective, the macrosystem—the cultural and historical context in which individuals grow up—is the outermost level of the environment. Major historical events such as Hurricane Katrina can transform all of the settings in which an individual develops.

macrosystem of modern-day industrialized society—where most people work in offices, the majority of individuals need to attend college in order to be competitive in the labor force, access to the Internet has become commonplace, and individuals from an array of cultural and religious backgrounds live in close proximity to one another.

Developmentalists who focus on the macrosystem have been especially interested in whether and how human development varies between societies (e.g., comparing development in different parts of the world), between ethnic groups (e.g., comparing development in different ethnic groups within the same society), between socioeconomic groups (e.g., comparing development in families living at different income levels), or across periods of time (e.g., before and after the events of 9/11).

How might the dropout rate of Hispanic American students be influenced by forces in the macrosystem? One possibility is that certain values and traditions that are widespread in Hispanic culture—part of the macrosystem in which Hispanic American children grow up—may end up making it more difficult for a Hispanic American youth to stay in school. The importance of the family—what some psychologists have called **familism** (Cuéllar, Arnold, & Gonzalez, 1995)—is especially valued in Hispanic culture, for instance, and compared with other children, Hispanic youngsters have high expectations to support and assist other family members, sacrifice their own individual needs for those of the family, and be involved in family activities (Fuligni, Tseng, & Lam, 1999). One way in which this sometimes manifests itself is that students often are expected to put family responsibilities before school. A junior high school student might be expected by her family to miss school in order to accompany an elderly, Spanish-speaking relative to the Social Security office, to serve as a translator. Another might be expected to complete household chores before attending to homework each day. Within Hispanic culture, these are perfectly reasonable expectations. But it is not hard to see how they could contribute to academic difficulties and, therefore, to the risk of dropping out of school. Indeed, some writers have suggested that one reason for the higher dropout rate of Hispanic students is that many more Hispanic than

familism Placing a high value on the interests of the family rather than the individual.

INTERIM SUMMARY 2.3

The Importance of Context	
The Ecological Perspective on Development	Bronfenbrenner was the pioneer of the ecological perspective, which provides a framework to organize the way we think about the contexts of development.
Microsystems	A **microsystem** is a setting in which the individual interacts with others face-to-face, such as a home or classroom.
The Mesosystem	The **mesosystem** refers to the ways in which microsystems are connected, such as the links between the home and school.
The Exosystem	The **exosystem** is made up of contexts outside the child's immediate, everyday experience, such as the neighborhood, as well as settings in which the individual him- or herself does not participate, such as the parents' workplace.
The Macrosystem	The **macrosystem** is the outermost layer of the context in Bronfenbrenner's model and includes influences such as culture and historical time.

non-Hispanic students leave school to help support their family (Suárez-Orozco & Suárez-Orozco, 2001).

In reality, there is considerable disagreement among experts about the true causes of the Hispanic American dropout problem—although few people disagree that it is a problem. In addition to the factors we discussed—a less authoritative parenting style, poorer quality schools, less support for achievement in the peer group, an incompatibility between the stress placed at home on cooperation and the emphasis on competition at school, the high unemployment rate in many Hispanic neighborhoods, and the strong sense of familism in Hispanic culture—many others have been suggested, from sheer poverty to language difficulties to discriminatory practices in school. And there is evidence, although not always conclusive, to support each of these accounts. In all likelihood, something as complicated as dropping out of school is not due to any one factor, but to the cumulative effects of many different ones. The value of the ecological perspective is that it provides a framework for looking at multiple contextual influences, at different levels of analysis. (For a summary of this section, see "Interim Summary 2.3: The Importance of Context.")

So far we have looked at the history of ideas about nature and nurture, at genetic influences on development (nature), and at contextual influences on development (nurture). In the last section of the chapter we look at ways to put nature and nurture together and show how they interact.

THE INTERPLAY BETWEEN GENES AND CONTEXT

There are four main types of interplay between genetic and environmental influences to consider when trying to understand children's development (Rutter, 2006). Each adds to our understanding of how genotypes (your inherited potentials and predispositions) are translated into phenotypes (how you actually turn out). These are:

1. Environmental effects on gene expression
2. Environmental effects on heritability
3. Gene-environment interactions
4. Gene-environment correlations

Environmental Effects on Gene Expression

Until recently, scientists thought that genes contained a fixed set of instructions and operated on set timetables. Now we know better. As we noted earlier in the chapter, the way that genes affect development is through the proteins they "instruct" the body to produce—what scientists refer to as **gene expression**. But, remember, the actual proteins that are produced—that is, the gene expression, rather than the gene—not only are a function of the particular set of instructions code for proteins contained in the gene, but also are dependent on factors such as temperature, light, available nutrients, and, importantly, other chemicals that are circulating in the body.

gene expression The process through which genes influence the production of specific proteins, which in turn influence the phenotype.

Maybe an example from the kitchen will help. The ingredients that go into a custard include milk, eggs, and some sort of flavoring (like vanilla and sugar). Most recipes have you beat the eggs and then add them to heated milk to make the base that you will eventually bake. So let's think of the eggs and milk as "genes" and the final product—the custard—as their manifestation. (Stay with us here.) But just as it would be wrong to think that genes alone can determine human traits, it is just as wrong to think that simply combining beaten eggs and hot milk will always produce a perfect custard. In fact, the environment in which you combine the milk and eggs can produce either a perfect, velvety product or a lumpy curdled mess. That's because if you heat the milk to too high a temperature before adding the beaten eggs, the eggs will cook and firm up before they have had a chance to blend with the milk. Moreover, there is no way to undo this. The environment in which the eggs and milk have "expressed" themselves makes all the difference—permanently.

The Nurturant Rat Manipulating the environment to see what happens to human gene expression is seldom ethical, of course. But scientists have studied this in animals, and it turns out that a change in environment can indeed affect genes. In a remarkable demonstration of this, a group of scientists examined how the biological processes that regulate rats' responses to stress could be permanently altered by changing the quality of mothering they received as newborns (Champagne et al., 2003; Meaney, 2001; Sabatini et al., 2007; Weaver et al., 2004). The scientists bred two strains of rats that differed in how the mothers treated their pups; one strain—the nurturant moms—licked and groomed their pups a great deal, and the other did not. As adults, the rats who were born to the nur-

Even if they have genes that predispose them to being fearful and anxious, rat pups raised by nurturant mothers do not show these characteristics. This is an example of how the environment can affect gene expression.

turant mothers were less fearful and anxious and showed less of a hormonal response to stress than the comparison group (the researchers were able to actually measure the biochemistry of the rats' stress response), and when they became mothers, they were more nurturant toward their own pups—no surprise, because the strain of nurturant rats had been bred with this trait in mind.

At this point, though, the researchers could not tell whether the differences between the two strains of rats in how they responded to stress were due to differences in their environments (which kind of mothering the rat received as a pup) or to differences in their genes (which mother's genes the rat inherited). So they did something very clever; they did a second experiment, in which they took rat pups born to "good moms" and transferred them to "bad moms" to be raised (a technique known as "**cross-fostering**"), and vice versa. Guess what? The rats raised by the bad moms turned fearful and anxious—despite their "better" genes—and the rats raised by the good moms were just the opposite. More important, the biochemical response that was usually associated with being raised by either a nurturant or non-nurturant mom changed as well. In other words, the expression of the gene regulating the stress response was altered by the way the rats were reared.

cross-fostering In animal research, the process of removing an offspring from its biological parents and having it raised by other adults, often with different attributes than the biological parents.

Environmental Effects on Heritability

Earlier we discussed the concept of "heritability," the extent to which a characteristic is influenced by genetic as opposed to environmental factors. As we explained, for decades scientists tried to attach a number—the heritability quotient—to all sorts of phenomena, from intelligence, to aggression, to self-esteem. There's a slight problem, though. No characteristic has one single heritability quotient that applies to everyone. In fact, recent studies have found that heritability varies from one group to another (e.g., from poor to middle-class families) (Bronfenbrenner & Morris, 2006). This means that it is impossible to pin down how much a trait (such as intelligence) is influenced by genes. The heritability of a trait depends on the environment.

Imagine that you have cuttings for two different strains of roses, one that has been genetically bred to produce lush blooms all summer, and one that has not. If you water and fertilize these cuttings as well as possible, the genetic differences between the plants will be clearly visible. However, if you deprive them, neither will thrive. In other words, one environment allows a genetic difference to shine through; another environment does not. If you were to compute the heritability of bloom production only looking at plants raised in the best environments, you would reach a very different conclusion (that bloom production is highly heritable) than if you were to do the same computation looking at these same plants in terrible environments (that bloom production is barely heritable).

And so it is with human potentials and predispositions. The way in which the environment changes the heritability of a trait is not always the same (Rutter, 2006). Many studies find, for example, that the heritability of intelligence is higher in more advantaged environments—presumably because under optimal contextual conditions, we can better see the result of differences in people's genetic endowment (not unlike the example of roses in the previous paragraph). Some studies also find that genetic factors matter less when the characteristic in question is already pretty much determined by the environment. If we were interested in estimating genetic influences on alcohol use, for instance, we would get an entirely different heritability quotient if we studied this question in a country in which alcohol use was illegal than we would in a country where it was easily available. In a place where using alcohol is illegal, even people with a very high genetic tendency to drink wouldn't be able to do so, so it would look as if genes had very little to do with drinking. But in a place where everyone has access to alcohol, our estimate of genetic influences would likely be much higher, because the open access allows people who don't have a genetic inclination to want to drink to avoid it, and people who have the genes for alcohol use to indulge themselves.

Gene-Environment Interaction

How a person's genotype becomes a phenotype depends on **gene-environment interaction**—that is, inherited traits lead to different characteristics in different contexts. An innately shy child might thrive in a peaceful home where her shyness is respected and she is encouraged (but not pushed) to be more outgoing and confident. The same child might become sullen and angry—a time bomb waiting to explode—in a family whose members fight, criticize and belittle one another, and constantly tease her. Likewise, a child with aggressive tendencies might become a bully in a home where he is punished physically but develop into a star athlete in a home where parents use "time-outs" and other nonconfrontational strategies to deal with his outbursts, at the same time channeling his anger into acceptable competitive outlets.

gene-environment interaction The process through which genotypes produce different phenotypes in different contexts.

The best way to look at inherited traits is as an array of possibilities, not fixed points—what scientists call a **reaction range** (see Figure 2.7). Height is an obvious example. Individuals do not inherit a specific height (there is no gene for being 5'10"); rather, they inherit a range of possible heights (say, from 5'7" to 5'11"). Where a person falls within that range—his or her actual (phenotypic) height—is influenced by the environment (especially prenatal and postnatal health and nutrition). But the influence of the environment is not limitless. No amount of good nutrition will increase someone's height beyond the maximum of his or her reaction range for that trait.

reaction range An array of phenotypic possibilities that a genotype has the potential to produce as a result of the context in which the organism develops.

The same is true for most other traits. Developmentalists see intellectual, personality, and behavioral traits as well as physical traits in terms of a reaction range. Someone who is genotypically clumsy may learn to play basketball competently, but probably will never become a professional all-star—or even make it into the pros to begin with.

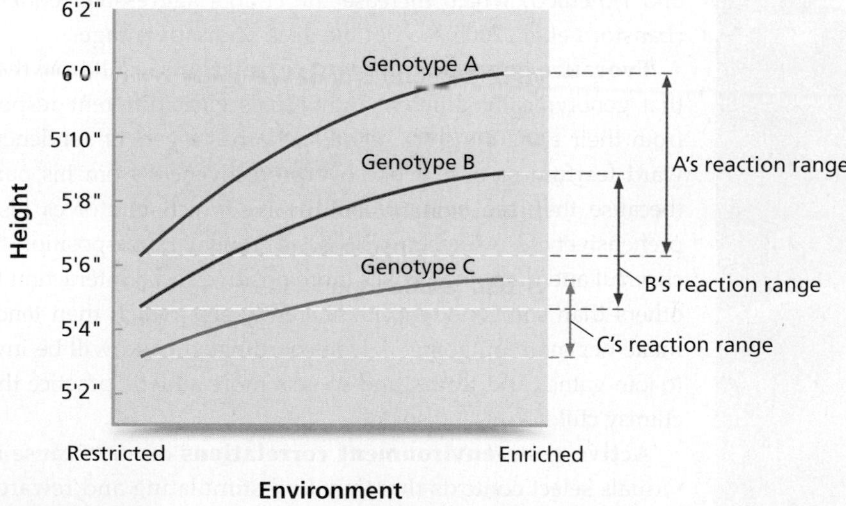

FIGURE 2.7

Reaction Range

The potential range of each person's height—the "reaction range"—is determined by his or her genotype. Person A has the potential to be anywhere from 5'6" to 6' tall, whereas person C's potential height ranges from 5'3" to 5'5". Although this reaction range is genetically determined, the environment is also very important. In an enriched environment (e.g., good prenatal care or nutrition), each person has a better chance of reaching the tallest potential height at the upper end of their reaction range.

Gene-Environment Correlation

So far we have been focusing on the effect of the environment on genes and genotypes. Sometimes overlooked is the impact of genotypes on the environment—that is, how the developing person shapes his or her world, just by being an individual. The idea of infants creating their environments, somehow getting the people around them to do exactly as they wish, might make a good horror movie. We're not talking about cause and effect, here, though, but rather correlations (see Chapter 1). Inherited traits and experience are not independent, unrelated influences but often go together (they are positively correlated).

passive gene-environment correlations Similarity between the results of genetic and environmental influences due to the fact that the same parents provide both genes and environments for their children.

evocative gene-environment correlations Similarity between the results of genetic and environmental influences due to the fact that genotypically different individuals elicit different responses from their environments.

Developmentalists have described three types of gene-environment correlations: *passive, evocative,* and *active* (Plomin, DeFries, & Loeblin, 1977; Scarr & McCartney, 1983).

Passive gene-environment correlations result from the fact that parents provide both genes and environments for their children. (This correlation is "passive" in that the child doesn't do anything; both are part of what has been passed down, either through parents' biology or behavior.) Reading is a good illustration. Children whose parents read to them often generally do well in school. This suggests that reading enhances intellectual development. But that is only half of the story. Parents who read to their children a lot probably enjoy reading and are good at reading to others. Thus their children not only are exposed to books, but also inherit "genes" for reading. They grow up to be book lovers (and do well in school) for both genetic and environmental reasons. Passive gene-environment correlations might be called the "double whammy effect." Children who grow up in intellectually stimulating environments probably have intelligent parents—a double dose of advantage. Similarly, a child whose parents are above average in aggression inherits a genetic predisposition in this direction and is also more likely to be spanked, threatened, and ridiculed, which increase the child's aggressive tendencies (Lansford et al., 2005)—a double dose of disadvantage.

Evocative gene-environment correlations result from the fact that genotypically different individuals elicit different responses from their environments. A child who has a genetic tendency toward fearfulness may evoke overprotectiveness from his parents (because they see how anxious he is), which reinforces his apprehensiveness. A person who has a genetic predisposition to be cheerful and outgoing evokes more positive social interaction from others than someone who is inherently shy, which then tends to make her more outgoing. A well-coordinated child will be invited to join games and teams, and so gets more athletic practice than a clumsy child does, and so on.

The fact that individuals select the contexts in which they spend time makes it difficult to distinguish between genetic and environmental influence. Someone who has inherited genes for musical ability spends time making music, which further strengthens the trait.

Active gene-environment correlations occur because individuals select contexts that they find stimulating and rewarding, a process called **niche-picking** (not to be confused with nitpicking, which is annoying). In other words, they choose to participate in contexts that tend to strengthen the traits that lead them to select those contexts. A child who is genetically inclined to be athletic chooses friends who enjoy the same active play she does, joins teams, practices and watches sports, chooses sports gear over other fashions, and so selects an athletic niche in her world. A child with artistic genetic tendencies chooses to play make-believe, create things from various items collected in his back-

INTERIM SUMMARY 2.4

The Interplay Between Genes and Context	
Environmental Effects on Gene Expression	The way that genes affect development is through the proteins they "instruct" the body to produce—what scientists refer to as **gene expression**. But gene expression is influenced by environmental factors.
Environmental Effects on Heritability	The heritability of a trait varies as a function of the environment. For example, some traits that appear highly heritable in advantageous environments appear less so in less advantageous ones.
Gene-Environment Interaction	Inherited traits lead to different characteristics in different contexts. The best way to view an inherited trait is as an array of possibilities—what scientists call a **reaction range**.
Gene-Environment Correlation	Genetic and environmental influences often work in the same direction, which makes it hard to separate their effects. Three types of gene-environment correlation are passive, evocative, and active.

yard, and spend time with a grandfather who is a sculptor, and in so doing, selects his context and experiences.

The importance of these different types of gene-environment correlations changes over the course of development (Scarr & McCartney, 1983). Not surprisingly, passive gene-environment correlations are most important for infants and young children. Adults choose contexts for small children. An infant can decide what to pay attention to but cannot select where he or she goes. Active gene-environment correlations become more important with age, as children develop skills and have more opportunities to choose contexts. A toddler plays with siblings, neighbors, or whomever her mother invites to play; a six-year-old makes her own friends in school; an adolescent makes friends from other schools and neighborhoods. Evocative gene-environment correlations are important throughout the lifespan. Infants influence the way others handle them, just as the way adults act toward others affects how others act toward them. (For a summary of this section, see "Interim Summary 2.4: The Interplay Between Genes and Context.")

active gene-environment correlations Similarity between the results of genetic and environmental influences due to the fact that children select contexts that they find rewarding, and that therefore tend to maintain or strengthen their genetically influenced traits.

niche-picking The process through which individuals select the environments in which they spend time.

SUMMING UP AND LOOKING AHEAD

In this chapter we described the long debate over whether nature (genes) or nurture (the environment) drives development. That debate is over. Developmentalists today know that nature works *with* nurture. Advances in our understanding of genetics (culminating in the human genome project) have shown that the interplay between genes and the environment is more complex, and gene expression more variable, than anyone suspected, even as recently as 15 or 20 years ago. Likewise, we are more aware of the different but overlapping effects of the contexts in which children become themselves. Thus, two historically separate approaches to development have become one.

Nowhere is this more visible or significant than in prenatal development, the subject of our next chapter, "Conception, Prenatal Development, and Birth."

HERE'S WHAT YOU SHOULD KNOW

Did You Get It?

After reading this chapter, you should understand the following:

- How views of ways in which genetic and environmental forces influence development have changed over time, and how contemporary scientists think about this issue
- What genes are, and how they influence development
- The difference between mitosis and meiosis
- Why a genotype and phenotype can differ
- The various levels of context as described in the ecological perspective on development
- The different ways in which genetic and environmental influences interact to influence development

Important Terms and Concepts

active gene-environment correlations (p. 60)
additive heredity (p. 47)
adoption studies (p. 39)
alleles (p. 47)
base pairs (p. 46)
bipedalism (p. 43)
canalization (p. 44)
chromosomes (p. 46)
cross-fostering (p. 58)
dominant/recessive heredity (p. 48)
epigenesis (p. 42)
eugenics (p. 38)
evocative gene-environment correlations (p. 60)
exosystem (p. 53)
familism (p. 55)
family relatedness studies (p. 40)
fraternal twins (p. 39)
gametes (p. 47)
gene (p. 46)
gene expression (p. 57)
gene-environment interaction (p. 59)
genetic determinism (p. 38)
genotype (p. 46)
heritability (p. 39)
human genome (p. 36)
identical twins (p. 39)
macrosystem (p. 54)
meiosis (p. 47)
mesosystem (p. 52)
microsystem (p. 51)
mitosis (p. 47)
mutations (p. 49)
nativism (p. 37)
natural selection (p. 42)
niche-picking (p. 60)
nonshared environment (p. 40)
passive gene-environment correlations (p. 60)
phenotype (p. 46)
preformationism (p. 37)
reaction range (p. 59)
regulator genes (p. 49)
shared environment (p. 40)
stem cells (p. 42)
survival of the fittest (p. 42)
tabula rasa (p. 38)
theory of evolution (p. 42)
twin studies (p. 39)

CHAPTER 3

Conception, Prenatal Development, and Birth

© Larry Williams/Corbis

3 Conception, Prenatal Development, and Birth

Is it a girl or a boy?

Sex is genetically determined at the moment of conception; we are either male or female from the very beginning—or so people assume. But the reality isn't that simple. Genes do not control prenatal sex development the way a playwright determines the lines for characters in a play, creating every detail. Genes are more like the director of a play. The director creates a basic plan, but the performance depends on how the actors interpret their roles, whether the lighting engineer and backstage hands perform their jobs, what the audience and the atmosphere in the theater are like, and so on. Throughout the performance, timing is also critical.

So it is with gender differentiation. Becoming male or female is not simply the unfolding of a genetic plan, but a dynamic, interactive process. The genes a developing person inherits from his or her parents create probabilities, but the context—the world inside the mother's womb and the outside world in which she lives—plays a critical role in the outcome. Moreover, the developing person plays a leading role in this drama.

This chapter seeks to address four main questions:

- What happens during the first nine months of development?
- Will the baby be normal?
- What should parents do during pregnancy to optimize the baby's health?
- What happens during the birth process?

THE FIRST 9 MONTHS

Lifespan development begins long before birth. Some of the most rapid and dramatic developments in the human lifespan occur in the first 9 months. **Gestation**—the period from conception to birth—takes about 280 days, counting from the mother's last menstrual period. During this time, a single cell, smaller than the period at the end of this sentence, develops into an approximately 7-pound, 20-inch-long baby boy or girl, a new and unique individual.

gestation The period from conception to birth that lasts about 280 days, counting from the mother's last menstrual period.

The following sections present information on the three main stages of prenatal development: the stage of the zygote (from conception to about 2 weeks); the stage of the embryo (from about 2 to 8 weeks); and the stage of the fetus (from about 8 to 40 weeks).

ovum (singular), **ova** (plural) Female sex cells (egg). Girls are born with about 2 million ova.

ovulation An event that occurs about every 28 days for women, in which a follicle in one of the ovaries ruptures, releasing a mature ovum to begin its 4- to 5-day journey down a fallopian tube toward the uterus.

Conception and the Zygote: The First 2 Weeks

The lifespan development of a new human being starts when a male's sperm pierces the membrane of a female's ovum, or egg. (In Latin, **ovum** is the singular for egg and **ova**, the plural.) Girls are born with about 2 million immature ova, each in its own sac or follicle. After puberty, a woman experiences **ovulation** about every 28 days; when a woman is ovulating, a follicle in one of her ovaries ruptures, releasing a mature ovum to begin its 4- to 5-day journey down a fallopian tube toward the uterus, or womb. (In some cases, two or, more rarely, several ova are released.) In puberty, a boy's body begins to produce an average of 2 million sperm per day.

During sexual intercourse, a man ejaculates up to 500 million sperm into the woman's body. Equipped with tails, sperm enter the vagina and attempt to swim through the cervix (the narrow opening between the uterus and vagina), into the uterus, and up the fallopian tubes. It's a difficult, upstream journey. Only a few hundred sperm will reach the fallopian tubes, and only one can fertilize the egg. After one sperm penetrates the ovum, the ovum instantly develops a protective coating that shuts out other sperm. This "winner-take-all" competition is a form of natural selection (see Chapter 2), in which weak or damaged sperm are eliminated. **Fertilization** is most likely if a couple has sexual intercourse on, or a few days before, ovulation. If fertilization does not occur, the sperm and ovum disintegrate and are expelled when the woman has her menstrual period.

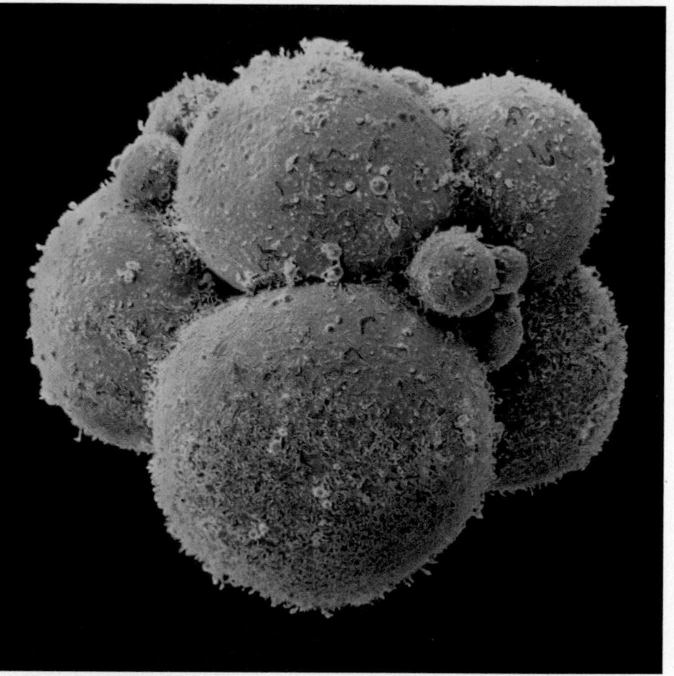

A colored scanning electron micrograph (SEM) of a human embryo at the eight-cell stage, 3 days after fertilization. The surface of each cell is covered in microvilli, microscopic cellular membrane protusions that increase the surface area of cells and are involved in a wide variety of functions, including absorption, secretion, and cellular adhesion. At this stage, the embryo has not yet implanted in the uterus (womb). Magnification: x900.

When conception occurs, development begins almost immediately. Within hours, the sperm and egg fuse to create a new cell, called a **zygote**. As discussed in Chapter 2, the 23 chromosomes from the mother's egg pair up with the 23 chromosomes from the father's sperm, creating a *genotype* (the unique genetic makeup of the individual) unlike any other, an inheritance that lasts throughout life. But development of the future child's *phenotype* (actual, observable characteristics) is only beginning.

As the zygote travels toward the uterus, the original cell divides and multiplies. By the end of the first week, *differentiation* begins—that is, the original stem cells begin to assume specialized roles. The zygote's outer cells will become a support system, including the **placenta**. The placenta—via the umbilical cord—provides food and oxygen to the developing child and carries waste products away. The zygote's inner cells will become the embryo.

During the second week, another critical event in pregnancy occurs: **implantation**. On reaching the uterus, the zygote embeds in the uterus's nutrient-rich lining (or endometrium), like roots of a growing plant into soil. But implantation is not automatic (Moore & Persaud, 2003).

When implantation is successful, a pregnancy has begun. But pregnancy eludes some couples.

fertilization Insemination of an ovum by a sperm.

zygote The new cell created when the sperm and egg fuse.

placenta The support system that—via the umbilical cord—provides food and oxygen to the developing child and carries waste products away.

implantation On reaching the uterus, the zygote embeds in the uterus's nutrient-rich lining (or endometrium), like roots of a growing plant into soil.

infertility Failure to conceive a child after 12 months of sexual intercourse without birth control.

Infertility and Reproductive Technology Every year, some 2 million U.S. couples seek medical help for **infertility**, the failure to conceive a child after 12 months of sexual intercourse without birth control. The risk of infertility depends on a variety of factors; three primary ones are the couple's overall health, lifestyle, and age. For example, infections—especially sexually transmitted diseases (STDs)—may interfere with conception and implantation. In addition, malnutrition at one extreme and obesity at the other reduce the chances of pregnancy. So do alcohol, smoking, and drugs (including some medications). A major life cycle factor is chronological age. A woman's fertility begins to decrease around age 32, and a man's declines after age 35. Because many young people in developed nations postpone marriage and parenthood to pursue higher education and establish careers (see Figure 3.1), infertility is more common today than in the past (Barber, 2001). But infertility is not sterility (permanent inability to conceive); often infertility is treatable.

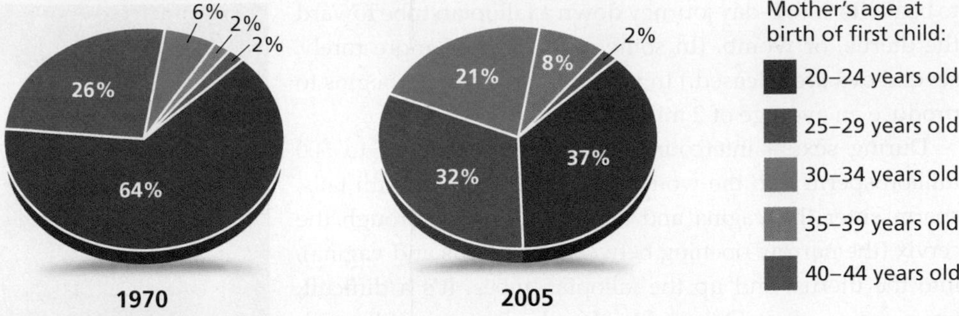

FIGURE 3.1

Changes Between 1970 and 2005 in the Age When Women Have Their First Child

In 1970, the majority of women (64%) were 20 to 24 years old when they had their first child; however, in 2005, fewer than 40 percent of women had their first child in their earlier 20s. Moreover, between 1970 and 2005, the percentage of women who had their first child at age 30 or older tripled from 10 percent to 31 percent.

Source: U.S. Department of Health and Human Services, Health Resources and Services Administration, Maternal and Child Health Bureau. *Child Health USA 2007*, Rockville, Maryland: U.S. Department of Health and Human Services, 2007.

The first step in treatment of infertility is to identify the cause. Perhaps the woman is not ovulating or her fallopian tubes are blocked (due to infections). Other causes may be that the woman has endometriosis (a buildup of tissue in the uterus over time, which interferes with implantation) or the man has a low sperm count or immobile, misshapen sperm (usually due to infections and age). In about a third of cases, no cause is found.

The simplest treatments are giving a woman hormone-based **fertility drugs** to stimulate ovulation (often of more than one egg) or performing surgery to repair a damaged part of the man or woman's reproductive system.

fertility drugs Hormone-based agents that enhance ovarian activity.

The most common treatment for male infertility is **artificial insemination**: inserting sperm directly into the woman's uterus with a syringe. This may be done with a concentration of the male partner's ejaculations or with sperm from an anonymous donor. Increasingly, lesbian couples and single women who want to become mothers without a male partner choose this route to pregnancy.

artificial insemination The most common treatment for male infertility, which involves inserting sperm directly into the woman's uterus with a syringe.

For couples with complex problems, more advanced reproductive technology is available. The best-known and most common procedure is **in vitro fertilization (IVF)**. First, the woman takes fertility drugs so that her body releases more than one egg. When tests show that she is at the point of ovulation, her ova are surgically extracted and mixed with her partner's sperm in a laboratory dish. (Literally, *in vitro* means "in glass.") After sperm fertilize the ova and cell duplication, or mitosis (see Chapter 2), has begun, one or more of the embryos is inserted into the woman's womb at the time in her cycle that implantation is most likely.

in vitro fertilization (IVF) The best-known and most common advanced reproductive technology procedure in which the woman takes fertility drugs so that her body releases more than one egg, her ova are surgically extracted at ovulation, and then are mixed with her partner's sperm in a laboratory dish.

Several variations on IVF are available, including the use of donated ova, sperm, or both. *Prenatal adoption,* as the latter is sometimes called, enables a couple to experience pregnancy and birth even though the developing child does not have their genes. If a woman cannot sustain a pregnancy, the couple may arrange for a **surrogate mother**, or "gestational carrier." The surrogate mother may be impregnated with the male partner's sperm through artificial insemination or with the couple's embryo, conceived in vitro. Technically, then, a child could have five parents: a sperm donor, an ova donor, a gestational mother, and the people the child calls Mom or Dad. But in the great majority of cases, couples use their own **gametes** (sex cells, or sperm and ova).

surrogate mother The woman who is impregnated with a male's sperm through artificial insemination or with the couple's embryo, conceived in vitro.

gametes Sex cells, the male sperm and female ova.

Reproductive technology does not increase the danger of birth defects (Shevell et al., 2005). The main "risk" is a multiple pregnancy (twins or more), which is linked to pregnancy complications, premature birth, low birth weight, and even infant death (Johnson, 2005). About 30 percent of IVF deliveries are twins, compared with only 1–2 percent of natural pregnancies. In January 2009, a California woman famously gave birth to octuplets (six boys and two girls) through IVF.

Another risk is failure of an IVF pregnancy to succeed, and that failure is compounded by the psychological stress of repeated cycles of hope and disappointment about eventually having a child for the would-be mother and father (Kopitzke & Wilson, 2000). Less than 30 percent of IVF and related procedures result in pregnancy and birth, often only after several attempts (www.sart.org, 2006).

The good news is that 1.4 million babies conceived with IVF have been born worldwide since the first "test-tube" baby was born in England in 1978. In 2000, 25,000 U.S. women became pregnant with technological help and gave birth to more than 35,000 babies, nearly 1 percent of the babies born in the United States that year. (Note that 10,000 were multiple births.)

Reproductive technology not only has permitted many people who would have remained childless to become parents, but also has created new types of relatedness (Golombok, 2002). When donated gametes are used, either the mother or the father is not genetically related to the child. Unlike stepfamilies, however, the couple goes through pregnancy together, rears the child from birth, and introduces him or her to other people as their own. The differences between parents who used IVF and those who conceived naturally tend to be small. In general, the children appear to be well adjusted in terms of their relationships with parents and peers and their social and emotional development.

For couples who conceive without extra help, embryonic development is a given; for couples who use reproductive technologies, it is a miracle.

The Embryo: Weeks 2 Through 8

The embryonic period begins about 2 weeks after conception, when the zygote is firmly attached to the wall of the uterus (Hamdoun & Epel, 2007). Already the embryo's cells have formed specialized layers. The outer layer (**ectoderm**) will become skin, nerves, and sense organs; the middle layer (**mesoderm**), muscle, bones, the circulatory system, and some organs; and the inner layer (**endoderm**), the digestive system, lungs, urinary tract, and glands. The **amniotic sac**, a protective membrane filled with warm liquid that cushions the tiny embryo, takes shape.

During the next 6 weeks, the basic structure for a human being appears, and organs begin to function. The embryo grows about 0.04 inches (1 millimeter) per day, but development is not uniform. Each organ system has its own program for lifespan development, and different parts of the body develop on different days. The first visible development is the appearance of a "primitive streak," a thin line down the center of the embryo that will become the central nervous system. A portion of the ectoderm folds over to form a neural tube, the beginning of the spinal cord. At 3½ weeks, the brain begins to form at the top of the neural tube. **Neurogenesis** (the production of neurons or nerve cells) begins. Almost all of the neurons in the human brain are generated during prenatal development. This means that an average of 250,000 neurons must be generated *each minute*, although the rate is not steady over the 9 months of gestation.

ectoderm The outer layer of an embryo's cells that will become fetal skin, nerves, and sense organs.

mesoderm The middle layer of an embryo's cells that will become muscle, bones, the circulatory system, and some organs.

endoderm The inner layer of an embryo's cells that will become the digestive system, lungs, urinary tract, and glands.

amniotic sac A protective membrane filled with warm liquid that cushions the embryo.

neurogenesis The production of neurons or nerve cells.

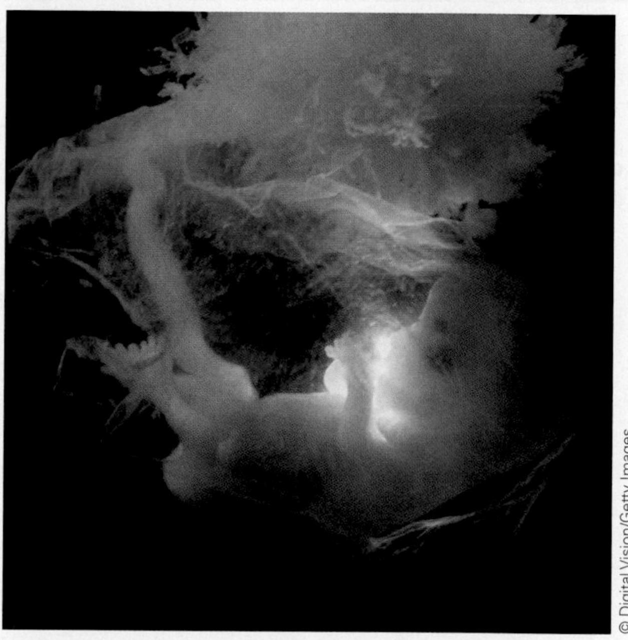

Even at an early stage of development, the human embryo has many anatomical features (such as eyes, hands, legs, and feet) that can be distinguished.

Two months after conception, the embryo is about 1 inch long (the length of the last joint of your thumb) and weighs just 0.04 ounces (one gram). Nevertheless, all of the major organs and body parts have formed. The head is rounded, and facial features are visible. Arm and leg buds are developing. The embryo's stomach produces digestive juices, its kidneys filter blood, and its heart beats. The respiratory system—designed for air, not the liquid environment of the womb—is the last to develop. The embryo's head is much larger in proportion to its body (about one-half the embryo's length) than at any other time in life.

The Fetus: Week 8 to Birth

The fetal period begins 2 months after conception, when major organ systems have formed. Now organs, muscles, and the nervous system become more organized and connected. Over the next 7 months, the size of the fetus (length and weight) increases twentyfold. Advances in form, function, and activity are even more pronounced.

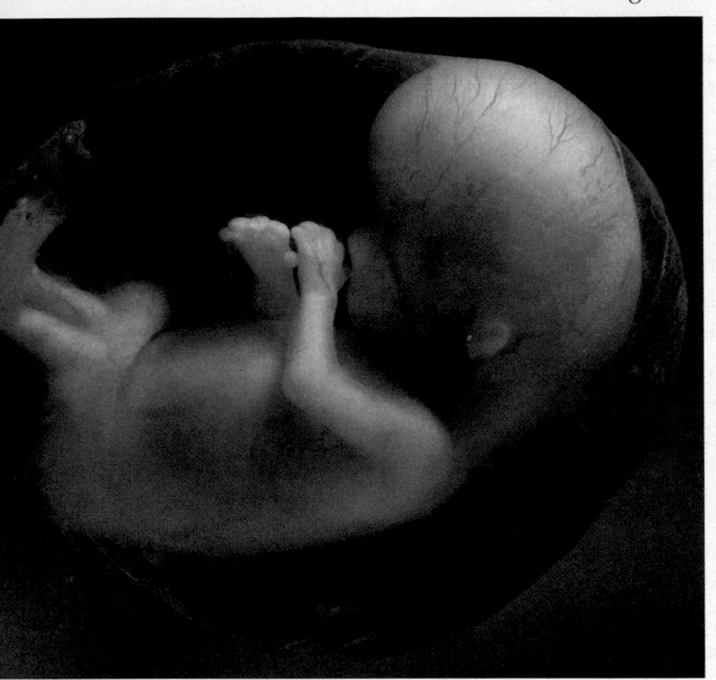
© Steve Allen/Brand X Pictures/JupiterImages

The human fetus floats in an amniotic protective sac inside the womb.

The embryo has almost all of its necessary parts, but they are still primitive. For example, the embryo has distinct but rudimentary arm buds. During the fetal period, arms lengthen, joints develop, fingers separate and grow nails, and a complex network of veins and muscles lays the foundation for the finely coordinated movements that continue to develop in childhood. The fetus can make a fist and may suck its thumb, the beginning of behavior and a sign that the brain is functioning.

The Brain and Behavior Brain development accelerates in the fetal period. By the end of the sixth month of pregnancy, neurogenesis is essentially complete. Now the brain begins to organize itself: Some neurons die off as others make new connections. Brain and neurological development continue throughout life, as we will show in later chapters. The key point here is that the central nervous system becomes active and responsive in midpregnancy.

The human fetus is not a passive voyager in the womb. Spontaneous movement begins at about 4 months and remains frequent up to and shortly after birth (Robertson & Bacher, 1995). The fourth month is the time of **quickening**, which refers to the first fetal movements the mother can feel.

quickening The first fetal movements the mother can feel.

The development of the brain and behavior is bidirectional (or two-way); that is, genetically determined brain development permits new behavior and interactions with the environment that, in turn, shape further brain development (Lecanuet et al., 1995). Prenatal behavior appears to play an important role in development. When chick embryos are immobilized, their muscles and joints do not develop normally—perhaps because their own pre-hatch movements would normally help to determine which neurons connect and which do not.

Although fetal behavior is at first random and infrequent, it becomes increasingly organized. At 3 months, the fetus swallows, urinates, kicks, curls toes, blinks, hiccups, and occasionally yawns. These activities show that the fetus's brain is sending signals to its muscles, and the muscles are responding. At 6 months, fetuses have been observed "breathing" (inhaling and exhaling amniotic fluid) and even "crying" when disturbed (Gingras, Mitchell, & Grattan, 2005). Brain waves show distinct waking and sleep states. Normally, fetal heart rate is tied to body movement and is higher during activity and lower during inactivity (DiPietro et al., 2002).

At 7 to 8 months, the fetus is less active but more vigorous. One reason is that fetal quarters are cramped; another, that the brain can now inhibit as well as initiate activity. At this age the fetus responds to sounds and vibrations. For example, a mother's walking may calm her fetus; and when the mother sits or lies down, the fetus may shift into a comfortable position. Sudden movements or vibrations cause the fetus to jump, and if the mother is frightened or anxious, the fetus's heart beats faster and movement increases (DiPietro et al., 2002).

Learning As the brain develops, fetuses are capable of simple learning; they start to recognize familiar sounds and rhythms (Hopkins & Johnson, 2005). In one study (DeCasper et al., 1994), pregnant women read nursery rhymes out loud each day for several weeks to their fetuses. At age 37 weeks, the fetuses' heart rate slowed (indicating heightened attention) when they heard audiotapes of their mother reading. They did not react this way when they were played tapes of another woman reading the same rhymes, before birth or after. Does this mean that if a mother listens to Mozart her child will be born with musical appreciation? No; this is modern folklore. If parents continue to play symphonies after the baby is born, he or she may develop musical appreciation, but whether the child becomes a skilled performer—much less a "genius" because of that—is highly doubtful. Research shows only that the fetuses recognize repeated, familiar sounds.

Individual differences Individual differences are already apparent in the fetal stage. A series of studies explored the possibility that fetal heart rates predict later, postnatal development (Bornstein et al., 2002; DiPietro et al., 2007). Fetal heart activity was measured at 24, 30, and 36 weeks' gestation. The same children's levels of language development and symbolic play were evaluated at 27 months after birth. Children who had higher heart rate variability *in utero* (in the womb) were more advanced in both language and play. One possible explanation is that these fetuses are more reactive, which translates into more advanced cognitive skills after birth; another is that some children use oxygen more efficiently, which has a positive effect on brain growth and later cognitive development. In either case, individual prenatal variations predicted later childhood differences.

In related studies, the same researchers looked at levels of fetal activity and **temperament**—a child's emotional and behavioral predispositions—at one and two years (DiPietro et al., 2002). Children who were more active as fetuses not only developed motor skills earlier, but also explored more and were more upset at being restrained at ages 1 and 2. Temperamentally, they were more confident and independent.

temperament A child's emotional and behavioral predispositions.

Developmental scientists have long viewed temperament as inborn or genetic, but these findings go further to suggest that the development of temperament is bidirectional. When fetal connections between the brain and the muscles develop rapidly, the fetus is more active. When the fetus is more active, connections are strengthened and refined, which make the fetus more active still, and so on in a cycle. Likewise, an infant who has advanced motor skills explores more; exploration enhances motor abilities, which builds confidence; and all of this influences both brain development and temperament. These infants are upset when they can't exercise their motor skills and their curiosity. Infants who were less active in the womb are easier in the sense of being more willing to accept limits on their activity.

Boy or Girl?

Gender differentiation begins at conception. Females have two X chromosomes, so all of a woman's ova have an X chromosome. Males have an X and a Y chromosome, so their sperm may contain either an X or a Y chromosome (see Chapter 2). Which sperm fertilizes an ovum determines whether the child will have a female (XX) or male (XY) genotype. But, as we said, this is just the beginning. The child's internal reproductive organs and external genitalia—much less masculine and feminine attitudes and behaviors—are not fixed the moment X meets X (or Y).

Prenatal gender development can be divided into four stages. The fact that an embryo has XX or XY chromosomes has little effect on stage one. For the first 1½ months after conception, the embryo is basically "unisex." All embryos have a similar *gonadal streak* and both Müllerian ducts (which may develop into female sex organs) and Wolffian ducts (which may develop into male sex organs). The only way to identify an embryo's sex is to examine its chromosomes.

In the second stage, physiological sex differences emerge. At about 7 weeks, a gene on the Y chromosome sends a signal that triggers the development of testes. A week or so later, the testes begin to produce two hormones: testosterone, which stimulates the development of male reproductive organs, and Müllerian inhibiting substance (MIS), which blocks the development of female reproductive organs. If the embryo does not receive this signal, and testosterone and MIS are not produced or absorbed, the fetus develops female reproductive organs, beginning with ovaries at about 10 weeks.

In the third stage (2½ to 3 months), external genitals form. Testosterone stimulates the development of testicles and a penis. If not present, the fetus develops a clitoris and vulva. Finally, in stage four, testosterone inhibits the rhythmic cycles of the hypothalamus and the pituitary, which regulate female ovulation.

Note that nature's basic plan seems to be to produce a female. The development of a male requires two extra steps. The first requirement is a signal from the Y chromosome. In **Turner's syndrome**, the embryo's cells have only one (X) chromosome. In the absence of a Y chromosome, the fetus develops into a female. The second requirement is testosterone. Without testosterone, development again follows the female pattern. A genetic defect called *testicular-feminizing syndrome* prevents a male (XY) fetus from utilizing testosterone. The embryo develops testes, but because it cannot respond to male hormones, it develops female external genitalia. Both conditions are rare.

Turner's syndrome A condition in which the embryo's cells have only one (X) chromosome.

Gender differences are not limited to anatomy, of course. Males and females act, talk, and to some degree think differently. Why? One possibility is that prenatal development is confined to physiology, and the development of masculine or feminine attitudes and behaviors is largely the result of socialization. Whether a baby has male or female genitals affects how parents and others treat him or her. And socialization guides the development of a gender identity and sex-typed behavior. Another possibility is that prenatal sex development affects the brain as well as the body. Prenatal experiences may program a boy's brain to respond to certain aspects of the environment, and a girl's brain to respond to other features of the environment. This does not mean that boys are naturally tough and girls are naturally sweet, but subtle differences may exist. Or both factors may operate together. . . .

Gender differentiation is normally continuous. Thus, a child who has an XY genotype develops a male reproductive system, is reared as a boy, has a male identity, and behaves in masculine ways. As a result, it is difficult to separate the effects of prenatal, biological development from those of postnatal socialization. Most likely males and females are *predisposed* to behave in somewhat different ways, and gender socialization brings out and reinforces their predispositions.

For example, boys typically engage in more rough-and-tumble play than girls do. Let's assume that males are genetically primed for physical aggression (a probability but not a certainty). Equally significant, parents are more physical with male than with female infants, strengthening this tendency. Dads tickle baby boys to excite them, but cuddle baby girls. In childhood, parents are more likely to accept and even encourage play-fighting in a son, whereas they discourage the same behavior in a daughter. Girls aren't "supposed" to fight physically, and boys aren't "supposed" to be afraid. Whether deliberate or unconscious, gender socialization reinforces genetic and hormonal predispositions (see Chapter 8). (For a summary of this section, see "Interim Summary 3.1: The First 9 Months.")

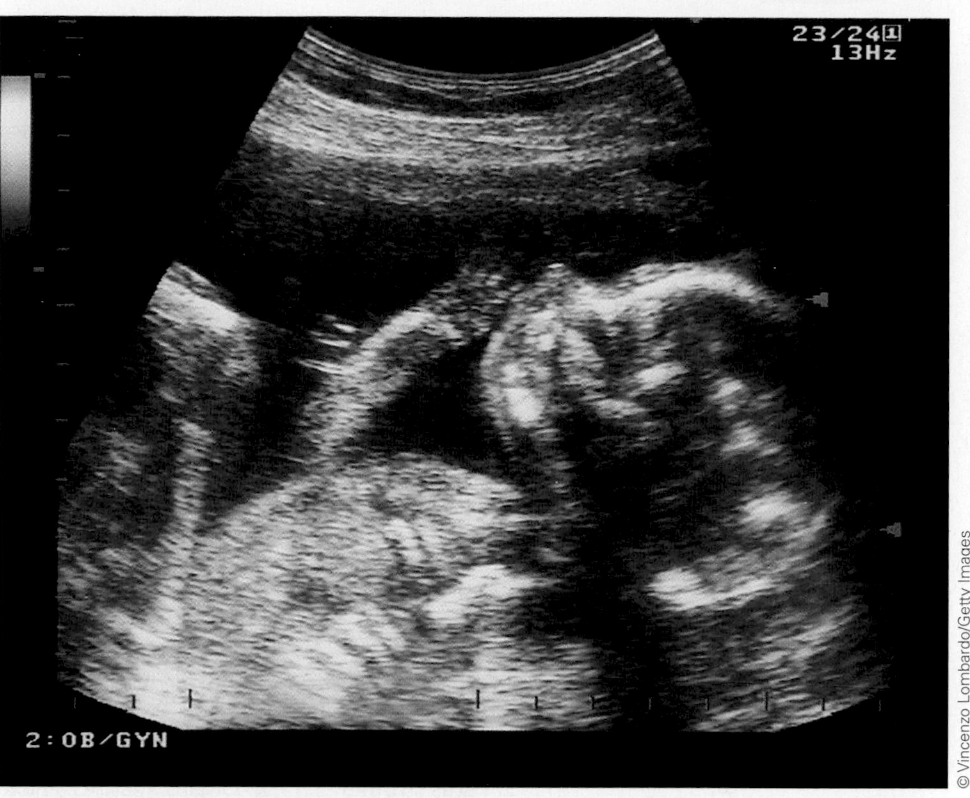

During an examination, ultrasound can be used to image the human fetus while still in utero. This one is 20 weeks old.

EVALUATING PRENATAL DEVELOPMENT

Twenty-five years ago, parents didn't know the health of their child until birth. Thanks to new technology, today we can monitor prenatal development almost from the beginning. A woman's doctor can assure her and her partner that the baby is developing normally or, when necessary, help them to prepare for complications.

One technology now used to see the fetus's structure and to watch behavior directly is **ultrasound imaging**, which provides a living picture of prenatal development (including sex differentiation at about 3 months). In this scanning process, high-frequency sound waves are directed at the womb, and a computer transforms their reflections or echoes into an image on a monitor, called a *sonogram* (Levi & Chervenak, 1998). A noninvasive procedure with no known risk to the mother or fetus, ultrasound is used routinely to assess the growth, development, and health of the fetus (Chervenak & McCullough, 1998; Garmel & D'Alton, 1994). Ultrasound scans can be performed as early as 8 weeks, but they are more accurate in later stages of pregnancy. They allow a physician to verify a baby's due date, predict multiple births, anticipate birth problems, and detect some fetal abnormalities.

ultrasound imaging A technology that provides a living picture of prenatal development (including sex differentiation).

The great majority of babies (95%) are healthy and normal at birth. "Nature" (or natural selection) eliminates most malformations before birth. Estimates are that half of all conceptions are not implanted, and a quarter of implanted embryos are spontaneously aborted in the next month or two, often before the mother knows that she was pregnant. Most of these are the result of genetic abnormalities. But fetuses with certain genetic disorders survive the prenatal period.

It is still rare for scientists to be able to link particular genes to specific disorders. Many problems—from dyslexia to depression—run in families. If a grandparent, aunt or uncle, or a sibling has the disorder, the risk that a new child in the family will be

INTERIM SUMMARY 3.1

The First 9 Months

Gestation	■ The stage from conception to birth, takes about 280 days.
Infertility	■ The failure to conceive a child after 12 months of sexual intercourse without birth control. ■ Treatments: fertility drugs, artificial insemination, in vitro fertilization (IVF)
Prenatal Development Periods	
1. Zygote (from conception to about 2 weeks)	■ Fertilization is the insemination of an ovum by a sperm. ■ A zygote is a new cell formed when the sperm and egg fuse together. ■ The 23 chromosomes from the mother's egg pair up with the 23 chromosomes from the father's sperm, creating a *genotype*.
2. Embryo (from about 2 to 8 weeks, beginning about 2 weeks after conception)	■ The embryo's cells form specialized layers: **ectoderm** (outer layer: skin, nerves, sense organs); **mesoderm** (middle layer: muscle, bones, the circulatory system, and some organs); **endoderm** (inner layer: digestive system, lungs, urinary tract, and glands). ■ The **amniotic sac**—a protective membrane that cushions the tiny embryo—takes shape.
3. Fetus (from 8 to 40 weeks)	■ Organs, muscles, and the nervous system become more organized and connected. ■ The size of the fetus (length and weight) increases twentyfold. ■ Spontaneous movement **(quickening)** begins at about 4 months (and remains frequent up to birth). ■ At 7 to 8 months, the fetus is less active but more vigorous. ■ Fetuses recognize familiar sounds and rhythms.
Gender Differentiation Begins at Conception	■ Females have two X chromosomes, so all of a woman's ova have an X chromosome. ■ Males have an X and a Y chromosome, so their sperm may contain either an X or a Y chromosome. ■ Which sperm fertilizes an ovum determines whether the child will have a female (XX) or male (XY) genotype. ■ The child's internal reproductive organs and external genitalia—and masculine and feminine attitudes and behaviors—are not fixed the moment X meets X (or Y).
Prenatal Sexual Development Can Be Divided into Four Stages	1. For the first 1½ months after conception, the embryo is basically "unisex." 2. In the second stage, physiological sex differences emerge. 3. In the third stage (2½ to 3 months), external genitals form. Testosterone stimulates the development of testicles and a penis. If not present, the fetus develops a clitoris and vulva. 4. In stage four, testosterone inhibits the rhythmic cycles of the hypothalamus and the pituitary, which regulate female ovulation.
	■ Gender socialization reinforces genetic and hormonal predispositions.

affected increases. But most are **multifactoral disorders**; that is, they are the result of interactions among multiple genes and between genes and the environment. Therefore, people can inherit a predisposition for the problem, but they may or may not manifest the problem. Next we look at abnormalities that have known causes and consequences.

multifactoral disorders Disorders that result from interactions among multiple genes and between genes and the environment.

Chromosomal and Genetic Abnormalities

Chromosomal Malformations Some abnormalities are caused by mutations or accidents during *meiosis* (the production of sperm and ova; see Chapter 2). The most common example is *Down syndrome*, also called *trisomy 21* because the child has three instead of the normal two 21st chromosomes. Down syndrome is linked to many factors, especially the mother's chronological age. About 1 in 2,000 babies born to 20-year-old women have the disorder, a rate that climbs to 1 in 20 for 45-year-old women. But there are genetic abnormalities (like Down syndrome) as well as other developmental disorders (like autism) that are linked to father's age as well (Bray, Gunnell, & Smith, 2006; Fisch et al., 2003; Reichenberg et al., 2006).

People with Down syndrome are usually short and stocky with small heads, round faces, slanted eyes, and flat noses. Most have medical problems, including heart and thyroid trouble, hearing loss, and muscle weakness. These children have moderate to severe learning handicaps, especially with language. They also tend to be exceptionally cheerful and affectionate. But no two people with Down syndrome are alike; individuals vary.

People with Down syndrome were once confined to institutions, where they received minimal attention and often died in their teens or early twenties. Today most remain with their families and attend public schools. With special attention they can develop reading, writing, and speaking skills. In adulthood they may hold jobs and live semi-independently, in group homes. With preventive health care, almost half live into their 50s and even 60s, though they may suffer from diseases of old age (such as Alzheimer's or heart disease) as early as their 30s.

Genetic abnormalities range from minor conditions like color blindness, to problems that can be corrected surgically (such as cleft palate or clubfoot), to still incurable physical and mental disabilities.

Recessive genes Most genetic disorders are carried on a recessive gene (see Chapter 2). *Sickle cell anemia* is an example. Children who inherit the sickle cell gene from both parents—homozygotes—suffer from problems ranging from chronic shortness of breath and fatigue to bouts of severe pain (from swollen joints) and frequent, sometimes fatal crises in which the heart, kidneys, and liver malfunction. But children who inherit the gene from only one parent—heterozygotes—rarely experience any symptoms. In homozygotes, all of the red blood cells are bent into a sickle shape and cannot carry adequate oxygen to the tissues and organs. In heterozygotes, only some blood cells are abnormal.

The sickle cell trait is found in populations that live, or that once lived, in tropical areas where malaria is common (Africa, the Caribbean, and Central America). Although lethal in a double dose, the sickle cell *protects* heterozygotes from malaria. About 1 in 10 African Americans and 1 in 20 Latin Americans carry the sickle cell gene.

Some recessive gene disorders are *sex linked*. Women carry the recessive gene but, because they have two X chromosomes, almost never suffer its effects. However, there is a 50-50 chance that they will transmit the genetic abnormality to their sons, who have only one X chromosome. The most common example is color blindness. (Baldness is also sex linked—carried by females, expressed in males—but is not a "disorder.")

The most famous sex-linked disorder is *hemophilia*, a disease in which the victim's body does not produce blood-clotting factor. For a person with hemophilia, even minor injuries can lead to hemorrhage, and early death is common. Hemophilia can be controlled (with injections of blood-clotting factor) but not cured. England's Queen Victoria (1819–1901) carried hemophilia—of particular significance because her children married into most of the royal houses of Europe. One of her sons, three of her grandsons, and six of her great-grandsons were hemophiliac. Historians believe that the Russian Revolution of 1917 succeeded in part because the tsar and tsarina (a granddaughter of Victoria) were preoccupied with their hemophiliac son's illness.

The Founder Effect The Amish have one of the highest rates of genetic defects in the United States. The reason is the *founder effect*. Today's 150,000 Amish are all descended from a few hundred Swiss-German settlers who came to America to found religious communities in the eighteenth century. Amish traditions forbid marriage with outsiders. Hence, over many generations of intermarriage, rare genetic disorders that lie dormant or die out in the wider population have surfaced among the Amish. Although the Amish shun such "modern" inventions as television and telephones, and even electricity and cars, like all parents, the Amish want their children to be healthy. Today their horse-drawn buggies line up outside local clinics that offer genetic counseling backed by cutting-edge technology.

Genetic Counseling

genetic counseling A profession designed to help couples understand how heredity might affect their child.

Genetic counseling is a relatively new profession, designed to help couples understand how heredity might affect their child. Health practitioners who specialize in hereditary disorders, genetic counselors function as diagnosticians, educators, and therapists. They may work alone or on a team to assist patients who have already conceived or those considering pregnancy. Who should seek genetic counseling? Generally, couples who would benefit from genetic counseling include those who belong to a group known to be at risk, those who already have a child or relatives with a genetic disorder, and those who have experienced miscarriage, stillbirth, or infertility. In addition, those couples in which the woman is age 35 or older might seek counseling.

A genetic counselor starts by taking a couple's family histories to assess whether a genetic abnormality runs in one partner's or both partners' families. The next step would be a DNA test or **karyotype**: a picture of the man and woman's chromosomes. Karyotypes are most useful in identifying recessive genetic defects.

karyotype A picture of the individual's chromosomes.

Genetic counselors help couples to understand how likely they are to have a child with a genetic disorder. For example, Tay-Sachs disease—most common among people of Eastern European Jewish heritage—is a fatal disorder characterized by steady mental and physical deterioration beginning at about six months. Homozygotes suffer seizures, muscle atrophy, and paralysis, and they rarely live beyond age 4. If only one partner carries the Tay-Sachs gene, there is no risk that a child will be affected. Only homozygotes suffer from the disorder. If both the man and woman are carriers, the risk that their child will inherit this disease is the same as the "risk" that a couple who have the recessive gene for blue eyes will have a blue-eyed child: one in four (or 25%). Each partner has one dominant, healthy gene, *A*, and one recessive, Tay-Sachs gene, *a*. Their child might be *AA* (neither afflicted nor a carrier); *Aa* or *aA* (an unafflicted carrier); or *aa* (afflicted). This does not mean that if a couple has four children, one will be affected and the other three healthy. Each pregnancy carries the same risk.

If both partners carry an abnormal recessive gene or the mother is 35 or older, they have several options. Some couples decide to adopt rather than risk bearing a child who will inevitably suffer or lead a limited life. An alternative is to conceive through IVF with donor eggs or sperm. Other couples decide to take the risk, hoping that they will conceive a healthy child. If prenatal testing reveals the fetus has a chromosomal or genetic abnormality, the couple may decide to terminate the pregnancy. Needless to say, none of these options presents an easy decision. A couple may rule out abortion, for religious or emotional reasons. They may worry about the impact of these decisions on their marriage or their other children, and they may doubt their emotional (and financial) ability to rear a disabled child. Consciously or unconsciously, they may feel ashamed and guilty about being "carriers." Genetic counselors can help parents understand the underlying causes and risks associated with different choices.

If the couple conceives, the next step is prenatal testing.

Prenatal Testing

Some (but not all) genetic defects can be identified before birth. Equally important, prenatal tests can relieve prospective parents of the anxiety of not knowing whether a baby will be normal. Most women who take prenatal tests receive the good news that their fetus does *not* have the disorder for which the test was given (March of Dimes, Pregnancy & Newborn Health Education Center, 2008).

Couples using IVF may elect to have **preimplantation genetic diagnosis**. In this screening, one or two cells are removed from a 3-day-old test-tube embryo; if the cell contains genes linked to fatal childhood disorders, that embryo is not used. In Britain, couples may also screen for genes linked to adult diseases, such as breast, ovarian, and colon cancer. (There are no regulations on preimplantation screening in the United States.)

preimplantation genetic diagnosis A screening technique that involves removing cells from a test-tube embryo to determine if the cell contains genes linked to fatal childhood disorders.

The most common prenatal test is **amniocentesis**. Using ultrasound as a guide, the doctor inserts a thin needle through the woman's abdomen into the uterus and withdraws a small amount of amniotic fluid, which contains skin cells from the fetus. These cells are cultured in a laboratory for 10 to 12 days and then tested for chromosomal or genetic abnormalities. Amniocentesis is usually done halfway through pregnancy, in the fourth month. Test results take 3 weeks. The main drawback is that the results are not known until the fifth month of pregnancy, when the fetus is relatively well developed. If the results show that the fetus has a severe disorder, the parents are faced with an emotionally and morally difficult decision: whether to give birth to a handicapped baby or to abort a fetus whose movements they may have already felt.

amniocentesis A prenatal test in which, using ultrasound as a guide, the doctor inserts a thin needle through the woman's abdomen into the uterus to withdraw amniotic fluid that contains skin cells from the fetus.

Newer tests permit earlier results. In **chorionic villi sampling** (CVS), the doctor uses a needle to remove a small piece of the villi, extensions that attach the amniotic sac to the wall of the uterus. Cells from the villi have the same genetic and biochemical makeup as the fetus. CVS can be done in the middle of the third month of pregnancy, and it yields preliminary results in about 10 days.

chorionic villi sampling A fetal test that involves removal of a small piece of the villi, extensions that attach the amniotic sac to the wall of the uterus.

Both amniocentesis and CVS can be used to diagnose chromosomal, metabolic, and blood-borne conditions; screen for sickle cell anemia; and identify congenital defects (such as muscular dystrophy) (Green & Statham, 1996; Robinson & Wisner, 1993).

These tests are not risk free, however. The American College of Obstreticians and Gynecologists claims that for every 200 to 400 amniocentesis procedures, approximately one miscarriage will occur, and there is a 1 in 50 to 100 chance after CVS. In addition, CVS has been linked to a slight (1 in 1,000–3,000) risk of deformed limbs (Olney et al., 1995). Neither are these tests foolproof. *False positives* (test results that show a disorder is present when it is not) and *false negatives* (test results that show a disorder is not present when it is) are possible. No test can *guarantee* a normal, healthy baby. (For a summary of this section, see "Interim Summary 3.2: Evaluating Prenatal Development.")

INTERIM SUMMARY 3.2

Evaluating Prenatal Development

Ultrasound Imaging Provides a Living Picture of Prenatal Development	■ It is noninvasive with no known risk to the mother or the fetus. ■ It allows a physician to verify a baby's due date, predict multiple births, anticipate birth problems, and detect some fetal abnormalities.
Genetic Abnormalities	■ These can range from minor conditions like color blindness, to problems that can be corrected surgically, to incurable physical and mental disabilities. ■ Some abnormalities are caused by mutations or accidents during meiosis, the most common being Down syndrome, also called *trisomy 21,* where the child has three instead of the normal two 21st chromosomes.
Recessive Gene Disorders	■ Most genetic disorders, such as sickle cell anemia, are carried on a recessive gene. ■ Children who inherit the sickle cell gene from both parents suffer from problems ranging from chronic shortness of breath and fatigue to bouts of severe pain and frequent, sometimes fatal crises in which the heart, kidneys, and liver malfunction. ■ Children who inherit the gene from only one parent rarely experience any symptoms. ■ Some recessive gene disorders are *sex linked,* such as hemophilia, a disease in which the victim's body does not produce blood-clotting factor.
Genetic Counseling	■ Helps couples understand how heredity might affect their child and how likely they are to have a child with a genetic disorder. ■ A counselor starts by taking a couple's family histories and then by doing a DNA test or **karyotype**: a picture of the man and woman's chromosomes.
Prenatal Tests	■ **Preimplantation genetic diagnosis** (screens cells from three-day-old test-tube embryos for genes linked to fatal childhood disorders). ■ **Amniocentesis** and **chorionic villi sampling** (CVS) (used to diagnose chromosomal, metabolic, and blood-borne conditions, screen for sickle cell anemia, and identify congenital defects).

PROTECTING THE FETUS

A healthy pregnancy begins before conception (Caviness & Grant, 2006; CDC, 2008). Therefore, women who want to become pregnant need to prepare their bodies. Smoking, for example, can reduce fertility (Akushevich, Kravchenko, & Manton, 2007). So can a case of mumps, if untreated. This applies to would-be fathers as well as mothers. It also applies to women who *might* become pregnant (women who are sexually active but do not use birth control). A woman who isn't planning to have a baby might not even suspect she is pregnant until 10 or 12 weeks after conception—and the fetus is most vulnerable to certain disorders during the first 4 to 10 weeks of pregnancy (CDC, 2006).

The guidelines for healthy living—eat your vegetables; don't smoke, drink, or use drugs—become imperative during pregnancy, because the main source of contact between the embryo and fetus and the outside world is the mother's bloodstream. The mother's blood does not flow directly into the fetus's veins but through the placenta to the umbilical cord. The placenta acts as a filter, protecting the fetus from some—but not all—harmful substances.

Regular visits during pregnancy to an obstetrician (a physician who specializes in pregnancy, delivery, and postnatal care) are essential. But young women, in particular, often take their health for granted . . . and take chances.

Pregnant mothers eat for two—for themselves and their developing baby—so following a healthy diet is doubly important.

Maternal Characteristics

Aside from genetic abnormalities, the well-being of the fetus depends first on the mother.

Age For different reasons, both younger and older women are more likely to have problematic pregnancies and birth complications than are women in their 20s. Mothers under age 18 have significantly higher rates of preterm (or premature) births and low-birth-weight babies than do mothers ages 20 to 24 of the same ethnicity, income level, and marital status (Bornstein & Putnick, 2007; Bornstein et al., 2006; Ekwo & Moawad, 2000). One reason is that teenage mothers typically wait longer to see a doctor when they think they might be pregnant and are less likely than older mothers to have regular prenatal checkups. Evidence shows even worse outcomes for teenagers' second preganancies (Reime, Schücking, & Wenzlaff, 2008).

Older mothers have an increased rate of birth complications. Even when medical risks and socioeconomic factors are taken into consideration, women age 30 or older are more likely than younger women to experience birth complications, to have cesarean sections (explained later), and to give birth to infants who need to be admitted to newborn intensive care units. Older women also have a greater risk of miscarriage, stillbirths, high blood pressure, and even death during childbirth than do mothers under age 30. As we mentioned earlier in this chapter, some harmful effects associated with fathers' advancing age have also been identified. On the positive side, the newborns of older women are as healthy as those of younger mothers, despite complicated pregnancies and delivery.

Diet and Nutrition According to an old saying, "a pregnant woman is eating for two." Like many sayings, this one contains a grain of truth. It doesn't mean that a mother-to-be should eat twice as much, but that she should eat twice as *well* (Leavitt, Tonniges, & Rogers, 2003). Nutrients are essential elements of health, the fuel that propels development. Women whose diets are rich in protein have fewer complications during pregnancy, go through shorter labors, and bear healthier babies. Deficiencies in zinc and folic acid, as well as protein, have been linked to central nervous dysfunction, prematurity, and low-birth-weight births (Keen, Bendich, & Willhite, 1993).

For some pregnant women, however, eating a balanced diet isn't an option. In many regions of the developing world, malnutrition is a chronic problem (UNICEF, 2007). Moreover, this problem isn't limited to poor countries. The U.S. Special Supplemental Food Program for Women, Infants, and Children (WIC) provides food packages, nutrition education, and healthy care to low-income pregnant women, new mothers, and young children. But funding is limited, and women who apply may be put on waiting lists. More than 8 million people get WIC benefits each month (U.S. Department of Agriculture, 2006). Severe malnutrition in early pregnancy (especially lack of folic acid, a B vitamin) increases the risk of neural tube defects—such as **spina bifida**, in which the spinal cord does not close completely, or **anencephaly**, in which part of the brain does not develop. Malnutrition later in pregnancy is associated with low birth weight. But the long-term prognosis for children chronically malnourished in utero is not entirely bleak. If children receive nutritious diets before age 2, they can rebound. Near the end of World War II, western (but not northern or eastern) Holland endured a food blockade that provided an unhappy but important natural experiment in public health. Unlike other famines, the so-called Dutch Hunger Winter struck during a precisely circumscribed time and place and in a society that kept comprehensive and meticulous health records. As a result, researchers later identified children who were exposed to fetal malnutrition in different trimesters and followed them through adolescence and well into adulthood. In general, children born during this time of famine did not suffer pervasive long-term physical or mental diabilities (Hoek, Brown, & Susser, 1999; Susser, Hoek, & Brown, 1998). Relative to those who received proper nutrition, however, these children did suffer more nervous system congenital abnormalities (which is how we know that folic acid is important to normal fetal development) as well as increased risk of schizophrenia (a psychiatric diagnosis that describes a mental disorder characterized by abnormalities in the perception or expression of reality, as in hallucinations, paranoid or bizarre delusions, or disorganized speech and thinking). Fetally malnourished individuals are most likely to recover their health as children or adolescents if they eat healthy diets *and* grow up in stable, supportive environments. But if malnutrition continues and the environment is deprived or chaotic, they are at risk for cognitive, behavioral, and social problems as children or adolescents. Furthermore, maternal malnutrition is rarely an isolated problem—it is usually compounded by poverty, poor health, inadequate medical care, low levels of education, and high levels of stress.

spina bifida A developmental condition in which the spinal cord does not close completely.

anencephaly A developmental condition in which part of the brain does not develop.

Stress Pregnancy is a time of many changes—in a woman's body, in her and her partner's emotions, and in their family life. Some tension and anxiety are normal. But constant or chronic stress, or sudden acute stress, can be harmful (Davis et al., 2004; DiPietro et al., 2006; Yehuda et al., 2005). Very high stress during pregnancy is associated with premature birth and birth defects; blood flow to the uterus can be restricted so that the fetus gets fewer nutrients, which tends to lower birth weight. One study looked at women who had been through an earthquake (Glynn et al., 2001). The earlier in their pregnancy the earthquake happened, the earlier they delivered their babies. On the positive side, women who were further along with pregnancy seemed better able to cope with stress. Children of mothers who experience severe stress (e.g., death of a close relative, diagnosis of cancer), especially in the first trimester, are at increased risk to develop schizophrenia. According to one population study of 1.3 million Danish births, children 10 and older of stressed mothers have a 67 percent higher likelihood of being diagnosed as schizophrenic than children of nonstressed mothers (Khashan, Abel, McNamee, Pedersen, Webb, Baker, Kenny, & Mortensen, 2008).

As with malnutrition, stress is often part of a package. Stress causes—and is caused by—too little rest or too little exercise, skipping meals or overeating, and headaches and backaches; in addition, stress is accompanied by smoking and drinking. Women who take care of themselves typically manage stress successfully.

Outside Influences

A **teratogen** is any substance that can have a negative impact on fetal development and, possibly, result in birth defects or even death. Viruses, drugs, and environmental pollutants fall into this category (Field, 1998; Kopera-Frye & Arendt, 1999). Almost all teratogens can be avoided or their effects can be reduced. Awareness is key. The best

teratogen Any environmental substance that can have a negative impact on fetal development and possibly result in birth defects or even death.

way for a woman to protect her fetus is to talk with her doctor and learn what is and is not safe.

Diseases The placenta protects the fetus from many bacteria, but not from viruses. Sexually transmitted diseases (STDs), smallpox, and measles all cross the placenta. **Rubella** (German measles) is a relatively mild disease in adults, but it can be devastating for the fetus. Women who contract rubella in the first 3 months of pregnancy have a 50 percent chance of bearing babies with cataracts, deafness, possible brain damage, and mental retardation (Moore & Persaud, 1993). During an outbreak in 1964–1965, more than 20,000 babies were born with defects, and an estimated 10,000 pregnancies ended in miscarriages and stillbirths.

rubella German measles, a disease that can be devastating for the fetus if the mother contracts it during the first 3 months of pregnancy.

The major threat today is **HIV** (human immunodeficiency virus), the virus that causes **AIDS** (acquired immunodeficiency syndrome). Even without treatment, a person may have HIV for as long as 10 years and not develop symptoms. With AIDS, the immune system breaks down, making the individual more susceptible to infections, certain cancers, and other, often life-threatening or fatal conditions.

HIV Human immunodeficiency virus that causes AIDS.

AIDS Acquired immunodeficiency syndrome.

Through 2002, more than 9,300 American children have contracted AIDS—nearly always from their mother during pregnancy, during labor and delivery, or through breastfeeding (CDC, 2006). About one in four HIV-infected infants develops AIDS symptoms shortly after birth—these symptoms include opportunistic bacterial infections such as pneumonia, internal organ abscesses, and meningitis (an inflammation of brain tissues). These children do not reach the developmental milestones of the first year and usually die in their fifth year. Very likely this group became infected during pregnancy, before their immune systems began to function. The remaining three in four, who probably became infected with HIV during birth, may not exhibit symptoms of AIDS until they are 5 years old and survive into adolescence. But neither of these outcomes is inevitable.

A pregnant woman can protect her fetus (and herself) by getting a test for HIV and, if she is HIV-positive, taking AZT (zidovudine) and other medications that slow or stop HIV duplication (Rutstein et al., 1998). With these new treatments, a mother can reduce the risk of transmitting HIV to her baby to 2 percent or less (Fogler, 2007). The prognosis for mothers and babies in the United States has improved dramatically, but worldwide more than 800,000 babies are infected with HIV by their mothers during pregnancy, childbirth, or breastfeeding each year. Most are in developing countries, where appropriate medications are not widely available (World Health Organization, 2008).

Medications In the developed world, medications of all sorts are widely available and widely used. The simple rule here is: pregnant women, beware. Whatever the mother takes, her fetus takes, too. For example, prescription and over-the-counter medications that are good for the mother can be harmful to the fetus. Even aspirin may cause blood clotting and bleeding in the fetus (Briggs, Freeman, & Sumner, 1994). A pregnant woman should not take any drugs, not even vitamins, before consulting her doctor. Even when she does, mistakes can happen.

In the 1950s and 1960s, hundreds of thousands of women were given DES (diethylstilbestrol) to prevent miscarriage. It took almost 30 years for the long-term effects of DES to be recognized. Grown women who were exposed before birth have a substantially increased risk of rare cervical and vaginal cancers. Men who were similarly exposed sometimes develop cysts near the ducts where sperm are stored and may have low sperm counts as well as misshapen sperm, leading to infertility. DES daughters also have higher than average rates of infertility and problem pregnancies. Even *their* daughters are thought to be at some risk for cancers—a case in which exposure of the grandmother is visited on the granddaughters!

To protect her fetus a woman should only take medications that are necessary for her health and that of the fetus.

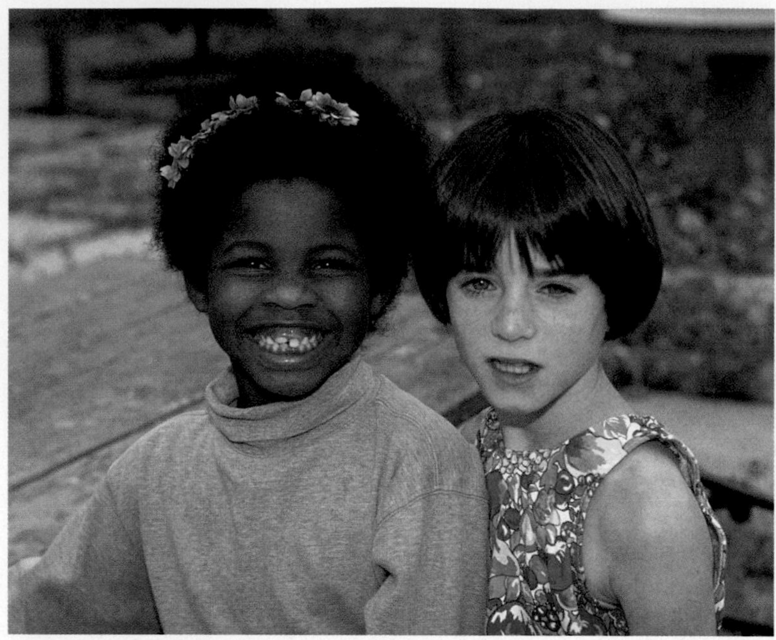

FIGURE 3.2

Fetal Alcohol Syndrome

Fetal alcohol syndrome affects internal development (of cognition and personality) as well as external development (as shown here in the facial anatomy of these two girls).

Drinking and Smoking Because alcoholic beverages are legal (with some restrictions) and woven into social occasions, from weddings to wakes, we don't usually think of alcohol as a drug. And even though public opinion has turned against smoking, which many adults—though not necessarily teenagers—now see as "uncool," cigarettes are widely available. Despite their acceptance as part of U.S. culture, it's important to remember that alcohol and nicotine *are* drugs: Both contain mood-changing, addictive substances that alter body chemistry.

Alcohol In 1973, Kenneth Lyons Jones and his colleagues identified a pattern of facial features and mental disabilities found in babies and children with alcoholic mothers, called **fetal alcohol syndrome** (FAS). Since then a large amount of research has supported their diagnosis (Fryer et al., 2007; Jones et al., 2006; Lowe, Handmaker, & Aragon, 2006).

FAS is the most common known cause of mental retardation. It is also entirely preventable. Yet every year between 1,000 and 6,000 babies in the United States are born with FAS (Bertrand, Floyd, & Weber, 2004). An estimated 40,000 are born with some alcohol-related problems (Sokol, Delaney-Black, & Deary, 2003).

fetal alcohol syndrome A pattern of disabilities found in babies and children of mothers who consumed alcohol during pregnancy.

fetal alcohol effects Fetal deformities that are the result of significant (but not chronic) prenatal exposure to alcohol.

Babies with FAS are small at birth and usually do not catch up with their peers as they grow older. They have small heads (microcephaly) and distinctive facial features, including small eyes, a narrow forehead, a low nasal bridge, and a thin upper lip (Astley & Claren, 1996; Roebuck, Mattson, & Riley, 1999) (see Figure 3.2). Many have brain and central nervous system abnormalities. Most have some degree of mental disability, including mental retardation, a short attention span, and emotional and behavioral disorders. Many also have low muscle tone and poor coordination. Babies with **fetal alcohol effects** (FAE), the result of significant (but not chronic) prenatal exposure to alcohol, have some but not all of these problems (Bertrand, Floyd, & Weber, 2004).

Does drinking *any* alcohol harm the fetus? This is a matter of dispute. FAS is clearly linked to alcohol *abuse* (having five or more drinks at a time, twice a week), and binge drinking during a sensitive period may be harmful, but questions surround very moderate drinking at other times (Ploygenis et al., 1998). This does not mean that moderate or social drinking has *no* harmful effects. Two drinks a day during the first and particularly the second trimester of pregnancy is associated with a seven-point drop in IQ at age 10 (Willford, Leech, & Day); moderate drinking predicts attention deficits in children and adolescents ages 4 to 14 (Streissguth et al., 2004). There's a reason bottles of wine and other alcoholic beverages have clear labels with the Surgeon General's warning to pregnant women (U.S. Department of Health and Human Services, 2005).

In numerous studies, the long-term effects of fetal exposure to alcohol include not only cognitive disabilities, but also high rates of criminal and sexualized behavior, depression, suicide, and parental neglect of children (Kelly, Day, & Streissguth, 2000). Clearly, there is no one-to-one correspondence between prenatal alcohol exposure and these later difficulties. But alcohol exposure and early disruptions in cognition, attention, and social behavior, if combined with unresponsive or harsh parenting, might lead to a maladaptive lifestyle later on.

One point is clear: No one has proven that alcohol consumption is *safe* for the fetus. The best way for mothers to protect their baby is to stop drinking when they think they *might* become pregnant. Women who have a drinking problem should get help *before* they become pregnant.

Nicotine Whether the nicotine in cigarettes during pregnancy places a child at risk for delays in cognitive and social and emotional development is not clear. It *is* clear that women who smoke during pregnancy have a higher risk than nonsmokers of miscarriage, preterm deliveries, and small, low-birth-weight, and otherwise compromised babies (Schuetze & Eiden, 2005; Zaskind & Gingras, 2006). The March of Dimes (2008) estimates that if all pregnant women in the United States stopped smoking, stillbirths would be reduced by 11 percent and newborn deaths by 5 percent. Staying smoke-free after a baby is born is equally important. Newborns whose parents smoke have higher rates of respiratory illnesses (such as bronchitis and pneumonia) and ear infections, and they may be at increased risk of developing asthma (March of Dimes, 2008).

Illicit Drugs Illegal or not, heroin, cocaine, marijuana, ecstasy, and other psychoactive drugs are part of our culture. Americans of all socioeconomic levels—in suburbs, small towns, and upscale urban neighborhoods—use "street" drugs.

But in most cases, drug use is usually embedded in a web of problems. As often as not, addicted mothers use multiple drugs (including alcohol and tobacco), continue using drugs after their baby is born, neglect their health and obtain little prenatal care, live in poverty, suffer from mental illness, and are neglectful as parents (Mayes & Truman, 2002). Children of addicts may be exposed to violence, abandonment, and homelessness. As infants, they often go through frequent separations, short-term foster home placements, and/or moves. In short, it is difficult to separate the effects of prenatal exposure to a drug from other, related conditions.

Heroin Babies born to heroin-addicted mothers are themselves addicted. Within 1 to 3 days after birth, they go into withdrawal, including tremors, irritability, vomiting, diarrhea, and sleep disturbances. Newborns also go through withdrawal when the mother is taking methadone, an oral medication used to wean adults from heroin. Many are born at low birth weights. Because heroin addicts usually inject the drug, and may share needles, these babies are also at risk for infection with HIV. Over the long term, heroin may be associated with lower IQ, attention disorders, and behavioral problems (Batshaw & Conlon, 1997). Most likely these problems also intensify with the interaction of prenatal exposure to the drug and ongoing exposure to the drug culture.

Cocaine Cocaine is of special concern (Jones, 2006). Abuse of cocaine (sometimes in the crystallized form of crack) has devastating effects on the fetus and newborn in the short term (Singer et al., 1999; Singer et al., 2005) and on the developing child and adolescent in the long term (Arendt et al., 2004; Bada et al., 2007; Bendersky et al., 2003; Dennis et al., 2006). In addition, cocaine use is widespread; in inner cities, as many as 10 to 18 percent of pregnant women use this drug (Schama et al., 1998).

Cocaine is a central nervous system stimulant that interferes with the reabsorption of neurochemicals associated with pleasure and movement. The "high," or euphoria, cocaine users experience is the result of constant stimulation. Cocaine passes quickly from the mother to the fetus. Cocaine increases the risk of miscarriage, stillbirths, and premature births. Prenatal exposure to cocaine has been linked to low birth weight, small head circumference and length, irritability, hypersensitivity, and lack of muscle and mood control, as well as an increased risk of **sudden infant death syndrome** (SIDS)—an unexplained death, usually during the night, of an infant under 1 year old (McKenna et al., 1994).

sudden infant death syndrome Unexplained death, usually during the night, of an infant under 1 year old.

Some research suggests that prenatal cocaine exposure results in small but significant problems with cognitive development and language. To clarify this picture, Linda Mayes, Marc Bornstein, and their colleagues conducted a series of developmental studies of infants exposed to cocaine in utero (Mayes et al., 1993, 2003). Compared with infants exposed to drugs (but not cocaine) as well as infants not exposed to drugs, cocaine-exposed infants scored low on tests designed to assess reflexes, motor skills, and general responsiveness at 3 and 6 months. In particular, they had problems with mood control, becoming highly distressed when presented with something new (Mayes et al., 1996).

The problems may be attributed to cocaine exposure alone, but they also may be complicated by the behavior of cocaine-using mothers. The researchers also studied face-to-face interactions between cocaine-abusing mothers and their infants at 3 and 6 months (Mayes et al., 1997). Compared with other mothers, cocaine-abusing mothers were less attentive to their infants, often looking away, distracting rather than responding to the infant, or simply withdrawing. Thus, unresponsive parenting may have compounded any cocaine effect on children. Some good news is that discontinuing cocaine may improve child development. In another study, 40 percent of children whose mothers abused cocaine during pregnancy and continued to do so after the baby was born had IQ scores of 85 or lower; among children whose mothers stopped using cocaine after they were born, only 15 percent scored this low (Scherling, 1994).

Environmental Toxins Environmental pollutants pose health risks for everyone, but unborn babies are especially vulnerable (Talan, 2007). For example, prenatal exposure to air pollution also affects cognitive development. An ongoing study has followed New York City children from before birth to age 3 (Perera et al., 2006). The researchers focused on polycyclic aromatic hydrocarbons (PAHs), a common byproduct of combustion engines, power plants, residential heating, and smoking. At age 3, children whose mothers were exposed to high levels of PAH during pregnancy were compared with children whose mothers were exposed to lower levels. The high-exposed children scored lower on mental tests and were more than twice as likely to score behind their peers in psychomotor development. Airborne concentrations of PAH could be reduced by antipollution technology that is currently available, greater energy efficiency, and use of alternative energy sources. But as things stand, pollution is a regular feature of the inner city. Poor children are more likely to be affected by PAH than are better-off suburban children.

Of the millions of chemical mixtures found in homes and workplaces, a few are known to be teratogens: lead, mercury, DDT (an insecticide), and PCBs (polychlorinated biphenyls, once used widely in manufacturing). The fetus can be exposed when a pregnant woman inhales, consumes, or absorbs these substances through her skin. Exposure to these pollutants can lead to lower birth weights, premature birth, small head circumference, muted reflexes, and long-term problems with memory and learning (Eskenazi et al., 2006). DDT, PCBs, and lead paint (the most common source of lead poisoning) have been banned in the United States since the 1970s. But residues are still found in the soil, water, air, and (especially lead) in older houses. Intrauterine and childhood exposure to lead is associated with shrinking of specific parts of the brain and with an increased risk for criminal behavior in adulthood. Researchers studied 15- to 17-year-olds who were born in a poor area of Cincinnati at a time when there was a high concentration of lead-contaminated housing (Cecil, Brubaker, Adler, Dietrich, & Altaye, 2008; Wright, Dietrich, Ris, Hornung, & Wessel, 2008). Those with the greatest lead exposure in childhood were those with the greatest brain volume loss (as shown by MRIs) and the hightest rates of criminal arrest in young adulthood. Pregnant women can protect themselves and the fetus by having their home tested, not drinking water from wells or old lead pipes, and wearing protective gloves when cleaning.

Fish are the leading source of mercury. Mercury entering the environment as industrial pollution is deposited into the water by rain, is converted by bacteria into a more dangerous form (methylmercury), and builds up in the fatty tissue of fish. PCBs may also be found in fish caught in contaminated streams, lakes, and coastal areas. Pregnant women can learn which fish are safe and which aren't from www.epa.gov.

The Importance of Timing

The impact of outside influences—from diseases to pollutants—depends on timing and duration, on when the exposure occurs and how long it lasts. Different body parts develop according to different timetables. Damage to the fetus is most severe during the time an organ or limb is developing fastest (Bornstein, 1989). For example, in the 1950s and 1960s, European doctors prescribed the sedative thalidomide for women who were suffering from morning sickness. Women who took thalidomide during weeks 6 or 7 of pregnancy, the period when limbs are developing, gave birth to babies with arm and leg buds rather than fully developed limbs (Newman, 1985). Taken at other times, thalidomide did not cause that damage. (Thalidomide was not approved for use in the United States.) As in this example, the effects of a teratogen depend as much or more on timing as on the nature of the teratogen itself. Two different toxins may have similar effects at the same phase of prenatal development, although neither affects development at other stages.

A **sensitive period** is the time during which the developing child is most vulnerable to teratogens (see Figure 3.3). During a sensitive period, outside influences—even if present for a short time—may alter anatomy or function, often irreversibly (Bailey, Bruer, Symons, & Lichtman, 2001; Bornstein, 1989). But body parts that develop earlier or later remain largely unaffected. The embryonic stage is one of high vulnerability because this is when the major organ systems develop. In general, the older fetus is less vulnerable, although oxygen supply is vital at this stage because the fetal brain has developed and is dependent on an oxygen supply.

sensitive period A time in development during which the organism is especially vulnerable to experience.

The impact of environmental factors may be immediately apparent, as when newborns whose mothers use heroin go through withdrawal. Or it may be chronic, such as the learning and behavioral problems in children with FAS. Some experiences have **sleeper effects**. For example, examinations of military recruits found that young men who were born during the Dutch Hunger Winter in World War II and experienced chronic malnutrition in the first trimester in utero had elevated rates of schizophrenia—suggesting that severe malnutrition caused subtle brain damage, the effects of which did not emerge until later in development (Hoek, Brown, & Susser, 1999). Twenty-one reproductive toxins and teratogenic agents have been reported as having been present in the environment of the first Gulf War, and so the offspring of Gulf War veterans may be at risk for birth defects (Doyle et al., 2004). In addition, exposure to teratogens may be ongoing. As mentioned previously, infants whose parents smoke are at risk for bronchitis, pneumonia, and asthma.

sleeper effect An outcome that is displaced in time from a cause.

Pregnancy and Parents-to-Be

The experience of pregnancy depends on timing, too. Mothers' and fathers' chronological age is important, as is where parents stand in terms of their educational and career plans, whether they feel able to support and care for a baby, how committed they are to each other, their relationships with their own families, and, above all, whether they want to become parents at this time.

In the first trimester of pregnancy, a woman tends to concentrate on her own well-being and taking care of herself. In the second trimester, she becomes more concerned about the welfare of her developing child. In the third trimester, she begins to experience the fetus as *real* and to bond with her baby (Heinicke, 2002).

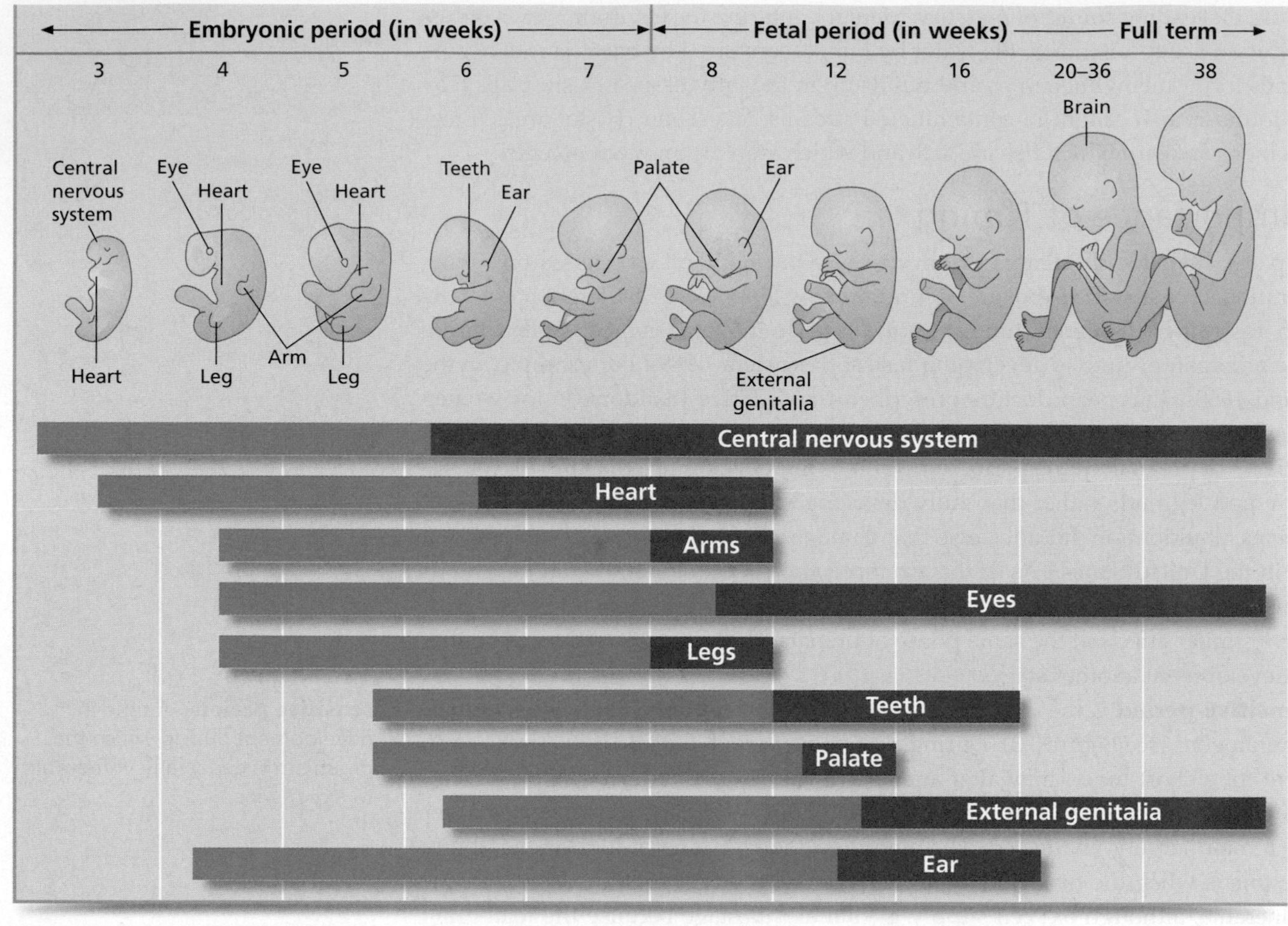

FIGURE 3.3

Sensitive Periods in Prenatal Development

Exposure to teratogens during prenatal development can be detrimental and result in major defects in the structure or function of organs and systems, especially if the exposure occurs during certain "sensitive periods." The green bars indicate the period of time in which the embryo or fetus is most susceptible to outside influences; the purple bars represent the time in which teratogenic effects might be less serious. Several structures, like the central nervous system and the eyes, remain sensitive to outside influences for most of prenatal development.

Source: This figure was published in *Before we are born: Essentials of embryology and birth defects,* 5/e by K.L. Moore & T.V.N. Persaud, Copyright Elsevier 1998. Reprinted by permission of Elsevier Ltd.

Pregnancy poses a series of social and emotional challenges for a woman (Barnard & Solchany, 2002). Learning that she is pregnant for the first time marks the beginning of a transformation to a new identity as a mother. Often it is a period of introspection. Her relationship with her own mother can change. Her mother's advice (whether sought or volunteered) can make a woman feel dependent, almost as if she were a child again. Yet, at the same time, she begins to see her mother as a peer and indentify herself as another mother. She may have feelings of loss: of her freedom and independence; her one-to-one relationship with her partner; and her youthful body and appearance. In addition, she may reexamine her feelings of competency, in light of a new and dependent person entering her life. Feeling that she made a choice can relieve these anxieties.

For couples, adaptation to pregnancy is multilayered (Heinicke, 2002). Parents-to-be cope best when they believe that a positive, sustained relationship is possible (based largely on their parents' relationships). Equally important is a positive partnership, including agreement on roles (who does what) and openness in communication. Good "co-parenting" is shown to be fundamental in child development (McHale, Khazan, Rotman, DeCourcey, & McConnell, 2002). How couples feel about pregnancy and parenthood depends on how they feel about themselves and whether they feel that being a couple, soon to be a family (or larger one), enhances or interferes with their personal goals. Finally, parenting only begins with the birth of a baby; *once a parent, always a parent.* Young children may affect their parents, but children are not really the major agents of their development. Parents have continuing responsibilities for children and need to remain forever vigilant. For example, babies are fed from plastic bottles, but those bottles are made of synthetic chemical resins (like Bisphenol A or BPA) which can leach into the contents. BPA is associated with brain damage. Although there is controversy about its long-term effects, in 2008 Canada banned the sale of baby bottles made with BPA. Parents need to judge which precautionary measures to take. Children used to play outside where they were exposed to the sun, a natural source of Vitamin D. As parents take precautions to shield their children from harmful sun exposure, and as children spend more time indoors and drink less milk, they are also deprived of Vitamin D. About 9 percent of children ages 1 to 21 now have Vitamin D levels so low they can be considered deficient (Kumar, Muntner, Kaskel, Hailpern, & Melamed, 2009; Misra et al., 2008). Low levels of Vitamin D are associated with long-term bone problems, heart disease, and diabetes, among other physical ailments. (For a summary of this section, see "Interim Summary 3.3: Protecting the Fetus.")

INTERIM SUMMARY 3.3

Protecting the Fetus

Guidelines for a Healthy Pregnancy	■ Eat well. ■ Don't smoke, drink, or use drugs. ■ See the obstetrician regularly. ■ Remember—the mother's blood flows into the fetus's veins through the placenta to the umbilical cord. The placenta acts as a filter, but it does not protect against the transmission of all harmful substances.
The Well-Being of the Fetus	Maternal characteristics play a role: ■ Age ■ Diet and nutrition ■ Stress Outside influences also play a role: ■ **Teratogens** are substances that can have a negative impact on fetal development and possibly result in birth defects or even death. ■ They include viruses (rubella and HIV), drugs (nicotine, alcohol, and illicit drugs such as heroin and cocaine), and environmental pollutants (lead, mercury, DDT, and PCBs). ■ A **sensitive period** is the time during which the developing child is most vulnerable to teratogens, such as the embryonic stage because this is when the major organ systems develop. ■ In general, older fetuses are less vulnerable, though oxygen supply is vital at this stage.

BIRTH

Birth can be seen as one transition in the ongoing *process* of development. There is little change in the way the central nervous system functions or in the baby's movements after delivery, for example. Though attached to the mother's bloodstream through the umbilical cord and placenta, the blood systems of mother and baby do not mix, and babies develop their own blood chemistry throughout gestation. Like fetuses, newborns depend on others—for example, to regulate their body temperature. They lack both the insulation (subcutaneous body fat) and neural capacity to do this on their own and so rely on their caregivers. Yet birth is also an *event* that brings profound changes. Suddenly, the baby has to breathe and obtain nourishment for him- or herself. After months of floating in the warm, dark, liquid, quiet of the womb, the baby is confronted with gravity, hunger, and totally new sights, sounds, and sensations.

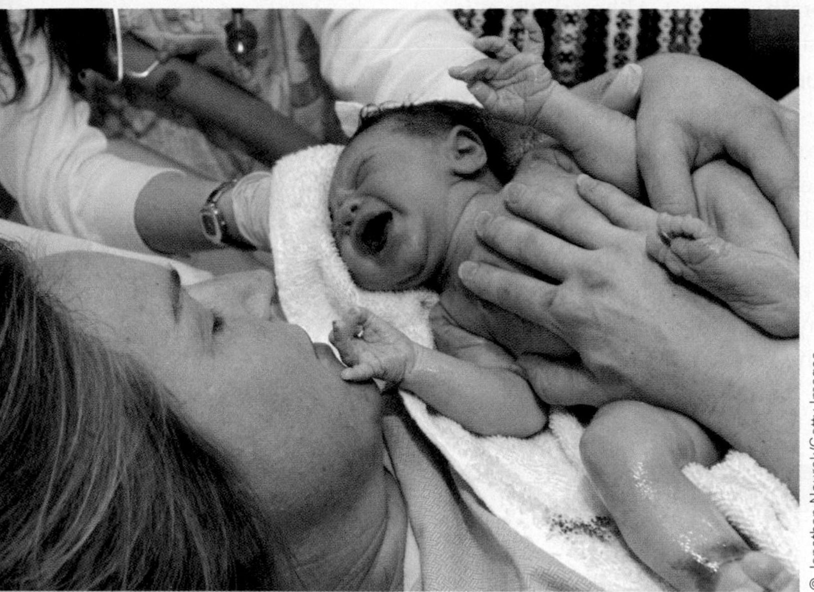
© Jonathan Nourok/Getty Images

New mothers typically get to hold their newborn baby as soon as the infant is delivered.

Labor and Delivery

Birth takes place 9 months after conception, give or take a week or two. (The average date is 280 days after conception.) We still do not know exactly why the birth process starts when it does, which explains why doctors cannot give a mother-to-be the exact date. What we do know is that the mother's pituitary gland releases the hormone **oxytocin**, which in turn triggers uterine contractions. The uterus is actually a muscle that expands to accommodate the growing fetus but keeps the cervix closed during pregnancy. Labor consists of involuntary contractions—at first in widely spaced intervals, then more and more frequently—that push the baby into the world.

oxytocin A maternal pituitary gland hormone that triggers uterine contractions.

In the first stage of labor, the uterine muscle pulls and tugs to open the cervix to the 4 inches (10 to 12 centimeters) required for the baby to pass through. In the second stage, contractions push the baby's head, and then body, into the birth canal. After the head and a shoulder have emerged, the rest of the body slips through. In the third stage, contractions expel the placenta, fetal membranes, and the remainder of the umbilical cord. At first appearance, newborns are red and battered, with misshapen heads as a result of being squeezed through the birth canal. These effects are temporary but useful: Although labor is just that for the mother, it is thought that it may be beneficial for the baby in that it triggers the release of hormones that promote healthy infant lung functioning, and the physical compression of labor removes amniotic fluid from the newborn's lungs. For first births, a normal delivery may take 16 to 17 hours. But some mothers and babies need additional help.

Birth Complications and Controversies

Just as births don't occur on schedule, so they don't always go according to plan. Complications may require medical intervention.

In the week or two before birth, most fetuses shift into position for birth, with their head against the cervix. But some are positioned with their feet or buttocks first (a *breech* position) or cross-wise (the *hammock* position). These positions complicate and prolong delivery.

anoxia Cutoff of the supply of oxygen through the umbilical cord before the baby can breathe independently.

One of the most serious birth complications is **anoxia**: The supply of oxygen through the umbilical cord is cut off before the baby can breathe independently. This may happen because the baby is in an unusual position for birth, the umbilical cord is pinched or twisted, or the placenta pulls away from the wall of the uterus (*placental abruption*) or blocks the baby's exit from the womb (*placenta previa*). A brief interruption in oxygen supply is not usually a problem, but long-lasting anoxia may cause brain damage and related problems, including seizures, cerebral palsy, and mental retardation.

If a baby is threatened, physicians can perform a **cesarean section** (or **C-section**), delivering the baby surgically through an incision in the mother's abdomen. C-sections are also used when the baby's head is very large and/or the mother's pelvis is narrow, to prevent infection with HIV or another disease, and sometimes when the mother is having multiple births. A cesarean section is major surgery and, like all surgery, carries risks—for the baby as well as the mother. Some evidence indicates that the anesthesia given to the mother makes babies listless and prone to breathing problems. Critics hold that many cesareans are performed for the mother's or doctor's convenience, not because of medical necessity. Neonatal mortality for cesarean deliveries among low-risk women is 1.77 deaths per 1,000 live births; the rate for vaginal delivery is 0.62 deaths per 1,000 live births (MacDorman, Declercq, Menacker, & Malloy, 2006.) The United States has the highest rate of cesarean sections in the world, which increased in frequency from 20.7 percent in 1996 to 29.1 percent in 2004. Medical malpractice claims may drive these numbers in part, as physicians opt to perform C-sections to avoid risks associated with birth complications.

cesarean section (or **C-section**) Method of delivering a baby surgically through an incision in the mother's abdomen.

In addition, women who deliver their children naturally may need or want help dealing with the pain of childbirth. The use of anesthesia during labor and delivery is controversial. Babies whose mothers use anesthesia score below average on a range of tests and are less active and alert than other infants. However, the differences are small and noticeable only for the first few days after birth. Local anesthetics—such as the epidural block, which numbs the woman's body only from the waist down—appear to be effective in reducing labor pain without harmful consequences for the infant (Albaladejo, Bouaziz, & Benhamou, 1998). Longer-term and larger-sample studies show no differences in learning-disorder outcomes for children delivered by C-section (and so exposed to anesthesia in the womb) and children delivered vaginally (Sprung et al., 2009).

At the same time, natural childbirth has grown in popularity as women—and men—are seeking ways to "demedicalize" childbirth. One of the oldest of these approaches is the Lamaze method (http://www.lamaze.org/). The couple attends childbirth classes in which the mother learns how to relax and to concentrate on breathing and pushing the baby into the world, and the partner learns how to be her coach, supporting her physically and psychologically. Today, so-called "birthing classes" are wildly popular and available in every community.

Newborns at Risk

Even term babies, who enjoyed a full 40 weeks' gestation, need a few days to adjust to life outside of the womb. Breathing and sucking are automatic reflexes, but newborns have frequent bouts of hiccups from doing both at once. Very small babies face more difficult challenges. Of the approximately 4 million babies born in the United States each year, about 12.5 percent are born too early (Davidoff, Dias, Damus, Russell, Bettegowda, Dolan, Schwarz, Green, & Petrini, 2006; MacDorman et al., 2007). Babies are considered **preterm** if born before the 37th week of pregnancy, and *very* preterm if born before 32 weeks of gestation. Less than 5½ pounds (2,500 grams) is a **low birth weight**, and less than 2½ pounds (1,500 grams) is a *very* low birth weight. (See Figure 3.4.) Not surprisingly, premature birth and low birth weight often go together.

preterm Babies born before the 37th week of pregnancy.

low birth weight Babies born weighing less than 5½ pounds (2,500 grams).

Babies may be born preterm for a number of reasons. For example, the mother may be unable to carry a baby to term because of abnormalities in her uterus or cervix. In other cases, the mother's reproductive system may be immature: Young teens have higher rates of preterm births than other age groups (Bornstein & Putnick, 2007; Bornstein et al., 2006). Or the mother may not have had enough time to recuperate from a previous

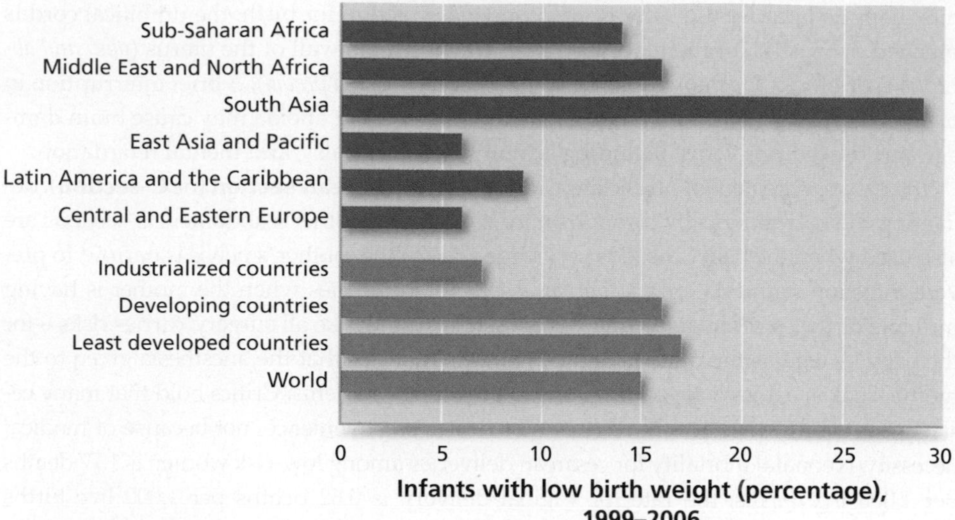

FIGURE 3.4

Comparing Rates of Low Birth Weight Around the World

The top part of this UNICEF graph shows the percentages of infants who were born with low birth weights between 1999 and 2006 in six world regions (South Asia has the highest percentage, followed by Africa; East Asia, Latin America, and Europe have the lowest). The bottom part of the graph compares three levels of country development (not surprisingly, industrialized countries have a lower percentage than developing and least developed countries). The world rate is about 15 percent.
Source: UNICEF (2007).

pregnancy (a birth interval of 1½ to 2 years is recommended). When the mother's or fetus's health is in danger, physicians may induce labor by breaking the amniotic sac and giving the mother synthetic oxytocin. Finally, disadvantaged living conditions—including poverty, malnutrition, and inadequate medical care—are linked to preterm births. So are smoking, drinking alcohol, and using drugs, which often go together.

Babies who are only slightly premature face little danger. But very small babies need help to survive. For these babies, medical complications are common. Preterm babies often suffer from **respiratory distress syndrome** (RDS) because their lungs do not produce enough *surfactin*, a soapy substance that helps to carry oxygen into, and carbon dioxide out of, the lungs. They may develop a chronic lung disease characterized by thickening and inflammation of the walls of the lungs, which reduces the amount of oxygen the baby can inhale (Vanhatalo et al., 1994). Because their immune systems are immature, preterm infants are particularly vulnerable to infection. Their nervous system may not be developed enough to perform basic functions such as sucking, so they may need to be fed intravenously or via a nasogastric tube. Very preterm, very low-birth-weight infants are in danger of brain complications, such as hemorrhages. Low-birth-weight infants are placed in an incubator or "isolette"—an antiseptic, temperature-controlled, covered crib with a high concentration of oxygen—for as long as 45 or 50 days.

respiratory distress syndrome A condition common to preterm babies whose lungs do not produce enough surfactin that helps to carry oxygen into and carbon dioxide out of the lungs.

Thanks to medical and technological advances in intensive neonatal care, the prognosis for small babies has improved dramatically (Bernbaum & Batshaw, 1997). In 1960, the survival rate for *all* preterm babies was less than 50 percent. Today, more than 9 in 10 infants with birth weights under 5.5 pounds (2,500 grams), two-thirds of infants between 1.65 and 2.2 pounds (750 and 1,000 grams), and one-third of infants between 1.1 and 1.65 pounds (500 and 750 grams) survive. However, their long-term prognosis is not altogether positive. Very preterm, very low-birth-weight infants have shown anatomical differences in the brain compared to term infants (Mewes et al., 2006; Woodward, Mogridge, Wells & Inder,

2004). They are at increased risk of diabetes and heart disease and are significantly more likely than term infants to have delayed language development, low IQs, and developmental and learning disabilities later on (Foster-Cohen, Edgin, Champion, & Woodward, 2007; Gayraud & Kern, 2007; Sansavini et al., 2006; Skenkin, Starr, & Deary, 2004). Smaller babies also grow up to be sadder adults in that birth weight has been linked to both depression and anxiety in a 40-year longitudinal study (Colman, Ploubidis, Wadsworth, Jones, & Croudace, 2007). But low birth weight is not the only reason for potential problems; gestational age at birth is a vital factor as well.

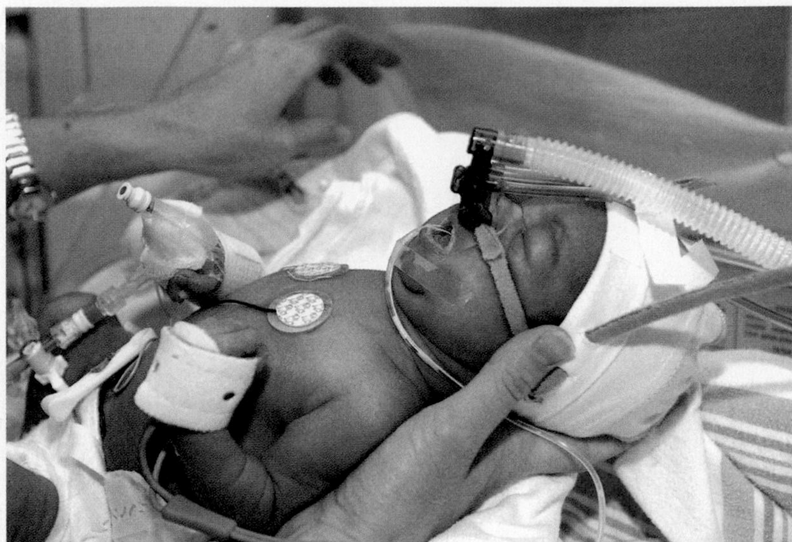

Preterm newborns, like this three-day-old baby, need all the help they can get. In addition to medical paraphernalia, they get much-needed human contact in the neonatal intensive care unit (NICU).

In the United States, a large proportion of very small babies are born to women who come from disadvantaged homes and return to these environments when they leave the hospital. One study of infants who weighed just over 2 pounds, on average, at birth, and were judged to be borderline delayed, found that most showed improvement in early childhood and scored within the normal range on intelligence tests at age 8. Children who improved the most lived in two-parent families, with mothers who had higher education, and had not suffered significant brain damage (Ment et al., 2003). Clearly, the caregiving environment made a difference.

Apgar test A delivery room test that assesses a newborn with a score of 0, 1, or 2 on each of five scales: **A**ppearance, **P**ulse, **G**rimace, **A**ctivity, and **R**espiration.

Neonatal Behavioral Assessment Scale A test for newborns that uses reflexes and social interaction to assess their overall well-being, including motor capabilities, state changes, attention, and central nervous system stability.

Infant Assessment

How do parents know whether their newborn is healthy and normal? Hospital personnel give the newborn a test in the delivery room, 1 minute and again 5 minutes after birth (see Table 3.1). The **Apgar test**, named for its originator Virginia Apgar (1953), gives a baby a score of 0, 1, or 2 on each of five scales, which are easy to remember because of the acronym: **A**ppearance, **P**ulse, **G**rimace, **A**ctivity, and **R**espiration. If the score is 7 or higher, the infant is not normally in danger; if the score is below 4, he or she is in critical condition.

The Apgar indicates if there is a need for immediate intervention, but there are questions it cannot answer. The **Neonatal Behavioral Assessment Scale** (NBAS; Brazelton

TABLE 3.1 The Apgar Test*

APGAR SCORING SYSTEM				
	SIGN	0	1	2
Appearance	Color of baby's body and extremities	Body is pale or blue	Body is normal color but hands and feet are blue	Body including hands and feet are nice and pink
Pulse	Baby's heart rate	No pulse	Less than 100 beats per minute	100 beats per minute or higher
Grimace	Baby's reflex response to suctioning with a bulb syringe	No response	Grimace	Active cry
Activity	Baby's muscle tone	Limp or no movement	Some movement of arms and legs	Actively moving arms and legs
Respiration	Baby's breathing	Not breathing	Slow or irregular	Breathing well/strong cry

*This test gives a baby a score of 0, 1, or 2 on each of five scales—Appearance, Pulse, Grimace, Activity, and Respiration.
Source: Apgar (1953).

INTERIM SUMMARY 3.4

Birth	
Birth Takes Place Nine Months after Conception, Give or Take a Week or Two	■ In the first stage of labor, the uterine muscle pulls and tugs to open the cervix to the four inches required for the baby to pass through. ■ In the second stage, contractions push the baby's head, and then body, into the birth canal. After the head and a shoulder have emerged from the mother, the rest of the body slips through. ■ In the third stage, contractions expel the placenta, fetal membranes, and the remainder of the umbilical cord.
Birth Complications	■ The baby may be in a breech (fetus positioned with buttocks first) or hammock position (fetus positioned crosswise). ■ The mother's pelvis may be too narrow or the baby's head too big. ■ The baby may have **anoxia**—the supply of oxygen through the umbilical cord is cut off before the baby can breathe independently.
Cesarean Sections, Anesthesia, and Natural Childbirth	■ Physicians can perform a **cesarean section** (or **C-section**) if warranted, delivering the baby surgically through an incision in the mother's abdomen. ■ The use of anesthesia is controversial, though local anesthesia such as the epidural is effective without harming the infant. ■ Natural childbirth is popular. The Lamaze method concentrates on the mother's breathing, with a partner acting as a supportive "coach."
Preterm and Low-Birth-Weight Babies	■ Babies are considered **preterm** if born before the 37th week of pregnancy, and **very** preterm if born before 32 weeks of gestation. ■ Less than 5½ pounds is a **low birth weight**, and less than 2½ pounds is a **very** low birth weight. ■ Preterm babies often suffer from **respiratory distress syndrome** (RDS). ■ They are particularly vulnerable to infection. ■ Their nervous system may not be developed enough to perform basic functions such as sucking, so they may need to be fed intravenously. ■ Very preterm, very low-birth-weight infants are in danger of brain complications, such as hemorrhages.
Assessing Infants—the Apgar and Neonatal Behavioral Assessment Scale (NBAS) Tests	■ The Apgar test is administered 1 minute and 5 minutes after birth and gives a baby a score of 0, 1, or 2 on each of five scales—**A**ppearance, **P**ulse, **G**rimace, **A**ctivity, and **R**espiration. ■ A score of 7 or higher means the infant is not normally in danger; if the score is below 4, he or she is in critical condition. ■ The NBAS uses reflexes and social interaction to assess the newborn's overall well-being.

& Nugent, 1995) uses reflexes and social interaction to assess the newborn's overall well-being, including motor capabilities, state changes (irritability, excitability, and ability to calm down), attention (alertness and responsiveness), and central nervous system stability.

Although the Apgar and the NBAS have been used widely for many years, they raise questions. Which test or test session represents the baby best? Do we want to measure average behavior or best performance? Is it better to assess spontaneous or elicited behavior? Despite these questions, newborn screening is a valuable tool for identifying infants who need immediate attention (Meisels & Atkins-Burnett, 2006; Zuckerman et al., 2004).

A baby who was born in 2006 can expect to live to be 78.1 years, a record high for Americans. Baby girls can expect to live to 80.7, and baby boys to 75.4. Many factors in addition to gender affect life expectancy, such as nationality, socioeconomic status, and ethnicity. (For a summary of this section, see "Interim Summary 3.4: Birth.")

SUMMING UP AND LOOKING AHEAD

This chapter has discussed some of the most rapid and dramatic developments in the human lifespan that occur in the first 9 months. The stages of prenatal development and gender differentiation were discussed. We also explored contemporary technologies to assess prenatal development and to protect the fetus. Finally, we discussed the delivery process and the screening tools used to evaluate newborns.

A newborn changes from moment to moment, slipping from an alert into a drowsy state (or the reverse) in a heartbeat. How does this new human being begin to adapt to his or her new environment? This is the subject of the next chapter, "Physical Development in Infancy."

HERE'S WHAT YOU SHOULD KNOW

Did You Get It?

After reading this chapter, you should understand the following:

- What happens during the zygote, embryo, and fetal stages of prenatal development
- What is involved in gender differentiation and the four stages of prenatal gender development
- Genetic counseling, genetic abnormalities, and types of genetic and prenatal tests
- What/who influences the well-being of the fetus
- What happens at birth, possible birth complications, and preterm and low-birth-weight babies
- Infant assessment tests—the APGAR test and Neonatal Behavioral Assessment Scale

Important Terms and Concepts

AIDS (p. 79)
amniocentesis (p. 75)
amniotic sac (p. 67)
anencephaly (p. 78)
anoxia (p. 86)
Apgar test (p. 89)
artificial insemination (p. 66)
cesarean section (C-section) (p. 87)
chorionic villi sampling (p. 75)
ectoderm (p. 67)
endoderm (p. 67)
fertility drugs (p. 66)
fertilization (p. 65)
fetal alcohol effects (p. 80)
fetal alcohol syndrome (p. 80)
gametes (p. 66)
genetic counseling (p. 74)
gestation (p. 64)
HIV (p. 79)
implantation (p. 65)
infertility (p. 65)
in vitro fertilization (IVF) (p. 66)
karyotype (p. 74)
low birth weight (p. 87)
mesoderm (p. 67)
multifactoral disorders (p. 73)
Neonatal Behavioral Assessment Scale (p. 89)
neurogenesis (p. 67)
ovulation (p. 64)
ovum (or ova) (p. 64)
oxytocin (p. 86)
placenta (p. 65)
preimplantation genetic diagnosis (p. 75)
preterm (p. 87)
quickening (p. 68)
respiratory distress syndrome (p. 88)
rubella (p. 79)
sensitive period (p. 83)
sleeper effect (p. 83)
spina bifida (p. 78)
sudden infant death syndrome (p. 81)
surrogate mother (p. 66)
temperament (p. 69)
teratogen (p. 78)
Turner's syndrome (p. 70)
ultrasound imaging (p. 71)
zygote (p. 65)

Part I Review

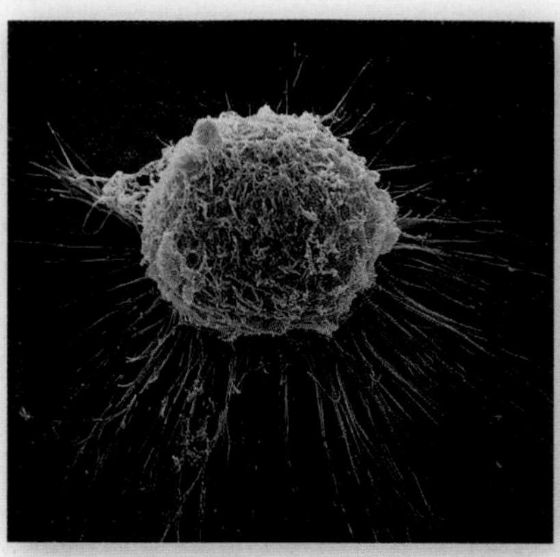

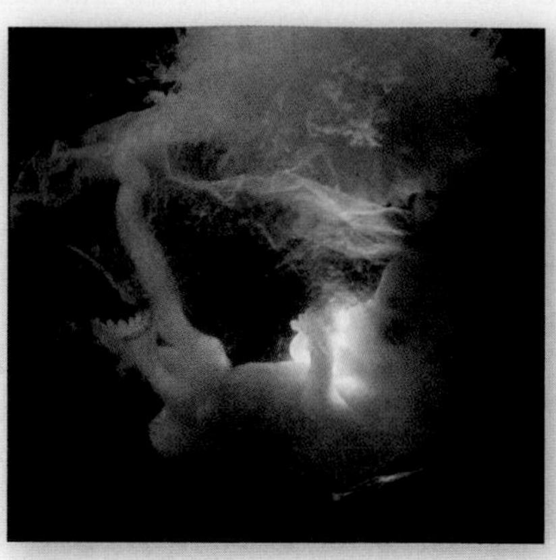

CHAPTER 1
The Study of Human Development

- Developmental research seeks to *describe* what people are like at different ages and how they change as a result of age, *explain* what causes such change, *predict* what an individual will be like based on past and present characteristics, and *intervene,* or use this knowledge to improve children's lives.
- Classical theories of development include psychoanalytic theory, learning theory, and cognitive-developmental theory.
- Contemporary theories of development include the ecological perspective, the sociocultural perspective, behavioral genetics, the evolutionary perspective, and dynamic systems theory.
- The scientific method is a systematic, step-by-step procedure for testing ideas. Researchers use three main ways to gather information about people: observational research, self-reports, and standardized tests.
- Most developmental research uses one of three research designs: case studies, correlational studies, and experiments.
- The three basic strategies for studying development over time are longitudinal studies, cross-sectional studies, and accelerated longitudinal studies.

CHAPTER 2
Nature with Nurture

- There are four main perspectives on nature and nurture: (1) development is driven by nature, (2) development is driven by nurture, (3) development is part nature, part nurture, and (4) development results from the interplay of nature and nurture.
- A **gene** is a segment of the chromosome that controls a particular aspect of the production of a specific protein. An individual's observable characteristics and behavior, or **phenotype,** depend on the genotype and environment. The outcome of the merger of the mother's and father's genes depends primarily on which genes from each parent are matched with the other's, referred to as **gene-gene interaction**.
- The environment or context plays an important role in development: Bronfenbrenner was the pioneer of the ecological perspective, which organizes the way we think about the contexts of development.
- There are four main types of interplay between genetic and environmental influences: (1) environmental effects on gene expression, (2) environmental effects on heritability, (3) gene-environment interaction, and (4) gene-environment correlation.

CHAPTER 3
Conception, Prenatal Development, and Birth

- The period from conception to birth takes about 280 days. There are three prenatal periods: zygote, embryo, and fetus.
- Prenatal sexual development can be divided into four stages: (1) unisex, (2) physiological sex differences emerge, (3) external genitals form, and (4) testosterone inhibits the rhythmic cycles of the hypothalamus and the pituitary, which regulate female ovulation.
- Most genetic disorders are carried on a recessive gene. Some recessive gene disorders are sex linked. Prenatal tests screen for certain disorders. These tests include preimplantation genetic diagnosis, amniocentesis, and chorionic villi sampling.
- Maternal characteristics (age and stress) and outside influences (teratogens, viruses) play a role in the well-being of a fetus.

part two

Infancy

© Mary Ellen Bartley/Getty Images

CHAPTER 4

Physical Development in Infancy

Did your parents keep a record of your height, either in a baby diary or as notched lines on a doorjamb? Count Philibert Guéneau de Montbeillard, who lived during the 1700s, kept one of his son. In April of 1759, he began a series of measurements of his son's growth. Although these data were gathered 250 years ago, their general pattern resembles that obtained using modern scientific measurement.

Count de Montbeillard not only recorded his son's absolute height, but also recorded how much his son's height changed at each age. In this way, he showed just how rapid growth is during infancy. Look at the right panel of Figure 4.1. During the first year of life, the count's son was growing at the rate of about 8.5 inches (22 centimeters) per year. By the end of infancy, his rate of growth had slowed to about about 2.5 inches (6 centimeters) annually. Growth once again becomes rapid as children enter puberty, as we shall see in Chapter 11 but it is never as rapid as in infancy.

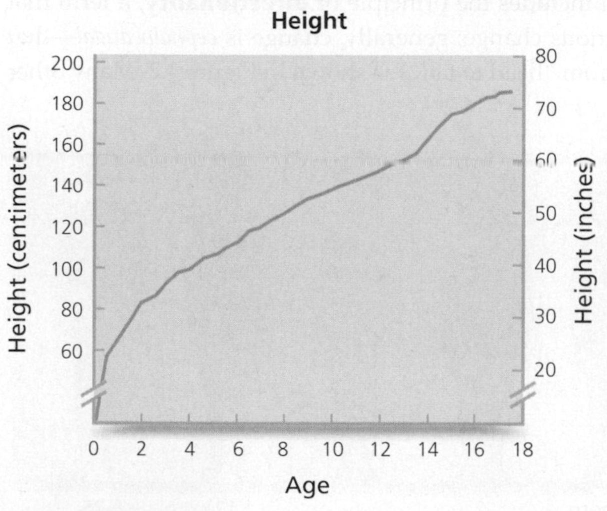

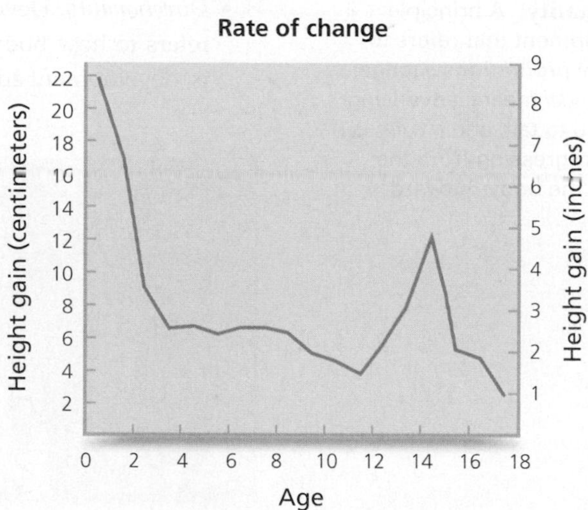

FIGURE 4.1

Growth Charts for the Son of Count Philibert Guéneau de Montbeillard

The panel on the left shows the height of the Count de Montbeillard's son in centimeters over the first 18 years of life between 1759 and 1777; at age 18, his son stood roughly 6 feet (185 centimeters) tall. The panel on the right shows just how much his son's height changed each year. In the first 2 years, growth is rapid. By age 3, he was only growing about 6 centimeters per year. Growth slowed considerably until a spike between ages 14 and 15, when he gained about 5 inches (13 centimeters); this period represents the "adolescent growth spurt."

Source: From J.M. Tanner, *Fetus into man: Physical growth from conception to maturity.* Copyright © 1990. Published by Harvard University Press.

By the end of the first year of postnatal life, the average American child weighs about 20 pounds (9 kilograms) and is about 30 inches long (76 centimeters)—more than double his or her height and weight at birth. (If that isn't impressive, just think about what you'd look like a year from now at twice your height and weight!) In this chapter, we look at physical growth and development during the first 2 years of life—not just at changes in the infant's size, but also at changes in the infant's brain, physical capabilities, and ability to perceive the world.

PHYSICAL GROWTH

Physical growth, which is easy to observe and quantify, tells us a lot about whether a child is developing normally. If a child suddenly stops growing, it is a concern. That's one reason that physical exams of people of all ages always include an assessment of height and weight. Even now, when you visit the doctor, he or she asks you to step on the scale.

Physical growth also has implications for development in many other psychological domains (Thelen & Smith, 2006). For example, when children start to walk, their parents change their own behavior in many ways, such as child-proofing the house, locking low cabinets, speaking to the child differently, and the like, which in turn affect the child's cognitive and socioemotional development. Although this chapter separates physical development from cognitive and socioemotional development, this is just a way of organizing information. In the real world, all three domains of development are closely linked.

General Principles of Physical Growth

Studies of physical growth reveal important general principles that apply to other realms of child development, including directionality, independence of systems, and canalization.

directionality A principle of development that refers to how body proportions change; *cephalocaudal* means advancing from head to tail, and *proximodistal* means progressing from the center of the body outward.

- *Directionality*. Development includes the principle of **directionality**, a term that refers to how body proportions change; generally, change is *cephalocaudal*—that is, development advances from "head to tail," as shown in Figure 4.2. Many other

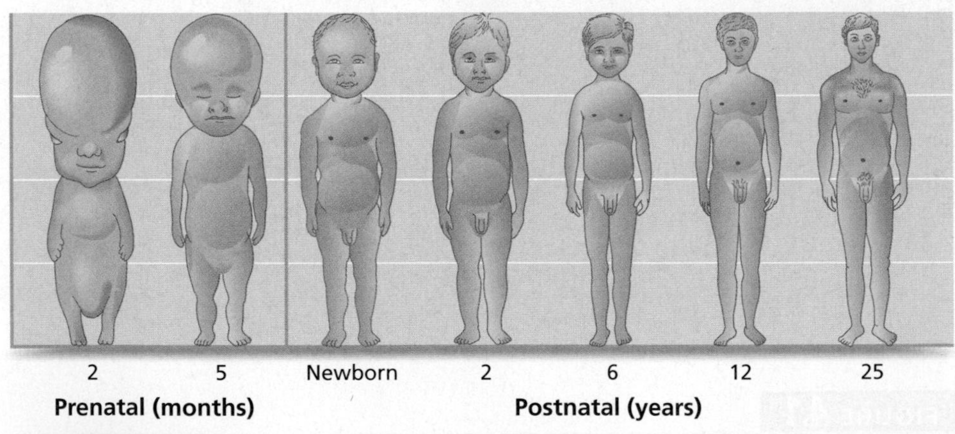

FIGURE 4.2

Changes in Body Proportions from Prenatal Development Through Adulthood

The human body develops from head to tail and from the center outward. Although a fetus appears to have an abnormally large head (in fact, the head is about the same length as the rest of the body in early prenatal development), over time, as the rest of the body grows, the head becomes much smaller relative to the rest of the body.

Source: Adapted from W.J. Robbins, S. Brody, A.G. Hogan, C.M. Jackson, & C.W. Green (eds.), *Growth.* Copyright © 1928. Reprinted by permission of the publisher, Yale University Press.

aspects of development also proceed top-down rather than bottom-up. The eyes mature earlier than the legs, and babies can look around sooner than they begin to walk. Physical development is also *proximodistal*—it progresses from the center of the body outward. Prenatally, the heart begins to beat long before fingers develop, just as postnatally, the child has control over large arm movements before finer hand ones.

- *Independence of systems*. The **independence of systems** principle asserts that not all parts of the body follow the same timetable. Figure 4.3 plots growth for three major components of the body. Some are developed at or soon after birth; others do not develop until much later. For example, by the time an infant is 2 years old, the nervous system has reached more than half of its mature form, whereas secondary sexual characteristics (such as pubic or underarm hair) do not appear until puberty.
- *Canalization*. Many systems in the body are genetically programmed to follow a standard and highly structured course of development, like water flowing in a canal (see Chapter 2). If something throws development off course, a course correction is made as soon as a change is possible. That's **canalization**. A well-known case study illustrates this nicely. The child was growing normally during his first year, but just before his first birthday the child became sick for approximately 1 year. During this time the child fell behind his normal and expected growth pattern. Following recovery, however, he returned to his projected growth path so that, by his fourth birthday, he was again well within the normal range. This *catch-up* illustrates the principle of canalization (Prader, Tanner, & von Harnack, 1963).

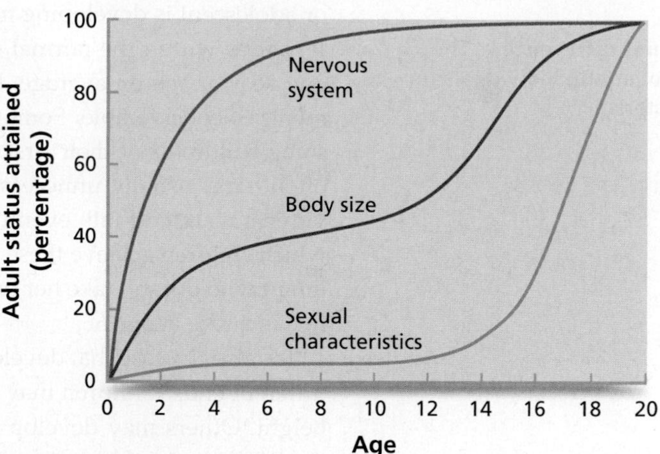

FIGURE 4.3

Differential Growth Rates in the Human Body

Not all body parts and systems develop at the same rate. The nervous system develops most rapidly in the first 5 years of life, while sexual characteristics remain fairly stagnant until puberty is reached in early adolescence. Body size changes quickly from birth to age 3 before slowing down, rapid growth occurs again beginning at puberty and continuing until full adult height is reached in late adolescence.

independence of systems A principle of development that asserts that different parts of the body develop along different timetables.

canalization Development tends to follow, and return to, a normative course.

Catch-up also seems to occur in cognitive development. For example, Ronald Wilson (1978) studied the canalization of intelligence in relation to low birth weight. He observed identical twins who had unequal birth weights, one normal and one considerably below normal. (Babies born at a low birth weight are usually at risk for poor cognitive outcomes.) Wilson found that across the course of development, the babies' shared genotype prevailed over their different birth weights. Although one twin was born at a distinct disadvantage, by 6 years of age, the children's IQs were almost identical. Very-low-birth-weight infants show deficits in reading comprehension at 9 years that are gone by 15 years (Samuelsson, Finnström, Flodmark, Gäddlin, Leijon, & Wadsby, 2006).

In short, physical development doesn't just mean straightforward growth; it is also directed, multifaceted, and sometimes self-correcting. Even though the overall blueprint for physical development is canalized, individuals (and contexts) vary.

Norms and Individual Differences

In studying physical development, scientists consider both norms and individual differences. **Norms** represent average outcomes on some characteristic. For example, very few adults are either 4 or 7 feet tall; many more stand between 5 and 6 feet. This distribution during the childhood and adolescent years tells us how height varies in the population and provides guidance for pediatricians to determine whether a child

norms Average outcomes on a characteristic.

individual differences The variation among individuals on a characteristic.

or adolescent is developing normally. But there is a wide variation in **individual differences** within the normal range. For example, infants first walk and talk at about one year of age on average. But the range of individual differences in both achievements is considerable. Some children first walk at 10 months, others at 18 months; some children say their first word at 9 months, others not until 29 months. Parents often—and usually unnecessarily—worry about "late" developers. All normal individuals walk and talk eventually—an example of canalization. Moreover, the age at which children achieve these milestones does not necessarily predict future skills. The infant who doesn't take her first steps until 18 months may be the first across the finish line in a race at age 6.

It's also the case that development can follow many different paths to the same or to different ends. Children may develop at different rates, but eventually reach the same height. Others may develop at the same rate, but stop growing at different heights. And different children may develop at different rates and reach different heights. All these paths illustrate individual differences.

Physical growth is strongly influenced by larger genetic and cultural factors. If you were born to a Pygmy family in Cameroon in Africa, you and your siblings might develop at different rates, but your genetic potential as a Pygmy would limit your ultimate height, no matter how fast you grew. (The average height of adult Pygmies is 4 feet.) Nutritional conditions, governed by culture, are also important. Before World War II, for example, Japanese diets were restricted to rice and small amounts of meat, fish, and vegetables. As a result, the average height of Japanese individuals at that time (including many great-grandparents still alive today) was diminutive. Since World War II, the Japanese diet has changed in terms of protein and other nutrients, altering average height among Japanese dramatically. A contemporary Japanese teenager would have seemed supersized in 1940.

At birth as well as through the first years of development, infants born in richer countries tend to be healthier, heavier, and longer than infants born in poorer countries. Furthermore, within wealthy countries (such as the United States), children born into poverty grow more slowly than those born into prosperity, and they do not reach equivalent levels of height and weight (Schroeder et al., 1995; Tanner, 1990). (For a summary of this section, see "Interim Summary 4.1: Physical Growth.")

We see the same interaction between genetic inheritance and environmental conditions in the development of the central nervous system.

INTERIM SUMMARY 4.1

Physical Growth	
General Principles of Physical Growth	■ **Directionality:** How body proportions change—generally *cephalocaudal* (advances from "head to tail") though also *proximodistal* (progresses from the center of the body outward). ■ **Independence of systems:** Different parts of the body develop along different timetables. ■ **Canalization:** Many systems in the body follow a standard, structured course of development. If something throws development off course, a correction back on course occurs as soon as a change is possible.
Norms vs. Individual Differences	■ Norms: represent average outcomes. ■ Individual differences—the range of variation among people.

THE DEVELOPMENT OF THE CENTRAL NERVOUS SYSTEM

In just 9 months, that single fertilized egg we met in Chapter 3 developed into a fetus with a complex and self-regulating nervous system that changes from relatively generalized to specialized during development. In just 9 to 12 months more, the newborn develops into a child who feels sad if you do, communicates wants and needs, and can act in ways that make her parents marvel.

None of these many achievements would be possible without the internal wiring of the brain and nervous system. The **central nervous system (CNS),** the division of the nervous system that consists of the brain and spinal cord, processes information and directs behavior. In adapting to the complexities of life, the CNS develops at many levels at the same time, from the overall structure of the brain at one end of the spectrum to individual cells at the other. Connections between brain and behavior do not travel in only one direction, however. In a circular way, genetically predetermined developments of the brain give rise to new behaviors, and new behaviors lead to new interactions with the environment that then foster brain development. As we have stressed, development is always the product of the reciprocal interplay between biology and experience, and brain development is no different.

central nervous system (CNS) The division of the nervous system, consisting of the brain and spinal cord, that processes information and directs behavior.

subcortical structures Brain components that control state of arousal.

limbic system The part of the nervous system that manages emotions.

cortex Thin layers of outer tissue that cover the brain.

association areas The parts of the brain concerned with awareness, attention, memory, and the integration of information.

hemispheres The two halves of the brain.

corpus callosum The connection between the two halves or hemispheres of the brain.

visual cortex The part of the brain that regulates sight.

auditory cortex The part of the brain that monitors hearing.

sensorimotor cortex The part of the brain concerned with touch.

motor cortex The part of the brain that controls voluntary movement.

frontal cortex The brain's command central responsible for thinking, planning, initiative, impulse control, and creativity.

Wernicke's area The region on the left side of the brain dedicated to language or speech comprehension.

Broca's area The region on the left side of the brain dedicated to language or speech production.

neurons Cells that carry information across the body and brain.

The Brain

The CNS begins as a layer of cells on the outer surface of the embryo and is already visible just one month after conception. **Subcortical structures** that control *state*—whether we are asleep, awake, or somewhere in between—and arousal emerge first during prenatal brain development. Components of the **limbic system** that manage emotions develop next. The **cortex** and **association areas** of the brain concerned with awareness, attention, memory, and the integration of information emerge last and do not completely develop until late adolescence or the early 20s in some individuals.

The brain is divided into two halves or **hemispheres**, connected by the **corpus callosum**. The cortex of the brain is made up of thin layers of tissue that cover the brain. (*Cortex* means "bark" in Latin.) Although only about 0.12 inch (3 millimeters) thick, the cortex contains 75 percent of the brain's cells (Sharpee et al., 2006). It is wrinkled and folded to fit billions of cells into a small space; otherwise, we would require giant-sized heads. The cortex of other mammals is smaller (relative to body weight) and smoother than ours is. (Nonmammals do not have a cortex.) The corpus callosum, which integrates activities of the two hemispheres by transferring information between them (Gazzaniga, Bogen, & Sperry, 1962), may not complete growth until 6 years of age (Thompson et al., 2000), and the cortex does not mature fully until adolescence.

Different areas of the cortex have specialized functions. The **visual cortex** regulates sight; the **auditory cortex** monitors hearing; the **sensorimotor cortex** processes touch; and the **motor cortex** controls voluntary movement. The **frontal cortex**—the brain's "command central"—is responsible for thinking, planning, initiative, impulse control, and creativity. In addition, two regions in the left cortex are dedicated to language comprehension (**Wernicke's area**) and language production or speech (**Broca's area**). (See Figure 4.4.)

In short, the brain is highly specialized. But it is also flexible, as we will discuss later in this chapter. First, we need a close-up view of how the brain functions at the cellular level.

Brain Cells

Your brain contains approximately 100 billion cells, a number equal to all of the stars in our galaxy (Nowakowski, 2006). **Neurons** are cells that carry information between

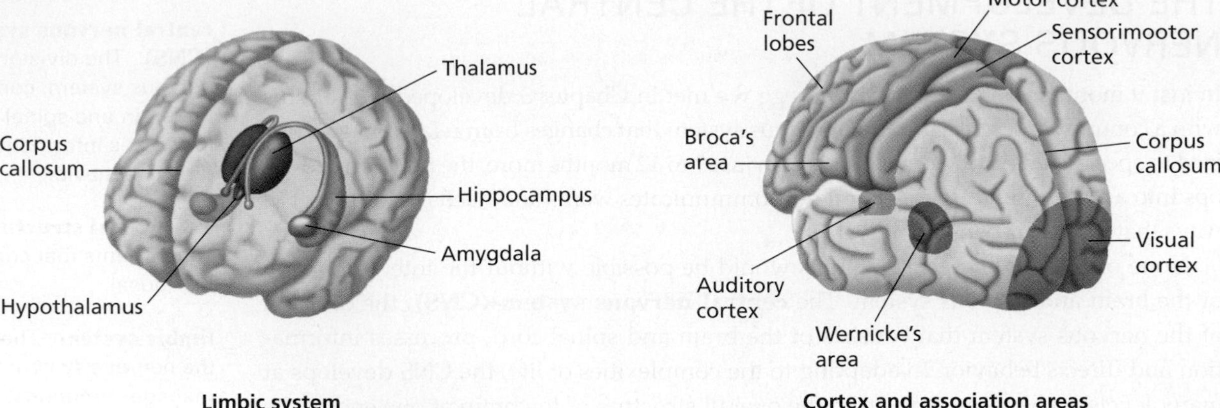

FIGURE 4.4

Areas of the Brain

Structures in the limbic system (shown on the left of the figure) are located deep within the cerebral hemispheres. Together, they oversee several important functions related to emotion, motivation, hormone secretion, and homeostasis (the tendency of physiological systems to maintain internal stability). The cerebral cortex (show on the right of the figure) is divided into four lobes (frontal, parietal, temporal, and occipital) based on the location of fissures, or folds, in the brain tissue. Each lobe contains areas specialized for different functions.
Source: From Bernstein/Penner/Clarke-Stewart/Roy. *Psychology,* 8E. © 2008 Wadsworth, a part of Cengage Learning, Inc. Reproduced by permission. www.cengage.com/permissions

the body and brain, as well as back and forth within the brain. Collectively, neurons and their connections compose the *gray matter* of the brain.

As shown in Figure 4.5, a neuron has three main parts: a cell body, dendrites, and an axon. The **cell body** contains the nucleus of the cell and the biochemical mechanisms to keep the cell alive and determine whether the cell will send out signals to other cells. The **dendrites** are like antennas that pick up signals from other neurons. (The word *dendrite* comes from the Greek for "little trees"; like trees, a neuron may have many branches.) The **axon** carries signals away from the cell body toward other neurons in the brain or nerves in the body. At their tips, axons usually divide into many *axon terminals.*

The connection between one neuron's axon and another neuron's dendrite is called a **synapse**. The two neurons do not actually touch; rather, there is a minuscule gap between them, and that gap is the synapse. Neurons communicate by means of chemicals called **neurotransmitters,** which carry the signal across the synapse from one neuron to the next. For the neuron to fire there is a change in an electrical charge inside the neuron called the **action potential**. When this charge travels along the axon and reaches the axon terminal, it stimulates the release of neurotransmitters (Kandel, 2007).

Neurons grow, move, and develop relations with one another to form stable interconnected pathways—many during the prenatal period (Bhardwaj et al., 2006; Muotri & Gage, 2006). Migrating cells move to particular locations or partner cells; that is, they seem to "know" their future addresses (Lewis, 2005). Scientists believe that migrating cells may be drawn to those points by the neurochemicals their partners produce. Whatever the process, it is swift and sure. By about the end of the sixth month of gestation (i.e., about 3 months *before* birth), cell migration within the brain is more or less complete (Nowakowski, 2006). At birth, the brain is about one-quarter the size of the adult brain, and virtually all of the neurons that will ever exist are in place. The dendrites, axons, and synapses are still developing, however. The development parents see in their baby—from first smiles to first steps—reflects these unseen changes.

cell body The part of the cell that contains the nucleus and biochemical mechanisms to keep the cell alive and determine whether the cell will fire.

dendrites Branched extensions of a neuron that act like antennas that pick up signals from other neurons.

axon The part of the cell that carries signals away from the cell body toward other neurons. At their tips, axons divide into many *axon terminals.*

synapse The connection between one neuron's axon and another neuron's dendrite.

neurotransmitters Electrochemicals through which neurons intercommunicate.

action potential An electrical charge inside the neuron.

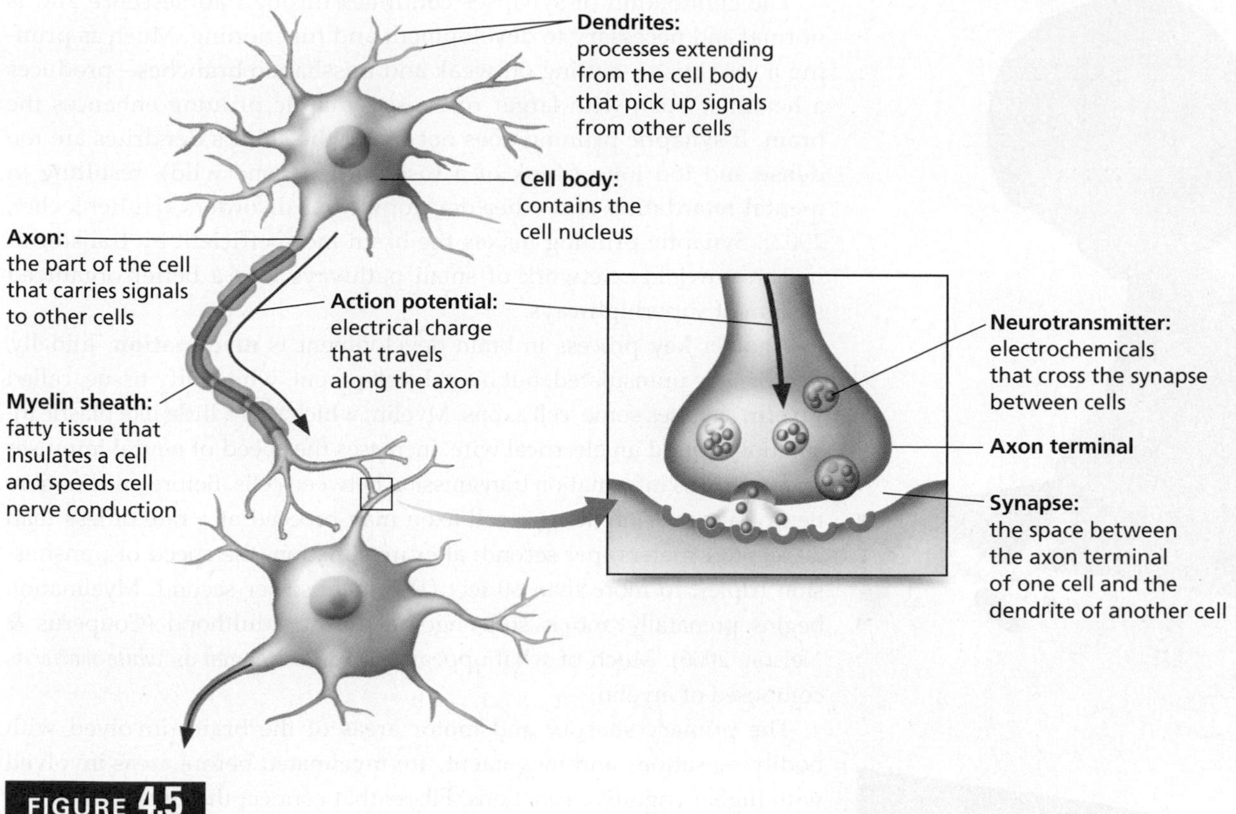

FIGURE 4.5

The Neuron and Synapse

Source: From Bernstein/Penner/Clarke-Stewart/Roy. *Psychology,* 8E. © 2008 Wadsworth, a part of Cengage Learning, Inc. Reproduced by permission. www.cengage.com/permissions

A key process in early brain development is **synaptogenesis**, the development of connections—synapses—between neurons through the growth of axons and dendrites. In just the first 6 months of life, 100,000 new synapses form every second! By age 2, a single neuron may have 10,000 connections to other neurons. No wonder scientists call this the "exuberant" phase of synaptogenesis. The rate of synaptogenesis peaks at about age one and slows down in early childhood, but synaptogenesis continues throughout life as children, adolescents, and adults learn new skills, acquire knowledge, build memories, and adapt to changing circumstances. The formation of some synapses is genetically programmed, but others depend on experience. The more a synapse is used, the stronger its pathway.

synaptogenesis The development of connections between neurons through the growth of axons and dendrites.

Initially the brain produces many more connections among cells than it will use. At one year of age, the number of synapses in the infant brain is about *twice* the number in the adult brain (Couperus & Nelson, 2006). However, soon after birth a complementary process to synaptogenesis begins. **Synaptic pruning** eliminates unused and unnecessary synapses on a principle of use-it-or-lose-it. As a general rule, we tend to assume that "more is better," but that's not the case here. Imagine hills and a meadow between two villages. Hundreds of lightly trodden paths connect one to the other (the unpruned brain). Over time people discover that one path is more direct than others. More people begin using this path more often, so it becomes wider and deeper. Because the other paths are not used anymore, the grass grows back and those paths disappear (synaptic pruning). The complementary processes of synaptogenesis and synaptic pruning are fundamental to brain **plasticity**—the capacity of the brain to be modified by experience (Sur & Rubenstein, 2005). (We'll discuss plasticity more later in this chapter.)

synaptic pruning The process of elimination of unused and unnecessary synapses.

plasticity The capacity of the brain to be modified by experience.

© Laura Dwight

A 19-month-old girl drawing with a marker. At first, her movements will be jerky, inexact, and uncontrolled, but over time they become controlled, exact, and directed.

The elimination of synapses continues through adolescence and is normal and necessary to development and functioning. Much as pruning a rose bush—cutting off weak and misshapen branches—produces a healthier bush with larger roses, so synaptic pruning enhances the brain. If synaptic pruning does not occur, the child's dendrites are too dense and too long (think of a rose garden gone wild), resulting in mental retardation and other developmental disorders (Huttenlocher, 2002). Synaptic pruning makes the brain more efficient by transforming an unwieldy network of small pathways into a better organized system of superhighways.

Another key process in brain development is **myelination**. Initially, neurons are uninsulated, but over development, white fatty tissue, called **myelin**, encases some cell axons. Myelin, which acts a little like plastic insulation around an electrical wire, increases the speed of neural impulses and improves information transmission between cells. Before myelination, neurotrans-mission along a cell axon may proceed at a rate of less than 20 feet (6.1 meters) per second; after myelination, the speed of transmission triples, to more than 60 feet (18.3 meters) per second. Myelination begins prenatally and is still ongoing during adulthood (Couperus & Nelson, 2006). Much of what appears on brain images as *white matter* is composed of myelin.

The primary sensory and motor areas of the brain, involved with bodily sensations and movement, are myelinated before areas involved with higher cognitive functions. Fibers that connect the **cerebellum** (associated with balance and control of body movements) to the cerebral cortex grow and myelinate through age 4, contributing to advances in motor control. Walking, running, and jumping become more synchronized. Myelination of the prefrontal cortex, which is associated with higher cognition, continues through middle and late childhood into adolescence and young adulthood (Kostovic, Judas, & Petankjek, 2008; Olson & Luciana, 2008). A tragic illustration of the importance of myelin is **multiple sclerosis**, a disease in which the autoimmune system strips neurons of myelin, leading to loss of motor control, deteriorating speech and vision, and eventually death.

myelinization The process through which cell axons become sheathed in myelin.

myelin The white fatty tissue that encases cell axons.

cerebellum The part of the brain associated with balance and control of body movements.

multiple sclerosis A disease in which the autoimmune system strips neurons of myelin, leading to loss of motor control.

For a number of reasons, for example the exuberance of connections among cells, the transmission of information among cells is at first *diffuse* or spread out, so that reactions to stimulation develop and end slowly, something like when the body shudders in response to the roll of thunder. In their more developed state, after pruning, connections among cells are more orderly and efficient. The same stimulation now produces a *phasic* reaction that is discrete and synchronous in time, like a startle. A simple illustration is the way younger versus older babies respond to a loud hand clap. Early on, a sudden sound like a clap elicits a gross response; the whole body shudders. Later, clapping leads to a clear-cut and much more efficient turn of the head.

Maturation alone does not account for improved communication among cells, however; experience plays a key role. When infants look at a form—a circle, for example—they scan it with their eyes and develop a mental representation that is related to eye movements as well as to the activity of cortical neurons excited by the form. Virtually identical cortical activity is excited every time they view a circle, which makes the circle progressively easier to identify. Thus, experience smoothes connections among cells to speed perceptual pathways. This is how babies come to recognize their mother's face, their father's voice, and the feel of their blanket.

Cell Activity

Individual cells in the CNS typically have highly specialized functions. The 1981 Nobel laureates David Hubel and Torsten Wiesel tried to find out how individual cells in the visual cortex respond to light, in a series of experiments with cats. Hubel had developed a special technique, called **microelectrode recording**, to measure the activity of individual cells. At the beginning of their research, he and Wiesel expected to find that shining a light in front of the cat's eyes would increase or decrease the activity of single cells in the cat's brain. Instead, they found that some cells only fired when a vertical line passed in front of the cat, other cells were excited by diagonal lines, and so on. Hubel and Wiesel even found these highly specialized cells in newborn kittens that had no visual experience! Apparently the brain is prewired in ways that assist visual perception.

microelectrode recording A technique used to measure the activity of individual cells.

We cannot observe or directly measure the activity of single cells in the brains of human beings. However, it is possible to measure the electrical activity of groups of cells. **Electroencephalographic (EEG) recordings** reflect spontaneous natural rhythms of electrical activity of the cortex of the brain. Neuroscientists use sensors that touch the scalp to pick up the electrical signals underneath. Broadly speaking, newborns have low-level, irregular brain activity, as though they are not processing stimulation completely. By the time they are 2 years old, however, children have high-amplitude and regular patterns of EEG activity much more like adult brain activity (Field et al., 2004; Otero et al., 2003).

electroencephalographic (EEG) recordings Measurements acquired with sensors at the scalp that show electrical activity of masses of individual cells.

Scientists examine EEG outputs to see how long it takes the brain to respond to stimulation and how focused that response is at different ages. **Event-related potentials (ERPs)** are specific patterns of brain activity evoked by a specific stimulus. The ERP is simple and takes a long time to develop in infancy, but it develops quickly and is more complex as the child matures (Parker et al., 2005; Wiebe et al., 2006). Responses to sensory stimuli (like a light or a sound) become more rapid and more focused as children grow older.

event-related potentials (ERPs) Specific patterns of brain activity evoked by a specific stimulus.

ERPs provide valuable information about the maturation of the brain. Reynolds and Richards (2005) made a close examination of the development of ERPs in infants 4 to 7 months of age and identified different underlying brain structures for different aspects of information processing. ERPs also help to determine how the senses are developing. Suppose a baby does not respond to a sound—for example, by turning his or her head. How would you learn whether the baby can hear? If that infant's ERP shows a similar pattern to a given repeated sound, you at least know that the infant's brain is responding; so, it is likely that the neuronal pathway from the ear to the brain is working. Not surprisingly, infants who have well developed auditory ERPs at birth have better language ability in later childhood (Molfese & Molfese, 1994).

Brain Plasticity

Some of our description of brain development may make it sound as though the infant's brain is entirely *pre*programmed. Developmental scientists have discussed this in terms of **experience-expectant processes**, those the brain is already prepared for. This is, of course, not the whole story. Brain development is far from complete. **Experience-dependent processes** involve the active formation of new synaptic connections in response to a person's unique experiences (Greenough, Black, & Wallace, 1987; Holtmaat et al., 2006). They contribute to our individuality. Experiences shape brain structure and alter brain function. Individual cells change and synapses grow or are pruned to improve the speed and efficiency of neural connections. For example, rats that are raised in complex environments (supplied with toys and

experience-expectant processes Prewired processes in the brain.

experience-dependent processes Brain processes that involve the active formation of new synaptic connections in response to the individual's unique experience.

opportunities for lots of play and exploration) develop heavier and thicker visual cortices (*cortices* is plural for *cortex*) than littermates raised in barren, standard laboratory cages; experienced rats also solve problems better (Greenough et al., 1987).

Of course, development is not just the result of an environment operating on a passive organism; in many respects we create our development though our active involvement with the environment. An experiment with kittens shows this (Held & Hein, 1963). The researchers yoked two kittens together. One was allowed to walk around and explore its environment. It also wore a harness that connected to a "gondola" that held another kitten with only its head sticking out. As one cat moved, the other cat moved; as one cat saw the world, the other cat saw the world. For one cat, exploration and vision depended on its own movement; the other cat was passive. Kittens that were allowed to physically explore their visual environments later, as adult cats, mastered visual tasks whereas their "yoked-control" littermates whose movement was restrained performed more poorly. In other words, active exploration of the environment facilitated and enriched subsequent development relative to passive exposure to the same stimulation. (We will return to other implications of this study later.)

As all these experiments show, the brain's structure (anatomy) and function (how it works) are *plastic*. They can be molded by experience. Our brain is programmed to respond to important features of our environment (experience expectancy), but adapts to the environment in which we find ourselves (experience dependency). Two kinds of plasticity in the nervous system are modifiability and compensation.

modifiability A principle of development that asserts that, although cells are predestined for specific functions, their function can be changed.

sensitive periods Times in development when the organism is especially open to environmental influence.

Modifiability means that, although cells are predestined for specific functions, their function can be changed. Sometimes change must occur at critical points in development, which, as you'll recall from Chapter 3, are called **sensitive periods** (Bornstein, 1989, 2003). The window of modifiability is opened early in life so that we can prepare ourselves quickly and efficiently for the particular environment in which we develop. Studies of kittens, for example, show that cells in the visual cortex that respond to visual stimuli at birth become more responsive to certain types of stimuli, depending on what the kitten sees during sensitive periods in visual development (Wiesel & Hubel, 1974). Indeed, the brain is so plastic early in life that some cells can be modified to serve a completely different purpose. Surgically moving a part of the brain to a different place in the brain will result in the transplanted part adapting to functions of its new location. Thus, cells from the auditory cortex moved to the visual cortex become responsive to visual stimuli. This must take place within a specific window of time, however; if transplanted after their sensitive period, the same cells will die.

compensation A kind of plasticity in which cells substitute for others, permitting recovery of function after loss or damage.

Compensation is a second kind of plasticity. In compensation, healthy cells substitute for others, permitting recovery of function after brain injury. Cells can compensate for defects in neighboring cells. After an injury—say, limb amputation—the parts of the brain that would be stimulated by the (now missing) limb are activated by other sources of stimulation. Indeed, new connections have been observed in as short a time as a day after amputation. Congenitally blind people compensate with improved hearing due to cells that would have processed visual information. Similarly, congenitally deaf people compensate with improved sight, which assists in decoding the visual motions of American Sign Language (Neville & Lawson, 1987). The ultimate version of compensation may be embryonic **stem cells**—the newest, youngest, and least developed cells of all—that can be grafted to repair damaged parts of the CNS or replace cells that have died. (Adult stem cells may have some of the same adaptive properties.)

stem cells The newest, youngest, and least developed cells that can be grafted to repair damaged parts of the CNS or replace cells that have died.

In summary, central nervous system development in infancy has been studied in terms of overall brain growth and structure as well as single-cell and gross electrical activity. The brain displays remarkable specificity of function, but at the same time has evolved the capacity and flexibility to adjust to the environment. An active interplay between maturation and experience transpires during the development of single cells and the brain as a whole. (For a summary of this section, see "Interim Summary 4.2: The Development of the Central Nervous System.")

INTERIM SUMMARY 4.2

The Development of the Central Nervous System

Central Nervous System (CNS)	■ The **CNS** processes information and directs behavior. ■ Brain development is always the product of reciprocal interplay between biology and experience.
The Brain	Anatomy of the brain: ■ The brain oversees several important functions related to motivation, memory, hormone secretion, and homeostasis. ■ The cerebral cortex is divided into four lobes (frontal, parietal, temporal, and occipital) based on their location. Each lobe contains areas specialized for different functions. ■ The **cortex**, or outer layer of brain tissue, has several association areas, including the visual cortex (sight), auditory cortex (sound), sensorimotor cortex (touch), and motor cortex (movement). **Wernicke's** and **Broca's areas** are specialized for language comprehension and language production, respectively.
The brain's structure and function (how it works) are plastic—cells are predestined for different functions but that changes sometimes at sensitive periods.	Two kinds of **plasticity:** 1. **Modifiability**—although cells are predestined for specific functions, they can be changed. 2. **Compensation**—cells can substitute for others, permitting recovery of function after loss or damage.
Brain development is not fixed.	We create our own development through our active involvement with the environment.
Neurons are cells that carry information across the body and brain.	Three main parts of a neuron: 1. **Dendrites:** Processes extending from the cell body that pick up signals from other cells. 2. **Cell body:** Contains the cell nucleus. 3. **Axon:** The part of the cell that carries signals to other cells.
A synapse is the connection between one neuron's axon and another neuron's dendrite.	■ **Neurotransmitters** are electrochemicals that cross the synapse between cells. ■ **Action potential** is an electrical charge that travels along the axon.

THE AUTONOMIC NERVOUS SYSTEM

Much of what very new babies do is survival oriented and may not yet be under conscious or voluntary control. The **autonomic nervous system (ANS)**, which regulates many body activities (such as breathing, blood flow, or digestion), reigns early on. In considering ANS development in infancy, we focus on *cycles* and *states.*

At first glance, a baby's activity appears random and chaotic. To a new parent, a baby seems to be constantly moving his or her mouth, eyes, hands, and feet and shifting unpredictably from alertness to sleep. Close examination tells a different story, however. Infants are much more regular than meets the eye. Many different systems **cycle** in identifiable and predictable rhythms (Rivkees, 2004).

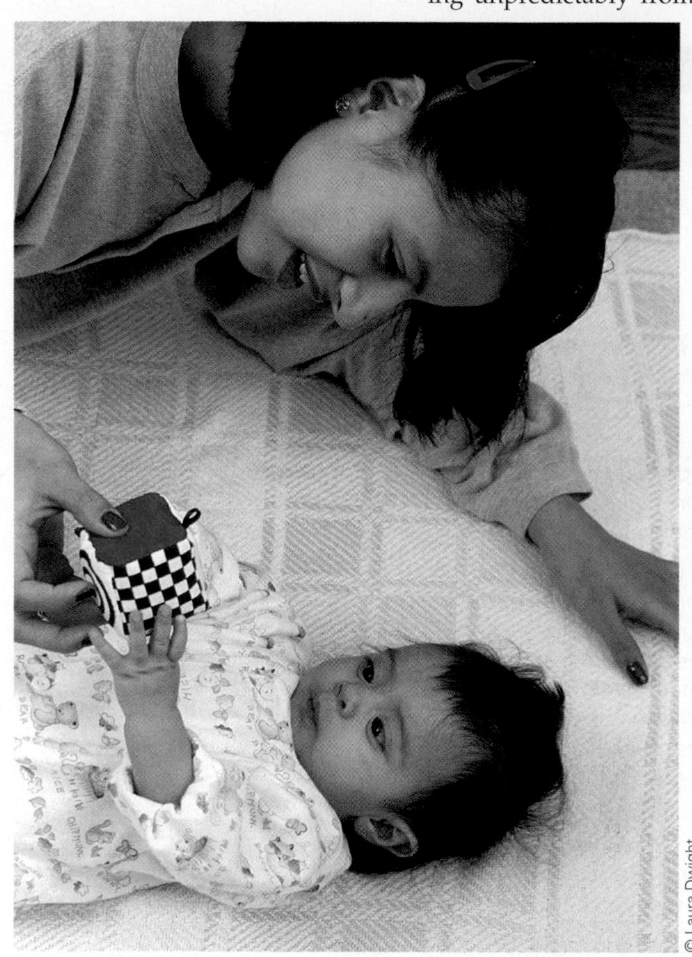

© Laura Dwight

A 4-month-old baby girl interested in a toy held out for her by her mother. Even simple visual stimulation at this age promotes infant brain development, and the interaction promotes mother-infant involvement.

Some activities repeat regularly and often, perhaps once or more every second. The heart beats, the lungs expand and contract, and, when appropriate, the infant sucks in rather fast rhythms. All these biological activities maintain life. Although less frequent, infant kicking and rocking also cycle quickly when they occur (Thelen & Smith, 2006). Other behaviors, like general body movements, cycle every minute or two (Groome et al., 1999). And still others, such as states of waking, quiet sleep (no rapid eye movements), and active sleep (with rapid eye movements, indicating dreaming) have cycles on the order of hours (Papoušek, 1996). Taken altogether, infant activity might appear unstructured and erratic. But actually what we see in the newborn at any one time is the simultaneous and independent cycling of several overlapping rhythms. It's as if the woodwind, percussion, and brass sections of an orchestra were all playing at the same time, but to different beats.

What purposes do these cycles serve? First, no one could keep moving all the time, so periods of activity are necessarily followed by periods of rest. Second, as we've said, development need not wait for external stimulation; sometimes babies make their own stimulation. Waving their arms or kicking their legs, for example, stimulates the development of neuronal connections—synapses—in regions of the brain responsible for these movements. Last, social activity is triggered by these cyclic behaviors. Rhythmic pauses in babies' sucking, and stages of the sleep-wake cycle, signal to adults when to caregive or initiate play.

States of arousal in young infants are not quite as regular as some other cycles, like breathing. You can be talking or playing with a little baby and suddenly he or she falls fast asleep! Infants shift frequently among states of sleep, drowsiness, alertness, and activity. It sometimes takes months to establish the predictable schedule of wake and sleep states that all parents crave. Infants vary tremendously in their sleep patterns and in the age at which they begin sleeping through the night (St. James-Roberts, 2007). One of us has a colleague whose two children are perfectly normal, but the first baby was sleeping through the night by 2 months, whereas her second child was still sleeping in 45-minute shifts when she was a 1-year-old.

The age at which infants begin to control or *regulate* their state has important implications for infant development and infant care (as well as parental well-being). State

autonomic nervous system (ANS) The division of the nervous system that regulates many body activities without our voluntary control, such as breathing, blood flow, or digestion.

cycle Moving in an identifiable and predictable rhythm.

regularity provides a window on the maturity of the infant's nervous system. Poor state regulation is common in preterm infants, for example. Equally important is an infant's state of arousal, which influences what will happen next. Adults rock and soothe distressed babies. They engage happy and alert babies in play and learning, showing them toys. Babies who frequently cry or fuss elicit different patterns of care than do babies who frequently smile and coo. In addition, state determines whether and how infants learn. When quietly alert, infants respond to touch and visual stimuli, and they may listen to a soothing voice that is ignored when they are crying. During these quiet moments, infants can examine and become familiar with their parents' faces or study the mobiles hanging over their crib. Thus, babies' states influence their perceptual and cognitive development.

As mentioned, organization of the sleep-wake cycle reflects neurological maturation and the developing ability of babies to regulate their own states (McKenna et al., 1994; Moon, Kotch, & Aird, 2006; Scher, Epstein, & Tirosh, 2004). However, the way a baby is cared for is also influential. Experiences around birth, parental caregiving, and cultural beliefs all affect infant sleep cycles. For example, infants who receive more sensitive caregiving (from a parent or nurse) spend more time in quiet sleep (Ingersoll & Thoman, 1999). Infants' sleep states are also affected by culture. Among the Kipsigis people in East Africa, infants sleep with their mothers and are permitted to nurse on demand. During the day they are strapped to their mothers' backs, accompanying them on their daily rounds of farming, household chores, and social activities. They often nap while their mothers go about their work, and, so, they do not begin to sleep through the night until many months later than U.S. children. Japanese infants generally have good state regulation and few sleep problems. The reason appears to be a function of—*surprise!*—nature and nurture: That is, this difference is due to a biological predisposition among Japanese infants to be less disturbed by noise during sleep *and* the custom among Japanese families of babies sleeping with their mothers (Kawasaki et al., 1994). *Co-sleeping*, which is practiced in much of the world, allows mothers to reach for and pull their infants close for feeding or comforting (McKenna et al., 1994). Western infants typically sleep in separate rooms from their parents. Although there are those who believe that co-sleeping may have advantages for the child and parent in terms of closeness and immediate responsiveness, there are also risks such as SIDS (Kemp et al., 2000; St. James-Roberts, 2007). (For a summary of this section, see "Interim Summary 4.3: The Autonomic Nervous System.")

REFLEXES AND MOTOR SKILLS

The development of movement during infancy is characterized by increasingly voluntary and controlled actions (Brandtstädter, 2006; von Hofsten, 2007). At birth, much infant movement is reflexive; by toddlerhood, the baby is largely in control.

INTERIM SUMMARY 4.3

The Autonomic Nervous System

The **autonomic nervous system (ANS)** regulates many body activities without our voluntary control (such as breathing, blood flow, or digestion).

- At any one time in newborns, you can see the simultaneous and independent cycling of several overlapping rhythms.
- The age at which infants begin to regulate their state provides a window on the maturity of the nervous system.

Reflexes

reflexes Simple, involuntary responses to certain stimuli that have (or had) adaptive significance.

Newborn babies look completely helpless, but they are not. They are good at a few special—if limited—behaviors, called "reflexes." **Reflexes** are simple, involuntary responses to certain stimuli. Many reflexes have *adaptive significance;* that is, they are designed to aid survival.

Reflexes are divided into three groups. The *approach reflexes* are concerned with intake, especially breathing and rooting, sucking, and swallowing. Babies show the rooting reflex in response to being stroked on the cheek; rooting entails turning the head toward the source of stimulation and beginning to suck. Rooting and sucking allow infants to locate and swallow food.

The *avoidance reflexes* include coughing, sneezing, and blinking. A common characteristic of avoidance reflexes is their all-or-nothing quality; when they are elicited, they occur in full-blown strength. It's almost impossible to stop or modify a sneeze!

A third collection of reflexes (simply referred to as *other reflexes*) seems to have had more meaning once upon a time in our evolutionary history than they do now. The *Palmer grasp* and *Moro response* are two examples. The Moro reflex is the tendency for babies to swing their arms wide and bring them together again across the middle of their body—as if around the body of a caregiver. This reflex can be elicited by a loud sound or when the baby suddenly loses support. Similarly, in the Palmer grasp, babies tighten their grip if whatever they are holding is suddenly raised; this allows babies to support their own weight for brief periods during the first few weeks of life. This reflex is also exhibited by many nonhuman primate newborns, who cling to their mother's body hair.

Although these other reflexes do not seem to serve their original function any longer, they provide an important means of assessing infant development. Indeed, eliciting reflexes are a part of most neonatal examinations and screening tests. Most reflexes develop before birth (preterm infants show them) and are normally present for 4 to 8 months after birth. Then, rather suddenly, they disappear. Why? As cortical processes develop, they inhibit subcortical ones. Thus, the disappearance of some reflexes reflects the emergence of higher cortical function; their disappearance is a sign that brain development is progressing normally. As is the case with synaptic pruning, sometimes maturation is indicated by the *disappearance* of something old, rather than the *emergence* of something new.

Motor Skills

The growth of motor function across infancy is as dramatic as physical growth (Adolph & Berger, 2005, 2006). Newborns can't even roll over, but toddlers are so fast at getting around that parents must monitor a 2-year-old's whereabouts constantly. Now the whole house needs to be childproofed! Like other aspects of development, development of motor skills depends on both physical maturation and the experiences infants have (von Hofsten, 2007). As motor systems develop, infants acquire the ability to move about and manipulate objects (Claxton, Keen, & McCarty, 2003; Keen et al., 2003).

Infant motor development follows a more or less predictable sequence. Until about 5 months, infants lie flat unless they're being held. By 6 months, most babies can sit up by themselves, an accomplishment that opens new vistas. Before, babies could only look at what was put in front of them; now they can look around. By 8 to 10 months, most infants begin crawling, which means they can move toward sights and sounds (unless restrained). First-time parents are often surprised at how quickly infants can scoot about. They also make active efforts to stand up and "cruise" with the support of a caregiver or piece of furniture, soon they begin to walk with help. On average, infants take their first, awkward, independent steps at age 1, though another year passes before their walking is smooth and steady. Remember that we are talking about norms. Individuals vary in their rate of development of motor skills. Some infants progress directly from sitting to walking at 9 or 10 months without crawling; others do not even attempt to stand

TABLE 4.1 Norms of Motor Development

Age	Gross Motor	Nonlocomotor	Fine Motor
1 month		Supports head. Can lift head from prone lying.	Will hold on to object placed in hand.
3–4 months		Stepping reflex pattern.	Plays with hands as a first toy.
5 months	Rolls over from front to back.	Holds head and shoulders erect when sitting.	Stretches out to grasp with increased accuracy.
6–8 months	May begin to crawl.	Sits unsupported.	Begins to be able to let go.
9 months	Can stand with support.	Pulls up to stand holding furniture.	Transfers objects from one hand to the other.
10 months	Crawling established.	Can bend to pick up objects when one hand is held.	Can use two hands doing different actions at the midline of the body.
1 year	Can crawl and stand alone, and may walk unaided. Uses step-together pattern to climb stairs.	Early walking. Starts games such as peekaboo.	Can build with bricks, pour water, eat finger food independently.
2 years	Can climb up and down stairs safely now using a passing-step pattern.	Problem solving—empties cupboards, dismantles toys.	Pulls on clothes. Can put on roomy garments—shoes on wrong feet. Increasing independence.

Source: Macintyre & McVitty (2004).

until 18 or 20 months. All are within the normal range. Table 4.1 shows the age norms for children's acquisition of basic motor milestones.

Do rates of motor development depend on maturation? Not entirely. Cross-cultural research shows that motor development can be influenced by parental expectations and childrearing practices. Hopkins and Westra (1988, 1990) questioned mothers and observed children in European cultures, Jamaica, and the West African nation of Mali. European mothers believed that motor skills development is driven by maturation, without special environmental or parental input. They see crawling as an important stage, between sitting independently and walking. In contrast, Jamaican and Mali mothers believed that motor skills development requires training and exercise. They viewed crawling as primitive, undesirable behavior; only animals move on all fours. They expected their infants to sit and walk at earlier ages than European mothers. Jamaican and Mali mothers also performed daily exercise routines with and massaged their infants. In European cultures, virtually all babies went through a crawling stage. Jamaican and Mali infants sat up and started walking at earlier ages. Surprisingly, 25 percent of Jamaican infants and 60 percent of Mali infants never crawled. Thus, parents or other caregivers can influence motor development, but only when an infant's nervous system and muscles are ready.

A toddler walking toward its mother. Development moves from unsure and unsteady to sure and steady and depends on motivation and experience.

FIGURE 4.6

Negotiating Motor Tasks in Infancy

In this laboratory paradigm, toys were placed at the bottom of a ramp in order to attract the infant. The angle of the ramp was adjusted to increase or decrease the steepness of the slope, and infants' behaviors are observed as they make their way down the ramp.

Source: Reprinted by permission of Karen Adolph.

It is not the case that infants automatically perform more complex motor acts as they mature. Experiences, too, are vital in shaping the course of motor development. Learning to move about and handle objects in infancy involves reciprocal relations between maturation and experience (Adolph & Berger, 2005, 2006). For example, an infant's success at negotiating a challenging motor task, such as descending a sloped surface, is not automatic. Infants take into account properties of the surfaces, such as the degree of slant, as well as their own abilities and explore different methods before settling on a specific way of descending (e.g., crawling forward or backward; see Figure 4.6). Infants who are already walking have to learn all over again how to come down the same slopes that they had mastered during crawling.

As we discussed in Chapter 1, **dynamic systems theory** asserts that change in one area of development influences others. Children's motor achievements affect many other, sometimes surprising, aspects of their psychological growth (Howe & Lewis, 2005; Thelen & Smith, 2006; van Geert & Steenbeek, 2005). For example, infants have depth perception (the ability to correctly judge distances) at 2 months, but they do not show fear of heights until they are able to crawl on their own, regardless of the age at which they begin to crawl (Bertenthal & Campos, 1990). Crawling (motor development) allows the infant to estimate distances more accurately than before (cognitive development), which later translates into fear (emotional development).

dynamic systems theory
A theory that asserts that change in one area of development impacts others.

autism spectrum disorder
A disorder characterized by difficulty in expressing needs and inability to socialize.

About 1 in 150 American children has some form of **autism spectrum disorder (ASD),** making autism an urgent public health concern (U.S. Centers for Disease Control and Prevention, 2007). Autism is a complex disorder characterized by difficulty in expressing needs and inability to socialize. The cause is not known. Clearly, early identification and intervention services are needed. The problem is that normally, autism cannot be diagnosed until children are around 3 years old. Movement disorders are considered one of the first signs of autism and may precede linguistic and social abnormalities. To get around the barrier of late diagnosis, Esposito, Venuti, Maestro, and Muratori (2009) applied a movement analysis to retrospective home videos parents had made in the first 5 months of life of children who were later diagnosed with ASD or with mental retardation versus children who developed normally. The researchers found a way to distinguish infants with ASD from the other infants by the asymmetric movements of ASD infants.

Each milestone in motor skills development also affects parent-infant interaction. When a baby first deliberately rolls over, stands upright, or walks, it is an occasion for joy and for telephone calls to grandparents. These achievements also signal all sorts of other cognitive and social changes at home as now the baby can get into all the cupboards. Toddlers are known for saying no often once they turn 2, but parents started saying no to these children long before, usually once the children started moving around on their own. Worse yet, the child's climbing out of his or her crib and going to the top of the stairs for the first time may cause panic as well as a trip to the hardware store to buy a baby gate the very next morning. (For a summary of this section, see "Interim Summary 4.4: Reflexes and Motor Development.")

INTERIM SUMMARY 4.4

Reflexes and Motor Development

Reflexes are divided into three groups and are important for providing external means of assessing development.	■ *Approach reflexes* are concerned with intake, especially breathing and rooting, sucking, and swallowing. ■ *Avoidance reflexes* include coughing, sneezing, and blinking. ■ *Other reflexes* such as the Palmar grasp and Moro response have more meaning in an evolutionary context.
Motor skills development is dependent on physical maturation and experience.	■ Until 5 months, infants are horizontal unless held. ■ By 6 months, most babies can sit up by themselves. ■ By 8–20 months, most babies begin to crawl. ■ On average infants take their first step at age 1.
Dynamic Systems Theory	■ This theory asserts that one change in development impacts others. Children's motor achievements affect many other aspects of their psychological growth.

SENSING AND PERCEIVING

We experience the world through our five senses—seeing, hearing, touching, tasting, and smelling. These sensory systems function *in utero*; they do not lie dormant until they are suddenly "switched on" at birth. By the second trimester of gestation, the eye and visual system, the ear and auditory system, the skin and tactile system, the nose and olfactory (smell) system, and the tongue and gustatory (taste) system are developing structurally, but they will not function at mature levels for some time.

The different senses appear to begin their road to development and achieve maturity at slightly different times. This staggered schedule has the possible biological advantage of permitting both biology and experience to "concentrate" on one system at a time.

Before we can begin to understand infant cognition and socioemotional development, we need to know what babies perceive. The short answer is, a good deal—but that's jumping ahead of our story. Understanding what babies see and hear or feel, taste, or smell is a challenge. After all, perception is private. That is, there is no way for the person sitting next to you to know what you perceive unless you tell him and infants are mute. To study babies we must infer what infants perceive from how they behave. (Developmental scientists have engineered ways around this barrier, which we will look at in some detail in Chapter 5.)

Seeing

We know most about the early development of sight, so let's begin there (Aslin, 2007; Kellman & Arterberry, 2006). The visual world is made up of pattern, depth, movement, and color. To see into the infant's visual world, we review early development along each of these dimensions (Livingstone & Hubel, 1988).

Pattern, Shape, and Form Not all that long ago, people believed that newborns could *not* see; like kittens, they were thought to be blind at birth. Indeed, some people in the world today (like rural peoples in Thailand) still think this way and place their babies in folding cloth hammocks with only a slit view of sky and ceiling to look at all day long. Now we know that newborns not only see, they actively seek visual stimulation, scanning the environment to find things to look at even when it is dark. When they do come

FIGURE 4.7

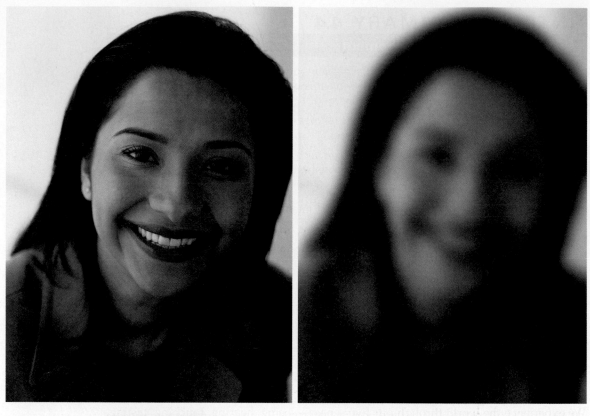

What the Infant Sees

Two photos of a female face that show how you, and how a baby, see another person.

across a pattern, newborns focus most on its boundaries, where the greatest amount of information is found (Conde-Agudelo, Rosas-Bermúdez, & Kafury-Goeta, 2006). Think of a Mondrian painting. You could look at a red or yellow or blue field, but then that's all you would see. What makes the painting dynamic are the intersections between the colored fields. If we track eye moments, younger infants scan patterns in a limited way, whereas older babies scan more of the patterns and do so more systematically.

Figure 4.7 provides an idea of how well newborn babies see, in comparison to the actual image. Visual acuity is relatively poor in newborns, but it improves rapidly and, by about 6 months of age, is almost the same as that of normal adults. The development of visual acuity is not wholly based on biological maturation. Off the west coast of Thailand, island preserves in the Andaman Sea are home to a tribe of so-called "sea gypsies," the Moken. These people dive to harvest clams, sea cucumbers, and other marine foods. Without goggles or other aids, sea gypsy children routinely spot even the smallest shellfish. As we all know, seeing underwater is usually difficult because water blurs our vision. Moken children have the same visual acuity on land as other children, but Moken children have better than twice the underwater resolving power—a level of underwater acuity thought to be impossible in humans. Mokens shrink the size of their pupils, the round black aperture through which light enters the eye, to be much smaller to increase their acuity. Mokens apparently learn this adaptive skill in childhood and do not simply inherit it as an inborn reflex (Gislen et al., 2003).

Infants are very attracted to faces, but it is not clear why. It could be that we have evolved an innate predisposition to attend to faces (Johnson, 2005). It could be that faces contain features that infants find intrinsically interesting (three dimensions, movement, sounds, and high contrast). It could be that infants learn to look at faces because they are associated with all things good—love, nourishment, and the like. Whatever its origins, though, face preference is real, strong, and present early in life (Bornstein & Arterberry, 2003; Gallay et al., 2006; Hunnius & Geuze, 2004; Turati et al., 2006). Sugita (2008) reared infant monkeys in isolation so they had no exposure to faces for the first 6 to 24 months of life. The people who fed them wore masks. When they were later tested, the monkeys showed a preference for both monkey and human faces relative to nonface objects, and they discriminated different faces, so it seems that the primate visual system has an experience-independent ability for face processing.

But when a newborn looks at her mother, does she see a face *or* the parts of a face (eyes, nose, mouth, and so forth)? In other words, do infants actually perceive whole forms or their separate pieces? If you know a baby, try this. Make a two-dimensional picture of a normal face pattern, a scrambled face pattern (i.e., with the parts of the face arranged in an unnatural way), and a blank oval, and then move each slowly in an arc-like path in front of a baby. More likely than not, even a newborn will look at and track the normal face pattern more than the scrambled face pattern (which have all the same elements as the normal face, so it's not the elements that make the face attractive, but the whole form). Infants also prefer the scrambled face pattern (it has more information) to the blank oval.

Infants not only see faces, they imitate facial expressions (happiness, sadness, surprise; Field et al., 1982). It is possible that newborns have a specialized brain mechanism for processing facial expressions (de Haan, 2008; Johnson, 2010) and that in the first week of life they can identify their mother (Pascalis, de Schonen, Morton, Fabre-Grenet, & Deruelle, 1995). This does not mean that infants' knowledge of faces is complete at birth. The ability to discriminate their mother's face from others, tell different facial expressions apart, understand that different expressions convey different emotions (see "Socioemotional Development in Infancy"), and discriminate between male versus female, or young versus old, faces are all products of everyday experience (Bornstein, Arterberry, & Mash, 2005).

Depth Parents put infants in cribs with side panels to keep them from falling out, just as they put gates at the top and bottom of stairways once babies start to crawl. Infants at the creeping and toddling stages are notoriously prone to falls from high (or even slightly elevated) places. Depth perception is crucial to determining the layout of the environment, recognizing objects, and guiding action. As their muscular coordination matures, infants begin to avoid such accidents on their own. Common sense might suggest that children learn to recognize depth through experience—that is, by falling and hurting themselves. "But is experience really the teacher? Or is the ability to perceive and avoid a brink part of the child's original endowment?" (Gibson & Walk, 1960, p. 64).

The story goes that two famous perceptual psychologists were on vacation with their infant daughter at the Grand Canyon when the baby began to scoot toward the edge. The mother was Eleanor Gibson, and this experience inspired the idea of creating a "visual cliff" to investigate depth perception in infants (Gibson & Walk, 1960). The visual cliff is a Plexiglas table (with protective sides) as you can see in Figure 4.8. On half the table, there is a checkerboard surface directly below the glass; on the other side, the checkerboard is several feet below the glass, making it appear as though the checkerboard floor is far away or a deep drop. Very few infants the researchers tested between 6 and 14 months of age actually crawled across the deep side when their mothers called to them. These results suggested that infants as young as 6 months of age perceive depth.

By 6 months, however, children may already have had experience falling. So other researchers studied precrawling babies by monitoring their heart rates when they were exposed to shallow or deep ends of the visual cliff (Bertenthal & Campos, 1990). Two-month-olds react to the deep side with a decrease in heart rate, indicating increased attention or interest. Thus, babies may perceive depth long before they themselves move about, but this does not mean they show fear of heights that early. It could be that the fear of drops shown by older infants results from the anxiety parents display when infants approach a drop rather than from infants' own experiences. Infants often

FIGURE 4.8

The Visual Cliff

The mother is gesturing for the baby to come across the "cliff"—will she go?

use their parents' emotional cues to help them interpret ambiguous events. (We'll say more about this *social referencing* in Chapter 6.)

More generally, when do infants see in depth, and how do we know? Several movement or *kinetic cues* help us see depth. When an object comes directly toward us, it grows in size and appears as though it will hit us, so we normally move to avoid the impending collision. Babies as young as one month consistently blink at approaching objects (Bornstein et al., 2005).

Movement Movement is important to perceiving. Things that move bring protection and nutrition, danger, and opportunities for exploration and play. So being able to perceive motion is an important survival tool. Infants will normally reach for objects in front of them even if the objects are moving. Indeed, babies as young as 4½ months will reach in a way that indicates they are good at targeting the object's next location if it moves in a predictable way (von Hofsten, 2007).

The infant's perception of motion is actually quite sophisticated (Arterberry & Bornstein, 2001). By 3½ months, infants distinguish between movement in different directions; by 5 months, they discriminate rotation (turning in a circle) from oscillation (swaying from side-to-side) (Ruff, 1982, 1985).

Indeed, movement perception is important for the recognition of objects. If you show a 4-month-old a stimulus such as that depicted in Figure 4.9 in common motion (i.e., the rod projecting from the top of the box, and the rod projecting from the bottom, moving together, at the same rate of speed, in the same direction, at the same time), infants mentally connect the two rods. Like you, they see it as a single rod that is partially blocked by the box rather than two separate rods that both happen to be moving.

Other studies also show the power of movement perception. An example is the so-called point-light walker display, which shows motion typical of human beings represented by moving points of light (see Figure 4.10). Imagine seeing the dots in panel A of the figure without the lines that connect them. When adults see the stationary display, the information is essentially uninterpretable; they don't think they are looking at anything in particular. But if the same set of lights starts to move in a way that mimics someone walking, adults can identify the object as a human figure in less than

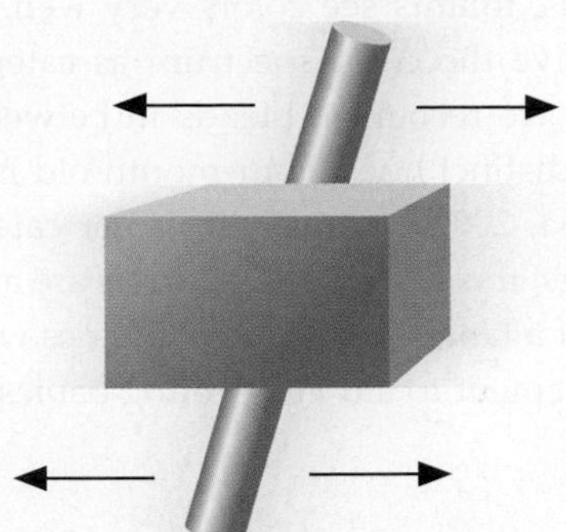

FIGURE 4.9

Infant Perception of Motion and Object Continuity

When infants as young as 4 months old are shown an image—like the one shown here in which a single rod appears to be moving left and right behind a box—they become surprised by (and look longer at) an image (not shown) of two separate short rods with no box in front of them. The fact that infants are surprised by the second image suggests that they mentally connected the top and bottom pieces of the rod and perceived it as one long rod (a whole object) moving behind the box, rather than as two separate shorter rods.

two-tenths of a second. Infants, too, are sensitive to biomechanical motion of this kind by 5 months of age (Arterberry & Bornstein, 2001). Experience and the brain play important roles in motion detection. Individual neurons in the adult monkey brain are sensitive to "biological motion."

In sum, infants in the first year of life see elements as parts of wholes. They also show developing sensitivity to the dimensions of spatial information of depth and movement. They even use movement to understand object form.

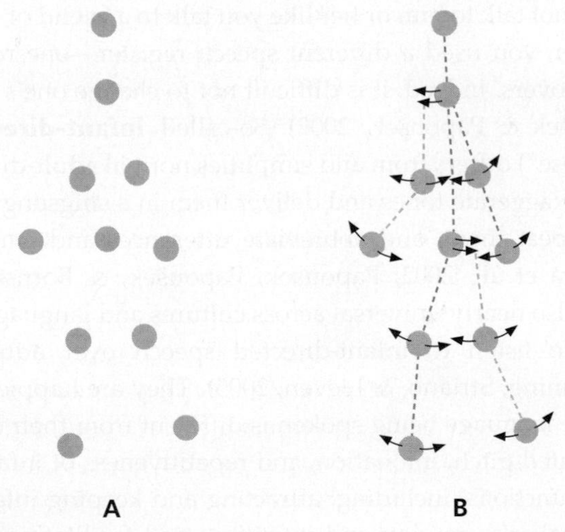

FIGURE 4.10

Point-Light Walker Display

When infants (or adults) see points of light, such as those in panel A, they are unable to make sense of them and therefore do not perceive them as any particular object or figure. However, when the lights are set in a "walking" motion such as in panel B, infants as young as 5 months old show evidence that they perceive the moving lights to represent a human walking.

Color Patterns and objects in the environment not only vary in terms of dimensions but also color. By 2 months, infants see colors very well. Adults do not merely see colors, however; we perceive the color spectrum as categories of hue: blue, green, yellow, and red. Although we recognize blends in between, we distinguish at least these four as qualitatively distinct hues. Four-month-old infants perceive color in the same way (Bornstein, 2006a, 2006b). Perceiving color categorically (i.e., recognizing that the color of robins' eggs, the sky, and blueberries are all in the same general color family, and that the color of a tangerine is not) combines with seeing pattern, locating in space, and tracking movement to aid very young babies in organizing and making sense of what they see.

Hearing

After vision, we know most about newborn and infant hearing. Fetuses respond to sounds beginning around the third month of gestation (Busnel, Granier-Deferre, & Lecanuet, 1992). Of course, the mother's abdominal wall and uterus lower the intensity of surrounding sounds somewhat, but they change other characteristics of the sounds surprisingly little. After birth, newborns are especially sensitive to sound frequencies that match those of human voices (Saffran, Werker, & Werner, 2006).

Obviously, newborns can hear sounds: Make a sudden loud noise, and a neonate will startle. But infants' hearing is so good that they distinguish high pitch sounds better than adults do (but not as well as dogs!) (Saffran et al., 2006). Infants can discriminate differences between melodies at 6 months of age (Trehub, Trainor, & Unyk, 1993). Furthermore, they show preference for music with common chords over music with uncommon chords. By 4 months of age, they reach in the direction of a sound even in the dark; by 6 months, their ability to locate the source of sound matches that of adults.

In other words, normal infants are equipped with good hearing. Almost immediately, infants apply their basic abilities to the much more complex tasks of perceiving, deciphering, and making sense of their world, especially speech. Certain characteristics of human speech attract babies. Adults (and older children) seem to know this intuitively. Remember the last time you spoke with your infant nephew or niece? We guess that you did not talk to him or her like you talk to a friend or like your professor talks to you. Rather, you used a different speech register—one reserved for babies, little animals, and lovers. Indeed, it is difficult not to change one's speech in addressing babies (Papoušek & Papoušek, 2002). So-called **infant-directed speech** (also known as "motherese") differs from and simplifies normal adult-directed speech in all sorts of ways. We exaggerate tones and deliver them in a singsongy rhythm, use simpler words and repeat them, and abbreviate utterances and employ less complex grammar (Kitamura et al., 2002; Papoušek, Papoušek, & Bornstein, 1985). Infant-directed speech is also nearly universal across cultures and languages.

infant-directed speech
A special speech register reserved for babies that simplifies normal adult-directed speech in many ways.

Infants prefer to listen to infant-directed speech over adult-directed speech (Fernald, 2001; Henning, Striano, & Lieven, 2005). They are happier listening to baby talk, even when the language being spoken is different from their own (Saffran et al., 2006). The exaggerated pitch, intonation, and repetitiveness of infant-directed speech may have several functions, including: attracting and keeping infant attention; communicating the speaker's emotion and intention; and facilitating recognition of the mother's voice.

Babies in the first year of life distinguish a great many different sounds of language (Saffran et al., 2006), even some that are not part of the language they hear every day. However, with continuous exposure to one particular language, infants' ability to distinguish sounds that are not part of their native language diminishes (Saffran et al., 2006). This reduced sensitivity to non-native sounds is probably not permanent, however, as adults can be trained to hear them.

Certain auditory perceptions seem to be universal and developed at birth; they are maintained by linguistic experiences but may be (at least partially) lost if children do not hear them in their language.

Touching

We know from everyday experience that soothing touches can quiet a fussy infant, whereas a vaccination shot almost invariably causes distress. In addition to the ability to feel things, infants use the sense of touch to learn about the world (Stack, 2001). Very young babies will look at an object without reaching for it; by the middle of the first year, however, babies reach for everything in sight. They must have it—whatever it is—in their hands. Piaget (who was discussed in Chapter 1 and who appears again as a central figure in the story of infant cognition, in Chapter 5) emphasized the significance of touch when he proposed that seemingly simple sensorimotor behavior constitutes the foundations of knowledge (Brainerd, 1996; Lourenco, 1996).

In the same way that infant looking is guided by an active search for information, once infants have the chance to explore an object in some detail, they will change patterns of exploration to acquire more information (Ruff, 1982, 1985). Infants respond to a change in the shape of an object by rotating the object more, and to a change in texture by fingering the object more. They throw and push away or drop new objects less often than familiar ones. Furthermore, infants explore complex objects longer than simple objects, and they are less distractible when they are engaged in object exploration than when they are not (Richard et al., 2004).

Infants are highly responsive to tactile stimulation (Blossfeld et al., 2006). Touch is also vital to establishing and maintaining intimacy and infant-parent attachment (Bowlby, 1969; Harlow, 1958). Regular touch promotes weight gain and growth in high-risk newborns, for example (Goldberg & DiVitto, 2002).

A baby exploring an interesting object through touching. Infants explore some objects in detail and will learn about them by looking at them, touching and manipulating them, and mouthing them.

Harlow's (1958) studies showed that contact comfort is a powerful motivator of infant behavior. Given a choice between a wire mother covered with padding and soft cloth and one equipped with a bottle, infant monkeys clung to the first. (Most infants would briefly leave, or, in a few cases, actually lean over from the cloth mother to drink milk from the bottle, and then go back to the cloth surrogate.) Contact comfort is universally perceived as reassuring by infants of nonhuman primates and human infants alike. Across cultures, the first instinctive reaction of a mother to her infant's distress is to embrace, rock, or pat, and then to sing or talk soothingly to the infant (Bornstein et al., 1992). The formation of a close attachment between infant and caregiver, which we examine in Chapter 6, is linked to touch, not just to providing nourishment.

So touch works with vision to inform infants about key properties of the physical world. Touch also appears to promote weight gain and normal development in preterm and at-risk infants and to be critical to the formation of infant-parent relationships.

Tasting and Smelling

Taste and smell have received less attention than have vision, hearing, and touch, but these senses play major roles in our lives from babyhood, including all-important decisions about what to eat and what to reject.

Newborn babies, even those who have tasted nothing but amniotic fluid, discriminate different tastes, and they prefer certain tastes over others. Neonates display characteristic facial expressions when sweet, sour, and bitter substances are placed on their tongues. A sweet stimulus evokes an expression of satisfaction, often accompanied by a slight smile and by sucking movements. A sour stimulus evokes lip pursing, often accompanied or followed by wrinkling the nose and blinking the eyes. A bitter fluid evokes an expression of dislike and disgust or rejection, often followed by spitting or even by gagging (Oster, 2005; Steiner, 1979). Distressed preterm and term infants alike can be soothed merely by giving them a sweet (glucose) solution to taste. Sweet tastes hold a high reward value for infants; this is adaptive, because it ensures that infants will take to breast milk, which is slightly sweet.

The olfactory (smell) system is highly developed at birth as well. If you place a cotton swab with a particular odor beneath the nose of even a newborn, the baby will display facial expressions and reactions appropriate to the odors (Steiner, 1979). It's easy to tell which smells neonates like and which they do not. Butter and banana odors elicit positive expressions; vanilla, either positive or indifferent expressions; a fishy odor, some rejection; and the odor of rotten eggs, unanimous rejection. Newborns' preferences mirror adult preferences.

Learning about odors, such as vanilla, is rapid in infants (Groubet et al., 2002). Indeed, their sense of smell is so good that newborn babies who breastfeed are able to identify their mothers' signature odor (Porter et al., 1992). Only 12 to 18 days after birth, breastfed and bottle-fed infants were exposed to pairs of gauze pads worn by an adult in the underarm area on the previous night. When the investigators gave infants the opportunity to turn their heads in one direction to smell their mother's odor or turn in the opposite direction to smell a stranger, as you probably guessed, the breastfed babies spent more time turning toward their mother's odor. Infants did not prefer their fathers' odor, though, and bottle-fed infants did not recognize their mothers' odor, suggesting that breastfeeding infants are exposed to and learn unique olfactory signatures. (By the way, mothers also recognize the scent of their babies after only 1 or 2 days.) The ability to recognize mothers very early in life—and vice versa—by scent alone might play an important role in the mother-infant relationship (Porter & Winberg, 1999). Some smells are also soothing. The presence of a familiar odor during a medical procedure has a calming effect on babies (Goubet et al, 2003).In sum, newborns taste and smell, and seem to be very discriminating. Just try to feed them a food they do not like! (For a summary of this section, see "Interim Summary 4.5: Sensing and Perceiving.")

INTERIM SUMMARY **4.5**

Sensing and Perceiving

Sensory systems—sight, hearing, touch, taste, and smell—develop *in utero*.

- Seeing—This sense involves pattern, depth, movement, and color. Newborns not only see but also actively seek visual stimulation.
- Hearing—Normal infants come with good hearing. Infants prefer to listen to **infant-directed speech** (a speech register reserved for babies) over adult-directed speech.
- Touch—Infants use the sense of touch to learn about the world and are highly responsive to tactile stimulation. Touch is vital to establishing and maintaining emotional intimacy and infant–parent attachment.
- Tasting and smelling—Newborn babies discriminate different tastes, and they prefer certain tastes over others. The olfactory (smell) system is also highly developed at birth.

MULTIMODAL AND CROSS-MODAL PERCEPTION

Although we have discussed different perceptions as though they were discrete and separate (to explain how each works), the senses do not work independently. Rather, our senses interact with one another and fuse perceptions into wholes. When we have sex, for instance, we see images that excite us, hear sounds that reinforce our passion, feel skin that scintillates, and so forth. These sensory impressions go together naturally to give rise to an integrated experience that is more intense than that from any one sensory input alone.

Objects and events in the world give rise to sights, touch, and sounds; that is, we experience **multimodal perceptions** that coordinate across two or more senses. Also, some information available in one modality can combine with information from other senses (Jordan & Brannon, 2006). What we learn about something through one sense (vision) is enhanced by what we experience through another (touch).

multimodal perceptions The perception of information about objects and events in the world that stimulates many senses at once.

The American philosopher William James (1924, p. 50) famously referred to the infant's world as a "blooming, buzzing confusion." But developmental science has shown that the world of the infant is not as disorganized as James believed. Information obtained by looking, listening, and touching is coordinated very early in life. For example, in one study, infants as young as 29 days of age successfully identified by sight an object they had previously explored by mouth alone (i.e., a pacifier with small nubs). When researchers put the pacifier with the nubs in the infants' mouths, let them suck on it for a while, and then showed them that pacifier and one that was smooth (with no nubs), infants looked longer at the familiar one than at the new one (Meltzoff, 1993).

The study of these kinds of cross-modal perception has led to insights about infants' developing sense of self—another illustration of how physical development and socioemotional development are linked. The earliest kind of self-knowledge might be based on the coordination of information from different perceptual systems (visual, tactile, and auditory) and motor actions (sucking, rooting, and orienting).

You know how you cannot tickle yourself? There is something about knowing that you are doing the touching that makes what otherwise would tickle you have no effect. Babies use similar knowledge as well. Normally, stroking an infant's cheek will evoke the rooting reflex. But the rooting reflex in 3- to 4-week-olds is stronger when their cheeks were touched by a researcher's finger or a pacifier than by the infants' own hand (Rochat, 1997). So, babies can tell the difference between (or at least they respond differently to) different kinds of touches. They can tell the difference between touches that come from a source external to their own bodies and self-touches (in which touch is felt both on their cheek and on their finger that is touching their cheek). (For a summary of this section, see "Interim Summary 4.6: Multimodal and Cross-Modal Perception.")

INTERIM SUMMARY 4.6

Multimodal and Cross-Modal Perception

Experience and Early Perceptual Development

- The senses do not work independently. Our **multimodal perceptions** are coordinated across senses.
- A baby's self-perception can come from different perceptual systems (visual, tactile, and auditory) and motor actions (sucking, rooting, and orienting).
- Babies can tell the difference between touches that come from a source external to their own bodies and self-touches.

EXPERIENCE AND EARLY PERCEPTUAL DEVELOPMENT

Perceptual abilities are remarkably well organized at birth. However, perceptual experience is just as critical for normal psychological growth and development. One early experiment with institutionalized babies showed that simply introducing a visually interesting object into the infant's otherwise bland environment at one month nearly doubled infants' visually directed reaching and visual attentiveness (White, Castle, & Held, 1964).

The everyday perceptual experiences that infants have matter to their development. In one experiment, 3-month-olds were tested in the laboratory for their sensitivity to smiling faces (Kuchuk, Vibbert, & Bornstein, 1986). A series of smiles that graduated in intensity were shown to babies, randomly one face at a time, and the amount of time babies looked at each one was recorded. In general, babies looked more at faces with more intense smiles, but babies showed individual differences. The investigators also went into the infants' homes and recorded mothers' interactions with their infants. Mothers who smiled at their babies more often themselves had infants who showed the most sensitivity to the smiling faces in the laboratory. In the experiment you read about earlier, monkeys that were first exposed to monkey faces preferred to look at monkey faces more than human faces, but monkeys that were first exposed to human faces preferred to look at human faces more than monkey faces (Sugita, 2008).

Adults who speak tonal languages (like Mandarin Chinese) process pitch with greater accuracy than do adults who speak non-tonal languages (like English). They can repeat a word on the same note or begin a song on the same note, and they are more likely to possess perfect pitch (Deutsch, Henthorn, & Dolson, 2004). Furthermore, language experience and early musical training work together. Early trained musicians with perfect pitch are more common among speakers of tonal than non-tonal languages (Deutsch, Henthorn, Marvin, & Xu, 2006).

Perceptual development in infancy provides multiple examples of the interplay between biology and experience. At birth, the brain and central nervous system, although far from mature, are developing quite rapidly and are in place to seek out and process information about the environment. Indeed, the basic sensory systems function at birth, and then—or soon after—infants perceive complex and sophisticated information. Moreover, infants perceive some information arriving via the different senses in a coordinated way, and information acquired via multiple senses can be processed simultaneously by the brain. An adaptive biological system interacts with an experience-providing environment. (For a summary of this section, see "Interim Summary 4.7: Experience and Early Perceptual Development.")

INTERIM SUMMARY **4.7**

Experience and Early Perceptual Development

Perceptual abilities are well organized at birth and illustrate the interplay between biology and experience.

- The everyday perceptual experiences that infants have matter to their development.
- At birth, the brain and central nervous system, although far from mature, are developing rapidly.
- The basic sensory systems function at birth, and then or soon after infants perceive some even complex and sophisticated information.
- Infants perceive some information arriving via the different senses in a coordinated way, and information acquired via one sense is available to other senses.

SUMMING UP AND LOOKING AHEAD

In this chapter, we traced the remarkable physical, motor, and perceptual growth that characterizes the first 2 years of life. The difference between what a newborn can do and what a 2-year-old is capable of in these areas is simply staggering. Part of this transformation is the result of a maturational plan encoded in our genes, but the real beauty of this plan is that it is a flexible one that is responsive to environmental stimulation. A prewired, unchangeable biological plan for maturation would be less adaptive, just as would be a totally flexible one that allowed only experience to shape development. The perfect combination of biological readiness and responsiveness to experience ensures that humans are able to develop in ways that are adaptive in the particular environment into which they are born. Biology assures that, in the absence of some sort of abnormality, infants are born able to hear, taste, and see. They are also born with sensory systems that are still maturing and that are plastic enough to develop preferences for their mother's voice, the particular foods available in their environment, and the sights they are likely to encounter in their world.

Intellectual development during the first 2 years is just as amazing. That journey is the subject of our next chapter, "Cognitive Development in Infancy."

HERE'S WHAT YOU SHOULD KNOW

Did You Get It?

After reading this chapter, you should understand the following:

- The general principles of physical growth
- The meaning of norms versus individual differences
- How the central nervous system develops
- The anatomy of the brain
- The autonomic nervous system
- The importance of reflexes
- The sequence of motor skills development in infancy
- The development of an infant's sensory and perceptual systems

Important Terms and Concepts

action potential (p. 100)
association areas (p. 99)
auditory cortex (p. 99)
autism spectrum disorder (p. 110)
autonomic nervous system (ANS) (p. 106)
axon (p. 100)
Broca's area (p. 99)
canalization (p. 97)
cell body (p. 100)
central nervous system (CNS) (p. 99)
corpus callosum (p. 99)
cerebellum (p. 102)
compensation (p. 104)
cortex (p. 99)
cycle (p. 106)
dendrites (p. 100)
directionality (p. 96)
dynamic systems theory (p. 110)
electroencephalographic (EEG) recordings (p. 103)
event-related potentials (ERPs) (p. 103)
experience-dependent processes (p. 103)
experience-expectant processes (p. 103)
frontal cortex (p. 99)
hemispheres (p. 99)
independence of systems (p. 97)
individual differences (p. 98)
infant-directed speech (p. 116)
limbic system (p. 99)
microelectrode recording (p. 103)
modifiability (p. 104)
motor cortex (p. 99)
multimodal perceptions (p. 114)
multiple sclerosis (p. 102)
myelin (p. 102)
myelination (p. 102)
neurons (p. 99)
neurotransmitters (p. 100)
norms (p. 97)
plasticity (p. 101)
reflexes (p. 108)
sensitive periods (p. 104)
sensorimotor cortex (p. 99)
stem cells (p. 104)
subcortical structures (p. 99)
synapse (p. 100)
synaptic pruning (p. 101)
synaptogenesis (p. 101)
visual cortex (p. 99)
Wernicke's area (p. 99)

CHAPTER 5

Cognitive Development in Infancy

© George Doyle

The baby being carried in the infant seat is not a passive voyager, seeing, hearing, feeling, tasting, and smelling. She must make sense of all of this input. This is where cognitive development comes in. Just how does the infant make sense of these sensations? How do we know what's going on inside her head?

In this chapter, we're going to review what developmental scientists have learned about the mind of the infant in just the last 50 years or so. (Before then, *whether* babies think, and *what* they thought, were the subjects of speculation.) The topics will include Piaget's views of cognitive development and some of the contributions of researchers who came after Piaget and questioned his views. (Piaget was a major figure in the field, and his writings energized the field of infant and child development. As often happens, however, those who followed him modified or revolutionized his thinking. Because he was so original, and his ideas formed a springboard to modern developments, we spend a little time with Piaget, even though the field has passed his specific work.) We then turn to cover mental representation in infancy, attempts to measure infant intelligence, and the development of communication. We consider norms and individual differences, how learning and cognition change over infancy, and how infants' interactions with objects and people influence their mental development—especially the ability to communicate with others. Equally important, we look at how researchers know what infants think; after all, infants cannot tell us what's on their mind.

HOW SCIENTISTS KNOW WHAT BABIES KNOW

How do researchers ask babies questions about what babies know, and how do babies answer them? Students of infancy have developed many different techniques and strategies to ask babies questions. Two techniques are based on the concepts of *habituation* and *novelty responsiveness* and use a similar approach. For example, a researcher shows a baby a picture once, and the baby will look at it for a while. But if the baby is shown the same picture over and over, the baby will look at it less and less. The first time, the picture was novel and attention grabbing. However, like you would, babies get "bored" with the same thing.

The baby's getting bored is perfect for the researcher, because then the researcher knows that the baby has developed some sort of *mental representation* of the picture—otherwise, why should the baby look at the picture less the tenth time it is shown? The loss of interest suggests that the baby *recognizes* the picture. Presumably, the baby is comparing each new picture presentation with a developing memory of the picture based on previous exposures. This process of getting to know about a stimulus is called **habituation**. What happens if the researcher now shows the bored (habituated) baby something new? If the baby looks more at a new picture than at the one she's been

habituation The process in which a baby compares each new stimulus with a developing memory of the stimulus based on previous exposures, thus learning about the stimulus.

© Laura Dwight

One of the ways developmental researchers test infants is by showing them stimuli and noting infants' reactions, like this 8-month-old baby boy looking at an image on a computer screen.

shown over and over—called **novelty responsiveness**—that tells the researcher that the baby not only recognizes the old picture but also can tell the difference between the old one and the new one (Bornstein & Colombo, 2010; Sirois & Mareschal, 2002). Specifically, novelty responsiveness following habituation occurs when a baby looks more at a new stimulus than at a familiar one.

Using habituation and novelty responsiveness, researchers can ask a variety of "yes-no" questions of babies. For example, can babies tell the difference between a smiling and a frowning face? To do your own experiment, get two pictures, preferably of the same person: one happy and another frowning. Show one to the baby until he or she stops looking, then show the two pictures together. If the baby looks longer at the novel facial expression, then he is telling you that he can tell the difference between smiling and frowning. How good is a baby's memory? By habituating (familiarizing) infants with a picture and testing them later with the same picture, it is also possible to study memory. (If the baby acts as if the picture is new, he obviously doesn't remember it.)

novelty responsiveness Following habituation, the process in which a baby looks more at a new stimulus than at a familiar one.

A third approach to infant perception and cognition involves learning. Again, try your own experiment. Put a baby in a crib with a mobile hanging overhead. Now, take a baseline reading of how often she kicks. Then attach the mobile by a ribbon to the baby's ankle so that, when the baby kicks, the mobile jangles. Babies quickly learn that their kicking moves the mobile. When attached to the mobile in this way, most babies kick at two to three times their baseline rate. Suppose now that you wait a day or two and then retest the baby. When an infant who has previously learned the association between kicking and mobile-moving *relearns* that association more rapidly than he or she did the first time, this tells us that the baby remembers (Rovee-Collier & Barr, 2001).

INTERIM SUMMARY 5.1

How Scientists Know What Babies Know

Four Different Approaches Used to Learn About Infant Perception and Cognition

1. **Habituation**—occurs when a baby compares each new stimulus with a developing memory of the same stimulus shown on previous exposures.
2. **Novelty responsiveness**—happens after habituation; if a baby looks more at a new stimulus than at the one shown repeatedly, the baby not only recognizes the old stimulus but also can tell the difference between the old and new.
3. **Learning**—an example is putting a baby in a crib with a mobile and taking a baseline reading of how often she kicks. Then conditions are changed, responses noted, and the baby is retested, which tells us about infant learning and memory.
4. **Imitation**—babies are shown a sequence of events and observed to see if they imitate the sequence.

Finally, scientists use a fourth approach to study what babies know by showing them a sequence of events and seeing whether they imitate the sequence. Consider this scenario. You are seated across the table from an older infant. You have a spoon, a small red box, and a larger blue box. While the baby is watching, you place the spoon inside the red box, and then place the red box inside the blue one. Then, you disassemble it all and do it again. Now, you give the baby the three objects. If the infant does exactly what you did, in the same order, this tells us she is able to observe and remember a sequence of events (Barr & Hayne, 2000).

Each of these ways of studying development has been used with the littlest infants. If you were to do some or all of these things with an infant you know, you'd rediscover what developmental scientists in the last half century have discovered. Although it might not always be apparent, infants have an active mental life. They are constantly learning, developing, and even testing—yes, *testing*—new ideas. (For a summary of this section, see "Interim Summary 5.1: How Scientists Know What Babies Know.")

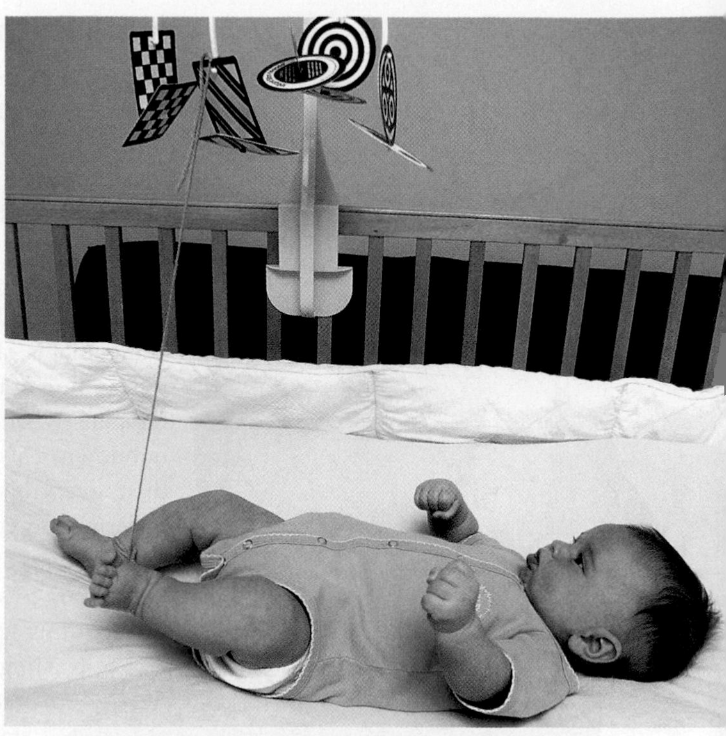

This baby is lying in a crib with a ribbon connecting his ankle to the mobile overhead so that when he kicks, the mobile jangles. In this way it is possible to study how infants react when they can control their environment.

PIAGET AND INFANT COGNITIVE DEVELOPMENT

Between 1925 and 1932, the Swiss biologist and philosopher Jean Piaget watched closely as his own three children—Jacqueline, Lucienne, and Laurent—developed from infancy, noting the enormous intellectual progress each made during the first two years of life. Soon afterward, Piaget (1936/1952) published the *Origins of Intelligence in Children*, a collection of his observations and informal experiments that led to a revolutionary theory of cognitive development in infancy (Brainerd, 1996; Bremner, 2001; Lourenco, 1996).

Piaget suggested that each infant constructs an understanding of the world—including space, time, causality, and substance—on the basis of his or her own actions in the world. At the time, other developmental scientists viewed children as well-equipped, but basically passive, recipients of information from the environment. Piaget did not think that knowledge derives from sensations or perceptions, or from information provided by others. Rather, Piaget wrote that infants *actively construct* what they know. This basic notion has shaped the study of infant cognition ever since.

What does it mean to "actively construct" knowledge? Imagine that you and a friend have driven to a new restaurant in a neighboring town. A month later, you want to eat there again, so you decide to drive back. If you were the driver the first time, you'll have an easier time remembering how to go than if you had been the passenger—because you actively constructed your knowledge of how to get there by doing the driving. Recall the kitten study conducted by Richard Held and Alan Hein (1963), which was discussed in Chapter 4. This study demonstrated the critical importance of self-produced activity for understanding the environment. The kittens that were allowed to move about on their own avoided the deep side of a visual cliff, stretched out their paws appropriately in preparation for contact with a solid surface, and blinked at approaching objects. By contrast, even after extensive transportation in the gondola, the passive cats failed to show such spatially sensitive behavior. To Piaget, an infant is the driver (not the passenger) in cognitive development; the active (not the passive) kitten.

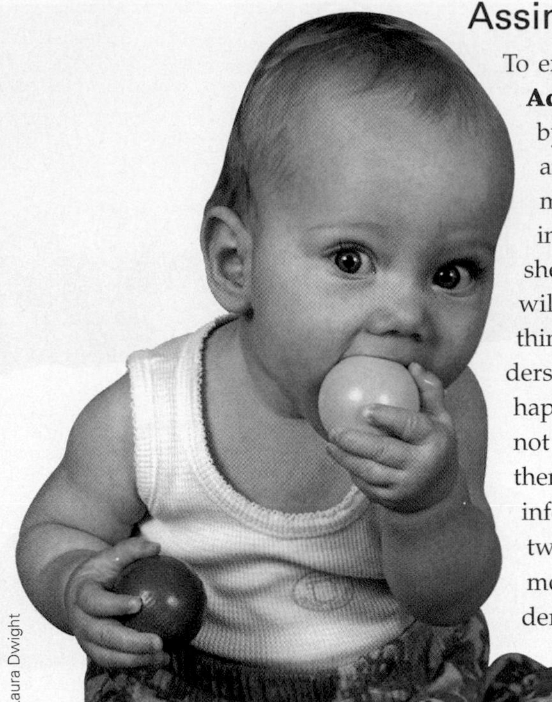

© Laura Dwight

To actively learn about their world, babies grasp, touch, and mouth objects just as this 9-month-old girl is doing.

Assimilation and Accommodation

To explain cognitive development, Piaget detailed the process of adaptation. **Adaptation**, in Piaget's theory, is the process whereby knowledge is altered by experience. Adaptation itself involves two complementary, interwined, and powerful processes: **assimilation** and **accommodation**. When information can be processed according to what the child already knows, the information is said to be *assimilated*. A child who understands that when she drops a rattle off her high chair, the toy falls downward onto the floor will easily understand that when she drops her Cheerios®, they do the same thing; that is, she can assimilate this new knowledge. At times, the child's understanding of the world does not permit assimilating new information. What happens when the child lets go of a balloon filled with helium? It goes up, not down. This violates the child's understanding of the world (because until then, everything that was dropped followed the same pattern). When new information cannot be assimilated into the child's existing understanding, two things can happen. One is that the child fails to assimilate and simply moves on to another activity. Alternatively, the child changes his or her understanding to permit new information to be processed. The modification of existing understanding to better accord with reality is termed *accommodation*; that is, children actively change so that they can understand the environment better. Following the experience with the helium balloon, the child understands that some objects rise or float and not all objects fall when released; through the process of accommodation, the baby has developed a new way of thinking.

Assimilation and accommodation are not separate processes, but alternatively occur so that the child's understanding can match reality. In assimilation, children use their existing understanding to make sense of the world. In accommodation, they modify their understanding to appreciate reality better and better.

adaptation The process whereby knowledge is altered by experience. Adaptation involves two complementary processes: assimilation and accommodation.

assimilation The process by which information can be incorporated according to what the infant already knows. Assimilation allows the infant to use existing understanding to make sense of the world.

accommodation The process by which the infant changes to reach new understanding; that is, the modification of existing understanding to make it apply to a new situation. Accommodation allows the infant to understand reality better and better.

sensorimotor period A developmental time, consisting of a six-stage sequence, when thinking consists of coordinating sensory information with motor activity.

object permanence The understanding that an object continues to exist even when it cannot be sensed.

Stage Theory

Perhaps the best-known feature of Piaget's theory is his *stages* of cognitive development. Piaget held that mental development unfolds in a fixed sequence of developmental steps. As a whole, the **sensorimotor period** occurs during infancy; it is followed, in Piaget's theory, by the preoperational, concrete operational, and formal operational periods of childhood, preadolescence, and adolescence, respectively (discussed in the chapters on physical development in early childhood, middle childhood, and adolescence). During the sensorimotor period, "thinking" consists of putting sensory information with motor activity. According to Piaget, infants learn through actions: looking, listening, touching, sucking, mouthing, and grasping. Within the sensorimotor period in infancy, Piaget proposed a sequence of six stages (see Table 5.1). The child's current stage defines the way the child views the world and processes information in it.

One more accomplishment during the sensorimotor period is learning that certain actions produce certain results (*causality*). For example, banging a spoon on a highchair tray produces a loud noise, attracts attention, and may bring dinner. Another major advance is **object permanence**. In early infancy, "out of sight is out of mind"—literally. The baby's world consists of what he or she can perceive in the here-and-now. If you give a 3-month-old an interesting toy, his attention perks up. But if you cover the toy with a cloth, he doesn't look for it; rather, he behaves as if the toy no longer exists. By 8 or 10 months, the infant is surprised when the toy disappears, and he searches for it. The infant realizes that something out of sight still exists (Bogartz, Shinskey, & Schilling, 2000; Krojgaard, 2003; Mash, Arterberry, & Bornstein, 2007; Xu, 2003). For Piaget, object permanence was a first step toward **mental representation**: No longer

TABLE 5.1 Stages of the Sensorimotor Period of Infancy

Stage	Approximate Age	What the Baby Can and Cannot Do	Example
Stage 1	Birth to 1 month	Infants do not accommodate, so mental development is minimal. Everything is assimilated into their existing understanding and very slowly.	They cannot recognize that stimuli belong to solid objects in the outside world—for instance, that sounds come from other things.
Stage 2	1 to 4 months	Infants coordinate different aspects of their understanding of the world.	They coordinate hand and mouth (deliberately putting their fingers in their mouth).
Stage 3	4 to 7 months	Infants are aware of relations between their own behavior and the environment.	When infants accidentally produce environmental events—kicking the side of the crib shakes the mobile that is attached to the railing, for instance—they may repeat them, suggesting that they want to review their effects on the environment.
Stage 4	7 to 10 months	Infants construct relations among environmental stimuli.	They coordinate a face and a voice as being from the same source.
Stage 5	10 to 18 months	Infants accommodate to the outside world and discover many unexpected relations among objects.	They attempt to see whether milk leaks out of a bottle at different rates depending on the angle of the bottle and the force with which it is squeezed.
Stage 6	18 to 24 months	Infants now can form a *mental representation*; for example, imagining the whereabouts of an invisible object.	When a ball rolls under a sofa, for example, a child will move around the sofa and anticipate the reemergence of the ball.

dependent on immediate sensory data, the infant has images or thoughts of objects (including people) in mind when the object (or person) is not physically present. Piaget believed that mental representation did not develop until the end of the sensorimotor period.

mental representation The ability to hold in the mind an image of objects (and people) that are not physically present.

Challenges to Piaget

Although Piaget's view of infant cognition has been extremely influential, many of his claims about infant development have been challenged by empirical research. In general, it seems that Piaget underestimated what infants know at different ages.

One major criticism, for instance, is that Piaget focused on the ways that infants learn through movement (i.e., the "motor" in sensorimotor) and ignored other ways in which infants learn. For example, one study showed that limbless children (whose mothers took the sedative thalidomide during the first trimester of pregnancy) developed a normal cognitive life despite the absence of normal sensorimotor experience in infancy (Décarie & Ricard, 1996). This suggests that Piaget overestimated the importance of active (mobile and tactile) exploration—and underestimated other sensory and organizational capacities of infants. Babies make a lot of sense of the world by looking and listening without physically manipulating things.

Other research shows that object permanence and the capacity for mental representation of the physical world (i.e., the ability to hold an image or thought of something in the mind) appear much earlier in development than Piaget supposed (Baillargeon, 2004). Indeed, infants can imitate some behaviors they see (for example, sticking out their tongue) soon after they are born, which says that they have some capacity to represent the external world at birth (Meltzoff & Moore, 1999).

Not only can infants imitate another person within the first months of life, as early as 6 months of age they can imitate a model's novel actions after a *delay*. For example, in one experiment, 6- to 9-month-old infants observed an adult model lean forward and

INTERIM SUMMARY 5.2

Piaget and Infant Cognitive Development

Jean Piaget was a Swiss biologist and philosopher who laid the foundation for the study of infant cognition today.

He believed that mental development unfolds in a fixed sequence of developmental stages. The **sensorimotor period** encompasses infancy.

Developmental scientists now agree that Piaget underestimated infants' perceptual and cognitive capacities.

Piaget's theory

- He believed children actively construct what they know on the basis of their own motor activity and interactions in the world.
- He believed **adaptation** is the process whereby knowledge is altered by experience.
- It involves **assimilation** (using existing understanding) and **accommodation** (modifying understanding).
- Advances in the sensorimotor period include causality (certain actions produce certain results) and **object permanence** (the understanding that an object continues to exist even though it cannot be sensed).
- Object permanence paves the way to **mental representation** (infants can hold in their mind images of objects and people that are not physically present).

press a panel with his forehead (a highly unusual, novel behavior) (Meltzoff, 1988). One week later, the infants who had viewed this behavior, and a control group of infants who had not, returned to the laboratory and were put in front of the panel. Infants who had not seen the experimenter never pressed their foreheads to the panel, whereas two-thirds of the infants who had previously witnessed this behavior did. So not only were babies able to imitate what they had seen, they were able to do so from memory!

Developmental scientists now agree that Piaget seriously underestimated infants' perceptual and cognitive capacities (Birney et al., 2005; Keil, 2006). Infants' competencies in understanding sequences of events, means-ends relations, space, causality, and number are all in evidence much earlier in development than Piaget predicted. Infants are more organized and sophisticated cognitively than Piaget thought. Nevertheless, his contributions—especially his beliefs that infants are active learners and that infants *think*, although differently from older children and adults—laid the foundation for the study of infant cognition today. (For a summary of this section, see "Interim Summary 5.2: Piaget and Infant Cognitive Development.")

MENTAL REPRESENTATION IN INFANCY

Piaget was interested in the broad picture—in the overarching features of cognitive development from birth through adolescence. Other developmentalists concentrate on specific elements of cognitive development—on what skills infants acquire and when. Students of infant cognition are particularly interested in categorization, memory, and pretend play. One reason is because each of these developments is related to representational thinking—the ability to think about objects and people that are not present. Piaget thought that this breakthrough did not occur until 18 to 24 months. Using different investigative techniques, though, contemporary researchers have found evidence of representational thinking at considerably younger ages.

Categorizing

Imagine going to a grocery store in which there is no rhyme or reason to the way that products are arranged. Chicken breasts are placed next to trash bags, which are alongside cream cheese. Chicken drumsticks are on the same shelf as toothpaste, which is right below the tangerines. What a nightmare shopping would be! Thankfully, though, grocery stores group similar or related objects near one another—into categories (poultry, cleaning supplies, dental products, fruits).

Categorization involves grouping separate items into a set according to some rule. A Ford, a Toyota, and a Mercedes-Benz are all cars. Oaks, elms, and pines are all trees. Sipping, slurping, and guzzling are all ways of consuming liquids. To better organize our experiences, we frequently treat different objects or events as similar; that is, we *categorize*. So do infants.

categorization A process that involves grouping separate items into a set according to some rule.

Categorization is important for a variety of reasons. It helps to simplify and order the infant's world in three ways (Bornstein, 1984). First, the infant comes to understand that his brown teddy bear is the same teddy bear in the light and in the dark, when it is nearby and faraway, and so on. The environment into which infants are born, and in which they develop, is constantly changing, producing an infinite variety of sensations. Moreover, infants experience the world in biological states that are frequently changing (e.g., from being drowsy to being awake). Categorization structures and clarifies perception.

Second, the infant doesn't have to remember every single aspect of every single object, such as every one of his or her mother's facial expressions to recognize her face. Categorization facilitates the storage and retrieval of information. It supplies a principle of organization that allows more information to be stored in one "file" for mother, rather than multiple files.

Third, the infant's learning that her family's dog barks can be applied to other dogs as well. With categorization, knowledge of an attribute of one member of a category provides information about other members of the same category. And new observations (dogs also have tails) can be added to the category and automatically applied to other members of the category.

Evidence that infants categorize comes from habituation and novelty responsiveness tasks. In the habituation/novelty responsiveness paradigm, infants are first familiarized with several examples from the same category (say, several cats) and are then presented with a novel example from the same category (a new cat) and with a novel example from a different category (a dog). We know infants categorize because they pay more attention to a novel out-of-category dog than to a novel in-category cat; that is, they treat one novel stimulus as familiar and another novel stimulus as new. To understand this concept, try this: Habituate a baby to pictures of a horse, a cow, and a cat. Then show the baby either a dog or a rocking chair. The baby will tend to look longer at the picture of the rocking chair because it is not an animal (Arterberry & Bornstein, 2001, 2002).

Studies of the way children play with objects from similar and different categories also show that categorization abilities progress during the first 3 years. Here's how it's done: Give a child eight small three-dimensional models (see Figure 5.1), four each belonging to two categories, say, animals (cow, dog, goose, and walrus) and vehicles (train, bus, motorbike, and all-terrain vehicle), and encourage the child to play with them. Close analysis in such studies reveals that children touch objects within a category one after the other more frequently (at greater than chance levels) than objects across categories. That is, in the preceding example, the baby plays with animals and then with the vehicles but does not mix both together. Categories also function at different levels of *inclusiveness*, and understanding how children use them tells us how children mentally represent information (Rakison & Oakes, 2003). By 1 year, children show that they have a grasp (so to speak!) of the most inclusive categories

© Laura Dwight

FIGURE 5.1

Categorization Abilities

To understand infants' categories of objects, researchers present them with plastic models—for example, four animals and four vehicles—and then analyze infants' patterns of holding and looking at the two groupings.

(e.g., animals vs. vehicles), but children have to be 1½ years old to recognize less inclusive categories (e.g., dogs vs. cats) and almost three to tell the least inclusive categories apart (e.g., two different kinds of cats).

Remembering

It is obviously important that infants attend to stimuli and events in their environment. But it is also crucial that they be able to store, retrieve, and use that information later. Memory representations underlie the child's awareness, experience, knowledge, and interpretation of the world.

For years, people believed that infants could not remember much of anything. You probably don't remember much of events that took place before you were 3 or 4 (see Bornstein, Arterberry, & Mash, 2004). Indeed, Sigmund Freud (1916/1917, 1966) coined the term **infantile amnesia** to describe this phenomenon, which he attributed to repression (excluding ideas from consciousness or holding them in the unconscious) of memories of traumatic events. Piaget (1954) also believed that memories may not be possible during the first year because infants do not have the capacity to encode information symbolically. We now know that this view is inaccurate. It is true that most adults may not be able to recall things from their first two or so years of life. But research shows that infants can remember previously experienced events. Whether adults accurately remember their infant experiences, and whether infants remember things from their very short past, are two different questions, with two different answers.

infantile amnesia The adult recollection of almost nothing of events that took place before the age of 3 or 4.

Human infant memory has been studied using many techniques. By habituating (familiarizing) infants with stimuli and testing them immediately afterward with the same stimulus, we can study *short-term memory* (i.e., see whether infants can tell the difference between something they've been shown and something new right away). Imposing a delay between habituation and a later test allows us to assess *long-term memory*. By varying the amount of delay between habituation and the subsequent test, it is possible to study the accuracy of infants' memory over different time intervals and to see if this changes with age. We can also vary how long the initial period of familiarization is to see if there are changes with age in how much an infant must be exposed to something (study time) to remember it.

Research shows that infants' ability to remember clearly improves with age. Infants habituate more quickly and more efficiently as they grow older. They also remember more information, across longer periods of time, as they get older and with helpful reminders (Hsu & Rovee-Collier, 2006; Sheffield & Hudson, 2006). **Deferred imitation**—showing children a series of actions, then seeing whether they reproduce these actions later—is even more advanced. One team of researchers used three events—pulling a mitten off a puppet's hand, shaking the mitten, and then putting the mitten back on the puppet's hand (Barr & Hayne, 2000). They found that recall of these actions after a 24-hour delay was lowest among 6-month-olds (who did not perform any better than infants who never observed the modeled sequence), intermediate among 12-month-olds, and highest among 18- and 24-month-olds. Babies did not require extremely long exposures to demonstrate short-term memory. In sum, as children grow they demonstrate an ability to hold events in memory for longer time spans, and they require fewer cues and shorter periods of familiarization to recall past events.

deferred imitation Reproducing a series of actions seen at an earlier time.

The study of very long-term memory in human infants poses challenges for another reason—you need to wait a long time for them to grow up! This is one of the reasons that some developmental scientists interested in early memory have turned to animals, like rats, whose lifecycles are substantially shorter. In one animal experiment, infant rats were stressed—they were deprived of nesting materials—and their ability to remember location and recognize objects was subsequently tested. In their young adulthood, memory was unaffected; by middle age, however, memory deficits appeared, and the deficits progressively worsened compared to unstressed rats (Brunson, Kramár, Lin, Chen, Colgin, Yanagihara, & Baram, 2006). Electrical activity in brain cells in stressed rats was adversely affected too. The suspicion is that, in human infants, stress caused by parental loss or abuse or neglect might likewise undermine long-term memory.

Playing

Play is fun and interactive, but also involves mental work—studying a doll, manipulating a busy box, building with a set of blocks, or interacting with an imaginary playmate at a make-believe tea party. Play frequently imitates life, and it is quite common to observe children reenacting in play specific events that they observed or participated in routinely (e.g., "driving" a toy car). Such behavior indicates that young children represent events mentally well enough to reproduce them.

Piaget proposed that play increases in sophistication as children mature, and that infants progress from exploratory play to symbolic, or pretend, play. In the first year, play is predominantly characterized by sensorimotor manipulation; infants' play appears designed to extract information about objects—what objects do, what perceivable qualities they have, and what immediate effects they can produce. This is commonly referred to as **exploratory play** because children's play activities are tied to the tangible properties of objects.

exploratory play Children's play in which activities are tied to the tangible properties of objects.

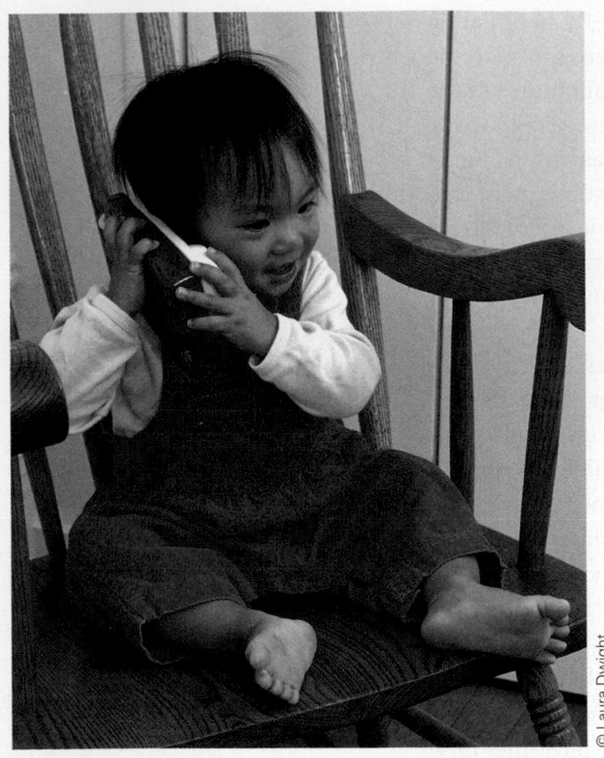
© Laura Dwight

FIGURE 5.2

Symbolic Play

Here's a 15-month-old girl pretending to talk on a telephone . . . just like mommy.

In the second year, children's play takes on a new quality: The cognitive goal of play now appears to be symbolic. In **symbolic play**, children enact activities performed by the self, others, and objects in simple make-believe scenarios, pretending to drink from empty teacups, to talk on toy telephones (as in Figure 5.2), and the like.

Most children pass through these two broad stages of play, but children of a given age vary greatly. On average, 15 percent of 1-year-olds' total play is symbolic. However, some 1-year-olds never exhibit symbolic play, whereas others spend as much as 50 percent of their time in symbolic play. At 2 years, 33 percent of toddlers' total play is symbolic on average. For some individual children as little as 2 percent is symbolic, whereas for others 80 percent is symbolic. (Elaborate pretend play such as dramatic sequences is typically not seen until early childhood, and is discussed in Chapter 7).

Play normally occurs in the context of social interaction. Children may initiate play, but adults influence its development by outfitting the play environment, engaging children actively, and responding to their overtures. How does adult social interaction affect play? When interacting with their mother, children's play is more sophisticated, complex, and varied than is their solitary play (Bornstein, 2007). In a longitudinal study of mother-child play interaction, researchers found that, when mothers responded to their 18-month-olds' object play in an "options-promoting" manner (i.e., encouraging, affirming, and/or expanding on the child's activities), the children engaged in higher levels of symbolic play at 40 months of age than did children whose mothers responded in an "options-limiting" manner (i.e., disapproving of or obstructing the child's play) (Stilson & Harding, 1997).

symbolic play Children's play that enacts activities performed by the self, others, and objects in pretend or make-believe scenarios.

In some cultures, infant play is viewed as predominantly a child's activity (e.g., in Mayan and many American Indian cultures), whereas other cultures assign an important role to parents as play partners (e.g., in middle-income U.S. culture). Differences between cultures also exist in views about the value of play (Göncü & Gaskins, 2007). Some cultures believe that play provides important development-promoting experiences; others see play primarily to amuse. Presumably, cultural beliefs about play affect the nature and frequency of children's play with parents, siblings, and peers.

Generally speaking, Japanese children and mothers tend to engage in more symbolic play than their U.S. counterparts, whereas U.S. children and mothers tend to engage in more exploratory play (Bornstein, 2007). In line with other social features of the culture, Japanese mothers organize infant-directed pretend play in ways that incorporate a partner into play. Japanese mothers encourage interactive (other-directed) activities (e.g., "Feed the dolly"), whereas U.S. mothers encourage self-exploration that is more functional ("Push the bus"). For Americans, play and toys are frequently the focus or object of communication. In contrast, for Japanese, the play setting and associated toys are used to promote mother-infant communication and interaction. This difference is consistent with cultural child-rearing practices more generally, which in Japan emphasize closeness and interdependency between people, and in the United States encourage interest in objects, interpersonal independence, and the acquisition of information.

In summary, infants' categorization, memory, and play reflect mental representation as well as broader cultural themes and values. These abilities do not develop in isolation; indeed, they are fostered during social interactions with parents when parents are attuned to their child's emotional cues and developmental level. (For a summary of this section, see "Interim Summary 5.3: Mental Representation in Infancy.")

INTERIM SUMMARY 5.3

Mental Representation in Infancy

Specific Areas of Cognitive Development

Categorization

- Grouping separate things together according to some rule.
- It facilitates the storage and retrieval of information.
- Infants learn to apply their knowledge of attributes to other members of the same category (for example, that his/her dog barking applies to other dogs as well).

Memory

- **Infantile amnesia** is not being able to remember much before the age of 3 or 4.
- Short-term memory has been studied by habituating infants and testing them afterward with the same stimulus.
- Long-term memory has been studied by imposing a delay between habituation and a later test.
- Infants' ability to remember improves with age—infants habituate more quickly and effectively as they grow older.
- **Deferred imitation** (showing babies a series of actions, then seeing whether they produce these actions later) is even more advanced.

Play

- Play is fun and interactive but also involves mental work.
- Play progresses from **exploratory play** (goal of extracting information about objects) in the first year to pretend or **symbolic play** (make-believe scenarios) in the second year.
- Play normally occurs in the context of social interaction and in some cultures is predominantly a child's activity, whereas in others parents play as partners.

INFANT "INTELLIGENCE"

Developmental scientists are also interested in how much children of a given age understand, and how much children of the same age vary in their "intelligence"—a quantitative approach to cognitive development (Siegler, 2002, 2007).

Infant Tests

Beginning in the 1920s, about the same time that Piaget began making notes on his own children's cognitive development, Nancy Bayley set out to measure mental and motor growth in infancy. She developed a scale of the performance of middle-income children, and they were tested regularly from birth through 18 years. The Bayley Scales of Infant Development have become the most widely used assessments of infant and early childhood development. Today, there are two scales: a Mental Development Index and a Psychomotor Development Index. They assess motor, sensation, perception, cognition, memory, language, and social behavior in infants and toddlers over the first years of life.

Measuring infant intelligence is challenging. If you wanted to assess the usefulness of an IQ measure, say, among college students, you might ask how well IQ scores tell you about performance on another index of intelligence, like achievement in school. From preschoolers to adults, standardized tests are appropriate (Lichtenberger, 2005), and there is modest agreement between IQ scores and other measures of intelligence. The degree to which a test measures what it was designed to measure—what is called the test's **validity**—is assessed by comparing test scores with independent measures

validity The degree to which a test measures what it was designed to measure.

predictive validity When performance at one time relates meaningfully to performance at a later time.

of the same or similar things. With infants, however, there is no definitive or obvious index of achievement with which to compare intelligence test performance. One way to assess the validity of infant tests is to compare infants' performance early in life with their performance years later, when they grow up to be children or even as adults. Logically, if infants who perform well on infant tests do well on IQ tests as children or adults, then the infant tests must be telling us something about "intelligence" in infancy. This is a particular type of validity, called **predictive validity** (the ability of measurements to predict later outcomes, i.e., for infant tests of intelligence to predict later IQ scores). When Bayley (1949) studied the same children over time, she found essentially no relation between test performance in the first 3 to 4 years and intelligence test performance of the same children at 18 years. Only after children reached about 6 years of age or so did an association between childhood scores and later adult scores emerge. The Bayley Scales are useful in detecting developmental problems in infants; a very poor score on the Bayley may indicate serious developmental delays. It is not, however, predictive of later intellectual functioning (Bornstein & Colombo, 2010).

The absence of a connection between infant intelligence and child and adolescent intelligence could be due to several different things. It could reflect a genuine discontinuity in intellectual development. Maybe being a smart baby has nothing to do with being an intelligent first-grader. Or the absence of a link between infant test performance and later test performance could reflect a problem with the instrument—maybe the Bayley test is not a very good measure of the things that should predict later intelligence. The Bayley Scales test babies' sensory capacities, and motor achievements, as well as responses that are influenced by the baby's emotional state, like orienting, reaching, and smiling. For an older child, very different items are used in evaluating intelligence—skills related to language, reasoning, and memory. On these grounds, the lack of predictive validity of the Bayley Scales to foretell later IQ scores is not surprising.

Perhaps measures of infant mental ability that are more purely cognitive and do not include motor or emotional components would make more appropriate tests and have more predictive validity. What might show us how well a baby is *thinking*? One way is to watch how he or she pays attention. Generally speaking, infants who process information more efficiently acquire knowledge more quickly. We can measure the efficiency of an infant's information processing with some of the tools described at the beginning of this chapter: habituation and novelty responsiveness.

Just as students vary in their ability to concentrate, so infants vary in the ways they perform on tests of habituation and novelty responsiveness. Studies find that those who are more efficient (i.e., who pay more attention to novel stimuli and less to familiar ones) also tend to explore their environment more competently and play in more sophisticated ways—two other indicators of infant cognitive competence. Furthermore, infants who are expected to show lower intelligence later in life—those with developmental disabilities such as Down syndrome—are poorer in managing attention when they are babies. Although infants' scores on the Bayley do not predict later intelligence, performance on tests of habituation and novelty responsiveness do. That is, infants who show efficient information processing tend to perform better on traditional assessments of cognitive competence in later childhood (Bornstein & Colombo, 2010; Kavšek, 2004; Strid et al., 2006; Tasbihsazan, Nettelbeck, & Kirby, 2003; Tsao, Liu, & Kuhl, 2004).

Both low- and high-risk preterm and low- and very-low-birth-weight (VLBW) infants and children are at risk for impaired developmental outcomes in motor skills and behavior as well as attention and cognition (Bhutta, Cleves, Casey, Cradock, & Anand, 2002; Saigal, 2000; Salt & Redshaw, 2006; Taylor, Klein, & Hack, 2000; van de

Weijer-Bergsma, Wijnroks, & Jongmans, 2008). For example, even low-risk preterms, at 3 to 4 years of age, achieve lower results in an intelligence test, in a visual perception test, in a location memory test, and in a sustained-attention test (Caravale, Tozzi, Albino, & Vicari, 2009). Longitudinal studies of VLBW children confirm that many differences from normal birthweight children at all ages up to adulthood remain stable over time (Breslau, Paneth, & Lucia, 2004; Saigal et al., 2000; Taylor, Klein, Minich, & Hack, 2000). However, differences and delays are not pervasive. Monset-Couchard, de Bethmann, and Kastler (2002) found some "catch-up" on language skills among VLBW children (we first encountered this developmental recovery phenomenon in Chapter 4). This finding received further support from two studies, one demonstrating catch-up in vocabulary development between 3 and 8 years of age by Ment et al. (2003) and the other in reading skills between 9 and 15 years of age by Samuelsson and his colleagues (2006).

So, intelligence is neither innate nor fixed in early life. Certainly genes contribute to general mental development (Johnson, Bouchard, McGue, Segal, Tellegen, & Keyes, 2007; Segal, McGuire, Havlena, Gill, & Hershberger, 2007), but experience in the world is a major contributing factor to all psychological functions, including intelligence, and to be inherited does not mean to be immutable or nonchangeable. Longitudinal studies of intelligence show that individuals definitely change over time. Even heritable traits depend on learning for their expression, and they are subject to environmental effects (Lerner, Fisher, & Gianinno, 2006). So, infant and child learning are assisted and guided by others. This is the *social context* of mental development in infancy (Bornstein, 1991; Bornstein & Bradley, 2003; Bronfenbrenner & Morris, 1998; Rogoff, 2003).

Infant Mental Development in Social Context

In cultural communities as far flung as Turkey, Guatemala, India, and the United States, children participate actively in culturally organized activities; in this way, they gain an understanding of the world they live in. As apprentices in daily living, infants must learn to think, act, and interact with others in their culture to live successfully.

One way to think about how the environment influences child development is to take an *ecological perspective*, which you read about in Chapter 2. As you recall, children's growth and development are influenced by some forces that are close at hand (parents, extended family, peers); other forces that are somewhat removed (their neighborhood, their parents' workplaces); and still other forces that are quite removed, although still influential (social class, culture). Closer influences are called *proximal*, and more remote influences are called *distal*. Generally speaking, distal forces influence child development through proximal forces.

We know, for example, that low socioeconomic status (a distal influence) is linked to poor intellectual development in children (McLoyd, Aikens, & Burton, 2006). For example, using data from the Panel Study of Income Dynamics, which followed approximately 2,400 children born from 1955 to 1970 into adulthood, Sharkey (2009) discovered that experiencing high neighborhood poverty throughout childhood (say, experiencing a poverty rate of 25 percent compared to a rate of 5 percent) raised the chances of a person's downward mobility by 52 percent. Growing up poor by itself isn't all that influences the child's IQ and life chances, though. In addition, fewer educated parents live in poor neighborhoods, and poorly educated parents typically provide their children with less verbal stimulation (Hoff, 2006) and fewer enriching life experiences (Bradley & Corwyn, 2002). These are proximal influences. In addition, other distal aspects of social life that are organized by geography exert coordinate influences. These include schools, government and electoral districts, and other local institutions. Public schools are partially funded by residential districts, so the quality of the educational opportunities afforded children depends directly on where they live. Similarly, the quality of parks and recreation centers, the effectiveness of the police, as well as exposure to violence, gangs, toxic soil, and polluted air all depend on one's neighborhood.

Risks associated with social deprivation early in life can be offset by intervention, as the long-term Carolina Abecedarian Project shows. Beginning in the 1970s, this project was administered to a group of predominantly African American children who were living with single mothers who had less than a high-school degree. The educational intervention started by age 3 months, and children in the treatment group received center-based child care for a full day, 5 days a week through kindergarten entry at age 5. Some services (nutritional supplements and medical care) were provided to the control group to ensure that those were not the factors accounting for different outcomes between the two groups. Experimental evaluations have found positive and lasting effects of this intervention on children's IQ, reading, and math scores first detected at 18 months of age. Children who participated in the intervention were also less likely to be retained in a grade or placed in special education, and they were more likely to be enrolled in or have graduated from college, than children in the control group. As young adults (age 21 years), treatment participants showed a reduction in teenaged pregnancy compared with controls. These findings suggest that sustained, high-quality, center-based interventions starting in infancy and continuing at least to school entry can produce long-term positive impacts (Campbell, Ramey, Pungello, Sparling, & Miller-Johnson, 2002).

Different social risks in early life (such as being born into poverty, to a single teenage mother, being low birth weight, etc.) tend to go together and add to one another to increase the long-term disadvantages (Burchinal, Roberts, Hooper, & Zeisel, 2000; Burchinal, Roberts, Zeisel, Hennon, & Hooper, 2006; Gutman, Sameroff, & Eccles, 2002). This is called *multiple risks*. One of those risks is the air children breathe. As noted in Chaper 3, polycyclic aromatic hydrocarbons (PAHs) are released into the air during incomplete combustion of fossil fuel, tobacco, and other organic material. Perera and her colleagues (2008, 2009) noticed delayed motor development at 2 years of age in a cohort of Chinese children exposed prenatally to PAHs from local coal-fired plant emissions. The effects were not seen in a second cohort conceived after the power plant had been shut. In a later study, they evaluated the relation between prenatal exposure to airborne PAHs and child intelligence. Children of nonsmoking African or Dominican American women residing in New York City were monitored from *in utero* to 5 years of age, with determination of prenatal PAH exposure through personal air monitoring by mothers during pregnancy and intelligence assessed at 5 years of age. After adjustment for maternal intelligence, quality of the home environment, environmental tobacco smoke exposure, and other potentially confounding factors, high prenatal PAH levels predicted lower childhood IQ scores. IQ scores of high-exposure children were 4 points lower than those of less-exposed children. Environmental PAHs at levels encountered in New York City air affect children's IQ adversely.

Children reared in more advantaged homes show superior mental development both because of genetic factors and environmental ones (Petrill et al., 2004). The influence of the family on infant cognitive development is not a one-way street, however. Infant and caregiver *jointly* contribute to developing cognitive competence. Although children learn from the experiences they have with their parents, the experiences that parents provide their children are affected by children's capabilities at various points in their development. In other words, the infant's cognitive development is a product of the constant interplay between the child's abilities and the environment, including experiences that their caregivers provide.

Parents influence their infants' intellectual development in many ways: via teaching skills, by being responsive to their needs, and by providing books and toys. In infancy, the vast majority of experiences stem directly from interactions within the family. Parents take principal responsibility for teaching their infants: They engage infants in early games as well as in turn-taking exchanges in play. As carpenters do in constructing a building, parents sometimes use temporary aids—a process referred to as **scaffolding**—to help their child advance (Vygotsky, 1978). Later, as the edifice of intellect grows and is solidified, the scaffold may be replaced or taken down (see Chapter 7).

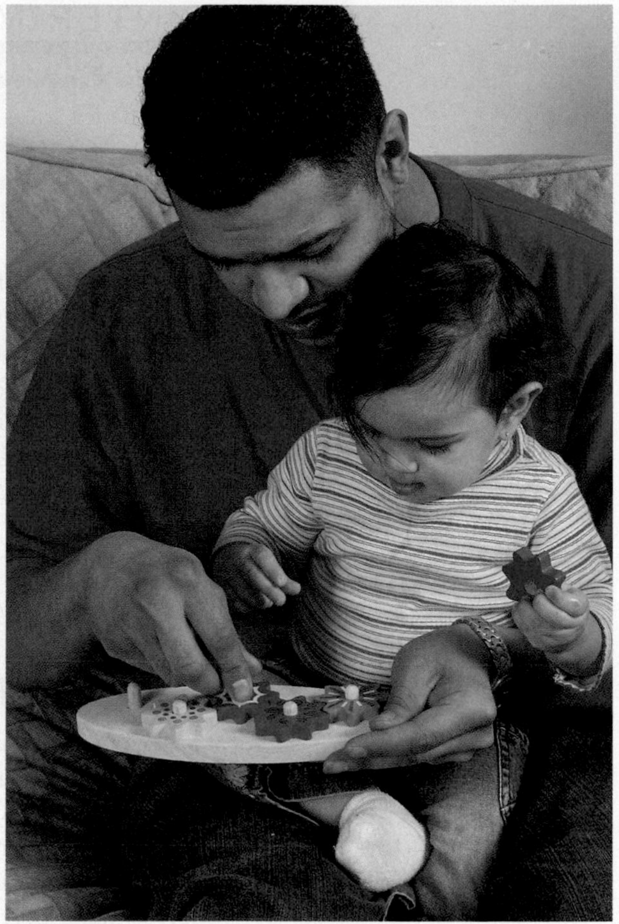

© Laura Dwight

Parents have important roles to play in their infants' learning about the world, as this dad shows in demonstrating for his 10-month-old girl how a new toy works.

Parents vary in the scaffolds they favor, and some scaffolding strategies may be more effective than others, depending on the nature and age of the child. Positive *stimulation* in the first 3 years (responsiveness, for example) is one kind of interaction that supports later motor, cognitive, and social development (Bradley, Corwyn, Burchinal, Pipes McAdoo, & Garcia Coll, 2001a, b; Saltaris, Serbin, Stack, Karp, Schwartzman, & Ledingham, 2004). *Joint attention* occurs when a caregiver and a child are focused on the same object and promotes cognitive development; joint attention has been linked to improved communication skills in infants (Butterworth, 2001; Mundy & Sigman, 2006). *Responsiveness* occurs when parents react appropriately, contingently, and promptly in response to interactions that their infants initiate; this is another effective scaffolding strategy that has long-term positive outcomes for children's cognitive and language development (Bornstein, 2002; Bradley et al., 2001b; Gros-Louis et al., 2006). For example, in their prospective study of a cohort of low-income, predominantly Caucasian mothers and their infants in Minneapolis, early care predicted reading and math achievement as measured at age 16 (Sroufe, Egeland, Carlson, & Collins, 2005). The *material environment* (toys and books) that parents provide for their infants is another effective scaffolding technique (Bradley, et al., 2001a, b; Gottfried, Fleming, & Gottfried, 1998). Toys that provide challenges and rewards (i.e., toys that infants can use with some help at first, but then by themselves) are ideal. Reading with children broadens their knowledge as well as developing prereading skills (see Chapter 7). The number of books and toys matters, but so does parental involvement with them. Generally, careful and considered early childhood stimulation programs have lasting positive effects into adult years (Reynolds, 2003).

scaffolding Providing learning opportunities, materials, hints, and clues when a child has difficulty with a task.

What motivates infants' parents to behave in the ways they do? Parental belief systems, called **ethnotheories**, help to determine how parents interact with their children. As a result, different approaches to scaffolding are seen around the world. For example, European American mothers tend to believe that physical development is the result of maturation but that knowledge comes from interaction with the environment. Kenyan Gisuii mothers tend to believe that physical development depends on interaction but that knowledge comes from observation. Not surprisingly, European American mothers tend to encourage infant exploration more than Gusii mothers as a way of developing their babies' cognitive skills, but Gisuii mothers deliberately encourage physical development more than their European American counterparts. (For a summary of this section, see "Interim Summary 5.4: Infant 'Intelligence.'")

ethnotheories Parents' belief systems that motivate them to behave in the ways they do.

INTERIM SUMMARY 5.4

Infant "Intelligence"

The Bayley Scales of Infant Development are used to assess infant motor, sensation, perception, cognition, memory, language, and social behavior:

- The **validity** (the degree to which a test measures what it was designed to measure) of these tests is problematic since there's no definitive external index of achievement with which to compare infant test performance.
- **Predictive validity** (validity over time)—compares infants' performance early in life with their performance years later as children or adults.
- The Bayley is still useful in detecting developmental problems in infants but not predictive of later intellectual functioning.
- Intelligence is not fixed in early life—genetics contribute but experience in the world or social context is a major contributing factor.
- An infant's cognitive development is always a product of the infant's abilities and the environment and experiences provided by caregivers.

LANGUAGE DEVELOPMENT IN INFANCY

The word *infant* derives from the Latin *in* + *fans*, which translated literally means "nonspeaker"; the word *baby* shares a Middle English root with "babble." Beginning to speak—and understand speech—is one of most impressive, and essentially human, developments during infancy.

Language depends on perceptual, cognitive, and social development, and it involves many overlapping levels of production and comprehension. Sounds must be produced and perceived (**phonology**). The meaning of words (**semantics**) must be learned. The grammar (**syntax**) of language defines the ways in which words and phrases are arranged to ensure correct and meaningful communication.

phonology Sounds in language that are produced and perceived.

semantics The meaning of words and sentences, or the content of speech.

syntax The rules that define the ways in which words and phrases are arranged to ensure correct and meaningful communication. Also called *grammar*.

Consider what the infant must do to understand his mother when she says, "Comeherelovelyforadrinkofjuice." The child must break up the sound stream into individual words, understand what each word means, and analyze the grammatical structure linking the words to decipher the overall meaning. To complicate matters further, these three types of decoding must take place as the mother is talking.

Scholars have disagreed over the relative contributions of biology and experience to the acquisition of language. Some theoreticians have argued that language learning is based solely on the child's experiences. In the fourth century, Saint Augustine wrote that children learn language by imitating their elders; in the twentieth century, B. F. Skinner (1957) argued that children acquire language through experience (learning). In contrast, other theorists have asserted that infants must come into the world with an inborn ability to acquire language (Chomsky, 1965; Jakobson, 1968). The truth is some combination of these two extremes. Language is too rich, unique, and complex a system for infants to learn through imitation and/or reinforcement, just as it is too rich, unique, and complex a system for infants simply to know without appropriate experience. The acquisition of language, like other developments, reflects a complex interaction between the child's developing competencies (biology) and adult-child social communication (experience).

Language Norms and Methods of Study

Figure 5.3 depicts some milestones of language development in infancy. As you can see, the first 2 years of life are a time of remarkable growth. In the first month of life, infants coo and babble; by their 24th month, toddlers can speak grammatically correct

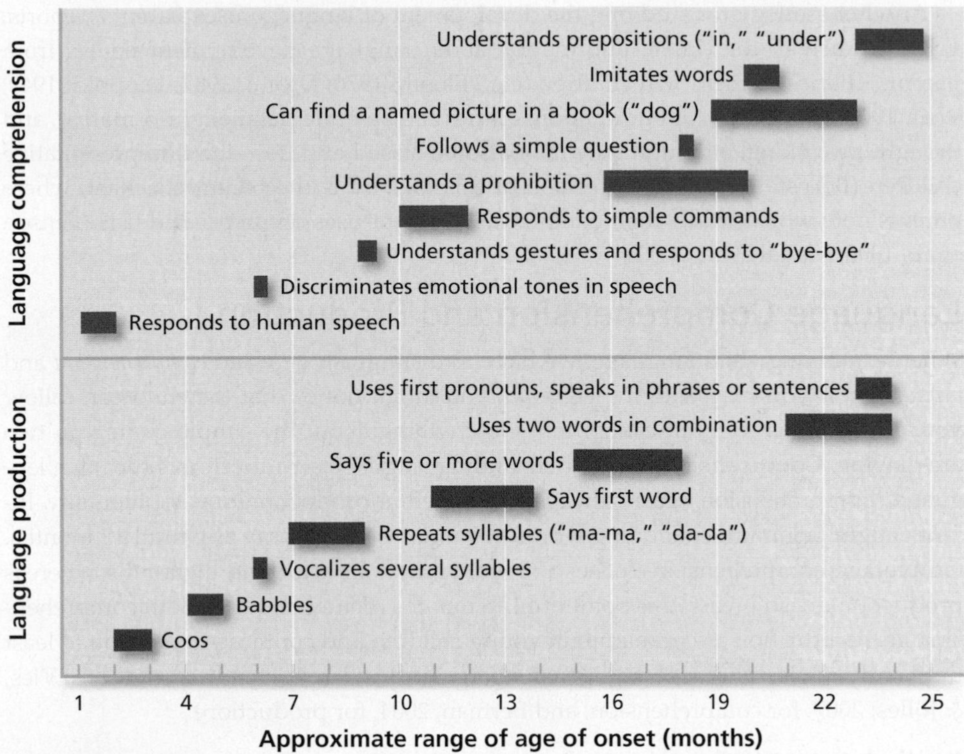

FIGURE 5.3

Milestones of Language Development in Infancy

The top half of the graph shows development of language comprehension. Across infancy, babies develop from simply responding to voices to understanding sophisticated phrases. The bottom half of the graph shows development of language production. Across infancy, babies develop from making cooing and babbling sounds to speaking in phrases and short sentences. The length of each bar represents the range of ages by which most infants achieve each ability, which is a reflection of individual differences in language development.

Source: Reprinted by permission of the publisher from *A First Language: The Early Stages* by Roger Brown, p. 57, Cambridge, Mass.: Harvard University Press, Copyright © 1973 by the President and Fellows of Harvard College.

sentences. In the first month, infants respond to the sound of the human voice; by their 24th month, toddlers comprehend the meaning of prepositions (e.g., *to, in, of*).

To understand how language develops in infancy, we might simply observe, record, and analyze what children seem to understand or say as they grow up. Recordings capture and reveal that the infants' early speech is more sophisticated than it sounds. For example, when children start saying words, it seems like they do not make certain distinctions clearly; a child might seem to pronounce the /*p*/ (pronounced "pa") and /*b*/ (pronounced "ba") at the beginnings of words in exactly the same way. However, close analyses of recordings of children's attempts at /*p*/ and /*b*/ sounds reveal that some children actually make the sounds differently—but not differently enough for adults to hear clearly. One important implication of this finding is that children's learning certain distinctions between sounds cannot be due solely to adult reinforcement, because adults are generally unable to hear children's initial improvements. Another implication is that our naked ears may underestimate children's abilities. This echoes a theme that arises again and again in the study of language development (and of cognitive development more generally): The roots of complex behaviors often exist long before those behaviors are clear and blossoming, and many capacities that seem to bloom overnight have in fact been developing for months.

Another strategy for studying the development of language uses parents' reports. In fact, much of the classic information about language development comes from parents' diaries of their own children (e.g., Bloom, 1976; Dromi, 1987; Leopold, 1949; Weir, 1962). As sources of information, diaries can be quite detailed, informative, and thought provoking, although they may also be biased and describe unrepresentative children (Bornstein, 2010). A variation of this method is the parent checklist, where parents note which words their child understands or uses on preprinted lists (Fenson et al., 1993; Maital et al., 2000).

Language Comprehension and Production

When examining child language, we have to distinguish between *comprehension* and *production*. If you play with a 1-year-old, you might notice that the child can follow your instructions well but cannot tell you anything about the simple game you two are playing. **Comprehension** is understanding language; **production** is speaking language. Comprehension nearly always comes before production developmentally. Infants might begin understanding words at 9 months but not say any until 12 months. On average, comprehension reaches a 50-word milestone at around 13 months, whereas production doesn't reach this point until 18 months (Benedict, 1979). Both comprehension and production are immature in young children and continue to develop at least until early adolescence (see, e.g., Wassenberg, Hurks, Feron, Hendriksen, Meijs, Vles, & Jolles, 2007, for comprehension, and Berman, 2004, for production).

comprehension Understanding language.

production Speaking the language.

Individual Variation in Language Development

Children of the same age vary dramatically on nearly every measure of language development (Bates & Carnevale, 1993). One researcher (Brown, 1973) traced speech development in three children—Adam, Eve, and Sarah—by indexing their verbal growth in terms of their *mean length of utterance*, measured in the number of **morphemes** (units of meaning, including spoken words, like *play*, and word parts, like the "ing" in *playing*). Figure 5.4 shows that all three children achieved common *goals* and that their growth *rates* were nearly equivalent. However, Eve began talking considerably earlier than did Adam or Sarah. For example, Eve used an average of three morphemes in an utterance at about 2 years of age, whereas Adam and Sarah did not do so until approximately 3 years of age—one-third of their lifetimes later.

morphemes Units of meaning in a language.

At 13 months, some toddlers produce no words, others 27 (Tamis-LeMonda & Bornstein, 1990, 1991). At 20 months, individual toddlers can range from 10 to 500 words in their productive vocabularies, and this is true across cultures (Bornstein et al., 2004). Over the course of early childhood, moreover, there is a fair amount of consistency within individual children: Infants who know more words at 1 year tend to know more words at 2 years. What is more, children who know more words may be at a long-term advantage. Knowing more words speeds learning to read, improves reading comprehension, and spills over into written language skills; vocabulary size at 2 years of age predicts linguistic and cognitive skills at 8 years (Marchman & Fernald, 2008).

Number of words and mean length of utterance are measures of quantitative differences among children; children also differ from one another qualitatively. Some children are **referential**; their vocabularies include a high proportion of nouns, and their speech provides information and refers to things in the environment ("ball," "kitty," "apple"). Other children are **expressive**; their early vocabularies have more verbs, and they use speech to communicate feelings and desires ("carry me," "hungry," "Mommy go"). One researcher video recorded two children at play with their mothers at home at 12, 15, and 18 months of age (Goldfield, 1985/1986). Johanna was a referential child. Of

referential A linguistic style hallmarked by vocabularies that include a high proportion of nouns and speech that provides information and refers to things in the environment.

expressive A linguistic style hallmarked by early vocabularies that have relatively more verbs and speech that uses social routines to communicate feelings and desires.

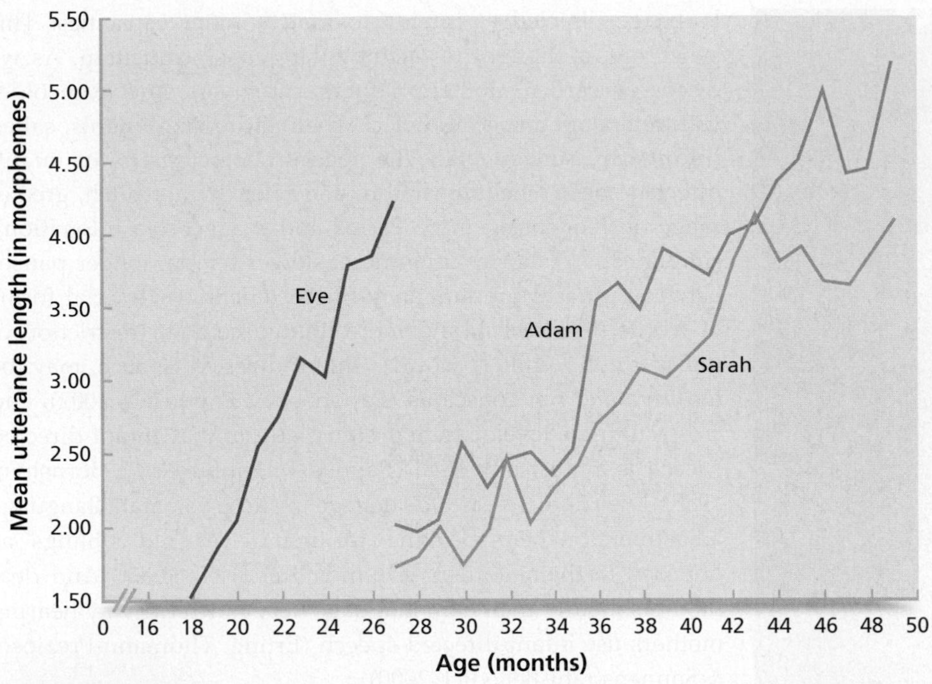

FIGURE 5.4

Individual Differences in Language Development

Although most children develop language abilities through a very similar sequence, there is a lot of individual variation in when the process begins and how fast the process occurs. For example, Eve was using four-morpheme utterances just after her second birthday, but Adam and Sarah did not do so until they were about 3½ years old.

Source: Reprinted by permission of the publisher from *A first language: The early stages* by Roger Brown, p. 57, Cambridge, Mass.: Harvard University Press, Copyright ©1973 by the President and Fellows of Harvard College.

Johanna's first 50 words, 49 were names for things. In play, approximately half of her attempts to engage her mother involved her giving or showing a toy, and reciprocally Johanna's mother consistently labeled toys for her. Caitlin was an expressive child. Nearly two-thirds of Caitlin's first 50 words consisted of social expressions, many of them in phrases. For referential youngsters, the purposes of language are to label, describe, and exchange information, whereas for expressive youngsters, language is to note or confirm activity. Caitlin and Johanna are extremes, of course; most children are both referential and expressive and their speech depends on the situation.

The Building Blocks of Language

One of the principal tasks of the first 2½ years of life is for the infant to develop into a conversational partner. Adult and infant alike are focused on this common goal, and infants come very far very fast. In learning language, the child is neither ill equipped nor, typically, alone. There are many elements of language that infants and their caregivers utilize, such as infant-directed speech, turn-taking, and gestures.

Infant-Directed Speech Think about the way you would speak to a baby: As we noted in Chapter 4, your inflection, speed, and choice of words are no doubt different from those you use in speaking to an adult. Although infants possess perceptual abilities that help in language learning (see Chapter 4), parents repackage the

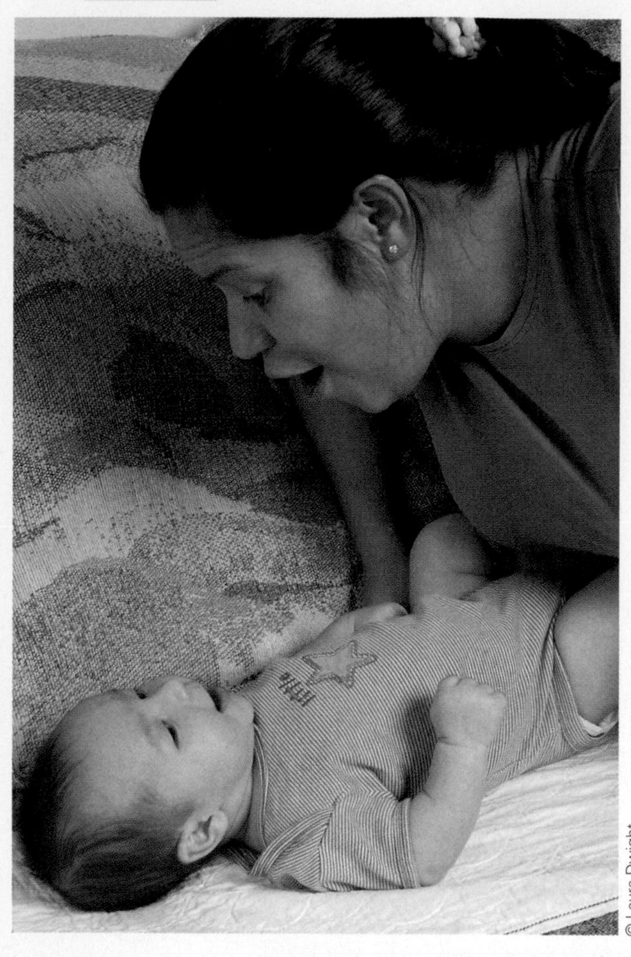

Even the youngest babies—this boy is only 2 months old—are interested in interacting with others; this mother is using infant-directed speech (sometimes called "baby talk") to keep their interaction going.

language directed at infants to match infant capacities. This synchrony is thought to facilitate language acquisition. As we discussed earlier, mothers, fathers, caregivers, and even older children adopt a special dialect when addressing infants, called **infant-directed speech**. The special characteristics of infant-directed speech include rhythm and tone (higher pitch, greater range of frequencies, more varied and exaggerated intonation); simplification (shorter utterances, slower tempo, longer pauses between phrases); redundancy (more repetition); special forms of words (like *mama*); and more limited content (restriction of topics to the child's world). Infant-directed speech may be intuitive and not conscious (Papoušek & Papoušek, 2002), and cross-cultural developmental study attests that infant-directed speech is almost universal (Papoušek, Papoušek, & Bornstein, 1985). Even 2- to 3-year-olds engage in such systematic language adjustments when speaking to their 1-year-old siblings as opposed to their mothers (Dunn & Kendrick, 1982). And deaf mothers modify their sign language very much the way hearing mothers use infant-directed speech (Erting, Thumann-Prezioso, & Sonnenstrahl-Benedict, 2000).

Turn-Taking Turn-taking is fundamental to adult dialogue. It is impolite to interrupt; rather, we wait our turn to speak. Setting manners aside, it is likely that turn-taking evolved because the human nervous system cannot simultaneously produce and understand speech. Mothers and their infants take turns with one another much more than speaking at the same time (Jasnow & Feldstein, 1986). After a mother or a baby vocalizes, each will next suppress vocalization to permit their partner to join the conversation. When adults use conversational give-and-take patterns, infants produce more speech-like than non-speech-like sounds (Bloom, Russell, & Wassenburg, 1987). Infants participating in such conversations also vocalize with sounds that are more like real speech.

infant-directed speech
A special speech register reserved for babies that simplifies normal adult-directed speech in many ways.

Gesture Gestures are a form of nonverbal communication and are often used to support spoken language (Blake et al., 2003; Goldin-Meadow, 2006; Locke, 2001). By the time infants are 9 months of age, parents already are labeling objects or events while pointing or gazing at them. Mothers use their hands to attract and maintain infant attention. For example, a mother might point and at the same time ask "What is that?"

Infants are more likely to look at objects previously pointed to and labeled than at objects that were not labeled (Baldwin & Markman, 1989). That is, pointing and labeling increase infants' attention to, and memory of, objects. At about 12 months, infants themselves start to point, although the age varies considerably: Some begin by 9 months, whereas others don't start until 19 months (Hoff, 2006). Infants whose mothers respond to infants' pointing by labeling ("Yes, that's the *moon*.") later become children with larger referential vocabularies.

Why do people use infant-directed speech, turn-taking, and gesture with babies? These strategies elicit the baby's attention, change the baby's state of arousal (by exciting him or her), communicate emotion, and, of course, facilitate language comprehension. For example, infants respond more to their own mother's voice when mothers use infant-directed speech; infants also prefer to listen to infant-directed speech than to adult-directed speech even when spoken by strangers (Kitamura et al., 2002). Indeed, Zangl and Mills (2007) reported that infant-directed speech boosts neural activity to unknown words in 6- and 13-month-olds. Certain features of mothers' speech are consistent across languages such as American English, German, and Mandarin Chinese. Mothers around the world use rising pitch to engage infant attention, falling pitch to soothe a distressed infant, and an up-then-down pattern to maintain infant attention (Papoušek & Papoušek, 2002; Papoušek et al., 1985). These adult modifications may make it easier for the baby to acquire language. For example, when presented with a sequence of syllables that contain some speech sounds (e.g., in English, the sound "bay" is a speech sound) and other sounds that are not a part of speech ("gwu"), infants discriminate speech sounds better in infant-directed speech than in adult-directed speech (Karzon, 1985).

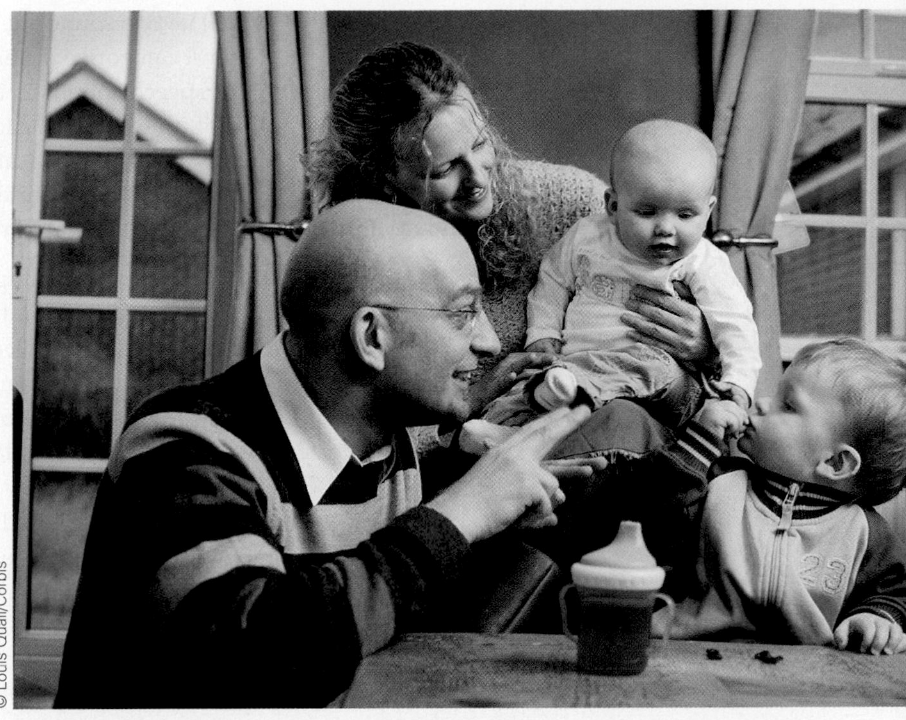

To overcome the loss of a communication channel, speech and hearing, families in the Deaf culture use visual and tactile means, like this dad signing to his infant son.

Making and Understanding Sounds

At the most basic level, language and communication involve sounds. When we speak we make sounds, and when we hear we listen to sounds.

Sound Perception As you read in Chapter 4, the auditory system is well developed before birth, and so newborns hear, orient to, and distinguish all sorts of sounds from the moment they are born. But babies seem especially primed to perceive and appreciate human speech. Consider the seemingly impossible task of segmenting the speech stream—knowing where one word ends and the next begins—before knowing any words or even what a word is. Imagine figuring out that "Comeherelovelyforadrinkofjuice" is "Come here, lovely, for a drink of juice," and not "Co mehere lo velyfor adrin kof jui ce"). Moreover, infants have to do this for different speakers and in different contexts. One competency that has evolved to address segmenting sounds and recognizing speech is categorization.

Parents use many different strategies to get and hold their infant's attention; gesturing to catch a baby's attention and pointing to direct attention are common.

Infants perceive *categories* of speech sounds. Because sounds vary so much from one language to another, many scholars once thought that meaningful distinctions among sounds must be shaped by experience. It appears, however, that many speech sounds are not experienced as wholly different from one another or as random; rather, many sounds fit into manageable categories that infants recognize from a very early age. The two sounds */b/* and */p/* are examples. Infants categorize different */b/*s as similar and categorize different */p/*s as similar, but distinguish */b/*s from */p/*s. Categorization of speech sounds is important to language acquisition for many reasons. For example, if infants heard each and every variant of */b/* as different, then learning "ball," "box," "bat," "bottle," and so forth would be more difficult, not to mention the challenges posed by the variations in */b/* produced by the same speaker at different times or by different speakers (mother and father).

Sound Production Infants pass through stages in early verbal development: a prelinguistic stage, a one-word stage, and a multiword stage.

Babies' first means of vocal communication—crying and babbling—are prelinguistic, but this hardly means that they are unimportant. Few adults can disregard a baby's cry. It compels us to respond (Bowlby, 1969), and the nearly universal response is to be nurturing in some way (Bornstein et al., 1992). The infant's cry is also a very revealing vocalization. Babies' cries are affected by many factors, including hunger and sleepiness, nutritional deficiency, respiratory disorder, prematurity, genetic disorders such as Down syndrome, and cocaine exposure during pregnancy. For example, parents perceive the cries of children with autism spectrum disorder (ASD), compared to typically developing children and children with developmental delay, as less mature and more negative (Esposito & Venuti, 2008).

If babies' cries inform parents about their unhappy state, babbling is the first significant nondistress communication. In babbling, there are frequent repetitions of the same syllable sound or syllable—for example, ba-ba-ba-ba—and this practice perfects the sounds, syllables, and sequences of syllables that later comprise full-blown speech. Babbling is typically accompanied by excitement and motor activity and alternates with attentive listening. Although babbling seems simple, there is more to it than first meets the ear (Dromi, 2001). Babbling is significant because it comprises infants' first structured vocalizations, because it sounds like fun, and because it follows crying so common in early infancy on the one hand, and the advent of intelligible words during toddlerhood on the other. Even deaf infants "babble" using sounds as well as hand signs (Petitto et al., 2001). We can conclude that having heard speech is not critical to babbling. The similarities in manual signing and vocal babbling indicate that babbling is an abstract language capacity of human beings related to expressive capacity.

Every child uses two sources of information when beginning to speak: the speech of others and feedback regarding his or her own speech. As might be expected, deaf infants' vocal babbles develop later than those of hearing infants (Oller, 2000). Auditory input is necessary for the normal and timely development of the ability to reproduce the full range of adult-like syllables; indeed, it is crucial to children developing normal vocalizations in their native language. Babbling in Chinese differs from babbling in French. Language experts and laypeople alike can identify the language of origin in samples of 6- to 10-month-olds' babbling, even though the infants will not be producing their native languages for quite a while (Boysson-Bardies, Sagart, & Durand, 1984). Thus, the prelinguistic speech of infants as young as 8 months of age is influenced by the language they hear. In sum, infants' very earliest sensitivities to sound and their earliest vocal expressions provide evidence of strong biological influences on language development. Very soon, however, both perception and production of sound are shaped by the linguistic experiences provided by parents and cultures.

How Infants Learn Words

Recall the "Comeherelovelyforadrinkofjuice" problem. To understand this simple statement, even after breaking it down into separate units correctly, the child (lovely) must determine which unit refers to him- or herself, which to objects (juice) in the environment, which to an action (come), and so forth. After all, connections between word sounds and word meanings are arbitrary, so the decoding task is challenging.

Once the baby speaks his or her first word around 12 months on average, the baby uses the word for all kinds of things. A **holophrase** is a single word that stands in for a phrase and has different meanings depending on the context—for example, "bear" can mean "that is a bear," "the bear fell," "I want my bear," or "my bear drinks milk."

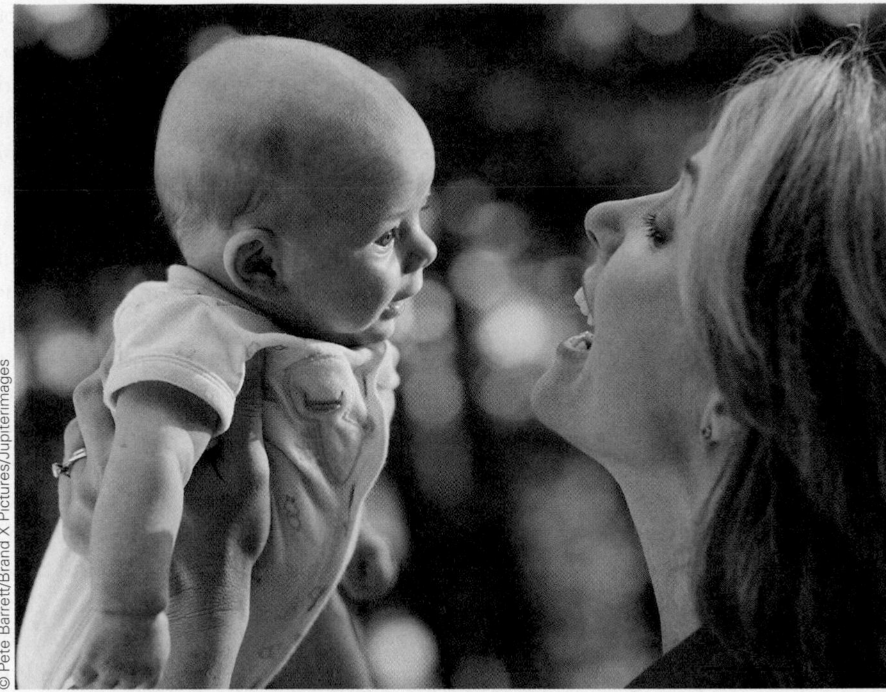
© Pete Barrett/Brand X Pictures/Jupiterimages

Being responsive to an infant, as this mother shows, is not only a major way of interacting, but is one way that parents show infants that infants can influence their environment.

After the child had attained one-word speech, word learning proceeds rapidly. The average 3-year-old possesses an estimated vocabulary of 3,000 words. Therefore, between approximately 12 and 36 months, the child acquires four new words per day on average (MacWhinney & Bornstein, 2003). Word learning is also developmentally important: Vocabulary is a key marker of children's development; vocabulary is a prominent component of child language that parents hear, attend to, and make judgments on; and size of vocabulary is an indicator of intelligence (Neisser et al., 1996). Thus, infants cry, babble, and gesture to communicate effectively, but these methods of communication are limited. A major step in language development is when infants begin learning the connections between sounds and meanings of their languages.

holophrase A single word that stands in for a phrase and has different meanings depending on the context.

To what do children's first words refer? One would think that children's first words might be those that they hear most often. But this is not altogether true—or at least the story is not this simple. The two most frequent English words said to infants are *you* and *the*, which are rarely among the first 50 words children produce. So word frequency is not predictive of early vocabularies, although all other factors being equal, frequency matters; American children learn *cat* before *cap* because they hear one much more frequently than the other. What about the grammatical class of early words? Nouns refer to concrete objects, verbs to actions, and adjectives to properties. Perhaps because notions like "dog" are easier to grasp than notions like "give" or "round," children around the world learn nouns earlier on than verbs or adjectives (Bornstein et al., 2004). One way word learning occurs is through **induction**, or using examples to draw conclusions about new cases. Suppose a child sees a cup referred to as "cup." For the child to recognize that the same word refers to other cups requires an induction using a learned example to make inferences about novel objects. This is not as simple as it sounds, and there are several problems to solve.

induction The process of using a limited set of examples to draw conclusions that permit inferences about new cases.

First, there is what we might call the *immediate reference problem*: Mommy is holding a mug of coffee and saying the word "cup." But what does the sound "cup" refer to? Sometimes the speaker will be pointing to an object when labeling it, but even in these seemingly clear cases there are many logical possibilities. The word might refer to the mug or its handle or the coffee in the mug or the act of drinking or that it is not appropriate for babies your age, or any of an infinite number of conceivable meanings. How do infants get it right?

Second is the *extension problem*: Once the infant has guessed what "cup" refers to, the child extends this word to other objects belonging to the same category unless the word is a proper name. (Having learned *bird*, a child will spontaneously use the same word for other members of the same object kind, but won't extend *Joan* to all girls.)

But what makes a cup a "cup"? Its shape? Color? Function? We cannot simply say that *cup* designates things that are similar to the original cup; and without defining *similar,* we're right back where we started. Children manage to figure out fairly quickly how to extend the use of words correctly if adults use words carefully. Once adults consistently name an object as few as nine times, children pick up that name for the object (Markman, 1999; Schafer & Plunkett, 1998; Woodward, Markman, & Fitzsimmons, 1994). That is, they map the sound onto the object, a phenomenon aptly called **fast mapping**.

fast mapping A phenomenon that refers to how easily children pick up words they have heard only a few times.

Children must have some rules to help them in their guesses about word meanings (Markman, 1999). An example is the **whole object assumption**. When an adult points to a novel object and labels it, the child is believed to initially think the novel label refers to the whole object and not to its parts, substance, or other properties (although it could very well refer to these other things). Another rule is **mutual exclusivity**: The child assumes that any given object has only one name.

whole object assumption A concept that refers to children's belief that a novel label refers to the "whole object" and not to its parts, substance, or other properties.

mutual exclusivity A concept that refers to an infant's assumption that any given object has only one name.

Children vary dramatically in their early vocabularies. In the fourth century, Emperor Constantine wrote that infants could not speak well or form words because their teeth had not yet erupted—which, if correct, should lead to earlier language development among infants with the fastest dental growth; this turns out not to be true, though. Most subsequent accounts have focused on differences in children's experience, primarily in the speech children hear from their parents. Parents who are lower in **socioeconomic status (SES)** talk substantially less to their children than more affluent parents, and as a consequence, infants from lower SES homes speak later and less than infants from higher SES homes. Hart and Risley (1995) estimated that children from high SES families have been exposed to around 44 million utterances by the age of 4 years, compared to 12 million utterances for low SES children (Huttenlocher, Vasilyeva, Cymerman, & Levine, 2002). But there is also a great deal of variation that SES does not account for. Even among mothers from the same SES group, some talk to their babies during as little as 3 percent of a typical home observation and others during as much as 97 percent (Bornstein & Ruddy, 1984). When both language amount (how much the parent talks) and verbal responsiveness (whether the parent's speech is responsive to the infant) are considered, verbal responsiveness is found to contribute more to children's emerging language than amount of speech (Bornstein, Tamis-LeMonda, & Haynes, 1999; Tamis-LeMonda & Bornstein, 2002). Moreover, children with verbally responsive mothers combine words into simple sentences sooner in development than do children with less verbally responsive mothers. When mothers teach infants a name for a novel toy, they tend to move the toy in synchrony with their labeling, which helps infants make the association (Gogate, Bahrick, & Watson, 2000). Thus, maternal verbal responsiveness facilitates the growth of infant language skills. Indeed, Connor, Morrison, and Katch (2004) estimated that the family environment is the major source of preparation for children's literacy skills at school entry.

socioeconomic status (SES) The education, occupation, and income of householders.

Is language development biologically programmed in our genes or determined by the environment? You probably know the answer to this: Language competence is, as you likely guessed, the product of genes *and* experience (Pruden et al., 2006; Waxman & Lidz, 2006). One-year-old adopted children are like their biological *and* adoptive parents in their language abilities, indicating genetic *and* environmental influences on language development (Hardy-Brown & Plomin, 1985).

How Infants Learn Grammar

grammar See *syntax.*

Grammar (or *syntax*) refers to the rules for combining words into meaningful and interpretable communications, and grammatical development is underway by just about the beginning of the child's second year (Bates, Devescovi, & Wulfeck, 2001). The speed with which children achieve grammatical competence is particularly remarkable in that children are able to detect syntactic rules and regularities as to their native languages even though these vary enormously across languages. In English, for example, subjects usually precede verbs, which in turn usually precede objects. Thus, when you hear "Larry, Marc, Deborah, and Karen wrote this book," you know the book was written by Larry, Marc, Deborah, and Karen. As English speakers, we are so accustomed to this word order that it seems natural, even logical. But a great many languages don't work this way. For example, in Welsh, the verb usually comes first. In Turkish and Japanese, many sentences place the verb last, but subjects and objects do not have a fixed order. Given that these rules vary across languages, one would think that they must be learned.

As to children's acquisition of syntax, Skinner (1957) argued that children learn grammatical rules by imitation and reinforcement. According to this way of thinking, children learn *transitional probabilities* among words, or which word is likely to come after which other word. "The dog ate my homework" is English, but "Homework my dog the ate" is not. According to this view, adults produce grammatical statements for children to imitate, and they also systematically reward children's grammatically correct statements.

However, Noam Chomsky (1965) argued that Skinner's account of grammatical development, with its emphasis on learned transitional probabilities, is far too simple. The grammatically correct use and meaning of an initial word in a sentence just as often depends on the end of the sentence (i.e., on an overall sentence plan) as it does on the next word. For example, "Colorless green ideas sleep furiously" is a grammatical sentence, although the transitional probabilities in the word string are nonsensically low. Thus, transitional probabilities cannot serve as a principle of the child's grammatical development.

Second, Skinner's notion of reinforcement requires parents to consistently reward children for producing grammatical utterances (and not for ungrammatical ones). In practice, though, parents do not do this; in fact, parents are much more likely to correct young children's factual errors than their grammar. If a child who is eating an apple says, "Me eat banana," parents are more likely to say, "No, that is an apple" than "No, say 'I am eating a banana'." Thus, parents do not directly teach children grammar the way schoolteachers do. (Also, children resist explicit correction of grammar; a child saying "Me eat banana" will not generally switch to "I am eating a banana" upon being corrected.)

Chomsky argued that a number of aspects of syntax are innate, built into every infant's brain in what he called **universal grammar**. Universal grammar accounts for the fact that, although children's language environments differ, children's syntactic outcomes are strikingly similar. Variation in the vocabulary size of English-learning children can be traced to environmental factors such as parents' verbal responsiveness, but variation in grammar among children learning the same language is miminal; poor, middle-class, and well-to-do U.S. children use the subject-verb-object syntax of American English when they speak, even if the numbers of nouns, verbs, and adjectives in their vocabularies differ dramatically. Chomsky likened learning language to the growth of an organ like the heart: As long as certain very basic preconditions are met, it (whether language or the heart) will develop in all children. The claim is not that language itself is innate (if it were, why would children in Boston learn the syntax of English and children in Berlin the syntax of German?). Rather, the claim is that children have innate abilities that facilitate grammatical development. The cross-language evidence suggests that, when children everywhere start to put two words together, they try to convey the same basic set of meanings, like possession and location, and as they progress from there the rate of grammatical errors is surprisingly small (Bates et al., 2001).

universal grammar Chomsky's term for aspects of syntax that are thought to be innate and built into every infant's brain.

Can biological structures that support language development be identified in the brain? At present it is not possible to give a complete answer to this question. We can say that no special area of brain tissue is wholly dedicated to language; however, certain structures in the brain are involved in particular aspects of language processing. It is well known that the left hemisphere of the brain is generally concerned with

Broca's area The region on the left side of the brain dedicated to language or speech production.

Wernicke's area The region on the left side of the brain dedicated to language or speech comprehension.

language processing. For example, injury to **Broca's area** (in the left frontal lobe) tends to cause problems in producing fluent speech and in comprehending syntactic structure; injury to **Wernicke's area** (in the left temporal lobe) tends to cause poor comprehension and fluent, but relatively meaningless speech (Sakai, 2005). (See Figure 4.4 for reference.)

When does brain lateralization begin in childhood? Mills, Prat, Zangl, Stager, Neville, and Werker (2004) examined auditory event-related potentials (ERPs) in response to words whose meanings infants knew and compared them with ERPs to words infants did not. From 14 to 20 months, ERP amplitude differences between known and unknown words could be observed over both the left and right hemispheres; by 20 months, the difference was limited to the left hemisphere, showing that word understanding is lateralized before children reach their second birthday.

INTERIM SUMMARY 5.5

Language Development in Infancy

Language depends on perceptual, cognitive, and social development. The acquisition of language reflects a complex interaction between the child's developing competencies (biology) and the larger context of adult-infant social communication (experience). Children of the same age vary dramatically on nearly every measure of language development, both quantitatively and qualitatively.	■ Sounds must be produced and perceived (phonology). ■ The meaning of words (semantics) must be learned. ■ The grammar (syntax) of the language defines the ways in which words and phrases are arranged to ensure correct communication. ■ Some children are **referential** (their vocabularies include a high proportion of nouns); some, **expressive** (their early language has more social routines).
Infant-Directed Speech	■ Individuals use a special dialect when addressing infants. ■ Turn-taking is used in parent-child dialogue as is gesture.
Making and Understanding Sounds	■ Infants perceive categories of speech sounds. ■ Infants pass through prelinguistic, one-word, and multiword stages in early verbal development. ■ Babies' first means of vocal communication are prelinguistic—crying and babbling.
How Infants Learn Words	■ Babies tend to use a single word (or **holophrase**) for many things when they first speak (around 12 months on average). ■ Between 13 and 36 months, infants acquire four new words a day on average.
How Infants Learn Grammar	■ Noam Chomsky argued that a number of aspects of syntax are innate, built into every infant's brain in a **universal grammar**. ■ Children have a natural inclination to develop grammatically structured communication.

Was there once just one language? Would all children initially speak the same language if they weren't influenced by their experience to speak the specific language they hear? The question of whether children possess a "natural language" has been asked with surprising frequency in history and by a surprising group of individuals, from pharaohs to phoneticians. James I of England (1566–1625), for example, posed the question and thought of how to address it. Long interested in the Bible—his is the King James version, of course—James sought to identify the original language of Adam and Eve. He proposed to place two infants on an otherwise uninhabited island in the care of a deaf-mute nurse. James reasoned that, if the two spontaneously developed speech, theirs would be the natural language of humankind. Although probably within his power, King James never (to our knowledge) conducted his study as such an experiment would be wholly unethical.

Natural experiments that approximate King James's conditions suggest that children develop their own grammar and vocabulary in the absence of formal linguistic experience. For example, deaf infants who are of normal intelligence but whose parents (for various reasons) have prohibited their learning sign language have essentially no experience with any formal language, but their other life experiences are normal. These children develop their own signs to refer to objects, people, and actions, and they combine signs into phrases to express relations among words in ordered ways. Their communication system is not only structured, it incorporates many properties found in hearing children's language. Clearly, in the absence of formal training and imitation, children develop syntactic rules: They sign nouns before verbs, and verbs before objects acted on.

Furthermore, the timing of deaf children's invention of communication systems is roughly the same as that of hearing children learning spoken languages—their first "words" appear at around 12 months, and their first combinations of words appear several months later. Even children in challenging circumstances reveal a natural inclination to develop grammatical communication. (For a summary of this section, see "Interim Summary 5.5: Language Development in Infancy.")

SUMMING UP AND LOOKING AHEAD

In the not too distant past, the notion that infants think would have been considered laughable. Today, however, we know better thanks largely to the work of Piaget and the decades of scientific study his work stimulated. Although Piaget's timetable for development in this period has been challenged, his general theory of the sequence of cognitive development still stands: Children are active learners, who use their eyes and ears, hands and mouth to investigate and make sense of their world. Infants seem predisposed to form categories, build memories, play, and communicate with others. They are drawn to novelty and are primed to develop language. Although maturation plays a central role in this process, what infants discover, and the rate at which they develop, are shaped by experience and context. Cognitive development is in large part a social process, stimulated and influenced by the interactions of children with parents, siblings, peers, and adults outside the family.

There is much cognitive development that takes place after infancy, which builds on the foundation of language developed during these early years. As you will read in Chapter 7, tremendous strides in language, information processing, mathematical thinking, and social understanding take place between ages 3 and 5. But we are getting ahead of ourselves. We still have one more broad domain of infancy to cover before we leave babyhood behind. The development of the infant as a social being—and the relationships he or she forms with others—is the subject of our next, and final, chapter on the first 2 years after birth.

HERE'S WHAT YOU SHOULD KNOW

Did You Get It?

After reading this chapter, you should know:

- The techniques and strategies that developmental scientists use to confirm that infants have an active mental life
- Piaget's contribution to the study of infant cognition, including his six stages of the sensorimotor period
- The development of infants' abilities of categorization, memory, and play
- Infant intelligence tests and their limitations
- The processes of language development in infancy

Important Terms and Concepts

accommodation (p. 126)
adaptation (p. 126)
assimilation (p. 126)
Broca's area (p. 148)
categorization (p. 129)
comprehension (p. 140)
deferred imitation (p. 131)
ethnotheories (p. 137)
exploratory play (p. 131)
expressive (p. 140)
fast mapping (p. 146)
grammar (p. 146)
habituation (p. 123)
holophrase (p. 145)
induction (p. 145)
infant-directed speech (p. 142)
infantile amnesia (p. 130)
mental representation (p. 127)
morphemes (p. 140)
mutual exclusivity (p. 146)
novelty responsiveness (p. 124)
object permanence (p. 126)
phonology (p. 138)
predictive validity (p. 134)
production (p. 140)
referential (p. 140)
scaffolding (p. 137)
semantics (p. 138)
sensorimotor period (p. 126)
socioeconomic status (SES) (p. 146)
symbolic play (p. 132)
syntax (p. 138)
universal grammar (p. 147)
validity (p. 133)
Wernicke's area (p. 148)
whole object assumption (p. 146)

CHAPTER 6

Socioemotional Development in Infancy

You've just had your first baby. You are excited, but also more than a little nervous. The responsibility is enormous, and you really want to get everything right. The baby seems so tiny, helpless, and demanding. A month passes, and he is crying almost every night. Is he hungry? Or wet? Is the baby afraid of the dark? Or scared because he's alone? Is this the baby's personality? Is my baby insecure? Have I done something wrong? What is it?

Most parents wonder what their baby is feeling and why (Bolzani Dinehart et al., 2005). Every parent worries about what a baby's behavior might mean—whether it reflects the baby's feelings at that moment (Why is my baby angry?), his basic personality (Why is my baby always so crabby?), or the way he relates to others (Why does my baby fuss so when my parents try to pick him up?).

Like parents, developmental scientists are interested in infants' emotions, temperament, and attachments. **Emotions** are feelings that provide strong and informative cues about the infant's current state. **Temperament** reflects stable, biologically based differences in behavior that impact the infant's interactions with the social and physical environment. **Attachments** are infants' specific, lasting, social relationships with others, especially parents and other caregivers. This chapter begins with questions concerning development of infants' emotional responses and sensitivity to the emotional cues of others. Next, we discuss temperament and consider how temperamental differences affect infants' behavioral functioning, as well as factors that might explain the stability of temperament from infancy into adolescence. We conclude by examining the topics of attachment and the nature of parent-infant interactions.

emotions Feelings that give strong and informative cues about one's current state.

temperament The biologically based source of individual differences in behavioral functioning.

attachments Infants' specific, lasting, social relationships with others, especially parents and caregivers.

emotional expression The communication of feelings to others through facial expressions, gestures, and vocalizations.

emotional understanding The interpretation (reading) of the emotional expressions of others.

INFANTS' EMOTIONS

Emotions—feelings as seemingly simple as happiness or sadness—pose challenging questions for developmental researchers (Bornstein, 2000; Halle, 2003; Saarni et al., 2006). Because infants cannot tell us what they are feeling, interpreting infants' emotions from their expressions is just about all researchers (and parents for that matter) have to go on. But the display of feelings is only part of the story. There are two sides to emotional behavior. One side is **emotional expression**—communicating feelings to others through facial expressions, gestures, and vocalizations. The other side is **emotional understanding**—reading the emotional expressions of others. Infancy is a time of great strides in both.

Development of Emotional Expressions

By the time their infants are only 1 month of age, 99 percent of mothers believe that their babies express interest; 95 percent, joy; 84 percent, anger; 75 percent, surprise; 58 percent, fear; and 34 percent, sadness (Johnson et al., 1982). Mothers base their judgments on infants' facial and vocal expressions, along with gestures and movements. Infants display some emotions—joy, surprise, sadness, anger, fear, and shyness—

reliably and in appropriate contexts (Izard & Malatesta, 1987). These are called **primary emotions** because they appear to be so deeply rooted in human biology and develop so early. Just as there is a timetable for physical and cognitive growth (infants sit before they stand, babble before they use words), so there is one for emotional growth. The primary emotions appear well before such **secondary emotions** as embarrassment, pride, guilt, shame, and envy, which do not emerge until well into toddlerhood. Secondary emotions depend on higher-level mental capacities. For example, to feel guilt or shame, you have to know that you have done something wrong (Lewis, 2000).

Babies wear their emotions on their faces, so it's easy to tell when they are happy, sad, or surprised, like this little girl with her father at the window.

Charles Darwin (1872/1975) observed that certain expressions are remarkably consistent across age and culture. Darwin believed in the universality of emotional expressions (Ekman, 2006). To the extent that they are culturally universal, some emotional expressions may be innate (Ekman, 1984). This suggests that they are biologically adaptive patterns that evolved early in the development of the human species to foster survival. For example, expressing distress in a way that all members of a species easily recognize makes it more likely that caregivers will attend to infants' needs. An infant's crying elicits concern; few adults can resist attempting to soothe her. Crying is programmed in babies; the response is programmed in us.

primary emotions The feelings of joy, surprise, sadness, anger, fear, and shyness that appear to be deeply rooted in human biology and develop early in life.

secondary emotions The feelings of embarrassment, pride, guilt, shame, and envy that emerge in the second and third years of life.

The face, which is full of muscles that can convey a broad range of expressions, is one of our primary means of evaluating another person's emotions. Researchers have devoted considerable effort to developing systems to measure facial expressions of emotion in infants. One example is the Maximally Discriminative Facial Movements Code, or MAX, as it is more commonly known (Izard, 1979; Izard & Dougherty, 1982). MAX allows users to identify 27 distinct facial patterns that, alone or in combination, express particular emotions (such as the way the baby's eyebrows are positioned, or how open or closed his mouth is. If you try right now to make a "surprised" face, you will probably raise your eyebrows and open your mouth; see the photo on this page.) Another system is BabyFACS (Facial Action Coding System for Infants and Young Children) with its 92 separate facial components (Oster, 2005). Such systems are useful, for example, in studying the baby's emotional reactions to social events—such as the approach of an unfamiliar adult.

How well do facial expressions identify underlying emotions in infants? Because we rely on facial expressions in our everyday estimates of others' emotions, these measures carry considerable "validity."

Infants express different emotions vocally as well, by cooing and babbling versus by fretting and crying. Adults respond to certain infant cries as more distressed and aversive than others: When babies cry with a high pitch, with great intensity, and for a long time they are more likely to elicit faster responses from adults than when they cry less intensely (Barr, Hopkins, & Green, 2000). Parents certainly think infants' cries are meaningful, and research suggests that parents can tell the difference among cries—say, ones that signal hunger versus ones that indicate pain (Sagi, 1981).

Infants also express their emotions with gestures and movements. Figure 6.1 shows drawings used in a study testing parents' and nonparents' identification of infants'

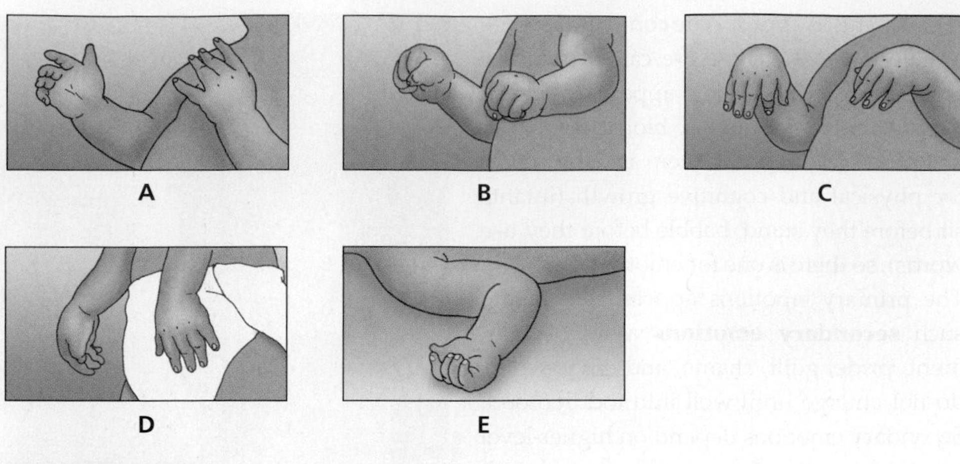

FIGURE 6.1

Identification of Infants' Behavior and Emotional States

See if you can match which hand position goes with each of the following states: transition to sleep, distress, sleep, alertness, and passive waking. Answers appear at the bottom of page 156.

Source: Papoušek, H., & Papoušek, M. (1978). Interdisciplinary parallels in studies of early human behavior: From physical to cognitive needs, from attachment to dyadic education. *International Journal of Behavioral Development, 1*, 37–49.

emotional states (Papoušek & Papoušek, 1978). See if you can match which hand positions go with which infant states: transition to sleep, distress, sleep, alertness, and passive waking. (Correct answers appear at the bottom of page 156—no peeking!)

Infants become very still when they are interested in an event, turn away from stimuli that evoke fear, show a slumped posture when sad, look intently (often with a double take) at stimuli that surprise them, and try to repeat or duplicate experiences they find joyful.

Emotional expressions can be observed during the newborn period, often in response to survival-related experiences, like pain or hunger. We already discussed neonates' emotional reactions to sour, sweet, and bitter tastes (see Chapter 4). Newborns clearly respond to a sweet taste with what adults interpret as positive facial expressions, and to other tastes with various negative expressions of disgust as if wanting to eliminate the noxious substance.

Expressions of fear and anger have been observed as early as 3 to 4 months (Lemerise & Dodge, 2000). For example, if an object looms in front of a 3-month-old, the baby will show fear. After 6 months, infants also begin to show fearful reactions to visual cliffs (see Chapter 4), approaching strangers, and sudden or unusual events. As infants grow, anger becomes increasingly typical in response to unpleasant or restricting events, like being buckled into a car seat. When 2-month-olds get a painful inoculation, they show distress; by 2 years, children get downright angry. Put a wanted toy in arm's reach and stop an infant from playing with it by restraining the infant's arms, and you'll see anger; have a noisy and unpredictable remote-controlled spider approach a child, and you'll see fear. Differences among children in the ways they behave are often accompanied by differences in emotional expressions, indicating that actions and emotions are coordinated: Children who withdraw from fear-inducing stimuli and look to their mothers more also show more intense facial expressions of fear; children who resist the arm restraint more, and work harder to distract themselves by focusing on another object, show greater intensity of anger.

Sadness has been observed in infants as young as 2½ months of age (Izard et al., 1995). When a person initially plays with their 3-month-old and then suddenly becomes unresponsive, the baby is likely to show signs of withdrawal, wariness, and sadness in both facial expression and posture (Bornstein, Arterberry, & Mash, 2005; Cohn & Tronick, 1983).

Although all infants show signs of sadness from time to time, some infants are sadder than others. Infants of depressed mothers are at particular risk. These infants show depressed social behavior not only when interacting with their mothers (acting withdrawn, immobile, and nonresponsive), but also when interacting with a stranger who knows nothing about the baby or his family. Infants of depressed mothers might have acquired their negative emotions in several ways: through shared genes, through reduced opportunities for positive social interaction at home, through imitation of the mother's behavior, or due to effects of the mother's depression on the baby (e.g., the baby's sense of helplessness that may have been learned through interacting with an unresponsive mother).

Researchers have often focused on negative emotions, such as fear, anger, or sadness, but obviously, not all of an infant's emotional life is gloom and doom. Young infants often express positive emotions (Lewis, 2000). Social interaction, such as the sound of a high-pitched human voice or the appearance of a nodding face, can elicit smiles in the first month of life. Clear expressions of joy have been observed by 2½ months, when infants are engaged in social play with their mothers and fathers; by 3 to 4 months, infants outright laugh, especially during social interaction.

As children grow older, they become capable of a broader range of emotional expressions and are responsive to a growing variety of conditions. Cognitive development contributes to emotional growth by enabling infants to evaluate situations in more sophisticated ways. Experiences that may not have elicited certain emotions earlier may now bring them out, because the child is processing more information at a higher level—playing peek-a-boo won't do much for a 1-month-old. Between 6 and 12 months, when the child acquires object permanence (see Chapter 5), this game elicits gales of laughter. Cognitive development also affects negative emotions. Toward the end of the first year, for example, an infant's reactions to a stranger entail not just an evaluation of the adult's unfamiliarity, but also of the context (mother's presence or absence), the setting (a comfortable and familiar home environment or an unfamiliar laboratory), and the stranger's appearance (male or female, child or adult) and behavior (approaching rapidly or slowly, looming high overhead or looking at eye level).

Children's social experiences play a significant role in shaping their emotional expressions (Saarni, 2000). Young adults report that their styles of emotional expression and communication skills are attributable to the emotional expressiveness of their families (Halberstadt, 1986; Halberstadt & Eaton, 2003). Typically, mothers change their facial expressions an average of seven to nine times a minute, and roughly 25 percent of the time, mothers respond to their infants' emotional expressions by imitating or responding to positive expressions and ignoring their negative expressions. This kind of contingent emotional responding reinforces the expression of positive emotions and mutes the expression of negative emotions. Thus, mothers who smile more have young infants who smile more (Kuchuk, Vibbert, & Bornstein, 1986). This result suggests that mothers may socialize their infants' expressive styles from the early months of life. Of course, it is also possible that these familial similarities in expressiveness reflect, for example, happy infants making their mothers happy or shared mother-infant genes.

As children become self-aware, a variety of self-conscious secondary emotions such as embarrassment, shame, and, later, guilt and pride appear (Lewis, 2000; Lewis et al., 1989). Infants who recognize themselves (e.g., when looking in a mirror, they will touch themselves as opposed to reaching out for the "person" in the mirror) also look embarrassed when, for example, they are effusively praised by an adult: They smile and look away and cover their faces with their hands. Children who do not recognize themselves do not exhibit these self-aware reactions to adult praise.

In summary, newborns and young infants express a variety of emotions that are related to specific eliciting conditions. With growth across different developmental domains, children's emotional repertoires continue to broaden, they become responsive to a greater range of stimuli and situations, and more complex emotions emerge. Emotional development includes not only these internal changes in responsiveness, but also children's responses to the emotional expressions of others, our next topic.

The Development of Sensitivity to Emotional Signals

Emotional development involves interpreting as well as sending emotional signals. Recognizing different facial expressions is not the same as understanding their meaning, which requires important interpretive as well as perceptual skills (Barna & Legerstee, 2005). In other words, just because a baby can tell the difference between a happy face and an angry one (something researchers can determine from habituation experiments), doesn't mean that the infant knows what either expression actually means.

To understand an emotional signal, you first need to be able to detect it. Visual acuity in early infancy is limited, though, making it hard for newborns to distinguish among different facial features and expressive patterns (see Chapter 4). At around 1½ to 2 months of age, infants begin to discriminate among different facial expressions of emotion (Bornstein & Arterberry, 2003) and can even distinguish variations in their intensity (Kuchuk et al., 1986). For example, if you show infants a series of smiles that are graded in intensity from just barely smiling to a broad toothy grin, infants tend to look longer at more intense expressions. This does not necessarily mean that infants understand the emotional meaning of the expression, but they do fuss or protest when their mothers adopt unresponsive "still-faces" (Cohn & Tronick, 1983). Infants seek emotional cues from others and are upset when they don't find them.

Infants respond to adults' emotions by sometimes matching facial expressions they see. Some of infants' earliest responses involve the babies spontaneously imitating another person's emotional expressions (Saarni, Mumme, & Campos, 1998). For example, infants display joy when adults show happiness or interest, and they display negative emotions when adults exhibit anger or fear. As we will explain in Chapter 7, scientists who study brain development have discovered that certain neurons—called **mirror neurons**—are activated both when we do something (like smile) *or* when we see someone else do the same thing (Rizzolatti et al., 1996). These neurons may play a special role in infants' responding to facial expressions and the development of empathy, feeling what others are feeling (Legerstee & Varghese, 2001). Perhaps mirror neuron circuts are involved in failures of appropriate social interaction characteristic of autism (Williams, Whiten, Suddendorf, & Perrett, 2001).

mirror neurons Cells in the brain that are activated both when we do something and when we see someone else do the same thing.

Infants also respond differently to different vocalizations of emotion (a laughing sound versus a crying sound, for instance), and their vocal and facial expressions are coordinated. For example, they recognize that laughing sounds and smiling faces go together—but that laughing sounds and angry faces do not. These newfound abilities imply that infants now comprehend the meaning of emotional expressions more fully.

Starting around 8 to 9 months of age, infants begin to use another person's emotional expressions to guide their own reactions to events, and so social referencing begins. **Social referencing** is the tendency to use another person's emotional expressions to interpret uncertain or ambiguous events (Campos & Stenberg, 1981). Remember the visual cliff in Chapter 4? When mothers beckon an infant across the "deep" side in a happy and playful way, older infants are likely to follow Mom's cues, and crawl across the glass. They will not follow directions, however, if Mom signals fear or fright.

social referencing The tendency to use others' emotional expressions to interpret uncertain or ambiguous events.

Correct answers: D, B, E, A, C.

Similarly, infants would not play with unusual toys when their mothers show or voice disgust as opposed to pleasure. When the same toys are presented a few minutes later, infants still avoided them, even when their mothers are silent and neutral (Hornik, Risenhoover, & Gunnar, 1987). Infants look to fathers as well as mothers for emotional cues (Dickstein & Parke, 1988; Hirshberg & Svejda, 1990), and even refer to previously unfamiliar adults for information (Klinnert et al., 1986).

Once they can be perceived clearly, facial and vocal expressions of emotion have great significance in a child's experience of the world. This is hardly surprising, as emotional expressions are social signals that greatly affect children's well-being. So, we should expect babies to become attuned to these signals from early in life. As they proceed through their second year, children become increasingly good at interpreting the emotions of others, and this skill enhances social competence and sensitivity. Their sensitivity to others' emotions can lead to *prosocial* behavior (e.g., sharing toys). It can also lead to conflict with siblings and other family members. Toddlers are capable of saying or doing things to elicit emotions, thus testing the limits of parental tolerance (Dunn, 2000).

In summary, from birth or shortly thereafter, infants are capable of expressing and, later, interpreting a range of different emotions in a variety of situations. Many primary emotions often appear early in life in survival-related situations. Some links between facial

INTERIM SUMMARY 6.1

Infants' Emotions

There are two sides to emotional behavior.	■ **Emotional expression**—communicating feelings to others through facial expressions, gestures, and vocalizations. ■ **Emotional understanding**—reading the emotional expressions of others.
Development of Emotional Expressions	■ **Primary emotions**—those deeply rooted in human biology (joy, anger, fear, and sadness)—develop early in infants. ■ **Secondary emotions** (embarrassment, pride, guilt, shame, and envy) develop later. ■ As infants develop cognitively, they grow emotionally, evaluating situations in more sophisticated ways, processing information at a higher level, and responding with more complex emotions.
Emotional development involves reading as well as sending emotional signals.	■ Newborns find it hard to distinguish among different facial features and expressive patterns. ■ At 1½–2 months, infants begin to discriminate among different facial expressions of emotion. ■ Infants respond to adults' emotions by matching expressions they see. ■ Infants respond differently to different vocalizations of emotion and coordinate vocal and facial expressions. ■ At around 8–9 months, infants begin to use others' emotional expressions to guide their own reaction to events—**social referencing**.

and vocal expressions and underlying feelings are likely innate; others depend on social experience, nervous system maturation, and a growing emotional repertoire, or all of them. Emotions organize how a child responds to events, and how parents respond to their children, whether they try to manage, pacify, or ignore them. Over the first 2 years of life, changes in a child's emotions—for example, the first smiles or the earliest indications of stranger wariness—are seen as developmental milestones. These emotional reactions are significant also because parents view them as signs of emerging individuality—cues to what the child's behavioral style is like now and will be like in future years. The origins of this individuality can be found in the infant's temperament. (For a summary of this section, see "Interim Summary 6.1: Infants' Emotions.")

INFANT TEMPERAMENT

Emotions change from moment to moment, but temperament is more enduring (Bornstein, 2000). Parents and other caregivers devote considerable energy to identifying, adapting to, and channeling the temperament of their infants, just as they try to interpret, respond to, and manage their infants' emotions. Almost all infants fuss when we change their routine or when unfamiliar people come too close. When fussiness is part of the baby's persistent style, though, we view it as one of the child's characteristics and a part of the child's temperament. Moreover, we don't think of short-term fluctuations in a child's emotional state as telling us about long-term consequences, but we view temperamental attributes as foreshadowing the child's later personality. It is difficult for parents to imagine a perpetually happy baby as growing into anything other than a perpetually happy child, and to a certain degree, they are correct.

Temperament is the biologically based source of individual differences in behavioral functioning. It emerges early in life and appears to be moderately consistent over time. A child's underlying temperamental characteristics tend to show themselves and endure even though overt behaviors may change. Thus, a temperamentally sociable child is likely to display ease and friendliness in different ways at different ages, for example, in smiles and reaching out as an infant; in approaching and exploring other people as a toddler; in animated conversation as a preschooler; and so forth into adolescence and adulthood.

Insights into the biological origins of temperament come from twin studies. Individual differences in temperamental factors such as activity level and sociability are heritable (Goldsmith & Lemery, 2000; Goldsmith et al., 2000). Whereas correlations between identical twins range up to .8, correlations between fraternal twins are .5 or less (remember from our discussion in Chapter 1 that correlations of .5 are considered moderate and .8 are strong). Temperament is based in biology, but it is not fixed or unaffected by experience; it is affected by the interaction between innate predispositions and experience (Rothbart & Bates, 2006). A child who starts out in life cheerful may continue to be so, but if her parents divorce when she is 4, that may dampen her happy outlook. By the same token, a temperamentally fearful child may become less shy and cautious if reared in a comforting environment where parents help the child learn to better manage his timidity. Culture matters as well, although cross-cultural comparisons cannot tell us the extent to which temperament is biologically versus contextually influenced (Gartstein, Kinsht, & Slobodskaya, 2003). Cross-cultural studies have found that, on average, infants of Asian descent are less easily upset, better able to soothe themselves, and less quickly aroused than their Caucasian counterparts (Kagan, 2006). Research on differences between girls and boys illustrates how difficult it is to disentangle the effects of genes and the environment on temperament. Systematic studies have not revealed many strong or consistent gender differences in temperament, although some research suggests that boys have a higher activity level than girls (Eaton & Enns, 1986). It is tempting to view such differences as genetically based (Roisman & Fraley, 2006; Rothbart, 2005). But parents and other caregivers treat male and female infants differently and in ways that are consistent with cultural stereotypes, including beliefs about the higher activity level of boys. Parents are likely to encourage rough-and-tumble play in a boy, but discourage it in a girl, regardless of the two children's individual temperaments.

© Girl Ray/Getty Images

Children differ in their temperaments, and show how they feel quite clearly, as does this little girl clinging to her mother's skirt.

Measuring Infant Temperament

How do scientists measure an infant's temperament? There are two basic ways. We can ask people who know the infant best what he or she is usually like ("How easily does your child get upset?"). Alternatively, we can observe infants ourselves and draw inferences from what we see, either during naturalistic observation (How often did we see the child get upset during play time?) or in situations designed to elicit temperamentally driven responses (How easily was the child upset when we deliberately tried to frustrate him?). Each approach has its pros and cons (Bornstein, 2008).

Parents are likely to provide highly insightful reports of their child's temperamental attributes based on their long-term and intimate experience with the child. However, parents' reports may be biased by their subjective views, their own personality, unique experiences, and other factors. A highly negative mother, for instance, or one who is under a lot of stress, may describe her child in more negative terms than would the more cheerful or stress-free mother of a temperamentally similar baby.

Observations by researchers unacquainted with children may provide less biased accounts, but they inevitably involve limited sampling (that is, an observer can only watch an infant for a given amount of time, whereas a mother is with the infant daily, often for long periods of time); observer effects (being with a stranger can change the infant's behavior); context effects (as in the difference between laboratory and home observations); and other potential biases (such as an observer's preconceptions about gender). For instance, the same behavior that is perceived as angry when viewed in a boy may be perceived as fearful when viewed in a girl. Generally speaking, the more information we can gather about an infant's temperament (different reporters, different situations, different contexts), the more certain we can be about it. So, researchers recognize the strengths and limitations of each method and try to combine methods when they study children's temperament (Bornstein, Gaughran, & Segui, 1991).

Approaches to Characterizing Infant Temperament

Most approaches to characterizing temperament have focused on identifying overarching dimensions of behavior, such as how active, how easily aroused, or how sociable an infant is. Many different formulations have been offered over the years, but two particular characterizations that have received considerable attention are **positive affectivity** (smiling, laughing, soothability, or attentiveness) and **negative affectivity** (fear or distress in response to restrictions or high levels of stimulation) (Putnam, Sanson, & Rothbart, 2002; Rothbart & Bates, 2006).

Two types of negatively affective children tend to raise the anxiety levels of parents, caregivers, and teachers the most. They are **inhibited children** (who are characteristically shy, fearful, and timid) and **difficult children** (who are easily irritated and hard to soothe). Because these types of children can pose significant challenges to parents, researchers have spent a lot of time studying them.

positive affectivity A dimension of temperament that reflects the extent to which a person feels enthusiastic and alert (e.g., cheerful, outgoing, etc.).

negative affectivity A dimension of temperament that reflects the extent to which a person feels distressed (sad, angry).

inhibited children Children who are characteristically shy, fearful, and timid.

difficult children Children who are easily irritated and hard to soothe.

The Behaviorally Inhibited Child Inhibited children are fearful, wary, and shy in situations where uninhibited children are generally outgoing (Schwartz et al., 2003). Emily, the participant in a large ongoing study of temperament, is an example (Fox et al., 2001). At 4 months, she showed high levels of motor activity and distress in response to sounds, smells, and visual images. At 14 and 21 months, she reacted fearfully to novel stimuli. By 4½ years, she showed little spontaneity and sociability with adults. By 7 years, Emily suffered symptoms of anxiety. Inhibition tends to be a stable characteristic, but it is not immutable. It can be changed through concerted efforts by parents (Kagan, 2006).

The Difficult Child Temperamental difficultness, irritability, and negativity also remain stable during the first few years of life (Rothbart & Bates, 2006). The majority (70%) of difficult infants go on to develop behavior problems in later childhood (although some 30% do not), whereas only 18 percent of "easy" infants do (Thomas, Chess, & Birch, 1970). Temperament is important in emotions and behaviors at later ages, in part because of the ways in which a child's temperament affects his or her parents' behavior. Steve is a difficult child; he reacts negatively to changes in the environment, is easily aroused, and sleeps very little. His irritability and distress often cause his parents to withdraw from him, to get angry, and to try coercive discipline techniques such as punishment (Bates, Pettit, & Dodge, 1995; van den Boom, 1991). As with inhibited children, parents can make a difference in whether a difficult temperament leads to problems later in development. A temperamentally difficult child whose parents anticipate and help their child cope with stress and/or minimize the sorts of situations that distress the child is less likely to develop problems than is a temperamentally difficult child whose parents are less sensitive and adaptive to the child's needs.

The Easy and Happy Child By identifying two kinds of unhappy temperaments, we don't mean to neglect the easy and happy child. Most babies have easy temperaments and are usually in good moods. They adjust easily and quickly to new situations and changes in routine. They usually eat on a regular schedule, and if they get hungry or experience some other form of discomfort, they usually react mildly. When babies with easy temperaments do get fussy, they are usually able to find ways to soothe or calm themselves. Where defiance and aggression in children contribute to later peer rejection, school problems, and other adjustment difficulties, and anxiety and inhibition in infancy are associated with poor peer relationships and loneliness and depression, positive emotionality and sociability in infancy are predictive of peer acceptance, school achievement, and psychological well-being (Dodge, Coie, & Lynam, 2006; Rubin, Burgess, & Coplan, 2002).

More generally, *prosocial* development, helping and sharing, increases from early toddlerhood to the early preschool years (Eisenberg, Fabes, & Spinrad, 2006), likely as a consequence of growing abilities at understanding how others think and feel. This facilitates more mature peer interactions. Over the first 3 years of life, coordinated activities between toddlers move from sporadic and coincidental to skilled and cooperative (Brownell, Ramani, & Zerwas, 2006).

Does Temperament Matter?

A baby's enduring temperament can influence his or her cognitive and personality development. For example, temperamentally sociable 6-month-olds do better in standardized tests than do temperamentally difficult infants (Wachs & Gandour, 1983). Furthermore, a difficult temperament in 12-month-olds interferes with infants' motivation to master structured laboratory tasks (Wachs, 1987). And shyness in 2-year-olds has been shown to inhibit social cognition, including role taking and self-recognition (Pipp-Siegel et al., 1997).

What accounts for these influences? On the one hand, certain temperamental attributes may promote the child's cognitive performance. Infants who are positive and persistent are likely to approach cognitive tasks more constructively than infants with more negative or distractible dispositions. On the other hand, these temperamental features may facilitate cognitive functioning both directly and indirectly, by evoking different responses from others. Parents and other caregivers may interact more positively with children who have sociable temperaments than with those who do not, enhancing intellectual and social development of these children. Alternatively, children with positive characteristics may receive better scores on cognitive tests because they respond better to strange examiners, adapt better to unfamiliar testing procedures, or are perceived more positively by testers.

Child temperament provides a foundation for adult personality. One longitudinal-epidemiological investigation from New Zealand, the Dunedin Study, has continuously observed 1,000 children born in 1972 to 1973. At age 3, children exhibited temperament types that, 23 years later, when they were reexamined, predicted facets of their adult personalities (Caspi, 2000; Caspi, Harrington, Milne, Amell, Theodore, & Moffitt, 2003). The Dunedin longitudinal data provide the longest and most robust confirmation that children's early emerging behavioral styles foretell their characteristic behaviors, thoughts, and feelings as young adults. These findings confirm that the foundations of personality are in place in the early years of life.

In infancy, socializing influences are only beginning, and thus the genetic and biological bases for temperamental individuality are most apparent. To the extent that we can see the person-to-be in the baby, we see the personality-to-be in the baby's temperament. Of course, temperament does not fix personality immutably, nor is temperament the only influence on personality development. Other factors play roles, including the way a child is socialized and the experiences the child has within and outside the family. For example, parental education appears to be influential in the child's developing social behaviors (Putnam et al., 2002; see Figure 6.2). Nevertheless, the biologically based temperament with which the infant enters the world exerts a significant and enduring influence over the child's emotional and social development. An inhibited child is not necessarily destined to develop a full-blown anxiety disorder as a teenager but is very unlikely to become a gregarious extravert. By the same token, an infant who comes into the world with a strong inclination toward cheerfulness is not inoculated against feeling sad later in life, but the odds are much greater that a highly positive infant will grow into an optimistic and happy adult than into a pessimistic and perpetually cranky one.

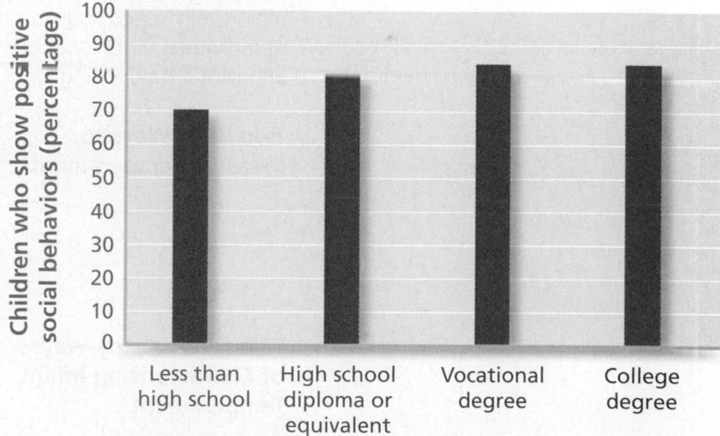

FIGURE 6.2

Parental Education Level and Children's Social Behaviors

Parenting plays a role in shaping temperament. More children of parents with a high school diploma or higher show positive prosocial behaviors when they start kindergarten compared with children whose parents had not completed high school.

Source: From *Early Child Development in Social Context: A Chartbook of the Commonwealth Fund,* September 2004. Reprinted by permission of the Commonwealth Fund.

Context Matters

Temperament is best thought of as a tendency or predisposition toward a certain personality, rather than a fixed guarantee. This is because the link between temperament and later personality is also influenced by the context in which the child develops. Temperamental inhibition or difficulty in infancy need not lead to parenting failures and child maladjustment. For example, mothers who restrict their difficult infants, but do not engage in physical discipline, have more positive results (Bates et al., 1998). That is, consistent and firm parental control, without physical coercion, is an adaptive parental response to temperamental difficulty and may foster the child's ability to self-regulate and develop internalized standards of conduct (Rothbart, Posner, & Kieras, 2006). In contrast, when parents respond to a difficult infant with hostility and anger, the infant is placed at even greater risk for later maladjustment than he is by his difficult temperament alone (Belsky, Hsieh, & Crnic, 1998).

goodness of fit A concept that refers to a match of the child's temperament and the demands of the environment.

These findings are consistent with the concept of **goodness of fit** (Chess & Thomas, 1996; Lerner, Theokas, & Bobek, 2005). Whether a child's long-term adjustment is favorable or unfavorable depends on the interaction between the child's temperament and the demands of the environment. Infant characteristics that some adults find difficult may not be difficult for others. Thus, "difficultness" is not only in the infant but also in the perceptions of the caregiver and in the situation. A child with a low activity level and poor adaptability fits well in a home or school setting that makes few demands. But such an environment is a poor fit for a highly active, distractible child. A temperamentally difficult child will not inevitably experience later problems if, say, parents understand and tolerate the child's behavioral style and can provide activities into which the child's characteristics can be channeled and valued. Conversely, even a temperamentally easy child will experience problems if parents impose excessive demands or ignore reasonable needs. As a consequence, the sensitivity and adaptability of parents to their child's temperament is an important predictor of long-term child adjustment.

In sum, a child's individual characteristics interact with environmental demands to shape and guide temperament. Contrary to views that easy temperaments lead to optimal development, and difficult or inhibited temperaments invariably predict later behavioral problems, it appears that the consequences of a particular temperamental profile for a child depend in part on the demands of the environments in which

INTERIM SUMMARY 6.2

Infant Temperament

Temperament is the biologically based source of individual differences in behavioral functioning.	■ A child's underlying temperamental characteristics endure even though the specifics may change. ■ Temperament is based in biology but is influenced by the environment and experience.
Two Basic Ways to Measure Temperament	1. Ask people who know the infant best what he or she is like. 2. Observe infants and draw inferences from what is seen, either in naturalistic observations or in situations designed to elicit temperamentally driven responses.
Two Noteworthy Ways of Characterizing Infant Temperament	1. **Positive affectivity**—when the infant characteristically smiles and laughs 2. **Negative affectivity**—when the infant typically displays fears or is easily distressed in response to restrictions or high levels of stimulation. ■ **Inhibited** children (characteristically slow, fearful, and timid) and **difficult** children (easily irritated and hard to soothe) are high in negative affectivity.
The consequences of a particular temperamental profile for a child depend on:	■ The demands of the environment in which the child is living. ■ The sensitivity and adaptability of the child's social partners within those settings. ■ How temperament guides the child's choice of activities and interpretation of experiences.

the child is living, including his or her culture, the sensitivity and adaptability of the child's social partners within those settings, and how temperament guides the child's choice of activities and his interpretations of experiences.

Infants shape their interactions with people through their emotions and through their temperament. At the same time, caregivers accommodate, interpret, and channel as well as shape the child's socioemotional characteristics. When the fit is good between the two, development is optimized. (For a summary of this section, see "Interim Summary 6.2: Infant Temperament.")

ATTACHMENT AND INFANT SOCIAL DEVELOPMENT

Developing fulfilling and dependable relationships with other people (mainly parents) is one of the most important aspects of social development in infancy. The infant's first social relationships, commonly referred to as attachments, appear to be universal (van IJzendoorn et al., 2006). There are differences in the types of attachment infants form with their parents, however, and these differences affect children's development. The quality of infant-parent attachments is influenced both by the harmony of infant-parent interaction and the infant's temperament.

An early explanation of the process of attachment was provided by John Bowlby, a psychoanalyst who drew on animal studies to understand interpersonal communication and the formation of social bonds. Bowlby (1969) assumed that how infants and parents behave toward one another is best considered in the context of the environment in which our species evolved. In that **environment of evolutionary adaptedness**, the survival of infants depended on their ability to remain close to protective adults to obtain nourishment, comfort, and security. Unlike the young of many other species, however, human infants cannot move closer or follow adults for several months after birth; they are even incapable of clinging to adults to stay in contact. (Human infants are not strong enough, and human parents are not hairy enough.) Instead, human infants rely on different kinds of *signals* to attract adults. For these signals to be effective, adults must be predisposed to respond to them. The best example of such a signal is the infant cry, which very effectively draws adults to approach, pick up, and soothe the infant (Barr et al., 2000; Bornstein et al., 1992). As they grow older, infants develop other means of achieving closeness or contact, including independent locomotion, and they gradually come to focus on people with whom they are most familiar.

environment of evolutionary adaptedness The context in which our species evolved.

Phases of Social Development

Bowlby (1969) described four main phases in the development of infant-parent attachments.

Phase 1: Indiscriminate Social Responsiveness (1 to 2 Months of Age) The baby develops a repertoire of signals like the *cry*. The common characteristic of these behaviors is that they all help to provide comfort and security by bringing a protective, caregiving adult close to the baby. Another potent attachment behavior in the baby's repertoire is *smiling*. Like crying, smiling is a signal that powerfully affects adult behavior. Cries encourage adults to approach the baby; smiles are effective because they encourage adults to stay near the baby.

From birth, babies are capable of affecting the social environment around them. However, in this early phase of

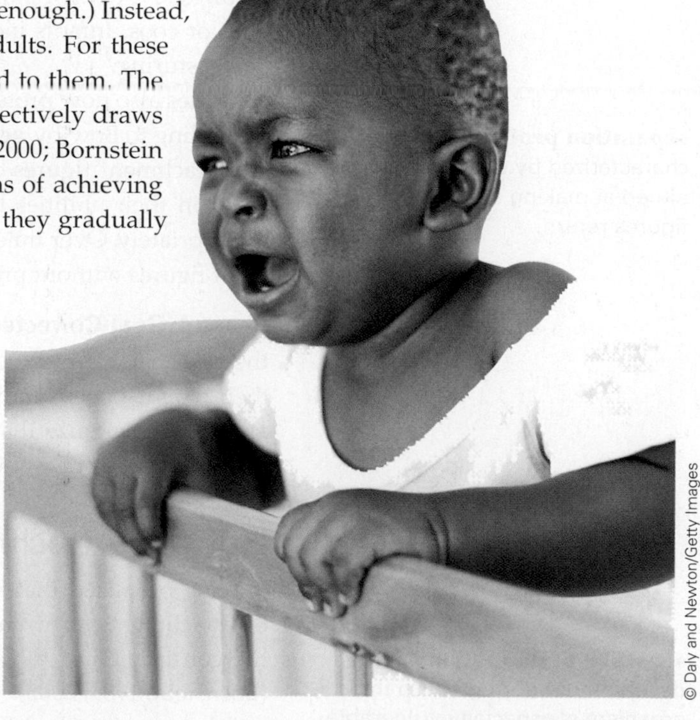
© Daly and Newton/Getty Images

Infants normally do not hide their emotions, but rather display them openly as an important means of communication, as this baby is doing. It's up to caregivers to interpret the infant's communications.

attachment development babies are indiscriminate in the use of proximity-promoting signals: They appear to be satisfied by whoever responds to their cries, smiles, or other signals. Adults, of course, respond selectively depending on their relatedness and responsibility. Because the caregivers who are close by can be felt, smelled, heard, and seen when infants are alert, babies may come to learn a great deal about them, and rapidly learn to associate their presence with alertness and the relief of distress (Thompson & Goodvin, 2005).

Phase 2: Discriminating Sociability (2 to 7 Months of Age)

Bowlby (1969) suggested that the ability to recognize specific people marked the transition to the second phase of attachment development. (Studies we described in Chapter 4 show that infants are able to recognize their own mothers' voice and smell within the first 2 weeks of life, however—much earlier than Bowlby believed.) Presumably because significant others (such as parents) have been associated with pleasurable experiences (such as feeding, cuddling, rocking, and play) and with the relief of distress, babies come to prefer to interact with familiar people. Initially, these preferences manifest themselves in fairly subtle ways: Certain people will be able to soothe the baby more easily and elicit smiles and coos more readily. They are special to the baby. Prior to this phase, the baby appeared to enjoy interacting with anyone without apparent preference.

During this second phase of attachment development, babies are also more coordinated behaviorally than they were earlier. Their arousal level is less variable, and they now spend larger proportions of their time in alert states. As a result, distress is less frequent, and interactions with adults more often involve play.

Phase 3: Attachments (7 to 24 Months of Age) The beginning of Phase 3 marks the time at which the first infant-adult attachments are thought to form. By 6 or 7 months of age, infants clearly understand and respect rules of reciprocity in their interactions and enjoy their newly acquired ability to creep around and to take responsibility for getting close to their parents, instead of waiting for others to come in response to their cries or coos. Infants increasingly initiate interaction using directed social behaviors like gesturing.

Babies also now protest (by crying) when left by people to whom they are attached. According to Bowlby, **separation protest** should be viewed as a signal aimed at making attachment figures come back to the baby. Infants become increasingly sophisticated in their abilities to behave intentionally, communicate verbally, and respond appropriately. Over time, infants can begin to tolerate a growing distance from attachment figures without protesting.

separation protest A signal, characterized by crying, that is aimed at making attachment figures return.

Phase 4: Goal-Corrected Partnerships (Year 3 Onward) According to Bowlby (1969), the next major transition occurs at the beginning of the third year, when children take their parents' needs into account when interacting with them. For example, they now appear to recognize that parents sometimes must attend to other activities, and that their own needs or wants must wait.

How Do Attachments Form?

Bowlby proposed that humans have a predisposition to form attachments. But how do attachments form, and to whom do infants become attached? According to Bowlby, the consistency of the adults' presence and availability during a **sensitive period** (Bornstein, 1989, 2003)—the first six postnatal months—determines to whom the baby will become attached. If there is no consistent caregiver over this period (as might occur in institutions like hospitals), the baby would not form attachments. Bowlby and his student Mary Ainsworth believed that most babies develop a hierarchy of attachment figures and that their primary caregivers—usually their mothers, but fathers as

sensitive period A time in development during which the organism is especially vulnerable to experience.

well, so long as they engage in caregiving—become primary attachment figures before any other relationships are formed. Once infants have this foundation, Bowlby and Ainsworth argued, infants may (and often do) form relationships with others, such as daycare providers and older siblings (van den Boom, 2001).

Obviously, there must be a minimal amount that these other individuals regularly interact with infants for attachments to form; we do not know what this minimum is, or how it varies across individual children. The amount of time adults spend with infants is not the only factor that determines whether infant-adult attachments will form: The *quality* of adult-infant interaction is also important. Bowlby and Ainsworth believed that an infant becomes attached to those people who have been associated over time with consistent, predictable, and appropriate responses to the baby's signals as well as to his or her needs (Ainsworth et al., 1978; Cummings & Cummings, 2002; Thompson, 2006; Thompson & Goodvin, 2005). With a vast network of cross-cultural colleagues, Rohner (2004) determined that children all around the globe understand the meaning of the simple statement "My mother makes me feel wanted and needed." West Bengali children know unmistakably that their mothers have expressed a very special feeling for them when they peel an orange and remove the seeds before giving it to them. Other behaviors signify maternal love and approval in other societies.

Mothers typically take a central role in attachment (Cummings & Cummings, 2002), but a number of individuals (other than mothers) directly influence the child (Parke, 2002). Studies of infant-mother and infant-father attachments indicate that infants show no systematic preference for either parent on attachment behavior measures (their propensity to stay near, approach, touch, cry to, and ask to be held by specific adults), although babies show preferences for parents over relatively unfamiliar adults. When babies are distressed, they increase displays of attachment behavior and organize their behavior around the parent who is present. When both parents are present, however, distressed infants typically turn to their mothers first.

Although it may be adaptive to be cautious when first encountering strange persons, it is not adaptive for human infants to refuse all interaction with nonattachment figures. People other than parents have a profound impact on children's psychosocial development, and most interactions involve people to whom children are not attached. From an evolutionary standpoint, it is not surprising that **stranger wariness**, the hesitancy that infants show at around 10 months when they are approached by unfamiliar people, diminishes rapidly over time, and infants eventually enter into friendly interactions with nonattachment figures (Bornstein et al., 1997; Bornstein et al., 2000). In fact, young children begin to organize attachment patterns to new caregivers (like foster parents) within days of placement (Stovall & Dozier, 2000).

stranger wariness The hesitancy that infants show at around 10 months when they are approached by unfamiliar people.

How Is Infant Attachment Measured?

The most popular technique for studying attachment is the so-called **Strange Situation** developed by Ainsworth and her colleagues. It can be used when infants are old enough to have formed attachments and are mobile, yet are not so old that brief separations and encounters with strangers are no longer noteworthy. As a result, the Strange Situation is appropriate for infants ranging in age from about 10 to 24 months. The procedure has seven episodes (see Table 6.1) designed to expose infants to increasing amounts of mild stress and observe their attachment behaviors around their parents when distressed. Stress is stimulated by an unfamiliar environment, the proximity of an unfamiliar adult, and two brief separations from the parent.

Strange Situation An experimental paradigm that reveals security of attachment.

The Strange Situation begins with the parent and infant alone in a room (episode 1). Researchers are generally present in an adjacent room, videorecording what happens through a one-way glass. The stranger's entrance (episode 2) usually leads infants to inhibit exploration and draw a little closer to the parent, at least temporarily. The parent's departure (episode 3) usually leads infants to attempt to bring them back by

TABLE 6.1 The Strange Situation

EPISODE	PERSONS PRESENT	CHANGE
1	Parent, infant	Parent and infant enter room
2	Parent, infant, stranger	Unfamiliar adult enters
3	Infant, stranger	Parent leaves
4	Parent, infant	Parent returns, stranger leaves
5	Infant	Parent leaves
6	Infant, stranger	Stranger returns
7	Parent, infant	Parent returns, stranger leaves

crying or searching and to reduced exploration. Following the parent's return (episode 4), infants typically seek to reengage in interaction and, if distressed, may wish to be cuddled and comforted. The same responses should occur, with somewhat greater intensity, following the second separation and reunion (episodes 5 and 7). In fact, this is precisely how about 65 percent of the infants studied in the United States behave in the Strange Situation (Thompson, 2006; Thompson & Goodvin, 2005). These infants (designated *type B*) are regarded as *securely attached.*

However, some infants do not view their parents as secure bases from which to explore an unfamiliar environment. Although they are distressed by their parents' absence, they behave ambivalently on reunion, seeking contact and interaction but angrily rejecting it when it is offered. These infants are conventionally labeled *insecure-resistant* or *insecure-ambivalent* (*type C*). They typically account for about 10 to 15 percent of the infants in U.S. American research samples (Thompson, 2006; Thompson & Goodvin, 2005).

A third group of infants seems little concerned by their parents' absence. Instead of greeting their parents on reunion, they actively avoid interaction and ignore their parents' overtures. These infants are said to exhibit *insecure-avoidant* attachments (*type A*); they typically constitute about 20 percent of the infants in U.S. samples (Thompson, 2006; Thompson & Goodvin, 2005).

A very small fourth group of infants has also been described; their behavior is *disoriented* and/or *disorganized* (*type D*; Brisch, 2002; Main & Solomon, 1990). These infants manifest incomplete or undirected movements, and appear confused or apprehensive about approaching their parents.

Are different types of infants consistent in their behavior? When researchers bring the same infant to the laboratory to participate in the Strange Situation on different occasions, they typically find consistency. According to one researcher, 48 out of 50 infants—96 percent—obtained the same classification on two separate occasions (Waters, 1978). Another study reported 84 percent stability between 12-month assessments in the Strange Situation and 6-year assessments using an observational procedure appropriate for older children (Main & Cassidy, 1988).

In some cases, attachment classifications on different occasions are not related to one another, but are related in understandable ways to changes in children's experiences. For example, a study of attachment stability in an economically disadvantaged sample of children found that many infants changed from one classification to another between 12 and 18 months of age, but the changes were systematic. That is, when the families had experienced considerable social stress during the 6-month period, secure (type B) attachments often changed to insecure-avoidant (type A) or insecure-ambivalent (type C). When families experienced a low degree of stress, however, type A or C attachments did not necessarily become secure (type B; Vaughn et al., 1979). Weinfield et al. (2000)

reported that adolescents who showed instability in their attachment security were those who had experienced inconsistency over time in the quality of maternal availability or sensitivity (e.g., physical and verbal abuse, neglect, unavailability).

Another experience that can affect attachment security is the birth of a second child, which predicts a decrease in attachment security among firstborn children. This decrease is not linked to changes in the mothers' sensitivity with their first-borns, psychiatric symptoms, or reports of marital harmony. Instead, the decrease in firstborn attachment security seems to reflect changes in children's perceptions of their relationships with their mothers in response to the introduction of new family members, who may be perceived as rivals for their parents' attention. These findings raise the question of the role of parent-infant interactions in the development of attachment security; at the very least, they suggest that the early experiences an infant has with a parent do not inoculate the child with an unchanging level of security or insecurity. The type of attachment between infants and parents can change: to become better or worse.

What happens when there is no attachment figure for infants, or attachment relationships are atypical? The poor prognosis of this circumstance has long been observed in certain institutions, like orphanages (Spitz, 1945; Tizard & Hodges, 1978; Tizard & Rees, 1975). Several groups have studied attachment of orphans in Romanian institutions (O'Connor, Rutter, & the English and Romanian Adoptees Study Team, 2000; Zeanah, Smyke, Koga, & Carlson, 2005). These children are reported to exhibit serious disturbances of attachment in later childhood. Developmentalists have also noted that early social deprivation contributes to significant problems in coping with stress later in childhood, for example (Fries, Shirtcliff, & Pollak, 2008).

Worse still in its effects on attachment is outright abuse or neglect in the early years. Adults who report having been exposed to four or more kinds of adverse childhood experiences—psychological, physical, or sexual abuse; violence against the mother; or living with household members who were substance abusers, mentally ill or suicidal, or ever imprisoned—compared to those who had experienced none of these, had a 4- to 12-fold increase in health risks such as alcoholism, drug abuse, depression, and suicide attempts; a 2- to 4-fold increase in smoking and poor self-rated health, and a 1.4- to 1.6-fold increase in physical inactivity and severe obesity (Felitti, Anda, Nordenberg, Williamson, Spitz, Edwards, Koss, & Marks, 1998). Resilience in the face of adversity depends on having experienced a supportive caregiving relationship at some (preferably early) point in development (Werner, 1971).

Parent-Child Interaction and Attachment Security

From repeated experiences in face-to-face play and distress-relief by caregivers, the child learns several important lessons. The first lesson is **reciprocity**: Children learn that, in social interaction, partners take turns acting and reacting to the other's behavior. Two- to 3-month-olds show they are learning this lesson because they respond with boredom, distress, or withdrawal when their mothers adopt unresponsive faces instead of behaving in their typical interactive fashion (Moore, Cohn, & Campbell, 2001). They are disconcerted over adults' failure to follow the rules of interaction, indicating they understand these rules, find synchronized and reciprocal interactions more enjoyable, and expect their partners to follow the same rules. A second lesson is **effectance**. The child learns that his or her behavior can affect the behavior of others in a consistent and predictable fashion. And the third lesson is **trust**: The child learns that the caregiver can be counted on to respond when signaled.

reciprocity A lesson in social interaction in which partners take turns acting and reacting to the other's behavior.

effectance A lesson in social interaction that involves learning that one's behavior can affect the behavior of others in a consistent and predictable fashion.

trust A lesson in social interaction that involves learning that another person can be counted on to respond when signaled.

Achieving reciprocity, effectance, and trust are major steps in the process of becoming social. As infants realize that their cries, smiles, and coos elicit predictable responses from others, they develop a coherent view of the social world and of themselves as individuals who can affect others. The degree to which babies feel confident in their predictions regarding the behavior of others—that is, the degree to which they trust or have faith in the reliability of specific people—in turn influences the security of their attachment relationships.

Individual differences in the amount of trust or perceived effectance each infant develops depend in part on individual differences in the sensitivity and responsiveness of the adults with whom the baby interacts. As we noted in Chapter 1, Sigmund Freud (1949) was by far the most prominent advocate of the importance of infancy in this regard, suggesting that the ways babies are treated establish lifelong orientations and personality traits. Erik Erikson, one of Freud's students, likewise believed that early experience is extremely influential, as you also read in that chapter. From early experiences, he suggested, children develop a degree of basic trust or mistrust in their caregiver. He also believed that the harmoniousness of early interactions has implications for the way the infant negotiates the next stage of development, in which the key issue is establishing autonomy (independence) or shame.

© Laura Dwight

Face-to-face and eye-to-eye contact are plain ways of connecting, as this dad and his 3-month-old baby girl show.

The Secure Base In the course of interaction with other people, babies have the opportunity to gain social competence and learn social skills. But the development of attachment relationships also facilitates the infant's physical and cognitive development. Interacting with a variety of individuals provides opportunities for infants to learn how to modulate their style of interaction in accordance with each individual's characteristic and unique interpersonal style. Infants also engage in interaction with their physical environment to develop competence and master it.

Infants count on attachment figures to protect them and to be accessible when needed, and so use them as a **secure base** from which to explore and interact with other people. Secure infants more readily explore objects in the environment, for instance. Sensitive parenting—that is, nurturant, attentive, nonrestrictive parental care—and attuned infant-mother interactions are associated with secure (type B) infant behavior in the Strange Situation. This appears to be true in cultures outside the United States as well as in U.S.-based samples (van IJzendoorn, 1997).

secure base The trustworthy place infants count on for protection and accessibility when needed as they explore and interact with other people.

Conversely, the mothers of infants who behave in either insecure-avoidant or insecure-resistant fashions manifest less socially desirable patterns of behavior. Insecure-avoidant attachments are associated with intrusive, overstimulating, rejecting parenting, whereas insecure-resistant attachments are linked to inconsistent, unresponsive parenting (De Wolff & van IJzendoorn, 1997).

People who perceive themselves to be rejected by attachment figures (e.g., by parents in childhood or by intimate partners in adulthood) are usually anxious and insecure, and likely develop distorted mental representations of self, of significant others, and of the world around them (Rohner, 2004). Studies in India and Turkey as well as the United States bear out associations between adult psychological adjustment and their experiences of acceptance and rejection in relationships with intimate adult partners (e.g., spouses and girlfriends/boyfriends) as well as with parents in childhood (Khaleque & Rohner, 2002; Parmar & Rohner, 2008; Varan, Rohner, & Eryuksel, 2008).

Although the antecedents of disorganized attachments are less well established, such attachments are more common among abused and maltreated infants and among infants exposed to other types of pathological caregiving (Azar, 2002; Brisch, 2002). These parental behaviors are frightening or disturbing to infants. Adverse events in early as well as later childhood (such as physical, sexual, or emotional abuse; loss of a parent; or living with a depressed or addicted adult) make for higher lifetime risks of many untoward outcomes (such as disorders of mental health and adult mortality) (Anda, Felitti, & Brenner, 2006; Hammen, 2005). Indeed, one prospective study from age 5 years through to age 21 found that individuals who had been physically abused in the first 5 years of life were at greater risk for being arrested as juveniles for violent, nonviolent, and status offenses; were less likely to have graduated from high school and more likely to have been fired from a job in the past year; were more likely to have become a teen parent and to have been pregnant or impregnated someone in the past year while not married (Lansford et al., 2007).

Children adjust to different types of caregiving, so parenting is regarded as a major source of individual differences in attachment styles, even into adulthood (Fraley & Shaver, 2000; Shaver & Mikulincer, 2002). As conceptualized in the attachment literature, early experiences are stored as relatively stable internal representations of how trustworthy others are, and how worthy one is of support, and these **internal working models** form the basis of relationships during the balance of the lifespan (Main, Kaplan, & Cassidy, 1985). Research on adolescent and adult memories of experiences with parents has revealed that securely attached individuals (low in anxiety) remember their parents as warm, accepting, engaged, and supportive individuals; those high on avoidance recollect their parents as rejecting and distant; and individuals high on anxiety recall their parents as overprotective, intrusive, and controlling (Hazan & Shaver, 1987; Kobak & Sceery, 1988; Levy, Blatt, & Shaver, 1998). Moreover, Swiss and Japanese mothers' behaviors predict their 3- to- 6 year-olds' attachment types (Behrens, Hesse, & Main, 2007; Miljkovitch, Pierrehumbert, Bretherton, & Halfon, 2004).

internal working models Children's thoughts about their caregivers and themselves with respect to their caregivers constitute internal working models of attachment.

In Chapter 5 we raised the issue of multiple risks. The same holds for socioemotional development. For example, a study conducted in Norway found that "double risk," signified by a combination of biological and sociodemographic risk factors when children were 7 months of age, predicted developmental problems at age 4 (Rostad, Nyberg, & Sivberg, 2008).

Attachment Security and Infant Temperament In early face-to-face interactions, the adult assumes major responsibility for keeping the interaction going, but babies are not simply passive partners. Adults respond to baby-initiated behaviors of all sorts and, so, infant temperament is another important influence on the parent-infant relationship. Temperament does not have a direct effect on whether infants are classified as type A, B, or C, but infant temperament has an indirect effect on infant Strange Situation behavior because it likely affects the quality of infant-parent interaction, which, in turn, affects security of attachment. In addition, temperament may affect how infants are influenced by their parents. Distractible babies, for example, may be less affected by their parents' behavior than are attentive babies. In this sense, the security of an infant's attachment is the product of three influences: the infant's temperament, the parent's behavior, and the nature of their interaction with each other.

Attachment Classifications One of the reasons developmentalists have been so interested in infant attachment is that there is cause to believe that the security of the baby's early relationships influences the ways in which he or she relates to others in later periods of development after infancy (van IJzendoorn, 2005). And indeed, infants' attachment classification appears to predict aspects of the child's future behavior. Babies who have developed trust in their attachment figures tend to regard new people they encounter as potentially trustworthy. Babies with secure attachments are more cooperatively playful than insecure infants when interacting with a friendly stranger. The quality of early attachment predicts social relationships with siblings and peers (Furman & Lanthier, 2002; Ladd & Pettit, 2002; Volling, 2003). Secure infants engage in more frequent, more prosocial, and more mature forms of interaction, sharing more and showing a greater capacity to initiate and maintain interactions, for example.Infants with secure attachment histories are more popular and socially competent in their peer groups in elementary school than are their insecurely attached peers (Sroufe, Egeland, Carlson, & Collins, 2005).

Secure infant-mother attachments at 12 or 18 months are also associated with superior problem-solving abilities in a variety of stressful and challenging contexts during the preschool years (Sroufe et al., 2005). Securely attached children persist longer and more enthusiastically in cognitively challenging situations than do insecurely attached children. Secure infants also seem to be more resilient when stressed or challenged and appear more socially competent and independent when they enter preschool. Early parental support is a strong predictor of mental health and freedom from disease well into later life (Shaw, Krause, Chatters, Connell, & Ingersoll-Dayton, 2004). Insecure attachment in infancy, and in particular the disorganized/disoriented classification, predicts antisocial behavior in later childhood (van IJzendoorn & Bakermans-Kranenburg, 2006).

Cross-Cultural Research on Infant Attachment Figure 6.3 shows that most babies in most cultures are secure, but the distribution of infants across the A, B, and C categories in many countries differs from that typically found in U.S. samples (even though

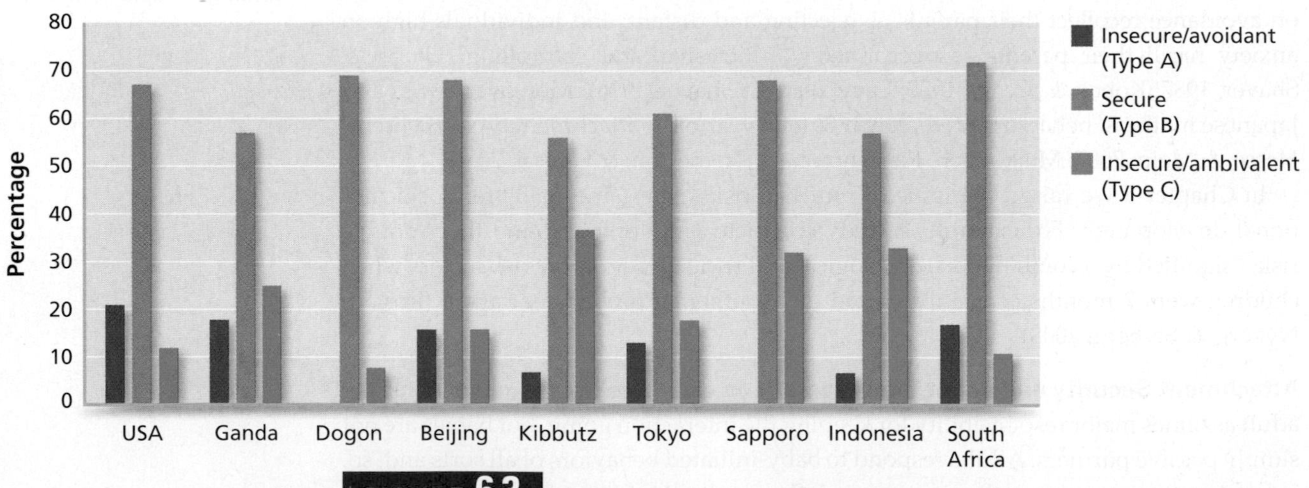

FIGURE 6.3

Attachment Styles Across Cultures

Across many cultures, secure attachments (type B) are the most common; however, in places like Israel (Kibbutz), Japan (Sapporo), and Indonesia, insecure/ambivalent attachments (type C) appear more often than in other places. This is most likely a result of cultural differences in parenting styles.

Source: Van IJzendoorn, M. H. & Sagi-Schwartz, A. (2008). Cross-cultural patterns of attachment: Universal and contextual dimensions. In J. Cassidy & P. R. Shaver (Eds.) *Handbook of attachment: Theory, research and clinical applications* (2nd edition). New York: Guildford Press.

researchers in different countries apply the same coding and classification criteria; True, Pisani, & Oumar, 2001; van IJzendoorn et al., 2006). This could mean that parents in other cultures are more or less sensitive than American parents, but this ethnocentric interpretation seems incorrect. Rather, the results may point to the importance of factors other than the quality of parent-child interactions. For example, proportionately more Japanese, Indonesian, and Israeli babies show high degrees of stress in the Strange Situation, and their reactions may have led to increases in the proportion of infants classified as insecure-ambivalent (type C) by researchers. These infants may appear distressed either because they have much less experience with separations from their mothers than U.S. infants typically have, or because their mothers are much more stressed by the procedures (recall the notion of social referencing, where infants look to others to help them figure out what sense to make of an ambiguous situation). In either case, the Strange Situation would not be psychologically similar for these other babies and U.S. babies. Or, possibly, for infants growing up in these places, encounters with total strangers are more unusual and thus elicit distress. In other words, even though the Strange Situation procedure is *structurally* the same for Japanese, Indonesian, Israeli, and U.S. infants, the *psychological* meaning of the procedure for infants from each culture may differ (Bornstein, 1995).

In summary, infants generally form attachments around the middle of the first year of life to those adults with whom they have had the most consistent and extended interaction. The function of attachment is to ensure that infants retain access to persons on whom they can rely for nurturance and protection. For the same reason that it is important for infants to ensure proximity to protective adults, it is of survival value to avoid encounters with unknown and potentially dangerous people and situations. Infants generally establish significant relationships with both of their parents, even though they tend to have more interaction with their mothers than fathers. Infants also form relationships with siblings, peers, and nonfamilial caregivers. These early relationships with mothers, fathers, brothers, sisters, and others all contribute to the rich social world of the young child. The facts that ratings of Strange Situation behavior are consistent over time and relate to measures of earlier infant-parent interaction and later child achievement and personality suggest that the Strange Situation measures some meaningful aspect of mother-infant attachment and has important implications for understanding and predicting child development. Keep in mind, though, that the relation between Strange Situation behavior in infancy and subsequent child behavior is found only when there is stability in caregiving arrangements and family circumstances, which maintain consistency in the quality of parent-child interaction. (For a summary of this section, see "Interim Summary 6.3: Attachment and Infant Social Development.")

Children often enjoy other children, and the pleasure is a two-way street, as these interacting siblings show.

INTERIM SUMMARY 6.3

Attachment and Infant Social Development

Differences in the types of **attachments** (infants' first social relationships) infants form with their parents affect children's development. John Bowlby, a psychoanalyst, assumed that how infants and parents behave toward one another is best considered in the context of the environment in which our species evolved (**environment of evolutionary adaptedness**). He described four main phases in the development of infant-parent attachment:	■ Phase 1: Indiscriminate social responsiveness (1 to 2 months)—the baby develops a repertoire of signals that help to provide comfort and security (crying) by bringing a protective, caregiving adult close. Babies then associate the presence of adults with alertness and the relief of distress. ■ Phase 2: Discriminating sociability (2 to 7 months)—babies come to prefer to interact with familiar people. ■ Phase 3: Attachments (7 to 24 months)—infants understand the rules of reciprocity in their interactions and increasingly initiate interaction using directed social behaviors and protest when left by people to whom they are attached (**separation protest**). ■ Phase 4: Goal-corrected partnerships (year 3 onward)—children take their parents' needs into account when interacting with them and so their own needs or wants must wait.
How do attachments form?	■ The consistency of the adults' presence and availability during a sensitive period—the first postnatal 6 months—determines the person to whom the baby will become attached, according to Bowlby and Ainsworth. ■ The *quality* of adult-infant interaction is important as babies become attached to people who have been associated over time with consistent, predictable, and appropriate responses to the baby's signals and needs. ■ Mothers play a central role in attachment but other individuals, such as fathers, siblings, peers, and nonfamilial caregivers, directly influence the child.
How is infant attachment measured?	■ The Strange Situation is a procedure with seven episodes that is designed to expose infants to increasing amounts of mild stress and observe how infants organize their attachment behaviors around their parents when distressed. ■ Stress is stimulated by an unfamiliar environment, the entrance of an unfamiliar adult, and two brief separations from the parent. ■ It measures meaningful aspects of mother-infant attachment and has important implications for understanding and predicting child development. ■ Even though the Strange Situation procedure is structurally the same for infants in different cultures, the psychological experiences or meaning for infants from each culture may differ.

(continued)

INTERIM SUMMARY 6.3 (continued)

Attachment and Infant Social Development

Attachment Security	■ Achieving reciprocity, effectance, and trust are steps in the process of becoming social. ■ Infants count on attachment figures to protect them and be accessible when needed and use them as a **secure base** from which to explore and interact with other people. ■ Secure attachments are associated with sensitive and responsive parenting. ■ Insecure-avoidant attachments are associated with intrusive, overstimulating, rejecting parenting. ■ Insecure-resistant attachments are associated with inconsistent, unresponsive parenting.

PARENTAL BEHAVIOR AND INTERACTION WITH INFANTS

Interactions between parents and infants are like an intricate dance, not only in rhythm, but in style. Mother or father does one kind of step and the infant may do the same, or a different step, and it is not always clear who is in the lead. Actually, most parents and infants engage in many kinds of dances. One is *social oriented*, in which their interactions focus exclusively on each other. Contact is an important feature of this dance. Babies need **contact comfort** from adults who love them. In his experiments designed to see whether infants' attraction to their mothers was simply because mothers were a source of food, Harlow (1958) removed infant rhesus monkeys from their mothers and gave them a choice of two substitute models, one constructed of wire and the other of terry cloth (see Figure 6.4). The young animals strongly preferred the cloth model, which they hugged and clutched much of the time. Contact with the material proved crucial.

contact comfort The gratification derived from touch.

Harlow's study helped pave the way for Bowlby's theory of attachment, which emphasized proximity and contact seeking rather than just feeding. It demonstrated that the parenting functions of childbearing and feeding are separate from those of protection and comforting. Furthermore, although the young monkeys thrived *physically* when they were supplied with milk in ordinary baby bottles attached to the front of the models, as the monkeys grew up and were permitted to join other monkeys, their social behavior proved abnormal, even psychotic. They were sometimes hyperaggressive and sometimes autistic, sitting withdrawn while rocking silently back and forth. They also cried a great deal and sucked their own fingers and toes. Simply put, mother's love (or caregiver love), which the monkeys lacked, is essential to normal development.

Within the first year of life, babies and their parents increasingly incorporate the outside world into their interactions (Bornstein, 2006). The *object-oriented* domain of interaction refers to interactions that turn outward from the dyad and a focus on properties, objects, and events in the environment, like playing together with a toy or taking a stroll around the neighborhood. Both social and object interactions have been observed in mothers and infants in many different countries, such as Argentina, France, Israel, Japan, and South Korea (Bornstein, 2006; Bornstein et al., 1991, 1992).

© Nina Leen

FIGURE 6.4

Harlow's Monkeys

The primatologist Harry Harlow demonstrated the importance of contact comfort by showing that infant monkeys preferred terry cloth "mothers" to wire "mothers" even though wire mothers provided milk.

Mothers and Fathers

From the very start, mothers and fathers engage their infants in interactions with different characteristics. Mothers kiss, hug, talk to, smile at, tend, or hold their infants more than fathers do. When video-recorded in face-to-face play with their one-half to 6-month-old infants, for example, fathers were more rambunctious in both physical stimulation and social play, whereas mothers are nurturant, rhythmic, and containing (Barnard & Solchany, 2002; Bornstein, 2002, 2006; Parke, 2002). Indeed, parent gender has a much more powerful influence than child care or employment status: Fathers and mothers tend to behave in their characteristic ways even in families where mothers work and/or fathers assume the major role in child care.

Almost anywhere in the world, mothers are likely to spend more time with infants than do fathers. Despite recent increases in the amount of time fathers spend with their infants, most fathers continue to assume little responsibility for their infants' care and rearing. Fathers typically see themselves as helpers rather than parents with a primary responsibility for caregiving (and most mothers tend to see them that way as well). Both mothers and fathers see breadwinning as the primary responsibility of fathers. However, because most infants become attached to their father as well as their mother, most infants must have enough quality interaction with their fathers to make up for the typically low quantity (Parke, 2002).

All that said, two caring parents are better than one when it comes to rearing an infant. If we ask, other things being equal, how infants who have two (biological or adopted) parents fare relative to infants who have one biological parent and/or one stepparent or no biological parents, the results for many aspects of children's development are clear. Figure 6.5 shows differences in self-control among infants reared in different types of families. As you can see, self-control in young children suffers to the extent that children are

© Polka Dot Images/Jupiterimages

Mothers and fathers play in different ways with infants and young children. Mothers are typically tender, soft, and nurturant, and fathers are typically more physical and vigorous.

reared in atypical families, where presumably the stresses on parents are greater. *Stress*, and not the number or marital status of the parents, is key. Stress on parents can undermine their ability to interact with their infants in ways that promote secure attachment and healthy socioemotional development.

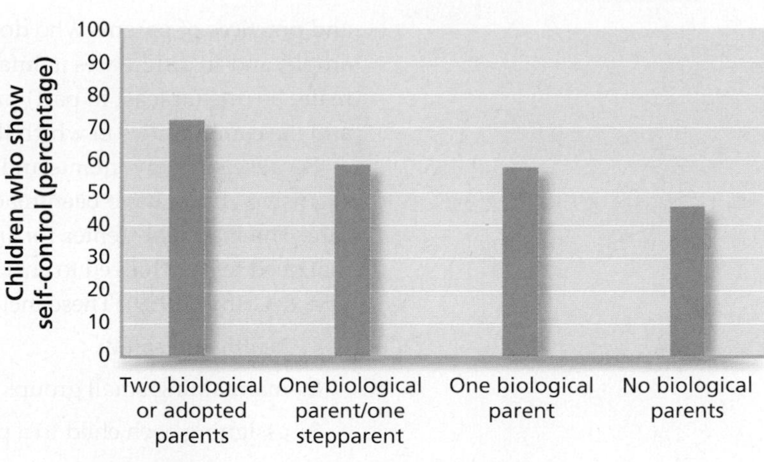

FIGURE 6.5

Family Structure and Children's Self-Control

Children's behavior often varies based on differences in experience, which include family structure. As this graph shows, levels of self-control were highest among children from two-parent (biological or adopted) households and lower among children with one stepparent, one biological parent, or no biological parent (e.g., foster family).

Source: From *Early Child Development in Social Context: A Chartbook of the Commonwealth Fund,* September 2004. Reprinted by permission of the Commonwealth Fund.

Nonparental Care

The majority of infants in the United States are now cared for by someone other than a parent at least some of the time (Clarke-Stewart & Allhusen, 2002; Honig, 2002). This situation may have a variety of effects on infant and child development. Families of all kinds need and use supplementary care for their infants, and these needs are most often driven by economic concerns and motives. Some babies are cared for in their own home by a relative or a "nanny," some in the homes of family daycare providers, and some in daycare centers (see Chapter 7).

It's impossible to generalize about the effects of nonparental child care on child development for several reasons. First, daycare environments, like home environments, vary so much. (Asking how infants are affected by child care is a bit like asking how children are affected by school—the answer to the first question depends on the child-care setting, just as the answer to the second depends on the school.) But it is also hard to generalize about the effects of child care because children are not randomly assigned to different care environments. The values

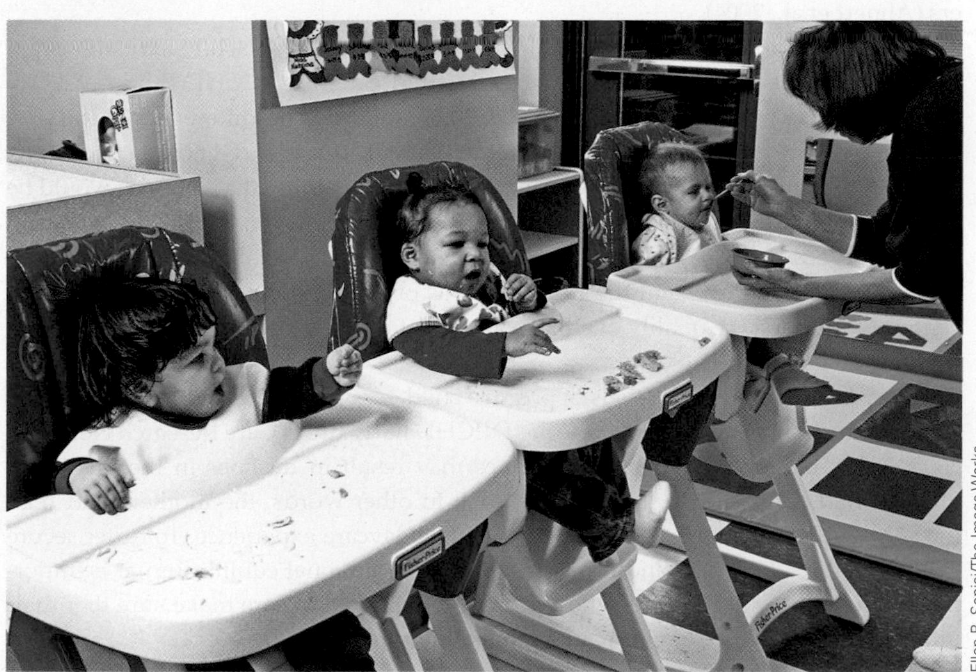

Ellen B. Senisi/The Image Works

Infant daycare is sometimes surprisingly regimented, as seen here in the assembly-line feeding method used.

and practices of parents who do or do not enroll their children in daycare differ, for example, and so differences in infants that might be attributed to daycare experience may really be due (at least in part) to differences in the values and behaviors of the parents and the communities in which they live.

Because so many infants and young children have been placed in nonparental care, extensive efforts have been made to conceptualize and measure the quality of infant care. The National Center for Infants, Toddlers, and Families identified eight criteria that need to be achieved to ensure high-quality nonparental care (Fenichel, Lurie-Hurvitz, & Griffin, 1999). These include:

1. health and safety,
2. maintaining small groups (no more than three to four infants per caregiver),
3. assigning each child to a primary caregiver,
4. ensuring continuity in care,
5. providing responsive caregiving,
6. meeting individual needs in the context of the larger group,
7. ensuring cultural and linguistic continuity, and
8. providing a stimulating physical environment.

Children are often distressed when they begin receiving care outside their homes. In fact, one study found that Italian infants enrolled full-time in high-quality centers remained unhappy (demonstrating negative affect, immobilization, and self-comforting) 6 months after enrollment (Fein, 1996; Fein, Gariboldi, & Boni, 1993). Similarly, German infants who were enrolled in child care between 12 and 18 months of age (late entry) were more irritable and negative than those enrolled before 12 months (early entry) (Rauh et al., 2000). To help children adjust, many European child-care centers have implemented adaptation programs in which mothers accompany their children during the transitional period of enrollment. When mothers familiarize their children to child care in a leisurely manner and accompany their children in the center, adjustment is easier (Rauh et al., 2000), especially when children are securely attached to their mothers (Ahnert et al., 2004).

Despite commonly held fears that daycare will disrupt the attachment relationship, the most comprehensive U.S. study of early child care, the NICHD Study of Early Child Care and Youth Development (2005, 2006), indicates no differences in the proportion of secure attachments based on children having experienced nonmaternal care. However, greater maternal sensitivity increased the probability that children would be classified as securely attached to their mothers, whereas children whose mothers were less sensitive were more likely to be insecurely attached, especially when the children spent long hours in care and the child care was of poor quality. Evidently, parenting continues to shape the quality of child-parent relationships even when children experience child care.

Maternal sensitivity and levels of positive child engagement decline when children spend many hours in child-care facilities (NICHD Early Child Care Research Network, 2005, 2006), though, and this circumstance may result in declines in the quality of mother-child relationships (Sagi et al., 2002). In other words, the mother-child relationship can be negatively affected by the child's daycare experience. To foster secure child-parent relationships and promote children's emotional equilibrium, it is important, for example, that parents who use a lot of nonparental care make sure that their interactions with their infant remain high-quality when they are home.

Children's relationships with their nonparental caregivers can also affect their socioemotional development. Israeli infants who behaved securely with care providers in the Strange Situation were more empathic, dominant, purposive, achievement oriented, and independent 4 years later than those whose attachments were insecure-resistant (Oppenheim, Sagi, & Lamb, 1988). The quality of their first attachment to care providers also predicts school children's perceptions of their relationships with teachers, underscoring the long-lasting impact of these early relationships (Howes, Hamilton, & Phillipsen, 1998). Although it is reassuring to know that infant attachment is not affected by nonparental care, one cause for concern that has surfaced in recent years involves the impact of extensive child-care experience on children's subsequent social behavior. The NICHD Early Child Care Research Network (2005, 2006) and Bornstein and his colleagues (Bornstein et al., 2006; Bornstein & Hahn, 2007) showed that the amount of time spent in nonmaternal care in the first 4½ years of life predicted children's level of problem behavior (including inappropriate assertiveness, disobedience, and aggression) displayed at home or in kindergarten. The elevated risk of behavior problems for children with extensive child-care histories was evident in reports by mothers, care providers, and teachers, and the effects remained significant even when the effects of maternal sensitivity, family background, and the type, quality, and stability of child care were taken into account. However, the difference between the behavior of children who were enrolled in early child care versus those who were not was very small, and few children who have had nonparental care early in life develop significant behavioral problems.

It is important to remember that the arrangements that parents make to care for their infants are greatly influenced by the broader ecology in which families live, including the availability of various alternatives. In most contemporary industrialized societies, the problem of how to care for an infant while two parents must or want to work is solved by using some sort of nonparental care. But in other cultures, parents bring their infants to work with them. For example, infants among the Aka foragers in the Central African Republic are held by their parents while the parents hunt, butcher, and eat game (Hewlett, 1992). Quechua infants who live high in the Andes mountains spend their early months wrapped in layers of woolen cloth and strapped to their mothers' backs to help them survive the exceedingly cold, thin, dry air surrounding them. Ache infants living in the rain forests of eastern Paraguay spend 80 to 100 percent of their time in physical contact with their parents and are almost never more than 3 feet away because this hunter-gatherer group does not make permanent camps in the forest, but moves frequently, clearing a space of stumps and roots that are hazardous for the children (Kaplan & Dove, 1987). "Take Your Child to Work" day is a once-a-year occurrence in modern-day America, but it is the norm, not the exception, in many nonindustrialized cultures.

Gender and Infant Socioemotional Development

Male and female infants are treated differently from birth. Newborn nurseries in maternity wards use color codes (blue for boys and pink for girls) to differentiate the sexes, and early presents given to infants by friends and family members often abide by similar gender-typed color codes. In addition, from birth onward, fathers appear to interact preferentially with sons and mothers with daughters (Parke, 2002). In a study of mothers' and fathers' behavior with male infants while shopping at a mall, fathers were more likely than were mothers to accompany their infants to toy stores than to clothing stores (Parke, 2002), lending support to the premise that fathers are more likely to pursue play activities with their male infants than are mothers. Fathers play more boisterous games with sons than with daughters, whereas mothers' interactions with both boys and girls tend to be nurturing. Mother-daughter interactions are characterized by greater levels of closeness and intimacy than are mother-son interactions.

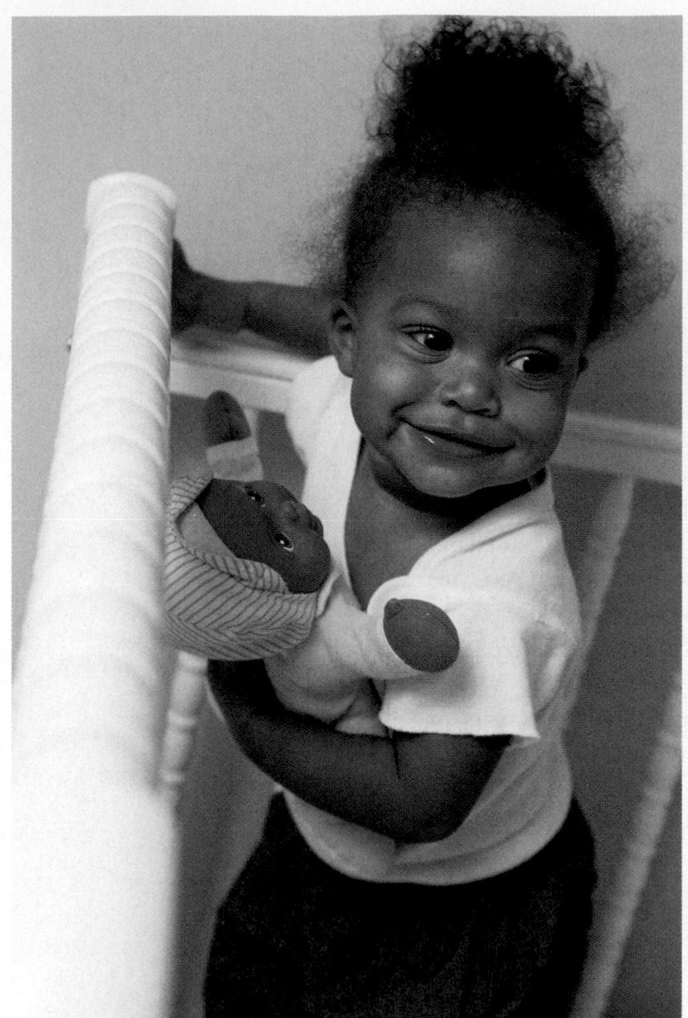
© Purestock

© Artiga Photo/Corbis

Many children—from a surprisingly early age—choose to play with same-sex-typed toys (often in spite of their parents' attempts at gender equality).

Whatever their origins, gender-typed differences in play are evident by the end of the first year and do not change much thereafter (Ruble, Martin, & Berenbaum, 2006).

The sex typing of infant-parent play is always fascinating because girls and boys gravitate in such different directions, regardless of parents' professed beliefs. Children, and especially boys, begin to show preferences for gender-typed toys (e.g., toy trucks for boys) as early as the second year of life. Furthermore, parents choose gender-typed toys for infants (Leaper, 2002). To determine the age at which toddlers begin to exhibit consistently stereotyped toy choices, and to investigate the association between parents' expectations and the children's own knowledge of gender-typed toys, two researchers observed the development of gender-typed play behavior in toddlers beginning at 18 months of age (O'Brien & Huston, 1985a, 1985b). Both boys and girls played significantly more often with gender-typed toys that matched their gender. Both had more own-gender-typed than cross-gender-typed toys in their homes, and parents felt that their children preferred to play with own-gender-typed toys (Alexander, 2003).

Gender-typed preferences seem to be promoted by the child's social environment from early in life, and parents certainly contribute to them. Mothers of 11-month-old male infants overestimated how well their babies would crawl down a sloped pathway, whereas mothers of 11-month-old female infants underestimated how well their

INTERIM SUMMARY 6.4

Parental Behavior and Interaction with Infants	
Harlow's monkey study paved the way for Bowlby's attachment theory and illustrated that babies need **contact comfort** from adults.	■ Harlow's study removed infant rhesus monkeys from their mothers and gave them a choice of substitutes—one model constructed of wire and the other of terry cloth.
Mothers and Fathers	■ Mothers and fathers engage their infants in different types of interactions with different characteristics. ■ Stress on parents can undermine their ability to interact with their infants in ways that promote secure attachment and healthy socioemotional development.
Nonparental Care	■ The majority of U.S. infants are now cared for by someone other than a parent at least some of the time. ■ It's impossible to generalize about the effects of nonparental child care on infant development because there are many variables, including the differences in environments from one daycare situation to another. ■ The National Center for Infants, Toddlers, and Families identified eight criteria that need to be achieved to ensure high-quality infant care: 1. Health and safety 2. Maintaining small groups 3. Assigning each infant to a primary caregiver 4. Ensuring continuity in care 5. Providing responsive caregiving 6. Meeting individual needs in the context of the larger group 7. Ensuring cultural and linguistic continuity 8. Providing a stimulating physical environment
Gender and Socioemotional Development	■ Gender-typed preferences seem to be promoted by the child's social environment from early in life, and parents contribute to them.

babies would do (Mondschein, Adolph, & Tamis-LeMonda, 2000). Guess what? Tests of crawling ability on the sloped path revealed no gender differences whatsoever in infant crawling. (For a summary of this section, see "Interim Summary 6.4: Parental Behavior and Interaction with Infants.")

SUMMING UP AND LOOKING AHEAD

Human infants enter the world primed to form relationships with others; ours is, by any standard, a very social species. As you've read, from a very early age, infants are able to express and discern different emotions and are masters at behaving in ways that elicit attention and nurturance from the adults around them. These capabilities provide the basis for the formation of attachments with parents and other caregivers—bonds that act as foundations for subsequent social relationships, not just in the family or with adults, but with the peers children encounter as their social world expands (Ladd & Pettit, 2002). By toddlerhood, children are more likely to socially imitate peers than adults (Ryalls, Gull, & Ryalls, 2000). Toddlers who leave infancy with a sense of security have a substantial socioemotional advantage over those whose attachments are insecure or disorganized.

The development of emotional and social competence during the first 2 years of life follows a predictable timetable, but there are important variations among infants in how they express their feelings and interact with others. There are two sides to emotional behavior: Emotional expressions communicate feelings to others through facial expressions, gestures, and vocalizations, and emotional understanding involves interpreting the emotional expressions of others.

Primary emotions—joy, anger, fear, sadness—are deeply rooted in human biology and develop early in infants; secondary emotions—embarrassment, pride, guilt, shame, and envy—develop during toddlerhood. While emotions are fleeting, temperament is a biologically based source of consistent individual differences in behavior that is evident very early in life. In combination with experience, an infant's temperament shapes the development of what will eventually become the individual's personality. Temperament is not destiny, of course, but a large measure of who we are as individuals—how shy or gregarious, how positive or negative, how energetic or calm—is apparent at a surprisingly early age.

Socioemotional development is rapid during the early years, but there is a tremendous amount of growth ahead in early childhood and beyond. Infants develop their first social relationships (attachments) with their parents, but differ in the security of their attachments. These differences affect children's later development. Among the highlights we will be looking at when we turn our attention to early childhood socioemotional development, in Chapter 8, are the emergence of a more sophisticated sense of self (Harter, 2006); increases in the child's ability to understand and regulate his or her emotional states; the first signs of behavior that is deliberately helpful to others; and the development of more complex relationships with others, especially with peers.

Our look at the first 2 years of life is now complete. It is time to move on to a new period of life—early childhood. We begin by discussing physical and cognitive development.

HERE'S WHAT YOU SHOULD KNOW

Did You Get It?

After reading this chapter, you should understand the following:

- The two sides of infant emotional behavior—*emotional expression* and *emotional understanding*
- How emotional expression develops from *primary* to *secondary emotions*
- What temperament is and how it is measured
- John Bowlby's theory of attachment
- How parents and children interact and the implications of these interactions

Important Terms and Concepts

attachments (p. 152)
contact comfort (p. 173)
difficult children (p. 159)
effectance (p. 167)
emotional expression (p. 152)
emotional understanding (p. 152)
emotions (p. 152)
environment of evolutionary adaptedness (p. 163)
goodness of fit (p. 162)
inhibited children (p. 159)
internal working models (p. 169)
mirror neurons (p. 156)
negative affectivity (p. 159)
positive affectivity (p. 159)
primary emotions (p. 153)
reciprocity (p. 167)
secondary emotions (p. 153)
secure base (p. 168)
sensitive period (p. 164)
separation protest (p. 164)
social referencing (p. 156)
Strange Situation (p. 165)
stranger wariness (p. 165)
temperament (p. 152)
trust (p. 167)

Part II Review

CHAPTER 4
Physical Development in Infancy

- The general principles of physical growth are *directionality, independence of systems,* and *canalization.*
- The **central nervous system** processes information and directs behavior. Brain development is the product of reciprocal interplay between biology and experience.
- The brain's structure and function is **plastic**—cells are predestined for different functions but that changes at sensitive periods. There are two kinds of plasticity: (1) **modifiability** and (2) **compensation.**
- The **autonomic nervous system** regulates many body activities (such as breathing) without our voluntary control.
- **Reflexes** are divided into three groups: (1) *approach reflexes,* (2) *avoidance reflexes,* and (3) *other reflexes* such as the Palmar grasp and Moro response.
- Motor development is dependent on physical maturation. Dynamic systems theory asserts that one change in development impacts others.
- Sensory systems develop in utero. Our **multimodal perceptions** of objects are coordinated across senses.

CHAPTER 5
Cognitive Development in Infancy

- There are four approaches used to learn about infant perception and cognition: (1) habituation, (2) novelty responsiveness, (3) learning, and (4) showing.
- Jean Piaget believed that mental development unfolds in a fixed sequence of stages. The **sensorimotor period** encompasses infancy. Advances in the sensorimotor period include causality and **object permanence,** which paves the way toward **mental representation.**
- Developmental scientists now agree that Piaget underestimated infants' perceptual and cognitive capacities.
- There are several specific areas of mental development: (1) **categorization,** (2) memory, and (3) play.
- The Bayley Scales of Infant Development are used to assess infant motor, sensation, perception, cognition, memory, language, and social behavior. The **validity** of these tests is problematic.
- The acquisition of language reflects a complex interaction between biology and experience. Some children are **referential;** some, **expressive.**
- Noam Chomsky argues that a number of aspects of syntax are innate, built into every infant's brain in what he called **universal grammar.**

CHAPTER 6
Socioemotional Development in Infancy

- There are two sides to emotional behavior: **emotional expression** and **emotional understanding. Primary emotions** develop early in infants. Secondary emotions develop later.
- **Temperament** is the biologically based source of individual differences in behavioral functioning. There are three characterizations: (1) **positive affectivity,** (2) **negative affectivity,** and (3) **inhibited and difficult children.**
- Differences in the types of **attachments** infants form with their parents affect children's development.
- John Bowlby assumed that how infants and parents behave toward one another is best considered in the context of the environment in which our species evolved **(environment of evolutionary adaptedness).**
- Harlow's monkey study illustrated that babies need **contact comfort** from adults.
- It's impossible to generalize about the effects of nonparental child care on development because there are many variables, including the differences in daycare environments.
- Gender-typed preferences seem to be promoted by the child's social environment from early in life.

part three

Early Childhood

© C Squared Studios/Getty Images

CHAPTER

7

Physical and Cognitive Development in Early Childhood

This chapter is the first of two on early childhood, sometimes called the "play" or "preschool" years, ages 2 to 5. Early childhood is a period of transformation. At age 1½, the child tottered across the grass on wobbly legs. At 6 she is a whirlwind of activity. She can run, skip, jump rope, catch a ball, and even ride a bicycle. She has moved from a high chair to a place at the table with a knife and fork. She can button her own blouse, zip her own jacket, and tie her own shoes. At age 2, she stacked blocks any which way. At 5 or 6, she can put a puzzle together, cut out shapes with scissors, play video games with a joystick, draw a picture of her family, and even print her own name (Case-Smith, 2005).

Thinking in early childhood is a mixture of impressive accomplishments and surprising shortcomings (Gelman, 2006). Young children learn thousands of words during this period—an average of 10 new words a day according to one estimate (Carey, 1978). They can count and understand basic arithmetic (Geary, 2006). They know that plants and animals grow, but that cars and clouds do not (Gelman & Kalish, 2006). Some are experts in a particular domain, such as dinosaurs or geography (Chi & Koeske, 1983). They become skilled in understanding and using symbols (DeLoache, 1995). But, as we will see, young children's thinking also is characterized by surprising blind spots.

PHYSICAL DEVELOPMENT

Body Growth

In this section we explain how the child's body and brain develop, and look at the rapid advances in mobility, coordination, and dexterity during this period. We will consider **normative development**: the pattern of development that is typical, or average. But we know that typical development, based on what occurs on average, is only part of the story because children who are the same age vary in body size and physical skills. Understanding development requires that we look at **individual differences,** or the variation among individuals on a characteristic, as well as what is typical or normative.

normative development A pattern of development that is typical, or average.

individual differences The variation among individuals on a characteristic.

The dramatic growth rate that characterizes infancy slows in early childhood (Mei et al., 2004). Children continue to grow, of course, but the most noticeable changes are in their proportions. The child's torso, arms, and legs grow longer, and the tummy, flatter. The head is smaller in proportion to the body than in infancy. The pudgy one-and-a-half-year-old cherub looks more like an elf at age 5. A typical preschooler is leaner than both his baby brother and his teenage sister.

The first scientific studies of physical growth were designed to establish **norms** or standards of what is "typical" for different ages (e.g., Gesell & Thompson, 1938). Studies of normative growth often use a cross-sectional research design (introduced in Chapter 1). Other researchers use a longitudinal research design, in which the same children are studied at different ages. Researchers measure the heights and weights of

norms Average outcomes rather than actual or even ideal ones.

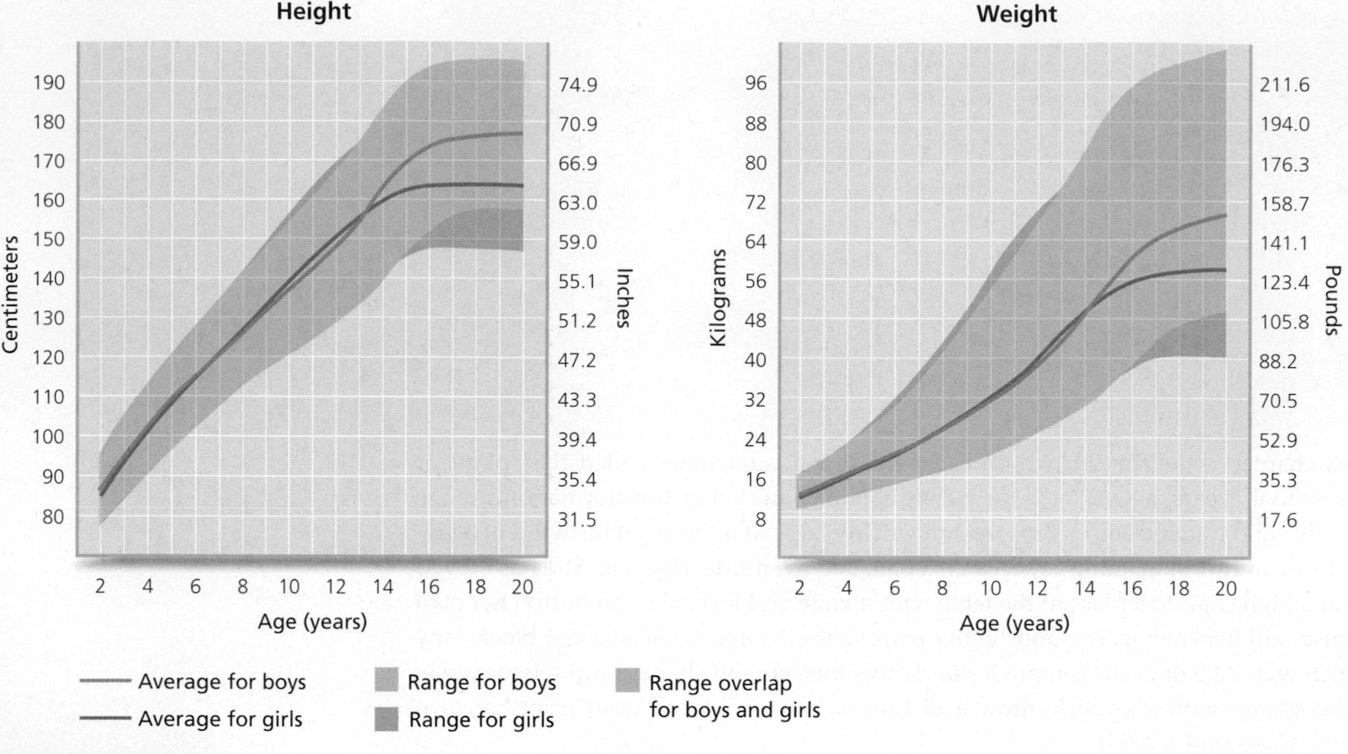

FIGURE 7.1

Growth in Height and Weight from Age 2 to Age 20

On average, children gain about 6 pounds and grow 2.5 inches per year in early childhood. As you can see from the area shaded in green, boys and girls are fairly similar in size during this period, but differences begin to appear in early adolescence.

Source: National Center for Health Statistics (2000a and 2000b).

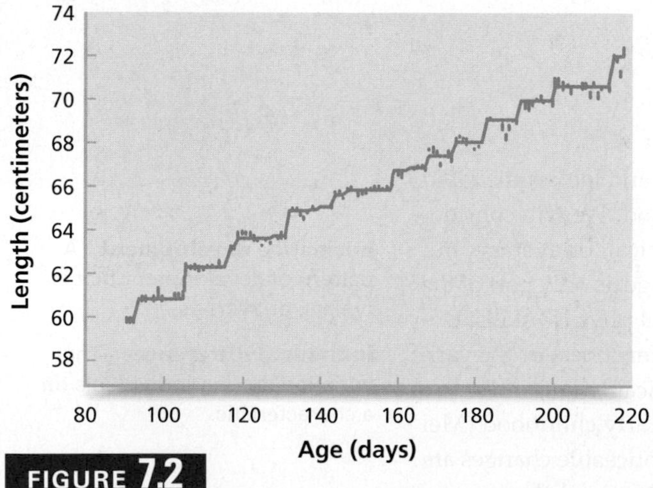

FIGURE 7.2

One Child's Growth Over 140 Days

In contrast to the smooth growth curves found when many children's scores are averaged, an individual child's growth has a choppy stop-and-start pattern.

Source: Adoph, K. & Berger, S. E. (2006). Motor development. In W. Damon & R. Lerner (Eds.) & D. Kuhn & R. S. Siegler (Vol. Eds.) *Handbook of child psychology: Vol. 2: Cognition, perception and language* (6th edition). New York: Wiley, p. 175.

a large number of children of different ages, and then average the results for 2-year-olds, 3-year-olds, and so on.

These studies have been used to create *growth curve tables* of normative development based on heights and weights of children of different ages. The growth curves suggest that physical development is slow and steady during early childhood. On average, children grow 2.5 inches and gain 6 pounds per year during early childhood (see Figure 7.1). Boys are slightly taller and heavier than girls, but the sexes are similar in body proportion (National Center for Health Statistics, 2000a, 2000b).

How does growth in early childhood compare in the United States and other countries? To answer this question, the World Health Organization conducted a study of approximately 8,500 children from different ethnic backgrounds and cultural settings (Brazil, Ghana, India, Norway, Oman, and the United States). The investigators concluded that children from these diverse parts of the world had very similar average growth patterns when provided healthy growth conditions in early life (Garza & de Onis, 2007).

But averages do not tell the whole story. As Figure 7.2 shows, studies of individual children show that growth is not smooth and continuous, but rather episodic, occurring in fits and starts (Adolph & Berger, 2006). In one set of studies, researchers measured individual children daily with precise instruments (Lampl & Emde, 1983). They found that brief periods (less than 24 hours) of growth were followed by periods during which no growth occurred for days or even weeks. This stop-and-start pattern characterizes growth in height, weight, head circumference, and other measures. The resulting picture is quite different from average growth curves shown in Figure 7.1. When a grandmother exclaims to her grandchild, "Why, you've grown over night!," she might be right!

Individual Differences Healthy babies are fairly similar in size and shape. In early childhood, children begin to show a wider range of individual differences in physical development than was true during infancy. Some children stand head and shoulders above most of their peers. Some are straight and slim, even "skinny," whereas others are stocky.

One way to measure children's physical development is by the **body mass index (BMI)**, which helps us to judge whether a child's weight is appropriate for his or her height. The BMI is calculated by dividing weight (measured in kilograms) by height (measured in meters) squared, or wt/ht^2. The BMI for a 4-year-old boy who weighs 36.75 pounds (16.69 kilograms) and is 40.5 inches (1.03 meters) tall is 15.8:

body mass index (BMI) BMI is calculated by dividing weight (measured in kilograms) by height (measured in meters) squared, or wt/ht^2.

$$16.69/(1.03)^2 = 15.8$$

Figure 7.3 shows the variability of BMI scores in boys, ages 2 to 10. An average boy at each age is in the 50th percentile, midway between 1 and 99. A boy in the 60th percentile for BMI is heavier than 60 percent but lighter than 40 percent of children his age, sex, and height. Boys in the 85th to 94th percentiles are considered overweight, and those in the 95th percentile or higher, obese. Boys in the 5th percentile or lower are clinically underweight for their height. For medical or other reasons, they are not thriving. But 80 percent of children—in all of their variety—are within the normal range.

What factors contribute to these differences? Heredity is an important source. Studies that have contrasted the growth of monozygotic or identical twins (who share 100% of their genes) and dizygotic or fraternal twins (who share, on average, 50% of their genes) find that about two-thirds of the statistical variations in height and weight can be attributed to genetic factors (Plomin, 2007). But heredity is only part of the story. Changes in diet and physical health have resulted in increases in height and weight within families in the last hundred years in the United States, Europe, and Asia. Nutrition is a significant issue—with long-term consequences—for pre-schoolers and their parents.

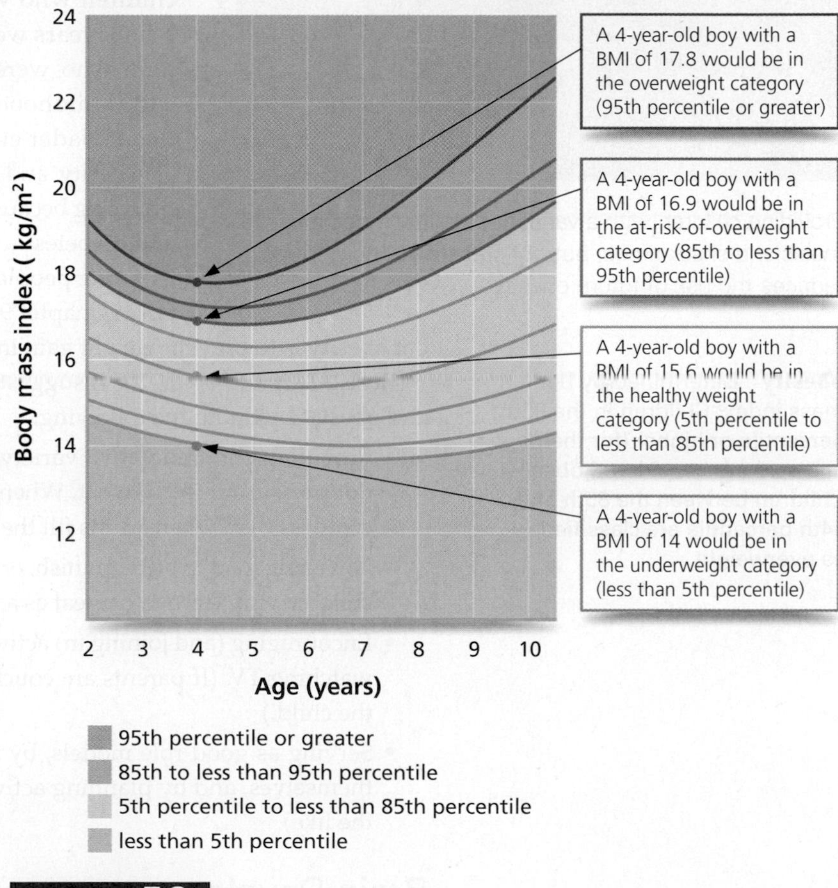

FIGURE 7.3

Body Mass Index (BMI) of Boys Who Are Overweight, Healthy Weight, and Underweight

Four-year-old boys who are considered to be in the healthy range of height-to-weight ratio have a BMI that is above 14 and below 16.9.

Source: National Center for Health Statistics (2000a and 2000b).

Diet and Nutrition Two changes in eating patterns coincide in early childhood. Because

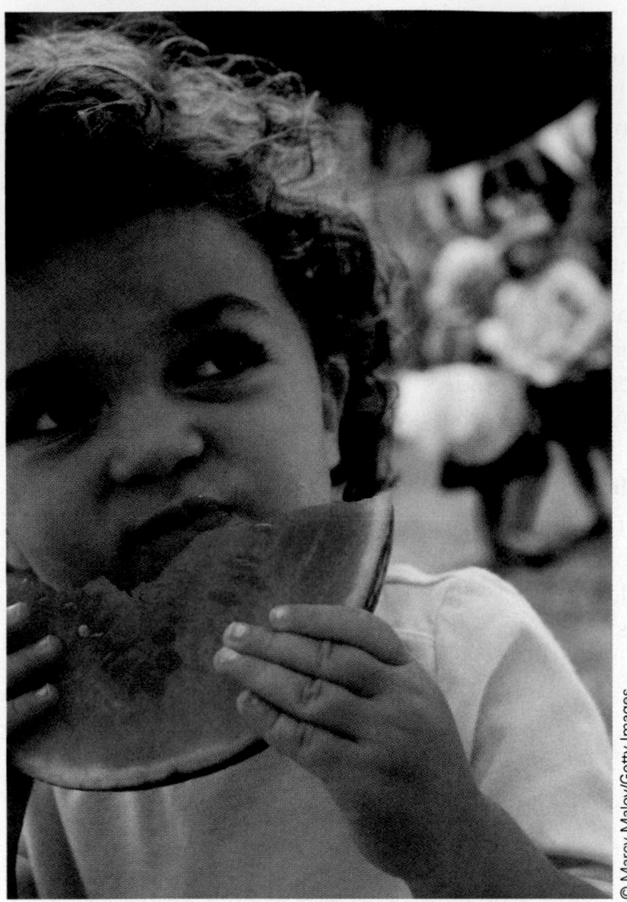
© Marcy Maloy/Getty Images

Providing children with a variety of healthy foods at meals and snack times, but *not* pressuring them to eat, reduces the risk of future obesity.

they are growing more slowly than they did as infants, children's appetites decrease. They don't need as many calories (in proportion to their size) as they did when they were babies (Kedesdy & Budd, 1998). And they aren't as hungry. At the same time, they are graduating from baby to adult food, though in smaller portions and bite-size pieces.

What young children will eat and how much they eat will vary from meal to meal, day to day. Allowed to eat only as much as they want, children compensate for eating very little at one meal by eating more at other times. When parents insist that children clean their plates, children don't learn to pay attention to internal cues of hunger and fullness.

The danger is not that children will starve themselves, but that they will learn to overeat. Childhood **obesity** has reached epidemic levels. Estimates are that 9 million U.S. children are obese and many more are at risk (overweight) (National Research Council, 2004). For many young children, being overweight is not simply a matter of having "baby fat" that they lose as they grow. One longitudinal study of more than 1,000 healthy U.S. youngsters found that 60 percent of children who were overweight at any time during the preschool years were overweight at age 12, and none of the children who were in the 50th percentile or lower for BMI in early childhood was obese at age 12—that's right, not one of them (Nader et al., 2006).

Obesity and overweight in early childhood is particularly troubling because serious health problems such as heart disease and diabetes—once adult illnesses—now are increasingly seen in young people. We will discuss childhood obesity in more detail in Chapter 9. The key point here is that the best way to combat obesity is to prevent weight gain in the first place.

obesity Determined by body mass index. Children in the 95th percentile or higher (for their age and sex) are considered obese. Children between the 85th and 94th percentile are classified as overweight.

Research (Faith et al., 2004) suggests that parents can lower the risk of overweight and obesity by doing the following:

- Providing children with a variety of healthy foods at meals and snack times, but not pressuring them to eat. When preschoolers serve themselves they eat 25 percent less than when adults fill their plates (Fisher, Rolls, & Birch, 2003).
- Not using food to bribe, punish, or entertain children. When food becomes an issue, children may learn to overeat as a way of rewarding or consoling themselves.
- Encouraging (and joining in) active play and limiting sedentary pastimes, such as watching TV. (If parents are couch potatoes, they are modeling this behavior for the child.)
- Serving as good role models, by practicing healthy eating habits and exercising themselves, and by planning active family time (raking leaves, bicycle rides, and the like).

Brain Development

During early childhood, the brain matures both structurally and functionally, a process that continues into adolescence and young adulthood (Nelson, Thomas, & de Haan, 2006). An important aspect of brain development in early childhood is establishing and fine tuning communications within the brain and between the brain and nervous system.

As we discussed in Chapter 4, a key process in brain development is the forming of connections between **neurons** through the growth of **dendrites**, which collect information and carry it to the body of the neuron, and **axons**, which transmit information away from the cell body (see Figure 7.4). The connection between one neuron's axon and another neuron's dendrite (called a **synapse**) enables information to pass from one neuron to another. The growth of synapses, a process called **synaptogenesis**, peaks at about age 1 year but continues into childhood, and, at lower levels, throughout life. The formation of some synapses is genetically programmed, but the formation of other synapses depends on experience (Couperus & Nelson, 2006). Conversing with young children, reading books, doing puzzles, and riding bikes are all activities that encourage the development of new synapses.

Synaptic pruning—the selective elimination of unused and unnecessary synapses—is an equally important part of brain development. The *over*production and later reduction of synapses are normal parts of brain development. Synaptic pruning begins in the first years and continues into young adulthood. From peak levels in early childhood, synaptic density is reduced by about 40 percent by adulthood (Couperus & Nelson, 2006). The "extra" synapses in a child's brain provide some "backup insurance" that supports brain plasticity (discussed later in this chapter); however, synaptic pruning also is needed. Selective elimination of some synapses while others are strengthened supports brain adaptation and plasticity by making the brain more efficient. An overabundance of synapses is too unwieldy in the long run (Couperus & Nelson, 2006).

neuron A cell that carries information across the body and brain, as well as back and forth within the brain.

dendrites Branched extensions of a neuron that pick up signals from other neurons.

axon The part of the cell that carries signals away from the cell body toward other neurons. At their tips, axons divide into many axon terminals.

synapse The connection between one neuron's axon and another neuron's dendrite.

synaptogenesis A key process in the brain involving the development of connections between neurons through the growth of axons and dendrites.

synaptic pruning The process of elimination of unused and unnecessary synapses.

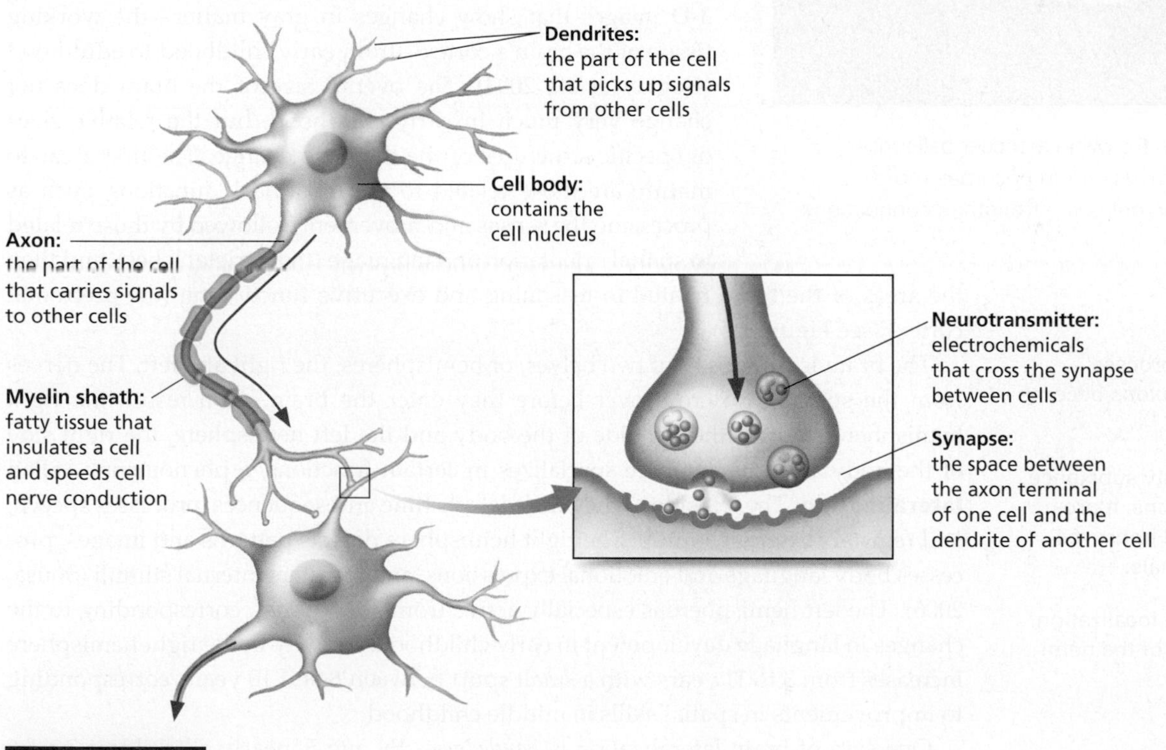

FIGURE 7.4

Parts of the Neuron

This diagram shows several important structures of the neuron, including the dendrites, cell body, and axons.

Source: From Bernstein/Penner/Clarke-Stewart/Roy. *Psychology,* 8E. © 2008 Wadsworth, a part of Cengage Learning, Inc. Reproduced by permission. www.cengage.com/permissions

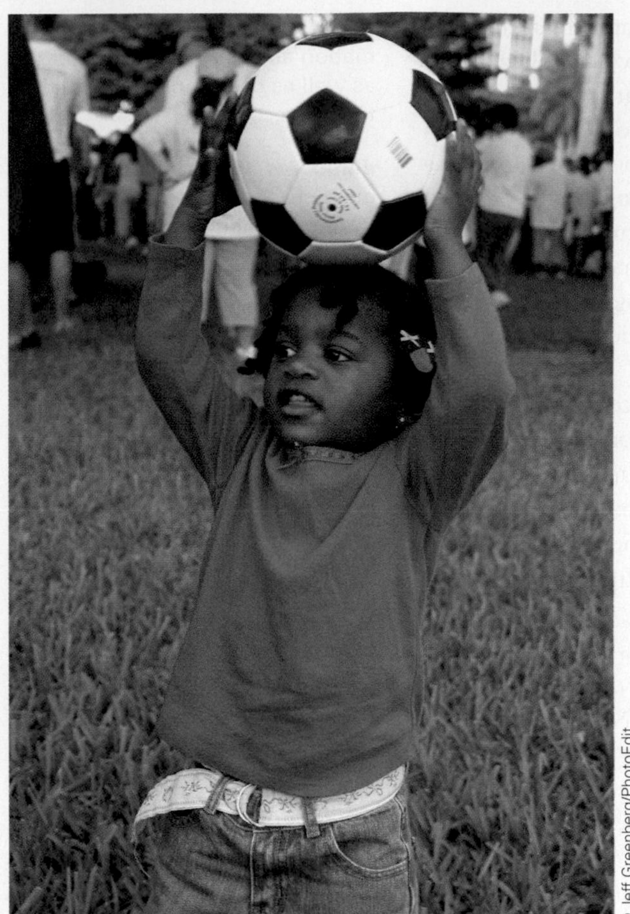
© Jeff Greenberg/PhotoEdit

With lots of practice, throwing a soccer ball while keeping both feet firmly planted becomes more automatic. Repetition helps to strengthen connections among synapses.

As we discussed in Chapter 4, another process that improves connections and communication within the brain is **myelination**. **Myelin** is a fatty substance that wraps itself around the axon. Not unlike the way in which plastic insulation helps keep electricity traveling along a wire, myelin increases both the speed and efficiency at which information travels across the brain's circuits (Webb, Monk, & Nelson, 2001).

Myelination of different areas of the brain occurs sequentially, beginning prenatally and continuing into young adulthood (Nelson et al., 2006). The areas of the brain involved with vision and movement are myelinated first. During early childhood, the fibers that connect the cerebellum to the cerebral cortex grow and myelinate. These changes improve children's balance and control of body movements. Walking, running, and jumping become more synchronized. Myelination in the regions of the brain that govern hand-eye coordination also continues through early childhood, enabling children to be able to print their name or use a crayon to color a picture. Myelination of the frontal lobes, perhaps the most plastic area of the brain, continues into late adolescence and early adulthood.

Brain Anatomy Important changes in brain anatomy occur during early childhood. Using brain imaging technology to document brain activity, researchers have created time-lapse 3-D images that show changes in gray matter—the working tissue of the brain's cortex—from early childhood to adulthood (Gogtay et al., 2004). The overall size of the brain does not change very much in early childhood, but the relative sizes of specific structures of the brain do change. The first areas to mature are those related to the most basic functions, such as processing the senses and movement, followed by those related to spatial orientation and language (the parietal lobes), and then the areas of the brain related to reasoning and executive functioning (the prefrontal cortex) (see Figure 7.5).

myelination The process through which cell axons become sheathed in myelin.

myelin A white fatty substance that encases cell axons. It provides insulation and improves transmission of signals.

lateralization The localization of a function to one of the hemispheres of the brain.

The brain is composed of two halves, or hemispheres, the right and left. The nerves from the spinal cord cross over before they enter the brain. As a result, the right hemisphere controls the left side of the body and the left hemisphere, the right side of the body. Each hemisphere specializes in certain functions, a phenomenon called **lateralization**. The left side of the brain detects time and sequences, processes speech, and registers external stimuli. The right hemisphere detects patterns and images, processes body language and emotional expressions, and registers internal stimuli (Sousa, 2006). The left hemisphere is especially active from 3 to 6 years, corresponding to the changes in language development in early childhood. Activity in the right hemisphere increases from 3 to 11 years with a small spurt between 8 and 10 years, corresponding to improvements in spatial skills in middle childhood.

One sign of brain lateralization is *handedness*. By age 5, nearly all children prefer using one hand more than the other, and 85 percent are right-handed. In almost all right-handers (close to 95 percent), the area of the brain that processes language is located in the left hemisphere; however, in left-handers, the incidence of right-hemisphere language dominance increases linearly with the degree of left-handedness, from 15 percent in ambidextrous individuals to 27 percent in strong left-handers (Knecht et al., 2000). In males, language development typically occurs in the left hemisphere. In females, the main area is in the left hemisphere, with additional processing in the right hemisphere (Cahill, 2005). Handedness has a genetic component, but cultural beliefs

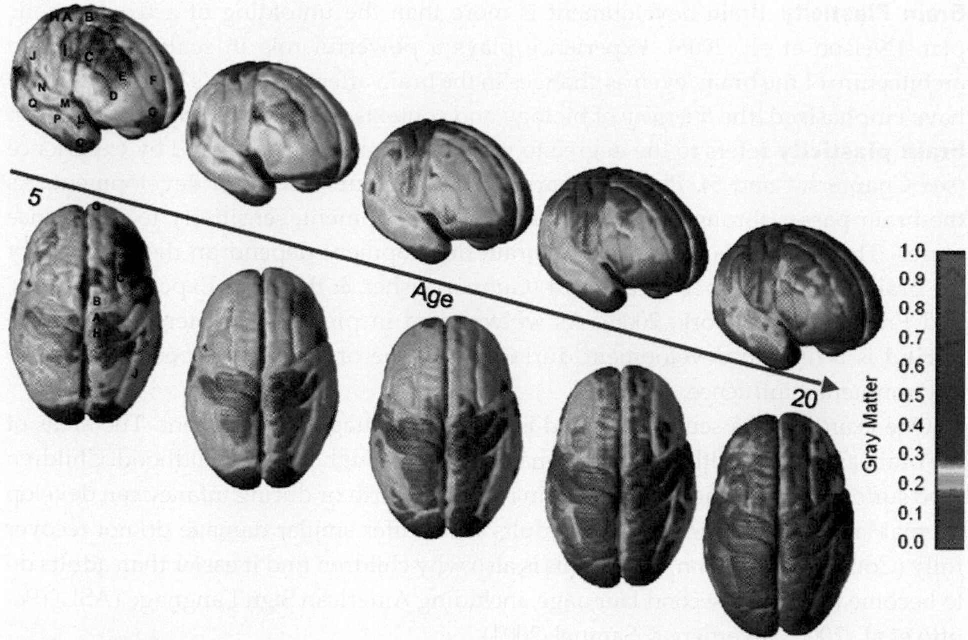

FIGURE 7.5

Right Lateral and Top Views of Gray Matter Maturation from Ages 5 to 20

Brain scans obtained from the same children over time reveal that parts of the brain mature at different rates. Areas involved with motor and sensory functions mature first, followed by speech and language areas, and then areas related to attention and planning.

Source: Gogtay, N., Giedd, J. N., Lusk, L., Hayashi, K. M., Greenstein, D., Vaituzis, A. C., et al. (2004, May). Dynamic mapping of human cortical development during childhood through early adulthood. *Proceedings of the National Academy of Sciences,* 101(21), 8174–8179. Copyright 2004 National Academy of Sciences, U.S.A.

and schooling also play a role (Annett, 2002). In the United States during the early twentieth century, left-handed children were forced to use their right hand for writing and punished for slipping into left-handedness. The bias even remains in our language today, for example, in the phrase "left-handed compliment."

Between ages 3 and 6 years, the **corpus callosum**—the large bundle of fibers that connects the two hemispheres—develops rapidly. Communication between the two halves of the brain facilitates quicker and smoother action, and the hemispheres can share information and learning. Incomplete or abnormal development of the corpus callosum is associated with mild to severe symptoms, including retardation, seizures, and inability to initiate or control muscle movements.

corpus callosum The connection between the two halves or hemispheres of the brain.

The **frontal lobes** make up the area of the brain that develops most in early childhood (Gogtay et al., 2004). Sometimes called the "executive" of the brain, the frontal lobes are responsible for planning and organizing new actions, problem solving, and regulating emotions, as well as focusing attention. Rapid growth occurs in the frontal lobes between ages 3 and 6. Everyday behavior provides evidence of frontal lobe development. For example, toddlers are impulsive. Sometimes their attention span is so short they fail to follow through and complete tasks such as putting away toys when asked by parents or teachers (Rothbart, Posner, & Kieras, 2006). Other times they find it difficult to stop an activity they have begun, whether singing a jingle over and over or banging two pot lids together. By age 6, however, maturation of the frontal lobes supports the development of more focused, planful, and goal-oriented behavior (Anderson et al., 2007).

frontal lobes Sometimes called the "executive" of the brain, the frontal lobes are responsible for planning and organizing new actions, problem solving, and regulating emotions, as well as focusing attention.

Brain Plasticity Brain development is more than the unfolding of a fixed genetic plan (Nelson et al., 2006). Experience plays a powerful role in sculpting the fine architecture of the brain, even as changes in the brain affect children's behavior. As we have emphasized, the *interplay* of biology and contexts drives development. The term **brain plasticity** refers to the degree to which the brain can be altered by experience (see Chapters 4 and 5). Plasticity varies over the course of brain development. As the brain passes through different stages of development, sensitivity to experience varies. The effects of experiences on brain development depend on the maturity of the brain when the experiences occur (Gunnar, Fisher, & the Early Experience, Stress, and Prevention Network, 2006). As we've noted in previous chapters, a **sensitive period** is a time in development during which the organism is especially open to environmental influence.

brain plasticity The degree to which the brain can be altered by experience.

sensitive period A time in development during which the organism is especially open to environmental influence.

One example of a sensitive period is seen in language development. The areas of the brain associated with language remain plastic through middle childhood. Children who suffer major damage to these brain regions at birth or during infancy can develop normal language abilities, whereas adults who suffer similar damage do not recover fully (Couperus & Nelson, 2006). This is also why children find it easier than adults do to become fluent in a second language, including American Sign Language (ASL) (Petitto et al., 2000; Silverberg & Samuel, 2004).

Motor Development

gross motor skills Abilities required to control the large movements of the arms, legs, and feet, or the whole body, such as running, jumping, climbing, and throwing.

fine motor skills Abilities required to control smaller movements of the hand and fingers, such as picking up small objects and tying one's shoes.

Motor development in early childhood occurs on two fronts. **Gross motor skills** are the abilities required to control the large movements of the arms, legs, and feet, or the whole body—such as running, jumping, climbing, and throwing (Case-Smith, 2005). **Fine motor skills** involve smaller movements of the hand and fingers—such as picking up small objects and tying one's shoes (Case-Smith, 2005).

© David Young-Wolff/PhotoEdit

The gross motor skills required to ride a tricycle reflect brain and muscular maturation as well as opportunity and experience.

Both gross motor skills and fine motor skills are inseparably linked to perception and cognition (Adolph & Berger, 2006). Achieving the balance needed to run or the coordination needed to button a shirt depends on perception. Movement and perception, in turn, provide the raw material for cognitive development. To a significant degree, young children learn by and through their actions or movement.

Gross Motor Skills Arnold Gesell and his colleagues at Yale University were the first scientists to catalog the development of gross motor skills in early childhood (Gesell & Thompson, 1938). Their normative standards for motor development (with refinements) are still in use today. The Bayley Scales of Infant Development (Black & Matula, 1999), for example, is based on norms for motor development, body control, and coordination at different ages. Like norms for height and weight, norms of motor development describe the "average child" at a given age, based on cross-sectional or longitudinal studies. Table 7.1 illustrates some milestones in normative gross motor development.

Physicians and physical therapists use this and other scales to assess whether a child is developing normally. As discussed in earlier chapters, scores on the Bayley Scales do *not* predict future intellectual or physical achievements in the normal range. But, especially in the lower range, they provide warning signs that a child may have developmental problems. If a child scores significantly below the age norm, further testing is called for.

TABLE 7.1 Some Milestones in Normative Gross Motor Development

2 years	Kicks a ball. Walks up and down stairs, two feet at a time.
2.5 years	Jumps with both feet, including off stairs. Can walk on tiptoe.
3 years	Climbs stairs using alternate feet. Can stand on one foot (briefly). Rides tricycle. Runs well.
4 years	Skips on one foot. Throws ball overhand. Jumps well from standing position.
5 years	Hops and skips. Has good balance. Can skate or ride a scooter.

Source: This table was published in J. Case-Smith, *Occupational therapy for children,* 5/e. Copyright Elsevier 2005. Used by permission of Elsevier.

Like physical growth charts, charts of motor development imply this is a smooth curve with one milestone leading to the next and then the next. But contemporary research shows that children often straddle two stages, sometimes revert back to an earlier stage, and show wide individual differences (Adolph & Berger, 2006). Also, maturation is only part of the story.

Motor development must be studied in context. In the real world, children acquire new skills with the help of their parents and child-care providers in different places with different objects, surfaces, and opportunities. The environment in which they develop and their access to different challenges, in turn, depends on the cultural and historic context (Adolph & Berger, 2006).

Fine Motor Skills Fine motor skills are smaller movements of the hands and fingers. To pour milk into a glass, button a sweater, draw a picture, or print one's name are some examples. These skills are complicated accomplishments that require motor control and coordination with the visual system. The development of fine motor skills during early childhood is a source of considerable pride and feelings of accomplishment. These skills are important steps toward independence that develop in early childhood.

Fine motor skills, like gross motor skills, depend in part on culture and experience. In other times and places, young children demonstrated skills that we would consider remarkable. In colonial America, for example, 4-year-old girls knitted mittens and socks while their 6-year-old sisters transformed raw wool into yarn on spinning wheels (Ogburn & Nimkoff, 1955). In the Mayan communities of Central America, children begin weaving rugs—an activity that requires considerable dexterity—between ages 4 and 6 (Rogoff, 2003). Table 7.2 illustrates some milestones in normative fine motor development in the United States.

Drawing—with crayons, markers, paint, or merely a stick in the dirt—is one of the fine motor skills that develops during early childhood in many cultures (Golomb, 2004). Between ages 18 months and 2 years, children begin scribbling—drawing lines, curves, loops, zigzags, and the like. These marks are not random. To the child, they convey action. A series of dots is a bunny hopping; a swirl is a plane moving through the sky (Wolf & Perry, 1988). Toddlers seem to enjoy the activity of drawing as much as (or more than) what they produce.

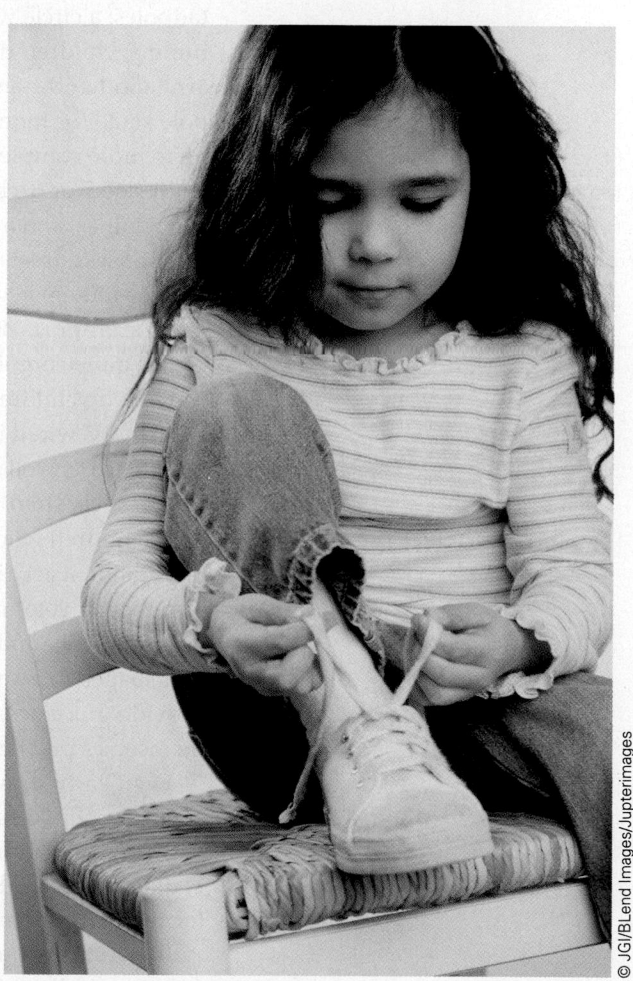

Do you remember learning to tie your shoes? It wasn't easy.

TABLE 7.2 Some Milestones in Normative Fine Motor Development in the United States

Age	Milestones
2 years	Builds a tower with six or seven blocks. Turns the pages of a book one at a time. Turns door knobs and untwists jar lids. Washes and dries hands. Uses spoon and fork well.
2.5 years	Builds tower with eight blocks. Holds pencil or crayon between fingers (instead of fist).
3 years	Builds tower with nine or ten blocks. Puts on shoes and socks and can button and unbutton. Carries a container without spilling or dropping (most of the time).
4 years	Except for tying, can dress him- or herself. Cuts with scissors (but not well). Washes and dries face.
5 years	Dresses without help and ties shoes. Prints simple letters.

Source: This table was published in J. Case-Smith, *Occupational therapy for children*, 5/e. Copyright Elsevier 2005. Used by permission of Elsevier.

Around age 3, children make spontaneous attempts to draw recognizable objects, usually beginning with a human figure (Golomb, 2004). These early efforts look like tadpoles: a circle with eyes for the head and dangling legs. When asked to include the tummy, children do so; when asked to draw a person holding a flower, they add an arm and hand—and then go back to their tadpoles. Some children remain in the tadpole stage for months, drawing the same picture over and over. Others quickly move on to more complete figures.

By age 5 or 6, children draw a body and head with arms and fingers, legs and feet, hair, clothes, and a smile—all in the right places. Complete scenes (with trees and flowers, houses, streets, and the members of their family or characters from a favorite cartoon or movie) begin to replace a single figure; distinct individuals appear in place of a single all-purpose human figure (Gardner, 1980; Golomb, 2004). Drawings at this age can be quite complex and detailed, as well as fanciful.

How do children learn to draw? Some experts have argued that drawing is a natural activity, wired into our brains. Human beings have an affinity for symbols—music and dance as well as pictures and words (Gardner, 1980). Around the world, in varied cultures, children draw similar tadpole-like human figures at age 3 to 4. Moreover, blind children who regain their sight and children in cultures with no tradition of representational art can draw a human figure after a few attempts (Millar, 1975).

Other developmental scientists (e.g., Kellogg, 1969) emphasize that drawing requires practice and instruction. Consciously or not, parents and others point out forms and shapes to a child; ask representation-oriented questions ("Is that the sun?"); and provide guidance ("That's a face? Here, let's draw the eyes and a smile"). Children themselves practice, observe, and experiment.

Even early drawings are influenced by culture. In Bali, children fill the page with small, repetitive designs that seem to echo a traditional Balinese dance (Gardner, 1980). Drawings by Japanese children feature simple elements spread across the page like a Haiku poem (see Figures 7.6 and 7.7). Drawings by U.S. children are sometimes free-form and fun, sometimes more mechanical.

In Western countries, interest in drawing and other forms of graphics tends to fade in middle childhood. Older children's drawings seem to be more conventional, with stock characters, themes, and techniques. By age 8 or 9, children become increasingly concerned about "getting things right": Their clothes have to match; their games are played and judged by rules; in school there are right and wrong answers.

Courtesy of Dr. Alexander Allend

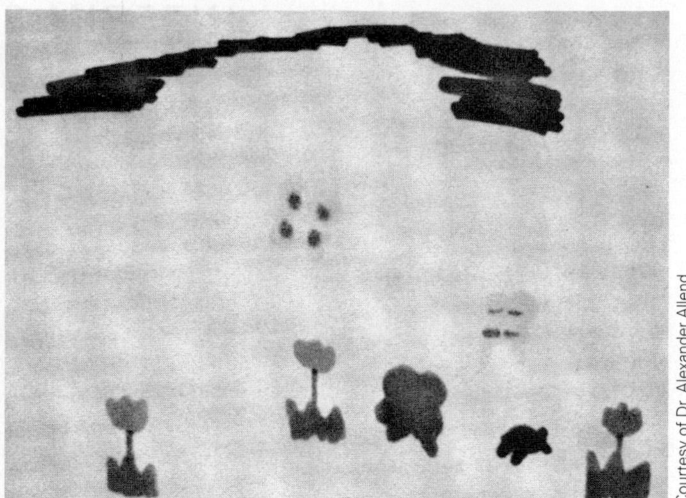

Courtesy of Dr. Alexander Allend

FIGURES 7.6 and 7.7

Cultural Differences Are Evident in Young Children's Drawings

There is strong evidence, even in the earliest drawings, of cultural influences. In Bali, children fill the space with repetitive forms drawn separately yet snugly across the page (left). In Japan, children's drawings feature simple elements spread across the page (right).

Representational art requires skill and practice that most Westerners do not receive in school.

Writing (or printing) is another fine motor skill that develops in early childhood. Like drawing, writing begins as scribbles. Around age 5, children begin to pay attention to the printed word, to distinguish writing from nonwriting, and to recognize and copy individual letters (Case-Smith, 2005). With encouragement, they begin to print their name and simple words (*cat, dog*), sounding out the letters as they work on their writing. (For a summary of this section, see "Interim Summary 7.1: Physical Development.")

PHYSICAL HEALTH AND WELL-BEING

Physical health is a prerequisite for many aspects of child development. Frequent illness or malnutrition can dull children's motivation and curiosity, as well as reduce the time they spend exploring and playing. These, in turn, slow cognitive and socioemotional development by reducing the amount of interaction children have with their environment and with other people. How healthy are today's children? How can we improve health and safety in early childhood?

Injuries and Illnesses

In the United States, unintentional injuries are the leading cause of death in early childhood (Grossman, 2000). More than 5,600 U.S. children die from injuries each year—an average of 15 children per day. Injuries also account for almost 14 million medical visits by U.S. children ages 14 and under (National SAFE KIDS Campaign, 2006).

Drownings lead the list of unintended injury deaths among children ages 1 to 4, followed by automobile accidents, fire and burns, and airway obstructions (National SAFE KIDS Campaign, 2006). Accidents may not be totally avoidable, but death and serious injury from accidents can be greatly reduced by simple precautions. Whenever small children are around water (including bathtubs), playing, or eating, they need adult supervision. Readily available safety equipment and safety measures also can

INTERIM SUMMARY 7.1

Physical Development	
Body Growth	■ Body Mass Index (BMI), the ratio of weight to height, is a common index of whether a child's weight is appropriate for his or her height. ■ Differences in BMI are influenced by heredity, diet, physical health, and exercise. The rate of physical development slows in early childhood compared with infancy. ■ Children from diverse parts of the world show similar growth patterns when provided healthy environments. ■ The incidence of obesity and overweight in early childhood is increasing. ■ Parents can lower the risk of obesity by providing healthy foods, not using food to bribe or entertain children, encouraging active play, and serving as good role models.
Brain Development	■ **Synaptogenesis** is the development of connections between **neurons** through the growth of **axons** and **dendrites**. ■ The more a synapse is used, the stronger it becomes. Unused synapses are eliminated. ■ **Myelination**, the development of a myelin coating around axons, increases the speed and efficiency of transmitting signals between neurons. ■ The left hemisphere is especially active from ages 3 to 6, corresponding to the changes in language development in early childhood. ■ Between ages 3 and 6, the **corpus callosum** (the large bundle of fibers that connects the two hemispheres) develops rapidly.
Motor Development	■ Gross motor skills involve large movements of arms, legs, feet, or the whole body. ■ Gross motor skills reflect maturation, cultural context, and opportunities. ■ Fine motor skills involve smaller movements of the hands and fingers. ■ Development of particular fine motor skills depends in part on culture and experience and in part on brain development.

prevent many of these deaths, including fences and self-locking gates around swimming pools, car safety seats and seat belts, bike helmets, and home smoke detectors. As a result of these measures and efforts, deaths from unintentional injuries in childhood dropped 40 percent between 1987 and 2000.

One reason that more U.S. children die from injuries than from illnesses is that successful immunization programs have almost eliminated some diseases such as polio and measles that previously claimed lives. The annual number of reported cases of measles in the United States, for example, has declined from 3 to 4 million cases before the introduction of a measles vaccine to fewer than a hundred cases a year

(Meissner, Strebel, & Orenstein, 2004). Vaccinations prevent an estimated 10.5 million disease cases and 35,000 deaths each year (Mitka, 2004).

However, medical personnel are concerned that these health advances are in danger of not being maintained because a large number of children in the United States are not fully immunized (Mitka, 2004). About 20 percent of infants and toddlers are missing one or more of the necessary set of immunizations. And, in one study, of the 80 percent who received the complete schedule in the first 2 years, 24 percent lacked essential immunizations as preschoolers (Chu, Barker, & Smith, 2004). There also are income disparities in who is fully immunized. Thirty-eight percent of low-income children in the United States lack essential immunizations compared with 7 percent in Great Britain and Canada (Chu et al., 2004).

One reason for the poorer immunization record in the United States is that many families lack health insurance, and their children do not have their own physicians who provide routine well-child visits. A second reason is that some parents believe that these immunizations increase the risk of conditions such as autism and multiple sclerosis (Mitka, 2004), Systematic review of the evidence by the National Academy of Science (National Research Council, 2004) has not found credible scientific evidence that immunizations cause these conditions. The Academy warns that children are under much greater risks of death and impairment from measles and polio if they are not properly immunized.

Although the incidence of some infectious diseases has decreased, other minor illnesses such as colds and upset stomachs continue to be a part of growing up. For example, in the United States, young children average 6 to 10 colds a year (National Institute of Allergy and Infectious Diseases, 2004). It is not possible to estimate the average number of gastrointestinal illnesses because they often go unreported. For well-nourished children with access to health care, these common illnesses are rarely serious.

A key factor contributing to these minor infections is coming into contact with other children. Children who attend child-care centers with other children are more likely to get sick than are children cared for at home or by a relative. A study of more than 1,100 children found that preschoolers enrolled in child-care groups with more than six children have higher rates of upper respiratory illness, diarrhea, and ear infections than do children cared for at home or in smaller groups (NICHD Early Child Care Research Network, 2003a). These minor illnesses in early childhood appear to boost immunity. Three-year-olds who have just entered child care are more likely to become ill than 3-year-olds who have been in care for a longer period.

A major risk is that an upper respiratory infection will lead to a middle-ear infection, called *otitis media*. Frequent ear infections can lead to social isolation because they make it difficult for a child to hear (Roberts et al., 2000). Hand-washing with soap and water, one of the simplest and most effective ways to stop the spread of the common cold, is an important practice in child-care settings as well as children's homes (National Institute of Allergy and Infectious Diseases, 2004).

Although child mortality rates are low in the United States, the picture in the poor countries of the developing world is quite different. Globally, 9.7 million children under age 5 die each year, the great majority from preventable or treatable infectious diseases (especially pneumonia and diarrhea).

In 2000, 189 countries endorsed the United Nations Millennium Declaration, which established global goals. One of the millennium goals is to reduce child mortality to two-thirds the 1990 level by 2015 (World Bank, 2006). Public health experts (Jones et al., 2003) believe that this goal can be achieved with a small number of well-known, cost-effective interventions, such as the following:

- Oral rehydration therapy (ORT), a solution of glucose, salt, and water that can eliminate most childhood deaths involving diarrhea

- Immunization for diseases such as measles and polio, which can be fatal for malnourished children
- The use of mosquito nets treated with insecticide to prevent malaria, which depresses the immune system and may prove fatal
- Education for mothers and other caregivers on good sanitary practices such as hand washing and proper nutrition for small children

Through systematic efforts in each of these areas, substantial progress has been made in meeting the goal (UNICEF and the World Health Organization, 2008). About 20 million children under the age of 5 died in 1960. Less than half that number (9.7 million) died in 2007. Several countries such as Vietnam and the Dominican Republic have had big drops in child mortality. However, there are still wide disparities around the world. In the United States and Western Europe, about 6 of every 1,000 children die before the age of 5. In West and Central Africa, that number is 150 of every 1,000 children, more than 20 times as many deaths.

Malnutrition is the underlying cause of more than half of all deaths of children under the age of 5 around the world (UNICEF and the World Health Organization, 2008). Malnutrition increases the chances that children will catch a disease, and the effects of the disease are more severe. When children are ill, their appetites are reduced and the amount of nutrition they absorb decreases, resulting in a vicious cycle of sickness and delayed growth.

kwashiorkor A form of malnutrition in which individuals have an adequate intake of calories, but an inadequate intake of protein.

marasmus A form of malnutrition in which individuals are not receiving enough protein or enough calories.

Malnutrition is more than lack of food. Children can feel "full" but still not get the amounts of protein (needed to build muscle), calories (needed for energy), iron (for proper blood cell function), and other nutrients they need to be healthy (Grigsby & Shashidhar, 2006). **Kwashiorkor** and **marasmus** are two forms of protein energy malnutrition. A child with marasmus is not receiving enough protein or enough calories, whereas a child with kwashiorkor has an adequate intake of calories but an inadequate intake of protein. In addition, malnutrition can occur when children's diets are deficient in micronutrients such as iron, iodine, zinc, and vitamin A.

In both developed and developing countries, childhood mortality is linked to poverty. Common sense says that poverty causes malnutrition and illness, but malnutrition and illness also cause poverty—in terms of lower school achievement, fewer years of schooling, reduced wages, and loss of income due to illness.

Sleep and Sleep Problems

Sleep patterns change in early childhood—from sleeping 12 to 13 hours at ages 2 and 3, to 10 to 11 hours at ages 4 through 6 (Donaldson & Owens, 2006). The toddler's need for afternoon naps fades around age 4 or 5, though rests are helpful.

Sleep problems are common in young children. Some have difficulty falling asleep and summon their parents for one, another, and another "curtain call" after lights out. They may wake during the night but are able to console themselves and fall back asleep. About half are awakened by nightmares (frightening dreams in which they or their family are threatened). Some also have night terrors (waking in a state of fright, with no memory of why) (Mindell, Owens, & Carskadon, 1999).

Sleep problems worry parents and result in sleep disruptions for the family. Occasional sleep problems are not a concern, and most children outgrow these problems in time. Chronic inability to fall asleep or frequent nightmares or night terrors, however, can be signs of daytime stress and a call for help.

Scientists are working to understand *why* sleep is so important (Azar, 2006). A number of possible explanations are being explored. Sleep may help young children to learn about their bodies. Twitches or muscle spasms during sleep tell the brain what is out there in the body (Dingfelder, 2006). Sleep also allows the brain to recharge (Azar, 2006). After a full day of stimulation and learning, with synapses constantly firing, the brain runs out of energy and needs time off. Sleep may help children to store memories by allowing new synapses to form and consolidate (Stickgold, 2005). Finally, sleep is essential to physical development because this is when growth hormone (GH) is released (Donaldson & Owens, 2006).

Parents can adopt several practices to promote their children's sleep hygiene (Donaldson & Owens, 2006). Young children develop (and to some degree depend on) regular bedtime rituals and routines: washing or bathing, being read to by a parent, and cuddling a favorite blanket or soft toy before falling asleep. Regular bedtime routines and consistent sleep schedules, plus a quiet time before lights out, help young children to sleep more soundly.

© Andrew Holbrooke/Corbis

Spending some quiet time with parents before lights out can help children to sleep more soundly.

Physiological Indicators of Stress

Stress is a normal and an inevitable part of life. Indeed, some stress is good for us; it keeps us on our toes. Coping with stress begins in the body. When we are under stress, levels of the hormone **cortisol** rise in our bloodstream (Levine, 2003). Cortisol signals our brains to be on guard and mobilizes the body for quick action in an emergency. When the threat has passed and we calm down, levels of cortisol decrease. But individuals' hormonal responses to events—their physiological coping mechanisms—vary (Gunnar, 2006).

cortisol A hormone secreted when individuals are exposed to stress.

Some differences in cortisol are related to children's temperament. Higher levels of cortisol and larger increases in cortisol across the day are observed in young children who have problems regulating their negative emotions and behavior (Dettling, Gunnar, & Donzella, 1999), in children who are fearful of unfamiliar situations (Watamura et al., 2003), and in children who have difficulties playing with peers (Watamura et al., 2003).

Cortisol levels also are linked to children's attachment security (see Chapter 6 for more information about attachment security). In general, children who are securely attached show different patterns and levels of cortisol in the Strange Situation than do insecurely attached children. When children with secure attachments to their mothers are challenged by the series of separations and reunions in the Strange Situation procedure (see Chapter 6 for a description of the procedure), their cortisol levels did not peak in the same way as did those of the insecurely attached children (Gunnar, 2000).

Lieselotte Ahnert and colleagues (2004) have measured children's cortisol when they began a new child-care arrangement. These researchers found children's reactions to the new child-care arrangement were related to their attachment security and whether their mothers were present or not. When mothers accompanied their young children to a new child-care program, children with secure attachment relationships did not show high elevations in cortisol as long as their mothers were with them. Children with insecure relationships showed elevations in cortisol even when their mothers were with them.

Finally, cortisol levels across the day are related to the quality of children's child-care settings. For children in poor-quality child care, cortisol increases across the day, whereas cortisol levels decrease across the day for children who attend high-quality child care. Increases across the day were steepest when children are in child-care settings with lots of children (Dettling et al., 2000).

Physical Abuse and Neglect

Decades of research have provided solid evidence that maltreatment in early childhood increases the risk of later problems, ranging from poor peer relations and low academic achievement in childhood, to delinquency and substance abuse in adolescence, to depression, criminal behavior, chronic health problems, and poor parenting as adults (Cicchetti & Manly, 2001). No one doubts that child abuse is bad for children. The question is why child abuse affects so many areas of behavior so long after the abuse has stopped.

Justin Paget/Shutterstock

Victims of childhood abuse and neglect are at increased risk for social and cognitive problems that extend into adulthood.

Developmental scientists are studying the impact of physical abuse and neglect as long-term and extreme stressors of young children (Gunnar, Fisher, & the Early Experience, Stress, and Prevention Network, 2006; Pollak, 2005). Studies of nonhuman animals indicate that these early patterns may become a permanent or semipermanent part of the animal's makeup—a case where experience molds biology (Levine, 2003). Evidence is accumulating that this may be true for children as well.

In a series of experiments, Seth Pollak studied how abused children process and read emotions. He found that abused children are more sensitive to cues of anger than other children are. In one study, children were asked to look at a series of computerized pictures of human faces that morphed from one emotion to another, such as happy to sad or fearful to angry (Pollak & Kistler, 2002). The abused children were much quicker to identify anger than the control, nonabused children. In another study, children were asked to look at two pictures on the screen and pick the one marked with an "X." Sometimes the abused children took longer to make a decision. Measures of brain waves showed that they paid more attention to the angry face, whether it had an "X" or not, as if they couldn't tear their eyes away from the angry person (Pollak et al., 2001).

Pollak hypothesizes that early emotional experiences, occurring when children's brains are still quite plastic, can exert a powerful and long-lasting influence. In a dangerous environment, where adults are unpredictable and abusive, being able to identify hints of anger quickly and respond by hiding or striking out is adaptive. However, when these children move to other settings, where adults are more consistently caring, oversensitivity to anger is maladaptive. These children perceive anger when it is not there or spend so much time looking for signs of anger that they ignore other, positive emotional cues. When they suspect a threat, they often become aggressive or, alternatively, withdrawn. Mild criticism by a teacher or teasing by a peer triggers an intense reaction. Whatever the setting, they experience the world as dangerous, other people as untrustworthy—and respond in kind. Whether such children can "unlearn" distorted perceptions and develop positive relationships with others is an open question. Research on different types of therapies is under way (Gunnar, Fisher, & the Early Experience, Stress, and Prevention Network, 2006).

Severely neglected children face other challenges. They are ignored and have few interactions with adults, rather than being the recipients of physical harm. These effects are being studied in a tragic "natural experiment." In the 1980s, hundreds of Romanian children were sent to orphanages where they were confined to cribs with minimal human contact beyond simple health care and feeding and where they had very little stimulation from toys or other children. The orphanages have been called "child warehouses" (Ames, 1990). After the fall of the Ceausescu government, the children's plight became known. Families from other countries, including the United States, Canada, and Great Britain, adopted many of the children. Some were young infants. Others were toddlers and preschoolers.

When they joined their new families, the orphanage children had difficulty identifying *any* emotions (Wismer Fries & Pollak, 2004). For example, they could not link a facial expression to a happy, sad, fearful, or angry scenario. The longer they were institutionalized, the greater their emotional impairment. In later chapters, we will return to the development of these children who suffered extreme neglect in their early years. (For a summary of this section, see "Interim Summary 7.2: Physical Health and Well-Being.")

INTERIM SUMMARY 7.2

Physical Health and Well-Being

Injuries and Illnesses	■ Drownings, auto accidents, fires and burns, and airway obstructions are the leading causes of death of young children in the United States. Many of these deaths are preventable. ■ Immunizations protect children from measles, polio, and other life-threatening diseases. ■ Hand-washing with soap and water is the most effective way to prevent the common cold. ■ 9.7 million young children die each year, many from preventable diseases. ■ Proven, cost-effective ways to improve child health and reduce child deaths are oral rehydration therapy (ORT), childhood immunization, mosquito nets treated with insecticides, and safe hygiene and proper nutrition. ■ Malnutrition is the underlying cause of more than half of all deaths of children under the age of 5.
Sleep and Sleep Problems	■ Sleep serves important functions, including giving the brain time to recuperate and to store memories. ■ Growth hormones (GH) are released during sleep. ■ Consistent bedtime routines help children to sleep more soundly.
Physiological Indicators of Stress	■ Amounts of, and changes in, cortisol are physiological indicators of stress. ■ Cortisol levels are related to children's temperament, sociability, attachment security, and quality of child care.
Physical Abuse and Neglect	■ Maltreatment increases the risk of social and academic problems. ■ Abused children are quicker than nonabused children to perceive angry expressions in others. ■ Severely neglected children have difficulties linking facial expressions to happy, sad, anger, and fear situations.

PIAGET, VYGOTSKY, AND BEYOND

Now we turn to cognitive development in early childhood: We begin this section by looking at Piaget's preoperational period and contemporary work that challenged his ideas. Then we describe Vygotsky's sociocultural theory and contemporary work that expanded his theory.

Piaget's Theory: The Preoperational Period

It's obvious that young children do not think like adults do. A child may use the word *horsie* for all large animals; he may be seduced by appearances when shown different-sized beakers of water. Jean Piaget (1896–1980) saw such mistakes as a window into the child's developing mind. Piaget (1929/1955, 1970) identified the second stage of cognitive development, from about age 2 to 7, as the **preoperational period**. He held that preoperational children do not just know "more" than sensorimotor children (up to age 2) or "less" than concrete operational children (roughly age 7 to 12). Rather, preoperational thinking is organized differently than cognition in the earlier and later stages. According to Piaget, cognitive development is more than quantitative change in how *much* children know; it also involves qualitative change in *how* children think. During this period, children acquire a mental storehouse of images and symbols, especially spoken and written words.

preoperational period The second stage in Piaget's theory of cognitive development, from about age 2 to 7, during which children acquire a mental storehouse of images and symbols, especially spoken and written words.

pretend play Make-believe play in which common objects are often used to symbolize other objects.

reversibility A logical operation that requires an understanding that relations can be returned to their original state by reversing operations—if nothing has been added or taken away.

Hallmarks of Preoperational Thinking One hallmark of the preoperational period that represents an advance from the sensorimotor period (see Chapter 5) is children's ability to think about objects and events that are not present in the here and now (Piaget, 1951/1962, 1947/1973). Children are able to represent (that is, *re*-present) previous experiences to themselves mentally. These symbolic representations may take the form of internalized activities, images, or words. A year earlier, the child understood the world only through direct sensory and motor contact and his actions; now he carries the world he has experienced in his head (Piaget, 1952). This is a giant step in cognitive development.

© Sean Justice/Corbis

Pretend play, a hallmark of the preoperational period, provides evidence of symbolic thinking. Pots and spoons are transformed into musical instruments. With a cape and a crown, identities can be transformed.

Language is one of the clearest examples of symbolic representation. Words are symbols: They stand for something else. For example, the word *bug* stands for a small creature that creeps, crawls, or flies, whereas the word *boy* represents a young male who walks, talks, and plays. Children's vocabularies expand dramatically during this period; so does their ability to combine words into original sentences. (We talk about language development and children's understanding of symbol-referent relations later in this chapter.)

Make-believe or pretend play, a favorite activity in early childhood, is another prime example of symbolic representation (Garvey, 1990; Piaget, 1951/1962). In **pretend play**, a block may stand for a telephone or a truck; a cardboard box becomes a fort or a tea table; a stick can serve as a magic wand, a broom, or a horse. Children also can assume different roles. In the housekeeping area at their preschool, they may take the role of baby one day and the role of mother the next day. They may be the horsie one day and pretend to ride the stick horsie the next day.

Language and pretend play demonstrate that the preoperational child is a symbolic thinker (no small feat), but she cannot, according to Piaget, reason logically (1941/1965, 1970). Her thinking does not yet include logical operations such as **reversibility** (understanding that an item that has been changed can be returned to its original state by reversing the process—for instance, that multiplying 5 by 3 to make 15 can be reversed by dividing 15 by 3 to make 5) or **classification** (the ability to divide or sort objects into different sets and subsets, and to consider their inter-relationships—for instance, that Peyton Manning is *both* a quarterback and a member of the Indianapolis Colts, or that a poodle is both a mammal and a dog). Hence Piaget's term preoperational.

classification The ability to divide or sort objects into different sets and subsets, and to consider their interrelationships.

Gaps in Preoperational Thought A major gap in preoperational thinking, according to Piaget (1941/1965), is the young child's inability to grasp **conservation**: the fact that some characteristics of objects (their volume, mass, and number) do not change despite changes in form or appearance. Piaget devised several tasks that test conservation.

conservation The understanding that some characteristics of objects (including volume, mass, and number) do not change despite changes in form or appearance when nothing is added or taken away.

In the *conservation of volume* task, shown in Figure 7.8, you show a child two identical beakers filled with water. Then you ask the child whether they have the same or different amounts. The child usually answers, "The same." Next, as the child watches, you pour the water from one beaker into a taller, thinner one. Again, you ask the child if they have the same or different amounts. Amazingly, the child answers that they are "different"; the taller beaker has more. With the child still watching, you pour the water back into the original beaker and repeat the question. Defying logic (which was Piaget's point), the child now asserts that they are "the same." Appearance (what the child sees and how the beakers look) trumps logic (nothing was added, nothing was taken away, so the two beakers must be holding the same amount).

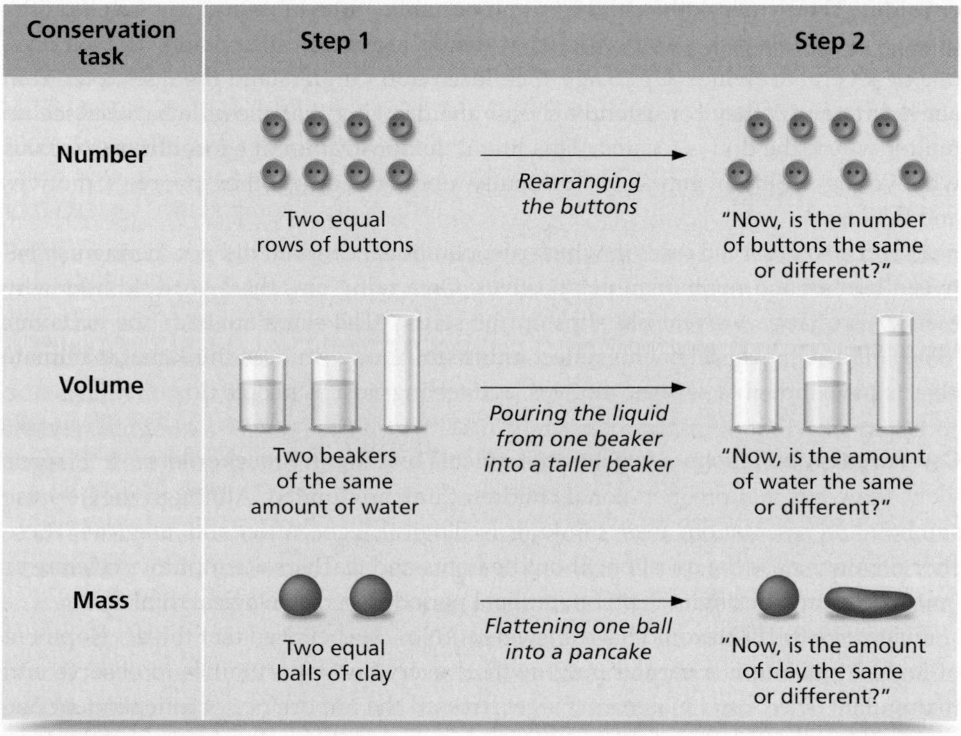

Conservation task	Step 1		Step 2
Number	Two equal rows of buttons	*Rearranging the buttons*	"Now, is the number of buttons the same or different?"
Volume	Two beakers of the same amount of water	*Pouring the liquid from one beaker into a taller beaker*	"Now, is the amount of water the same or different?"
Mass	Two equal balls of clay	*Flattening one ball into a pancake*	"Now, is the amount of clay the same or different?"

FIGURE 7.8

Conservation Tasks in Preoperational Children

Conservation of number (top): When the buttons in the lower row are spread out, a preoperational child will say that the lower row contains more buttons than the upper row. *Conservation of volume* (middle): Even after a preoperational child watches the experimenter pour liquid from one beaker to the other, the child will typically say that the taller beaker contains more water than the shorter beaker. *Conservation of mass* (bottom): If one of the two balls is flattened into a pancake shape while the child is watching, a preoperational child will say that the flattened ball is bigger than the round ball.

Why can't small children grasp conservation? Piaget gave several reasons. First, preoperational children are seduced by appearances. If something *looks* different, then it must *be* different. Second, their thinking is one-dimensional. They focus on one feature (how tall the beaker is), ignoring other features (how wide the beaker is). Piaget called the focus on only one aspect *centration*. Third, a preoperational thinker does not recognize that operations are *reversible*. A child of 7 or 8 years (in the concrete operational stage) might laugh at the questions. "Of course it's the same." Why? "Because it came from the same glass and you could pour it back." The older child is thinking logically. She reasons that because nothing has been added or subtracted, the amount must be the same. According to Piaget, the preoperational child is pre-logical.

egocentrism In Piaget's theory of cognitive development, egocentrism refers to the child's inability to see other people's viewpoints.

Much as the preoperational child does not take into account more than one dimension at a time (e.g., focusing only on the height of the beaker not the width), so he does not consider different points of view. Piaget (1923/1955) called this **egocentrism**, which means, literally, self-centeredness. Piaget did not mean that preoperational children are "selfish" in the sense of wanting everything for themselves. Rather, preoperational children see the world from their own perspective and do not realize that other people *have* different points of view.

Children's performance on the *three mountain task* illustrates egocentrism (Piaget & Inhelder, 1967). You show the child a three-dimensional model of a mountain scene and encourage him or her to walk around the table, looking at the model from different sides. Then you ask the child to sit on one side of the table and put a doll on the other. The child's task is to decide what the doll sees from its position by selecting one of several drawings. Up to age 4, children don't understand the question. From age 4 to about 7, they consistently choose the drawing that shows what *they* see no matter where the doll is located. This literal demonstration of egocentrism explains why young children may have difficulty understanding other people's motives and beliefs.

animism Belief that inanimate objects are alive and have thoughts, feelings, and motives like humans.

Piaget also observed cases in which preoperational children did not distinguish between human and nonhuman perspectives. On a rainy day, the 3-year-old asks why the sky is crying. A 4-year-old slips on the stairs. "The stairs are bad," he exclaims. "They *hit* me!" Such statements reflect **animism**. Young children think that inanimate objects have thoughts, wishes, motives, and feelings just as people do.

Can Parents and Teachers Accelerate Logical Thinking in Preschoolers? In Piaget's view, the ways that preoperational children think are limited. Although they do use symbolic representation, their thinking is illogical, egocentric, and magical. These shortcomings raise the question, Should parents and teachers attempt to accelerate or "push" children through the preoperational period to become logical thinkers?

Piaget (1948/1972) would have answered, "No." He believed that the development of logical thinking is a natural outgrowth of everyday opportunities to observe and manipulate objects and materials. Piaget stressed the importance of independent discovery (Flavell, 1963; Piaget, 1948/1972). In his view, children develop logical thinking primarily through their own explorations and actions. He believed that efforts to teach logical operations to young children would result in empty verbalizations and rote memorization, without true understanding.

Whereas Piaget questioned whether interactions with adults can promote cognitive development, he believed that interactions with other children might serve that function. Disagreements and arguments with peers about appearances versus reality, he believed, could force a child to accommodate (i.e., to change her way of thinking in response to new information she cannot assimilate; see Chapter 5). So, in Piaget's view, peers might promote cognitive development in ways that adults (parents and teachers) cannot.

Contemporary Challenges to Piaget's Theory

Piaget revolutionized the way that we look at children by focusing on how they think rather than how much they know. But like many pioneers, Piaget inspired other scientists to conduct research about his theory, which ultimately challenged many of his conclusions. In general, these scientists have found that the stages of cognitive development are not as clear-cut as Piaget believed (Gelman & Kalish, 2006; Halford & Andrews, 2006). Piaget saw functioning at each period—sensorimotor, preoperational, concrete operations, formal operations—as a unified whole, in which different domains of thinking within each stage fit together.

Contemporary scientists think cognitive development is better described as a series of overlapping waves than as discrete and distinctly different periods (Siegler, 1996, 2006). Some contemporary scientists also argue that using logical reasoning as an endpoint for correct reasoning is not appropriate (Halford & Andrews, 2006). Children's (and adults') responses and solutions may be based on different representations of the problem that do not involve logical deduction.

Perhaps most critical, we have learned from many careful studies that young children understand more than Piaget credited them for (Gelman, 2006). How young children perform on Piaget's tasks depends on how familiar they are with the topic, the situation in which the questions are posed, who asks the questions, and how they ask the questions. Young children may be animistic about the sun or the sea but realistic about other things. They know that people are alive and that rocks and dolls are not. They know that rocks do not have thoughts or feelings and that dolls cannot move on their own (Gelman & Kalish, 2006).

Preschoolers also aren't as consistently deceived by appearances as Piaget suggested. For example, if an experimenter pours a glass of milk and then places it behind an orange screen, they know it is still *really* milk, even though it *looks like* orange juice (Flavell, Flavell, & Green, 1983). When the experimenter asks what the glass *really* holds versus what it *looks like*, they understand the question and answer correctly. They also recognize conservation when the test involves a small number of familiar objects, such as dolls and doll beds.

Theory of Mind Piaget's view that preoperational children are egocentric has drawn particular attention. Are young children really locked into their own point of view? Do they really take appearances literally? A number of contemporary developmental scientists (Astington, 1993; Barr, 2006; Flavell et al., 1983; Wellman, 2002) think not. These scientists are interested in children's **theory of mind**—that is, the ability to attribute mental states—beliefs, intents, desires, knowledge—to oneself and others and to understand that others have beliefs, desires, and intentions that are different from one's own,

theory of mind The ability to attribute mental states—beliefs, intents, desires, knowledge—to oneself and others and to understand that others have beliefs, desires, and intentions that are different from one's own.

Young children aren't always egocentric. For example, when talking to a baby, 3- and 4-year-olds (like adults) use shorter sentences, simpler words, and a higher intonation to capture the infant's attention (Shatz & Gelman, 1973). They seem to recognize that babies do not understand speech the way older children and adults do. Three-year-olds also distinguish between real and pretend events. For example, they know the difference between a boy who is thinking about a cookie and a boy who has a cookie; they know which boy can touch, eat, or share the cookie (Astington, 1993).

Age 4 is considered a watershed in the development of a theory of mind (Barr, 2006; Flavell et al., 1983). The classic demonstration is the *false-belief task*. A child is shown, say, a Band-Aids box and asked what is inside. Naturally enough, she answers "Band-Aids." But when she opens the box, she finds it contains crayons. The experimenter tells her that another child, who hasn't seen this demonstration, will be asked to guess what is in the box. What will that child think? Most 3-year-olds respond that the other child will guess crayons, assuming that he knows what they know (and confirming Piaget's notion of egocentrism). However, most 4-year-olds predict the other child will be fooled as they were and guess that the box contains Band-Aids. Variations of the false-belief task have been tried on children in many cultures with similar results, although sometimes a theory of mind is evident in 5- and 6-year-olds rather than in 4-year-olds (Barr, 2006).

An understanding that other people can have false beliefs arises from the realization that what is inside a person's head may be different from what is outside; that thoughts and beliefs are mental representations, which can sometimes be wrong. Four-year-olds understand that different people can see or hear different versions of the same object or event. But not until about age 6 do children recognize that different people who see or hear the *same* thing may remember it differently (Pillow & Henrichon, 1996).

What causes children to begin developing a theory of mind? Researchers are learning that cognitive and language abilities play a part (Barr, 2006). But experiences with adults and older children also are important, as Judy Dunn and her colleagues observed in young children's interactions with their mothers and siblings (Dunn, 1991; Dunn et al., 1991). She found that 1½- to 2-year-olds sometimes smiled or laughed as they repeated behavior that had been forbidden (dropping a toy from their high chair; spilling juice on the carpet)—as if they enjoyed their power to provoke a reaction from their mother. On other occasions, they hid from their mother before engaging in a forbidden act, or they blamed a sibling for a mishap. The young children also would tease their siblings and seemed well aware of actions that would be particularly distressing for their sibs. Thus, the children demonstrate a sophisticated understanding of what their mother and siblings know (or didn't know), what they will tolerate (or not tolerate).

Vygotsky's Sociocultural Theory

Russian developmental scientist Lev Vygotsky (1896–1934) also challenged Piaget's views. Although Vygotsky (1978, 1986) shared Piaget's belief that children are motivated learners who actively seek to understand their world, he disagreed with Piaget's other basic assumptions. Piaget saw the child as a solitary scientist and focused on what the child could do working alone, without assistance. Vygotsky (1978) saw the child as embedded in a social context and focused on what she could do with the assistance of adults or older, more skilled children. For Vygotsky, cognitive development was the result of *collaboration* in a particular sociocultural setting. In effect, the child is an apprentice. Vygotsky also measured development in terms of the child assuming more important social roles and responsibilities, not the child's use of logic. Finally, Vygotsky saw cognitive development as continuous, not as distinct stages.

zone of proximal development (ZPD) The gap between what a child can do alone and what a child can do with assistance.

scaffolding Providing learning opportunities, materials, hints, and clues when a child has difficulty with a task.

Zone of Proximal Development At the heart of Vygotsky's theory was an idea called the *zone of proximal development.* The **zone of proximal development (ZPD)** is the area between what a child can do alone and what a child can do with assistance. The ZPD is made up of skills, ideas, and understandings that are just beyond the child's reach, that the child is beginning to perform and can do with support or assistance from adults or more skilled peers. As you read in Chapter 5, the parent or older child's role is to support the child's efforts with **scaffolding**; that is, to provide learning opportunities, materials, hints, and clues when the child gets stuck (Bruner, Jolly, & Sylva, 1976). A key feature of effective scaffolding is that the parent provides only as much support as the child needs; once skills are mastered, the parent withdraws the "scaffold" or support (because that particular support is not needed).

When reading picture books, parents (ideally) adjust their prompts to the child's ZPD. With 15-month-olds, parents point to illustrations and ask leading questions that supply the answer: "Is that an elephant?" When the child is able to label familiar objects, parents begin to ask for information that is not visible on the page ("What do bees make?"), providing clues that lead the child to an answer ("What does Winnie-the-Pooh like to eat?" "Honey, that's right. Bees make honey. You knew."). Through these interactions in the ZPD, parents scaffold early literacy activities. Helping the child to come up with the right answer herself, providing assistance when it is needed, and allowing the child to "do it herself" when she can are part of the scaffold.

© Big Cheese Photo/Jupiterimages

A key feature of effective scaffolding is that the parent provides only as much support as the child needs. Once a particular skill is mastered, the parent withdraws the "scaffold" or support because that particular support is no longer needed.

Guided Participation Barbara Rogoff (2003) has expanded Vygotsky's sociocultural theory and the idea of the ZPD to include **guided participation,** or the varied ways children learn their society's values and practices through participation in family and community activities. Guided participation goes beyond actions intended to be instructional. It includes times when children watch adults going about their business and listen to adults talking among themselves, participate in cultural rituals and everyday activities, listen to family stories or their culture's mythology, play traditional games, and so on. When adults or older children praise, shame, or laugh about a child's behavior, they are guiding participation by providing a frame of how to behave and how *not* to behave.

For example, middle-class Euro-American families (directly and indirectly) prepare children for their future role as student. With toddlers, parents combine play with vocabulary lessons. They often ask *known-answer questions*, such as "What is this?" (holding up a toy) or "Where is your bellybutton?" Both the parent and child know the answer, so the question isn't a request for information. Rather, parents are teaching the format used for test questions in school. At the dinner table, parents ask children to talk about their day and, as in school, each child gets a turn. When a child hesitates, they prompt the child with questions such as "What did you do?" "Who was there?" "And then . . ." "And after that . . ."—providing a scaffold for the narrative format used in school (when, where, what, who, and why). Even before they learn to read, middle-class Euro-American children learn to "talk like a book" (Gauvain, 2001; Rogoff, 2003).

guided participation The varied ways children learn their society's values and practices through participation in family and community activities.

Children learn some social and cultural lessons on their own, simply by observing. In one example, a U.S. mother was working at home, spending hours every day transcribing tape-recorded conversations onto her computer for a research project, while her 3-year-old daughter played nearby. One day the little girl set up her own "office."

> She had pulled her small director's chair up to her bed, which served as a desk. It held her "computer" (really a toy typewriter), as well as her small plastic tape recorder. She would play a section of *Star Wars,* and then stop the recording to bang out a message on the plastic keys of her typewriter. Back and forth she went between the recorder and her "computer," playing and typing, playing a new section and typing again, in a way more than a little reminiscent of my efforts at transcription. (Wolf & Heath, 1992, pp. 11–12)

Guided participation is seen in other cultures (Rogoff, 2003). In a Mayan village in Guatemala, for example, a young child watched her mother make tortillas each morning. One day the mother rolled a small ball of dough, flattened it a little, and gestured to her daughter to continue. After the child seemed to be doing her best, the mother began demonstrating techniques to make the play tortilla thinner and more even—an example of scaffolding. Emulating adults is one way children actively seek knowledge and skills.

Just as the content of guided participation varies, so do the rules for participation. In some cultures children are expected to learn by listening and holding their tongues. For example, in Native American communities, asking direct questions often is considered rude because it obliges the other person to reply. Silence is the appropriate response when a person does not have a reply or wish to make one. The Inuit of Arctic Quebec say, "The more intelligent [children] become, the quieter they become" (Freeman, 1978, p. 21). Euro-American teachers find these children's silence unnerving, even disrespectful. To some degree these children must *un*learn the manners they acquire at home to succeed in schools where Euro-American standards prevail and where how children talk can be as important as what they say. In classrooms, non-Inuit teachers ask children to speak up, in contrast to their parents' expectations. This clash surfaced in a parent-teacher conference:

NON-INUIT TEACHER: Your son is talking well in class. He is speaking up a lot.

INUIT PARENT: I am sorry. (Crago, 1992, p. 496)

Language and Thought Both Piaget and Vygotsky were interested in the relationship between language and thought. Piaget (1923/1955) believed that the development of thought precedes language—that is, we think and then we communicate. In Piaget's view, children in the sensorimotor period have impressions or rudimentary ideas about objects and people before they are able to speak, and they must form mental representations before they consistently attach names to things. Thought comes first.

In contrast, Vygotsky (1986) argued that thought and language develop together. He held that the child's first attempts to speak are efforts to establish and maintain social contact. When an infant says, "Bow-wow," the mother responds, "Yes! That's a dog." Using a word elicits and maintains social interaction, which is the child's primary goal (though she may be expressing excitement, too). These interactions served to place the child in a zone of proximal development. So-called social speech is all-important at this stage.

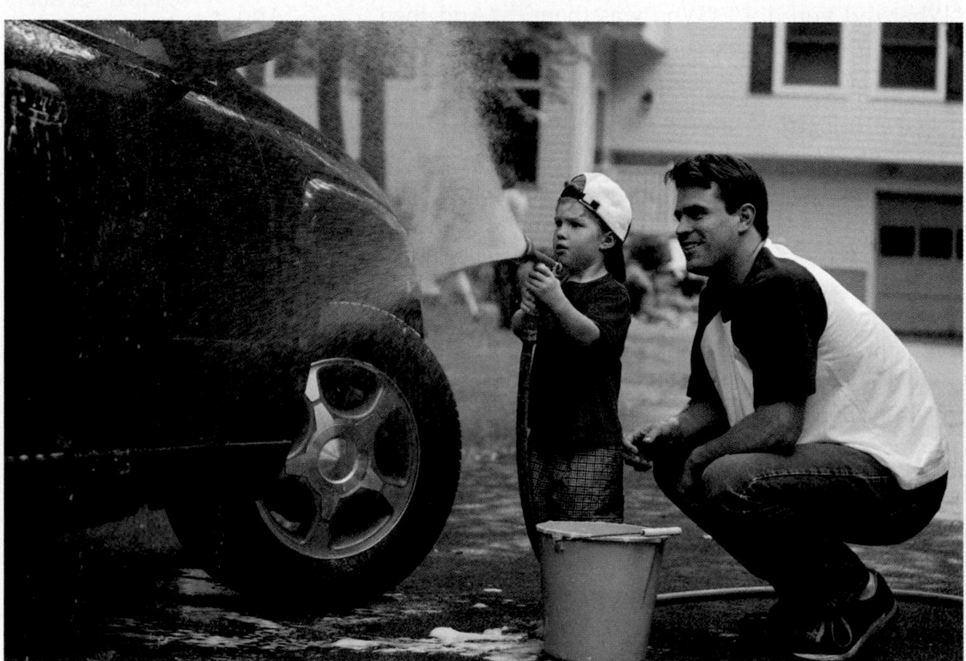

© Comstock Images/Jupiterimages

Children learn about their society's values and practices as they participate in everyday activities.

Around age 3 or 4, according to Vygotsky, children begin to use the language they developed for social purposes as a tool to organize their thoughts and actions. Faced with a problem, they talk out loud to themselves. Thus, language facilitates problem solving and thought. The self-directed talk helps children to recall what they know and to plan and organize what they want to do. "I want to draw a tree. I need the green pencil for the leaves. But I need a brown pencil, too, for the tree trunk," and so on. Gradually, private speech becomes silent or inner talk. The child runs through possible solutions in her mind instead of talking out loud. Vygotsky held that adult thought is an advanced version of inner talk. Of course, adults also talk to themselves out loud, usually when no one else is around. "Great! I got it. Now, what next?" (For a summary of this section, see "Interim Summary 7.3: Piaget, Vygotsky, and Beyond.")

INTERIM SUMMARY 7.3

Piaget, Vygotsky, and Beyond

Piaget's Theory: The Preoperational Period	■ Hallmarks of preoperational thinking include being able to think about objects and events that are not present. ■ **Pretend play** is another hallmark. ■ Gaps in preoperational thinking include **egocentrism**, **animism**, and an inability to conserve. ■ Piaget believed that adults should not try to teach conservation or other types of logical thinking. Instead, he argued that development occurs through independent discovery, active manipulation of materials, and interactions with peers.
Contemporary Challenges to Piaget's Theory	■ Research on young children's **theory of mind** indicates that they are not as egocentric as Piaget thought. ■ Theory of mind refers to individuals' awareness of their own and other people's thought processes and mental states. ■ Performance on false belief tasks indicate that age 4 is a watershed in the development of a theory of mind. ■ Young children only gradually develop an understanding of symbols, where an entity can stand for something other than itself. ■ There is not a discrete qualitative shift in symbolic thinking of the sort that Piaget proposed.
Vygotsky's Sociocultural Theory	■ The **zone of proximal development (ZPD)** (the area between what a child can do alone and what a child can do with assistance) is at the center of Vygotsky's theory. ■ **Scaffolding** refers to how parents or older peers can support a child's learning by providing assistance or help when it is needed. ■ **Guided participation** refers to the varied ways children learn their society's values and practices through participation in family and community activities. ■ Vygotsky believed that language and thought develop in tandem. ■ Young children begin by using language for social purposes. Gradually, self-directed talk becomes silent or inner speech. ■ Piaget believed that thought precedes language. In his view, children must first form mental representations before they consistently attach names to things.

OTHER ADVANCES IN COGNITIVE AND LANGUAGE DEVELOPMENT

Other scientists have focused on specific aspects of children's thought and language in early childhood. These studies document changes in attention, memory, language, literacy, and mathematics, competencies that help to prepare children for success at school.

Information Processing

The information-processing approach to cognitive development deals with basic questions about how people acquire, encode, store, and use information (Munakata, 2006). By analogy, the brain is similar to a computer. When you work on a computer, you encode information by typing on the keyboard. To store the information, you press keys that save the information on a disk. Similarly, our brains acquire and select information (perception and attention), store and retrieve information (memory), and use information to cope with the present situation or plan for the future (problem solving) (see Figure 7.9). The question for developmental scientists is, how do these elements of information processing (perception, attention, memory, and problem solving) change over the course of development?

We discussed perception in Chapter 5 when we described the development of infant cognition. Here we will look at attention and memory. Being able to focus selectively on specific information (attention) and then being able to store and retrieve that information (memory) are essential to all types of learning. The two work together: to remember something you have to pay attention to it. What do young children notice? How much do they recall?

continuous performance task (CPT) A laboratory task designed to assess attentiveness and impulsivity by pushing a button when a specific object appears on the computer screen.

impulsivity As measured by CPT, how often a child incorrectly pushes a button designating that an object is on the screen.

sensory memory A subconscious process of picking up sensory information—sights, sounds, smells, touch—from the environment.

working memory Conscious, short-term representations of what a person is actively thinking about at a given time.

long-term memory The collection of information that is mentally encoded and stored; it is believed to have potentially unlimited capacity and no time limits.

generic memory A script or general outline of how familiar activities occur based on experience.

Attention Attention consists of focusing on particular information while ignoring other information. One classic measure of attention is the **continuous performance task (CPT)** (Rosvold et al., 1956; see Figure 7.10). In this exercise, the child is asked to push a button whenever a particular object (say, a chair) appears on a computer monitor. The researcher flashes a series of pictures (chairs and other things) over a 7-minute period. By design, the task is fairly boring; maintaining attention requires effort. On the CPT, attention is measured by how many times the child pushes the button when a chair is on the screen. **Impulsivity** is measured by how often the child (incorrectly) pushes the button when another object is on the screen. Three-year-olds and most 4-year-olds perform poorly; some 4- and most 5-year-olds get more right than wrong answers; and 6-year-olds make only a few mistakes (Ruff & Capozzoli, 2003).

Improvements in attention are linked to the maturation of the brain's prefrontal cortex and basal ganglia (Nelson, Thomas, & de Haan, 2006). But individual differences in CPT scores show that the child's environment and experience with parents are also important (NICHD Early Child Care Research Network [ECCRN], 2003b). Children from stimulating homes with warm, responsive parents gain control of their attention earlier than do children from less supportive homes. Why? One reason may be that frequent conversations with parents provide young children with guided opportunities to observe and practice concentration and self-regulation.

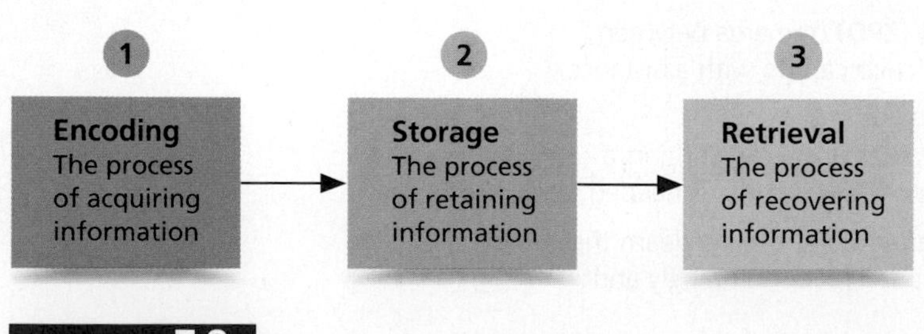

FIGURE 7.9

Information-Processing Model

Three steps involved in the information-processing model of cognitive development—encoding, storage, and retrieval—are analogous to creating a document on your computer. You begin by typing in the information (encoding) and then it is saved onto the hard drive (storage); when you need the information, you can open the saved document (retrieval).

Memory We tend to think of memory as a mental record of something we experienced, witnessed, heard, or read—much like a photograph or video recording. But there is far more to memory than pushing a save button in our minds. The information-processing model identifies three steps in memory processing: sensory memory, working memory, and long-term memory (Martinez, 2010; Pressley & Hilden, 2006). **Sensory memory** is the entryway. It is a subconscious process of picking up sensory information from the environment (sights, sounds, smells, and touch). Sensory memory consists of fleeting impressions. This information is either forgotten or transferred to **working memory**: conscious representations of what a person is actively thinking about at a given time. It depends on the child (or adult) paying attention and encoding the impression in some way—for example, attaching it to a known word or image. Working memory improves during early childhood from recall of two numbers at age 2½ years to five numbers at age 7, and about seven numbers in adulthood (Kail, 2003).

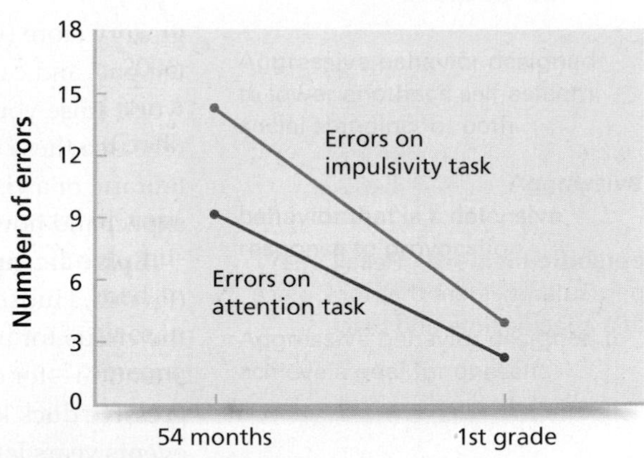

FIGURE 7.10

Errors on Impulsivity and Attention Tasks by Age

As children get older, their success on the Continuous Performance Task (CPT) improves. When 4½-year-olds were retested in first grade, the number of errors they made on tests of impulsivity (that is, clicking that the item had appeared on the screen when it had not) declined. Errors in attention (failing to click when the item appeared on the screen) also declined, indicating that older children are better at regulating these processes than younger children.

Source: NICHD Early Child Care Research Network. (2003). Do children's attention processes mediate the link between family predictors and school readiness? *Developmental Psychology,* 39, 581–593.

Part of the reason for the improvements in working memory is biological; part, social. As discussed previously, the prefrontal cortex and corpus callosum, which provide the "hardware" for short-term memory, are developing during early childhood and provide the capacity that supports an expanded working memory (Nelson et al., 2006). And, as is the case with attention, the development of working memory is accelerated by warm, stimulating interactions with parents at home and by attending preschools or child-care centers that are high quality (NICHD ECCRN, 2002).

Working memory lasts at most a few minutes. The information either fades or is stored in **long-term memory**, which has a potentially unlimited capacity and no time limitations (Martinez, 2010). *Long-term memory* can store a vast amount of interconnected information, encoded in a variety of formats. Access to long-term memory may take the form of *recall* (summoning up stored information) or *recognition* (identifying something as the same as, or similar to, something encountered before). For most people (children included), recognition is easier than recall (Martinez, 2010).

Some researchers (Pressley & Hilden, 2006) have used hiding and finding games to learn about young children's memory strategies. Preschoolers can be very strategic when it comes to remembering where objects have been hidden when the situations are very familiar to them—for example, finding a Big Bird doll in a living room setting (DeLoache, Cassidy, & Brown, 1985). In more difficult and less familiar tasks, such as finding a candy hidden under one of six cups on a turntable that would spin quickly, some preschoolers (but not all) are able to use directive prompts from an experimenter to develop strategies (such as marking the right cup with a gold star) that help them find the hidden candy (Ritter, 1978).

Scientists distinguish among several types of long-term memory (Bauer, 2006). **Generic memory**, which begins at about age 2, is a script or general outline of what happens when, based on experience (Nelson, 2006). Children have scripts for going to the

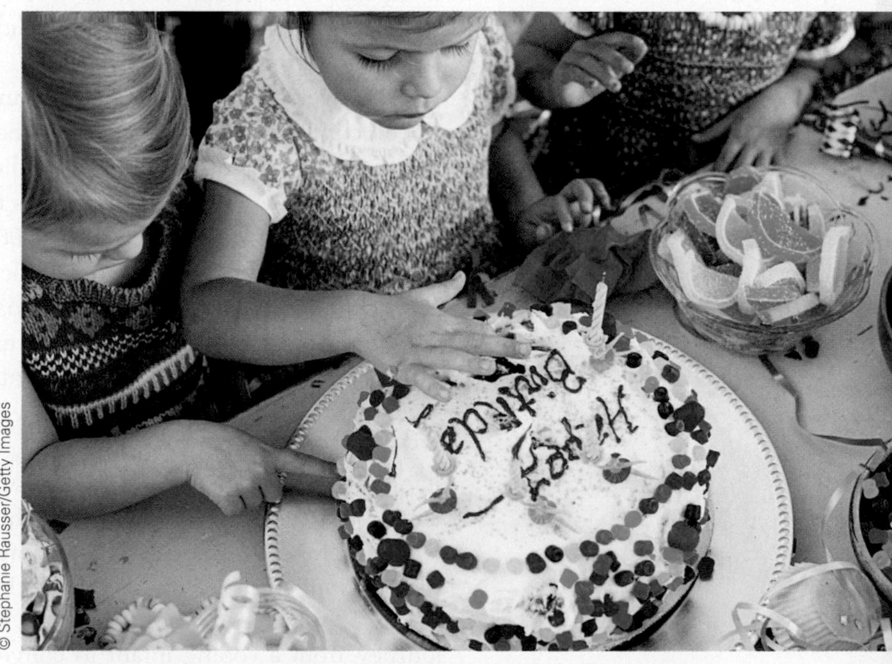

Many young children in the United States have well-developed scripts for events such as attending a birthday party (you arrive, give presents, sing "Happy Birthday," and eat cake).

grocery store (you get a cart, put in items from the shelves, go to the check-out counter, pay, and carry your groceries away in bags), going to school (you sit at a desk, do work, raise your hand to ask a question), and other familiar activities. Often children rehearse these scripts in pretend play, re-creating a trip to the doctor, a meal in a restaurant, or a visit to grandparents from memory. Scripts help children to know what to expect and how to behave in common situations.

episodic memory Recall of a particular incident that took place at a specific time and place.

Episodic memory is recall of a particular incident at a specific time and place (Fivush, Hudson, & Nelson, 1984). Three-year-olds may remember details of a trip to the circus for a year or more. They also recall events that particularly captured their attention—for example, a visit to the river to feed the ducks when one particularly aggressive duck kept all the others away from the bread—sometimes remembering these events years later.

autobiographical memory Recall of individual episodes that are personally meaningful, which begins at about age 4 and may last for decades.

Autobiographical memory, recall of individual episodes that are personally meaningful, begins at about age 4 and may last for decades (Nelson & Fivush, 2004). Autobiographical memories become part of the child's developing self-concept or self-image (see Chapter 8). Beginning in early childhood, each of us constructs a personal history, a life story we revise and edit as we grow older to describe ourselves and explain our attitudes and behavior, to ourselves as well as to others.

Why do some early memories last while others fade? One factor is the uniqueness of the event—for example, the death of a grandparent. It may be the child's first experience of death, of the loss of someone she is close to and the emotional climate and rituals surrounding death. Another factor is personal participation, as opposed to watching. For example, riding a pony is more memorable than watching a riding class. Perhaps most important is talking to a parent or another adult about an event.

The development of memory in early childhood is partly a social process, guided by parents and others. Mary Gauvain (2001, p. 102) uses the example of Molly, age 5. At a family holiday dinner, someone asked Molly about her first day at school. After some hesitation, Molly responded, "It was fun." A long silence indicated that she was finished. Then relatives began asking questions (based on their own scripts for school). "Who's your teacher? Is she nice?" "Did you have a snack? A nap?" and so on. After a lively half-hour discussion, Molly's mother thanked her for telling everyone about her day. "Yes," Molly exclaimed, "and I did it all myself!" She did, but with considerable scaffolding from her family.

The development of memory and language work hand in hand. To become verbally fluent, children need to learn (remember) many words; words, in turn, make it easier to store and recall memories. When children are able to put memories into words, they are better able to hold these memories in mind, think about them, and compare them to other people's memories (Bauer, 2006).

Long-term memories, which include recollections that may last a lifetime, begin in early childhood. These memories are part of a complex selective constructive process. Children do not remember or recall exactly what happened, but rather *construct* a memory out of what caught their attention (Bauer, 2006).

Language

Language development, which begins one word at a time in infancy, takes off in early childhood (Tomasello, 2006). During this period, children progress from one- and two-word utterances ("Daddy eat") to simple sentences ("Daddy eat breakfast") to complex grammatical forms and a rich vocabulary ("Why didn't Daddy eat his cereal?"—which combines a question, a negative [did*n't*], and a possessive [*his*]). The journey from a cooing infant to conversationalist illustrates the interplay of innate characteristics and experience (Goldin-Meadow, 2006).

Developmental scientists chart language development in early childhood by looking at several different phenomena: vocabulary (the words we know and their associated

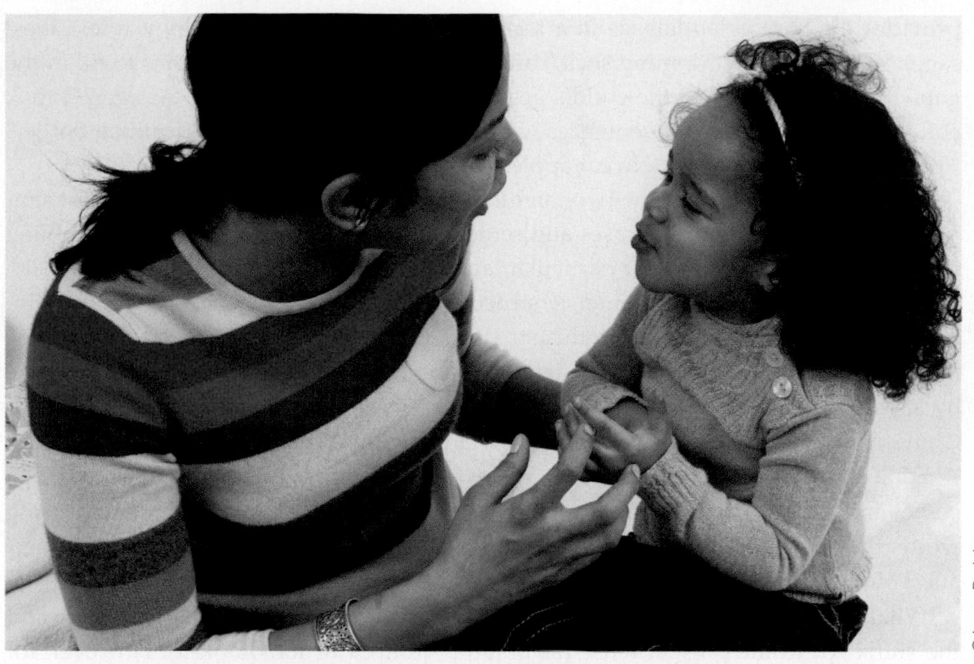

© Laura Dwight

The more speech children are exposed to from parents and teachers, the faster their vocabularies grow. Conversations help to fuel language development.

knowledge), morphology and syntax (our understanding of the rules we use to put words together), and semantics (our understanding of what words and sentences mean) (Hoff, 2006).

Around age 2, young children's vocabularies begin to expand rapidly. 2-year-olds know about 200 words. At age 3, they understand and can use 900 to 1,000 words. By age 6, they have vocabularies of 8,000 to 14,000 words (Carey, 1978). How can children do this?

As we discussed in Chapter 5, a key to vocabulary growth is **fast mapping**, a phenomenon that refers to when children pick up words they have heard only a few times (Carey & Bartlett, 1978). Children intuit meanings from the context, the topic of conversation, similar words, and their understanding of what kinds of words go where. For example, a child may grasp that *tomorrow* means something like "not now" before he understands the relationship between the words *yesterday*, *today*, and *tomorrow*. As children hear a word used more often and try using it themselves, their definition becomes more refined.

fast mapping A phenomenon that refers to how easily children pick up words they have heard only a few times.

The more speech children are exposed to from parents and teachers, the faster the rate at which their vocabularies grow (Hart & Risley, 1995). Mothers in high-income families are likely to have higher levels of education than mothers in low-income families and so have wider vocabularies. They talk more to their children and often follow the child's interests, rather than dictating the subject. In part, this explains why poor children may be a year or more behind better-off children in vocabulary at age 4 (Hoff, 2006). First-born children, who are exposed to more talk from parents, generally have larger vocabularies than do later-born children (Hoff-Ginsburg, 1998). Children who attend child-care centers with a high caregiver-to-children ratio that permits more adult/child conversations have richer vocabularies than children whose child-care center has a low caregiver-to-child ratio (NICHD Early Child Care Research Network, 2000b).

Between about 18 and 36 months, children begin putting two words together in simple utterances called **telegraphic speech** (Bloom, 1970). The young speaker

telegraphic speech Simple, meaningful two-word utterances spoken by young children.

provides the bare essentials, as in a telegram (or in modern technology, a text message): "Throw ball," "Mommy sock," and "Baby drink." The listener has to fill in the gaps from the context or the child's gestures and facial expressions. At age 2½ to 3, children advance to longer sentences with more information: "Baby drinking bottle," "That Mommy sock," and "No eat apple."

What is revealing about the two- and three-word stage is that children are not simply repeating or imitating phrases and sentences that they've heard, but are applying some of the basic rules of their particular language (Goldin-Meadow, 2006; Tomasello, 2006). In English, the basic sentence structure is agent-verb-object (as in "I ate dinner"). "Throw ball" conforms to this structure (verb-action), as does "No eat apple" (verb-object, implying "Me" as the agent). Young children rarely violate this structure by saying "Ball throw" or "Apple no eat." Likewise, children who speak French or Chinese use the correct word order of their languages (Waxman & Lidz, 2006).

overregulation When children mistakenly apply regular grammatical rules to irregular cases.

semantics The meaning of words and sentences, or the content of speech.

Some of the best evidence that children extract and apply rules from their language comes from the mistakes children make. Around age 2½ to 3, children begin using words they never said or heard before, such as "He taked my toy," "I seed a horsie," and "Mommy goed to work."

What's happening? In English, the general rule for forming the past tense is to add the suffix *–ed* to the present tense (as in jump/jump*ed* or look/look*ed*). However, for some common English verbs the past tense is irregular (as in take/*took*, go/*went*, and see/*saw*). When children discover the regular rule for the past tense, they mistakenly apply it to all verbs, including irregular verbs. Young children also make mistakes with irregular plurals (e.g., calling geese *gooses* or feet *foots*). **Overregulation**, as this is called, is not a step backward but a step forward—it's a sign that children are learning the underlying structure of their language, not just mimicking what they hear (Clark, 1998). By the end of early childhood, most children learn that general rules have exceptions, though 5- and 6-year-olds still make mistakes.

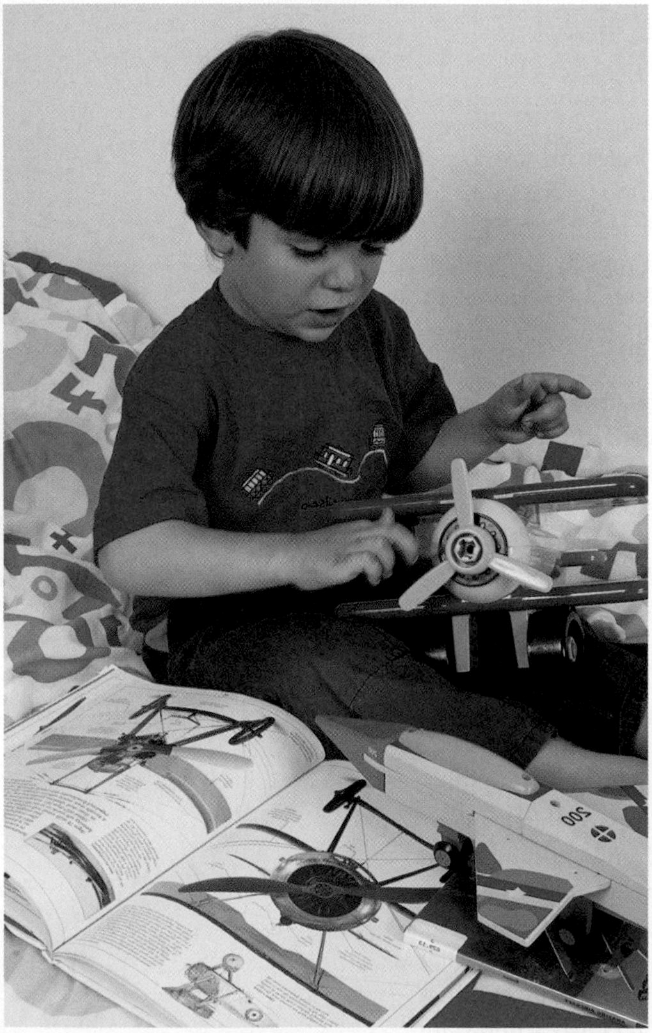

Semantics refers to the *meaning* of words and sentences, or the content of speech (Hoff, 2006). There is more to semantics, however, than learning which word applies to which person, object, activity, or trait. In learning what words mean, children are also learning how their culture uses concepts to organize their perceptions of the world. A *concept* is a mental representation or category, a general notion that applies to many individual cases. Concepts help a young child simplify, sort, and group the many things in the environment (Gelman, 2006).

Children do not build concepts one case at a time, but rather take their cues from "authorities," adults and older children (Gelman & Kalish, 2006). When a father says, "That birdie is a cardinal," the child grasps that a "cardinal" is a type of bird, not a synonym for bird (Mervis, Pani, & Pani, 2003). When the child sees a new bird, she already knows something about it. She can think and talk about birds even when one isn't present, can remember birds she saw in the past, and can imagine birds she will see in the future.

Current research indicates that young children's concepts are more advanced than Piaget believed. They not only have concrete concepts about things they can see or touch (birds, flowers, cars) but also have abstract concepts (Gelman, 2006).

© Laura Dwight

Child experts have extensive knowledge in specific areas that accelerate the development of hierarchical concepts in those areas.

For example, they know that common objects, like spoons and scissors, were designed for a purpose (Keleman, 2004). They understand that germs can cause illness, even though you can't see them (Kalish, 1996). If they learn something new about a brontosaurus, they are more likely to apply this to a triceratops (another dinosaur, but the two look quite different) than to a rhinoceros (which is quite similar to a brontosaurus in appearance, but not a dinosaur) (Gelman, 2006). This is the opposite of what Piaget would have predicted for a preoperational child. As you read earlier, Piaget believed that preoperational thinking was driven by the way things look. Although this is true a lot of time, it isn't true all the time, especially in situations where children have specialized knowledge about the subject matter.

Specialized knowledge accelerates the development of concepts in particular areas (Gelman, 2006). Child experts in dinosaurs, construction vehicles, or chess have richer, more defined, and hierarchical concepts for their particular field than do adult novices. Expertise (at any age) is not a reflection of general intelligence, but rather of knowledge of a specific topic or domain. Exposure is clearly important: A child cannot become an expert on birds without opportunities to bird watch, guidance from someone who is knowledgeable, and perhaps binoculars and bird books.

Emergent Literacy

Foundations of literacy are seen during early childhood (National Research Council, 1998; NICHD ECCRN, 2005c). A typical 3-year-old knows how to hold a book and turn pages; listens when read to; understands the pictures in books and names characters and features; may distinguish pictures from print; and perhaps recognizes a few letters. A typical 4-year-old can recite the alphabet and recognize some letters; relates stories to "real life" (his or her own experiences); enjoys rhymes and word play; and may pretend-write in play. A typical 5-year-old may track the print when being read a simple, familiar book; spontaneously talks about the content of story and information

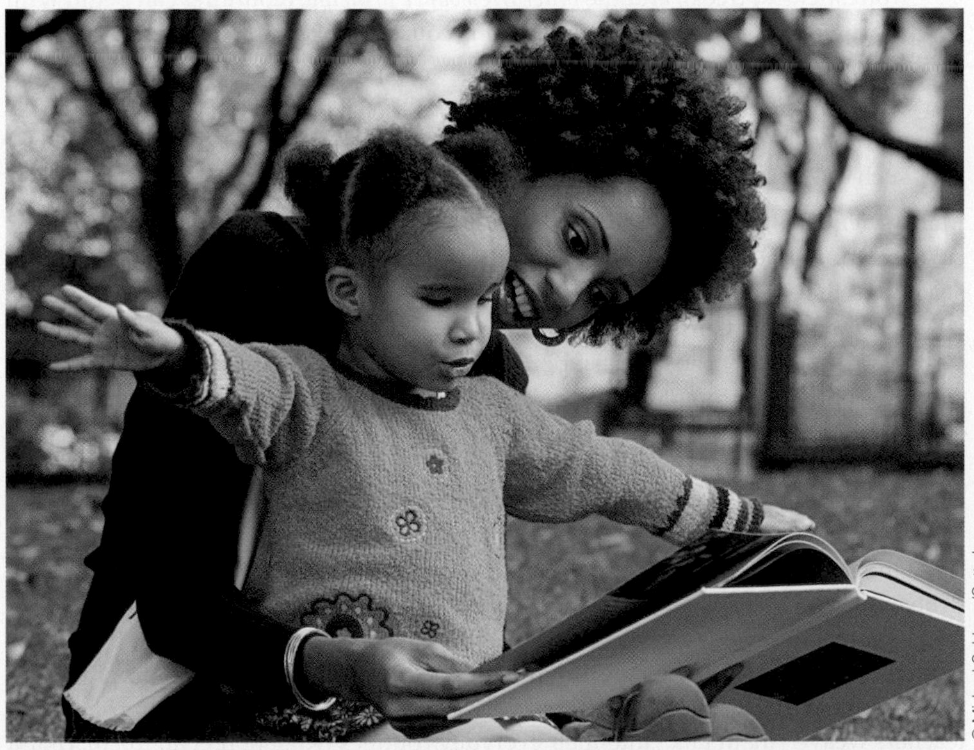

Parents can promote literacy by reading with children, talking about the story content, pointing out letter–sound correspondence, and playing language sound games.

books; can identify all, and write most, letters; recognizes and can spell some simple words (including his or her name); but mostly uses invented spellings when writing (Snow, 2006).

Whether being an accomplished reader in kindergarten is beneficial (because it gives children a fast start) or detrimental (because it is done at the expense of other more developmentally appropriate activities such as pretend play) is still being studied and debated (Hirsh-Pasek & Golinkoff, 2003). But there is agreement among researchers and practitioners about the value of exposure to books and language (Snow, 2006).

Early Mathematical Thinking

Like emergent literacy, everyday mathematical knowledge and reasoning develop in ordinary environments, often without special instruction, and earlier than you might imagine. During early childhood, before they enter first grade, youngsters master a number of basic mathematical concepts, including the following:

- *Magnitude*: Three-year-olds understand the meaning of "a lot," whether applied to a bowl of cherries or cars in a parking lot (Wagner & Walters, 1982), and recognize which of two groups of objects has "more" (Ginsburg & Baroody, 2003).
- *Numbers*: Although the first 10 numbers are essentially nonsense syllables that have to be memorized, 2- and 3-year-olds can recite them—though not always in the right order, as in "one, three, two, seven" (Ginsburg, 1989).
- *Counting*: Two- and 3-year-olds can count very small sets (up to four objects) (Ginsburg et al., 2006). Three-year-olds understand the basic rules of counting—the *one-to-one principle* (one and only one number word should be assigned to each object; i.e., a single teddy bear can't be number 2 *and* number 3); the *stable order principle* (number words should be said in the same order all of the time); the *cardinality principle* (the last number in a counting sequence indicates the quantity of items in a set); the *abstraction principle* (anything can be counted, from sticks to trees); and the *order irrelevance principle* (counting can begin with any item in a set as long as each item is counted once and only once).
- *Addition and subtraction*: Three- and 4-year-olds understand the general idea that adding increases and subtracting decreases the size of a set (Bertelli, Joanni, & Martlew, 1998). They can also perform calculations involving small numbers, such as 2 + 1 or 3 – 1 (Starkey & Gelman, 1982).

Many scientists (Gelman, 2000; Ginsburg et al., 2006) believe that there is a biological basis for mathematical concepts. Children are born with number-relevant mental structures that promote the development of counting and basic geometry (Geary, 2006; Gelman, 2000; Ginsburg et al., 2006).

But—as is usually the case—experience also counts. Ordinary physical and social environments promote the development of mathematical thinking (Ginsburg et al., 2006). Every human environment has objects to count, shapes to recognize, locations to identify, and so forth. In addition, almost all cultures offer children counting systems (Zaslavsky, 1973), as well as games and activities that promote mathematical thinking.

At the beginning of kindergarten, children vary widely in mathematical knowledge (Klibanoff et al., 2006). As with language, children from middle-class families score much higher, on average, on tests of math achievement than do children from poor families. Moreover, children enrolled in full-time, high quality preschool programs are more mathematically proficient (Campbell et al., 2001). What matters most is that teachers weave "math talk" into their everyday routines (Klibanoff et al., 2006). (For a summary of this section, see "Interim Summary 7.4: Other Advances in Cognitive and Language Development.")

INTERIM SUMMARY 7.4

Other Advances in Cognitive and Language Development

Information Processing	■ Attention refers to how we are able to focus on some information while ignoring other information. ■ Improvements in attention are linked to the maturation of the prefrontal cortex and basal ganglia. ■ Children whose parents are cognitively stimulating, warm, and responsive are better at controlling their attention than children whose parents do not act in these ways. ■ **Sensory memory** is a subconscious process of picking up sensory information from the environment and lasts only a few seconds at most. ■ **Working memory** consists of conscious, short-term representations of what a person is actively thinking about at a given time. ■ Working memory lasts at most a few minutes. The information either fades or is stored in long-term memory. ■ Maturation of the prefrontal cortex and corpus callosum provide the capacity that supports an expanded working memory. ■ **Long-term memory** can store a vast amount of interconnected information, encoded in a variety of formats. Three types of long-term memory have been identified: **generic, episodic,** and **autobiographical**.
Language	■ During early childhood, children progress from simple sentences to complex grammatical forms and a rich vocabulary. ■ Children develop complex rule-governed language, and the sequence and the timetable of language development appear universal. ■ At around age 2, young children's vocabularies begin to expand rapidly. A key to this growth is fast mapping. ■ Between 18 and 36 months, children began putting two words together in simple utterances called **telegraphic speech**. ■ **Semantics** refers to the *meaning* of words and sentences, or the content of speech. In learning what words mean, children are also learning how their culture uses concepts to organize their perceptions of the world. ■ A concept is a mental representation or category—a general notion that applies to many individual cases. Concepts help a young child simplify, sort, and group the many things in the environment.
Emergent Literacy	■ A typical 3-year-old knows how to hold a book and turn pages; listens when read to; understands the pictures in books; can name characters and features; and perhaps recognizes a few letters. ■ A typical 4-year-old can recite the alphabet and recognize some letters; relates stories to real life; enjoys rhymes and word play; and may pretend-write in play. ■ A typical 5-year-old may track the print when being read a simple, familiar book; spontaneously talks about the content of story and information books; can identify all, and write most, letters; and recognizes and can spell some simple words but mostly uses invented spellings when writing. ■ Adults can promote literacy by regularly reading to and reading with young children.
Early Mathematical Thinking	■ During early childhood, children demonstrate rudimentary understanding of fundamental mathematical concepts including magnitude, addition, and subtraction. ■ There is a biological basis to the development of mathematical concepts, but experience also matters.

CHILD CARE AND EARLY EDUCATION PROGRAMS

Clearly, parents play an important role in children's cognitive and language development, including memory, attention, conceptual development, and emerging literacy. But parents are not the only influence on their children's cognitive development. As noted in Chapter 6, young children in the United States also typically spend part of their day in other care settings.

Child care comes in many shapes and sizes (Clarke-Stewart & Allhusen, 2005; Mulligan, Brimhall, & West, 2005). Arrangements include in-home care, child-care homes, and child-care centers and preschools. (See Figure 7.11.)

in-home care Child care that occurs in the child's own home with a relative, nanny, or babysitter.

In-home care occurs in the child's own home. In some cases the caregiver is a relative (often a grandmother); in others she (the overwhelming majority of child-care providers are female) is a nanny or a babysitter. In-home care allows the child to remain in a familiar, safe place and the caregiver to provide individual attention to one or more siblings. It tends to provide more flexibility in terms of parents' work hours. But it does not provide professionally trained educators or frequent opportunities to interact with other children.

child-care homes Child-care settings in which a caregiver takes from one to six children into his or her home.

Child-care homes (also called *family day care*) are often chosen for infants and toddlers. The caregiver (often a neighbor) may take from one to six children into her home. Sometimes the parents and provider have a close, personal relationship. This arrangement provides the continuity of a home setting and a "mother figure," combined with the experience of interaction with other children, often of different ages.

Nonparental child care	Description	Benefits	Limitations
In-home care	Child is cared for by relative or nonrelative (e.g., nanny, babysitter) in his or her own home	Familiar environment ■	Caregivers are generally not professionally trained; fewer opportunities to interact with other children
Child-care home/ Family day care	Child is cared for in the home of an adult caregiver alone or in a small group	Home-like setting, with a "maternal" figure ■ ■	Caregiver may or may not have professional training
Child-care center	Children attend a program at a facility outside of the home (church, school, etc.) and are often divided into groups with same-age peers	Age-appropriate activities directed by staff who are generally trained in early childhood development ■ ■	In larger centers children tend to receive less individualized attention

Benefits key:
■ Individual attention
■ Opportunities for social interaction
■ Professionally trained caregivers

FIGURE 7.11

Common Child-Care Arrangements in the United States

Child-care arrangements vary in the amount of individual attention and/or social interaction a child receives, and some settings are more likely to have trained professionals than others.

Source: Mulligan, G. M., Brimhall, D., & West, J. (2005). Child care and early education arrangements of infants, toddlers, and preschoolers: 2001 (NCES 2006-039). U. S. Department of Education, National Center for Education Statistics. Washington, DC: U.S. Government Printing Office.

The provider may or may not have professional training in child care or plan activities around educational goals.

Child-care centers and preschools are a third type of care. Child-care centers are preferred by the majority of parents of children ages 3 to 5 (Clarke-Stewart & Allhusen, 2005). They may be operated by nonprofit organizations (such as a church), individual entrepreneurs, national chains, local school districts, or the federal government. Usually children are divided into classes or groups of same-age children, and activities are designed for their particular level of development. Staff members tend to have more education and special training in early childhood development than in-home care and family day care. Centers are usually equipped with an array of blocks, books, dolls, costumes, puzzles, paints, and pets, and offer instruction as well as free play.

child-care centers Child-care settings generally run by trained staff in which children are divided into classes or groups of same-age children, and activities are designed for their particular level of development.

Families use child care for many reasons—to promote cognitive and academic skills, to promote social skills, and to provide supervision while parents are at work. Today almost 60 percent of small children in the United States—about 12.2 million in all—are in child care, ranging from 40 percent of infants to 80 percent of 4- and 5-year-olds (Mulligan, Brimhall, & West, 2005). Given the widespread use of child care, parents, educators, and social policy makers are asking about the impact of child care on children's development.

structural quality Characteristics of child-care settings, such as group size, child/adult ratios, and caregiver education and training.

process quality An assessment of children's interactions and experiences in child-care settings. Higher process quality is characterized by more sensitive and caring interactions with adults, rich conversations, and stimulating materials and activities.

Child-Care Quality Matters

What is the quality of children's experiences in these different child-care settings, and do these experiences "matter" for the children's cognitive and social development?

To answer these questions, the National Institute of Child Health and Human Development (NICHD)—part of the National Institutes of Health—sponsored a detailed study of the child care of more than 1,300 U.S. children. Beginning shortly after birth and until the children entered kindergarten, mothers reported what types of child care their child attended and how much time the children spent in care each week. In addition, trained observers visited the child-care settings to evaluate the quality of the child care (NICHD ECCRN, 2000a, 2005a).

The researchers measured quality in two ways. **Structural quality** referred to characteristics of the child-care setting, such as the number of children per adult (the child/adult ratio), group size or how many children there were in the classroom or care setting, and the level of the caregivers' education and specialized training. The researchers also looked at children's experiences with caregivers, peers, and materials as indicators of **process quality** (NICHD ECCRN, 1996, 2000a; Vandell & Wolfe, 2000). High process-quality care is characterized by sensitive and warm interactions with adults, rich conversations, and a variety of stimulating materials and activities. Low process-quality care, in contrast, is characterized by disengaged, unresponsive caregivers, negative interactions with caregivers, and children wandering aimlessly.

Structural quality and process quality are related (Lamb & Ahnert, 2006; Vandell, 2007; Vandell & Wolfe, 2000). The fewer children in a group or class, the less restrictive and more

Well-designed centers and preschools offer age-appropriate activities and materials. Staff have specialized training in child development and education.

sensitive caregivers are to individual children's needs. The more education and training caregivers have, the better they organize material, the more age-appropriate the activities they offer, and the richer their language when they interact with the children.

Quality of child care is linked to children's cognitive development. Children who attend higher-quality child care—child care in which caregivers' are sensitive and stimulating—obtain higher scores on tests of memory, vocabulary, and math development. These higher scores are evident prior to kindergarten and carry over through elementary school (Belsky et al., 2007; NICHD ECCRN, 2005b). Poor quality child care is associated with poorer vocabulary, language comprehension, and memory development.

Effects of Different Types of Care Settings

Findings from the NICHD Study of Early Child Care indicate that experiences in different types of child care also matter. On average, children who attend child-care centers score higher on standardized tests of memory and preacademic skills at ages 2, 3, and 4½ than do children in in-home care and child-care homes (NICHD ECCRN, 2000b, 2002). This may be because centers include materials, conversations, and lessons related to emergent literacy and emergent mathematics.

Programs for Economically Disadvantaged Children

Children who are growing up in low-income families often start school with less advanced cognitive skills than children whose families have more economic resources (Dearing, Berry, & Zaslow, 2006). According to one estimate, two-thirds of poor, urban children are not ready to learn when they enter first grade (Zigler, 1998). Can preschool programs help these economically disadvantaged children to catch up and start school on a more equal footing with their better-off peers? Several studies say that the answer is yes.

Two well-known demonstration projects—the Perry Preschool Project in Michigan (Schweinhart et al., 1993, 2005) and the Abecedarian Project in North Carolina (Campbell & Ramey, 1995; Ramey, Campbell, & Blair, 1998)—collected long-term information about the effects of high-quality preschool programs. Both studies used an experimental design to test the program effects. Participants from low-income families in the same neighborhoods were randomly assigned to an experimental group (who enrolled in the high-quality preschool program) or a control group (who received "care as usual" in their communities). The researchers followed these children from preschool to young adulthood.

Children in the high-quality preschool programs scored higher on IQ tests and on math and reading achievement tests than the control group in both elementary and high school. They were less likely to be placed in special education classes or to be held back a year. As adults, they were less likely to be arrested or to receive public assistance. Thus, both studies found that high-quality early education can have a *lasting* impact. However, the numbers of participants in each program were small and the interventions were mounted in only one location for each program, leaving open the possibility that they could not be "brought to scale"—that is, broadly implemented at other locations.

A third project, a study of the Chicago Parent-Child Centers (Reynolds et al., 2001), followed more than 1,500 children who lived in central Chicago. Roughly half of the children (the treatment group) attended federally funded early childhood programs; others (the control group) lived in the same neighborhoods but did not attend the programs. The Chicago Parent-Child Centers taught basic skills in language and math, hired teachers with college degrees, and emphasized parent involvement. Children who attended the Parent-Child Centers programs achieved significantly higher scores than the control group in math and reading achievement at ages 5, 8, and 14. At age 20, children in the treatment group were more likely to have completed high school. (See Figure 7.12 for comparisons of the results of the preceding projects.)

These three projects show that high-quality programs *can* make a difference for low-income children. The question is whether these goals can be achieved on a national scale. **Head Start,** launched in 1965 as part of President Lyndon Johnson's War on Poverty, is one such national project. It provides nutritious meals, medical and dental care, as well as center-type experiences to foster learning (language, math readiness, and reading readiness) and good classroom behavior (paying attention, listening to teachers, taking turns, and following rules). The program serves more than 900,000 children nationwide at a cost of $6 billion each year (Love et al., 2006). To date, 21 million Americans are Head Start graduates.

Head Start A comprehensive preschool program for economically disadvantaged children.

The Head Start Impact Study compared the academic development of more than 2,500 3-year-olds who were randomly assigned to either an experimental group, who were enrolled in Head Start, or to the control group, who received other services in the

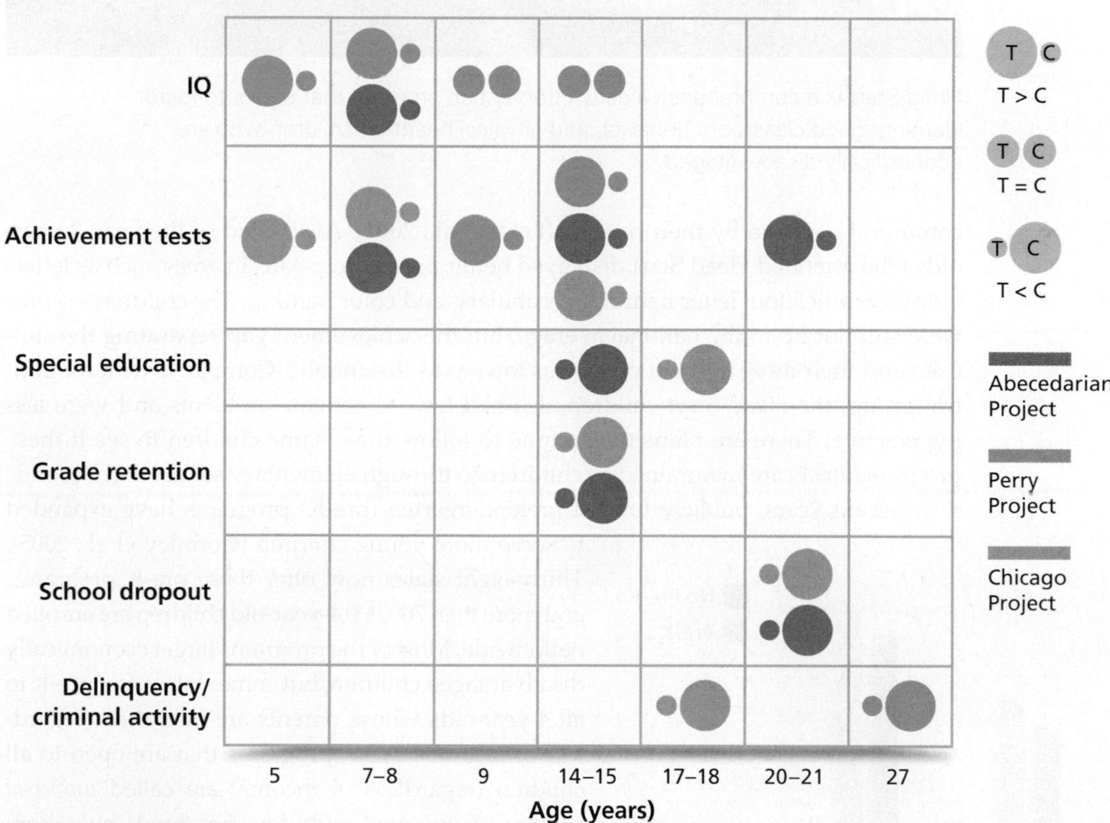

FIGURE 7.12

The Impact of Early Intervention on Later Outcomes

This grid shows the positive results found from three early childhood intervention projects: The Abecedarian Project, Perry Preschool Project, and Chicago Parent-Child Centers Project. For each pair of circles, the one on the left shows the effect of attending a preschool program (e.g., the treatment group "T"), while the one on the right represents the control group ("C"), who did not attend preschool. Circles of equal size show that the outcome for both the treatment and control groups was equivalent; however, a larger circle indicates that one of the groups had higher scores in that particular category compared to the other group.

Source: Gormley et al. (2005). The effects of universal Pre-K on cognitive development. *Developmental Psychology, 41*, 872–884, published by American Psychological Association. Reprinted with permission.

© Laura Dwight

Head Start is a comprehensive early intervention program that seeks to foster learning, good classroom behavior, and physical health of children who are economically disadvantaged.

community, chosen by their parents (Love et al., 2006). At the end of the year, 3-year-olds who attended Head Start displayed better prereading skills in areas such as letter-word identification, letter naming, vocabulary, and color naming. The children's scores were still not up to the national average, but the achievement gap separating the children and their more affluent peers was lowered substantially. Compared with the control group, the Head Start children also had fewer behavior problems and were less hyperactive. There are plans to continue to follow these same children to see if these program effects are maintained as children go through elementary school and beyond.

In recent years, publicly funded prekindergarten (pre-K) programs have expanded to serve more young children (Gormley et al., 2005). Thirty-eight states now offer these pre-K programs, and more than 700,000 4-year-old children are enrolled nationwide. Most of the programs target economically disadvantaged children, but some states offer pre-K to all 4-year-olds whose parents are interested (regardless of income). Pre-K programs that are open to all children (regardless of income) are called *universal programs*. Compared with day care, pre-K puts more emphasis on teaching the skills, knowledge, and behavior linked to success in elementary school.

William Gormley and colleagues (2005) have found pre-K programs have positive impacts on children's reading, math, and spelling skills (see Figure 7.13). Hispanic, African American, Caucasian, and Native American children all benefited from the pre-K program, as did children of all income groups. Further research is needed to learn exactly whether these positive short-term effects have a lasting impact. (For a summary of this section, see "Interim Summary 7.5: Child Care and Early Education Programs.")

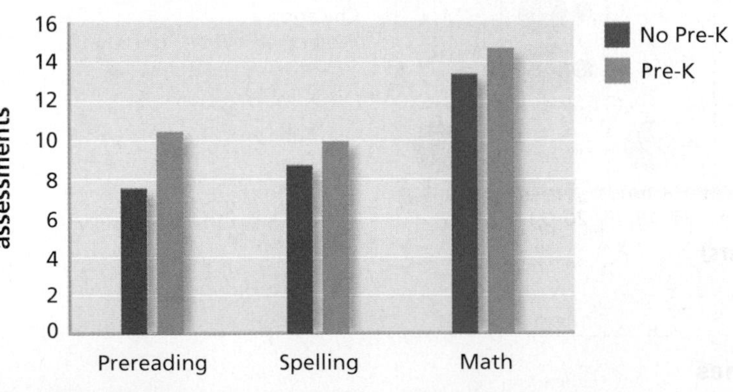

FIGURE 7.13

Academic Benefits of Prekindergarten

Researchers found that children who attended prekindergarten programs had higher scores on reading, spelling, and math assessments when they started kindergarten compared with their peers who did not attend pre-K programs.

Source: Gormley et al. (2005). The effects of universal Pre-K on cognitive development. *Developmental Psychology, 41*, 872–884. Published by American Psychological Association. Reprinted with permission.

INTERIM SUMMARY 7.5

Child Care and Early Education Programs	
Child-Care Quality Matters	■ Almost 60% of American children under age 5 are in routine nonparental child care. ■ **Structural quality** is measured by group size, child/adult ratios, and caregiver education and training. High-quality environments have a lower child/adult ratio and better-trained caregivers. ■ **Process quality** is measured by assessing children's experiences in the child-care settings. Higher process quality is characterized by more sensitive and caring interactions with adults, rich conversations, and stimulating materials and activities. ■ Child-care quality is linked to children's vocabulary, memory, and mathematics ability.
Effects of Different Types of Care Settings	■ Formal child-care settings (preschools, pre-K) are linked to cognitive and language development. ■ On average, preschool-age children who attend high-quality child-care centers score higher on standardized tests of memory and preacademic skills.
Programs for Economically Disadvantaged Children	■ Low-income children often begin elementary school with poorer preacademic skills in reading and math. ■ **Head Start** and pre-K programs can improve early literacy and mathematical thinking.

SUMMING UP AND LOOKING AHEAD

Physical growth slows in early childhood, but impressive accomplishments in motor development continue. By the end of this period, the young child is running and climbing, drawing and beginning to print. In large part these advances are due to the maturation of the brain. But experience plays an important role in shaping the brain, which is still quite plastic at this age. And so it is with motor development. Physical skills depend on the interactions of nature and nurture, biological readiness and practice. Each influences the other.

Individual children vary in size and shape, coordination and dexterity, eating and sleep patterns, and reactions to stress, but most fall within the normal range for their age. Tragically, the "norm" in many poor countries is a cycle of malnutrition and illness that delays physical development and learning and can lead to early death. With global effort and simple medical precautions, progress is being made in reducing child mortality rates. Likewise, in the United States, available safety devices and procedures are reducing serious injury and death from childhood accidents.

In this chapter, you learned about impressive accomplishments in children's thought and language, but also gaps. Unlike babies, preoperational children use mental images and symbols. But unlike older children, they do not think logically. Contemporary developmental scientists have found that preschoolers are more sophisticated than Piaget believed, especially in familiar situations such as interactions with their parents and siblings. Studies of attention and memory show that cognitive development is more cumulative than stage-like.

One of the most impressive accomplishments during this period is language development. At age 2, children use words like signals—a juvenile Morse Code. By age 6, they are fluent, chatting about past, present, future, and maybe. In between, children pick up new words, grammatical rules, and basic concepts naturally, without formal instruction. The same is true of fundamental mathematical concepts. Thus, children seem predisposed to use what culture provides.

Even so, the specific context matters. Learning language is a social process, with adults and older children providing scaffolding. Children whose parents talk *with* them—listening, prompting, and encouraging—advance faster than children whose parents talk *at* them. Today parents are not the only influence on cognitive development. Most children attend some form of preschool before age 6. In addition to school readiness, high-quality day care, child centers, and pre-K promote social and emotional development, the subject to which we now turn.

HERE'S WHAT YOU SHOULD KNOW

Did You Get It?

After reading this chapter, you should understand the following:

- The major features of physical growth and development in early childhood, and the impact of nutrition on growth and development
- The ways in which the brain matures during early childhood, structurally and functionally
- The major accomplishments during early childhood in the realms of gross and fine motor skills
- The most common physical illnesses and problems in early childhood
- The ways in which development in early childhood is affected by problems in sleep, the exposure to stress, and abuse or neglect
- The characteristics of preoperational thinking, including both its strengths and limitations
- The ways in which Piaget's theory of cognitive development in early childhood has been criticized, amended, and extended
- What is meant by the "theory of mind"
- The main features of Vygotsky's sociocultural perspective on cognitive development
- The information-processing approach to cognitive development
- The ways in which memory and attention improve in early childhood
- How children progress in their language development and mathematical thinking in early childhood
- The impact of child care and early childhood education on children's development

Important Terms and Concepts

animism (p. 204)
autobiographical memory (p. 212)
axon (p. 189)
body mass index (BMI) (p. 187)
brain plasticity (p. 192)
child-care centers (p. 219)
child-care homes (p. 218)
classification (p. 203)
conservation (p. 203)
continuous performance task (CPT) (p. 210)
corpus callosum (p. 191)
cortisol (p. 199)
dendrites (p. 189)
egocentrism (p. 204)
episodic memory (p. 212)
fast mapping (p. 213)
fine motor skills (p. 192)
frontal lobes (p. 191)
generic memory (p. 210)
gross motor skills (p. 192)
guided participation (p. 207)
Head Start (p. 221)
impulsivity (p. 210)
individual differences (p. 185)
in-home care (p. 218)
kwashiorkor (p. 198)
lateralization (p. 190)
long-term memory (p. 210)
marasmus (p. 198)
myelin (p. 190)
myelination (p. 190)
neurons (p. 189)
normative development (p. 185)
norms (p. 185)
obesity (p. 188)
overregulation (p. 214)
preoperational period (p. 202)
pretend play (p. 202)
process quality (p. 219)
reversibility (p. 202)
scaffolding (p. 206)
semantics (p. 214)
sensitive period (p. 192)
sensory memory (p. 210)
structural quality (p. 219)
synapse (p. 189)
synaptic pruning (p. 189)
synaptogenesis (p. 189)
telegraphic speech (p. 213)
theory of mind (p. 205)
working memory (p. 210)
zone of proximal development (ZPD) (p. 206)

CHAPTER 8

Socioemotional Development in Early Childhood

At a university-based preschool, a 4-year-old girl was playing in the housekeeping corner. Back and forth she went, from the play refrigerator where she selected several plastic "ingredients," to the play stove where she stirred a pot, to the cupboard where she gathered up dishes to set the dinner table. Periodically, she walked over to a cradle to cuddle a baby doll. All the while, a boy classmate sat at the table, becoming increasingly fidgety. Finally, he stood up, went to the play stove, and began to stir the pot. She rebuffed him in no uncertain terms. "Go back to the table. Mommies cook; daddies don't cook!" Looking downcast, the boy returned to the table. One might assume that the girl was re-creating her home life. She wasn't. Her mother, a medical intern, rarely cooked; her father was the family chef (Vandell, personal observation, 2006).

In early childhood, children become more themselves. They have their own ideas—including gender stereotypes that surprise their parents. Just as they are picky about their vegetables, so they have likes and dislikes for specific clothes, videos, people, and activities. Parents see 2-year-olds as more capable and intentional or willful than they were as infants, and they begin expecting more obedience and cooperation. **Socialization** (Parsons & Bales, 1956)—the process of developing cultural values and rules for behavior—becomes more explicit. At the same time, as we saw in Chapter 7, children begin spending more time with peers in preschools and other settings. Learning how to get along with other children is a central challenge. How they respond to new demands for emotional and social self-control is influenced by temperamental differences, cognitive competencies, cultural values, and ongoing social experiences with their parents, siblings, and peers.

socialization The process of developing cultural values and rules for behavior.

In this chapter, we look at the major socioemotional developments of early childhood. First, we examine the child's changing sense of self, both with respect to how children evaluate and think about different aspects of who they are, and with respect to how much children like themselves. Next, we look at gender development—changes in children's beliefs and behaviors that reflect and influence their developing awareness of what it means to be a boy or a girl. Our third topic is emotional development: how children learn about and learn to manage their feelings. Following this, we look at children's helpful and hurtful sides—their prosocial behavior and aggression. We conclude with an examination of children's experiences with parents, siblings, and peers in early childhood.

THE DEVELOPMENT OF THE SELF

In early childhood, the child not only knows that he or she is someone, but begins to form a sense of *who* he or she is. The self is both a cognitive construction that reflects the child's level of mental development and a social construction that reflects the child's interactions and experiences with other people, especially parents (Harter,

2006; Thompson, 2006). The young child who has begun to form mental representations now has the tools to think about herself. She learns through social interaction what qualities and activities matter in her social world.

Self-Conceptions and Self-Esteem

Children's **self-conceptions** are evaluative judgments about specific areas such as sports ("I am a fast runner"), physical appearance ("I am big"), and cognitive ability ("I am a good reader") (Harter, 2006), whereas **self-esteem** refers to more global assessment of self-worth—"I am special"; "I am worthless" (Coopersmith, 1967). More than a simple catalog of self-conceptions, self-esteem sets the tone for inner experiences and outward behavior.

self-conception A cognitive construction that reflects the child's level of mental development and a social construction that reflects the child's interactions and experiences with other people.

self-esteem A global assessment of self-worth.

Young children's self-conceptions are composed primarily of concrete, observable characteristics: physical appearance (blue eyes), possessions (a kitty), specific skills ("I know my ABCs"), and preferences (for pizza) may all be part of the picture. Here is one child's self-description:

> I am almost 3 years old and live in a big house with my mother and father and my brother, Jason, and my sister, Lisa. I have blue eyes and a kitty that is orange and a television in my own room. I know all of my ABCs, listen: ABC . . . XYZ. I can run real fast. I like pizza and have a nice teacher at preschool. I can count up to 100, want to hear me? I love my dog Skipper. I can climb to the top of the jungle gym, I'm not scared! I'm never scared! I am always happy. I have brown hair and I go to preschool. I'm really strong. I can lift this chair, watch me! (Harter, 2006, p. 513)

This boy's self-conception might include the specific skill, "I can open the van door all by myself!" His confidence and initiative are behavioral indications of self-esteem.

Conceptions at this age tend to be unrealistically positive. Susan Harter (2006), a scientist who studies early development of the self, sees this as normal. Young children fail Piaget's conservation test because they cannot consider two dimensions (such as the height and width of a beaker filled with water) simultaneously (see Chapter 7). In much the same way, they do not think of themselves as being good at some things but not at others, or as happy sometimes and sad other times. They tend to underestimate the difficulty of tasks and overestimate their own abilities, and they do not distinguish between their actual and ideal selves. All-or-none thinking ("I'm *never* scared! I'm *always* happy!") is typical. They have difficulty contrasting their own performance with others' performance, and they have difficulty differentiating between their actual performance and their desired performance (Harter, 2006). The young child's self-image is a bit disjointed, with separate bits of information pasted together.

Young children's self-esteem, or feelings of global self-worth, reveals itself in behavior. According to a survey of preschool teachers, children high in self-esteem are confident, curious, and independent (Harter, 2006). They take initiative and set goals independently, enjoy challenges, explore and ask questions, and eagerly try new things. They describe themselves in positive terms and take pride in their accomplishments. They also adapt well to change or stress. They adjust to transitions (e.g., from home care to preschool), persevere in the face of frustration, and are able to cope with criticism or teasing. In contrast, children low in self-esteem lack confidence, curiosity, and independence. Uncertain about their own ideas, they rarely take the initiative and rarely explore or ask questions. In the face of challenges, they withdraw, hanging back, sitting apart, and watching only. They describe themselves in negative terms and do not take pride in their accomplishments, even when praised. They have difficulty adjusting to stress or change, reverting to immature behavior during transitions and giving up in the face of frustration, criticism, or teasing.

One surprise is that self-esteem is not related to actual competence at this age (Harter, 2006). Children who are high in self-esteem are not necessarily more accomplished than their peers at cognitive skills (knowing their ABCs), playground prowess (climbing to the top of the jungle gym), or in other areas. Nonetheless, they feel good about themselves. Likewise, children who are low in self-esteem are not necessarily behind their peers in specific domains (though they may be more hesitant to "show off"). This suggests that the origins of confidence in early childhood are not directly linked to abilities, but lie elsewhere.

Initiative Versus Guilt

initiative versus guilt The third stage in Erikson's theory of psychosocial development during which mastery of new skills becomes a primary goal.

Erik Erikson (1963) identified the development of **initiative versus guilt** as central to children's developing sense of self during early childhood. Mastering new skills—from learning to count to climbing up a slide—becomes a primary goal, and young children want to do things for themselves. Adults react to these changes in different ways. Erikson (1963) observed that children whose parents accept and encourage their efforts, without being pushy or interfering, eagerly try new activities. These children, according to Erikson, develop a sense of themselves as capable of initiative. Children whose parents repeatedly restrict, ridicule, or criticize their efforts give up more quickly and blame themselves for failing. These children, according to Erikson, develop a sense of themselves as failures who are unworthy and who feel guilt.

As was noted, children do not engage in much social comparison at this age—that is, they do not judge themselves by what their peers can do. Rather, young children's sense of self is rooted in their everyday interactions with adults who are important in their lives—especially their mothers and fathers, but also grandparents, other family members, and child-care providers (Thompson, 2006). Children see themselves through the looking glass of their parents' and other adults' eyes (Cooley, 1902)

Internal Working Models

internal working model A child's evaluation of his or her worth as a person, growing out of attachment relationships.

Attachment researchers also have studied young children's sense of self, in this case, children's **internal working models** of the self (Bowlby, 1982; Bretherton & Mulholland, 1999). Similar to Erikson, these researchers see the quality of the parent-child relationship as central to the young child's developing sense of self. But attachment researchers see the internal working models as growing out of attachment relationships. When parents are sensitive, supportive, warm, and emotionally available, children are more likely to become securely attached. They also develop a working model of self as a person of value who is worthy of love. Conversely, when parents are rejecting, remote, or interfering, children are likely to develop insecure attachments. Their internal working model of self is one who is unworthy of love.

Still, these models are *working* models, according to attachment theorist John Bowlby. Based on their ongoing experiences with their parents, children's models of self can and do change. As discussed in an earlier chapter, if parent-child relations worsen—due to loss of income, marital conflict, maternal depression, or other factors—children may move from a secure to an insecure attachment or to a disorganized attachment, and a more negative, disjointed and incoherent sense of self (Thompson, 2006). If the quality of parent-child interaction improves—because the family's financial situation improves, marital relations are better, or another helpful adult joins the household, for example—children can move from an insecure to a secure attachment, which also is manifested in a more positive, coherent, and articulated internal working model of the self. (See Figure 8.1.)

Abused and severely neglected children provide an extreme example of problematic internal working models. Abused children have less self-awareness and less coherent self-concepts than do other children (Toth et al., 2000). Much as young children whose parents are generally supportive tend to think of themselves as "all good," children who are maltreated may have a more fragmented and disjointed sense of self. They also may come to think of themselves as "all bad" (Harter, 2006).

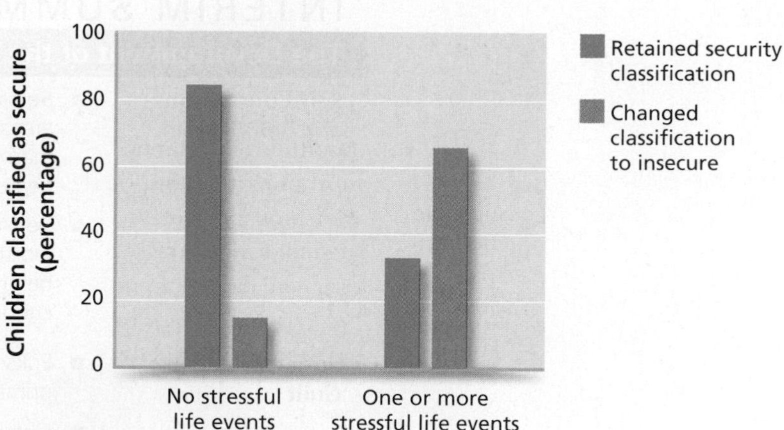

FIGURE 8.1

Stability and Change of Attachment Classifications from 12 Months to 21 Years

Experience can play a role in the stability of attachment classifications. In one study, participants' attachment security was assessed when they were 12 months old and again when they were 21 years old. When no stressful life experiences occurred, the majority of people who were securely attached at 12 months continued to have secure attachment relationships as young adults. However, two-thirds of those who had been classified as secure as infants but who experienced one or more stressful life events were classified as insecure in early adulthood.

Source: From Everett Waters, Susan Merrick, Dominique Treboux, Judith Crowell, and Leah Albersheim, *Child Development*, May/June 2000, Vol. 71, Number 3, pp. 684–689. Copyright © 2000. Reprinted by permission of Wiley/Blackwell through Rightslink.

Family Stories

Family narratives or stories that are told and retold also contribute to the child's developing sense of self (Fivush, 2001). At first, parents include children by telling stories about them. "When you were a baby . . . ." Gradually, children assume a more active role. The construction of autobiographical memories is a collaborative process, with adults providing the scaffolding (see Chapter 7). By asking questions and providing hints ("Who was there?" "What did you do?" "Was there a birthday cake?"), parents help children to develop narratives for themselves. Such memories anchor and enrich a child's self-concept. When parents ignore or dismiss children's experiences, the result can be an "impoverished self" with no grounding in the past and few hopes for the future (Harter, 1999).

In telling and listening to stories, children acquire knowledge about their culture and their place in it—what people consider worth learning and remembering (or best forgotten), what different events mean, and how their own experiences are both personal and shared, making them both unique individuals and members of a cultural community (Gauvain, 2001). Families in all cultures talk about children's misbehavior, but the message varies (Miller et al., 1997). The Taiwanese see impolite or improper acts as bringing dishonor on the family. Irish Americans are more likely to wink: A mischievous child is considered "spunky." Parents' everyday comments to children—"You're a big girl now," "You're so smart," "Big boys don't cry"—reinforce cultural norms and values and provide a grounding for the child's self-concept within his or her particular culture (Nelson, 1993). (For a summary of this section, see "Interim Summary 8.1: The Development of the Self.")

© Michael Newman/PhotoEdit

By asking questions, telling family stories, and providing their own comments, parents help children to develop personal narratives as well as acquire knowledge about their culture and their place in the world.

INTERIM SUMMARY 8.1

The Development of the Self	
Self-Conceptions and Self-Esteem	■ **Self-conceptions** are evaluative judgments about specific areas. Young children's self-conceptions are composed primarily of concrete, observable characteristics. They tend to be unrealistically positive. ■ **Self-esteem** refers to a more global assessment of self-worth. In early childhood, self-esteem is manifested by behavior. Children high in self-esteem tend to be confident, curious, and independent.
Initiative Versus Guilt	■ Erikson's third stage in which mastery of new skills is the primary challenge. ■ Children whose parents accept and encourage their efforts without being pushy or interfering are more likely to develop initiative.
Internal Working Models	■ Attachment researchers argue that **internal working models** are developed in conjunction with attachment relationships. ■ When parents are sensitive, responsive, and accepting, children are more likely to become securely attached and to develop an internal working model of self who is worthy of love. ■ When parents are rejecting, remote, and interfering, children are likely to develop insecure attachment relationships. Their working model of self is one who is unworthy, unloved, and incompetent.
Family Stories	■ Family stories that are told and retold also play a role in children's developing sense of self. In telling and listening to stories, children acquire knowledge about their culture—what people consider worth learning and remembering, what different events mean, and so on.

GENDER DEVELOPMENT

Being a boy or a girl has profound implications for young children everywhere (Ruble, Martin, & Berenbaum, 2006). Virtually all cultures expect males and females to differ in many ways: appearance, mannerisms, temperament, dreams, and values. Their activities at home and in preschool often differ. Expectations for the two sexes also vary from one culture to another, although most cultures follow what we consider "typical" gender roles (Maccoby, 1999).

Gender Awareness, Identity, and Constancy

How do children come to think of themselves as boys or girls? Gender awareness develops early. Even before they can walk and talk, infants discriminate between males and females (Martin, Ruble, & Szkrybalo, 2002). Two-year-olds choose the correct picture when a researcher asks them to select a boy or girl, man or woman (Campbell, Shirley, & Candy, 2004). They also look longer at gender-inconsistent pictures, such as a man putting on makeup, as if they are puzzled (Serbin, Poulin-Dubois, & Eichstedt, 2002).

gender identity A person's sense of self as male or female.

By age 2½, if not sooner, most children can label themselves and others by sex (Fagot & Leinbach, 1989). This is the beginning of a **gender identity**: a person's sense of the self as male or female (Ruble et al., 2006). But gender is only a label at this age—only "skin deep." Young children believe that a girl can become a boy if she dresses and acts like a boy.

Not until age 6 or 7 do most children understand **gender constancy**: that gender is permanent and immutable, that "I am a boy and always will be a boy" (Kohlberg, 1969). Preschoolers believe that one can choose to grow up as a mommy or a daddy. The development of gender constancy parallels the development of conservation. Children come to realize that just as the amount of water remains the same when it is poured from a short, wide beaker into a tall, thin one, a woman remains a woman when she dresses in overalls and a hard hat and works in construction.

gender constancy The concept that gender is permanent and immutable.

A small proportion of young children (2–5%) display gender identity disorders of childhood (GIDC). Beginning in the preschool years, these children express strong wishes to be the other sex and engage in cross-sex behavior (Zucker, 2004). For example, a boy with GIDC wants to go to preschool in a pink dress and pigtails, plays with dolls, prefers girls as playmates, and likes to be called "she." How to respond to these children is controversial (Brown, 2006). Some parents, educators, and mental health professionals advocate allowing these children to "be themselves" and follow their inclinations (to promote security and self-esteem), whereas others recommend the opposite (if only to protect them from social rejection). No one has identified the cause of GIDC. It's also rare. Still, it illustrates the degree to which children develop their own ideas about gender identity.

Behavioral Differences

By age 3, most boys and girls are moving in different directions toward gender typical—often stereotypical—behavior. These differences are seen in their choices of toys, their play styles, and their playmates (Ruble et al., 2006). They spend most of their time playing with children of their own sex (Fabes, Hanish, & Martin, 2007; Lederberg et al., 1986) and generally have a higher opinion of their own than of the opposite sex (Ruble & Martin, 1998). Young children tend to avoid toys that are linked to the opposite sex (Emmerich & Shepard, 1982).

Boys' and girls' styles of play also differ, as seen in Figure 8.2. On average, boys are more physically active, especially with groups of other boys in familiar settings (Fabes et al., 2007). They engage in more active and physical play, with more attempts to establish dominance. In observations conducted in many cultures, young boys tend to play farther away from adults and so with less supervision (Maccoby, 1999). Boys, on average, are more physically aggressive than girls (Dodge, Coie, & Lynam, 2006)—a subject to which we will return later in this chapter.

In general, preschool boys like transportation toys, construction sets like Lego, and action figures. Their fantasy play revolves around heroes, combat, and danger (Ruble et al., 2006). In keeping with these themes, boys spend more time than girls playing video games (Huston et al., 1999). Girls play more with dolls, tea and kitchen sets, and dress up. Their fantasy play often involves household roles, glamour, and romance. At preschool, many make a beeline for the dress-up area to deck themselves out in tulle and tiaras.

In general, girls tend to play in pairs or threesomes, whereas boys spend more time playing in larger groups (Fabes et al., 2007). Compared with boys, their play is more cooperative than competitive (Eisenberg & Fabes, 1998). Girls are more likely to play indoors or close to home; to choose quieter activities, such as drawing or pretend cooking; and to seek adult approval while they play (Maccoby, 1999).

	Girls	Boys
Group dynamics	Cooperative	Competitive
Physical aggression	Lower	Higher
Number of playmates	Two or three	Larger groups
Role playing	Household roles, romance	Heroes, combat
Toys	Dolls, dress-up, kitchen sets	Action figures, toy vehicles
Proximity to adults	Closer	Farther away

FIGURE 8.2

Gender Comparisons in Children's Play

Gender differences are often seen in play during early childhood, including types of play activities, number of playmates, and levels of physical aggression.

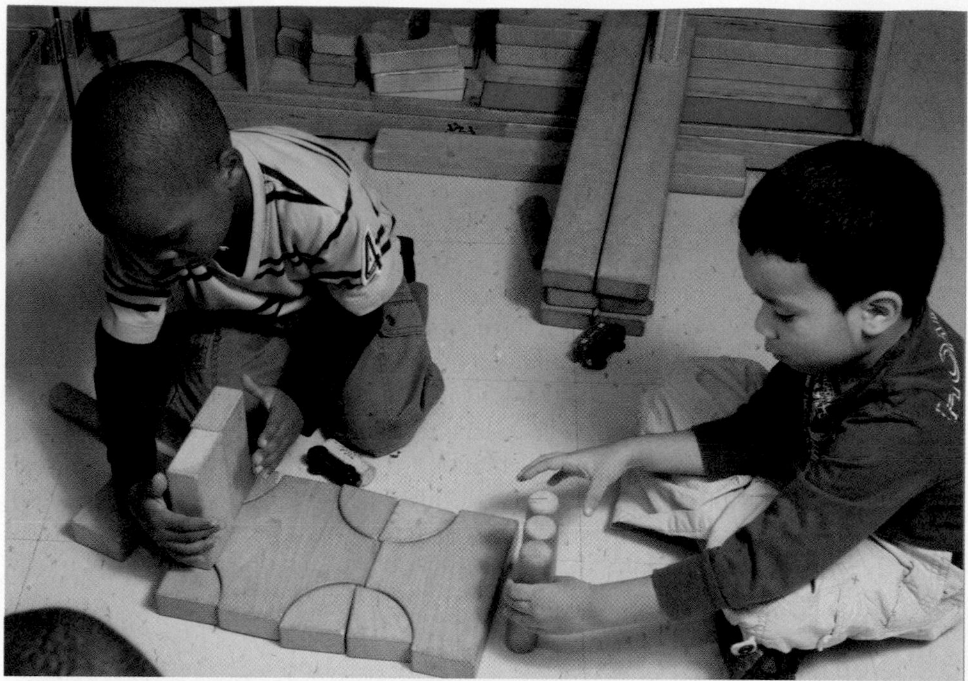

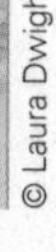

Young children spend most of their time playing with same-sex peers, often engaging in gender stereotypic activities.

Sources of Gender Differences

Where do these gender differences come from? The puzzle is that parents who don't conform to gender stereotypes themselves, and who actively try to raise their children in nonstereotyped ways, often find that their preschoolers adopt—and even insist on—stereotypes. Why, then, are sex differences so pronounced in early childhood? Developmental scientists are finding that multiple factors—biological differences, socialization, and cognition—play a role.

Biological Differences Children's sex is determined at conception by a gene on one of the 23 pairs of chromosomes (see Chapter 2). Girls have two X chromosomes, and boys have one X and one Y chromosome, with gene SRY on the Y chromosome (Ruble et al., 2006). At around the sixth or seventh week of gestation, SRY initiates the development of testes in males (Grumbach, Hughes, & Conte, 2002). From this point, physical differentiation is largely dependent on hormones, particularly **androgens**, which control the development of masculine characteristics (the most important androgen is the hormone **testosterone**, secreted by testicles in males and ovaries in females). Males have larger concentrations of androgens, which cause the male external genitalia to develop 7 to 8 weeks prenatally.

androgens Hormones that control the development of masculine characteristics, generally found in higher levels in males than females.

testosterone An androgen secreted by the testicles (in males) or ovaries (in females).

Hormones also contribute to sexual differentiation of the brain and behavior (Wallen, 2005). Most of the research on differentiation has been conducted by manipulating hormone levels in animals at different developmental periods. But much also has been learned by "natural experiments" of children and adults whose hormone levels were atypical for their sex. These natural experiments occur as a result of genetic diseases or mothers' use of drugs during pregnancy.

One example is congenital adrenal hyperplasia (CAH)—a condition caused by fetal exposure to androgens early in pregnancy. In early childhood, girls with untreated CAH show a strong preference for traditionally male toys, male playmates, and male activities (Pasterski et al., 2005). The girls like to play with trucks, are not very interested in dolls or babies, and enjoy rough, outdoor play, whereas their unaffected sisters prefer typically female play. In one study, 50 percent of the girls with CAH chose a transportation toy to keep, whereas none of the control girls did (Berenbaum & Synder, 1995). Parents' attempts to encourage CAH girls to engage in more feminine activities are often unsuccessful. Clearly, hormones play a role in gender differences, but they are not the full story. Read on.

Sex differences also may lie, in part, in "his" and "her" brains. At age 5, boys' brains have relatively more white matter in the cerebral cortex. There also are some differences in the hypothalamus and amygdala, areas of the brain related to emotion and emotional regulation (Ruble et al., 2006). Brain scans of preschool girls suggest greater neuronal density and a relatively larger **corpus callosum**, the brain structure that connects the brain's left and right hemispheres (Baron-Cohen, 2004). These areas of the brain are linked to physical activity, self-regulation, and effortful control, consistent with the argument that brain differences are contributing to behavioral differences. However, because the brain is changing in early childhood, it also could be that differential experiences are influencing brain development.

corpus callosum The connection between the two halves or hemispheres of the brain.

Gender Socialization Consciously or unconsciously, subtly and not so subtly, parents and teachers give boys and girls different messages (Gelman, Taylor, & Nguyen, 2004; Ruble et al., 2006). Mothers talk more to their daughters than to their sons, especially about emotions (Fivush et al., 2000). When girls are playing, mothers provide directions and suggestions, and they respond positively when asked for help. Parents allow—and expect—boys to be more independent. A boy who often asks for help may be seen as "whiny"; one who follows his mother around, as "clinging." With girls, parents emphasize sharing; with boys, parents are more likely to support competition (Keenan & Shaw, 1997).

Girls also are given more approval than boys are for dancing, dressing up, playing with dolls, following parents around, and asking for help, and more disapproval for jumping and manipulating objects (Lytton & Romney, 1991). Boys receive more encouragement for running, climbing, wrestling, and playing with male-typical construction and transportation toys, and more discouragement for engaging in activities considered feminine. In general, parents—especially fathers—seem to be more actively and personally concerned about appropriate sex role behavior in boys than in girls

(Ruble et al., 2006). A boy playing dress up with feminine clothes is more likely to be discouraged than a girl who plays with construction vehicles.

gender socialization Social norms conveyed to children that concern characteristics associated with being male or female.

During everyday interaction—reading a book, going to a store, or just chatting—parents contribute to **gender socialization** by providing gender labels ("That's a girl"; "You're a big boy"), by contrasting males and females ("Is that a girl job or a boy job?"; "How is my little princess today?" versus "What's happening, champ?"), and by giving approval for children's stereotyped statements ("That's right, daddies like football") (Gelman et al., 2004). Grandparents, teachers, and strangers do the same. But adults are not the only influence on the development of ideas about gender.

rough-and-tumble play Physically vigorous behaviors such as chasing, jumping, and play fighting that are accompanied by shared smiles and laughter.

Carol Martin and Richard Fabes (2001) find that interactions with peers also contribute to gender socialization. In their observations of young children on the playground and in preschool classrooms, they found gender differences increased across the school year. Boys became more physically active and participated in more **rough-and-tumble play** (physically vigorous play such as chasing, jumping and play fighting that is accompanied by shared smiles and laughter) as the school year progresses, whereas the girls became less physically active. Additionally, as the school year progresses, the boys spent more time playing in larger groups with other boys. The girls spent more time playing in close proximity to teachers. Those preschool children who spent more time playing with same-sex peers early in the school year had greater increases in gender-typed behaviors later in the school year.

gender schema A mental network of beliefs and expectations about males versus females.

Gender Schema Children are not merely passive recipients of biological and social influences. They also are actively constructing their own ideas of what it means to be male or female (Bussey & Bandura, 1999; Martin et al., 2002). **Gender schemas** are mental networks of beliefs and expectations about males versus females. As children develop a gender identity, they begin to classify people, activities, and interests as male or female. Children first become aware of stereotypic differences in appearance, then possessions, and then behavior.

As noted earlier, knowledge of activities typically associated with gender increases rapidly between ages 3 and 5. Once children have gender schemas, they try to match their own behavior to what boys and girls in their culture are supposed to do. They also use gender schemas to organize incoming information. Focusing on external signs of gender, they try to fit everyone into one or the other category. At this stage they tend to see deviations from gender stereotypes as "bad" behavior.

INTERIM SUMMARY 8.2

Gender Development

Gender Awareness, Identity, and Constancy	■ By age 2½, most children can label themselves and others by sex, which is the beginning of a **gender identity**. ■ Around age 6 or 7, children understand **gender constancy**—that gender is permanent and immutable. This understanding parallels the development of conservation.
Behavioral Differences	■ By age 3, styles of play often differ. Boys tend to play in larger groups, be more physically active, and be more physically aggressive than girls. ■ Preferred toys and activities also differ.
Sources of Gender Differences	■ Biology, socialization, and cognition all play a role in gender development. ■ **Gender schemas** are mental networks of beliefs and expectations about males versus females.

Gender stereotyping peaks between ages 5 and 6, and then becomes more flexible in middle childhood (Ruble et al., 2006). One reason for this early rigidity may be that young children have not yet grasped gender constancy. If sex depends on appearances, it makes sense to want to look and act as feminine or masculine as possible, dressing in spangles or playing with toy sabers to reinforce one's female or male identity. Once children master gender constancy—when they understand that gender is not altered by superficial changes in appearance—they are more able to accept that males and females can *share* traits and activities. (For a summary of this section see "Interim Summary 8.2: Gender Development.")

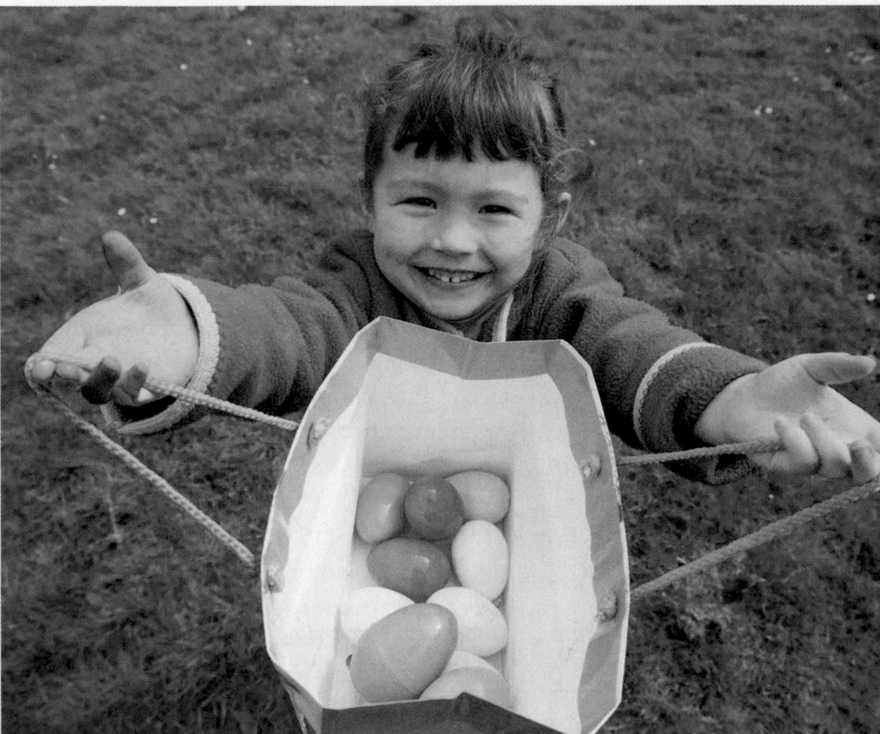

© Don Mason/Workbook Stock/Jupiterimages

Self-conscious emotions such as pride develop in early childhood.

EMOTIONAL DEVELOPMENT

Emotional development in early childhood is marked by advances in children's awareness of their own and others' emotional states and in children's ability to regulate their emotional expressions (Saarni et al., 2006). We examine these advances in turn.

Understanding Emotions

Being aware of one's own emotions and the emotions of others is a step in the direction of emotional understanding. Between ages 2 and 3, children begin to label their own and other people's subjective feelings (Bloom, 1998). Preschoolers generally are able to identify their peers' facial expressions of emotion such as sad, happy, mad, surprised, or fearful (Fabes et al., 1991). The number of emotional terms in their vocabulary increases (Ridgeway, Waters, & Kuczaj, 1985), and they begin to identify the object or target of their feeling: "I'm mad *at* you"; "I'm afraid *of* dogs"; "I'm happy *about* the party" (Harris, 2000).

Over early childhood, young children also develop a more accurate and nuanced understanding of the causes and consequences of emotion. For example, they predict that an angry child is more likely to hit, whereas a happy child will share (Lagattuta, Wellman, & Flavell, 1997). Like self-awareness, other-awareness is grounded in cognitive advances. To understand other people's feelings, children need to comprehend that other people have intentions, beliefs, and subjective experiences of their own; that certain people tend to be more positive or negative than others; and what situations commonly evoke emotions (Saarni et al., 2006).

Secondary or **self-conscious emotions**, including pride, guilt, shame, and embarrassment, develop in early childhood (Lewis, 2000). Self-conscious emotions are complex. They require an objective sense of the self as distinct from others; awareness of standards for behavior; an evaluation of one's own performance in terms of these standards; and a sense of responsibility for success or failure. In some cases, an emotion is linked to specific acts: "I did a good job" (pride) or "I did a bad thing" (guilt). In other cases the emotion is more global and linked to self-esteem: "I am a bad person" (shame).

self-conscious emotion An emotion that involves evaluation of oneself, such as embarrassment or pride.

Lewis and Ramsay (2002) identified two types of embarrassment in 4-year-olds. One type occurs when the child is an object of positive attention, such as when teachers or parents provide public recognition of a new accomplishment. (In one experiment, for example, these researchers induced embarrassment by having children dance and bang on a tambourine by themselves while others were watching them.) Another type of self-evaluative embarrassment occurs when a child fails a task. Children show elevated cortisol, indicating a stress reaction, only with the second type of embarrassment.

emotional intelligence The ability to monitor one's own and others' feelings and to use that information to guide thinking and action.

Individual children vary in their ability to recognize and understand emotions. Some children display considerable **emotional intelligence**, defined as the ability to monitor one's own and others' feelings and to use that information to guide thinking and action (Salovey & Mayer, 1990). Children who demonstrate emotional intelligence are rated as more likable by their peers (Denham et al., 1990; Walden & Knieps, 1996). Indeed, this is a key factor in their popularity. Children who are biased toward seeing anger in ambiguous situations are rated as more hostile and are often avoided by peers (Barth & Bastiani, 1997). Socially isolated, they have fewer opportunities to observe and practice emotional self-regulation, which compounds the problem.

Some evidence indicates that young girls are better than young boys at decoding emotions (Stipek, 1995). Part of the reason may be that mothers spend more time talking with daughters than with sons about emotion states and feelings, or that girls spend more time than boys do in joint pretend play, which requires negotiation and compromise (Youngblade & Dunn, 1995). Or perhaps subtle differences in brain functioning lead girls to tune into emotions as well as actions, bring up the topic more in conversation, and choose games that allow them to "try on" other perspectives.

During early childhood, family conversations play a key role in emotional socialization (Thompson, 2006). Young children talk with family members about expectations of how they will feel and how they did feel. When parents use scaffolding, children learn the deeper meanings of emotion labels. "Why did you hit him? Were you *angry*? Why?" "How would you *feel* if someone tore up your painting?" "It was *sad* that Kendra tripped during the school play. I remember being so *embarrassed* when that happened to me once. How would you feel?" This sort of conversation draws attention not only to the child's feeling but also to others' emotions. When mothers talk about feelings and negotiate compromises (thus acknowledging the child's point of view) with their 2½-year-olds, the children are more advanced in emotional understanding (Laible, 2004). Talking with parents also introduces children to cultural expectations (a subject to which we will return).

In the absence of warm, supportive family relations, emotional understanding may be impaired. Young children who are exposed to physical abuse and family violence are hypervigilant, always on the alert for signs of danger (Pollak et al., 2005), as seen in Figure 8.3. They have difficulty understanding social cues and controlling their emotions. They interpret neutral behavior as hostile and often react aggressively. This can become a self-fulfilling prophecy. As a result of this

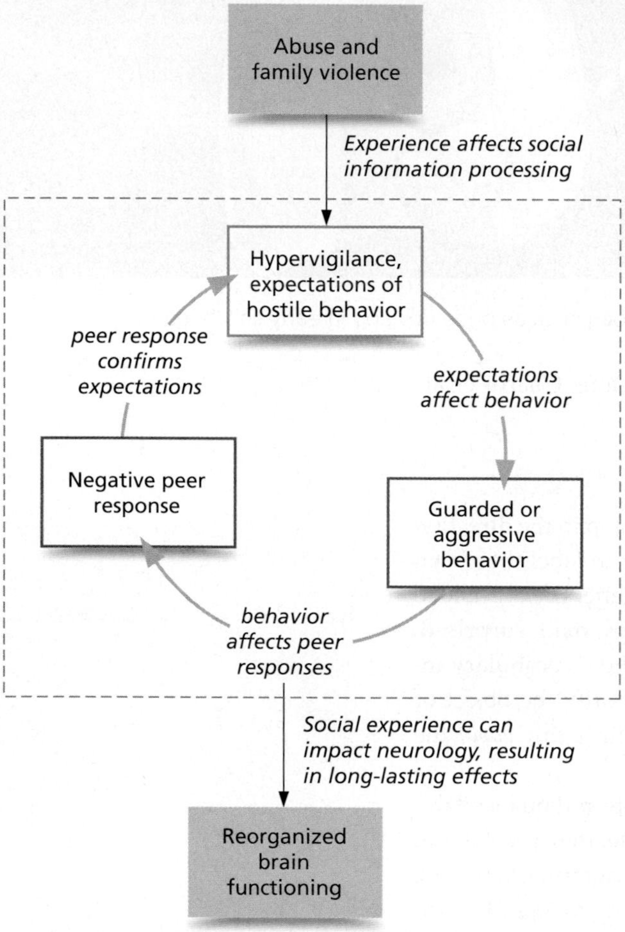

FIGURE 8.3

Links Between Experiences of Abuse in Childhood and Later Brain Functioning

Abuse and family violence can affect the way a child perceives social information. Children may become hypervigilant and perceive neutral behavior as hostile, leading them to react aggressively. Peers respond accordingly, confirming the child's initial expectations for hostile behavior. Over time, this cycle of self-fulfilling prophecies can lead to the reorganization of neural pathways in the brain.
Source: Pollack et al., 2005.

behavior, children may be avoided by peers and singled out by teachers. Recent findings in neuroscience suggest that these social experiences can reorganize and alter brain functioning, which may explain, in part, the long-lasting effects of child abuse (Pollak et al., 2005).

Children who have been neglected also have difficulty discriminating between different emotions (Pollak & Kistler, 2002; Pollak et al., 2001). We mentioned in an earlier chapter the Romanian children who were institutionalized in orphanages from infancy, where they had little interaction with others. Tested as preschoolers, after they had been adopted by middle-class U.S., Canadian, or British families, the Romanian orphans had problems identifying facial expressions or scenes as happy, sad, or fearful (Camras et al., 2006).

Young children whose mothers are chronically depressed have other difficulties (Zahn-Waxler & Radke-Yarrow, 1990). They may experience too much empathy and too many feelings of responsibility. Children of depressed mothers sometimes hold themselves responsible for their mothers' sadness. They express more shame and guilt and apologize more often than other children.

Regulating Emotions

Emotional regulation refers to the ability to inhibit, enhance, maintain, and modulate emotional arousal to accomplish a goal (Eisenberg, Fabes, & Spinrad, 2006). We see important gains in early childhood in children's emotional regulation. Parents and caregivers play key roles in helping infants and toddlers to regulate their emotions. In comparison, 5-year-olds have more self-control. They can be frustrated without striking out; happy without going over the top; frightened but still willing to approach a new situation. When children can "down-regulate" or de-escalate internal arousal, they are better able to negotiate solutions to conflicts with parents and peers (Gottman, Katz, & Hoover, 1997). They are also more flexible in approaching situations they once feared.

emotional regulation The ability to inhibit, enhance, maintain, and modulate emotional arousal to accomplish a goal.

Effortful control—the ability to withhold a dominant response in order to make a nondominant response, to engage in planning, and to regulate reactive tendencies—contributes to young children's ability to modulate their emotions (Kochanska, Coy, & Murray, 2001; Rothbart & Bates, 2006). With effortful control, children can inhibit some actions (such as touching an attractive but forbidden toy) and can perform actions they would prefer *not* to do (such as putting away their toys). Effortful control enables children to think about others' feelings as well as their own without being overwhelmed by their emotional reactions. A lack of effortful control is linked to **externalizing problems** such as impulsively striking out at people or objects that the child sees as standing in his way (Eisenberg et al., 1994).

effortful control The ability to withhold a dominant response in order to make a nondominant response, to engage in planning, and to regulate reactive tendencies.

externalizing problems Psychosocial problems that are manifested in outward symptoms, such as aggression or noncompliance.

The development of effortful control in early childhood reflects children's individual predispositions or temperament, as well as their social experiences (Rothbart & Bates, 2006). Researchers have found continuity between early individual differences in infants' ability to focus and sustain attention and effortful control when the children are preschoolers (Kochanska & Knaack, 2003; Vaughn, Kopp, & Krakow, 1984), suggesting that effortful control is a temperamental dimension rooted in early emotional reactivity and control systems (Rothbart & Bates, 2006).

But this is only part of the story. The association between poor self-regulation and externalizing behaviors is greater when children experience hostile and intrusive parenting (Rubin et al., 2003) (see Figure 8.4), whereas positive parenting (to be discussed in more detail later in this chapter) helps to offset the negative effects of poor regulation (Bates & Pettit, 2007). Among children who have poor self-regulation skills, those whose parents are hostile and intrusive are more likely to "act out," compared with children whose parents provide authoritative parenting that combines warmth with firm control.

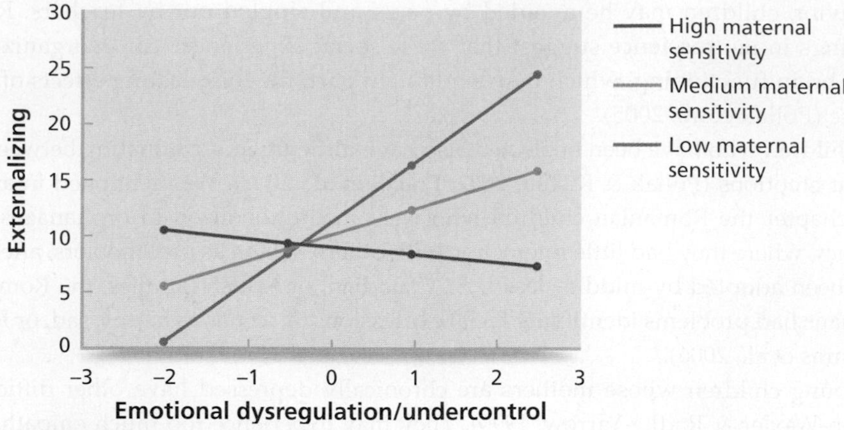

FIGURE 8.4

The Importance of Maternal Sensitivity for Children with Emotional Regulation Difficulties

Children who have trouble regulating their emotions often show higher levels of aggressive, or "externalizing," behavior than their peers. Children who score high on a measure of emotional dysregulation have lower levels of externalizing behavior if their mothers are sensitive. Children who have difficulty regulating their emotions show higher levels of externalizing behaviors if their mothers are hostile, controlling, and insensitive.

Source: From K.H. Rubin, K.B. Burgess, K.M. Dwyer & P.D. Hastings. Predicting preschoolers' externalizing behaviors from toddler temperament, conflict, and maternal negativity. *Developmental Psychology,* 39, 2003, pp. 164–176, published by American Psychological Association. Reprinted with permission.

Emotions in a Cultural Context

Emotional regulation occurs in a cultural context. In contemporary mainstream American culture, expressing and talking about one's emotions is encouraged. But the idea that the open expression and discussion of emotions is healthy is not universal (Trommsdorff, 2006). In some cultures, the display of emotions (especially anger) is considered rude, immature, or even deranged (Kitayama, 2001).

Much of the cross-cultural research on emotional development has focused on the differences between *individualistic* (usually Western) cultures that emphasize self-development and *collectivist* (usually Asian) cultures that emphasize social harmony (Trommsdorff, 2006). Whereas individualistic cultures value independence, collectivist cultures value *inter*dependence; the self is defined less in terms of inner, personal traits than in terms of social relations and behavior.

These different models of the self have implications for the cultural meaning of certain emotions. In individualistic cultures, pride is considered a positive emotion that signals individual accomplishment, validates the independent self, and is associated with feelings of well-being (Mesquita & Karasawa, 2004). In individualistic cultures, shame is seen as a negative emotion, a blow to self-esteem. In collectivist cultures, however, pride is linked to social disengagement and dishonor, and shame is considered a positive emotion. Shame signals group involvement, striving for conformity, and motivation to perform better in the future (Trommsdorff, 2006).

Culture shapes socialization (Wang, 2006; Wang & Fivush, 2005). Consider the comparison in Table 8.1 of a conversation between a European American mother and her preschooler versus a Chinese mother and her preschooler.

TABLE **8.1** Two Cultures, Two Conversations

EURO-AMERICAN MOTHER-CHILD DYAD	CHINESE MOTHER-CHILD DYAD
M: . . . Do you remember doing some crying?	M: . . . Do you remember why Dad spanked you last time?
C: Why did I cry?	C: Chess!
M: I'm not quite sure why you cried. But do you remember where you were?	M: Why chess? What did you do with chess?
C: I cried because I had any, no any balloon.	C: Not obedient!
M: They had no balloon. But then, you were also crying because, did you not want to go home?	M: How were you not being obedient?
C: Yeah.	C: (I) threw the pieces on the floor.
M: Where were you?	M: All over the floor, right? And did you do it on purpose?
C: At Stewart Park!	C: Umm. I'll be careful next time!
M: (Laughs). You did cry a lot at Stewart Park, but, um, this was in Joe's parking lot. Do you remember Joe's Restaurant parking lot? Do you remember standing by the door and crying?	M: Right! That's why Dad spanked your bottom, right? . . . Did you cry then?
C: Yeah	C: (I) cried.
M: You do?	M: Did it hurt?
C: Yeah.	C: It hurt.
M: What were you crying about?	M: It hurt? It doesn't hurt anymore, right?
C: 'Cause I didn't wanted to leave yet; it was because I wanted to eat.	C: Right. I'll be careful next time.
M: Oh, you wanted to eat some more (laughs); is that why?	M: Umm, be careful.
C: Yeah.	. . .
M: Hmm. I remember Mommy tried to pick you up and you put up a little bit of a fight. You were crying real hard. Maybe it was 'cause the balloon and maybe it was 'cause you were hungry. But we knew that you could get another balloon, right?	
C: Yep.	
. . .	

Source: Reproduced by permission of SAGE Publications Ltd., London, Los Angeles, New Delhi, Singapore and Washington, DC, from Q. Wang, Developing emotion knowledge in cultural contexts, *International Journal of Behavioral Development,* 30(Suppl. 1), p. 9, Copyright © SAGE Publications Ltd., 2006.

As a rule, European American mothers encourage children to "share" their emotions, in the belief that burying emotions is harmful. Chinese mothers see emotional displays as disruptive and believe that they should be controlled (Wang, 2006). Chinese mothers' conversations with children focus on the proper way to behave, obedience, and the consequences of misbehavior. In different ways, though, all parents become concerned with moral development during this period.

As we will see in the next section, young children's emotional understanding and self-regulation set the stage for other areas of development in early childhood: prosocial behaviors, conscience, and the control of aggression. (For a summary of this section, see "Interim Summary 8.3: Emotional Development.")

INTERIM SUMMARY 8.3

Emotional Development	
Understanding Emotions	■ Between ages 2 and 3, children begin to label their own and other people's subjective feelings. ■ Secondary or **self-conscious emotions**, such as pride, guilt, and shame, develop in early childhood. ■ Individual children vary in their ability to recognize and understand emotions. Some children display considerable **emotional intelligence** (the ability to monitor one's own and others' feelings and to use that information to guide thinking and emotion). ■ In the absence of warm, supportive family relations, emotional understanding may be impaired.
Regulating Emotions	■ **Emotional regulation** refers to the ability to inhibit, enhance, maintain, and modulate emotional arousal to accomplish a goal. ■ **Effortful control**—the ability to withhold a dominant response in order to make a nondominant response—contributes to young children's ability to modulate their emotions. ■ Lack of effortful control is linked to **externalizing problems**. ■ The link between poor self-regulation and externalizing behaviors is greater when children experience hostile and intrusive parenting.
Emotions in a Cultural Context	■ Pride and shame are viewed differently in individualistic and collectivist cultures. ■ Cultures differ in their views about whether emotional expressiveness is a positive or negative trait.

PROSOCIAL BEHAVIORS, CONSCIENCE, AND AGGRESSION

One goal of socialization in many cultures is to encourage children's moral development—to adopt their society's conception of right and wrong and to behave in ways consistent with that understanding. Children's moral development has been studied using two distinct approaches. One approach considers the ways children think about moral dilemmas and changes in moral reasoning that take place as children become more cognitively advanced (Kohlberg, 1969; Piaget, 1932). In Chaper 10 we will examine this approach in more detail.

In the second approach (and the topic of this section), researchers are primarily interested in children's prosocial behaviors (actions such as helping another child or comforting a person in distress) and in their ability to control aggression. As we will see in this section, children make great strides in these areas in early childhood.

Prosocial Behaviors

prosocial behavior A voluntary action intended to benefit another person.

Prosocial behaviors are voluntary actions intended to benefit another person (Eisenberg et al., 2006). Sharing, cooperating, helping, defending, and comforting someone who is upset or in pain all fall into this category. People are prosocial for many reasons, including self-interest (to win praise, look good, make friends, and achieve mutual goals) and altruism (aid that is motivated by concern without expectation of reward or escape from punishment).

Prosocial behavior also may be motivated by **conscience**: an internalized sense of right and wrong that makes us feel good about doing the right thing and bad about doing something wrong. When values and standards are truly internalized, children feel guilt or shame for going against their conscience—even when no one is watching.

conscience An internalized sense of right and wrong that invokes positive feelings about doing the right thing and negative feelings about doing something wrong.

empathy Understanding and sharing another person's feelings.

Early Signs of a Conscience

Nazan Aksan and Grazyna Kochanska (2005) devised several tasks to assess the development of conscience in early childhood. The first dealt with guilt. The researchers staged a mishap that led the preschooler to believe she had damaged a special, highly valued object. They then observed the child's response. Indications of guilt included avoiding the experimenter's gaze and various signs of tension: squirming, hunched shoulders, head down, and covering the face with hands. Afterward, the experimenter assured the child that no harm had been done by showing her the "fixed object" (an exact but intact replica of the damaged one), so that no child left the laboratory feeling guilty.

A second task dealt with **empathy**, or understanding and sharing another person's feelings. While the child was playing with toys that were placed in the observation room, a female experimenter "accidentally" dropped a large box of neatly sorted cards on her foot. Empathy was measured by whether the child looked sad, stopped playing, and showed signs of tension.

A third task, assessing children's compliance and internalization, occurred at the end of the session. The mother was instructed to have the child help pick up the toys in the playroom. Then the mother left the room and asked the child to finish the job while she was gone (a test of internalization). Here, the researchers recorded how many toys the child put away.

Young children are sensitive to others' emotions and will seek to comfort peers who are in distress.

The researchers found evidence of the beginnings of conscience, as evident by signs of guilt, empathy, and internalization, in children as young as 33 months and increases in empathy and in the internalization of standards at 45 months. Longitudinal studies indicate that children who score high on measures of conscience at an early age remain so in the school years (Kochanska & Aksan, 2007).

Factors Associated with the Development of Conscience

What are the factors associated with the development of conscience? Earlier we mentioned the development of *effortful control*—the ability to willingly suppress a dominant response (e.g., grabbing a desired toy out of another child's hands) in order to engage in a nondominant one (e.g., asking to play with the desired toy). Kochanska and Askan (2007) find effortful control to be related to conscience in early childhood. Children who scored high on effortful control (measured by tasks such as waiting for candy that could be seen under a transparent cup, drawing a line slowly, lowering their voice, and recognizing small shapes hidden in a large shape) at 2½ years displayed more empathy, and expressed feelings of guilt and shame in conscience assessments at age 4.

Emotional regulation also is related to prosocial behavior. Children who have less emotional control are less sympathetic and helpful (Eisenberg et al., 2006). Children who are sociable, assertive, and good at controlling their emotions are likely to help, share, and comfort peers and adults (Eisenberg & Fabes, 1998).

To some degree, prosocial behaviors are intrinsically motivated. In a classic study (Eisenberg-Berg, 1979), preschoolers were asked why they had done something nice. Most mentioned need ("He was hungry") or said simply that they wanted to do it. Some referred to friendship, wanting approval, or mutual benefit. None cited the fear of punishment or the expectation of reward from adults.

This does not mean that experiences with their parents and other adults are unimportant. Children with secure attachments to their mothers in infancy are more sympathetic as preschoolers (Waters, Hay, & Richters, 1986) and show more concern for others (Kestenbaum, Farber, & Sroufe, 1989). Parental warmth and acceptance serves as a pathway for early conscience for children who are temperamentally inhibited or fearful (Kochanska, 1995).

Experiences in child care also have been linked to children's prosocial behaviors. One team of researchers compared children who attended programs with small classes and a low child/adult ratio (in line with American Public Health Association Guidelines) to children who attended programs with larger classes and a higher child/adult ratio (NICHD Early Child Care Research Network, 1999). According to mothers, children who went to the first engaged in more prosocial behavior, and had fewer behavior problems, than children who went to the second. In other analyses, preschoolers whose caregivers were more emotionally supportive, stimulating, and responsive tended to be more cooperative and sociable with peers (NICHD Early Child Care Research Network, 2001).

Finally, children's prosocial behaviors reflect the larger culture in which they live. Prosocial behavior is more common in collectivist societies in which people live in extended families and children are assigned household tasks at an earlier age than in individualistic societies (Whiting & Whiting, 1975). Parents in rural Mexico, a collectivist society, were more likely to punish children's use of aggression toward peers than were parents in more individualistic societies such as suburban New England (Minturn & Lambert, 1964).

aggression Actions that are intended to harm or injure another person.

physical aggression Behaviors such as hitting, pushing, and biting that are intended to harm another.

verbal aggression Aggressive behavior such as threats and name calling.

Aggression

Researchers also have studied aggression in young children. **Aggression** is any action that is intended to harm or injure other people. The key element in this definition is *intentionality*. Accidental injury, due to clumsiness or ignorance, doesn't count. In early childhood, aggression can take different forms, including **physical aggression** (fighting or damaging another child's possessions), **verbal aggression**

© Laura Dwight

Tussles over toys are examples of instrumental aggression that decline as children become more skilled in negotiating toy exchanges.

(threatening someone or name calling), and **relational aggression** (attempting to lower another child's social standing or relations with others) (Dodge et al., 2006; Vitaro, Brendgen, & Barker, 2006). Ignoring another child, refusing to let a child join a group, or threatening to end a friendship are examples of relational aggression (Crick, Casas, & Mosher, 1997).

relational aggression Aggressive behavior designed to lower another's self-esteem, social standing, or both.

All three types of aggression (physical, verbal, and relational) may occur for various reasons. **Reactive aggression** is a defensive response to provocation (e.g., hitting someone who has been hitting you). **Instrumental aggression** is designed to achieve a goal for oneself (e.g., pushing someone aside in order to get a better place in line), and **hostile aggression** intends harm as its primary goal (e.g., hitting someone because you want to hurt them). Sometimes aggression may occur for more than one reason; for example, it may be both instrumental and hostile.

reactive aggression Aggressive behavior that is a defensive response to provocation.

instrumental aggression Aggressive behavior designed to achieve a goal for oneself.

hostile aggression Aggressive behavior that intends harm as its primary goal, in contrast to instrumental aggression that has the primary goal of achieving some end or controlling resources.

Nothing infants do is true aggression. Granted, babies can pull (hard) on their mothers' dangling earrings and their grandmothers' large noses, but these actions appear motivated by curiosity and exploration, not the intent to hurt mother or grandmother. Similarly, infants will poke their finger in a peer's eye, or topple over a peer as both reach for an attractive toy, but the hurt is not intentional (Hay, Nash, & Pedersen, 1983; Mueller & Vandell, 1979). The term that researchers use for behavior that inflicts unintentional harm is **agonism**.

agonism Behaviors by very young children that may unintentionally hurt or harm another person.

Like infants, toddlers are sometimes agonistic, but other times their behavior is clearly aggressive, especially when they seek possession or control of desirable toys (acts that appear to be instrumental aggression). About *half* of toddlers' interactions with peers involve behaviors that might be perceived as either agonistic or aggressive—putting sand in a peer's hair, taking a toy, pushing a peer out of the way, as well as hitting (Mueller & Vandell, 1979). But aggression and prosocial behavior are not opposite sides of the same coin. In fact, some 2-year-olds are high in aggression *and* high in prosocial behavior (Brownell, 1990). The reason is simply that they are more socially active than other children. Outgoing, they make more efforts to engage with other children—which makes them friends but also gets them into fights.

Between ages 2 and 4, acts of physical aggression such as hitting and pushing typically decrease, whereas verbal aggression increases (Dodge et al., 2006). This is not a surprise: Children's vocabularies and verbal skills are growing rapidly in this period. Words ("Give it to me!! It's my turn!") can now substitute for actions such as hitting or pushing someone in order to get something.

The reasons for conflict also change. For toddlers, conflicts typically revolve around resources and toys. For preschoolers, conflicts also can involve differences of opinion (Laursen & Hartup, 1989; Rubin, Bukowski, & Parker, 2006). Children as young as age 3 may engage in relational aggression, but this is far more common among older children and adolescents (Crick & Grotpeter, 1995; Underwood, 2003).

Toddlers have limited abilities to understand other people's intentions and motives, to control their emotional reactions, and to formulate alternative strategies to get what they want. By age 4 or 5, most have developed a broader array of strategies for resolving conflicts (such as taking turns) and voicing their feelings ("That's not fair!")—or for getting what they want through verbal threats ("I won't be your friend")—rather than grabbing toys. Some young children are better at controlling aggression than others.

Does aggression in early childhood predict later aggression? Investigators in one large study of over 1,000 children collected reports of children's aggression at multiple times from age 2 through 9 (NICHD Early Child Care Research Network, 2004). They identified five groups of children (see Figure 8.5) based on different developmental trajectories of aggression over the 7-year period. (A **developmental trajectory** describes the patterns of change in performance in an individual over a relatively long period [Nagin & Tremblay, 2005].) The largest group (45% of the children) showed

developmental trajectory A pattern of changes in an individual over a relatively long period.

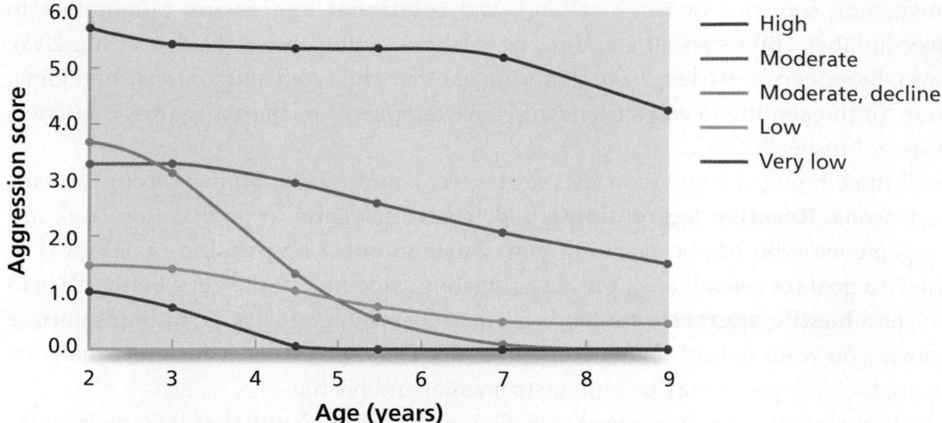

Group sizes		
Group 1	Very low = 45%	n = 547
Group 2	Low = 24%	n = 302
Group 3	Moderate, decline = 12%	n = 132
Group 4	Moderate = 15%	n = 184
Group 5	High = 3%	n = 30

FIGURE 8.5

Developmental Trajectories of Physical Aggression in Childhood

Each line in the figure represents the pattern of change in aggressive behavior for a group of children who followed a similar trajectory between ages 2 through 9. The majority of children showed low levels of aggression at all ages. An additional 12 percent started at a slightly higher level that declined over time. Fifteen percent of children showed moderate levels of aggression at all ages, and a small group (3%) had high levels of aggression that remained stable from toddlerhood through middle childhood. This last group also had problems in other domains, including poor peer relations and higher levels of psychological maladjustment.

Source: NICHD Early Child Care Research Network (2004).

very low aggression at all of the ages. Other children displayed somewhat low aggression at all ages, moderate aggression that decreased sharply when they began elementary school, or consistently moderate aggression. A fifth group (3% of the sample) was high in aggression at all of the ages.

It was this fifth group, the children who were highly aggressive at all of the assessment ages, who were at greatest risk for later problem behaviors. In elementary school, this small group had more problems with school and with peers, demonstrated more externalizing problems (acting out behavior problems such as physical aggression and rule violations) and more **internalizing problems** (behavior problems that are directed inward, such as depression and anxiety), and had fewer friends than any other group (Campbell et al., 2006). At lowest risk for later problem behaviors were the children who were consistently very low in aggression. For other children, aggression in early childhood is a phase, the result of temporary social difficulties. Children with moderate-declining aggression were better adjusted in elementary school than were children who consistently showed somewhat elevated aggression over time.

internalizing problems
Psychosocial problems that are manifested in inward symptoms, such as depression and anxiety.

Differences in the amount and types of aggression in early childhood reflect multiple influences, including children's temperament, gender, and social experiences.

- **Temperament:** In general, preschoolers who are low in effortful control and emotional regulation display more reactive aggression than other children (Dodge et al., 2006; Eisenberg et al., 2001). If they feel threatened, they react, without stopping to calm themselves or to think about alternatives.
- **Gender:** Boys engage in far more physical aggression than girls. In the large-scale study reported above, three out of four of the children who were consistently high in aggression were boys (NICHD Early Child Care Research Network, 2004). Preschool girls, in contrast, are more likely to use relational aggression (Crick et al., 1997).
- **Socialization:** An old saying declares, "Spare the rod, spoil the child." Research paints a different picture. Coercive, punitive, and harsh parental discipline in early childhood is associated with high levels of both physical and verbal aggression in early childhood and beyond (Gershoff, 2002).
- **Child care:** The amount of time children spend in child care as well as the type of care setting has been linked to aggressive behaviors in early childhood. In one study, children in child care for 45 hours a week or more from age 3 months to 54 months had more externalizing problems (including aggression) than children who attended fewer hours (NICHD Early Child Care Research Network, 2002). In follow-up analyses, the investigators found hours in settings with large numbers of peers, but not with smaller peer groups, was linked to parent and teacher reports of aggression (NICHD Early Child Care Research Network, 2008).

Scientists are studying young children's interactions with peers and caregivers in larger group settings to see *why* this might be and identify possible preventative strategies. One possibility comes from the research that measured cortisol levels. These studies found that cortisol increased on days when children were in centers (the opposite of the typical circadian rhythm of cortisol), but not on days when the same children were at home (Watamura et al., 2003). The largest increases in cortisol were observed in children who had the most difficulty regulating negative emotions and behavior (Dettling, Gunnar, & Donzella, 1999), who were more fearful (Watamura et al., 2003), and who were less involved in peer play (Watamura et al., 2003). These findings suggest that toddlers and preschoolers, who are learning to negotiate with peers for the first time, experience large peer groups as socially demanding and stressful. Reducing group sizes in early child-care programs is one way to reduce the stress associated with early care. Explicitly working with young children to help develop ways to play cooperatively and to regulate emotional arousal are others. (For a summary of this section, see "Interim Summary 8.4: Prosocial Behaviors, Conscience, and Aggression.")

SOCIAL RELATIONSHIPS IN EARLY CHILDHOOD

Socioemotional development in early childhood is a transactional process that reflects interplay between children's own dispositions and their experiences with others. The child's own dispositions and capacities form the core. But these are tried and tested in interactions with others. Parents are a primary influence in early childhood, but siblings and peers become increasingly important.

Parenting Styles and Children's Development

In an influential study conducted more than 40 years ago, Diana Baumrind (1967, 1971) observed middle-class, European American children at home with their parents and at preschool with peers. Baumrind wanted to learn whether different parenting styles

INTERIM SUMMARY 8.4

Prosocial Behaviors, Conscience, and Aggression	
Prosocial Behaviors	■ **Prosocial behaviors** are voluntary actions intended to benefit another person.
Early Signs of Conscience	■ **Conscience** is an internalized sense of right and wrong. ■ Laboratory measures of guilt, empathy, and internalized standards indicate the beginnings of conscience as early as 33 months.
Factors Associated with the Development of Conscience	■ Children who display more effortful control and emotional regulation also demonstrate behavioral manifestations of conscience. ■ Children with secure attachment relationships are more sympathetic with their peers. ■ Preschoolers with emotionally supportive, stimulating, and responsive caregivers tend to be more cooperative and sociable with peers.
Aggression	■ **Aggression** is behavior that is *intended* to harm or injure other people. **Physical aggression** (fighting or damaging another child's possessions), **verbal aggression** (threatening someone), and **relational aggression** (attempting to lower another child's social standing or relations with others) are evident in early childhood. ■ Aggression can occur for various reasons: **reactive aggression** is a defense response to provocation; **instrumental aggression** is designed to achieve a goal for oneself; **hostile aggression** is designed to hurt or "put down" another person. ■ Boys engage in more physical aggression than girls. ■ Preschoolers who are low in effortful control and emotional regulation display more reactive aggression than other children. ■ Coercive, punitive, and harsh parental discipline is associated with high levels of physical and verbal aggression in early childhood and beyond. ■ High hours in child care and large group sizes are associated with higher levels of aggression in early childhood.

affect social competence. She identified two critical parenting dimensions—*warmth/acceptance* and *control*—that occurred in different combinations and were exhibited in different styles of parenting (see Figure 8.6).

authoritative parenting Parenting style characterized by high warmth and high control.

- **Authoritative parenting** is high in both warmth/acceptance AND in control. Authoritative parents have high expectations, set standards, and enforce rules, but they also convey that the child is valued, loved, and accepted. Affectionate and understanding, they enjoy their child's company and take pride in his accomplishments.

authoritarian parenting Parenting style characterized by low warmth and high control.

- **Authoritarian parenting** is high in control, but is low in warmth/acceptance. Authoritarian parents set strict standards. They rarely display affection and rarely take pride in the child's accomplishments. Their word is law, and rules are not explained or discussed.

- **Permissive parenting** is high in warmth/acceptance but low in control. Affectionate and indulgent, permissive parents often as not let the child have her way. They make few demands for responsibility or order in the home, avoid confrontations, and impose little discipline.

These different styles of parenting reflect different underlying beliefs about the nature of children and the role of parents. Authoritarian parents act as if children are "wild creatures" who need to be "tamed"—they value obedience. Permissive parents act as if children are like the seeds of beautiful flowers that only need love and care to flourish. Permissive parents value freedom and self-expression. The third group, authoritative parents, provides a balance of strong support and high expectations. Authoritative parents value responsibility.

Eleanor Maccoby described a fourth style, **disengaged parenting**, characterized by low warmth/acceptance and low control (Maccoby & Martin, 1983). These disengaged parents focus on their own needs, not the child's, and do whatever is necessary to minimize the costs in time and effort to interact with the child. They might not set a bedtime . . . and not notice or care that the child has fallen asleep, fully dressed, on the couch.

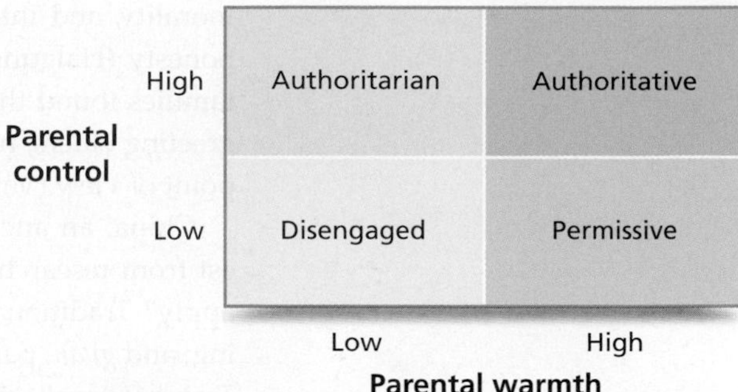

FIGURE 8.6

Parenting Style Classifications

Researchers who study parenting behaviors have identified four categories based on parental levels of warmth/responsiveness and control. Parents who are firm but also warm with their children are categorized as "authoritative," and this style has been associated with children's positive adjustment. Although this is one way of classifying parenting styles, it is important to keep in mind that family values and parenting behaviors can vary across cultures, and different ways of classifying parents may make more sense in different cultural contexts.

permissive parenting Parenting style characterized by high warmth and low control; also known as "indulgent" parenting.

disengaged parenting Parenting style characterized by low warmth and low control.

The Influence of Parenting Styles on Social Competence

Parenting styles are linked to socioemotional development. Children of authoritative parents generally are independent, self-controlled, cheerful, and cooperative. As a rule, they are popular with peers. Children of authoritarian parents tend to have high levels of both externalizing (acting out) and internalizing (withdrawing) behavior problems. Boys are often defiant while girls are often dependent and clinging. Children of permissive parents tend to be impulsive, lacking self-reliance and self-control. According to Baumrind, control without warmth/acceptance (*authoritarian parenting*) or warmth/acceptance without control (*permissive parenting*) has negative effects on development. Children thrive on a balance of the two (*authoritative parenting*).

One criticism of Baumrind's research is that she did not consider that different children may *elicit* different styles of parenting (Harris, 1998). A parent may be permissive with a child who is quiet and shy, authoritarian with a child who is aggressive and noncompliant, and authoritative with a child who is competent and reasonable. Today, most researchers conceptualize the parent-child relationship as transactional, with parents affecting children and children affecting parents.

Another criticism is that Baumrind's work was based on the study of only one social group—middle-class European American families. There has been much lively debate about whether her conclusions apply in other cultural contexts, such as different ethnic groups in the United States, or in other countries (Sorkhabi, 2005).

Cultural Differences in Parenting

Although many of Baumrind's findings have now been replicated across many different cultural contexts, a growing body of research has identified other values and beliefs that also can influence parenting. Studies of Hispanic families reveal distinctive core values reflected in their parenting, including *la familia*—maintaining strong extended family ties, feelings of loyalty to the family, and putting commitment to the family ahead of individual needs; *respeto*—maintaining harmonious interpersonal relationships through respect for self and others; and *educación*—training in responsibility, morality, and interpersonal relationships, emphasizing good manners, warmth, and honesty (Halgunseth, Ispa, & Rudy, 2006). A study of Mexican American immigrant families found that children as young as age 4 had internalized rules such as politely greeting elders, not interrupting an adult conversation, and not challenging an adult's point of view (Valdes, 1996).

China, an ancient culture with collectivist traditions, has attracted a lot of interest from researchers. Do standards developed for an individualistic, Western society apply? Traditional Chinese parenting is based on two principles: *chia-shun*, or training; and *guan*, parental involvement and investment in children (Chao & Tseng, 2002). Training emphasizes the value of hard work, self-discipline, achievement, family honor, and obedience. Parents tend to see their child's schoolwork as a parental responsibility and to take low grades or failure personally. Displays of affection primarily take the form of praise for a child's achievements, not unconditional love (a distinctively Western concept). In the Chinese context, this parenting style—*chia-shun* and *guan*—is associated with high academic achievement.

Some developmental scientists (e.g., Chao & Tseng, 2002) see this as evidence that authoritative parenting is not the best approach in all cultures; and that, in China, authoritarian parenting (high control, low warmth/acceptance) is more effective. Other developmental scientists (e.g., Chen et al., 2000) hold that Chinese parenting *is* authoritative but expressed differently. In that cultural context, children see training as just and parental involvement as an expression of love.

Sibling Interactions and Relationships

Sibling interactions and relationships represent another important social experience in early childhood. Interactions with siblings tap a wide array of emotions—laughter and shared joys but also tears and heated fights. Disagreements and reconciliations are common, everyday occurrences.

In African, Polynesian, Mexican, and Mayan cultures, children (especially girls) become caregivers and teachers for younger siblings as early as age 4. In European American families, an older sibling's role is less prescribed, but still important.

As noted in Chapter 7, interactions among siblings provide fertile ground to develop a theory of mind and social understanding. Sibling relationships also serve as a model for relations with friends. Children who have highly conflictual relationships with their siblings also tend to have highly conflictual relationships with peers (Dunn, 2002). Those who are skilled at negotiating with siblings tend to be skilled negotiators with peers. Older siblings act as tutors, managers, or supervisors of younger children, and sometimes as gatekeepers who can expand or limit opportunities to interact with other children and the world outside the family (Brody, 1998). If at times "worst enemies," siblings can serve as buffers from adjustment problems for children experiencing social isolation in the outside world.

Interactions with siblings also provide opportunities to practice social skills learned from parents. Having a sibling in the household creates occasions for young children to observe their parents interacting with another child and to be challenged by complex emotions including jealousy, pride, guilt, and disappointment. At other times, siblings can serve as allies during conflicts or disruptions within the family (Vandell & Bailey, 1992).

Peers

peers Age-mates who are equals in terms of skills and maturity.

Early childhood is a period in which relationships with peers blossom. **Peers** are age-mates who are equals in terms of skills and maturity. They provide a unique set of opportunities for social growth that children cannot obtain from their parents or their siblings (Hartup, 1989). With a peer, children can present their own opinions and assert themselves more freely than they do with an "all-knowing and all-powerful" adult or older child. Peers are equals who do not have the authority to order another around ("You're not the boss of me!"). Furthermore, children can choose their playmates, but not their parents and siblings. If siblings get into a bitter argument, they still remain siblings. Friends (at any age) do not have this guarantee. As a result, maintaining relationships with peers encourages developing skills in negotiation, compromise, and management.

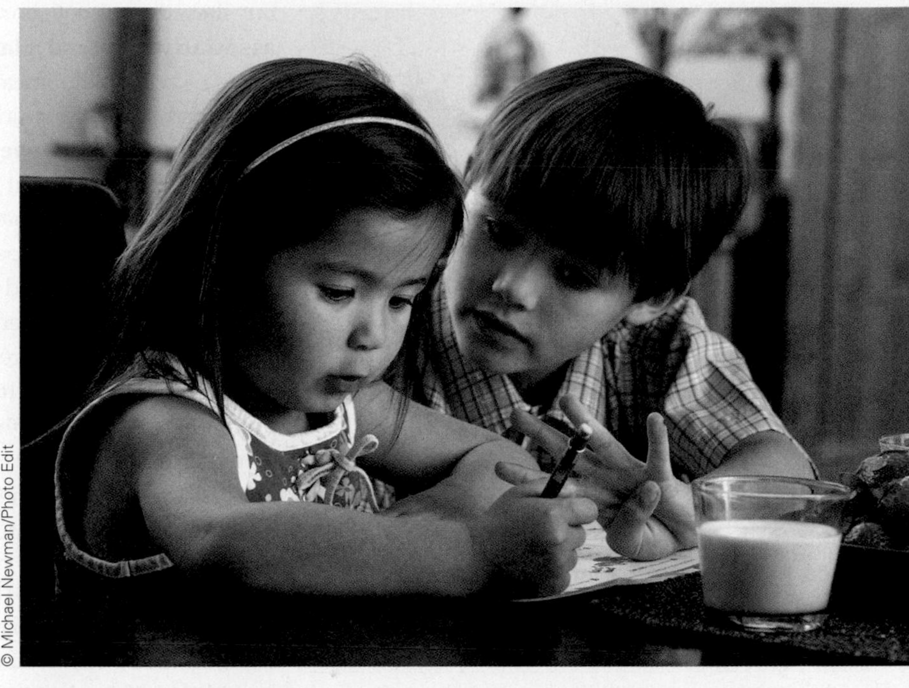

© Michael Newman/Photo Edit

Older siblings act as tutors and supervisors of younger children, providing opportunities for cognitive and social growth for both.

During the preschool period, interactions with peers increase in their frequency and their complexity. Interactions extend over several minutes as children talk about Halloween plans, work together to build forts out of blankets and pillows, and negotiate who is getting to wear which dress-up clothes. Piaget (1923/1955) portrayed preoperational children as egocentric communicators who fail to recognize other's perspectives. But detailed linguistic analyses reveal that most (60%) of preschoolers' utterances are directed toward other children, are comprehensible, and result in an appropriate response or dialogue (Levin & Rubin, 1983; Mueller, 1972).

In her observations of children's play in nursery schools conducted more than 70 years ago, Mildred Parten (1932) recorded six different types of play-related behaviors. A visit to a local child care center will reveal very similar play behaviors in the twenty-first century. These categories of play are:

1. **Unoccupied**: Wandering aimlessly or staring into space. Not engaged in play, exploration, or social interaction.
2. **Solitary play**: Playing alone, with no reference to what others are doing.
3. **Onlooker**: Watching others as they play.
4. **Parallel play**: Playing (with a similar toy in a similar way) next to another child, but without conversing.
5. **Associative play**: Involves social interactions and playing with others but children are not working toward a common goal.
6. **Cooperative play**: Involves social interactions in which one child's behavior is coordinated with another child's behavior, as children work toward common goals. Some examples of cooperative play are working together to build a sand castle and playing stick ball.

Parten observed all six levels of play in young children, but parallel play was relatively more common in 2-year-olds and cooperative play was relatively more common in 5- and 6-year-olds. Onlooker behavior often sets the stage for associative and cooperative play, as children move from watching others to joining in the play.

Pretend Play Carollee Howes (Howes, 1984, 1992; Howes & Matheson, 1992) used Parten's play categories to describe social pretend play in early childhood (see Figure 8.7). At first, young children play side by side, pretending to "eat" from a cup or "sleep" on a pillow. In this **simple pretend play**, they watch and sometimes mimic one another,

simple pretend play Fantasy play behavior in which children watch or mimic each other but do not collaborate in any organized way.

Type	Behavior
Simple	Children play side by side without collaboration
Associative	Children create stories/scripts with sequences of actions
Cooperative	Children create scripts and play reciprocal roles

FIGURE 8.7

Developments in Social Pretend Play in Early Childhood

The development of cognitive and social skills in early childhood is reflected in how children engage in pretend play together. Young children often play side by side, but true reciprocal interactions in which both children co-create pretend scenarios do not occur until children are older.

associative pretend play Social fantasy play in which children create a story or script with a series of actions in a meaningful sequence.

cooperative pretend play Social fantasy play in which children develop a script and play reciprocal roles (e.g., mother and baby).

but they do not collaborate in any organized way. In the next stage, **associative pretend play**, two children create a story or script with a series of actions in a meaningful sequence. For example, both children are superheroes, "rescuing" damsels and others in distress. The most advanced stage is **cooperative pretend play**, in which children not only develop a script but also play reciprocal roles. Julia "feeds" Emma with a bottle, and Emma "drinks" and "cries" like a baby. Thus, how Emma plays her role depends on Julia and vice versa.

Cooperative pretend play provides unique opportunities for young children to understand and rehearse the roles of people with whom they interact in real life (such as Mommy and Daddy) as well as fantasy characters. They can practice regulating their emotions by pretending to be brave or afraid or angry; learn how to express and convince others of their ideas; and explore issues such as dependency and trust (by playing the baby, e.g.)—all in a nonthreatening context. After all, it's only pretend.

Friendships During early childhood, most young children develop one or more friendships. Researchers identify friends by asking children to list their friends; if two children name one another, they're considered "friends." A study of children who attended a university preschool found that 75 percent had at least one reciprocated friendship in the fall; 85 percent did in the spring (Walden, Lemerise, & Smith, 1999). Moreover, friendships—usually between same-age, same-sex peers—were generally stable over the school year.

Children direct more social overtures, engage in more interactions, and play in more complex ways with friends than with nonfriends (Gottman, 1983; Hinde et al., 1985). Preschool friends also have more conflicts with one another than with nonfriends, but these conflicts are resolved differently: Friends are more likely to negotiate a solution, to stay together, and to continue playing (Hinde et al., 1985). Preschool friends also provide emotional support and act as a secure base during stressful times, such as the birth of a sibling (Gottman & Parker, 1986), the transition to a new school, or the beginning of a new school year (Ladd & Kochenderfer, 1996). Kindergarten students adjust more easily to school when they have a friend in the class, and even show more cognitive improvement over the school year (Ladd & Price, 1987).

Peer Groups Even in early childhood, peer groups have an underlying structure or organization in which some children are "popular" and others are not. A study of preschool classrooms found stable dominance hierarchies based on struggles over objects, threats, and conflicts (Strayer & Strayer, 1976). Children who lost an object struggle rarely initiated conflicts again with the winners. As a result, overall conflict in the classroom decreased over time.

Other researchers have found early indications of peer social status in the preschool classroom based on classmates' nominations of those they like to play with and those they do not like to play with (Ladd, Price, & Hart, 1988). These ratings, too, are relatively stable over time—suggesting that peer acceptance and peer rejection begin at a young age.

Influences on Early Peer Relations What factors influence the quality of early peer relationships? One factor that has received considerable attention is the quality of children's relationships with their parents. Children who were securely attached to their mothers as toddlers are more socially competent and popular with classmates as well as less aggressive with friends during early childhood (Schneider, Atkinson, & Tardif, 2001). In contrast, children who were insecurely attached as infants show more negative emotions, hostility, and aggression, and less assertive control with peers in early childhood (McElwain et al., 2003; Rubin et al., 2006).

Parenting styles and particular behaviors serve as a model for early peer relations. Children whose interactions with their parents include balanced turn-taking are rated by teachers as being more socially competent (Lindsey, Mize, & Pettit, 1997). Cooperation and communication in the parent-child dyad is associated with more responsive communication with peers, which in turn predicts greater peer acceptance (Black & Logan, 1995).

Attachment security and opportunities to develop social competencies during well-scaffolded interactions are only two of the ways that parents influence their young children's peer relations. A third way is by providing opportunities for children to interact with peers and offering advice about play strategies. Parents who arrange "play dates" for their young children and who indirectly supervise those dates have children who are better liked by peers, exhibit more prosocial behaviors, and have more friends (Kerns, Cole, & Andrews, 1998; Parke et al., 2002). There also is evidence that "like attracts like," a process

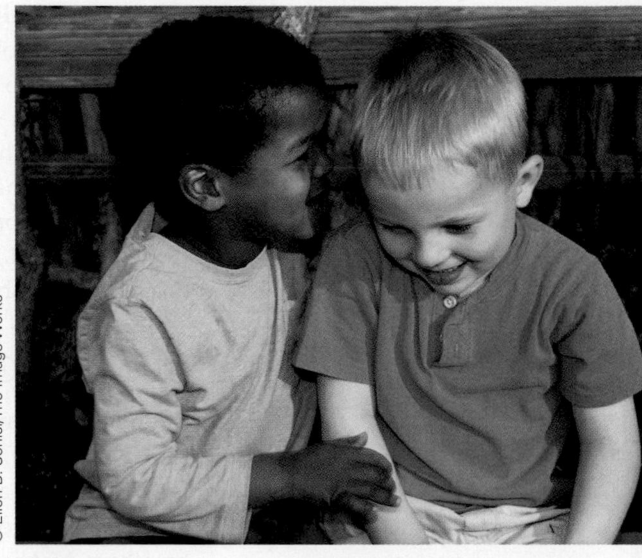

Contrary to Piaget's view, preschoolers are often skilled communicators who have extended conversations. Here, two 4-year-olds are conversing at a bilingual English-Spanish preschool.

INTERIM SUMMARY 8.5

Social Relationships in Early Childhood

Parenting Styles and Children's Development	■ Two key parenting dimensions are warmth/acceptance and control. **Authoritative parents** are high in both warmth/acceptance and control. **Authoritarian parents** are high in control but low in warmth/acceptance. **Permissive parents** are high in warmth/acceptance but low in control. **Disengaged parents** are low in control and low in warmth/acceptance. ■ These parenting styles have been linked to child developmental outcomes. Children of authoritative parents generally are independent, self-controlled, cheerful, and cooperative. Children of authoritarian parents tend to have higher levels of externalizing and internalizing problems. Children of permissive parents tend to be impulsive, lacking self-reliance and self-control.
Cultural Differences in Parenting	■ Studies of Hispanic families demonstrate other aspects of parenting: *la familia, respeto* and *educación*. ■ Chinese parenting reflects other principles: *chia-shun* and *guan*.
Sibling Interactions and Relationships	■ Relationships with siblings are some of the most enduring and intense of all relationships. ■ Interactions with siblings provide opportunities to develop social understanding and to hone social skills.
Peers	■ Peers are age-mates who are equals in skills and maturity. ■ Maintaining relationships with peers encourages developing skills in negotiations, compromise, and management. ■ Social pretend play, one of the hallmarks of early childhood, provides opportunities to coordinate complex roles in a nonthreatening context. ■ Most young children develop one or more friendships. These friendships can provide emotional support and act as a secure base.

homophily The tendency of individuals to associate and bond with others who are similar or "like" themselves.

called **homophily**. Children who were securely attached as toddlers tend to form positive playgroups with one another as preschoolers, whereas insecurely attached children tend to form playgroups with other insecurely attached children (Denham et al., 2001). In a sense, children re-create with their friends the security—or the insecurity—of their relations with their parents. The quality of parent-infant attachment is more highly related to children's friendships (another close relationship) than to their popularity or social status, which depend more on other social skills (Schneider et al., 2001). (For a summary of this section, see "Interim Summary 8.5: Social Relationships in Early Childhood.")

SUMMING UP AND LOOKING AHEAD

Brain maturation, as well as cognitive gains (especially in attention, memory, and perspective-taking), set the stage for socioemotional development in early childhood. Infants may exert a strong pull on their parents' heartstrings (and glasses, earrings, and other appendages); they are not entirely passive. But their lives are largely controlled by others. Not so with young children. Although they are still closely supervised, they are far more independent in body and mind than infants.

The emerging sense of self (though rudimentary and unrealistically positive) is the foundation for other advances. Self-conscious emotions, such as pride and embarrassment, appear. Preschoolers develop a gender identity and beliefs (often highly stereotyped) about what it means to be a boy or girl. We see the beginnings of self-control—or "effortful control"—and emotional regulation. We also see the emergence of actions deliberately intended to help—or to hurt—others. The "self" has motives.

The context in which the young child is growing up (including child care and preschool), interacting with the child's temperament and early experiences, especially at home, contribute to individual variations. Parents and others now actively attempt to shape social and emotional development, the process of socialization. Families—and cultures—have different values and different styles of parenting. And children respond in different ways. Some children are secure and develop a strong sense of initiative, whereas others feel unworthy of love and develop a sense of guilt (reflecting differences in self-esteem). Some are able to manage their emotions and actions; others respond to the slightest stress with a meltdown or tantrum (reflecting differences in self-regulation). Some find it easy to make friends or join a play group, but others are wary and hesitant, and still others are disliked (because they are pushy, overly aggressive, or do not fit in for other reasons), reflecting differences in social competence. Peer pressure does not begin in adolescence. Gender nonconformity is a particular social liability at this age.

As you will see in Chapter 10, the same themes continue in middle childhood: the further development of a more realistic and integrated sense of self, more sophisticated strategies for self-control, and more advanced social skills (though some children experience rejection or victimization). The major change in middle childhood is in context. The child's social horizons—and challenges—expand: to school, where achievement counts more than getting along with peers; to peer groups that are increasingly independent of adult supervision (so that children have to negotiate rules and standards among themselves); and to a whole new set of influences, including organized after-school and weekend programs, the neighborhood, and the mass media.

We've completed our discussion of development in early childhood and are ready to move on to the next stage of life. Our next chapter looks at children's physical and cognitive development during middle childhood.

HERE'S WHAT YOU SHOULD KNOW

Did You Get It?

After reading this chapter, you should understand the following:

- What the self is and the characteristics of young children's self-conceptions
- How biology, socialization, and cognition play a role in gender development
- Major aspects of emotional development in early childhood, including the development of secondary emotions and emotional intelligence
- What prosocial behaviors are and how they indicate the development of a conscience
- How parents, siblings, and peers influence development in early childhood
- How different parenting styles are linked to children's development

Important Terms and Concepts

aggression (p. 242)
agonism (p. 243)
androgens (p. 233)
associative pretend play (p. 250)
authoritative parenting (p. 246)
authoritarian parenting (p. 246)
conscience (p. 241)
cooperative pretend play (p. 250)
corpus callosum (p. 233)
developmental trajectory (p. 243)
disengaged parenting (p. 247)
effortful control (p. 237)
emotional intelligence (p. 236)
emotional regulation (p. 237)
empathy (p. 241)
externalizing problems (p. 237)
gender identity (p. 230)
gender constancy (p. 231)
gender schema (p. 234)
gender socialization (p. 234)
homophily (p. 252)
hostile aggression (p. 243)
initiative versus guilt (p. 228)
instrumental aggression (p. 243)
internal working model (p. 228)
internalizing problems (p. 244)
peers (p. 248)
permissive parenting (p. 247)
physical aggression (p. 242)
prosocial behavior (p. 240)
reactive aggression (p. 243)
relational aggression (p. 243)
rough and tumble play (p. 234)
self-conscious emotion (p. 235)
self-conception (p. 227)
self-esteem (p. 227)
simple pretend play (p. 250)
socialization (p. 226)
testosterone (p. 233)
verbal aggression (p. 242)

Part III Review

CHAPTER 7
Physical and Cognitive Development in Early Childhood

- During early childhood, the brain matures structurally and functionally. A key process is the development of connections between neurons that occurs through the growth of axons and dendrites **(synaptogenesis).**
- Motor development occurs on two fronts in early childhood: (1) gross motor skills and (2) fine motor skills.
- Jean Piaget identified the second stage of cognitive development, from about age 2 to 7, as the **preoperational period.** In contrast to Piaget, Lev Vygotsky argued that thought and language develop together. The **zone of proximal development (ZPD)** is at the center of his theory.
- The **information-processing approach** deals with basic questions about how people acquire, encode, store, and use information. The approach identifies three steps in memory processing: **sensory memory, working memory,** and **long-term memory.**
- The quality of child care is linked to children's cognitive development. High-quality programs can benefit the development of emergent literacy and mathematical thinking.

CHAPTER 8
Socioemotional Development in Early Childhood

- The **self** is a cognitive and social construction that reflects a child's level of mental development and interactions and experiences with others.
- **Self-conceptions** are evaluative judgments about specific areas such as cognitive ability. **Self-esteem** refers to a more global assessment of self-worth.
- Biology, socialization, and cognition each play a role in **gender development.** By age 2½ years, most children can label themselves and others by sex, which is the beginning of a **gender identity.** By age 3, styles of play often differ by gender. Around age 6 or 7, children understand **gender constancy.**
- Emotional development in early childhood is marked by advances in children's awareness of their own and others' emotional states and in their ability to regulate their emotional expressions.
- Parents, siblings, and peers influence development in early childhood, Different parenting styles (authoritative, authoritarian, permissive, and disengaged) are linked to children's development.

part four

Middle Childhood

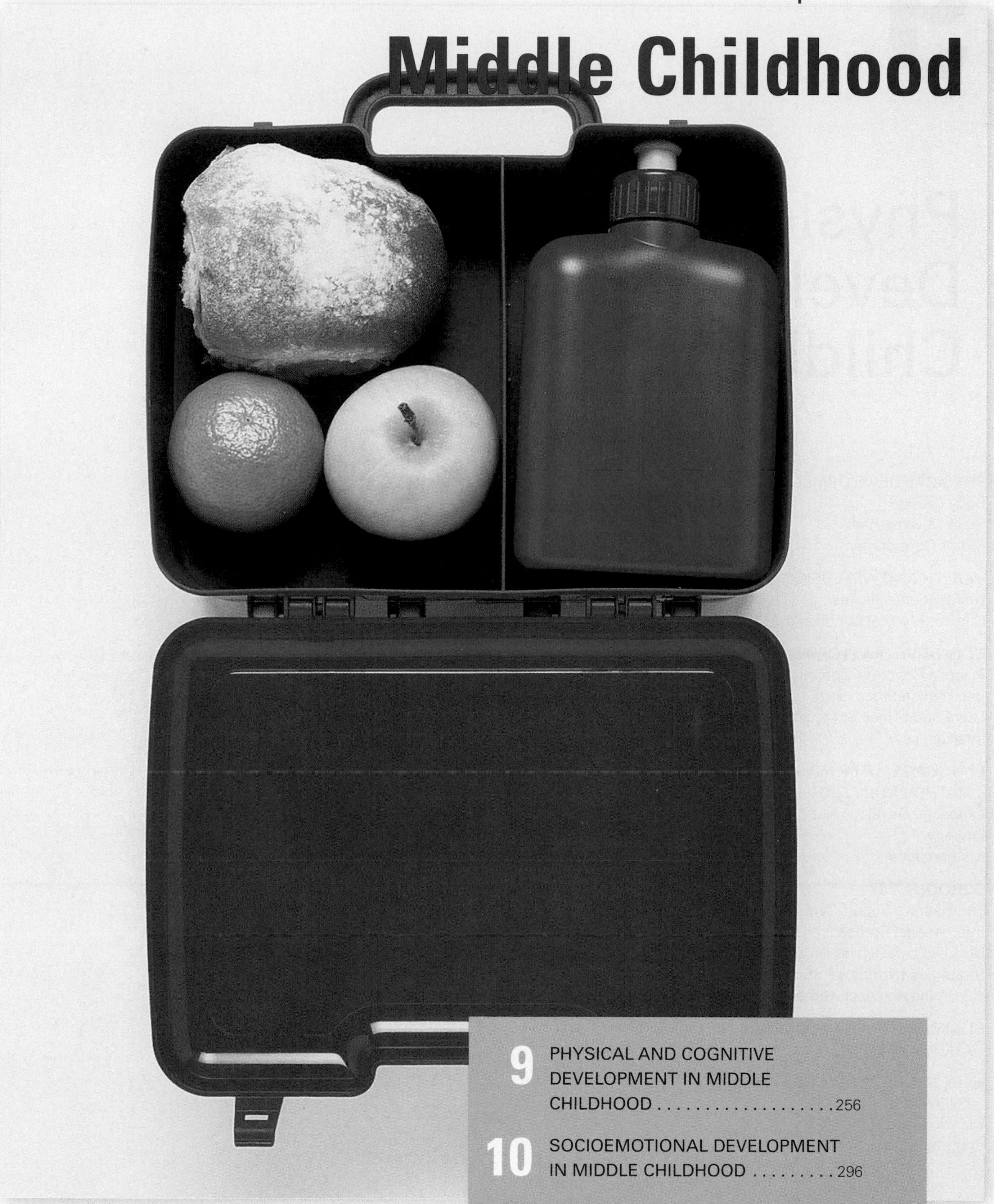

CHAPTER

9

Physical and Cognitive Development in Middle Childhood

© Brand X Pictures / Jupiterimages

This is the first of two chapters on middle childhood, spanning ages 5 to 12 and sometimes called "the school years." Children become increasingly independent during this period. They wash and dress themselves, make their own snacks, and find their way around their neighborhood. As their brains and bodies mature, children begin acquiring skills that may last a lifetime—not only in school but also in out-of-school activities such as sports and the arts. Their thinking becomes more logical as they categorize and organize material in ways that enable them to process increasing amounts of information faster and to remember more of it. Their knowledge of the world beyond their immediate experience expands, not only from school but also through mass media. During middle childhood, children spend more time with peers and less time with their families. Friends and the peer group become an important influence on their self-esteem as well as their tastes and behavior.

PHYSICAL DEVELOPMENT

In this section, we look at both **normative development** (typical changes in body size and shape) and **individual differences** (variations within individuals of the same age). We also consider how social change is affecting the physical development of today's children. How are they different from previous generations?

normative development A pattern of development that is typical, or average.

individual differences Variations within individuals of the same age.

Body Growth

In many parts of the world, today's children are growing faster and bigger than earlier generations, thanks to better health and nutrition. In such far-flung places as Canada, China, and Greece, children are taller and heavier, with a higher **body mass index (BMI),** than previous generations (Hoppa & Garlie, 1998; Magkos et al., 2005; Zhen-Wang & Cheng-Ye, 2005). (As discussed in Chapter 7, BMI is calculated by dividing weight [measured in kilograms] by height [measured in meters] squared, or wt/ht^2.)

body mass index (BMI) BMI is calculated by dividing weight (measured in kilograms) by height (measured in meters) squared, or wt/ht^2.

On average, school-age children in the United States gain 2 to 3 inches and 5 to 7 pounds per year. At age 7, the average American child (boys and girls) is 4'0" tall and weighs 50 pounds. By age 11, the average girl is 4'9" tall and weighs 82 pounds, whereas the average boy is 4'8½" tall and weighs 78 pounds (Kuczmarski et al., 2000).

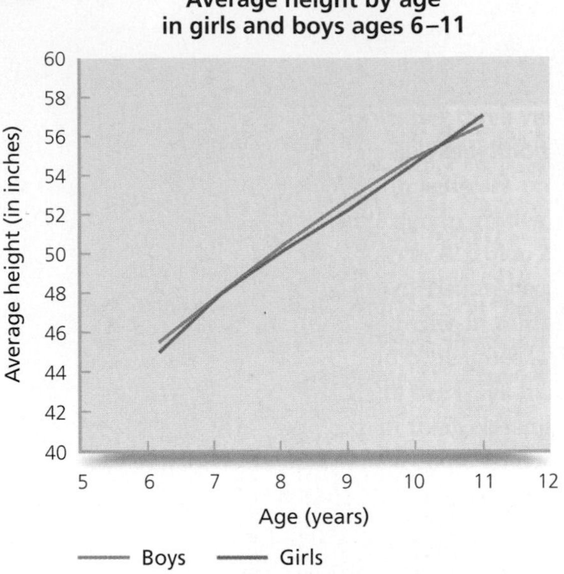

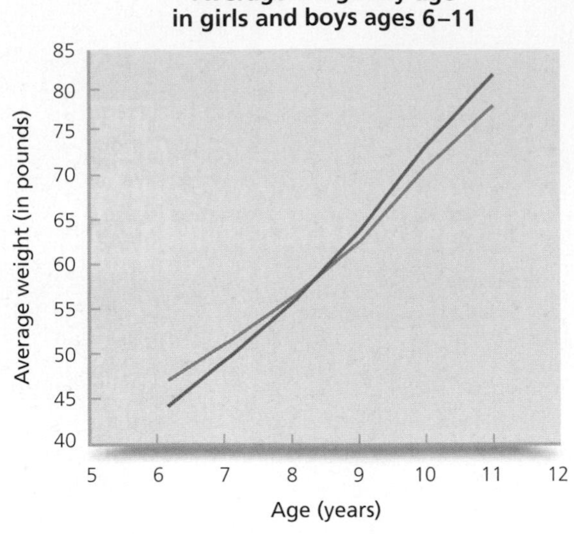

FIGURE 9.1

Increases in Height and Weight During Middle Childhood

At age 7, boys and girls are similar in height and weight, but with an earlier onset of puberty, girls are heavier than boys at age 11.

Source: Kuczmarski et al. (2000).

(See Figure 9.1.) These differences, although small, reflect the earlier onset of puberty in girls (see Chapter 11). Their adolescent growth spurt is beginning. From here on, girls have more body fat, whereas boys have more lean body mass per inch of height.

As was the case in early childhood, growth in middle childhood occurs in spurts rather than gradually. There are brief periods (24 hours) of very rapid growth followed by days or weeks when no growth occurs. Within these spurts, growth is most rapid at night while the child is lying down, rather than during the day when he or she is up and active (Adolph & Berger, 2006).

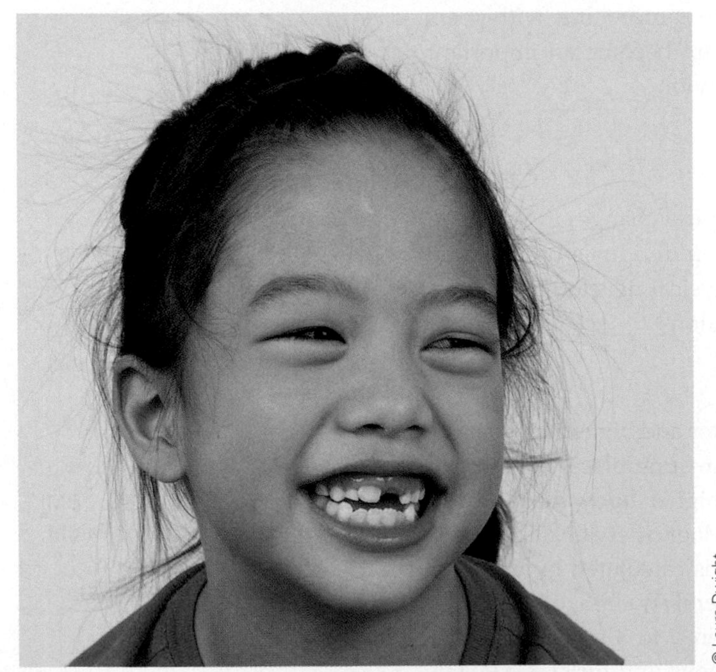

© Laura Dwight

Middle childhood is the period when children lose their primary teeth.

Body proportions are also changing. The torso becomes slimmer, bones (especially in the arms and legs) are longer and broader, and the center of gravity shifts to the pelvic area. Because the lower half of the body grows fastest, school-age children often appear long-legged. Ligaments are not yet firmly attached to the bones, which gives children great flexibility. Back-bends and cartwheels are easy.

Children lose their primary ("baby") teeth during this period, typically beginning with the front middle teeth at age 6 or 7, followed by the molars at age 10 to 12 (keeping the "tooth fairy" busy). Permanent teeth come in at the rate of about four a year, so that most are in place by the end of middle childhood (Moorrees, 1959). Because the lower part of the face grows gradually, these teeth may look too big for the child's face at first.

Children's eyes are also maturing in size and function. Myopia, or nearsightedness, is rarely diagnosed before first grade, but often develops between age 6 and adolescence (Saw et al., 2002). The reason may be that no one notices nearsightedness in the preschool years, but now a teacher notices that a child has difficulty seeing the chalkboard. Or growth (especially of the eyeball) may cause myopia. All told, more than one in five children ages 6 to 11 has a vision problem, a number that increases with age (Ganley & Roberts, 1983). Children in higher-income families are more likely to have corrective lenses (29.9%) than children who are poor and near-poor (19%), most likely because more affluent children have better access to medical care. ("Poor" is defined as a family of four whose income is less than $20,000 a year. "Near-poor" is defined as a family of four whose income is between $20,000 and $40,000 a year.) This difference needs to be addressed because vision problems can contribute to problems at school. Children who can't see the material on the blackboard can't read the blackboard.

Obesity In the past, lack of food was a problem for many. Today, children suffer from another problem: too much food of the wrong sort. Childhood obesity is on the rise. In 40 years, the percentage of 6- to 11-year-olds who are overweight in the United States has increased from 4 percent to 19 percent (National Center for Health Statistics, 2007) (see Figure 9.2). An additional 18 percent of children are now at risk for overweight (Ogden et al., 2006). All told, almost 40 percent of U.S. children—about 25 million—are either overweight or at risk for overweight.

Childhood obesity has become so commonplace that health experts believe the current generation of children could have a shorter lifespan than their parents due to obesity-related deaths in adulthood (Blom-Hoffman, George, & Franko, 2006). As noted in Chapter 7, health problems once seen only in adults are now being diagnosed in children, including Type 2 diabetes (discussed later in this chapter), high blood pressure, and high cholesterol. Overweight children are also more likely to suffer from asthma (discussed below) than are normal-weight children.

Unfortunately, many children do not "outgrow" pudginess. To the contrary, overweight and risk of overweight increase with age. In a longitudinal study conducted by Marion O'Brien and colleagues (2007), the proportion of children who were overweight at 24 months was 15 percent; this increased to 18 percent at 36 months, 25 percent at 54 months, 26 percent at first grade, 31 percent at third grade, and 34 percent at fifth and sixth grades.

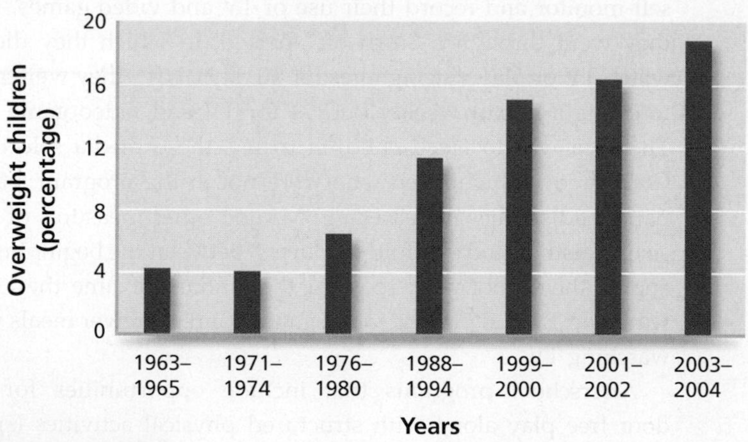

FIGURE 9.2

A Dramatic Increase in Proportion of Children Who Are Overweight: 1963 to 2004

Almost 20 percent of U.S. children are overweight, in contrast to only 4 percent in 1963.
Source: National Center for Health Statistics (2007).

Watching TV and gaining weight go hand-in-hand because children are less physically active *and* more likely to snack.

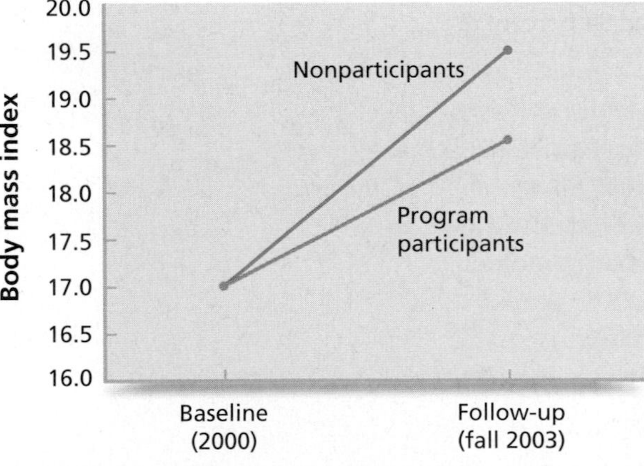

FIGURE 9.3

Changes in Body Mass Index (BMI) for Afterschool Program Participants and Nonparticipants

Although the BMI of afterschool participants and nonparticipants did not differ at baseline, program participants showed significantly lower BMI at follow-up compared to nonparticipants.
Source: Mahoney, Lord, & Carryl (2005).

Extra pounds are a social and emotional hazard. Boys and girls who are overweight are subject to teasing and more likely to be excluded from friendship groups (O'Brien et al., 2007). Overweight children also tend to have less confidence in their athletic competency, social skills, and appearance, and they have lower opinions of their overall self-worth (Bradley et al., 2008). They score lower than normal-weight children on measures of their quality of life in physical, emotional, social, and school domains (Schwimmer, Burwinkle, & Varni, 2003). Not surprisingly, overweight children are prone to internalizing problems, such as depression and anxiety (Bradley et al., 2008). Overweight girls, in particular, are more likely to develop depressive symptoms (Erikson et al., 2000). Even as early as age 5, overweight girls have more negative self-images than normal-weight peers (Davison & Birch, 2001).

Efforts to Reduce Childhood Obesity The link between physical inactivity and being overweight is clear. Children who are less physically active between the ages of 9 and 12 are more likely to become overweight by age 12 than are children who are more physically active (O'Brien et al., 2007). They spend more of their afterschool time watching TV (and snacking), a virtual recipe for gaining weight. Efforts to reduce childhood obesity often seek to increase physical activity and reduce snacking.

Several interventions have slowed the increase in BMI typically seen in middle childhood. In one, a nurse taught a curriculum focused on reducing consumption of soft drinks to elementary school children (James et al., 2004). Over a year, the prevalence of overweight among children who took the course stayed the same, but increased 7 percent in the control group of children who did not receive instruction.

Another intervention tried reducing the amount of time third- and fourth-graders spend watching TV and playing video games (Robinson, 1999). Taught by classroom teachers, the program lasted most of the school year. First, the children were taught to self-monitor and record their use of TV and video games. Next, they went through a "turn off" period, in which they did not watch TV or play video games for 10 days. Last, they were asked to create a 7-hour weekly budget for TV and video game time. The idea was to teach children to use these media selectively. Compared with children who were not in the program, participants had smaller increases in BMI and other measures of body size (waistline and skinfold thickness) between the beginning and end of the school year; reduced the amount of time they spent watching TV and playing video games; and ate fewer meals while watching TV.

Afterschool programs that include opportunities for outdoor free play along with structured physical activities (sports, dance, and fitness classes) are another promising strategy. Joseph Mahoney and colleagues compared children who attended an afterschool program with classmates who did not (Mahoney, Lord, & Carryl, 2005). In kindergarten, the two groups were similar in BMI. After 3 years in the afterschool program, participants had lower BMIs (see Figure 9.3) and were less likely to be overweight than nonparticipants. Very likely, the more time that children spent in the program, the less time they had for TV and video games and the fewer soft drinks they consumed.

Brain Development

Processes of brain development described in Chapter 7 continue in middle childhood. **Dendrites** and **axons** (the specialized extensions that carry information to and from the main body of the neurons) are still growing, branching, and establishing new **synapses** in response to new experiences. **Myelin** (the white fatty substance that encases cell axons that improves the speed and efficiency of transmission) also increases across middle childhood. The strengthening of synapses that are used regularly, and pruning of unused synapses to eliminate "clutter"—a process called **competitive elimination**—accelerates the speed with which children can process information (Lenroot & Giedd, 2006).

Synaptic pruning (the selective elimination of some synapses) leads to increased **lateralization** during middle childhood, with the left and right hemispheres becoming more differentiated in the brain processes for which they are responsible. At the same time, the **corpus callosum** (the band of nerve fibers connecting the two hemispheres) thickens, which improves communication between the left and right hemispheres, so even if the "left hand" and "right hand" are doing different things, they know what each other is up to (Lenroot & Giedd, 2006). These refinements in the brain's structure, rather than an increase in sheer size or weight, are linked to the strides in cognitive development that we'll discuss in this chapter.

Magnetic resonance imaging (MRI) has been used to document growth and development in different parts of the brain. Brain growth during early childhood is concentrated in areas at the front of the brain. Then, during middle childhood, significant growth occurs farther back in the brain. Across all cortical areas, the growth of **gray matter** (neuron cell bodies) follows a pattern that resembles a ∩ shape, with a proliferation of neurons and their connections increasing, reaching a peak, and then decreasing (Giedd et al., 1999; Lenroot & Giedd, 2006) (see Figure 9.4).

The timetable of peaks and valleys in particular areas of the brain corresponds to developmental changes in specific cognitive abilities (Fischer, 2008). Periods of

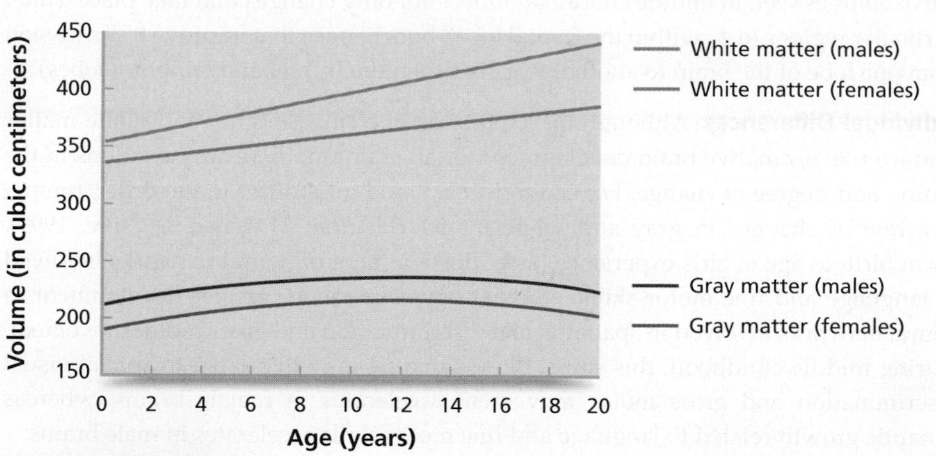

FIGURE 9.4

Changes in White and Gray Matter

The volume of white matter increases linearly with age. In contrast, the volume of gray matter shows an upside-down U shape, increasing during middle childhood and then decreasing in adolescence.

Source: Giedd et al. (1999).

dendrite Branched extension of a neuron that picks up signals from other neurons.

axon An extension of the cell that carries signals away from the cell body toward other neurons.

synapse The connection between one neuron's axon and another neuron's dendrite.

myelin A white fatty substance that encases cell axons. It provides insulation and improves the transmission of signals.

competitive elimination A process that strengthens synapses that are used regularly, and prunes unused synapses to eliminate clutter. It accelerates the speed with which children can process information.

synaptic pruning The process of elimination of unused and unnecessary synapses.

lateralization The localization of function in one of the hemispheres of the brain.

corpus callosum The connection between the two halves or hemispheres of the brain.

gray matter Refers to nerve cell bodies (neurons, axons, and dendrites). Gray matter is contrasted to the white matter or myelinated nerve fibers in the brain.

development characterized by large-scale competitive elimination in specific brain regions are also the periods in which there are dramatic gains in ability to perform the functions associated with those areas. The region of the brain responsible for vision, for instance, undergoes major changes in gray matter during infancy when visual acuity is improving dramatically but not in middle childhood when eyesight doesn't change very much (Lenroot & Giedd, 2006).

The areas of change in middle childhood are those regions of the brain related to higher-level information-processing skills. The **frontal lobes**, which are responsible for critical thinking and problem solving, undergo a growth spurt between ages 6 and 8. Gray matter in the **prefrontal cortex**, the seat of planning and emotional regulation, increases slowly until about age 8, followed by rapid growth until age 14 (Kanemura et al., 2003). As the prefrontal cortex develops, cognitive skills such as attention, planning, and short-term (working) memory improve (Giedd et al., 1999).

frontal lobe Part of the brain located in front of the parietal lobe and above the temporal lobe that is involved in recognizing future consequences, overriding unacceptable social responses, and remembering emotional experiences

prefrontal cortex The part of the brain involved in higher-order cognitive skills, such as decision making and planning. It is located in front of the brain, right behind the forehead.

temporal lobe The part of the brain that is involved in speech, memory, and hearing. It is located at the side of the brain.

parietal lobe The part of the brain associated with movement, orientation, recognition, and perception of stimuli.

white matter Refers to myelinated nerve fibers in the brain.

There also is marked change in gray matter in the **temporal lobes** and **parietal lobes** of the brain in middle childhood (Giedd et al., 1999), areas that play important roles in memory and information processing. Within these lobes, regions where the amount of gray matter peaks relatively early are responsible for simpler cognitive functions, whereas those areas that show a later peak contribute to more advanced functions. For example, in the temporal and parietal lobes, regions of the brain responsible for coordination and integration of different aspects of information processing mature later than areas responsible for specific components of information processing (Lenroot & Giedd, 2006). This helps to explain why first-graders and teenagers can perform similarly on relatively simple tasks (e.g., recalling a list words that includes a jumbled mix of animals and vegetables) but not on relatively more complicated ones (e.g., recalling the same list of words and sorting them into categories while doing so).

The growth of **white matter**—myelin—also continues during middle childhood, but it follows a different pattern than gray matter (Giedd et al., 1999). Whereas gray matter shows the inverted-U shape we've described, white matter increases linearly during middle childhood and well into adulthood. Because white matter insulates brain circuits, the continued growth of white matter allows for better communication within and across brain regions (Lenroot & Geidd, 2006). Many of the advances in cognitive abilities seen in middle childhood reflect not only changes that take place *within* particular regions (e.g., within the frontal lobe), but changes that improve transmission from one lobe of the brain to another (e.g., between the frontal and temporal lobes).

Individual Differences Although these patterns of change in gray and white matter characterize normative brain development for all children, there are variations in the timing and degree of change. For example, boys and girls differ in the order, timing, and rate of changes in gray and white matter (Hanlon, Thatcher, & Cline, 1999). From birth to age 6, girls experience faster development of neural networks involved in language and fine motor skills, whereas boys experience greater development in neural networks involved in spatial-visual discrimination and gross motor movement. During middle childhood, this shifts. Now, synaptic growth related to spatial-visual discrimination and gross motor movement accelerates in female brains, whereas synaptic growth related to language and fine motor skills accelerates in male brains.

There are sex differences in brain volume, with male brains close to 10 percent larger, on average, than female brains—a difference that is not simply due to the fact that males' bodies are larger than females' in virtually all respects (Lenroot & Giedd, 2006). But bigger is not necessarily smarter—in fact, children of equal cognitive ability can have brains that differ in size by as much as 50 percent.

Other brain differences are correlated with differences in intelligence, although these relations are more complicated than you might expect. What seems to be important is not the absolute size of the brain, but the pattern of change over time, especially as measured by the thickness of the **cerebral cortex**. Measuring cerebral cortex thickness is a way of tracking the proliferation and pruning of gray matter.

cerebral cortex The outer layer of the brain, largely responsible for higher brain functions, including sensation, voluntary muscle movement, thought, reasoning, and memory.

In a longitudinal study of more than 300 children, Shaw and colleagues (2006) charted patterns of brain development and compared those observed among children whose performance on a standard IQ test was either superior (IQ range 121–149), high (IQ range 109–120), or average (IQ range 83–108). They did not include any children whose IQ scores were below average. At age 7, children who had IQ scores in the superior range had a thinner cortex than the high or average intelligence groups, but showed a rapid increase in gray matter during middle childhood, followed by a rapid decline during adolescence. For children in the superior IQ range, the proliferation and then the pruning of redundant or unused synapses (competitive elimination) resulted in a more orderly organization of the synapses, which in turn enhances information-processing speed. In contrast, children in the other groups showed no increase in cortical gray matter during middle childhood and, especially among the average children, only a gradual decline in gray matter during adolescence. The difference in patterns was most pronounced in the prefrontal cortex, the brain region responsible for many of the higher-order cognitive abilities that are measured on IQ tests. In other words, superior intelligence is correlated with a pattern of brain development that suggests greater than average proliferation of gray matter during middle childhood, as well as a relatively more rapid pruning of gray matter during adolescence. It may be the rate of change (in either direction) rather than absolute degree of change that is crucial.

Attention Deficit Hyperactivity Disorder **Attention deficit hyperactivity disorder (ADHD)** is a condition that is linked to brain functioning and development. About 6 percent of school-age children have been diagnosed with ADHD, with about twice as many boys as girls receiving the diagnosis (Bloom, Dey, & Freeman, 2006). The American Psychiatric Association (2000) identifies three subtypes of ADHD: predominantly inattentive (IA); predominantly hyperactive-impulsive (HI); and a combination of the two (C). Girls most often have the IA form, with low levels of hyperactivity and externalizing behavior, but high levels of cognitive disability.

attention deficit hyperactivity disorder (ADHD) A condition in which children have difficulty getting organized, focusing on a task, or thinking before acting.

ADHD is most often diagnosed at ages 7 to 9, the years in which children are expected to exhibit self-control, especially in school. However, symptoms may be visible in toddlers (Lehn et al., 2007). About half of children diagnosed with ADHD continue to have problems with impulsivity, concentration, and restlessness in adolescence and adulthood (Whalen, 2000). Some children with ADHD have difficulty getting organized, focusing on a task, or thinking before acting (Whalen, 2000). Unable to sit still, they have trouble paying attention and attending to details. They do not modulate their emotions, or their energy, to fit the situation. They perform poorly in school and on tests. Other children with ADHD disorders are oppositional and noncompliant with adults, disruptive and aggressive with peers, and have difficulty making friends. They often provoke intense, negative emotions in others (parents, teachers, and peers).

Because ADHD is so variable, some scientists believe that it is unlikely that the disorder has a single cause. Scientists are looking for differences in the brains of children diagnosed with ADHD and those without the disorder to see if the different subtypes are actually separate and distinct disorders (Diamond, 2005). They are finding differences in the **cerebellum,** which is associated with coordination of motor movements and such other functions as timing and attention (Krain & Castellanos, 2006). Others have found evidence of differences in neurotransmitters and brain metabolism (Whalen, 2000).

cerebellum The part of the brain associated with balance and control of body movements.

Some scientists are investigating whether ADHD is related to delayed brain maturation. In one recent study (Shaw et al., 2007), magnetic resonance imaging (MRI) was used to measure the thickness of the cortex (gray matter) at more than 40,000 points in the brain in children diagnosed with ADHD and children who were developing more

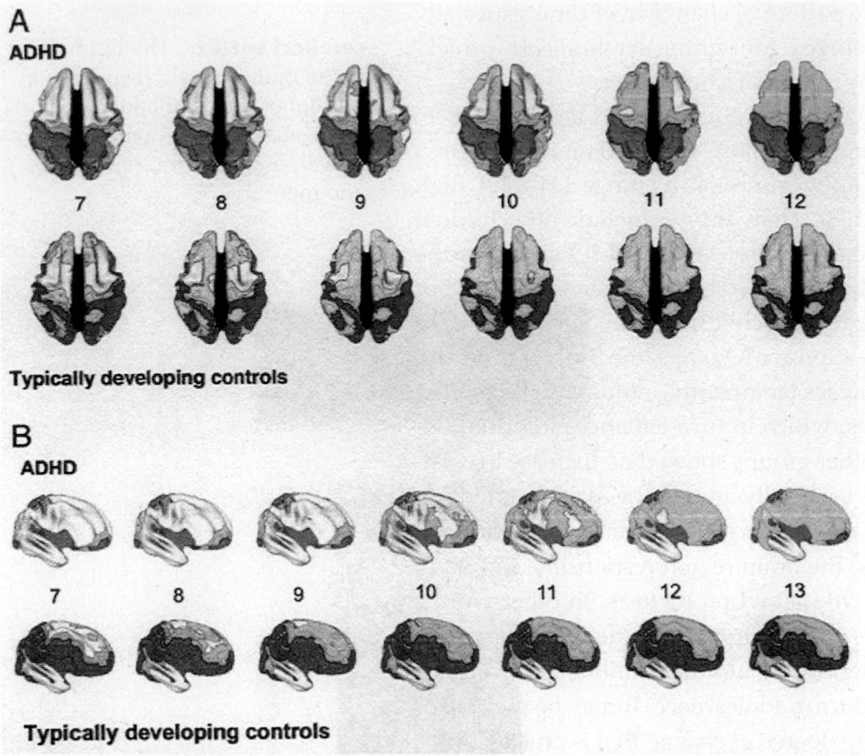

A
ADHD

7 8 9 10 11 12

Typically developing controls

B
ADHD

7 8 9 10 11 12 13

Typically developing controls

FIGURE 9.5

Cortical Development in Children with ADHD and without ADHD

Children with ADHD show a similar sequence of cortical thickening as children without ADHD, but the timing of attaining peak cortical thickness differs. ADHD children show considerable delay in attaining this marker.

Source: Shaw et al. (2007).

typically. (Recall that growth in gray matter during middle childhood follows a ∩-shaped pattern, with gray matter increasing until it reaches a peak, and then decreasing as competitive elimination occurs.) Each child's brain was scanned two to four times; the average time between each scan was 2.8 years. The researchers calculated the age at which different areas of the brain reached peak cortical thickness (see Figure 9.5).

The ADHD and non-ADHD children followed the same overall pattern of brain development, with sensory and motor areas of the brain achieving peak cortical thickness before areas associated with higher-level skills, but there were differences in the timing of gray matter peaks. The ADHD children reached the peak in gray matter about 3 years later than the non-ADHD children (10½ years versus 7½ years). The largest differences in the children were found in the prefrontal cortex (the area of the brain associated with attention, planning, and short-term memory), where cortical thickness peaked about 5 years later in the ADHD group compared with the non-ADHD group. Differences also were found for the motor cortex, where the ADHD group reached the peak slightly *earlier*, at 7 years, compared with 7.4 years among the typically developing children. These findings may explain why some ADHD children "age out" of the disorder and function more typically in late adolescence and adulthood.

Motor Development

Muscle strength, hand-eye coordination, and stamina all improve greatly during middle childhood. For example, very few preschoolers can hit a tennis ball with a racket, dribble a basketball, or jump rope, but most 10- and 11-year-olds can develop these skills with some practice. Few preschoolers can play chords on the piano or write in script, skills that older children can master with practice. Middle childhood is a time of great strides in both gross and fine motor skills.

gross motor skills Abilities required to control large movements of the arms, legs, and feet, or the whole body, such as running, jumping, climbing, and throwing.

Gross Motor Skills **Gross motor skills**, or large motor movements, become smoother and more coordinated in middle childhood (Case-Smith, 2005). Actions the preschooler performed clumsily—running, jumping, hopping, and throwing and catching a ball—become more refined. Improved flexibility, balance and coordination, agility, and strength enable children to engage in new, more complex physical activities: bike riding, skating, swimming, gymnastics, and other sports. Reaction time also improves steadily (see Table 9.1).

Some children report "growing pains" during this period, characterized by pain in the thigh and calf as well as behind the knee. Contrary to common wisdom, these aches are not caused by growth itself. Rather, they are the result of increased physical activity (running, climbing, jumping) and using developing muscles in new ways (Mayo Clinic, 2006).

TABLE 9.1 Improvement in Gross and Fine Motor Skills

	EARLY CHILDHOOD, AGES 4–5	MIDDLE CHILDHOOD, AGES 6–10
Gross motor skills	Jumps down from high step; jumps forward; hops for 4–6 steps; skips with good balance	Jumps, hops, and skips with ease
	Throws ball and hits target	Throws ball well at long distances
	Catches ball with two hands	Catches ball with accuracy
Fine motor skills	Traces letters; begins to copy letters	Precision and motor planning evident in drawing
	Completes puzzles of 10–20 pieces	Motor planning evident in completion of complex puzzles
	Strings ¼-inch beads	Good dexterity for crafts and construction with small objects

Source: Case-Smith (2005).

Historically, school-age boys have been reported to be better than girls at throwing (both distance and speed) and running, whereas girls have been reported to be more flexible and to have greater balance (e.g., Thomas & French, 1985). It is unclear, however, whether these findings represent true physiological differences or whether they result from the different types of motor experiences boys and girls have. Home and family characteristics such as parental education, father's involvement in sports, and the amount of time spent watching TV are linked to how far boys and girls are able to throw a ball (East & Hensley, 1985). Nurture—sociocultural factors and experiences within the family—plays a significant role in the development of children's motor skills in middle childhood.

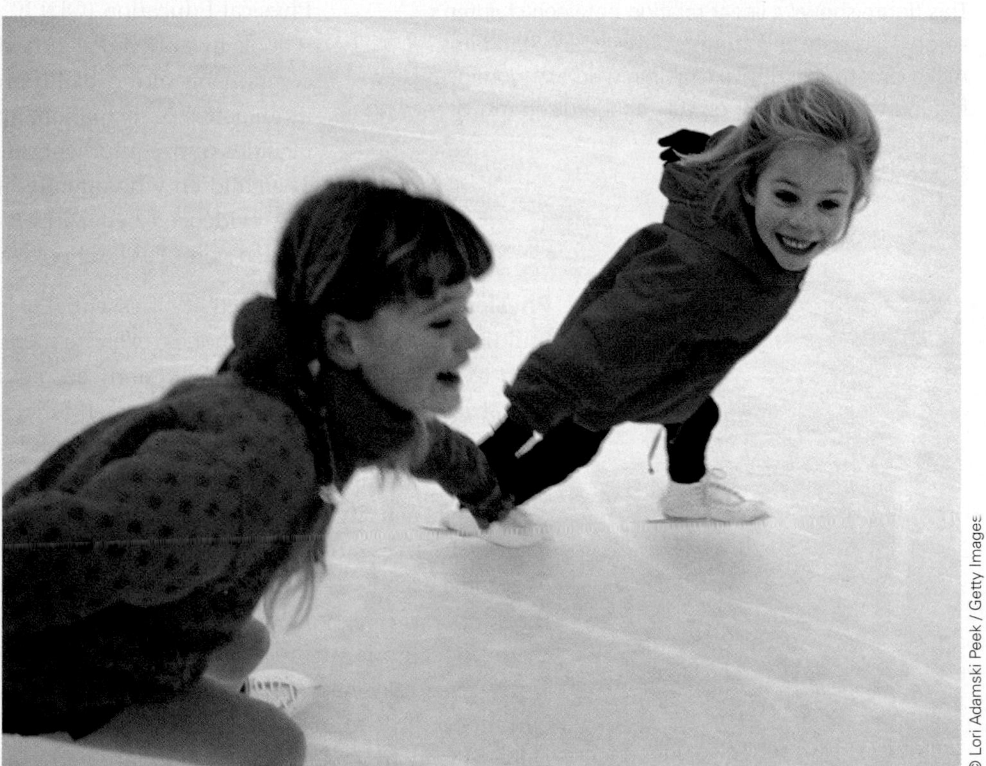

Physical activities like ice skating become smoother and more refined in middle childhood as a result of improved flexibility, balance, strength, and practice.

A more recent study reported no sex differences in fundamental movement skills (e.g., running, skipping, hopping, jumping) among elementary-age children in grades K–2 (Butterfield, Lehnhard, & Coladarci, 2002). These findings may reflect the greater inclusion in recent years of young girls in sports and other activities that contribute to motor development. This broader participation may have some long-term effects on the girls' proficiencies.

Through practice and repetition, children develop "motor skills programs" that are stored in long-term memory (Martinez, 2010). These memories are what allow us to ride a bike after a long period without riding. It's as if the memories were stored in our muscles, though, more accurately, it is the brain's nonverbal commands to our muscles

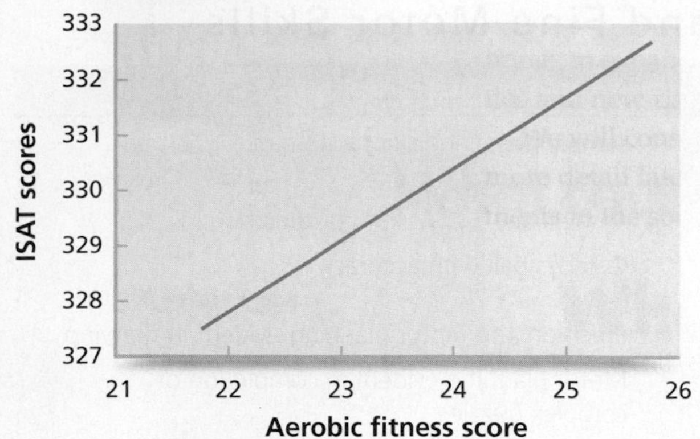

FIGURE 9.6

Relation Between Aerobic Fitness and Academic Achievement in Middle Childhood

This figure shows a linear relation between children's aerobic capacity and scores on the Illinois Standards Achievement Test (ISAT). Children who are more physically fit tend to score higher on this standardized test of reading and math.

Source: Castelli (2005).

that remain accessible. To some degree, middle childhood is a sensitive period in the development of motor skills. Learning to ride a bike, swim, or skate later in life (say, age 25) is possible but more difficult.

For some children, motor development problems can be significant during middle childhood. One contributor to poor gross motor skills is obesity. In a study conducted in Canada, gross motor skills that included running, galloping, hopping, leaping, horizontal jumping, skipping, and sliding were studied in children ages 5 to 10 (Marshall & Bouffard, 1997). The researchers found that obese children were less aerobically fit and less competent in these skills than children who were not obese.

These deficits in gross motor skills can be remediated, at least in part, by high-quality physical education at school. In the Canadian study of locomotor skills just described, the researchers compared children who attended schools that offered the Quality Daily Physical Education (QDPE) program and children who attended schools that offered standard PE two or three times per week. The components of the QDPE program included daily PE class, maximum active participation, fitness activities in each class, adequate facilities and equipment, and qualified and competent teachers. The children who attended the QDPE schools, whether obese or not, evidenced better locomotor skills than the children who attended non-QDPE schools (Marshall & Bouffard, 1997).

Physical Activity Physical activity is essential to growth and maturation. In addition to building strong muscles and bones, exercise increases energy and alertness, helps children to maintain a healthy weight, and can reduce stress. Health and fitness experts, pediatricians, and policymakers recommend that school-age children get a minimum of 60 minutes of vigorous physical activity every day, doing activities such as swimming, bike riding, jumping rope, running, or playing sports (Corbin & Pangrazi, 1998).

Physical activity may even stimulate brain growth and academic achievement. In a recent study, researchers compared the MRIs of adults taken before and after 3 months of aerobic exercise (Pereria et al., 2007). Exercise increased the flow of blood (and hence the supply of oxygen) to the brain and also resulted in the creation of new neurons in the hippocampus, an area of the brain linked to learning and memory.

Exercise may have similar effects on brain development and learning in middle childhood. Indeed, researchers have found relationships between being more physically fit and higher scores on standardized math and reading tests (Castelli, 2005; Castelli et al., 2007) (see Figure 9.6). Of five fitness measures, aerobic capacity was most highly related to academic achievement (Castelli, 2005).

During a typical school day, children have two opportunities for physical activity: physical education/PE classes and recess (Beighle et al., 2006). Unfortunately, PE classes have been cut back in many schools because of budget cuts and pressure to meet standardized test score requirements. In the United States, only 8 percent of elementary schools, 6.4 percent of middle schools, and 5.8 percent of high schools provide daily PE for all students during the full school year (Burgeson et al., 2001).

In one large national study (NICHD ECCRN, 2003), elementary school children had only two 33-minute PE classes on average each week. Out of the 66 minutes devoted to PE, children were engaged in moderate to vigorous activity for only 25 minutes. The remaining time (41 minutes) was devoted to instruction, class management, and waiting one's turn. All told, PE provided only 6 percent of children's recommended amount of weekly physical activity.

Recess is another opportunity for children to be physically active. Using a pedometer to measure activity, Beighle and colleagues (2006) found that children are quite active during recess, but recess lasted only 15 minutes. And, many schools have a single 15-minute recess each day.

Put together, these studies suggest that school-age children have limited chances to be physically active during the school day. In fact, experts believe that children are receiving less than half of the vigorous physical activity that they need each day (Nader et al., 2008). This makes the afterschool hours and weekends particularly important for meeting children's needs for physical activity. Counteracting the social trend to ride instead of walk, and watch instead of play, are youth sports.

Youth Sports Since the founding of Little League baseball in 1954, organized sports in the out-of-school hours have become a rite of childhood in the United States. Nine million children between ages 6 and 11 are in basketball leagues. Eight million play soccer; 4.6 million, baseball; and 2.9 million, volleyball. All told, almost 70 percent of all U.S. children participate in one sport or another, with participation peaking around age 12 (Ewing & Seefeldt, 2002).

Conventional wisdom holds that sports are good for children. In this view, sports provide exercise and teach physical skills while building character, leadership, sportsmanship, and achievement motivation (Bandura, 1997). But sports may also expose children to anxiety and stress and build up the best players to the exclusion of average players who are left sitting on the bench. Much depends on the context, especially coaches and parents.

Frank Smoll and Ron Smith's research is classic. In their early work, they observed Little League coaches in over 200 games involving 500 players (Smith, Smoll, & Curtis, 1978). Children were most likely to enjoy the sport and to like the coach when the coach was positive and gave technical instruction rather than just making general comments. Not surprisingly, children disliked the coach and the sport when the coach was punitive.

Drawing on these findings, Smoll and Smith (2002) developed a Coach Effectiveness Training (CET) program that emphasized four principles: (1) "Winning isn't everything, nor is it the only thing; (2) Failure is not the same thing as losing; (3) Success is not equivalent to winning; and (4) Success is found in striving for victory." The basic goal of the training is to teach coaches to emphasize fun and effort over winning, and to provide support in the face of failure.

CET-trained coaches are more consistent in praising children when they do well, handle mistakes by providing encouragement and technical instruction, and avoid punitive responses to children's behavior. The young players with CET-trained coachers like their coaches, their teammates, and the sport more in comparison to children with untrained coaches. They also show more gains in self-esteem. Studies of other sports, such as competitive swimming (Black & Weiss, 1992), have reported similar findings.

Ask coaches what their biggest problem is and many will say, "parents." When parents are supportive and enthusiastic—but not pushy—children are more likely to report enjoying the sport, looking forward to the next practice and game, and not feeling overly anxious about their own performance (Stearn, 1995). When parents were over-involved, interfering, and focused on the child winning (in an individual sport) or starring (in a team sport), children were more likely to report that they weren't having fun, felt under considerable stress, and wanted to drop out of the sport.

Fine Motor Skills **Fine motor skills** involve refined use of the small muscles controlling the hands, fingers, and thumbs, often coordinated with the eyes (Case-Smith, 2005). The development of these skills sets the stage for new accomplishments in middle childhood, including cursive handwriting; drawings with lots of details; using a joy stick and

fine motor skills Abilities required to control small movements of the hands and fingers, such as picking up small objects and tying one's shoes.

© Richard Hutchings / PhotoEdit

Further development of fine motor skills in middle childhood enables children in this period to begin to master a musical instrument.

mouse; typing; sending text messages; knitting, cooking, measuring, cutting, and sewing; building models; playing piano, violin, and flute; and more. All of these contribute to a child's growing sense of competence and industry (see Chapter 8). (For a summary of this section, see "Interim Summary 9.1: Physical Development.")

INTERIM SUMMARY 9.1

Physical Development	
Body Growth	■ Children are growing faster and bigger in many parts of the world. ■ Almost 40% of U.S. children (about 25 million) are overweight or at risk for becoming overweight. ■ The obesity epidemic can be traced to changes in lifestyle, including unhealthy diets and less physical activity. ■ Overweight children are more likely to develop physical ailments and socioemotional difficulties. ■ Reducing soft drink consumption, limiting TV viewing, and increasing physical activity are effective in slowing the increase in BMI.
Brain Development	■ **Competitive elimination** occurs when regularly used synapses are strengthened and unused synapses are pruned to eliminate "clutter." ■ The growth of **gray matter** follows a pattern that resembles a ∩ shape. Neutrons and their connections increase, reach a peak, and then decrease. ■ The growth of **white matter**—myelin—increases linearly. ■ In comparison to children with average intelligence, children with superior intelligence show more rapid growth of gray matter during middle childhood and more rapid pruning of gray matter during adolescence.

(continued)

INTERIM SUMMARY 9.1 (continued)

Physical Development	
Motor Development	■ Running, jumping, hopping, throwing, and catching a ball are **gross motor skills** that become more refined in middle childhood. ■ Experiences at home and in school influence the development of gross motor skills. ■ Examples of **fine motor skills** in middle childhood include cursive handwriting, drawings with lots of details, using a joy stick, and writing text messages. ■ Experts recommend that school-age children get at least 1 hour of vigorous physical activity every day. ■ Overall, school-age children get about half the recommended amount of exercise for their age during a typical school week. ■ When coaches are positive and give technical instruction rather than make general comments, children are more likely to enjoy the sport and like the coach. ■ When parents are supportive and enthusiastic—but not pushy—children are more likely to report enjoying the sport.

HEALTH AND WELL-BEING

Physical health is important in middle childhood. However, injuries, chronic ailments, and acute diseases during this period pose threats to children's development and well-being.

Unintentional Injuries

Unintentional injuries are a serious threat to physical well-being in middle childhood (see Figure 9.7). Motor vehicle accidents are the leading cause of death for children in the United States. More than 1,400 children die in car crashes, and approximately 203,000 are injured—an average of four deaths and 556 injuries each day (Centers for Disease Control, 2007). The tragedy is that many of these deaths and injuries could have been prevented. Having children who are under 4'9" sit in the back seat and wear a safety belt could cut these numbers by half.

Drowning is the second most common cause of injury death in childhood (CDC, 2005). And for every child who drowns, five others require emergency room treatment for near-drownings. Again, safety procedures save lives. These include secure fences equipped with alarms around pools, adult supervision whenever children are playing in or around water, and swimming in a lake or at a beach only when lifeguards are present.

The drowning rate for 5- to 14-year-old African American children is 3.2 times higher, and for American Indians and Alaskan Natives 2.6 times higher, than that for Caucasian children. In these subcultures, learning to swim is not considered a routine part of growing up, so children who fall into the water cannot help themselves or count on their friends to help them get to safety (Branche et al., 2004). City parks

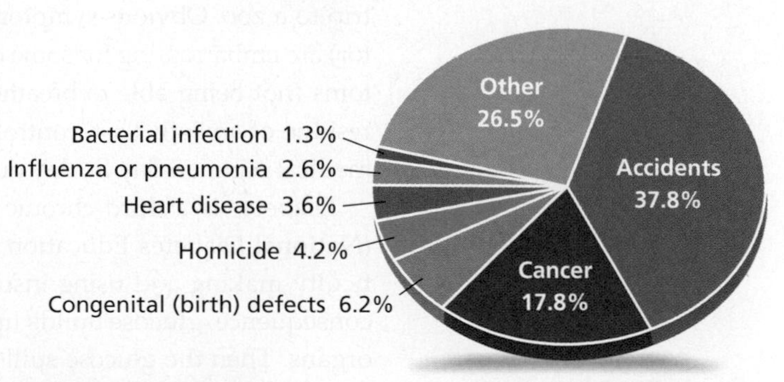

FIGURE 9.7

Leading Causes of Death in Middle Childhood

Injuries from accidents (motor vehicles and drowning) are the leading cause of death in this period. Many of these deaths are preventable. *Source:* Heron (2007).

and recreation programs, the Red Cross, and the YMCA are introducing programs in some urban neighborhoods, but many more are needed.

Chronic Medical Conditions

asthma A chronic respiratory condition that causes sudden attacks of wheezing, coughing, and shortness of breath.

Although acute illnesses like measles and mumps have declined sharply, some chronic conditions have become more common. **Asthma** is a chronic respiratory condition that causes sudden attacks of wheezing, coughing, and shortness of breath. During an attack, the airways to the lungs contract and produce excess mucus. Severe attacks can result in difficulty speaking in complete sentences (McQuaid, Mitchell, & Esteban, 2006). Asthma attacks can be triggered by lung infections, allergic reactions to airborne substances, stress, exercise, and cold weather. It is the leading cause of school absenteeism in the United States (McQuaid et al., 2006).

Almost 10 percent of U.S. children ages 5 to 11 suffer from asthma (Bloom et al., 2006). It is more common for boys than for girls and for African American children and Puerto Rican children than for Caucasian children. Poor children have higher rates than affluent children (Mannino et al., 2002). The incidence of asthma in U.S. children in this age range increased 65 percent between 1980 and 1996 (Mannino et al., 2002). The reasons for this sharp increase are difficult to pin down. Researchers have pointed to higher levels of air pollution and to the dust levels in better-insulated, airtight housing as likely suspects. Some (but not all) of the increase may be due to changes in the questions on health surveys.

allergy An exaggerated immune response or reaction to substances that are generally not harmful.

Allergies also are common in middle childhood. Allergies occur when the immune system overreacts to substances in the environment, such as dust, pollen, or smoke (McQuaid et al., 2006). About 12 percent of children ages 5 to 11 have respiratory (as opposed to food or skin) allergies (Bloom et al., 2006). Symptoms include a runny nose, sneezing, congestion, and a scratchy throat and eyes. Allergies have become more common, possibly due to greater exposure to indoor allergens, or to frequent antibiotic use, which reduces exposure to infection and hence the buildup of immunities (McQuaid et al., 2006). They are more frequently diagnosed in Caucasian children than in African American and Hispanic children, and in children whose parents have more education (Bloom et al., 2006). Obviously, education doesn't "cause" allergies, but educated parents may be more likely to seek medical attention for their children.

Having asthma or allergies affects a child's (and her family's) quality of life (McQuaid et al., 2006). The child may have difficulty concentrating in school as the result of active symptoms, poor sleep, or medication side effects. Asthma and allergies also can impose social limitations, such as not being able to participate in sports or go on a field trip to a zoo. Obvious symptoms and public use of medication (such as a bronchodilator) are embarrassing for some children. Moreover, acute attacks, with frightening symptoms (not being able to breathe) and visits to hospital emergency rooms, may leave a residue of anxiety. Last, controlling asthma and allergies often means following a strict medical regimen day in, day out. Colds go away; asthma and allergies don't.

Diabetes is a third chronic condition that is common among school-age children (National Diabetes Education Program, 2006). Children who have diabetes have difficulty making and using insulin, a hormone that converts glucose into energy. As a consequence, glucose builds up in the bloodstream, causing damage to the tissues and organs. Then the glucose spills over into urine and is excreted, depriving the body of its primary source of fuel.

Type 1 diabetes A type of diabetes where the immune system destroys the beta cells in the pancreas so that pancreas produces little or no insulin.

There are two main forms of diabetes. In **Type 1 diabetes**, the immune system destroys the beta cells in the pancreas that produce insulin. Type 1 diabetes appears suddenly, most often in children, adolescents, and young adults. It is not related to being overweight. People with Type 1 diabetes need daily injections or supplements of insulin throughout their lives. Even with treatment they are at risk for long-term complications, including damage to the cardiovascular system, which may result in heart attacks or strokes; kidney damage, which may require dialysis or transplant; poor circulation, particularly in the feet and legs, which makes people more vulnerable to infections that may lead to amputations; nerve damage; and blindness.

Type 2 diabetes used to be called "adult-onset diabetes" because it occurred mainly in adults who were overweight and age 40 or older. Now, with more children who are overweight and inactive, rates are rising among children. In Type 2 diabetes, the body cannot use insulin efficiently. At first the pancreas produces more insulin to compensate for this, but after several years this is not enough and the person requires insulin-boosting medications and perhaps, later, insulin injections. Type 2 diabetes develops slowly and may not show symptoms for some time, so monitoring populations at risk is essential. Complications such as poor circulation and nerve damage can begin 10 to 15 years after onset, but they can be delayed or even prevented through diet and exercise. At present, about 177,000 Americans under age 20 have diabetes. Most have Type 1 diabetes, but rates of Type 2 diabetes have risen from less than 5 percent in 1994 to an estimated 30 to 50 percent of new, youthful diabetes cases today. The earlier onset of Type 2 diabetes means the earlier development of complications (when people are in their 30s and 40s, not their 50s and 60s). Although no ethnic group is untouched, the disease is more common among American Indian, African American, Mexican American, and Pacific Islander youth.

Type 2 diabetes A type of diabetes in which the body does not use insulin efficiently. Type 2 diabetes is brought on by a combination of genes, overweight, and inactivity.

Managing diabetes—measuring blood glucose level, taking medication and perhaps giving injections, following a strict diet, and exercising—is difficult to sustain (Kleinfield, 2006). Children with Type 1 diabetes need help and support from parents and school nurses, but many schools do not have full-time nurses. Children with Type 2 diabetes do not always follow the rules of their treatment. Many are in denial: They feel fine so insist that the doctor must be wrong, they don't have diabetes. Warned about the complications they might suffer 10 or 15 years later, when they will be in the prime of life, they shrug. They don't worry about things that might happen when they are 30 or 40, which seems like "old age" to them. Right now, following a diet and exercise program feels like punishment. Getting children (and adults) to take diabetes very seriously, as a potentially debilitating, life-shortening disease, is a major challenge. (For a summary of this section, see "Interim Summary 9.2: Health and Well-Being.")

INTERIM SUMMARY 9.2

Health and Well-Being

Unintentional Injuries	■ Accidents are the leading cause of death for children in the United States. ■ Motor vehicle accidents are the most common single cause of accidental death, followed by drowning. ■ Many of these deaths are preventable.
Chronic Medical Conditions	■ **Asthma** is a chronic respiratory condition that causes sudden attacks of wheezing, coughing, and shortness of breath. ■ **Allergies** occur when the immune system overreacts to substances in the environment, such as dust, pollen, or smoke. ■ Children who have diabetes have difficulty either making (**Type 1 diabetes**) or using insulin (**Type 2 diabetes**), a hormone that converts glucose into energy.

COGNITIVE DEVELOPMENT

In this section, we will look at changes in children's thinking in middle childhood. Piaget's theory emphasizes the development of concrete operations. Studies of children's information processing are more concerned with understanding specific components such as attention and memory that are part of the sequential processing of information. Standardized tests are used to measure individual (and group) differences in general cognitive abilities or intelligence.

Piaget's Concrete Operational Period

concrete operations The third stage of cognitive development in Piaget's theory when mental activities become more logical with respect to actual (i.e., *concrete*) objects and materials.

Concrete operations is the third stage of cognitive development in Piaget's theory (Piaget, 1983; Piaget & Inhelder, 1967). It is during this period (roughly between ages 7 and 12) that children's mental activities (or *operations* in Piaget's terminology) become more logical with respect to actual (i.e., *concrete*) objects and materials.

According to Piaget, concrete operational thinking is *qualitatively* different from preoperational thinking. (Recall that qualitative differences are differences in type or kind, whereas quantitative differences are differences in amount.)

The hallmarks of the concrete operational period are five interrelated competencies—classification, class inclusion, seriation, transitive inference, and reversibility—that underlie logical reasoning (see Table 9.2). The development of these competencies allows the concrete operational child to apply logic across a variety of situations—on tests of conservation in the psychologist's lab, in the classroom, at home, and with friends. School-age children understand that some characterisitics—including volume, mass, and number—do not change despite superficial changes in form or appearance.

classification The ability to divide or sort objects into different sets and subsets and to consider their interrelationships.

As noted in an earlier chapter, **classification** is the ability to divide or sort objects into different sets and subsets and to consider their interrelationships. It includes the ability to group items along multiple dimensions (Inhelder & Piaget, 1964). Harry Potter, for instance, can be classified as a wizard, a boy, a member of Gryffindor house, and a Quidditch player, among other qualities.

class inclusion A logical operation that recognizes that a class (or group) can be part of a larger group.

Class inclusion is a logical operation that recognizes that a class (or group) can be part of a larger group. If a preoperational child is shown seven dogs and three cats and is asked if there are more dogs or more animals, she will say "more dogs." She is comparing dogs to cats and not to the larger class ("animals"). The concrete operational

TABLE 9.2 Hallmarks of Cognitive Development in the Concrete Operational Period

OPERATION	DEFINITION	EXAMPLE
Classification	Dividing objects into sets and subsets and examining relationships between them	Separating objects into groups by color and shape: red triangles, blue triangles, red circles, blue circles
Class inclusion	Recognition that one group can be part of a larger group	Motorcycles and trucks are both recognized as "vehicles"
Seriation	Arranging items in sequence according to particular properties	Arranging sticks in order from shortest to longest
Transitive inference	Comparing two sets of relationships to each other	If stick 1 is shorter than stick 2, and stick 1 is longer than stick 3, the child knows that stick 2 is longer than stick 3
Reversibility	Reversing operations in order to turn relations to their original state	A ball of clay that has been flattened out can be re-formed into a ball

child, in contrast, will say "more animals." Class inclusion requires that children understand that dogs and cats can be part of a broader concept of animals.

Math classrooms in the primary grades (kindergarten through Grade 3) sometimes use what are called "attribute blocks" to provide children with opportunities to develop understanding of classification and class inclusion. These small blocks vary in size (small, medium, large), shape (square, triangle, circle), and color (red, black, blue, yellow). Most second-graders (7- and 8-year-olds) are able to sort these blocks in various ways on their own—by color, by shape, by size; and some can sort by color and shape simultaneously. Others, however, are not yet able to do this task. When asked to form a group of blocks that go together, they simply look perplexed. In a classroom observed by one of the authors when she taught young children, a student looked around as he saw others moving the blocks to create separate groups. He then proceeded to create two groups on his desk, looked up proudly, and announced, "This one's the messy group. And this one is the not so messy group"—a perceptually based response characteristic of a preoperational thinker.

Children's collections provide them with many opportunities to organize and classify objects along different dimensions.

School-age children enjoy classification, as seen in their intense interest in collections of all sorts—baseball cards, stamps, rocks, dolls, and action figures. When they play with their collections, they organize and reorganize them, over and over. Baseball cards can be sorted and organized by teams, player positions, years, rarity, and so forth. Rocks can be sorted by type, origin, color, size, and so on.

seriation The ability to arrange items in a sequenced order according to particular properties.

Seriation, a third operation that is acquired during middle childhood, is the ability to arrange items in a sequenced order according to particular properties (Inhelder & Piaget, 1964). Concrete operational children are able to organize items along various dimensions such as height (shortest to tallest) or color (lightest to darkest). An everyday application of seriation occurs when children organize themselves by height for their class photograph. Seriation requires that children simultaneously recognize two-way relations—Juan is taller than Jason but shorter than George. Preoperational children struggle with relational concepts, such as *taller than* or *bigger than*. They don't seem to grasp that object A can be both bigger than object B and smaller than object C. Concrete operational children "get it."

transitive inference A logical operation that builds on an understanding of seriation. It requires that two relations are combined to derive a third relation.

Transitive inference builds on an understanding of seriation. For example, we know that George is taller than Juan and Juan is taller than Jason. Is George taller than Jason? The concrete operational child can compare two relations ("George > Juan" and "Juan > Jason"), put the two together ("George > Juan > Jason"), and arrive at the answer. This ability becomes increasingly important in the development of math skills, as you can well imagine.

reversibility A logical operation that requires an understanding that relations can be returned to their original state by reversing operations—if nothing has been added or taken.

Reversibility is the fifth operation Piaget (1983) described. Reversibility is the understanding that relations can be returned to their original state by reversing operations—

if nothing has been added or taken away. For example, the child understands that if 10 pennies = 1 dime, this relation can be reversed: 1 dime = 10 pennies. Reversibility is one of the keys to understanding conservation, one of the crowning achievements of the concrete operational period.

The development of basic logic means that school-age children are able to think about the world using basic principles of logic, not just report what they see. But the use of logical operations during middle childhood is limited to concrete materials and tasks; not until adolescence will individuals be able to apply the same logical reasoning abilities to things that they cannot directly experience. Children in the concrete operational stage think about the real world, not abstract concepts such as *democracy*, *justice*, or *social class*. This is one of the reasons that math teachers in elementary school use "manipulatives"—materials such as an abacus or the attribute blocks described earlier—to provide hands-on experience with addition, subtraction, multiplication, division, fractions, and place value. Of course, many children discover that their fingers (and their toes) are also useful manipulatives for solving some addition and subtraction problems!

Piaget recognized that children's reasoning does not instantly shift from preoperations to concrete operations. Children are able, typically, to successfully solve conservation of matter problems before they can successfully do conservation of number (see Chapter 7). Inhelder and Piaget (1964) called this differential performance in logical thinking **horizontal decalage**.

horizontal decalage Differences in performance on conceptually related Piagetian tasks. For example, children typically understand conservation of mass before they understand conservation of number.

Experiences That Foster the Development of Concrete Operations Piaget (1964) believed that concrete operational thinking is a natural outgrowth of children's opportunities to manipulate materials and objects and to "experiment" with these materials. He did not think that logical operations need to be explicitly taught. Other researchers, however, have found that concrete operational thinking can be fostered by particular experiences. For example, in a study of number conservation, simply asking children to explain their reasoning helped to prompt the more rapid development of more advanced reasoning (Siegler, 1995). Reasoning based on length (a typical preoperational response) decreased over time, whereas reasoning based on counting and reversibility increased.

Formal schooling, in general, fosters concrete operational thinking. Mathematics instruction often incorporates explicit lessons about properties of numbers such as reversibility and transitivity. Language arts and reading classes include exercises in class inclusion. "Cars are vehicles; buses are vehicles; trucks are vehicles. Can you think of any other vehicles? What are some characteristics of vehicles?" "Broccoli is a vegetable. Green beans are vegetables. Can you think of any other vegetables?"

Although schooling can foster concrete operational thinking, it is not required. Child street vendors in Brazil (who have very little formal schooling) do poorly on Piaget's classic class inclusion problems when tested by experimenters. However, they demonstrate an understanding of class inclusion when the questions are worded in ways that tap knowledge they need in their businesses. For example, when a customer asks to buy a peach, it is better to offer a nectarine if there are no peaches left than to offer a bag of nuts because peaches and nectarines are members of the same general class (Ceci & Roazzi, 1994; Nunes, Schliemann, & Carraher, 1993).

Information Processing

The information-processing perspective provides another approach to understanding cognitive development in middle childhood. Here, researchers study how children come to attend to relevant information (attention), or remember the information, and then use the information to reason and solve problems (Munakata, 2006). Attention, memory, and problem solving all improve in middle childhood, which makes reasoning and strategic thinking possible.

Processing Speed One way to study how children process information is to look at the speed and accuracy with which information is analyzed (Kail & Ferrer, 2007). *Visual matching* and *cross out* are two procedures that researchers have used. In the visual matching procedure, a task card consists of 60 rows of six digits (e.g., 8 9 5 2 9 7). The child is asked to circle two rows that are identical. Processing speed is then measured as the number of task cards that a child can complete correctly in a set amount of time. In the cross-out procedure, a task card has 30 rows of geometric figures. At the left of each row is the target figure (for example, a triangle with a circle in the middle). To the right are 19 similar geometric figures, five of which are identical. Here, the child is asked to cross out the five identical figures. Processing speed is measured by the number of rows the child can complete in a set period (see Figure 9.8).

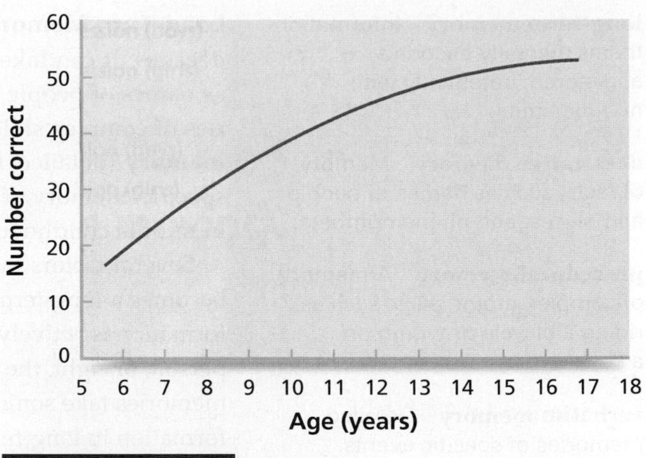

FIGURE 9.8

Processing Speed in Childhood and Adolescence

Processing speed, measured as the number of task cards completed correctly, improves more rapidly in middle childhood than in adolescence.

Source: Adapted from Kail & Ferrer (2007).

Longitudinal studies of children ranging in age from 5 to 18 have studied changes in processing speed (Kail & Ferrer, 2007). In general, improvements in processing speed are especially rapid during middle childhood. Processing speed tends to reach a plateau in adolescence. Faster, more efficient information processing in middle childhood helps to set the stage for advances in information processing that we see in working memory and long-term memory (Halford, 2004).

Working Memory As discussed in Chapter 7, **working memory** refers to conscious, short-term representations of what a person is actively thinking about at a given time. Working memory is clearly relevant for teachers and parents because it provides an upper limit to how many items children can keep in mind when being taught or when given a list of things to remember ("When you get home from school, I want you to clean up your room, walk the dog, set the table for dinner, and do your homework."). One way of assessing working memory is the **digit span task**, a research procedure in which people are asked to repeat in order a series of rapidly presented items—numbers, letters, or words (Schneider, 2004). Two-year-olds have a memory span of about two items. Five-year- olds can remember about four items; 7-year-olds, about five items; and 9-year-olds, about six items. The average for adults is about seven items (Miller, 1956).

working memory Conscious, short-term representations of what a person is actively thinking about at a given time.

digit span task A research procedure in which people are asked to repeat in order a series of rapidly presented items.

This small number of items is not as huge a limitation on how much information children can retain and use as you would think, however. Part of the reason is that children become more skilled at chunking bits of information into larger units that can then serve as an item (Pressley & Hilden, 2006). For example, a parent's cell phone number has ten units (e.g., 312-555-1212), which is beyond the short-term memory capacity of a 7-year-old. But these numbers can be chunked and recalled as three units: the area code (312), the prefix (555), and the number (1212). Children (and adults) are more likely to chunk material that is familiar or has special meaning.

One of the things that distinguishes experts from novices is their ability to chunk information. Expert chess players (both children and adults) are able to see common patterns of play across several turns and remember these patterns as single units of meaningful information (Chase & Simon, 1973). Child chess experts are able to outperform adult novices on chess moves, but not on the standard digit span task (Schneider et al., 1993).

long-term memory Information that is mentally encoded and stored, potentially with no time limits.

declarative memory Memory of facts, such as names of people and places, and phone numbers.

procedural memory A memory of complex motor skills, such as riding a bicycle or typing on a keyboard.

verbatim memory Detailed memories of specific events.

gist memory A generalized, rather than specific, memory of common occurrences.

false memory A memory that is a distortion of an actual experience, or a confabulation of an imagined one.

Deese-Roediger-McDermott (DRM) procedure An experimental task that demonstrates the creation of false memories; participants often recollect or recall words that they have not heard because they make associations based on conceptual commonalities.

Long-Term Memory **Long-term memory** can span from minutes after an event to decades. It can take different forms: **declarative memory** (memories of facts, such as names of people and places, phone numbers, etc.), **procedural memory** (memories of complex skills such as riding a bicycle and typing on a keyboard), **verbatim memory** (detailed memories of specific events), and **gist memory** (a general, not specific, memory of common occurrences). Each of these types of memory improves in middle childhood.

Several factors influence whether a piece of information held in working memory becomes a long-term memory (Martinez, 2009). One is the length of time that the information is actively attended to. The more time a child focuses on the thought, word, person, or sight, the more likely that it will be stored in long-term memory. Long-term memories take some recording time—roughly a minute to record a single piece of information in long-term memory (Martinez, 2009).

False Memories As much as we like to think that our memories are unerringly factual and accurate records ("I heard you say that you were putting out the trash," "I saw the man entering the house"), this is actually not the case. The process of constructing memories can result in memory distortions and **false memories** (Brainerd et al., 2006; Brainerd & Reyna, 2004).

One way that scientists demonstrate the construction of false memories is through the use of the **Deese-Roediger-McDermott (DRM) procedure** (Deese, 1959; Roediger & McDermott, 1995). Suppose you were presented with the following list of words: bed, rest, awake, tired, dream. After taking the list away, you are asked either to recall the words or to select the words you heard off a list that includes the original words plus some new ones (a recognition task).

Adults typically recalled and recognized words that were not presented (e.g., *sleep*) about as often as words that were presented. This is because adults made associations about the conceptual or semantic commonalities among words, which then led them to include *sleep*, a word that they had not actually heard.

Eleven-year-olds create false memories that are similar to those created by adults (Dewhurst & Robinson, 2004). Like adults, the 11-year-olds "remember" non-presented words that were conceptually or semantically related to the words that they did hear. Findings for younger children are different, and they tell us something about how their minds are organized. Five-year-olds tend to falsely "remember" nonpresented words that rhyme with the presented words, making associations based on sounds (phonology) rather than on meaning (semantics). The 8-year-olds studied made the most errors of all because they made both phonological and semantic associations to nonpresented words!

Children's memories also can be affected by misinformation. In one study, children were read a story about a girl named Loren, who went to her first day of school and had a stomachache after eating too quickly (Ceci, Ross, & Toglia, 1987). The next day, children were asked questions about the story. The treatment group was given misinformation: "Do you remember the story about Loren who had a headache because she ate her cereal too fast?" Two days later, the children were given a test that pitted true events against misinformation. Misinformation (that Loren had a headache) was related to false memories in all age groups (3-, 5-, 8-, and 10-year-olds), although the size of the effect decreased with age. Younger children were more susceptible than older children to misinformation.

So, it looks like how questions are worded can create and modify memories over time. Gist memories (which are more global and undifferentiated) are more likely to be distorted or changed following misinformation than are verbatim memories (Brainerd & Reyna, 2005).

Learning to Think Strategically

Other scientists are studying how children learn to think strategically. These scientists often use a technique called **microgenetic analysis**. Microgenetic analysis involves close-up (*micro*) study of development (*genesis*) across trials within a single session as well as performance across sessions. Siegler and Stern (1998) provide an example of this type of approach. Second-grade students were asked to solve math problems in the form of $A + B - B = ?$ An example of such a problem is, $16 + 7 - 7 = ?$ If a child solves this problem using a simple computation strategy, she adds the first two numbers together and then subtracts the third number ($16 + 7 = 23$; $23 - 7 = 16$.) This strategy takes about 16 seconds to execute. A second strategy, the shortcut strategy, takes less than 4 seconds. The shortcut involves reasoning that $B - B = 0$ so the answer must be A—regardless of what numbers are in the equation. By studying children's computation time, Siegler and Stern documented children's progression from using the computation strategy to an unconscious use of the shortcut strategy to conscious use of the shortcut strategy over a series of sessions.

microgenetic analysis A research strategy that involves frequent, detailed observations of behavior.

Microgenetic analyses have been applied to a wide variety of domains, including mathematical reasoning, scientific thinking, and memory. Across these studies, consistent patterns of learning and strategic thinking are seen (Siegler, 2006). In contrast to the stage-like and consistent performance suggested by Piaget's theory (i.e., if a child is in the concrete operational period, he will usually demonstrate concrete operational thinking, regardless of the problem), microgenetic studies show that children's behavior is much more variable. A given child uses different strategies for different problems and sometimes uses different strategies for the same problem. Children's performance is most variable during periods of rapid learning. For most types of learning, older and more knowledgeable children learn more quickly and use more appropriate generalizations than younger children do.

Memory strategies are mental or behavioral activities that can improve recall and recognition of material. The simplest, often used by children, is rehearsal or repetition (Pressley & Hilden, 2006). Practicing spelling words and multiplication tables with flash cards are examples of this common rehearsal strategy in middle childhood. As students and parents have discovered, practice distributed over several days is more effective than one day of intensive practice. Written notes ("to-do lists") also can improve long-term memory (Martinez, 2009). That's one of the reasons that it is so helpful for teachers to write assignments on the blackboard (or, nowadays, on a website) and for students to record the assignments in their logbooks. Writing something down requires effort and is a more advanced way of rehearsing.

memory strategy Mental or behavioral activities that can improve recall or recognition of material.

Explicitly relating new information to prior knowledge also increases the likelihood that the new material is remembered (Pressley & Hilden, 2006). Suppose that a child is asked to learn new facts about her state (the state bird, flower, tree, capital, largest city, etc.). She is more likely to remember the new information if she adds it to other knowledge that she has about the state. Another memory strategy is to organize pictures or words into meaningful categories. Suppose a child is given a randomly ordered list of words to memorize: shoes, hat, cat, table, cow, pants, chair, dress, raccoon, desk. This task is easier for children in middle childhood than in early childhood because the older children can mentally sort the objects into categories: *clothes* (shoes, hat, pants, dress); *animals* (cat, cow, raccoon); and *furniture* (table, chair, desk). Organizing the items (class inclusion, to use Piaget's terminology) creates chunks, and the category labels act as retrieval cues.

In middle childhood, children may not explicitly and mindfully use these sorts of strategies on their own, but they can be taught to do so, sometimes with improvements in performance (Bjorkland et al., 1997). Interestingly, preschoolers typically do not use

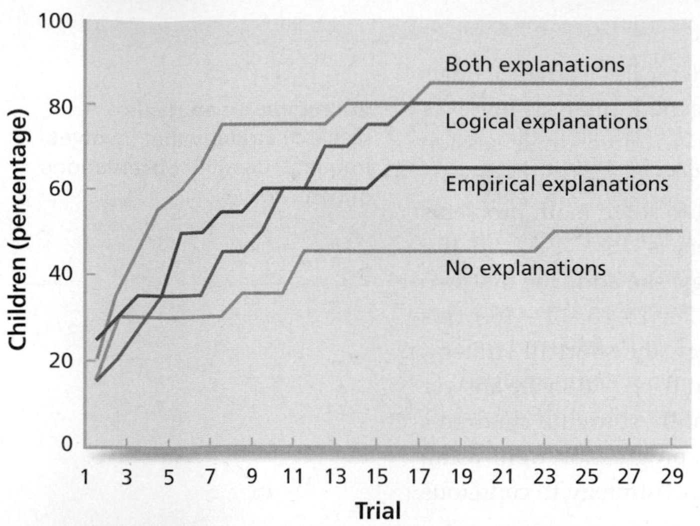

FIGURE 9.9

Cumulative Percentage of Children Who Reached Discovery Criterion at Different Trials

Children's performance jumps from near chance level to more skilled performance very quickly instead of showing a pattern of slow, steady improvement over many trials (Siegler, 2006).

Source: Siegler & Svetina (2006).

these deliberate strategies even after specific instructions (Miller & Seier, 1994). Or, if they use the strategy, they do not appear to benefit from using it. Preschoolers' recall of material is not improved by teaching them the memory strategies that are so effective in middle childhood.

Microgenetic analyses of individual children's performance indicate that the development of strategies is not the result of slow, steady growth (Siegler, 2006). In one study, only 8 percent of the children showed gradual steady increases in their use of organizational strategies. Over 80 percent of the children jumped from chance level to near perfect performance, a pattern consistent with a qualitative shift (Siegler, 2006) (see Figure 9.9).

Intelligence

A fourth approach to understanding cognitive development uses standardized tests to measure individual (and group) differences in general cognitive abilities or intelligence (Sternberg, 2004).

Sir Francis Galton, a cousin of Charles Darwin, was one of the first scientists to attempt to measure intelligence. Galton (1907) tried (unsuccessfully) to use simple cognitive tasks such as reaction times to assess intelligence. Other European scientists of the day, such as Alfred Binet and Theodore Simon (1908), argued that a broader approach was needed because intelligence involves people making complex evaluations of what has to be done and how to do it, weighing different strategies, and critiques of thoughts and actions.

Binet and Simon's ideas were brought to the United States by Louis Terman (1916), a professor at Stanford University, who created early versions of a test that became known as the Stanford-Binet Intelligence Test. Revised and updated, this test is still used today. It has separate parts that measure verbal reasoning, quantitative reasoning, abstract visual reasoning, and short-term memory. Intelligence quotients (IQ) are computed based on a relative performance within an age group. The average or mean score on the Stanford Binet is 100, with a standard deviation of 15 points. Seventeen percent of children score above 115, and 17 percent score below 85 (see Figure 9.10).

Another commonly used test is the Wechsler Intelligence Scale for Children (WISC-III; Wechsler, 1991), which has two main scales—a performance scale and a verbal scale. The performance scale includes tasks such as rearrangements of a scrambled set of cartoon-type pictures to tell a story and the identification of missing parts of a picture. The verbal scale includes vocabulary, similarities, and understanding of common social customs.

The adequacy of these tests is assessed by examining their **reliability** and **validity.** A reliable test is one in which individuals receive similar or consistent scores each time they are tested. Another indicator of reliability is items that "hang together," and children who do well on one item tend to do well on other items on the same scale. Valid tests are ones that assess what the test developer claims to be measuring. On average, IQ scores tend to be relatively consistent over time (that is, reliable), and the scores are related to measures of school performance (an indication of validity). By these criteria, the Stanford-Binet and WISC are "good" tests.

Critics of IQ tests have raised broader questions about the meaning and nature of intelligence, how it is manifested, and whether it can be modified.

One influential contemporary theorist is Howard Gardner (1999), who has proposed a theory of **multiple intelligences**. Gardner argues that there are at least eight

reliability A reliable test is one in which individuals receive similar or relatively consistent scores each time they are tested.

validity The extent to which a test measures what it was designed to measure.

multiple intelligences Gardner's theory that intelligence has at least eight distinct forms: linguistic, logical-mathematical, spatial, musical, bodily-kinesthetic, interpersonal, intrapersonal, and naturalistic.

distinct forms of intelligence: (a) linguistic intelligence, which is used when reading a book, writing, or speaking; (b) logical-mathematical intelligence, which is used when arguing a case and solving math problems; (c) spatial intelligence, which is used in reading maps and in doing things like loading the dishwasher efficiently; (d) musical intelligence, which is used in playing a musical instrument and singing; (e) bodily-kinesthetic intelligence, which is used in dancing, playing sports, surfing, and skateboarding; (f) interpersonal intelligence, which is used in relating to others, (g) intrapersonal intelligence, which reflects an awareness of oneself; and (h) naturalistic intelligence, which reflects an understanding of the natural world.

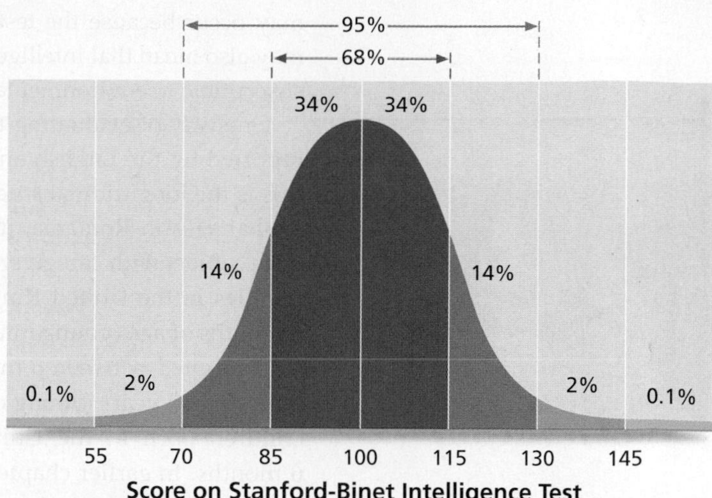

FIGURE 9.10

The Distribution of IQ Scores

The distribution of the scores on the Stanford-Binet and other commonly used IQ tests is set so the mean is 100 and the standard deviation is 15.

Gardner finds that these different intelligences are relatively independent and are associated with different areas of the brain. Thus, from the perspective of the theory of multiple intelligences, professional athletes and ballet dancers possess bodily-kinesthetic intelligence, and successful salespersons are interpersonally intelligent.

Robert Sternberg (1988, 1999) is a second contemporary theorist who studies intelligence. Sternberg proposed the **triarchic theory of successful intelligence**, which identified three broad components of intelligence: (a) analytical abilities to critique, judge, and evaluate; (b) creative abilities to invent, discover, and imagine; and (c) practical abilities to utilize and implement ideas in the real world. Research suggests that these components are relatively independent statistically, and that children apply them to different kinds of problems. Some children are more intelligent about concrete practical problems. Others are more intelligent about abstract academic problems, and still others are better at inventing, discovering, and imagining. An intelligent child, according to Sternberg (1999), is not necessarily one who succeeds in all aspects of intelligence. Instead, an intelligent child is one who knows his or her strengths and weaknesses and finds ways to capitalize on strengths and compensate for weaknesses. A child strong in verbal skills and weak in math skills may want to become a writer, not an engineer.

triarchic theory of successful intelligence Sternberg's theory that intelligence is composed of three broad components: analytical abilities, creative abilities, and practical abilities.

Intelligence in Different Social Contexts Another question concerns the extent that IQ scores are an accurate measure of underlying abilities or are dependent on the social context and experience. Critics of standard IQ tests observe that items on the tests favor Caucasian, middle-class children (Greenfield, Suzuki, & Rothstein-Fisch, 2006). Knowing the meaning of words such as *banister* is, no doubt, greater in multistory households in which there are banisters and opportunities to talk about them.

Tests that draw on children's experiences can make a difference. As we noted earlier, Brazilian children who are street vendors can do complex math computations when selling items on the street but have difficulty on standardized tests that measure the same abilities (Nunes et al., 1993).

How Malleable Are IQ Scores? A third question concerns just how malleable (or potentially changeable) IQ scores are. Between infancy and early childhood, we see considerable movement in individual children's test scores (up and down) (McCall, Appelbaum, & Hogarty, 1973). This may be because items on the infant tests are less reliable, or it may be that young children's general cognitive abilities (intelligence) are more susceptible to environmental influences. In middle childhood and adolescence, IQ scores are more stable. Children who receive high scores at one administration tend to receive high scores at subsequent administrations of related tests. This consistency may occur because the tests are better (i.e., items are more reliable or consistent). It may also mean that intelligence has become more consolidated as a single trait and less susceptible to environmental influences.

One way of evaluating these alternative explanations is to look at recent findings reported by the English and Romanian Adoptees Study (Beckett et al., 2006). Recall this is the longitudinal study of children who spent varying amounts of time in state orphanages in Romania, under conditions of extreme deprivation, where they had little contact with caregivers or environmental stimulation, and were then adopted by families in the United Kingdom and Canada. One group of children was less than 6 months of age (young infants) when placed with their new families. A second group was adopted between 6 months and 2 years (older infants), and a third group was older than 2 years (young children) when adopted. A comparison group consisted of children born in the United Kingdom who were adopted as young infants by 6 months. In earlier chapters, we talked about the effects of this natural experiment on children's biological and social emotional development. Here, we look at the children's IQ scores.

At 6 years, the IQ scores of Romanian children who were adopted as young infants were similar to the UK children who were adopted as young infants (an average score of 102 versus 105). However, those older infants had significantly lower scores (an average of 86) and those who had been adopted as young children had the lowest scores (an average of 77). At age 11, the IQ scores of the early adopted Romanian (average score = 101) and UK (average score = 105) children continued to differ from the children adopted when they were older (average scores of 86 for the older infants and 82 for the group adopted as young children). These findings suggest that early severe deprivation can have long-term effects on children's general intelligence.

Others have studied the effects of high-quality, early intervention programs on children at risk for environmentally based mental retardation (Ramey & Ramey, 2004). A group of children who were living in deep poverty in rural North Carolina participated in the Abecedarian Project, a high-quality comprehensive early intervention project that started in infancy and continued through early childhood (see Chapter 7). When compared with children in the control group who did not participate in the program, the treatment group had significantly higher IQ scores at age 8. These findings indicate that early environments (both early severe deprivation and enrichment) can exert profound effects (20 points or more) on intelligence as measured by standard IQ tests.

Very High and Very Low IQ Scores Go back and take a look at Figure 9.10. You will see that some children are at the extremes of the distribution of IQ scores and have either very high or very low IQ scores. Let's look more closely at these children.

giftedness Indicated by extraordinary creativity or performance in music, sports, or art, as well as traditional academic subjects.

There are several definitions of **giftedness** (Sternberg, 2004). One definition, based on IQ scores, categorizes children with scores in the top 1 percent (roughly IQ scores of 135 or above) or top 2 percent (roughly 132 or above) as "gifted." Others supplement IQ scores with other measures of motivation, commitment, and achievement (Csikszentmihalyi, Rathunde, & Whalen, 1993; Renzulli, 1986; Sternberg, 1988).

Still others, such as Howe (2002), have described geniuses (perhaps the *most* talented and gifted), like Leonardo da Vinci or Albert Einstein. These individuals have several features in common: intense curiosity, dedication to their work, sustained diligence, and broad capacities that open up opportunities for new discoveries. Consistent with the broader definitions of intelligence, giftedness is indicated by extraordinary creativity or performance in music, sports, or art, as well as traditional academic subjects. Both genes and enriched environments contribute to giftedness (Geschwind &

Galaburda, 1987). For example, a study of high mathematics ability in 10-year-olds found substantial genetic and moderate environmental influences (Petrill et al., 2009).

Other children have very low scores on standardized tests of intelligence. The Individuals with Disabilities Act is a landmark federal law that defines mental retardation as significantly below average general intellectual functioning that is accompanied by deficits in adaptive behavior and that has adverse effects on educational performance (34 *Code of Federal Regulations* §300.7[c][6]). This definition has been operationalized as an IQ score of less than 70 or 75 accompanied by deficits in daily living skills, communication skills, and social skills relative to other children of the same age.

Some forms of mental retardation, such as **Down syndrome** and **fragile X syndrome**, have genetic origins. Children with Down syndrome have all or a part of an extra chromosome 21 (Chapman, 1997). Children with fragile X syndrome have a change in a single gene on the X chromosome (Abbeduto et al., 2001). These two conditions are the most common genetic causes of intellectual disabilities, but hundreds of other rarer mutations have been identified as having effects on general intelligence (Inlow & Restifo, 2004). Other forms of mental retardation, such as that observed in the Romanian orphans and impoverished rural communities discussed earlier, are linked to severe environmental deprivation. As noted earlier, longitudinal studies suggest that attending high-quality early education can raise IQ scores of children growing up in impoverished homes (Ramey & Ramey, 2004).

Down syndrome A condition in which children have a third copy of chromosome 21; one of the most common genetic causes of mental retardation.

fragile X syndrome A condition in which children have a change in a single gene on the X chromosome; one of the most common genetic causes of mental retardation.

In summary, intelligence testing has a long history and some unanswered questions. Is intelligence one general capability or are there multiple intelligences? How are scores influenced by the social context? Is intelligence fixed or malleable? In the next section, we turn to children's skills in specific areas that are also often related to success—language, literacy, and mathematics. (For a summary of this section, see "Interim Summary 9.3: Cognitive Development.")

Children with Down syndrome vary in their intellectual functioning, ranging from mild to severe impairments. Early educational interventions can make a difference in their performance and achievement.

INTERIM SUMMARY 9.3

Cognitive Development

Piaget's Concrete Operational Period	■ Hallmarks of the period are **classification, class inclusion, seriation, transitive inference,** and **reversibility**. ■ These cognitive operations enable children to perform conservation tasks and formal mathematics. ■ Piaget believed that concrete operational thinking is a natural outgrowth of children's opportunities to manipulate materials and objects. ■ Others have studied ways to foster concrete operations: Asking children to explain their thinking can increase logical thinking. ■ Formal schooling also encourages concrete operational thinking.
Information Processing	■ Improvements in processing speed are steep during the school years and tend to reach a plateau in adolescence. ■ Faster processing speed and more efficient information processing help to set the stage for advances in both **working memory** and **long-term memory**. ■ Two-year-olds have a memory span of about two items. Five-year-olds can remember about four items; 7-year-olds about five items, and 9-year-olds about six items. The average for adults is about seven items. ■ Chunking bits of information into larger units increases the size of working memory. ■ Long-term memory includes **declarative, procedural, verbatim,** and **gist memories,** all of which improve in middle childhood. ■ Long-term memory is influenced by the length of time that the information is actively attended to, rehearsal or repetition, written notes, relating new information to prior information, and organizing information into meaningful categories. ■ Adults and older children create **false memories** around conceptually related information.
Learning to Think Strategically	■ **Microgenetic analysis** involves close-up (*micro*) study of development (*genesis*) across trials within a single session as well as performance across sessions. ■ Microgenetic analyses have been applied to a wide variety of domains, including mathematical reasoning, scientific thinking, and memory. Across these studies, consistent patterns of learning and strategic thinking are seen. ■ **Memory strategies** are mental or behavioral activities that can improve recall and recognition of material. The simplest, often used by children, is rehearsal or repetition.
Intelligence	■ Intelligence tests like the Stanford-Binet Intelligence Test measure skills such as verbal reasoning, quantitative reasoning, abstract visual reasoning, and short-term memory. ■ Howard Gardner has proposed eight distinct forms of intelligence: linguistic, logical-mathematical, spatial, musical, bodily-kinesthetic, interpersonal, intrapersonal, and naturalistic. ■ Robert Sternberg's **triarchic theory** posits three separate components of intelligence: analytical, creative, and practical. ■ Genius has been defined by very high scores on IQ tests, but also by intense curiosity, sustained diligence, and broad capacities that open up opportunities for new discoveries. ■ Mental retardation is operationalized as an IQ score of less than 70 or 75, accompanied by deficits relative to other children of the same age.

LANGUAGE, LITERACY, AND MATHEMATICS

What cognitive operations and experiences support the dramatic growth in academic skills in middle childhood? How do teaching strategies and school organization influence academic skills? Do experiences at home and after school contribute to these skills? Let us now turn to these questions.

Language Development

Beginning at about 1 year of age, children start to add about two root words a day to their vocabularies (Biemiller & Slonim, 2001). These **root words** must be learned, whereas derived and compound words build on root words. (*Fish* is a root word; *fishy* is a derived word. *Fishhook* is a compound word.) By the time children are in second grade (around age 7), they have amassed root vocabularies of 5,200 words on average. Between second and fifth grade, their root vocabularies expand even more rapidly, as they add about three root words each day. By fifth grade, they have about 8,400 root words in their vocabulary. With this growth of vocabulary, their words become more precise (see Figure 9.11).

root words Vocabulary that must be learned, in contrast to derived and compound words that build on root words.

In middle childhood, sentence structures become more complex, with more use of subordinate clauses (e.g., The girl *who is a fast runner* entered two races). Stories become longer and more complex, including more details about the setting and time period. Children come to enjoy and appreciate jokes, puns, and riddles. They begin to use metaphors and similes.

Children become adept at **code switching**, changing their speech to reflect who they are talking to (Rickford & Rickford, 2000). They are more skilled in their use of *formal codes* of speaking at school and with unfamiliar adults. This formal code avoids colloquialisms and contractions and provides more elaboration, details, and background material. When speaking with friends and family in informal settings, children become adept at *informal codes* that presume a common body of shared history and popular expressions. African American children may use Standard English in the classroom,

code switching Changing speech to reflect the audience and situation.

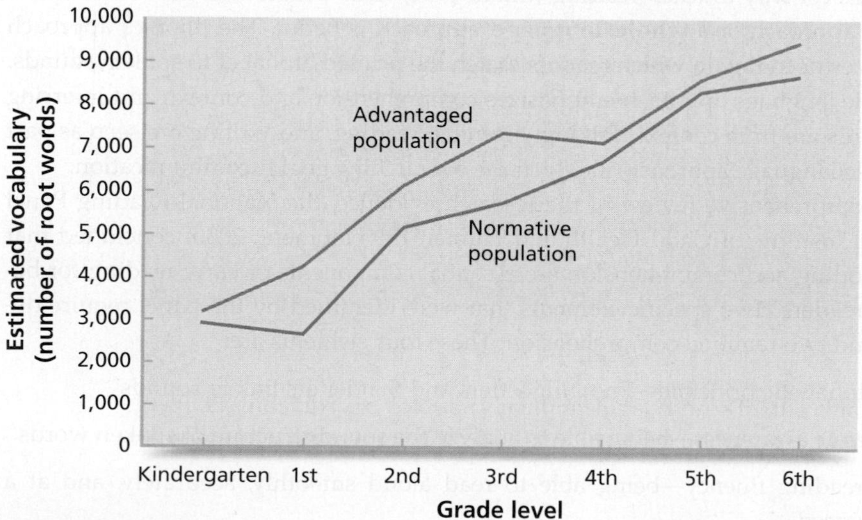

FIGURE 9.11

Growth of Root Word Vocabulary in Normative and Advantaged Children

Although root vocabularies increase substantially in both groups, children growing up in more advantaged homes maintain larger root vocabularies throughout middle childhood.

Source: Data from Biemiller & Slonim (2001).

© Robert Warren / Getty Images

Children become adept at code switching, using an informal speech code with friends and family and a more formal speech code with unfamiliar adults.

but Black English with friends and family (Rickford & Rickford, 2000). Children whose parents are first- and second-generation immigrants who do not speak English may serve as their parents' translators (O'Malley, 2006; Orellana et al., 2003).

Children's language reflects their experiences at home. Vocabulary is linked to variations in families' total amount of dinner table conversation, the number of different words used by parents, and the proportion of words not in the child's vocabulary. The more sophisticated words that children hear, embedded in helpful or instructive interactions, the more advanced their vocabularies in middle childhood (Weizman & Snow, 2001).

Literacy

One of the great challenges and accomplishments of middle childhood is becoming a skilled reader. Reading is a complex activity that involves two broad sets of competencies—those related to decoding and those related to comprehension (NICHD Early Child Care Research Network, 2005a; Snow, Burns, & Griffin, 1998). **Decoding** is applying knowledge of letter-sound relationships to read written words. **Comprehension** refers to understanding what you have read.

decoding Applying knowledge of letter-sound relationships to read written words.

comprehension Understanding what is read or said.

phonics Emphasizes decoding in which readers match the printed alphabet to spoken sounds.

whole language Emphasizes comprehension and context, and inferring what words are from context.

For almost 50 years, there was a debate, sometimes called "the reading wars," about the best way to teach reading (Chall, 1970). This debate was about whether a **phonics** approach or a **whole language** approach is better. The phonics approach emphasizes decoding in which readers match the printed alphabet to spoken sounds. The whole language approach emphasizes comprehension and context, and inferring what words are from context. Talking, listening, reading, and writing are seen as part of a whole language approach, in which the overarching goal is communication.

In a comprehensive review of the research evidence, the National Reading Panel (National Institute of Child Health and Human Development, 2000) concluded that both decoding and comprehension are essential components of early reading for beginning readers. Two specific elements that were identified by the panel require decoding and two required comprehension. These four elements are:

1. The alphabetic principle—knowing letters and that letters link to sounds
2. Phonemic awareness—being able to analyze the sound structure of spoken words
3. Oral reading fluency—being able to read aloud smoothly, accurately, and at a good speed
4. Vocabulary comprehension—understanding words and text meaning

Skills in decoding and comprehension start to develop in early childhood (see Chapter 7) and these skills set the stage for reading performance in elementary schools (NICHD Early Child Care Research Network, 2005a). Some children enter kindergarten able to recognize and name all of the letters and to isolate beginning and ending sounds in simple words. Children who can sound out words in first grade are usually good readers later on. By third grade, these good readers are able to look at and process most of the letters in almost all of the words on a page. They can independently read chapter books fluently, and with excellent comprehension (Snow & Kang, 2006).

Children learn the alphabet and letter-sound connections (the first two components identified by the National Reading Panel) relatively quickly and easily. But, although learning the alphabet and understanding letter-sound connections are necessary skills, they are not sufficient for becoming a good reader. Vocabulary and comprehension, which take longer and require more effort, are equally important. This means that a more structured approach that emphasizes phonics in first grade is more effective for some students who have limited decoding skills, but by third grade, more and more attention needs to be devoted to comprehension and vocabulary (Morrison & Connor, 2002). So, the reading wars have ended in a truce: both phonics and whole language understanding are fundamental to literacy (Snow, Burns, & Griffin, 1998). Both have a place in reading instruction, depending on the developmental stage of the readers (see Figure 9.12).

Difficulties Learning to Read Children from low-income backgrounds, whose parents have low literacy skills or learning disabilities, and whose homes have few books and reading materials are at special risk for reading problems (Snow & Kang, 2006). Individual problems, such as language delay or hearing loss, also contribute to problems learning to read.

But schools and families can make a difference. In one study of low-income children who were in the bottom 30th percentile for reading skills, 30 percent showed substantial improvement from first grade to third grade (Spira, Bracken, & Fischel, 2005). These were children whose first-grade teachers spent more time on literacy and language instruction (Downer & Pianta, 2006). Successfully addressing early problems in reading has implications for other areas of development. Poor literacy achievement in the early grades is linked to poor academic achievement *and* increased aggressive behaviors in later grades (Miles & Stipek, 2006).

Dyslexia Children with **dyslexia** also have difficulty learning to read. Dyslexia is a learning disability characterized by difficulties with word recognition and by poor spelling and poor decoding skills. Despite average or above-average intelligence, instruction, and environmental opportunities, most children with dyslexia have phonological difficulties (Snowling, 2004). As preschoolers, children who later are dyslexic had equal vocabulary to preschoolers who did not develop the disability, but they made

dyslexia A learning disability characterized by difficulties with word recognition and by poor spelling and decoding skills.

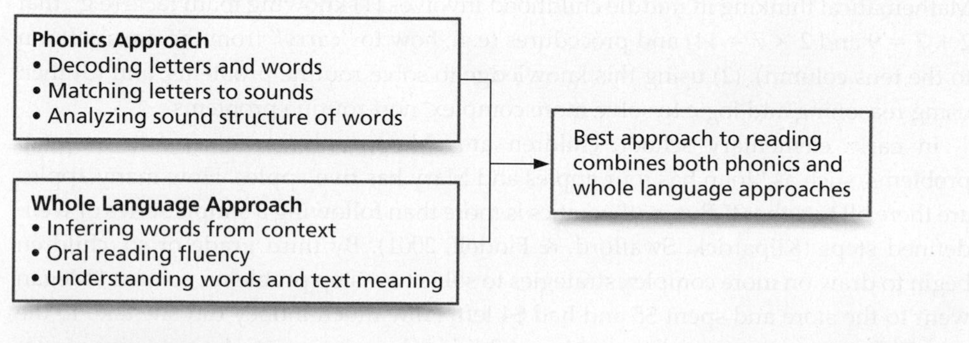

Phonics Approach
• Decoding letters and words
• Matching letters to sounds
• Analyzing sound structure of words
Whole Language Approach
• Inferring words from context
• Oral reading fluency
• Understanding words and text meaning
Best approach to reading combines both phonics and whole language approaches

FIGURE 9.12

Both Phonics and Whole Language Understanding Contribute to the Development of Skilled Readers

more speech errors and were poorer at rhyming. Some adults with childhood dyslexia are fluent readers but still have spelling problems and difficulty decoding words they have not seen before. Today, the majority of students with dyslexia and other special needs spend most of the school day in regular classrooms (called **inclusion**).

inclusion Placement of children with special needs in regular classrooms.

English Language Learners The number of children in the United States who speak a language other than English in their homes more than doubled from 1979 to 2005—an increase from 3.8 million students to 10.6 million students. States vary widely in their strategies for meeting the educational needs of **English language learners (ELLs).** Ballot referenda reducing access to bilingual education have passed in some states (California, Arizona, and Massachusetts), but failed in others (e.g., Colorado).

English language learner (ELL) Child for whom English is a new language.

What does research tell us about the development of English language learners in the United States? Findings across multiple studies are consistent (Snow & Kang, 2006). Some may surprise you.

- In most cases, children's first language is at some risk for loss or decline under the influence of the second language (English).
- Continued development of the first language is more likely if parents are bilingual and/or highly educated.
- Homes that provide high-quality support for literacy development (by reading with children and having books and reading materials in the house) have children who become better, more skilled readers. This home support can be in either the first language or the second language.
- Using the first language at home does not interfere with literacy development in English as long as English is also used at home.
- Having an older sibling who speaks English and can help with homework accelerates this process.
- Children who already know how to read in a first language have an easier time learning to read in English.
- Older children typically learn English faster than younger children, perhaps because of their better developed literacy skills.

As the number of ELLs in the United States continues to grow, developing strategies to better support the children's literacy and academic development needs to be a priority for schools and families. We now turn to another national priority, the development of mathematical thinking.

Mathematics

Mathematical thinking in middle childhood involves (1) knowing math facts (e.g., that $2 + 7 = 9$ and $2 \times 7 = 14$) and procedures (e.g., how to "carry" from the ones column to the tens column), (2) using this knowledge to solve routine problems, and (3) then using reasoning and logic to solve more complex, non-routine problems.

In early elementary school, children are able to solve most simple one-step problems, such as "John has four apples and Mary has five apples. How many apples are there all together?" But mathematics is more than following a simple series of well-defined steps (Kilpatrick, Swafford, & Findell, 2001). By third grade or so, children begin to draw on more complex strategies to solve two-step problems, such as "Megan went to the store and spent $5 and had $4 left. How much money did she take to the store?" To solve more complex problems, children become more adept at using strategies such as working backward from the answer, breaking the problem down into subproblems, and trying to think of a related problem.

Children also need to be able to know if their solutions are "in the ballpark" and to reflect, "Does the problem make sense? Does the solution make sense?" This kind of reflective questioning is hard to develop. For example, in one study, children were presented with this story problem: "There are 26 sheep and 10 goats on a ship. How old is the captain?" A large majority provided an answer (most often, "36"), seemingly unaware that the question could not be answered. Another aspect of mathematical proficiency, which is unfortunately rare, is an inclination to see mathematics as sensible, useful, and worthwhile.

Gender Differences Researchers have studied gender differences in mathematics performance (as measured by report card grades) and mathematics achievement (as measured by scores on standardized tests). School-age girls consistently receive better grades than do boys in math and science. Different approaches to school work, self-efficacy, and motivation have all been identified as playing a role in gender differences in math (Halpern et al., 2007). Girls, on average, put forth more effort and refrain from disruptive behavior in the classroom (Kenney-Benson et al., 2006). Boys are less compliant to teacher requests. They talk more to classmates and annoy their teachers more. As a result, boys typically earn lower grades than girls do. Historically boys tended to score higher than girls on standardized tests in science and some areas of math (Hyde et al., 1990), but these differences are not evident in more recent studies (Hyde et al., 2008). What accounts for these discrepancies? Hyde and colleagues believe that girls' wider participation in higher level mathematics coursework has eliminated the earlier differences that favored boys.

In the next section, we look at how well schools are providing instruction in math, reading, and other subjects. (For a summary of this section, see "Interim Summary 9.4: Language, Literacy, and Mathematics.")

Cooking and baking provide children with hands-on experiences in mathematics.

SCHOOLS

More than 40 million children are enrolled in elementary schools across the United States, an all-time high (National Center for Education Statistics, 2008). These children and their classrooms are much more ethnically and racially diverse than in previous generations. For example, in 1970, only 21 percent of students were children of color, whereas 47 percent were students of color in 2007. Students who speak a language other than English at home more than doubled during this period (National Center for Education Statistics, 2008).

One demographic characteristic has not changed appreciably. Poverty rates have remained persistently high, with two out of every five students qualifying as either "poor" (defined as a family of four with an income of less than $20,000 a year) or "near-poor" (defined as a family of four with an income between $20,000 and $40,000 a year). How well are our schools doing in educating this large, diverse group of students?

The Nation's Report Card

Since the early 1970s the National Assessment of Educational Progress (NAEP) has been measuring student achievement in nationally representative samples of students in fourth grade (about age 9), eighth grade (around age 13), and twelfth grade (around age 17). In effect, NAEP is a national report card indicating what U.S. students know and can do in reading, math, history, and science.

The NAEP findings suggest that U.S. schools are failing many children. Fully 36 percent of fourth graders are scoring *below* basic skills in reading (in essence failing the test).

INTERIM SUMMARY 9.4

Language, Literacy, and Mathematics

Language Development	■ Root vocabularies expand rapidly in middle childhood, as children add about three **root words** each day between ages 7 and 10. ■ Children become adept at **code switching.** ■ Sentence structure becomes more complex.
Literacy	■ Reading is a complex activity that involves **decoding** and **comprehension**. ■ "The reading wars" grew out of disagreements about whether a **phonics** or a **whole language** approach is better. Research shows that both sets of competencies are needed. ■ Children from low-income backgrounds, whose parents have low literacy skills, and whose homes have few reading materials are at risk for reading problems. ■ Children whose teachers spend more time on literacy and language instruction show greater gains in reading achievement and phoneme knowledge. ■ **Dyslexia** is a learning disability characterized by difficulties with word recognition and by poor spelling and decoding skills (despite average or above average intelligence). ■ For **English language learners,** development of the first language is more likely if parents are bilingual and/or highly educated. ■ Children who already know how to read in a first language have an easier time learning to read in the second language. ■ Older children typically learn a second language faster than younger children, perhaps because of their better developed literacy skills. ■ Homes that provide high-quality support for literacy development have children who become better, more skilled readers.
Mathematics	■ Mathematical competence in middle childhood involves knowing math facts and computational procedures, using this knowledge to solve routine problems, and using reasoning and logic to solve more complex, non-routine problems. ■ Children need to be able to know if their solutions are "in the ballpark" and to reflect, "Does the problem make sense?"

Only 31 percent are scoring as proficient or advanced in reading. There is much more room for improvement. The NAEP assessments also document significant differences in the scores of low-income, African American, and Hispanic students versus middle income, Caucasian, and Asian students. These differences, called the **achievement gap**, indicate that many students of color and low-income students are not on track to be successful in secondary school, high school, college, and well-paying careers (see Figure 9.13). Historically, U.S. schools have been viewed as an institution that provides children with access and opportunities to develop the skills to achieve their dreams. The achievement gap indicates that this is not happening for many children.

achievement gap An observed disparity on educational measures between the performance of groups of students, especially social class and ethnic disparities.

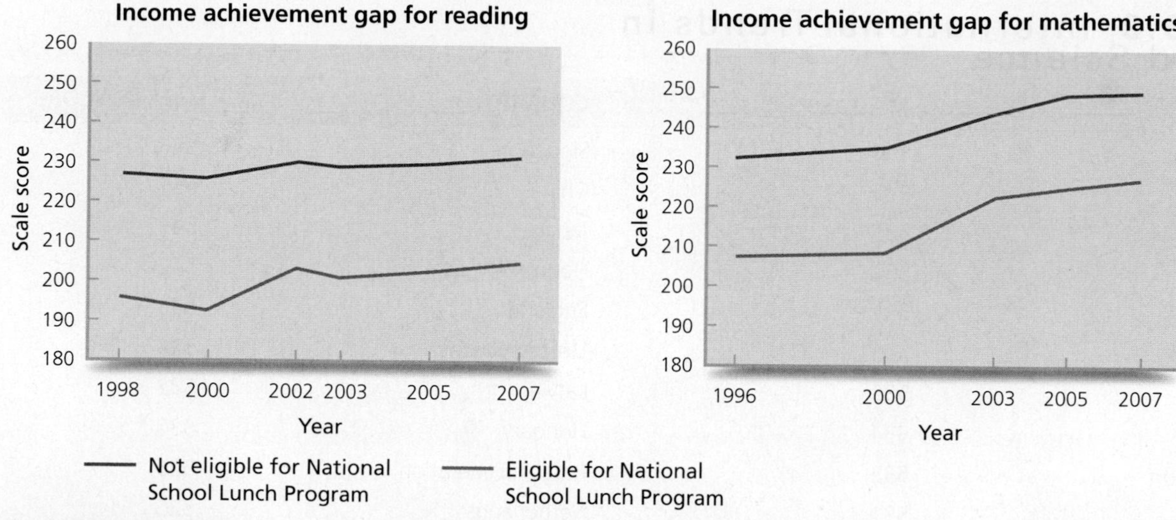

FIGURE 9.13

Average Reading Test Scores of Students by Eligibility for National School Lunch Program

On average, students who are eligible for the school lunch program have significantly lower reading test scores than students who do not qualify for the school lunch subsidy. This difference is referred to as the *achievement gap*.

Source: National Center for Education Statistics (2007). The Condition of Education 2007. http://nces.ed.gov/pubsearch/pubsinfo.asp?pubid=2007064. Accessed March 3, 2010.

International Comparisons

When they are adults, today's children will be competing in a global market for jobs that require high-level skills, especially in math and science (Committee on Prospering in the Global Economy, 2007; Friedman, 2007). How do U.S. students measure up to those in other countries? The Trends in International Mathematics and Science Study (TIMSS) has compared students' mathematics performance in fourth grade. As shown in Table 9.3, U.S. students score in the middling ranks in mathematics and (slightly) above average in science. Fourth-grade students in the United States performed better than those in Slovenia, Cyprus, and Iran, but worse than those in England, Hong Kong, and Singapore.

An influential report by the National Academy of Science in 2007 called *Rising above the Gathering Storm* makes the case that being "average" in math and science means that the United States is falling behind and will not be competitive in a knowledge- or technology-based global economy of the future. The report predicts that companies will go to other countries for highly skilled workers who can make advances in new technologies, taking those well-paying jobs and prosperity with them if improvements in U.S. education do not occur.

No Child Left Behind (NCLB)

The achievement gap, coupled with poor scores on international comparisons, has led to reform efforts at the local, state, and federal levels. Perhaps the best known is the federal law commonly known as **No Child Left Behind (NCLB)**. NCLB requires that states meet specific goals as measured by standardized achievement tests. These are sometimes referred to as **high stakes tests** because failure to meet specific performance standards can result in sanctions against a school and loss of federal funds. NCLB requires

No Child Left Behind (NCLB) A federal law that holds schools accountable for student performance and requires that states meet specific goals as measured by standardized achievement tests.

high stakes test A test that results in serious sanctions if performance standards are not met.

TABLE 9.3 International Trends in Math and Science

COUNTRY	AVERAGE MATH SCORE	COUNTRY	AVERAGE SCIENCE SCORE
Singapore	594	Singapore	565
Hong Kong SAR	575	Chinese Taipei	551
Japan	565	Japan	543
Chinese Taipei	564	Hong Kong SAR	542
Belgium-Flemish	551	England	540
Netherlands	540	**United States**	**536**
Latvia	536	Latvia	532
Lithuania	534	Hungary	530
Russian Federation	532	Russian Federation	526
England	531	Netherlands	525
Hungary	529	Australia	521
United States	**518**	New Zealand	520
Cyprus	510	Belgium-Flemish	518
Moldova, Republic of	504	Italy	516
Italy	503	Lithuania	512
Australia	499	Scotland	502
New Zealand	493	Moldova, Republic of	496
Scotland	490	Slovenia	490
Slovenia	479	Cyprus	480
Armenia	456	Norway	466
Norway	451	Armenia	437
Iran, Islamic Republic of	389	Iran, Islamic Republic of	414
Philippines	358	Philippines	332
Morocco	347	Tunisia	314
Tunisia	339	Morocco	304

Note: Countries were required to sample students in the upper of the two grades that contained the largest number of 9-year-olds. In the United States and most countries, this corresponds to grade 4.
Source: Adapted from National Center for Education Statistics (2003).

that children be tested in reading and math starting in third grade. All children, including members of minority groups, those who are economically disadvantaged, disabled children, and children who speak English as a second language, are tested and held to the same standards.

Some educators have questioned whether NCLB has boosted student achievement in elementary school (Fuller et al., 2007). They note that gains in reading and math achievement, measured by NAEP scores, have tended to slow since the passage of the law in 2002. Progress in narrowing the achievement gap, they argue, also has largely disappeared since the passage of NCLB. Other criticisms of NCLB have been that the law places too much attention on test scores, forcing teachers to devote too much time to drills and other test preparation at the expense of more thought-provoking classroom activities (Nichols & Berliner, 2007). Whether these criticisms will result in substantial changes in the law remains to be seen.

Strategies to Improve Student Learning and Achievement

The achievement gap and poor performance in international comparisons indicate that "something" needs to be done. The question is, what?

Research has identified several promising strategies for narrowing the achievement gap, and for improving overall student performance and learning. Policymakers and school districts will likely need to consider multiple strategies because it is unlikely that any single strategy alone can result in the needed improvements.

Class Size Smaller class sizes in elementary school (13–17 students versus 22–26 students) improve student achievement scores, and there are larger benefits for low-income children and students of color (Ehrenberg et. al, 2001; Finn & Achilles, 1999). Smaller classes tend to have fewer disruptions and more student-centered learning. As class size increases, classrooms become more structured and more teacher-directed.

Teacher Quality Teacher quality makes a difference (Darling-Hammond, 2008). Effective teachers are more knowledgeable about the subjects they teach. They have strong beliefs that their students can learn, and they have a large toolkit of teaching strategies and materials to draw on. When one approach does not work with students, they readily adapt and use other strategies. Having a very effective teacher versus an average teaching predicts substantial differences in both reading and math achievement (Ehrenberg et al., 2001).

Efforts to increase the supply and retention of effective teachers are under way. In some universities, teacher education programs are partnering with the science and math departments to develop ways for science and math majors to simultaneously earn teaching credentials. School districts and states also are experimenting with strategies to reward high-quality teaching and gains in student performance (Wallis, 2008).

Lengthening the School Year The structure of the school calendar in the United States harkens back to a time when children were needed to help their families with farm chores (Wallis & Steptoe, 2006). Because summer was a time for planting and harvesting, the school "year" was only 9 months. The school year in most industrial countries is considerably longer—7 weeks of summer vacation instead of 12 weeks.

Summer breaks are hard on children's mathematical computation skills. Both middle-income and low-income students lose about 2 months of grade-level skills in math over summer vacation (Cooper, 2004). Low-income students also lose about 2 months of achievement in reading, whereas middle-class students post modest gains, presumably because middle-class parents are able to provide their children with more opportunities to read. Trips to the library, summer book clubs, and access to the family computer may all play a role.

Having an effective teacher makes a difference in daily experiences at school and in how much children learn.

Some afterschool programs feature sports and arts; others feature science, math, and reading enrichment. The particular focus is less important than that the activities are chosen by the students, are engaging to students, and allow students to build skills over time.

These summer differences tend to accumulate over time. According to one estimate, fully two-thirds of the achievement gap separating lower income and higher income students can be explained by unequal access to summer learning opportunities (Alexander, Entwisle, & Olson, 2007). Some schools districts, communities, and organizations are testing different strategies to foster summer learning, including alternative school calendars that result in shorter break periods and tuition-free summer camps for students.

Lengthening the School Day Another holdover from our agrarian past is the length of the school day (Wallis & Steptoe, 2006). Because children were needed to do chores on the farm before dark, the school day needed to end by 3:00 P.M. or so. Now many working parents are not home before dark, leaving a gap of some 2 to 3 hours between the time that school ends and parents arrive home. In our discussion of adolescence, we'll see that having all this unstructured, unsupervised time may contribute to problem behavior, such as experimentation with drugs and alcohol. Some states, like Massachusetts, are experimenting with lengthening the school day. However, what goes on during the added hours matters. If the extra time is devoted to enriched learning, students benefit. However, using extra hours just to drill children on basic skills is stressful for teachers as well as students (Nichols & Berliner, 2007).

Afterschool Programs Participation in high-quality afterschool programs predicts gains in work habits and task persistence, skills that underlie academic performance. Such programs also predict improvements in academic outcomes, such as grades and standardized test scores (Mahoney, Lord, & Carryl, 2005; Pierce, Bolt, & Vandell, in press). The quality of the programs and how frequently young people attend the programs are key. High-quality programs are characterized by positive relationships between staff and students and by high levels of student engagement in activities. The particular focus of these activities (community service, music, sports, arts, chess, computers, newspaper) is less important than that they are chosen by the students, are engaging to students, and allow students to build skills over time. Afterschool programs of this sort appear especially beneficial for low-income youth, perhaps due to a lack of other extracurricular enrichment opportunities.

Reorganizing the School Curriculum Some schools are reorienting their curricula to include writer's workshops, art, music, and Spanish as well as traditional subjects (mathematics, literature, social studies, and science). Instead of teaching these subjects as discrete and disconnected, teachers encourage students to integrate what they are learning using higher-level concepts such as trends over time, paradoxical thinking, universal concepts, and ethics. Teaching is project based rather than subject oriented.

Collaborative and original research are used to help children to examine their work from different perspectives, such as from the point of view of a sociologist or political scientist, and to document evidence of their understanding.

Early Childhood Education Another strategy for improving academic achievement is high quality early childhood education programs that can help to prepare children to come to elementary school ready to learn. Kindergarten teachers report that 10 percent of their students come to kindergarten with "serious problems," and an additional 35 percent have "some problems" in preacademic skills, attention, and relations with peers (Rimm-Kaufman, Pianta, & Cox, 2000). As we discussed in Chapter 7, high-quality early education programs can reduce these deficits and increase the numbers of children who are ready to learn when they start kindergarten.

Family Involvement in School Family involvement in the school (defined as attending parent-teacher conferences and performances and volunteering in the classroom or for field trips) is related to children's academic success. In one longitudinal study that followed children from kindergarten to fifth grade, Dearing and colleagues (2006) found that increases in family involvement predicted gains in literacy. In addition, although there was an achievement gap in average literacy performance between children of more and less educated mothers when family involvement was low, this gap was nonexistent when family involvement levels were high. These results add to other evidence on the value of family involvement in school, especially for low-income children, and suggest that efforts to support family involvement might be part of a comprehensive effort to improve student learning. (For a summary of this section, see "Interim Summary 9.5: Schools.")

INTERIM SUMMARY 9.5

Schools	
The Nation's Report Card	■ The National Assessment of Educational Progress (NAEP) measures student achievement in nationally representative samples in the United States. ■ NAEP documents significant differences in the scores of low-income, African American, and Hispanic students versus middle-income, Caucasian, and Asian students. These differences have been called the **achievement gap**.
International Comparisons	■ The Trends in International Mathematics and Science Study compares mathematics performance in different countries. ■ U.S. students score in the middling ranks in mathematics and (slightly) above average in science.
No Child Left Behind (NCLB)	■ The federal law known as **No Child Left Behind (NCLB)** has sought to improve children's academic skills by holding schools accountable for student performance on standardized achievement tests.
Strategies to Improve Student Learning and Achievement	■ Strategies that have narrowed the achievement gap include smaller class sizes, more effective teachers, a longer school year, a longer school day, afterschool programs, a reorganized curriculum, early childhood educational programs, and increased family involvement.

SUMMING UP AND LOOKING AHEAD

Children grow taller and heavier in middle childhood. With practice, a child can become adept at playing ice hockey or playing the piano at this age. Not surprisingly, out-of-school sports leagues and music lessons are quite popular. Changes in the frontal lobes, prefrontal cortex, temporal lobes, and parietal lobes all help to set the stage for advances in higher-order thinking and fine and gross motor skills that are seen in middle childhood.

Many school-age children are healthy and fit, but some are not. The dramatic increase in obesity among school-age children illustrates how social and cultural change—the broader context—affects individual development. Fast food and soft drinks have become part of the American way of life. With today's hectic lifestyles, families take less time to prepare home-cooked meals from fresh ingredients. Tight budgets have forced schools to cut back on healthy menus, recess, and PE classes. Many neighborhoods lack safe places for children to run and play outdoors. So, too, many children fill their afterschool hours with sedentary pastimes—not only TV but also video games and computers. In addition to obesity, rates of chronic illness, such as asthma and diabetes, have increased in recent years. Moreover, formerly adult diseases—such as Type 2 diabetes—are now being diagnosed in children.

Good health and physical activity are essential not only to growth but also to cognitive development. Cognitive development in middle childhood is nothing short of an "intellectual revolution." Not only do children acquire basic skills—reading, writing, and mathematics—but also the *way* they think changes. No longer seduced by perception, they use logical operations to organize information and probe beneath the surface. They develop strategies for analyzing problems and remembering large chunks of information. Given opportunities, children this age are avid learners. At the same time, however, their thinking is limited to real or "concrete" objects and events. It is not until adolescence that individuals can reliably apply these logical tools to abstract concepts.

School plays a pivotal role in middle childhood. Ready or not, it's time to learn. These is much debate about what and how to teach children, from the reading wars to the length of the school year. This debate is fueled by the achievement gap between poor and better-off students within the United States, and by this country's middle ranking in international comparisons.

Of course, cognitive development is not confined to school learning. What children do when they are not in school, their family life, neighborhoods in which they live, and the media are all powerful influences, as we will see in the next chapter. Middle childhood is a time of change in the way children see themselves, in how they relate to their parents and siblings, in how they interact with their peers, and in their experience of the wider world.

HERE'S WHAT YOU SHOULD KNOW

Did You Get It?

After reading this chapter, you should understand the following:

- The major features of physical growth and development in middle childhood, and the physical and mental impact of obesity
- How the brain develops during middle childhood
- The major accomplishments during middle childhood in the realms of gross and fine motor skills
- The most common threats to physical health and well-being in middle childhood
- What the concrete operational period is and the characteristics of concrete operational thinking
- What microgenetic analysis involves and what these studies show about children's behavior
- The development of processing speed and working and long-term memory in middle childhood
- What false memories are
- An overview of the efforts to measure intelligence and what IQ scores mean
- The propositions of Gardner's theory of multiple intelligences and Sternberg's triarchic theory
- How children progress in their language development and mathematical thinking in middle childhood
- Strategies to improve U.S. schools

Important Terms and Concepts

achievement gap (p. 288)
allergies (p. 270)
asthma (p. 270)
attention deficit hyperactivity disorder (ADHD) (p. 263)
axon (p. 261)
body mass index (BMI) (p. 257)
cerebellum (p. 263)
cerebral cortex (p. 263)
class inclusion (p. 272)
classification (p. 272)
code switching (p. 283)
competitive elimination (p. 261)
comprehension (p. 284)
concrete operations (p. 272)
corpus callosum (p. 261)
declarative memory (p. 276)
decoding (p. 284)
Deese-Roediger-McDermott (DRM) procedure (p. 276)
dendrite (p. 261)
digit span task (p. 275)
Down syndrome (p. 281)
dyslexia (p. 285)
English language learner (ELL) (p. 286)
false memory (p. 276)
fine motor skills (p. 267)
fragile X syndrome (p. 281)
frontal lobe (p. 262)
giftedness (p. 280)
gist memory (p. 276)
gray matter (p. 261)
gross motor skills (p. 264)
high stakes test (p. 289)
horizontal decalage (p. 274)
inclusion (p. 286)
individual differences (p. 257)
lateralization (p. 261)
long-term memory (p. 276)
memory strategies (p. 277)
microgenetic analysis (p. 277)
multiple intelligences (p. 278)
myelin (p. 261)
No Child Left Behind (NCLB) (p. 289)
normative development (p. 257)
parietal lobe (p. 262)
phonics (p. 284)
prefrontal cortex (p. 262)
procedural memory (p. 276)
reliability (p. 278)
reversibility (p. 273)
root words (p. 283)
seriation (p. 273)
synapse (p. 261)
synaptic pruning (p. 261)
temporal lobe (p. 262)
transitive inference (p. 273)
triarchic theory of successful intelligence (p. 279)
Type 1 diabetes (p. 270)
Type 2 diabetes (p. 271)
validity (p. 278)
verbatim memory (p. 276)
white matter (p. 262)
whole language (p. 284)
working memory (p. 275)

CHAPTER 10

Socioemotional Development in Middle Childhood

For Alexander Williams, son of a lawyer and a high-level manager, weekends are jam-packed. Alexander plays soccer, basketball, and baseball; goes to Sunday school; sings in the church choir and a university choral group; takes private piano lessons; and studies guitar at school. He sometimes has five or more formal, scheduled events between Friday and Monday.

For Billy Yandell, son of a house painter and a domestic worker, weekends are leisurely. He has few scheduled activities except for attending church. He spends his weekends visiting with relatives, playing street ball, riding his bike, watching TV, playing video games, going to the store for a snack, and just hanging out with other kids in his neighborhood.

Alexander and Billy were part of sociologist Annette Lareau's (2003) ethnographic study of school-age U.S. children. Ethnographers conduct fieldwork in which they gain access to a group and carry out intensive observations over a period of months or years. Lareau was interested in how children spend their out-of-school time and in how social class shapes the content and pace of their daily lives. She observed that the middle-class children spent much of their out-of-school time in ways that were preparing them for their roles as high-achieving students and for future careers. Their activities were organized and emphasized mastering skills and performing for an audience, whether at bat or in a music recital. At soccer practice, for example, they lined up, performed drills according to the coach's instructions, occupied the spotlight when they had the ball (much as they do at school when a teacher asks them a question), and likewise were judged by their performance. They also were "in training" for careers and family lives that demand skill in managing a crowded schedule.

The lives of the working-class children were more relaxed and informal. They were more likely to play in improvised, mixed-age groups, without adult supervision. As long as they stayed within the physical boundaries their parents set, they had autonomy and social space apart from adults. The working-class children were less dependent on their parents to chauffer them from here to there than middle-class children were. Their weekends were more kin centered, often including visits with nearby grandparents, aunts, uncles, and cousins. With few organized, structured activities, they had few performance expectations, limited opportunities "to shine," and less experience learning how to juggle competing demands. Lareau noted that these differences in out-of-school time were shaped more by social class than by race. For example, in the case of the two boys just described, Alexander Williams is African American; Billy Yandell is Irish American.

Lareau's study highlights that social and emotional development in middle childhood take place within different contexts. The immediate family is still important and provides children with widely varying opportunities, economic and social resources, and cultural expectations. In addition, peer contexts (both friendships and larger peer groups) are increasingly salient, as is the broader neighborhood context. Children's exposure to the world outside of their immediate neighborhood and community continues to expand. Television, video games, and computers open new social opportunities and new risks.

We will consider the family, the peer group, organized activities, and technology in more detail later in this chapter. First, though, we look at several notable accomplishments in the socioemotional domain that occur during middle childhood.

THE DEVELOPING SENSE OF SELF

The advances in the physical and cognitive domains (described in Chapter 9) help set the stage for socioemotional development in middle childhood. In this section, we consider three aspects of socioemotional development that reflect a more differentiated conception of self, feelings of industry versus inferiority, and gender.

Conception of Self

In early childhood, the child's conception of self is generally positive (see Chapter 8). In middle childhood, this conception has become more balanced and nuanced. One girl described herself this way:

> I'm in fourth grade this year, and I'm pretty popular, at least with my girl friends. That's because I am nice to people and helpful and can keep secrets. Mostly I am nice to my friends, although if I get in a bad mood I sometimes say something that can be a little mean. I try to control my temper, but when I don't, I'm ashamed of myself. I'm usually happy when I'm with friends, but I get sad if there is no one around to do things with. At school, I'm feeling pretty smart in certain subjects like language arts and social studies. I got A's in these subjects on my last report card and was really proud of myself. But I'm feeling pretty dumb in math and science, especially when I see how well a lot of other kids are doing. Even though I'm not doing well in these subjects, I still like myself as a person, because math and science just aren't that important to me. How I look and how popular I am are more important. I also like myself because I know my parents like me and so do other kids. That helps you like yourself. (Harter, 2006, p. 526)

Unlike a preschooler, this fourth-grader doesn't see herself as "all good" (or "all bad"), but describes her strengths and weaknesses in comparison to "other kids." Accomplishments are important, but she also sees social relationships as central to her life. Interpersonal terms have replaced the concrete descriptions of the younger child. This girl is able to recognize and reconcile conflicting traits (*smart* in some subjects, but *dumb* in others) and contradictory emotions (*happy* in some situations, but *sad* in others). More conscious of how other people see her, she begins her self-description, "I'm pretty popular. . . ." But she doesn't see herself through rose-colored glasses: sometimes she's "proud"; other times she's "ashamed."

The sense of self in middle childhood builds on cognitive advances that we described in Chapter 9. Children are now able to consider two different concepts or dimensions (such as *nice* and *mean*) at the same time. This means they can compare their ideal and real self (*always nice* vs. *sometimes mean*), as well as compare themselves to others. They use higher-order generalizations such as "smart" rather than mention specific skills ("I know my ABCs") and, reversing this process, analyze the components of generalizations (popularity = nice + helpful + keeping secrets).

In middle childhood, children's conception of self becomes more multifaceted, reflecting the views of their parents and peers. Children with more positive self-appraisals are more likely to have parents who are accepting, affectionate, and involved in their activities (Harter, 2006). Parents who set excessively high and unrealistic standards undermine children's sense of self, resulting in a tarnished image of self as unlovable, incompetent, and unworthy (Erikson, 1963). Children's self-appraisals also reflect their standing and reputation among classmates and teammates, as we saw in the girl's self-description. At this age, peer groups rank with parents as influences on self-concepts and self-esteem (Harris, 1995).

Societal views and standards also play a role. By middle childhood, youngsters have internalized many of their culture's values. Physical appearance is an example. Children who don't measure up to cultural ideas of physical attractiveness, in body shape or facial features, suffer from lower self-esteem and from symptoms of depression (Harter, 2006; Huesmann & Taylor, 2006). Becoming aware of others' perceptions and evaluations may provide a more realistic sense of self, but also leads to greater vulnerability.

Industry Versus Inferiority

Erik Erikson's (1963) fourth stage of psychosocial development—**industry versus inferiority**—describes another aspect of the developing sense of self in middle childhood. According to Erickson, children develop a view of themselves as industrious (and worthy) when they win recognition by producing things beside and with others. Striving for recognition for their accomplishments, children develop skills and perform tasks that their society values. From these efforts, they come to appreciate (and even enjoy) persistence and hard work that leads to their success and recognition.

industry versus inferiority Erikson's fourth stage of psychosocial development in which children develop a view of themselves as industrious (and worthy) versus inferior. Striving for recognition for their accomplishments, children develop skills and perform tasks that their society values.

Elementary school children are graded for their school work and often for their industry under the label "Work Habits" or "Study Skills." But opportunities to develop industry are not confined to school. Performing tricks on a skateboard, reaching the next level in online games like World of Warcraft, organizing a magic show, and selling Girl Scout cookies also require effort and diligence and contribute to children's growing sense of industry.

The danger, according to Erikson, is when parents and teachers undermine industry by failing to recognize accomplishments. By being overly critical of children's efforts, parents and teachers can leave children with an abiding sense of inferiority.

The social context also affects the development of industry. Alexander Williams, one of the boys described at the beginning of this chapter, had ample opportunities to win recognition in his organized music and sports activities; Billy Yandell had fewer of these experiences. It is important to remember that, although school is probably the main context in which children develop (or fail to develop) a healthy sense of industry, it is not the only setting where this aspect of the development of the self unfolds. Many children who have difficulty achieving in school demonstrate mastery in other arenas.

Gender Development

Gender functions as an organizing framework in middle childhood. It provides a context for children to think about themselves in relation to others; a basis for choosing interests, activities, and friends; and a guide for behavior and even emotions. Gender consciousness is not limited to middle childhood, of course, but solidifies during this period.

By age 8 or 9, children's self-concepts reflect gender norms (see Table 10.1.) The differences are not large; boys in self-descriptions emphasize skill in math and sports. Girls highlight verbal/reading ability, music, and social competence (being nice and being popular) (Eccles et al., 1993).

Gender differences in global self-esteem appear in mid- to late childhood, with girls (on average) exhibiting lower self-esteem than boys (Kling et al., 1999). A cross-cultural study of more than 3,000 school-age children found that academic self-conceptions usually matched achievement (Stetsenko et al., 2000). However, girls who achieved top grades and test scores typically said they were "as good as boys," not crediting

TABLE 10.1 Gender Differences in Middle Childhood

DOMAIN	BOYS	GIRLS
Competencies reflected in self-descriptions	Math ability, sports	Verbal/reading ability, music, social skills
Personality traits	Instrumental; emphasis on accomplishments and action	Expressive; emphasis on communication and collaboration
Play	Rough-and-tumble play all over the playground	Social games on the sidelines
Media preferences	Science fiction, sports, comic books	Adventures, ghost stories, romances, animal themes
Self-esteem	Slightly higher than girls	Slightly lower than boys

themselves for being better than boys, despite demonstrated superiority. In math and science classes, on the basketball court, and elsewhere, a girl might be told "You're really good" but internalize a different message, "You're good—*for a girl*" (Gelman, Taylor, & Nguyen, 2004).

instrumentality A personality trait that is characterized by a focus on action and accomplishments.

expressivity A personality trait that is marked by a "caring" orientation; a focus on communication, collaboration, and conciliation.

Gender-linked personality traits become more apparent during this period (Ruble, Martin, & Berenbaum, 2006). **Instrumentality** is a "can do" orientation, focused on action and accomplishments. **Expressivity** is a "caring" orientation, focused on communication, collaboration, and conciliation. Parents and peers tend to encourage instrumentality in boys (Richards & Larson, 1989). The reverse is true for girls. Instrumental girls are "bossy." Girls who talk about their talents and victories are seen as "bragging." But boys who do the same are viewed as assertive. As a consequence, boys learn to make direct statements, whereas girls learn to make polite suggestions or hints (Tannen, 1994). In mixed-sex interaction, boys don't hear the hints and ignore the girls' efforts to influence activities, one possible reason that girls have lower self-esteem (Kling et al., 1999).

rough-and-tumble play Physically vigorous behaviors such as chasing, jumping, and play fighting that are accompanied by shared smiles and laughter.

Different orientations are both a cause and consequence of separate lives. Gender segregation, which we first saw in early childhood, intensifies during middle childhood (Ruble et al., 2006). Visit an elementary school playground. Most likely, the boys are playing with other boys and taking up most of the space on the playground. Their play is more likely to involve **rough-and-tumble play**—which, as we discussed in an earlier chapter, includes physically vigorous behaviors such as chasing, jumping, and play fighting, accompanied by shared smiles and laughter. Girls are on the sidelines, most often talking and playing with other girls.

Neither sex wants much to do with the other. Each sees his or her own sex as the in-group and the other sex as the out-group (Maccoby, 2003). Put another way, what is "in" for girls is off limits for boys, and vice versa. In a typical in-group/out-group pattern, children perceive more positive traits in their own sex and negative traits in the other. They exaggerate both the similarities among members of their own sex and the differences between themselves and the other sex. And so the notion of the *opposite* sex takes root.

In-group identity is echoed in gender-stereotypic preferences in reading and media (Ruble et al., 2006). Girls prefer adventure, ghost, romance, and social relationship themes, animal stories, and poetry. Boys read science fiction, sports, war/spy stories, comic books, and joke books. Girls write stories about affection; boys, about aggression. Girls draw human figures, butterflies, and flowers. Boys draw mechanical objects (often cars) and battle scenes. Alone and in groups, then, girls and boys create different worlds for themselves (Blatchford, Baines, & Pellegrini, 2003).

At the same time, **gender schemas**—the conceptualization of what it means to be male or female—become more complex (Ruble et al., 2006). Rigid, simplistic sex stereotypes decline after a peak at about age 6. In general, girls are more flexible about gender norms and sex roles than boys are. Both sexes are more likely to accept girls who like "masculine" activities such as playing sports than boys who like "feminine" activities such as sewing. Actually, by the end of middle childhood, both boys *and* girls find boy-type activities (especially sports) more interesting than girl-type activities (McHale et al., 2004). This doesn't mean that they play together, though. Girls join all-girl soccer leagues and boys join all-boy leagues. Hispanic and Asian American children are more likely to conform to sex stereotypes, and African Americans less likely, than are European American children (Corsaro, 2006; Ruble et al., 2006).

gender schema A conceptualization of what it means to be male or female.

Clearly, in the mind of the school-age child, differences between the sexes are strong and real. But how accurate are children's perceptions? Literally hundreds of studies have compared boys' and girls' performances during middle childhood (Blakemore, Berenbaum, & Liben, 2008). This means that the odds are that one or another study has detected a statistically significant difference by chance. For this reason, researchers have turned to meta-analysis to weigh the evidence. **Meta-analysis** is a statistical technique that combines the findings of multiple studies, taking into account the number of children in each of the individual studies and the magnitude of the result (for instance, the size of the sex difference) reported in each one. By pooling the results of many, many studies, meta-analyses help us to be more confident that findings are robust and reliable.

Girls' participation in organized sports has increased dramatically since the passage of Title IX, a law passed in 1972 that requires gender equity for boys and girls in all educational programs that receive federal funding.

meta-analysis A statistical technique that combines the findings of multiple studies, taking into account the number of children in each of the individual studies and the magnitude of the effect reported in each one.

For the most part, meta-analyses of research on sex differences indicate that boys are more active and more physically aggressive than girls. Boys have better spatial abilities as reflected in their skills at mental rotations. Boys have better gross motor skills (such as hitting a target with a ball) (Blakemore et al., 2008; Ruble et al., 2006). Girls, on the other hand, have better verbal skills, including speech, fluency, and verbal memory. Girls also are better at reading emotions.

However, Janet Hyde (2005) has cautioned that these meta-analyses also reveal a lot of overlap between boys and girls in all of these areas. Look at Figure 10.1. You see that boys, on average, have a slight edge in their self-esteem, but many girls have scores that are higher than boys'. In fact, there is about an 85 percent overlap in the

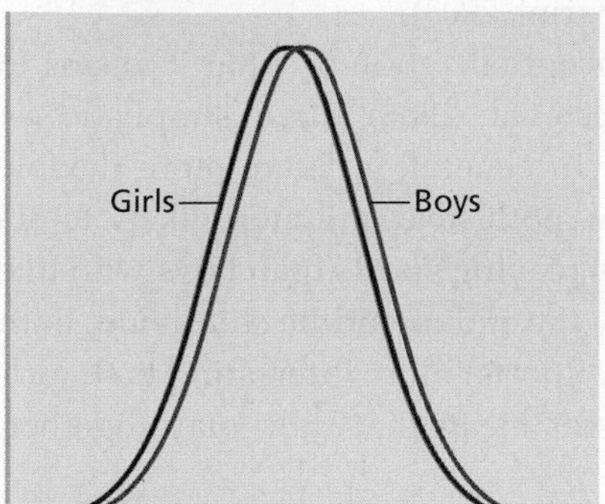

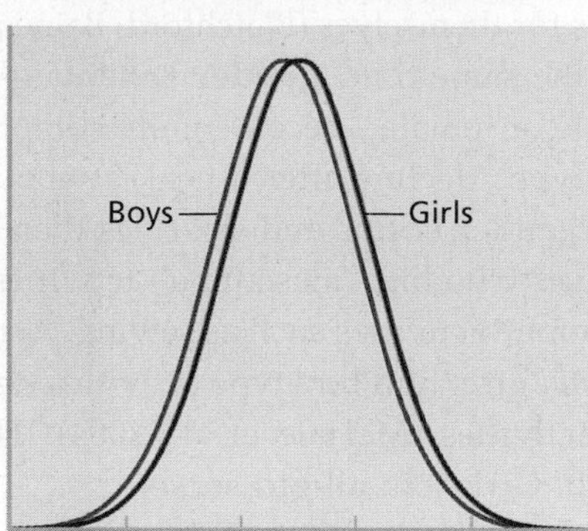

FIGURE 10.1

The Overlap in the Performances of Boys and Girls

Boys, on average, have a slight edge in terms of self-esteem, but many girls have scores that are higher than boys. In fact, there is about an 85 percent overlap in the distributions of the scores for boys and girls.

Source: Hyde (2005).

distributions of the scores for boys and girls. In contrast, girls, on average, have a slight edge in verbal abilities. But many boys have higher verbal abilities than many girls (again, about an 85% overlap). In other areas such as physical activity, the average differences between boys and girls are larger, although there is still a lot of overlap (67%).

In summary, objective measures show that school-age boys and girls are more alike than different. But they see themselves almost as belonging to different "tribes" and act in ways that accentuate and even create gender differences. Gender structures their sense of self as well as their social lives. (For a summary of this section, see "Interim Summary 10.1: The Developing Sense of Self.")

INTERIM SUMMARY **10.1**

The Developing Sense of Self

Conception of Self	■ Self-concepts become more balanced and nuanced in middle childhood than in early childhood. These conceptions are influenced by parents, peers, and societal standards.
Industry Versus Inferiority	■ Erikson's fourth stage of psychosocial development, **industry versus inferiority,** occurs in middle childhood. Children develop a view of self as industrious (and worthy) versus inferior when they obtain recognition for their accomplishments.
Gender Development	■ Gender provides an organizing framework for children to think about themselves in relation to others. Children's self-concepts reflect gender norms. ■ **Meta-analyses** indicate that boys are more active, are more physically aggressive, and have better spatial abilities and better large motor skills. Girls have better verbal skills and are better at reading emotions. ■ Most of the differences are small, and there is considerable overlap between the scores of boys and girls.

MORAL DEVELOPMENT

During middle childhood children are involved in multiple groups: the family, the school class, informal friendship groups, and often teams and clubs. All of these groups have standards, rules, and sanctions that provide rewards for conformity and punishments for nonconformity. Understanding standards, playing by the rules, and deciding what is fair are part of group life. These social experiences, interacting with cognitive development and genetic factors, propel moral development (Pinker, 2008). They also provide contexts for behaving kindly and for behaving aggressively. In this section, we will first look at how children evaluate moral dilemmas.

Moral Reasoning

How do children this age think about right and wrong? Lawrence Kohlberg's theory long dominated the study of moral reasoning (Kohlberg, 1976; Turiel, 2006). In this approach, researchers assess children's level of moral reasoning by examining responses to hypothetical moral dilemmas about real-world situations, such as the following:

> Judy was a twelve-year-old girl. Her mother promised her that she could go to a special rock concert coming to their town if she saved up from baby-sitting and lunch money to buy a ticket to the concert. She managed to save up the fifteen dollars the ticket cost plus another five dollars. But then her mother changed her mind and told Judy that she had to spend the money on new clothes for school. Judy was disappointed and decided to go to the concert anyway. She bought a ticket and told her mother that she had only been able to save five dollars. That Saturday she went to the performance and told her mother that she was spending the day with a friend. A week passed without her mother finding out. Judy then told her older sister, Louise, that she had gone to the performance and had lied to her mother about it. Louise wonders whether to tell their mother what Judy did.
>
> Should Louise, the older sister, tell their mother that Judy lied or should she keep quiet?

According to Kohlberg, whether or not you think that Louise should tell her mother is less important than the reasoning behind your answer. Kohlberg theorized that individuals' reasoning about moral issues becomes more sophisticated with development. Specifically, Kohlberg held that there are three main levels of moral reasoning: **preconventional**, which is dominant during most of childhood; **conventional moral reasoning**, which is usually dominant during late childhood and early adolescence; and **postconventional** (sometimes called "principled moral reasoning"), which emerges sometime during the adolescent or young adult years (see Table 10.2).

Preconventional moral reasoning is not based on society's standards, rules, or conventions. Rather, children at this stage focus on the rewards and punishments associated

preconventional moral reasoning In Kohlberg's theory, reasoning that focuses on the rewards and punishments associated with different courses of action, not societal standards.

conventional moral reasoning In Kohlberg's theory, reasoning that focuses on receiving the approval of others or maintaining the social order.

postconventional moral reasoning In Kohlberg's theory, reasoning guided by principles such as justice, fairness, and sanctity of life.

TABLE 10.2 Kohlberg's Theory of Moral Reasoning

LEVEL	DESCRIPTION
Preconventional	Moral decisions are based on the rewards and punishments that could be associated with an action or behavior.
Conventional	Morality is judged by whether the behavior conforms to social rules and whether it will be approved of by others.
Postconventional	Societal rules are considered relative; principles such as justice, fairness, and the sanctity of life guide decisions about moral behavior.

with different courses of action. Here, a child might reason that Louise shouldn't tell on her sister Judy because Judy will be angry and get back at her *or* Louise should tell on her sister because Louise will get in big trouble if her mother finds out that Louise had not told what her sister had done.

Conventional moral thinking focuses not so much on tangible rewards and punishments but on how an individual will be judged by others for behaving in a certain way. One behaves properly because, in so doing, one receives the approval of others and helps to maintain the social order. Here, a child might reason that Louise should tell on her sister because lying is wrong and Judy lied *or* Louise should not tell on her sister because her sister trusted her. Individuals at this level do not question society's rules. They see these rules as coming from a higher authority and leading to the greater good.

At the *postconventional* level of reasoning, which is not seen prior to adolescence, society's rules and conventions are seen as relative and subjective rather than absolute and definitive. One may have a duty to abide by society's standards for behavior—but only insofar as those standards support and serve moral ends. Occasions arise in which conventions ought to be questioned; when more important principles—such as justice, fairness, keeping one's word, or the sanctity of human life—take precedence over established social norms. Post-conventional thinkers might reason that Louise shouldn't tell on her sister because their mother *promised* Judy she could go to the concert if she saved enough money but then broke her promise.

Many studies have confirmed Kohlberg's belief that moral reasoning becomes more principled over the course of childhood and adolescence (Eisenberg & Morris, 2004). According to Kohlberg, development into higher stages of moral reasoning occurs when the child is developmentally "ready"—when his or her reasoning is predominantly at one stage but partially at the next higher one—and when he or she is exposed to the more advanced type of reasoning by other people, such as parents or peers (Eisenberg & Morris, 2004). This has led to the development of many curricula designed to stimulate the growth of advanced moral reasoning.

Kohlberg's work has been criticized because he interviewed only boys from Caucasian, middle-class backgrounds. Whether the results can be generalized to all children is questionable. Carol Gilligan (1982) argued that girls and women employ a morality of care, emphasizing nurturance and compassion, as opposed to a morality of justice, which is more evident in boys. Kohlberg's work also has been criticized because he focused on moral reasoning and not on actions or behavior. Although moral reasoning and moral behavior are related, they are not perfectly so. For instance, you know full well that it is important to have traffic laws in order to protect individuals from injuring themselves or others, but there probably have been times when you have knowingly violated the law because you were in a hurry to get someplace. Others are now studying the links between moral reasoning and prosocial behaviors in middle childhood in different cultural contexts.

Prosocial Development

prosocial behaviors Voluntary actions such as sharing, cooperating, helping, and comforting that are intended to benefit another person.

The sheer number of **prosocial behaviors**—actions such as sharing, cooperating, helping, and comforting that are intended to benefit another person—increases from the preschool period through middle childhood (Eisenberg, Fabes, & Spinrad, 2006). This increase occurs, in part, because school-age children are better able to read emotional cues and to understand other people's emotional states and thought processes (Garner, 1996). They also are better at regulating their own emotional states so that they are less likely to be overwhelmed by their feelings (Eisenberg et al., 2006).

The increase also reflects developmental changes in children's motivations or reasons for helping (Bar-Tal, Raviv, & Leiser, 1980). When presented with hypothetical moral dilemmas (e.g., helping an injured child versus going to a party), children have been asked what they would do and why. In early childhood, children typically use **hedonistic reasoning** that focuses on their own wishes and needs. In middle childhood, children's reasoning becomes other oriented and aimed at winning social approval and enhancing interpersonal relationships. Children this age want to be seen as "good." **Altruism**—helping behaviors that are motivated by helping as an end in itself, without expectation of reward or recognition—begins to emerge in late elemetary school (Bar-Tal et al., 1980).

© Ellen B. Senisi / The Image Works

Prosocial behaviors, such as providing comfort and assistance, increase in frequency from early to middle childhood.

Cross-Cultural Variations Societies differ in the degree to which prosocial and cooperative behaviors are normative or expected (Grusec, Davidov, & Lundell, 2002). In individualistic (westernized, urban) cultures, a higher value is placed on spontaneous acts of kindness than on doing one's duty. Prosocial behaviors are thought of as an expression of personal values and individual personality. Duty is obligatory; altruism is heartfelt. Socialization emphasizes empathy (feeling *with* others) and sympathy (feeling *for* others). In collectivist (traditional Asian, African, and Latin American, rural and semiagricultural) cultures, doing one's duty is valued above spontaneous acts. Social harmony is thought to depend on individuals performing their social roles, not individual motivation. Socialization emphasizes propriety and reciprocity.

hedonistic reasoning Moral reasoning that focuses on one's own wishes and needs.

altruism Helping behaviors that are motivated by assistance as an end in itself, without expectation of reward or recognition.

Laboratory studies in which children decide about sharing prizes with a peer highlight cultural differences. Chinese children are more willing than European American children to donate gifts or share food with classmates (Rao & Stewart, 1999; Stewart & McBride-Chang, 2000). They've been taught from an early age that food is not private property ("mine" or "yours") but communal property ("ours"). Mexican American children whose parents grew up in traditional communal villages are more generous with their peers than are European American children (Knight, Kagan, & Buriel, 1981). But the difference fades in third-generation immigrants, whose behavior more closely resembles their European American peers (Knight & Kagan, 1977), a pattern that suggests that acculturation to conventional U.S. norms may lead children to become less prosocial.

Within-Culture Variations Other developmental scientists have studied individual variations within cultures. The likelihood that children are prosocial shows relative continuity over childhood. In one study, Chinese children who were relatively helpful (in comparison to their peers) when they entered kindergarten remained relatively helpful 6 years later, at the beginning of adolescence (Chen, French, & Schneider, 2006). The same was true of children who are relatively self-centered and uncooperative. This evidence is particularly significant because different teachers rated children at different ages.

This continuity may reflect biological factors (genes and brain structures) as well as cultural and family expectations. Identical twins are more similar to each other than fraternal twins, suggesting that genetic factors predispose some children toward prosocial behaviors (Knafo & Plomin, 2006).

Aggression

"I was sitting on the bus one day and a boy came up and hit me for no reason." (12-year-old boy)

"Three boys called me a rat and harassed me and hit me with a broom." (12-year-old girl)

"I started hanging out with another girl, they didn't like her, they said, 'We won't be your friend anymore if you hang with her.'" (12-year-old girl)

physical aggression Acts such as hitting or pushing with an intent to harm.

verbal aggression Behavior such as threats, name calling, and yelling with an angry voice.

social aggression Behavior that is directed toward damaging another's self-esteem, social status, or both.

relational aggression Any behavior that is intended to harm someone by damaging or manipulating relationships with others.

As these interviews reported by Julie Paquette and Marion Underwood (1999) illustrate, aggression in middle childhood takes different forms, which you'll recall from an earlier chapter: **physical aggression** (hitting, pushing), **verbal aggression** (threats, name calling, yelling with an angry voice), and **social aggression** or **relational aggression** (acting in ways to undermine another's position in a group).

The amount of physical aggression declines in middle childhood (Dodge, Coie, & Lynam, 2006). By the time they have entered elementary school, children have expanded their array of strategies and skills for coping with conflicts, including better reading of social cues (being able to read frustration in someone's face), being able to delay a response (holding back before hitting someone), emotional self-regulation (calming oneself down), negotiation (working out a compromise with someone), and the use of the other forms of aggression, like verbal aggression, which means they have alternatives to pushing and hitting (Rubin, Bukowski, & Parker, 2006). There are, however, a small number of children (mostly boys) who continue to pick fights (Loeber et al., 1998).

In one large longitudinal study of more than 1,200 children, the most common form of early aggression (hitting others) was reported for about 70 percent of the children at age 2, for about 20 percent of the children at age 5, and for about 12 percent of the children at age 8 (NICHD Early Child Care Research Network, 2004b). Researchers have found that highly aggressive children process social information differently (Gifford-Smith & Rabiner, 2004). They are more likely to perceive ambiguous encounters or comments as hostile and respond in kind. For example, they interpret an accidental bump in the hallway as a deliberate shove, to which they respond with an even stronger shove.

Children who are highly aggressive at this age usually have a history of aggression in early childhood (Campbell et al., 2006). High levels of physical aggression in middle childhood also are associated with poverty (Bradley & Corwyn, 2002; McLoyd, 1990), coercive or harsh parenting, and parental use of physical discipline (spanking, hitting) (Dodge, Pettit, & Bates, 1994).

Social aggression is directed toward damaging another's self-esteem, social status, or both (Galen & Underwood, 1997). *Relational aggression* is an attempt to harm someone by manipulating or damaging their peer relationships (Crick & Grotpeter, 1995). These types of aggression may take the form of threatening to end a friendship unless the child does what the aggressor wants; excluding a peer from social gatherings or conversations; or spreading rumors designed to cause others to reject the child. Whereas physical aggression becomes less common in middle childhood (for both boys and girls), social and relational aggression does not decline (Underwood, Beron, & Gentsch, 2007). Indeed, there are some suggestions that social aggression becomes more common in girls during the transition between middle childhood and early adolescence (Cairns, Cairns, & Neckerman, 1989).

Stereotypes hold that boys are tough and girls are mean. Is social and relational aggression the female equivalent of physical aggression among boys? Yes and no. Boys do engage in more physical aggression than girls (Broidy et al., 2003), and girls do engage in more relational than physical aggression (Crick & Grotpeter, 1995). And some

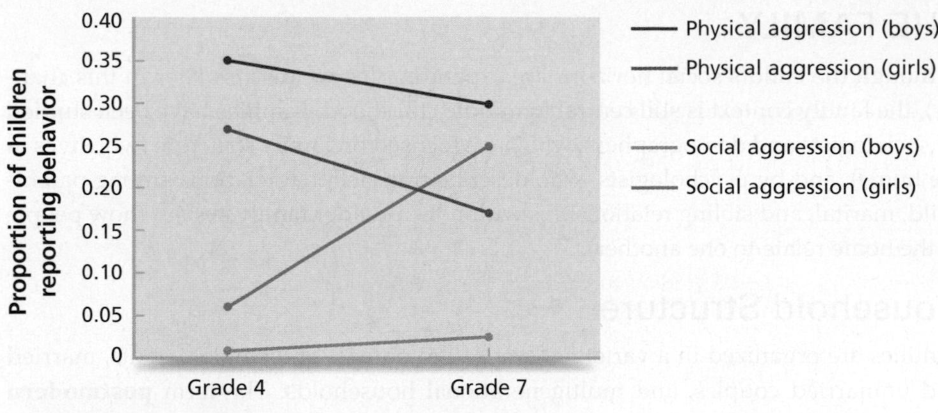

FIGURE 10.2

Differences in Social Versus Physical Aggression by Age and Gender

Physical aggression is less common in grade 7 than in grade 4 for both boys and girls. In contrast, social aggression is more common in girls in grade 7 than in grade 4. Boys displayed little social aggression at either age.

Source: Cairns, Cairns, & Neckerman (1989).

studies find that girls are more likely than boys to use social aggression (see Figure 10.2). However, boys also gossip, spread rumors, and practice exclusion (Crick, Casas, & Nelson, 2002; Underwood, 2002). To the extent that girls are more concerned about social relationships than boys are, they may suffer more from relational victimization (Crick, Ostrov, & Werner, 2006). (For a summary of this section, see "Interim Summary 10.2: Moral Development.")

INTERIM SUMMARY 10.2

Moral Development	
Moral Reasoning	■ Kohlberg identified three main levels of moral reasoning: **preconventional**, **conventional**, and **postconventional**. ■ Preconventional reasoning is based on rewards and punishments. ■ Conventional thinking focuses on how an individual will be judged by others. ■ Postconventional reasoning is guided by principles such as justice, fairness, and sanctity of life.
Prosocial Development	■ **Prosocial behaviors** (sharing, cooperating, helping, etc.) increase from early childhood through middle childhood. ■ The increase reflects better skill at reading others' emotional cues and better regulation of one's own emotions. ■ Prosocial behaviors also reflect cultural values and biological factors.
Aggression	■ Aggression can take several forms: **physical aggression**, **verbal aggression**, and **social or relational aggression**. ■ Physical aggression (hitting, pushing, etc.) displayed by children declines in middle childhood. ■ Social and relational aggression does not decline, and may even increase in middle childhood.

THE FAMILY

Although the child's social horizons are expanding (as we discuss later in this chapter), the family context is still central in middle childhood. Families have been studied by sociologists and demographers, who have focused on family structure (who lives in the home), and by psychologists, who describe transactional relations among parent-child, marital, and sibling relationships within the broader family system (how people in the home relate to one another).

Household Structure

postmodern family A term that describes the variation in modern-day families—two parents and single parents, married and unmarried couples, and multigenerational households.

Families are organized in a variety of ways: two parents and single parents, married and unmarried couples, and multigenerational households. The term **postmodern family** captures some of this variety (see Figure 10.3).

The *postmodern family* is not only varied but also fluid. A child may live in two or more types of households in the course of growing up. For example, she may live in a nuclear family with both biological parents in a home of their own (about one-quarter of the households). If her parents divorce (as do about half of married couples), she may live with her single mom for a time, and then her mom may remarry (typically within 3 to 4 years).

According to the U.S. Census (see Figure 10.3), 70 percent of children live in households with two married parents—counting biological, adoptive, and stepparents. (This count excludes two parents who are not married.) About one-quarter of children live with a single parent. Single parents may be divorced, widowed, or never married; that is, any parent who is not currently living with a spouse. According to the U.S. Census Bureau, 3.3 million children (5% of all children) live in step- or blended families, although the actual number is higher because the Census Bureau does not include cohabiting couples or families in which the noncustodial parent remarries. Some 3.9 million households are multigenerational families composed of three or more

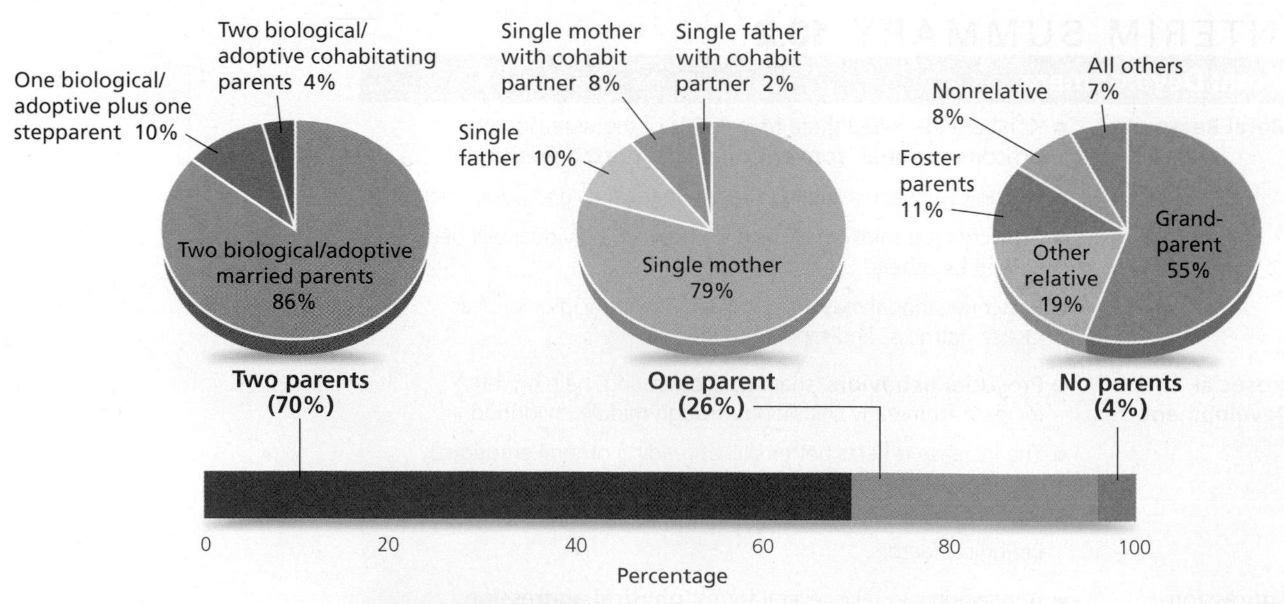

FIGURE 10.3

Proportion of U.S. Children Who Live in Different Types of Households

Postmodern families include a diverse array of households.

Source: Federal Interagency Forum on Child and Family Statistics (2007).

generations of parents and their families. Multigenerational households are more common in immigrant families, communities where price of housing is high, and households in which single parents need assistance with child care (U.S. Census Bureau, 2004).

These differences in household structure have implications for families' economic and social resources, and they also are linked to differences in parenting and children's development.

Two-Parent and One-Parent Households

Two-parent families have several built-in advantages (Hay & Nash, 2002). They enjoy higher incomes than single-parent families, and levels of education backgrounds tend to be higher. Their jobs are more stable, as are their living arrangements (Bumpass & Lu, 2000). They move less often and are more likely to own their homes.

Given these advantages, it is probably not surprising that mothers in two-parent households report fewer symptoms of depression and anxiety (Hay & Nash, 2002). Their parenting practices are more likely to be authoritative, rather than authoritarian or permissive. Children in two-parent households fare better, on average, than children in single-parent households. Their grades and test scores are higher. As a group, they have fewer internalizing and externalizing behavior problems.

This is not to say that growing up in a two-parent household is "good" and growing up in a single-parent household is "bad." There is considerable overlap in the two groups in parents' income, education, emotional well-being, and parenting styles. And there also is considerable overlap in children's academic performance, social competences, and behavior problems. Quality of parenting is a key factor in both two-parent and single-parent households.

Divorce Parents underestimate the intensity of their children's reactions to divorce (Clarke-Stewart & Brentano, 2006). Six- to eight-year-olds express grief and fear; they long for their parents to be reunited. Older school-age children react more with anger, often directed at the parent they hold responsible for the divorce. Acting out and rumination (repeatedly dwelling on the divorce) are common. One study found that a year later, 40 percent of children reported that they still thought about the divorce at least once a day (Weyer & Sandler, 1998).

Paul Amato (2001) conducted a meta-analysis of the effects of divorce on children, drawing on 67 different studies conducted in the 1990s. This analysis was used to supplement an earlier one that combined analyses across 92 studies. (Recall that meta-analyses combine findings across studies, taking into account sample sizes and effect sizes.) From these analyses, Amato concluded that the children of divorced parents score lower on measures of academic achievement, conduct, psychological adjustment, self-concept, and social relations, although there was substantial overlap between the two groups. For example, between 17 percent and 25 percent of the children of divorced families display elevated behavior problems compared with 10 percent to 15 percent of children in nondivorced households (Greene et al., 2006).

It is hard to generalize about the effects of divorce on children, because much depends on the conditions surrounding the event. Children fare better when there are amicable relations between ex-spouses, when their parents use authoritative parenting, and when child support arrangements are complied with. On the other hand, several factors increase the likelihood of negative effects of divorce on children's development (Clarke-Stewart & Brentano, 2006). The most important risk factors include the following:

- *A dramatic decrease in family income.* Even among couples who were relatively well off before they split up, divorce means a drop in income, averaging 13 percent to 35 percent per person (one reason is that families must maintain two households on the same amount of income) (Peterson, 1996). Children who experience a sharp decline in their family's income are twice as likely to develop behavior problems compared to other children of divorce.

- *Abandonment (or fear of abandonment).* Children take their parents' presence for granted, as part of the natural order. When a parent moves out, this security is undermined. About one-third of fathers have no contact with their children at all following a divorce. Only one-quarter see their children as often as once a week, and contact decreases with time.
- *Diminished parenting.* In the year after a divorce, newly single parents tend to be preoccupied with their own issues, less attentive to their children, inconsistent, and irritable (Belsky & Jaffee, 2006). Often they are less concerned about household routines, such as regular family meals. They are less likely to be involved in school-related activities. Authoritative parenting often gives way to authoritarian, permissive, or detached parenting (see Chapter 8 for a description of these parenting styles).
- *Parental conflict.* The conflicts that led the couple to end their marriage may spill over into postdivorce relations. Children are caught in the middle and may be pressured by both parents to choose sides.
- *Dislocation.* Divorce typically means that the child moves to a new home—or two new homes in cases of joint custody—often in a new neighborhood and school district. At a time when he or she needs stability, the child is cut off from familiar, everyday sources of social support and is required to make new friends, meet new neighbors, and so on. Dislocation compounds other problems.

Longitudinal studies indicate that the negative effects of divorce generally resolve 1 to 2 years after the divorce (Hetherington, Cox, & Cox, 1982). Fear, disbelief, and the fantasy that parents will reunite fade. Behavior problems, especially aggression, decline markedly. One exception to this general rule concerns boys' academic performance, which does not rebound. Even 5 years later, boys whose parents split up have test scores and grades that are below the average for boys from intact families (Sun & Li, 2001, 2002).

Other Postmodern Families

Postmodern families also include blended families, adoptive families, and those with same-sex parents. Are these different family environments related to differences in child developmental outcomes?

Blended Families The composition of blended families varies. A child may have a stepfather, a stepmother, stepbrothers and stepsisters, and half-sisters and half-brothers. They may or may not live together, full- or part-time. In general, preschoolers adapt more readily to a new family than school-age children and adolescents do, for several reasons (Clarke-Stewart & Brentano, 2006). Preschoolers don't have as long a history living with both parents. Older children are becoming more independent and peer oriented, and they don't necessarily want another adult authority in their lives. Daughters usually have more difficulty accepting remarriage than do sons (Hetherington & Clingempeel, 1992). The happier a mother and her new partner are, the more negative parent-child relationships are (the opposite of the pattern in intact families). Children do not easily or willingly share their parent with someone new.

On average, children in blended families have somewhat lower grades and scores on achievement tests, and report more symptoms of depression, than do children in intact, nuclear families. But the difference is small, with substantial overlap between the groups (Clarke-Stewart & Brentano, 2006). As we saw in our earlier discussion of sex differences in personality and interests, very often the similarities among children from different groups (for instance, those from intact versus blended families) are more impressive than the differences.

Adoption More than 1 million U.S. children are adopted, and nearly that many adults are seeking to adopt. In the past three decades, the stigma for being an unwed parent has declined, and the number of healthy infants available for adoption in the United States has dropped. As a result, international adoptions (notably from China, Russia, Guatemala, and South Korea) have tripled. In 2004, Americans adopted about 75,000 children—52,000 from within the United States and 23,000 from abroad (Child Welfare League of America, 2007). In addition, larger numbers of older children, children with special needs, and sibling groups are being adopted—by married couples, committed but unmarried couples, and singles (Wrobel, Hendrickson, & Grotevant, 2006).

Like families in general, adoptive families are more diverse than ever before.

Do adopted children differ from nonadopted children? To answer this question researchers have compared adopted children to their biological siblings who have remained with their biological parents. They have also compared adopted children to their adoptive siblings who were born to the adopting parents. A meta-analysis of these studies found that adoptees had significantly higher scores on IQ tests, and higher grades in school, than their biological siblings who remained with their biological parents (van IJzendoorn & Juffer, 2005). Comparison of the adopted children with their adoptive siblings are mixed (see Figure 10.4). Their IQs are similar to those of their siblings in their adopted family, but they lag behind them in school performance. They are twice as likely as their adoptive siblings to be referred for special education. Others report that adoptees are more likely than other children to be in counseling or psychotherapy (Miller et al., 2000; Wrobel, Hendrickson, & Gortevant, 2006).

The problems of some adoptees and their families do not mean that adoption is "bad" for children and should be discouraged (Miller et al., 2000). Adoption clearly is good for children who might otherwise live in a series of foster homes or with families who are not able to care for them or do not want them. And a majority of young adoptees are functioning well. However, adoption policies and practices might be changed to provide long-term resources for adoptive parents, should they need them.

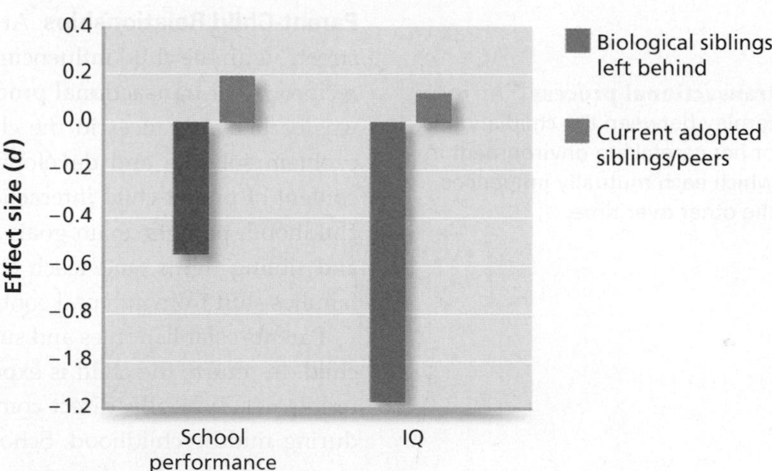

FIGURE 10.4

School Performance and IQ of Adopted Children Compared with Biological Siblings Left Behind and Current Nonbiological Siblings

The negative *d*s mean that the adopted children showed better school performance and higher IQ scores than their biological siblings left behind. The positive *d*s mean that the adopted children scored lower than their current nonbiological siblings. Larger *d*s mean larger differences.

Source: van IJzendoorn, Marinus, Juffer, & Femmie (2005).

Gay and Lesbian Parents Other households are headed by gay, lesbian, or bisexual parents. More than one-third of lesbian women have given birth, and one in six gay men has either fathered or adopted a child. An estimated 65,500 adopted children (4% of all adopted children in the United States) are living with a gay or lesbian parent, as are approximately 14,100 foster children (3% of the total) (Gates et al., 2007).

Developmental scientists have studied children of homosexual parents, mostly lesbian mothers.

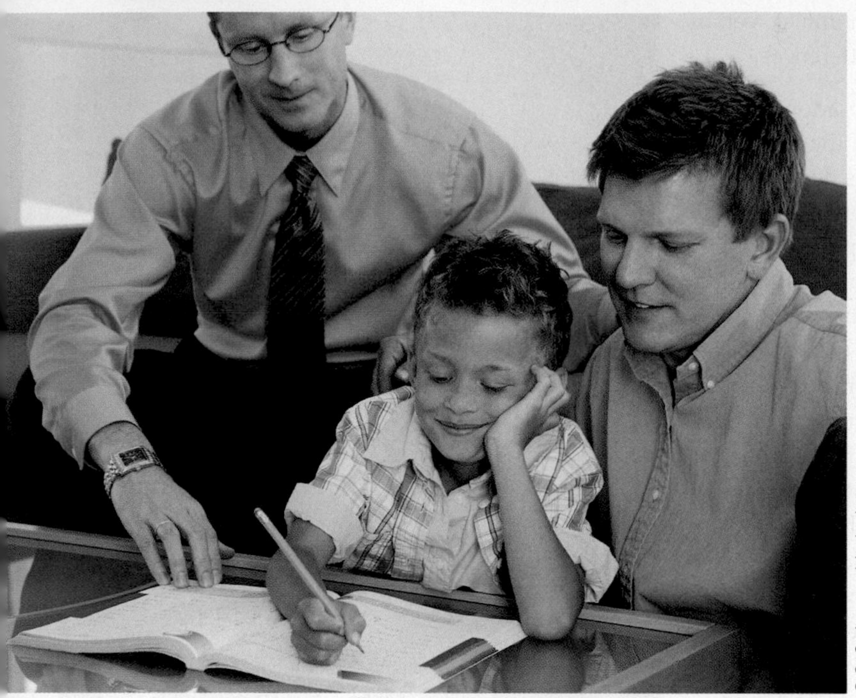

Postmodern families include children who are growing up with same-sex parents.

Children of same-sex parents are similar to children of opposite-sex parents in self-concepts, preferences for same-sex playmates and activities in childhood, social competence, school grades, and quality of family relationships (Patterson, 2006; Wainright, Russell, & Patterson, 2004). Further research of larger, nationally representative samples is needed, however, before definitive conclusions can be made because current research has utilized relatively small community-based samples.

The Family System

Urie Bronfenbrenner (1979) is an influential theorist whose work we discussed in Chapters 1 and 2. Bronfenbrenner argued that looking at static "social addresses" such as single-parent and two-parent households is not enough. To understand development, he contended, researchers needed to study the dynamic interplay between individuals, their surroundings, and psychological processes over time (Bronfenbrenner & Morris, 1998). It is to a more dynamic systemic analysis of families that we now turn.

The family can be conceptualized as an overarching *system* of relationships composed of several subsystems (parent-child relationships, parent-parent relations, and sibling relations) that have their own features and implications for children's development, while being part of the family as a whole (see Figure 10.5).

transactional process An interplay between the child and his or her caretaking environment in which each mutually influences the other over time.

Parent-Child Relationships At every age, the parent-child relationship is a "two-way street," with the child influencing the parent and the parent influencing the child. This reciprocity or **transactional process** becomes more visible in middle childhood than it was earlier. Advances in the child's cognitive and social skills (perspective taking, problem solving, and developing ideas of fairness) require parents to adjust. The content of parent-child interaction changes (Russell, Mize, & Bissaker, 2002). In early childhood, parents' main goals are to establish routines, control emotional outbursts and sibling fights, and teach children to care for themselves. In middle childhood, families shift from parental control to *co-regulation*.

Parents establish rules and supervise, but they leave many daily decisions up to the child. In return, the child is expected to keep them informed of his or her plans (and problems). Typically, direct commands decrease, and reasoning and debate increase during middle childhood. School-age children are more likely than preschoolers to argue, and when they lose, to sulk, mope, or give parents the silent treatment.

Common sources of conflict and negotiation include how much time the child watches TV and talks on the telephone, homework (when, where, and how it is done), and getting along with others (especially siblings). Ideally, parents and children begin to solve problems together and make joint decisions, achieving a balance between connectedness and closeness on the one hand, and independence and autonomy on the other (Cox & Paley, 2003).

In middle childhood, as in early childhood (see Chapter 8), parental styles vary (Belsky & Jaffee, 2006). How parents establish and enforce rules, and the overall tone of parent-child interactions, are linked to both the child's adjustment and achievement. Parental warmth, emotional support, and appropriate expectations are associated with children's competence, social skills, academic achievement, positive self-image, and healthy emotion regulation (NICHD Early Child Care Research Network, 2008). In contrast, parental harshness, coercion, and punitiveness is linked to aggression and other externalizing behavior (including bullying), as well as depression and other internalizing problems (Dearing, 2004; Pettit et al., 2001; Shumow, Vandell, & Posner, 1998). This pattern is observed in Western, individualistic societies such as the United States as well in as Eastern, collectivist societies such as China (Chen et al., 2001; Zhou et al., 2004).

Another change in relations between parents and children in middle childhood is in the amount of time they spend together. Children are developing lives of their own. Parents spend about half as much time supervising, entertaining, and caring for children in middle childhood as they did in early childhood, although there is lots of variability (Russell et al., 2002).

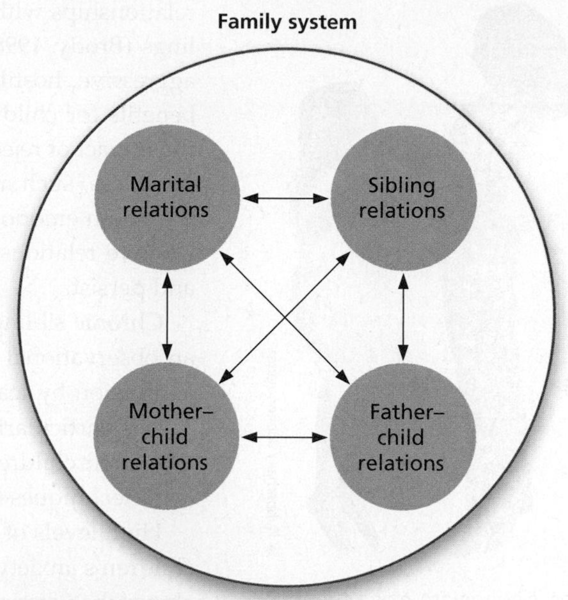

FIGURE 10.5

The Family System

The family system is composed of subsystems (parent-child, parent-parent, and sibling relationships) that influence and are influenced by other relationships within the family.

Source: Parke & Buriel (2006).

Marital Relationships The quality of the parents' relationship with each other is another aspect of the family system that has implications for children's development in middle childhood. Marital hostilities can lead to diminished parenting because parents are short-tempered, depressed, or otherwise psychologically unavailable (Cummings & Davies, 1994; Grych & Fincham, 2001). At the same time, problems in parenting can lead to marital conflict. A couple may not agree on how best to raise a child. An especially difficult child or a child who is chronically ill may put added strains on the marriage.

Marital problems have both direct and indirect effects on children. Exposure to unresolved marital conflicts and frequent, hostile confrontations between parents can depress children's moods (Katz & Gottman, 1993; Kerig, 1996) and undermine both short-term coping skills and long-term adjustment (Grych & Fincham, 2001). However, not all marital conflicts are associated with negative developmental outcomes. Family expressiveness helps children to interpret and convey emotions in constructive ways (Parke & Buriel, 2006). When parents disagree in low to moderate tones and resolve conflicts in a warm, supportive family context, children observe how to negotiate and settle disagreements without rupturing relationships (Cummings & Davies, 1994).

Sibling Relationships For families that have more than one child, sibling relationships are another component of the family system. These relationships run the gamut (Dunn, 2002). Some sibling pairs are affectionate, cooperative, and supportive. Others are irritating, hostile, and aggressive toward one another. Some ignore one another. Many are ambivalent, vacillating between cooperative and antagonistic interchanges.

What explains differences in sibling pairs? Temperament is one factor. The closer the match between siblings, the more likely their social interactions will be affectionate, conflicted, or both (Brody, 1998; Munn & Dunn, 1989). Gender also makes a difference. From middle childhood on, sisters exhibit more warmth and intimacy than do brothers or brother-sister pairs (Brody, 1998). For brothers, "close" means doing things together; for sisters, it means sharing secrets. As you will read later, a similar difference characterizes boys' and girls' friendships outside the family.

Consistent with predictions of a family systems perspective, the quality of parent-child relationships is associated with the quality of sibling relationships. More positive

Some siblings are close friends who seek one another out as playmates. Others have frequent disagreements and conflicts. And some have emotionally intense relationships that combine positive and negative emotions.

relationships with parents are linked to warmer and friendlier relations between siblings (Brody, 1998). Conversely, harsh parent-child relationships are associated with aggressive, hostile sibling relations. Harmonious sibling relationships have tangible benefits for children's development. A positive relationship with a sibling can mute the impact of rejection and isolation by peers (East & Rook, 1992). During stressful experiences, such as a parental illness or relocation, siblings can provide one another with both emotional and instrumental, practical support (Dunn, 2002). Children with positive relationships are higher in self-regulation and the ability to set goals, plan, and persist.

Chronic sibling conflict is associated with both short- and long-term problems. In an observational study, Patterson (1986) found that siblings reinforce one another's aggression by teasing, taunting, fighting back, and otherwise escalating the conflict. This is particularly true when parents fight a lot and do not intervene in siblings' battles. Such children are doubly handicapped: They learn to use coercion and do *not* learn techniques for de-escalation, compromise, and reconciliation.

High levels of sibling conflict in middle childhood are associated with increases in children's anxiety, depressed mood, and delinquent behavior in adolescence, over and above that explained by parental hostility or marital conflict (Stocker, Burwell, & Briggs, 2002). However, some sibling conflict—balanced with supportiveness, in an atmosphere of general goodwill—is beneficial (Brody, 1998). Conflict provides opportunities for siblings to vent their emotions and to express their feelings openly—without fear of loss, as might be the case with a classmate or friend. Reciprocal self-assertion, discussion, and compromise are lessons in anger management. Siblings can learn from each other how to express themselves and why it's important to consider another's feelings, as well as techniques for breaking tension. (For a summary of this section, see "Interim Summary 10.3: The Family.")

PEERS

Talking and gossiping in the school cafeteria, hanging out at the mall or a playground, watching TV, playing video games, singing in a youth choir—peers are an important part of life in middle childhood. Peer groups are less closely supervised by adults now and occur in more varied settings, including schools, playgrounds, churches, shopping malls, and skating rinks.

Time spent socializing and playing competitive games—both formal and informal—increases. Games with rules are one of the significant advances in peer play from early childhood (Piaget, 1962). To play basketball, for example, a child must be able to see the game not only from her own position as guard, but also from the other players' points of view. She needs to anticipate what the other players will do, as well as what they expect from her (an example of multiple perspective-taking). Athletic leagues organized and managed by adults provide practice in playing by the rules.

The pickup games children organize on their own require different social and cognitive skills. Children have to improvise the rules and decide such issues as how to select teams so the game is fair, what to do about an odd number of participants, and what constitutes "out-of-bounds" on their own, through negotiation. No one child has authority over the others; they have to work things out together. Time spent on the playing fields provides rich opportunities to hone social and cognitive competencies as well as physical skills.

Friendships

Friendships are an important part of children's experience of middle childhood (Rubin et al., 2006). These relationships are defined by reciprocity and mutuality. Each child particularly likes the other and counts the other as a "friend" (Hartup, 1992; Newcomb

INTERIM SUMMARY 10.3

The Family	
Household Structure	■ Refers to the types and numbers of individuals who live in a household; examples include single-parent and two-parent households and multigenerational families.
Two-Parent and One-Parent Households	■ On average, two-parent households have higher incomes, more education, more stable jobs, and more stable living arrangements. Mothers in two-parent households report less depression and anxiety. They are more likely to use authoritative parenting. ■ Children in two-parent households (on average) have higher grades and fewer behavior problems. ■ Negative effects of divorce generally resolve 1 to 2 years after the divorce.
Other Postmodern Families	■ On average, preschoolers adapt more readily to a parent's remarriage than do older children, and sons typically adjust more readily than daughters. Children in blended families have somewhat lower grades and achievement test scores than other two-parent families, but there is lots of overlap between the two groups. ■ Children who are adopted have higher IQ scores and school grades than biological siblings who remain with biological parents, but their grades tend to be lower than those of their siblings in their adopted family. ■ Children of same-sex parents are similar to children of opposite-sex parents in self-concepts, playmate preferences, social competence, school grades, and quality of family relationships.
The Family System	■ The family can be conceptualized as a system composed of interrelated subsystems (parent-child, parent-parent, and sibling relationships) that affect and are affected by other subsystems. Each subsystem also has its own features and implications for child development. ■ Parent-child relationships are a "two-way street" in which the child influences the parent and the parent influences the child. This reciprocity or **transactional process** becomes more visible in middle childhood than it was earlier. ■ Relationships with siblings run the gamut from highly positive to highly negative. Some siblings have relationships that are highly charged with both positive and negative emotions.

& Bagwell, 1995). Friendships are voluntary relationships, chosen by the children, unlike the children whose parents invite for play dates in early childhood or familial relations with siblings or cousins (Hartup & Abecassis, 2002). Children expect their friends to provide more companionship and intimacy than other classmates.

Friendship expectations change over middle childhood (Rubin et al., 2006). At the beginning of this period (ages 7 to 8), perceptions about friendships and selections of friends are based on rewards and costs (Bigelow, 1977). Friends are fun to be with (the reward); nonfriends are difficult or uninteresting (the costs). There also is an element of convenience in early friendship, such as living near the other child. Friendships deepen toward the end of middle childhood (ages 10 to 11), as shared values and shared social understandings become more important. Friendships among preadolescents are more

© David Papazian / Corbis

Children's impromptu games provide opportunities for perspective taking, problem solving, and negotiation.

exclusive, individualistic, and stable than those of younger children (Berndt, 2004).

Boys' friendships and girls' friendships differ qualitatively (Rubin et al., 2006). Girls' friendships are characterized by intimacy, self-disclosure, and validation ("I know just what you mean/how you feel"). Boys' friendships are characterized more by physical activity, which doesn't require self-disclosure, and often develop in the context of larger social networks. Because they are so close, girls' friendships also are more fragile (Benenson & Christakos, 2003). A violation of confidences may end the relationship.

How do children pick one another as friends? Children are drawn to other children who are "like them." Researchers call this **homophily**. Friends tend to be similar not only in sex and age, but also in academic performance, interests, shyness, sociability, popularity, and ethnicity (Rubin et al., 2006). There is no evidence that opposites attract (Hartup & Abecassis, 2002). Which characteristics draw friends together depends on what interests them most (Hamm, 2000). For example, academic performance is most similar among friends who consider academic achievement important. Friends also have similar ideas about people and relationships.

Children are more likely to maintain friendships that are higher in quality. Higher-quality friendships are ones that are mutually supportive and cooperative, and are less conflictual. Friendships are more likely to terminate when the children's conversations are negative and nonsupportive, although sometimes friendships cease when children simply stop interacting (Hartup & Abecassis, 2002; Rizzo, 1989). Losing a friend can have important consequences. One study found that 10-year-olds who lost a best friend and did not replace that friend during the school year were at risk for victimization by classmates (Wojslawowicz et al., 2006).

homophily The tendency of individuals to associate and bond with others who are similar or "like" themselves.

peer group A group of children who interact frequently and who see themselves, and are seen by others, as having a common identity. Peer groups have boundaries that define who is in and who is out of the group, a structure or hierarchy, and norms about what is acceptable or unacceptable among the group members.

peer group status An indication of children's relative standing in the peer group as measured by peer nominations of acceptance and rejection.

sociometric nomination A research method used by developmental scientists to determine peer group status. Typically children are asked to nominate or select three classmates they like and three classmates that they do not like.

Peer Groups

A **peer group** is a collection of children who interact frequently and who see themselves, and are seen by others, as having a common identity—for example, Mrs. Jones's third-grade class, the Strikers soccer team, or "the popular kids" (Rubin et al., 2006). Like other social groups, peer groups have boundaries defining who is inside and who is outside (other classes and grades); a structure or hierarchy (e.g., children who are leaders or followers, popular or unpopular); and their own norms or rules about what is acceptable or unacceptable behavior among the ranks.

Some writers, such as Judith Rich Harris (1995), hold that peer groups play a central role in socialization during this period. Children want to be accepted and liked by their peers, a member of a peer group. They act and dress and talk in ways that allow them to fit in. They also evaluate themselves in comparison to others in the group. Whether Harris is correct that peers are more influential than family at this age is debatable (Collins et al., 2000; Vandell, 2000), but peers are clearly significant.

In elementary school classrooms, some children are better liked by classmates than are others. Developmental scientists determine a child's **peer group status** by asking classmates questions like "Who are three children you like to play with?" and "Who are three children you do not like to play with?"—a research procedure called **sociometric nomination**. From these nominations, researchers can study peer acceptance (based on how many positive nominations a child receives) and peer rejection (based on many negative nominations a child receives). This makes it possible to divide children into five categories: popular, rejected, controversial, average, and neglected (Coie, Dodge, & Coppotelli, 1982), as seen in Table 10.3.

TABLE 10.3 Sociometric Status Differences in Peer Acceptance and Peer Rejection

		PEER ACCEPTANCE (POSITIVE NOMINATIONS)		
		HIGH		LOW
PEER REJECTION (NEGATIVE NOMINATIONS)	HIGH	Controversial		Rejected
			Average	
	LOW	Popular		Neglected

Source: Coie, Dodge, & Coppotelli (1982).

Popular children receive many positive nominations and few negative nominations. Studies of these children conducted in a variety of settings show that they are skilled at initiating and maintaining positive interactions with their peers (Dodge, McClaskey, & Feldman, 1985). They are successful at joining groups of children on the playground because they focus on the group's activity rather than trying to call attention to themselves. They can be assertive but usually do not interfere with the actions or goals of other children. They are good at recognizing emotions, acknowledging their own feelings, and identifying the cause of their own or another's emotions (Edwards, Manstead, & McDonald, 1984). Teachers and observers, as well as other children, see them as cooperative, friendly, and helpful (Pakaslahti, Karjalainen, & Keltikangas-Jarvinen, 2002). About 12 percent of children are classified as "popular" (Terry & Coie, 1991).

There is a distinction between children who are widely *liked* as playmates or accepted by their peers (sociometric popularity) and children who are nominated as "most popular" (prestige popularity). Children who receive a lot of nominations of "most popular" can be somewhat aggressive—they like to get their own way—whereas children who are widely liked by their classmates are not pushy or antagonistic (Rubin et al., 2006).

Rejected children receive few positive nominations and many negative nominations. Sociometric studies conducted in the laboratory, classroom, and playground indicate that rejected children typically have a number of shortcomings—limited perspective-taking, poor communication skills, a tendency to perceive ambiguous social situations as hostile, and low academic achievement (Newcomb, Bukowski, & Pattee, 1993). About 12 percent of children are classified as rejected (Terry & Cole, 1991).

Many rejected children are aggressive (Haselager et al., 2002). They have acquired reputations for spoiling games with disruptive behavior, negative behavior (such as verbal insults), and physical aggression. They are viewed as troublemakers. But some rejected children are the opposite: withdrawn. They ignore social overtures and keep to themselves. School-age children, who value social interaction and social competence, see them as weird.

Developmental outcomes for rejected children are worrisome. Peer rejection predicts later problems at school, including being held back a grade, truancy, and dropping

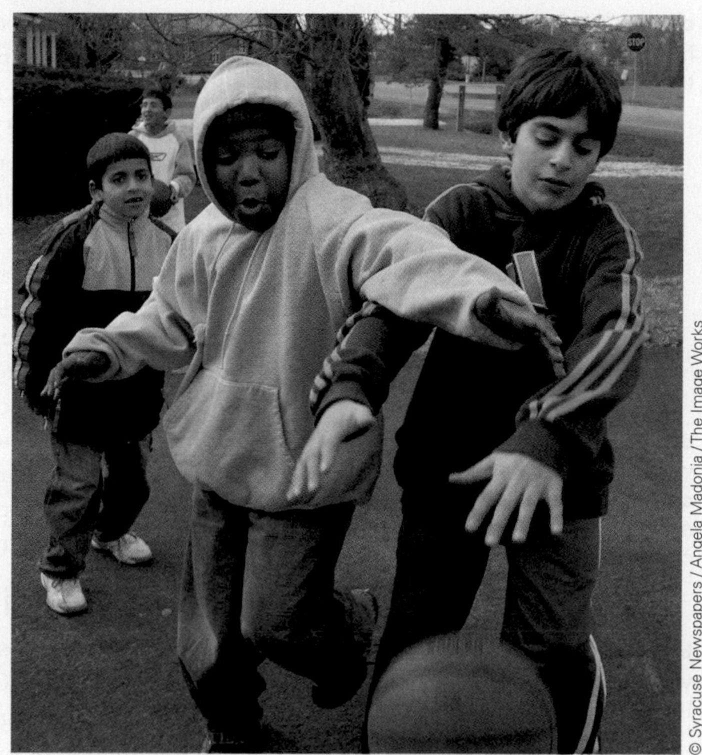

Boys' friendships are often characterized by physical activity in the context of larger peer groups.

out (Hymel et al., 2002). There also is evidence that aggressive rejected children band together, forming deviant cliques that encourage delinquency (Patterson, Capaldi, & Bank, 1991). Withdrawn rejected children, in contrast, are at risk for internalizing problems, including depression and loneliness (Hymel et al., 2002). These serious consequences of peer rejection have led schools, parents, and clinicians to develop social competence coaching programs to improve skills in perspective-taking and emotional modulation (Bierman, 2004).

Controversial children receive many positive and many negative nominations. This group shares characteristics with both popular and rejected children. They can be aggressive and disruptive, but also helpful, cooperative, and even sensitive to others. This classification is rare (6-7% of children) (Hymel et al., 2002).

Neglected children are low in both positive and negative nominations. Only about 6 to 7 percent of children fall in this group at any one time (Terry & Coie, 1991). This classification is often temporary, with considerable movement between the average and neglected group classifications (Newcomb et al., 1993; Terry & Coie, 1991). Not surprisingly, then, neglected children tend to be similar to average children in sociability and aggression (Newcomb et al., 1993). Chronic neglect by one's peers, on the other hand, is associated with timidity, lack of social skills, and internalizing behavior problems.

Average children (58–60% of children) receive some positive and some negative peer nominations. Moderately sociable (not aggressive or withdrawn), with adequate cognitive skills, they do not stand out in the group (Newcomb et al., 1993).

Average, popular, and rejected children are more likely than neglected and controversial children to maintain their peer group status over time (Cillessen, Bukowski, & Haselager, 2000; Hymel et al., 2002). In one study, about 41 percent of elementary students had the same status 1 year later. About one-quarter of the students maintained the same classification over a 4-year period. Reputations in the group, as well as the children's behaviors, contribute to this stability.

Networks and Cliques

cliques Voluntary, friendship-based peer networks, generally of the same sex and age.

During elementary school, children organize themselves in clusters, or **cliques**, that are voluntary, friendship-based peer networks (Bagwell et al., 2000). The key word here is "voluntary," which distinguishes cliques from peer groups that schools or clubs create. Typically a clique is made up of three to nine children of the same sex and race. By age 11, most children report that they are part of a clique and that most of their peer interactions take place within this clique (Rubin et al., 2006).

Cliques are based on similarities. Studies in many countries (Canada, Finland, the United States, and China, among others) find that clique members are similar in the levels of, and attitudes about, aggression, bullying, school motivation, and school performance (Chen, Change, & He, 2003; Rubin et al., 2006). Given self-selection, similarities, and children's desire to fit in, cliques tend to reinforce minicultures of their own. Some cliques reinforce academic achievement, involvement in music or sports, or particular hairstyles or clothes, all in an effort to fit in. Of concern is **deviancy training**, in which friends or clique members praise, encourage, model, and reward one another for aggression or antisocial behavior (Dishion, Poulin, & Burraston, 2001). Membership in these cliques is linked to increases in misconduct and delinquent acts.

deviancy training A process in which clique members praise, encourage, model, and reward one another for aggression or antisocial behavior.

Bullies and Victims

bullying Aggression by an individual that is repeatedly directed toward particular peers (victims).

Bullying refers to aggression by an individual that is repeatedly directed toward particular peers (victims) (Olweus, 1993; Rubin et al., 2006). Bullying may be physical (hitting, kicking, shoving, tripping), verbal (teasing, harassing, name-calling), or social (public humiliation or exclusion). Bullying differs from other forms of aggression in that it is characterized by specificity (bullies direct their acts to certain peers) and by an imbalance of power between the bully and the victim (Olweus, 1993; Rigby, 2002). An older child bullies a younger one; a large child picks on a small, weaker one; a verbally assertive child torments a shy, quiet child. It is not bullying when equals have an occasional fight or disagreement. Bullies are more likely to use force unemotionally and outside of the flow of an ongoing conflict (Perry, Perry, & Kennedy, 1992).

About 1 in 10 children are the victims of bullying (Olweus, 1993). Research has revealed two distinct types of victims (Rubin et al., 2006). The first are children who are shy, anxious, and socially withdrawn, which makes them easy prey. Often they do not have friends to protect them. But other victims are high in aggression themselves and engage in irritating behavior that elicits aggression. Other children see them as "asking for it." Thus, bullying and victimization sometimes go hand in hand. These two types of victims have been seen in North America, South Asia, and East Asia (Schwartz et al., 2002).

Ordinarily we think of bullying as a male problem, but girls also can be bullies. With girls, bullying is more often relational; that is, the threat or actual betrayal of confidences, or shutting the victim out of social groups (Underwood, 2002). Bully–victim relationships in middle childhood usually occur between same-sex pairs, although boys may harass girls and girls may pick on boys (Rigby, 2002).

A study of bullies and victims found three broad styles of coping with victimization (Wilton, Craig, & Pepler, 2000). Some victims responded with aggression, anger, and contempt, which was not effective in stopping the bully; others, with passive capitulation or submissive avoidance, which wasn't effective, either. Very few (only 8%) responded with adaptive and constructive strategies such as getting help. Overall, the best protection against bullies is to have buddies or friends. (For a summary of this section, see ("Interim Summary 10.4: Peers.")

INTERIM SUMMARY 10.4

Peers	
Friendship	■ Friendships are defined by reciprocity in which each child counts the other as a "friend." Friendships deepen toward the end of middle childhood as shared values and shared social understandings become more important. Friends tend to be similar in sex, age, ethnicity, academic performance, interests, sociability, and popularity.
Peer Groups	■ A **peer group** is a group of children who interact frequently and who see themselves, and are seen by others, as having a common identity. ■ **Peer group status** is assessed by **sociometric nominations** in which children identify classroom peers they like and do not like. Based on their positive and negative nominations, five types of peer group status have been identified: popular, rejected, controversial, neglected, and average.
Networks and Cliques	■ **Cliques** are voluntary, friendship-based peer groups. Like friends, members of cliques tend to be similar in attributes, attitudes, and behaviors. Cliques tend to reinforce mini-cultures of their own. Some cliques reinforce academic achievement, involvement in music or sports, or particular hairstyles or clothes; others reward one another for agression or antisocial behavior.
Bullies and Victims	■ **Bullying** is aggression that is repeatedly directed from an individual to particular peers (victims). It is characterized by specificity and an imbalance of power between the bully and the victim. ■ Some victims are shy, anxious, and socially withdrawn, which makes them easy prey. Others are high in aggression and engage in irritating behavior that elicits aggression from others.

THE BROADER SOCIAL CONTEXT

Children's horizons expand during this period. Children are going to school full time, spending much more time with peers, and participating in a variety of activities away from their families. Most have extensive exposure to television, computers, and video games. They know their way around the neighborhood and often the Internet as well. The broader social context has more direct impact on development now than in early childhood.

To call middle childhood "the school years" would be telling only part of the story. There is more to childhood than going to school! Even on school days, children spend only about 50 percent of their waking hours in classrooms (Hofferth & Sandberg, 2001). Of course, schooling is critically important, as we discussed in Chapter 9. It's just that what happens outside of school during the other 50 percent of their time also is important. What are children doing after school and on weekends and in the summer?

Organized Activities

The majority of school-age children participate in at least one organized, out-of-school activity supervised by adults other than their parents (Vandell, Pierce, & Dadisman, 2005). These activities may be scheduled monthly, weekly, or even several times a week. Although employed parents may enroll children in activities to ensure that they are supervised while parents are at work, the primary goal of these activities is the child's enrichment and enjoyment.

Children can play in baseball leagues, belong to the 4-H and Scouts, take violin lessons or gymnastics, sing in a church choir. Some, like Alexander Williams, one of the boys described at the beginning of this chapter, participate in multiple activities. Sports are the most common organized activity, but other activities are also common, as shown in Figure 10.6 (National Center for Education Statistics, 2006).

Participation varies somewhat for boy and girls and for younger (grades K–2) and older (grades 3–5) children. Boys are more likely to participate in sports, whereas girls are more likely to participate in clubs and take lessons (Carver & Iruka, 2006). Volunteer work and academic activities are more common for older children. Participation also differs for different ethnic groups. African American children are more likely to participate in religious activities, Asian children in music activities, and Caucasian and Hispanic children in sports.

Whether children participate in organized activities depends in large part on the family's economic resources, because activities are often funded by fees paid by the family. Children whose families have higher incomes, more parental education, and two parents are more likely to participate in organized activities than children who are less well-off (Carver & Iruka,

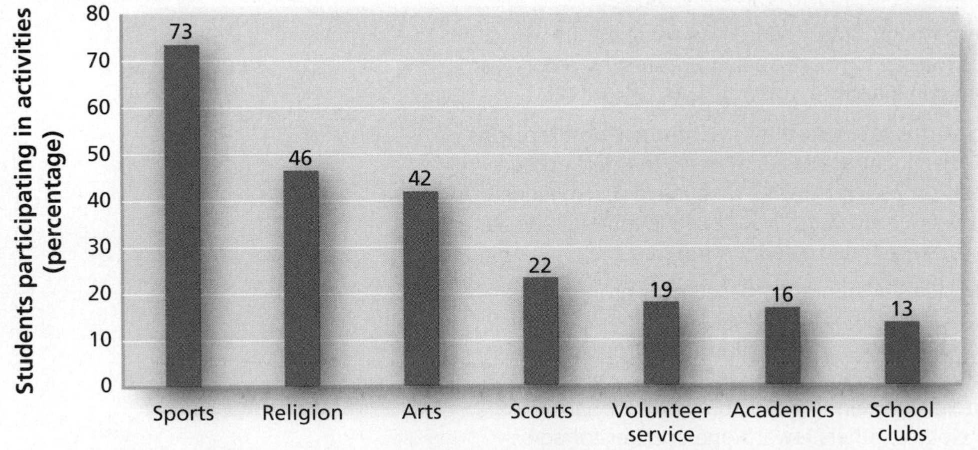

FIGURE 10.6

Percentages of U.S. Students (K–Grade 8) Who Participate in Different Types of Afterschool Activities

Organized sports, religious activities, and arts activities (music and dance lessons) are the most common afterschool activities for students (kindergarten through Grade 8).

Source: Carver & Iruka (2006).

2006). In one survey, 75 percent of children from "non-poor" families participated in sports, lessons, or clubs compared with 57 percent of "poor" families (National Center for Education Statistics, 2006).

Participation in organized activities is linked to improvements in both academic and social skills. In one longitudinal study of more than 900 children, those who consistently participated in an organized activity during kindergarten and first grade obtained higher math achievement test scores than did children who did not participate in these activities, controlling for child and family factors and children's earlier math skills (NICHD Early Child Care Research Network, 2004a). In another study, low-income urban children who participated in organized activities in grades 3 to 5 displayed higher test scores and better emotional adjustment in grade 5 (Posner & Vandell, 1999).

Others have found evidence that participation in organized activities outside of school improved peer acceptance scores of children who had been rejected by classmates the previous year, perhaps because the activities provided rejected children with opportunities to learn social norms and skills, and to showcase skills that were not visible in the classroom (Sandstrom & Coie, 1999).

Researchers have identified several factors that may be contributing to these positive outcomes. Mathematical reasoning is embedded in sports, music, art, cooking, and cookie sales. Many of these activities require teamwork and cooperation with peers. Because the activities are voluntary and of interest to the children, they provide opportunities for extended periods of engagement, effort, concentration, and enjoyment, which foster positive youth development (Larson, 2000; Vandell et al., 2005).

Some writers have worried that children are overscheduled with organized activities, a phenomenon labeled "the hurried child" (Elkind, 2001). Although some children have little downtime, this is the exception, not the rule. School-age children spend, on average, about 13 hours a week watching television and 12 hours a week playing, fully half of their discretionary free time (Hofferth & Curtin, 2005). They spend, on average, about 5 hours in sports and 1 hour in religious activities. Low-income and working-class children spend considerably less time in organized activities and considerably more time watching TV.

Afterschool Programs

Afterschool programs are a particular type of organized group activity that is held 4 or 5 days a week between the end of the school day and 5:00 to 6:00 P.M. Typically, they offer an array of activities (sports, arts and crafts, games, music, drama, and homework time). A primary goal of many programs is to provide supervision to children while their parents are at work.

In the 1990s, most afterschool programs were located in child-care centers, community centers, and churches (Vandell et al., 2005). Parents paid fees or tuition for a child to attend. Today, most programs are located in schools and receive some local, state, and federal monies to support their operations. A well-known example is 21st Century Community Learning Centers, a $40 million demonstration project started in 1998 that is now a $1 billion program serving more than 1 million students in 6,800 schools (Mahoney & Zigler, 2006). This program is free of charge (or has only a small fee), which allows larger numbers of low-income children to attend. The emphasis has shifted from recreation to hands-on extended learning opportunities and academic enrichment along with sports, music, and art.

Effects of the programs on children's developmental outcomes are related to the programs' quality and how often individual children attend. Programs are more likely to report positive effects on social competencies and academic achievement when program quality is high; that is, relationships between staff and students are emotionally supportive, activities are engaging and interesting, and children attend 3 to 4 days a week (Pierce, Bolt, & Vandell, in press).

Time Without Adult Supervision

self-care Refers to children caring for themselves without adult supervision.

Public support for afterschool programs and organized activities is based, in part, on concerns about the risks children face when they are without adult supervision. In this section, we consider three variations of unsupervised time. **Self-care** refers to children caring for themselves without adult supervision. Two percent of children in grades K–2 (ages 5–7) are in self-care on a regular basis, averaging about 5 hours a week. Seven percent of children in grades 3–5 (ages 8–10) are in self-care, typically for about 4 hours each week (Carver & Iruka, 2006).

Self-care is worrisome because of the immediate risks to children's health and safety. In addition, self-care in middle childhood is linked to later social and academic problems. Pettit and colleagues (1997) have reported that children who were in self-care for 4 or more hours per week in first grade were less socially and academically competent in grade 6 than their classmates. More hours in self-care in middle childhood also is linked to antisocial behavior (Vandell & Ramanan, 1991), externalizing behavior (Marshall et al., 1997), and feelings of loneliness (Belle, 1999).

Another form of unsupervised time is hanging out with peers away from adult supervision. It, like self-care, is linked to a variety of problems in middle childhood, including poor grades and academic achievement, misconduct, externalizing behavior, alcohol and tobacco use, and a greater likelihood of dropping out of school later on (Jordan & Nettles, 2000; McHale, Crouter, & Tucker, 2001). The direction of effects is ambiguous, however. McHale and colleagues (2001) reported that adjustment at age 10 (poorer grades, poorer emotional adjustment, more behavior problems) was a better predictor of time hanging out with peers at age 12 than hanging out at age 10 was of adjustment at age 12. This suggests that self-selection may be a factor. Children with behavior problems may be choosing to spend their time with unsupervised peers as opposed to more developmentally positive contexts such as structured activities.

A third form of "lack of adult supervision" is care by child siblings. In traditional agricultural societies, older children (particularly girls) routinely care for younger siblings, typically with adults close by (Weisner & Gallimore, 1977; Whiting & Whiting, 1975). Older siblings also provide care for younger siblings in the United States, where almost one-quarter of children in grades K–8 are cared for by a sibling on a regular basis during the afterschool hours (National Center for Education Statistics, 2006). Sibling care is more common in Hispanic families and in two-parent households in which mothers are employed.

Children in grades 4 through 6 who are cared for by older siblings during the out-of-school hours report lower social acceptance and lower self-worth than children who are supervised by adults or home alone, even after controlling for child gender, family income, and race (Berman et al., 1992). Berman and colleagues speculate that this is because the older siblings have limited knowledge about child care. Being cared for after school by a sibling for an extended period of time (2 or more years) is also linked to participation in risky behaviors (Pettine & Rosén, 1998). Children in the care of older siblings report greater tolerance for risky behaviors compared with children in self-care at home alone. Older siblings' delinquent activities predict the younger siblings' delinquent activities concurrently and more strongly 3 years later (Slomkowski et al., 2001). The links between sibling-care and engaging in problem behavior are particularly strong in unsafe neighborhoods (Lord & Mahoney, 2007).

Neighborhoods

Parents have long recognized that neighborhoods can be sources of risk as well as sources of support for their children. When asked about what's important about neighborhoods, parents talk about availability of good schools, good neighbors, and safe places for their children to play (Leventhal & Brooks-Gunn, 2000). Those living in high-crime neighborhoods are more likely to keep their children indoors and out of harm's way and to be more restrictive in their parenting practices (Weir, Etelson, & Brand, 2006).

One way that scientists study neighborhoods is by using information from the U.S. Census to measure *structural* (or demographic) *characteristics*. Disadvantaged neighborhoods are characterized by high percentages of low-income residents, female-headed households, unemployed men, by high rates of crime, and by residential instability (Leventhal & Brooks-Gunn, 2000; Nettles, Caughy, & O'Campo, 2008). In contrast, advantaged neighborhoods are characterized by high percentages of residents who are college educated, hold professional positions, and earn high incomes. Advantaged neighborhoods have more two-parent households and low crime rates.

These structural characteristics are related to developmental outcomes in middle childhood (Nettles et al., 2008). Children growing up in disadvantaged neighborhoods are more likely to hang out with deviant peers (Brody et al., 2001), to display more frequent externalizing problems (Leventhal & Brooks-Gunn, 2000), and to report more psychological distress (Shumow, Vandell, & Posner, 1999). In a study of almost 3,000 school-age children in Chicago, concentrated neighborhood disadvantage was associated with mental health problems, even after accounting for family demographic characteristics, maternal depression, and earlier child mental health scores (Xue et al., 2005). Twenty-two percent of children in the poorest neighborhood were above the clinical threshold for internalizing behavior problems (depression, anxiety, withdrawal, and somatic problems), whereas only 12 percent of children in more advantaged neighborhoods were.

Another way to study neighborhoods is to look at residents' *perceptions* of where they live. How safe do they feel? How connected do they feel to others in their neighborhood? Do they think they could go to neighbors for material or psychological help? Mothers' perceptions are more predictive of their behaviors than are the neighborhood's actual characteristics (Christie-Mizell et al., 2003). Mothers who feel their neighborhoods are unsafe place stricter limits on their children's activities than mothers who feel secure in their neighborhood (O'Neil et al., 2001).

A challenge for scientists is how to disentangle neighborhood effects from other factors. Parental depression might be the *reason* a family lives in a disadvantaged area, not a reaction to living in a bad neighborhood. As we've said often, correlational studies do not identify cause and effect. Experiments do.

The Move to Opportunity (MTO) program, a project funded by the U.S. Department of Housing and Urban Development, provided one such experimental test. The program offered poor families a chance to move from public housing in high-poverty neighborhoods to private housing in low-poverty neighborhoods, in the hope of improving their educational and employment opportunities. All of the families had volunteered to join the MTO program. Most said the main reason they wanted to move was "gangs and drugs."

By random assignment, some families were given housing vouchers and assistance in finding new homes. This was the experimental, or treatment, group. Other families were provided some assistance but remained in housing projects in the original neighborhood (the control group). Three years after the move, boys' scores on achievement tests were comparable to girls' scores, whereas in the control group girls' scores were ten points higher than boys'. Greater school safety and more time spent on homework partially account for this gain. Moving out of a high-poverty neighborhood also had a positive impact on mothers' mental health (Leventhal & Brooks-Gunn, 2003). Further study of the MTO program is needed to determine longer-term effects. A 7-year follow-up of the Yonkers Project, a study of a court-ordered desegregation in Yonkers, New York, for example, found beneficial effects in middle childhood and early adulthood, but not adolescence (Fauth, Leventhal, & Brooks-Gunn, 2007).

Media: Television, Video Games, and Computers

The last 50 years have witnessed an explosion in the role of electronic media in children's lives (Comstock & Scharrer, 2006; Roberts & Foehr, 2008). Television, with more than 1,000 cable channels, has been joined by video consoles and games,

© Andersen Ross / Getty Images

Videogames have introduced new formats for play in middle childhood and beyond.

media multitasking The simultaneous use of multiple forms of media.

computers and the Internet, CDs, VCRs, DVDs, and iPods®, digital cameras, and who knows what next year. The world beyond the child's neighborhood is only a click away, and most children are tuned in.

One national survey of 2,000 children and youth found that the typical U.S. home has three TV sets, three tape players, three radios, two VCRs, two CD players, one video game console, and one computer (Roberts & Foehr, 2004). The survey also asked about direct access to media in the children's own rooms. Eighty-eight percent had a CD player; 86 percent, a radio; 65 percent, a television; 45 percent, a game console; 36 percent, a VCR; and 21 percent, a computer for their personal use. This technology-rich world has created new forms of communication, learning, and entertainment.

Media multitasking—the simultaneous use of multiple forms of media—is common (Roberts & Foehr, 2008). Children watch TV while surfing the Internet, listen to iPods while text-messaging friends, and play online games while sending digital images on their cell phones. To be successful in the global economy, students will need to be technologically savvy and able to seek out and evaluate the information obtained from the Internet (Liu et al., in press).

TV is the single most popular form of media used by school-age children, even when they have access to other technology. Viewing starts before age 2 and peaks at about age 12 (Roberts & Foehr, 2008). On average, school-age children spend about 3½ hours a day watching television, although their total media exposure is upward of 8 hours a day. Watching TV is highest in homes where there are few books and magazines, and the TV is turned on most of the time (Comstock & Scharrer, 2006).

There is a small negative relation between the amount of time that children spend watching television and academic achievement, but this relation often disappears once factors such as socioeconomic status are controlled (Schmidt & Vandewater, 2008). Much more important is the *content* of the electronic media. Educational programming, such as Sesame Street, is associated with long-term academic benefits (Anderson et al., 2001). A recent meta-analysis found viewing prosocial programming was related to tolerance of others and altruism, with effects peaking at age 7 and then declining (Mares & Woodard, 2005).

Many TV shows, movies, and video games feature violence. What impact does this have on children's behavior and attitudes? In general, experiments have found that showing school-age children violent behavior on film or TV increases the likelihood that they will behave aggressively immediately afterward (Wilson, 2008). For example, in one experiment, 7- to 9-year-old boys were randomly assigned to watch either a violent or nonviolent film before playing a game of floor hockey (Josephson, 1987). In some games, the referee carried a walkie-talkie identical to one used in the violent film. The combination of the violent film and the cue from the film stimulated significantly more assaultive behavior than the other conditions.

Research studies also find longer-term relations between regularly watching violent media and children's behavior. Children who watch more violent media day in and day out are more aggressive than other children (Wilson, 2008). And the relations are persistent. In a longitudinal study spanning several years, children who had a preference for violent media in middle childhood were more aggressive than their peers in adolescence (Huesmann et al., 2003). Direction of effects is difficult to disentangle. Children who are aggressive with peers may prefer to watch violent shows.

Children may also assimilate gender stereotypes from TV. Those who watch a lot of TV (25 hours or more a week) have more stereotyped ideas about men's and women's roles than children who watch a little TV (10 hours or less per week) (McGhee & Frueh, 1980). However, the number of shows a child views that depict women in nonstereotyped positions—as doctors, police officers, or farmers—can counteract this trend, opening children's minds to possibilities. The same is true for racial and ethnic stereotypes (Huesmann & Taylor, 2006).

Finally there is evidence that TV influences eating patterns and body image. The more TV children watch, the more likely they are to be seduced by ads and to prefer junk food (Gable & Lutz, 2000). Female TV and film stars are usually exceptionally thin, which may lead to excessive dieting or excessive eating (in despair) among girls.

Computers at Home Home computers are commonplace. More than 86 percent of families with youth between 8 and 18 years own a computer (Roberts & Foehr, 2008). More educated families, higher-income families, and those with parents who value or excel in math and science are more likely than others to have computers in their homes.

Children use computers in a variety of ways—to search for information, to communicate with peers via e-mail and instant messaging, and to participate in chat rooms. The **digital divide** refers to the gap between these children and other children who do not have access to computers and related materials in their homes (Warschauer, 2003).

digital divide The gap between those families that have access to computers and related materials in their homes and those that do not.

Studies find links between having computers in the home and academic success in science and math (Jackson et al., 2006). But these data do not tell us whether the computer itself boosts academic achievement or whether other factors are involved (remember that correlation is not the same as causation). One experimental study of the HomeNetToo project sought to establish this causal link experimentally. The treatment group consisted of children of low-income families who were provided with a home computer and Internet access. The control group did not receive these materials (Jackson et al., 2006). The researchers studied patterns of computer use and measured children's academic performance (grades) and achievement (test scores).

Children who participated in the project spent about 30 minutes a day on the computer, typically searching the Internet. They used the Internet less for communication purposes, such as e-mail or instant messaging, probably because friends and family did not have access to the technology. The project found a positive association between Internet usage and grade-point average and reading comprehension scores 6 months later. Contrary to what some pre-technology adults think, surfing the Internet is not a waste of time.

Computers in a School Setting Computers are playing a much larger role in elementary schools than in years past, but some schools are still struggling to make effective use of technology.

To be effective, school-based computers need to be embedded in high-quality teaching. Positive effects on student learning and achievement are more likely when technology is used to support five fundamentals of learning (Roschelle et al., 2000):

- Children are actively engaged in the digital activity.
- Children work in groups rather than alone.

The mere presence of computers in classrooms does not ensure their effective use.

- Children have frequent interaction and feedback from teachers around technology.
- There are clear connections to real-world contexts.
- There is systematic evaluation of learning.

The mere presence of computers in classrooms does not ensure their effective use. (For a summary of this section, see "Interim Summary 10.5: The Broader Social Context.")

INTERIM SUMMARY 10.5

The Broader Social Context

Organized Activities	■ Children whose families have higher incomes, more parental education, and two parents are more likely to participate in organized activities than children who are less well-off. ■ Participation in organized activities is linked to improvements in higher test scores and better emotional adjustment. Although some children are "over-scheduled" and lack free time, this is the exception rather than the rule.
Afterschool Programs	■ Publicly supported afterschool programs have increased in recent years. ■ Programs are more likely to report positive effects on social competencies and academic achievement when interactions between staff and students are emotionally supportive, activities are engaging and interesting, and students attend 3 to 4 days a week.
Time Without Adult Supervision	■ **Self-care** refers to children who care for themselves without adult supervision. ■ Hanging out with unsupervised peers is linked to poor grades, misconduct, and externalizing behavior problems although the direction of these effects is not clear. ■ Extensive and extended sibling care is linked to participation in risky behaviors.
Neighborhoods	■ Structural or demographic characteristics such as percentages of low-income residents, female-headed households, and unemployed men are one way to describe neighborhoods as disadvantaged. ■ These structural characteristics are related to child developmental outcomes beyond individual and family factors. ■ Neighborhoods also can be described in relation to perceptions of safety and support.
Media: Television, Video Games, and Computers	■ The last 50 years have witnessed an explosion in the role of electronic media in children's lives. ■ Children who watch more violent media day in and day out are more aggressive than other children. ■ Children assimilate attitudes about gender, body image, and tolerance of others from the particular programs that they view on TV. ■ Computers and technology are more likely to support student learning when students are actively engaged in the activity, students participate in groups as opposed to working alone, students have frequent interaction and feedback from teachers around technology, there are clear connections to real-world contexts, and there is systematic evaluation.

SUMMING UP AND LOOKING AHEAD

Themes that we saw in early childhood continue in middle childhood: the further development of a more realistic and integrated sense of self; more sophisticated strategies for self-control; and more advanced social skills. To a large degree, verbal, social, and relational aggression replaces physical, instrumental aggression. The family, whatever its configuration, plays a central role in whether children develop industry or inferiority. In addition, children's self-images are beginning to be influenced by their friends and their standing in the peer group. We looked at why some children are popular with peers and others are rejected or victimized.

A major change in middle childhood is in context. The child's social horizons—and challenges—expand: to school, where achievement and getting along with peers both count; to peer groups that are increasingly independent of adult supervision (so that children have to negotiate rules and standards among themselves); and to a whole new set of influences, including organized afterschool and weekend programs, the neighborhood, and the mass media.

Changes in the context of socioemotional development occur as the school-age child moves into adolescence. The balance of power in the family shifts (often after a bumpy period). Peers take on even more importance, and romantic relationships become an important focus. School becomes more challenging, and how well (or poorly) students perform takes on much great importance.

These are just some of the many changes that take place during adolescence, the next stop in our journey.

HERE'S WHAT YOU SHOULD KNOW

Did You Get It?

After reading this chapter, you should understand the following:

- The characteristics of children's self-concepts in middle childhood
- The characteristics of gender development in middle childhood
- Kohlberg's three main levels of moral reasoning: preconventional, conventional, and postconventional
- How the increase in prosocial behaviors reflects multiple factors
- The forms of aggression—physical, verbal, social, and relational
- The impact of the family system and one- and two-parent households on development
- How friendships change in middle childhood, what peer groups are, and how networks and cliques influence behavior
- The impact of neighborhoods, the media, and how children spend their out-of-school time on development

Important Terms and Concepts

altruism (p. 305)
bullying (p. 318)
cliques (p. 318)
conventional moral reasoning (p. 303)
deviancy training (p. 318)
digital divide (p. 325)
expressivity (p. 300)
gender schema (p. 301)
hedonistic reasoning (p. 305)
homophily (p. 316)
industry versus inferiority (p. 299)
instrumentality (p. 300)
media multitasking (p. 324)
meta-analysis (p. 301)
peer group (p. 316)
peer group status (p. 316)
physical aggression (p. 306)
postconventional moral reasoning (p. 303)
postmodern family (p. 308)
preconventional moral reasoning (p. 303)
prosocial behaviors (p. 304)
relational aggression (p. 306)
rough-and-tumble play (p. 300)
self-care (p. 322)
social aggression (p. 306)
sociometric nomination (p. 316)
transactional process (p. 312)
verbal aggression (p. 306)

Part IV Review

CHAPTER 9

Physical and Cognitive Development in Middle Childhood

- In middle childhood, marked changes in **gray matter** occur in the brain. The growth of **white matter—myelin—** increases linearly. Synapse growth shifts and girls show faster growth in spatial-visual discrimination and **gross motor skills,** and boys show faster growth in language and **fine motor skills.**
- Hallmarks of cognitive development in middle childhood include **classification, class inclusion, seriation, transitive inference,** and **reversibility.** These cognitive operations enable children to perform **conservation** tasks and formal mathematics.
- Faster processing speed and more efficient information processing help set the stage for advances in **working memory** and **long-term memory.**
- Root vocabularies expand rapidly in middle childhood. Children from low-income backgrounds whose parents have low literacy skills and whose homes have few reading materials are at risk for reading problems.
- Mathematical competence in middle childhood involves knowing math facts and computational procedures, using this knowledge to solve routine problems, and using reasoning and logic to solve more complex, nonroutine problems.

CHAPTER 10

Socioemotional Development in Middle Childhood

- Erikson's fourth stage of psychosocial development, **industry versus inferiority,** occurs in middle childhood. Self-concepts also become more balanced, and gender provides an organizing framework for children to think about themselves in relation to others.
- Social experiences interacting with cognitive development and genetic factors propel moral development during middle childhood. **Prosocial behaviors** increase during this time, although aggression (**physical aggression, verbal aggression, social** or **relational aggression,** and **bullying**) also takes place.
- The family context is still central in middle childhood. The family can be conceptualized as a social *system* composed of interrelated subsystems (parent-child, parent-parent, and sibling relations) that have different implications for child development.
- Friendships deepen toward the end of middle childhood, and **peer group status** and membership in **cliques** become important issues.
- The broader social context (including participation in organized activities, afterschool programs, time without adult supervision, neighborhoods, and digital media) has a more direct impact on development in middle childhood than in early childhood.

part five

Adolescence

© Thomas Barwick/Getty Images

CHAPTER

11

Physical and Cognitive Development in Adolescence

Photodisc/Getty

Benjamin Franklin once remarked that "In this world, nothing is certain but death and taxes." He was only partly right. To Franklin's list we should probably add puberty—the physical changes of adolescence. Not all adolescents experience identity crises, rebel against their parents, or fall head over heels in love, but virtually all undergo the biological transition from childhood to adolescence. Some might say that without puberty, there would be no adolescence. In this chapter, we look at the physical changes of puberty and how they affect individuals, including their impact on sleep, psychological functioning, sexual development, and body image.

However, puberty is not the only important physical transformation of adolescence that has implications for psychological development. Adolescence is also a period of dramatic brain development, with profound implications for individuals' thinking and behavior. Not only do teenagers know more than children, they actually think in different ways—ways that are more advanced, more efficient, and more effective. As you'll read in this chapter, the changes that take place during adolescence in the way individuals think have far-reaching implications—not only for what they like to watch on television or think lofty thoughts about, but also for how they perform in school, their social relationships, and their day-to-day decision making.

PUBERTY AND ITS CONSEQUENCES

Technically, "puberty" refers to the period during which an individual becomes capable of sexual reproduction. More broadly speaking, however, **puberty** encompasses all the physical changes that occur in the growing girl or boy as the individual passes from childhood into adulthood.

puberty The biological changes of adolescence.

Puberty has five chief physical components (Marshall, 1978):

- A *rapid acceleration in growth,* resulting in dramatic increases in both height and weight
- The *development of primary sex characteristics,* including the further development of the gonads, or sex glands, which are the testes in males and the ovaries in females
- The *development of secondary sex characteristics,* which involve changes in the genitals and breasts, and the growth of pubic, facial, and body hair, and the further development of the sex organs
- *Changes in body composition,* specifically in the quantity and distribution of fat and muscle
- *Changes in the circulatory and respiratory systems,* which lead to increased strength and endurance

Each of these sets of changes is the result of developments in the endocrine (hormone) and central nervous systems, many of which begin years before the external signs of puberty are evident—in fact, some occur even before birth (Susman & Dorn, 2009).

endocrine system The system of the body that produces, circulates, and regulates hormones.

hormones Highly specialized substances secreted by one or more endocrine glands.

glands Organs that stimulate particular parts of the body to respond in specific ways to particular hormones.

set point A physiological level or setting (of a specific hormone, e.g.) that the body attempts to maintain through a self-regulating system.

pituitary gland One of the chief glands responsible for regulating levels of hormones in the body.

hypothalamus A part of the lower brain stem that controls the functioning of the pituitary gland.

gonads The glands that secrete sex hormones: in males, the testes; in females, the ovaries.

testes The male gonads.

ovaries The female gonads.

HPG (hypothalamic-pituitary-gonadal) axis The neuropsychological pathway that involves the hypothalamus, pituitary gland, and gonads.

androgens A class of sex hormones secreted by the gonads, found in both sexes but in higher levels among males than among females following puberty.

estrogens A class of sex hormones secreted by the gonads, found in both sexes but in higher levels among females than among males following puberty.

leptin A protein produced by fat cells that may play a role in the onset of puberty.

adrenarche The maturation of the adrenal glands that takes place in preadolescence.

The Endocrine System

First, a few definitions. The **endocrine system** produces, circulates, and regulates levels of hormones in the body. **Hormones** are highly specialized substances secreted by one or more endocrine glands, after which they enter the bloodstream and travel throughout the body; hormones influence the functioning of different body organs. **Glands** are organs that stimulate particular parts of the body to respond in specific ways to particular hormones.

The endocrine system doesn't have a mind of its own, however. It receives its instructions to increase or decrease circulating levels of particular hormones from the brain. Think of a thermostat. Hormonal levels are "set" at a certain point, which may differ depending on the stage of development, just as you might set a thermostat at a certain temperature (and use different settings during different seasons or different times of the day). When you set your room's thermostat at 65°F, you are instructing your heating system to go into action when the temperature falls below this level (or your air conditioning to kick on when the temperature rises above this level). Similarly, when the level of a hormone in your body dips below the endocrine system's **set point** for that hormone, at that stage of development, secretion of the hormone increases; when the level reaches the set point, secretion temporarily stops. And, as is the case with a thermostat, the set point for a particular hormone can be adjusted up or down, depending on environmental or internal bodily conditions.

Such a *feedback loop* becomes increasingly important at the onset of puberty. Long before early adolescence—in fact, prenatally—a feedback loop develops involving the **pituitary gland** (which controls hormone levels in general), the **hypothalamus** (the part of the brain that controls the pituitary gland), and the **gonads** (in males, the **testes**; in females, the **ovaries**), a feedback loop known as the **HPG axis** (for **h**ypothalamus, **p**ituitary, **g**onads). The gonads release the "sex" hormones—**androgens** and **estrogens** (see Figure 11.1). Androgens and estrogens, in turn, stimulate sexual maturation and other aspects of physical growth.

The HPG axis is active before birth, but it is relatively quiet during much of childhood. During middle childhood, though, something happens that reawakens the HPG axis and signals it that the body is ready for puberty. Some of this is due to a puberty clock whose "alarm" is genetically programmed (as we discuss later, the age at which puberty begins is largely inherited). But some of the reawakening of the HPG axis at puberty is due to environmental signals that tell the brain that it is time to start thinking about having children. Some of these signals include whether there are sexually mature mating partners in the environment (exposure to sexually mature individuals is one of the triggers for puberty), whether a female adolescent has sufficient nutritional resources to support a pregnancy, and whether the individual is physically mature and healthy enough to begin reproducing. Some evidence indicates that rising levels of a protein produced by fat cells, **leptin**, may be the most important signal, at least in females (Susman & Dorn, 2009). This idea is consistent with observations that individuals may not go through puberty until they have accumulated a certain amount of body fat; it is consistent as well with research showing that puberty can be delayed by illness, nutritional deficiencies, excessive exercise, or excessive thinness (Frisch, 1983; McClintock, 1980).

Puberty is not all about sexual development, though. During and just before puberty, the pituitary, instructed by the hypothalamus, also secretes hormones that act on the thyroid and on the adrenal cortex and that stimulate bodily growth more generally. The thyroid and adrenal cortex, in turn, secrete hormones that cause various bodily changes to take place at puberty.

Do you remember the first time you felt a tingle of sexual attraction to someone? Research indicates that early feelings of sexual attraction may be stimulated by maturation of the adrenal glands, called **adrenarche**. Most individuals, not only in the United States but around the world, report that their first sexual attraction took place at the

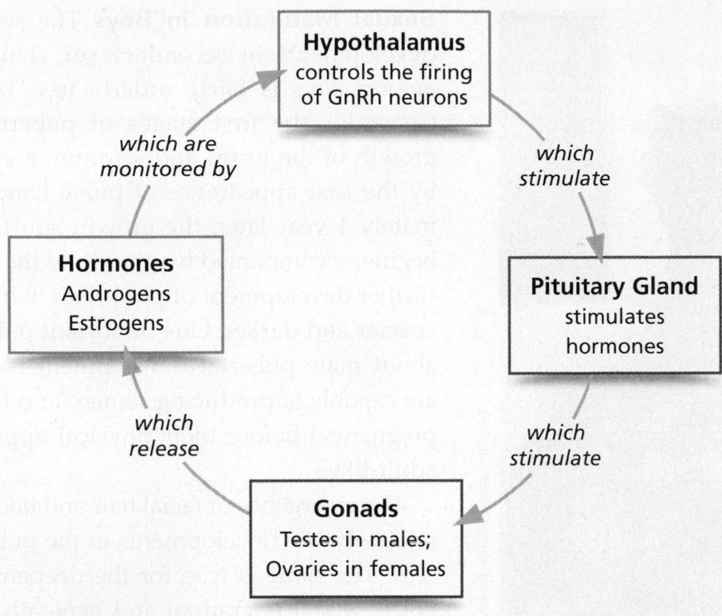

FIGURE 11.1

The Onset of Puberty

The onset of puberty is controlled by a feedback loop involving the hypothalamus, pituitary gland, and gonads. When levels of sex hormones drop below a certain set point, a signal is sent that stimulates their secretion.

"magical age of 10," before they went through puberty (Herdt & McClintock, 2000). Changes at puberty in the brain system that regulates the adrenal gland are especially important because this is the brain system that also controls how we respond to stress. One reason adolescence is a time for the onset of many serious mental disorders (depression, schizophrenia, substance abuse, and eating disorders are seldom seen before adolescence, for instance) is that an adverse side effect of the hormonal changes of puberty is to make us more responsive to stress (Steinberg et al., 2006; Walker, Sabuwalla, & Huot, 2004). This leads to excessive secretion of the stress hormone **cortisol**, a substance that, at high and chronic levels, can cause brain cells to die.

cortisol A hormone produced when we are exposed to stress.

Changes in Height, Weight, and Appearance

The triple whammy of growth hormones, thyroid hormones, and androgens stimulates rapid acceleration in height and weight, commonly referred to as the **adolescent growth spurt**. Both the absolute gain of height and weight that typically occurs at this time and the speed with which these increases take place are remarkable. Think for a moment of how quickly infants and toddlers grow, which we described in Chapter 4. During the adolescent growth spurt, individuals grow at the same rate as a toddler. For boys, the rate averages about 4 inches (10.3 centimeters) per year; for girls, it averages about 3½ inches (9.0 centimeters) annually. That's a lot of growing (imagine if you were to grow 4 inches taller over the next 12 months). On average, girls begin puberty about 2 years earlier than boys.

adolescent growth spurt The dramatic increase in height and weight that occurs during puberty.

Puberty also brings with it a series of developments associated with sexual maturation. In both boys and girls, the development of the **secondary sex characteristics** (the signs of sexual maturation, such as breast development or facial hair) is typically divided into five stages, often called **Tanner stages** after the British pediatrician who devised the categorization system.

secondary sex characteristics The manifestations of sexual maturation at puberty, including the development of breasts, the growth of facial and body hair, and changes in the voice.

Tanner stages A widely used system to describe the five stages of pubertal development.

© David Young-Wolff/PhotoEdit

One relatively late manifestation of puberty in boys is the emergence of facial hair.

Sexual Maturation in Boys The sequence of developments in secondary sex characteristics among boys is fairly orderly (see Table 11.1). Generally, the first stages of puberty involve growth of the testes and scrotum, accompanied by the first appearance of pubic hair. Approximately 1 year later, the growth spurt in height begins, accompanied by growth of the penis and further development of pubic hair, which is now coarser and darker. One important point to note about male pubertal development is that boys are capable of producing semen (and fathering a pregnancy) before their physical appearance is adult-like.

The emergence of facial hair and body hair are relatively late developments in the pubertal process. The same is true for the deepening of the voice, which is gradual and generally does not occur until very late adolescence. During puberty, there are changes in the skin as well; the skin becomes rougher, especially around the upper arms and thighs, and there is increased development of the sweat glands, which often gives rise to acne, pimples, and oily skin.

menarche The time of first menstruation, one of the important changes to occur among females during puberty.

rite of passage A ceremony or ritual marking an individual's transition from one social status to another, especially marking the young person's transition into adulthood.

Sexual Maturation in Girls The first sign of sexual maturation in girls usually is the elevation of the breast, although in about one-third of all adolescent girls the appearance of pubic hair comes first. The development of pubic hair follows a sequence in females similar to that in males—generally, from sparse, downy, light-colored hair to more dense, curled, coarse, darker hair. **Menarche**, the beginning of menstruation, is a relatively late development that reflects the culmination of a long series of hormonal changes (Dorn et al., 1999). Generally, a girl does not ovulate regularly until about 2 years after menarche, and she does not become fertile until several years after her first period (Hafetz, 1976). Unlike boys, who can father a child even though they look immature, girls generally appear physically mature before they are capable of becoming pregnant.

TABLE 11.1 The Sequence of Physical Changes at Puberty

BOYS		GIRLS	
Characteristic	*Age of First Appearance (Years)*	*Characteristic*	*Age of First Appearance (Years)*
1. Growth of testes, scrotal sac	10–13.5	1. Growth of breasts	7–13
2. Growth of pubic hair	10–15	2. Growth of pubic hair	7–14
3. Body growth	10.5–16	3. Body growth	9.5–14.5
4. Growth of penis	11–14.5	4. Menarche	10–16.5
5. Change in voice (growth of larynx)	About the same time as penis growth	5. Underarm hair	About two years after pubic hair
6. Facial and underarm hair	About two years after pubic hair appears	6. Oil- and sweat-producing glands	About the same time as underarm hair
7. Oil- and sweat-producing glands, acne	About the same time as underarm hair		

Source: Goldstein (1976).

The Psychological and Social Impact of Puberty

Puberty can affect the adolescent's behavior and psychological functioning in a number of different ways (Brooks-Gunn, Graber, & Paikoff, 1994) (see Figure 11.2). First, the biological changes of puberty can affect behavior directly. The increase in sex drive that occurs at puberty is the direct result of hormonal changes (Halpern, Udry, & Suchindran, 1996). Second, the biological changes of puberty can cause changes in the adolescent's self-image, which in turn may influence his or her behavior. A young teenager who looks in the mirror and sees the face of an adult may begin to demand more adult-like treatment and greater independence from his or her parents. Finally, changes in the adolescent's appearance may, in turn, elicit changes in how *others* react to the teenager. In some nonindustrialized societies, adolescents undergo a formal **rite of passage** when they go through puberty, a ceremony that certifies them as adult members of the community and confers new privileges and responsibilities on them. Although contemporary industrialized societies use chronological age to distinguish between adolescents and adults, in many nonindustrialized societies, a person's physical maturity is the deciding factor.

FIGURE 11.2

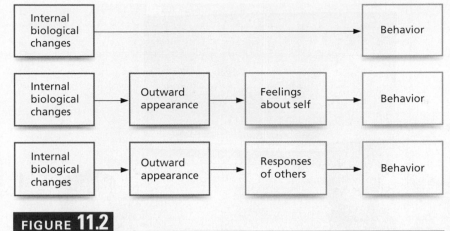

How Puberty Affects Adolescent Behavior

The impact of puberty on the adolescent's behavior occurs through multiple pathways. Some effects are direct, some occur through their impact on the adolescent's self-conceptions, and some occur through the reactions that the pubertal changes provoke in others.

delayed phase preference A pattern of sleep characterized by later sleep and wake times, which often emerges during puberty.

Puberty and the Adolescent's Emotions Many people believe that the "raging hormones" of puberty wreak havoc on the adolescent's emotions and mental health. But although research suggests that puberty is potentially stressful with temporary adverse psychological consequences, this is only likely when puberty occurs simultaneously with other changes that require adjustment, like changing schools (Simmons & Blyth, 1987). In this respect, the impact of puberty on adolescents' psychological functioning is to a great extent shaped by the social context in which puberty takes place (Susman, 1997).

When studies do find a connection between hormonal changes at puberty and adolescent mood or behavior (and not many of them do), the effects are strongest early in puberty, when the system is being activated and when hormonal levels are fluctuating more than usual. For example, *rapid* increases in many of the hormones linked with puberty may be associated with increased irritability, impulsivity, aggression (in boys), and depression (in girls), especially when the increases take place very early in adolescence. There is also evidence that important changes take place around the time of puberty in regions of the brain that play major roles in the processing of emotions, social information, and rewards.

Changes in Patterns of Sleep Many parents complain that their teenage children go to bed too late in the evening and sleep in too late in the morning. The emergence of this pattern—called a **delayed phase preference**—is driven by the biological changes of puberty (Carskadon et al., 1997), although as you will read, it is certainly helped along by having access 24/7 to all sorts of electronic entertainment.

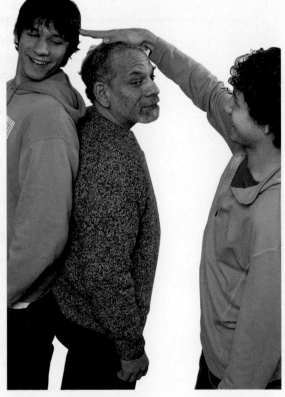

At least some of the psychological impact of puberty results from changes in the ways in which others respond to the adolescent's new appearance.

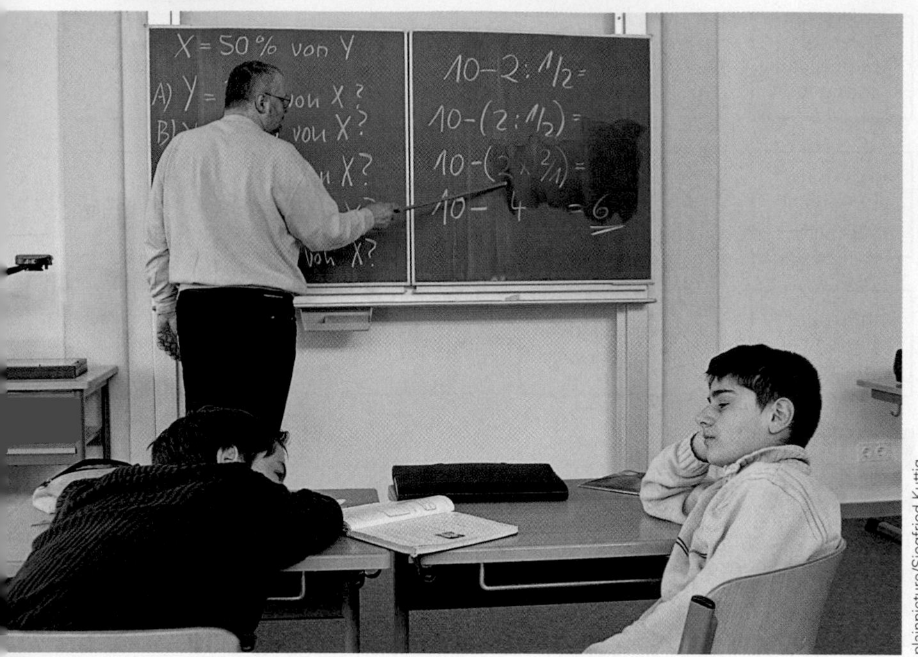

plainpicture/Siegfried Kuttig

Experts agree that most American teenagers do not get enough sleep. Falling asleep in school is one symptom.

Falling asleep is caused by a combination of biological and environmental factors. One of the most important influences on sleepiness is a hormone in the brain called **melatonin**. Melatonin levels change naturally over the course of the 24-hour day, mainly in response to the amount of light to which we're exposed. As melatonin rises, we feel sleepier, and as it falls, we feel more awake.

The time of night at which melatonin levels begin to rise changes at puberty, becoming later and later as individuals mature physically (Carskadon & Acebo, 2002). As a result of this shift, individuals are able to stay up later before they start to feel sleepy. In fact, when allowed to regulate their own sleep schedules (as on weekends), most teenagers will stay up until around 1:00 A.M. and sleep until about 10:00 A.M. It's not just nighttime sleepiness that is affected, however. Because the *whole cycle* of melatonin secretion is shifted later at puberty, adolescents who have gone through puberty are sleepier early in the morning than those who are still prepubertal. (Now you know why you felt so tired during that first-period class you had in eighth grade. You probably thought it was the teacher.)

melatonin A hormone present in the brain that causes sleepiness.

Of course, if getting up early the next day was not an issue, staying up late would not be a problem. Unfortunately, most teenagers need to get up early on school days, and the combination of staying up late and getting up early leads to sleep deprivation and daytime sleepiness. Indeed, one study found that adolescents were least alert between the hours of 8:00 and 9:00 A.M. (when most schools start) and most alert after 3:00 P.M., when the school day is over (Allen & Mirabell, 1990).

Although individuals' preferred bedtime gets later as they move from childhood into adolescence, the amount of sleep they need each night remains constant, at around 9 hours. Few teenagers get this much sleep, however. Scientists agree that most teenagers are not getting enough sleep, and that inadequate sleep in adolescence is associated with poorer mental health (more depression and anxiety) and lowered school performance (Fredriksen et al., 2004).

Early and Late Maturation

Puberty can begin as early as the age of 7 in girls and 9½ in boys, or as late as 13 in girls and 13½ in boys. In girls, the interval between the first sign of puberty and complete physical maturation can be as short as a year and a half or as long as 6 years; in boys, from about 2 years to 5 years (Tanner, 1972). The long and short of it (pun intended) is that within a totally normal population of young adolescents, some individuals will have completed the entire sequence of pubertal changes before others have even begun. Visit a junior high school or middle school and see for yourself!

Genetic and Environmental Influences on Pubertal Timing Differences in the timing and rate of puberty among individuals growing up in the same general environment result chiefly, but not exclusively, from genetic factors (Dick et al., 2001; Mustanski et al., 2004). In all likelihood, every individual inherits a predisposition to develop at a certain rate and to begin pubertal maturation at a certain time. But this predisposition is best thought of as an upper and lower age limit, not a fixed deadline.

The two most important environmental influences on pubertal maturation are nutrition and health. Simply put, puberty occurs earlier among individuals who are better nourished throughout their prenatal, infant, and childhood years. Because health and nutrition have improved considerably during the past two centuries, we would expect to find a decline in the average age at menarche over time, and indeed we do. This pattern is referred to as the **secular trend**. In most European countries, where this has been most extensively tracked over time, the age of puberty has dropped by about 3 to 4 months every decade (see Figure 11.3). Scientists disagree about whether the secular trend has continued in the United States in recent years and, if so, whether the trend toward earlier puberty is greater in some ethnic groups than in others. In general, though, most scientists agree that any changes in the average age of puberty have been much less dramatic in recent decades than they were in the early twentieth century.

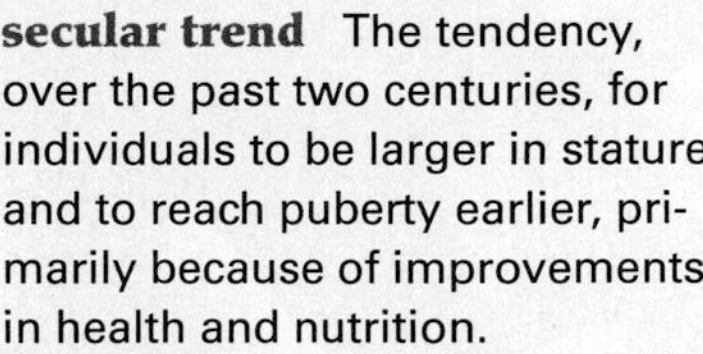

secular trend The tendency, over the past two centuries, for individuals to be larger in stature and to reach puberty earlier, primarily because of improvements in health and nutrition.

How does maturing early or late affect the adolescent's psychological health and well-being? The answer depends on whether the adolescent in question is male or female.

Early Versus Late Maturation Among Boys Over the past 50 years, research on boys' pubertal timing has found that early-maturing boys feel better about themselves and are more popular than their late-maturing peers, probably because of the role that athletics plays in determining a boy's social standing (Graber, 2009). Consistent with this, boys who are more physically mature than their peers more frequently report good moods, being popular, and feeling strong (Richards & Larson, 1993).

However, early-maturing boys are more likely than their peers to get involved in antisocial or deviant activities, including truancy, minor delinquency, and problems at school (Duncan et al., 1985). They are also more likely to use drugs and alcohol and

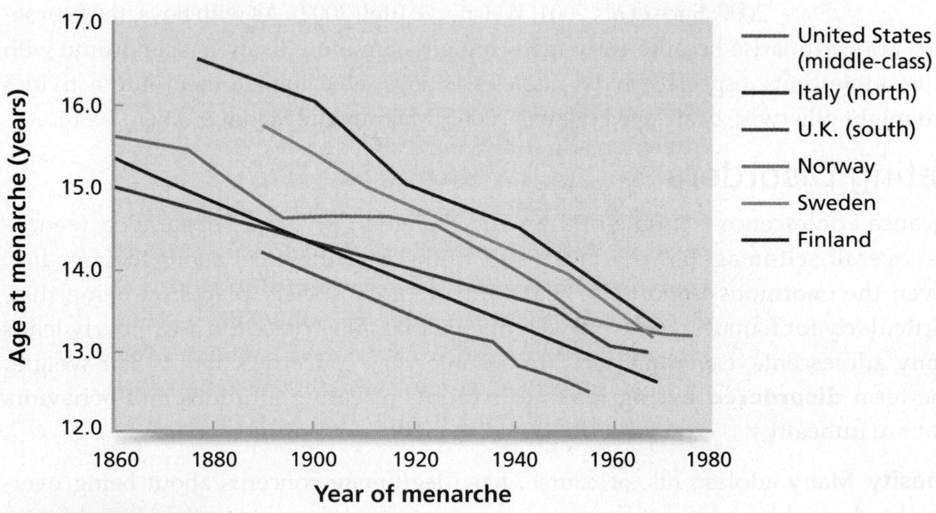

FIGURE 11.3

The Secular Trend

The average age of pubertal onset has dropped substantially in the industrialized world, due mainly to improvements in health and nutrition. This decline is referred to as the "secular trend."

Source: Reprinted by permission of the publisher and Castlemead Publications from *Fetus into Man: Physical Growth from Conception to Maturity* by J. M. Tanner, p. 160, Cambridge, Mass.: Harvard University Press, Copyright © 1978, 1989 by J. M. Tanner.

© Laura Dwight

The wide variability in the timing and tempo of puberty can create middle school classrooms in which students of the same age have very different appearances.

engage in other risky activities (Dick et al., 2001). The most widely accepted explanation for this is that boys who are more physically mature develop friendships with older peers and that these friendships lead them into activities that are problematic for the younger boys (Andersson & Magnusson, 1990).

Early Versus Late Maturation in Girls In contrast to the generally positive impact that early maturation has on the psychological well-being of boys, early-maturing girls have more emotional difficulties than their peers, including lowered self-image and higher rates of depression, anxiety, eating disorders, and panic attacks (Ge et al., 2003; Stice, Presnell, & Bearman, 2001). These difficulties seem to have a great deal to do with girls' feelings about their weight (Petersen, 1988). Early maturation in girls also may lead to heightened emotional arousal, which may leave girls more vulnerable to emotional problems (Graber, Brooks-Gunn, & Warren, 2006).

Although some early-maturing girls may have self-image difficulties, their popularity with peers is generally not jeopardized. Indeed, some studies indicate that early maturers are more popular than other girls, especially if the index of popularity includes popularity with boys (Simmons, Blyth, & McKinney, 1983). Ironically, it may be in part because the early maturer is more popular with boys that she reports more emotional upset: At a very early age, pressure to date and, perhaps, to be involved in a sexual relationship may take its toll on the adolescent girl's mental health, an issue we discuss in Chapter 12.

Like their male counterparts, early-maturing girls are also more likely to become involved in problem behavior, including delinquency and use of drugs and alcohol; more likely to have school problems; and more likely to experience early sexual intercourse (Dick et al., 2000; Stice et al., 2001; Weisner & Ittel, 2002). As with boys, these problems appear to arise because early-maturing girls are more likely to spend time with older adolescents, especially older adolescent boys, who initiate them into activities that might otherwise be delayed (Haynie, 2003; Magnusson, Statin, & Allen, 1986).

Eating Disorders

Because adolescence is a time of dramatic change in physical appearance, teenagers' overall self-image is very much tied to the way they feel about their bodies. Given the enormous importance that contemporary society places on being thin, particularly for females, the usual weight gain that takes place during puberty leads many adolescents, especially girls, to become very concerned about their weight. The term **disordered eating** refers to patterns of eating attitudes and behaviors that are unhealthy.

disordered eating Patterns of unhealthy eating attitudes and behaviors.

Obesity Many adolescents, of course, have legitimate concerns about being overweight. According to recent surveys, 16 percent of adolescents in the United States are obese, and another 15 percent are at great risk for obesity (Institute of Medicine, 2006), a rate that has *tripled* since 1980 (see Figure 11.4). The average 15-year-old boy today is 15 pounds heavier, and the average 15-year-old girl is 10 pounds heavier than was the case in the mid-1960s—increases that cannot be explained by the fact that people have gotten a little taller since then. Today, obesity is the single most serious public health problem afflicting U.S. teenagers. Although it is true that genetic factors contribute to how much we weigh, the dramatic increase in the prevalence of adolescent obesity over such a short time period indicates that the problem has strong environmental causes.

Anorexia Nervosa and Bulimia Health care professionals are concerned not only about adolescents who are obese but also about adolescents of normal or even below-normal weight who have unhealthy attitudes toward eating and about their body (French et al., 1995). More than half of all adolescent girls consider themselves overweight and have attempted to diet (Fisher et al., 1995). One recent study found that 14 percent of undergraduate women were so concerned about eating that they were embarrassed to go into a store and buy a chocolate bar (Rozin, Bauer, & Catanese, 2003)!

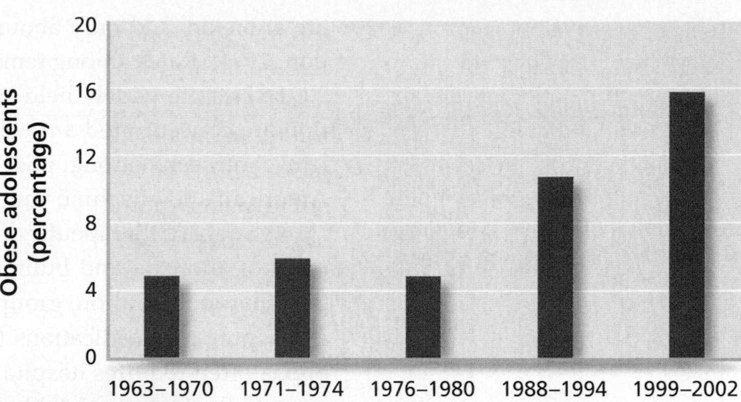

FIGURE 11.4

The Obesity Epidemic

The rate of obesity among U.S. adolescents nearly quadrupled during the last two decades of the twentieth century.

Source: Food marketing to children and youth: Threat or opportunity? Reprinted with permission from Institute of Medicine, 2006 by the National Academy of Sciences, Courtesy of the National Academies Press, Washington, DC.

Some adolescent girls and young women become so worried about gaining weight that they take drastic—and dangerous—measures to become or remain thin. They might go on eating binges and then force themselves to vomit to avoid gaining weight, a pattern associated with an eating disorder called **bulimia**. In more severe cases, young women who suffer from an eating disorder called **anorexia nervosa** actually starve themselves in an effort to keep their weight down. Adolescents with these sorts of eating disorders have an extremely disturbed body image, seeing themselves as overweight when they actually are underweight. Some youngsters with anorexia lose between 25 percent and 50 percent of their body weight. If untreated, bulimia and anorexia frequently lead to a variety of very serious physical problems; in fact, nearly 20 percent of anorexic teenagers starve themselves to death.

bulimia An eating disorder found chiefly among young women, characterized primarily by a pattern of binge eating and self-induced vomiting.

anorexia nervosa An eating disorder found chiefly among young women, characterized by dramatic and severe self-induced weight loss.

Although unhealthy eating and unnecessary dieting are widespread among adolescents, careful studies indicate that the incidence of genuine anorexia and genuine bulimia is much lower than most people think (and very small when compared with rates of obesity) (Fisher et al., 1995). Fewer than one-half of 1 percent of adolescents

© Karen Kasmauski/Corbis

About one-third of U.S. teenagers are obese, and another third are extremely overweight.

are anorexic, and only about 3 percent are bulimic (American Psychiatric Association, 1994). Rates among females are 10 times higher than among males (Jacobi et al., 2004). Despite widely held stereotypes that disordered eating and body dissatisfaction are concentrated among middle-class Caucasian and Asian youth, these problems are seen among poor, as well as affluent, teenagers, and among African American and Hispanic youth as well (Jacobi et al., 2004).

A variety of therapeutic approaches have been employed successfully in the treatment of anorexia and bulimia, including individual psychotherapy and cognitive-behavior modification, group therapy, family therapy, and, more recently, the use of antidepressant medications (Agras et al., 1989; Killian, 1994). The treatment of anorexia often requires hospitalization initially to ensure that starvation does not progress to fatal or near fatal levels (Mitchell, 1985). (For a summary of this section, see "Interim Summary 11.1: Puberty and Its Consequences.")

INTERIM SUMMARY 11.1

Puberty and Its Consequences

What is puberty?	Puberty refers to the set of bodily changes that takes place during the transition from childhood to adolescence. It has five chief components: 1. A rapid acceleration in growth 2. The development of primary sex characteristics 3. The development of secondary sex characteristics 4. Changes in body composition 5. Changes in the circulatory and respiratory systems
The Endocrine System	■ The **endocrine system** produces, circulates, and regulates levels of hormones in the body. **Hormones** are highly specialized substances secreted by one or more endocrine glands, after which they enter the bloodstream and travel throughout the body. ■ During the prenatal period, a feedback loop develops involving the **pituitary gland**, the **hypothalamus**, and the **gonads**, known as the **HPG axis**. The gonads release the "sex" hormones—**androgens** and **estrogens**. Androgens and estrogens, in turn, stimulate sexual maturation and other aspects of physical growth. ■ Other important changes at puberty involve the thyroid and the adrenal gland. ■ The onset of puberty is triggered by both genetic and environmental factors. There is some evidence that rising levels of a protein produced by fat cells, **leptin**, may be the most important trigger, at least in females. ■ Puberty can be delayed by illness, nutritional deficiencies, excessive exercise, or excessive thinness.
Changes in Height, Weight, and Appearance	■ Growth hormones, thyroid hormones, and androgens stimulate rapid acceleration in height and weight, commonly referred to as the **adolescent growth spurt**. ■ In both boys and girls, the development of the **secondary sex characteristics** (the signs of sexual maturation, such as breast development or facial hair) is typically divided into five stages, called **Tanner stages**.

(continued)

INTERIM SUMMARY **11.1** *(continued)*

Puberty and Its Consequences

	■ The first stages of puberty in boys are the growth of the testes and scrotum, accompanied by the first appearance of pubic hair. The growth spurt in height begins approximately one year later. The emergence of facial and body hair, and the lowering of the voice, are relatively late developments. ■ The first sign of sexual maturation in girls usually is the elevation of the breast, although in about one-third of all adolescent girls the appearance of pubic hair comes first. **Menarche**, the beginning of menstruation, is a relatively late development.
The Psychological and Social Impact of Puberty	■ In some nonindustrialized societies, adolescents undergo a formal **rite of passage** when they go through puberty. ■ The direct connection between hormones and adolescent mood is weak; observed links between hormones and mood tend to be strongest early in puberty, when hormone levels are fluctuating most. ■ The biological changes of puberty lead to a **delayed phase preference** in adolescents, which is a sleep pattern of staying up late and awakening late.
Early and Late Maturation	■ Puberty occurs earlier among individuals who are better nourished throughout their prenatal, infant, and childhood years. Because health and nutrition have improved considerably during the past two centuries, the average age of the onset of puberty has declined over time. This pattern is referred to as the **secular trend**. ■ Early-maturing boys feel better about themselves and are more popular than their late-maturing peers but early maturers are more likely than their peers to get involved in antisocial or deviant activities. ■ Early-maturing girls have more emotional difficulties than their peers and are more likely to become involved in problem behavior.
Eating Disorders	■ **Disordered eating** refers to patterns of eating attitudes and behaviors that are unhealthy. ■ Close to one-third of U.S. adolescents are either obese or at risk for obesity. ■ The major contributors to the epidemic of obesity among contemporary adolescents are inadequate exercise and poor nutrition. ■ Individuals who suffer from **anorexia** starve themselves to lose weight. ■ Individuals who suffer from **bulimia** go on eating binges and then force themselves to vomit to avoid gaining weight. ■ The incidence of genuine bulimia and anorexia is much smaller than most people think, but the rates among females are substantially higher than among males. ■ A variety of therapeutic approaches have been used successfully in the treatment of bulimia and anorexia, including individual psychotherapy and cognitive-behavior modification, group therapy, family therapy, and antidepressant medications.

© MedioImages/Corbix

Most U.S. adolescents have had experience in a sexual relationship by the time they enter high school.

SEXUAL ACTIVITY DURING ADOLESCENCE

For most individuals, adolescence marks the onset of sexual activity. This section discusses the stages of adolescent sexual activity as well as many of the issues involved in teens' sexuality: sexual intercourse, contraceptive use, sex education, and teen pregnancy.

Stages of Sexual Activity

The typical adolescent's first experience with sex is alone (Katchadourian, 1990). (This isn't sad, though. As Woody Allen once said, "Don't knock masturbation—it's sex with someone I love.") Different surveys yield different estimates, depending on the age of the respondents and how the questions are worded, but about half of all adolescent boys and about one-fourth of all adolescent girls masturbate prior to age 18 (Savin-Williams & Diamond, 2005).

By the time adolescents have reached high school, most of them have made the transition to sexual activity with another person. You may be interested to know that the developmental progression of sexual behaviors, from less intimate to more intimate, has not changed very much over the past 50 years, and the sequence in which males and females engage in various sexual activities is remarkably similar. Holding hands comes first, followed by (in this order) kissing, making out, feeling breasts through clothes, feeling breasts under clothes, feeling a penis through clothes, feeling a penis under clothes or while naked, feeling a vagina through clothes, feeling a vagina under clothes or while naked, and intercourse or oral sex. Whether intercourse precedes oral sex or vice versa varies from study to study (Savin-Williams & Diamond, 2004).

Sexual Intercourse During Adolescence

Although there has been a slight drop since the mid-1990s in the proportion of sexually experienced teenagers, more adolescents are sexually active at an earlier age today than several decades ago (see Figure 11.5). In other words, slightly fewer adolescents are having sexual intercourse, but those who are do so at a somewhat earlier age (Santelli et al., 2000; Singh & Darroch, 1999). The best estimates we have are that, by the end of their sophomore year in high school, more than 40 percent of American adolescents have had heterosexual vaginal intercourse (these estimates, which are based on large national surveys, do not include same-sex intercourse or other types of sex, like oral or anal sex). By age 18, this number has risen to about two-thirds (Centers for Disease Control and Prevention, 2006).

There are substantial ethnic differences in age of sexual initiation, especially among males (Warren et al., 1998). Among African American males, the average age of first intercourse is 15; among Caucasian and Hispanic American males, 16½; and among Asian American males, 18 (Upchurch et al., 1998). Ethnic differences in the age of sexual initiation are far smaller among females, although Hispanic American and Asian American females generally have their first sexual intercourse at a later age than African American and Caucasian females (Grunbaum et al., 2000). One reason for the relatively high rate of early sexual activity among African American males is the higher proportion of African American youth who grow up in single-parent homes and in poor neighborhoods, both of which are risk factors for early sexual activity (Brewster,

1994; Lauritsen, 1994). In general, Mexican American youngsters who were born in Mexico are less likely to be sexually active at an early age than Mexican Americans who are U.S.-born, reflecting differences in norms between the two countries (Aneshensel et al., 1990).

Many studies show that sexual activity during adolescence is decidedly *not* associated with psychological disturbance (Savin-Williams & Diamond, 2004). However, *early* sexual activity (i.e., having intercourse before age 16) is associated with experimentation with drugs and alcohol, a low level of religious involvement, tolerance of deviant behavior, less engagement in school, and greater desires for independence (Halpern et al., 2000; Martin et al., 2005). In contrast, studies of adolescents who become sexually active at age 16 or later do not find major differences between these youth and their virginal counterparts.

It is not uncommon for young adolescents to engage in sex play with members of the same sex, to have sexual fantasies about people of the same sex, or to have questions about the nature of their feelings for same-sex peers (Savin-Williams & Diamond, 2004). According to the national (and confidential) Add Health survey, about 8 percent of boys and 6 percent of girls reported having had strong same-sex attractions or having engaged in same-sex activity during adolescence. (Males are more likely to experiment with same-sex activity during adolescence, whereas females are more likely to experiment in young adulthood, often during college.) A smaller number of adolescents—between 3 and 4 percent—identify themselves as gay, lesbian, or bisexual, a number that increases to about 8 percent among adults (Michael, Laumann, & Kolata, 1994; Savin-Williams & Diamond, 2004).

Proportion of students who have had sexual intercourse
70
60
50
40
30
20
10
0
9 10 11 12
Grade

FIGURE 11.5

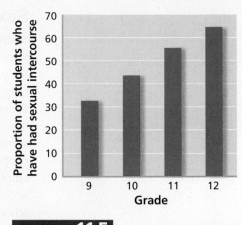

Sexual Intercourse in Adolescence

The proportion of U.S. high school students having sexual intercourse rose dramatically between 1960 and 1980. It has declined only slightly since then. Today, about 40 percent of U.S. teenagers have had sexual intercourse before the end of their sophomore year.

Source: Steinberg, 2008.

Contraceptive Use

One reason adults worry about the sexual activity of adolescents is that many sexually active young people don't use contraception regularly. Nearly one-third of older adolescent males report using either no contraception or an ineffective method (e.g., pulling out before ejaculating) the first time they had sex (Manning, Longmore, & Giordano, 2000). Perhaps more important, between 20 and 30 percent of young people did not use contraception the last time they had sex, either (Coleman, 1999; Hogan, Sun, & Cornwell, 2000; Santelli et al., 2000).

Among adolescents who do use contraception, the most popular method by far is condoms, which are used by close to 60 percent of sexually active teenage couples, followed by the birth control pill, which is used by about one-fifth of couples (Everett et al., 2000). (About 20% of girls who are on the pill report that their partner uses a condom as well [Santelli et al., 1997].) Pulling out, a highly *in*effective method of preventing pregnancy, unfortunately is still used by a large number of teenagers, as is the rhythm method (calculating when a female is likely to get pregnant). The rhythm method requires more regular menstrual cycling than many teenagers have and more careful monitoring than most teenagers are willing or able to do. Studies also show that a large proportion of condom users do not use condoms correctly (e.g., putting the condom on before first entry and holding on to the condom while withdrawing) (Oakley & Bogue, 1995).

There are several reasons that so few adolescents use contraception regularly and effectively. More than 25 percent of nonusers of contraception report that they or their partners simply did not want to use birth control. Perhaps most important, many adolescents fail to use birth control because doing so means admitting that they are choosing to be sexually active and are planning ahead for it (Miller & Moore, 1990). Going on the pill or purchasing a condom requires an adolescent to acknowledge that he or she is having or expects to have sexual relations.

Sex Education

Many adolescents receive some sort of classroom instruction about sex—whether through high school health classes, biology classes, classes designated exclusively for the purpose of sex education, or educational programs administered through youth or religious organizations. Evaluations of school-based sex education programs have shown them to have no effect on adolescents' sexual activity but a small impact on their use of contraceptives (Franklin et al., 1997). (That is, classroom programs don't seem to dissuade adolescents from having sex, but they do seem to get some young people to have safer sex.) Most traditional sex education programs fail because they emphasize the biological over the emotional aspects of sex (and therefore don't help adolescents make decisions about sexual involvement); they come too late in high school; and they focus primarily on changing students' knowledge rather than their behavior (Landry, Singh, & Darroch, 2000).

During the mid-1980s, the emphasis in sex education shifted from encouraging "responsible" sex to encouraging sexual abstinence, an emphasis that still prevails in many school districts (Landry, Kaeser, & Richards, 1999). It was hoped that by encouraging sexual abstinence these programs would also have the effect of reducing teenage pregnancy. Unfortunately, careful evaluations of these programs have shown that they too are not successful, either in changing adolescents' sexual behavior or in reducing rates of nonmarital pregnancy (Christopher, 1995; Kirby et al., 1997; Leiberman et al., 2000).

Does anything work? One approach that makes experts cautiously optimistic involves a combination of school-based sex education and community-based health clinics through which adolescents can receive information about sex and pregnancy as well as contraception. Some evaluations indicate that this combination of sex education and clinics may diminish the rate of teen pregnancy, even within inner-city communities characterized by high rates of adolescent pregnancy and childbearing (Christopher, 1995; Frost & Forrest, 1995; Tiezzi et al., 1997).

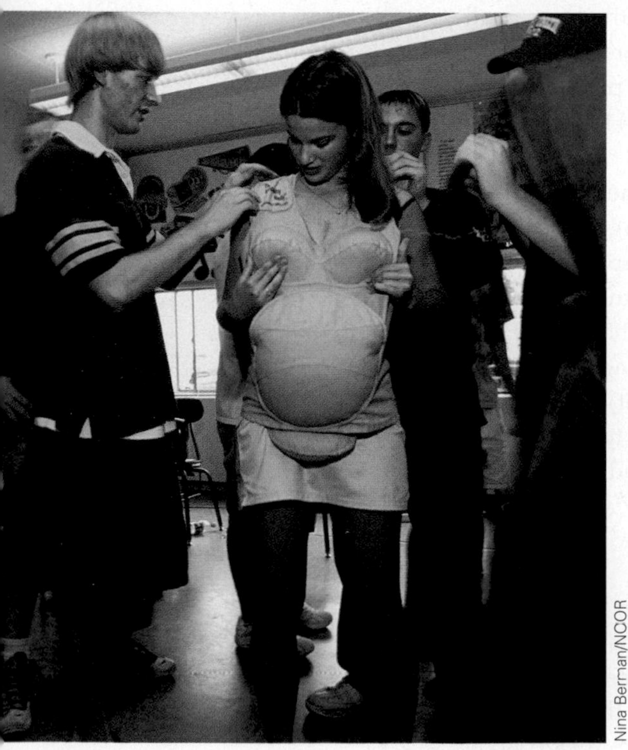
Nina Berman/NCOR

Research on school-based sex education indicates that it influences adolescents' knowledge and beliefs much more than their level of sexual activity.

Teenage Pregnancy

The high rate of sexual activity and erratic contraceptive use among today's adolescents results in many young women becoming pregnant before the end of adolescence. Each year, between 800,000 and 900,000 U.S. adolescents become pregnant—giving the United States the highest rate of teen pregnancy in the industrialized world (Alan Guttmacher Institute, 2004). Nearly one-third of U.S. young women become pregnant at least once by age 20, although rates of teen pregnancy vary considerably by ethnicity: The rate is twice as high among African American youth as among Caucasian youth, and rates of teen pregnancy among Hispanic teenagers fall somewhere between (Alan Guttmacher Institute, 2004).

Not all adolescent pregnancies result in childbirth, of course. In the United States, about one-third of all teenage pregnancies are aborted, and slightly more than one-sixth end in miscarriage (Centers for Disease Control and Prevention, 2004). Among U.S. adolescents who do not abort their pregnancy, the vast majority—over 90 percent—keep and raise the infant, whereas only 1 in 10 chooses to have the child adopted. In other words, about 45 percent of teenage pregnancies end in abortion or miscarriage, about 50 percent result in the birth of an infant who will be raised by his or her mother (with or without the help of a partner or other family members), and about 5 percent result in the birth of an infant put up for adoption (Coley & Chase-Lansdale, 1998) (see Figure 11.6).

Because ethnic minority adolescents are more likely to grow up poor, and teenage childbearing is more common in economically disadvantaged communities, adolescent parenthood is especially high in nonwhite communities. Among Caucasian adolescents, nearly two-thirds of all births occur outside of marriage, but a large proportion of these births occur within the context of cohabitation; among African American adolescents, virtually all childbirths are out of wedlock, and relatively few of these occur among cohabiting couples (Manning & Landale, 1996; Schellenbach et al., 1992). The rate for Hispanic teenagers falls somewhere in between; interestingly, young Mexican American women are more likely to bear their first child within marriage, whereas young Puerto Rican women are more likely to bear children out of wedlock but within the context of cohabitation (Darabi & Ortiz, 1987; East & Blaustein, 1995; Manning & Landale, 1996). (For a summary of this section, see "Interim Summary 11.2: Sexual Activity During Adolescence.")

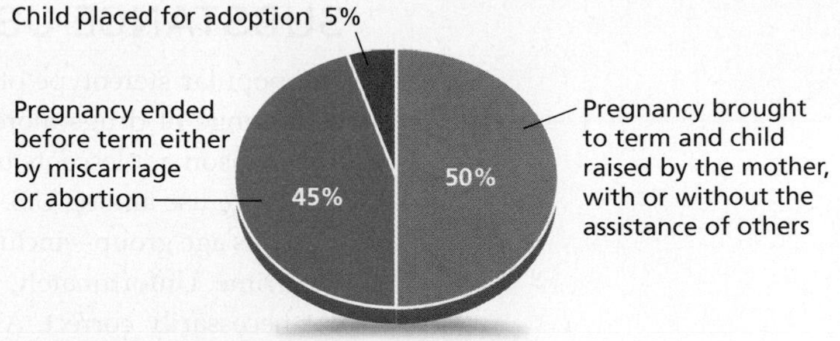

FIGURE 11.6

Outcomes of Teen Pregnancies

In about half of all cases, teen pregnancy in the United States results in the birth of a child raised by the teen parent. The vast majority of the other teen pregnancies end in miscarriage or by abortion. Very few teen pregnancies result in the birth of a baby who is put up for adoption.

INTERIM SUMMARY 11.2

Sexual Activity During Adolescence

Stages of Sexual Activity	■ Most adolescents are sexually active by the time they enter high school. ■ The developmental progression of sexual behaviors, from less intimate to more intimate, has not changed very much over the past 50 years.
Sexual Intercourse During Adolescence	■ By the end of their sophomore year in high school, more than 40 percent of U.S. adolescents have had intercourse. By age 18, this number has risen to about two-thirds. ■ Slightly fewer adolescents are having sexual intercourse today than in recent years, but those who are do so at a somewhat earlier age. ■ *Early* sexual intercourse (i.e., before age 16) is associated with a range of problem behaviors, but sexual intercourse after this age is not.
Contraceptive Use	■ The most popular contraceptive method among adolescents is condoms, followed by the birth control pill. ■ Few adolescents use contraception regularly, however.
Sex Education	■ Most evaluations of school-based sex education programs have shown them to have no effect on adolescents' sexual activity but a small impact on their use of contraceptives. ■ One approach that makes experts cautiously optimistic involves a combination of school-based sex education and community-based health clinics through which adolescents can receive information about sex and pregnancy as well as contraception.
Teenage Pregnancy	■ Each year, between 800,000 and 900,000 U.S. adolescents become pregnant. ■ About 45 percent of teenage pregnancies end in abortion or miscarriage, about 50 percent result in the birth of an infant who will be raised by his or her mother, and about 5 percent result in the birth of an infant put up for adoption.

SUBSTANCE USE AND ABUSE IN ADOLESCENCE

The popular stereotype of contemporary young people is that they use and abuse a wide range of drugs more than their counterparts in previous generations; that the main reason adolescents use drugs is peer pressure; and that the "epidemic" level of substance use among U.S. teenagers is behind many of the other problems associated with this age group—including academic underachievement, early pregnancy, suicide, and crime. Unfortunately, what we would like to believe about adolescent drug use is not necessarily correct. Although there are grains of truth to many of the popular claims about the causes, nature, and consequences of teenage substance use and abuse, there are many widely held misconceptions about the subject, too.

Prevalence of Substance Use and Abuse in Adolescence

Although adults tend to worry a lot about adolescents' use of illegal drugs, such as marijuana, cocaine, or LSD, the Monitoring the Future surveys consistently find that the two major legal drugs—alcohol and nicotine—are by far the most commonly used and abused substances. By the time they are seniors in high school, three-fourths of teenagers have tried alcohol and half have smoked cigarettes. Experimentation with marijuana is also common: 45 percent of all seniors have tried marijuana, one-third have smoked marijuana at least once within the last year, and 25 percent have done so within the past 30 days. After marijuana, however, the percentage of young people who have tried various other drugs drops significantly: Only about 10 percent of teenagers have used any illicit drug other than marijuana (Monitoring the Future, 2005) (see Figure 11.7).

binge drinking Consuming five or more drinks in a row on one occasion, an indicator of alcohol abuse.

It is one thing to have tried alcohol or marijuana, but it is something else to use either of these substances so often that one's life and behavior are markedly affected. Cigarettes are the only substances used daily by a substantial number of high school seniors (about one-sixth smoke daily). Of the remaining drugs, only alcohol and marijuana are used this frequently by even a modest percentage of teenagers (alcohol is used daily by about 3% of high school seniors; marijuana is used daily by about 5%). On this indicator, then, things don't look as bad as one might expect. But although daily use of alcohol is relatively infrequent, the occasional abuse of alcohol is not. Nearly 30 percent of all seniors, 20 percent of all tenth-graders, and 10 percent of all eighth-graders report having had more than five drinks in a row, referred to as **binge drinking**, at least once during the past two weeks (Monitoring the Future, 2005).

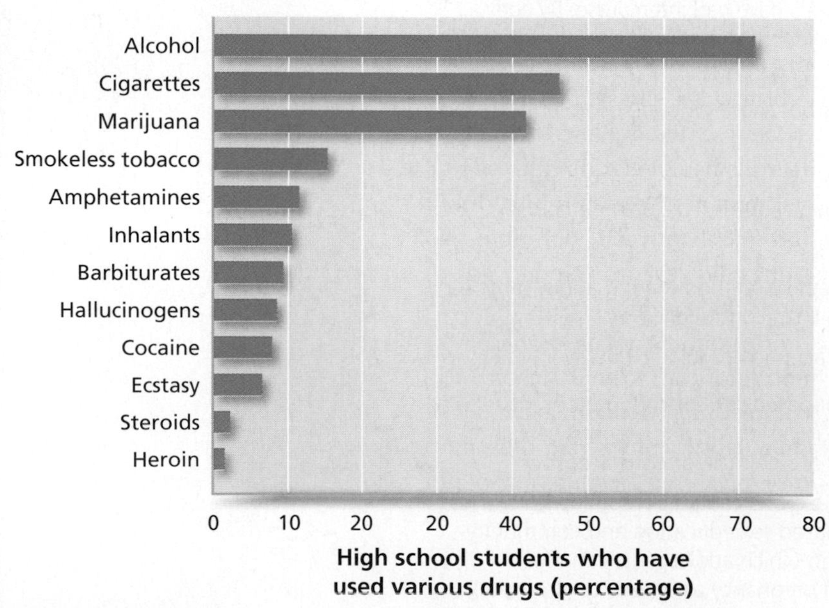

FIGURE 11.7

Substance Use in Adolescence

This figure shows percentages of U.S. high school students who have ever used various drugs, according to data from Monitoring the Future, an annual survey of a representative sample of American teenagers.

The overall picture indicates that most adolescents have experimented with alcohol and marijuana, that many have used one or both of these drugs regularly, that alcohol is clearly the drug of choice among teenagers (a substantial minority of whom drink to excess), and that most teenagers have not experimented with other drugs. From a health and safety standpoint, education about alcohol and cigarette use and abuse is more urgently needed and

© Laura Dwight

Alcohol and nicotine (in the forms of cigarettes and smokeless tobacco) are by far the most commonly used and abused substances by U.S. teenagers.

may potentially affect a larger percentage of young people than education about any other drug type.

Causes and Consequences of Adolescent Substance Use and Abuse

Psychologists distinguish between two levels of severity of pathological substance use: **substance abuse**, using drugs in a way that causes significant problems at home, school, work, or with the law, and **substance dependence**, where the individual is physically addicted. All individuals who are substance dependent by definition have substance abuse, but the reverse is not true.

substance abuse The misuse of alcohol or other drugs to a degree that causes problems in the individual's life.

substance dependence The misuse of alcohol or other drugs to a degree that causes physical addiction.

Research clearly shows that occasional alcohol and marijuana use has become normative among U.S. high school students and, consequently, that there are plenty of normal, healthy young people who have experimented with these drugs at least once. Substance abuse during adolescence, in contrast, is associated with a host of other problems. Young people who abuse alcohol, tobacco, and other drugs are more likely to experience problems at school, experience psychological distress and depression, have physical health problems, engage in unprotected sexual activity, abuse alcohol as young adults, and become involved in dangerous or deviant activities, including crime, delinquency, and truancy (Chassin et al., 2009; Holmen et al., 2000; Kandel et al., 1997; Wu & Anthony, 1999). Alcohol and other drugs are often implicated in adolescent automobile crashes, the leading cause of death and disability among U.S. teenagers (Lang, Waller, & Shope, 1996; O'Malley & Johnston, 1999), and in other fatal and nonfatal accidents, such as drownings, falls, and burns (Irwin, 1986; Wintemute et al., 1987). Adolescent substance abusers also expose themselves to the long-term health risks of excessive drug use that stem from addiction or dependency; in the case of cigarettes, alcohol, and marijuana, these risks are substantial and well documented—among them, cancer, heart disease, and kidney and liver damage. Also, it is now well established that heavy cigarette smoking during adolescence can exacerbate feelings of emotional distress and lead to depression and anxiety disorders (Goodman & Capitman, 2000).

risk factors Factors that increase individual vulnerability to harm.

Which adolescents are most likely to become substance abusers? Generally, four sets of **risk factors**—psychological, familial, social, and contextual—for substance abuse have been identified. The first set of risk factors is psychological. Individuals with certain personality characteristics—which typically are present before adolescence—are more likely to develop drug and alcohol problems than their peers. These characteristics include *anger, impulsivity,* and *inattentiveness* (Chassin et al., 2009). Second, individuals with *distant, hostile,* or *conflicted family relationships* are more likely to develop substance abuse problems than are their peers who grow up in close, nurturing families (Dishion, Capaldi, & Yoerger, 1999; Sale et al., 2005). Third, individuals with substance abuse problems also are more likely to have *friends who use and tolerate the use of drugs,* both because they are influenced by these friends and because they have others with whom to use them (Ennett et al., 2006). Finally, adolescents who become substance abusers are more likely to live in a *social context that makes drug use easier,* such as the easy availability of drugs, community norms tolerating drug use, lax enforcement of drug laws, and positive portrayals of drug use in the mass media (Chassin et al., 2009). The more risk factors that are present for an individual, the more likely he or she is to use and abuse drugs (Petraitis, Flay, & Miller, 1995).

Prevention and Treatment of Substance Use and Abuse

Efforts to prevent substance use and abuse among teenagers focus on one of three factors: the supply of drugs, the environment in which teenagers may be exposed to drugs, and characteristics of the potential drug user (Newcomb & Bentler, 1989). Today, the consensus among experts is that it is more realistic to try to change adolescents' motivation to use drugs and the environment in which they live, since it has proven virtually impossible to remove drugs totally from society. After all, the two most commonly used and abused drugs by teenagers—cigarettes and alcohol—are both legal and widely available, and as you may know from firsthand experience, laws prohibiting the sale of these substances to minors are not well enforced (Centers for Disease Control and Prevention, 2006). Research does show, however, that raising the price of alcohol and cigarettes reduces adolescents' use of them (Gruber & Zinman, 2001).

Many different types of drug abuse prevention interventions have been tried, either alone or in combination. In programs designed to change some characteristic of the adolescent, drug use is either targeted indirectly by attempting to enhance adolescents' psychological development in general or by helping adolescents to develop other activities and interests that will make drug use less likely, such as getting involved in athletics. The idea behind these sorts of efforts is that adolescents who have high self-esteem, for example, or who are involved in productive activities, will be less likely to use drugs. In other programs, the intervention is more directly aimed at preventing drug use. These programs include educating adolescents about the dangers of drugs, teaching adolescents how to turn down drugs, and some combination of informational and general psychological intervention (in which adolescents are educated about drug abuse and exposed to a program designed to enhance their self-esteem, for instance) (Newcomb & Bentler, 1989).

Generally speaking, the results of research designed to evaluate these sorts of individual-focused approaches have not been especially encouraging (Dielman, 1994; Leventhal & Keeshan, 1993). Careful evaluations of Project DARE (Drug Abuse Resistance Education), for example—the most widely implemented drug education program in the United States—show that the program is largely ineffective (Ennett et al.,

1994). Experts are now fairly confident that drug education alone, whether based on rational information or scare tactics, does not prevent drug use.

The most encouraging results have been found in programs that do not focus just on the individual adolescent but, rather, combine some sort of social competence training (e.g., training in how to resist peer pressure) with a communitywide intervention aimed not only at adolescents but also at their peers, parents, and teachers (so that antidrug messages are consistent across these sources of information). These multifaceted efforts have been shown to be effective, especially if the programs begin when youngsters are preadolescents and continue well into high school (Bruvold, 1993; Dielman, 1994; Ellickson, Bell, & McGuigan, 1993; Flynn et al., 1994; Perry et al., 1996). (For a summary of this section, see "Interim Summary 11.3: Substance Use and Abuse in Adolescence.")

INTERIM SUMMARY 11.3

Substance Use and Abuse in Adolescence

Prevalence of Substance Use and Abuse in Adolescence	■ Alcohol and nicotine are by far the most commonly used and abused substances by teenagers, although experimentation with marijuana is also common. ■ Although daily alcohol use is relatively infrequent, occasional abuse is not. Many adolescents engage in **binge drinking**. ■ Recent surveys indicate that drug experimentation begins at an earlier age today than previously.
Causes and Consequences of Adolescent Substance Use and Abuse	■ Psychologists distinguish between two levels of severity of pathological substance use: **substance abuse** (using drugs in a way that causes significant problems at home, school, work, or with the law) and **substance dependence** (where the individual is physically addicted). ■ There are four sets of risk factors for substance abuse: 1. Having certain personality characteristics, including anger, impulsivity, and inattentiveness 2. Having distant, hostile, or conflicted family relationships 3. Having friends who use and tolerate the use of drugs 4. Living in a social context that makes drug use easier ■ Substance abuse is associated with other problems, such as psychological distress and depression, problems at school, physical health problems, unprotected sexual activity, dangerous or deviant activities, and the long-term health risks of excessive drug use.
Prevention and Treatment of Substance Use and Abuse	■ Efforts to prevent substance use and abuse focus on one of three factors: the supply of drugs, the environment in which teenagers are exposed to drugs, and characteristics of the potential drug user. ■ Most experts agree that efforts designed to simply change the potential adolescent drug user without transforming the environment in which the adolescent lives are not likely to succeed. ■ The most encouraging programs combine some sort of social competence training (how to resist peer pressure) with a community-wide intervention aimed at adolescents, their peers, parents, and teachers.

THE ADOLESCENT BRAIN

Scientists once believed that brain maturation was more or less complete by the end of childhood. No longer. We now know that important changes in the brain occur throughout adolescence (and even into young adulthood).

Brain Maturation in Adolescence

First, there appears to be considerable "remodeling" of the brain through the processes of synaptic pruning and myelination, both of which you've read about in previous chapters. Although, as you now know, synaptic pruning takes place throughout infancy, childhood, and adolescence, different regions of the brain are pruned at different points in development. The part of the brain that is pruned most in adolescence is the **prefrontal cortex**, the region that is most important for various sorts of advanced thinking abilities, such as planning, thinking ahead, weighing risks and rewards, and impulse control (Casey et al., 2005). As you read in earlier chapters, synaptic pruning eliminates unused connections in the brain, reducing clutter. Myelination of the prefrontal cortex also continues throughout adolescence, improving the efficiency of communication between neurons (Paus et al., 1999; Sowell et al., 2002).

prefrontal cortex The part of the brain responsible for many higher-order cognitive skills, such as decision making and planning.

dorsolateral prefrontal cortex The outer and upper areas of the front of the brain, important for skills such as planning ahead and controlling impulses.

ventromedial prefrontal cortex The lower and central area at the front of the brain, important for gut-level decision making.

orbitofrontal cortex The region of the brain located directly behind the eyes, important for the evaluation of risk and reward.

We now know that maturation of the prefrontal cortex takes place gradually over the course of adolescence and is not complete until the mid-20s (Casey et al., 2005; Hooper et al., 2004; Segalowitz & Davies, 2004). Of special importance are developments in the **dorsolateral prefrontal cortex**, the outer and upper areas of the front of the brain, which is important for skills such as planning ahead and controlling impulses (Casey et al., 2005); the **ventromedial prefrontal cortex**, the lower and central area of the front of the brain, which is important for more gut-level, intuitive decision making, and which has strong connections with the limbic system, where emotions and social information are processed (Bechara, 2005); and the **orbitofrontal cortex**, the area of the brain directly behind the eyes, which is important for evaluating risks and rewards (May et al., 2004) (see Figure 11.8).

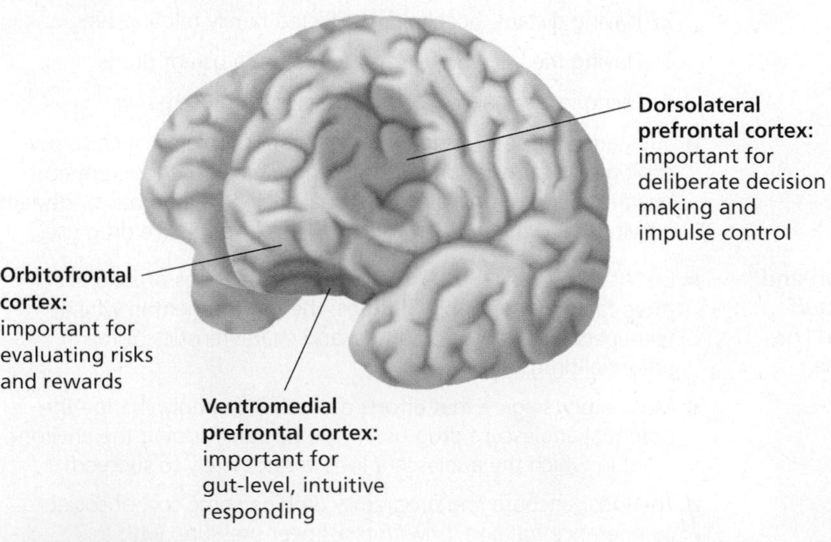

FIGURE 11.8

The Prefrontal Cortex

Important changes take place during adolescence in the dorsolateral prefrontal cortex, the orbitofrontal cortex, and the ventromedial prefrontal cortex. These regions are important for planning, thinking ahead, weighing risks and rewards, and impulse control.

Imaging studies have also shown that there is a significant increase in connectivity between the prefrontal cortex and other areas of the brain, including the limbic system, suggesting better "communication" between brain regions as individuals mature (Cunningham, Bhattacharyya, & Benes, 2002; Luna et al., 2001). Second, around the time of puberty, there are changes in levels of several **neurotransmitters** (the chemicals that permit the transfer of electrical charges between neurons), including dopamine and serotonin, in the parts of the brain that process rewards as well as emotional and social stimuli, most notably, areas of the **limbic system**. These changes may make individuals more emotional, more responsive to stress, and more interested in sensation seeking. Changes in the limbic system are also thought to increase individuals' vulnerability to substance abuse (because they seek higher levels of reward), depression (because of their increased vulnerability to stress), and other mental health problems (because of their easily aroused emotions, including anger and sadness) (Steinberg et al., 2006).

neurotransmitters Chemical substances in the brain that carry electrical impulses across synapses.

limbic system An area of the brain that plays an important role in emotional experience and processing social information.

Implications for Adolescent Behavior

The relatively late maturation of the prefrontal cortex, particularly in relation to the changes that take place in the limbic system at puberty, has been the subject of much discussion among those interested in risk taking and behavioral problems in adolescence (Steinberg, 2007). It appears that the brain changes in ways that may provoke individuals to crave novelty, reward, and stimulation several years before the complete maturation of the brain systems that control judgment, decision making, and impulse control. This gap may help explain why adolescence is a period of heightened experimentation with risk. In the words of one team of writers, it's like "starting the engines with an unskilled driver" (Nelson et al., 2002, p. 515).

Drugs and the Adolescent Brain

Researchers had long hypothesized that, because the brain is still very malleable early in adolescence, experimentation with drugs was especially harmful at this point in development. Until fairly recently, this was mainly speculation. But in the past several years, experimental studies, in which researchers have compared the brains of animals that have been exposed to drugs either close to the time of puberty or after reaching full maturity, have shown that the potential for addiction to both nicotine and alcohol is much greater in adolescence than in adulthood (Schochet, Kelley, & Landry, 2004, 2005; Sturmhöfel & Swartzwelder, 2004; Volkow & Li, 2005). Compared with individuals who delay drinking until they are 21, people who begin drinking in early adolescence (before age 14) are *seven times* more likely to binge drink as teenagers and *five times* more likely to develop a substance abuse or dependence disorder at some point in their life (Hingson, Heeren, & Winter, 2006). Similarly, individuals who begin smoking regularly before age 14 (which, as we noted, is when most smokers begin) are at greater risk for nicotine dependence as adults than those who start in late adolescence (Orlando et al., 2004). How many exposures to a drug does it take to permanently alter the adolescent's brain? No one knows for sure, and the answer varies from person to person, largely because of genetic factors (this is why some people are more likely to develop addictions than others).

And it's not just that the potential for addiction is higher in adolescence. The effects of nicotine and alcohol on brain functioning actually are worse in adolescence than in adulthood—again, because the brain is more vulnerable at this point in development. One area of the adolescent brain that appears especially susceptible to the harmful effects of alcohol is the **hippocampus**, which is important for memory and, along with the prefrontal cortex, for "putting the brakes" on impulsive behavior (Sturmhöfel & Swartzwelder, 2004; Walker et al., 2004). We also know that alcohol has harmful effects on the development of regions of the brain involved in higher-order cognitive abilities, such as planning, and in the regulation of impulses (Butler, 2006). (For a summary of this section, see "Interim Summary 11.4: The Adolescent Brain.")

hippocampus A structure in the brain's limbic system that is especially important for memory and controlling impulsive behavior.

INTERIM SUMMARY 11.4

The Adolescent Brain

Brain Maturation in Adolescence	■ There is considerable "remodeling" of the brain during adolescence through the processes of synaptic pruning and myelination. ■ The part of the brain that is pruned most in adolescence is the **prefrontal cortex**, the region responsible for many advanced thinking abilities. ■ Maturation of the prefrontal cortex takes place gradually over the course of adolescence and is not complete until the mid-20s. ■ Developments take place in the **dorsolateral prefrontal cortex**, which is involved in skills such as planning ahead and controlling impulses, in the **ventromedial prefrontal cortex**, which is involved in more gut-level, intuitive decision making, and in the **orbitofrontal cortex**, which is important for evaluating risks and rewards. ■ There also are important changes in the **limbic system** at puberty, which influence sensation-seeking, mood, and attentiveness to social stimuli.
Implications for Adolescent Behavior	■ The brain changes in ways during adolescence that may provoke individuals to crave novelty, reward, and stimulation several years before the complete maturation of the brain systems that control judgment, decision making, and impulse control. This gap may help explain why adolescence is a period of heightened experimentation with risk.
Drugs and the Adolescent Brain	■ The effects of nicotine and alcohol on brain functioning are worse in adolescence than in adulthood because the brain is especially vulnerable during this stage. Individuals who are exposed to drugs early in adolescence are much more likely to develop substance abuse problems than those whose exposure is delayed until late adolescence. ■ The **hippocampus**, which is important for memory and for controlling impulsive behavior, is especially susceptible to the harmful effects of alcohol.

HOW THINKING CHANGES IN ADOLESCENCE

Brain development in adolescence, of course, has an impact on the way individuals think. Five important sets of changes in thinking take place during adolescence:

- We become more able to think about what is possible, not just about what actually is.
- We become more able to think in sophisticated ways about abstract concepts, like love, democracy, and justice.
- We become better at thinking about the process of thinking.
- We improve in our ability to think about things from multiple vantage points at the same time.
- We start to see things as relative rather than absolute.

Let's take a look at each of these changes in detail.

Thinking About Possibilities

Children's thinking is oriented to things and events that they can observe directly. But adolescents are able to consider what they observe against a backdrop of what is possible. Children do not wonder, the way adolescents often do, about the ways in which their personalities might change in the future or how they might have been different had they grown up with different parents or under different economic circumstances. For the young child, you simply are who you are. Not so for teenagers: Who you are is just one possibility of who you could be.

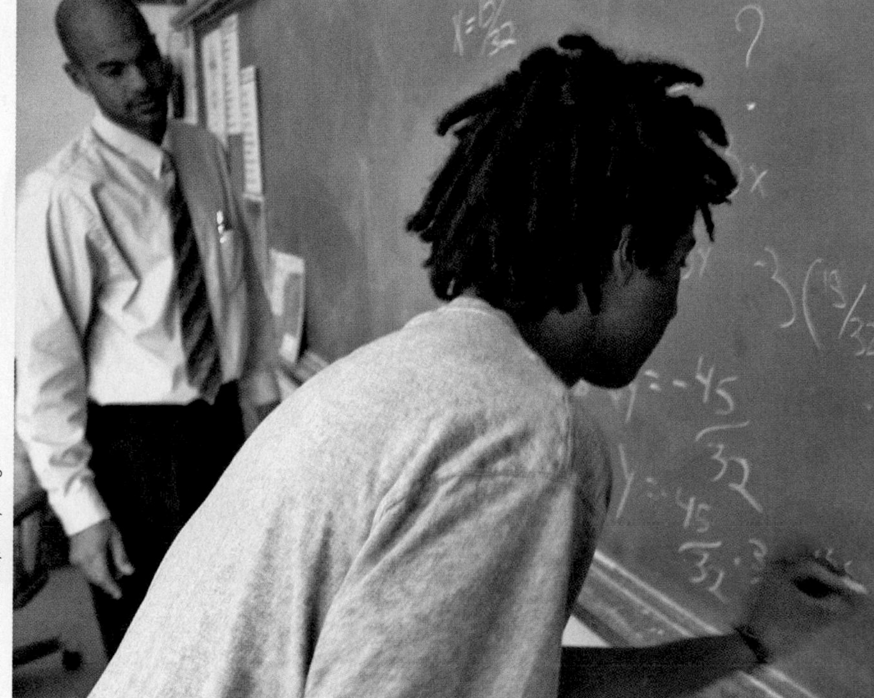

© Christina Kennedy/Getty Images

Improvements in abstract reasoning abilities enable adolescents to learn algebra.

One important manifestation of the adolescent's increased facility with thinking about possibilities is the development of **deductive reasoning**. Deductive reasoning is a type of logical reasoning in which you draw logically necessary conclusions from a general set of premises, or givens. For example, consider the following problem:

All soccer players wear shin guards.
Chris is a soccer player.
Does Chris wear shin guards?

Individuals who can reason deductively understand that the correct conclusion (that Chris wears shin guards) necessarily follows from the first two statements. No additional knowledge about soccer, or about Chris, or about shin guards is necessary to reach the correct answer. By the same token, adolescents are also better able than children to recognize when a logical problem doesn't provide sufficient information and to respond by saying that the question can't be answered with any certainty. Suppose we were to change the problem to read like this:

deductive reasoning A type of logical reasoning in which one draws logically necessary conclusions from a general set of premises, or givens.

All soccer players wear shin guards.
Chris is wearing shin guards.
Is Chris a soccer player?

If you answer this type of question quickly, without thinking it through, you might say that Chris indeed is a soccer player. But this is not necessarily the case. Whereas children are easily fooled by such problems, adolescents are more likely to say that there is no way of knowing whether Chris plays soccer or not, because we are not told that the *only* people who wear shin guards are soccer players. Deductive reasoning is seldom seen before adolescence, because deductive reasoning requires us to think systematically about possibilities (Klaczynski & Narasimham, 1998; Morris & Sloutsky, 2001).

Related to the development of deductive reasoning is the emergence of **hypothetical thinking**, or "if-then" thinking, as it is sometimes called. Being able to plan ahead, to see the future consequences of an action, and to provide alternative explanations of events are all dependent on being able to hypothesize effectively. The ability to think through hypotheses is an enormously powerful tool. For example, thinking in hypothetical terms allows us to suspend our beliefs about something in order to argue in the abstract.

hypothetical thinking Thinking that is based on what is possible, and not just what is real; sometimes referred to as "if-then" thinking.

Hypothetical thinking also has implications for the adolescent's social behavior. It helps the young person to take the perspective of others by enabling him or her to think through what someone else might be thinking or feeling, given that person's point of view. ("If someone treated me the way she was just treated, I would feel pretty angry.") Hypothetical thinking therefore helps in formulating and arguing one's viewpoint, because it allows adolescents to think a step ahead of the opposition—a cognitive tool that comes in quite handy when dealing with parents. ("If they come back with 'You have to stay home and clean out the garage,' then I'll remind them about the time they let my brother go out when *he* had chores to do.") Hypothetical thinking also plays an important role in decision making, because it permits the young person to plan ahead and to foresee the consequences of choosing one alternative over another. ("If I choose to go out for the basketball team, then I am going to have to give up my job at the mall.") Scientists now believe that the development of the ability to plan ahead and foresee the future consequences of one's actions is closely tied to the maturation of the prefrontal cortex, a development that you read about earlier in this chapter.

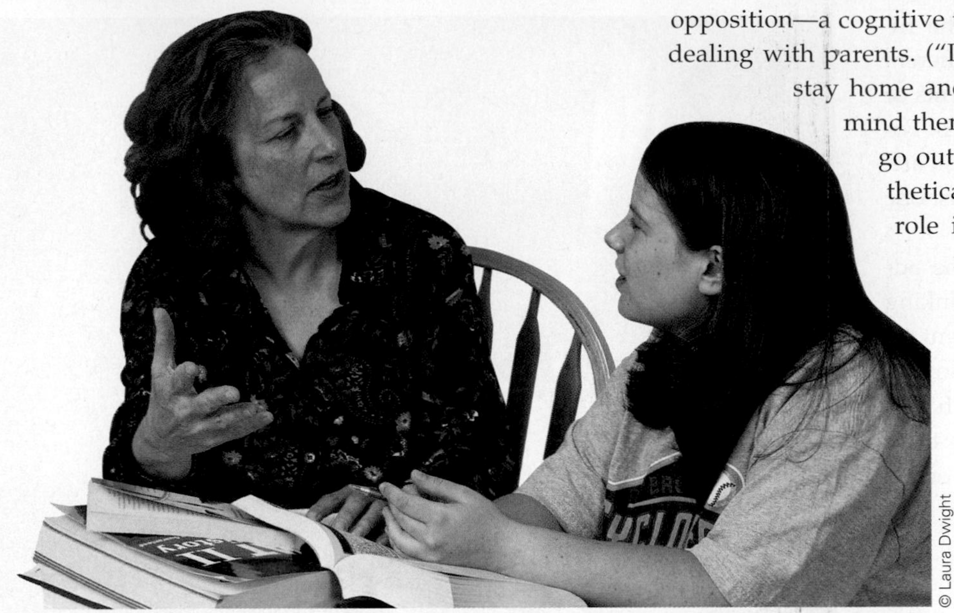

© Laura Dwight

Adolescents' ability to engage in hypothetical thinking may make them seem argumentative to their parents. In actuality, what adolescents may be are just better arguers.

Thinking About Abstract Concepts

The appearance of more systematic, abstract thinking is a second notable aspect of cognitive development during adolescence. For example, adolescents find it easier than children to comprehend the sorts of higher-order abstract logic inherent in puns, proverbs, metaphors, and analogies. The adolescent's greater facility with abstract thinking also applies to interpersonal and philosophical matters. This is clearly seen in the adolescent's increased capacity and interest in thinking about relationships, politics, religion, and morality—topics that involve such abstract concepts as friendship, democracy, faith, and honesty. As some writers have pointed out, the ability to think abstractly may prompt many adolescents to spend time thinking about the meaning of life itself (Hacker, 1994).

Thinking About Thinking

metacognition The process of thinking about thinking itself.

A third noteworthy gain in cognitive ability during adolescence involves thinking about thinking itself, the process sometimes referred to as **metacognition**. Metacognition often involves monitoring one's own cognitive activity during the process of thinking—when you consciously use a strategy for remembering something (such as *HOMES*, for the names of the Great Lakes—in case *you* don't remember, they are Huron, Ontario, Michigan, Erie, and Superior), or when you appraise your own comprehension of something you are reading before going on to the next paragraph. Not only do adolescents "manage" their thinking more than children, but they are also better able to explain to others the processes they are using. When asked, adolescents can explain not only *what* they know but also *why* knowing what they know enables them to think differently and solve problems more effectively (Reich, Oser, & Valentin, 1994).

One fascinating way in which thinking about thinking becomes more apparent during adolescence is in increased introspection, self-consciousness, and intellectualization. These intellectual advances may occasionally result in problems for the young adolescent, particularly before he or she adjusts to having such powerful cognitive tools. Being able to introspect, for instance, may lead to periods of extreme self-absorption—a sort of "adolescent egocentrism" (Elkind, 1967). **Adolescent egocentrism** results in two distinct problems in thinking that help to explain some of the seemingly odd beliefs and behaviors of teenagers (Goossens, Seiffge-Krenke, & Marcoen, 1992).

adolescent egocentrism The tendency for adolescents to be extremely self-absorbed, thought to result from advances in thinking abilities.

The first, the **imaginary audience**, involves having such a heightened sense of self-consciousness that you think your behavior is the focus of everyone else's concern and attention. For example, a teenager who is going to see the New Orleans Saints play the Philadelphia Eagles, with 68,000 other people in the stadium, may worry about dressing the right way because "everybody will notice." Given the cognitive limitations of adolescent egocentrism, it is difficult to persuade a young person that the "audience" is not all that concerned with his or her behavior or appearance. (Of course, if you were to wear a Saints jersey and the game were being played in Philadelphia, you'd be making a very big mistake.)

imaginary audience The belief, often brought on by the heightened self-consciousness of early adolescence, that everyone is watching and evaluating one's behavior.

A second problem resulting from adolescent egocentrism is the **personal fable**. The personal fable revolves around the adolescent's egocentric (and usually erroneous) belief that his or her experiences are unique. For instance, a teenager who just broke up with his girlfriend might tell his mother that she could not possibly understand what it feels like to break up with someone—even though breaking up is something that most people experienced often during their adolescent and young adult years. Adherence to a personal fable of uniqueness provides some protective benefits, in that it enhances adolescents' self-esteem and feelings of self-importance. But sometimes holding on to a personal fable can actually be quite dangerous, as in the case of a sexually active adolescent who believes that pregnancy simply won't happen to her or a reckless driver who believes that he will defy the laws of nature by taking hairpin turns on an icy road at breakneck speed. Although we associate this type of thinking with adolescence, studies show that susceptibility to the personal fable actually may appear not only in adolescence but also in adulthood (Goossens et al., 1992; Quadrel, Fischhoff, & Davis, 1993). Just ask any *adult* cigarette smoker if he or she is aware of the scientific evidence linking cigarette smoking with heart and lung disease.

personal fable A person's belief that he or she is unique and therefore not subject to the rules that govern other people's behavior.

Thinking in Multiple Dimensions

A fourth way in which thinking changes during adolescence involves the ability to think about things from different vantage points at the same time. Children tend to think about things one aspect at a time. Adolescents can see things through more complicated lenses, though. For instance, when a certain hitter comes up to the plate in a baseball game, a preadolescent who knows that the hitter has a good home-run record might exclaim that the batter will hit the ball out of the park. An adolescent, however, would consider the hitter's record in relation to the specific pitcher on the mound and would weigh both factors, or dimensions, before making a prediction (perhaps this player hits a lot of home runs against left-handed pitchers but strikes out often against righties).

As is the case with other gains in cognitive ability, the increasing capability of individuals to think in multiple dimensions also has consequences for their behavior and thinking in all sorts of settings. Adolescents describe themselves and others in more differentiated and complicated terms ("I'm both shy and extraverted") and find it easier to look at problems from multiple perspectives ("I know that's the way you see it, but try to look at it from her point of view"). Being able to understand that people's personalities are not one-sided, or that social situations can have different interpretations, depending on one's point of view, permits the adolescent to have far more sophisticated—and far more complicated—relationships with other people and self-conceptions, two topics we discuss in Chapter 12.

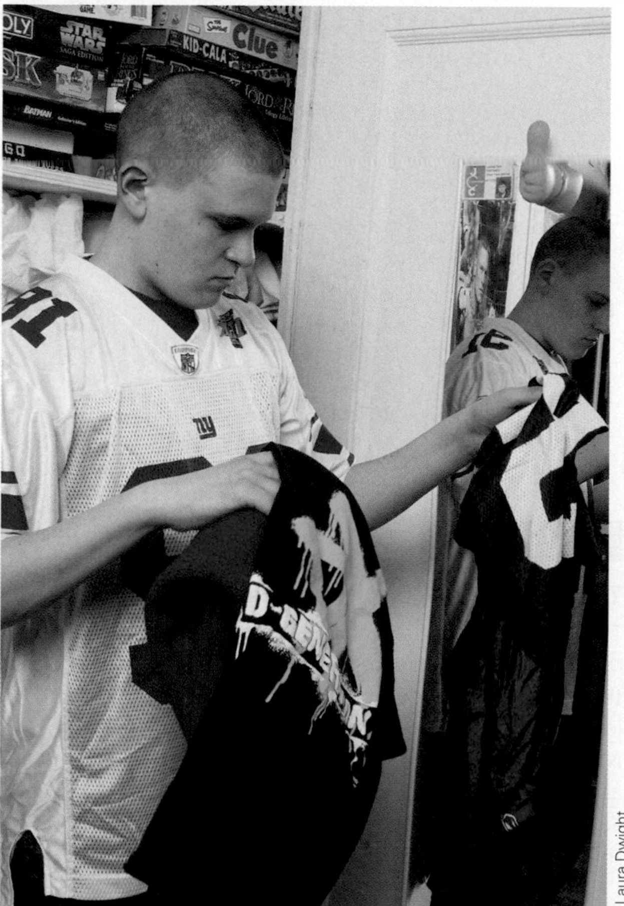

One manifestation of adolescent egocentrism is the "imaginary audience," which leads to the belief that one is the focus of everyone else's attention.

Adolescent Relativism

A final aspect of cognition that changes during adolescence concerns the way in which adolescents look at things. Children tend to see things in absolute terms—in black and white. Adolescents, in contrast, tend to see things as relative. They are more likely to question others' assertions and less likely to accept "facts" as absolute truths.

This increase in relativism can be particularly exasperating to parents, who may feel as though their adolescent children question everything just for the sake of argument. Difficulties often arise, for example, when adolescents begin seeing parents' values that they had previously considered absolutely correct ("Moral people do not have sex before they are married") as completely relative ("Welcome to the twenty-first century, Dad").

Theoretical Perspectives on Adolescent Thinking

The two theoretical viewpoints that have been especially important in the study of cognitive development in adolescence are Piaget's perspective and the information-processing perspective. Although these two views of adolescent thinking begin from different assumptions about the nature of cognitive development, they each provide valuable insight into why thinking changes during adolescence.

Piaget's View of Adolescent Thinking As you have read in previous chapters, Piaget theorized that intellectual development proceeds through stages, and that the stage of formal operations characterizes adolescence. Formal operational thinking is based in abstract logical principles.

The shift from concrete operational thinking, which characterizes middle childhood (see Chapter 9), to formal operational thinking appears to take place in two steps. During the first step, characteristic of early adolescence, formal thinking is apparent, but it has a sort of "Now you see it, now you don't" quality to it. Young adolescents may demonstrate formal thinking at some times but at others may only be able to think in concrete terms; use formal operations on some tasks but not on others; and reason formally under some but not all testing situations (Markovits et al., 1996). Virtually all adolescents go through this period of "emergent formal operations" (Kuhn et al., 1977). It is not until middle or even late adolescence that formal operational thinking becomes consolidated and integrated into the individual's general approach to reasoning (Markovits & Valchon, 1989).

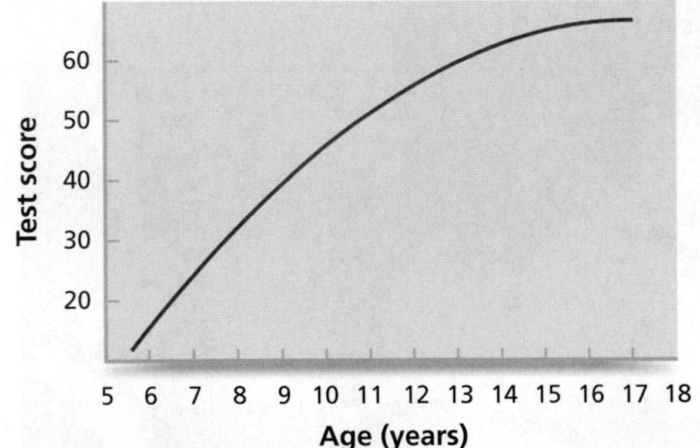

FIGURE 11.9

The Growth of Cognitive Abilities

The growth of cognitive abilities, as measured by standardized tests, is rapid between birth and age 16, and then levels off. Although there is little change in basic information processing after middle adolescence, there is continued development of more sophisticated thinking abilities in late adolescence.

Source: From *Journal of Genetic Psychology* by N. Bayley. Copyright 1949 by Taylor & Francis Informa UK Ltd.—Journals. Reproduced with permission of Taylor & Francis Informa UK Ltd. in the format Textbook via Copyright Clearance Center.

Piaget's perspective on adolescent cognition helps to explain why adolescents are better able than children to think about possibilities, to think multidimensionally, and to think about thoughts. Where Piaget's perspective on adolescent cognitive development falls short is in its claim that cognitive development proceeds in stages and adolescents' thinking should be thought of as qualitatively different from that of children (Kuhn, 2009). Rather, research suggests that advanced reasoning capabilities develop gradually and continuously from childhood through adolescence and beyond, probably in more of a quantitative fashion than was proposed by Piaget (i.e., more like a ramp than like a staircase).

The Information-Processing View of Adolescent Thinking Just what is it about the ways that adolescents think about things that makes them better problem solvers than children? This question has been the focus of researchers working from the information-processing perspective.

Studies of changes in specific components of information processing have focused on five areas in which improvement occurs during adolescence: attention, working memory, processing speed, organization, and metacognition. Improvements in all of these areas take place as individuals move from childhood through middle adolescence, with only very slight improvements after age 15 (and basically no improvements after age 20) (see Figure 11.9) (Demetriou et al., 2002; Keating, 2004; Luciana et al., 2005). (In other words, your memory, attention, and reasoning ability are no better now than when you were a junior in high school—and they may even be a little worse.) Don't despair, though: Cognitive development continues beyond age 15 and into young adulthood in more sophisticated skills, such as planning ahead or judging the relative costs and benefits of a risky decision. We also become better at coordinating cognition and emotion, when, for instance, one's feelings might interfere with logical reasoning (e.g., when you have to make a decision when you are angry, or in the face of peer pressure). (For a summary of this section, see "Interim Summary 11.5: How Thinking Changes in Adolescence.")

INTERIM SUMMARY 11.5

How Thinking Changes in Adolescence

Thinking About Possibilities	■ Adolescents are more able than children to think about what is possible, not just about what actually is. Two important manifestations of this are improvements in **deductive reasoning** and in **hypothetical thinking**. ■ Scientists believe that the ability to plan ahead and foresee the future consequences of one's actions is closely tied to the maturation of the prefrontal cortex.
Thinking About Abstract Concepts	■ Adolescents find it easier than children to comprehend the sorts of higher-order abstract logic inherent in puns, proverbs, metaphors, and analogies. ■ The adolescent's greater facility with abstract thinking also applies to interpersonal and philosophical matters, reflected in the adolescent's increased capacity and interest in thinking about relationships, politics, religion, and morality.
Thinking About Thinking	■ Improvements in **metacognition**, thinking about thinking, enable adolescents to explain what they know and use why they know what they know to solve problems more effectively. ■ Increased introspection, self-consciousness, and intellectualization may lead to periods of extreme self-absorption—a sort of "**adolescent egocentrism**" that contributes to the **imaginary audience** and the **personal fable**.
Thinking in Multiple Dimensions	■ Adolescents experience improvements in the ability to think about things from different vantage points at the same time, which permits them to have far more sophisticated and far more complicated self-conceptions and relations with other people.
Adolescent Relativism	■ Whereas children tend to see things in absolute terms, adolescents tend to see things as relative. ■ As a consequence, adolescents are more likely to question others' assertions and less likely to accept "facts" as absolute truths.

(continued)

INTERIM SUMMARY 11.5 *(continued)*

How Thinking Changes in Adolescence	
Theoretical Perspectives on Adolescent Thinking	■ According to Piaget, the stage of formal operations characterizes adolescence. Formal thinking is apparent in early adolescence but it is not until middle or even late adolescence that formal operational thinking becomes consolidated and integrated into the individual's general approach to reasoning. ■ Researchers working from the information-processing perspective focus on what it is about the ways that adolescents think about things that makes them better problem solvers than children. ■ Improvements in attention, working memory, processing speed, organization, and metacognition all take place during early adolescence. ■ Most basic information-processing skills level off around age 15, with only slight improvements after that. Cognitive development does continue beyond age 15 and into young adulthood, however, in more sophisticated skills such as planning ahead, weighing risks and rewards, and coordinating cognition and emotion.

SCHOOLING AND WORKING

One of the most important settings in which the cognitive developments of adolescence play out is school. In this section, we examine schools for adolescents, as well as why some individuals achieve more than others. We also look at the impact of having a job during the school year.

The Transition to Secondary School

Virtually all U.S. students make the transition from elementary school to secondary school (either middle school, junior high school, or high school) sometime in early adolescence. Generally speaking, research suggests that school transitions, whenever they occur, can disrupt adolescents' academic performance, behavior, and self-image. This disruption is generally temporary, however; over time, most youngsters adapt successfully to changing schools, especially when other aspects of their life—the family and peer relations, for example—remain stable and supportive and when the new school environment is well suited for adolescents (Eccles & Roeser, 2009).

Some experts believe that middle and junior high schools fail to meet the particular developmental needs of young adolescents (Eccles & Roeser, 2009). Not only are these schools larger and less personal, but teachers are less likely to trust their students and more likely to emphasize discipline, which creates a mismatch between what students at this age desire (more independence) and what their teachers provide (more control) (Midgley, Berman, & Hicks, 1995). It is little surprise that students experience a drop in achievement motivation when they enter middle or junior high school. The issue, according to some, is not that adolescents have to change schools. Rather, it is the nature of the change they must make.

Generally speaking, both adolescents and teachers are more satisfied in classes that combine a moderate degree of structure with high student involvement and high teacher support (Vieno et al., 2005; Wentzel, 2002). In these classes, teachers encourage their students' participation but do not let the class get out of control. Classes that are too task oriented—particularly when they also emphasize teacher control—tend to make students feel anxious, uninterested, and unhappy (Moos, 1978). Students do best when their teachers spend a high proportion of time on lessons (rather than on setting up equipment or dealing with discipline problems), begin and end lessons on time, provide clear feedback to students about what is expected of them and about their performance, and give ample praise to students when they perform well (Rutter, 1983).

Of course, student achievement is not solely in the hands of their teachers. Adolescents' own attitudes and motivation also play a role.

Making the transition from elementary school to middle school can be a challenge for many adolescents.

Achievement Motivation and Beliefs

Individuals differ in the extent to which they strive for success, and this difference in striving—which can be measured independently of sheer ability—helps to account for differences in actual achievement. Two students may be of equal intelligence, but if one student tries much harder than the other to do well in school, their grades will probably differ.

The extent to which an individual strives for success is called his or her **need for achievement** (McClelland et al., 1953). One of the oldest findings in the study of adolescent development is that adolescents who have a strong need for achievement have parents who have set high performance standards, rewarded school success in the past, and encouraged autonomy and independence (Rosen & D'Andrade, 1959; Winterbottom, 1958). Equally important, this training for achievement and independence needs to takes place in the context of a warm parent-child relationship (Shaw & White, 1965).

need for achievement A need that influences the extent to which an individual strives for success in evaluative situations.

Adolescents' behavior in school is also influenced by their judgments about their likelihood of succeeding or failing. Students who believe that they are good at math, for instance, will take more and more difficult math courses than their peers. But because course selection influences subsequent achievement (students who take more challenging math classes perform better on math tests), and achievement in turn influences students' beliefs about their abilities (students who do well on math examinations come to see themselves as better math students), a cycle is set in motion in which students' beliefs, abilities, and actual achievement have a reciprocal influence on each other (Marsh & Yeung, 1997).

A number of studies indicate that students' beliefs about their abilities exert a particularly strong influence on their motivation and effort, which in turn influences their scholastic performance (Mac Iver, Stipek, & Daniels, 1991; Pintrich, Roeser, & De Groot, 1994). To understand this process, it is necessary to draw a distinction between **intrinsic motivation** (sometimes referred to as *mastery motivation*) and **extrinsic motivation** (sometimes referred to as *performance motivation*). Individuals who are intrinsically motivated strive to achieve because of the pleasure they get out of learning and mastering the material. Individuals who are extrinsically motivated strive to achieve because of the rewards they get for performing well and the punishments they receive for performing poorly (see Figure 11.10).

intrinsic motivation Motivation based on the pleasure one will experience from mastering a task.

extrinsic motivation Motivation based on the rewards one will receive for successful performance.

Jeff Greenberg/The Image Works

Students who are intrinsically, rather than extrinsically, motivated, perform better and achieve more in school.

You probably know individuals who are genuinely interested in what they learn in school, and others whose main concern is really just their grade-point average. It turns out that these two approaches to achievement have very different psychological correlates and consequences. Adolescents who believe that they are competent are more likely to be intrinsically motivated and to maintain their efforts to do well in school (Pintrich et al., 1994). In contrast, adolescents who have doubts about their abilities are more likely to be extrinsically motivated and to be more susceptible to feelings of anxiety and hesitation in the face of challenge. Although extrinsically motivated adolescents want to do well in school, the source of their motivation puts them on shaky ground.

Parents and teachers also can affect adolescents' motivation to do well in school. It is also true that adults affect the extent to which an adolescent's achievement motives are intrinsic or extrinsic. When adults attempt to control an adolescent's achievement behavior through rewarding good grades (e.g., by giving prizes or money), punishing bad grades (e.g., by restricting privileges), or excessively supervising their performance (e.g., by constantly checking up on whether they are doing their homework), adolescents are more likely to develop an extrinsic orientation and, as a result, are less likely to do well in school.

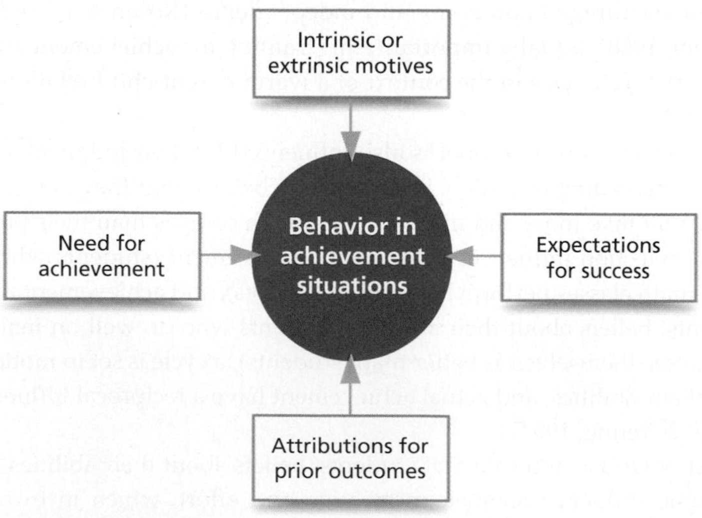

FIGURE 11.10

Influences on Achievement

Adolescents' behavior in achievement situations is influenced by their attitudes, expectations, beliefs, and motives. Students who have a strong need for achievement, expect to succeed, believe that success comes from working hard, and are intrinsically motivated are more likely to be high achievers.

In contrast, adolescents whose parents encourage their autonomy, provide a cognitively stimulating home environment, and are supportive of school success (without rewarding it concretely) tend to perform better in the classroom (Deci & Ryan, 1985; Ginsburg & Bronstein, 1993; Gottfried, Fleming, & Gottfried, 1998).

How students interpret their successes and failures—what psychologists refer to as **achievement attribution**—is also important (Dweck & Wortman, 1980). Generally speaking, individuals attribute their performance to a combination of four factors: ability, effort, task difficulty, and luck. When individuals succeed and attribute their success to internal causes, such as their ability or effort, they are more likely to approach future tasks confidently and with self-assurance. If individuals attribute their success to external factors outside their control, however—such as luck or an easy assignment—they remain unsure of their abilities. Not surprisingly, scholastically successful individuals, who tend to be high in achievement motivation, are likely to attribute their successes to internal causes (Carr, Borkowski, & Maxwell, 1991; Randel, Stevenson, & Witruk, 2000) (see Figure 11.11).

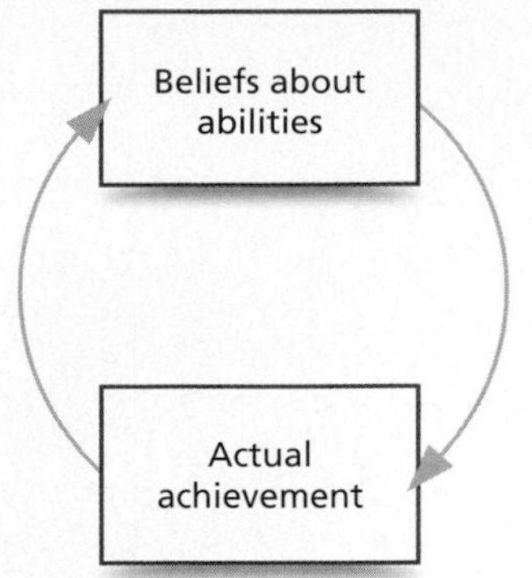

FIGURE 11.11

The Reciprocal Relation Between Beliefs and Achievement

The links between students' beliefs about their abilities and their actual achievement work in both directions. Students' school performance affects how they view their abilities, which in turn affects their subsequent performance.

How youngsters interpret their failures is also important. Some youngsters try harder in the face of failure, whereas others withdraw and exert less effort. When individuals attribute their failures to a lack of effort, they are more likely to try harder on future tasks (Dweck & Licht, 1980). But individuals who attribute their failure to factors that they feel cannot be changed (bad luck, lack of ability, task difficulty) are more likely to feel helpless and to exert less effort in subsequent situations. One important implication of this is that parents and teachers should encourage students to view their performance in school as primarily due to effort, rather than ability. That way, when they don't succeed (as is the case for all students from time to time), their response will be to try harder. In contrast, students who are told that they haven't done well because of a lack of ability ("You've never been good at foreign languages," "Girls just aren't as good at science as boys") see trying harder the next time as pointless.

achievement attribution The belief one holds about the causes of one's successes and failures.

Environmental Influences on Achievement

Ability, beliefs, and motivation may play a large role in influencing individual performance, but context also matters (Eccles & Roeser, 2009). Many of the differences in achievement that are observed among adolescents result from differences in the schools and classrooms where their abilities, beliefs, and motives are expressed, and in the home and neighborhood contexts in which these factors develop.

School environments differ markedly—in physical facilities, in opportunities for pursuing academically enriched programs, and in classroom atmospheres. Unfortunately, many school districts, plagued with shrinking tax bases, are characterized by decaying school buildings, outdated equipment, and textbook and teacher shortages. In some schools, problems with crime and discipline are so overwhelming that attention to these matters takes precedence over learning and instruction. As a result, many young people who genuinely want to succeed are held back not by a lack of talent or motivation but by a school environment that makes academic success virtually impossible. Students who attend schools with a high concentration of poor minority students are especially disadvantaged, as are students who attend schools with a high proportion of students from single-parent families (Bankston & Caldas, 1998; Pong, 1998).

The school, of course, is not the only environment that makes a difference in adolescents' achievement; indeed, few would argue that schools alone should accept full responsibility for adolescents who do not perform up to their abilities. If anything, the evidence suggests that important aspects of the home environment are better predictors of adolescents' academic achievement than are features of the school environment (Coleman et al., 1966; Steinberg, 1996). Studies have shown that adolescents' achievement is directly related to their parents' values and expectations (Jodl et al., 2001).

Parents who encourage school success set higher standards for their child's school performance and homework and have higher aspirations for their child, which in turn contributes to school success (Entwisle & Hayduk, 1988; Wilson & Wilson, 1992).

Parents who encourage school success also have values that are consistent with doing well in school, and they structure the home environment to support academic pursuits. Thus, the messages children receive from their teachers are echoed at home (Jodl et al., 2001; Kurdek & Sinclair, 1988; Sui-Chu & Willms, 1996). Parents who encourage success are likely to be more involved in their child's education—more likely to attend school programs, to help in course selection, to maintain interest in school activities and assignments, and the like—all of which contribute to students' success (Hill et al., 2004; Hoover-Dempsey & Sandler, 1995; Shumow & Miller, 2001).

There is also evidence that friends influence adolescents' achievement. Indeed, some studies suggest that friends, not parents, are the most powerful influences on adolescents' day-to-day school behavior, such as doing homework and exerting effort in class (Steinberg, 1996). Parents are stronger influences on long-range educational plans, but what adolescents do in school on a daily basis is more affected by their friends. Unfortunately, in the contemporary United States, the influence of the peer culture on academic achievement is more often negative than positive (Bishop et al., 2003; Steinberg, 1996). Perhaps because of this, adolescents with an extremely high orientation toward peers tend to perform worse in school (Fuligni & Eccles, 1993). As they move into middle school, adolescents become increasingly worried about their friends' reactions to success in school. One study found, for example, that by eighth grade, students did not want their classmates to know that they worked hard in school, even though they knew that it would be helpful to convey this impression to their teachers (Juvonen & Murdock, 1995).

Ethnic Differences in Educational Achievement

Among the most controversial—and intriguing—findings in research on adolescents' achievement are those concerning ethnic differences in school success. On average, the educational achievement of African American and Hispanic American students lags

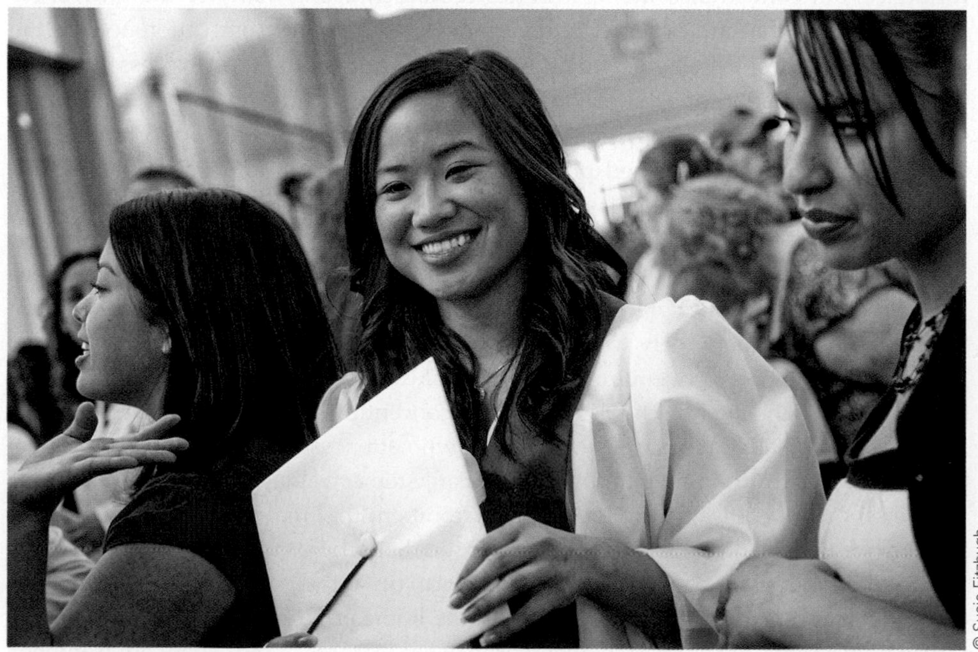

© Susie Fitzhugh

There are significant ethnic differences in adolescent achievement. Many studies find that Asian-American students are more successful in school than their peers.

behind that of Caucasian students, and all three groups achieve less in school than do Asian American students. These group differences persist even after socioeconomic factors are taken into account (Chen & Stevenson, 1995; Goyette & Xie, 1999; Hedges & Nowell, 1999; Mickelson, 1990; Steinberg, Dornbusch, & Brown, 1992). The academic superiority of Asian American students tends to emerge during the transition into junior high school—when most other students' grades typically decline—and persists through high school and into college (Fuligni, 1994; Fuligni & Witkow, 2004). What has been most puzzling to social scientists, though, is that even though African American and Hispanic students have educational aspirations and attitudes that are similar to those of Asian American and Caucasian students, they have significantly poorer academic skills, study habits, and school-related behavior (Ainsworth-Darnell & Downey, 1998). If African American and Hispanic students have the same long-term goals as other students, why do they not behave in similar ways?

Several explanations have been offered. Some writers have argued that even though they have high aspirations in the abstract, many African American and Hispanic youth do not genuinely believe that educational success will have substantial occupational payoff for them, because of prejudice against their ethnic group (Mickelson, 1990; Ogbu, 1974). Although intuitively appealing, this theory has not received convincing empirical support. It is true that adolescents who believe they have been victims of discrimination, or who believe that their opportunities for occupational success are unfairly limited by society, achieve less in school and report more emotional distress than do peers who do not hold these beliefs (Fisher, Wallace, & Fenton, 2000; Taylor et al., 1994). It is not true, however, that African American or Hispanic youngsters are more likely than other adolescents to believe that their opportunities for success are blocked (Steinberg et al., 1992). Indeed, several studies indicate that African American and Hispanic youth may actually have more optimistic beliefs and positive feelings about school than other students (e.g., Ainsworth-Darnell & Downey, 1998; Voelkl, 1997).

If anything, it may be adolescents' fear of failure, rather than their desire (or lack of desire) to succeed that matters most (Steinberg et al., 1992). Asian American youngsters not only believe in the value of school success but also are very anxious about the possible negative consequences of not doing well in school, both in terms of occupational success and in terms of their parents' disappointment (Eaton & Dembo, 1997; Steinberg et al., 1996). In addition, Asian cultures tend to place more emphasis on effort than on ability in explaining school success and are more likely to believe that all students have the capacity to succeed (Stevenson & Stigler, 1992). It is also important to note that Asian students—both in the United States and in Asia—spend significantly more time each week on homework and other school-related activities, and significantly less time socializing and watching television, than do other youth (Asakawa & Csikzentmihalyi, 2000; Steinberg et al., 1996). Studies of ethnic minority youngsters also show that foreign-born adolescents as well as those who are children of immigrants tend to achieve more in school than do minority youngsters who are second- or third-generation Americans (Fuligni, 1997; Kao, 1999). One explanation for this has been that part of becoming acculturated to U.S. society—at least among teenagers—may be learning to devalue academic success.

Dropping Out of High School

Today, how many years of schooling one completes is a powerful predictor of adult occupational success and earnings. Not surprisingly, high school dropouts are far more likely than graduates to live at or near the poverty level, to experience unemployment, to depend on government-subsidized income maintenance programs, to become pregnant while still teenagers, and to be involved in delinquent and criminal activity (Rumberger, 1995).

The proportion of individuals who have not completed high school has declined steadily over the past half century, to about 12 percent. There are huge variations in dropout rates from region to region, however; indeed, in some urban areas, well over 50 percent of all students leave school prematurely (Alexander, Entwisle, & Kabbani, 2001). African American youngsters drop out of high school at a rate only slightly greater than that of Caucasian youngsters (both are near the national average), but Hispanic youngsters drop out at more than twice the rate of other youth (U.S. Bureau of the Census, 2006) (see Figure 11.12). One reason for this is the large proportion of Hispanic youth who are not English-speaking; among Hispanic youth, a lack of proficiency in English is a major reason for dropping out (Stanton-Salazar & Dornbusch, 1995).

Adolescents who leave high school before graduating are more likely to come from lower socioeconomic levels, poor communities, large families, single-parent families, permissive or disengaged families, and households where little reading material is available (Alexander et al., 2001; Rumberger, 1995). Coupled with this disadvantage in background, adolescents who drop out of high school also are more likely to have had a history of poor school performance, low school involvement, multiple changes of schools, poor performance on standardized tests of achievement and intelligence, negative school experiences, and a variety of behavioral problems, such as excessive aggression (Rumberger & Larson, 1998). Specific events may trigger a student's final decision to leave school—a suspension for misbehavior, a failed course, an unintended pregnancy, or the lure of a job. But by and large, dropping out is a process characterized by a history of repeated academic failure and increasing alienation from school (Jordan, Lara, & McPartland, 1996).

Working During the School Year

Although most individuals do not enter into full-time employment until they are young adults, many teenagers, especially in the United States, hold part-time jobs while in high school. More high school students are working today than ever before, and

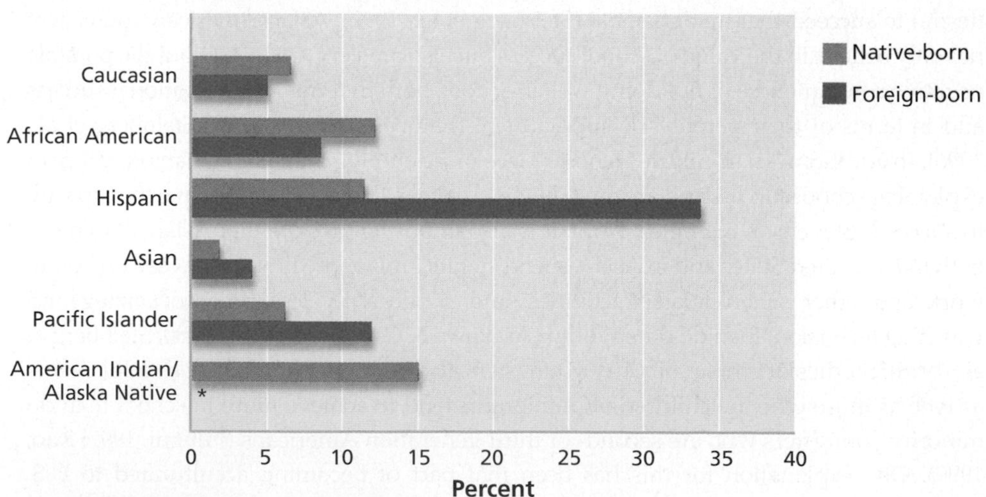

FIGURE 11.12

Ethnic Differences in the Rate of Dropping Out of School

There are substantial ethnic differences in dropout rates. Hispanic students are far more likely to leave school early than their African American or Caucasian peers. Although the dropout rate of Asian American students has not been tracked over as long a period, current dropout rates among Asian American students are substantially lower than in any other group.

those who do are working for considerably more hours than adolescents have in the past (Mortimer, 2003; National Research Council, 1998) (see Figure 11.13). The average high school sophomore puts in close to 15 hours per week at a job, and the average senior works about 20 hours per week (Mortimer, 2003).

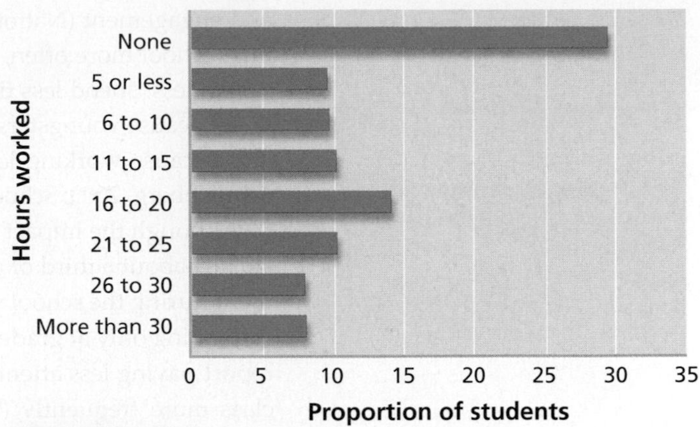

FIGURE 11.13

Working During the School Year

A dramatic increase occurred between 1940 and 1980 in the proportion of U.S. students who work during the school year. Today, the average high school sophomore puts in close to 15 hours per week at a job, and the average senior works about 20 hours per week.

Working and Adolescent Development Most people believe that working builds character, teaches adolescents about the real world, and helps young people prepare for adulthood. These assumptions are not generally supported by research, however. Indeed, studies indicate that the benefits of working during adolescence have probably been overstated and, moreover, that intensive employment during the school year may even have some costs to young people's development and preparation for adult work.

Studies of contemporary youth, for example, generally do not support the view that holding a job makes adolescents become more personally responsible and "learn the value of a dollar" (Mortimer & Johnson, 1998; Wright, Cullen, & Williams, 1997). Because the average working teenager earns around $400 each month, holding a job potentially provides many opportunities for learning how to budget, save, and use money responsibly. Few teenagers exercise a great deal of control when it comes to managing their wages, however. The majority of working teenagers spend most of their wages on their own needs and activities. Few adolescents who work save a large percentage of their income for their education, and fewer still use their earnings to help their families with household expenses. Instead, wages are spent on designer clothing, expensive stereo equipment, movies, and eating out (Steinberg, Fegley, & Dornbusch, 1993). Ironically, the very experience that many adults believe builds character may, in reality, teach adolescents undesirable lessons about work and the meaning of money (Steinberg et al., 1982). Adolescents who work long hours (20-plus hours weekly) are less satisfied with their lives than are adolescents who work fewer hours (Fine, Mortimer, & Roberts, 1990). In smaller doses (less than 20 hours per week), however, working does not seem to have either a positive or negative effect on adolescents' psychological development (Staff et al., 2009).

What can we make of these findings? Why would working long hours make youngsters more cynical about work and less satisfied with their lives? Perhaps the answer has something to do with the nature of the work most adolescents perform. Think for a moment about the job environment of most teenagers—or perhaps the environment you worked in as a teenager if you had a job: wrapping burgers at a fast-food restaurant, bagging groceries, staffing the cash register at a store in the mall. The work generally is dull, monotonous, and sometimes stressful (Greenberger & Steinberg, 1986). Even if you have never held such a job, you can certainly imagine that working under these conditions could make people feel cynical and protective of their own interests.

Working and Achievement A second question that has received a fair amount of research attention concerns the impact of working on adolescents' involvement in other activities, most notably, schooling. Here studies indicate that the issue is not whether a teenager works, but how much (Staff et al., 2004). Many experts now believe that working more than 20 hours a week may jeopardize adolescents' school performance and engagement (National Research Council, 1998). Youngsters who work long hours miss school more often, are less likely to participate in extracurricular activities, enjoy school less, spend less time on homework, and earn lower grades. These results occur both because youngsters who are less interested in school choose to work longer hours, and because working long hours leads to disengagement from school (Safron, Sy, & Schulenberg, 2003; Schoenhals, Tienda, & Schneider, 1998; Warren, 2002).

Although the impact of working on students' grades and achievement test scores is small—about a third of a letter grade—several studies indicate that extensive employment during the school year may take its toll on students in ways that are not revealed by looking only at grade-point averages. Students who work a great deal, for example, report paying less attention in class, exerting less effort on their studies, and skipping class more frequently (Steinberg & Dornbusch, 1991). Additionally, when students work a great deal, they often develop strategies for protecting their grades. These strategies include taking easier courses, cutting corners on homework assignments, copying homework from friends, and cheating (Greenberger & Steinberg, 1986). Teachers express concern about the excessive involvement of students in afterschool jobs (Bills, Helms, & Ozcan, 1995), and some teachers may respond to an influx of students into the workplace by lowering classroom expectations, assigning less homework, and using class time for students to complete assignments that otherwise would be done outside of school (Bills et al., 1995).

Working and Problem Behavior Some studies have asked if keeping teenagers busy with work will keep them out of trouble. Contrary to popular belief, employment during adolescence does not deter delinquent activity (Steinberg & Cauffman, 1995). In fact, several studies suggest that working long hours may actually be associated with *increases* in problem behavior (Gottfredson, 1985; Rich & Kim, 2002; Wright et al., 1997), although at least one study reports that the higher rate of problem behavior among working adolescents is due to the fact that delinquent youth are simply more likely to choose to work long hours than their peers (Paternoster et al., 2003). Many studies also have found that smoking, drinking, and drug use is higher among teenage workers than nonworkers, especially among students who work long hours (Mihalic & Elliott, 1997; Mortimer & Johnson, 1998; Wu, Schlenger, & Galvin, 2003). Alcohol and drug use both leads to, and follows from, intensive employment. That is, students who use alcohol and other drugs are more likely to want to work long hours, but increases in work hours lead to increases in cigarette, drug, and alcohol use (Paschall, Flewelling, & Russell, 2004; Safron et al., 2003; Steinberg et al., 1993).

Why should working lead to smoking, drinking, and drug use? The impact of extensive employment on adolescent drug and alcohol use probably reflects the fact that adolescents who work long hours have more discretionary income to spend on drugs and alcohol. In addition, drug and alcohol use are more common among adolescents who work under conditions of high job stress than among their peers who work for comparable amounts of time and money but under less stressful conditions. But the reality is that many adolescents work in stressful work settings, like fast-food restaurants (Greenberger, Steinberg, & Vaux, 1981). Whatever the reason, the impact of school-year employment on drug and alcohol use persists over time. Individuals who worked long hours as teenagers drink and use drugs more in their late twenties than their peers who worked less or not at all (Mihalic & Elliott, 1997). (For a summary of this section, see "Interim Summary 11.6, Schooling and Working.")

INTERIM SUMMARY **11.6**

Schooling and Working

The Transition to Secondary School	■ Making the transition from elementary school to secondary school can disrupt the academic performance, behavior, and self-image of adolescents. ■ Students who have more academic and psychosocial problems before making this school transition cope less successfully. ■ Generally speaking, both adolescents and teachers are more satisfied in classes that combine a moderate degree of structure with high student involvement and high teacher support.
Achievement, Motivation and Beliefs	■ The extent to which an individual strives for success is called the **need for achievement**. Adolescents who have a strong need for achievement have parents who set high performance standards, reward school success, and encourage autonomy and independence. ■ Adolescents' behavior in school is also influenced by their judgments about their likelihood of succeeding or failing, their motivation, and their attributions for success and failure. ■ Intrinsically motivated individuals strive to achieve because of the pleasure they get out of learning and mastering the material. Extrinsically motivated individuals strive to achieve because of the rewards they get for performing well and the punishments they receive for performing poorly. ■ When individuals attribute their failures to a lack of effort, they are more likely to try harder on future tasks. Individuals who attribute their failure to factors that they feel cannot be changed are more likely to feel helpless and to exert less effort in subsequent situations.
Environmental Influences on Achievement	■ Context also influences performance—school environments differ markedly in ways that affect student success. ■ Important aspects of the home environment are better predicators of adolescents' academic achievement than are features of the school environment. ■ Studies have shown that adolescents' achievement is directly related to their parents' values and expectations. In addition, the socioeconomic status of the adolescents' family impacts educational achievement. ■ Adolescents who are friends with high-achieving students do better in school, whereas those whose friends perform poorly in school do worse.

(continued)

INTERIM SUMMARY 11.6 *(continued)*

Schooling and Working	
Ethnic Differences in Educational Achievement	■ On average, the educational achievement of African American and Hispanic students lags behind that of Caucasian students, and all three groups achieve less in school than do Asian American students. ■ Studies have linked these differences to ethnic differences in beliefs about the causes of success and failure and to differences in beliefs about the consequences of doing poorly in school. ■ Studies of ethnic minority youngsters also show that foreign-born adolescents as well as those who are children of immigrants tend to achieve more in school than do minority youngsters who are second- or third-generation Americans.
Dropping Out of High School	■ High-school dropouts are far more likely than graduates to live at or near the poverty level, to experience unemployment, to depend on government-subsidized income-maintenance programs, to become pregnant while still teenagers, and to be involved in delinquent and criminal activity. ■ Dropping out of high school is not so much a discrete decision as the culmination of a long history of repeated academic failure and increasing alienation from school.
Working During High School	■ The majority of U.S. high school students work during the school year, with the average sophomore putting in close to 15 hours per week at a job and the average senior working about 20 hours per week. ■ Studies indicate that the benefits of working during adolescence have probably been overstated and that intensive employment during the school year may even have some costs to young people's development. ■ Many experts believe that working more than 20 hours a week may jeopardize adolescents' school performance and engagement and may increase delinquency and substance use.

SUMMING UP AND LOOKING AHEAD

Physical development in adolescence is dramatic. Boys and girls enter adolescence looking like children and leave looking like adults, not only taller and bigger, but with their sexual maturity in full view and their libido up and running. And of course, there are those physical changes inside the skull that are not as easy to see (at least without an expensive machine that images the brain) but that are equally important. We are only beginning to map out the course of brain development in adolescence and beyond, but already our view of what is happening inside the teenager's head has been radically transformed. A lot more development is taking place during adolescence than anyone had ever imagined. Scientists are just now beginning to understand the consequences of this for individuals' behavior, psychological development, and mental health.

In this chapter we looked at several aspects of adolescent functioning that are directly linked to the physical changes of the period—sleeping, having sex, dieting, and using alcohol and other drugs. (That combination sounds like a parent's nightmare, doesn't it?) Perhaps the safest thing we can say about developments in these domains is that adolescence is a time of risk, but it is also a time of opportunity. Yes, there are teenagers who are sleep deprived, promiscuous, obese, and substance-dependent. But there are plenty of young people who are well rested, sexually responsible, physically fit, and resistant to forces that lead others toward substance abuse. One of the most important things to keep in mind about physical health and well-being in adolescence is that the most significant threats to youngsters' health are self-imposed, and therefore avoidable. The challenge facing individuals who work with teenagers is to help them learn how to be, and how to stay, healthy.

We've also seen how brain maturation and the growth of advanced thinking abilities transforms many aspects of individuals' lives as they move into, through, and out of adolescence. The child who enters adolescence focused on the immediate, who thinks concretely about right and wrong, and whose ability to see things from others' points of view grows into the adolescent who thinks about the future, questions authority, and interacts with others in ways that take into account the fact that different people can look at the same event from different vantage points—and all be correct. By the time they are 16, teenagers can think just about as well as adults, at least with regard to their basic information-processing and logical reasoning abilities.

At the same time, however, adolescents' thinking is still limited in important ways, especially during early adolescence. They often suffer from a distinctive type of egocentrism, in which they believe that they are not only unique but also the focus of everyone else's attention. Their judgment, although better than it was during childhood, is still immature, and they often make impulsive and risky decisions. In some respects, then, there is still much cognitive development ahead.

The biological and cognitive changes of adolescence set the stage for equally profound changes in the ways in which adolescents view themselves and relate to family members and peers. That's where our examination of development in adolescence takes us next.

HERE'S WHAT YOU SHOULD KNOW

Did You Get It?

After reading this chapter, you should understand the following:

- The major physical changes in males and females at puberty, and the process that triggers the onset of puberty
- The ways in which early and later maturation affect adolescents' psychological development
- Basic facts about sexual behavior during adolescence, including patterns of sexual activity, contraceptive use, pregnancy, and the impact of sex education
- The most common forms of disordered eating in adolescence
- The main ways in which the brain changes during adolescence and the impact of these changes on adolescent thinking and behavior
- Basic facts about substance use in adolescence, including patterns of use, risk factors for problems, and approaches to treatment and prevention
- The major ways in which thinking changes during adolescence, and the Piagetian and information-processing accounts of these changes
- Important influences on adolescents' school achievement, as well as basic facts about patterns of educational attainment
- The impact of work experience on adolescent development

Important Terms and Concepts

achievement attribution (p. 361)
adolescent egocentrism (p. 354)
adolescent growth spurt (p. 333)
adrenarche (p. 332)
androgens (p. 332)
anorexia nervosa (p. 339)
binge drinking (p. 346)
bulimia (p. 339)
cortisol (p. 333)
deductive reasoning (p. 353)
delayed phase preference (p. 335)
disordered eating (p. 338)
dorsolateral prefrontal cortex (p. 350)
endocrine system (p. 332)
estrogens (p. 332)
extrinsic motivation (p. 359)
glands (p. 332)
gonads (p. 332)
hippocampus (p. 351)
hormones (p. 332)
HPG (hypothalamic-pituitary-gonadal) axis (p. 332)
hypothalamus (p. 332)
hypothetical thinking (p. 353)
imaginary audience (p. 355)
intrinsic motivation (p. 359)
leptin (p. 332)
limbic system (p. 351)
melatonin (p. 336)
menarche (p. 334)
metacognition (p. 354)
need for achievement (p. 359)
neurotransmitters (p. 351)
orbitofrontal cortex (p. 350)
ovaries (p. 332)
personal fable (p. 355)
pituitary gland (p. 332)
prefrontal cortex (p. 350)
puberty (p. 331)
risk factors (p. 348)
rite of passage (p. 334)
secondary sex characteristics (p. 333)
secular trend (p. 337)
set point (p. 332)
substance abuse (p. 347)
substance dependence (p. 347)
Tanner stages (p. 333)
testes (p. 332)
ventromedial prefrontal cortex (p. 350)

CHAPTER

12

Socioemotional Development in Adolescence

© Spencer Grant/PhotoEdit

By virtually any indicator, adolescence is longer than it has ever been before, because young people go through puberty (one marker of the beginning of adolescence) earlier, and because they enter into adult roles of work and family (one way to define the end of adolescence) later.

In previous eras, when puberty occurred around 15, and when individuals left school and entered the world of work just a few years later, adolescence, at least by these markers, was only a few years long. Today, though, young people are caught between the world of childhood and the world of adulthood for an extremely long time, often longer than a decade. The lengthening of adolescence as a developmental period has had important implications for how young people see themselves, relate to others, and develop psychologically.

Here's an illustration of why this matters. If someone older tells you that people should "wait until they're married before having sex," you might point out that this was a lot easier when they (or their parents) were growing up. A woman who was born in 1930 went through puberty when she was about 14½ and probably got married when she was around 20. So if she "waited" before losing her virginity, she waited for about 5½ years. Today, the average girl goes through puberty around 12 and will probably get married when she is in her late 20s. She'll have to wait three times as long!

In this chapter, we look at some of the main psychosocial developments of the adolescent period. We begin with what many consider to be the central psychological task of adolescence—developing an independent identity. Next, we look at two of the main contexts in which psychosocial development takes place: the family and the peer group. Following this, we turn to a discussion of two sets of problems that aren't universal during adolescence, but that affect a large number of teenagers: externalizing problems, like delinquency and aggression, and internalizing problems, like depression and suicide.

Before we begin, though, we're going to start with what may strike you as an odd question: Have there always been adolescents?

THE INVENTION OF ADOLESCENCE

Although this question seems like a simple one with an obvious answer, it actually is pretty complicated. Naturally, there have always been individuals between 10 and 20 years old, who have gone through puberty, and whose prefrontal cortex was still maturing. But adolescence as we know it in contemporary society did not really exist until the middle of the nineteenth century (Fasick, 1994). Prior to that time, children were viewed as miniature adults, and the term "child" referred to anyone under the age of 18 or even 21. The main difference between "children" and "adults" was not their age or their abilities but whether they could own property (Modell & Goodman, 1990). Thus there was little reason to label some young people as "children" and others as "adolescents." In fact, the word *adolescent* was not widely used before the nineteenth century.

With the Industrial Revolution in the late nineteenth century, however, came profound changes in work, schooling, and family life, and adolescents were among those most affected. Because the economy was moving away from the simple and predictable life known in farming societies, the connection between what individuals learned in childhood and what they would need to know in adulthood grew uncertain. Parents, especially in middle-class families, encouraged their teenagers to prepare for adulthood in school, rather than on the job. Before industrialization, adolescents spent their days working with their parents and other adults close to home. Now they were increasingly likely to spend their days in school with peers of the same age.

Industrialization also changed adolescents' standing in the work force. One outcome of industrialization was a shortage of jobs, because new machines replaced many workers. Adolescents were now competing with adults for a limited supply of jobs—and adults didn't like it one bit. A convenient way of dealing with this competition was to remove adolescents from the labor force by turning them into full-time students. To accomplish this, society needed to rationalize differentiating between individuals who were "ready" for work and those who still needed to go to school. Teenagers, who earlier in the century would have been working side by side with adults, were now seen as too immature or too unskilled to carry out similar tasks—even though the adolescents themselves hadn't changed in any meaningful way (Enright et al., 1987). No one wants to admit it, but one reason we force teenagers to go to high school for as long as they must is to make sure that they don't take jobs away from adults! (Kind of puts that awful class you endured as a high school sophomore in a new light, doesn't it?)

Some adults were genuinely interested in protecting adolescents from the dangers of a changing society, of course. Families were moving from small, traditional farming communities, where everyone knew everyone else, to large, crowded, turbulent urban areas. The "evils of city life" (crime and vice) loomed large. Furthermore, factories were hazardous working environments, filled with new and unfamiliar machinery. **Child protectionists** argued that young people needed to be sheltered from the labor force for their own good (Modell & Goodman, 1990).

child protectionists Individuals who argued, early in the twentieth century, that adolescents needed to be kept out of the labor force in order to protect them from the hazards of the workplace.

Whatever the reason, it was not until the late nineteenth century—a little more than 100 years ago—that adolescence became what it is today: a long period of preparation for adulthood, in which young people remain economically reliant on their parents and spend most of their time in school or in leisure activities with people of the same age. As you can imagine, the way adolescence is structured by society gives it a distinctive psychological flavor. Many of the things we take for granted as inherent features of adolescence—peer pressure, struggles with parents over independence, having an

INTERIM SUMMARY 12.1

The Invention of Adolescence

- Adolescence, as we know it in contemporary society, did not really exist until the middle of the nineteenth century.
- As a result of the Industrial Revolution, teenagers were encouraged to prepare for adulthood in school rather than on the job, and over time, adolescents were removed from the labor force.
- Today adolescence is a long period of preparation for adulthood in which young people remain economically reliant on their parents and spend most of their time in school or in leisure activities with people of the same age.

"identity crisis"—are new phenomena. Far more than in previous times, today, one of the most important socioemotional tasks of adolescence is to develop a clearer sense of who you are and where you are headed. (For a summary of this section, see "Interim Summary 12.1: The Invention of Adolescence.")

DEVELOPING AN INDEPENDENT IDENTITY

More novels, movies, television shows, and plays have probably been written about "coming of age"—making the transition from adolescence to adulthood—than any other subject. The list is endless, and as diverse as adolescents themselves: *Hamlet, The Catcher in the Rye, I Know Why the Caged Bird Sings, The House on Mango Street, My So-Called Life, American Graffiti, Y Tu Mamá También, The Bluest Eye, The Joy Luck Club, Stand By Me, The Wonder Years*. In all of these stories, an adolescent has a series of experiences that leads to a reevaluation of who he or she is and where he or she is headed. It's not surprising that this theme is so popular—adolescence is one of the most important periods for the development of an independent identity. The dominant view in the study of adolescent identity development is that proposed by Erik Erikson. Although developing a coherent sense of identity appears to take place at a later age than Erikson thought when he first wrote about it, in the 1950s (it probably happens in the early 20s or mid-20s for most people today), his theory of the adolescent identity crisis remains extremely influential.

Erikson's Theoretical Framework

identity versus identity diffusion According to Erikson, the normative crisis characteristic of the fifth stage of psychosocial development, predominant during adolescence, during which a coherent and unique sense of self is formed.

As you read in Chapter 1, Erikson viewed the developing person as moving through a series of eight psychosocial crises over the course of the lifespan. He believed that resolving the crisis of **identity versus identity diffusion** is the chief psychosocial task of adolescence. Before adolescence, the child's identity is like a jigsaw puzzle with many pieces that have not yet been connected. But after this crisis is successfully resolved, these pieces will be joined to form a coherent picture that is unique to the adolescent. According to Erikson, it is not until adolescence that individuals have the mental or emotional capacity to tackle this task. Of the many social roles available in contemporary society, which fits them? The key to resolving the identity crisis, he argued, lies in the adolescent's interactions with others. Responding to the reactions of people who matter, the adolescent selects and chooses from among the many facets that could conceivably become a part of who he or she really is. The other people with whom the young person interacts serve as a sort of mirror that reflects back information about who the adolescent is and who he or she ought to be. Through others' reactions, we learn whether we are graceful or clumsy, nice-looking or unattractive, socially competent or clueless. Perhaps more important, we learn from others what it is we do that we ought to keep doing, and what it is that we ought to stop.

Social Context and Identity Development The social context has a tremendous effect on the nature and outcome of the process of identity development. Clearly, if adolescents' identities grow out of others' responses to them, society will play an important role in determining which sorts of identities are possible alternatives, and of those identities that are genuine options, which are desirable and which are not. As a result, the course of identity development varies across cultures, among different groups within the same society, and over different historical epochs (Kroger, 1993). For example, in the past, most young women assumed that their adult identity would revolve around being a wife and mother. But many more alternative identities are open to women today, and as a result, choosing among different alternatives (What's more important to me, marriage and family or a career? Should I pursue higher education?

What occupation should I aim for? When do I want to get married? Have children?) has become much more complicated.

The rapid rate of social change in today's world has raised new sets of questions for young people (both males and females) to consider—questions not only about their occupation but also about their values, lifestyle, and relationships. Consequently, the likelihood of going through a prolonged and difficult identity crisis is probably greater today than it has ever been.

The Psychosocial Moratorium According to Erikson, the complications inherent in identity development in modern society have created the need for a **psychosocial moratorium**—a "time-out" during adolescence from responsibilities and obligations that might restrict the young person's pursuit of self-discovery. Most adolescents in the contemporary United States are given a moratorium of sorts by being encouraged to remain in school for a long time, where they can develop plans for the future without making decisions that are impossible to undo.

psychosocial moratorium A period of time during which individuals are free from excessive obligations and responsibilities and can therefore experiment with different roles and personalities.

During the psychosocial moratorium, adolescents can experiment with different roles and identities in a context that permits and encourages this sort of exploration. They can try on different postures, personalities, and ways of behaving. One week, an adolescent girl will spend hours engrossed in *Vogue* or *Seventeen*; the next week she will insist to her parents that she is tired of caring so much about the way she looks. An adolescent boy will come home one day with a tattoo and pierced ear; a few weeks later he will discard this image for Abercrombie & Fitch or Polo (although he may discover that getting rid of the tattoo and piercing is not so simple). Although many parents worry about their teenage children going through phases like these, much of this behavior is actually normal experimentation with roles and personalities.

© Andrew Holbrooke/Corbis

Adolescence is often a time for experimentation with different roles and identities.

The moratorium Erikson described is an ideal, however, perhaps even a luxury of the affluent. Many young people—possibly most—do not have the economic freedom to enjoy a long time-out before taking on adult responsibilities. For many, alternatives are not open in any realistic sense, and introspection only interferes with the more pressing task of survival. You may know people who have had to drop out of college and take a job they really did not want because of financial pressures. According to Erikson, without a chance to explore, to experiment, and to choose among options for the future, these young people may not realize all that they are capable of becoming. Some might even say that the most important part of going to college is not what you learn in class, but what you learn about yourself.

Determining an Adolescent's Identity Status

Psychologists use the term **identity status** to refer to the point in the identity development process that characterizes an adolescent at a given time. Most researchers who study identity development this way use an approach developed by James Marcia (1966), which focuses on identity exploration in three areas—work, ideology (values and beliefs), and relationships. Based on responses to an interview or questionnaire,

identity status The point in the identity development process that characterizes an adolescent at a given time.

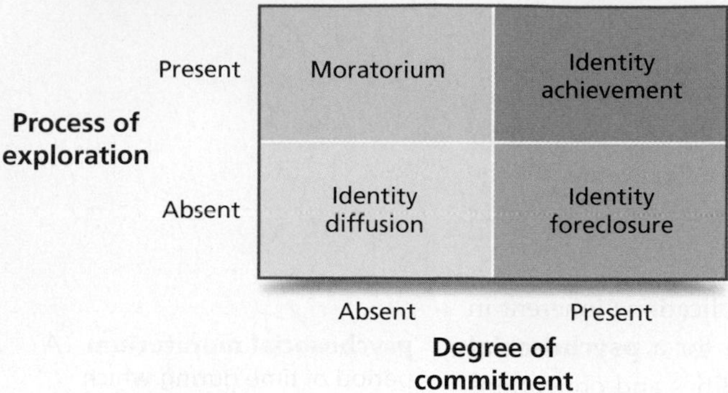

FIGURE 12.1

Identity Status Categories, as Defined by Exploration and Commitment

Psychologists study the development of identity by interviewing adolescents about work, ideology, and relationships, and then assigning them to one of four identity status categories.

individuals are rated on two dimensions: (1) the degree to which they have made commitments and (2) the degree to which they engaged in a sustained search in the process. Researchers then assign individuals to one of four categories: *identity achievement* (after a period of exploration, the individual has established a coherent sense of identity); *moratorium* (the individual is in the midst of a period of crisis and experimentation); *identity foreclosure* (the individual has made commitments but without a period of crisis or experimentation); and *identity diffusion* (the individual does not have firm commitments and is not currently trying to make them) (see Figure 12.1).

Generally speaking, research employing this approach has supported many aspects of Erikson's theory (Meeus et al., 1999). Identity achievers score highest on measures of achievement motivation, moral reasoning, intimacy with peers, reflectiveness, and career maturity. Individuals in the moratorium category score highest on measures of anxiety, show the highest levels of conflict over issues of authority, and do not have a firm set of values and beliefs. Individuals in the foreclosure group are the most authoritarian and most prejudiced, have the highest need for social approval and the lowest level of autonomy, and are especially close to their parents. Individuals in a state of identity diffusion display the most psychological and interpersonal problems, are the most socially withdrawn, and report the lowest level of intimacy with peers (Adams, Gullotta, & Montemayor, 1992).

The Development of Ethnic Identity

ethnic identity The aspect of one's sense of identity concerning ancestry or racial group membership.

For adolescents who are not part of the majority culture, integrating a sense of **ethnic identity** into their overall sense of personal identity is an important task of late adolescence, perhaps as important as establishing a coherent occupational, ideological, or interpersonal identity (Newman, 2005; Phinney & Alipuria, 1987). Over the past two decades, the process through which ethnic identity develops has received a great deal of research attention, as has the link between ethnic identity and psychological adjustment. Ethnic identity has been studied in samples of African American, Hispanic, American Indian, Asian American, and Caucasian youth (Spencer & Markstrom-Adams, 1990). In America, Caucasian youth generally have a weaker sense of ethnic identity than their non-Caucasian peers, but many Caucasian adolescents identify strongly with a particular ethnic group (e.g., German, Irish, Italian, Jewish) and derive part of their overall sense of self from this identification (Martinez & Dukes, 1997; Roberts et al., 1999).

The process of ethnic identity development follows the general process of identity development: An event or series of events makes the adolescent realize that others see him as "different," which upsets the unquestioning view he had of himself as a child (Cross, 1978; Kim, 1981, cited in Phinney & Alipuria, 1987). As a result of the crisis, the individual may become immersed in his or her own ethnic group and may turn against the majority culture. Eventually, as the value of having a strong ethnic identity becomes clear, the adolescent establishes a more coherent sense of self that includes this ethnic identity, and with growing confidence he or she attempts to help others deal with their own struggles with similar issues. Consistent with this, a recent study of ethnic identity development found that inner-city adolescents' feelings about their own ethnic group became more positive during both early and middle adolescence (when ethnic identity first becomes salient and individuals become immersed in their own culture) but that actual identity exploration did not really begin until middle adolescence (French et al., 2006).

Do members of ethnic minorities have more difficulty than Caucasian adolescents in resolving the identity crisis? The little research that has been done suggests more similarities than differences. One difference, though, appears to be quite important, if maybe unsurprising: Having a strong ethnic identity is associated with higher self-esteem, stronger feelings of self-efficacy, and better mental health among minority youngsters, whereas the link between ethnic identity and psychological functioning is weaker among Caucasian youth (DuBois et al., 2002; Martinez & Dukes, 1997).

As many writers have noted, however, developing a coherent sense of identity is much more complicated for minority adolescents than for their majority counterparts (Spencer & Dornbusch, 1990). Because identity development is so influenced by the social context in which the adolescent lives, the development of minority adolescents must be understood in relation to the specific context in which they grow up (Garcia Coll et al., 1996). All too often, this context includes racial stereotypes, discrimination, and mixed messages about the costs and benefits of identifying too closely with the majority culture.

For ethnic minority youth, developing a sense of ethnic identity is an important challenge.

According to psychologist Jean Phinney, an expert on this issue, minority youth have four possibilities open to them for dealing with their ethnicity: *assimilation* (i.e., adopting the majority culture's norms and standards while rejecting those of one's own group); *marginality* (i.e., living within the majority culture but feeling estranged and outcast); *separation* (i.e., associating only with members of one's own culture and rejecting the majority culture); and *biculturalism* (i.e., maintaining ties to both the majority and the minority cultures) (Phinney et al., 1994).

Advice on which of these paths is most preferable has changed considerably. In the past, minority youth were encouraged, at least by majority society, to assimilate as much as possible. Assimilation, however, has not proven to be as simple as many nonminority individuals imagine (Gil, Vega, & Dimas, 1994). First, although minority youth are told to assimilate, they may be nonetheless excluded from majority society because of their physical appearance or language (Vega et al., 1995). This leads to a situation of marginality in which the minority youth is on the edge of majority society but is never really accepted as a full-status member.

Second, minority youth who do attempt to assimilate are often scorned by their own communities for trying to "act white." Partly in reaction to this, many minority youth in predominantly Caucasian schools adopt strategies of separation and biculturalism, especially as they get older (Hamm & Coleman, 2001). This is particularly common among African American adolescents, who are often the victims of intense discrimination and prejudice (Sellers et al., 2006; Spencer, 2005) (see Figure 12.2).

A few studies have compared the ethnic identity orientations of Asian American, African American, Hispanic, and Caucasian adolescents. In one such study (Rotherham-Borus, 1990), as expected, Caucasian youngsters were more likely to characterize themselves as assimilated (or "mainstream") than were minority students, who were more likely to characterize themselves as bicultural (between 40% and 50%) than as either assimilated or embedded solely within their ethnic group (separated). African American and Puerto Rican adolescents are relatively more likely to be ethnically embedded, whereas Mexican American and Asian American adolescents are more likely to be bicultural (e.g., Phinney et al., 1994). In general, positive mental health among ethnic minority adolescents is associated with having a strong and positive ethnic identity and a healthy awareness of the potential for discrimination, but not with outright rejection of the mainstream culture (Umaña-Taylor, 2004; Yasui, Dorham, & Dishion, 2004).

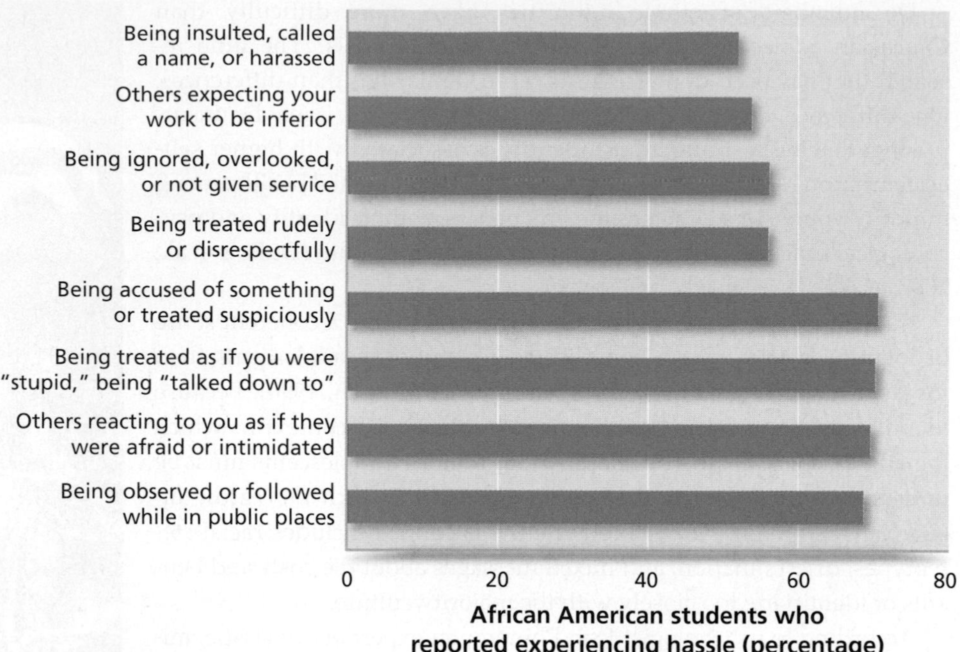

FIGURE 12.2

African American Students' Reports of Race-Related Hassles

Many African American students report that they are the victims of discrimination.

Source: "Racial identity matters: The relationship between racial discrimination and psychological functioning in African American adolescents" by R.M. Sellers, N. Copeland-Linder, P.P. Martin, and R.L. Lewis, *Journal of Research on Adolescence,* 16, pp. 187–216. Copyright © 2006 by Blackwell Publishing Ltd. Reproduced by permission of Blackwell Publishing Ltd.

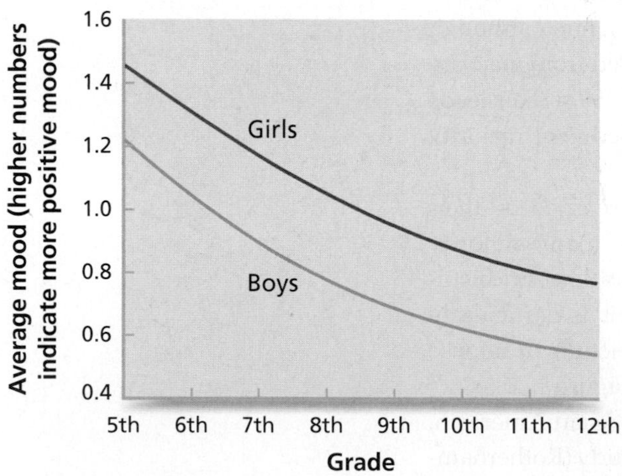

FIGURE 12.3

Changes in Self-Evaluations in Adolescence

Early adolescence is a time of heightened self-consciousness and greater fluctuation in self-image, which may make a teenager's mood become more negative.

Source: From "Continuity, stability, and change in daily emotional experience across adolescence" by R. Larson, G. Moneta, M.H. Richards, & S. Wilson, *Child Development, 734,* pp. 1151–1165. Copyright © 2002. Reprinted by permission of Wiley/Blackwell through Rightslink.

Changes in Self-Esteem

Researchers interested in identity development have also studied self-esteem in adolescence, although studies have not yielded consistent findings. Some studies find that individuals' feelings about themselves decline over the course of adolescence (e.g., Jacobs et al., 2002), but others find that they increase (Cole et al., 2001). In general, however, *changes* in self-perceptions (whether positive or negative) are greater during early adolescence than during middle or late adolescence; from middle adolescence through young adulthood, self-esteem either remains at about the same level or increases (Harter, 1998).

More specifically, fluctuations in adolescents' self-image are most likely to occur between the ages of 12 and 14. Compared with older adolescents (15 years and older) and with preadolescents (8 to 11 years old), early adolescents are more self-conscious and have a more unstable self-image than other youngsters (see Figure 12.3). Younger adolescents are also more prone to feel ashamed than older individuals, which may result from and contribute to their heightened self-consciousness (Reimer, 1996). Generally speaking, the small but reliable differences between the preadolescents and the early adolescents are greater than those between the younger and the older adolescents, which indicates that the most marked fluctuations in self-image occur during the transition into adolescence, rather than over the course of adolescence itself (Simmons, Rosenberg, & Rosenberg, 1973). As you will read in the next section, early adolescence is also the time of the most dramatic changes in family relationships. (For a summary of this section, see "Interim Summary 12.2: Developing an Independent Identity.")

INTERIM SUMMARY 12.2

Developing an Independent Identity

Erikson's Theoretical Framework	■ Erikson believed that resolving the crisis of **identity versus identity diffusion** is the chief psychological task of adolescence. ■ Erikson believed that the complications inherent in identity development in modern society have created the need for a **psychological moratorium**—a "time-out" during adolescence from responsibilities and obligations that might restrict the young person's pursuit of self-discovery. ■ During this moratorium, adolescents can experiment with different roles and identities in a context that permits and encourages this sort of exploration.
Determining an Adolescent's Identity Status	■ The term **identity status** refers to the point in the identity development process that characterizes an adolescent at a given time. ■ Most researchers who study development this way use an approach that focuses on identity exploration in three areas—work, ideology, and relationships. ■ Based on responses to an interview or questionnaire, individuals are assigned to one of four categories: identity achievement, moratorium, identity foreclosure, or identity diffusion.
The Development of Ethnic Identity	■ For adolescents who are not part of the majority culture, integrating a sense of **ethnic identity** into their overall sense of personal identity is an important task of adolescence. ■ Having a strong ethnic identity is associated with higher self-esteem, stronger feelings of self-efficacy, and better mental health among minority youngsters, whereas the link between ethnic identity and psychological functioning is weaker among Caucasian youth. ■ According to one model, minority youth have four possibilities open to them for dealing with their ethnicity within the context of the larger society: assimilating, remaining marginal, separating, and becoming bicultural. ■ In general, positive mental health among ethnic minority adolescents is associated with having a strong and positive ethnic identity, but not with outright rejection of the mainstream culture.
Changes in Self-Esteem	■ Some studies find that individuals' feelings about themselves become more negative over the course of adolescence, but others find that they increase. ■ Compared with older adolescents and with preadolescents, early adolescents are more self-conscious and have a more unstable self-image.

FAMILY RELATIONSHIPS IN ADOLESCENCE

Have you ever noticed that your relationships with others sometimes alternate between periods when things are very smooth and predictable and times when they are not? The same is true in families. Not surprisingly, relationships in families change most dramatically when individual family members or the family's circumstances are changing, since that's when the family's previously established equilibrium will be upset. One period in which family relationships often become unstable is adolescence. A study of interactions between adolescent boys and their parents found that the peak time for this disequilibrium was around ages 13 and 14. The researchers speculate that, because some of this transformation may be driven by puberty, in families with girls, this "disequilibrium" is more likely to occur earlier, around 11 or 12 (Granic et al., 2003).

Adolescents' Relationships with Parents

In most families, there is a shift during adolescence away from patterns of influence and interaction that are unequal to ones in which parents and their adolescent children are on more equal footing (Collins & Laursen, 2009). And some evidence indicates that early adolescence—when this shift first begins—may be a time of temporary disruption in the family system. In particular, studies of family interaction suggest that in early adolescence, young people begin to try to play a more forceful role in the family, but their parents may not yet acknowledge the adolescents' input. As a result, young adolescents may interrupt their parents more often but have little impact. By middle adolescence, however, teenagers act and are treated much more like adults. They have more influence over family decisions, but they do not need to assert their opinions through interruptions and similarly immature behavior (Grotevant, 1997).

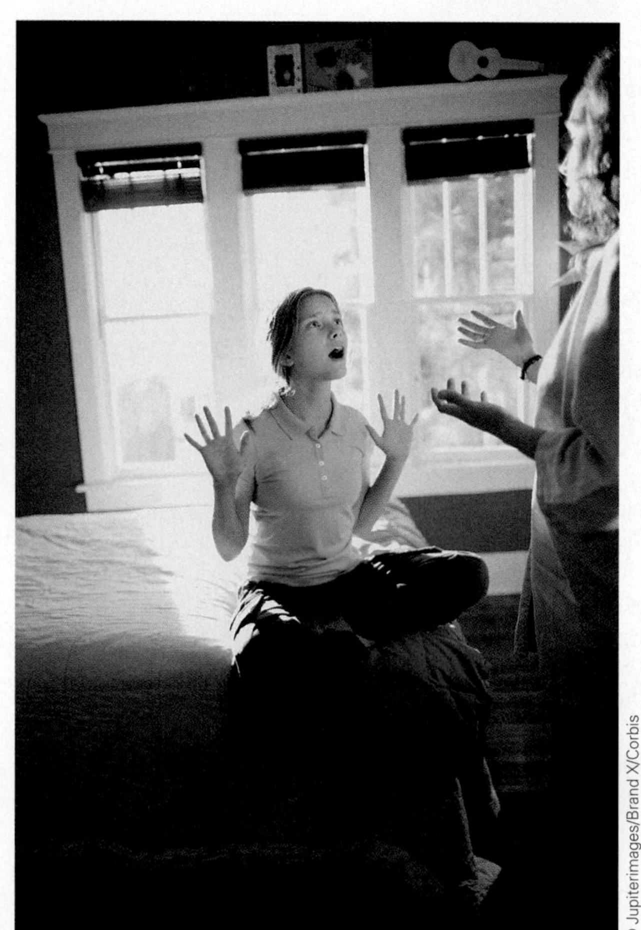
© Jupiterimages/Brand X/Corbis

Early adolescence may be a challenging time for the family, as teenagers begin to assert their influence.

To adapt to the changes triggered by the child's entrance into adolescence, family members must have some shared sense of what they are experiencing and how they are changing. Yet in many families, parents and children live in "separate realities," perceiving their day-to-day experiences in very different ways (Larson & Richards, 1994). Suppose that a mother and son have a conversation about the boy's schoolwork. She may experience the conversation as a serious discussion, while he may perceive it as an argument. One interesting finding to emerge from recent research on brain maturation in adolescence is that young adolescents may be especially sensitive—perhaps even overreactive—to the emotional signals transmitted by others. A parent may speak to an adolescent in a serious voice, but the adolescent may experience it as anger (Nelson et al., 2005).

Several researchers have studied how the sorts of changes in cognitive abilities you read about in Chapter 11 may reverberate throughout the family. Early adolescence is a time of changes in youngsters' views of family relationships and in family members' expectations of one another (Lanz et al., 2001). For example, one study asked adolescents of different ages to compare their actual family with their view of an ideal one in terms of how close and dominant different family members were (Feldman & Gehring, 1988). With age, the gap between adolescents' actual and ideal portraits widened, indicating that as they became older, adolescents became more aware of their families' shortcomings.

Although adolescence is a time of transformation in family relationships for the majority of households, some families adapt more successfully than others to this challenge. In several studies, families have been asked to discuss a problem together, and their interaction is taped and later analyzed. Researchers have found that families with psychologically competent teenagers interact in ways that permit family members to express their autonomy and individuality while remaining attached, or connected, to other family members (Grotevant, 1997). In these families, verbal give-and-take is the norm, and adolescents (as well as parents) are encouraged to express their own opinions, even if this sometimes leads to disagreements. At the same time, however, the importance of maintaining close relationships in the family is emphasized, and individuals are encouraged to consider how their actions may affect other family members (Rueter & Conger, 1995a, 1995b). Indeed, adolescents who are permitted to assert their own opinions within a family context that is secure and loving develop higher self-esteem and more mature coping abilities. Adolescents whose autonomy is stifled are at risk for developing feelings of depression and low self-esteem, whereas those who do not feel connected are at risk for behavior problems (Barber, 1996). These studies remind us that it is important to distinguish between separating from one's parents in a way that nevertheless maintains emotional closeness in the relationship (which is healthy) versus breaking away from one's parents in a fashion that leads to alienation, conflict, and hostility (which is unhealthy) (Beyers et al., 2003).

Adolescents' Relationships with Siblings

Far more is known about adolescents' relations with their parents than about their relations with brothers and sisters. In general, sibling relationships during adolescence have characteristics that set them apart from other family relationships (such as those between adolescents and their parents) as well as from relationships with peers (such as those between adolescents and their close friends) (East, 2009). Adolescents rate their sibling relationships as similar to those with their parents in companionship and importance, but as more like friendships with respect to power, assistance, and their satisfaction with the relationship.

Young adolescents often have emotionally charged relationships with siblings that are marked by conflict and rivalry, but also by nurturance and support (Lempers & Clark-Lempers 1992). Conflict between siblings increases as children mature from childhood to early adolescence (Brody, Stoneman, & McCoy, 1994), with adolescents reporting more negativity in their sibling relationships compared with their relationships with peers (Buhrmester & Furman, 1990) and less effective conflict resolution than with their parents (Tucker, McHale, & Crouter, 2003). Over the course of adolescence, adolescents' relationships with siblings, and especially with younger siblings, become more egalitarian but more distant and less emotionally intense (Buhrmester & Furman, 1990; Cole & Kerns, 2001). Fortunately, sibling relationships improve as individuals leave adolescence and move into young adulthood, perhaps because they are less likely to compete with each other for resources or attention (Scharf, Shulman, & Avigad-Spitz, 2005).

There are important links among parent-child, sibling, and peer relations in adolescence. In fact, it is helpful to think of the adolescent's interpersonal world as consisting of a web of interconnected relationships rather than a set of separate ones. Having a positive parent-adolescent relationship is associated with less sibling conflict and a more positive sibling relationship (e.g., Hetherington, Henderson, & Reiss, 1999). In contrast, adolescents who experience parental rejection and negativity are more likely to fight with their siblings.

Similarly, children and adolescents learn much about social relationships from sibling interactions, and they transfer this knowledge and experience to friendships outside the family (Brody et al., 1994; Updegraff, McHale, & Crouter, 2000). In poorly functioning families, aggressive interchanges between unsupervised siblings may provide a training ground within which adolescents learn, practice, and perfect aggressive behavior (Snyder, Bank, & Burraston, 2005). The reverse is true as well—the quality of adolescents' relationships with their friends, for better or worse, influences how they interact with their siblings (Kramer & Kowal, 2005).

The quality of the sibling relationship also affects adolescents' adjustment (Stocker, Burwell, & Briggs, 2002). Positive sibling relationships contribute to school success, sociability, autonomy, and self-esteem (e.g., Hetherington et al., 1999; Yeh & Lempers, 2004). Having a close sibling relationship can partially buffer the negative effects of not having friends in school (East & Rook, 1992), and siblings can serve as sources of advice and guidance (Kramer & Kowal, 2005; Tucker, McHale, & Crouter, 2001). Of course, siblings can influence the development of problems as well (Bank, Burraston, & Snyder, 2004; Conger, Conger, & Scaramella, 1997). For example, siblings influence each other's drug use and antisocial behavior (Ardelt & Day, 2002; Bullock & Dishion, 2002; Rowe et al., 1989). And, younger sisters of childbearing adolescents are more likely to engage in early sexual activity and to become pregnant during adolescence themselves (East & Jacobson, 2001).

Although the family is certainly an important influence on adolescent development, another context—the peer group—takes on new and special significance in this stage of life. (For a summary of this section, see "Interim Summary 12.3: Family Relationships in Adolescence.")

PEER RELATIONSHIPS IN ADOLESCENCE

A visit to an elementary school playground will reveal that peer groups are an important feature of the social world of childhood. But even though peer groups exist well before adolescence, during the teenage years, they change in significance and structure. Four specific developments stand out.

First, there is a sharp increase during adolescence in the sheer amount of time individuals spend with their peers and in the relative time they spend with peers versus

INTERIM SUMMARY **12.3**

Family Relationships in Adolescence	
Adolescents' Relationships with Parents	■ In most families, there is a shift in adolescence away from patterns of influence and interaction that are unequal to ones in which parents and their adolescent children are on more equal footing. ■ Early adolescence is a time of changes in youngsters' views of family relationships and in family members' expectations of each other. ■ It is important to distinguish between separating from one's parents in a way that maintains emotional closeness in the relationship, versus breaking away from parents in a fashion that leads to alienation, conflict, and hostility.
Adolescents' Relationships with Siblings	■ Sibling relationships in adolescence differ both from other family relationships and from relationships with friends. ■ Young adolescents have emotionally charged relationships with siblings that are marked by conflict and rivalry but also by nurturance and support. Over the course of adolescence, adolescents' relationships with siblings become more egalitarian but more distant and less emotionally intense. ■ Having a positive parent-adolescent relationship is associated with less sibling conflict and a more positive sibling relationship. ■ The quality of sibling relationships also affects adolescents' adjustment, in both positive and negative ways.

adults. If we count school as a setting in which adolescents are mainly with age-mates, well over half of the typical U.S. adolescent's waking hours are spent with peers; only 15 percent of their time is with adults—including their parents. (A good deal of the remaining time is spent alone or with a combination of adults and age-mates.) When asked to list the people in their life who are most important to them, nearly half the people adolescents mention are people of the same age. By sixth grade, adults other than parents account for less than 25 percent of the typical adolescent's social network—the people he or she interacts with most regularly (Brown, 1990).

Second, during adolescence, peer groups function much more often without adult supervision than they do during childhood, partly because adolescents are simply more mobile than children but partly because adolescents seek, and are granted, more independence (Brown, 1990). Groups of younger children typically play where adults are present, or in activities that are organized or supervised by adults (e.g., Little League, Youth Soccer, Brownies), whereas adolescents spend more time on their own. A group of teenagers may go off to the mall or to the movies, or will choose to congregate at the home of someone whose parents are not around.

Third, adolescents have increasingly more contact with opposite-sex friends. During childhood, peer groups are highly sex segregated. This is especially true of children's peer activities in school and other settings organized by adults, although somewhat less so of their more informal activities, such as neighborhood play (Maccoby, 1990). During adolescence, however, a growing proportion of an individual's significant others are opposite-sex peers, even in public settings (Brown, 2009). Part of this is due to the emergence of romantic relationships, but part is due to an increase in nonromantic friendships with other-sex peers.

Finally, whereas children's peer relationships are limited mainly to pairs of friends and relatively small groups—three or four children at a time, for example—adolescence marks the emergence of larger collectives. In junior high school cafeterias, for example, the "popular" crowd sits in one section of the room, the "brains" in another, and the "druggies" in yet a third (see Eder, 1985). These crowds typically develop their own minicultures, which dictate particular styles of dressing, talking, and behaving. It is not until early adolescence that individuals can confidently list the different crowds that characterize their schools and reliably describe the stereotypes that distinguish the different crowds from one another (Brown, Mory, & Kinney, 1994). (Movies like *The Breakfast Club* or *Heathers* illustrate this nicely.)

Cliques and Crowds

It is helpful to think of adolescents' peer groups as organized around two related, but different, structures (Brown, 2009). As noted earlier in the chapter, a **clique** is a small group of between 2 and 12 individuals—the average is about 5 or 6—generally of the same sex, and, of course, the same age. Cliques can be defined by common activities (e.g., the "drama" group, a group of students who study together regularly) or simply by friendship (e.g., a group of girls who have lunch together every day or a group of boys who have known one another for a long time). The clique is the social setting in which adolescents hang out, talk to each other, and form close friendships. Some cliques are more closed to outsiders than others (i.e., the members are, well, "cliquish"), but virtually all cliques are small enough so that the members feel that they know one another well and appreciate one another more than people outside the clique do (Brown, 2009).

clique A small, tightly knit group of between 2 and 12 friends, generally of the same sex and age.

Adolescents' cliques are usually composed of individuals who are in the same grade in school, from the same social class, and of the same race, in part because cliques usually develop in schools or neighborhoods, which are often race segregated or class segregated. But what about factors beyond these? Do members of a clique also share certain interests and attitudes? Generally speaking, they do. Three factors appear to be especially important in determining adolescent clique membership and friendship

© Jeff Greenberg/PhotoEdit

Bob Daemmrich/PhotoEdit

Because the clique is based on activity and friendship, it is the important setting in which the adolescent learns social skills. In contrast, because crowds are based on reputation and stereotype, and not interaction, they probably contribute more to the adolescent's self-conceptions and less to the development of social competence.

patterns: orientation toward school, orientation toward the teen culture, and involvement in antisocial activity (Crosnoe & Needham, 2004). Adolescents who don't care much about doing well in school and who would rather spend time drinking and doing drugs usually have friends who feel the same way, whereas "nerds of a feather" usually flock together.

crowd A large, loosely organized group of young people, composed of several cliques and typically organized around a common shared activity.

Cliques are quite different in structure and purpose than crowds. Membership in a **crowd** is based mainly on reputation and stereotype, rather than on actual friendship or social interaction. This is very different from membership in a clique, which, by definition, hinges on shared activity and friendship. In contemporary U.S. high schools, typical crowds are "jocks," "brains," "nerds," "populars," "druggies," and so on. The labels for these crowds may vary from school to school ("nerds" versus "geeks," "populars" versus "preps"), but their presence is commonplace, at least in the United States and Canada. (Can you can recall the main crowds that existed in your high school?) In contrast to cliques, crowds are not settings for adolescents' intimate interactions or friendships but, instead, serve three broad purposes: to locate adolescents (to themselves and to others) within the social structure of the school, to channel adolescents into associations with some peers and away from others, and to provide contexts that reward certain lifestyles and discourage others (Brown, 2009). According to recent estimates, close to half of high school students are associated with one crowd, about one-third are associated with two or more crowds, and about one-sixth do not clearly fit into any crowd (Brown, 2009).

In concrete terms—and perhaps ironically—an adolescent does not have to actually have "brains" as friends, or to hang around with "brainy" students, to be one of the "brains." If he dresses like a "brain," acts like a "brain," and takes honors courses, then he is a "brain," at least as far as his crowd membership goes. The fact that crowd membership is based on reputation and stereotype can be very difficult for individual adolescents, who—if they do not change their reputation early on in high school—may find themselves stuck, at least in the eyes of their peers, with a label that they do not wish to have (or that they do not see themselves as deserving) (Brown et al., 1992).

Crowds are not simply clusters of cliques; the two different structures serve entirely different purposes. Because the clique is based on activity and friendship, it is the important setting in which the adolescent learns social skills—how to be a good friend to someone else, how to communicate with others effectively, how to be a leader, how to enjoy someone else's company, or even how to break off a friendship that is no longer satisfying. These and other social skills are important in adulthood as well as in adolescence. In contrast, because crowds are based on reputation and stereotype, and not interaction, they probably contribute more to the adolescent's sense of identity and self-conceptions—for better and for worse—than to his or her actual social development.

Because the adolescent's peer group plays such an important role as a source of identity, the nature of the crowd with which an adolescent affiliates can have an important influence on his or her behavior and activities (Prinstein & La Greca, 2002). Although most adolescents feel pressure from their friends to behave in ways that are consistent with their crowd's values and goals, the specific nature of the pressure varies from one crowd to another. Adolescents who are part of the "druggie" crowd report much more peer pressure to engage in misconduct, for example, than do adolescents from the "jock" crowd (Clasen & Brown, 1985).

Crowd membership can also affect the way adolescents feel about themselves. Adolescents' self-esteem is higher among students who are identified with peer groups that have relatively more status in their school. In one high school, in which the "jocks" and "socies" were highest in status, and the "druggies" and "toughs" were lowest, students who were identified with the higher-status groups had higher self-esteem than did those who were identified with the lower-status groups (Brown & Lohr, 1987). Another study found that over the course of adolescence, symptoms of psychological distress declined among the "populars" and "jocks" but increased among the "brains" (Prinstein & La Greca, 2002). Of course, the longer-term consequences of crowd membership during adolescence is not necessarily the same as its immediate impact. One study of the young adult outcomes of high school crowd membership found that "brains" as well as "jocks" showed the most favorable patterns of psychological adjustment over time (Barber, Eccles, & Stone, 2001). Not surprisingly, individuals who had been members of antisocial crowds fared the worst.

Responding to Peer Pressure

As adolescents come to spend more time outside the family, the opinions and advice of others—not only peers but adults as well—become more important. Adolescents are often portrayed as being extremely susceptible to the influence of peers—more so than children or young adults—and as being stubbornly resistant to the influence of their parents. Is peer pressure really more potent, and parental influence much weaker, during adolescence than during other stages?

Researchers have looked at this question by putting adolescents in situations in which they must choose either between the pressures of their parents and the pressures of their peers or between their own wishes and those of others. In a typical study of this sort, an adolescent might be told to imagine that he and his friends discover something that looks suspicious on the way home from school. His friends tell him that they should keep it a secret. But the adolescent in the imaginary scenario tells his mother about it, and she advises him to report it to the police. The adolescent study participant then would be asked by the researcher to say what he would do.

In general, studies that contrast parents' and peers' influences indicate that it is hard to generalize about who is more important. In some situations, peers' opinions are more influential, but in others situations, parents' opinions matter more. Adolescents are more likely to conform to their peers when it comes to short-term, day-to-day, and social matters—styles of dress, tastes in music, choices among leisure activities, and so on. This is particularly true during junior high school and the early years of high school. Teenagers are primarily influenced by their parents, however, when it comes to long-term questions concerning educational or occupational plans, or to questions of values, religious beliefs, or ethics (Steinberg, 2008).

Researchers also have studied how adolescents respond when placed between the pressure of their friends and their own opinions of what to do. An adolescent might be asked whether she would go along with her friends' pressure to shoplift, even if she did not want to do so (Berndt, 1979). The age pattern found in these studies depends on the type of behavior under pressure. In particular, conformity to peer pressure to do something antisocial is higher during early and middle adolescence (it peaks around age 14) than before or after (Berndt, 1979; Steinberg & Silverberg, 1986). But when peer pressure is not specifically to do something wrong—for instance, pressure simply to change one's opinion about music or clothing—studies find that individuals' ability to stand up to the influence of their friends increases steadily during adolescence, most sharply between ages 14 and 18 (Steinberg & Monahan, 2007) (see Figure 12.4).

Although conformity to peer pressure is greater during early adolescence than later, it is not exactly clear just why this is so. One possibility is that adolescents are more susceptible to peer influence during this time because of their heightened orientation toward the peer group. Because they care more about what their friends think of them, they are more likely to go along with the crowd to avoid being rejected (Brown, Clasen, & Eicher, 1986). It is possible that this heightened conformity to peer pressure during early adolescence is a sign of a sort of emotional "way station" between becoming emotionally autonomous from parents and developing an independent sense of identity (Collins & Steinberg, 2006). In other words, the adolescent may become emotionally autonomous from parents before he or she is emotionally ready for this degree of independence and may turn to peers to fill this void.

Popularity and Rejection in Adolescent Peer Groups

Thus far, our discussion has focused on how and why crowds and cliques serve as the basis for adolescents' social activities and self-conceptions. But what about the internal structure of peer groups? Within a clique or a crowd, what determines which adolescents are popular and which ones are disliked?

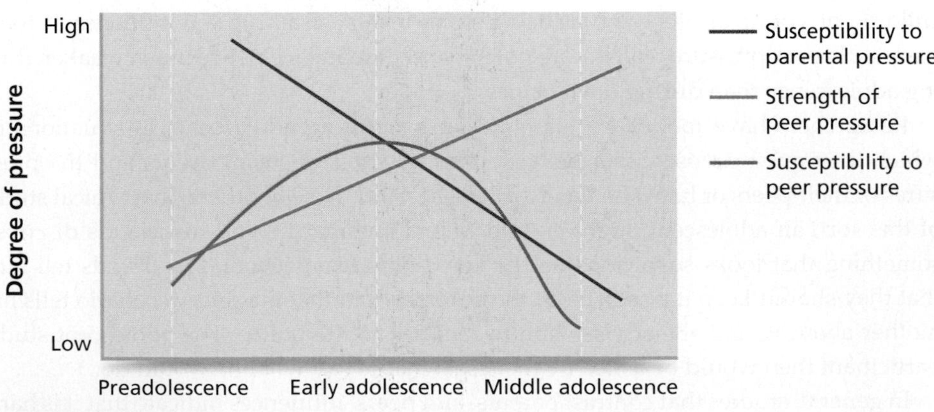

FIGURE 12.4

Changes in Susceptibility to Parental and Peer Influence in Adolescence

During adolescence, susceptibility to pressure from parents declines, whereas susceptibility to peer pressure rises, then declines. The fact that peer pressure itself grows stronger, even while susceptibility to their influence is declining, reflects the growth of independence.

The main determinant of a youngster's popularity during adolescence is his or her social competence. Popular adolescents act appropriately in the eyes of their peers, are skilled at perceiving and meeting the needs of others, and are confident without being conceited. Because of their social skill, popular adolescents also are good at adjusting their behavior to maintain their favored social standing when peer group norms change; if, for instance, smoking marijuana becomes something that is valued by the peer group, popular adolescents will start getting high more regularly (Allen et al., 2005). Although many determinants of popularity are common across cultures (e.g., having a good sense of humor), some differ. Shyness, for example, which is clearly a social liability in U.S. peer groups, may be an asset in China (Chen, Rubin, & Li, 1995).

What about unpopular adolescents? Social scientists have shown that it is important to distinguish among three types of adolescents who are disliked by their peers (Bierman & Wargo, 1995; Coie et al., 1995; Parkhurst & Asher, 1992). One set is overly aggressive; they are likely to get into fights with other students, are more likely to be involved in antisocial activities, and often are involved in bullying. A second set is withdrawn; these adolescents are exceedingly shy, timid, and inhibited and, actually, are themselves more likely to be the *victims* of bullying. A third group of unpopular youngsters combine both liabilities: They are aggressive and withdrawn. Like other aggressive youngsters, aggressive-withdrawn children have problems controlling their hostility; but like other withdrawn children, they tend to be nervous about initiating friendships with other adolescents.

Sex Differences in Adolescents' Friendships

Friendships become closer and more intimate during adolescence, but there are striking sex differences in intimacy. When asked to name the people who are most important to them, adolescent girls—particularly in the middle adolescent years—list more friends than boys do, and girls are more likely to mention intimacy as a defining aspect of close friendship. In interviews, adolescent girls express greater interest in their close friendships, talk more frequently about their intimate conversations with friends, and express greater concern about their friends' faithfulness and greater anxiety over rejection. Consistent with stereotypes, sitcoms, and stand-up comedy shtick, females place greater emphasis than males do on emotional closeness in their evaluation of romantic partners (Feiring, 1999; Parker et al., 2005). Girls are more likely than boys to make distinctions in the way they treat intimate and nonintimate friends, fight more about relationship issues, and appear to prefer to keep their friendships more exclusive and are less willing to include other classmates in their clique's activities (Berndt, 1982).

There also are interesting sex differences in the nature of conflicts between close friends. Boys' conflicts with their friends are briefer, typically over issues of power and control (e.g., whose turn it is in a game, who gets the last piece of pizza), more likely to escalate into physical aggression, and settled without any explicit effort to do so, often by just "letting

© David Young-Wolff/PhotoEdit

By most indicators, adolescent girls' friendships are more intimate than boys' friendships.

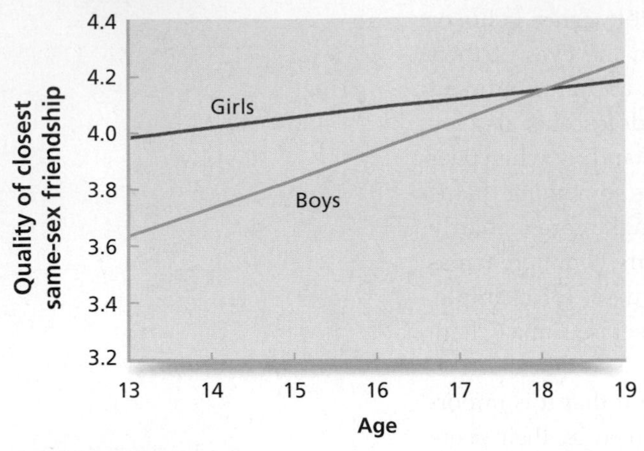

FIGURE 12.5

Males' and Females' Reports of Friendship Quality

Sex differences in friendship quality are substantial early in adolescence, but negligible by the time individuals are 18. There are considerable sex differences in the ways that males and females express intimacy, however.

Source: "Trajectories of perceived friendship quality during adolescence: The patterns and contextual predictors" by N. Way & M.L. Greene, *Journal of Research on Adolescence, 16*, pp. 293-320. Copyright © 2006 by Blackwell Publishing Ltd. Reproduced with permission of Blackwell Publishing Ltd.

things slide." Girls' conflicts, in contrast, are longer, typically about some form of betrayal in the relationship (e.g., breaking a confidence, ignoring the other person), and only resolved when one of the friends apologizes (Raffaeli, 1997).

Although intimacy is a more conscious concern for adolescent girls than for boys, this does not mean that intimacy is absent from boys' relationships—it just is expressed differently. In general, boys' friendships are more oriented toward shared activities than toward the explicit satisfaction of emotional needs; hence, the development of intimacy between adolescent males may be a more subtle phenomenon that doesn't entail a lot of verbal expression (McNelles & Connolly, 1999). A group of adolescent boys might backpack together without much conversation but feel the same degree of closeness as a result of their trip as a group of girls who stayed up all night talking. In addition, the development of close friendships among males may start at a later age than it does among females (generally speaking, girls mature earlier emotionally as well as physically). There are substantial sex differences in adolescents' reports of friendship quality at age 13, but by 18 these sex differences are gone (Way & Greene, 2006) (see Figure 12.5).

The importance of intimacy as a defining feature of close friendship continues to increase throughout early and middle adolescence (Berndt & Perry, 1990; McNelles & Connolly, 1999; Phillipsen, 1999). But an interesting pattern of change occurs around age 14. During middle adolescence (between ages 13 and 15), particularly for girls, concerns about loyalty and anxieties over rejection become more pronounced (Berndt & Perry, 1990). Girls show a significant increase in jealousy over their friends' friends during early adolescence (Parker et al., 2005). Ironically, the relatively greater intimacy enjoyed by girls with their friends compared to boys is both an asset and a liability—girls get the benefits of having confidantes with whom they can easily talk about their problems, but their friendships are more fragile and easily disrupted by betrayal. As a consequence, girls' friendships on average do not last as long as boys' do (Benenson & Christakos, 2003). As we'll see in a later section, some theorists believe that this may also explain why girls are at relatively greater risk for depression than boys.

Dating and Romantic Relationships

In earlier eras, dating during adolescence was not so much a recreational activity (as it is today) but a part of the process of courtship and mate selection. Individuals would date in order to ready themselves for marriage, and unmarried individuals would play the field—under the watchful eyes of chaperones—before settling down (Montgomery, 1996). The function of adolescent dating changed, however, as individuals began to marry later and later—a trend that began in the mid-1950s and continues today (U.S. Bureau of the Census, 2006). This, of course, gives adolescent dating a whole new meaning, because today it is clearly divorced from its function in mate selection. Adults continue to regulate and monitor adolescent dating in order to prevent rash or impulsive commitments to early marriage (Laursen & Jensen-Campbell, 1999), but in the minds of most young people, high school dating has little to do with marriage.

Today, the average adolescent begins dating around age 13 or 14, although nearly half of all adolescents have at least one date before they turn 12. By age 16, more than

90 percent of adolescents of both sexes have had at least one date, and during the later years of high school, more than half of all students average one or more dates each week (Feiring, 1993). By age 18, virtually all adolescents have dated once, and three-fourths have had at least one steady boyfriend or girlfriend (Neemann, Hubbard, & Masten, 1995). Moreover, and contrary to stereotypes of adolescents' romances as being short-lived, one-fifth of adolescents 14 or younger, one-third of 15- and 16-year-olds, and more than half of 17- and 18-year-olds who are in dating relationships have been dating the same person for nearly a year. Girls tend to become involved with boys who are slightly older, whereas boys tend to become involved with girls who are the same age or younger. Asian American adolescents are less likely than other adolescents to date, but the prevalence of dating at different ages is very similar among African American, Hispanic, Native American, and Caucasian adolescents (Collins, 2003).

The Meaning of Dating in Adolescence "Dating" can mean a variety of different things, of course, from group activities that bring males and females together (without much actual contact between the sexes); to group dates, in which a group of boys and girls go out jointly (and spend part of the time in couples and part of the time in large groups); to casual dating in couples; to serious involvement with a steady boyfriend or girlfriend. Generally speaking, casual socializing with opposite-sex peers and experiences in mixed-sex groups generally occur before the development of romantic relationships (Connolly, 2009).

Even for adolescents with a history of successful and intimate friendships with same- and other-sex peers, the transition into romantic relationships can be difficult. In one recent study, adolescents were asked to discuss social situations they thought were difficult. Themes having to do with communicating with the other sex were mentioned frequently. Many adolescents discussed difficulty in initiating or maintaining conversations, both face-to-face (e.g., "He will think I am an idiot." "Sometimes you don't know, if you're like sitting with a guy and you're watching a basketball game or something, you don't know if you should start talking or if you should just sit there") and on the phone ("I think it is hard to call. After it's done with, you don't know how to get off the phone"). Others mentioned problems in asking people out ("Asking a girl out on a first date—complete panic!") or in turning people down ("How about if you go on a date and you're really not interested, but he keeps calling?"). Still others noted problems in making or ending romantic commitments ("You don't know if you are going out with someone or if you are just seeing them," "It is hard to say, 'so, are we gonna make a commitment?,'" "I avoided [breaking up] for two weeks because I was trying to think of what to say") (Grover & Nangle, 2003, pp. 133–134).

The Impact of Dating on Adolescent Development Does dating have any impact on adolescents' social and emotional development? Like most influences on development, the impact of dating depends on the context in which it occurs. In this specific case, the "contextual" factor that matters most is the adolescent's age.

Early and intensive dating—for example, becoming seriously involved before age 15—has a somewhat stunting effect on psychosocial development (Neemann et al., 1995) and is associated with increased alcohol use, delinquency, and, not surprisingly, sexual activity (Davies & Windle, 2000). This is probably true for males and females alike, but researchers have focused primarily on girls because boys are less likely to begin serious dating quite so early. Compared with their peers, girls who begin serious dating early are less mature socially, less imaginative, less oriented toward achievement, less happy with who they are and how they look, more depressed, and more superficial—a finding that has been reported consistently for at least 40 years (Neemann et al., 1995).

© James Hardy/PhotoAlto Agency

By age 16, more than 90 percent of adolescents of both sexes have had at least one date.

This is not to say that dating is not a valuable interpersonal experience for the adolescent, only that dating may have different effects in early adolescence than in middle and late adolescence (Neemann et al., 1995). Although early involvement in serious romance has its costs, adolescent girls who do not date at all show their own signs of delayed social development, as well as excessive dependency on their parents and feelings of insecurity (Douvan & Adelson, 1966). In contrast, adolescents who date and go to parties regularly are more popular, have a stronger self-image, and report greater acceptance by their friends (Connolly & Johnson, 1993). Stopping or cutting back on dating after having dated heavily is associated with a drop in self-esteem and an increase in depression (Davies & Windle, 2000).

All in all, experts agree that a moderate degree of dating—and delaying serious involvement until age 15 or so—appears to be the most potentially valuable route. Perhaps adolescents need more time to develop the capacity to be intimate through same-sex friendships and less pressured group activities before they enter intensively into the more highly ritualized relationships that are encouraged through dating.

Regardless of the impact that dating does or doesn't have on the adolescent's psychosocial development, studies show that romance has a powerful impact on the adolescent's emotional state. Adolescents' real and fantasized romances trigger more of their strong emotional feelings during the course of a day (one-third of girls' strong feelings and one-fourth of boys') than do family, school, or friends. Although the majority of adolescents' feelings about their romantic relationships are positive, more than 40 percent are negative, involving feelings of anxiety, anger, jealousy, and depression (Larson, Clore, & Wood, 1999). Adolescents who have entered into a romantic relationship in the past year report more symptoms of depression than do those who have not (Joyner & Udry, 2000), perhaps because many adolescents who are involved romantically also experience breakups during the same time period (Collins, 2003). Breaking up is the single most common trigger of the first episode of major depression, which, as you will read, often occurs for the first time in adolescence (Monroe et al., 1999). (For a summary of this section, see "Interim Summary 12.4: Peer Relationships in Adolescence.")

INTERIM SUMMARY 12.4

Peer Relationships in Adolescence

Cliques and Crowds	■ **Cliques** are small groups of between 2 and 12 individuals, generally of the same sex and age, and are usually composed of individuals who are in the same grade, from the same social class, and of the same race. ■ Orientation toward school, orientation toward teen culture, and involvement in antisocial activity are important influences on clique membership.

(continued)

INTERIM SUMMARY 12.4 *(continued)*

Peer Relationships in Adolescence

	■ Membership in a **crowd** is based mainly on reputation and stereotype rather than on actual friendship or social interaction. ■ Crowds locate adolescents within the social structure of the school, channel adolescents into associations with some peers and away from others, and provide contexts that reward certain lifestyles and discourage others. ■ Whereas the clique is important for learning social skills, crowds contribute more to the adolescent's sense of identity and self-conception.
Responding to Peer Pressure	■ Adolescents may be especially susceptible to peer pressure because they have a heightened orientation toward the peer group during this time. ■ Adolescents are more likely to conform to their peers when it comes to short-term matters such as style of dress and leisure pursuits and to their parents for more long-term questions concerning education or occupational plans. ■ Conformity to antisocial peer pressure is higher during early and middle adolescence than before or after. When peer pressure is not specifically to do something wrong, studies find that individuals' ability to stand up to the influence of their friends increases steadily during adolescence.
Popularity and Rejection in Adolescent Peer Groups	■ Popular adolescents act appropriately in the eyes of their peers, are skilled at perceiving and meeting the needs of others, and are confident without being conceited. ■ Social scientists distinguish between three types of adolescents who are disliked by their peers: those who are overly aggressive, those who are withdrawn, and those who are both aggressive and withdrawn.
Sex Differences in Adolescents' Friendships	■ The importance of intimacy as a defining feature of close friendship increases throughout early and middle adolescence. ■ Intimacy is a more conscious concern for adolescent girls than for boys, but this does not mean that intimacy is absent from boys' relationships—it just is expressed differently. In general, boys' friendships are more oriented toward shared activities than toward the explicit satisfaction of emotional needs.
Dating and Romantic Relationships	■ High school dating has little to do with marriage in the minds of most young people. ■ Generally speaking, casual socializing with opposite-sex peers and experiences in mixed-sex groups generally occur before the development of romantic relationships. ■ Early and intensive dating has a somewhat stunting effect on psychosocial development and is associated with increased alcohol use, delinquency, and sexual activity. ■ Experts agree that a moderate degree of dating and delaying serious involvement until age 15 or so appears to be the most potentially valuable route. ■ Adolescents' real and fantasized romances trigger more of their strong emotional feelings during the course of a day than do family, school, or friends. Breaking up is the single most common trigger of the first episode of major depression.

SOCIOEMOTIONAL PROBLEMS IN ADOLESCENCE

Although the vast majority of young people move through adolescence without experiencing major difficulty, some encounter serious psychological and behavioral problems that disrupt not only their lives but also the lives of those around them. Problems such as substance abuse, delinquency, and depression are not the norm during adolescence, but they do affect a worrisome number of teenagers. In this concluding section of the chapter, we look at some of the problems that are most often associated with adolescence.

Before we begin, though, we need to make some general observations about problems in adolescence that apply to a range of issues.

Some General Observations About Problems in Adolescence

First, let's distinguish between occasional experimentation and enduring patterns of dangerous or troublesome behavior. Although the vast majority of teenagers do something during adolescence that is against the law, very few of these young people develop criminal careers. Similarly, the majority of adolescents experiment with alcohol sometime before high school graduation, and the majority will have been drunk at least once; but relatively few teenagers will develop drinking problems or will permit alcohol to have a negative impact on their school performance or personal relationships.

Second, there's a difference between problems that have their origins and onset during adolescence and those that have their roots in earlier periods of development. Many individuals who develop depression during adolescence suffered from other types of psychological distress, such as excessive anxiety, as children. In other words, simply because a problem may be displayed during adolescence does not mean that it has adolescent origins.

Third, many of the problems experienced by adolescents are relatively transitory and resolved by the beginning of adulthood, with few long-term repercussions in most cases. The fact that some of the problems of adolescence disappear on their own with time does not make their prevalence during adolescence any less worrisome, but it should be kept in mind when rhetoric is hurled back and forth about the inevitable decline of civilization at the hands of contemporary youth.

Finally, problem behavior during adolescence is virtually never a direct consequence of going through the normative changes of adolescence itself. Popular theories about "raging hormones" causing adolescent craziness have no scientific support whatsoever, for example, nor do the widely held beliefs that problem behaviors are manifestations of an inherent need to rebel against authority, or that bizarre behavior results from having an identity crisis. When a young person exhibits a serious psychosocial problem, such as depression, the worst possible interpretation is that it is a "normal" part of growing up. It is more likely to be a sign that something is wrong (Steinberg, 2008).

externalizing problem A psychosocial problem that is manifested in a turning of the symptoms outward, as in aggression or delinquency.

internalizing problem A psychosocial problem that is manifested in a turning of the symptoms inward, as in depression or anxiety.

Experts on the development and treatment of psychosocial problems during adolescence typically distinguish among three broad categories of problems: substance abuse (which we looked at in Chapter 11), externalizing problems, and internalizing problems (Achenbach & Edelbrock, 1987). To review, an **externalizing problem** is one in which the young person's problems are turned outward and are manifested in antisocial behavior—behavior that is intended to harm others or deliberately violates society's norms. Common externalizing problems during adolescence are delinquency, antisocial aggression, and truancy. An **internalizing problem** is one in which the young person's problems are turned inward and are manifested in emotional and cognitive distress, such as depression, anxiety, or phobia.

Externalizing Problems

The most common externalizing problem, and the one that has been most researched, is **delinquency**, which refers to acts committed by juveniles that violate the law. Both violent crimes (such as assault, rape, robbery, and murder) and property crimes (such as burglary, theft, and arson) increase in frequency between the preadolescent and adolescent years, peak during the late high school years (slightly earlier for property than for violent crimes), and decline during young adulthood. The onset of serious delinquency generally begins between the ages of 13 and 16 (Farrington, 2009) (see Figure 12.6).

delinquency Juvenile offending that is processed within the juvenile justice system.

In general, the earlier an adolescent's delinquency begins—in particular, if it begins before adolescence—the more likely he or she is to become a chronic offender, to commit serious and violent crimes, and to continue committing crimes as an adult (Farrington, 2004). Conversely, the older an adolescent is when the delinquent activity first appears, the less likely criminal behavior will become a lasting problem. For purposes of discussion, therefore, it is helpful to distinguish between youngsters who begin misbehaving before adolescence and those whose delinquent activity first appears during adolescence.

One of the most influential ways of characterizing these two groups of delinquents has been suggested by psychologist Terrie Moffitt (2006), who has distinguished between **life-course-persistent offenders** and **adolescence-limited offenders**. The first group demonstrates antisocial behavior before adolescence, is involved in delinquency during adolescence, and is at great risk for continuing criminal activity in adulthood. The second group engages in antisocial behavior *only* during adolescence. Experts agree that the causes and the consequences of delinquent behavior that begins during childhood or preadolescence are quite different from those of delinquency that begins—and typically ends—during adolescence (e.g., McCabe et al., 2001).

life-course-persistent offenders Individuals who begin demonstrating antisocial or aggressive behavior during childhood and continue their antisocial behavior through adolescence and into adulthood (contrast with *adolescence-limited offenders*).

adolescence-limited offenders Antisocial adolescents whose delinquent or violent behavior begins and ends during adolescence (contrast with *life-course-persistent offenders*).

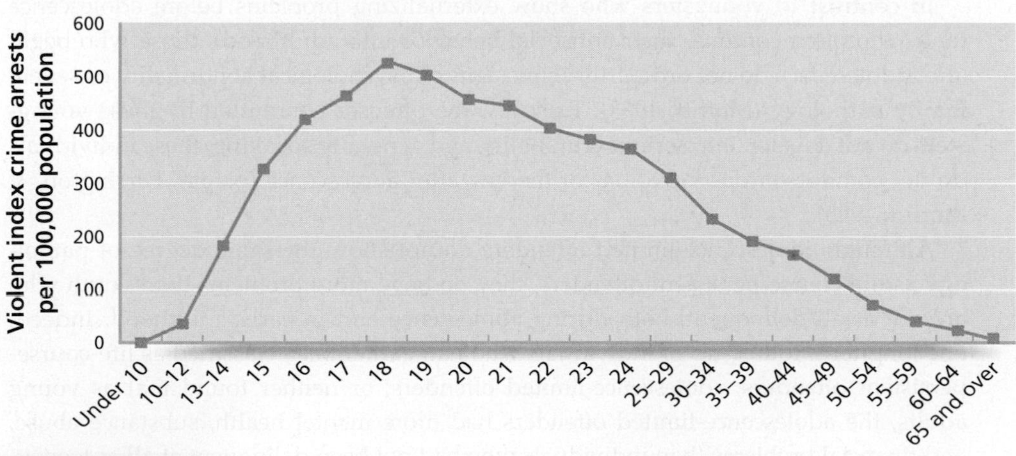

FIGURE 12.6

The Age-Crime Curve

Violent crime peaks around age 17 or 18 and then declines steadily in early adulthood. Although the vast majority of antisocial adolescents are "adolescence-limited" offenders, a small minority become "life-course-persistent" offenders and continue criminal activity into adulthood.

Youngsters whose externalizing problems begin before adolescence are often psychologically troubled. Most of these individuals are male, many are poor, and a large number come from homes in which divorce has occurred (Farrington, 2009). More important, a large and consistent body of research shows that chronic delinquents typically come from disorganized families with hostile, inept, or neglectful parents who have mistreated their children and failed to instill in them proper standards of behavior or the psychological foundations of self-control (Laub & Sampson, 1995).

In addition to family factors, there are individual characteristics that distinguish persistently delinquent youngsters from their peers at a relatively early age. First and most important, children who become delinquent—especially those who engage in violence—have histories of aggressive and antisocial behavior that were identifiable as early as age 8 (Brody et al., 2003). It is important to keep in mind, though, that the majority of children who have histories of aggressive behavior problems do not grow up to be delinquent. (If this seems confusing, think about it this way: The majority of delinquents probably have eaten French fries at some point in their childhood, but the majority of children who eat French fries do not grow up to be delinquent.)

Second, studies show that many children who become persistent offenders have problems in self-regulation—they are more impulsive, less able to control their anger, and more likely than their peers to suffer from hyperactivity, or as it is technically known, **attention deficit/hyperactivity disorder (ADHD)** (Farrington, 2004). Although ADHD does not directly cause antisocial behavior, it does elevate the risk for other family and academic problems, which in turn increase the likelihood of an adolescent developing externalizing problems (Nagin & Tremblay, 1999).

attention deficit / hyperactivity disorder (ADHD) A biologically based psychological disorder characterized by impulsivity, inattentiveness, and restlessness, often in school situations.

Third, children who become chronically delinquent are more likely to score low on standardized tests of intelligence and neuropsychological functioning and to perform poorly in school (Raine et al., 2005). Some of this is due to genetic factors, but some is also due to conditions surrounding their birth and prenatal care. A disproportionate number of persistently violent adolescents were born to poor mothers who abused drugs during pregnancy and had medical complications during delivery that likely affected their baby's neuropsychological and intellectual development (Piquero & Chung, 2001).

In contrast to youngsters who show externalizing problems before adolescence (and who often continue their antisocial behavior into adulthood), those who begin after adolescence do not ordinarily show signs of psychological abnormality or severe family pathology (Moffitt, 1993). Typically, the offenses committed by these youngsters do not develop into serious criminality, and generally speaking, these individuals do not commit serious violations of the law after adolescence (Nagin, Farrington, & Moffitt, 1995).

Although adolescence-limited offenders do not show the same degree of pathology as life-course-persistent offenders, they do have more problems than youth who are not at all delinquent, both during adolescence and in early adulthood. Indeed, one long-term follow-up of individuals who had earlier been classified as life-course-persistent offenders, adolescence-limited offenders, or neither found that as young adults, the adolescence-limited offenders had more mental health, substance abuse, and financial problems than individuals who had not been delinquent at all as teenagers (Moffitt et al., 2002). In other words, their delinquent behavior may be limited to adolescence, but they may have other problems that persist into early adulthood.

The two main risk factors for adolescence-limited offending are *poor parenting*, especially poor monitoring, and *affiliation with antisocial peers* (Ary et al., 1999; Lacourse, Nagin, & Tremblay, 2003). The first of these (poor parenting) usually leads to the second (hanging around with antisocial peers) (Dishion et al., 1991; Lansford et al., 2003). The role of the peer group in adolescence-limited offending is extremely important. One of the strongest predictors of delinquency and other forms of problem behavior is the amount of time the adolescent spends in unsupervised, unstructured activities with peers—activities like hanging out, driving around, and going to parties.

Internalizing Problems

In some instances, the changes and demands of adolescence may leave a teenager feeling helpless, confused, and pessimistic about the future. Although minor fluctuations in self-esteem during early adolescence are commonplace, it is not normal for adolescents (or adults, for that matter) to feel a prolonged or intense sense of hopelessness or frustration. Such young people are likely to be psychologically depressed and in need of professional help.

depression A psychological disturbance characterized by low self-esteem, decreased motivation, sadness, and difficulty finding pleasure in formerly enjoyable activities.

Depression In its mild form, **depression** is the most common psychological disturbance during adolescence (Graber, 2009). Although we typically associate depression with feelings of sadness, there are other symptoms that are important signs of the disorder; sadness alone, without any other symptoms, may not indicate depression in the clinical sense of the term. Depression has emotional symptoms, including dejection, decreased enjoyment of pleasurable activities, and low self-esteem. It has cognitive symptoms, such as pessimism and hopelessness, and motivational symptoms, including apathy and boredom. Finally, depression usually has physical symptoms, such as a loss of appetite, difficulty in sleeping, and loss of energy. The symptoms of major depression are the same in adolescence as in adulthood and among males and females, although, as you will read, there are sex differences in the prevalence of the illness (Lewinsohn, Pettit, et al., 2003).

Many people use the term *depression* imprecisely. It is important to distinguish among depressed mood (feeling sad), depressive syndromes (having multiple symptoms of depression), and depressive disorder (having enough symptoms to be diagnosed with the illness) (Graber, 2009). All individuals experience periods of sadness or depressed mood at one time or another; far fewer report a wider range of depressive symptoms. At any one point in time, close to 10 percent of U.S. teenagers report moderate or severe symptoms of depression—about 5 percent have the symptoms of a depressive syndrome, and approximately 3 percent meet formal diagnostic criteria for depressive disorder (Compas, Ey, & Grant, 1993). Some studies estimate that as many as 25 percent of individuals will experience at least one bout of depressive disorder by the end of adolescence (Forbes & Dahl, 2005).

There is a dramatic increase in the prevalence of depressive feelings around the time of puberty; depression is half as common during childhood as it is during adolescence (Avenevoli & Steinberg, 2001). Symptoms of depression increase steadily throughout adolescence, and then start to decline—making late adolescence the period of greatest risk (Wight, Sepúlveda, & Aneshensel, 2004). There are ethnic differences in the prevalence of depression during adolescence, with significantly more Mexican American teenagers reporting depressive symptoms than their Caucasian, African American, or Asian American peers, especially within samples of girls (Siegel et al., 1998). At this point it is not known why this is or whether similar patterns are found when the Hispanic comparison group is drawn from other subpopulations (e.g., Puerto Rican or Dominican adolescents). Individuals who develop internalizing disorders such as depression and anxiety in adolescence are at elevated risk to suffer from these problems as adults (Lewinsohn, Rhode, et al., 2003; Pine et al., 1998).

At any one point in time, close to 10 percent of U.S. teenagers report moderate or severe symptoms of depression.

A variety of theories have been proposed to account for the onset of depression and other types of internalizing problems during adolescence. The current consensus is that internalizing problems result from interacting

diathesis-stress model A perspective on disorder that posits that problems are the result of an interaction between a preexisting condition (the diathesis) and exposure to a stressful event or condition.

neuroendocrine Referring to hormonal activity in the brain and nervous system.

environmental conditions and individual predispositions rather than either alone. Today, most experts endorse a **diathesis-stress model** of depression, which posits depression may occur when individuals who are predisposed toward internalizing problems (the term *diathesis* refers to this predisposition) are exposed to chronic or acute stressors that precipitate a depressive reaction (Hilsman & Garber, 1995; Lewinsohn, Joiner, & Rohde, 2001). Individuals without the diathesis—who are not predisposed toward depression—are able to withstand a great deal of stress, for instance, without developing any psychological problems. Other individuals, who have strong predispositions toward the disorder, may become depressed in the face of stressful circumstances that most of us would consider to be normal. Research on depression in adolescence has focused both on the diathesis and the stress. Two categories of predispositions have received the most attention. First, because depression has been found to have a strong genetic component, it is believed that at least some of the predisposition is biological and may be related to problematic patterns of neuroendocrine functioning (**neuroendocrine** refers to hormonal activity in the brain and nervous system). As you read in Chapter 2, scientists have discovered that abnormalities in one gene, in particular, may make some individuals more likely to develop depression in the face of stress (Caspi et al., 2003).

Other researchers have focused more on the cognitive style of depressed individuals, suggesting that people with tendencies toward hopelessness, pessimism, and self-blame are more likely to interpret events in their lives in ways that make them depressed—to them, the proverbial glass is always half-empty (Prinstein & Aikins, 2004; Robinson, Garber, & Hilsman, 1995). These sorts of cognitive sets, which may be linked to the ways in which children think they are viewed by parents, and later by peers, develop during childhood and are thought to play a role in the onset of depression during adolescence (Cole & Jordan, 1995; Nolen-Hoeksema, Girgus, & Seligman, 1992).

Researchers who have been more concerned with the stress component of the diathesis-stress model—that is, with environmental influences on depression—have focused on three broad sets of stressors (Lewinsohn, Rohde, & Seeley, 1994). First, depression is more common among adolescents from families characterized by high conflict and low cohesion, and it is higher among adolescents from divorced homes. Second, depression is more prevalent among adolescents who are unpopular or who have poor peer relations. Third, depressed adolescents report more chronic and acute stress than nondepressed adolescents do. There is also evidence that academic difficulties are correlated with depression, especially among adolescents from Asian and also affluent families, who place a good deal of emphasis on achievement (Chan, 1997; Greenberger et al., 2000; Luthar & Becker, 2002).

You read earlier that the prevalence of depression rises during adolescence. Can diathesis-stress models of depression account for this increase? For the most part, they can. Biological theorists can point to the hormonal changes of puberty; as you read in Chapter 11, one of the effects of pubertal hormones is to make individuals more sensitive to stress (Walker, Sabuwalla, & Huot, 2004). Many studies show that the increase in depression in adolescence is more closely linked to puberty than age (Hayward et al., 1999), although it is difficult to pinpoint puberty as the cause of the problem, since many other changes typically occur around the same time (e.g., the transition out of elementary school). Cognitive theorists can point to the onset of hypothetical thinking at adolescence, which may result in new (and perhaps potentially more depressing) ways of viewing the world (Keating, 2004). And theorists who emphasize environmental factors draw attention to the new environmental demands of adolescence, such as changing schools, beginning to date, or coping with transformations in family relationships—all of which may lead to heightened stress (Graber, 2009). Thus, there are many reasons to expect that the prevalence of depression would increase as individuals pass from childhood into adolescence.

Sex Differences in Rates of Depression One of the most consistent findings to emerge in the study of adolescent depression involves the emergence of a very large sex difference in rates of depression in early adolescence. Before adolescence, boys are somewhat more likely to exhibit depressive symptoms than girls, but after puberty the sex difference in prevalence of depression reverses. From early adolescence until very late in adulthood, twice as many females as males suffer from depressive disorder, and females are somewhat more likely than males to report depressed mood (Compas et al., 1997). The increased risk for depression among girls emerges during puberty, rather than at a particular age or grade in school (Angold, Costello, & Worthman, 1998). Although sex differences in major depression persist beyond adolescence, both sexes report less depression in their mid-20s than late teens, but the decline is steeper among females, which results in a smaller sex difference (Galambos, Barker, & Krahn, 2006; Stoolmiller, Kim, & Capaldi, 2005).

Psychologists do not have a certain explanation for the emergence of sex differences in depressive disorder at adolescence. Although the association of depression with puberty suggests a biological explanation, there actually is little evidence that the sex difference in depression is directly attributable to sex differences in hormones (Rutter & Garmezy, 1983). Instead, four main explanations have received scientific support.

First, the emergence of sex differences in depression seems to have something to do with the social role that the adolescent girl may find herself in as she enters the world of boy-girl relationships (Wichstrøm, 1999). As you've read, this role may bring heightened self-consciousness over one's physical appearance and increased concern over popularity with peers. Since many of these feelings may provoke helplessness, hopelessness, and anxiety, adolescent girls may be more susceptible to depressive feelings. Consistent with this, studies show that depression in girls is significantly correlated with having a poor body image (Wichstrøm, 1999).

Second, early adolescence is generally a more stressful time for girls than boys (Rudolph & Hammen, 1999). This is because the bodily changes of puberty, especially when they occur early in adolescence, are more likely to be stressful for girls; because girls are more likely than boys to experience multiple stressors at the same time (e.g., going through puberty while making the transition into junior high school); and because girls are likely to experience more stressful life events than boys, such as sexual victimization (Graber, 2009).

Third, girls are more likely than boys to react to stress by turning their feelings inward—for instance, by ruminating about the problem and feeling helpless—whereas boys are more likely to respond either by distracting themselves or by turning their feelings outward, in aggressive behavior or in drug and alcohol abuse (Sethi & Nolen-Hoeksema, 1997). As a result, even when exposed to the same degree of stress, girls are more likely to respond to the stressors by becoming depressed (Rudolph & Hammen, 1999).

A final explanation emphasizes girls' generally greater orientation toward and sensitivity to interpersonal relations, which we noted earlier in our discussion of intimacy in adolescent friendships (Cyranowski & Frank, 2000). Females may invest more in their close relationships than males, but this may make them more distressed by interpersonal difficulties and breakups. Because adolescence is a time of many changes in relationships—in the family, with friends, and with romantic partners—the capacity of females to invest heavily in their relationships with others may be both a strength and a potential vulnerability.

Suicide According to recent national surveys, in any given year more than 10 percent of U.S. female high school students and more than 6 percent of males attempt suicide; about one-third of these attempts are serious enough to require treatment by a

suicidal ideation Thinking about ending one's life.

physician or nurse. A much larger proportion—close to 20 percent—think about killing themselves (referred to as **suicidal ideation**), and the vast majority of these have gone so far as to make a plan (Centers for Disease Control and Prevention, 2006). Suicidal ideation increases during early adolescence, peaks around age 15, and then declines (Rueter & Kwon, 2005) (see Figure 12.7). Adolescents who attempt to kill themselves usually have made appeals for help and have tried but have not found emotional support from family or friends. They report feeling trapped, lonely, worthless, and hopeless (Kidd, 2004).

The most common method of suicide among adolescents is with a firearm, followed by hanging. Drug overdoses and carbon monoxide poisoning are also common (Judge & Billick, 2004). The suicide rate is highest among American Indian and Alaskan Native adolescents and lowest among African Americans; rates among Caucasian, Hispanic, and Asian adolescents fall in between these extremes (Judge & Billick, 2004). Systematic studies have identified four established sets of risk factors for attempting suicide during adolescence: having a *psychiatric problem*, especially depression or substance abuse; having a *history of suicide in the family*; being under *stress* (especially in the areas of achievement and sexuality); and experiencing *parental rejection, family disruption*, or *extensive family conflict* (Judge & Billick, 2004). Adolescents who have one of these risk factors are significantly more likely to attempt suicide than their peers, and adolescents who have more than one risk factor are dramatically more likely to try to kill themselves. Adolescents who have attempted suicide once are at risk for attempting it again (Lewinsohn et al., 1994). Adolescents are also more likely to attempt suicide if one of their friends or someone else in their community has committed suicide (Bearman & Moody, 2004; Gould, Wallenstein, & Kleinman, 1990).

The adolescent suicide rate increased alarmingly between 1950 and 1990, fueled by the increased use of drugs and alcohol and the increased availability of firearms (Judge & Billick, 2004). The rate peaked and declined somewhat during the 1990s, as new forms of antidepressant medication became more widely prescribed to adolescents (Zito et al., 2002). Although some reports have indicated that antidepressants may actually *increase* the risk of suicide among children and adolescents, more recent studies have found that when prescriptions of antidepressants drop (after articles linking antidepressants and suicide receive a lot of attention), the number of children attempting suicide increases, suggesting that taking antidepressants off the market likely does more harm than good (Bridge et al., 2007). You may have read that suicide is a leading cause of death among young people, but this is primarily because very few young people die from other causes, such as disease. Actually, suicide is a much more common cause of death among adults than it is among young people, largely because very few suicide attempts by adolescents are successful. But hints or threats of suicide, by anyone at any age, should be taken seriously. (For a summary of this section, see "Interim Summary 12.5: Socioemotional Problems in Adolescence.")

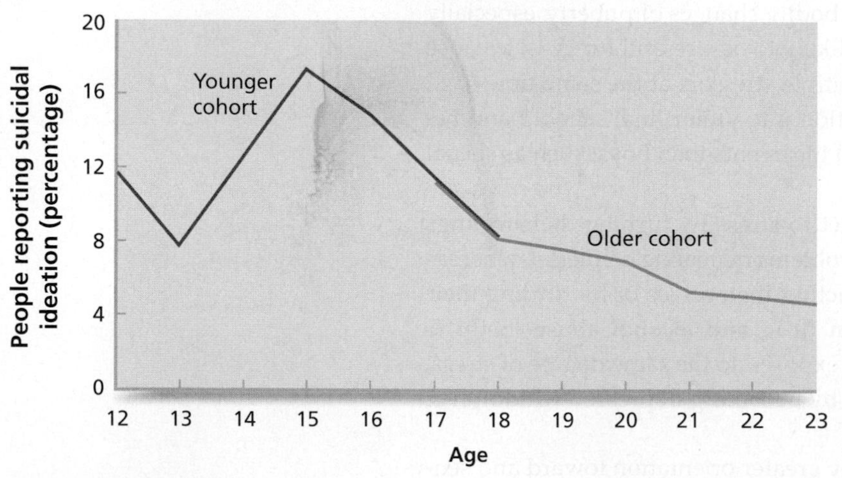

FIGURE 12.7

Age Differences in Suicidal Ideation

Depression is the most common internalizing problem in adolescents. Middle adolescents are more likely to think about suicide than younger or older individuals.

Source: "Developmental trends in adolescent suicidal ideation" by M. Rueter & H. Kwon, *Journal of Research on Adolescence,* 15, pp. 205–222. Copyright © 2005 by Blackwell Publishing Ltd. Reproduced by permission of Blackwell UK through Rightslink.

INTERIM SUMMARY 12.5

Socioemotional Problems in Adolescence

Some General Observations About Problems in Adolescence	■ Problems such as substance abuse, delinquency, and depression are not the norm during adolescence, but they do affect a worrisome number of teenagers. ■ It is important to distinguish between occasional experimentation and enduring patterns of dangerous or troublesome behavior. ■ Many of the problems experienced by adolescents are relatively transitory and resolved by the beginning of adulthood. ■ Problem behavior is virtually never a direct consequence of going through the normative changes of adolescence itself.
Externalizing Problems	■ **Delinquency** generally begins between the ages of 13 and 16 and declines during young adulthood. ■ The earlier an adolescent's delinquency begins, the more likely he or she is to become a **life-course-persistent offender**. Conversely, the older an adolescent is when delinquency activity first appears, the more likely his or her criminal behavior will be **adolescence-limited**. ■ Youngsters whose offending starts before adolescence often have long histories of aggressive and antisocial behavior, problems in self-regulation, and are more likely to score low on tests of intelligence and neuropsychological functioning. ■ Adolescents whose externalizing problems begin and end in adolescence do not ordinarily show signs of psychological abnormality or severe family pathology. However, they often have been exposed to poor parenting and antisocial peers.
Internalizing Problems	■ **Depression** is the most common internalizing problem during adolescence. ■ Depression has emotional symptoms, physical symptoms, and cognitive symptoms. ■ It is important to distinguish between depressed mood, depressive syndromes, and depressive disorder. ■ There is a dramatic increase in the prevalence of depressive feelings around the time of puberty. Symptoms of depression increase steadily throughout adolescence and then start to decline, making late adolescence the period of greatest risk. ■ Most experts posit a **diathesis-stress model** of depression, which suggests that depression may occur when individuals who are biologically or cognitively predisposed toward internalizing problems are exposed to chronic or acute stressors. ■ From early adolescence until very late in adulthood, twice as many females as males suffer from depression. ■ In any given year, more than 10 percent of U.S. female high school students and more than 6 percent of males attempt suicide. Suicidal ideation increases during adolescence, peaks around age 15, and then declines.

SUMMING UP AND LOOKING AHEAD

Although the final section of this chapter ended with a discussion of socioemotional problems in adolescence, we don't want to leave you with the impression that adolescence is an inherently or inevitably difficult time. It's crucial that you keep in mind that most individuals emerge from adolescence with positive feelings about themselves and their parents; with the ability to form, maintain, and enjoy close relationships with same- and opposite-sex peers; and with the basic capabilities needed to take advantage of a range of educational, occupational, and recreational opportunities. Most adolescents settle into adulthood relatively smoothly and begin establishing their work and family careers with little serious difficulty. Although the transition into adulthood may appear forbidding to the young adolescent approaching many weighty decisions about the future, statistics tell us that, for a remarkably high proportion of youth, the transition is relatively peaceful.

Adolescence is, above all, a remarkable period for the development of psychological maturity. Individuals enter with only a faint idea of who they are (and with few reasons to even question this) and leave well on the way toward developing a clear (if still changing) sense of identity. Relationships with family members are transformed, and a new equilibrium and balance of power is established—if perhaps after a temporary period of difficulty and distance. Relationships with friends change even more dramatically, with the development of closer and more intimate relationships with same- and opposite-sex peers, the ascendance and decline of peer groups, and the increasing importance of romantic relationships.

Development doesn't end with adolescence, of course. As individuals begin the transition to adulthood, they experience new challenges as they enter new roles and settings. Relationships with parents change as individuals start the process of establishing an independent residence (even as many still depend on their parents for financial assistance). Adolescent romances give way to more serious commitments, and career plans begin to take shape.

Young adulthood is also a time of continued physical and cognitive change, as we shall see in our next chapter.

HERE'S WHAT YOU SHOULD KNOW

Did You Get It?

After reading this chapter, you should understand the following:

- How adolescence as we know it today came to be "invented"
- Erikson's theory of adolescent identity development, and the ways in which scientists who study identity assess it
- Why the development of ethnic identity is important, and the different pathways associated with it
- How self-evaluations change in adolescence
- How family and sibling relationships change in adolescence
- How peer relationships change in adolescence, and the significance of cliques, crowds, and romantic relationships
- Basic facts about common externalizing and internalizing problems, including the factors that contribute to them

Important Terms and Concepts

adolescence-limited offenders (p. 393)
attention deficit/hyperactivity disorder (ADHD) (p. 394)
child protectionists (p. 373)
clique (p. 383)
crowd (p. 384)
delinquency (p. 393)
depression (p. 395)
diathesis-stress model (p. 396)
ethnic identity (p. 376)
externalizing problem (p. 392)
identity status (p. 375)
identity versus identity diffusion (p. 374)
internalizing problem (p. 392)
life-course-persistent offenders (p. 393)
neuroendocrine (p. 396)
psychosocial moratorium (p. 375)
suicidal ideation (p. 398)

Part V Review

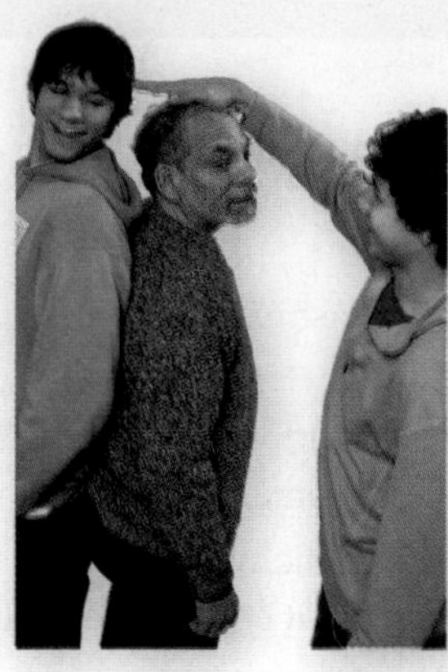

CHAPTER 11
Physical and Cognitive Development in Adolescence

- During **puberty,** there is a rapid acceleration in growth, development of primary and secondary sex characteristics, and changes in body composition and in the circulatory and respiratory systems.
- By the end of their sophomore year in high school, more than 40 percent of U.S. adolescents have had intercourse. By age 18, this number has risen to about two-thirds. Sexual intercourse before age 16 is associated with a range of problem behaviors, but sexual intercourse after this age is not.
- Alcohol and nicotine are the most commonly used and abused substances by teenagers. Their effects on brain functioning are worse in adolescence than in adulthood because the brain is especially vulnerable during this period.
- There is considerable "remodeling" of the brain during adolescence, especially in the **prefrontal cortex,** the region responsible for many advanced thinking abilities. There also are important changes in the **limbic system** at puberty, which influence sensation-seeking, mood, and attentiveness to social stimuli.
- **Deductive reasoning** and **hypothetical thinking** improve during adolescence and are tied to the maturation of the prefrontal cortex. Adolescents have an increased capacity and interest in thinking about relationships, politics, religion, and morality.

CHAPTER 12
Socioemotional Development in Adolescence

- Adolescence, as we know it in contemporary society, did not really exist until the middle of the nineteenth century. As a result of the Industrial Revolution, teenagers were encouraged to prepare for adulthood in school rather than on the job, and over time, adolescents were removed from the labor force.
- Erikson believed that resolving the crisis of **identity versus identity diffusion** is the chief psychological task of adolescence. Compared with older adolescents and with preadolescents, early adolescents are more self-conscious and have a less stable self-image.
- In most families, there is a shift in adolescence away from patterns of influence and interaction that are unequal to ones in which parents and their adolescent children are on more equal footing. Early adolescence is a time of changes in youngsters' views of family relationships and in family members' expectations of each other.
- During adolescence, peer relationships are oriented around cliques and crowds. Friendships also become more intimate during this time.
- An **externalizing problem** is one in which the adolescent's problems are turned outward and are manifested in antisocial behavior that is intended to harm others or that violates society's norms. During adolescence, depression is the most common **internalizing problem**—problems that are turned inward and are manifested in emotional and cognitive distress.

part six

Young Adulthood

Brian Leatart/Getty Images

CHAPTER 13

Physical and Cognitive Development in Young Adulthood

John Giustina/Getty Images

Having looked closely at the first 18 years of the lifespan, we now turn our attention to the next 60 to 70 years. In fact, given the increase in the number of people living beyond the age of 100 (Himes, 2001), we might be looking at an even longer period. As you will see in this chapter and those that follow, our tour through the long stretch of time that we call adulthood will take us through an amazing number of changes.

PERSPECTIVES ON ADULTHOOD

Because adulthood spans so many years, you may wonder whether or how development differs in adulthood compared to the earlier life periods you have learned about. Does development continue in adulthood, or does development simply peak and stop at some point? Do people tend to develop in much the same way in adulthood, or is development in this life stage highly variable? Do people in their 20s develop in similar or fundamentally different ways from those in their 40s, 60s, or 80s?

Guiding Principles and Assumptions

Lifespan developmental psychologists have wrestled with exactly such questions, and they offer some guiding principles and assumptions that can help us think about development in adulthood. Before we begin our journey through adulthood, let's consider these principles, which build on and extend the principles of development you read about in Chapter 1.

Development Continues into Adulthood You might be inclined to think that most of the action, from a development perspective, occurs in childhood and adolescence. In fact, as we noted in Chapter 1, early theorists held exactly this view. Freud (1910) believed that personality crystallizes by the age of 5 or 6, with little change occurring thereafter. Piaget (1970) regarded cognitive development as reaching its peak in early adolescence. More generally, adulthood has been viewed as a time when relatively little change occurs beyond modest refinements of existing abilities. However, Erikson (1968) broke ranks with these theorists, describing adulthood as unfolding through three psychosocial stages, each with its own unique concerns and challenges. Today, contemporary theorists regard development as a lifelong process (Baltes, Lindenberger, & Staudinger, 2006; Heckhausen, Wrosch, & Schulz, 2010).

As you'll see in this and subsequent chapters, adulthood is a time of tremendous change. In young adulthood, changes are set in motion by the many decisions that must be made—where to live, what kind of education to pursue, what kinds of jobs to seek, what kinds of social relationships to form, whether and when to launch a family, how to maintain ties with parents and siblings, and how best to juggle responsibilities among all these different roles and commitments. These choices both reflect and fuel the ongoing development of the individual throughout adulthood.

interindividual variability Variability between people.

The Paths of Development Are More Variable and Self-Directed Than in Earlier Life Periods The distinctive life trajectories that are set in motion by such choices and life transitions vary tremendously, so much so that people come to differ from each other more in adulthood than they did earlier in life (Cohen et al., 2003; Nelson & Dannefer, 1992). That is, **interindividual variability**—variability between individuals—increases in adulthood, as biology (physical maturation) plays a less dominant role in shaping the course of development, and the sociocultural environment and, particularly, the individual assume greater importance.

As biology becomes a less dominant determinant of development in adulthood (at least until later adulthood), there is greater potential for people to act as *agents of their own development*, particularly in societies in which decisions are based more on individual choice than on strict conventions and traditions (Heckhausen, 1999; Heinz, 2002). This means that development tends to be more self-directed in adulthood. Not surprisingly, researchers who study adulthood have a keen interest in the processes by which people decide upon their major life goals, set out to pursue those goals, and adapt to challenges and setbacks encountered as their lives unfold (Heckhausen, 1999; Lerner, Freund, DeStefanis, & Habermas, 2001). We explore these processes in upcoming chapters.

Development in Adulthood Involves More Than Growth Development in adulthood is not simply a matter of making choices or acting on one's preferences, however. Adults often face constraints and obstacles as they pursue their personal goals. Constraints can limit the choices they make, and obstacles can interfere with their efforts to realize goals. Constraints can be socially imposed, as when people face discrimination in the workplace. Constraints can also be imposed by biology. A young man with the lifelong goal of being a police officer may have to give up that dream when he discovers that limited physical agility disqualifies him for the role. An older woman may be forced to leave the comfort and familiarity of her home when physical frailty makes it impossible for her to climb stairs or manage household chores. In fact, you will see in Chapters 17 and 18 that biology looms large again in later adulthood in shaping the developmental outcomes and experiences of older people.

From this perspective, development in adulthood involves not only *growth* but also *maintaining stability* and, when necessary, *adapting to declines and losses* (Baltes, 1987; Baltes, Lindenberger, & Staudinger, 2006). This makes it important to understand not only how people seek to pursue personal goals but also how they respond to the obstacles and setbacks they inevitably experience at various points in their lives. Efforts to attain important goals may need to be intensified. At other times, the goals may need to be modified or even abandoned, and losses may need to be accepted.

Growth, maintaining stability, and adapting to loss play roles in each life period, but their relative importance shifts across the lifespan (Baltes, Lindenberger, & Staudinger, 2006). Young adults do not experience gains exclusively, nor do older adults experience losses exclusively. For example, young adults may have to give up many of their leisure activities when they become working parents; older adults may gain a new perspective on their marital relationship that makes them more patient and accepting. In general, though, gains tend to be more common and losses less common in young adulthood, whereas the opposite is true in later adulthood, as shown in Figure 13.1.

As a result, how we use our personal (physical and psychological) resources changes over time. Young adults direct their time and energy primarily toward growth, whereas older adults direct their time and energy primarily toward maintaining their current circumstances and activities and, when that is not possible, adapting to loss (Heckhausen, 1997). Middle adulthood represents an intermediate period, in which resources are directed less toward growth and more toward maintaining and enhancing

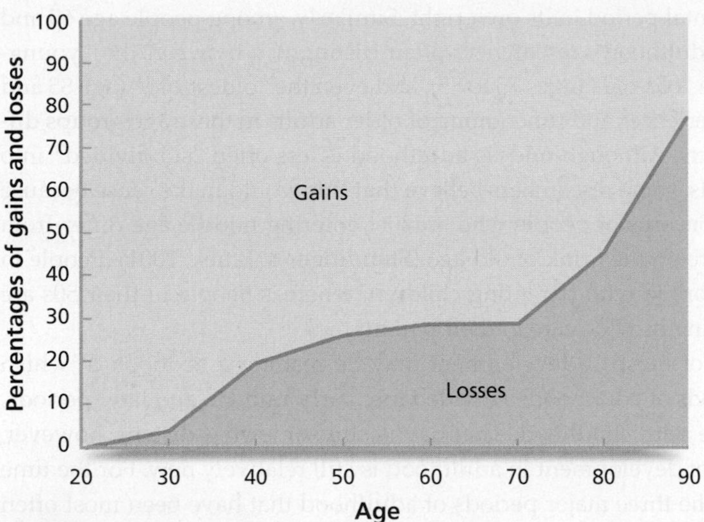

FIGURE 13.1

Ratio of Gains to Losses Over the Lifespan

Participants in this study rated life experiences and personal attributes they believed to show gains or losses at different ages. The grey area shows the percentage of ratings that reflect losses, and the tan area shows the percentage of ratings that reflect losses. A person at age 20, for example, is perceived to experience nearly all gains and very few losses. A person at age 40, in contrast, is perceived to experience about 80 percent gains and 20 percent losses. The ratio of gains to losses decreases further with age.

Source: Heckhausen, J., Dixon, R. A., & Baltes, P. B. (1989). Gains and losses in development throughout adulthood as perceived by different adult age groups. *Developmental Psychology, 25*(1), 109–121.

current achievements and preventing loss. The upcoming discussion of these major periods of adulthood in later chapters explores why and how these shifts occur.

Development Is Cumulative Although the periods of adulthood are sometimes discussed as if they were discrete stages of life, they are interconnected. Development in one period builds upon capacities established and choices made in earlier periods and, in turn, influences development in subsequent periods (Baltes et al., 2006). Developing the capacity for intimacy, for example, paves the way for the formation of satisfying love relationships. Acquiring critical thinking skills helps make it possible for people to assume cognitively challenging jobs, which, in turn, may contribute to further cognitive development. Engaging in risky health behaviors can affect not only current health but also future health. We will see many such examples of links over time as we explore adulthood.

The Three Major Periods of Adulthood

Adulthood is often divided into three major periods—young adulthood (ages 18 to 40), middle adulthood (ages 40 to 65), and later adulthood (ages 65 and older). However, considerable variability exists within each of these life periods, and some researchers make further distinctions within these periods.

For example, the earliest stage of young adulthood, or the period of transition from adolescence to adulthood (ages 18 to 25), has come to be called **emerging adulthood**. In fact, psychologist Jeffrey Arnett (2000, 2006) argues that this period is characterized by such unique developmental challenges and changes that it should be considered a

emerging adulthood The period of transition from adolescence to adulthood (ages 18 to 25) in which the individual begins to establish independence from parents and to assume adult roles.

distinctive developmental period in its own right. Similarly, among people age 65 and older (those in later adulthood), researchers often distinguish between the "young-old" (ages 65 to 75), the "old-old" (ages 75 to 85), and even the "oldest-old" (age 85 and older) because the experiences and functioning of older adults in these age groups differ in important respects. Although middle adulthood is less often "subdivided" into earlier and later periods, some researchers believe that this would make sense because the experiences and concerns of people who are just entering middle age differ from those of people who are on the brink of old age (Staudinger & Bluck, 2001). People in their 40s are often absorbed with parenting children, whereas people in their 50s are often involved in helping provide care to their parents.

Someday, students of lifespan development may be reading a textbook in which each of the major periods of adulthood is divided into early, middle, and later periods, as is currently the case with childhood. That day is still somewhat distant, however, as the scientific study of development in adulthood is still relatively new. For the time being, we emphasize the three major periods of adulthood that have been most often distinguished by researchers, but we will illustrate important developmental differences between "younger" and "older" adults within each of these periods.

We begin our exploration of adulthood in young adulthood. In this chapter, we consider what it means to become an adult and how the transition to adulthood has changed. Next we explore young adults' physical and sexual development. We then examine cognitive development, and how it is shaped by the social roles and responsibilities that people often assume in young adulthood. In this as in other periods of development, context is critical. (For a summary of this section, see "Interim Summary 13.1: Perspectives on Adulthood.")

INTERIM SUMMARY 13.1

Perspectives on Adulthood

Guiding Principles and Assumptions	■ Early theorists such as Freud and Piaget viewed adulthood as a time when relatively little change occurs. Erikson broke ranks with these theorists, describing adulthood as unfolding through three psychosocial stages. Contemporary theorists regard development as a lifelong process. ■ **Interindividual variability** increases in adulthood, as biology plays a less dominant role, and the sociocultural environment and the individual assume greater importance. ■ Development in adulthood involves not only *growth* but also *maintaining stability* and *adapting to declines and losses*. ■ Development in one period of adulthood builds upon experiences and capacities established in earlier periods and affects development in subsequent periods.
The Three Major Periods of Adulthood	■ Adulthood is often divided into three major periods: young adulthood (ages 18 to 40), middle adulthood (ages 40 to 65), and later adulthood (ages 65 and over). ■ Considerable variability exists within each of these life periods, and some researchers make further distinctions within these periods. ■ The earliest stage of young adulthood (ages 18 to 25) has come to be called **emerging adulthood**.

THE TRANSITION TO ADULTHOOD

Many of the most significant events that people will experience in their lifetimes occur during young adulthood (Tanner, 2006). For most people, some or all of the following occur between age 18 and the late 30s: leaving home and establishing an independent residence, pursuing higher education or vocational training, entering the work force, forging intimate relationships and friendships, marrying, and having children. The decisions made and events experienced during this life period often have effects that ripple throughout the rest of adulthood, setting people on paths that influence their future health status, financial security, social relationships, and psychological well-being.

Markers and Meanings of Adulthood

When does a person actually become an adult? Many societies confer some adult privileges when a person reaches a particular age, such as the right to vote at age 18 or the ability to drive at age 16. Some cultures observe coming-of-age rituals or celebrations that are treated as markers of a young person's passage to adulthood, such as the bar mitzvah in Jewish religion that celebrates a 13-year-old boy's transition to manhood or the Quinceañera celebration in Hispanic culture that marks a 15-year old girl's transition to womanhood. However, these ceremonies do not automatically confer adult status, for two main reasons.

First, in many societies, people are not considered adults until they become self-sufficient. In the United States, young people are considered adults when they make their own decisions, accept responsibility for their actions, and attain financial independence from their parents (Arnett, 2000). Second, becoming an adult is usually a gradual process, not a single event. Thus a young person may be "adult" in some ways but not in others. Consider some examples. A young woman has launched a career and maintains her own apartment, but she calls her mother almost every night to ask for advice. A college student lives in a dorm but brings his laundry to his parents' house on weekends. Each has one foot in adulthood, but neither has attained full self-sufficiency.

The self-perceptions of young people often reflect this mixed status. In one study, people of different ages were asked whether they considered themselves to be adults. As you can see in Figure 13.2, over 50 percent of those aged 18 to 25 replied "in some respects yes, in some respects no" (Arnett, 2001). This is not surprising, given that some of the key criteria for adult status, such as accepting responsibility, are largely subjective. Deciding when one has become an adult is not necessarily a simple or straightforward task (Arnett, 2001).

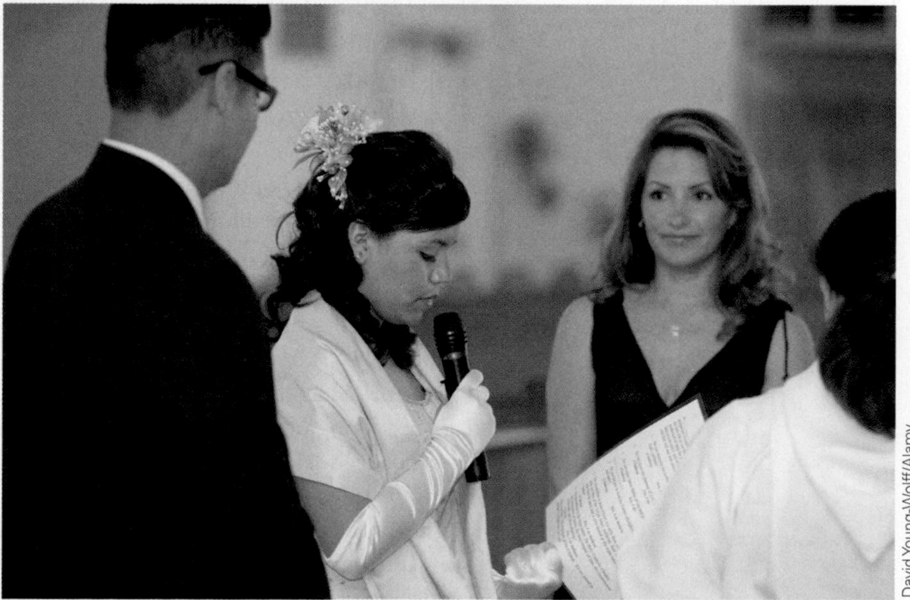
David Young-Wolff/Alamy

In some cultures, specific celebrations—such as this Quinceanera celebration—mark a young person's passage to adulthood. In other cultures, young people are not considered adults until they become self-sufficient.

It may be a somewhat simpler task, though, in societies in which specific social roles are seen as conferring adult status. In China, for example, getting married is a key marker of adult status. Because people tend to marry at a younger age in China than

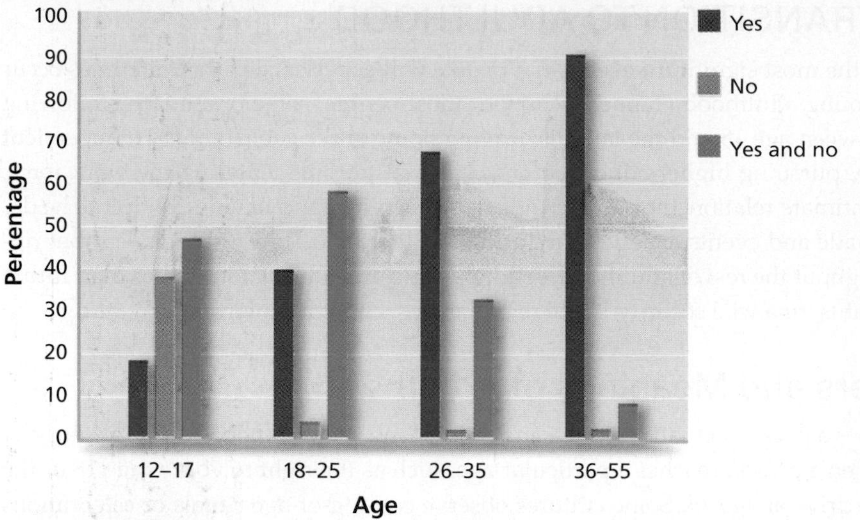

FIGURE 13.2

Views of One's Own Adult Status, by Age

Study participants were asked the question, "Do you feel you have reached adulthood?"

Source: Arnett, J. J. (2000). Emerging adulthood: A theory of development from the late teens through the twenties. *American Psychologist, 55*(5), 469–480.

in the United States, Chinese young people define themselves as adults at an earlier age. In a recent study, 59 percent of Chinese college students regarded themselves as adults, compared with only 28 percent of U.S. college students (Badger, Nelson, & Barry, 2006).

The Longer Transition to Adulthood

The transition to adulthood is a gradual process that has been growing longer in most economically developed societies (Arnett, 2000). In the past—for example, the 1950s—most young Americans finished their schooling in their teens, entered the work force shortly thereafter (especially if they were male), and then got married, established their own homes, and became parents—all in the space of a few years.

The transition to adulthood is lengthening in part because young adults today need more extensive education and training to compete in the work force (Arnett, 2000, 2006). The kinds of jobs that allow young people to establish independent households and become financially independent of their parents increasingly require higher education. As a result, the proportion of men and women attending college and graduate school has increased (Hamilton & Hamilton, 2006), and the process of settling into an occupation occurs at later ages (Cohen, Kasen, Chen, Hartmark, & Gordon, 2003). For similar reasons, young people are remaining in their parents' homes for a longer time and often return home for interim stays even after they have lived on their own (Mitchell, 2006). Young people are also marrying and becoming parents at later ages than was true in the past, as shown in Figure 13.3 (Arnett, 2006; Matthews & Hamilton, 2009).

At the same time, however, the age at which young people assume these adult roles has become more variable. For example, compared to young adults from affluent (high socioeconomic status [SES]) backgrounds, those from poor (lower SES) backgrounds are more likely to be working full-time, to be married, and to have children by age 25.

These variations are partly due to financial resources—some young people simply cannot afford to delay their entry into the work force. They may also be partly due to personal preferences. Some young people want to "enjoy life while they are young" and postpone commitments (if they have the means to do so). Others choose to assume adult roles one at a time—finishing their education before they get married, and getting established in a career before they have children. Chapter 14 explores research on the personal and societal timetables people have in mind as they try to plan when they will take on major social roles such as marriage and parenthood.

How do these life changes affect young adults? The answer is not simple. On the one hand, as young people become more autonomous and begin to establish lives separate from their parents, the freedom to experiment can be stimulating, and the opportunity to make decisions for themselves can enhance feelings of self-efficacy. On the other hand, some developmental psychologists believe that the passage to adulthood in modern society is too long, too vague, and too rocky (Chisholm & Hurrelmann, 1995). The lack of clear structure during this passage and the need to negotiate new environments, roles, and relationships can be stressful or even bewildering at times for young people.

Whether such stress contributes to psychological distress in young adulthood is a question that will be examined in the next chapter, when we explore young adults' emotional health. For now, we turn to physical development and health in young adulthood. (For a summary of this section, see "Interim Summary 13.2: The Transition to Adulthood.")

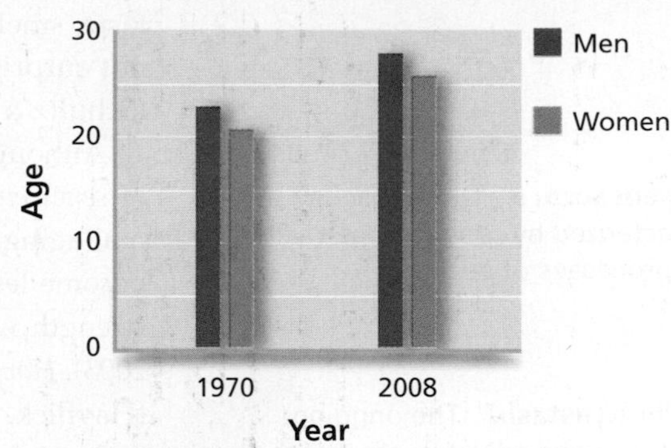

FIGURE 13.3

Age at First Marriage, 1970 vs. 2008

Source: Adapted from U.S. Bureau of the Census (2006, September 21). *Table MS-2. Estimated Median Age at First Marriage, by Sex: 1890 to the Present.* Retrieved April 2, 2010 from www.census.gov/population/socdemo/hh-fam/ms2.pdf

INTERIM SUMMARY 13.2

The Transition to Adulthood

Markers and Meanings of Adulthood	■ Although conceptions of adulthood vary, most emphasize the idea that to be an adult requires a person to become self-sufficient ■ Becoming an adult is a gradual process, not an event, in most economically developed societies.
The Longer Transition to Adulthood	■ Becoming an adult is a process that has become longer in recent years. This is due in part to the fact that young adults today need more education and training to compete in the work force. ■ People are entering the work force, marrying, and becoming parents at later ages than in the past. ■ Some developmental psychologists believe that the passage to adulthood in modern society is too long, vague, and rocky, and may cause stress and confusion.

PHYSICAL DEVELOPMENT AND HEALTH

How much has your body changed since you were 18? How much do you expect it to change by the time you are 35? As we'll see in this section, our bodies change in many ways throughout young adulthood.

Physical Functioning

For most people, young adulthood is a time when their physical functioning will be at its peak. People typically reach their maximum height in their early 20s, and continue to gain muscle mass and physical strength until about age 30. The cardiovascular, respiratory, immune, neuroendocrine, digestive, and other bodily systems function at their greatest capacity and efficiency in young adulthood. The senses (vision, hearing, taste, smell, touch, and balance) also tend to be sharp during young adulthood. It is not surprising that athletes often reach their peak performance in their 20s and 30s (Schultz & Curnow, 1988).

senescence Normal aging, characterized by gradual, age-related processes of decline.

Although young adulthood is generally a time of peak physical functioning, signs of *senescence* begin to appear gradually during this life period. **Senescence**, or normal aging, involves gradual, age-related processes of decline. Lung tissues begin to become less elastic, for example, and respiratory muscles begin to lose some of their strength when people are in their 20s and 30s (Sharma & Goodwin, 2006; Zeleznik, 2003). *Homeostasis* also begins to become slower and less efficient in young adulthood (Hayflick, 1994). **Homeostasis** refers to the automatic adjustments that the human body makes constantly to maintain equilibrium, such as adjusting body temperature to variations in room temperature. In young adulthood, the impact of such changes on everyday life is minimal because the changes are typically small and gradual.

homeostasis The ongoing, automatic adjustments that the human body makes to maintain physiological equilibrium.

Physical Health

Like physical functioning, overall physical health tends to be robust in young adulthood. The vast majority of young adults in the United States—over 96 percent—describe their physical health as good to excellent, and fewer than 5 percent have health problems that interfere with their daily activities (Park, Mulye, Adams, Brindis, & Irwin, 2006). In general, the physical illnesses that young adults experience tend to be brief, such as the flu or common cold.

Yet risks for some young adults can also be seen against this general backdrop of physical fitness and health. We examine several of these risks next, including obesity-related chronic illness, health risk behaviors, violence, and limited access to health care. (See Chapter 11 for a discussion of eating disorders that can threaten health by leading people to be severely underweight.)

Obesity-Related Chronic Illness Rates of obesity have risen sharply in the United States, taking a toll on Americans' health (Centers for Disease Control and Prevention, 2008a; Ferraro, Thorpe, & Wilkinson, 1995). Obesity, which is usually defined as having a body mass index (or BMI—ratio of weight to height) above 30, affects nearly one in six young adults in the United States (Park et al., 2006), with higher rates among African American, Hispanic, and Native American young adults. The United States is not alone in facing this public health threat, as an epidemic of obesity has emerged in many developed nations and is beginning to appear in developing nations such as India and China as well (Prentice, 2006; World Health Organization, 2010).

© GUANG NIU/Reuters/Corbis

Obesity has become a concern in many developed and developing nations, and it contributes to many chronic illnesses later in life.

Obesity substantially increases the risk of serious chronic illnesses, such as cardiovascular disease, type 2 diabetes, and cancer. As we discussed in earlier chapters, already, rates of type 2 diabetes (once called adult-onset diabetes) have burgeoned among children and adolescents (Goran, Ball, & Cruz, 2003). The epidemic of obesity in the United States, with its clear connection to chronic diseases, has led some researchers to worry that the current generation of young people may be the first to have a shorter life expectancy than that of their parents (Olshansky et al., 2005). There have always been some people who entered young adulthood with existing chronic illnesses (Williams, Holmbeck, & Greenley, 2002), but the number who face this prospect appears to be rising rapidly. How the burden of chronic disease may affect not only individuals but society as a whole remains to be seen.

Health Risk Behaviors Chronic conditions associated with obesity are not the only threat to health in young adulthood. Some threats stem from young adults' health risk behaviors. Researchers often distinguish between **health-promoting behaviors** (such as good nutrition, regular physical exercise, and adequate sleep) and **health-damaging behaviors** (such as cigarette smoking, alcohol and drug abuse, and unsafe sex). The latter are sometimes referred to as "health risk behaviors" because they increase the risk of illness, injury, and even death. Cigarette smoking, for example, peaks in young adulthood and contributes to the risks for cancer, cardiovascular disease, and respiratory disease, all of which are leading causes of death later in life (Centers for Disease Control, 2009).

health-promoting behaviors Behaviors that contribute to better physical health, such as proper nutrition, regular physical exercise, and adequate sleep.

health-damaging behaviors Behaviors that contribute to worse physical health, such as cigarette smoking and excessive alcohol consumption.

Experimentation with cigarettes, alcohol, and drugs usually begins in adolescence and increases when young people leave home (Chen & Kandel, 1995; Everett et al., 1999). Typically, smoking, drinking, and use of illicit drugs increase in emerging adulthood (ages 18 to 25), a time when young people are free from parental monitoring and eager for novel experiences (Bachman, Wadsworth, O'Malley, Johnston, & Schulenberg, 1997). Hazardous alcohol use by college students is also common, as few restraints on drinking exist on many college campuses, and students often embrace social traditions that involve drinking (Zamboanga, Olthuis, Horton, McCollum, Lee, & Shaw, 2009).

Such novelty seeking can be dangerous. Unintentional injury is the leading cause of death in young adulthood, and nearly 70 percent of such injury-related deaths involve motor-vehicle accidents (Park et al., 2006). Alcohol use—particularly driving under the influence—contributes to more fatal accidents (and nonfatal injuries) in early adulthood than in later periods. When alcohol use is coupled with the failure to wear a seatbelt, the results are often deadly.

Fortunately, the increase in health risk behaviors in adolescence and early adulthood tends to be short-lived. Figure 13.4, for example, shows that rates of binge drinking increase from the teens through the early 20s and then decline steadily thereafter. Cigarette smoking follows a similar pattern, although it declines more slowly in young adulthood (Chen & Kandel, 1995).

Assuming new social roles—such as entering the work force full-time, marrying, and becoming a parent—brings many new responsibilities that often lead people to curtail health risk behaviors (Bachman et al., 2002; Maggs & Schulenberg, 2004). This decline in health risk behaviors as adult roles are assumed is sometimes referred to as **maturing out** (Bachman et al., 1997). But not all young adults follow this pattern. Some show little decline or even increase their consumption over time (Flora & Chassin, 2005). Young people whose substance use persists or increases through young adulthood are at high risk for drug and alcohol dependence (Flora & Chassin, 2005).

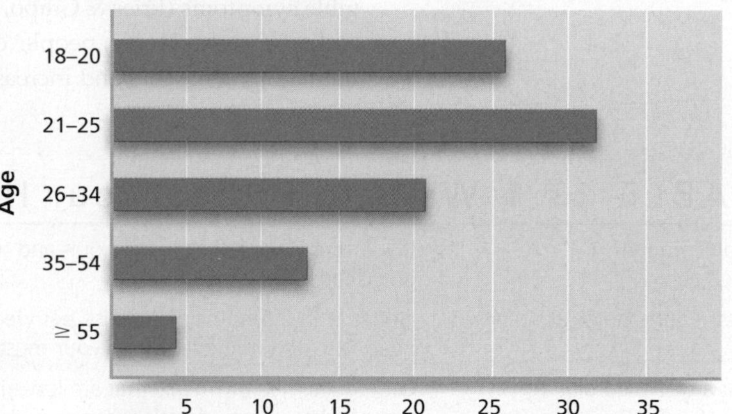

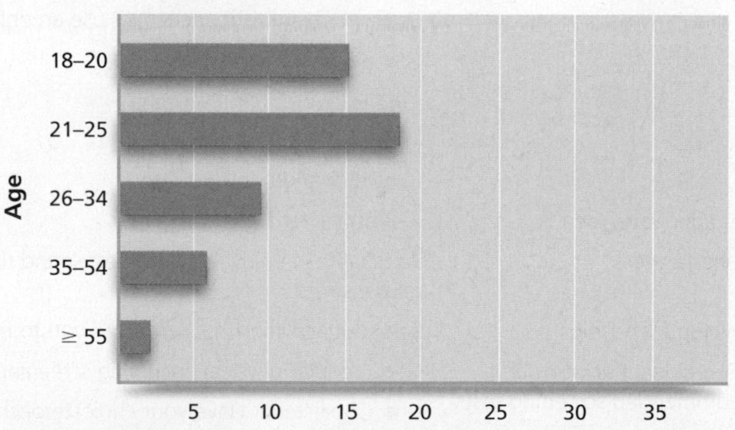

FIGURE 13.4

Rates of Binge Drinking in Adulthood

Note: Binge drinking is defined as having consumed five or more drinks on one occasion.

Source: Naimi, T. S., Brewer, R. D., Mokdad, A., Denny, C., Serdula, M. K., & Marks, J. S. (2003). Binge drinking among U.S. adults. *Journal of the American Medical Association, 289*(1), 70–75.

Young adults' health behaviors affect not only their current health, but also their future health. This makes young adulthood an important time for establishing health behaviors that will reduce the risk of chronic illness and disability later in life

maturing out A decline in health risk behaviors in young adulthood that occurs as adult roles are assumed.

(Holmbeck, 2002). A number of chronic diseases begin to develop in young adulthood, slowly and without noticeable symptoms. Cardiovascular disease—the leading cause of death worldwide—begins to develop among smokers and people with high-fat diets as early as their 20s, with the development of elevated cholesterol (Fries & Crapo, 1981). Because they do not experience symptoms at this stage, young adults have little motivation to change their behavior. As the disease progresses, plaque (made up of cholesterol and fatty substances) begins to form in the walls of coronary arteries, building up over time until it eventually restricts the flow of oxygen to the heart, causing shortness of breath or chest pain. Further progression may result in a heart attack or stroke, with the possibility of lingering physical limitations, disability, or even death. The precursors of other diseases in which poor health behavior plays a role, such as lung cancer, also often begin to develop in early adulthood, frequently without tangible symptoms (Fries & Crapo, 1981).

Fortunately, young people can do something about this by decreasing health-damaging behaviors and increasing health-promoting behaviors (see Table 13.1). Just

TABLE 13.1 Ways to Protect Your Health

Don't smoke	If you do smoke, take steps to quit and find tips at www.smokefree.gov or www.healthfinder.gov (search for "smoking").
Get regular physical activity	Get at least 2.5 hours of exercise per week. Include activities that increase your breathing and heart rate and that strengthen your muscles.
Eat a balanced diet	Eat regular, healthy meals that are low in fat and include fruits and vegetables. Choose complex carbohydrates, include adequate calcium, and avoid excess salt and sugar.
Maintain a healthy weight	Avoid body weight extremes (being underweight or overweight). Balance calorie intake with calories burned off through physical activity. Calculate your body mass index (BMI): weight (in pounds) / height^2 (in inches) or use an online calculator (e.g., www.nhlbisupport.com/bmi). ■ Below 18.5: underweight ■ 18.5–24.9: normal ■ 25.0–29.9: overweight ■ 30.0 and above: obese
Get adequate sleep	7–8 hours per night
Manage stress	Participate in enjoyable activities, spend time with friends, or find other healthy ways to relieve stress.
Develop friendships	Seek out activities that will allow you to meet people with similar interests.
Get regular check-ups and recommended screening tests	Get a regular physical, including screening tests for: ■ Cholesterol: Have your cholesterol checked regularly starting at age 35 (earlier if you have risk factors for heart disease, such as smoking, diabetes, high blood pressure, or a family history of heart disease). ■ Blood pressure: Have your blood pressure checked every 2 years. High blood pressure is 140/90 or higher. ■ Skin cancer: Check your skin regularly for irregular moles and other possible signs of skin cancer. ■ Pap smear and mammogram (women): Have regular pap smears and discuss with your doctor when to have mammograms. ■ Screening for sexually transmitted diseases: Discuss with your doctor whether you should be tested for any sexually transmitted diseases.

Sources: Adapted from http://www.ahrq.gov/ppip/healthymen.htm; http://www.ahrq.gov/ppip/healthywom.htm; http://www.cdc.gov/family/college/; Choi, C. Q. (2007), Five New Year's resolutions you owe yourself. *Scientific American 17,* 82–85; and Hazzard, W. R. (2001). Aging, health, longevity, and the promise of biomedical research: The perspective of a gerontologist and geriatrician. In E. J.. Masoro & S. N. Austad (Eds.), *Handbook of the biology of aging* (5th ed., pp, 445–456.). San Diego, CA: Academic Press.

like health-damaging behaviors, health-promoting behaviors may influence both current and future health. Physical exercise, for example, promotes the growth and maintenance of bones and muscles, reduces the risk of obesity and obesity-related chronic conditions, helps to relieve stress and reduce depression and anxiety, and may enhance cognitive functioning (Centers for Disease Control, 2006a; Dubbert, 2002). Getting adequate rest is less often thought of as a health-enhancing behavior, but researchers have documented the restorative benefits of sleep. Individuals who are sleep deprived are more susceptible to illness than those who get their regular 8 hours (Cacioppo et al., 2002).

Violence Young adulthood is also characterized by spikes in the rates of physical violence, including homicide, suicide, and sexual assault (discussed more fully below). Young people can be both the targets and the perpetrators of such violence. Homicide rates in the United States peak in young adulthood and then decline thereafter (Park et al., 2006). The risk is greater for men; young men are nearly six times more likely to die from homicide than are young women. African American men are especially at risk for death by homicide (Park et al., 2006). Figure 13.5 illustrates this troubling rise in physical violence in early adulthood as compared to adolescence.

Violence committed by young adults is a problem with complex roots and multiple causes. In some cases, it is an escalation of aggression and poorly controlled behavior that was evident in childhood. Family factors, such as a history of violence in the family, particularly child abuse, may play a role. Situational factors, such as having a heated argument while under the influence of alcohol, can trigger violence in people who have little prior history of violence. Social conditions—such as high rates of poverty, deteriorating neighborhoods, easy access to guns, and exposure to violence in the media—may interact with these other factors to contribute to an increased risk of violence (Krug, Dahlberg, Mercy, Zwi, & Rafael, 2002). Spikes in rates of violence in early adulthood are seen not only in the United States but in many other countries, leading the World Health Organization (Krug et al., 2002) to describe this as a significant public health threat that wreaks havoc in the lives of too many young adults.

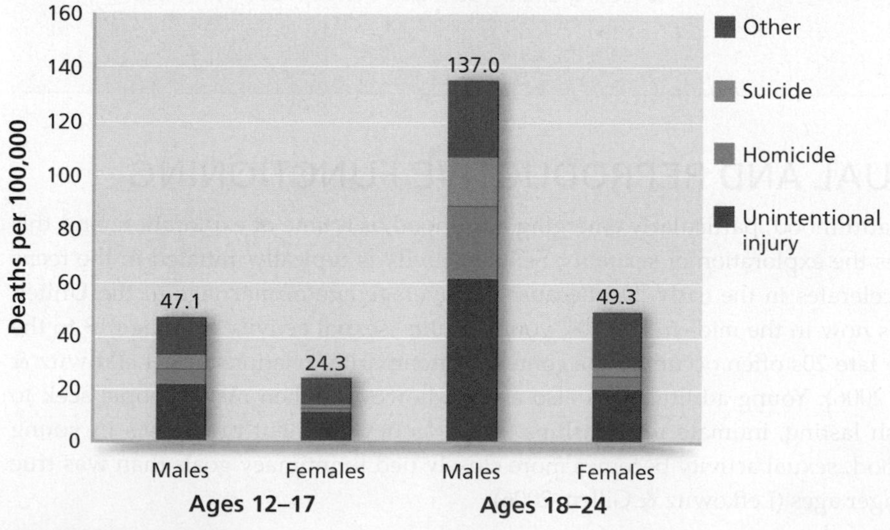

FIGURE 13.5

Rates of Violence from Adolescence to Young Adulthood

Source: Park, M. J., Mulye, T. P., Adams, S. H., Brindis, C. D, & Irwin, C. E. (2006). The health status of young adults in the United States. *Journal of Adolescent Health, 39,* 305–317.

Access to Health Care Access to adequate health care clearly is important in addressing the health problems that some young adults experience. Yet young adults have the lowest rates of health insurance of any age group (Park et al., 2006). One reason for this is that they become ineligible for their parents' health insurance coverage during the transition to adulthood (Park et al., 2006). In a recent study, 31 percent of women and 38 percent of men ages 18 to 24 had been without health insurance for at least some part of the preceding year (Park et al., 2006). The problem is more severe among members of ethnic minority groups, the poor, nonstudents, and those with less education (Park et al., 2006). It is not unusual for uninsured young adults to forego seeking needed medical care. (For a summary of this section, see "Interim Summary 13.3: Physical Development and Health.")

INTERIM SUMMARY 13.3

Physical Development and Health

Physical Functioning	■ For most people, young adulthood is a time of peak physical functioning. ■ Still, small signs of **senescence**, or normal aging, do begin to appear at this time. **Homeostasis** also begins to become slightly slower and less efficient. ■ The impact of such changes tends to be minimal because the changes are typically small and gradual.
Physical Health	■ Overall physical health tends to be robust in young adulthood. However, the risk of chronic illness in young adulthood is increasing, and many chronic conditions that will not cause symptoms until later in life begin to develop in young adulthood. ■ Prevalence of **health-damaging behaviors** (such as smoking, alcohol and drug abuse, and unsafe sex) rises and then falls in young adulthood. ■ Young adulthood is an important time for establishing **health-promoting behaviors** that will reduce the risk of chronic illness and disability later in life ■ Young adulthood is also characterized by increasing rates of physical violence and limited access to health care for some.

SEXUAL AND REPRODUCTIVE FUNCTIONING

Young adulthood, particularly emerging adulthood, is a time of exploration, and this includes the exploration of sexuality. Sexual activity is typically initiated in the teens and accelerates in the early 20s. Because the average age of marriage in the United States is now in the mid- to late 20s, young adults' sexual activity from age 18 to the mid- to late 20s often occurs in the context of nonmarital relationships (Lefkowitz & Gillen, 2006). Young adulthood is also a time, however, when many people seek to establish lasting, intimate relationships. Thus, as development progresses in young adulthood, sexual activity becomes more closely tied to intimacy goals than was true at younger ages (Lefkowitz & Gillen, 2006).

Sexual Attitudes and Behavior

Attitudes toward sex, including casual sex, become more accepting and open-minded in young adulthood. Consistent with this, the majority of young adults are sexually active. Approximately half of young people are sexually active by age 18, and nearly all have become sexually active by age 25 (Lefkowitz & Gillen, 2006). Members of ethnic minority groups tend to become sexually active at younger ages, although the opposite is true for Asian Americans, who tend to become sexually active later and to have fewer sexual partners (McLaughlin, Chen, Greenberger, & Beiermeir, 1997).

Some young adults prefer to abstain from sexual activity, however, for reasons ranging from religious convictions to fears of negative outcomes (e.g., unwanted pregnancy, sexually transmitted diseases) to the desire to wait for the right relationship (Lefkowitz & Gillen, 2006). Moreover, not all sexual activity necessarily involves sexual intercourse; kissing and other forms of physical affection can be meaningful expressions of sexuality in young adulthood.

Gender Differences Compared to young women, young men report greater sexual desire, greater acceptance of casual sex, and, not surprisingly, having had more sexual partners. Women appear to be more selective about their partners, preferring to experience closeness before they have sex (and assigning greater importance to committed relationships as a context for sex) (Peplau, 2003). Consider the comments of two young heterosexual adults who participated in a study on the meaning of sexual desire (Regan & Berscheid, 1996, p. 116):

> *Male participant:* "Sexual desire is wanting someone . . . in a physical manner. No strings attached. Just for uninhibited *sexual intercourse.*" [italics in original]
>
> *Female participant:* "Sexual desire is the longing to be emotionally intimate and to express love for another person."

This gender difference has often been attributed to cultural factors—women typically have been socialized to confine their sexual feelings and behaviors to close relationships. But new research suggests that biology plays a role as well. **Oxytocin** is a hormone that is involved in nurturing behavior, as well as sexual excitement and orgasms, particularly among women. Women have more oxytocin circuits in their brains, and the oxytocin circuits in women's brains are located closer to the circuits involved in nurturing behavior. Nurturing behaviors—touching, affection, and expressions of emotional closeness—are therefore more likely to stimulate sexual arousal among women than among men. Women also release more oxytocin during orgasms. These biological factors, coupled with cultural factors, may explain why sexuality is more closely linked to feelings of intimacy and attachment among women (Diamond, 2004; Peplau, 2003).

oxytocin A maternal pituitary gland hormone that is involved in affiliation and nurturing behavior as well as sexual excitement and orgasms.

Sexual Minorities For lesbian, gay, bisexual, and transgendered (LGBT) individuals, initial experiences of same-sex attraction and same-sex behavior, as well as self-labeling as LGBT, typically occur in adolescence (Lefkowitz & Gillen, 2006). But most LGBT individuals experience their first same-sex relationship (as opposed to experimentation) during young adulthood (Lefkowitz & Gillen, 2006). Research also suggests that LGBT individuals often begin to disclose their sexual orientation, or "come out," to others, such as friends and family members, during young adulthood (Lefkowitz & Gillen, 2006). Gender differences among LGBT young adults mirror those observed among heterosexual young adults. For example, compared to lesbians, gay men report a greater acceptance of casual sex, report more sexual partners, and assign less importance to monogamy in a relationship (Peplau & Beals, 2001).

What determines a person's sexual orientation? The answer to this question is complex, but most researchers believe that sexual orientation is determined by the interaction of biological, cognitive, and environmental factors (American Psychological Association, 2005). For example, homosexuals are more likely than heterosexuals to have a homosexual relative, which suggests that genes play a role (Peplau & Garnets, 2000). Scientists have soundly rejected early ideas that homosexuality reflects psychological maladjustment or inverted sex roles (Herek & Garnets, 2007). Research indicates that gay men and lesbians are as well adjusted psychologically as heterosexuals, although

Queerstock, Inc./Alamy

Research has shown that gay men and lesbians are as well adjusted psychologically as heterosexuals, although prejudice and discrimination can detract from their well-being.

their psychological health can suffer as a result of experiencing prejudice and discrimination (Herek & Garnets, 2007; Meyer, 2003). Homosexuals are no more or less likely than heterosexuals to have feminine or masculine traits (Peplau & Garnets, 2000). Research indicates, moreover, that sexual orientation falls along a continuum, from exclusively heterosexual to exclusively homosexual, with various forms of bisexuality (attraction to members of both the opposite sex and one's own sex) in between.

New research suggests that the sexual orientation of women is more fluid, or changeable, than that of men (Diamond, 2004; Peplau, 2001). Longitudinal studies indicate that women are more likely than men to change their sexual orientation over time, alternating between lesbian and heterosexual identities. The distinction between lesbian and bisexual identities, moreover, is less sharp among women (Peplau, 2001). The greater fluidity of women's sexual orientation may reflect the role of oxytocin in linking emotional closeness with sexual desire among women, as discussed earlier. This stronger link makes falling in love with a friend far more common among lesbians than among gay men (Diamond, 2004). In one study, for example, 70 percent of lesbians but only 5 percent of gay men in the United States reported that their first same-sex experience had occurred within an established friendship (Diamond & Savin-Williams, 2000).

Sexual Risk Behavior

sexually transmitted diseases (STDs) Diseases that are spread through sexual contact.

sexual risk behaviors Risky sexual behaviors such as engaging in unprotected sex, failing to disclose that one has a sexually transmitted disease (STD), and failing to inquire whether a new partner has an STD.

Much research on sexual behavior in young adulthood, like research on health behavior, has emphasized risk taking and resulting threats to health. Given the dangers of **sexually transmitted diseases (STDs)**, this emphasis makes sense, but it is important to remember that engaging in sexual activity during this life stage is normative and can contribute to the development of intimacy (Lefkowitz & Gillen, 2006). This said, some young adults take more risks than others. **Sexual risk behaviors** include engaging in unprotected sex, failing to disclose that one has an STD, and failing to inquire whether a new partner has an STD. Consuming alcohol along with sexual activity compounds these risks and also increases the risk of sexual assault (Reed, Amaro, Matsumoto, & Kaysen, 2009).

As you read in Chapter 11, adolescents are erratic in their use of contraception. Unfortunately, this pattern of inconsistent use continues into young adulthood. Although young adults generally appear to recognize that condoms offer protection during sexual intercourse (Oncale & King, 2001), they nonetheless use condoms inconsistently and, sometimes, incorrectly (Lefkowitz & Gillen, 2006). Moreover, the actions of their sexual partner play a role in condom and contraceptive use. As many as 30 percent of young men and 41 percent of young women report having had a sexual partner try to persuade them not to use a condom (Lefkowitz & Gillen, 2006). Notably, more people in their early 20s report using condoms to avoid pregnancy than to prevent STDs (Cooper, Agocha, & Powers, 1999). Such findings, coupled with the fact that some STDs can exist without symptoms for many years, have led some researchers to worry that young adults may underestimate the risks associated with sexual activity (Lefkowitz & Gillen, 2006).

chlamydia The most frequently reported STD; it often has only mild symptoms or no symptoms. It is treatable with antibiotics, but if untreated it can lead to infertility.

Sexually Transmitted Diseases Sexually transmitted diseases are distressingly common in adolescence and young adulthood: approximately half of all new cases of STDs in the United States occur among people ages 15 to 24 (Weinstock, Berman, & Cates, 2004). **Chlamydia** is the most frequently reported STD. It is an infection that often has only mild symptoms or no symptoms, but if untreated it can lead to infertility.

Fortunately, it can be treated effectively with antibiotics. **Human papilloma virus (HPV) infection** can also be symptomless for many years, but it may be riskier for young adults because it cannot be treated with antibiotics, and it tends to be poorly understood by young adults (Lefkowitz & Gillen, 2006). This is worrisome because HPV is the major cause of cervical cancer in women.

In contrast to their limited knowledge of HPV, young adults have more extensive knowledge of **HIV,** the human immunodeficiency virus that can lead to **AIDS** (acquired immune deficiency syndrome). Young adults perceive the risk of HIV infection to be greater than that of other STDs, but they also tend to believe that HIV is something that happens to "other people," not themselves—an example of an optimistic bias that often characterizes how young adults think about their personal risk for various health threats (Kalichman & Cain, 2005; Younge, Salem, & Bybee, 2008). Moreover, knowledge of the risks for HIV infection does not in and of itself lead to behavior that would reduce these risks (Gerrard, Gibbons, & Bushman, 1996; Polacek, Hicks, & Oswalt, 2007). HIV infection and AIDS diagnoses and deaths have declined in the United States since the mid-1990s (Karon, Fleming, Steketee, & DeCock, 2001), yet as many as 56,000 Americans may become infected with HIV each year, many of whom are under the age of 25 (Hall et al., 2008; see Figure 13.6).

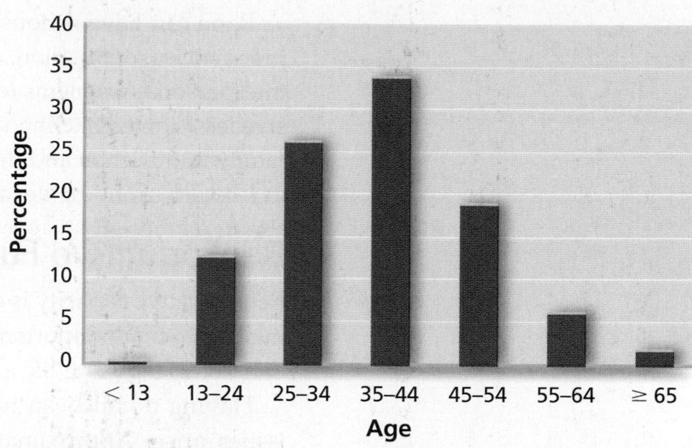

FIGURE 13.6

Rates of HIV Infection or AIDS Diagnoses by Age in 2004

Note: The data shown are for cases of HIV infection or AIDS diagnoses in the United States for 1 year, 2004.

Source: Centers for Disease Control and Prevention (2008b). *HIV/AIDS among youth*. Retrieved from http://www.cdc.gov/hiv/resources/factsheets/youth.htm.

Given young adults' relatively high rates of sexual risk behaviors and their uneven knowledge of the links between these behaviors and STDs, programs designed to limit the spread of HIV infection continue to be important. The AIDS epidemic riveted public attention when it first appeared in the early 1980s, but it is no longer a "new"—or newsworthy—epidemic (Kelly & Kalichman, 2002). This shift, coupled with the reduction in AIDS-related deaths due to antiretroviral medications, could lead to dangerous complacency. Maintaining a sense of urgency about this global epidemic is important: it already has led to the deaths of over 16 million people worldwide and continues to claim many lives (Kelly & Kalichman, 2002).

human papillomavirus (HPV) infection A sexually transmitted disease that is often symptomless and cannot be treated with antibiotics.

HIV Human immunodeficiency virus; the virus that causes AIDS (acquired immunodeficiency syndrome).

AIDS Acquired immunodeficiency syndrome, a disease that compromises the immune system and is spread through sexual contact.

Sexual Assault Unfortunately, sexual behavior sometimes involves aggression and violence. **Rape** refers to forcible intercourse (vaginal, anal, or oral) with someone who does not give consent. Estimating how often rapes occur is difficult because fear or shame sometimes leads victims to forgo reporting that they were raped. In fact, rape is one of the most underreported crimes (Tjaden & Thoennes, 2006), but it is a serious problem worldwide, particularly for women. In the United States, a survey of 16,000 men and women revealed that 18 percent of women reported having been raped at some point in their lives, and another 3 percent reported having been the victim of an attempted rape (Tjaden & Thoennes, 2006). The corresponding figures among men in the survey were 2.1 percent and 0.9 percent.

rape Forcible intercourse (vaginal, oral, or anal) with someone who does not give consent.

Date rape or **acquaintance rape**, which involves forced sexual activity with someone the victim knows at least casually, is of special concern for young adults, as it is most common in this age group. A large study of sexual assault among female college students revealed that one-third of the women had experienced unwanted or uninvited sexual contact, most of which involved classmates, friends, current or former boyfriends, or acquaintances (Fisher, Cullen, & Turner, 2001). Higher estimates have been reported in other studies (e.g., Watts & Zimmerman, 2002).

date (or acquaintance) rape Forced sexual activity with a date or acquaintance whom the victim knows at least casually.

Rape can have serious and long-lasting consequences, including STDs, unwanted pregnancies, depression, anxiety, posttraumatic stress disorder, eating disorders, and interpersonal problems (e.g., loss of trust in others, loss of sexual desire and responsiveness, lower likelihood of marriage) (Tjaden & Thoennes, 2006). The support of family and friends and the assistance of mental health professionals can be important in recovery from the devastating effects of rape.

Reproductive Functioning

Reproductive capacity is at its peak in young adulthood. Becoming pregnant and having children are important life goals for many young adults, and the transition to parenthood is a pivotal life experience, as will be discussed in Chapter 14.

Having a child can become a difficult goal to achieve, however, when fertility issues arise. Approximately 7 percent of couples in the United States experience **infertility**, defined as failing to conceive a child after a year or more of trying without contraceptive use (Chandra, Martinez, Mosher, Abma, & Jones, 2005). Infertility has become a more common experience among married couples as the decision to marry and have children has been postponed to older ages. Fertility declines and rates of miscarriage begin to rise sharply among women, for example, by age 35 (Balen & Rutherford, 2007).

infertility Failing to conceive a child after a year or more of trying without contraceptive use.

Infertility is often deeply disappointing to couples and can lead to depression and anxiety, as well as feelings of shame and inadequacy (Clay, 2006). This distress may be compounded by stereotypes that attribute the failure to conceive a child to the couple's stress or personal failings. Such stereotypes are not warranted; research suggests that the major causes of infertility are biomedical rather than psychological in nature (Stanton, Lobel, Sears, & DeLuca, 2002). Common causes include blocked fallopian tubes in women and low sperm count in men. Men and women are equally likely to be the source of infertility problems in a couple (American Society of Reproductive Medicine, n.d.).

Surgery often can correct minor physical problems. In other cases, women can be helped to conceive a child through **donor insemination,** which involves injecting sperm from a donor (often anonymous) into the woman's uterus. This procedure results in a pregnancy about 75 percent of the time (Botchan et al., 2001). **Assisted reproductive technologies** may be an option for couples with ample financial resources because these technologies are expensive and are seldom covered by insurance. **In vitro fertilization** is one of the more common technologies. It involves extracting eggs from the woman's ovaries, fertilizing them with sperm in a laboratory, allowing them to grow for a period of about 48 hours, and then transferring the most viable embryos to the woman's uterus. Successful pregnancies result 30 to 40 percent of the time among women under the age of 35, although multiple births are common, producing twins, triplets, or more children all at once (Centers for Disease Control, 2006b). Multiple births can pose risks to the health of mothers and their babies. In addition, although couples are usually thrilled to overcome their infertility, the physical, emotional, and financial challenges of parenting are magnified by multiple births (Bryan, 2003).

donor insemination A form of assisted reproductive technology in which sperm from a donor (often anonymous) is injected into a woman who wishes to become pregnant.

assisted reproductive technologies Technologies that assist infertile couples to conceive a child.

in vitro fertilization A form of assisted reproductive technology that involves extracting eggs from a woman's ovaries, fertilizing them with sperm in a laboratory setting, allowing them to grow for a period of about 48 hours, and then transferring the most viable embryos to the woman's uterus.

Treating infertility can be more difficult at older ages. The success rate for in vitro fertilization, for example, drops to 4 percent among women in their early 40s (Centers for Disease Control, 2006b). Some couples, though, do not recognize they have a fertility problem in time to pursue treatment. Adoption is an option for them. Adoption and assistive reproductive technologies are options, as well, for gay and lesbian couples and for single individuals who want to have children. (For a summary of this section, see "Interim Summary 13.4: Sexual and Reproductive Functioning.")

INTERIM SUMMARY 13.4

Sexual and Reproductive Functioning

Sexual Attitudes and Behavior	■ Most young adults are sexually active, and attitudes toward sex become more accepting and open-minded in young adulthood. ■ Gender differences in sexual attitudes and behavior are common in young adulthood, with young men reporting greater sexual desire and more sexual partners than women. ■ Most lesbian, gay, bisexual, and transgendered individuals experience their first same-sex relationship during young adulthood.
Sexual Risk Behavior	■ **Sexual risk behaviors** include engaging in unprotected sex, failing to disclose that one has a **sexually transmitted disease (STD),** and failing to inquire whether a new partner has an STD. ■ Young adults use condoms inconsistently and are often not knowledgeable about the risks of STDs. ■ Estimates of rates of **rape** and **date (or acquaintance) rape** among young adult women suggest that it is a serious problem in the United States.
Reproductive Functioning	■ Reproductive capacity is at its peak in young adulthood. However, fertility declines and rates of miscarriage begin to rise sharply among women by age 35. ■ Approximately 7 percent of couples in the United States experience infertility. **Assisted reproductive technologies** such as **in vitro fertilization** may be an option for infertile couples.

COGNITIVE DEVELOPMENT

Imagine a situation like this: A man realizes as he returns home from work that he forgot that today is his wedding anniversary. (This can happen as the years go by!) Worried that he will hurt his wife's feelings by not having a present to give her, he tells her a white lie—he has made reservations for dinner at a special restaurant for the upcoming weekend. She is happy, he is relieved, and the next day he makes reservations at a restaurant that they have both wanted to try for a long time. Was he wrong to lie to his wife?

Ask an 11-year-old this question and you are likely to get a simple "yes" answer—the man should not have lied. Ask a 30-year-old the same question, and you are likely to get a very different answer, one that emphasizes the different ways of thinking about the man's dilemma and his hasty solution: "Well, it's not good to lie, but it was more important for the man to protect his wife's feelings. So what he did was not really bad." What accounts for such a difference between the child and the young adult? Would this difference have implications for their ability to function in the world?

These are examples of issues that interest developmental researchers who study cognitive development in adulthood. More generally, these researchers are concerned with four broad questions:

1. Does thinking in adulthood undergo significant qualitative changes, as is true in childhood and adolescence?

2. How does intelligence develop in adulthood—does it increase, remain stable, or decline?

3. Does our ability to process and remember information change over the course of adulthood?

4. To what extent is cognitive functioning in adulthood malleable? Can declines in cognitive functioning be prevented or reversed?

We discuss the first of these questions in this chapter because brain development, coupled with the challenges and opportunities of adult roles, stimulate new ways of thinking in young adulthood. The second question becomes more important in middle and later adulthood, when changes in some aspects of intelligence become apparent. The third and fourth questions have special importance in later adulthood, when changes in information processing and memory functioning are prominent. Those questions, therefore, are addressed in subsequent chapters.

New Ways of Thinking

Influenced by Piaget's views, researchers once believed that cognitive development essentially ended with the emergence of formal operations in adolescence, as discussed in Chapter 11. Piaget (1970, 1980) held that adolescents and young adults think in ways that are qualitatively similar, even though young adults are capable of more advanced logic. In other words, formal operations improve with use, but the underlying principles remain the same. Contemporary researchers, in contrast, believe that cognition continues to develop in young adulthood: many (though not all) young adults engage in more complex modes of thought, referred to as **postformal thought** (Commons et al., 1990; Labouvie-Vief, 1980; Reigel, 1973; Sinnott, 1984).

postformal thought A type of thinking that is relativistic, flexible, pragmatic, tolerant of ambiguities and contradictions, and integrated with emotion.

Two key factors contribute to continued cognitive development in young adulthood. First, the brain continues to develop in ways that allow for more efficient and complex thought processes. The prefrontal cortex continues to mature through the mid-20s, contributing to increases in young adults' information-processing efficiency, ability to comprehend and evaluate abstract material, and ability to integrate emotion and cognition (Fischer & Pruyne, 2003; LaBouvie-Vief, 2006; Steinberg, 2005). As we discussed in previous chapters, synaptic pruning and myelination occur in the prefrontal cortex in late adolescence, and these changes continue in young adulthood. Synaptic pruning is the brain's way of discarding synaptic connections that are no longer used. Myelination, on the other hand, is a way of strengthening neuronal connections that are still needed by increasing their insulation (Kuhn, 2006), as captured in the handy saying "Neurons that fire together, wire together" (Casey, Giedd, & Thomas, 2000, p. 246). Together, synaptic pruning and myelination increase the efficiency of cognitive processing in young adulthood (Kuhn, 2006; Steinberg, 2005).

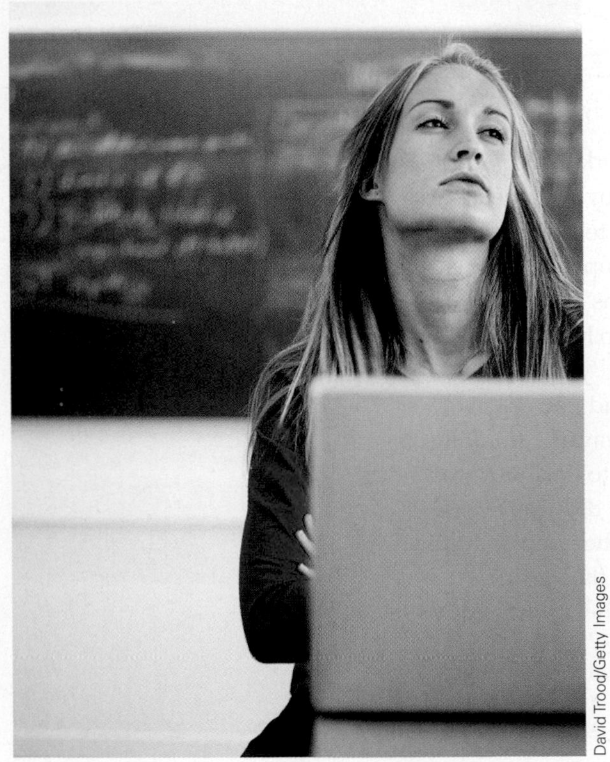
David Trood/Getty Images

Many, though not all, young adults engage in postformal thought.

A second impetus to cognitive development in young adulthood is immersion in social roles and contexts that require more complex thought processes (Fischer, & Pruyne, 2003; Kitchener, King, & DeLuca, 2006). As you have seen many times by now, development results from the constant interplay of biology and the environment. We will consider some of the important life contexts—college, work, parenting—that may foster cognitive growth in young adulthood later in this chapter. First, though, we will take a closer look at these new ways of thinking and their implications for everyday problem solving and moral reasoning and behavior.

Postformal Thought What is postformal thought? Many definitions exist, but they have several features in common. In contrast to the formal operations of adolescence, a style of thinking characterized by a search for absolute truths and "correct" solutions to problems, the postformal thought of adulthood is more:

- relativistic,
- flexible and pragmatic,
- tolerant of ambiguities and contradictions, and
- integrated with emotion.

People who are capable of postformal thought realize that "truth" can be relative, and that a given set of facts can be explained in different ways, depending on one's point of view *(relativistic thinking)*. They realize that a solution that works in one situation may not work in another situation and that most solutions are imperfect, making it necessary at times to aim for reasonable—rather than ideal—solutions to life's problems *(flexible and pragmatic thinking)*. Postformal thinkers are more comfortable in situations characterized by uncertainty, and life is full of such situations. For example, how should one weigh the pros and cons of staying in a secure but dull job versus leaving for a riskier but potentially satisfying job? How does one decide on the best course of action when a medical condition with an unknown prognosis develops?

Adults come to understand that uncertainties and contradictions are unavoidable in life, and they become more skilled at functioning in ambiguous situations *(tolerance of ambiguities and contradictions)*. They are helped in this regard by another feature of postformal thought, the ability to *integrate emotions and reasoning* in their decision making and planning. Labouvie-Vief (1997, 2006) refers to this as **cognitive-affective complexity**. Many situations in life, such as arguments or disputes with others, can be emotionally charged, and adolescents find it more difficult than adults to integrate their feelings and thoughts as they search for ways to manage such situations.

cognitive-affective complexity Ability to integrate emotions and reasoning in decision making and planning.

reflective judgment A type of thinking that involves the capacity to reflect on knowledge itself and to understand that knowledge is uncertain, must be critically evaluated, and sometimes needs revision.

metacognition The ability to monitor and regulate one's own cognitive processes.

Reflective Judgment An important feature of this new way of thinking in young adulthood is the capacity to reflect on knowledge itself. Children and adolescents tend to view knowledge as concrete and certain—a collection of facts to be gleaned from authorities. In young adulthood, this view begins to change. Knowledge comes to be seen as uncertain and constructed from evidence that must be carefully and critically evaluated, which means that existing knowledge sometimes must be revised (Fischer & Pruyne, 2003; Kitchener & King, 1981; Kitchener, King, & DeLuca, 2006). Such critical thinking emerges gradually, as people encounter complex or controversial problems for which simple solutions often do not exist. For example, should people have to pay more for their health insurance if they engage in unhealthy behavior? Is affirmative action a fair and effective means of promoting equal access to higher education?

People must make informed decisions about such questions, and the questioning mode of thought that is the hallmark of **reflective judgment** is useful in this regard. Compared to adolescents, adults are more aware of, and better able to regulate, their own thought processes (Vukman, 2005). In other words, **metacognition,** or the ability to monitor and regulate one's own cognitive processes, becomes more advanced in young adulthood. Fostering the capacity for reflective thinking is one of the goals of higher education, and it seems to accomplish this goal, as you will see later in this chapter.

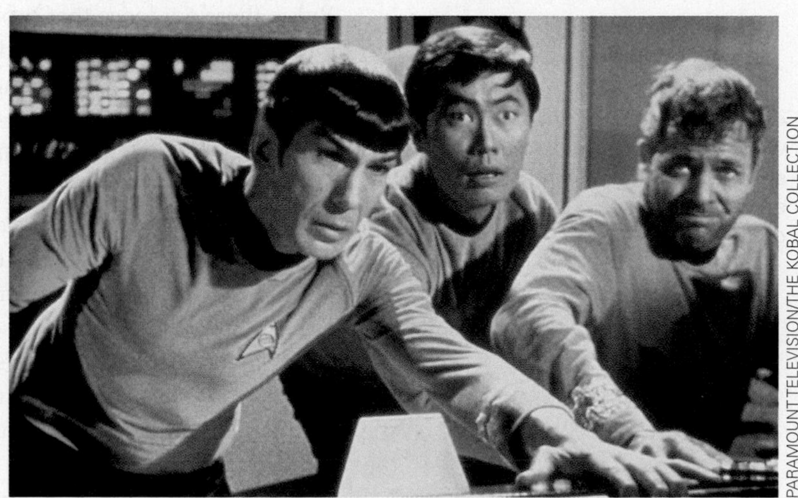

Spock, the famous character from the TV series *Star Trek,* could not experience emotions and so relied solely on logic to solve problems, much to the chagrin of his shipmates on the starship *Enterprise.* Spock was not capable of cognitive-affective complexity.

These shifts in ways of thinking are well suited to, and are actually spurred by, the complexities and uncertainties that young adults encounter in their daily lives. Take a minute to consider the bewildering choices and decisions that young adults face as they establish lives separate from their parents—choices about education and work, housing, intimate relationships and friendships, launching a family, managing finances, and much more. Young adults often have to make these decisions with incomplete information, while at the same time juggling competing interests and demands. Given such complexity, objectively "right" or "wrong" decisions can be difficult to discern through rational analysis alone. Moreover, as young adults' lives become closely intertwined with those of their intimate partners, they learn the value of taking the perspectives of others into account in making decisions and solving problems.

Not all researchers agree that cognitive development in adulthood is characterized by distinct stages, but most agree that cognition does mature gradually in adulthood, though adults do not engage in advanced modes of thought in all life domains. Postformal thought and reflective judgment are adaptive in many life circumstances and, at the same time, life experiences foster the emergence of these modes of thought (Sinnott, 2002). In the next sections we will look at how these advances influence everyday problem solving and moral reasoning and behavior.

Everyday Problem Solving

Daily life is full of large and small problems, and being able to engage in flexible, pragmatic, and integrative ways of thinking may give adults an advantage over adolescents when it comes to generating effective solutions. Much of the research examining this possibility has focused on adults' capacity to integrate emotion and reasoning (that is, their cognitive-affective complexity). Why might this capacity be especially useful in solving problems? First, it increases awareness of others' motivations and emotional needs, and this contributes to open-mindedness and tolerance in dealing with others. Additionally, cognitive-affective complexity helps people manage intense emotions that they may experience in real-life dilemmas, allowing them to think more clearly about possible solutions (Labouvie-Vief & Gonzales, 2004). For these reasons, people who are more adept at integrating emotion and reasoning have been found to be effective in solving marital conflicts—they are better able to understand their spouse's point of view and are less likely to experience resentment as they work on a solution (Katz, Kramer, & Gottman, 1992).

But is there evidence that problem-solving abilities actually improve as adult cognition matures? Studies of age differences in everyday problem solving suggest that the answer is yes, through young and middle adulthood (Thornton & Dumke, 2005). **Everyday problem solving** refers to the ways that people seek to generate solutions to the problems they encounter in the course of their daily lives. Researchers typically study this by asking people of different ages how they would handle hypothetical everyday problems. For example, Denny and her colleagues (Denny & Palmer, 1981; Denny & Pearce, 1989) asked participants who ranged in age from 20 to 80 to explain how they would handle problems such as being sold a defective item by a traveling salesman or needing to drive somewhere in severe weather. Participants' answers were evaluated by trained raters, with higher ratings given to those who generated more solutions that were safe and effective. The results revealed that the quality of participants' problem solving improved with age.

everyday problem solving The ways that people seek to generate solutions to the problems they encounter in the course of their daily lives.

Other research provides clues that cognitive-affective complexity may play a role in everyday problem solving in adulthood. Psychologist Fredda Blanchard-Fields (1986) demonstrated this in an early study in which high school students, college students, and middle-aged adults were asked to generate solutions to three hypothetical dilemmas that varied in the extent to which they were emotionally charged. One dilemma considered low in emotional charge involved a dispute between two historians' accounts of a past conflict between two countries. The dilemma considered intermediate in emotional charge involved a family disagreement about visiting a grandparent, and the dilemma considered high in emotional charge involved a dispute between a man and a woman about an unintended pregnancy. The study participants' answers were scored by trained raters for the level of reasoning exhibited (Blanchard-Fields, 1986; see Figure 13.7). Blanchard-Fields found that the middle-aged participants exhibited the best reasoning across all three dilemmas, but differences between the adolescents and young adults depended on the emotional nature of the dilemma. For the least emotional dilemma, the adolescents' level of reasoning was roughly equivalent to that of the young adults. For more emotional dilemmas, however, the young adults exhibited better reasoning. The findings suggest that emotions interfere with the problem solving and decision making of adolescents, but this interference decreases in adulthood, as people become more adept at integrating their thoughts and emotions.

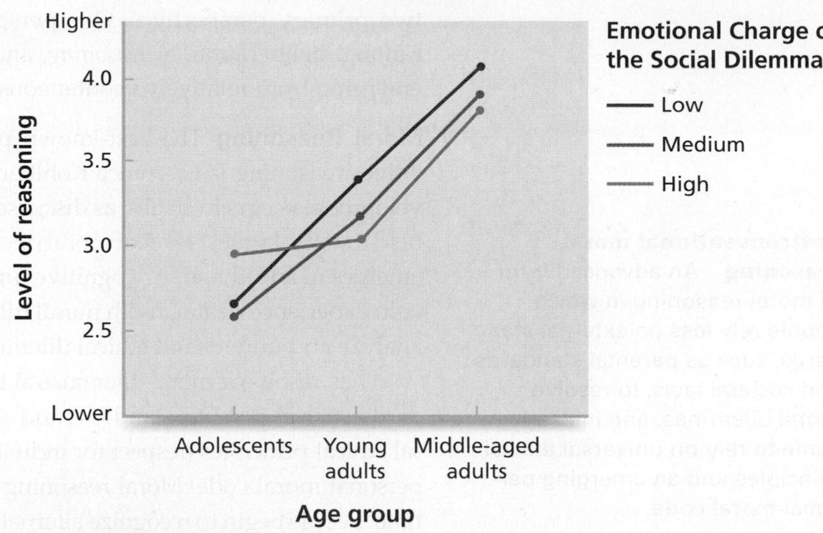

FIGURE 13.7

Age Differences in Problem Solving for Dilemmas Varying in Emotional Charge

Source: Adapted from Blanchard-Fields, F. (1986). Reasoning on social dilemmas varying in emotional saliency. *Psychology and Aging, 1*, 325–333.

Think about the implications of this research for the spike in risk-taking behavior during the transition from adolescence to early adulthood. Strong emotions may override cognition during emerging adulthood, for example when young people make decisions about whether to drive after drinking or whether to have unprotected sex (Steinberg, 2005).

Moral Development

The kind of problem solving that we have discussed so far deals largely with such questions as "What is the most effective way to solve this problem?" and "What do I want to do in this situation?" Another important kind of problem solving involves such questions as "What is the right thing to do in this situation?" and "What should I do if I believe a rule or law is simply wrong?" The latter questions are concerned with **moral development**.

moral development The development of moral judgment and behavior.

In 2009, an honors student at a Chicago high school was beaten to death while a group of young people stood by watching (Mack, 2009). In the same year, a 15-year old girl was gang raped outside of a high-school dance for over 2 hours, and no one stepped forward to help her (Lee & Tucker, 2009). Worse, witnesses to both crimes were reluctant to give the police information that might help solve the crime because they did not want to be "snitches" (Mack, 2009). Were these cases of moral lapses? Corporate greed may have played a role in the economic downturn that began in 2007. Were moral lapses at work here too?

Issues of morality and the need to make decisions about what constitutes "good" or "bad" behavior abound in our lives, often in less dramatic ways than these. Think about a time when you had to make a moral decision. Maybe you witnessed someone cheating on a test or defacing public property. Perhaps you felt conflicted at some point about needing to lie to a friend or your parents. What did you do in such situations? We make moral judgments all the time in the course of our daily lives, but how do we arrive at them? Developmental researchers are keenly interested in understanding the processes that underlie **moral judgment** and how these processes may change from childhood to adulthood. Researchers have investigated moral judgment from

moral judgment Reasoning and decision making about moral issues.

two primary perspectives. One perspective sees moral judgment as emerging from rational deliberation, or *reasoning*, and the other perspective sees moral judgment as emerging from relatively spontaneous emotional reactions, or *intuition*.

postconventional moral reasoning An advanced form of moral reasoning in which people rely less on external standards, such as parental standards and societal laws, to resolve moral dilemmas, and instead come to rely on universal ethical principles and an emerging personal moral code.

Moral Reasoning The best-known proponent of the view that moral judgment involves reasoning is Lawrence Kohlberg (1969, 1976). Kohlberg believed that moral development occurs in stages, as discussed in earlier chapters and shown in Table 13.2. He held that the highest level of moral development, **postconventional moral reasoning,** emerges in adulthood. As cognitive functioning becomes more advanced and as people gain experience dealing with moral dilemmas in the course of their lives, their ability to analyze and understand ethical dilemmas from new perspectives improves.

When resolving moral dilemmas at this highest level, people rely less on external standards, such as parental standards and society's laws, and, instead, come to rely on universal ethical principles (respect for individual rights and human dignity) and an emerging personal moral code. Moral reasoning becomes more complex as this shift occurs over time. People begin to recognize alternative courses of moral action, even prompting them at times to question the validity of societal laws as the best means of achieving justice and protecting human rights. Some ethical principles are perceived to transcend laws: when a conflict exists between law and conscience, people who reason at the postconventional level will act on their conscience. According to Kohlberg, then, as moral reasoning progresses, people shift in how they think about moral issues, from a concern with "What rules should I follow to avoid punishment?" (preconventional level), to a concern with "What rules should I follow to be a good person?" (conventional level), and, ultimately, to a concern with "What makes for a good and just society?" (postconventional level).

Perhaps you can see the parallels between postconventional reasoning and post-formal thought and reflective judgment. Both modes of thought require a questioning mindset and the capacity to evaluate the validity of particular claims or, in this case, rules and laws. In fact, Kohlberg argued that moral development cannot advance beyond a person's current level of cognitive development. He did not expect all people to reach the highest level of moral development, but he did expect moral development to unfold in the sequence proposed in his theory.

To test his ideas about moral development, Kohlberg asked people to respond to hypothetical scenarios that presented ethical dilemmas. Their responses were then coded for the level of moral reasoning they reflected. Here is one of the dilemmas from Kohlberg's test. As you read, think about how you would respond.

TABLE 13.2 Kohlberg's Levels of Moral Development

LEVEL OF DEVELOPMENT	STAGE	APPROXIMATE AGES
Preconventional	**Stage 1:** Obeying authority and avoiding punishment. **Stage 2:** Willingness to obey rules if doing so serves one's self-interests and yields rewards.	Childhood
Conventional	**Stage 3:** Willingness to obey rules in order to please others or gain their approval. **Stage 4:** Willingness to obey rules because they benefit society at large.	Early adolescence through young adulthood
Postconventional	**Stage 5:** Desire to follow rules that benefit society and preserve human rights; recognition that rules and laws are social contracts that can be changed if they are unfair. **Stage 6:** Following one's own ethical conscience even if it means violating rules or laws; universal principles of respect for individual rights and human dignity come to form the core of an ethical conscience.	Young adulthood and beyond

Source: Adapted from Kohlberg (1969, 1976, 1986).

A woman is near death from cancer. A druggist has discovered a drug that doctors believe might save her. The druggist is charging $2,000 for a small dose—10 times what the drug costs him to make. The sick woman's husband, Heinz, borrows from everyone he knows but can scrape together only $1,000. He begs the druggist to sell him the drug for $1,000 or let him pay the rest later. The druggist refuses, saying "I discovered the drug, and I'm going to make money from it." Heinz, desperate, breaks into the man's store and steals the drug. Should Heinz have done that? Why or why not? (Kohlberg, 1969).

Some of the participants in Kohlberg's study felt that Heinz should not have stolen the drug because he risked being punished or sent to jail. Such responses reflect a *preconventional level* of moral reasoning. Other people felt that Heinz should not have stolen the drug because it is important to obey the law. Responses like this reflect a *conventional level* of moral reasoning. Other study participants felt that Heinz was right to have stolen the drug because saving a person's life is more important than simply obeying the law; this last group of participants, then, exhibited a *postconventional level* of moral reasoning.

A key issue for Kohlberg's theory is whether the level of moral reasoning increases with age. Some of his own research and that of others suggests that it does. In an early longitudinal study, a group of preteen and teenage boys was followed for 20 years, with their moral reasoning evaluated every 3 to 4 years (Colby, Kohlberg, Gibbs, & Lieberman, 1983). Moral reasoning did generally improve with age, and advanced moral reasoning was evident only when people were in their 20s or older. Even then, advanced reasoning was relatively rare (found only in about 10 percent of the men studied), consistent with Kohlberg's view that not everyone will reach the highest level of moral reasoning. Other longitudinal studies using hypothetical moral dilemmas have revealed a similar developmental progression (Dawson, 2002).

Yet Kohlberg's theory of moral development has also been criticized. Carol Gilligan (1982) argued, for example, that Kohlberg overlooked potential differences in how men and women approach ethical dilemmas. She believed that men emphasize *justice* (moral obligations to treat others fairly), whereas women emphasize *care* (moral obligations to help others in need). She speculated that because women are socialized to place greater importance on social relationships, care has greater relevance to women's moral reasoning. Studies testing this idea, however, have found few gender differences in the bases (justice or care) for moral judgment (Jaffee & Hyde, 2000). Still, Gilligan's work was important in highlighting that considerations other than justice can underlie moral judgments, a theme that has carried forward into critiques of Kohlberg's theory from cross-cultural studies (Gibbs, Basinger, Grime, & Snarey, 2007; Miller, 2006). Studies across very diverse cultures have produced evidence for the first three stages in Kohlberg's model, but evidence for the other stages is much more rare and, in fact, Stage 6 is seldom seen (Jensen, 2008; Krebs & Denton, 2005; Snarey, 1985). One reason may be that Kohlberg considered concerns with justice and individual rights to underlie the highest moral reasoning, but that is not true in all cultures. Upholding one's duty to one's community and adhering to religious or spiritual standards are key moral concerns in some cultures (Shweder, Much, Mahapatra, & Park, 1997), but these concerns receive little attention in Kohlberg's model.

Moral Intuition A second major perspective on moral judgment also reflected some dissatisfaction with Kohlberg's approach—specifically, his neglect of the role of emotion in moral judgment. For Kohlberg, the key process involved in moral judgment is *reasoning*. Other researchers, however, believe that *emotion* is the key process involved in many kinds of moral judgments. They argue that many moral judgments and decisions involve nearly instantaneous emotional reactions (Greene & Haidt, 2002; Haidt, 2007). We react immediately with disgust or anger to a statement like "He slapped his young daughter across her face." Think back to the moral dilemma involving Heinz and the druggist—did you form a very quick impression of whether Heinz was right or wrong to have stolen the drug?

moral intuition An immediate, emotion-laden reaction of approval or disapproval regarding the rightness or wrongness of someone's conduct.

New research suggests that this is how adults often make moral decisions in real life. They have an immediate, emotional reaction of approval or disapproval regarding someone's conduct—a **moral intuition**. Then, after making a quick, intuitive judgment, people muster cognitive arguments that justify their initial impression. From this perspective, then, moral reasoning comes into play after the fact—to justify the original, emotion-driven moral judgments (Haidt, 2007). Research supports the view that emotions play a role in moral judgments (Green & Haidt, 2002; Haidt, 2007). For example, brain imaging studies indicate that regions of the brain that are responsible for emotions show increased activity when people are responding to moral dilemmas (Ciaramelli, Muccioli, Ladavas, & di Pellegrino, 2007; Greene, Sommerville, Nystrom, Darley, & Cohen, 2001). Moreover, people with damage to these regions of the brain can perform well on tests of cognitive ability, but they often exhibit a low level of moral reasoning and tend to engage in more antisocial behavior such as lying, stealing, and aggression (Damasio, 1994; Green & Haidt, 2002).

Both emotion and reason play important, but different, roles in moral judgment (Haidt, 2001, 2007). Moral intuition is fast, automatic, and emotional. When we encounter something for the first time, we tend to form a very quick impression of how much we like or dislike it even before we have consciously begun to think about it. Our intuitions help us process information fast, allowing us to react quickly in many situations. Imagine that you witness a man stealing something in a store. He is about to exit the store, and you must decide quickly whether to intervene. We often form quick impressions about the guilt or innocence of a person linked to a crime. If the mother whose daughter is missing does not shed tears, we might rush to conclude that she was involved in her daughter's disappearance (Mandel, 2009).

Yet the speediness of first reactions can contribute to errors in judgment (Reyna & Farley, 2006; Sunstein, 2005). Moral reasoning, which involves slower, methodical deliberation and analysis, is important in preventing or correcting such errors. We need moral reasoning to evaluate complex evidence and arrive at decisions when a great deal is at stake. Initial intuitive reactions can be overridden by carefully analyzing the various perspectives on a moral dilemma and by talking to others who may suggest new perspectives (Haidt, 2007).

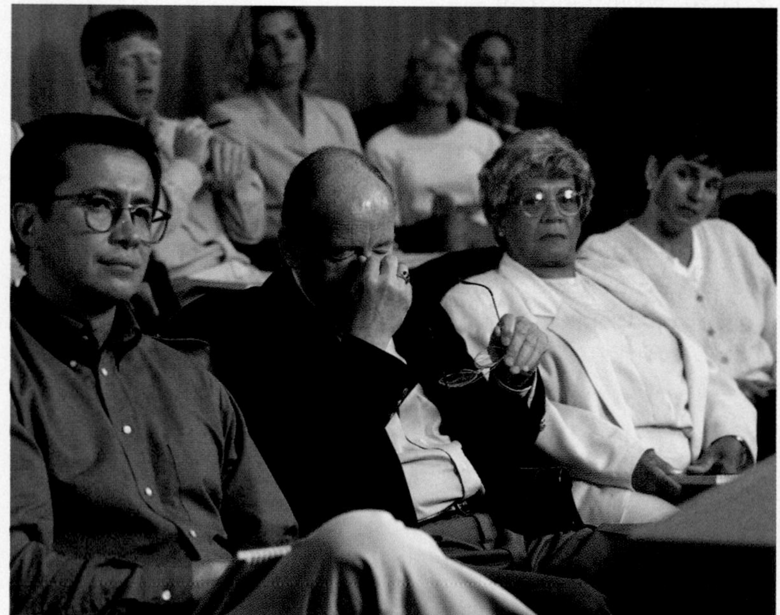
© Guy Cali/Corbis

Serving as a juror is a good example of a situation in which emotions need to be harnessed and moral judgments reached though careful analysis and weighing of the evidence.

Moral Behavior and Identity Moral development involves more than judgments about the morality of our own or others' actions—it also involves *moral behavior*. People who endorse moral values do not necessarily engage in moral conduct. For example, a person may agree that marital infidelity is immoral but nonetheless may engage in the behavior. Abstract moral principles (e.g., "Do unto others . . .") are not always sufficient to motivate moral behavior—emotions may be needed, too. Empathy—being able to perceive and actually feel another person's emotional distress—has been found to increase our willingness to help others (Hoffman, 2008; Tagney, Stuewig, & Mashek, 2007). Imagine seeing a young boy being ridiculed to the point of tears by a group of other children. If you experience empathy—actually feeling his misery—the odds are high that you would step forward to try to end his torment. Here is something to think about: Do people engage in immoral behavior because they are unable to tell right from wrong or because they lack the capacity to feel others' suffering?

Finally, **moral identity**—the integration of moral values and commitments into one's self-concept—is also an important aspect of moral development (Matsuba & Walker, 2004). People for whom being moral is an important part of their identity are more likely to self-monitor and reinforce their own moral conduct. For example, a young man who considers being honest an important part of his identity can more easily resist tempting but dishonest behavior, such as pocketing money that someone has inadvertently dropped or failing to report an erroneously high score that he received on an exam. Maintaining one's identity as a moral person thus strengthens the connections between moral judgments and moral behavior (Hardy, 2006). Moral development in all of these respects—judgment, behavior, and identity—is fostered not only by cognitive and emotional maturation but also experience gained in grappling with moral issues in various contexts in the course of one's life. (For a summary of this section, see "Interim Summary 13.5: Cognitive Development.")

moral identity The integration of moral understanding and commitment into one's self-concept.

INTERIM SUMMARY 13.5

Cognitive Development	
New Ways of Thinking	■ Contemporary researchers believe that cognition continues to develop in young adulthood: many young adults engage in more complex modes of thought, referred to as **postformal thought** and **reflective judgment**. ■ Two factors are primarily responsible for this continued cognitive development: (1) the brain develops in ways that allow for more complex thought processes, and (2) young adults are immersed in social roles and contexts that require more complex thought processes.
Everyday Problem Solving	■ **Everyday problem solving** refers to the ways that people seek to generate solutions to the problems they encounter in their daily lives. Studies show that problem-solving abilities improve through young adulthood. ■ Emotions appear to interfere with adolescents' problem solving and decision making, but this interference decreases with age, as people become more adept at integrating their thoughts and emotions.
Moral Development	■ Developmental researchers have investigated **moral judgment** from two primary perspectives: one sees moral judgment as emerging from *reasoning*, the other from spontaneous emotional reactions, or *intuition*. ■ Kohlberg believed that moral development is connected to reasoning. He held that the highest level of moral development, **postconventional reasoning**, emerges in adulthood. ■ New research suggests that **moral intuition** plays a role in moral judgment. ■ Some contemporary researchers think that emotion and reason play *complementary* roles in moral judgment. ■ Moral development also involves *moral behavior* and **moral identity**—the integration of moral understanding and commitment into one's self-concept. ■ Moral development in all of these respects—judgment, behavior, and identity—is fostered by cognitive and emotional maturation and by experience.

COGNITIVE DEVELOPMENT IN CONTEXT

Cognitive development in young adulthood—as in childhood and adolescence—results from the constant interplay of biology and the social context (or environment). In the process of becoming adults, young people must learn to make important decisions, to develop and carry out plans, and to juggle the responsibilities of adult roles, often in contexts that are relatively new to them (such as college, a first full-time job, or a first romantic relationship). Having to deal with this complexity contributes to the emergence of pragmatic, questioning modes of thought in young adulthood. Similarly, responding to the ethical dilemmas that arise in these different contexts can spur moral development. Three contexts may be especially important as catalysts for cognitive growth in young adulthood: college, work, and parenting. We'll discuss these next. In the next chapter, we explore how experiences in these contexts may affect personality development and emotional well-being in young adulthood.

Higher Education

Why are you going to college? To improve your mind? To get a better job? Having a college degree usually contributes to economic well-being, as well (see Figure 13.8). In fact, having a college degree plays a key role in reducing the likelihood of experiencing poverty. Higher education is also strongly linked to better physical health (Baum & Ma, 2007). So who attends college, who graduates (and why), and how college influences cognitive development are all important issues with real-life implications.

Nearly two-thirds of high-school graduates in the United States enroll in college, a figure that has risen steadily over the past several decades (Bureau of Labor Statistics, 2009; Pew Research Center, 2009). More women, minority students, and older students are now attending college, making college campuses more diverse than ever (Harvey & Anderson, 2005). However, gaps in rates of college enrollment persist. Minority college enrollment still trails well behind that of Caucasians, and gains in rates of college participation among Hispanics are smaller than gains seen among

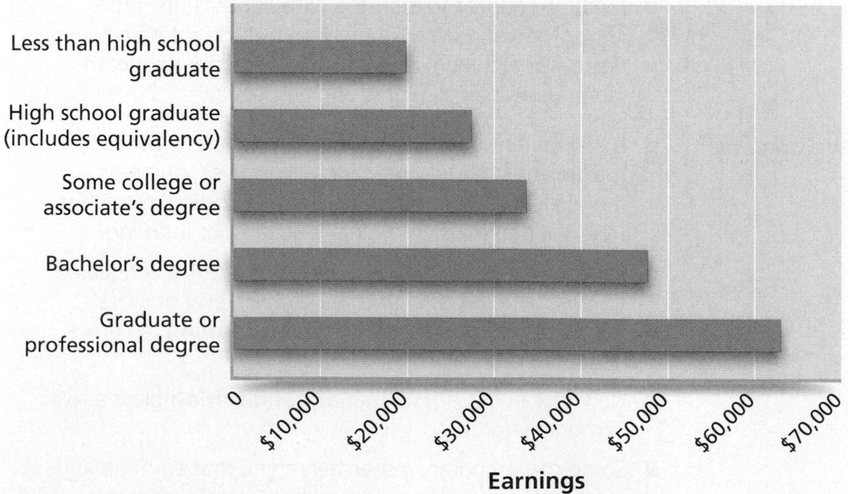

FIGURE 13.8

Average Annual Earnings by Education Level

Note: Figures are based on U.S. workers with earnings, ages 25 and older.

Source: U.S. Bureau of the Census (2008). Educational Attainment Data Set: 2006–2008 American Community Survey 3-Year Estimates. Retrieved from http://factfinder.census.gov/servlet/STTable?_bm=y&-geo_id=01000US&-qr_name=ACS_2008_3YR_G00_S1501&-ds_name=ACS_2008_3YR_G00_

African Americans. Other research indicates that rising rates of college enrollment among women have outpaced those of men in every group (Caucasians, African Americans, Hispanics, and Asian Americans; Harvey & Anderson, 2005).These findings indicate that access to higher education in the United States has been increasing but not at the same rate for everyone.

College enrollment rates tell only part of the story because dropout rates remain high. In one recent study, just over half of U.S. students who entered college had completed a bachelor's degree within 5 years (Wirt et al., 2004). Graduation rates tend to be lower for African American and Hispanic students, and higher for Asian American and Caucasian students. What influences the likelihood of finishing college to earn a bachelor's degree? Financial aid plays a role, but so do parental encouragement, making plans to attend college early in high school, taking courses in high school that prepare one for college (particularly math courses), and a supportive campus climate that helps students feel socially and academically integrated (Pascarella, & Terenzini, 1979; Swail, Redd, & Perna, 2003).

People who attend college generally have higher incomes and better health over the course of their lives, but does college also influence the way they think? Perry (1970, 1981) investigated this question in one of the first studies that tracked changes in thinking across the college years. He followed a group of undergraduates closely, interviewing them about their experiences at the end of each year in college. At the start of college, the students exhibited somewhat rigid, inflexible ways of thinking and looked to authority figures to impart absolute truths. One college freshman commented, "When I went to my first lecture, what the man said was just like God's word, you know? I believed everything he said because he was a professor. . . ." (Perry, 1999, p. 68). As time passed, the college students were exposed to new ideas and different points of view, and they came to understand that knowledge is created, uncertain, and subject to frequent revision. Through their experiences in college, the students became more questioning and independent in their thinking and also more open to diverse perspectives on a problem. Do you feel that your own thinking has changed as a result of going to college?

Higher education helps students gain new skills and bodies of knowledge, but beyond this, it helps them forge a new orientation to knowledge itself—one that acknowledges the relative and uncertain nature of knowledge and the validity of alternative points of view (Fischer & Pruyne, 2003).

College fosters cognitive growth not only by introducing students to new bodies of knowledge and training them in critical thinking, but also by bringing together people with different backgrounds and perspectives (Pascarella & Terenzini, 2005). College students in one study were assigned to work on a problem-solving task in small groups that included either only people familiar to themselves or a mix of unfamiliar and familiar people. Students in the more diverse groups (those with a mix of familiar and unfamiliar participants) performed better on the problem-solving task. They actually thought more deeply about the different perspectives that surfaced in the group discussions, a cognitive benefit of diversity (Phillips, Liljenquist, & Neale, 2009).

Corbis Premium RF/Alamy

Interacting with people from different backgrounds can stimulate cognitive growth in young adulthood.

Interacting with people from diverse backgrounds can also help to break down stereotypes that sometimes cause the ideas and abilities of particular groups of people to be devalued unfairly (Rudman, Ashmore, & Gary, 2001). Negative stereotypes can actually hurt the performance of stereotyped individuals. People who are aware of a negative stereotype about a group to which they belong and who fear that their behavior could confirm the stereotype often experience **stereotype threat** (Schmader, Johns, & Forbes, 2008; Steele, Spencer, & Aronson, 2002).

stereotype threat Awareness of a negative stereotype about a group to which one belongs and fear that one's behavior could confirm the stereotype.

Psychologist Claude Steele and his colleagues documented the harmful effects of stereotype threat in a classic study in which they compared the performance of African American and Caucasian college students on a test of verbal ability that either was or was not described as assessing the students' intellectual abilities. The researchers reasoned that the African American students would know that African Americans are often stereotyped as intellectually inferior, would worry about confirming this negative stereotype, and would actually perform worse when the test was described as assessing intellectual abilities. This is exactly what the results showed (Steele & Aronson, 1995) (see Figure 13.9). When the test was portrayed as measuring intellectual abilities, the African American students did not perform as well as the Caucasian students. When the test was not portrayed as measuring intellectual abilities, the two groups performed equally well. Stereotype threat appeared to harm the performance of the African American students, most likely by causing stress, self-consciousness, and anxiety that consumed some of the cognitive resources needed for optimal test performance (Schmader et al., 2008). In contrast, the Caucasian students were unlikely to have experienced negative stereotypes about the intellectual abilities of Caucasian individuals and, as a result, were unaffected by the test description.

The harmful effects of stereotype threat have since been documented in many different groups and situations—detracting, for example, from Hispanics' as well as African Americans' performance on tests of cognitive abilities, from women's performance on math tests, and from older adults' performance on memory tests (Nguyen & Ryan, 2008; Schmader et al., 2008; Walton & Cohen, 2003). Recurring experiences of stereotype threat can lead some individuals to alter their career goals and aspirations. Fortunately, researchers are beginning to develop strategies for reducing or eliminating stereotype threat (e.g., Alter, Aronson, Darley, Rodriguez, & Ruble, 2010; Ambady, Paik, Steele, Owen-Smith, & Mitchell, 2004; Walton & Cohen, 2007).

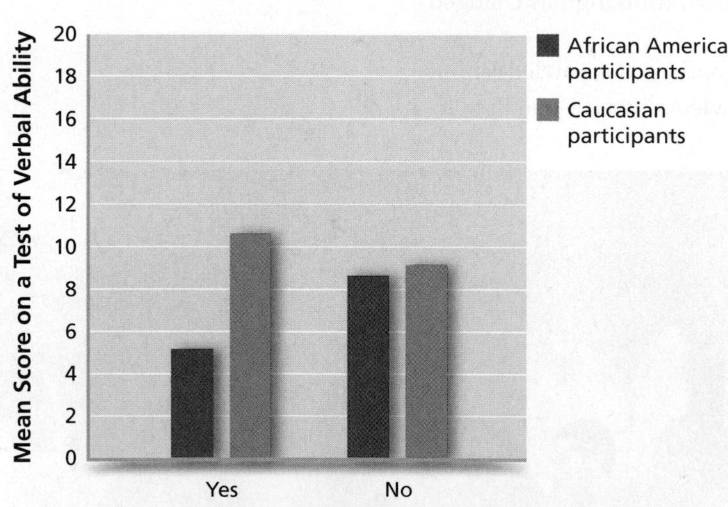

FIGURE 13.9

Influence of Stereotype Threat on Test Performance

Describing the test as measuring intellectual activity was believed to activate stereotype threat for African American students but not for Caucasian students.

Source: Steele & Aronson (1995).

Work

College is not the only context in which cognitive abilities develop in young adulthood. Some young adults do not attend college, and work instead. Many others hold jobs while they attend college. Can work experiences spur cognitive growth? Most evidence suggests that they can, so long as the work itself is mentally challenging. Work experiences that require independent thinking and judgment can foster cognitive development in young adults, and the benefits of complex work for cognitive functioning extend into middle and later adulthood (Kohn & Schooler, 1982; Schooler, Mulatu, & Oates, 1999). More complex work tends to be associated with more flexible thinking—although it is possible that more flexible thinkers are drawn to such work in the first place. Evidence also points to a spillover effect—having more complex work experiences is associated with engaging in more intellectually challenging leisure activities, regardless of the workers' income or educational level (Miller & Kohn, 1983; Schooler, 1984). Cognitive development in adulthood, therefore, may be stimulated by complex or challenging work or leisure activities.

Responsibility for Others

Cognitive growth in young adulthood, which allows young people to understand and integrate diverse points of view, paves the way for potential growth in moral judgment. In fact, attending college has been found to be associated with better moral reasoning (King & Mayhew, 2002). Real-life experiences dealing with moral dilemmas and conflicts are considered essential, however, for actual moral development. Having meaningful and sustained responsibility for the welfare of others is required for true moral growth, according to Kohlberg (1973). In young adulthood, significant responsibility for the welfare of others often arrives with parenthood: ethical decisions regarding children cannot be postponed. Other roles and contexts that entail significant responsibilities and obligations to others—such as teaching, military service, or working in the health care and mental health professions—can also expose young adults to ethical dilemmas and, in the process, spur them to forge new perspectives on moral issues. (For a summary of this section, see "Interim Summary 13.6: Cognitive Development in Context.")

INTERIM SUMMARY 13.6

Cognitive Development in Context	
	■ Cognitive development in young adulthood illustrates the core principle that development results from the constant interplay of biology and the social context (or environment).
Higher Education	■ Having a college degree is an important determinant of economic well-being and physical health over the lifespan. ■ Access to higher education in the United States has been increasing but not at the same rate for everyone. ■ College appears to foster cognitive growth by bringing together people with different backgrounds and perspectives, as well as by providing training in critical thinking.
Working	■ Work experiences can foster cognitive development in young adults so long as the work is challenging and requires independent thinking and judgment. ■ Having more complex work experiences is also associated with young adults engaging in more intellectually challenging leisure activities.
Responsibility for Others	■ Real-life experiences dealing with moral dilemmas and conflicts are considered essential for actual moral development in young adults. ■ Roles and contexts that entail significant responsibilities to others—such as parenting, teaching, and military service—can expose young adults to ethical dilemmas and spur them to forge new perspectives on moral issues.

SUMMING UP AND LOOKING AHEAD

In this chapter we have examined young adulthood, noting that the transition to adulthood (called *emerging adulthood*) is lengthening. It involves a time of increased freedom and exploration as young people leave behind the structured and supervised worlds of high school and living with parents and learn to function on their own in new settings. Adult status is considered to be attained when young adults make their own decisions, accept responsibility for their actions, and achieve financial independence. This period of life is important, as choices made at this time have important and lasting implications for health and well-being later in life.

Physical health and functioning peak in young adulthood. Signs of senescence do begin to emerge during this period, but they have little impact on everyday functioning. The epidemic of obesity in the United States may require this conclusion to be modified in the future, however, as obesity is contributing to rising rates of chronic disease in childhood and adolescence, as well as adulthood. Health risk behaviors initially increase in emerging adulthood but later decrease as adult roles and responsibilities are assumed. Sexual activity and exploration increase in young adulthood, but sexual behavior also becomes more closely tied to intimacy and the formation of romantic relationships. Risky sexual behaviors are relatively common in young adulthood, as are sexually transmitted diseases (STDs).

Cognitive development and moral development continue in young adulthood, fostered by higher education, work, and caring for others. A lot happens to young people as they leave childhood and adolescence behind and begin to establish themselves in a new phase of life—adulthood. The next chapter examines how their socioemotional development is affected by this process of settling into adulthood.

HERE'S WHAT YOU SHOULD KNOW

Did You Get It?

After reading this chapter, you should understand the following:

- The three major periods of adulthood
- What is involved in becoming an adult
- The physical changes that take place in young adults
- The sexual attitudes and behaviors of young adults
- What sexual risk behaviors include
- What developments in cognition occur in young adults, and why
- What moral development involves
- The impact that higher education, working, and responsibility for others have on the cognitive development of young adults

Important Terms and Concepts

AIDS (p. 419)
assisted reproductive technologies (p. 420)
chlamydia (p. 418)
cognitive-affective complexity (p. 423)
date (or acquaintance) rape (p. 419)
donor insemination (p. 420)
emerging adulthood (p. 407)
everyday problem solving (p. 424)
health-damaging behaviors (p. 413)
health-promoting behaviors (p. 413)
HIV (p. 419)
homeostasis (p. 412)
human papilloma virus (HPV) infection (p. 419)
in vitro fertilization (p. 420)
infertility (p. 420)
interindividual variability (p. 406)
maturing out (p. 413)
metacognition (p. 423)
moral development (p. 425)
moral identity (p. 429)
moral intuition (p. 428)
moral judgment (p. 425)
oxytocin (p. 417)
postconventional moral reasoning (p. 426)
postformal thought (p. 422)
rape (p. 419)
reflective judgment (p. 423)
senescence (p. 412)
sexual risk behaviors (p. 418)
sexually transmitted diseases (STDs) (p. 418)
stereotype threat (p. 432)

CHAPTER 14

Socioemotional Development in Young Adulthood

moodboard/Alamy

Imagine a group of 20-year-old college students sharing ideas about how their lives may unfold in the next decade. They are excited to be free of parental control, but uncertainty creeps into the conversation as they wonder how their studies will conclude, what kinds of job opportunities lie ahead, whether they will find soul mates and establish families of their own, and whether they will be happy in the future. Maybe questions like this are on your mind.

In this chapter, we explore how life paths begin to take hold in young adulthood. This doesn't happen overnight, and the process involves a good deal of experimentation. College students often switch majors. Graduates may change jobs frequently before they find an occupation that feels right. They may fall in—and out—of love several times before they find a partner with whom they want to make a long-term commitment. This experimental period can enable young adults to become clearer about their personal interests, goals, and values. Although some young adults flounder during this period, others gradually narrow their exploration of options, align their choices realistically with opportunities and constraints in the environment, and ultimately commit themselves to specific goals that begin to mold their life trajectories (Arnett, 2000). The first step in socioemotional development in young adulthood is becoming self-sufficient. Through a process called *recentering*, control shifts from parents to young adults as they begin to take charge of their own lives, set their own goals, make their own plans and decisions, and learn to deal with the consequences. The second step in socioemotional development in young adulthood is making social and emotional commitments (Tanner, 2006).

In this chapter, we take a look at the major changes in social roles and responsibilities that occur in young adulthood. We start by considering the developmental tasks, timetables, and processes that influence young adults' goals and plans. We then explore three major life domains in which many of the transforming changes of young adulthood occur: love relationships and friendships, families, and work. Finally, we consider how these changes affect young adults' personalities and emotional well-being.

DEVELOPMENTAL TASKS, TIMETABLES, AND PROCESSES IN YOUNG ADULTHOOD

How do young adults go about leaving their parents' homes and setting out on their own? Where do they start? Are there particular things they should be doing?

Some developmental theorists believe that each stage of life, young adulthood included, is characterized by specific developmental tasks that people need to accomplish to be well adjusted and to have an accepted place in society. These tasks give direction to young adults' efforts to launch independent lives. Other developmental theorists focus not so much on *what* tasks need to be accomplished but, rather, *when* they need to be accomplished. For these theorists, a societal timetable influences the age at which young people finish college, get married, or enter the workforce. Still other theorists emphasize *how* life goals are prioritized, pursued, adjusted, or even relinquished. These theorists focus on the processes by which people seek to direct, or regulate, the course of their own lives. We discuss each of these perspectives below.

Developmental Tasks

Robert Havighurst (1952, 1953) was one of the first theorists to introduce the idea of **developmental tasks**, or specific achievements that people are expected to accomplish in a given life period. According to Havighurst, each life period is characterized by key tasks that arise from biological (physical maturation), social (norms and expectations), and personal (needs and aspirations) forces. Successfully accomplishing developmental tasks considered appropriate for a particular life period contributes to feelings of happiness and self-worth. Failure to accomplish these tasks, in contrast, contributes to unhappiness, disapproval by others, and difficulty with future tasks.

developmental tasks Specific achievements and tasks that people are expected to accomplish in a given life period.

Developmental tasks are considered "normative" in the sense that they are either tasks that people *should* accomplish in a given life period (Hagestad & Neugarten, 1985; Havighurst, 1952), or tasks that people commonly accomplish in a particular life period (Schulenberg, Bryant, & Schulenberg, 2004). They are also sequential. In Havighurst's model, the developmental tasks of adolescence include acquiring problem-solving skills, becoming socially responsible and developing an ethical code of conduct, and preparing for adult roles. The developmental tasks of young adulthood involve initiating adult roles—making a long-term commitment to a partner, launching a family, beginning a career, and becoming involved in one's community. The developmental tasks of middle adulthood, in contrast, revolve around preserving one's social roles and relationships, whereas the important tasks of later adulthood involve dealing with declining health and the approaching end of one's life. You can see in Table 14.1 that people of different ages in one study identified life goals that mesh well with Havighurst's ideas about the key developmental tasks for different life periods (Nurmi, 1992).

While theorists like Havighurst emphasized developmental tasks that involve establishing oneself in social roles that are valued by society, Erik Erikson (1963, 1968) emphasized developmental tasks that are more psychological in nature—specifically, tasks that involve developing strengths in oneself by resolving key psychosocial challenges. As you recall from Chapter 1, Erikson proposed that each life period presents a unique psychosocial crisis, or challenge—a struggle between two opposing tendencies

TABLE 14.1 Percent of People with Future Life Goals in Particular Areas, by Age

		AGE GROUP				
Content	**Overall**	**19–24**	**25–34**	**35–44**	**45–54**	**55–64**
Occupation	46.3	43.8	58.6	42.6	48.4	36.0
Family	34.6	58.5	48.3	24.1	14.5	12.0
Education	29.1	79.8	34.5	8.3	0.0	4.0
Health	28.5	7.9	19.5	26.9	50.0	72.0
Leisure activities	12.8	13.5	4.5	12.0	14.5	28.0
Retirement	4.3	0.0	0.0	0.0	19.4	16.0

Source: Adapted from Nurmi, J. E. (1992). Age differences in adult life goals, concerns, and their temporal extension: A life course approach to future-oriented motivation. *International Journal of Behavioral Development, 15*(4), 487–508.

in oneself. Resolving the crisis successfully allows the person to develop an important new strength that provides a foundation for further development. Failure to resolve the crisis, in contrast, makes further development more difficult.

intimacy versus isolation The key psychosocial crisis or struggle in young adulthood, according to Erikson.

As you can see in Table 14.2, in Erikson's model, three of the eight stages of psychosocial crisis occur in adulthood. In young adulthood, the key struggle is that of **intimacy versus isolation**. The capacity to be involved in an intimate, loving relationship requires a sufficient sense of self and sufficient trust to be willing to reveal oneself truthfully to another person. It also requires having genuine concern for the other person's needs and being willing to set aside one's own needs at times. People who cannot develop the capacity for intimacy are vulnerable to social isolation.

It can be useful to think about development in a particular life period as partly organized around key developmental tasks or challenges, or goals, but it is important to realize that the nature of these tasks may vary across cultures and historical periods (Helson, Mitchell, & Moane, 1984; Schulenberg et al., 2004). For example, becoming a parent may be considered a crucial task for young adults in some cultures but not in others. Similarly, norms can change over time, and in the United States and elsewhere, some developmental tasks once considered normative are becoming more a matter of individual choice. For example, increasing numbers of adults are choosing to remain single rather than to marry (DePaulo & Morris, 2005). Societal norms about developmental tasks provide a roadmap, but in societies that allow personal freedom, these norms do not impose a rigid set of requirements that must be strictly followed (Heckhausen, 1999).

Developmental Timetables

As noted earlier, another perspective on developmental tasks focuses not so much on *what* these tasks are as *when* they occur. Bernice Neugarten and her colleagues (Neugarten, Moore, & Lowe, 1965; Neugarten & Neugarten, 1987) were among the first to propose that development in adulthood is influenced not only by the kinds of social role changes and other life events that occur but also by their timing. Consider the following two individuals:

- At age 34, Adam is in his last year of college. He lives with his parents, who have supported him financially during his years in college. Adam is looking forward

TABLE 14.2 Erikson's Theory of Psychosocial Stages of Development

AGE	PSYCHOSOCIAL CONFLICT	ADAPTIVE STRENGTH THAT DEVELOPS FROM RESOLUTION OF THE CONFLICT
Infancy	Basic trust vs. basic mistrust	Hope
Early childhood	Autonomy vs. shame, doubt	Will
Play age	Initiative vs. guilt	Purpose
School age	Industry vs. inferiority	Competence
Adolescence	Identity vs. confusion	Fidelity
Young adulthood	Intimacy vs. isolation	Love
Adulthood	Generativity vs. self-absorption	Care
Old age	Integrity vs. despair	Wisdom

Source: From *Vital involvement in old age: The experience of old age in our time* by Erik H. Erikson, Joan M. Erikson, and Helen Q. Kivnick. Copyright © 1986 by Joan M. Erikson, Erik H. Erikson, and Helen Q. Kivnick. Used by permission of W.W. Norton & Company, Inc.

to graduating soon, and, with a B.A. in business, he expects to get a job that will allow him to move out of his parents' home in another few years.

- At age 22, Raul is looking forward to graduating from college with a B.A. in sociology and getting a good job that will allow him to start paying off his student loans. He will keep his current apartment and may seek a roommate to help with expenses. With the money saved, Raul hopes to enter an M.A. program in 2 years.

What are your reactions to Adam and Raul? Perhaps you feel that Adam is too old to be living with his parents, much less depending on them financially. Adam's behavior violates what researchers refer to as the **social clock**, or social norms that specify the age by which important life events are expected to happen, such as leaving home, entering the workforce, or marrying.

social clock Social norms that specify the age by which important life events are expected to have occurred.

People are considered **on time** when they experience key life events at the expected, or normative, age. They are considered **off time** when they experience key life events at a non-normative age. A woman who has her first child in her mid-20s would be considered on time, whereas a woman who has her first child in her 50s or 60s would be considered off time. For example, a woman in the United States stirred intense public controversy not long ago when she became a mother at age 63 through in vitro fertilization (Kolata, 1997). It is also possible to be off time when an event occurs "too early," as when someone becomes a parent as a teenager or retires from work at age 40. Life events can be perceived to be on or off time in middle or later adulthood, too, although the social clock may tick more loudly in young adulthood.

on time Experiencing a key life event at the expected, or normative, age in a particular society.

off time Experiencing a key life event at an atypical, or non-normative, age in a particular society.

The timing of major life events is not always completely under our control, of course, but people may try to conform to social timetables for several reasons (Neugarten, 1979; Rook, Catalano, & Dooley, 1989). First, people whose life events occur too early or too late may experience disapproval or criticism from others. Second, even if they do not experience social disapproval, they may suffer a decline in self-esteem as they compare themselves to their peers. Third, experiencing a major life event off time is stressful because fewer peers will be experiencing the same event, and, as a result, there may be fewer people to turn to for guidance and support. Fourth, social institutions are often organized around social clocks. For example, teenagers who have babies have a difficult time, in part because high schools are not equipped to accommodate mothers and their babies. Many colleges and workplaces, in contrast, have day-care facilities or flexible work programs to help parents with young children. Going against the social clock can be difficult for all of these reasons.

Does scientific evidence support the existence of a social clock? Research indicates that people do have ideas about the optimal timing of life events, yet these ideas have become less rigid in recent decades. In the mid-1960s, people tended to have similar views of the ages at which particular life events should occur. For example, 80 to 90 percent of the participants in one study agreed that people should marry in their early 20s, finish school and go to work by age 22, and settle on a career by their mid-20s (Neugarten et al., 1965). More recent studies have revealed much less consensus, suggesting that age norms are loosening. Fewer than half of the participants in one such study agreed that people should marry in their early 20s, and even fewer agreed on the ideal ages for people to finish school, enter the workforce, or settle on a career (Passuth, Maines, & Neugarten, 1984).

Recent studies also indicate that people do not perceive significant negative repercussions for themselves or others if the timing of key educational, work, or family life events is later than average (Settersten, 2003; Settersten & Hagestad, 1996a, 1996b). The actual timing of major life events has become more variable in recent years, as we discussed in the previous chapter. Some young adults leave their

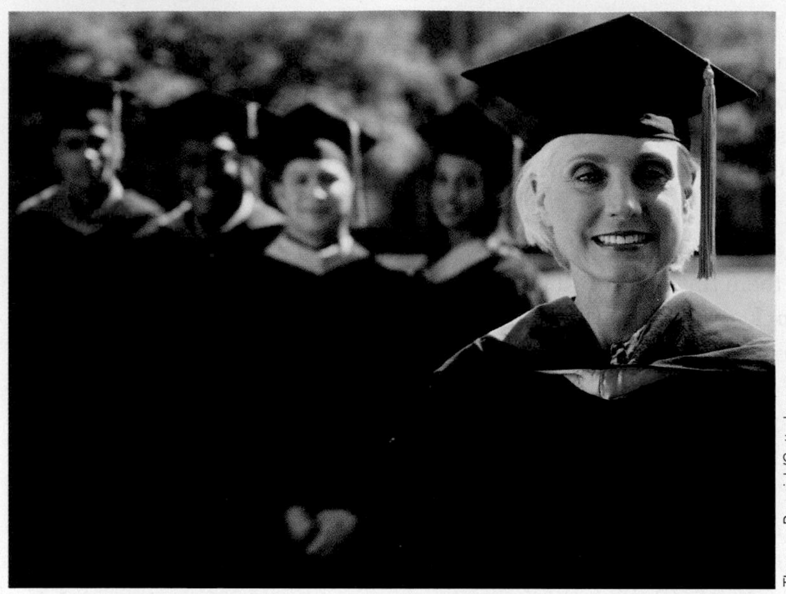
Thomas Barwick/Getty Images

Is the United States moving toward an age-irrelevant society in which age norms do not govern when particular life goals should be achieved?

parents' home, finish their schooling, enter the workforce, marry, and start families in their early to mid-20s; others are deferring these events to later ages or foregoing some of them altogether without experiencing the stigma that would have been likely in earlier eras.

What can we conclude from this research? It seems that people continue to perceive optimal timetables for assuming major roles and experiencing major events during their lives, but these timetables are flexible. Evidence of loosening age norms led Neugarten to suggest later in her career that the United States is moving toward an **age-irrelevant society** in which the passage through adulthood is not governed by strict social timetables (Neugarten & Neugarten, 1987). Take a look around any college campus, and you'll see far more diversity in students' ages than you would have seen 25 years ago.

Processes of Developmental Regulation: The Theory of Selective Optimization with Compensation

age-irrelevant society A society in which the passage through adulthood is not constrained by strict societal age norms and timetables.

theory of selective optimization with compensation A theory that proposes that successful development results from the use of three basic processes of developmental regulation: selection, optimization, and compensation.

selection A process of developmental regulation that involves choosing life goals that are manageable given one's resources and sociocultural opportunities.

optimization A process of developmental regulation that involves using and enhancing one's resources to pursue one's goals.

compensation A process of developmental regulation that involves developing alternative strategies to pursue one's goals when one's resources decline.

Our discussion of developmental tasks has focused up to this point on the content and timing (the "what" and "when" aspects) of developmental tasks. Another important perspective concerns the *processes* by which people seek to accomplish these tasks—how they make choices, how they invest their energies, and how they deal with setbacks when goals prove to be difficult or impossible to attain. A prominent theory of lifespan development, the **theory of selective optimization with compensation** (Baltes & Baltes, 1990; Baltes, Lindenberger, & Staudinger, 1998; Freund & Baltes, 2002), addresses these processes.

Successful development, according to this theory, depends on three interrelated processes: selection, optimization, and compensation, as shown in Figure 14.1. **Selection** involves choosing life goals to pursue that are manageable given one's resources and opportunities. Resources include one's physical, cognitive, and emotional capacities, as well as one's social (e.g., social support) and material (e.g., financial) assets. **Optimization** involves using and enhancing one's resources to pursue one's goals. **Compensation** involves finding alternative ways to pursue one's goals and maintain one's current level of functioning when one's resources decline. Let's take a closer look at each of these processes.

Selection comes into play when people must make choices among an array of possible goals or options they could pursue. Because one's resources (e.g., time, energy, abilities) are finite, only a few of these possible goals can actually be pursued. Consider a young college student who is torn between studying art, psychology, or computer science. Pursuing three different majors is not realistic; at some point, he must make a choice.

The process of selection involves more than just personal preferences. Constraints on one's preferences may come from the environment or from limitations of one's resources. The young man may truly want to major in art, but he may give up that goal because his parents pressure him to pursue a more "practical" major or because job opportunities for artists are scarce (examples of environmental constraints). Or he may realize that his artistic abilities are somewhat limited or that the time needed to make a living as an artist would leave too little time to realize his family goals (examples of

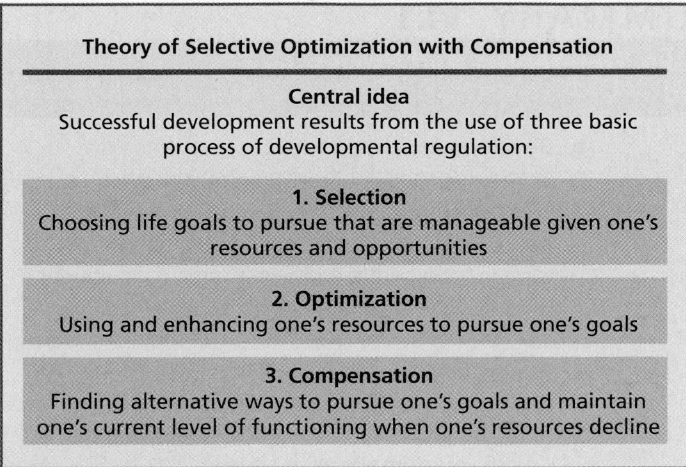
Theory of Selective Optimization with Compensation
Central idea
Successful development results from the use of three basic process of developmental regulation:
1. Selection
Choosing life goals to pursue that are manageable given one's resources and opportunities
2. Optimization
Using and enhancing one's resources to pursue one's goals
3. Compensation
Finding alternative ways to pursue one's goals and maintain one's current level of functioning when one's resources decline

FIGURE 14.1

Theory of Selective Optimization with Compensation

Source: Adapted from Riediger, M., Lindenberger, U., Li, S-C., Baltes, P. B., & Ebner, N. C. (2004). Research Project 4: Selection, optimization, and compensation (SOC): Regulation of goals and preferences in lifespan development. In the Annual Report 2004, Center for Lifespan Psychology, Max Plank Institute. Retrieved from http://www.baltes-paul.de/SOC.html; http://www.baltes-paul.de/LIP_annual_report_2004.pdf.

resource constraints). A loss of resources can also affect the goals that one is able to pursue. Financial resources may run out before one can complete a degree program, or a chronic illness may rule out a career that requires physical stamina.

Optimization comes into play after people have identified their key goals and now seek to pursue them by using and enhancing their resources, such as their skills and knowledge. For example, professional athletes practice every day and work with professional trainers to improve their performance. In the workforce, employees may invest long hours and work hard to improve their skills in order to earn promotions. New parents may read books, attend classes, or watch experienced parents closely to bolster their parenting skills. These are all examples of people optimizing their resources (e.g., physical competency, expertise, knowledge) to increase their likelihood of achieving and maintaining personal goals.

Compensation becomes relevant when the existing means of pursuing one's goals and activities are no longer viable because of a decline or loss of one's resources. For example, a young woman who enjoyed jogging every day to stay physically fit suffers an injury that makes jogging painful. She may decide to take up swimming or bicycling as a different means of staying in shape. Or a couple who has tried repeatedly to conceive a child may decide to pursue adoption in order to fulfill their dream of having a family.

Together, these three processes—selection, optimization, and compensation—help people define and manage their life plans and, in doing so, direct the course of their own development throughout adulthood. You'll see in later chapters that these processes of developmental regulation are important not only in young adulthood but also in middle and later adulthood. For now, we consider how the process of selection leads young adults to explore a wide range of possibilities before identifying a narrower, manageable set of goals and commitments that help them forge a life path. As we'll see, most of this exploration revolves around love relationships and friendship, marriage and family, and work. (For a summary of this section, see "Interim Summary 14.1: Developmental Tasks, Timetables, and Processes in Young Adulthood.")

INTERIM SUMMARY 14.1

Developmental Tasks, Timetables, and Processes in Young Adulthood	
Developmental Tasks	■ **Developmental tasks** are achievements that people are expected to accomplish in a given life period. ■ The developmental tasks of young adulthood involve initiating adult roles—making a commitment to a partner, launching a family, beginning a career, and becoming involved in one's community. ■ Erikson emphasized psychological tasks that need to be completed in different life periods, and in young adulthood this task involves resolving the struggle of **intimacy vs. isolation.** ■ Developmental tasks can vary across cultures and historical periods. In societies that afford personal freedom, norms about developmental tasks provide a roadmap rather than a rigid set of requirements to be followed.
Developmental Timetables	■ The **social clock** refers to the age by which important life events are expected to happen. People are considered **on time** when they experience these events at the normative age and **off time** when they experience them at a non-normative age. ■ Research indicates that people do have ideas about the optimal timing of life events, yet these ideas have become less rigid.
Processes of Developmental Regulation: The Theory of Selective Optimization with Compensation	■ The **theory of selective optimization with compensation** concerns the *processes* by which people seek to accomplish developmental tasks. ■ Successful adult development, according to this theory, depends on three processes: **selection** (choosing manageable life goals), **optimization** (using and enhancing one's resources to pursue one's goals), and **compensation** (developing other strategies to pursue goals when one's resources decline).

LOVE RELATIONSHIPS AND FRIENDSHIPS IN YOUNG ADULTHOOD

The need to belong—to form and maintain close relationships with others—is a fundamental human need that exists in all cultures and age groups (Baumeister & Leary, 1995). Throughout most of human history, people lived in small groups, which offered advantages for survival—in building shelter, finding food, fending off predators and other threats, bearing and raising offspring, and receiving care during times of illness or injury (Brewer & Caporael, 1990). The benefits of social bonds have been so important throughout human evolution that the need to belong became "hard-wired" in our brains (Bugental, 2000; Buss & Kenrick, 1998).

But what about modern times? Do social relationships remain so important in our lives today? Five kinds of research findings suggest that the answer is a resounding *yes.* First, social relationships help to buffer people from the harmful effects of stress by providing social support (comfort, advice, practical aid) in times of need (Cohen

& Wills, 1985). Second, people with strong social ties have better physical health and even live longer (Berkman, Glass, Brissette, & Seeman, 2000; Cohen, 2004). An early and influential study found that adults who had more close relationships and ties to the community were more likely to be alive at a 9-year follow-up (Berkman & Syme, 1979). Third, the quality of one's social relationships is a strong and consistent predictor of life satisfaction and happiness, mattering as much or more than money and material possessions in many studies (Diener & Seligman, 2004; Klinger, 1977). Fourth, people who have satisfying social relationships are less prone to depression and other psychological problems (Hammen, 1999). In fact, complaints about relationships are among the most common concerns of people seeking psychotherapy (Horowitz & Vitkus, 1986). Finally, losing a close relationship can affect us profoundly. The intense grief and sense of loss that people experience following the death of a loved one provide further evidence of the centrality of close relationships in our lives.

A person does not need a large set of social relationships, or a large *social network*, to experience these benefits. It is the quality, rather than the quantity, of social ties that matters most (Rook, 1984). Someone with one or two close friends may be happier than someone else with many friends who are not very close. We will see later that social networks tend to shrink as people grow older, but this does not jeopardize their health and well-being so long as the inner core of their network remains relatively intact (Carstensen, Fung, & Charles, 2003). This inner core includes a person's closest, most supportive relationships—most often spouses or partners, close friends, and family members.

People typically enter young adulthood with the social network that will accompany them through life partly established. They usually have ties to parents and siblings, and some friendships that will continue into their adult lives. But during young adulthood, they forge the rest of their social networks, establishing relationships with a primary partner, new friends, and a nuclear family of their own. We begin with a topic on the minds of many young adults—finding love.

Finding Love

Imagine that at age 16 your parents informed you that they had chosen the person you would marry. They expected you to understand that your preferences could not be taken into account and to trust that they had made a good choice for you. "Never!" you say. "That's crazy." Especially in matters of love, you are in charge of your own destiny. Your indignation reflects the American ideology that marriage should be based on love. This ideology is not universal, however. In many cultures, arranged marriages are still common, and love may be regarded as irrelevant (Ghimire, Axinn, Yabiku, & Thornton, 2006; Heine, 2008). Views of the connection between love and marriage also have varied historically. The ancient Greeks, for example, regarded passionate feelings of attraction as a form of madness that had no place in marriage (Brehm, Miller, Perlman, & Campbell, 2002). In their view, platonic (nonsexual) love was vastly superior to passionate love. The idea that love is a necessary precondition for marriage is a relatively recent cultural invention of Western societies. But what exactly is love?

Philip Bigg/Alamy

In many cultures, arranged marriages are still common, and love may be regarded as irrelevant.

Cultural metaphors provide some clues. Love is "falling head over heels" for someone or being "swept away." Love involves "chemistry" and "makes the world go 'round." Powerful stuff, indeed! These metaphors do capture one common meaning of love—feelings of passion

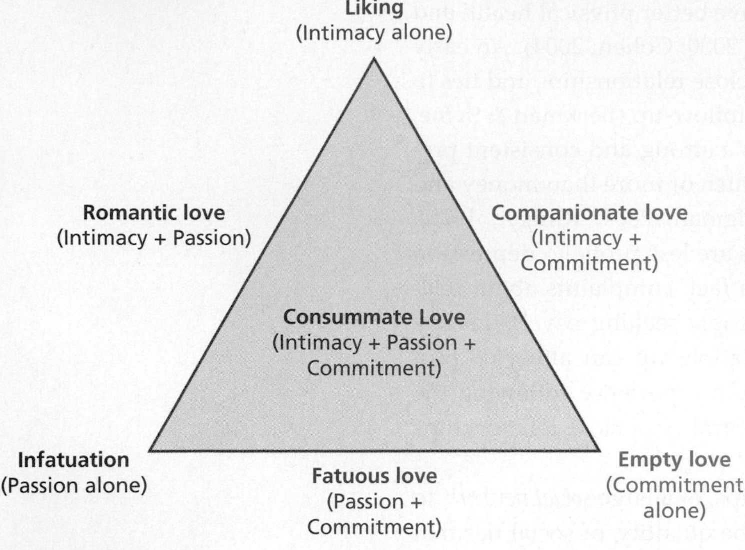

FIGURE 14.2

Sternberg's Triangular Theory of Love.

Different kinds of love result from different combinations of passion, intimacy, and commitment.

Source: From *The psychology of love* by R.J. Sternberg & M.L. Barnes (Eds.), p. 122. Copyright © 1988. Reprinted by permission of the publisher, Yale University Press.

and strong physical attraction for another person. But is there more to love than this? Unique feelings of closeness and trust often develop in a relationship with someone we love. But there is more. We all know people who have been deflated when a partner said, "I love you, but I'm not ready to settle down." Despite the partner's intention to be reassuring, the person on the receiving end of a statement like this often does not feel truly loved. So it seems that love may involve not only physical attraction and closeness but also commitment.

Psychologist Robert Sternberg (1986) proposed the **triangular theory of love,** which includes three components: *passion* (physical arousal, desire), *intimacy* (closeness, trust), and *commitment* (decision to stay in the relationship for the long term). These components can vary in intensity, resulting in different kinds of love (see Figure 14.2). For example, relationships based solely on sexual attraction, without intimacy or commitment, reflect *infatuation.* When people feel ready to commit to each other based on feelings of intense physical attraction, even though they have little intimacy, they are experiencing *fatuous love.* Fatuous love might lead people to get married after a brief whirlwind of passionate dating, a decision that can be risky for the longevity of the relationship (Sternberg, 1988). A relationship that persists despite that absence of passion and intimacy, in contrast, typifies *empty love.* A marriage maintained solely by the spouses' fear of being alone or their belief (often mistaken) that they should stay together for the sake of their children is an example of empty love. *Consummate love* exists when passion, intimacy, and commitment are all high. This is the kind of love to which most of us aspire, but maintaining such love is not easy because the components of love shift over time (Sternberg, 1986).

triangular theory of love A theory of love that emphasizes the idea that different kinds of love result from different combinations of three key components: passion, intimacy, and commitment.

The beginning stages of romantic relationships are often characterized by *romantic love,* or a combination of passionate feelings (strong physical arousal) and emotional intimacy, but the newness of the relationship makes a commitment seem premature. After people decide to commit to the relationship, they may enjoy *consummate love* for a while, but feelings of passion tend to subside as time passes. Researchers have found that excitement and arousal most often occur in situations characterized by novelty and uncertainty (Mandler, 1975, 1997), but as two partners get to know each other, they become more familiar and predictable. As a result, it is common for romantic love to decline over time and for *companionate love* to remain stable or increase (Baumeister & Bratslavsky, 1999; Sprecher & Regan, 1998). Companionate love involves affection, trust, caring, laughter, and shared activities; it is like a close friendship with the added element of commitment (Hatfield, 1988). Companionate love characterizes many long-term relationships after the initial flames of passion have subsided but feelings of closeness and devotion remain strong.

If this sounds disappointing, we leave you with two hopeful thoughts. First, although passionate love may bring couples together, evidence suggests that companionate love is what keeps them together over time (Acker & Davis, 1992; Sternberg 1988). Second, researchers are discovering ways that feelings of passion can be rekindled in long-term relationships, as we will discuss in Chapter 16, when we look at close relationships in middle adulthood. For now, though, we turn to the question of how people find their mates in the first place.

Attraction, Courtship, and Mate Selection

What draws two people together? What do you seek in a mate? How do people progress from being virtual strangers to becoming lovers? It may begin with something as simple as a flirtatious smile, but read on.

Interpersonal Attraction Three major factors emerge repeatedly in studies of interpersonal attraction: *proximity, similarity,* and *physical attractiveness* (Berscheid & Reis, 1998). We tend to choose our friends and lovers from the people who are nearby. When we consider residential *proximity,* even a few feet can make a difference. Festinger and his colleagues (Festinger, Schachter, & Back, 1950) discovered this in a classic study of friendship formation conducted in student housing at the Massachusetts Institute of Technology. Residents were randomly assigned to live in one of 17 different apartment buildings on campus. Over time, people who lived near each other were much more likely to become friends then were those who lived farther apart. Remarkably, people living on the same floor just doors apart were less likely to become friends than people who lived next door to each other. Proximity plays a strong role in the formation of love relationships, too—take a look at any Match.com profile and you'll see that people often specify the geographic distance they are willing to consider. Today, the Internet provides new ways for people to meet potential mates (Bargh & McKenna, 2004), but proximity still influences who actually gets together.

Why does proximity have this effect on relationship formation? It reduces the costs associated with getting together. More time, energy, and money are required to maintain a relationship with someone who lives far away. It may be romantic to think that we would go to the ends of the earth to be with a soul mate, but the truth is that most often we become involved with people who live nearby or work in the same setting. Cupid's wings, it seems, were not designed to fly very far (Rubin, 1973).

How does similarity play a role in interpersonal attraction? Do birds of a feather flock together, or do opposites attract? It turns out that we tend to be attracted to potential friends and mates who are similar to us (Byrne, 1971; Selfhout, Denissen, Branje, & Meeus, 2009). It was once thought that people with complementary, rather than similar, personalities might be attracted to each other (Kerckhoff & Davis, 1962). A dominant person might prefer to be with a submissive person, or perhaps an extravert would enjoy being with an introvert (a shy person). Over the years, however, little scientific support has emerged for this idea. Rather, similarity seems to rule the day in matters of love and friendship. Moreover, similarity influences not only who gets together but also how satisfied they are with their relationships. What kind of similarity matters? People tend to look for others who are like themselves in *demographic characteristics* (age, sex, ethnicity, religion, education, social class), *attitudes and values* (regarding political issues, moral standards, social controversies), *interests* (preferred activities, hobbies), and *personality characteristics* (extraversion, optimism, conscientiousness, assertiveness).

Why does similarity play such an important role in interpersonal attraction? Several explanations exist (Berscheid & Reis, 1998). It is affirming to meet others who share our interests and values. Similar others also are apt to reciprocate our liking, reducing the risk of rejection. In a related vein, mutual understanding is greater between similar partners, and it is rewarding to feel understood. Finally, similarity makes partners more predictable to each other, making their interactions smoother and less prone to conflicts.

A third major factor that influences interpersonal attraction is *physical attractiveness*. A person's looks influence our first impressions,

Alan Thornton/Getty Images

People tend to be attracted to others who have similar demographic characteristics, attitudes and values, interests, and personality characteristics.

and, for better or worse, research clearly indicates that we react more favorably to people who are attractive (Sprecher, 1989). Not everyone values physical attractiveness to the same extent, however. Studies show that, while both sexes value physical attractiveness, men place more importance on appearance than women do (Buss, 1989). In a national sample of Americans, for example, men expressed less willingness than women to marry someone who was not "good looking" (Sprecher, Sullivan, & Hatfield, 1994). Women, on the other hand, assign more importance to a potential partner's status and financial resources. In the same national sample, women expressed more interest in marrying someone with higher education, stable employment, and a good income (Sprecher et al., 1994). This gender difference has been documented in many cultures, Eastern as well as Western (Buss, 1989; Shackelford, Schmitt, & Buss, 2005), and it has been found in studies of homosexual as well as heterosexual individuals (Lippa, 2007).

Yet these same studies reveal many similarities between the sexes. Both men and women express a strong desire for their partners to be intelligent, kind, honest, to have a sense of humor, and to be in good health. Neither good looks nor good financial prospects are ranked as the *most* important characteristics of a potential mate by either men or women. We should be careful not to exaggerate gender differences when it comes to matters of the heart: despite the appeal of popular books that proclaim that men are from Mars and women from Venus, or stand-up comedians who draw stark contrasts between males and females, scientific research finds that men and women seek many of the same things in romantic relationships (Impett & Peplau, 2006).

Courtship So far we have discussed the *kinds of people* who we might want to court, but not how the *process of courtship* actually begins. Not surprisingly, it often starts with flirtation—a signal of interest exchanged between two people, such as meaningful eye contact or a flirtatious smile. In one study, 90 percent of college students who had recently fallen in love indicated that they had received a signal of some kind that the other person was attracted to them (Aron, Dutton, Aron, & Iverson, 1989). Of course, if such signals of interest are too intrusive, the sender risks being rejected (Shaver & Mikulincer, 2006). This may explain why reciprocation of liking—receiving an indication of interest from the other person in response to our own signal of interest—is important in getting a fledgling relationship off the ground (Aaron et al., 1989).

Self-disclosure, the willingness to share personal information and feelings with a partner, deepens the connection between the two individuals as they begin to date, so long as they pace their disclosures carefully (Altman & Taylor, 1973). A person who discloses too much personal information at the beginning of a relationship can make the other person uncomfortable. On the other hand, a person who is too inhibited about disclosure can convey a lack of trust in the partner, jeopardizing the relationship. New relationships develop more smoothly when the two individuals show genuine interest in each other's concerns and disclose information at a pace and depth that match that of the partner (Shaver & Mikulincer, 2006).

As time passes, the partners in a romantic relationship often progress from "falling in love" to "loving each other" (Shaver & Mikulincer, 2006, p. 259). Couples begin to spend more time together, not only in dates but also in informal, day-to-day activities, and their discussions go beyond exchanging intimate information and personal concerns to exploring whether they can be happy and can achieve shared goals together in a long-term relationship. Flirtation, passion, and sexual intimacy become less important, and their capacity to be caring and emotionally supportive to each other becomes more important. If partners learn that they can comfortably seek support and count on each other to be responsive, trust in the relationship develops. These changes lay the foundation for a lasting, committed, and mutually supportive relationship. In short, the partners are in the process of becoming primary attachment figures for each other (Shaver & Mikulincer, 2006).

Attachment Styles Our first encounter with the concept of "attachment" was in our discussion of infancy. Attachment relationships in adulthood serve many of the same basic functions as attachment relationships between children and their parents in early childhood (Hazan & Shaver, 1987)—providing comfort and aid in the face of threats and providing a secure base from which to explore the world. In the words of John Bowlby (1988, p. 129), attachment figures are important "from the cradle to the grave." As you may recall from Chapter 6, some children develop secure attachments with their parents, whereas other children develop insecure attachments. The same is true in adulthood. Some adults develop secure relationships with romantic partners, and others develop insecure ones. These parallels are not coincidental. Instead, our early relationships with parents lead us to form attachment styles that influence our close relationships in adulthood (Shaver & Mikulincer, 2006).

Early experiences with caregivers (usually parents) lead people to develop general expectations about what others are like and how they will be treated by others. These expectations, in turn, produce distinctive ways of thinking, feeling, and behaving that are called **attachment styles** (Shaver & Mikulincer, 2006). Researchers have identified four attachment styles that reflect whether people are high or low on two dimensions—*avoidance* of intimacy and dependence on others and *anxiety* about rejection and abandonment by others (see Figure 14.3; Brennan, Clark, & Shaver, 1998; Fraley & Shaver, 2000):

attachment styles Distinctive ways of thinking, feeling, and behaving in close relationships that result from one's early attachment experiences.

1. *Secure* individuals, about 60 percent of the adult population (Mickelson, Kessler, & Shaver, 1997), are low on both anxiety and avoidance. They believe that others can be counted on to be responsive and caring, and they feel comfortable depending on others when they feel needed and close to them.
2. *Preoccupied* individuals are high on anxiety and low on avoidance. They want to be close to others, but they worry about being rejected. They often have doubts about their partner's commitment to them and need frequent reassurance that they are loved.
3. *Fearful-avoidant individuals* are high on both anxiety and avoidance. They tend to distrust others and anticipate that others will reject them. As a result, they are often uncomfortable with closeness.
4. *Dismissive-avoidant individuals* are low on anxiety and high on avoidance. They tend to have high self-regard and do not care much whether others accept them. They perceive others to be unreliable and so tend to be self-sufficient.

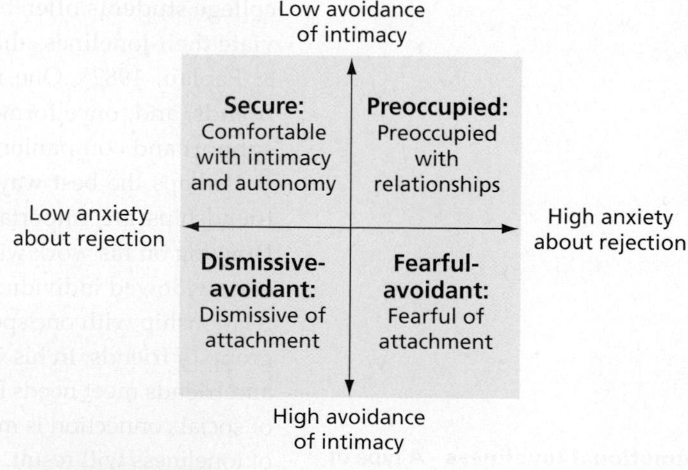

FIGURE 14.3

Attachment Styles in Adulthood

Source: Adapted from: Bartholomew, K., & Horowitz, L. M. (1991). Attachment styles among young adults: A test of a four-category model. *Journal of Personality and Social Psychology, 61*(2), 226–244; Fraley, R. C., & Shaver, P. R. (2000). Adult romantic attachment: Theoretical developments, emerging controversies, and unanswered questions. *Review of General Psychology, 4*(2), 132–154.

Overall, secure individuals experience greater emotional and sexual intimacy, greater happiness, and stronger commitment in their romantic relationships than insecure individuals (Shaver & Miklunicer, 2006). Not surprisingly, secure individuals tend to be more satisfied with their romantic relationships, a finding that has been confirmed in dozens of studies that measured attachment styles and relationship satisfaction in a variety of different ways (Mikulincer, Florian,

Cowan, & Cowan, 2002). Secure adults also have longer-lasting relationships and are less likely to get divorced (Morgan & Shaver, 1999). If they do experience a relationship breakup, secure individuals are less likely to engage in poor coping responses (such as rumination, inability to reflect constructively on the relationship, and use of alcohol and drugs) and more likely to make a healthy adjustment to the loss of the relationship (Davis, Shaver, & Vernon, 2003; Saffery & Ehrenberg, 2007).

Attachment styles tend to be fairly stable over time, but they are not carved in stone. Bowlby (1988) believed that attachment styles can change over the course of one's life as a result of transforming experiences in important relationships, and research supports his view (Kirkpatrick & Hazan, 1994; Mikulincer & Shaver, 2007a). A relationship with a caring, supportive partner, for example, may help someone with an insecure attachment style feel more confident of the partner's love and more comfortable being intimate and turning to the partner for comfort. An intriguing new line of research is demonstrating that even small interventions—such as priming people unconsciously to see others as compassionate and caring—can produce short-term increases in attachment security and emotional health (Mikulincer & Shaver, 2007b). Evidence that attachment styles are malleable offers the hope that insecurely attached individuals can be helped to feel more secure in their close relationships.

Friendship

We have emphasized intimate relationships with romantic partners up to this point, but we should not overlook the important role that friends play in contributing to psychological well-being. Friends provide emotional support and companionship, which is especially helpful when young adults leave home to live, study, and work in new environments. Loneliness is common when people must establish new social networks (Rook & Peplau, 1982). As many as 40 percent of college students, for example, report having no new friends during their first semester away from home (Collins & Madsen, 2006). By the second semester, however, most do make new friends, and their feelings of loneliness subside. Ironically, lonely college students often believe that finding a romantic partner will do more to alleviate their loneliness than making friends, but the opposite seems to be true (Rook & Peplau, 1982). One reason may be that more opportunities exist for making friends, and, once formed, friendships provide a reliable and reassuring source of support and companionship.

Perhaps the best way to think about this is that both romantic relationships and friendships are important to our psychological well-being, but in different ways. Drawing on his work with many different groups of lonely adults (e.g., divorced parents, widowed individuals), Robert Weiss (1973) argued that people need both a close relationship with one special person (often a romantic partner or spouse) and ties to a group of friends. In his view, a close relationship meets needs for emotional intimacy, and friends meet needs for camaraderie and a sense of group belonging. If either kind of social connection is missing in a person's life, according to Weiss, one of two types of loneliness will result. People who lack an intimate relationship are likely to experience **emotional loneliness,** characterized by feelings of utter aloneness and abandonment. In contrast, people who lack ties to a circle of friends experience **social loneliness**, characterized by feelings of boredom, exclusion, and social marginality. Weiss argued further that loneliness cannot be relieved by substituting one type of relationship for the other. Even a highly satisfying relationship with an intimate partner, therefore, cannot compensate for the absence of a set of friends, and vice versa. If we are fortunate, then, our social networks will include both intimate partners and good friends as we move through life. (For a summary of this section, see "Interim Summary 14.2: Love Relationships and Friendships in Young Adulthood.")

emotional loneliness A type of loneliness that results when a person lacks an intimate partner, reflected in feelings of utter aloneness and abandonment.

social loneliness A type of loneliness that results when a person lacks ties to a group of friends, reflected in feelings of boredom, exclusion, and social marginality.

INTERIM SUMMARY 14.2

Love Relationships and Friendships in Young Adulthood

	■ People typically enter young adulthood with a social network already partly established via ties to parents, siblings, and friends. However, during young adulthood, people forge the rest of their social networks, often establishing relationships with a primary partner, new friends, and a nuclear family of their own.
Finding Love	■ Views of the connection between love and marriage vary across cultures and historical periods. The idea that love is a prerequisite for marriage is a recent cultural invention of Western societies. ■ Sternberg proposed a theory of love that includes *passion, intimacy,* and *commitment.* These components vary in intensity in different relationships, resulting in different kinds of love.
Attraction, Courtship, and Mate Selection	■ Three major factors emerge in studies of interpersonal attraction: *proximity, similarity,* and *physical attractiveness.* We tend to be attracted to people who are near us, similar to us, and who are physically appealing. ■ Researchers have identified four **attachment styles** that reflect whether people are high or low on two dimensions: *anxiety* about rejection and abandonment by others and *avoidance* of intimacy and dependence on others. ■ Attachment styles tend to be fairly stable over time, but can change as a result of transforming experiences in important relationships.
Friendship	■ Friendship is especially important to young adults, as friends provide emotional support and companionship when young adults leave home to live, study, and work in new environments. Friends also help young adults ward off feelings of loneliness. ■ Weiss distinguished two kinds of loneliness: **emotional loneliness** and **social loneliness.**

MARRIAGE AND FAMILY IN YOUNG ADULTHOOD

After a period of exploring relationships with different partners, young adults often feel ready to establish a long-term partnership. This frequently takes the form of marriage, although the types of partnerships and families that young adults form, and the number of young adults who remain single, are changing.

Marrying, Cohabitating, or Remaining Single

One indication of changes in patterns of partnership and family formation is that rates of marriage among young adults have declined in recent decades. For example, the proportion of people who remained unmarried by their mid-20s more than doubled from the 1970s to the 1990s (Saluter & Lugalia, 1998). This shift is partly explained by the fact that people began to marry later during this period. The average ages of first marriage were 20 and 23, respectively, for women and men in 1960; the corresponding figures were 26 and 28 in 2009 (U.S. Bureau of the Census, 2009).

cohabitating Living together in an intimate relationship outside of the context of marriage.

Another factor is a sharp increase in the proportion of couples who are **cohabiting**—living together outside the context of marriage. Cohabitation was relatively rare before the 1970s, but now as many as half of women have cohabited by their mid-30s (Chandra, Martinez, Mosher, Abma, & Jones, 2005). Social acceptance of cohabitation has grown. Research indicates that young adults are coming to view cohabitation—whether as a prelude or an alternative to marriage—as a normal part of the life course (Manning, Longmore, & Giordano, 2007). Moreover, in the United States, the transition to parenthood now often occurs among cohabiting couples, who account for 40 to 50 percent of nonmarital births (Bumpass & Lu, 2000).

Some social critics worry that declining rates of marriage among young adults, coupled with the growing popularity of cohabitation and high rates of divorce, mean that Americans are abandoning the institution of marriage (Bellah, Madsen, Sullivan, Swidler, & Tipton, 1985). Findings from multiple surveys, however, indicate that the majority of Americans still view marriage as a personal goal and an important component of a good life (Axinn & Thornton, 2000; Coontz, 2007). In fact, respect for marriage may underlie the decision of some young adults to act cautiously, waiting to marry until they have a relatively secure occupational and financial foundation or until they have tried out a relationship through cohabitation (Huston & Melz, 2004). Whether their instincts are correct or not, young adults who defer marriage for such reasons often do so with the hope that their eventual unions will be long-lasting.

Although some people remain single by choice, others do so because they have difficulties finding mates with similar educational and social backgrounds. For example, only about 65 percent of African American women have married by their late 30s, and those who do experience high rates of divorce and relatively low rates of remarriage (Teachman, Tedrow, & Crowder, 2000). Does this mean that African American women place less value on marriage? Research shows that African Americans strongly endorse the idea that a happy marriage is a central life goal, and unmarried African Americans and Hispanics express greater interest in marrying than do unmarried Caucasians (Huston & Melz, 2004). What, then, is the explanation?

African American women are considerably more likely than African American men to obtain a B.A. degree, which, to the extent that people choose mates with similar educational backgrounds, makes their pool of eligible mates smaller (Ryu, 2009). Additionally, African American women are more likely to live in communities where men have less education, less job stability, and lower earnings. (Bear in mind, too, that rates of incarceration are higher among African American men than among Caucasian or Hispanic men; Bonhomme, Stephens, & Braithwaite, 2006). In considering potential mates, women do weigh a man's financial resources, as we noted earlier. Rates of marriage are higher not only among African Americans but also among Caucasians and Hispanics when rates of male employment are high (Landale & Oropesa, 2007; Teachman et al., 2000).

Not all intimate partnerships involve marriage, of course. Some long-term unions formed in young adulthood involve homosexual partners, who are prohibited from entering into legal marriage in most states. Because of the social stigma associated with homosexuality, obtaining accurate data on the number of gay and lesbian couples in the United States is challenging. However, current estimates suggest that one in nine unmarried, cohabiting couples are same-sex couples (Kurdek, 2005). Heterosexual and homosexual relationships have much in common, although gay and lesbian couples tend to have a less traditional division of labor in their households (Peplau & Fingerhut, 2007). Researchers have found that the long-term relationships of gay men and lesbians are characterized by feelings of love and satisfaction as strong as those of heterosexuals (Kurdek, 2004; Peplau & Fingerhut, 2007).

Not everyone wants to establish an intimate partnership with another person. Some people prefer to remain single, and the number of adults making this choice has risen steadily over the past decade. Adults who remain single and who have close friendships have been found to be as happy and well adjusted as people who get married (DePaulo & Morris, 2005). They derive emotional support and companionship from their close friends, siblings, and neighbors, and they tend to place less importance on having an intimate partnership (Dykstra, 1995; Pinquart, 2003). Feelings of personal mastery and self-sufficiency also contribute to the psychological well-being of adults who remain single over the course of their lives (Bookwala & Fekete, 2009). Here is a wrinkle, though: Research that has focused specifically on young adulthood suggests that single young adults have lower life satisfaction than dating, cohabiting, or married young adults (Dush & Amato, 2005; Soons & Liefbroer, 2008). The role of intimate partnerships in one's life may depend on a complex mix of factors that include developmental tasks and norms specific to one's life stage (Erikson, 1963, 1968; Soons & Liefbroer, 2008), personal preferences and self-sufficiency (Bookwala & Fekete, 2009; Dykstra 1995; Dykstra & Fokkema, 2007), and the adequacy of emotional support and companionship from sources other than a primary partner.

Marital Satisfaction

When two people do decide to marry or cohabit, they usually embark on a life together with strong feelings of love and great hopes for the future. Do these blissful feelings last? Longitudinal studies shed light on how marital quality changes over time. One consistent finding is that marital satisfaction tends to decline relatively early, often within the first 2 to 4 years of marriage, with wives expressing unhappiness before their husbands (Bradbury, & Karney, 2004; Huston, Niehuis, & Smith, 2001; Kurdek, 1999) (see Figure 14.4). Cohabiting couples fare no better, and, in fact, declines in their relationship satisfaction are even steeper and occur more quickly (Smock, 2000).

This evidence of a decline in marital satisfaction may seem discouraging, but it is important to put it in perspective. First, it may be inevitable for spouses to experience some decline in marital satisfaction as they habituate to each other and their initial excitement and feelings of attraction subside (Berscheid & Ammazzalorso, 2004; VanLaningham, Johnson, & Amato, 2001). Second, even though marital satisfaction declines, married individuals are generally happier and healthier than divorced and widowed individuals (Marks & Lambert, 1998). Third, the research documenting downward trends in marital quality reflects group averages. Not all marriages decline in quality over time, and researchers have discovered some of the factors that affect marital satisfaction.

Factors Affecting Marital Satisfaction Negative behavior by spouses, particularly during conflicts, plays an important role in eroding marital satisfaction (Gottman, 1994; Koerner & Jacobson, 1994). John Gottman (1994) observed many married couples interacting together in laboratory and naturalistic settings, and he concluded from this work that four types of negative behavior during conflicts are especially damaging: *criticism* (attacking the partner's personality or values), *contempt* (insulting the partner's sense of self), *defensiveness* (deflecting the

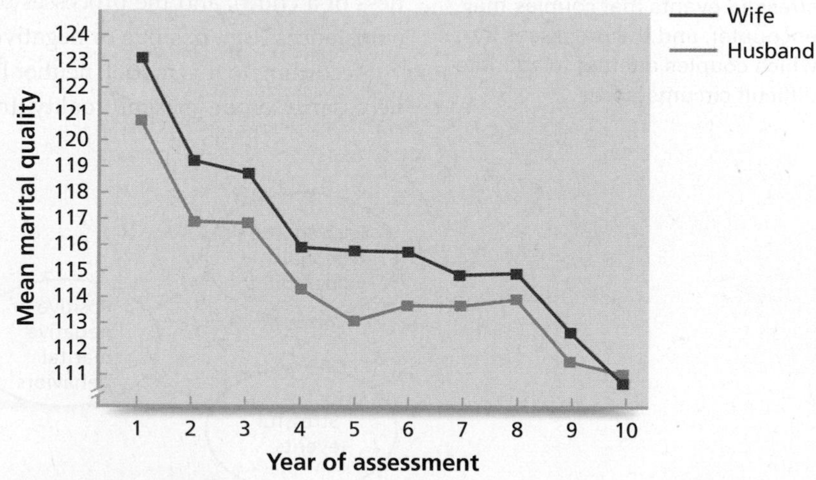

FIGURE 14.4

Longitudinal Change in Marital Satisfaction in the First 10 Years of Marriage

Source: Kurdek, L.A. (1999). The nature and predictors of the trajectory of change in marital quality for husbands and wives over the first 10 years of marriage. *Developmental Psychology 35* (5), 1283–1296.

partner's complaints by presenting oneself as the victim), and *stonewalling* (refusing to engage with the partner, or "the silent treatment"). Negative behavior keeps the couple's problems from being resolved and can cause their conflicts to escalate. An important goal of many marital therapies is to help couples learn to resolve their disagreements in nondestructive ways, so that feelings of resentment do not build up.

Reducing negative behavior in couples' interactions may not be enough, though—positive behavior is typically what drew spouses together in the first place, and maintaining positive behavior over time is crucial for marital happiness (Fincham, Stanley, & Beach, 2007; Huston et al., 2001; Karney & Bradbury, 1995) and for sustaining sexual desire (Impett, Strachman, Finkel, & Gable, 2008). Happier couples provide each other with support, express affection and closeness, seek out fun activities to do together, and are willing to forgive each other when misunderstandings occur.

Some couples face more serious problems than others, of course, including problems outside the marriage, such as job pressures, financial burdens, or illness. Even common life transitions, such as becoming parents, can be a source of stress. Life stress depletes spouses' energies, making it difficult for them to be positive and contributing to greater hostility and more negative perceptions of the partner's behavior (Conger & Donnellan, 2007; Neff & Karney, 2004). Spouses are affected not only by their own stress, but also by the stress their partners experience. Problems that one spouse experiences at work, for example, can lead to increased psychological distress in the other spouse (Neff & Karney, 2007). The transmission of stress from one spouse to another is called the **stress-crossover effect** (Larson & Almeida, 1999). It is nearly impossible to avoid life stress altogether, but spouses who support each other through difficult times can limit the toll of stress—on their own psychological health and, importantly, on the health of their relationship.

stress-crossover effect The transmission of stress from one spouse to another.

The Vulnerability-Stress-Adaptation Model These different influences on marital quality have been woven together in the **vulnerability-stress-adaptation model of marriage** (Bradbury & Karney, 2004; Karney & Bradbury, 1995). According to this model, shown in Figure 14.5, marital quality is affected by long-standing personal vulnerabilities that spouses may bring to a marriage (e.g., poor social skills, insecure attachment style), stressful events that couples may encounter (e.g., unemployment, illness of a child), and the processes by which couples attempt to adapt to difficult circumstances (e.g., positive or negative marital behavior).

vulnerability-stress-adaptation model of marriage A model that suggests that marital quality is affected by long-standing personal vulnerabilities that spouses may bring to a marriage, stressful events that couples may encounter, and the processes by which couples attempt to adapt to difficult circumstances.

According to this model, neither life stress nor personal vulnerabilities alone would necessarily erode marital quality. Instead, it is the combination—life stress *and* per-

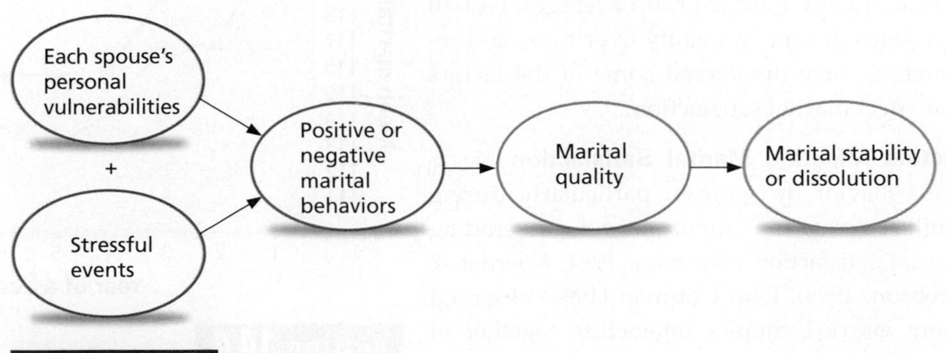

FIGURE 14.5

The Vulnerability-Stress-Adaptation Model of Marriage

Source: Adapted from Karney, B. R., & Bradbury, T. N. (1995). The longitudinal course of marital quality and stability: A review of theory, methods, and research. *Psychological Bulletin, 118*(1), 3–34.

sonal vulnerabilities—that erodes marital quality by causing spouses to engage in more negative marital behaviors and fewer positive marital behaviors. Imagine a couple facing serious financial problems. According to this model, if neither member of the couple has significant personal vulnerabilities, they may be able to weather the stress of their financial problems without fighting or otherwise hurting their marriage. On the other hand, if one or both spouses tends to be insecure, pessimistic, or angry, or to have some other personal vulnerability, the couple may be less able to cope with the stress of their financial problems without criticizing each other, becoming defensive or withdrawn, or engaging in destructive marital behaviors.

Helping to alleviate persistent stress in a couple's life *or* helping them overcome personal vulnerabilities that lead to corrosive marital behavior would be likely to strengthen their marriage. This is an important point because current approaches to marital intervention mostly emphasize teaching people how to communicate positively and resolve conflicts constructively with their partners. These interventions were generally developed for use in relatively affluent communities. Couples in low-income communities might benefit as much or more from programs that help to alleviate chronic stressors in their daily lives, such as poverty, unemployment, drugs, and crime (Karney & Bradbury, 2005).

Breakups and Divorce

Some marriages and cohabiting relationships deteriorate to the point that one or both members of the couple decide that breaking up is the best option. What leads couples to move from "I do" to "I don't"?

Divorce rates soared in the United States in the 1970s and 1980s. During this time, changing laws made divorce easier, divorce became more socially acceptable, and women had begun to gain considerable economic independence through increased participation in the workforce (Cherlin, 1992). Divorce rates did eventually level off and, more recently, have begun to decline (Goldstein, 1999). Approximately 50 percent of marriages currently end in divorce in the United States. This figure varies across different groups, however, as these examples indicate:

- Women who have a college degree are far less likely to divorce (36 percent) than women who are high-school dropouts (60 percent).
- People who have more financial resources and other resources needed to establish an independent household generally have stable marriages (Martin & Parashar, 2006).
- People who marry in their mid-20s or later have lower divorce rates than people who marry in their teens or early 20s (Raley & Bumpass, 2003).
- Adult children of divorced parents have an elevated risk of divorce both because they are less committed to the norm of lifelong marriage and because they may have fewer of the interpersonal skills needed to preserve a marriage (Amato, 1996; Amato & DeBoer, 2001).

Divorce is not a single event (Coleman, Ganong, & Leon, 2006). It begins with a decline in marital satisfaction that persists until one or both partners begin to consider separation. If significant improvement does not occur, divorce is likely to result. This downward cascade may be accelerated by an increase in conflict and an erosion of positive behavior (Caughlin & Huston, 2006; Gottman, 1994).

The aftermath of divorce often continues beyond its legal finalization. Given the high hopes with which people enter into marriages in Western societies and the protracted downward slide that often precedes divorce, it is not surprising that divorce is such a distressing experience for most people. Divorced individuals experience declines in happiness and self-esteem, increased psychological distress, increased alcohol consumption, worse physical health, and even a greater risk of mortality (Amato,

2000). Divorce often results in a lower standard of living, particularly for women. Divorce can also trigger property disputes, residential relocation, changes in relationships with friends, and feelings of social isolation. For parents, divorce brings new strains in their efforts to raise their children, as well as worries about how their children are being affected (a topic we discussed in Chapter 10). The psychological effects of divorce generally tend to subside after several years, however, particularly when people form new relationships or remarry (Marks & Lambert, 1998). Unfortunately, rates of divorce among remarriages are as high, or higher, than those among first marriages (Cherlin, 1992).

In thinking about the negative effects of divorce, it is important to bear in mind that ending a marriage ultimately can be preferable to staying in a conflict-ridden marriage (Hawkins & Booth, 2005). It is seldom beneficial to preserve a chronically unhappy marriage for the sake of children. In addition, divorced individuals are generally resilient. Most tend to make a satisfactory adjustment over time (Coleman et al., 2006).

Earlier we mentioned that a key reason couples decide to cohabitate rather than marry is to "try out" their relationship—to get to know each other better before committing to marriage. Does this strategy work? Unfortunately, the answer seems to be no. Cohabiting relationships appear to be less stable than marital relationships (Binstock & Thornton, 2003). As many as half of cohabiting relationships in the United States end within a year (Seltzer, 2004). Those who go on to marry after cohabiting tend to experience less marital happiness than people who marry without first cohabiting (Dush, Cohan, & Amato, 2003).

Before you jump to the conclusion that premarital cohabitation *leads to* later marital dissatisfaction, consider this: People who choose to cohabitate may have characteristics that increase the likelihood of relationship dissatisfaction. (As we have noted many times, correlation is not the same as causation.) People in cohabiting relationships are more likely to have parents who divorced, have more accepting attitudes toward divorce, and have more unconventional values (e.g., more politically liberal, less religious; Axinn & Thornton, 1992). But other research suggests that the experience of cohabiting seems to erode relationship quality. The fact that cohabiting couples begin their lives together with an uncertain commitment may lead them to invest less in their relationship (Dush et al., 2003). They also face fewer legal barriers to breaking up, which may have been one of their reasons for deciding to cohabit rather than to marry. Ironically, for some cohabiting couples—particularly those with children—the breakup may lead to conflicts over property, finances, and future child-rearing plans that are quite messy and intense precisely because they lack legal obligations and protections.

Less is known about the longevity of gay and lesbian partnerships. Many gay and lesbian couples enjoy satisfying relationships for many years—even decades—but the existing evidence suggests that they may break up at rates that are somewhat higher than those of married couples but comparable to those of heterosexual cohabiting couples (Kurdek, 2004; Peplau & Fingerhut, 2007). The absence of legal barriers to ending the relationship may play a role, since the legal recognition of gay and lesbian unions remains rare (Peplau & Fingerhut, 2007).

Despite the disappointment of seeing a marriage or other partnership end, the experience of having formed an intimate union with another person represents a milestone in most young adults' lives, and many will seek to remarry or cohabit again.

Launching a Family

Launching a family is another major milestone in the lives of many people. Although some people start a family later in life, for many this life change occurs in young adulthood.

Becoming a parent is a transforming event, one that introduces joys as well as challenges to parents' lives. It can enrich parents' self-concepts and bring a great sense of accomplishment, even as it adds to the role strains that couples experience. Let's explore how this transition unfolds and how mothers, fathers, and their relationship as a couple are affected by the new challenges it brings.

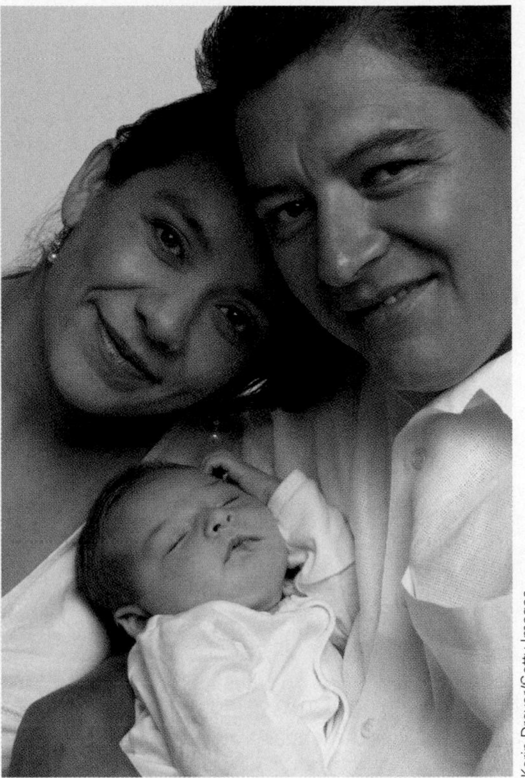
Karin Dreyer/Getty Images

Parenthood brings new responsibilities, but also many rewards.

The Transition to Parenthood Couples make the decision to start a family for several reasons. A primary reason is the desire to have a close bond with a child and to be able to watch a child grow and develop over time. Other common reasons include anticipated benefits to personal development (such as a sense of being grown up) and to the couple's development (increased closeness and a sense of achievement). Encouragement from family members and friends can also influence a couple's decision to start a family (Cowan & Cowan, 1992). Young couples often prefer to delay pregnancy until they feel relatively established in terms of their educational, work, and financial goals, and until they feel that their relationship has a solid foundation (Feeney et al., 2001). Older couples, aware of the ticking biological clock, may accelerate their plans to start a family.

The transition to parenthood marks a major change not only in the life of each spouse but also in their life together as a couple. They must grapple with the challenge of providing round-the-clock care for a newborn, often even as they juggle work and household responsibilities. Couples generally do not spend less time together, but the way they spend their time changes considerably (Feeney et al., 2001). With a newborn in the house, couples have less time for shared leisure activities, such as going out to eat or getting together with friends. Sexual intimacy may decrease as a lack of sleep and general fatigue cause sexual desire to wane. The increased workload associated with having a new baby and changes in the couple's relationship can trigger conflicts and disagreements (Namaguchi & Milkie, 2003; Twenge, Campbell, & Foster, 2003).

But becoming a parent involves many exhilarating and rewarding experiences, too. Parents report joy and a sense of achievement at being a family unit, as well as excitement at watching their baby develop. These shared experiences can increase feelings of closeness in new parents, even during this stressful time (Cowan & Cowan, 1992; Feeney et al., 2001).

How does this mix of experiences affect couples' feelings about their marriage overall? A number of longitudinal studies have documented a decline in marital satisfaction following the birth of a baby (Doss, Rhoades, Stanley, & Markman, 2009; Feeney et al., 2001; Hirschberger, Srivastava, Marsh, Cowan, & Cowan, 2009; Lawrence, Rothman, Cobb, Rothman, & Bradbury, 2008). These declines—which have been documented in European and Asian countries as well as in the United States (Doss et al., 2009)—most likely result from the increased workload and marital tensions noted above.

Yet not all couples experience a drop in marital satisfaction after becoming parents (Belksy & Rovine, 1990; Shapiro, Gottman, & Carrère, 2000). In one study, marital satisfaction was preserved when new parents showed affection and admiration for each other and refrained from expressing negativity or disappointment in the marriage (Shapiro et al., 2000). In other research, couples fared better when the pregnancy was planned (Lawrence et al., 2008) and when they understood that the arrival of the new baby would restrict their shared activities and would bring added responsibilities that might strain their relationship for a time (Belsky & Kelly, 1994). Realistic expectations may help couples weather the stress of launching a family. Bear in mind, too, that a dip in marital satisfaction may be offset by the rewards of positive coparenting experiences (Lawrence et al., 2008).

Camille Tokerrud/Getty Images

Single parenting is increasingly common, especially among African American women.

Variations in the Impact of Parenthood Becoming a parent is not an identical experience for all parents. Mothers tend to find new parenthood more stressful than fathers, and their marital satisfaction tends to suffer sooner (Cowan & Cowan, 1992; Feeney et al., 2001; Namaguchi & Milkie, 2003). Whether intended or not, the arrival of a new baby often contributes to a gender-based division of labor, with new mothers devoting considerably more time than new fathers to house work and infant care. Women also are more likely than men to reduce their hours of paid employment or to take a leave of absence, which can contribute to their feeling isolated.

Characteristics of the infant, the individual parents, the marriage, and the couple's social network also play a role in the adjustment to parenthood (Belsky & Pensky, 1988). Babies who are irritable or who have a physical handicap or illness are more difficult to care for, making parents' adjustment more difficult. Parents with psychological problems prior to the baby's birth or with unrealistic expectations of parenthood have a more difficult adjustment. Similarly, couples who are less satisfied with their marriages before the baby arrives or who are less satisfied with the division of labor after the baby comes home adjust less well (Lawrence et al., 2008). Finally, adjusting to parenthood is often easier if the couple's friends and family members, especially their parents, provide encouragement, advice, and practical assistance.

Alternative Routes to Parenthood The transition to parenthood does not always occur in the context of heterosexual unions. Perhaps as many as 20 percent of gay and lesbian couples have children, and evidence suggests that, as parents, they are as devoted and effective as heterosexual parents (Tasker, 2005). Children raised by gay or lesbian parents are generally well adjusted as a result, even though they may experience discrimination because of their parents' sexual orientation (Wainwright, Russell, & Patterson, 2004).

Single adults can become parents, too. Single parenthood is increasingly common among African American women, as the shortage of eligible partners with strong financial prospects leads many to opt to have children on their own (Teachman et al., 2000). The young women's mothers and male relatives often pitch in to help with child-rearing tasks. Such support is especially valuable because single mothers are less likely than divorced mothers to receive child support payments from the biological father (Wu, Bumpass, & Musik, 2001).

Having biological children is not the only route to parenthood, of course. Some adults adopt children or become stepparents through remarriage or cohabitation. Adopted children and stepchildren constitute about 8 percent of all children in the United States (Krieder, 2003). Nearly 30 percent of U.S. children live in stepfamilies at some point in their lives (Bumpass, Raley, & Sweet, 1995). Both adoptive families and stepfamilies go through several phases of adjustment as they form bonds with the nonbiological child, but, in the end, most manage to forge satisfying relationships and an effective family identity.

Being a parent is a major adult role, and it confers a sense of adult status and social identity. Even though it can be a demanding or difficult role at times, it also offers great rewards, and the majority of U.S. parents have long regarded it as a major source of satisfaction and meaning in their lives (Hoffman & Manis, 1979; Twenge et al., 2003). (For a summary of this section, see "Interim Summary 14.3: Marriage and Family in Young Adulthood.")

INTERIM SUMMARY 14.3

Marriage and Family in Young Adulthood

Marrying, Cohabiting, or Remaining Single	■ Rates of marriage among young adults have declined in recent decades. However, the majority of Americans still see marriage as a personal goal and a key to happiness. ■ There has been a sharp increase in the proportion of couples who are **cohabiting**. ■ The number of adults choosing to remain single has risen steadily. Having close friends may explain why single people are as happy as married people.
Marital Satisfaction	■ Marital satisfaction tends to decline relatively early in many marriages, with wives expressing unhappiness before their husbands. ■ Four types of negative behavior during conflicts are especially damaging to marital satisfaction: *criticism, contempt, defensiveness,* and *stonewalling*. ■ Job pressures, financial burdens, illness, and new parenthood can be sources of stress on a marriage. Spouses can also transmit stress to each other (the **stress-crossover effect**). ■ According to the *vulnerability-stress-adaptation model of marriage,* marital quality is affected by personal vulnerabilities, stressful events, and the processes by which the couple adapts to difficult circumstances.
Breakups and Divorce	■ Approximately 50 percent of U.S. marriages end in divorce. ■ Factors that improve a couple's economic resources and ability to establish an independent household make it easier for them to form a stable marriage. ■ Divorced individuals experience declines in happiness and self-esteem, increased psychological distress, increased alcohol consumption, worse physical health, and a lower standard of living. ■ Studies suggest the breakup rates of homosexual couples are higher than those of married heterosexual couples but comparable to those of cohabiting heterosexual couples.
Launching a Family	■ The transition to parenthood most often occurs in young adulthood and marks a major change not only in the life of each spouse but also in their life together. Parenthood is challenging, but the majority of U.S. parents view it as a source of satisfaction and meaning in their lives ■ Women find new parenthood more stressful than men, and their marital satisfaction takes a toll sooner. Realistic expectations of parenthood help couples weather the stress of launching a family. ■ Having biological children within a marriage is not the only way to become a parent. Single parenthood and gay parenthood are options, as are becoming a stepparent or adopting a child.

ENTERING THE WORKFORCE

Work is a major aspect of most adults' lives. It is not only a source of *income,* but also a source of *identity* for many people. When adults meet each other for the first time, especially in contemporary industrialized society, they move quickly from exchanging their names and hometowns to sharing information about the kind of work they do.

Even retirees, long after they leave the workforce, often continue to describe themselves in terms of the jobs they once held. Since people spend so much of their daily lives at work, it should come as no surprise that work can affect their health and well-being. Finally, work can be an important context for development and growth, allowing people to develop new competencies and an increased sense of mastery.

Occupational Choices and Aspirations

What makes one individual choose to become an attorney and another decide to be a nurse? As you think about your own life, what factors have influenced your occupational goals?

The Role of Personality Factors and Work Values One approach to understanding why people enter particular occupations emphasizes the role of *personality* factors, such as traits and interests, in career selection (Holland, 1997). Certain occupations are especially well suited to individuals with particular personality characteristics. Someone who is outgoing and assertive might be better suited to a career in sales than in accounting. Someone who enjoys helping others might be attracted to a career in teaching or social work. From this perspective, successful career choice requires matching a person's unique interests and personality with a vocation that allows these traits to be expressed.

A different approach to understanding vocational choice focuses on *work values*, which reflect the kinds of rewards individuals seek from their work (e.g., Johnson, 2002). When you finish your education, what will you look for in a job? For example, are you most interested in making a lot of money, in having a secure job, or in having a job with a lot of vacation time? According to theories of work values (Johnson, 2001), four key types of work rewards exist: *extrinsic rewards* (e.g., income, job security), *intrinsic rewards* (e.g., being able to be creative or to learn things from work), *altruistic rewards* (e.g., helping others, making a contribution to society), and *social rewards* (e.g., working with people you like). Individuals choose jobs based on the relative importance of these various work rewards to them.

Theories of career choice based solely on personality traits or work values have limitations, however. First, interests and abilities are not fixed in young adulthood (Mortimer & Lorence, 1979). They continue to develop and change during the adult years (Johnson, 2001). In fact, work itself changes people in some ways. By working in a job that emphasizes certain personality characteristics, requires certain abilities, or provides particular types of rewards, individuals begin to change their personality, skills, and values. A job that may seem like a bad match during early adulthood may become a better fit over time. For example, a tight job market might lead someone who is not especially interested in social interaction to take a sales position. Over time, the more he or she interacts with potential customers, the more appealing the interpersonal aspects of the job may become. Eventually, that person may come to value having opportunities for social interaction on the job.

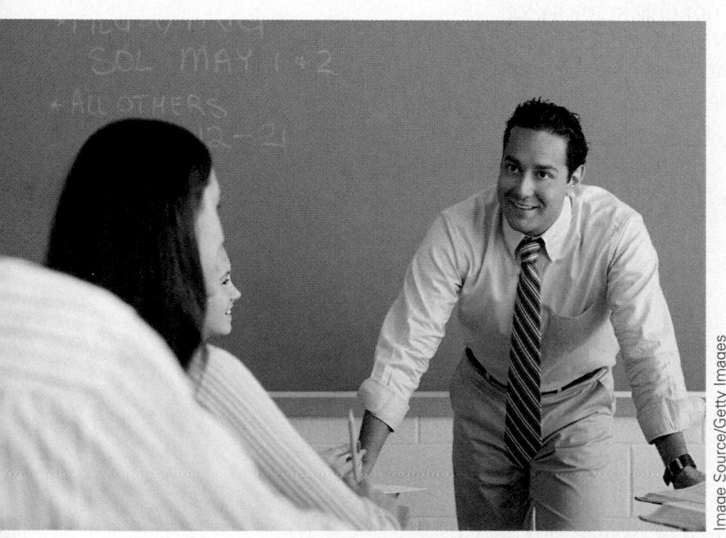

Image Source/Getty Images

Personality characteristics can influence occupational choices. For example, someone who likes helping others might be interested in becoming a teacher.

Another problem with theories of career choice that emphasize personality traits or work values is that they may underestimate the importance of other factors that shape occupational decisions. Many career decisions are influenced as much by individuals' beliefs about the kinds of jobs that are feasible for them as by their interests and preferences (Johnson, 2002). A young man may discover that he is drawn to a career in medicine, but the realization is of little value if he cannot afford the cost of college or medical school. A young woman may take a vocational preference test and learn that she is well suited for work in construction or engineering but find that her parents, friends, or others discourage her from pursuing a "masculine" line of work. Put most simply, career choices are not determined solely on the basis of preferences and personality traits, but, rather, by an interaction of these individual characteristics with other forces. Let's take a look at two of these important forces—socioeconomic status and employment opportunities.

The Role of Socioeconomic Status and Employment Opportunities As is the case with school achievement, a major determinant of occupational choice is socioeconomic status. As a result, the occupational ambitions and achievements of young people resemble those of the people in their lives (Duncan, Featherman, & Duncan, 1972). Young adults with middle-class parents and friends are more likely than less advantaged young adults to aspire to, and eventually enter, middle-class occupations. Socioeconomic status also influences work values, with individuals from middle- and upper-income backgrounds more likely to value intrinsic rewards of work. Young people from disadvantaged economic backgrounds, in contrast, often place more emphasis on extrinsic rewards—income and job security (Johnson, 2002). Low-income youths who were interviewed about their occupational goals in one study reported that they had received a clear message from their families that work had one primary goal: to earn money (Chaves et al., 2004). Social class influences what people look for in their jobs from adolescence through adulthood (Johnson, 2002).

An important aspect of the broader social environment also influences young adults' occupational aspirations: the nature of the employment opportunities they encounter as they venture into the workforce. Students are often very aware of the prospects for employment in different fields by the time they reach the end of their formal schooling. One study of inner-city youth found that many had developed strong ideas about their future job prospects even by the time they were in second grade (Cook, Church, Ajanaku, Shadish, Kim, & Cohen, 1996). Young people in such circumstances often tailor their plans in response to opportunities presented by the labor market and the acceptability of particular occupational choices within their community.

The Transition into the Workforce

So far we have discussed how occupational choices and aspirations develop, but what about the actual transition to full-time employment? As you learned in the previous chapter, this transition now takes longer for many people, as jobs increasingly require higher education and advanced training. How does the transition into adult work roles unfold?

Stage Models Stage models of career development describe this transition as a step in the process by which people explore and ultimately establish themselves in careers they will pursue throughout their work lives. An early and influential stage model, developed by Donald Super and his colleagues over a 40-year period (Savickas, 2001; Super, 1957, 1992; Super, Savickas, & Super, 1996), proposed that career development unfolds across the lifespan in five stages, as shown in Table 14.3. According to Super's model, adolescence and early adulthood are times when people explore, and ultimately crystallize, their occupational interests and goals. They also learn about and "try out" different types of work before settling on a career and obtaining the necessary education and training to pursue it. In middle adulthood, according to Super, people work on maintaining and enhancing their careers. In later adulthood, people prepare to disengage from, and eventually exit, the workforce.

This model helps us understand how people discover their occupational interests and then establish themselves in careers. Questions exist, however, about how well it

TABLE 14.3 Super's Lifespan Model of Career Development

STAGE	AGE	KEY TASKS AND ACTIVITIES
Growth	4–14	Developing a self-concept, interests, and attitudes; forming a general understanding of what it means to work
Exploration	15–24	Trying out and exploring occupational interests and possibilities; implementing a tentative occupational choice
Establishment	25–44	Settling into an occupation; building skills and experience to solidify one's position
Maintenance	45–64	Continuing to acquire skills and knowledge to preserve and improve one's position
Decline	65 and older	Beginning gradual disengagement from work; planning for retirement

Source: Adapted from Super, D. E. (1957). *Psychology of careers*. New York: Harper.

applies to the career development of women and ethnic minorities in the United States and to people in other cultures. Career opportunities and barriers—not just personal interests, skills, and knowledge—may influence how careers unfold (Fouad, 2007; Leong & Serafica, 2001). Family responsibilities, for example, often affect women's work lives, leading their career development to follow a different timetable and sequence of steps than men's career development (Sullivan, 1999). In addition, career development is not always as orderly and linear as Super's stage model implies. Super (1984, 1992) himself acknowledged that people sometimes "recycle" through the phases of exploration, establishment, and maintenance when they change career directions. As we discuss later, many people today are starting to experience less linear, orderly career paths because the world of work itself is changing.

The Transition from School to Full-Time Work Many young adults attend college before entering the workforce full-time. The transition from school to work can be somewhat bumpy for several reasons. First, young people often have unrealistic and overly optimistic ideas about the rewards they will derive from their future work. The sad truth is that many aspire to levels of work rewards they are unlikely to attain (Reynolds, Stewart, MacDonald, & Sischo, 2006; Schneider & Stevenson, 1999). Young adults tend to rate almost all work rewards very highly, optimistically believing that they can find jobs that satisfy multiple needs simultaneously. When they actually enter their first full-time adult jobs, though, they soon discover that it is very difficult to have a career in which one makes a lot of money, is creative, helps other people, enjoys job security, and has a lot of free time. Over the course of young adulthood, people become somewhat disillusioned, but also more focused and pragmatic, about what they want from a job, abandoning the unrealistic notion that one can "have it all" (Roberts, O'Donnell, & Robins, 2004).

In addition, the system of higher education in the Unites States, unlike some European countries, is not geared specifically toward preparing young people to enter the workforce. Germany provides an interesting comparison (Kerckhoff, 2003). The purpose of higher education in Germany is seen as preparing students for the workforce, whereas the purpose of higher education in the United States is seen as preparing students for adult life. The German system emphasizes vocational education and credentials; students typically complete a 3- to 4-year apprenticeship that prepares them for a specific occupation. The U.S. system, in contrast, emphasizes a strong general education and provides credentials that tend to be academic rather than vocational. Although many U.S. students work while they attend college, they usually do so in provisional jobs, rather than jobs that prepare them for their future careers. The transition from school to work for German students is highly structured and predictable—they usually know what job they will hold and whom they will work for when they leave school. This transition is far less structured and predictable for U.S. students—they must navigate their way into available jobs largely on their own and with vague knowledge of what employers desire in prospective employees (Kerckhoff, 2003).

For all of these reasons, in the United States, young adults' initial experiences in the workforce after leaving school are often disappointing. They may need to try different jobs or return to school for more education before they finally identify an occupation that provides a satisfactory fit with their interests and skills (Kerckhoff, 2003). For most, job satisfaction increases as they pare back unrealistic aspirations to match the realities of the workplace (Gottfredson, 1996; Johnson, 2001). In addition, with more job experience, young adults often gain confidence in their abilities and develop specific skills that are valued by their employers. As you learned in the previous chapter, cognitive development in young adulthood often increases tolerance for uncertainty, which helps young adults deal with some of the inevitable ambiguities and uncertainties of the workplace. These psychological adjustments, together with increased job confidence and competence, help many young adults settle into adult work roles.

There is an important exception to this pattern, however. If valued job rewards are unattainable because an employer is unfair or discriminatory, job dissatisfaction is likely to increase (Johnson, 2001). This is particularly true for individuals who are likely to experience discrimination in the workforce, such as women and members of minority groups.

The Changing Nature of Work

The world of work is changing in the United States and elsewhere, and this change may affect how young adults prepare for their work lives and how their work lives unfold over time. As recently as 20 to 30 years ago, it was common for workers to stay with one or two employers for the bulk of their work lives and for employers to make a similar long-term commitment to their employees. This **lifetime employment model** is becoming rare (Settersten, 2003). The increasingly competitive global economy creates pressures for employers to downsize their workforce or to outsource jobs to lower-paid workers in other countries.

lifetime employment model A model of employment common in the past in which people worked for one or two employers for the bulk of their work lives, and employers made a similar long-term commitment to their employees.

Rapidly changing technologies can also cause workers' job skills to become obsolete (Sullivan, 1999), threatening job security. The types of jobs available to Americans are changing as well. Jobs in manufacturing have become scarce; employment opportunities increasingly are concentrated in the service and retail sectors of the economy (see Figure 14.6). A college education and specialized training are often needed to compete for these positions. This puts young adults who do not obtain a college degree at a distinct disadvantage. Union jobs offering good salaries and benefits (for example, in the auto or steel industries) were once an option for people with less education, but that is far less true today (Hall & Mivris, 1996; Sullivan, 1999). Auto workers were among those hardest hit by job layoffs during the economic downturn that began in 2007. General Motors alone cut more than half of its factory workforce from 2006 to early 2009 (Kim, 2009).

What do these changes mean for young adults who are entering the workforce? Young adults need to be prepared for the possibility that they may have multiple employers, may need to change their lines of work, and may need to obtain additional education or training at various points in their lives to be competitive. Diverse skills and flexibility, as well as the ability to manage time pressures, will be needed to adapt to the contemporary labor market (Brandstadter & Rothermund, 2003). Here is something to consider: although it is often criticized for not being sufficiently career-oriented, the U.S. system of higher education, which helps students acquire a broad education and a diverse set of competencies rather than specific vocational training, actually may offer advantages to young adults who will need to be adaptable in a changing labor market.

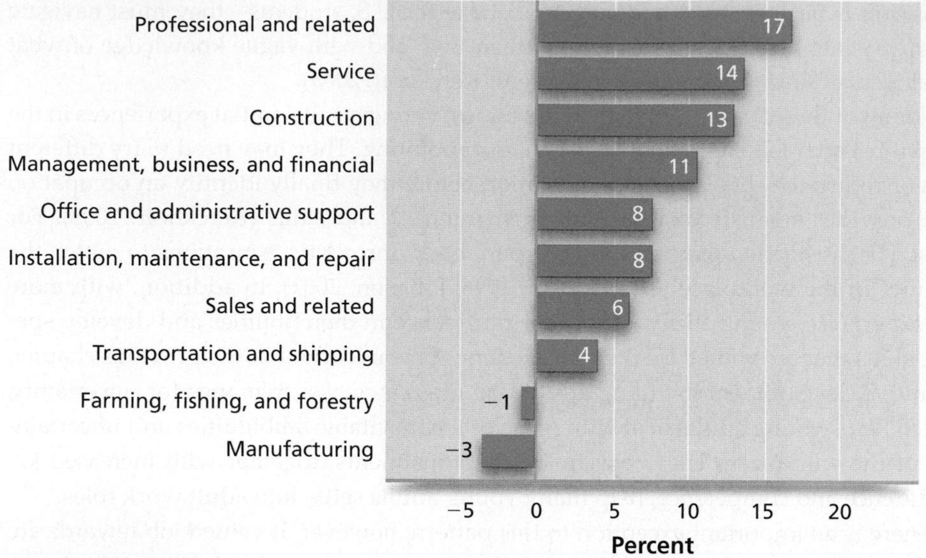

FIGURE 14.6

Projected Percent Change in Total Employment for Different Occupational Groups, 2008-18

Source: Bureau of Labor Statistics, *Occupational Outlook Handbook, 2010–11 Edition.* Retrieved January 7, 2010 from *http://www.bls.gov/oco/oco2003.htm#occupation* (see Chart 6)

Challenges Facing Dual-Earner Families: Combining Work and Family

As young adults make efforts to establish themselves in adult work roles, they are often adjusting to other new roles at the same time, such as the roles of spouse and parent. The vast majority of children in the United States live in families in which both parents work. Combining work and family can have advantages, but it can also present unique challenges.

Work gives parents the income needed to support a family, and it can also contribute to a more equal relationship between the spouses (Barnett, 1999). Yet role strain is also common as parents juggle work and family responsibilities, particularly when parents experience pressures at work (Crouter, Bumpus, Maguire, & McHale, 1999). Working mothers typically shoulder a greater share of the household and childcare tasks (Batalova & Cohen, 2002) and so are more likely than working fathers to experience stress. Role strain is even greater among low-income working mothers because they are less able to afford child care and less likely to work in settings that offer family-friendly work policies.

Perceptions of the fairness or unfairness of the division of labor between two spouses affects their marital satisfaction. If working mothers perceive the division of labor with the spouse to be fair, even if they spend more time on childcare and housework, they are less apt to feel resentful (Impett & Peplau, 2006). The perceived fairness of the division of labor is particularly important to women who have egalitarian rather than traditional sex-role attitudes (Greenstein, 1996). The attitudes of young men as well as young women have become more egalitarian in recent decades, as indicated in surveys of high-school seniors, college students, and working adults. The shift has been especially noticeable among men. For example, 77 percent of men surveyed in 1977 felt that the appropriate role for women was to take care of the home and children, whereas only 43 percent of men felt this way in 2002 (Bond, Thompson, Galinsky, & Protas, 2003). Both men and women today express strong support for family-friendly policies in the workplace (Barnett, 2004).

Family-friendly policies and programs that reduce the burdens on working parents include paid childbearing leave, flexible work hours, time off to care for sick children, opportunities to work from home, job sharing, affordable child-care facilities, and afterschool programs for children. Having such options reduces role strain and stress-related illnesses among working parents (Halpern, 2005). Employers derive benefit, too, from family-friendly work policies, including greater employee productivity and job satisfaction, lower employee turnover and absenteeism, and reduced employee recruitment and training costs (Halpern, 2005; Kossek & Distelberg, 2009; Swody & Powell, 2007). These programs are not for women only. Both men and women have capacities for nurturance and achievement, and supportive workplace programs help both men and women to pursue their goals as partners, parents, and workers, without sacrificing one role for the other (Barnett, 2004). (For a summary of this section, see "Interim Summary 14.4: Entering the Workforce.")

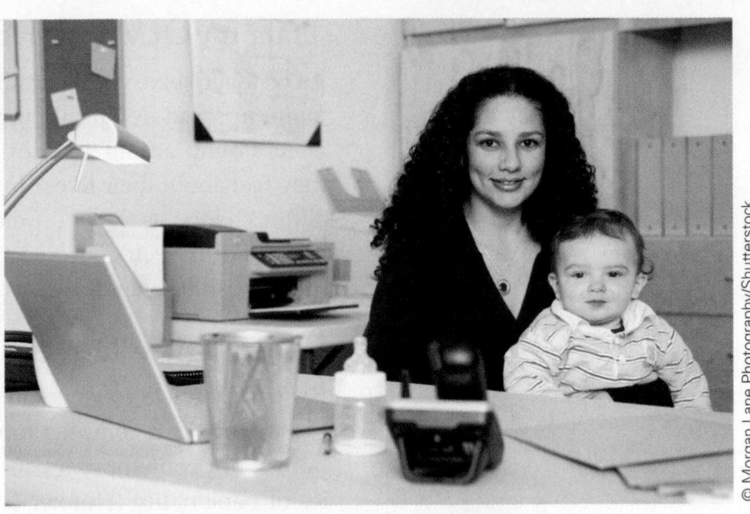

Family-friendly work policies, such as employer-sponsored day care, help workers manage job and family responsibilities.

INTERIM SUMMARY 14.4

Entering the Workforce

	■ Work is not only a source of *income*, but also a source of *identity* for many young adults. ■ Work can affect young adults' health and well-being and can be an important context for development and growth.
Occupational Choices and Aspirations	■ Theories that address why people enter different occupations have examined the role of *personality traits* and *work values* in career selection. These theories have limitations, however, as interests, abilities, and aptitudes are not fixed in young adulthood. ■ Another problem is that the theories may underestimate the importance of such factors as socioeconomic status and employment opportunities.
The Transition into the Workforce	■ Stage models of career development describe the transition into the workforce as one of a series of stages by which people explore and establish themselves in careers. ■ For most young adults, job satisfaction increases as they gain confidence and skills and as they adapt unrealistic aspirations to match the realities of the workplace.
The Changing Nature of Work	■ The nature of work is changing in the United States, with the **lifetime employment model** becoming rare, global competition increasing, and technology affecting jobs. The changes may affect young adults' preparation for work and the course of their work lives.
Challenges Facing Dual-Earner Families: Combining Work and Family	■ As young adults establish themselves in work roles, they are also often juggling family responsibilities, particularly when both parents work. ■ Working mothers typically shoulder a greater share of the household and childcare tasks. However, attitudes toward division of labor have become more egalitarian in recent decades. ■ Family-friendly policies that reduce the burdens on working parents reduce their role strain and improve their productivity.

THE EVOLVING PERSON IN YOUNG ADULTHOOD

As we have seen, young adulthood is a time of major life changes and transitions, with many ups and downs along the increasingly lengthy journey. How do these changes affect young adults' interior lives—who they are becoming as individuals and how they feel about their lives? In this section, we examine whether young adults' personalities change as they assume adult roles and responsibilities. We also examine how young adults' self-concepts and emotional health fare during the tumultuous process of establishing themselves as adults.

Personality Development

Personality refers to a person's characteristic ways of thinking, feeling, and behaving. Personality is a complex topic that has been studied from many different vantage points, but contemporary researchers distinguish between the structure and dynamics of personality (Hooker & McAdams, 2005; Staudinger, Freund, Linden, & Maas, 1999). *Structure* refers to the content and organization of personality, and it is reflected in individuals' key **personality traits**, or the behavioral dispositions they exhibit across many different situations. When you describe someone's personality, you very likely refer to traits. You might describe a friend as hotheaded, for example, meaning that he is quick to anger in many situations. You might describe another friend as shy because you see her as hesitant in many social settings. Personality traits are similar, then, to temperament in childhood. The *dynamics* of personality, in contrast, refer to the characteristic ways that people adapt to the challenges they encounter in the course of their lives; these are captured in **self-regulatory capacities**, or the ways that people manage their emotions, evaluate and adjust their behavior, and cope with stress and other challenges.

personality traits The behavioral dispositions a person exhibits across many different situations.

self-regulatory capacities The ways that people manage their emotions, evaluate and adjust their behavior, and cope with stress and other challenges.

Whether personality remains stable or changes over the lifespan is a hotly debated topic, and we will take a close look at that debate in Chapter 16, when we discuss socioemotional development in middle adulthood. A good deal of evidence suggests that personality is quite stable over time. Yet against this general backdrop of stability, evidence of change can also be found, and some important changes occur in young adulthood, as we discuss next.

Personality Traits Longitudinal studies of personality indicate that people tend to become more conscientious, agreeable, and socially dominant during young adulthood, with some of these gains extending into middle and later adulthood (see Figure 14.7; Roberts, Walton, & Viechtbauer, 2006; Srivastava, John, Gosling, & Potter, 2003). Not all young adults show such changes, however, and whether they do depends on their experiences in taking on such roles as spouse, parent, and worker. Research that has examined the link between work experiences and personality development provides an illustration. A study that tracked young adults from age 18 to 26 found that those whose work led to greater financial security, greater job satisfaction, and more objective job successes (e.g., higher earnings, more job prestige, greater authority on the job) became more emotionally stable, happier, and more committed to the work role. In contrast, young adults who by age 26 were struggling to pay their bills, had not found satisfying work, and experienced fewer objective job successes were less emotionally stable, less happy, and less committed to the work role (Roberts, Caspi, & Moffit, 2003). This study also revealed that participants' personality traits as adolescents predicted their futurework experiences. Those who were more alienated and hostile as adolescents encountered more problems in their efforts to enter the adult world of work, and those problems reinforced their negativity (Roberts et al., 2003).

These findings underscore that development is a reciprocal process, as we discussed in Chapter 1: characteristics of individuals influence the contexts in which they conduct their lives, and these contexts in turn influence their development. The major life

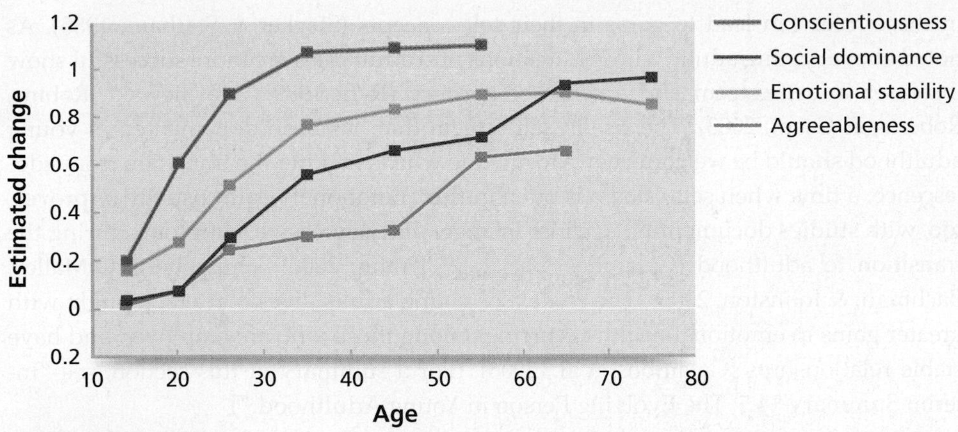

FIGURE 14.7

Changes in Personality Traits in Adulthood

The estimates are based on a meta-analysis of many studies, and fewer studies assessed social dominance and agreeableness in oder adults. The patterns shown, therefore, reflect the best estimates of age-related change in these traits based on existing data.

Source: Adapted from Roberts, B. W., Walton, K. E., & Viechtbauer, W. (2006). Patterns of mean-level change in personality traits across the life course: A meta-analysis of longitudinal studies. *Psychological Bulletin, 132*(1), 1–25.

transitions that are common in young adulthood—establishing intimate relationships, launching families, and settling into the workforce—are influenced by existing personality traits, and these traits, in turn, are deepened by experiences in these important roles (Caspi, Roberts, & Shiner, 2005; Helson & Kwan, 2000; Roberts et al., 2003). In many respects, we become more like ourselves as we age.

Self-Regulatory Capacities Young adulthood is a time when one's abilities to meet the demands of competing roles, to manage emotions, and to cope with stress are put to the test. Perhaps you know this from personal experience. Do self-regulatory capacities evolve from adolescence to young adulthood? This is a relatively new area of research, but here, too, the findings generally point to gains. During young adulthood, people generally become better at controlling impulses and strong emotions, using cognitive strategies to cope with stress or solve problems, and initiating efforts to pursue important goals (Consedine & Magai, 2006; Skinner & Zimmer-Gembeck, 2006; Steinberg, 2005).

These self-regulatory capacities do not necessarily peak in young adulthood, however; some continue to evolve in middle and later adulthood. Other capacities, such as the ability to coordinate different life goals and to deal with setbacks, do not appear to be well developed until relatively late in young adulthood or beyond (Riediger, Freund, & Baltes, 2005; Wrosch, Scheier, Carver, & Schulz, 2003). In one study, young adults who were able to relinquish unattainable goals and redirect their energies toward more realistic goals were better adjusted than young adults who could not let go of the unattainable goals. Yet young adults in this study were less skilled than older adults at modifying their goals (Wrosch et al., 2003). As you'll see in later chapters, older adults are more often faced with the need to scale back or relinquish goals when their physical capacities or other resources decline.

Self-Concept and Emotional Health

What do the changes discussed above imply for self-concept and emotional health in young adulthood? People form their self-concepts, in part, from the feedback they receive from others about their performance in key social roles, and positive experiences in these roles can lead to gains in their self-concepts (Stryker & Statham, 1985). As noted above, young adults whose transitions into adult roles are more successful show increases in self-esteem and a sense of mastery (Ryff, 1989; Trzesniewski, Robins, Roberts, & Caspi, 2003). The rise in self-esteem that has been documented in young adulthood should be welcome news to anyone who is making the transition from adolescence, a time when self-esteem is often in flux. Emotional health usually improves, too, with studies documenting declines in anger and depressive symptoms during the transition to adulthood (Galambos, Barker, & Krahn, 2006; Schulenberg, O'Malley, Bachman, & Johnston, 2005). The context of young adults' lives matters, though, with greater gains in emotional health occurring among those who are employed and have stable relationships (Galambos et al., 2006). (For a summary of this section, see "Interim Summary 14.5: The Evolving Person in Young Adulthood.")

INTERIM SUMMARY 14.5

The Evolving Person in Young Adulthood

Personality Development	■ Personality is studied in terms of both structure and dynamics. *Structure* refers to the content and organization of personality; it is reflected in **personality traits**. The *dynamics* of personality refer to the characteristic ways that people adapt to the challenges they encounter in their lives; these are captured in **self-regulatory capacities**. ■ Longitudinal studies of personality indicate that people tend to become more conscientious, agreeable, and socially dominant during young adulthood. ■ The major life transitions common in young adulthood are influenced by existing personality traits, and these traits are deepened by experiences in these roles. ■ Self-regulatory capacities evolve in young adulthood. Gains can be seen in the ability to control impulses and strong emotions, to use cognitive strategies to cope or solve problems, and to initiate efforts to pursue goals.
Self-Concept and Emotional Health	■ Self-esteem and emotional health tend to increase in young adulthood, particularly for young adults whose transitions into adult roles are more successful.

SUMMING UP AND LOOKING AHEAD

As we have seen repeatedly, development is shaped by the historical and social contexts in which it occurs. Today the transition to adulthood is taking longer than it once did, and is less rigidly structured by social norms and timetables than was once the case, giving young people more freedom, but also more responsibility, to direct the course of their own development. Finding love, making a commitment to a partner, becoming a parent, and settling into an occupation are achievements but also challenges. In different ways, these major changes all require young adults to give up unrealistic expectations and adjust to realities. Some young adults fare well during this process, but others—saddled by long-standing personal limitations, limited opportunities in the environment, or both—fare less well.

The life paths that take shape in young adulthood are not set in stone, but they define the key contexts in which experiences in midlife unfold, as we explore in the next two chapters. We begin that exploration by examining how physical and cognitive capacities develop in middle adulthood.

HERE'S WHAT YOU SHOULD KNOW

Did You Get It?

After reading this chapter, you should understand the following:

- The developmental tasks and timetables of young adulthood
- The three processes of developmental regulation and how they affect young adults
- The key roles friendships and love relationships play in the lives of young adults
- Attachment styles and how they influence intimate relationships
- Factors affecting young adults' decision to get married and divorced
- Factors affecting marital satisfaction in young adulthood
- How launching a family affects young adults
- The work challenges and transitions facing young adults
- How personality and self-concept develops in young adults

Important Terms and Concepts

age-irrelevant society (p. 440)
attachment styles (p. 447)
cohabiting (p. 450)
compensation (p. 440)
developmental tasks (p. 437)
emotional loneliness (p. 448)
intimacy versus isolation (p. 438)
lifetime employment model (p. 461)
off time (p. 439)
on time (p. 439)
optimization (p. 440)
personality traits (p. 464)
selection (p. 440)
self-regulatory capacities (p. 464)
social clock (p. 439)
social loneliness (p. 448)
stress-crossover effect (p. 452)
theory of selective optimization with compensation (p. 440)
triangular theory of love (p. 444)
vulnerability-stress-adaptation model of marriage (p. 452)

Part VI Review

CHAPTER 13

Physical and Cognitive Development in Young Adulthood

- Development in adulthood involves not only *growth* but also *maintaining stability* and *adapting to declines and losses.* Adulthood is often divided into young adulthood, middle adulthood, and later adulthood. Development in each period builds upon experiences and capacities established in earlier periods and affects development in subsequent periods.
- Conceptions of adulthood vary, but most emphasize the idea that to be an adult requires a person to become self-sufficient.
- For most people, young adulthood is a time of peak physical functioning, although small signs of *senescence*, or normal aging, begin to appear at this time. *Homeostasis* also begins to become slightly slower and less efficient.
- Most young adults are sexually active, and attitudes toward sex become more open-minded in young adulthood. Reproductive capacity is also at its peak in young adulthood.
- Cognitive development continues in young adulthood, with the emergence of a new mode of thought, referred to as **postformal thought. Reflective judgment** is an aspect of this new way of thinking. These gains in cognitive development are associated with gains in problem-solving skills. **Moral development** also continues in young adulthood, as the capacity for moral reasoning increases.
- Higher education, complex work, and experiences in close relationships can all contribute to cognitive and moral development in young adulthood.

CHAPTER 14

Socioemotional Development in Young Adulthood

- The **developmental tasks** of young adulthood involve initiating adult roles—making a commitment to a partner, launching a family, beginning a career, and becoming involved in one's community. Successful adult development, according to the **theory of selective optimization with compensation,** depends on **selection** (choosing manageable life goals), **optimization** (using and enhancing one's resources to pursue goals), and **compensation** (developing other strategies to pursue goals when resources decline).
- During young adulthood, people continue to forge their social networks, establishing relationships with a primary partner, new friends, and their own nuclear family.
- The transition to parenthood often occurs in young adulthood and marks a change not only in the life of each spouse but also in their life together.
- Work can affect young adults' health and well-being and can be an important context for development and growth.
- The major life transitions that are common in young adulthood are influenced by existing personality traits, and these traits are deepened by experiences in these roles. In young adulthood, gains are often seen in **self-regulatory capacities,** including the ability to control impulses and strong emotions, to use cognitive strategies to solve problems, and to initiate efforts to pursue goals.

part seven

Middle Adulthood

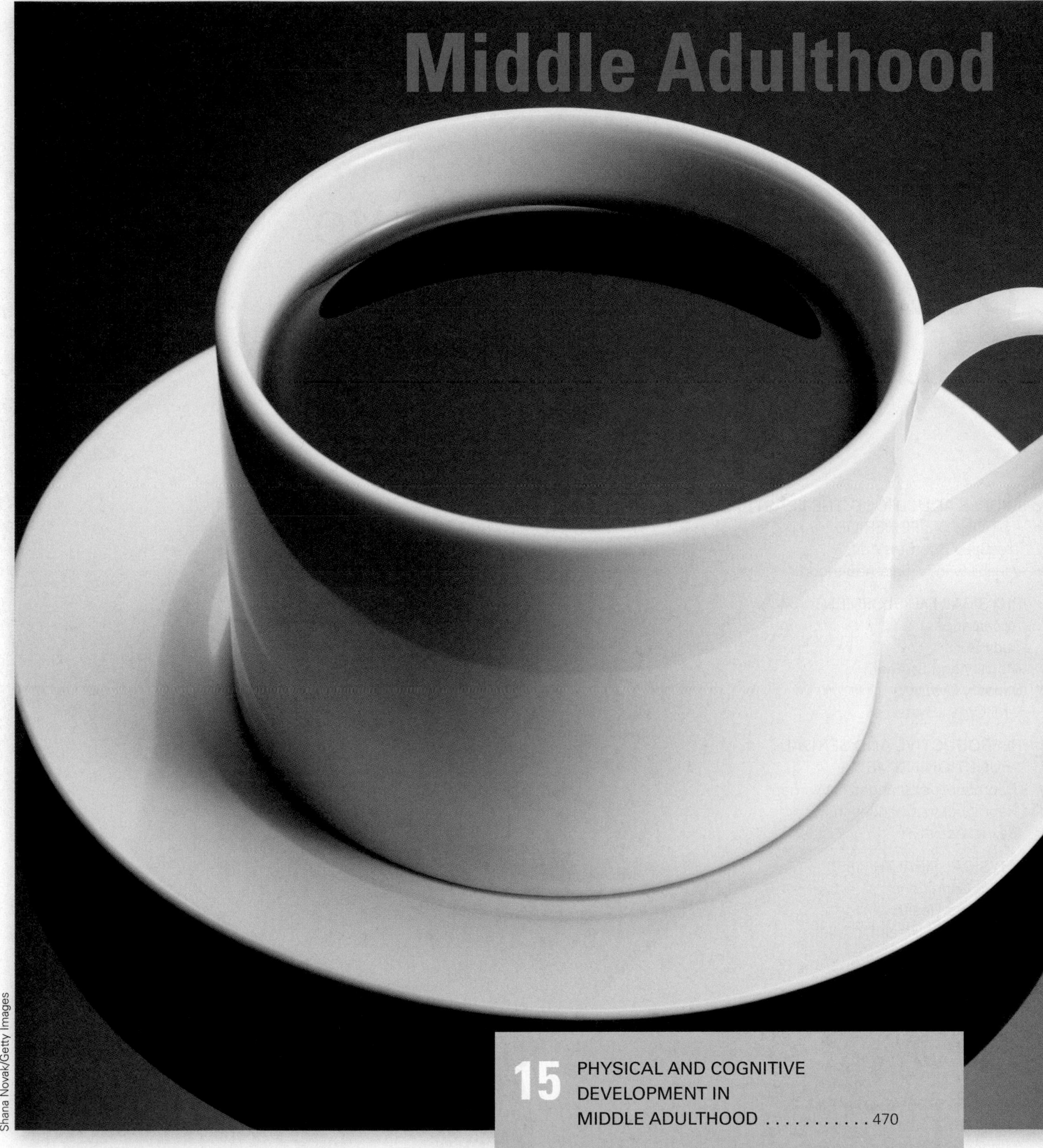

Shana Novak/Getty Images

CHAPTER 15

Physical and Cognitive Development in Middle Adulthood

Blue Jean Images/Alamy

What comes to mind when you think about middle-aged adults? You may conjure up images of people doggedly battling their gray or thinning hair, or waging determined—but not entirely successful—campaigns against expanding waistlines. So perhaps self-consciousness about signs of aging is a distinctive feature of middle adulthood. Or you may think about people who rise more slowly from their chairs than they once did or whose conversations are increasingly peppered with health tidbits and advice. So perhaps physical challenges and health concerns are distinctive features of midlife. What else comes to mind? Do you suppose that middle-aged adults face unique developmental tasks and experience life transitions as dramatic as those of young adulthood? If you found the last question harder to answer, you're not alone. Middle adulthood is a somewhat murkier life period than those we have discussed so far because it has received less attention from developmental researchers.

When does a person enter middle adulthood? This question is not so easy to answer. Common life events help to mark the transitions to young adulthood (such as marrying or getting a first job) and older adulthood (such as retiring from the workforce), but few life events mark the transition to middle adulthood. Even researchers differ in how they define middle adulthood. Some define it as the age range 40 to 60, but others define it as the age range 40 to 65 (as we do), and still others suggest lower (e.g., 35) or higher age boundaries (e.g., 70). Given the fuzziness of the boundaries that define middle adulthood, it is not surprising that the age at which people consider themselves to be middle-aged is highly variable (Lachman, 2004). If people remain healthy and active into their 60s and 70s, they may continue to see themselves as middle-aged. In fact, nearly half of the people ages 65 to 74 and one-quarter of those age 75 and older defined themselves as middle-aged in one study (Cutler, Whitelaw, & Beattie, 2002). And middle-aged and older adults tend to feel about 10 years younger than they actually are (Montepare & Lachman, 1989). It often takes a decline in health for people to acknowledge their own aging (Lachman, 2004).

The task for developmental scientists is both to find common threads and to explain variations in middle age. This chapter examines physical changes and physical health in midlife as well as intellectual changes and the links between work and intellectual development. A major theme in this chapter is how the times in which people are born and grow into adulthood influence their development. In the next chapter we will turn to socioemotional development in midlife.

MIDDLE ADULTHOOD: THE LEAST STUDIED LIFE PERIOD

Orville Brim, a sociologist who studied adult development, once described midlife as the "last uncharted territory in human development" (1992, p. 171). Until fairly recently, middle adulthood was rarely the subject of scientific attention. But that is beginning to change. Can you guess why? If you suspect that it has something to do with the Baby Boom generation, you are correct. This is the largest generation ever to reach middle age in Western society (Whitbourne & Willis, 2006), and it has provided a significant impetus to the study of this important life period.

The Baby Boomers

Baby Boom generation The generation born between 1946 and 1964, which resulted from an 18-year surge in birth rates that began after World War II.

The **Baby Boom generation** is the result of an 18-year "splurge of births" after World War II—specifically, from 1946 to 1964 (Eggebeen & Sturgeon, 2006; Lachman, 2004). Birthrates had been declining steadily for several decades before the 1940s. But the postwar period was a time of economic growth and prosperity, and after the hardships and dislocations of the war, people were eager to get on with their lives. As a result, couples married in record numbers and at younger ages, and they had children sooner and had more of them (Eggebeen & Sturgeon, 2006). The huge Baby Boom cohort began to emerge—a boon for diaper manufacturers and toymakers and, later, a decades-long project for researchers and marketers who sought to chart the Boomers' development over time and to cater to their consumer impulses. Today, all the Baby Boomers have reached middle age, and some are on the brink of old age. They currently make up about one-third of the U.S. population (Whitbourne & Willis, 2006).

Interest in tracking the Baby Boomers' progress from young to middle adulthood has helped to expand our knowledge about development in midlife. We have to bear in mind, though, that the midlife experiences of the Baby Boomers are unlikely to mirror those of past or future cohorts of middle-aged adults. As you learned in Chapter 1, a **cohort** refers to a group of people who were born at roughly the same time. A cohort is very similar to a generation. The main difference is that members of a generation share an identity (Alwin, McCammon, & Hofer, 2006)—for example, being a member of the "Greatest Generation" (Americans born in the first quarter of the 20th century who fought in World War II or contributed to the war effort on the home front) or "Generation X" (Americans born from the mid-1960s to the early 1980s). Because the terms *cohort* and *generation* have similar meanings, we use them interchangeably. As the members of a cohort grow up, they are likely to be affected by many of the same pivotal historical and social events. **Cohort effects** refer to the impact of such events on an individual's development. Let's examine this idea more closely.

cohort A group of people born at roughly the same time.

cohort effects The impact of pivotal historical and sociocultural events on an individual's development.

If you are in your early 20s, you and the members of your generation will grow up experiencing the same major historical and social events, and these events will differ from those your parents or grandparents experienced when they were growing up. Televisions were just being introduced into U.S. homes when many of today's middle-aged adults were children, and personal computers and the Internet had yet to be invented when they were in high school. Sophisticated technology has very likely been part of your life from a young age and may continue to influence your development in distinctive ways. Some of your parents, when they were young adults, lived through the assassination and resignation of presidents, as well as the tumultuous Civil Rights and feminist movements of the 1960s and 1970s. Events such as these may have influenced not only their attitudes, political views, and outlook on life, but also their educational and employment opportunities. Different historical and social events will affect the lives of members of your cohort and the cohorts that come behind you.

Even the *size* of a generation may affect the life prospects of its members. Members of very large generations—like the Baby Boomers—experience greater competition for jobs, which can contribute to psychological distress and increased crime during difficult economic times (Easterlin, 1987; Piazza & Charles, 2006).

Some aspects of midlife development, then, are universal, such as menopause (the cessation of menstruation), or nearly universal, such as the pursuit of central life goals related to family, friendship, and work. Other aspects of midlife development may vary across cohorts. Compared to earlier cohorts of middle-aged adults, the Baby

© Bettman/Corbis

© Bernd Obermann/Corbis

The historical and social events that shape our lives differ from one cohort to another. What events are shaping the lives of your cohort?

Boomers have enjoyed much greater access to higher education, which may have enhanced their cognitive development and life prospects. Future middle-aged cohorts may experience better health, as possible medical breakthroughs improve our control of chronic diseases, or worse health, as the current epidemic of obesity unfolds. You can think of aging as unfolding on a moving platform of historical time: some aspects of aging are universal across generations, but other aspects differ across generations, shaped by the unique historical contexts of their lives (Sweet, 2007).

Variability in Middle Adulthood

Development in midlife varies not only *across* cohorts, but also *within* cohorts. Age itself is an important source of variability within a cohort of middle-aged adults. Middle adulthood spans a period of 25 years (from age 40 to 65), and the health and well-being, life goals, and social roles of people in their early 40s differ in important respects from those of people in their late 50s or early 60s. (When you were in your teens, you surely would have found it odd to be grouped together with 5-year-olds in discussions of "young people"!) Developmental researchers have not yet distinguished systematically between younger and older middle-aged adults, but we will point out from time to time when particular conclusions apply more to the younger group than the older group, and vice versa.

Gender, race, and socioeconomic status also contribute to variability in development in midlife, and this chapter explores the effects of some of these factors as well. In

interindividual variability Variability between individuals in the ways that various aspects of development unfold.

intraindividual variability Variability within a person in the ways that various aspects of development unfold.

addition, development across the lifespan is *cumulative:* as the effects of the myriad life choices and paths that people pursue begin to accumulate over time, individuals become increasingly different from each other (Lachman, 2004). **Interindividual variability** (variability between individuals) increases, then, from young adulthood to middle adulthood.

Considerable in*tra*individual variability also exists in middle adulthood. **Intraindividual variability** refers to variability *within* a person in the ways that various aspects of development unfold. Different bodily systems and functions may change at different rates over time. A middle-aged man in his late 50s may have lost much of his hair and may now need glasses to read, yet he may remain a fierce competitor on the tennis court and may be more productive than ever at work. His development in midlife is characterized by intraindividual variability. This example also illustrates that developmental gains as well as losses can occur in middle adulthood. Although the ratio of developmental gains and losses begins to shift gradually in middle adulthood, with losses becoming more common, gains still occur. We will see examples of such developmental gains in this chapter and in the next chapter. (For a summary of this section, see "Interim Summary 15.1: Middle Adulthood: The Least Studied Life Period.")

INTERIM SUMMARY 15.1

Middle Adulthood: The Least Studied Life Period

The Baby Boomers	■ The **Baby Boom generation** is the result of the U.S. population explosion between 1946 and 1964. Today, Baby Boomers have reached middle age or are on the brink of old age. ■ Some aspects of midlife development are universal, such as menopause, or nearly universal, such as the pursuit of central life goals. Other aspects of midlife development vary across **cohorts**. **Cohort effects** refer to the impact of pivotal historical and societal events on development.
Variability in Middle Adulthood	■ Development in midlife also varies *within* cohorts. Middle adulthood spans a period of 25 years (from ages 40 to 65), and the health, goals, and roles of people in their early 40s differ from those in their late 50s or early 60s. ■ Gender, race, and socioeconomic status also contribute to variability in midlife development. ■ Development across the lifespan is *cumulative:* as the effects of life choices accumulate, individuals become increasingly different from each other. **Interindividual variability** (variability between individuals) increases from young adulthood to middle adulthood. ■ Considerable **intraindividual variability** also exists in middle adulthood and refers to variability *within* a person in the ways that various aspects of development unfold.

PHYSICAL DEVELOPMENT

Imagine the many tasks the body has to perform. Even as you are reading this page, your senses are busy perceiving information in the environment, and your brain is deciding which information should be retained (e.g., the material in this chapter) and which information can be ignored (e.g., the sound of a dog barking in the distance). Your muscles, joints, and bones are working together to make movement possible, such as turning a page in this book or getting up for a glass of water. Your lungs are taking in oxygen and removing carbon dioxide, and your heart is pumping blood and distributing oxygen and nutrients throughout your body. Your digestive system may be busy turning your breakfast into fuel for your body, and sending wastes to your excretory system. Your immune system is on the patrol for infections that may be trying to establish themselves in your body, and your endocrine system is controlling other organ systems, telling them whether to speed up or slow down. Your nervous system is integrating all of this information, and sending signals that control other bodily systems and your behavior.

Amazing—and you thought you were just reading! But does the body perform these functions unfailingly over the decades, or do changes become evident as people grow older? As you'll see in this section, changes in appearance, body build, and mobility (the ability to move physically), and in the functioning of the body's systems, occur gradually from young adulthood to middle adulthood. For the most part, these changes are relatively minor. A notable exception is menopause (the cessation of menstruation, and, therefore, a woman's reproductive potential) in midlife. Changes are more noticeable and have more implications for day-to-day functioning and physical health among many people in their 50s and early 60s, compared to people in their 40s.

But not all of the changes we will discuss are inevitable aspects of aging. Some age-related changes do result from inevitable, intrinsic processes of aging—referred to as **primary aging.** Other age-related changes result from the accumulated effects of disease, bodily abuse or disuse, or environmental hazards—referred to as **secondary aging**. Because people often have some control over the causes of secondary aging, such as unsound health practices, they may be able to affect the rate of decline in their physical functioning (Whitbourne, 2001). This chapter explores the common physical changes that occur in middle adulthood as a result of both primary and secondary aging.

primary aging Age-related changes that result from inevitable, intrinsic processes of aging.

secondary aging Age-related changes that result from the accumulated effects of disease, bodily abuse or disuse, or environmental hazards.

Jim Smeal/WireImage/Getty Images

Jon Kopaloff/FilmMagic/Getty Images

Although people age at different rates, by middle adulthood, most people exhibit visible signs of aging.

Appearance

Can you tell just by looking when someone is middle-aged? If you answered this question "Yes," what attributes came to mind? Wrinkles? Bald heads? Bulges here and there? Although people age at different rates, and some people look youthful through their 40s and 50s, aging does eventually leave its mark on our appearance. Hair tends to become gray, and eventually white, as the production of hair pigment (melanin) declines (Merrill & Verbrugge, 1999). Thinning of the hair and hair loss are also common, particularly among men, with over half of men experiencing moderate to extensive hair loss by age 50 (Rhodes et al., 1998). Products to dye gray hair and to combat baldness are big business.

The skin also changes with aging, becoming drier, less elastic, and more prone to wrinkles and sagging. Age spots (small areas of pigmentation in the skin) begin to appear, often caused by repeated sun exposure over the course of a lifetime. Here, too, products abound to address people's concerns about these visible signs of aging. *Botox*, for example, became something of a craze—albeit one with health risks—in the 1990s and early 2000s. Botox is a toxic protein that paralyzes facial muscles when injected, smoothing facial wrinkles, but it has been known to cause difficulty swallowing, weakness, and breathing problems in some people (Food and Drug Administration, 2008).

Body Build

osteoporosis A condition in which bones become brittle and susceptible to fracture.

Height and weight undergo changes as well. People tend to retain the maximum height they reached in young adulthood until their mid- to late 50s, when the loss of bone material in the vertebrae causes the spine to shorten, contributing to a very gradual loss of height. Women lose bone more rapidly than men. As a result, women lose more height as they age, and they are much more vulnerable to **osteoporosis**, a condition in which bones become brittle and susceptible to fractures. Eighty percent of people with osteoporosis are women (National Osteoporosis Foundation, 2007). Caucasian and Asian American women have a greater risk of developing osteoporosis than African American and Hispanic women (Barrett-Connor et al., 2005). Osteoporosis is a particularly serious health threat in later life, when falls become more common and increase the risk of bone fractures, as we discuss in greater detail in Chapter 17.

Osteoporosis is partly determined by genes, but people can reduce their risk for this condition by consuming foods that are high in calcium (such as dairy products, green leafy vegetables, and calcium-enriched cereals and juices), ensuring adequate Vitamin D intake, and engaging in regular exercise. Weight-bearing exercises (such as walking and jogging) and strength and resistance training are especially helpful. Smoking and drinking alcohol, in contrast, tend to accelerate bone loss. Adopting good health practices early in life helps to ensure that one's bones are as strong as possible by the time they reach their peak density in one's 20s or 30s (Gass & Dawson-Hughes, 2006). Maintaining these practices over time helps to slow the rate of bone loss when it begins to increase in midlife (National Osteoporosis Foundation, 2007). If osteoporosis is detected in middle adulthood or later, medication may help slow its progression.

While height begins to decrease gradually in middle adulthood, weight often increases (see Figure 15.1). The percentage of people who are overweight or obese tends to be higher among African Americans and Hispanics than among Caucasians, with the lowest rates found among Asian Americans (Ogden, Yanovski, Carroll, & Flegal, 2007). The amount of body fat tends to increase, often being deposited around the midsection, producing "middle-age spread." Weight gain and increased body fat not only wound middle-aged pride, but also pose a health threat (Jones, Whitbourne, & Skultety, 2006). The risk of stroke among women ages 35 to 54 has tripled in recent years, and some scientists suspect that the rising rate of abdominal obesity among women is the culprit (Towfighi, Saver, Engelhardt, & Ovbiagele, 2007). To reduce the risk of heart disease and stroke, women and men are advised to maintain a waist size no more than 35 and 40 inches, respectively (Weight Control Information Network, 2008).

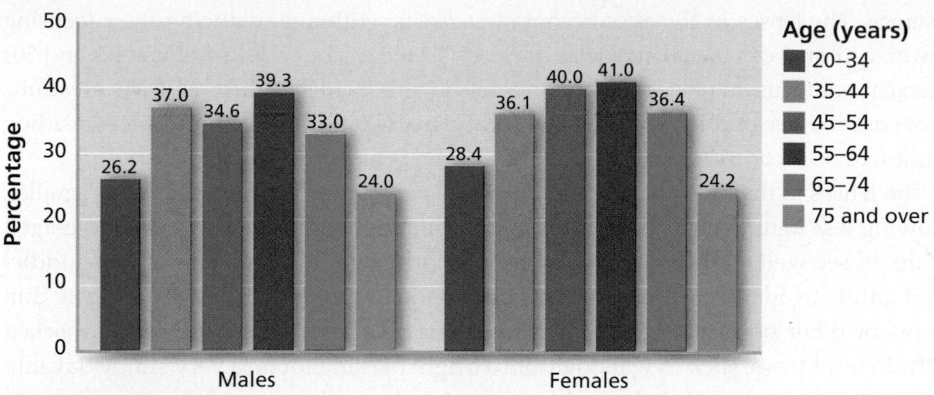

FIGURE 15.1

Prevalence of Obesity by Age and Gender

Note: Obesity is defined as a BMI of 30 or greater.

Source: National Center for Health Statistics. (2009). *Health, United States, 2008.* Hyattsville, MD: National Center for Health Statistics. Retrieved November 30, 2009 from http://www.cdc.gov/nchs/data/hus/hus08.pdf

Being overweight or obese also increases the risk of **metabolic syndrome**, a cluster of risk factors that occur together, including excess abdominal fat, elevated blood pressure, elevated blood sugar, high levels of "bad" cholesterol (**LDL, low-density lipoprotein**), and low levels of "good" cholesterol (**HDL, high-density lipoprotein**) (Eckel, Grundy, & Zimmet, 2005; Grundy, 2008). Metabolic syndrome doubles the risk of heart disease and increases the risk of type 2 diabetes five-fold (Grundy, 2008).

metabolic syndrome A cluster of risk factors that occur together, including excess abdominal fat, elevated blood pressure, elevated blood sugar, high levels of "bad" cholesterol (LDL, low-density lipoprotein), and low levels of "good" cholesterol (HDL, high-density lipoprotein).

low-density lipoprotein (LDL) A type of cholesterol that is considered "bad" because at high levels it increases the buildup of plaque in the arteries, elevating the risk of heart attacks or stroke.

high-density lipoprotein (HDL) A type of cholesterol that is considered "good" because at high levels it appears to reduce the risk of heart attack.

Mobility and Strength

Most of us take for granted being able to move at will. Our musculoskeletal system (which includes our muscles, bones, joints, tendons, and ligaments) makes this possible. Beginning in middle adulthood, though, gradual age-related declines in our musculoskeletal system begin to affect our strength, speed, and mobility. Muscle loss occurs at the rate of 1 to 2 percent per year among people over age 50, causing gradual declines in strength among middle-aged and older adults (Marcell, 2003). This progressive age-related loss of muscle mass and strength is called **sarcopenia**. Strength (or resistance) training helps to reduce sarcopenia, even among elderly individuals (Hunter, McCarthy, & Bamman, 2004).

sarcopenia Progressive, age-related loss of muscle mass and strength.

Joint pain and stiffness become more common as cartilage that protects the joints deteriorates gradually over time. Joint problems are aggravated, moreover, by obesity. As many as 38 percent of Americans ages 45 to 64 report some degree of joint pain or stiffness, compared to 18 percent of those ages 18 to 44 (National Center for Health Statistics, 2009). Flexibility training increases the joints' range of motion, and resistance training helps to strengthen muscles that support the joints (Hunter et al., 2004).

Sensory Systems

The senses become less sharp as people age, with declines in vision and hearing becoming apparent in middle adulthood. Fortunately, most middle-aged adults can adapt to these declines by wearing corrective glasses or hearing aids and by using extra care in environments in which they have difficulty seeing or hearing.

Vision You may have observed middle-aged adults trying to read a newspaper by holding it at arm's length. This is not an eccentric habit that people tend to acquire in midlife! Instead, it is a response to declines in near vision, a common change in eyesight called **presbyopia**. Presbyopia makes it difficult for people to focus on objects at a close

presbyopia A decline in the ability to focus on objects at a close distance.

distance. The lenses in the eyes become less elastic with age, reducing their focusing power. Children can focus on objects as close as 2 inches, but adults in their 40s and 50s often cannot focus on objects within an arm's length (Schieber, 2006). Nearly all adults have some degree of presbyopia by age 50, and many middle-aged adults need reading glasses, bifocals, or trifocals to read or see clearly (Schieber, 2006).

The lenses in the eyes also become less transparent and the pupil becomes smaller, allowing less light to enter the eye and requiring brighter conditions for middle-aged adults to see well (Scheiber, 2006). These changes make it more difficult for middle-aged adults to adapt to shifts from bright to dark environments and to navigate dim rooms or other poorly lit settings. Think about how your vision adjusts to marked shifts in brightness, such as walking from a bright parking lot on a very sunny day into a dimly lit restaurant or movie theater. It may take just a few seconds for your vision to adjust; this process is slower in midlife.

glaucoma A condition that develops when fluid builds up in the eye, putting pressure on the blood vessels that deliver oxygen and nutrients to the optic nerve.

These changes in vision are a normal part of aging (that is, primary aging), but some eye diseases also become more common as people age. **Glaucoma** is a condition that develops when fluid builds up in the eye, putting pressure on the blood vessels that deliver oxygen and nutrients to the optic nerve. If untreated, the blood vessels may break, causing damage to the optic nerve and leading to a loss of peripheral vision, and, eventually, blindness. The fluid buildup occurs either when the eyes produce too much fluid or when the fluid cannot drain properly. More than 2 million adults age 40 and over have glaucoma in the United States. Higher rates are found among African Americans (for reasons not yet known), diabetics, and people with a family history of glaucoma (Friedman, Wilson, Liebmann, Fechtner, & Weinreb, 2004). Fortunately, even though glaucoma has no symptoms in its early stages, it can be detected fairly easily through eye-pressure checks conducted as part of regular eye examinations and can be managed with medication and, as needed, laser surgery (Singh, 2005).

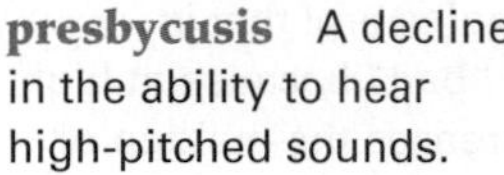

presbycusis A decline in the ability to hear high-pitched sounds.

Hearing Hearing, too, gradually becomes less sharp with age, beginning in middle adulthood. The eardrum becomes less elastic, decreasing its sensitivity to sound. Auditory acuity (the clarity or sharpness of one's hearing) also declines as hair cells, or *cilia*, within the inner ear are lost, because these cells are responsible for transmitting sound vibrations to the brain. The most common form of hearing loss in middle adulthood is **presbycusis**, or a decline in the ability to hear high-pitched sounds (Fozard & Gordon-Salant, 2001). Rates of hearing loss rise steadily with age, as shown in Figure 15.2. Exposure to noise can cause hearing loss, as well. Some young people may be at elevated risk of developing hearing loss later in life as a result of exposure to loud noise through MP3 players, video games, and concerts (Morata, 2007).

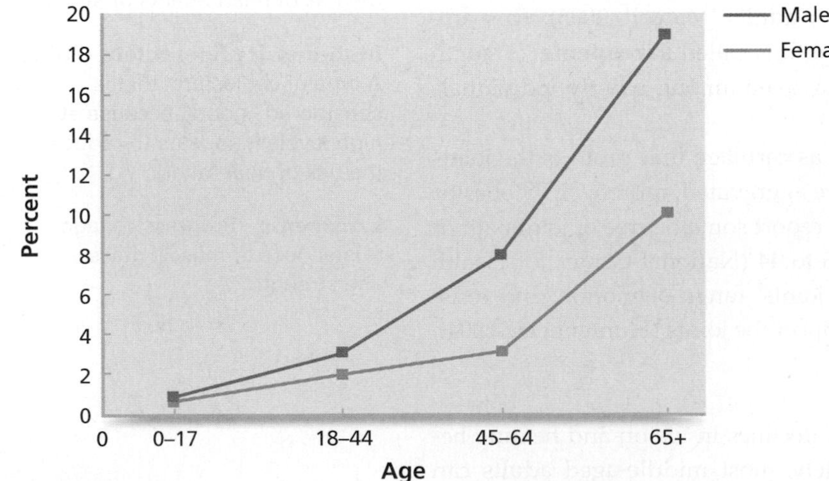

FIGURE 15.2

Prevalence of Hearing Loss by Age

Source: National Academy on an Aging Society. (1999). *Demography is not destiny.* Washington, DC: Author. Retrieved July 7, 2003 from http://www.agingsociety.org/agingsociety/publications/demography/destiny1999.pdf

Vital Organ Systems

By midlife, changes begin to emerge in some of the vital organ systems of the body, including the cardiovascular, respiratory, and urinary systems. These changes reflect both primary and secondary aging, and some—particularly those involving the cardiovascular system—have significant implications for health.

The Cardiovascular System The cardiovascular system has a tall order—it must pump enough blood to distribute oxygen and nutrients throughout the body on a continuous basis. During an average day, the human heart pumps nearly 2,000 gallons of blood (American Heart Association, n.d.). By middle adulthood, structural changes in the cardiovascular system begin to make this task more effortful. Fatty deposits, cholesterol, and calcium have accumulated in the arteries over time, leading to a build-up of **plaque**—a process called **atherosclerosis**. As plaque increases and hardens, the arteries become narrower, restricting blood flow. The heart must pump harder as a result, increasing the risk of **hypertension**, or chronically high blood pressure. Obesity, smoking, lack of exercise, and excessive salt intake increase the risk of hypertension. Stress also may contribute to high blood pressure and other health problems, as discussed later. Hypertension is a dangerous disease because it has no obvious symptoms, and people may fail to seek treatment. Regular blood pressure monitoring is important for this reason.

plaque Deposits (made of fat, cholesterol, calcium, and other substances) that form in the inner lining of the main arteries through the process of atherosclerosis, causing the arteries to become narrow and less elastic; this increases the risk of hypertension and, in turn, heart attack and stroke.

atherosclerosis A process by which fatty deposits, cholesterol, calcium, and other substances build up over time in the inner lining of the main arteries; the result of this build-up is called *plaque*.

hypertension Chronically high blood pressure.

If untreated, hypertension can damage blood vessels and increase the risk of heart attack and stroke. Heart attacks are more common in middle and later adulthood, as you can see in Figure 15.3. Historically, middle-aged men in the United States have had a greater risk of heart disease and stroke than middle-aged women, but this gender difference has begun to narrow in recent years as the risk of stroke among middle-aged women has risen (Towfighi et al., 2007).

Fortunately, diet, exercise, stress management, and avoiding tobacoo use can reduce the risk of heart disease, particularly if a healthy lifestyle is adopted early in life. In one large study of young adults who were followed over a 15-year period, those who were physically fit reduced their future risk of high blood pressure and diabetes by nearly 50 percent (Yan et al., 2003). And it is not too late to improve one's health behaviors in midlife. Middle-aged adults in one study who adopted a healthy lifestyle (diet with five or more servings of fruits and vegetables daily, regular exercise, maintenance of moderate body mass index, and no smoking) had fewer coronary disease events and were more likely to be alive 4 years later (King, Mainous, & Geesey, 2007).

The Respiratory System Lung capacity tends to decline gradually, beginning when people are in their 20s and 30s, as the respiratory muscles and lung tissue lose their ability to expand and contract efficiently. Lung capacity diminishes by about 40 percent from age 20 to 70 (National Institute on Aging [NIA], 1996). The effects of declining lung

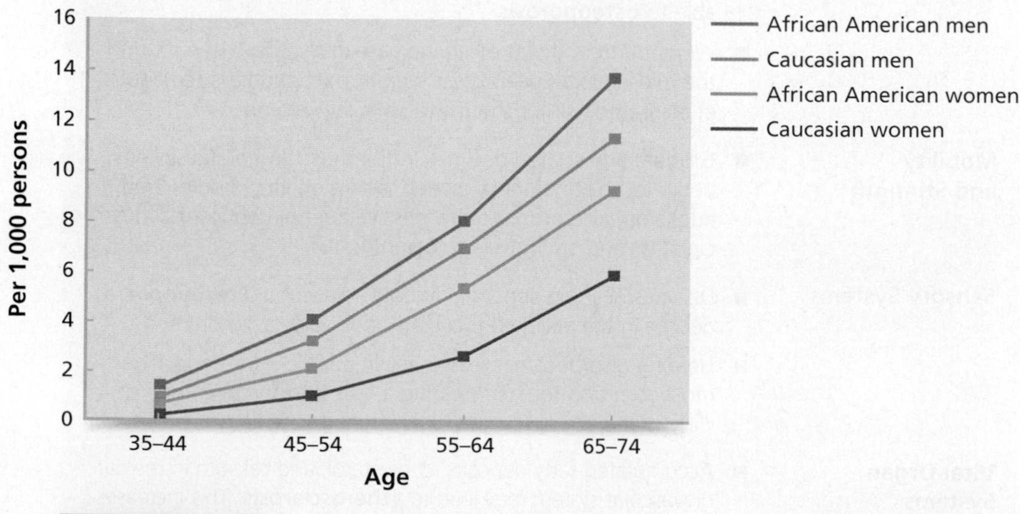

FIGURE 15.3

Rates of First Heart Attack by Age, Sex, and Race

Source: American Heart Association. (2009). *Heart disease and stroke statistics 2009 update: A report from the American Heart Association Statistics Committee and Stroke Statistics Subcommittee.* Circulation, 119, e21-e181. Retrieved December 8, 2009 from http://circ.ahajournals.org/cgi/reprint/CIRCULATIONAHA.108.191261. Chart 4-3, page e67.

capacity are most evident when people exert themselves—for example, when they are climbing a steep hill. Lung capacity declines more rapidly among people who smoke. Fortunately, smokers who give up the habit can slow the rate of decline, although they will still lose lung capacity faster than people who never smoked (Chinn et al., 2005). Weight loss and reducing body fat among overweight people also help to slow the rate of decline in the respiratory system (Chinn et al., 2005; Pistelli et al., 2008).

prostate gland Part of the male reproductive system that produces semen.

The Urinary System The urinary system is responsible for eliminating the waste products of metabolism from the body. With age, however, the bladder becomes less elastic, decreasing the efficiency with which it retains or expels urine (Siroky, 2004). Enlargement of the **prostate gland** also becomes more common as men grow older, and this gland's location on top of the bladder can put pressure on the bladder. Both men and women often begin to experience more frequent or intense urges to urinate as they age (Boyle et al., 2003). Urinary incontinence (loss of control over urination) is rare among middle-aged adults, but a common concern among elderly adults. (For a summary of this section, see "Interim Summary 15.2: Physical Development.")

INTERIM SUMMARY **15.2**

Physical Development	
	■ Minor changes in appearance, body build, mobility, and body system functioning occur gradually from young adulthood to middle adulthood. Changes are more noticeable among people in their 50s and early 60s. ■ Some age-related changes result from inevitable, intrinsic processes of aging (**primary aging**). Other changes result from the accumulated effects of disease, bodily abuse, or environmental hazards (**secondary aging**).
Appearance	■ In midlife, graying and thinning of hair are common, and the skin becomes drier, less elastic, and more prone to wrinkles.
Body Build	■ People tend to retain their maximum height until their mid to late 50s. Women experience greater height loss then men because they lose bone more rapidly, making them vulnerable to **osteoporosis**. ■ Weight and body fat often increase in midlife, often around the midsection. Such excess weight puts middle-aged adults at increased risk for the **metabolic syndrome**.
Mobility and Strength	■ Gradual age-related declines in the musculoskeletal system begin to affect strength, speed, and mobility. Middle-aged adults are also prone to progressive age-related loss of muscle mass and strength (**sarcopenia**).
Sensory Systems	■ Declines in vision appear in middle adulthood. **Presbyopia,** a decline in the ability to focus on close objects, is common. ■ Hearing also becomes less sharp in middle adulthood. The most common form of hearing loss is **presbycusis**, or a decline in the ability to hear high-pitched sounds.
Vital Organ Systems	■ Accumulated fatty deposits, cholesterol, and calcium in the cardiovascular system may lead to **atherosclerosis**. This increases the risk of **hypertension**, or chronically high blood pressure. ■ Lung capacity tends to decline gradually, beginning in young adulthood. ■ Enlargement of the **prostate gland** becomes more common as men grow older. Both men and women often begin to experience more frequent or intense urges to urinate as they age.

REPRODUCTIVE AND SEXUAL FUNCTIONING

Middle adulthood is a time when fertility declines, and, for women, eventually ends. Does sexual activity also decline, or does it remain important in the lives of middle-aged men and women? We explore these issues next.

Reproductive Changes in Women

Beginning in their late 40s or early 50s, women experience gradual declines in the female sex hormones (estrogen, progestin), which cause their menstrual cycles to become shorter and irregular, and eventually to stop. This process of change is called the **climacteric** (also called "perimenopause"). The climacteric unfolds gradually over a period of about 3 to 5 years on average, and culminates in **menopause**, the cessation of menstruation and the end of the woman's reproductive capacity (her ability to bear children). When a woman's menstrual periods have stopped for 12 consecutive months, she is said to have experienced menopause (National Institutes of Health [NIH], 2005). The duration of the climacteric varies, but 80 percent of U.S. women complete this transition and reach menopause by age 55 (Avis, 1999).

climacteric Gradual declines in the female sex hormones (also called *perimenopause*).

menopause The cessation of menstruation and the end of a woman's reproductive capacity (her ability to bear children).

The decline in hormones during this transition causes some women to experience physical or psychological symptoms, although women vary considerably in how much discomfort they report (Melby, Lock, & Kaufert, 2005; NIH, 2005). The most common symptom is **"hot flashes"** (called "night sweats" when they occur while a woman is sleeping)—periodic sensations of heat that can trigger sweating and reddening of the face, neck, and chest. In one study, 81 percent of menopausal women reported hot flashes, but fewer than 20 percent of those who experienced this symptom found it to be bothersome (Avis, 1999). Hot flashes tend to diminish, and eventually cease, over time. Vaginal dryness and sleep disturbances are also often associated with menopause. Vaginal tissues become thinner and drier during menopause, sometimes contributing to discomfort during sexual intercourse, but these symptoms have been found to subside over time without treatment in as many as half of postmenopausal women (Huang et al., 2010). In addition, the widespread belief that menopausal women are prone to irritability or negative moods is not well substantiated in the United States (NIH, 2005). The view of menopause that emerges from scientific studies is more positive than the view suggested by stereotypes that portray menopausal women as irritable and despondent that they are no longer "complete women" (Rossi, 2004).

hot flashes Periodic sensations of heat that can trigger sweating and reddening of the face, neck, and chest among menopausal women.

How do women feel about menopause? Here, too, the scientific evidence might surprise you. Women's attitudes toward menopause are largely neutral or positive rather than negative. Many women experience relief at not having menstrual periods any longer and enjoy the freedom to engage in sex without having to worry about pregnancy (Avis, 1999). In societies in which birth control is infrequently practiced and women spend most of their reproductive years either pregnant or lactating, menopause is often viewed as a welcome event (Leon, Chedraui, Hidalgo, & Ortiz, 2007). Similarly, in societies in which taboos restrict women's freedom of movement during menstruation (such as the freedom to go out in public), women often look forward to menopause (Avis, 1999; McMaster, Pitts, & Poyah, 1997). This is an example of a developmental loss—loss of reproductive capacity—that actually results in a developmental gain for some women—an increased sense of freedom. In Eastern cultures, menopause is often regarded as a natural phenomenon, and views of menopause tend to be more positive (Cheng, Wang, Wang, & Fuh, 2005). In general, although menopause was once viewed as a disorder or even a disease, it is now viewed as a normal part of aging that most women cope with quite well. Nevertheless, the declines in estrogen and progestin that cause menopause may have long-term implications for women's health.

Health Implications of Menopause Bone loss and the risk of osteoporosis increase after menopause, as we noted earlier. Menopause has been linked to increases in LDL ("bad") cholesterol and decreases in HDL ("good") cholesterol, changes that increase

Kevin Schafer/Getty Images

Women in some cultures, such as this woman from Ecuador, view menopause as a welcome event.

the risk of cardiovascular disease among women (Brown et al., 1993). Rates of hypertension rise more steeply in midlife among women than among men, although the exact role of menopause in the sex difference is unclear (Coylewright, Reckelhoff, & Ouyang, 2008).

Hormone Replacement Therapy **Hormone replacement therapy (HRT)** was introduced over 60 years ago to relieve symptoms of menopause, such as hot flashes, and it was later seen as a strategy for reducing the risk of chronic diseases among postmenopausal women (Barrett-Connor & Grady, 1998; Mendelsohn & Karas, 1999). The popularity of HRT has seen some wild swings since that time (Barrett-Connor, Grady, & Stefanick, 2005). High expectations about the benefits of HRT led to the widespread administration of estrogen to menopausal women in the 1960s. But prescriptions plunged in the 1970s, when estrogen use was linked to an increased risk of uterine cancer. HRT rose again when the combination of progestin and estrogen was believed to prevent this increased risk. Observational studies—in which postmenopausal women on HRT were compared to postmenopausal women not on HRT—seemed to indicate that the health benefits of HRT outweighed the risks.

By 1999, as many as 90 million prescriptions for HRT were filled annually, making it the most widely prescribed medication in the United States (Barrett-Connor, Grady, & Stefanick, 2005). But enthusiasm for HRT declined again dramatically in 2002 when the results of the first large randomized clinical trials began to emerge. Unlike the observational studies, women in these clinical trials were randomly assigned to receive either HRT or a **placebo** (e.g., a sugar pill), and their health was monitored over time. Two major clinical trials—the Women's Health Initiative (WHI) and the Heart and Estrogen/Progestin Replacement Study (HERS)—both found an increased, rather than decreased, risk of heart attack, stroke, blood clots, and breast cancer among those women receiving HRT (Hulley et al., 1998; Hulley & Grady, 2004). Among older women (those in their 60s and 70s), HRT was associated with an increased risk of Alzheimer's disease and other forms of cognitive impairment. These clinical trials were halted to avoid further risks to the women receiving HRT. After 2002, the use of HRT by middle-aged and older women again plummeted.

hormone replacement therapy (HRT) Treatment that involves the administration of estrogen and/or progestin to reduce menopausal symptoms and the risk of osteoporosis. Evidence is mixed regarding the risks and benefits of this treatment.

placebo An inert agent, such as a sugar pill, that is administered in clinical trials in order to compare its effects with those of a medication.

These dramatic ups and downs in the history of HRT have left many women in a quandary. Evidence suggests that HRT does produce some relief from hot flashes and vaginal symptoms and, over the long-term, reduces bone loss and fractures (Barrett-Connor et al., 2005), but these benefits are offset by significant health risks. Today, women must closely evaluate their family history and other risks for heart disease and breast cancer and consider a variety of options with their physicians before embarking on a course of HRT. Exercise, diet, and stress management may provide relief from symptoms of menopause, in addition to offering long-term health benefits (NIA, 2009; Vallance, Murray, Johnson, & Elavsky, 2010). Lubricants can be used to reduce discomfort that may be caused by vaginal dryness during sexual activity. In the meantime, medical researchers have not given up entirely on HRT and continue to investigate whether better outcomes can be achieved by prescribing lower doses or targeting younger women at the beginning of menopause, when their heart disease risk is lower (Barrett-Connor et al., 2005).

Reproductive Changes in Men

We have focused so far on women's reproductive changes in midlife. What about men? Do they experience a marked change like menopause? The answer is no, although men do experience a gradual decline in **androgens**, the hormones that are responsible for the development of male sexual characteristics. Men also experience a decline in the production of sperm beginning in midlife (Feldman et al., 2002; Tan & Culberson, 2003).

androgens Hormones that are responsible for the development of male sexual characteristics.

These changes in the male reproductive system have sometimes been referred to as **andropause** (also called the "male climacteric"). But this term, and its implied equivalence to menopause, are controversial (Handelsman & Liu, 2005; Hijazi & Cunningham, 2005). In contrast to the significant decline in estrogen and loss of fertility experienced by women, most men experience only a small decline in testosterone (the most important of the male sex hormones), and they usually remain capable of fathering children until well into their later years (Tan & Culberson, 2003).

andropause The gradual decline of androgens in men.

Age-related declines in testosterone reflect normal aging (as is the case for menopause), although factors such as elevated cholesterol, high body fat, and smoking can contribute to declines in testosterone (Travison, Araujo, Kupelian, O'Donnell, & McKinlay, 2007). Declining testosterone is sometimes viewed as causing changes in body build (reduced muscle mass, increased body fat, reduced bone density), sleep difficulties, negative mood, declines in cognitive functioning, and reduced sex drive. Like many of the purported effects of menopause, however, it is not clear whether age-related declines in testosterone actually have such effects (Tan & Culberson, 2003). Claims about the negative effects of declining testosterone frequently have been based on studies documenting physical symptoms among younger men who have abnormally low levels of testosterone (for example, because of disease or injury). Generalizing these findings to healthy middle-aged and older men who are experiencing small, naturally occurring declines in testosterone is risky. Researchers are continuing to investigate possible health risks of age-related declines in testosterone, but in the meantime, claims about such health risks need to be scrutinized very carefully (Handelsman & Liu, 2005).

Testosterone Replacement Therapy **Testosterone replacement therapy** involves administering testosterone supplements through pills, injections, or skin patches. It is rarely warranted for healthy men, particularly since it has side effects that include an increased risk of enlarged prostate gland, prostate cancer, and elevated red blood cell production (Calof et al., 2005; Tan & Culberson, 2003). Current evidence suggests that it should be used only by those who have a clear hormone deficiency. Yet in just the 5-year period from 1997 to 2002, prescriptions for testosterone increased by 500 percent in the United States, with most given to men in their 40s and 50s (Marshall, 2007). The widespread embrace of medication to treat physical changes in midlife may, once again, be outpacing the science regarding long-term risks and benefits (O'Donnell, Araujo, & McKinlay, 2004).

testosterone replacement therapy Treatment that involves administering testosterone supplements through pills, injections, or skin patches.

Erectile Dysfunction **Erectile dysfunction (ED),** difficulty achieving or maintaining an erection, becomes more common as men age, with as many as 40 to 50 percent of men experiencing at least occasional ED by age 60 (Kingsberg, 2002). Compared to men in their 20s, men in their 50s are three times more likely to experience ED (Laumann, Paik, & Rosen, 1999). Declines in testosterone may not be responsible for changes in sexual functioning, however. Among men who seek treatment for ED, relatively few actually have abnormal hormone profiles (Marshall, 2007). Other factors may be responsible for their ED, such as reduced blood flow (due to circulatory problems), stress, and social factors (e.g., anxiety about sexual performance or relationship problems) (Laumann et al., 1999). Diseases such as diabetes and hypertension, and the medications prescribed for various diseases, can also increase the risk of ED. In fact, ED sometimes can be a warning sign of underlying heart disease (Mayo Clinic, 2008). Fortunately, many more options now exist for treating ED than was true in the past (Qaseem et al., 2009).

erectile dysfunction (ED) Difficulty achieving or maintaining an erection.

Sexual Activity

You learned in Chapter 13 that sexual intimacy is an important part of young adults' lives, as they form relationships with long-term partners and launch families. What role does sexual intimacy play in the lives of middle-aged adults? Research on this topic is scarce, reflecting the fact that the scientific literature on middle adulthood has emerged only recently (perhaps coupled with stereotypes of middle-aged adults as disinterested in sex). But the available studies do point to a few general patterns.

First, research in the United States suggests that people engage in sexual activity less frequently and feel somewhat less satisfied with their sexual lives as they reach their 40s and 50s (Rossi, 2004). Evidence from one of the largest studies of middle adulthood—the study of Midlife in the United States (MIDUS) (Brim, Ryff, & Kessler, 2004)—found that when middle-aged adults were asked to evaluate different domains of their lives, they gave the least positive ratings to their sexual lives (Fleeson, 2004). But it is important to put this in perspective. The middle-aged participants' average rating of their sexual lives was above the midpoint of the rating scale, so it did not reflect deep dissatisfaction with their sexual lives.

Declines in the frequency of sexual activity in midlife may occur for a variety of different reasons. Physical factors—such as illness, the side effects of medication, or alcohol—sometimes play a role. The lack of a partner sometimes limits women's sexual activity because, as you'll see in the next chapter, women are less likely than men to remarry after a divorce in midlife. Other causes can include life stress, role demands that leave little time for sexual activity, and anxiety about sexual performance (Rossi, 2004). Stereotypes of middle-aged adults as less interested in sex also have the potential to become self-fulfilling prophecies (Rossi, 2004). Research challenges those stereotypes, as adults remain interested in, and capable of, sexual intimacy well into their later years. In a recent study of 1,682 people age 45 and older (Jacoby, 2005), 66 percent of the men and 48 percent of the women reported that they considered a satisfying sexual relationship to be important to their quality of life. Although sexual intercourse may become less common as people grow older, affection, caressing, and other forms of sexual intimacy can continue. As one participant in this study commented, "When you care, you find that there are all sorts of ways to express sensuality" (Jacoby, 2005). (For a summary of this section, see "Interim Summary 15.3: Reproductive and Sexual Functioning.")

INTERIM SUMMARY **15.3**

Reproductive and Sexual Functioning

Reproductive Changes in Women	■ Women experience gradual declines in female sex hormones in midlife, causing their menstrual cycles to stop eventually. This process (the **climacteric**) culminates in **menopause**, the cessation of menstruation. ■ In general, women's attitudes toward menopause are positive. However, there are health implications of menopause, including increased risk of osteoporosis and high cholesterol. ■ Some women use **hormone replacement therapy (HRT)** to relieve symptoms of menopause, but many believe its benefits are offset by its risks.
Reproductive Changes in Men	■ In midlife, men experience a gradual decline in the production of sperm and **androgens**, the hormones responsible for the development of male sexual characteristics. ■ Testosterone levels also decline in mid-life. **Testosterone replacement therapy** is warranted only for those who have a significant hormone deficiency. ■ **Erectile dysfunction (ED),** difficulty achieving or maintaining an erection, becomes more common as men age.
Sexual Activity	■ Declines in the frequency of sexual activity in midlife are caused by physical issues, lack of a partner, life stress, role demands that leave little time for sexual activity, and anxiety about sexual performance. ■ Although sexual intercourse may become less common in midlife, affection, caressing, and other forms of sexual intimacy can continue.

PHYSICAL HEALTH

Health has a major impact on our emotional well-being and ability to function in the world. Think back to the last time you had a bad cold or flu bug. You probably felt miserable and may have been confined to bed for a while. In young adulthood, such threats to health tend to be short-lived. Good health is something many young adults can take for granted. Fortunately, middle-aged adults generally enjoy good health, too, but midlife is a time when some health problems begin to linger longer and when aches and pains do not go away as quickly as they once did (Lachman, 2004). And some middle-aged adults do develop serious illnesses or disabilities that limit their activities (Lachman, 2004).

Health Conditions

One way to describe people's health status is to think about the kinds of health conditions they tend to have. You might be surprised to learn that middle-aged adults are less susceptible than young adults to **acute illnesses**, or illnesses that have a rapid onset and short duration. The common cold and influenza are examples. Chronic illnesses, in contrast, become more common and are more likely to cause activity limitations, especially as middle-aged adults reach their mid 50s and beyond (see Figure 15.4).

acute illnesses Illnesses that have a rapid onset and short duration.

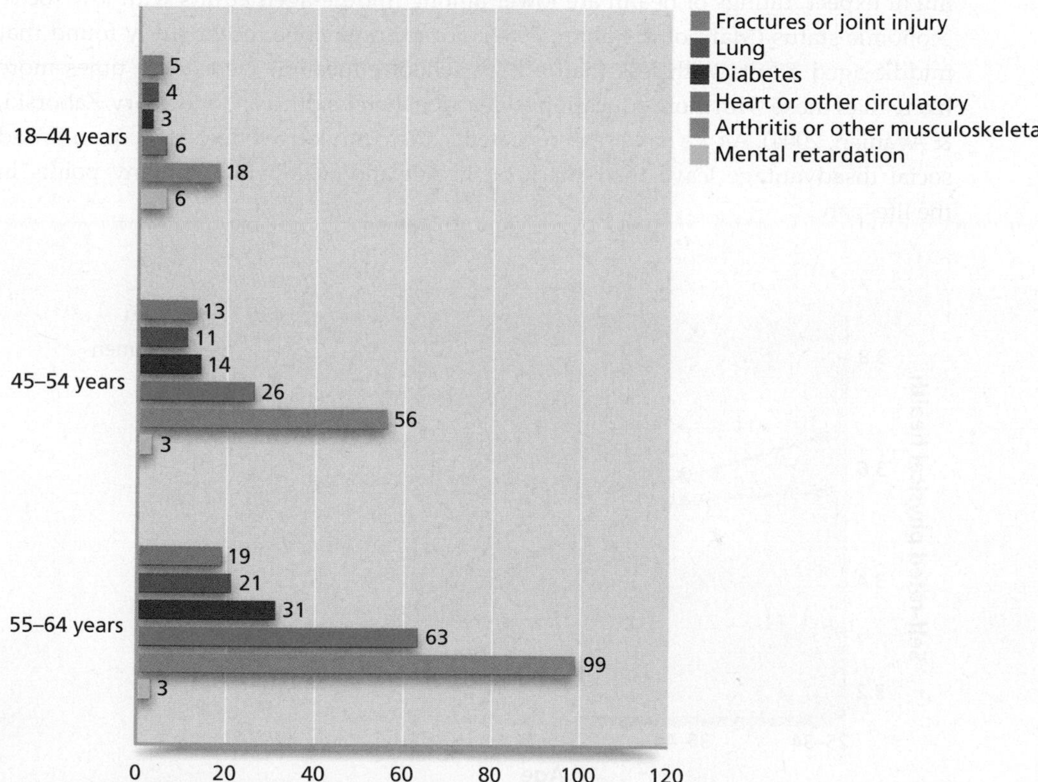

FIGURE 15.4

Chronic Conditions that Cause Activity Limitations by Age

Note: Data are for the civilan noninstitutionalized population. Adults with more than one chronic health condition were counted in each category.

Source: National Center for Health Statistics (2009). *Health, United States, 2008.* Hyattsville, MD. Retreived November 30, 2009 from http://www.cdc.gov/nchs/data/hus/hus08.pdf

chronic illnesses Illnesses that have a slow onset and long duration.

Chronic illnesses have a slow onset and long duration. Some chronic conditions, such as heart disease, are potentially fatal; others, such as arthritis, cause discomfort but are not fatal. Heart disease is the leading cause of death among middle-aged and older adults (Heron, 2007).

disability A physical or mental impairment that significantly limits one's life activities.

Although chronic conditions are more common in middle adulthood than in young adulthood, rates of **disability**—a physical or mental impairment that significantly limits one's life activities—are relatively low. Among people in their 40s, 7 percent have a disability of some kind, a figure that rises to 16 percent among people in their 50s and 30 percent among people in their 60s (Bumpass & Aquilino, 1995). Rates of chronic illness and disability are higher among people with low socioeconomic status (Lachman, 2004).

Self-Rated Health

Health conditions provide only a partial picture of someone's health status. How they *feel* about their health is another important part of the picture. Middle-aged adults generally rate their health favorably, despite their various aches and pains and growing health concerns (Lachman, 2004). Roughly 85 percent of middle-aged adults in the United States rate their health as "excellent" or "very good" (Schiller & Bernadel, 2004). Nonetheless, ratings of physical health are lower in middle adulthood, for both men and women, than in young adulthood, as you can see in Figure 15.5. And, as you might expect, ratings of health are lower among middle-aged adults with low socioeconomic status (Marmot & Fuhrer, 2004). For example, one recent study found that middle-aged adults with less than a high school education were three times more likely than those with more education to describe their health as poor (Cleary, Zaborski, & Ayanian, 2004). As we have seen repeatedly, the cumulative effects of economic and social disadvantage leave their mark on health and well-being at many points in the lifespan.

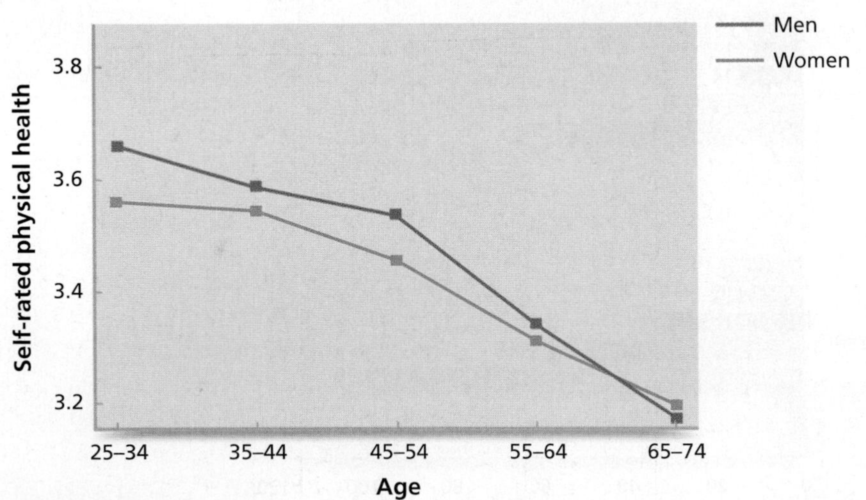

FIGURE 15.5

Self-Rated Physical Health by Age

Note: Self-ratings of physical health were made on a 5-point scale from 1 = poor to 5 = excellent.

Source: "Sex differences in health over the course of midlife" by P.D. Cleary, L.B. Zaborski, and J.A. Ayanian. From *How healthy are we?: A national study of well-being at midlife* by O.G. Brim, Carol D. Ryff, & Ronald C. Kessler (eds.) Copyright © 2004. Reprinted by permission of the publisher, The University of Chicago Press.

Influences on Health in Middle Adulthood

What influences a person's health in middle adulthood? This is a complex question that does not have a simple answer. But researchers generally have emphasized three major sources of influence on health: genes, behavior, and the environment.

Genes The genes we inherit from our parents influence our risk of developing particular diseases. When you hear people talking about a disease that "runs in the family," they are very likely referring to a disease with an inherited component (although family members may share unhealthy lifestyles and environments, as well as genes). Some forms of heart disease and cancer—two of the leading causes of death in middle and later adulthood—have a hereditary component. Other common but less lethal conditions, such as arthritis and glaucoma, also tend to be hereditary.

Behavior Although genes partly determine our risk of developing particular diseases, health behaviors and lifestyles generally play an even larger role (Merrill & Verbrugge, 1999). We have discussed many of these behaviors already in this chapter and in previous chapters, such as lack of exercise, poor diet, smoking, and drug or alcohol abuse. It is important to remember that these health-risk behaviors have cumulative effects over time. What matters, for example, is not just how many packs of cigarettes a middle-aged man currently smokes but also how long he has been a smoker.

Other behaviors that affect health in midlife, and that we have not yet discussed, include getting an adequate amount of sleep and finding effective ways to manage stress (Cacioppo & Bernston, 2007). Most people need 7 to 9 hours of sleep each night, but many Americans routinely get much less sleep than that (Lovgren, 2005). Sleep serves an important restorative function, allowing the systems of the body to repair themselves and restore homeostasis after responding to challenges and demands during the course of the day (Cacioppo & Bernston, 2007). Chronic sleep deficits interfere with cognitive functioning, harm the immune system, and contribute to obesity (Lovgren, 2005). Sleep deficits also cause levels of the stress hormone **cortisol** to become elevated, which may have harmful health effects (Van Cauter, Leproult, & Plat, 2000). We explore the links between stress and health later, but we leave you with this thought for now: Behavioral influences on health include not only specific health practices but also personality characteristics that affect how people deal with stress. Some people are quite easily upset by everyday life stress or even seem to generate stress in their lives. So some personality characteristics can jeopardize health over time (Smith, 2006).

cortisol A stress hormone.

The Environment Environmental factors can pose threats to health, from unsafe working conditions to dangerous pesticides or other toxins in the environment. In some poor communities, inadequate living conditions and persistently high rates of crime, unemployment, and discrimination are chronic sources of stress that can erode health over time (Geronimus, Bound, Waidmann, Hillemeier, & Burns, 1996). People in such communities often lack access to safe public parks and recreation centers where they could exercise and relieve stress. Instead, they sometimes try to manage their stress by drinking, smoking, and eating "comfort foods" that tend to be high in fats and carbohydrates. Yet the very actions that provide some relief from the chronic stress in their lives also elevate their risk of chronic disease over time. Psychologist James Jackson and his colleagues (Jackson & Knight, 2006; Jackson, Knight, & Rafferty, 2009) believe this process explains why poor health behaviors and chronic diseases, such as hypertension and diabetes, are more common among African Americans than Caucasians. Even though African Americans tend to experience more chronic stress throughout their lives, they have the same or lower rates of mental illness as Caucasians (Jackson et al., 2009). Paradoxically, the actions they take to reduce stress may be preserving their mental health at the expense of their physical health.

Environmental hazards, such as air pollution from factories and power plants, can pose threats to health.

You can see from this example why health problems in midlife sometimes have their origins in the interaction of environmental and behavioral factors. Efforts to promote health in our society and others will need to address environmental as well as behavioral risks.

Stress and Health

Stress is an unavoidable aspect of modern life, more so for some people than others. We have seen that it has the potential to harm our health. But what exactly is stress? **Stress** is the response to perceived threats or demands in the environment, called **stressors** (McEwen, 2006; Selye, 1983). When a threat is perceived, the body responds by releasing stress hormones that boost heart rate and breathing and increase glucose in the blood stream (providing fuel for the body's muscles). This is the body's way of preparing for a "fight or flight" response to the threat (Canon, 1932). If you have ever felt a rush of adrenaline when you were alarmed by an unexpected stressor—such as a car that suddenly swerved into your lane while you were driving—this was your body releasing stress hormones to help you deal with the stressor. At the same time, to conserve energy for the "fight or flight" response, the hormone cortisol signals other bodily functions—such as digestion, reproduction, and immune defenses—to slow down or stop temporarily. The human stress system is self-regulating. Ordinarily, if stress is short-lived, the release of stress hormones slows and other bodily functions resume (Cacioppo & Bernston, 2007; Ursin & Eriksen, 2004).

stress The response to perceived threats or demands (stressors) in the environment.

stressors Perceived threats or demands in the environment.

The Problem of Chronic Stress But what if stress is prolonged—for example, as a result of living or working in chronically stressful circumstances or having a conflict-ridden marriage? When stress persists or recurs repeatedly, stress hormones remain elevated, damaging some bodily systems and elevating the risk of acute illnesses, such as the common cold (Cohen et al., 1998) as well as chronic diseases, such as heart disease, diabetes, and even some cancers (Miller & Blackwell, 2006; Robles, Glaser, & Kiecolt-Glaser, 2005). This is why college students are more likely to get the flu or a cold at the end of a semester, after they have been pushing themselves to complete course assignments and prepare for final exams.

The stress response system evolved to help our earliest human ancestors deal with acute threats to survival, such as predators, but many of the stressors we experience in modern life are chronic in nature. Ironically, a system that once worked well in human evolution now can be a cause of illness and disease (Cacioppo & Bernston, 2007). Researchers have coined the term **allostatic load** to refer to the accumulated wear and tear on bodily systems that results from having to adapt to stressors repeatedly (McEwen & Stellar, 1993; Seeman, Singer, Rowe, Horwitz, & McEwen, 1997). The threat to health in midlife that stems from life stress is not simply a function of how much stress middle-aged people are currently experiencing, but rather how much stress they have repeatedly experienced over the course of their lives—a reminder, again, that health risks are cumulative. And there is another wrinkle in all of this—it is not only major life stressors, such as the death of a loved one or the loss of a job, but also minor

allostatic load Accumulated wear and tear on bodily systems that results from having to adapt to stressors repeatedly.

stressors and daily hassles, such as traffic congestion, arguments at work, or broken plumbing, that increase allostatic load and threaten health over time (DeLongis, Folkman, & Lazarus, 1988; Kamarck et al., 2005; McEwen, 2006).

In light of all of this, it is not hard to see why adequate sleep and restorative breaks for the body are important for health, particularly during times of stress (Cacioppo & Bernston, 2007). You can also see why people who do not deal well with stress may be especially vulnerable to its harmful effects.

Personality and Stress Personality characteristics play a role in the stress that people experience and, in turn, their risk of illness (Smith & MacKenzie. 2006). Let's explore these links in the context of heart disease.

Do you know someone who you would describe as "uptight"? If so, your uptight acquaintance may be at greater risk of developing heart disease because of a **Type A personality.** People with Type A personalities tend to be impatient, competitive, and easily angered (Friedman & Rosenman, 1959). Type As are driven—they seem to work at a breakneck pace, often juggling multiple tasks simultaneously, and they can become hostile if they encounter obstacles to achieving their goals. People with a **Type B personality**, in contrast, tend to be patient, noncompetitive, and less likely to become angry or hostile. They have less sense of urgency about accomplishing their goals, and they are less likely to take out their frustrations on others if their goals prove to be difficult to attain. As discussed in Chapter 13 (and as we will discuss in the next chapter), knowing when to disengage from unattainable goals can help to protect people from psychological distress. It appears to have health benefits, too, because the unrelenting pursuit of elusive goals can lead to exhaustion, lack of sleep, and rumination about failure—all factors that increase the risk of illness (Miller & Wrosch, 2007).

Type A personality A stress-prone personality type characterized by impatience, competitiveness, and hostility.

Type B personality A less stress-prone personality type characterized by patience, non-competitiveness, and less tendency toward hostility.

From this comparison, you can begin to understand why people with Type A personalities are more stress-prone. Their competitiveness and sense of urgency generate stress. They also react more intensely to setbacks. Type As experience greater physiological arousal in stressful situations, causing more stress hormones to be released and heart rate and blood pressure to rise more markedly (Sundin, Öhman, Palm, & Ström, 1995; Williams, Barefoot, & Schneiderman, 2003). The more frequently and more intensely they react to stress over time, the more likely Types As are to damage their cardiovascular systems. Early studies (which often focused on men) indicated that Type As are twice as likely as Type Bs to have heart disease (Haynes, Feinleib, & Kannel, 1980). Later studies yielded more mixed findings, leading researchers to wonder whether a particular trait in the Type A personality is most responsible for the increased risk of heart disease. The bulk of evidence suggests that the tendency to become hostile is the real culprit (Smith, 2006; Smith et al., 2007). In both men and women, hostility is linked to the development of atherosclerosis and hypertension, and to an increased risk of heart attacks and stroke (Smith & MacKenzie, 2006).

So it seems that some personality characteristics—such as proneness to hostility—can increase the risk of chronic disease in midlife. But the news is not all bad: some individual differences can protect people from the harmful effects of stress.

Protective Factors Optimism—having positive beliefs about the future—helps people deal with adversity and is associated both with a lower risk of heart disease and greater longevity (Giltay, Kamphuis, Kalmijn, Zitman, & Kromhout, 2006; Kubzansky, Sparrow, Vokonas, & Kawachi, 2001). Conscientiousness—the tendency to be dependable, planful, and prudent—also has been linked to better health and greater longevity (Friedman, 2007). Having supportive social relationships helps buffer people from the harmful effects of stress and is associated with better cardiovascular and immune functioning (Cohen, 2004; Kiecolt-Glaser, McGuire, Robles, & Glaser, 2002; Uchino, 2006). Close relationships not only provide comfort and aid in difficult times, but also help people relax, laugh, and enjoy companionship (Rook, 1987). The relaxation and positive emotions experienced by spending time with good friends facilitate recovery from stress and contribute to better health (Pressman & Cohen, 2005). Regular physical exercise can also be an antidote to stress and a boost to mood. In addition, by the time people reach midlife, they have had ample experience dealing with stressful life events off and on over the years, and this helps many middle-aged adults develop strong coping skills (Aldwin & Levenson, 2001; Lachman, 2004).

And here is another encouraging thought: As discussed in Chapter 13, personalities are not set in stone, and people whose personalities threaten their health may be able to change. Meyer Friedman, who helped to discover the link between Type A personality and heart disease, was, by his own admission, a Type A. After suffering a heart attack at age 55, he made a concerted effort to slow down, relax, and enjoy life. This decision appears to have paid off, as he lived to be 90 (Wargo, 2007). (For a summary of this section, see "Interim Summary 15.4: Physical Health.")

INTERIM SUMMARY 15.4

Physical Health

Health Conditions	■ Midlife is a time when some health problems begin to linger longer and when aches and pains do not go away as quickly as they once did. ■ **Chronic illnesses** become more common in midlife.
Self-Rated Health	■ Middle-aged adults generally rate their health favorably. However, ratings of health are lower among middle-aged adults with low socioeconomic status, as the cumulative effects of economic and social disadvantage take their toll.
Influences on Health in Middle Adulthood	■ Researchers emphasize three major sources of influence on health: genes, behavior, and the environment. ■ The genes we inherit influence our risk of developing particular diseases. ■ Behavior generally plays an even larger role in health. Lack of exercise, poor diet, smoking, and drug or alcohol abuse have cumulative effects. Getting an adequate amount of sleep and managing stress also affect health in mid-life. ■ Environmental factors such as unsafe working or living conditions, pollution, crime, and unemployment also can affect health.
Stress and Health	■ **Stress** is the response to perceived threats or demands in the environment, called **stressors**. When stress persists or recurs repeatedly, stress hormones damage some bodily systems and elevate the risk of acute illnesses and chronic diseases. ■ **Allostatic load** refers to the accumulated wear and tear on bodily systems that results from having to adapt to stressors repeatedly. ■ Personality characteristics affect the stress people experience and their risk of illness. People with **Type A** personalities are more stress-prone than those with **Type B** personalities. ■ Optimism and conscientiousness are associated with better health and longevity. Other factors that protect against stress are supportive social relationships, physical exercise, and coping skills.

COGNITIVE DEVELOPMENT

By the time people have lived 40 or 50 years, they have acquired a remarkable storehouse of information. This surely must mean that people become more intelligent by midlife. Or does it? There may be more to intelligence than factual knowledge. Being able to analyze and solve a problem not previously encountered may be important. What about the role of higher education? Perhaps you are the first generation in your family to attend college. Will this make you more intelligent than your parents? This section explores how cognitive abilities change with age, focusing on intelligence, expertise, and creativity. Chapter 17 discusses how memory changes with age, an issue that has special relevance to the lives of older adults.

Intelligence

Examining the relationship between intelligence and age seems like a straightforward task, but it has been more challenging than you might imagine. One reason is that different types of studies have yielded different conclusions. The earliest studies of intelligence and age used cross-sectional designs, in which people of different ages were tested at the same time. These studies suggested that intelligence declines steadily as people grow older (Schaie, 1958), a finding that surely would be discouraging to middle-aged and older adults. But cohort effects, rather than age differences per se, may have been responsible for the pattern observed in this research. Think about the possible role of education. Until recently, middle-aged and older adults were much less likely than younger adults to have attended college and to have reaped the cognitive benefits of higher education. As a result, cross-sectional studies may *underestimate* the intelligence of middle-aged and older adults, because they confound, or confuse, the effects of age and education.

Longitudinal studies, on the other hand, suggested that intelligence *increases* from young adulthood to middle adulthood and declines only modestly thereafter (Cunningham & Owens, 1983; Schaie, 1994). This pattern would be more reassuring to middle-aged and older adults. But longitudinal studies have some limitations, too. Some people drop out of longitudinal studies over time, and those who do tend to have worse health and lower intellectual functioning (Cooney, Schaie, & Willis, 1988; Schaie, 1996). The people who remain in longitudinal studies are a somewhat select group, and their age-related gains in intelligence may not generalize to the overall population. People may also become more comfortable or skilled at taking intelligence tests over time, causing their scores to rise for reasons unrelated to age. Longitudinal studies, therefore, may *overestimate* the intelligence of middle-aged and older adults.

Another kind of study overcomes the limitations of the cross-sectional and longitudinal designs by using an accelerated longitudinal design that combines features of cross-sectional and longitudinal studies (see Chapter 1). Such studies are powerful but quite expensive, and, as a result, are relatively rare. One of the most well known, the Seattle Longitudinal Study (SLS) (Schaie, 1994, 2005), focused on the development of cognitive abilities in adulthood. The study has been in progress for decades and has administered tests of cognitive abilities every 7 years to people ages 20 to 70. Based on this study, we now know that the relationship between age and intelligence lies somewhere between the overly pessimistic estimates of the cross-sectional studies and the overly optimistic estimates of the longitudinal ones. This is because intelligence is *multidimensional*, and the different dimensions of intelligence change in different ways as people age.

Crystallized and Fluid Intelligence Developmental researchers often distinguish between two broad kinds of cognitive abilities that make up intelligence (Horn & Cattell, 1966). **Crystallized intelligence** refers to the ability to use knowledge and skills acquired through life experience and education. For example, if you were asked to name the capital of Virginia or to explain to someone how to operate a car, you would be using crystallized intelligence. **Fluid intelligence** refers to the ability to solve novel problems,

crystallized intelligence The ability to use knowledge and skills acquired through life experience and education (also referred to as the pragmatics of intelligence).

fluid intelligence The ability to solve novel problems, recognize patterns, and draw inferences in ways that do not require prior knowledge or experience (also referred to as the mechanics of intelligence).

recognize patterns, and draw inferences in ways that do not require prior knowledge or experience ("on-the-spot" reasoning). Fluid intelligence does not depend on education or accumulated knowledge. Instead, think of it as your raw brainpower for processing, analyzing, and responding quickly to new information. Your fluid intelligence would be tapped if you were asked to generate as many ways as possible to use a paper clip or to predict the next letter that should appear in the following sequence: N_P_R_T.

Some researchers make a similar distinction between the *pragmatics* and *mechanics* of intelligence (Baltes, Staudinger, & Lindenberger, 1999). The pragmatics of intelligence, like crystallized intelligence, refer to the knowledge acquired from one's culture. The mechanics of intelligence, like fluid intelligence, refer to basic information processing and problem solving. As shown in Figure 15.6, these researchers predict that the pragmatics of intelligence (or crystallized intelligence) increase until middle adulthood, as people's knowledge and skills accumulate, and then level off. In contrast, they predict that the mechanics of intelligence (or fluid intelligence) peak in young adulthood, when the functioning of the sensory and central nervous systems peaks, and then decline as age-related declines in these systems occur.

Findings from the Seattle Longitudinal Study largely confirm these views. Crystallized intelligence increases from young adulthood through midlife and generally remains intact until people are well into in their 60s or 70s, when declines become evident. Fluid intelligence, in contrast, peaks in young adulthood and generally declines fairly steadily thereafter (Horn, 1970). These age-related changes in specific cognitive abilities are shown Figure 15.7. You can see, for example, that verbal memory (or vocabulary), which reflects crystallized intelligence, increases somewhat through midlife, and then declines. In contrast, perceptual speed, which reflects fluid intelligence, declines fairly steadily after young adulthood.

Reasons for Age-Related Change Scientists currently know more about *what* cognitive abilities change with age than *why* these changes occur (Salthouse, 2004). One widely cited explanation, however, is that a generalized cognitive slowing with age underlies age-related cognitive decline. This is particularly true for tasks that require a series of operations to be performed in sequence, such as perceiving and processing

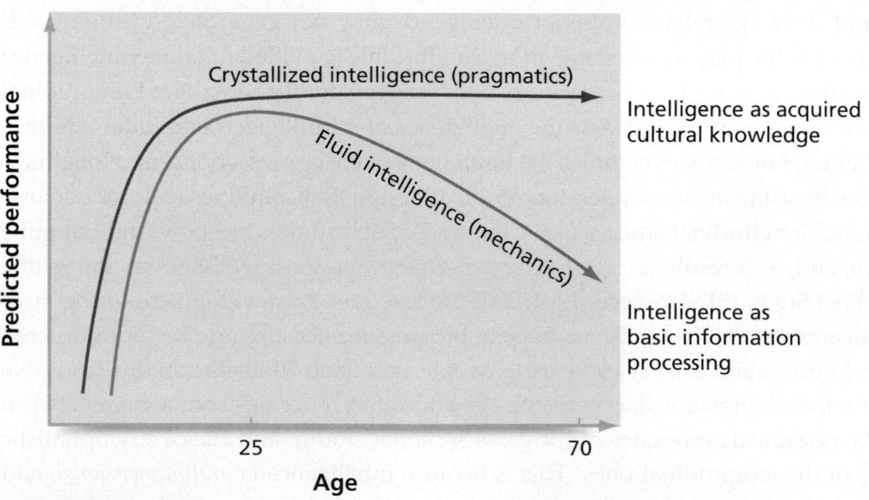

FIGURE 15.6

Predicted Association Between Age and Crystallized Intelligence (Pragmatics of Intelligence) versus Fluid Intelligence (Mechanics of Intelligence)

Source: Annual Review Of Psychology. Volume 50 by Baltes, Studinger, and Lindenberger. Copyright 1999 by *Annual Reviews, Inc.* Reproduced with permission of *Annual Reviews, Inc.* in the format Textbook via Copyright Clearance Center.

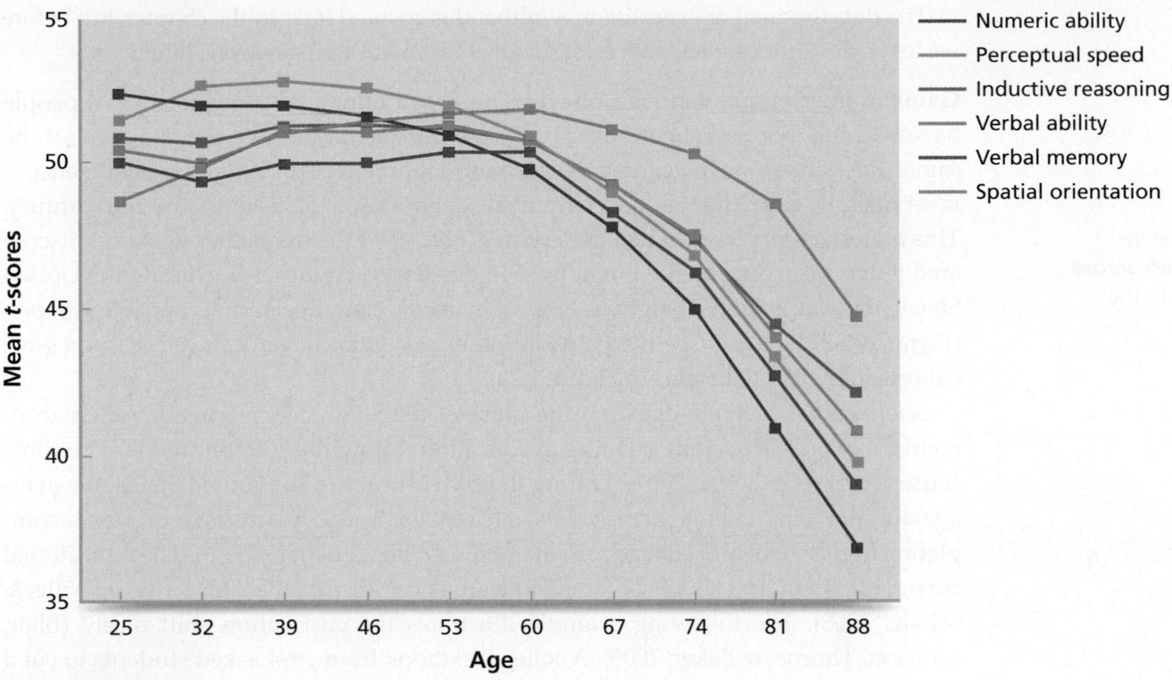

FIGURE 15.7

Longitudinal Change in Basic Cognitive Abilities with Age

Note: Higher mean *t*-scores indicate better performance.

Source: Developmental influences on adult intelligence: The Seattle Longitudinal Study by K.W. Schaie, 2005, p. 127. By permission of Oxford University Press, Inc., www.oup.com

information in the environment, evaluating alternative responses, and then deciding on and executing a response. When the overall time to perform the task is limited—whether it is a timed intelligence test in the laboratory or a real-life situation that calls for quick action—less time is left for the operations that come later in the sequence. As a result, task performance suffers (Salthouse, 1996). Another explanation is that the brain undergoes structural changes with age that contribute to cognitive decline (Zook & Davalos, 2006). The most well-documented change is a gradual age-related decline in the prefrontal cortex, which has been linked to declines in fluid intelligence (Bugg, Zook, DeLosh, Davalos, & Davis, 2006; Raz, 2000).

Implications for Everyday Functioning Even though declines in fluid intelligence occur with age, they generally have few implications for the ability of middle-aged and older adults to function in their daily lives. How can this be? Salthouse (2004) offers four reasons why age-related cognitive declines do not have more noticeable negative consequences:

1. Cognitive ability is not the only factor that determines how well people function in everyday life; motivation, effort, and personality characteristics play a role, too.
2. Most everyday situations do not require people to perform at their maximum level of cognitive functioning; in many instances, a moderate level of functioning is sufficient.
3. People often adapt to declining abilities by modifying their activities and ways of performing tasks, as we will see later when we consider how people function in the workplace as they grow older.
4. As people acquire more experience and expertise with age, they may have less need for the kind of novel problem-solving ability that declines with age. By midlife, people have accumulated a rich base of knowledge and familiar routines that serve them well in everyday situations.

The development of expertise in adulthood is covered later in the chapter, but before we leave the topic of intelligence, let's look at historical shifts in levels intelligence.

Flynn effect Gains in intelligence observed across successive cohorts in the 20th century.

Gains in Intelligence Across Cohorts: The Flynn Effect Would you say that people have become more intelligent over time, less intelligent, or have remained about the same? Researchers have documented striking cohort effects in studies of intelligence—most notably, gains in intelligence from one cohort to the next across the 20th century. This pattern of increases, called the **Flynn effect**, after the researcher who first discovered it, has been documented in at least 14 developed countries, including the United States, the Netherlands, Belgium, France, Norway, New Zealand, Canada, and Japan (Flynn, 1987). You can see the gains in intelligence that have occurred in successive cohorts in the United States in Figure 15.8.

Scientists are actively debating the cause of the Flynn effect. Some favor environmental explanations, citing changes in education during the 20th century as a possible cause (Dickens & Flynn, 2001). During the 20th century in the United States, the average duration of schooling increased by at least 4 years, and the number of people completing high school and college rose markedly (Willis & Schaie, 2006). The educational curriculum in many schools became more advanced during the 20th century (Willis & Schaie, 2006). The following example illustrates the curriculum shift nicely (Blair, Gamson, Thorne, & Baker, 2005): A college textbook from 1894 asked students to cut a two-dimensional triangle from a piece of paper and fold it into a polyhedron (a three-

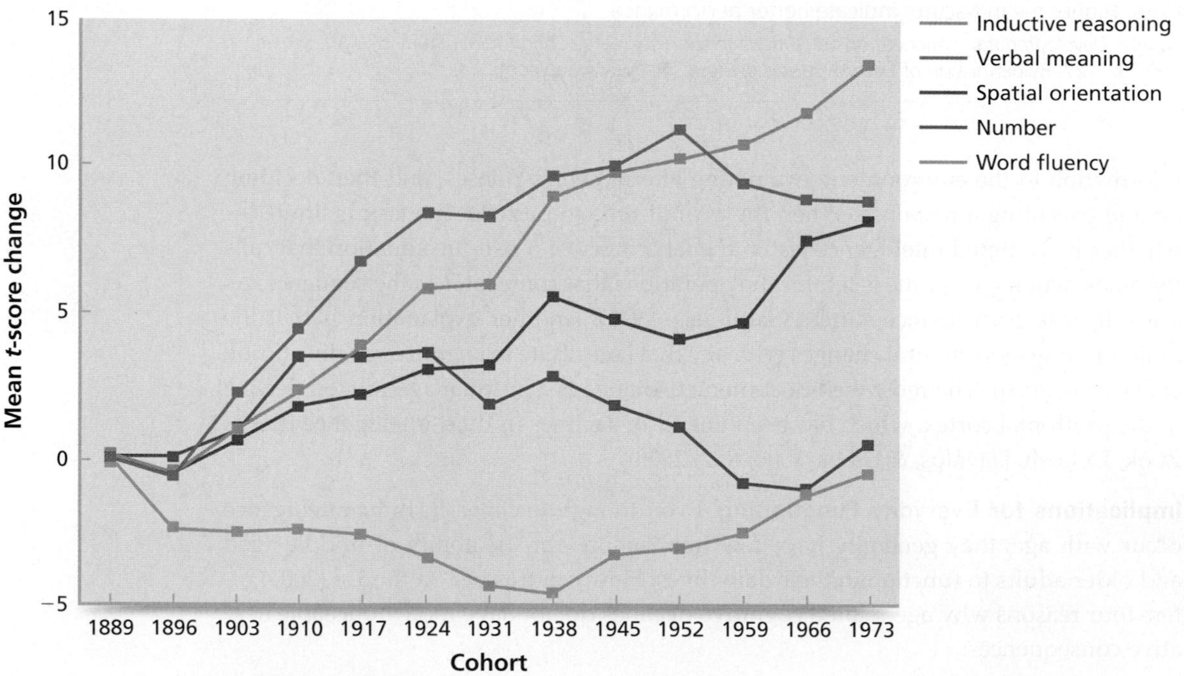

FIGURE 15.8

Gains in Various Dimensions of Intelligence in Successive Cohorts over the 20th Century

Note: Higher mean *t*-scores indicate better performance. Across 13 different cohorts—from those born in 1889 to those born in 1973—gains can be seen across multiple, though not all, cognitive abilities. Numerical abilities may have suffered when electronic devices for doing calculations began to be widely available.

Source: Schaie, K. W. (2005). *Developmental influences on adult intelligence: The Seattle Longitudinal Study.* New York: Oxford University Press, p. 144.

dimensional shape with flat surfaces). This same assignment appeared in a seventh-grade textbook by 1955, a third-grade textbook by 1971, and a first-grade textbook by 1991! Longer and more advanced schooling experiences may have contributed to the rise in intelligence documented over the 20th century. Other scientists favor biological explanations for the Flynn effect (such as improved nutrition, which enhances brain development and functioning), and still other scientists argue that both environmental and biological factors may be at work (Dickens & Flynn, 2001).

Expertise

If you could choose the person to pilot your next airplane flight, would it be the fresh, young 30-year-old right out of flight school or the 55-year-old veteran who has been a pilot for over 25 years? If you are inclined to opt for the older pilot, you may be counting on his additional years of experience to have helped him develop expertise in flying. **Expertise** refers to an organized set of skills and knowledge in a particular area acquired through extensive experience and practice (Bosman & Charness, 1996; Ericsson & Ward, 2007). Your hunch is probably that the older pilot would know how to react quickly and decisively if rough weather or technical problems were encountered during the flight. Veteran airline pilot "Sully" Sullenburger's remarkable landing on the Hudson River in 2009 is an example.

expertise An organized set of skills and knowledge in a particular area acquired through extensive experience in a particular domain.

Research on expert cognition bears out your hunch. Based on their years of experience, experts seem to be able to process information automatically and to draw upon their intuition about what will or will not work in order to solve a problem efficiently (Lewandowsky & Thomas, 2009). Experts are able to focus their attention on the information that is most critical in a particular situation, and they are less distracted by interruptions (Meade, Nokes, & Morrow, 2009). Often experts cannot explain exactly how they arrived at their solutions—instead, they are likely to say that a solution just felt right, based on past experience in similar situations. Beginners, in contrast, need to rely on formal training and rules to determine what to do in a given situation.

Not all middle-aged adults develop expertise in a particular area, but they are more likely to do so than young adults, because acquiring expertise takes time. In many areas, it takes 10 years or more of sustained practice to develop expertise (Ericsson & Ward, 2007). Having expertise in a particular area may help to compensate for some of the declines in cognitive and sensory functioning that occur with age (Horton, Baker, & Schorer, 2008). For example, accomplished middle-aged tennis players may lack the physical agility of younger players but may be able to continue playing well by relying on their instincts about what moves their opponent is likely to make during a game. By the same token, in many occupations, middle-aged and older workers often continue to function quite well despite age-related declines because of the expert skills and knowledge they have acquired over the years (Horton et al., 2008; Taylor, Kennedy, Noda, & Yesavage, 2007).

Creativity

Creativity is important in our lives in many ways. We enjoy the results of others' creative activity when we go to the movies or become engrossed in an interesting novel, and when we open a featherweight laptop or see a loved one's life saved by an organ transplant. And we draw on our own creative abilities when we take a photo, ponder how to rearrange the living room furniture, or try to think of a new approach to a vexing problem in a close relationship. You may know people who you consider to be especially creative. But what exactly is creativity?

Creativity has two defining characteristics (Sternberg and Lubart, 1999). It is the ability to produce work or a solution to a problem that is both *novel* (original, unexpected) and *appropriate* (useful, adaptive). Creativity is not the same thing as intelligence. Although a certain level of intelligence is required for creativity, additional

creativity The ability to produce work or a solution to a problem that is both novel (original, unexpected) and appropriate (useful, adaptive).

intelligence does not make a person more creative (Simonton, 2000). And simply having a creative insight is not the same thing as producing a creative work. It often takes well-developed skills and knowledge, strong intrinsic motivation to work hard, and an emotional investment in the work to produce a creative achievement (Keegan, 1996). For example, a medical breakthrough was announced in early 2008 that may have the potential to restore vision to many people who suffer from genetically based blindness (Maguire et al., 2008). The breakthrough began in the mid-1980s with a creative idea about implanting particular healthy genes in the retinas of blind individuals, but it took over 20 years to make this gene therapy a reality (Avril, 2008).

Is there an age when creativity flourishes and reaches a peak? This question has long intrigued researchers. Can you think of ways that a researcher might investigate the relationship between age and creativity? Perhaps you thought of bringing people of different ages into a laboratory and giving them tasks that assess their creativity. Or perhaps you thought of analyzing the creative works of prominent scientists, writers, artists, or musicians to discover when they were the most productive. These are exactly the strategies that creativity researchers have used to examine the relationship between age and creativity. Both strategies have yielded similar conclusions. Creative output tends to peak in early midlife, when people are in their early 40s, and then tends to decline gradually afterward. The prefrontal cortex appears to play an important role in creativity, as this is roughly the age when the prefrontal cortex matures (Dietrich, 2004). The age of peak creativity varies across disciplines, however, with creative achievements peaking earlier in the sciences than in the arts (Dietrich, 2004). In addition, creativity does not always decline after middle adulthood—some people continue to produce many creative works through later adulthood.

A decline in the *quantity* of creative output in older adulthood does not necessarily mean there is a decline in *quality* (Simonton, 1991). In fact, some researchers believe that gains in quality may offset declines in quantity. Simonton (1989) examined the "swan songs" of 172 classical composers—musical compositions written in the last years of their careers—and found that these compositions, although shorter and simpler, more often were among the most popular and important works they produced in their lifetimes. (For a summary of this section, see "Interim Summary 15.5: Cognitive Development.")

INTERIM SUMMARY 15.5

Cognitive Development	
Intelligence	■ **Crystallized intelligence** increases from young adulthood through midlife and generally remains intact until people are well into their 60s or 70s. **Fluid intelligence** peaks in young adulthood and generally declines fairly steadily thereafter. These changes may be due to a generalized slowing of cognitive processes with age, and to structural changes in the brain that occur. ■ Declines in fluid intelligence tend to have relatively few implications for the ability of middle-aged adults to function.
Expertise	■ Although not all middle-aged adults develop **expertise** in a particular area, they are more likely to do so than young adults because the acquisition of expertise often takes many years.
Creativity	■ Creative output tends to peak in early midlife, and then tends to decline gradually. Maturation of the prefrontal cortex in midlife may explain the midlife peak in creativity. A decline in the *quantity* of creative output in late middle adulthood and beyond does not necessarily mean there is a decline in *quality*.

COGNITIVE DEVELOPMENT IN CONTEXT

We saw in Chapter 13 that cognitive development in young adulthood is influenced by the cognitive stimulation and demands that young adults encounter in their daily lives, such as in college or in the workplace. Does the environment continue to influence cognitive development in midlife? And how does cognitive development in midlife influence the ability of middle-aged adults to deal with the cognitive challenges they encounter in the environment? We explore these questions next, focusing on work as a key context in midlife that may affect, and be affected by, the cognitive functioning of middle-aged adults.

Influence of Work on Cognition

Occupations vary in their cognitive complexity. Some jobs are fairly routine, with workers performing the same tasks every day, and experiencing few opportunities for initiative, decision making, or problem solving. Other jobs are much more complex—workers are required to supervise others, make plans, come up with original ideas, find solutions to unforeseen problems, and analyze and apply technical knowledge. Jobs of the latter type are considered to be high in **cognitive complexity**, and they have implications for intellectual functioning in adulthood.

cognitive complexity Type of thinking required in some life contexts (e.g., certain occupations) that involves initiative, decision-making, problem-solving, and analysis and application of technical knowledge.

In countries as diverse as the United States, Japan, Poland, and Ukraine, adults who work in jobs that are high in cognitive complexity have been found to show gains in intellectual functioning. Adults who work in jobs that are low in cognitive complexity, in contrast, tend to exhibit declines in intellectual functioning (Schooler, Mulatu, & Oates, 1999). A longitudinal study spanning a 20-year period revealed that cognitive complexity at work may benefit middle-aged and older workers even more than younger workers (Schooler et al., 1999; Schooler, Mulatu, & Oates, 2004). Not all middle-aged adults are involved in cognitively complex work, of course, but members of the Baby Boom generation are more likely than previous generations of middle-aged adults to work in professional, managerial, and technical positions (Willis & Schaie, 2006). Such positions typically entail the kind of cognitively complex work that contributes to better intellectual functioning.

Exactly how cognitively complex work contributes to enhanced intellectual functioning is not yet known, although workers who are rewarded at work for a high level of cognitive effort may be motivated to develop their intellectual abilities (Schooler et al., 1999). Brain changes may play a role, too, as suggested by studies showing that animals exposed to complex environments develop enhanced neurobiological functioning (Kempermann, Kuhn, & Gage, 1997). Finally, although much evidence suggests that complex work actually enhances intellectual functioning, it is also possible that people with stronger intellectual abilities are attracted to, and remain in, relatively more complex work in the first place (Dickens & Flynn, 2001).

Klaus Tiedge/Corbis

Cognitively complex work is associated with gains in intellectual functioning.

Influence of Cognition on Work

How well do the intellectual abilities of middle-aged adults allow them to function in the workplace? This issue is important in the lives of middle-aged and older adults who face the pressures of an increasingly competitive labor market and the prospect of ageist attitudes and age discrimination in the workplace. This issue is also important for society as the enormous Baby Boom generation approaches retirement age, raising concerns about the solvency of Social Security and Medicare. Most U.S. Boomers will be eligible for full Social Security benefits at age 66 or 67. But some experts project that if the Boomers were to remain in the workforce just 3 years longer—for example, by raising the age of eligibility for benefits to 69 or 70—the financial deficits now looming over the Social Security system could be eliminated within 75 years; this would help to keep the system solvent for future generations (Willis & Schaie, 2006). This potential solution to a worrisome societal problem depends, however, on the ability of middle-aged and older workers to remain in the workforce longer than previous cohorts have done (Willis & Schaie, 2006).

Can aging workers remain effective in their work roles even as they experience declines in fluid intelligence? The answer may lie in two of the developmental processes we have discussed previously—selection and optimization. Selection often leads people to specialize in a particular line of work, and over time, middle-aged adults often acquire expertise that allows them to perform tasks efficiently and to draw on past experience to solve difficult problems. Optimization may also help middle-aged adults remain effective at work, even as they experience such changes as slowing of performance. Older typists, for example, have been found to make up for declines in their typing speed by expanding the span of their gaze each time they view the material to be typed. Because they have to look at the material less often, their overall typing efficiency remains high even though the speed with which they move their fingers has declined (Salthouse, 1984). So both selection and optimization may help aging workers continue to function effectively in their jobs.

There is a catch, though: The changing world of work may mean that fewer people remain in the same line of work for many years. To the extent that it takes time to become an expert, acquiring expertise in a particular job may become more difficult. In addition, having expertise in a specific job may not be so advantageous when the job is eliminated or altered dramatically. Computer skills, for example, are now considered to be very, even extremely, important in over 40 percent of jobs (Johnson et al., 2007). Middle-aged and older workers will need to be adaptable in the rapidly changing world of work. The next chapter discusses career strategies that may be helpful to them. (For a summary of this section, see "Interim Summary 15.6: Cognitive Development in Context.")

INTERIM SUMMARY **15.6**

Cognitive Development in Context	
Influence of Work on Cognition	■ **Cognitive complexity** at work is of benefit to middle-aged and older workers.
Influence of Cognition on Work	■ Aging workers often are able to remain effective in their work roles, even as they experience declines in fluid intelligence. ■ Selection often leads people to specialize in a particular line of work, and middle-aged adults often acquire expertise that allows them to perform tasks efficiently and to draw on past experience to solve problems. ■ Optimization may also help middle-aged adults remain effective at work, even as they experience such changes as slowing of their performance.

SUMMING UP AND LOOKING AHEAD

We have seen how middle adulthood—the least studied period of the lifespan—straddles youth and old age. Declines in physical functioning, health, and cognitive abilities begin to emerge gradually as people move through middle adulthood, although gains in various areas of functioning are evident, too. Age-related changes may be noticeable to adults in early midlife, but they generally do not result in physical disabilities or interfere with daily functioning. By late midlife, more notable changes in sexual and reproductive functioning often have occurred, and health concerns become more salient. The cumulative effects of health behaviors, lifestyle choices, and life stress begin to be evident by late midlife, increasing the risk of chronic illness. Still, there is much that middle-aged adults can do to maintain their health. Moreover, they can draw upon their expertise and strong coping abilities in order to adapt to age-related changes in physical and cognitive functioning. In the next chapter, we explore how developmental tasks, social roles and relationships, and personality evolve in middle adulthood.

HERE'S WHAT YOU SHOULD KNOW

Did You Get It?

After reading this chapter, you should understand the following:

- What middle adulthood is, and the variability that takes place within it
- Physical changes that take place in middle-aged adults
- Reproductive and sexual functioning changes that take place in middle-aged adults
- Health conditions that affect middle adulthood
- How stress and health interact in the lives of middle-aged adults
- The cognitive changes that take place in middle adulthood
- How work and cognition influence the cognitive development of middle-aged adults

Important Terms and Concepts

acute illnesses (p. 485)
allostatic load (p. 488)
androgens (p. 482)
andropause (p. 483)
atherosclerosis (p. 479)
Baby Boom generation (p. 472)
chronic illnesses (p. 486)
climacteric (p. 481)
cognitive complexity (p. 497)
cohort (p. 472)
cohort effects (p. 472)
cortisol (p. 487)
creativity (p. 495)
crystallized intelligence (p. 491)
disability (p. 486)
erectile dysfunction (ED) (p. 483)
expertise (p. 495)
fluid intelligence (p. 491)
Flynn effect (p. 494)
glaucoma (p. 478)
high-density lipoprotein (HDL) (p. 477)
hormone replacement therapy (HRT) (p. 482)
hot flashes (p. 481)
hypertension (p. 479)
interindividual variability (p. 474)
intraindividual variability (p. 474)
low-density lipoprotein (LDL) (p. 477)
menopause (p. 481)
metabolic syndrome (p. 477)
osteoporosis (p. 476)
placebo (p. 482)
plaque (p. 479)
presbycusis (p. 478)
presbyopia (p. 477)
primary aging (p. 475)
prostate gland (p. 480)
sarcopenia (p. 477)
secondary aging (p. 485)
stress (p. 488)
stressors (p. 488)
testosterone replacement therapy (p. 483)
Type A personality (p. 489)
Type B personality (p. 489)

CHAPTER

16

Socioemotional Development in Middle Adulthood

Tom Morrison/Getty Images

After reaching midlife, comedian Jack Benny claimed on every birthday from that point forward that he had just turned 39. He dealt with the challenge of becoming middle-aged by simply denying it! Most of us have neither his powers of denial nor the ability to stop the clock, and our 40th, 50th, and 60th birthdays do eventually arrive. Are there reasons to dread these milestones, as Jack Benny apparently did? Or is middle age not so bad, perhaps even a good time of life?

Conflicting images and stereotypes of life in middle adulthood abound. On the one hand, midlife is seen as a time when people have settled into their lives and become proficient in many of their major social roles. This might make middle adulthood a relatively comfortable and satisfying period of life. On the other hand, midlife is seen as a time when family and work responsibilities mount, adding to daily pressures and demands. This could mean that middle adulthood is a stressful and unsatisfying period of life. Another common image is that midlife is a time when people become increasingly aware of their own aging, leading some to engage in reckless actions to preserve fleeting feelings of youthfulness—an extramarital affair or an impulsive purchase of a sports car. This image of middle adulthood is reflected in widespread beliefs about the "midlife crisis." These are puzzlingly different views of middle age. Are any of these images correct? In this chapter, we will examine what scientific evidence tells us about socioemotional development in middle adulthood.

We begin, as we did in our discussion of young adulthood, by considering whether development in middle adulthood is influenced by particular tasks or timetables. We also examine whether the processes people use to influence their own development begin to change in midlife—that is, whether shifts occur in the relative importance of the three processes we discussed when we looked at socioemotional development in young adulthood: selection (choosing manageable life goals), optimization (using and enhancing one's resources to pursue one's goals), and compensation (developing other strategies to pursue goals when one's resources decline). We then continue our journey through three major life domains—marriage and friendship, family relationships, and work—examining how experiences in each of these domains tend to unfold in middle adulthood. Finally, we explore how these experiences may affect the personalities and emotional well-being of middle-aged adults.

As we explore development in midlife, bear in mind that the developmental challenges and experiences that are common early in midlife (e.g., when people are in their 40s) may differ from those that are common later in midlife (e.g., when people are in their 50s and early 60s). Researchers have not yet charted the periods of adulthood in as much detail as they have infancy through adolescence, but when appropriate, we will provide examples of the developmental variations that exist within middle adulthood itself.

DEVELOPMENTAL TASKS, TIMETABLES, AND PROCESSES IN MIDLIFE

We saw in our discussion of young adulthood that societal norms regarding developmental tasks and timetables have loosened in recent decades but have not vanished altogether, serving as guidelines rather than rigid requirements for development in particular life periods. What are the primary developmental tasks of middle adulthood? Do middle-aged adults have timetables in mind as they pursue important goals? Do the ways that people seek to regulate their development shift from young adulthood to middle adulthood? We examine these *what*, *when*, and *how* aspects of developmental regulation in midlife next.

Developmental Tasks

A key idea in most stage theories of development is that the tasks accomplished in one life period lay a foundation for tasks that are undertaken in subsequent life periods. It is not surprising, then, that the developmental tasks of middle adulthood build upon the life paths that were initiated in young adulthood. Middle-aged adults seek to preserve their achievements and prevent losses in the key life domains in which they have invested their motivation, time, and energy (Havighurst, 1952).

Research confirms that age-related shifts occur in the key life tasks with which people grapple over the course of adulthood. For example, in a study that investigated age differences in adults' views of their primary life goals, young adults emphasized their future education, partnerships and family, friends, and occupation (Nurmi, 1992). Middle-aged adults, in contrast, emphasized securing what they already had established, fostering their children's future development, and dealing with property-related concerns. Goals related to preserving health also were noted by some middle-aged participants and were even more common in the oldest age group (a shift we will explore more fully in Chapter 18). In other words, young adulthood is a time in which new social roles are acquired, whereas middle adulthood is a time in which existing roles are maintained and strengthened.

generativity versus stagnation The key psychological struggle in middle adulthood, according to Erikson.

generativity The desire to contribute to one's family, community, and society by nurturing and guiding the next generation.

This does not mean, though, that the lives of middle-aged adults are static. Their roles as parents change as their children become teenagers and, later, leave home to launch independent lives. Their relationships with their spouses evolve, in turn, as their attention shifts from the shared tasks of parenting to their life together as a couple. Their connection to work may change in their late 50s and early 60s as they begin to anticipate retirement. Their roles as adult children often change as their parents age and begin to need assistance. In addition, in midlife, people often begin to reflect on their lives and what they have contributed to society. This process of reflection, and the actions it may kindle, are at the heart of Erikson's ideas about the chief psychosocial crisis of middle adulthood, **generativity versus stagnation**.

As you learned earlier, Erikson (1968) believed that a distinctive psychosocial crisis characterizes each life period. The key challenge in middle adulthood, in his view, involves the struggle between generativity and stagnation. **Generativity** refers to the desire to contribute to one's family, community, and society by nurturing and guiding

Jose Luis Pelaez/Getty Images

Generativity, the desire to nurture and guide the next generation, becomes an important concern for many middle-aged adults.

the next generation. Actions that reflect concern for the next generation benefit society and also benefit adults, by helping them to look beyond their own concerns and to feel that their contributions will endure after their lives have ended (McAdams, 2001). Adults in midlife who focus exclusively on their own needs may experience **stagnation**, a sense of self-absorption and lack of meaning.

stagnation A sense of self-absorption and lack of meaning that results when adults focus only on their own needs.

Consider an ambitious 56-year-old businessman who has worked his way to the top of the corporate ladder, becoming admired (and perhaps feared, as well) by his colleagues in the process. His successes have allowed him to own a beautiful home and an expensive car and to take luxurious vacations. But a divorce 5 years earlier has left him alone, with strained relationships with his adult children, who blame him for the divorce. These days he experiences gnawing doubts about what all the hard work has been for and what his life will have meant after he dies. This is an example of what Erikson meant by stagnation.

Erikson believed that this struggle is most salient in middle adulthood because it is in this life stage that people have the most skills and resources to be able to contribute to the well-being of others, if they can find ways to express generativity. A famous example is Bill Gates, co-founder and chairman of Microsoft. At midlife, Gates cut back on his corporate responsibilities to devote more time to the foundation he and his wife established to fund initiatives designed to improve the health and opportunities of poor people around the globe. Adults can be generative in a variety of different ways. Investing in efforts to improve the lives of one's children is perhaps the most common, but generativity can also be expressed by teachers, workplace mentors, community volunteers, and artists and others who create works of public benefit (McAdams, 2001).

Is generativity a more important concern in midlife than in other periods? Some evidence suggests that the answer may be yes. Researchers have studied generativity by asking people to rate themselves on generative characteristics (see examples in Table 16.1), and also by asking people to describe their lives and then coding the descriptions for generative themes (McAdams & de St. Aubin, 1992). In cross-sectional and longitudinal studies, middle-aged adults score higher on generativity than young and older adults (McAdams, 2001). Volunteer work, which reflects generativity, also increases in middle and later adulthood (Hart, Southerland, & Atkins, 2003). Erikson believed that successfully resolving the struggle between generativity and stagnation would contribute to better psychological health, and research bears out his prediction.

TABLE 16.1 Sample Items Used to Assess Generativity in Adulthood

- I try to pass along the knowledge I have gained through my experiences.
- I feel as though I have made a difference to many people.
- I have made and created things that have had an impact on other people.
- I have important skills that I try to teach others.
- I have made many commitments to many different kinds of people, groups, and activities in my life.
- I have a responsibility to improve the neighborhood in which I live.
- I feel as though my contributions will exist after I die.

Note: These items are from a 20-item survey that asks research participants to rate how much each item describes them, from 0 *not at all like me* to 4 *very much like me*.

Source: Adapted from McAdams. D. P., & de St. Aubin, Ed. (1992). A theory of generativity and its assessment through self-report, behavioral acts, and narrative themes in autobiography. *Journal of Personality and Social Psychology, 62*, 1003–1015.

Highly generative individuals report greater life satisfaction, less depression and anxiety, and greater happiness with their social relationships (de St. Aubin & McAdams, 1995; Keyes & Ryff, 1998). The developmental tasks of middle adulthood, then, revolve around maintaining existing roles and relationships, taking stock of one's life, and finding ways to make contributions to others.

Developmental Timetables

Is there a timetable or social clock that propels middle-aged adults to accomplish key developmental tasks within a particular time frame? This seems to be less true than in young adulthood, because the key tasks of middle adulthood generally involve ongoing activities in established roles and relationships rather than specific events with clear beginnings and endings. Timetables apply more to well-defined events, such as having a child or getting a first job, than to ongoing tasks, such as being a good parent or advancing in one's career. Because the developmental tasks of middle adulthood are less apt to be punctuated by distinct beginnings and endings, they are less likely to be governed by a social clock.

Does this mean that middle-aged adults are not monitoring the passage of time and gauging their progress toward life goals accordingly? Not at all. In fact, an interesting psychological shift in the perception of time begins to occur in midlife and continues into later life. Middle-aged adults become aware that the time they have left to live, and therefore the time left to accomplish life goals, is limited (Lachman, 2004). Bernice Neugarten (1979; Neugarten & Datan, 1974) was one of the first theorists to point out that our subjective sense of time can affect us in important ways. As you read on, you might think about your own subjective sense of time and whether it reflects your stage in life.

Early in life, one's time horizon seems to stretch indefinitely, and life's possibilities seem unconstrained by time. But by middle age, people begin to gauge time not in terms of how long they have been alive, but in terms of how much longer they have to live. Middle-aged adults start to view time as a finite resource, and, as a result, they often feel the need to reevaluate and reprioritize their goals (Carstensen, Isaacowitz, & Charles, 1999). Life goals that they have postponed, or attempted but not yet achieved, often take on special urgency (Heckhausen, 1999). At the same time, they may come to view other goals as simply unrealistic, given the time and energy required—resources that become limited as people age. At midlife, a woman who has always wanted to own a home may realize there is no time to waste in getting her finances in order if she is to achieve this goal. Or a man in his 50s who has long dreamed of taking skiing lessons may realize that it would take years to become a good skier, and he isn't as agile as he used to be. He might give up this goal to pursue something less demanding. The recognition that time is limited affects the processes by which middle-aged adults manage their lives and, in doing so, influences their development (Carstensen et al., 1999; Neugarten, 1979; Staudinger & Bluck, 2001).

Processes of Developmental Regulation

The process of deciding which life goals remain desirable, and viable, may remind you of one of three key processes described in the theory of selective optimization with compensation: *selection* (Baltes & Baltes, 1990; Baltes, Lindenberger, & Staudinger, 1998). Selection operates throughout the lifespan, but it can take on a different meaning as people grow older.

elective selection The process of selection that is directed toward choosing among alternative goals that are attractive and that seem attainable.

In young adulthood, the process of selection involves choosing among alternative life goals that are seen as attractive and attainable. This is called **elective selection**. People in their early 40s (early in middle adulthood), may still be engaged in elective selection, as they seek opportunities and weigh options for improving their life circumstances and those of their family members (Helson, Soto, & Cate, 2006;

Staudinger & Bluck, 2001). As people move through middle adulthood and reach old age, however, selection more often involves scaling back or relinquishing goals that no longer seem attainable, because either one's own capacities and resources or one's opportunities have declined (Helson et al., 2006; Staudinger & Bluck, 2001). This is called **loss-based selection** (Freund & Baltes, 2002). People in late middle age (those in their late 50s and early 60s) can still initiate new life goals, of course, but more often they focus on maintaining existing goals and paring back or giving up unattainable goals.

This shift with age was found in a study of 510 young, middle-aged, and older adults who were asked to describe their five most important hopes, goals, and plans for the next 5 to 10 years (Heckhausen, 1997). The goals they reported were classified by the researchers as oriented toward achieving gains (e.g., getting a better paying job, improving an important social relationship) or avoiding losses (e.g., avoiding a job layoff, preventing problems). As you can see in Figure 16.1, with age, the number of gain-oriented goals decreased and the number of loss-oriented goals increased. The middle-aged and older adults also were less optimistic than the young adults about the likelihood of obtaining their personal goals.

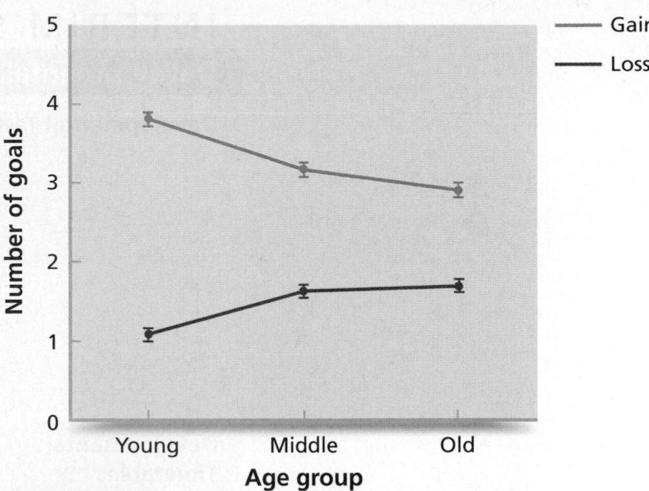

FIGURE 16.1

Life Goals that Involve Striving for Gains versus Avoiding Losses Across Age Groups

Source: Heckhausen, J. (1997). Developmental regulation across adulthood: Primary and secondary control of age-related challenges. *Developmental Psychology, 33,* 176–187.

Relinquishing goals that are perceived to be unattainable can be adaptive, as it keeps people from ruminating and feeling distressed about their unfulfilled aspirations. It also helps them redirect their energies toward other goals (Heckhausen, 1999; Wrosch & Freund, 2001). Goals sometimes become unattainable because of declining biological capacities. The **biological clock**, for example, limits the period of time in a woman's life during which she can bear children. In one study, middle-aged women who wanted to have children and who knew their biological clock was running out greatly increased their efforts to become pregnant (Heckhausen, Wrosch, & Fleeson, 2001). Among the women who remained childless after their biological clock had run out, those who could not let go of their dream experienced more symptoms of depression than those who were able to relinquish the goal. Being able to disengage from unattainable goals can be adaptive at any point in the lifespan, but it becomes a more important strategy of developmental regulation in middle and later adulthood as declining resources and opportunities begin to make more goals more difficult to achieve (Heckhausen & Schulz, 1995; Heckhausen, Wrosch, & Schulz, 2010).

loss-based selection The process of selection directed toward scaling back or relinquishing goals that are no longer attainable because of declines in one's resources for goal pursuit.

biological clock A woman's awareness that there is a finite period of time in her life during which she is biologically capable of bearing children, sometimes leading to a subjective sense of a deadline for bearing a first child.

The idea that midlife is a time when people direct many of their energies toward maintaining existing goals suggests that another process of developmental regulation—*optimization*—may take on special importance. The focus in midlife is on preserving gains that have been achieved in various life domains and preventing losses. Preserving one's resources, such as keeping up one's job skills at work, is an important strategy for this purpose.

Compensation, the third process in the theory of selective optimization with compensation, can be important at any point in the lifespan, but it assumes increasing importance as physical and cognitive resources begin to decline with age. Workers in their 50 and 60s, for example, sometimes compensate for declines in the speed with which they complete job tasks by increasing the accuracy of their work. (For a summary of this section, see "Interim Summary 16.1: Developmental Tasks, Timetables, and Processes in Midlife.")

INTERIM SUMMARY 16.1

Developmental Tasks, Timetables, and Processes in Midlife	
Developmental Tasks	■ The developmental tasks of middle adulthood build upon the life paths initiated in young adulthood. Middle-aged adults seek to preserve their achievements and prevent losses in the key life domains in which they have invested their motivation, time, and energy. ■ Erikson believed the key challenge in middle adulthood was the struggle of **generativity vs. stagnation**. **Generativity** refers to the desire to contribute to one's society by nurturing the next generation. **Stagnation** refers to a sense of self-absorption and lack of meaning.
Developmental Timetables	■ Because the developmental tasks of middle adulthood are less apt to be punctuated by distinct beginnings and endings, they are less likely to be governed by a social clock. However, middle-aged adults become aware that the time they have left to live and accomplish their goals is limited.
Processes of Developmental Regulation	■ Adults in their early 40s may be engaged in **elective selection** as they continue to seek ways to improve their lives. Later in midlife, the process of selection is more often directed toward scaling back or relinquishing goals. This is called **loss-based selection**. ■ Goals sometimes become unattainable because of declining biological capacities. The **biological clock**, for example, limits the time in a woman's life during which she can bear children. ■ Because people direct their energies toward maintaining existing goals in midlife, *optimization* may take on special importance. ■ *Compensation* also assumes increasing importance as physical and cognitive resources begin to decline in midlife.

MARRIAGE AND FRIENDSHIP IN MIDLIFE

Relationships in midlife are more variable today than they were in the past. Many people are now choosing to cohabitate rather than to marry, and the number of people opting to remain single has been rising. Gay and lesbian couples often form long-term unions that offer many of the same satisfactions and challenges as marriage. Divorce is becoming more common in middle adulthood, sometimes followed by another marriage that creates a **blended family**, one with children from the current marriage and stepchildren from a prior marriage. Given the later age for both first and second marriages, some middle-aged couples may be newlyweds. Other couples may have been together for 20 to 30 years, or even longer. Let's explore what is known about the quality of intimate partnerships in midlife.

blended family A family with children from a current marriage as well as stepchildren from a prior marriage.

Marital Satisfaction in Midlife

As you have learned, declines in marital satisfaction typically emerge fairly early in the course of a couple's life together. But what happens after couples have been together for decades? Does marital satisfaction continue to decline in middle adulthood, or does it level off or perhaps even improve?

Changes in Marital Satisfaction If you lean toward the most optimistic pattern—the idea that marital satisfaction improves after couples have been together for a long time—then your hunch matches what was once conventional wisdom. For many years, scientists felt that marital satisfaction is high at the beginning of a marriage, declines in midlife when the responsibilities of work and parenting intensify, and then rebounds later when children are grown and leave home. This view implied that marital quality would follow a U-shaped pattern over time, reaching a low point in middle adulthood (Orbuch, House, Mero, & Webster, 1996; Spanier, Lewis, & Cole, 1975).

Karte M. Deioma/PhotoEdit Inc.

Family forms are more diverse today than ever. Blended families include parents and children from the current marriage and the prior marriage of one or both parents.

This view was based largely on cross-sectional studies that assessed young, middle-aged, and older couples' views of their marriages at one point in time. One problem with such studies is that by midlife, the most troubled marriages are likely to have ended in divorce. The apparent rebound in marital satisfaction after midlife could simply reflect the fact that unhappy couples were no longer in the studies. It is also possible that cohort differences could have affected the results. The older adults in these early cross-sectional studies grew up during a time when expectations for marital happiness were much more modest. Marriages were not expected to be the primary source of satisfaction and personal fulfillment in couples' lives (Coontz, 2007). As a result, older adults may have been spared from feeling that their marriages were not achieving these ideals. If so, then the apparent increase in marital satisfaction in later adulthood would reflect a *cohort effect* (the impact of important historical and sociocultural events and norms on an individual's development) rather than a consequence of how long respondents had been married (Glenn, 1998).

Recent longitudinal studies that have tracked individuals over time are suggesting new views of the course of marital satisfaction. In one study, the marital happiness of over 2,000 adults was assessed multiple times over a 17-year period (VanLaningham, Johnson, & Amato, 2001). In contrast to the U-shaped pattern documented in earlier studies, this study found that marital satisfaction declined gradually, but steadily, over time. Another large longitudinal study spanning an 8-year period found that participants' positive marital experiences (e.g., feeling loved and cared for) decreased and their negative marital experiences (e.g., having disagreements and conflicts) increased over time (Umberson, Williams, Powers, Chen, & Campbell, 2005). Feelings of marital love among middle-aged adults declined over a 7-year period in another study, although overall marital satisfaction leveled off after an initial period of decline (Whiteman, McHale, & Crouter, 2007). This longitudinal research, therefore, suggests that marital quality either declines fairly steadily over time or declines initially and then levels off, as shown in Figure 16.2 (Doyle, 2006).

You've probably heard of couples who became parents in order to improve their marriage, but does having children have this effect? Research challenges this idea, as marital quality has been found to decline more sharply among adults with very young children or children who were reaching puberty and less sharply among adults who experienced the "empty nest" (children leaving home) (Umberson et al., 2005; Whiteman et al., 2007). But even though marital quality may suffer somewhat in young and middle adulthood from the strains of parenting, the opposite may be true in later life: Having adult children is associated with positive marital experiences (Umberson

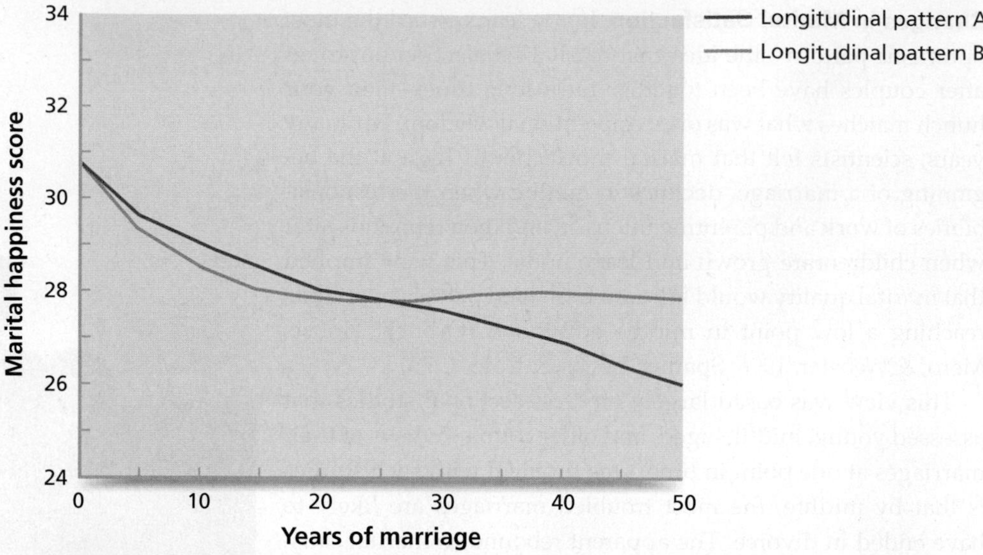

FIGURE 16.2

Longitudinal Estimates of the Association Between Years of Marriage and Marital Happiness

Note: Current estimates of the relationship between years of marriage and marital happiness reflect either longitudinal pattern A or longitudinal patttern B.
Source: Doyle, R. (2006, March). By the numbers: The honeymoon is over. *Scientific American*, p. 34.

et al., 2005). Adult children can provide support to their aging parents, reducing their stress and facilitating positive marital interaction. Marriages are not static—they change as family relationships, roles, and patterns of interaction change.

Enhancing Marital Satisfaction Although you may feel discouraged about the fact that couples' happiness usually starts to drop once they leave the altar (or, at the very least, soon after), it is important to keep in mind that research documenting declines in marital satisfaction over time reflect group trends, and there are exceptions to every rule. Many people remain happily married over time, and researchers are learning about the factors that help to preserve marital quality into midlife. What have developmental scientists discovered about happy couples?

Spouses in long-term happy marriages express affection toward each other and describe their marriages as emotionally close and caring. They are less likely to communicate with each other negatively and are more likely to express warmth and use humor in their problem-solving discussions (Bradbury & Karney, 2004; Huston, Caughlin, Houts, Smith, & George, 2001). Happily married individuals also have a sense of "we-ness"—they think about what is good for the relationship and not just what is good for themselves (Carrére, Buehlman, Gottman, Coan, & Ruckstuhl, 2000).

In many ways, marriages in which people treat each other like very good friends—companionate marriages—seem to be the most satisfying and stable over time (Gottman & Silver, 1999; Huston et al., 2001). While campaigning in 2008 for his wife's nomination to run for President, Bill Clinton expressed this view at a campaign stop when asked by a 5-year-old boy what marriage is like. Although he and his wife certainly had their own well-publicized share of marital difficulties, the 61-year-old former President noted the importance of friendship in marriage when he replied: "If you're really lucky . . . then your husband or wife becomes your best friend, and you get to live with your best friend for the rest of your life."

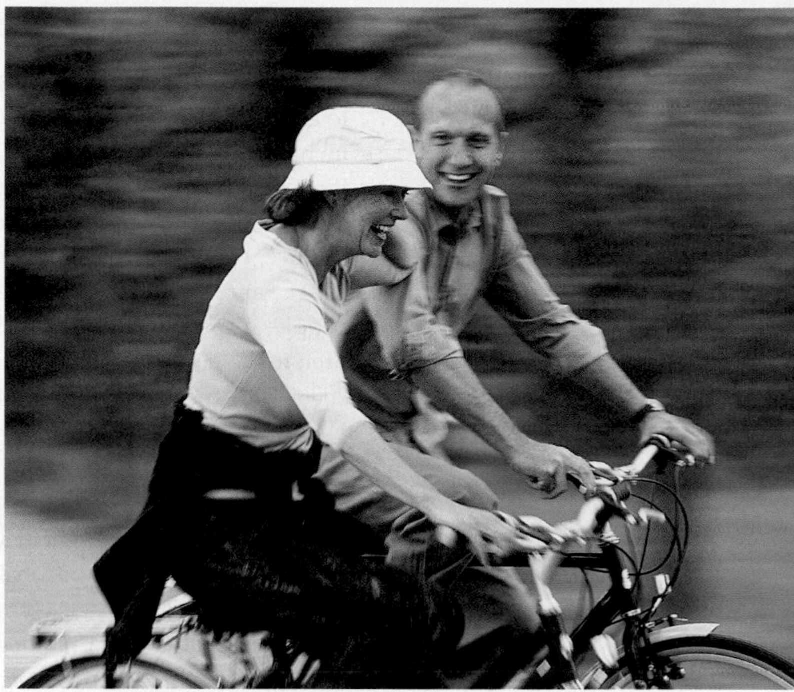

Couples who find ways to share adventures and stimulating activities together can help to keep the sparks of love alive in their relationship.

Researchers also are discovering ways that people in long-term marriages can rekindle feelings of excitement and passion in their relationship. Social psychologist Art Aron and his colleagues (Aron, Norman, Aron, McKenna, & Heyman, 2000) have found in both laboratory and field studies that couples who engage in novel, stimulating activities together experience increased feelings of love, compared to couples who engage in pleasant, but familiar, activities. Couples who vary their routines to include not only familiar activities, such as going to a movie or going out to eat, but also less typical activities, such as going to a concert or going hiking or dancing together, experience a boost in their feelings about their relationship.

Before we leave our discussion of marital satisfaction, it is useful to remember that commitment is a key component of love, as highlighted in Sternberg's triangular theory of love, which we discussed during our look at close relationships in young adulthood (Sternberg, 1986). Some marriages in middle adulthood thrive because the spouses are committed to each other or to the institution of marriage itself (Pruchno & Rosenbaum, 2003). Many people in long-term marriages or cohabiting relationships understand that juggling family and work roles may take a toll on their relationship, but they prefer to stay together nonetheless. For some couples, feelings of commitment and a shared sense of accomplishment in raising a family together are more important than the ebb and flow of feelings of personal satisfaction. And, as is true of young adults, middle-aged adults who are married tend to be happier and healthier, on average, than divorced and widowed individuals (Marks & Lambert, 1998).

Divorce in Midlife

People in long-term relationships of chronically low quality, of course, experience marked declines in well-being (Hawkins & Booth, 2005). For some, this leads to divorce. The majority of divorces occur relatively early in the course of a marriage, but divorces among middle-aged couples are becoming more common (Bramlett & Mosher, 2002; Heidemann, Suhomlinova, & O'Rand, 1998). Some researchers attribute the rising rates of divorce in midlife to women's greater involvement in the workforce, which has increased their economic and psychological independence, making it easier for them to end troubled marriages (Furstenberg, 1990; Heidemann et al., 1998).

Marital problems develop in middle adulthood for many of the same reasons as they do in young adulthood. Persistent marital conflict, coupled with life stress, erodes feelings of love and goodwill in both age groups. And, as is true in young adulthood, divorce in midlife is harmful to psychological and physical health, taking a toll on longevity as well (Dupre & Meadows, 2007). Even people for whom divorce brings relief from marital turmoil and conflict experience stress as they adjust to a new way of living (Dupre & Meadows, 2007). Whether the impact of divorce differs in midlife as compared to young adulthood is unclear. Some research suggests that divorce is harder on middle-aged adults (Antonucci, Akiyama, & Merline, 2001; Berardo, 1982), but other research suggests that middle-aged adults have more resources and are more adaptable than young adults, factors that might cushion the impact of divorce (Marks & Lambert, 1998).

Gender plays a role, as middle-aged men are more likely than middle-aged women to experience worse health following divorce (Williams & Umberson, 2004). Divorced men experience a loss of emotional support and support for a healthy lifestyle, and they are more likely to engage in poor health behaviors (Dupre & Meadows, 2007). On the other hand, women often suffer a marked decline in their financial resources after divorce, creating financial hardship that may persist into later life (Antonucci et al., 2001). Family factors play a role, too. The aftermath of divorce appears to be harder for people—especially women—with young children in the home, and having young children in the home also reduces the likelihood of remarriage (Goldscheider & Kaufman, 2006; Williams & Dunne-Bryant, 2006).

Remarriage in Midlife

The negative impact of divorce generally declines as time passes, and remarriage often contributes to a recovery of psychological well-being. The majority of people who divorce eventually marry (or cohabit) again, usually within 5 years (Cherlin & Furstenberg, 1994). Rates of remarriage are lower in midlife than in young adulthood, however, particularly among women. Among women under age 25, 90 percent remarry after divorce; among divorced women over age 40, in contrast, only about 30 percent remarry (Bramlett & Mosher, 2002). A primary reason for this difference is that the **marriage market** differs for men and women (De Graaf & Kalmijn, 2003). Societal norms make it acceptable for men to marry younger women, but women are discouraged from marrying younger men. In addition, women tend to outlive men. For both of these reasons, middle-aged women have a smaller pool of potential mates than middle-aged men, leading to women's lower rates of remarriage (Cherlin & Furstenberg, 1994).

marriage market The idea that prospects for marriage or remarriage may differ for men and women due to sex differences in longevity and to social norms regarding the suitable age of a partner.

What does this mean for someone who would like to be married in midlife but cannot find a compatible partner? As we've seen, successful development requires people to adjust their goals to fit the realities of their circumstances. Support for this idea emerged in a study in which recently divorced young and middle-aged adults were asked to list their most important personal goals for the next 5 to 10 years (Wrosch & Heckhausen, 1999). The middle-aged adults listed fewer goals related to forming an intimate relationship and reported making fewer efforts to find a partner. When asked how they would respond if they were unable to form a new partnership, the middle-aged adults indicated that they would focus their attention on other goals and on ways in which their lives compared favorably with those of other people. In a memory test, after being asked to read a series of statements about positive and negative aspects of marriage, the middle-aged adults recalled fewer positive and more negative statements.

These findings suggest that the divorced middle-aged adults were disengaging—consciously and unconsciously—from the goal of remarrying. Moreover, as the theory of selective optimization with compensation would predict, disengaging from an elusive goal appeared to be adaptive for the middle-aged adults. At a follow-up 15 months later, the researchers found that disengaging from the goal of remarrying was associated with improved psychological well-being among middle-aged adults but with declines in well-being among young adults (see Figure 16.3). One way of interpreting this is that goal disengagement is

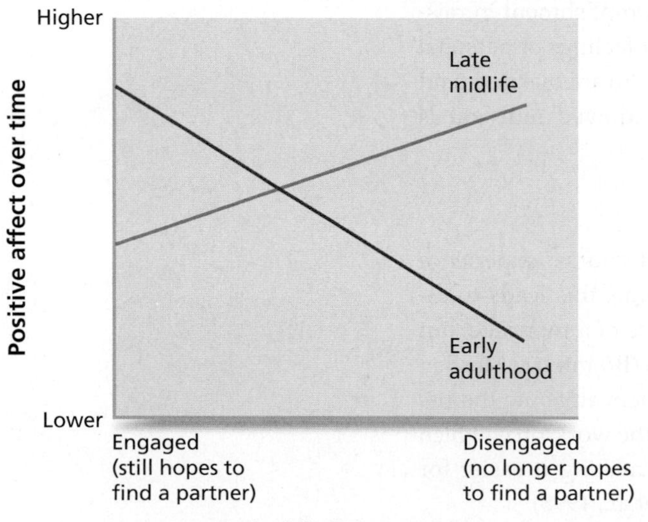

FIGURE 16.3

Disengaging from the Goal of Finding a Partner in Late Midlife versus Early Adulthood as a Predictor of Psychological Well-Being over a 15-Month Period

Source: Adapted from Wrosch, C., & Heckhausen, J. (1999). Control processes before and after passing a developmental deadline: Activation and deactivation of intimate relationship goals. *Journal of Personality and Social Psychology, 77,* 415–427.

self-protective when a goal has little prospect of being attained. Giving up on potentially attainable life goals too soon, however, can be problematic, as indicated by the data for the young adults in this study. Having an intimate partnership is a particularly important life goal in young adulthood (Erikson, 1968), and young adults who relinquish this goal prematurely may experience psychological distress. In other words, the same decision (whether to pursue or relinquish a life goal) can have very different consequences for mental health depending on one's life stage.

Friendship in Midlife

Friends make important contributions to well-being throughout adulthood, including middle adulthood. Getting together with friends is a common way that people relax, enjoy themselves, and take their minds off the stresses of the day. Friends also provide support during difficult life transitions, such as marital separation and divorce (Ginsberg, 1986). And as we saw in our discussion of socioemotional development in young adulthood, friendship is a key reason that never-married adults are often satisfied with their lives and well-adjusted psychologically; their needs for intimacy and companionship are met by close friends, siblings, and others (DePaulo & Morris, 2005). Friends are also distinctly important to gay men and lesbians, especially if their family members do not provide support (Peplau & Fingerhut, 2007).

Contact with friends tends to decrease over the course of adults' lives. In one study of time use patterns, adolescents spent nearly 29 percent of their time awake with friends, compared to 7 percent among middle-aged adults and 9 percent among older adults (Hartup & Stevens, 1999). Other studies have found a similar decrease in the frequency of contact with friends, with dips seen in early adulthood and again in midlife (from age 40 to 50; Carstensen, 1992), as you can see in Figure 16.4. If you look at Figure 16.4, you'll also see that even though adults spend less time with their friends than adolescents do, they feel close and satisfied with their friendships. The high quality of interaction with friends makes up for declines in the quantity of interaction. As people age, they increasingly choose to spend time with the people they enjoy most, a shift that we explore more closely when we discuss older adults' social relationships later in the book. (For a summary of this section, see "Interim Summary 16.2: Marriage and Friendship in Midlife.")

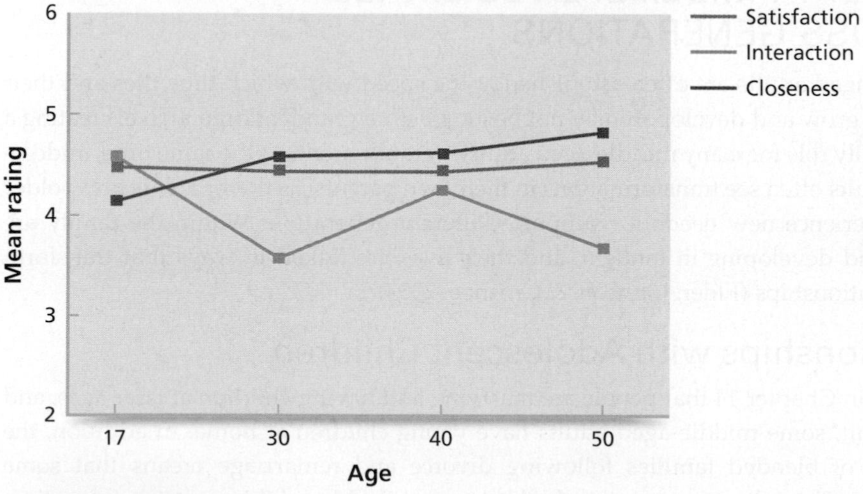

FIGURE 16.4

Ratings by Age of Interaction Frequency, Satisfaction, and Emotional Closeness with Close Friends

Source: Carstensen, L. L. (1992). Social and emotional patterns in adulthood: Support for socioemotional selectivity theory. *Psychology and Aging, 7,* 331–338.

INTERIM SUMMARY 16.2

Marriage and Friendship in Midlife	
Marital Satisfaction in Midlife	■ Changes in marital quality over time exhibit either a steady decline or an initial decline that eventually levels off. Marital quality declines among childless couples as well as those with children. ■ Spouses in long-term happy marriages express affection toward each other and describe their marriages as emotionally close. They communicate with each other less negatively and express greater warmth and use more humor in problem-solving.
Divorce in Midlife	■ The majority of divorces occur relatively early in the course of a marriage, but divorces among middle-aged couples are becoming more common. ■ Marital problems develop in midlife for many of the same reasons as they do in young adulthood. As is true in young adulthood, divorce in midlife is harmful to psychological and physical health.
Remarriage in Midlife	■ Rates of remarriage are lower in midlife than in young adulthood, particularly among women. A primary reason for this is that the **marriage market** differs for men and women. Societal norms make it more acceptable for men to marry someone younger than themselves. In addition, women tend to outlive men, making their pool of potential partners smaller.
Friendship in Midlife	■ Friends make important contributions to well-being in midlife, and although the contact with friends tends to decrease over the course of adults' lives, their feelings of closeness with friends remains high.

FAMILY IN MIDLIFE: LIVES LINKED ACROSS GENERATIONS

Middle-aged adults are often astonished at the speed with which time flies and their children grow and develop. It may not be long before grandchildren arrive, creating a new family role for many middle-aged adults—grandparent. At the same time, middle-aged adults often see transformations in their own parents, as their parents grow older and experience new needs for support. Different generations within the family are aging and developing in tandem, and their lives are linked in ways that transform their relationships (Elder, Johnson, & Crosnoe, 2003).

Relationships with Adolescent Children

We saw in Chapter 14 that people are marrying and having children at later ages, and as a result, some middle-aged adults have young children at home. In addition, the creation of blended families following divorce and remarriage means that some middle-aged adults are parenting both young and older children at the same time (Umberson, 1996). A nearly universal experience for parents at some point in midlife, however, is raising teenagers. Are the relationships between middle-aged parents and their adolescent children inevitably stormy? This is certainly a common image in the popular media, and it is a view that dominated early scientific thought about relationships between parents and their teenagers.

Why might parent-child relationships be strained when the children reach adolescence? Several possible explanations exist. First, teenagers' desire for autonomy and the increased time they spend either alone or with peers may lead to clashes with parents (Laursen, Coy, & Collins, 1998; Silverberg & Steinberg, 1990). Second, watching their children mature physically and sexually may increase middle-aged adults' awareness of their own aging and of possible declines in their physical and sexual attractiveness (Gould, 1972; Hamill & Goldberg, 1997). Third, as their children begin to date and fantasize about marriage and future careers, middle-aged adults may be prompted to evaluate the life choices they have made and whether their own hopes and dreams have been realized. In addition, as we mentioned earlier, in midlife, people begin to realize that their own time horizon for achieving life goals is limited. In contrast, the time horizon for their children is expansive. This comparison, too, might stimulate feelings of discomfort or envy in parents, perhaps straining their relationships with their teenagers. For these and other reasons, some of which we discussed in earlier chapters, many developmental scientists have wondered whether adolescence is a time of heightened conflict in the family.

Researchers have attempted to answer this question by examining whether parent-child conflict increases during adolescence. These studies indicate that the answer to this question is complicated. On the one hand, studies challenge the view that parents' relationships with their teenage children are conflict-ridden. In fact, the frequency of parent-child conflict declines, rather than rises, during adolescence. At the same time, though, the emotional intensity of parent-child conflicts increases during adolescence (Laursen et al., 1998). Perhaps the particularly intense and unpleasant nature of the arguments parents and teenagers have makes it feel as if these conflicts erupt frequently.

Why do conflicts between middle-aged parents and children occur less often but with greater emotional intensity during adolescence? Part of the explanation stems from the fact that, as noted above, children spend less time with their parents when they reach adolescence, spending more time alone and with peers, so there are fewer opportunities for disagreements to occur (Laursen et al., 1998). Yet—and this is the other part of the explanation—the disagreements that do occur are intense because adolescents are more emotionally volatile than children and because struggles over autonomy are troubling to both teenagers and their parents (Steinberg, 1990). Teenagers do not want their parents interfering in their personal and social lives; parents worry that their teenager might get involved in unsafe activities. Given these different agendas, discussions about where the teenager is allowed to go and curfews can become high-stakes battles. Adjusting to their children's passage through adolescence is more challenging for some parents than others, of course. Single parents and remarried parents appear to have a harder time, for example, than parents in satisfying marriages (Silverberg, Marczak, & Gondoli, 1996; Steinberg & Steinberg, 1994).

Although occasional unpleasant interactions occur, middle-aged parents generally manage to weather their children's adolescence (Steinberg, 1990). They then face a significant transition, as their children prepare to leave home and establish independent lives.

Relationships with Adult Children

If you moved away from home to attend college, you may have wondered how this affected your parents. If you happened to be the youngest child in your family, your departure would have emptied the parental nest. What do you suppose happened after you left? Did your parents break out the champagne and celebrate, or did they sink into a deep chasm of despair?

empty nest A transition experienced by parents when their last child leaves home.

When the Parental Nest Empties (and Refills) The "**empty nest**"—the phase of life that occurs when children are grown and the last child leaves home—was once thought to be a difficult time for middle-aged adults. Parents, especially mothers, were thought to experience feelings of sadness and a loss of identity. But we now know that these studies were flawed. The impression that parents adjust poorly to the empty nest came from studies that used small, nonrepresentative samples (including clinical samples, such as women seeking help for depression; e.g., Deykin, Jacobson, Klerman, & Solomon, 1966; Pillay, 1988). In addition, the early studies frequently used cross-sectional designs, which can make interpreting findings difficult, as we saw in our earlier discussion of marital satisfaction.

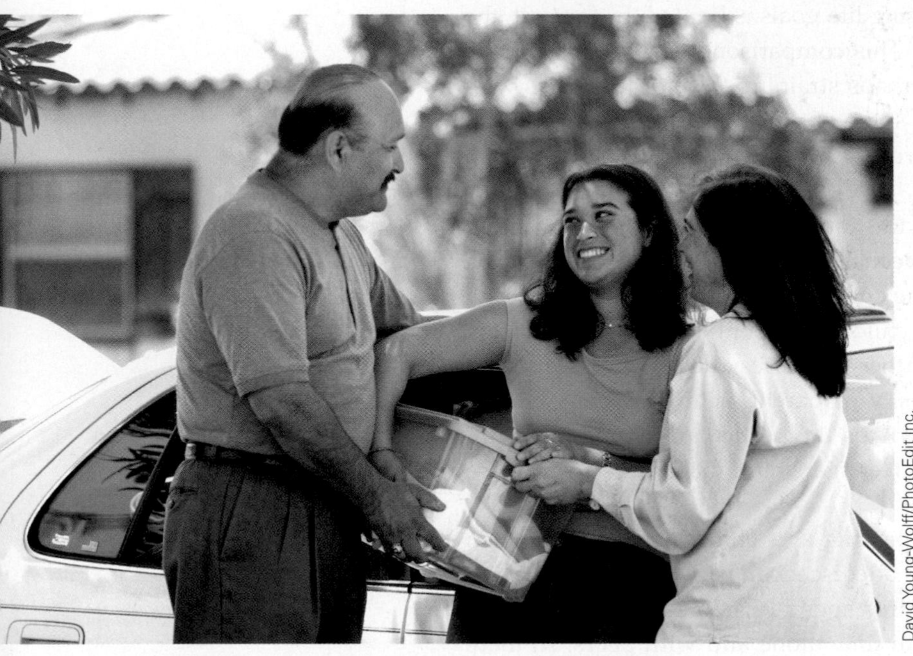

The nest is emptying for this middle-age couple as their youngest child leaves for college. How are they likely to adjust to this event?

More recent research using representative samples and longitudinal designs paints a different picture. Although middle-aged parents often feel twinges of sadness when the last child leaves home, these feelings tend to be short-lived, and parents' overall adjustment to this new phase of family life typically is quite positive (Dennerstein, Dudley, & Guthrie, 2002; White & Edwards, 1990). Middle-aged parents anticipate the transition to the empty nest, prepare for it, and generally do not find it to be stressful (Dennerstein et al., 2002). Empty nesters have more time together as a couple, as well as more time for friends, leisure, classes, or pursuing goals—such as attending college—that might have been put on hold while the children were being raised.

Of course, for some middle-aged adults, the nest empties more slowly than they had expected, and having young adult children who falter in their efforts to become independent and assume adult roles can detract from parents' well-being (Pillemer & Suitor, 1991). Other parents find that their children leave home, only to return to live with them for one or more extended stays. This phenomenon of **boomerang children** has become more common in recent years (Goldscheider, Goldscheider, St. Clair, & Hodges,1999; Mitchell, 2006). In 2009, roughly 16 percent of males and 10 percent of females ages 25 to 34 were living with a parent (U.S. Bureau of the Census, 2009). The reasons are often financial. Young adults may return home because the costs of higher education are unaffordable otherwise, because they have become unemployed or have low-paying jobs, or because they find it difficult to make ends meet after a marital separation or divorce (Casper & Bianchi, 2002).

boomerang children Young adults who return home to live with their parents after a period of living on their own.

Parents' reactions to a child returning home vary. Parents, especially single mothers, generally react more favorably if the child works and makes a contribution to the household. Fathers tend to be disapproving if the child is unemployed, but mothers often express more sympathy for the child's circumstances (Acquino, 1996). In general, though, parents and their adult children report feeling satisfied with their shared living arrangement, and negative effects on the parents' marital relationship appear to be rare (Pudrovska, 2008; Ward & Spitze, 2004).

The Quality of Relationships with Adult Children Middle-aged parents typically remain involved with their children after their children leave home, with close contact maintained through regular visits and phone calls. The majority of middle-aged parents and their adult children report that they enjoy each other's company and can rely on each other for emotional or practical support (Bengston, 2001). Middle-aged parents often provide extensive emotional support and aid as their adult children make their own transition to parenthood (Ward & Spitze, 2004). Middle-aged parents report greater psychological well-being if they have good relationships with their adult children, but the opposite is true as well—troubled parent-child relationships detract from the well-being of both mothers and fathers (Koropeckyj-Cox, 2002).

Parents' well-being is also associated with how their children turn out (Greenfield & Marks, 2006; Keyes & Ryff, 1999). Parents take pride in their children's accomplishments and experience greater self-esteem and life satisfaction when their children are doing well. They worry less and experience fewer recurring requests for assistance when their children are doing well. Their children's successes or problems also reflect on the middle-aged adults' own performance as parents. For all of these reasons, middle-aged parents experience greater emotional well-being when their children have fewer problems (Greenfield & Marks, 2006). This is particularly true among single parents, as you can see in Figure 16.5. When you learned about middle childhood in earlier chapters, you saw that parents' psychological health and marital quality can affect the development and functioning of their children. Now you can see that children's functioning also affects parents' psychological health, and this association persists over decades (Elder, Johnson, & Crosnoe, 2003).

Relationships with Grandchildren

Becoming a grandparent—on average, at age 48 in the United States (AARP, 2002)—is loaded with meaning for middle-aged adults. It can be an occasion to celebrate the maturation of one's own children as well as the continuation of the family into the future. But it can also be a tangible reminder of one's own aging.

Significance of the Grandparent Role How middle-aged adults take to the role of grandparent depends on many factors, including the grandparent's sex, employment status, and obligations to other family members. Women are more often the "kinkeepers"

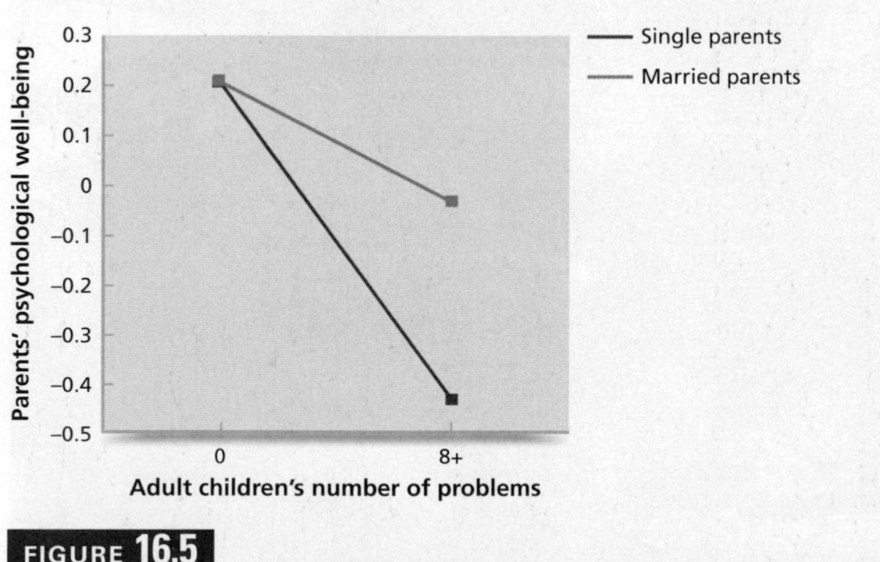

FIGURE 16.5

Adult Children's Problems and Parents' Psychological Well-Being

Note: As adult children have more problems, their parents' psychological well-being declines; this is especially true for single parents.

Source: From *Journal of Marriage and Family, 68*, pp. 442–454. Copyright © 2006. Reprinted by permission of Blackwell/Wiley through Rightslink.

than men, staying in touch with family members and orchestrating family gatherings; this extends to their role as grandparents, too. As a result, grandmothers tend to be closer to their grandchildren and somewhat more involved in their lives than are grandfathers (Putney & Bengston, 2001). Age matters, too. Younger middle-aged adults may still be working full time, leaving them less time to spend with grandchildren or to assist with childcare. Older middle-aged adults may be providing care to their aging parents, requiring them to juggle the support they provide each generation. Being a grandparent is a role that may span several decades, as many middle-aged adults will live long enough to see their grandchildren grow up and become adults (Reitzes & Mutran, 2004).

Family forms in the United States and elsewhere have become more varied and complex, and this means that grandparents' relationships with their grandchildren have also become complex. When an adult child's marriage ends in divorce, the breakup may affect the grandparents' involvement in the lives of their grandchildren. Because mothers usually receive custody of their children after divorce, maternal grandparents tend to be more involved with the grandchildren than are paternal grandparents (Cherlin & Furstenberg, 1986; Myers & Perrin, 1993). When their adult child remarries after a divorce, grandparents may experience challenges in forming bonds with step-grandchildren, especially if the step-grandchildren are older when the remarriage occurs (Longino & Erler, 1996). If the grandparents' own marriage ends in divorce, they have to forge new arrangements regarding access to their grandchildren. Although the legal rights of grandparents are in flux, most states in the United States grant visitation rights to grandparents.

skipped generation family
A family comprised of grandparents and their grandchildren without the children's parents being present.

Grandparents Raising Grandchildren Throughout the world, grandparents are an important source of aid with childcare, but in recent years, an increasing number of grandparents have become the primary caregivers for young grandchildren (Kinsella & Veroff, 2001). The term **skipped generation family** refers to households in which grandparents and grandchildren live together without the middle generation. These

AFP/Getty Images

Grandparents are raising grandchildren around the world. As many as half of the children orphaned by AIDS in Sub-Saharan Africa are being raised by their grandparents.

households form when an adult child cannot manage parenting responsibilities because of problems such as a drug or alcohol addiction, serious physical or mental illness, poverty, incarceration, or even death. The pandemic of AIDS in Sub-Saharan Africa has made orphans of as many as 10 million children under age 15, more than 50 percent of whom are being raised by grandparents (UNICEF, 1999; 2006). In the United States, 4.5 million children lived in homes headed by grandparents in 2000, a 30 percent increase from 1990 (Goyer, 2006). Such surrogate parenting can take a toll on the health and well-being of grandparents, many of whom did not expect to be raising children at this stage of their lives (Wang & Marcotte, 2007).

In our discussion of young adulthood, you learned that *off-time events* (events experienced at a non-normative age) can disrupt people's life plans. Conflicted feelings of love and resentment toward the adult child and additional strains on their own marriage can add to the stress experienced by grandparents who are raising grandchildren. It takes money to raise children, too, and grandparents living on fixed incomes often face unexpected financial difficulties. In the United States, grandparents who are raising grandchildren are disproportionately likely to be female, poor, and African American or, more recently, Hispanic (AARP, 2003a; Wang & Marcotte, 2007). Despite hardships, though, these grandparents usually commit themselves to their unexpected parental role and generally succeed in providing their grandchildren with much-needed security, stability, and nurturance.

Relationships with Aging Parents

Middle-aged adults' lives also are linked, in anticipated and unanticipated ways, not only to the younger generations in their family but also to the older generation—their parents. Relationships between middle-aged adults and their parents are usually warm and affectionate, based on frequent contact and mutual support. Research has shown that contact and closeness with parents tend to increase from young adulthood through midlife (Carstensen, 1992). Relationships between mothers and daughters tend to be especially close (Fingerman, 2001).

The parents of middle-aged adults often enjoy good health, but with advancing age they may begin to need assistance with some of the day-to-day tasks of living. Older adults turn first to their spouses for such aid, but when spouses are unavailable or unable to provide assistance, they turn to their adult children (Cantor, 1979). Throughout the world, adult daughters provide the bulk of care to aging parents and parents-in-law, although sons are becoming more involved in providing such care. In one recent study in the United States, 64 percent of the adults who were providing care to aging parents were daughters (Spillman & Black, 2005). Adult children who do not live near their parents and cannot provide in-person assistance nonetheless tend to be quite involved from a distance in trying to coordinate care for their parents.

The Sandwich Generation? Because U.S. families are smaller on average than they were in the past, adult children tend to have fewer siblings with whom to share the tasks of providing care to elderly parents (Kinsella & Velkoff, 2001). As a result, caregiving can be a demanding role, sometimes requiring working women to reduce their hours of employment, take a leave from work, or even quit their jobs (Marks, 1998). How stressful the caregiving role is depends on the nature of the parents' needs. Some parents may need help with meals, personal care (e.g., bathing, grooming), and transportation. Older parents with serious cognitive impairment may need round-the-clock supervision as well as help with these tasks. The title of a book written for caregivers—*The 36-Hour Day* (Mace & Rabins, 2006)—captures just how demanding it can be to care for a seriously ill or impaired older person.

Caregivers often have other responsibilities, too. As we noted earlier, some middle-aged adults who are caring for aging parents still have teenagers or young children at

sandwich generation The idea that middle-aged adults may be squeezed between the needs of the older and younger generations in their families or between work responsibilities and the needs of older generations.

home, and as a result, they are juggling multiple responsibilities. The term **sandwich generation** was coined to capture the image of middle-aged adults being squeezed, or sandwiched, between the needs of the older and younger generations in their families (Brody, 1985; Schwartz, 1977). Adults in the middle generation were thought to ricochet from one caregiving task to another, becoming emotionally and physically exhausted in the process. Yet the number of adults in midlife who are actually providing care simultaneously to children and to older parents turns out to be smaller than was once thought—only about 6 to 10 percent of middle-aged men and women (Rosenthal, Matthews, & Marshall, 1996; Spillman & Pezzin, 2000). Such findings have led some researchers to conclude that the sandwich generation is largely a myth (Putney & Bengston, 2001). At the very least, its prevalence has been greatly exaggerated.

Feeling squeezed between the needs of younger and older generations may have been a more common experience for middle-aged adults in an earlier era, when their elderly parents were more likely to have had health problems. As you will see in the next chapter, many older adults today often enjoy relatively good health and have little need for assistance until they are well into their 70s or 80s. By the time their elderly parents need assistance, then, middle-aged adults are unlikely to have children or teenagers still living at home. At the same time, though, many middle-aged women now have full-time jobs, and they may feel squeezed between work responsibilities and caring for elderly parents (Putney & Bengston, 2001). Viewed this way, as many as one-third or more of middle-aged women could be classified as being in the sandwich generation—not sandwiched between caring for their children and parents simultaneously, but sandwiched between work and caring for aging parents (Perrig-Chiello & Hopflinger, 2005; Spillman & Pezzin, 2000).

But are they as squeezed psychologically as the metaphor suggests? The evidence here is encouraging because it speaks to the adaptability of middle-aged adults. In general, middle-aged adults cope well with their dual sets of responsibilities (Loomis & Booth, 1995). They experience strain, but most feel able to manage this stress, and many feel grateful for the opportunity to repay their parents for the many years of support and care their parents provided to them (AARP, 2001; Putney & Bengston, 2001).

AFP/Getty Images

Adult children, especially daughters, provide a tremendous amount of care to their aging parents.

Death of a Parent The death of one or both parents is a sad, but common, reality for many middle-aged adults. Early in midlife, nearly half of adults have both parents alive, but by the end of midlife, over three-quarters of adults have no living parents (Lachman, 2004). The death of one's parents is not only often an anguishing experience for middle-aged adults but also one that often prompts self-reflection and a re-examination of their own life goals and priorities as they confront their own mortality (Umberson, 2003). Symbolic ties to their parents may persist for many years, even as they struggle to come to grips with the loss and with a revised identity, as the role of being someone's child has ended for them (Moss & Moss, 1983; Umberson, 2003). Feelings of grief eventually do subside, though, and the parents' death can be a kind of turning point for middle-aged adults who reinvest in their remaining relationships and redouble their efforts to make the best use of the time they have left to live (Umberson, 2003). (For a summary of this section, see "Interim Summary 16.3: Family in Midlife: Lives linked Across Generations.")

INTERIM SUMMARY 16.3

Family in Midlife: Lives Linked Across Generations

Relationships with Adolescent Children	■ A nearly universal experience for parents at some point in midlife is raising teenagers. Conflicts between middle-aged parents and children occur less often but with greater emotional intensity than during adolescence.
Relationships with Adult Children	■ The "**empty nest**" period was once thought to be a difficult time for middle-aged adults, but recent research suggests that parents' adjustment to this phase of life is positive. ■ Many parents see their children leave home only to return to live with them again. This phenomenon of **boomerang children** has become more common in recent years. In general, parents and their adult children report feeling satisfied with their shared living arrangement. ■ Middle-aged parents typically remain involved with their children after their children leave home, and often provide emotional support and aid as their adult children become parents.
Relationships with Grandchildren	■ How middle-aged adults take to the role of grandparent depends on a variety of factors, including the grandparent's sex, age, employment status, and obligations to other family members. ■ Most middle-aged adults consider grandparenthood to be a central role and an important source of life satisfaction. ■ In recent years, an increasing number of grandparents have become the primary caregivers for their grandchildren. The term **skipped generation family** refers to households in which grandparents and grandchildren live together without the middle generation.
Relationships with Aging Parents	■ The parents of middle-aged adults often enjoy good health, but with advancing age they may need assistance. Adult daughters provide the bulk of care to aging parents and parents-in-law, although sons are becoming more involved. ■ The term **sandwich generation** refers to middle-aged adults who are caring for their parents and are also caring for their own children or managing work responsibilities. ■ Early in midlife, nearly half of adults have both parents alive, but by the end of midlife, over three-quarters of adults have no living parents.

WORK IN MIDLIFE

Work is a major social role in midlife and a central context in which development unfolds. Approximately 70 to 80 percent of people in their 40s and 50s are employed (Bureau of Labor Statistics, 2009; Sterns & Huyck, 2001) (see Figure 16.6). Moreover, middle-aged and older workers will be an increasingly important part of the workforce as the Baby Boom generation continues to age. Currently, adults ages 55 and older make up about 12 percent of the workforce, but this figure is expected to rise to 20 percent by the year 2020 (Nyce, 2007).

Satisfaction with Work in Midlife

By middle age, many adults will have spent 20 to 30 years or more in the workforce. How do they feel about work, and what challenges do they face? Is the changing nature of work, which we discussed in Chapter 14, affecting middle-aged as well as young adults?

Work serves multiple functions in adults' lives, as you have already learned, from providing a source of income to serving as a context for personal growth. Research on the meaning of work for middle-aged and older workers suggests that it meets four basic needs (Mor-Barak, 1995):

1. *Social contact* (interaction and friendship with coworkers),
2. *Personal needs* (feelings of pride and self-worth),
3. *Financial needs* (income and health benefits), and
4. *Generativity* (the opportunity to pass on one's knowledge and skills to younger adults).

Most middle-aged workers continue to find meaning in their jobs, and the intrinsic rewards of work (such as a sense of accomplishment and purpose) assume greater importance in midlife (Sterns & Huyck, 2001). A recent survey found that roughly 50 to 60 percent of middle-aged workers reported that they derive feelings of pride from their work, compared with only 37 percent of young-adult workers (Harris Interactive,

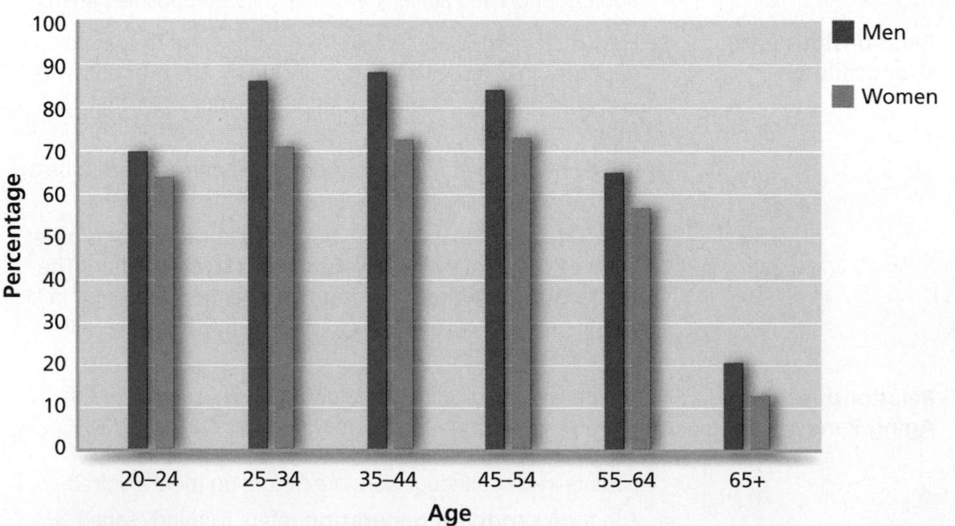

FIGURE 16.6

Percent of Men and Women Employed in the Labor Force by Age

Note: Data are for participation in the civilian labor force in 2008.

Source: Data from Bureau of Labor Statistics, "Employment Status of the Civilian Noninstitutional Population by Age, Sex, and Race." Retrieved April 2, 2010 from http://www.bls.gov/cps/cpsaat3.pdf

2005). In another recent survey, nearly 90 percent of workers ages 50 and older reported that they enjoyed work and were satisfied with their jobs overall (Nelson, 2007; Smyer & Pitt-Catsouphes, 2007). One might think that after long participation in the workforce, many people would feel "burnt out," but the reverse seems to be true.

What accounts for these generally positive feelings about work in midlife? Middle-aged and older adults have extensive work experience and skills, and over the years they have learned how to use their knowledge to solve practical problems and become efficient at their job (Sterns & Huyck, 2001). They usually have advanced well beyond the trainee or apprentice status that is typical of young workers and hold positions of greater authority in the workplace, often supervising or mentoring newer workers. Earnings frequently reach a peak in late middle age, as well. These various aspects of their work lives contribute to middle-aged workers' feelings of job competence and job satisfaction.

Challenges of Work in Midlife

Not all middle-aged workers have such positive experiences in the workplace, however. Some face obstacles that limit their career development. In addition, the global economy and changing nature of work are creating new uncertainties and demands to which middle-aged workers must adapt.

Challenges Facing Women and Minorities Women and individuals from ethnic minority groups face special challenges that may affect their work trajectories and financial status by midlife (Hansson, DeKoekkoek, Neece, & Patterson, 1997). First, sex discrimination and race discrimination—resulting in unfair decisions about hiring, firing, compensation, or working conditions based on a person's sex or race—are still common in the workplace. Discrimination limits the occupational opportunities available to women and ethnic minorities and the accomplishments they are able to achieve in the course of their work lives.

Although progress has been made in recent decades, women and minorities continue to encounter obstacles in the workplace. Some experience a **glass ceiling**—an invisible barrier that, because of discrimination, keeps them from being promoted at work beyond a particular level of responsibility or pay (Maume, 2004). Even though women's earnings have begun to improve as they have assumed jobs in traditionally male fields (such as law, medicine, and business), they still earn only about 77 percent of what men make (DeNavas-Walt, Proctor, & Smith, 2009) (see Figure 16.7). Members of minority groups also earn less on average than Caucasians, and this is true among men as well as women. For example, African American men currently earn about 72 percent and Hispanic men about 57 percent as much as Caucasian men. In an exception to this pattern, Asian American men and women have higher incomes on average than any other group (DeNavas-Walt et al., 2009). Bear in mind that these income differences are based only on people who are in the workforce; unemployment rates are considerably higher among African Americans, Hispanics, and Native Americans than among Caucasians.

glass ceiling An invisible barrier that, because of discrimination, keeps an employee from being promoted at work beyond a particular level of responsibility or pay.

Women's career development is also affected by the fact that they traditionally have been more likely than men to adjust their work goals and involvement to meet family needs. For example, Golan (1986) identified four different patterns of career development among professional women:

1. Some women follow a career path that has typically been more conventional among men—entering and staying in the workforce continuously after finishing school, known as the **regular career pattern**.
2. Some women leave the workforce when they have children, returning several years later when their children are older, a pattern referred to as the **interrupted career pattern** (Golan 1986).

regular career pattern A pattern of career development in which women enter and stay in the workforce continuously after finishing school.

interrupted career pattern A pattern of career development in which women leave the workforce when they have children, returning to the workforce later when the children are older.

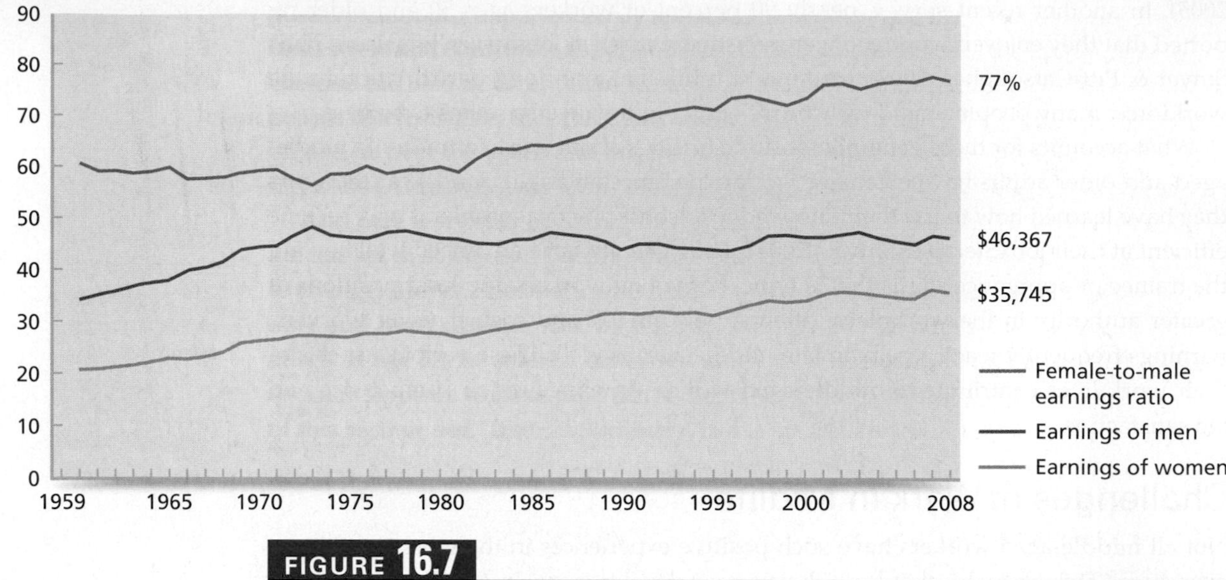

FIGURE 16.7

Ratio of Female Earnings to Male Earnings and Median Earnings of Full-Time Workers by Sex from 1960 to 2008

Source: DeNavas-Walt, C., Proctor, B. D., & Smith, J. C. (2009). *Income, poverty, and health insurance coverage in the United States: 2008*. U. S. Census Bureau, Current Population Reports, P60-236. Washington, DC: U. S. Government Printing Office. Retrieved December 13, 2009, from http://www.census.gov/prod/2009pubs/p60-236.pdf, page 11.

3. Other women defer their professional training and entry into the workforce until their children are grown, the **second career pattern.**

second career pattern
A pattern of career development in which women defer their professional training and entry into the workforce until their children are grown.

4. Still other women work part-time when their children are young and then move to full-time work after the children are grown, the **modified second career pattern**.

modified second career pattern
A pattern of career development in which women work part-time when their children are young and then move to full-time work after the children are grown.

Some women follow the regular career pattern, but the other patterns may lead to less orderly career development. In fact, compared to men, women are more likely to shift between periods with and without full-time paid employment (Settersten & Hagestad, 1996). In addition, women historically have worked in jobs that pay less and offer fewer opportunities for training and advancement. And, caring for aging parents, as we discussed earlier, sometimes requires women to reduce their work hours or quit working altogether.

For women and minorities, then, discrimination in the workplace, coupled with more variable work histories, can have the cumulative effect of leaving them with fewer financial resources in middle and later adulthood.

age discrimination Involves unfair practices regarding hiring, firing, compensation, or working conditions based on a person's age.

Age Discrimination in the Workplace Age can also be a basis for discrimination in the workplace. **Age discrimination** involves unfair practices regarding hiring, firing, compensation, or working conditions based on a person's age. One does not have to be truly "old" to experience age discrimination. Nearly two-thirds of complaints filed with the U.S. Equal Employment Opportunity Commission are filed by people ages 40 to 59 (AARP, 2003b). (The Age Discrimination in Employment Act, which makes age discrimination in the workplace illegal, protects workers age 40 and over.) Moreover, age discrimination complaints have increased as the Baby Boom generation has reached middle-age—jumping by 41 percent in just one 3-year period (AARP, 2003b) (see Figure 16.8). Because middle-aged and older workers alike can experience age discrimination, our discussion here focuses on this shared problem experienced by both age groups, whom we refer to as "mature workers."

Subtle and not-so-subtle forms of age discrimination occur in the workplace. Employers can give mature workers particularly difficult tasks and then use evidence of poor job performance to withhold promotions or terminate employment. Or they can withhold job offers from mature workers, claiming that younger workers are needed to represent the organization or to bring in fresh ideas (Nelson, 2007). Experimental studies have shown that age alone can unfairly influence hiring decisions. In one study, prospective employers were sent identical resumes for hypothetical younger and older job applicants; despite these identical qualifications; the younger applicants were 40 percent more likely to be called for an interview (Lahey, 2005).

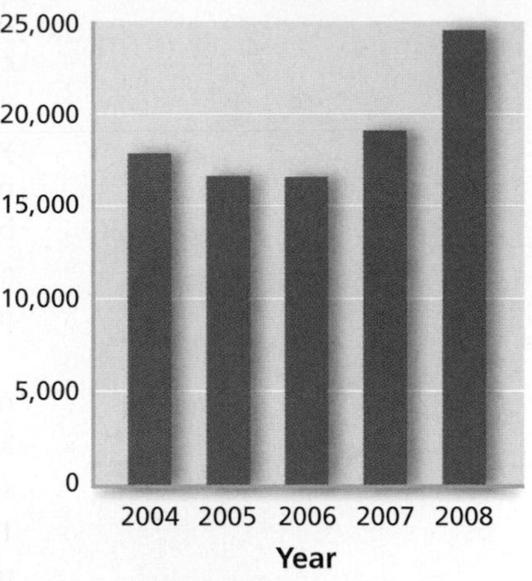

FIGURE 16.8

Charges Filed for Age Discrimination in the Workforce

Source: Data from Equal Employment Opportunity Commission. Retrieved April 2, 2010 from http://www.eeoc.gov/eeoc/statistics/enforcement/adea.cfm

Age discrimination in the workplace may stem from stereotypes of mature workers as less productive, less adaptable, and less suitable for training programs than younger workers (Ng & Feldman, 2008; Taylor & Walker, 1998). But research refutes these stereotypes. Mature workers have been found to be as productive as younger workers except in physically demanding jobs (Johnson et al., 2007). Mature workers generally can learn new skills, such as new computer skills, as effectively as younger workers, although it may take them longer (Charness, Czaja, & Sharit, 2007). Moreover, other evidence suggests that mature workers often are more accurate, better able to control their emotions at work, and less likely to engage in counterproductive behavior than younger workers (Ng & Feldman, 2008). They also have lower rates of absenteeism and exhibit greater commitment to the organization (Ng & Feldman, 2008; Rhodes, 1983).

Age discrimination makes middle-aged and older workers vulnerable to job loss. They are especially likely to be the focus of cost-saving measures, such as workforce downsizing, for several reasons (Sterns & Huyck, 2001). First, they are perceived (erroneously, as we have seen) to be less productive than younger workers and so are more likely to be laid off or fired during an economic squeeze. Second, they are more likely to hold managerial positions that increasingly are being eliminated as companies move toward leaner organizational structures. Third, mature workers often earn higher wages than younger workers, and to save costs, companies may eliminate their positions or offer incentives for early retirement. Mature workers who are displaced from their jobs face tough challenges trying to get back into the workforce, and many have to settle for lower-paying jobs with fewer benefits.

Challenges from the Changing Nature of Work The rapidly changing nature of work in the new economy is adding to the job pressures and insecurities faced by many middle-aged and older adults. As manufacturing jobs have become scarce and service jobs have increased, workers need to have different skills. Manufacturing jobs require mechanical intelligence and muscle; service jobs require specialized knowledge, interpersonal skills, and, often, computer savvy. In fact, more than one-third of jobs today require strong cognitive and interpersonal skills, compared to only one-quarter 35 years ago (Johnson, Mermin, & Resseger, 2007). Mature workers who once faced the challenges of physically demanding jobs are now more likely to face the challenges of stressful, cognitively demanding jobs (Johnson et al., 2007).

These new challenges come at a time in life when mature workers often are beginning to experience gradual age-related declines in sensory capacities and some cognitive slowing (Robson & Hansson, 2007). As you learned in the previous chapter, fluid cognitive abilities (grappling with new information and problem-solving tasks) tend to decline with age, but crystallized abilities (drawing upon accumulated knowledge) remain intact. However, mature workers may be able to use strong verbal abilities to compensate for a decline in fluid abilities (Johnson et al., 2007). For example, in one study, hotel reservation clerks age 50 and older actually were more productive than younger clerks, even though the older clerks handled fewer phone calls. Why? The mature workers' superior communication skills allowed them to make more hotel bookings per call (McNaught & Barth, 1992). This is a good example of compensation—a goal (being productive) was achieved through the use of alternative means (communication skills) despite a decline in speed.

In another study, middle-aged workers over age 49 maintained effective job performance by using selection (specializing in particular job tasks), optimization (practicing and updating job skills), and compensation (completing job tasks using alternative strategies when previous strategies had become ineffective) (Abraham & Hansson, 1995). The younger middle-aged workers in the study (ages 40 to 48) did not need to rely on these strategies as much to maintain their job performance because they had not yet experienced physical or cognitive declines that required adaptive strategies.

Here is an interesting wrinkle, however. While these strategies appear to be adaptive for workers *within* a particular job, they may be less adaptive for mature workers who need to *change* jobs (Robson & Hansson, 2007). Skills that have been well honed for a particular job may not transfer to other jobs and work settings. A high degree of specialization could be a liability, then, in a changing economy that may require more workers to pursue multiple career paths over the course of their lives.

What should mature workers do to remain employable? Researchers agree that mature workers must adapt to the realities of the new economy by maintaining and updating their general knowledge and skills, even as they acquire specialized skills for particular jobs (Robson & Hansson, 2007). Workers of all ages will need to become more responsible for directing their careers, but this may be especially important for mature workers because they are more vulnerable to organizational downsizing and job layoffs. Seniority in an organization no longer guarantees job security.

Researchers have identified a number of strategies that mature workers report using to function effectively in the workplace (Robson & Hansson, 2007). As you can see from Table 16.2, workers make use of strategies that maintain their productivity and

TABLE 16.2 Strategies Used by Mature Workers to Succeed at Work

STRATEGY	EXAMPLES
Relationship Development: Developing good business and work relationships	Meeting new people in one's field; offering to help coworkers
Skill Extension: Taking steps at work to build on existing skills	Accepting new projects when offered; seeking assignments outside of one's specialty
Continuous Learning: Seeking additional training and education to improve work-related knowledge, skills, and abilities	Attending workshops or classes to update one's knowledge and skills; staying up to date with developments in one's field
Conscientiousness: Working to increase one's job productivity and performance	Working hard to exceed standards; making continual efforts to be more productive
Career Management: Pursuing ways to improve one's future career	Communicating one's career goals to employers; seeking feedback about one's performance
Stress Relief: Finding ways to reduce stress on a regular basis	Participating in regular exercise, leisure activities, and other ways to relieve stress

Source: Adapted from Robson, S. M., & Hansson, R. O. (2007). Strategic self-development for successful aging at work. *International Journal of Aging and Human Development*, *64*, 331–339.

reduce stress in their current jobs *and* that keep their skills and social network connections updated to enhance their employability for future jobs.

Unemployment in Midlife

Unfortunately, some workers either cannot adapt to the demands of the new economy or face obstacles beyond their control, such as an unexpected disability that forces them to leave work or a company closure that causes mass job layoffs. Unemployment can be a devastating experience, one that is associated with an increased (and long-lasting) risk of physical health problems as well as depression, anxiety, and even suicide (Dooley, Catalano, & Rook, 1988; Kposowa, 2001). These negative effects become worse as the period of unemployment lengthens. Middle-aged adults in one study described six key ways that their quality of life and hopes for the future had suffered after becoming unemployed (Ranzijn, Carson, Winefield, & Price, 2006):

1. *Financial strains.* "Money hadn't been an object with me for all my working life. And now to be on the dole is devastating. . . . I'm drawing on reserves now, all the time, I've gone into my shell, I don't go out, nothing . . . can't afford it."

2. *Loss of self worth.* "If you meet someone socially one of the first questions they are going to ask you is 'What do you do for a [living]?' That is how you identify yourself. 'Oh, I'm a teacher.' I can't say that anymore, I'm not a teacher anymore. If you haven't got that label for yourself, your self-worth isn't as strong as it was. . . ."

3. *Inability to use one's talents and make a contribution.* "I cannot seem to find an outlet [for my] skills. . . . I feel the need to be a part of community, not just a job seeker."

4. *Loss of social contacts with peers.* "You don't have any office interaction. . . . [and] if someone says to me 'Hey, You want to [go out for] dinner . . . ?' I want to say, 'Yeah, cool, great idea.' But then I think [how much it will cost] and so I say 'Ah, no, got something else on, I've got to do this or that, can't make it tonight.' So you become increasingly isolated."

5. *Impact on family relationships.* "Having to say, 'No we can't do that' purely and simply because we don't have a spare . . . $15 to do it with, when it's your kids, it really hurts."

6. *Concerns about the future.* "Yes, it would be frightening [not to get another job], it would be very, very frightening. And I think that is something that [one] cannot afford . . . to be complacent about."

Being unemployed is difficult at any age, but it may be even harder in midlife. Middle-aged adults are likely to be unemployed longer and have a harder time finding new employment than younger workers (Neumark, 2009). Midlife is ordinarily a time when people enjoy high job satisfaction, increasing financial security, and the anticipation of retirement. It is also a time when people expect to be able to help launch their children into the world and to care for aging parents. Unemployment can shatter these expectations and wreak havoc with one's life plans and dreams.

The outlook for mature workers may improve in the future as projected labor force shortages increase their value to employers. In the meantime, job skills training programs for mature workers can help to reduce the likelihood of unemployment and make it easier for those who do lose their jobs to reenter the workforce (Ranzijn et al., 2006). (For a summary of this section, see Interim Summary 16.4: Work in Midlife.")

INTERIM SUMMARY 16.4

Work in Midlife	
Satisfaction with Work in Midlife	■ Work is a major social role in midlife and a central context in which development unfolds. ■ Research on the meaning of work for middle-aged workers has found that it meets four basic needs: *social contact*, *personal needs*, *financial needs*, and *generativity*. ■ Middle-aged workers experience greater feelings of job satisfaction because they have experience and skills, hold positions of greater authority, and are paid more.
Challenges of Work in Midlife	■ Some middle-aged workers have less positive experiences in the workplace, however. ■ Women and individuals from ethnic minority groups face special challenges, including sex discrimination, race discrimination, and a **glass ceiling** that keeps them from being promoted beyond a particular level of responsibility or pay. ■ Women's career development is further affected by the fact that they are more likely than men to adjust their work goals and involvement to meet family needs. ■ **Age discrimination** complaints are increasing as the Baby Boom generation reaches middle age. ■ In addition, the global economy and changing nature of work are creating new uncertainties and demands to which middle-aged workers must adapt.
Unemployment in Midlife	■ Unemployment is associated with an increased risk of physical health problems as well as depression, anxiety, and suicide. ■ Middle-aged adults are likely to be unemployed for longer periods and to have a harder time finding new employment than younger workers.

THE EVOLVING PERSON IN MIDLIFE

Imagine this situation: you are 43 years old and planning to attend your 25th high school reunion in a few months. Will your former classmates have the same personalities or will they have changed over the years? You have seen some important changes in yourself. Will your former classmates recognize these changes in you?

Personality Development in Midlife

By middle adulthood, people have experienced many changes in their lives—establishing and sometimes dissolving intimate relationships, seeing their children grow up and their parents grow old, and navigating their way through the changing world of work. Unexpected events may have occurred, too—such as injuries or illness, financial losses, or the death of a loved one. Do experiences such as these lead to personality change in adulthood? This issue is at the very heart of a vigorous debate in psychology.

Personality Traits Some personality researchers firmly believe that personality solidifies relatively early in life because personality traits, like temperament in childhood, are biologically based. From this perspective, genes partly determine what our personalities are like and contribute to stability over time (McCrae & Costa, 2003). Current estimates, however, suggest that genes account for no more than about 50 percent of individual variability in personality (Krueger, Johnson, & Kling, 2006). This leaves 50 percent to be explained by other factors, such as the person's experiences (Kreuger et al., 2006). According to this contextual perspective, personality can change because it is affected by the settings in which individuals' lives unfold (Roberts & Caspi, 2003).

As you can see, these two perspectives make different predictions about how personality evolves over time. What does the scientific evidence tell us about the merits of these two perspectives? To investigate whether personality traits change over time, scientists first had to come up with a manageable set of traits to examine. Think of all the different adjectives and terms you or other people might use to describe personality. If we compiled all of these terms, the complete list could be almost endless. Researchers have discovered, however, that most of these terms can be grouped into five basic personality factors, known as the **Big Five** (John & Srivastava, 1999; McCrae & Costa, 2003). You can think of a factor as a cluster of related personality characteristics. The Big Five factors are: *openness to experience, conscientiousness, extraversion, agreeableness*, and *neuroticism* (see Table 16.3). (One way to remember these factors is to note that they form the acronym OCEAN.) Even though some researchers argue that additional factors should be examined, most agree that these five factors capture key dimensions of personality. And it is striking that the same five factors have emerged in studies conducted in more than 30 different countries (McRae, 2002). In fact, quite remarkably, even animal species as diverse as chimpanzees, cats, dogs, pigs, donkeys, octopuses, and guppies have been found to exhibit some of the Big Five traits such as extraversion, agreeableness, and neuroticism (John & Srivastava, 1999).

Big Five A model of personality that groups personality traits into five basic clusters: openness to experience, conscientiousness, extraversion, agreeableness, and neuroticism.

Are the Big Five traits stable over time? Longitudinal studies—some spanning 40 years—have been conducted to answer this question (Roberts, Walton, & Viechtbauer, 2006). The results of these studies point to several conclusions. First, individuals' personalities become more consistent over time (Roberts & DelVecchio, 2000). For example, someone who is outgoing, dependable, and inquisitive at age 25 is likely to be that way at age 35, and even more likely to be that way at age 45. This consistency is evident in studies based on self-reports (people describing their own personalities) and on the reports of others (e.g., spouses or peers describing someone else's personality), and it is found in studies of men as well as women (Costa & McCrae, 1988). Because consistency increases as people mature, their personalities may be solidifying

TABLE 16.3 The Big Five Personality Traits

TRAIT	PEOPLE WHO SCORE HIGH ON THIS TRAIT TEND TO BE:
Openness to experience	Imaginative, curious, interested in a variety of experiences, insightful, unconventional
Conscientiousness	Organized, planful, thorough, reliable, responsible
Extraversion	Energetic, assertive, enthusiastic, outgoing, talkative
Agreeableness	Kind, compassionate, trusting, good-natured, forgiving
Neuroticism	Emotional and vulnerable; prone to negative moods, anxiety, and tension

Adapted from: John, O. P., & Srivastava, S. (1999). The Big-Five trait taxonomy: History, measurement, and theoretical perspectives. In L. A. Pervin & O. P. John (Eds.), *Handbook of personality: Theory and research* (2nd ed., pp. 102–139). New York: Guilford; McCrae, R. R., & Costa, P. T., Jr. (2003). *Personality in adulthood: A five-factor theory perspective*. New York: Guilford; and McCrae, R. R. & John, O. P. (1992). An introduction to the five-factor model and its applications. *Journal of Personality, 60*, 175–215.

with time, in part because the contexts in which they choose to spend time tend to reinforce their existing traits. According to Paul Costa and Robert McRae (1994), personality generally crystallizes by about age 30 and changes relatively little thereafter.

Second, even though the degree of consistency found in these studies is high, it is not perfect. This leaves room for some personality change. Two kinds of change have been documented: *mean-level change*, in which the average (or mean) level of a trait rises or falls in the overall population, and *individual differences in change*, in which individuals' personalities change in unique and idiosyncratic ways (Roberts, Walton, & Viechtbauer, 2006). We saw that people generally tend to become more socially dominant, more conscientious, more agreeable, and less neurotic from young adulthood through middle age (Roberts, Walton, & Viechtbauer, 2006; Roberts & Wood, 2006). This is an example of mean-level change, because the majority of people in the population exhibit these shifts.

These shifts tend to be relatively small in magnitude, but they have been documented in many studies conducted not only in the United States but in countries as diverse as Italy, Germany, Spain, Croatia, Turkey, and Korea (McCrae et al., 1999; McCrae et al., 2004). Because the central activities of adult life (finding a partner, launching a family, establishing a career) are similar across most cultures, they serve as catalysts for similar kinds of personality change (Helson, Kwan, John, & Jones, 2002; Roberts et al., 2006). Researchers taking a biological perspective, however, offer a different explanation. They argue that since these cultures differ in so many ways, biology must underlie the developmental shifts that occur in personality. Specifically, the overall trend toward greater psychosocial maturity and emotional adjustment in adulthood may reflect genetic programming that evolved in humans to facilitate the upbringing of children (Costa & McRae, 2006; McRae et al. 1999).

What about individual differences in personality change? Although there is little doubt that biologically determined temperament contributes to differences between individuals, unique life experiences can also contribute to individual differences in how personality might change over time. Becoming disabled, being out of work for months or years, or being trapped in a conflict-ridden marriage could cause a previously agreeable and optimistic person to become disagreeable and pessimistic. Positive transformations can occur, too. People with insecure attachment styles who manage to form a long-term relationship with a caring and responsive partner show a gradual change toward a more secure attachment style (Hollist & Miller, 2005).

A relatively new and powerful method for investigating how personality evolves over time involves identifying each individual's trajectory of personality development and then investigating what accounts for variations in the trajectories—to understand, for example, why one person becomes more agreeable over time, why another becomes less agreeable, and why still another person fluctuates between being agreeable and disagreeable over time. One recent study examined individual personality trajectories over a 12-year period in a large sample of middle-aged and older men and found that variations in these trajectories were due, in part, to life events. For example, many of the men showed a decline in neuroticism over time (as you might expect from our discussion above), but the rate of decline was greater among men who experienced a positive life event, such as marrying for the first time or becoming remarried after a divorce (Mroczek & Spiro, 2003).

Existing research, then, provides evidence of both stability and change in personality in adulthood. Genes partly determine the personality traits that people develop, and genes contribute to stability, but they are not the whole story. Biology and the environment interact constantly to influence development. Personality traits have genetic roots, but they are adjusted and fine-tuned by the environment. Personalities are not so malleable that extreme changes occur overnight, but neither are personalities so rigidly fixed by biology that people are unable to adapt to changing circumstances in their lives.

So far, our discussion has focused primarily on the *structure* of personality, or the set of traits that make up someone's personality. As you have learned, we can also consider personality development in terms of the *dynamics* of personality—how people manage their emotions and cope with stress and other challenges. Do these self-regulatory capacities change as people reach midlife?

Self-Regulatory Capacities Personality dynamics have been studied less extensively than personality traits, but the available evidence points to gains in self-regulatory capacities in midlife. Middle-aged adults, like younger adults, hope for improvements in various aspects of their lives, but they are better able than young adults to adjust their expectations when their hopes and dreams begin to become unattainable. More generally, the ability to reduce expectations and modify goals and strategies increases from young adulthood to middle adulthood (Heckhausen, 1999, 2001). Middle-aged adults also have an improved capacity to examine the sources of their emotions and, as a result, they can more effectively manage their emotional reactions to various life events. A study that tracked a sample of college students intensively from their 20s through their 40s and 50s found evidence of greater emotional control in midlife (Helsonet al., 2006). Coping skills also improve in midlife, as adults become more flexible, resourceful, and pragmatic and better able to handle life stresses effectively (Aldwin & Levenson, 2001; Chiriboga, 1997; Helson & Wink, 1992). In fact, feelings of control and mastery over one's life generally peak in midlife (Clark-Plaskie & Lachman, 1991; Keyes & Ryff, 1999). **Anticipatory coping**—the ability to anticipate and prevent stressful life events from happening in the first place—also tends to improve over the course of adulthood (Aldwin & Levinson, 2001).

anticipatory coping The ability to anticipate and prevent stressful life events from happening in the first place.

Self-Concept and Emotional Health in Midlife

What do these changes suggest for middle-aged adults' self-concepts and emotional health? A common image of midlife is that it is a time when people struggle with self-doubts and disillusionment. This image has taken hold in the popular imagination, due in part to influential publications from the 1960s and 70s (Jacques, 1965; Levinson, 1977; Sheehy, 1976). In his book *Seasons of a Man's Life*, Daniel Levinson and his colleagues (Levinson, Darrow, Klein, Levinson, & McKee, 1978) described each stage (or "season") of adulthood as involving key issues and transitions. Middle adulthood, in their view, is a time when people become aware of their own aging, grasping that life is finite and that some dreams may never be realized. As a result, middle-aged adults begin to question their lives and experience remorse over their past choices. This reassessment of one's life leads to uncertainty and self-doubt—inner turmoil that has been called the **midlife crisis**. Levinson's initial theorizing was based on intensive interviews conducted with a sample of only 40 men. He later studied women, but again, only a small sample. As a result, critics questioned whether the midlife crisis is universal (McRae & Costa, 1990; Stewart & Ostrove, 1998).

midlife crisis Stressful period of doubt and uncertainty believed to be triggered by the reevaluation of one's life in middle adulthood.

We can all probably generate examples of people whose behavior in midlife seems to reflect a midlife crisis—an affair with someone much younger or a driven quest to look younger through maniacal workouts or plastic surgery. But despite such examples, and the seductive nature of the concept, scientific evidence suggests that midlife crises are, in fact, rare. Middle-aged adults generally tend to be content with their lives, rather than dissatisfied (Lachman, 2004; Wethington, 2000). Indeed, young adults are just as likely as middle-aged adults to report symptoms stereotypically associated with the midlife crisis, and young adults actually express more dissatisfaction with various areas of their lives than middle-aged adults do (Costa & McRae, 1980; Farrell & Rosenberg, 1981). Some middle-aged adults may experience a crisis of uncertainty and doubt as they take stock of their lives, but more often, crises in midlife result from disruptive life events, such as unemployment or serious illness

Juice Images/Alamy

Some middle-age adults may experience anxiety and uncertainty about their lives that leads them to seek ways to feel young and vigorous. For most middle-aged adults, however, a midlife crisis is rare.

(Lachman, 2004). Disruptive life events, which can be experienced at any age, are not more common in middle adulthood.

Why are beliefs in the midlife crisis so widespread and persistent? Heckhausen (2001, p. 378) offered the intriguing idea that the belief in midlife crisis persists, despite research challenging its existence, because people benefit from it: "they expect the worst at midlife, and [are] pleasantly surprised by [their] own comparatively smooth sail." Although it is a less compelling story, middle-aged adults' appraisals of their lives are more likely to be mature and balanced than anxiety-ridden and remorseful. Some middle-aged adults do make adjustments after reflecting on their lives, but the process is more like midcourse correction than a dramatic overhaul (Hermans & Oles, 1999; Stewart & Ostrove, 1998). (For a summary of this section, see "Interim Summary 16.5: The Evolving Person in Midlife.")

INTERIM SUMMARY 16.5

The Evolving Person in Midlife

Personality Development in Midlife	■ Some researchers believe that five factors (the **Big Five**) capture the key dimensions of personality: *openness to experience*, *conscientiousness*, *extraversion*, *agreeableness*, and *neuroticism*. ■ Existing research provides evidence of both stability and change in personality in adulthood. ■ Available evidence points to gains in self-regulatory capacities from young adulthood to middle adulthood. ■ Coping skills also improve in midlife. Some researchers find that **anticipatory coping**—the ability to anticipate and prevent stressful life events from happening—improves over the course of adulthood.
Self-Concept and Emotional Health in Midlife	■ Scientific evidence suggests that the **midlife crisis** is more fiction than fact. Middle-aged adults generally tend to be content with their lives, rather than dissatisfied.

SUMMING UP AND LOOKING AHEAD

We have seen that middle adulthood does not deserve the bad rap it usually receives. Although it is a time when some physical and cognitive capacities begin to decline, the changes tend to be modest and generally do not interfere with middle-aged adults' ability to function effectively in their day-to-day roles and activities. Middle adulthood is also a time when gains can be experienced. Problem-solving and coping skills improve, and feelings of competence tend to increase. Middle-aged adults have acquired the ability to compensate for declines in order to maintain high productivity and high levels of functioning in many areas of their lives. Although not all middle-aged adults are so fortunate, most feel more confident and accomplished in their major social roles than they did as young adults. Many middle-aged adults also have learned how to adjust their expectations to minimize the negative impact of goal setbacks and disappointments. A growing recognition that time is a finite (rather than limitless) resource leads some middle-aged adults to reappraise their life goals and priorities, but this rarely provokes an emotional crisis. This shift in time perspective also leads to an increased concern with generativity, often expressed by supporting and mentoring younger generations but also by providing care to aging parents. Across middle adulthood, both continuity and change can be seen in personality characteristics and processes. In many ways, the person at age 50 is very much the same person he or she was at age 30. But changes also occur, as personality characteristics evolve in response to the requirements of the social contexts in which middle-aged adults leave their lives.

The life experiences and physical, cognitive, and socioemotional capacities that evolve in midlife provide the foundation from which middle-aged adults move on to the last period of adulthood—later life. This is a stage of life in which changes nearly as dramatic as those of childhood and adolescence once again occur, and this is where our journey through the lifespan takes us next.

HERE'S WHAT YOU SHOULD KNOW

Did You Get It?

After reading this chapter, you should understand the following:

- The developmental tasks and timetables of middle adulthood
- How the three processes of developmental regulation affect middle-aged adults
- The key roles friendships and love relationships play in middle adulthood
- How relationships with children and grandchildren affect middle-aged adults
- Special issues that relationships with aging parents pose in middle adulthood
- Sources of satisfaction and challenges that work life presents to middle-aged adults
- How personality and self-concept develop in middle adulthood

Important Terms and Concepts

Part VII Review

CHAPTER 15
Physical and Cognitive Development in Middle Adulthood

- Development in midlife varies across **cohorts**. Middle adulthood spans 25 years (ages 40 to 65), and the health, goals, and roles of people in their 40s differ from those in their 60s.
- Minor changes in appearance, body build, mobility, and body system functioning occur gradually from young adulthood to middle adulthood. Some age-related changes result from inevitable, intrinsic processes of aging (**primary aging**). Other changes result from the effects over time of disease, bodily abuse, or environmental hazards (**secondary aging**).
- Women experience declines in female sex hormones in midlife, culminating in **menopause**. Men experience a decline in the production of sperm and **androgens**. Research indicates that people tend to engage in sexual activity less frequently in midlife, but they remain interested in, and capable of, sexual intimacy.
- Three major sources of influence on health are genes, behavior, and the environment. People who experience persistent **stress** are more susceptible to health problems like **atherosclerosis** and **hypertension**.
- **Crystallized intelligence** increases through midlife and generally remains intact until people are well into in their 60s or 70s. **Fluid intelligence** peaks in young adulthood and generally declines thereafter.
- Cognitively complex work is associated with gains in intellectual functioning in middle-aged adults.

CHAPTER 16
Socioemotional Development in Middle Adulthood

- The developmental tasks of middle adulthood build upon the life paths initiated in young adulthood. Middle-aged adults seek to preserve their achievements and prevent losses, although they often reevaluate their priorities as they become aware that the time they have left to accomplish their goals is limited. Adults in their early 40s may be engaged in **elective selection** as they seek ways to improve their lives. Later in midlife, the process of selection is more often directed toward scaling back or relinquishing goals **(loss-based selection)**.
- Divorces among middle-aged couples are becoming more common, but rates of remarriage are lower in midlife than in young adulthood.
- Middle-aged parents typically remain involved with their children after their children leave home, and most middle-aged adults consider grandparenthood to be a source of satisfaction. By the end of midlife, over three-quarters of adults have no living parents.
- Work is a major social role in midlife and a central context in which development unfolds.
- Research provides evidence of both stability and change in personality in middle adulthood, and gains in self-regulatory capacities are common. The **midlife crisis** is more fiction than fact, as the majority of middle-aged adults are content with their lives.

part eight

Later Adulthood

Digital Vision/Getty Images

CHAPTER

17

Physical and Cognitive Development in Later Adulthood

© MBI/Alamy

Most of us assume we will reach old age, even if that life stage seems distant to people in their 20s, 30s, or 40s. Yet, remarkably, the very existence of old age as a life stage is a relatively new phenomenon in human history. Had you been born 100 years ago, the probability that you would live to old age would have been quite slim. Only recently have large numbers of people in many societies begun to live long enough to reach this life stage. In some parts of the world today, living long enough to reach old age is still a rare experience.

What is it like to be old? Some common beliefs about older people appear in Figure 17.1. Some of these beliefs may be familiar to you, yet it turns out that none of the statements in Figure 17.1 are true. Instead, they are examples of stereotypes that reflect both lack of knowledge about later adulthood as well as **ageism**. Ageism refers to prejudice and discrimination toward people on the basis of their age alone (Butler, 2001; Bytheway, 2005). Ageism can be directed toward younger age groups, but it is most often directed toward the elderly (Nelson, 2002). Ageist stereotypes can lead people to avoid or react negatively to older adults. They can also cause older adults to experience discrimination in employment opportunities, housing, and other services. Older adults sometimes internalize negative stereotypes about their competence in ways that adversely affect their functioning (Bugental & Hehman, 2007; Hess, 2005; O'Brien & Hummert, 2006).

ageism Prejudice and discrimination toward people on the basis of their age.

Later adulthood presents many paradoxes that challenge prevailing stereotypes. For example, declines in physical and cognitive functioning are common, yet socioemotional functioning is well preserved—and may even improve—in later life (Carstensen, Mikels, & Mather, 2006). In addition, the declines that do occur tend not to be so great—at least until very late in life—that they interfere with older adults' daily lives. Moreover, older adults are adept at finding ways to compensate for many of the declines they experience. It is also important to realize that some age-related declines can be slowed or prevented, and others may be reversed to some extent. Older adults today are generally healthier and more active than older adults were even a few decades ago (Carstensen & Charles, 2003). So, it seems that later life is not the bleak life stage implied by the statements in Figure 17.1.

Yet at the same time we have to acknowledge that age-related losses and declines do accumulate over time, and by very advanced old age they can seriously challenge older adults' biological and psychological adaptability (Baltes & Smith, 2003). Age itself is a key source of variability in later life, and the health and functioning of the **young-old** (those ages 65 to 79) often differs from that of the **old-old** (those age 80 or older; Neugarten, 1974; Suzman, Willis, & Manton, 1992). It is often not until people are in their 80s or older that age-related physical and cognitive changes begin to take a significant toll.

young-old Older adults ages 65 to 79.

old-old Older adults ages 80 and older.

FIGURE 17.1

10 Common Beliefs about Older Adults: True or False?

❑ True ❑ False 1. In general, most older people tend to be pretty much alike.

❑ True ❑ False 2. Older people are sick, frail, and dependent on others.

❑ True ❑ False 3. The majority of older people are senile (they have defective memories, are disoriented, or are demented).

❑ True ❑ False 4. Older people are generally lonely and alone.

❑ True ❑ False 5. Serious depression is more common among older people than younger people.

❑ True ❑ False 6. Psychotherapy is usually ineffective with older patients.

❑ True ❑ False 7. Older workers are more often absent from work than are younger workers.

❑ True ❑ False 8. Older adults are rigid and have difficulty adapting to change.

❑ True ❑ False 9. The majority of older people have no interest in, nor capacity for, sexual relations.

❑ True ❑ False 10. Older people tend to experience fewer positive emotions and lower life satisfaction than younger adults.

Note: None of the statements above are true.
Source: Adapted from Palmore, E. B. (1988). *The facts on aging quiz: A handbook of uses and results.* New York: Springer; and from American Psychological Association (1998). *Older adults' health and age-related changes: Reality versus myth.* Retrieved April 2, 2010 from http://www.apa.org/pi/aging/resources/guides/older-adults.pdf.

Human aging, therefore, has two faces: gains and losses (Baltes & Smith, 2003). We will examine both gains and losses that occur with age as we explore physical and cognitive development in later adulthood in this chapter and socioemotional development in the next chapter. We begin, though, by looking at how later adulthood emerged as an expected life period.

LATER ADULTHOOD: THE NEWEST LIFE PERIOD

To set the stage, imagine traveling back in time to ancient Rome when Julius Caesar was in power, about 45 B.C. Had you been alive during that time, how long do you think you might have lived? Now travel forward to the Middle Ages, about 1250. Had you been born in that era, how long do you think you might have lived? And now jump to the year 1900. Had you had been born then, how long might you have lived?

Life Expectancy

life expectancy The average number of years that a person can expect to live.

To compare your figures with researchers' estimates of life expectancy in different historical eras, look at Figure 17.2. **Life expectancy** refers to the average number of years that a person born in a particular year can expect to live. In Figure 17.2, you can see that life expectancy in ancient Rome was extremely short—only about 20 years. Zooming forward over 1,000 years to the Middle Ages, life expectancy had increased to only

33 years. It changed little until the twentieth century, when something rather extraordinary began to happen. As you can see in Figure 17.2, life expectancy in the United States was only 48 years in 1900 (American Administration on Aging, 2009; He, Sengupta, Velkoff, & DeBarros, 2005). By 1970, however, life expectancy had increased to 71 years (He et al., 2005). In just the 70-year period from 1900 to 1970, gains in life expectancy far exceeded the gains that had occurred in the preceding 2,000 years. In 1900, only 4 percent of Americans lived to age 65 or older; by 1970, this figure had more than doubled, to 10 percent (He et al., 2005).

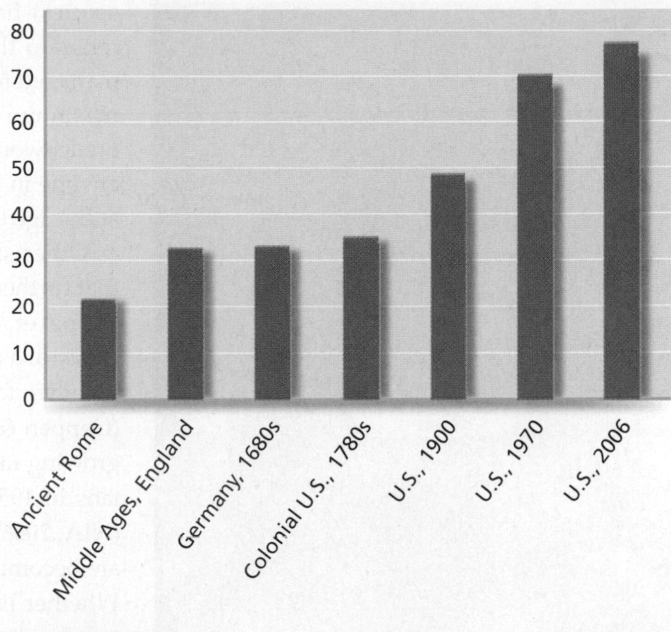

FIGURE 17.2

Life Expectancy: Past to Present

Source: Estimates derived from American Administration on Aging, 2009; Hayflick, L. (1994). *How and why we age*. New York: Ballantine Books; He, W., Sengupta, M., Velkoff, V. A., & DeBarros, K. A. (2005). *65+ in the United States: 2005.* U.S. Census Bureau, Current Population Reports, P23–P209. Washington, DC: U.S. Government Printing Office.

The United States does not lead the world in life expectancy. With a life expectancy of just over 78 years, the U.S. ranked 50th in a recent comparison of 224 nations (CIA, 2009). Japan, Singapore, Hong Kong, and Australia have some of the longest life expectancies, at approximately 82 years (CIA, 2009). Nor has the United States experienced the greatest population aging in the world. **Population aging** refers to an increase in the proportion of people within a population who are elderly (Kinsella, 2000). Italy is the "oldest" country in the world in terms of its age composition, with an estimated 18 percent of the population over age 65 (Kinsella & Velkoff, 2001). In the United States, the population ages 65 and older is just under 13 percent, but this figure is expected to increase to nearly 20 percent by 2030 (American Administration on Aging, 2008b, 2008c; He et al., 2005). The elderly segment of the population in the United States is not only growing but is also becoming more diverse, with particularly large increases expected in the number of older Hispanics and Asian Americans (He et al., 2005).

population aging The aging of the population in a society such that an increasing proportion of people in the population are elderly.

What explains these remarkable increases in life expectancy? People often assume that breakthroughs in treating the chronic diseases that affect the elderly are primarily responsible. Yet improved control over infectious diseases that once claimed the lives of many children actually played a larger role in extending life expectancy (Hayflick, 2004). Economic development in a society often brings about improvements in nutrition, sanitation, water quality, and the availability of antibiotics and vaccinations. These public health measures reduce the threat of infectious conditions (such as tuberculosis, pneumonia, influenza, diarrhea, and diphtheria) that once caused mortality rates among infants and children to be very high. The main force driving gains in life expectancy in economically developed societies has been the declines in mortality among children, which has allowed more children to survive to old age (Lee, 2003). Only in recent years has progress in treating the chronic, degenerative diseases of later life—such as heart disease and cancer—begun to contribute to further gains in life expectancy (Lee, 2003).

However, not all nations have the economic resources to implement public health programs that reduce deaths from infectious diseases. Life expectancy remains alarmingly low in some parts of the world. People seldom live past age 45 in the poorest countries of Africa and the Middle East (United Nations, 2009). Demographers—researchers who study the characteristics of populations in different societies—predict that life expectancy will increase with economic development in these countries.

Maximum Lifespan

Will further increases in life expectancy as dramatic as those that took place in the 20th century occur in the future? Scientists are hotly debating this question. Some believe that life expectancy cannot increase indefinitely because humans (and other species) have a maximum lifespan (Fries, 2003). **Maximum lifespan** refers to the maximum number of years that people could live if they managed to avoid all accidents and diseases. These scientists estimate the maximum human lifespan to be approximately 125 years (Coles, 2004). Frenchwoman Jeanne Calment, who is believed to have lived longer than anyone in recorded history, came close to this maximum when she died at the age of 122 in 1997 (National Institute on Aging [NIA], 2002).

Other scientists dispute the idea of a maximum lifespan and argue that further gains in life expectancy are possible (Oeppen & Vaupel, 2002; Vaupel et al., 1998). They predict that life expectancy will continue to increase at a rate of 2 to 3 years per decade, and that **centenarians**—people who live to be 100 or older—will become commonplace in our lifetimes (Oeppen & Vaupel, 2002). In fact, the number of centenarians is already growing rapidly. In the United States. there were roughly 3,000 centenarians in 1950, but that figure is expected to approach 1,000,000 by 2050 (NIA, 2006). **Supercentenarians**—people living to be 110 or older—also are becoming more common in some countries (Robine & Vaupel, 2002). Whether life expectancy will continue to increase markedly has important implications for projections about the future health status of the elderly population, as discussed later. (For a summary of this section, see "Interim Summary 17.1: Later Adulthood: The Newest Life Period.")

AP Photo

Jeanne Calment, the longest living person in recorded history, lived to be 122, very close to what some scientists regard as the maximum human lifespan of 125 years. Aging did not slow her down much. She took up fencing lessons at age 85 and was still riding a bicycle at age 100.

BIOLOGICAL THEORIES OF AGING

Why do we age? This simple question does not have a simple answer. Many different hypotheses and theories have been offered to explain aging, but they can be grouped into three basic categories: programmed theories, evolutionary theories, and random damage theories.

Programmed Theories of Aging

According to **programmed theories of aging**, a program or built-in clock of some kind causes us to age and, eventually, die (Bergeman, 1997; Cristafalo et al., 1999). One view, for example, is that a genetic code may be written into our DNA that programs cells to die. But while many scientists agree that development is genetically programmed *early* in life, they do not believe this is true *later* in life. They dispute the idea that aging and death are genetically programmed. A more widely accepted view is one that integrates evolutionary theories of aging with random damage theories of

maximum lifespan The maximum number of years people could live if they managed to avoid all accidents and diseases.

centenarian A person who lives to be at least 100 years old.

supercentenarian A person who lives to be 110 or older.

programmed theories of aging Theories that postulate the existence of a program or built-in clock of some kind that causes us to age and, eventually, die.

INTERIM SUMMARY 17.1

Later Adulthood: The Newest Life Period	
Life Expectancy	■ **Life expectancy** refers to the average number of years a person can expect to live. Life expectancy in the United States has increased in the last 100 years. ■ The main force driving gains in life expectancy in economically developed societies has been the decline in mortality among infants and children. Progress in treating chronic diseases has begun to contribute more recently to further gains in life expectancy.
Maximum Lifespan	■ Some scientists believe that life expectancy cannot increase indefinitely because humans have a **maximum lifespan** of about 125 years. Other scientists argue that further gains in life expectancy are possible.

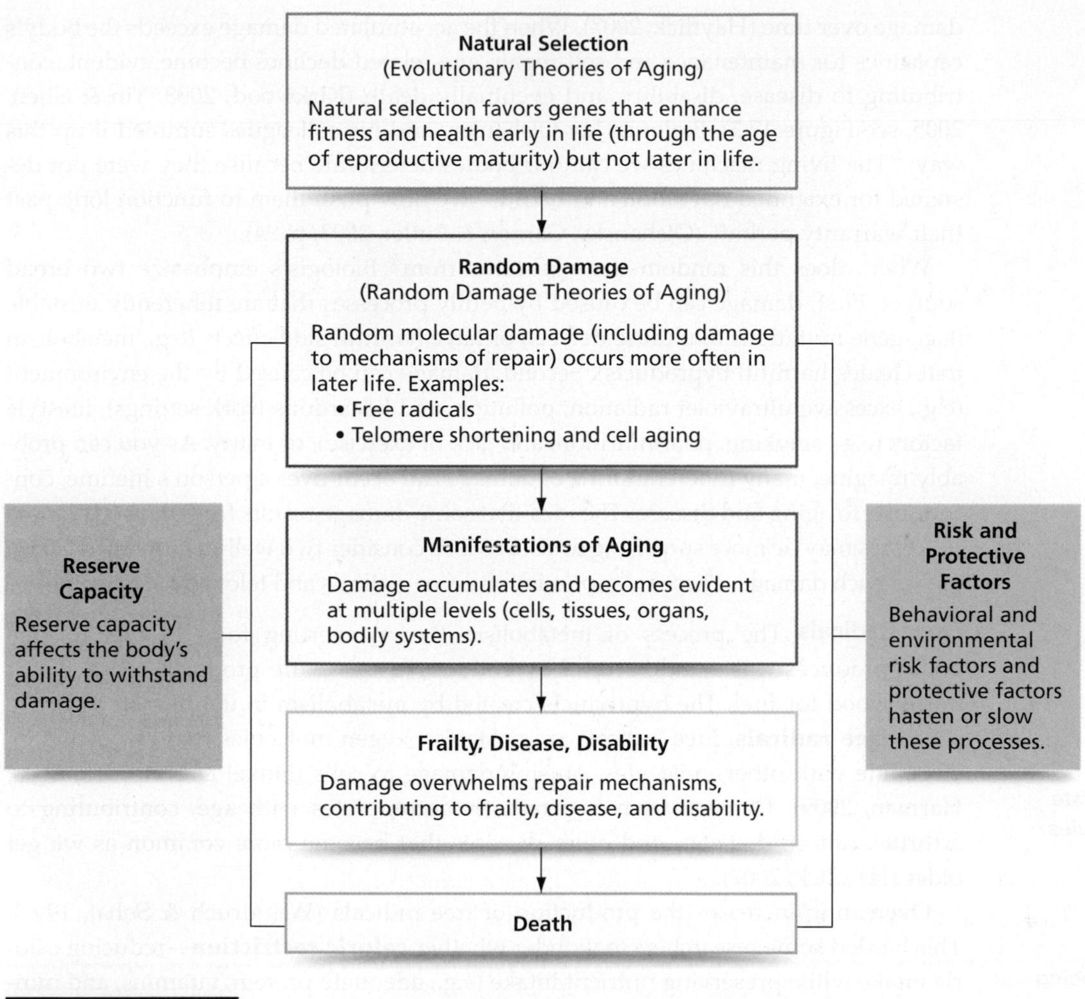

Natural Selection
(Evolutionary Theories of Aging)
Natural selection favors genes that enhance fitness and health early in life (through the age of reproductive maturity) but not later in life.
Random Damage
(Random Damage Theories of Aging)
Random molecular damage (including damage to mechanisms of repair) occurs more often in later life. Examples:
• Free radicals
• Telomere shortening and cell aging
Reserve Capacity
Reserve capacity affects the body's ability to withstand damage.
Manifestations of Aging
Damage accumulates and becomes evident at multiple levels (cells, tissues, organs, bodily systems).
Risk and Protective Factors
Behavioral and environmental risk factors and protective factors hasten or slow these processes.
Frailty, Disease, Disability
Damage overwhelms repair mechanisms, contributing to frailty, disease, and disability.
Death

FIGURE 17.3

Integrative View of the Causes of Aging

aging (Hayflick, 2007; Kirkwood, 2008; Olshansky & Hayflick, & Carnes, 2002; Rattan, 2007; Troen, 2003; see Figure 17.3).

Evolutionary Theories of Aging

According to **evolutionary theories of aging**, discussed in the first chapter of this book, natural selection favors genes that increase the likelihood that people will live long enough to reproduce and care for their offspring. Genes that contribute to fitness and health through the period of reproductive maturity (typically in the first half of life) are likely to be passed on to future generations. Living beyond the age of reproductive maturity, however, does not benefit survival of the species, and, as a result, genes that would confer fitness and health in the second half of life have not been selected through evolution (Rattan, 2007). Without this genetic advantage, according to evolutionary theories of aging, older adults have less capacity to withstand random damage to genes and other cells that are essential for life (Hayflick, 2007; Yin & Chen, 2005).

evolutionary theories of aging Theories that postulate that natural selection favors genes that confer fitness and increase survival through the age of reproductive maturity (first half of life), but not beyond the age of reproductive maturity (second half of life); without this advantage, older adults are less able to withstand random damage to genes and other essential cells.

Random Damage Theories of Aging

According to **random damage theories of aging**, damage accumulates as people grow older, gradually affecting cells, tissues, organs, and bodily systems (Kirkwood, 2008). Even the body's capacities for maintenance and self-repair experience random

random damage theories of aging Theories that postulate that damage accumulates as people grow older; when the accumulated damage exceeds the body's capacities for maintenance and self-repair, age-related declines become evident, contributing to disease, disability, and eventually death.

damage over time (Hayflick, 2007). When the accumulated damage exceeds the body's capacities for maintenance and self-repair, age-related declines become evident, contributing to disease, disability, and eventually death (Kirkwood, 2008; Yin & Chen, 2005; see Figure 17.3). Biologist Jay Olshanksy and his colleagues summed it up this way: "The living machines we call our bodies deteriorate because they were not designed for extended operation and because we now push them to function long past their warranty period" (Olshansky, Carnes, & Butler, 2003, p. 94).

Where does this random damage come from? Biologists emphasize two broad sources. First, damage can be caused by bodily processes that are inherently unstable (e.g., gene mutations that cause defects) or have harmful side-effects (e.g., metabolism that creates harmful byproducts). Second, damage can be caused by the environment (e.g., excessive ultraviolet radiation, pollution, and hazardous work settings), lifestyle factors (e.g., smoking, poor nutrition, and lack of exercise), or injury. As you can probably imagine, many different forms of damage can occur over a person's lifetime, contributing to aging and disease. The idea that some damage results from the body's own processes may be more surprising to you, so let's consider two well-documented examples of such damage. These examples involve free radicals and telomere shortening.

Free Radicals The process of metabolism (i.e., converting food to fuel for the body) produces waste and harmful byproducts, just as a fire produces soot when it burns wood for fuel. The byproducts created by metabolism in the human body are called **free radicals**. Free radicals are unstable oxygen molecules that can penetrate or collide with other molecules, causing damage to cells (Finkel & Holbrook, 2000; Harman, 2009). Damage from free radicals accumulates with age, contributing to arthritis, cancer, diabetes, and other diseases that become more common as we get older (Hayflick, 2007).

free radicals Unstable oxygen molecules produced during metabolism that can penetrate or collide with other molecules, causing damage to cells.

Overeating increases the production of free radicals (Weindruch & Sohal, 1997). This has led some researchers to wonder whether **caloric restriction**—reducing calorie intake while preserving nutrient intake (e.g., adequate protein, vitamins, and minerals)—could reduce the damage caused by free radicals (Gredilla & Barja, 2005; Yu, 1996). Experimental studies have found that caloric restriction increases the lifespan of flies, worms, fish, and rodents by postponing the onset or slowing the progression of many chronic diseases (Fontana & Klein, 2007; Masoro, 2005). Laboratory rats and mice, for example, live up to 40 percent longer than usual when they are fed a nutrient-rich diet that contains only 70 percent of their normal calorie intake (NIA, 2006).

caloric restriction An experimental intervention being investigated in animal studies to determine whether reducing calorie intake while preserving nutrient intake (e.g., adequate protein, vitamins, and minerals) extends longevity.

Experimental studies with humans are scarce, but nonexperimental evidence provides intriguing clues. During World War II, food shortages in some European countries were linked to sharp decreases in rates of cardiovascular disease—rates that later increased after the war ended and food became more plentiful (Fontana & Klein, 2007). Similarly, Okinawa, Japan, has an unusually large number of centenarians, and the Okinawan diet contains fewer calories than average but is highly nutritious (Willcox, Willcox, Todoriki, Curb, & Suzuki, 2006). In fact, a popular Okinawan saying is *hara hachi-bu*, "Eat until you are 80 percent full" (Willcox et al., 2006). Caloric restriction is being investigated as a possible strategy for improving health and longevity (Masoro, 2005), but scientists caution that experimental studies of long-term effects in humans need to be conducted before the benefits and risks can be fully understood (Olshansky et al., 2002).

Telomere Shortening When cells in our bodies become defective, they are replaced through the process of cell division. This process helps to replenish the body's tissues and organs. In the 1960s, however, cell biologist Leonard Hayflick discovered that human cells do not divide and replicate indefinitely, but rather slow down and eventually stop dividing with age. (Stem cells are an exception to this principle.) Hayflick demonstrated that human cells grown in ideal laboratory conditions—with a steady supply of nutrients, a constant temperature, and protection from environmental hazards—stopped replicating at some point, usually after about 50 divisions (Hayflick, 1965). Many other studies have confirmed the existence of a point at which cells stop dividing and replicating (Campisi, 1997). This point has come to be known as the **Hayflick limit**.

Hayflick limit The number of times a normal cell will divide and replicate before it stops due to telomere shortening.

What controls the number of times cells divide? The answer may lie with our **telomeres**, the protective tips on the ends of our chromosomes (a bit like the protective tips on the ends of shoestrings) (see Figure 17.4). These tips become shorter each time cells divide. Eventually, when the telomeres have nearly disappeared, the cells stop dividing, causing the cells to age and deteriorate (Harley, Futcher, & Greider, 1990). You might be inclined to think this means that the body has a built-in clock that controls the length of life by limiting cell reproduction. However, scientists view this process not as a clock, but rather as a mechanism that may have developed through evolution to prevent the growth of tumors early in life (Campisi, 2005). This mechanism would have been beneficial when human life expectancy was short, but it has become costly as life expectancy has increased, because cells that cannot be replenished will age and become defective over time (Troen, 2005).

telomeres Protective tips at the of ends of our chromosomes.

The rate of telomere shortening, like the production of free radicals, can be influenced by life experience and lifestyle factors. Chronic stress hastens telomere shortening and contributes to premature aging in animals and humans (Epel, 2009). Evidence has begun to link low socioeconomic status to accelerated telomere shortening, even after taking into account obesity, smoking, and exercise (Cherkas et al., 2006). You might think about the role of telomere shortening when you read later about the shorter life expectancies of socially disadvantaged groups.

Genes and Longevity

Emphasizing random damage (produced by the body's own internal processes and by external factors) as a fundamental cause of aging does not mean that genes are irrelevant to how long we live. Although genes do not dictate the aging process (as in a genetic program that causes us to age), they do play a role in determining longevity by influencing the reserve capacity of various organ systems (Hayflick, 2004; 2007). **Reserve capacity** refers to an excess physiological capacity built into many

reserve capacity An excess physiological capacity that allows organs and bodily systems to continue functioning even though age-related declines have begun to occur.

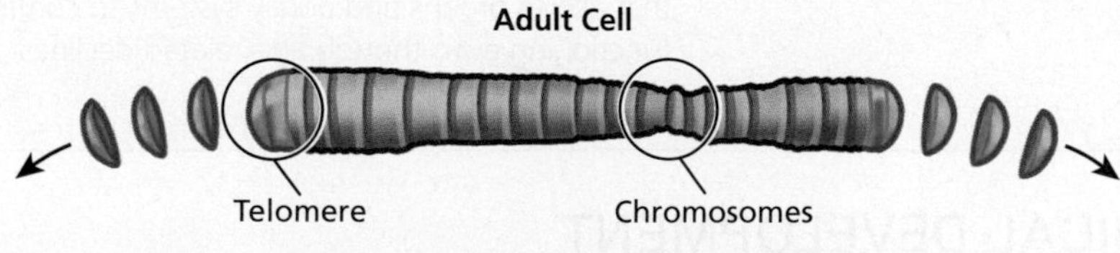

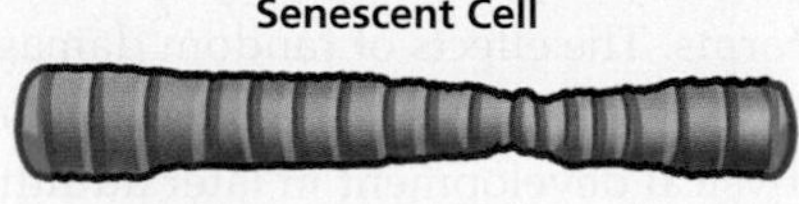

FIGURE 17.4

Telomere Shortening with Age

Telomeres, the protective tips on the ends of our chromosomes, become shorter each time cells divide. When the telomeres have nearly disappeared (as shown in the senescent cell), the cells stop dividing, causing the cells to age and deteriorate.

Source: Adapted from National Institute on Aging. (2006). *Aging under the microscope: A biological quest.* U.S. Department of Health and Human Services: National Institutes of Health. Retrieved April 2, 2010 from http://www.nia.nih.gov/HealthInformation/Publications/AgingUndertheMicroscope

organ systems that allows the body to respond to physical challenges even though age-related declines have begun to occur.

Having larger reserve capacity increases the likelihood of surviving long enough to reproduce and raise offspring. As a result, genes that increase reserve capacity would have been selected through evolution and passed from one generation to another. A fringe benefit of greater reserve capacity is being better able to withstand the effects of the random damage in the second half of life. People whose genes enhance reserve capacity live longer because the random damage that accumulates over time takes longer to cause organs or bodily systems to fail (Hayflick, 2007). Longevity tends to run in families for this reason (Hayflick, 2004, 2007). Genes don't tell the whole story, but there is some truth to the old expression that if you want to live a long life, you should choose your parents wisely. (For a summary of this section, see "Interim Summary 17.2: Biological Theories of Aging.")

INTERIM SUMMARY **17.2**

Biological Theories of Aging	
Programmed Theories of Aging	■ According to **programmed theories of aging**, a program or built-in clock of some kind causes us to age and eventually die.
Evolutionary Theories of Aging	■ According to **evolutionary theories of aging**, older adults have less capacity to withstand random damage to genes and other cells that are essential for life.
Random Damage Theories of Aging	■ According to **random damage theories of aging**, damage accumulates as people grow older. When the accumulated damage exceeds the body's capacities for maintenance and self-repair, age-related declines become evident, leading to death. ■ Sources of random damage include the body's internal processes (e.g., **free radicals** and **telomere shortening**) and external factors (environmental factors, lifestyle, injury).
Genes and Longevity	■ Genes do not dictate the aging process, but they do play a role in determining longevity by influencing **reserve capacity**—an excess physiological capacity that allows organs and bodily systems to continue functioning even though age-related declines have occurred.

PHYSICAL DEVELOPMENT

The various theories of aging help explain why the physical changes that occur in later life can take such varied forms. The effects of random damage to the body's cells, tissues, organs, and regulatory systems accumulate over time in unique ways for different people. This makes physical development in later adulthood more varied than in any earlier life period, and no two people age in exactly the same way. Try to think of two older adults who are about the same age but whose appearance, physical abilities, and health differ greatly. Now try to think about two infants or children who differ as greatly from each other in their physical development as this pair of older adults. The second task is more difficult, because physical development early in life *is* genetically programmed, and therefore unfolds in more similar ways across different children. This is not true in later life (Hayflick, 2007).

As you read about the physical changes that occur with age, it is important to keep a few key points in mind. First, these changes often *interact* with each other to affect an older person's functioning, which can magnify their impact. For example, declines in bone density, muscle strength, and the sense of balance can interact in ways that greatly increase the risk of falls and bone fractures in later life (Davison & Marrinan, 2008). Similarly, declines in vision, coupled with a general slowing of reaction times, can affect an older person's ability to drive an automobile safely (Anstey, Wood, Lord, & Walker, 2005).

Second, as discussed earlier, even when older adults experience physical declines, they can often still carry out their daily activities because many vital organs and bodily systems have a built-in reserve capacity. This reserve capacity is similar to the spare gallon or two of gasoline in a car's gas tank that allows the car to keep operating even when the tank registers as empty. The extra physiological capacity built into our vital organs and bodily systems allows them to keep functioning even though age-related declines have occurred.

Jose Azel/Getty Images

Reserve capacity in the cardiovascular system may allow an elderly person to enjoy daily walks, but not to shovel snow or lift a heavy box as easily, as such demanding activities could overwhelm the cardiovascular system and increase the risk of a heart attack.

When older people encounter very stressful life circumstances or extreme environmental conditions, however, the demands on their organ systems may overwhelm even this built-in reserve capacity, leading to organ failure. Reserve capacity in the cardiovascular system may be sufficient to allow an elderly person to enjoy daily walks, for example, but not to shovel snow or lift a heavy box, either of which might increase the risk of a heart attack (Rook, Charles, & Heckhausen, 2006). Reserve capacity itself is not a static resource, moreover, but tends to decline with advancing age (Fries, 1980; Rowe & Kahn, 1998). This decline helps to explain why the elderly are affected more severely by, and can even die from, health conditions such as influenza or pneumonia that are rarely lethal at younger ages (Koivula, Sten, & Makela, 1999).

Third, compensation reduces the impact of age-related biological decline. **Compensation** is an adaptive process of developmental regulation that involves using alternative strategies to pursue an important goal when one's physical capacities or resources decline (Baltes, Lindenberger, & Staudinger, 2006; Freund & Baltes, 2002). Therefore, the body's own systems sometimes compensate for age-related declines. For example, although the heart's ability to pump blood rapidly during periods of cardiovascular demand (such as exercise) declines with age, the volume of blood pumped with each heartbeat increases with age. As a result, overall blood flow declines relatively little as we get older (NIA, 2005). The brain is capable of reorganizing its functioning to compensate for age-related declines, as discussed later. In addition, people actively use compensation as a strategy to cope with declines or losses, as emphasized by the theory of selective optimization with compensation (Baltes & Baltes, 1990; Baltes et al., 2006; see Chapter 13).

compensation An adaptive process of developmental regulation that involves the use of alternative strategies to pursue an important goal when one's physical capacities or resources decline.

Developmental researcher Orville Brim once told an interviewer how his father adapted to vision loss late in life—a story that nicely illustrates the strategy of compensation (Cromie, 1997). His father loved working on a small farm after he retired. When this proved to be difficult as he grew older, he focused his attentions on a small garden patch. At age 90 he became blind, but he still pursued his love of gardening by arranging to have a window box installed in his bedroom in which he was could grow flowers.

Finally, some age-related physical declines can be slowed or even reversed, illustrating the **plasticity,** or malleability, of development (Baltes et al., 2006). For example, in the absence of exercise, muscle mass declines by more than 20 percent for both

plasticity The idea that development is malleable (like plastic); applied to the brain, plasticity refers to the ability of the brain to reorganize its structure and function.

men and women from age 30 to age 70, but regular exercise helps to preserve muscle strength (NIA, 1996).

Appearance and Body Build

The outward signs of aging that begin to become noticeable in midlife—wrinkled skin, grey hair, patches of baldness—continue into later life. Skin becomes drier and more wrinkled, and hair becomes entirely white or, among many men, entirely gone. Fortunately, no one ever died of wrinkles, gray hair, or baldness (Hayflick, 1998), and in some parts of the world, these signs of aging are associated with maturity, wisdom, and nurturance (Han, 1996; Muscarella & Cunningham, 1996).

Declines in bone density that begin in midlife continue into later adulthood, causing gradual loss of height and an increasing risk of osteoporosis (see Figure 17.5). Falls experienced by older people are more likely to cause serious bone fractures, a problem that is compounded by declines in the sense of balance. Fortunately, tai chi and other strength- and balance-training programs appear to be helpful in reducing the risk of falls in the elderly (Kannus, Sievänen, Palvanen, Järvinen, & Parkkari, 2005; Low, Ang, Goh, Chew, 2008; Straus, 2008).

Weight gain is common in midlife, but this trend reverses itself in later life, when unintentional weight loss becomes more common (Alley, Ferrucci, Barbagallo, Studenski, & Harris, 2008). Weight loss in later life is caused by a loss of muscle and bone and by a decline in nutrient intake by older adults (Alley et al., 2008; Chapman, 2007). You might think that such weight loss would be associated with improved health, but in later life it tends to be associated with poor outcomes, including frailty, disability, and even death (Alley et al., 2008). **Frailty** refers to a state of increased vulnerability to stressors that results from diminished reserve capacity and impaired functioning of *multiple* body systems (Bortz, 2002; Fried, Ferrucci, Darer, Williamson, & Anderson, 2004). Frailty in older adults is characterized by unintentional weight loss (usually 10 or more pounds), general muscular weakness, slow walking speed, low physical activity, and a reduced ability to withstand acute illness and emotional or physical stress (Fried et al., 2001; Gillick, 2001). Relatively few of the young-old,

frailty A state of increased vulnerability to stressors that results from diminished reserve capacity and impaired functioning of multiple bodily systems.

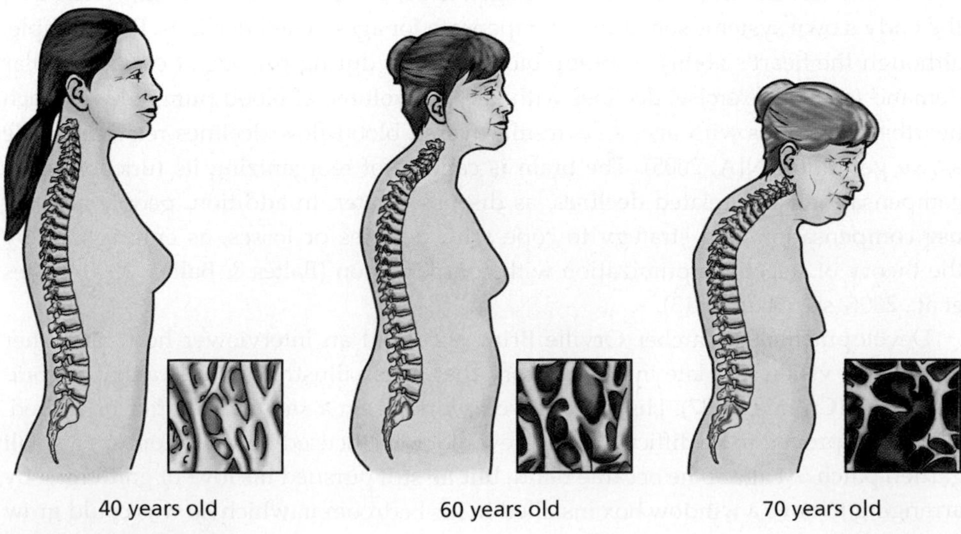

FIGURE 17.5

Progression of Bone Thinning with Age

but as many as 40 percent of the old-old, are frail (Fried et al., 2004). Frailty tends to worsen over time and is linked to a cascade of problems that include increased risks for falls, injuries, hospitalization, nursing-home placement, and mortality (Fried et al, 2004; Hamerman, 1999).

Exactly what causes frailty in later life is not yet known, but active lifestyles that preserve muscle strength may help to slow the development of frailty (Bortz, 2002). In one study of nearly 3,000 initially healthy people in their 70s, those who engaged in more physical exercise were much less likely to become frail over a 5-year period (Peterson et al., 2009). It's never too late to exercise. Even among the very old, carefully prescribed physical exercise can improve muscle strength and help to prevent frailty (Heath & Stuart, 2002).

Mobility and Strength

Mobility and strength decline gradually as we age. You may have observed elderly relatives walk stiffly or unsteadily. This may reflect declines in muscle strength, coupled with joint pain and stiffness (Ayis, Ebrahim, Williams, Juni, & Dieppe, 2007). Preserving muscle strength—especially lower body strength—is important for retaining independence in later life (Goodpaster et al., 2006; Onder et al., 2005). In one large study, older adults who performed well on tests of lower body strength (e.g., walking a short distance, getting in and out of a chair, standing with one's feet together) were much less likely to need nursing home care in the next 4 years (Gurlanik et al., 1994). "Leg power" may be as important for physicians to monitor in older adults as the standard vital signs of heart rate, breathing, temperature, and blood pressure (Bortz, 2002).

Sensory Systems

Declines in sensory systems in later life affect not only vision and hearing but also smell, taste, touch, and balance. For many older adults, these sensory declines cause only minor inconveniences, but for others—especially the very old—sensory declines are more severe and can interfere with their ability to carry out their daily activities safely and effectively (Guralnik & Simonsick, 1993).

Vision About 18 percent of people ages 70 and older report impaired vision (blindness in one or both eyes or difficulty seeing even with glasses; Crews & Campbell, 2004). As we discussed in Chapter 15, some vision changes may have begun in midlife, such as difficulty focusing on near objects, seeing well in dimly lit settings or settings with a lot of glare, and adjusting to bright-dark shifts. Other changes emerge in later life. As people grow older, they often see distant objects less clearly and have worse depth perception (NIA, 2007a). As you can imagine, such vision limitations could increase the risk of falls and accidents in the home and elsewhere. Driving a car often becomes more difficult, especially at night (Klein, Klein, Lee, & Cruickshanks, 1998). In fact, vision problems are the most common reasons why older adults limit or give up driving (Freeman, Muñoz, Turano, & West, 2006). Corrective eyewear (eyeglasses, contact lenses) and the use of large-print books or magnifiers can address some vision limitations, although one-third of adults in their mid-80s or older have difficulty seeing even with corrective eyewear (Desai, Pratt, Lentzner, & Robinson, 2001).

Some eye diseases become more common as people age. We discussed glaucoma in Chapter 15 (see also Figure 17.6, top right panel). Even though this largely asymptomatic condition becomes more common with age, it can be managed with medication and surgery if it is detected early enough.

Cataract disease affects as many as half of adults age 65 and older (Desai et al., 2001). **Cataracts** are cloudy areas that form gradually in the lens of the eye, causing blurry, distorted vision, and increasing sensitivity to glare (see Figure 17.6, lower-left

cataracts Cloudy areas that form gradually in the lens of the eye, causing blurry, distorted vision, and increasing sensitivity to glare.

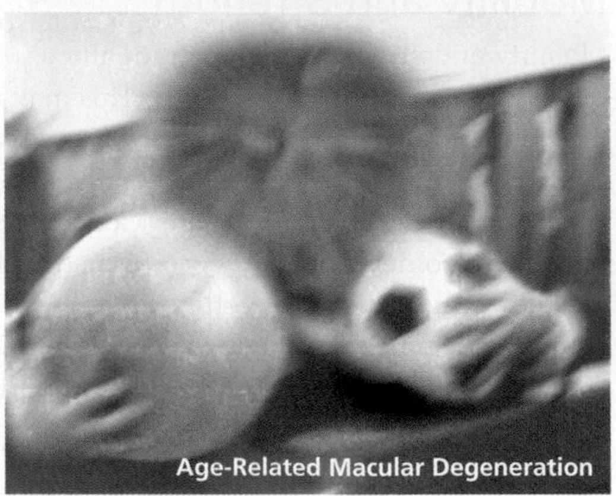

Photos courtesy of National Eye Institute/National Institutes of Health

FIGURE 17.6

Normal Vision versus Vision with Glaucoma, Cataracts, or Macular Degeneration

panel). As cataracts grow larger, they can interfere with daily activities, such as reading, watching television, engaging in hobbies, and doing household tasks. Fortunately, cataracts usually can be treated effectively with a short surgical procedure in which the affected lens is removed and a new lens implanted (Desai et al., 2001; National Eye Institute, 2009).

macular degeneration A condition in which the center of the retina, or macula, deteriorates, causing loss of central vision.

The leading cause of blindness in later life is **macular degeneration,** an eye disease that causes the center of the retina—the macula—to deteriorate (Jager, Mieler, & Miller, 2008). Central vision is lost as a result (see Figure 17.6, bottom-right panel). This condition is more common in advanced old age, affecting about 15 percent of the old-old (Oneill, Jamison, McCulloch, & Smith, 2001). Unlike cataracts, treatment options for macular degeneration are more limited, but promising medical research suggests that effective treatments may be on the horizon (Oneill et al., 2001).

Hearing Changes in hearing, like changes in vision, become more pronounced from midlife to later life, although, again, it is the old-old who are most affected. Hearing problems affect about half of those age 75 and older (Pleis & Lethbridge-Çejku, 2006). Hearing problems can make it difficult for older adults to follow conversations, especially when background noise is present (Weinstein, 1994). Interference with social interaction is an especially troubling aspect of hearing loss, causing some older adults to become hesitant when interacting with others or to avoid interaction altogether (Desai et al., 2001). Problems communicating with a hearing-impaired older person can frustrate others or lead them to view the older person as confused or incompetent, reactions that can undermine the older person's confidence or feelings of self-worth (Kampfe & Smith, 1998). It does not help to shout when communicating with a hearing-impaired older person. Instead, it is best to find a quiet location, face the person directly, and speak just a little louder than usual (National Institute on Aging, 2009a).

Hearing aids can help older adults compensate for hearing loss, even if they do not always completely correct the problem (Schneider & Pichora-Fuller, 2000). Many hearing aids today are small enough that they are not readily visible to others, reducing their stigma. Even so, older people are sometimes reluctant to wear hearing aids for fear of looking old or being perceived as disabled (Erler & Garstecki, 2002; Wallhagen, 2010). Combatting negative stereotypes of older adults may help older adults feel more comfortable using aids that help them in the course of their daily lives.

Smell and Taste Some of life's pleasures, often taken for granted, come from our senses of smell and taste. As we age, small but discernible declines in these senses occur (Murphy, Schubert, Cruickshanks, Klein, Klein, & Nondahl, 2002). The number of taste buds in the tongue does not change much with age, but taste sensitivity declines, possibly due to smoking, exposure to environmental pollutants, medication side effects, and even dentures (which can block taste receptors) (Schiffman, 1997). One consequence is that food sometimes tastes bland to older adults (Hetherington, 1998). Spices and other food seasonings may help to compensate for this loss of taste sensitivity. Our senses of taste and smell also serve safety functions, warning us about spoiled food, gas leaks, or fires. Smoke and gas detectors in the home benefit people of all ages, but may be especially important for older adults (Wysocki & Gilbert, 1989).

Touch and Pain Sensitivity to touch declines with age, especially in the hands and feet, due to declines in the functioning of touch receptors in the skin and poorer blood circulation to the body's extremities (Hayflick, 1994). As a result, it can be harder for older adults to grasp and manipulate objects and to do handiwork (such as needlework or other hobbies).

Does the age-related decline in the sense of touch mean that older adults are less likely to experience pain? The answer is not straightforward, in part because pain is influenced by psychological factors (Turk & Okifuji, 2002). Some people, regardless of age, tolerate pain better or are less inclined to admit their pain. Older people also sometimes mistakenly regard painful symptoms that could be due to disease as inevitable aspects of aging, leading them to forego or delay seeking medical care (George, 2001; Leventhal & Prohaska, 1986; Stoller, 1993). Among older adults who have chronic health problems, however, pain is often a persistent problem that can interfere with their daily activities and even their performance on tests of cognitive functioning (Weiner, Rudy, Morrow, Slaboda, & Lieber, 2006)—something you may have experienced if you have taken an exam on a day when you did not feel well. This is worth bearing in mind when age differences in cognitive performance are discussed later in this chapter.

Balance Many people probably fail to appreciate the important role played by the sense of balance until it begins to decline in later life. The sense of balance receives and sends information about the body's position when a person is standing or walking, so that continual adjustments can be made to prevent falls. With age, declines occur in receptors in the inner ear that monitor the body's position, and nerves that carry messages from these receptors to the brain decline (Park, Tang, Lopez, & Ishiyama, 2001). Standard tests of balance—such as standing on one foot with eyes closed—that are simple for younger people can be very challenging for people in their 70s or 80s.

Declines in the sense of balance greatly increase the risk of falls in later life (Davison & Marrinan, 2007). This problem is magnified by declines in vision because older adults may misgauge the depth of stairs or curbs or may not see hazards in the environment that could cause them to trip. Weaker muscles, medication side effects, and cognitive impairment can further increase the risk of falling in later life (Morley, 2002). More than one-third of adults age 65 and older fall annually, with the risk of falls being greatest among the old-old (Centers for Disease Control and Prevention [CDC], 2009). Falls can be very serious for older adults, causing fractures nearly 50 percent of the time (Davison & Marrinan, 2007) and often resulting in disability, hospitalization, nursing-home placement, and death. In fact, falls are the leading cause of death from injury in later life (CDC, 2009). Older women are especially likely to break bones when they fall because they often have osteoporosis, a condition that causes their bones to become brittle (CDC, 2006; see Chapter 15).

Given the severe consequences of falls, it is not surprising that older adults—especially the old-old—sometimes limit their activity for fear of falling (Cumming, Salkeld, Thomas, & Szonyi, 2000). Unfortunately, this lack of activity can make matters worse by contributing to further muscle loss and social isolation (Morley, 2002). Once again, physical exercise is crucial—early and later in life—to preserve bone health and reduce muscle loss (and to achieve other benefits for physical and cognitive health, as discussed later).

Vital Organ Systems

Changes in the body's vital organ systems that first become evident in midlife often continue into later life, and new changes appear as well. In the cardiovascular system, atherosclerosis continues to lead to the buildup of plaque in the artery walls, increasing the risk of heart attacks and strokes in later life (National Institutes on Health, 2005). Artery walls become less elastic (a process called **arteriosclerosis**), requiring the heart to pump harder and increasing the risk of **hypertension** (high blood pressure).

arteriosclerosis A process that causes artery walls to become less elastic, requiring the heart to pump harder and increasing the risk of hypertension (high blood pressure).

hypertension High blood pressure (a threat to health when it is chronic).

In the respiratory system, lung tissue similarly becomes less elastic, making breathing more effortful and causing older adults to become fatigued more easily during physical activity (National Institute on Aging, 2007; Zeleznik, 2003). This leads some older adults to reduce their physical activity, which only hastens declines in cardiovascular and respiratory function (Cousins, 2000).

Changes in the kidneys cause renal functioning to become less efficient (Tedla & Friedman, 2008). As a result, older adults are less able to excrete medication, causing medications to circulate in the bloodstream longer than usual (Turnheim, 2003). This makes it very important to monitor medication side effects in the elderly.

Changes in the urinary system tend to reduce the volume of urine the bladder can hold (Ouslander, 1997). **Urinary incontinence** (an inability to control urination) causes embarrassment and declines in older adults' quality of life, but medication and physical exercises help to reduce the problem (Minassian, Drutz, & Al-Badr, 2003).

urinary incontinence An inability to control urination.

Bodily Control Systems

With age, important changes also occur in our **bodily control systems**, which monitor and regulate the functioning of all organs and systems in the body. These control systems are the nervous system, immune system, and endocrine system. Chapter 15 discussed age-related changes in the endocrine system that trigger hormonal changes. The following discussion, therefore, focusses on the nervous and immune systems.

bodily control systems Bodily systems (nervous system, immune system, and endocrine system) that monitor and regulate the functioning of all organs and systems in the body.

Nervous System The nervous system—which consists of the brain, the spine, and nerves that fan out to all parts of the body—is responsible for integrating information received from the senses, muscles, and organ systems and for sending commands that regulate functions throughout the body. The nervous system controls many bodily functions outside of our awareness (e.g., respiration and digestion), but it is also the site of all conscious thoughts, emotions, and responses. The nervous system becomes less efficient and slows down with age (Salthouse, 1996). Physical coordination declines and cognitive functioning becomes slower as a result. In fact, an age-related slowing of **reaction time**—the length of time needed to respond to a stimulus—is one of the most reliable findings in research on aging (Madden, 2001). This increase in reaction time has been demonstrated in studies in which people of different ages are asked to respond as quickly as they can to experimentally presented stimuli, such as auditory tones or visual symbols.

reaction time The length of time that is needed to respond to a stimulus.

Why does reaction time become slower with age? One reason is that nerves that conduct information to and from the brain become less efficient, requiring more time for sensory information to reach the brain and for commands from the brain to reach the body's muscles in order to execute a response (Cerella, 1990; Ball, Edwards, & Ross, 2007). In addition, changes in the brain lengthen the time needed to process and respond to incoming information. The production of neurotransmitters, the chemical messengers that transmit information between neurons, declines with age, and the neurons themselves shrink in size as their connective structures (axons, dendrites, and synapses) are lost (Raz, 2000; Volkow et al., 1998). Brain volume declines with age, although the rate of decline varies across different areas of the brain. The prefrontal cortex and hippocampus (areas that are especially important for memory functioning) show the greatest declines in volume (Raz, 2000). Brain imaging studies also have shown that with aging there is less activation of the prefrontal cortex when memory tasks are being performed (Rajah & D'Esposito, 2005; Reuter-Lorenz, & Lustig, 2005).

Skip Nall/Getty Images

Slower reaction times may make it more difficult for an older person to react quickly to dangerous driving conditions.

Yet the aging brain is adaptive, and as these declines occur, compensatory changes are triggered that help to preserve cognitive and motor functioning (Greenwood, 2007; Hess, 2005; Reuter-Lorenz, & Lustig, 2005). New dendrites grow to improve the connectivity among neurons, and healthy neurons may take over some of the functions previously performed by adjacent neurons that have deteriorated (Greenwood, 2007). A particularly striking example of the brain's adaptive potential is that both hemispheres of the brain are activated during some cognitive tasks in later adulthood. Only the right hemisphere, in contrast, is typically activated during such tasks in young adulthood (Cabeza et al., 1997; Grady et al., 1995; Grady, Bernstein, Beig, & Siegenthaler, 2002; Reuter-Lorenz et al., 2000). The activation of both hemispheres is associated with improved memory in later life (Morcom, Good, Frackowiak, & Rugg, 2003; Rosen et al., 2002). The apparent plasticity—or malleability—of the aging brain is an important and hopeful discovery, and we return to this theme of plasticity later when we discuss interventions designed to enhance cognitive functioning in later life.

Not everyone experiences age-related declines in the nervous system at the same rate. Factors that can hasten age-related declines in brain structures and functions include hypertension, diabetes, and chronic stress (Raz & Rodrigue, 2006; Waldstein, 1995). Factors that slow the rate of age-related declines, in contrast, include cardiovascular fitness and physical exercise, especially aerobic exercise (Colcombe et al., 2006; Greenwood, 2007; Kramer et al., 2004; Raz & Rodrigue, 2006).

Immune System The job of the **immune system** is to detect, isolate, and destroy foreign substances (e.g., viruses, bacteria, and toxins) that might invade the body and cause illness. This is a tall order, because the immune system must be able to

immune system A bodily control system that detects, isolates, and destroys foreign substances (e.g., viruses, bacteria, toxins) that might invade the body and cause illness.

respond to an unknown variety of foreign substances while managing to distinguish these foreign substances from the body's own cells (Cacioppo & Bernstein, 2006). The immune system also must not overreact, because the powerful chemicals it releases to combat foreign substances have the potential to harm the body's own tissues. It must be able to recognize when an infection has ended, so that it can withdraw its immune defenses. A careful balancing act is required for the immune system to do its job properly.

With age, the immune system changes in several ways that, paradoxically, can increase (rather than decrease) susceptibility to illness and disease (Gupta, Agrawal, Agrawal, Su, & Gollapudi, 2006; Licastro et al., 2005). First, some of the specific weapons in the immune system's arsenal become less effective (Miller, 1996). **T cells** (so named because they develop in the thymus gland) are immune cells that patrol for foreign substances, lock onto any that are identified, and then either destroy them or mobilize other immune cells to destroy them. T-cell functioning declines progressively with age, making it more difficult for older adults to combat infections and disease (Aw, Silva, & Palmer, 2007; Gupta et al., 2006; Pawelec et al., 2002). Second, the body's ability to distinguish between foreign substances and its own cells declines with age, increasing the risk of **autoimmune diseases.** Autoimmune diseases develop when the immune system mistakenly attacks the body's own cells, damaging or destroying healthy tissues. Autoimmune diseases, such as rheumatoid arthritis, become more common with age (Doran, Pond, Crowson, O'Fallon, & Gabriel, 2002).

t cells Immune cells produced in the thymus gland that patrol for foreign substances, lock onto any that are identified, and then either destroy them or mobilize other immune cells to destroy them.

autoimmune diseases Diseases that develop when the immune system mistakenly attacks the body's own cells, damaging or destroying healthy tissues.

inflammation Part of the immune system's attempt to destroy foreign substances by rushing blood and immune cells to affected tissues.

Perhaps the most significant age-related change, however, is a tendency for the immune system to be chronically activated, producing chronic **inflammation** (Finch, 2007; Licastro et al., 2005). Inflammation is part of the immune system's response to foreign substances. It rushes blood and immune cells to the affected tissues—causing swelling, redness, and heat—all in an attempt to surround and destroy the foreign substances and to initiate healing. The redness and swelling you may have noticed when you have had an insect bite, for example, was your immune system's effort to isolate and neutralize the toxin from the bite and to help the affected tissues begin to heal.

But prolonged inflammation can damage the body's tissues. The aging immune system—perhaps because of repeated activation and deactivation over a lifetime or because of damage caused by stress—becomes overactive, causing chronic inflammation (Finch, 2007; Licastro et al., 2005). When the chemicals dispatched by the immune system as part of this chronic inflammatory response circulate persistently throughout the bloodstream, they can cause damage to *any* tissues and organs in the body. This is why some biologists now believe that chronic inflammation plays a key role in the development of *all* of the degenerative diseases of later life: cardiovascular disease, diabetes, cancer, Alzheimer's disease, and sarcopenia (a disease that leads to the loss of muscle mass) (Finch, 2007; Licastro et al., 2005). As one biologist commented, "Age-related diseases are the price we pay for a life-long active immune system" that loses its fine tuning over time (Licastro et al., 2005).

Sexual Functioning

The idea of older adults being sexually active sometimes provokes raised eyebrows or uncomfortable squirming. After all, it is widely assumed that the elderly cannot really be interested in or capable of sexual activity. But such ageist views do not match the realities of older adults' needs and desires. Sexual activity does decline as people age, but many older adults continue to value sexual intimacy, viewing it as an important element of an emotionally close relationship (Gott & Hinchliff, 2003).

Older couples generally maintain a steady level of interest in and satisfaction with their sexual activity (Zeiss & Kasl-Godley, 2001). As an older man commented in one study, "Why should there be a sudden stop [when you] get to 75?...I mean it's just a natural thing when you love somebody, isn't it?" (Gott & Hinchliff, 2003, p. 1621). Still, some older adults encounter barriers to sexual intimacy, including the lack of a partner and poor physical health (Ginsberg, Pomerantz, & Kramer-Feeley, 2005; Gott & Hinchliff, 2003; Zeiss & Kasl-Godley, 2001). Older participants in one study commented that sex was the last thing on their mind when their health was poor (Gott & Hinchliff, 2003). Cultural stereotypes also present barriers to sexual intimacy in later life (Zeiss & Kasl-Godley, 2001). An investigation of sexual practices in 106 cultures revealed that older adults remained sexually active in cultures in which sexual activity in later life was seen as normal and appropriate. Older adults curtailed their sexual activity, in contrast, in cultures in which sexual activity in later life was viewed negatively (Winn & Newton, 1982).

When older adults describe how they adapt to changes in their sexual functioning, the processes of developmental regulation can be seen at work. For example, although many older adults in one study reported that sex remains important to them, those who lacked a partner and who did not expect to have a partner again in their lifetime reported that sex is unimportant to them (Gott & Hinchliff, 2003). The views of the latter group can be regarded as an example of **loss-based selection** (see Chapter 16), an adaptive process of developmental regulation in which goals are reprioritized and those perceived to be unattainable are relinquished (Freund & Baltes, 2002).

loss-based selection An adaptive process of developmental regulation in which goals are reprioritized and those perceived to be unattainable are relinquished.

Similarly, when age-related physiological changes such as decreased erections or vaginal dryness make sexual intercourse more challenging, older adults often adapt by taking a broader view of sexuality, one that encompasses cuddling and touching as expressions of sexual intimacy (Gott & Hinchliff, 2003; Zeiss & Kasl-Godley, 2001). As an older man commented on his reduced capacity to have sexual intercourse, "Obviously, as you get older you act differently and you adjust to your age, but I consider that a cuddle is sex, isn't it?" (Gott & Hinchliff, 2003, p. 1624). This shift to other expressions of sexual intimacy can be seen as an example of compensation.

Ronnie Kaufman/Getty Images

Physical intimacy and affection remain important to many older adults.

Many of the basic physical changes that occur with age, then, call upon older adults' adaptive capacities to preserve their well-being. Such adaptive capacities help older adults preserve their emotional well-being when they experience changes in sexual functioning, and also help older adults adapt to changes in areas such as mobility, strength, and sensory functioning. As discussed later, older adults' adaptive capacities also play a role in how they respond to changes in their physical health. (For a summary of this section, see "Interim Summary 17.3: Physical Development.")

INTERIM SUMMARY 17.3

Physical Development	
	■ Physical changes in later life often interact with each other, magnifying their impact. ■ The impact of physical declines on older adults' ability to carry out their daily activities is reduced by a reserve capacity in many vital organs and bodily systems and by older adults' use of **compensation**. ■ Some age-related physical declines can be slowed or even reversed, illustrating the **plasticity**, or malleability, of development.
Appearance and Body Build	■ Declines in bone density continue into later adulthood, causing loss of height and increased risk of osteoporosis. Unintentional weight loss also becomes more common. ■ **Frailty** is characterized by unintentional weight loss, muscular weakness, slow walking speed, low physical activity, and a reduced ability to withstand acute illness and emotional or physical stress.
Mobility and Strength	■ Mobility decreases in later adulthood as a result of declines in muscle strength, coupled with joint pain and stiffness. Physical exercise can help preserve mobility and muscle strength.
Sensory Systems	■ Declines in sensory systems in later life affect vision, hearing, smell, taste, touch, and balance. For some, these declines can interfere with daily living.
Vital Organ Systems	■ In the cardiovascular system, atherosclerosis increases the risk of heart attacks and strokes, and artery walls become less elastic (**arteriosclerosis**), requiring the heart to pump harder and increasing the risk of **hypertension**. ■ In the respiratory system, lung tissue becomes less elastic, making breathing more effortful. ■ Renal functioning also becomes less efficient, and changes in the urinary system reduce bladder capacity, sometimes leading to **urinary incontinence**.
Bodily Control Systems	■ Important changes occur in **bodily control systems**: the nervous, immune, and endocrine systems. ■ The nervous system becomes slower and less efficient, reducing physical coordination and slowing cognitive functioning. **Reaction time** also slows as a result of declines in brain efficiency. The aging brain is adaptive, though, and can compensate for some declines in functioning. ■ The **immune system** changes in ways that increase susceptibility to illness and disease. **T cell** functioning declines, the risk of **autoimmune diseases** increases, and chronic **inflammation** plays a role in the development of degenerative diseases.
Sexual Functioning	■ The frequency of sexual activity declines as people age, but many older adults continue to value sexual intimacy. ■ If physiological changes make sexual intercourse challenging, older adults often adapt by taking a broader view of sexuality (an example of compensation).

PHYSICAL HEALTH

If you are a young or middle-aged adult, good health may be something you tend to take for granted—you may realize its importance only when an illness disrupts your activities and plans. In the first half of life, illnesses tend to be short-lived, allowing people to resume their activities after a brief period of discomfort and inconvenience. What about later life? The previous discussion has explored age-related physical changes and biological processes that contribute to the development of health problems in later life, but what health problems are most common? How do they affect older adults' daily lives or their views of their health? These questions are explored next (reserving our discussion of older adults' emotional and mental health for the next chapter).

Common Health Conditions

Older adults experience both acute and chronic health conditions. Acute illnesses—which have a rapid onset and short duration—are less common in later life but often require more bed rest and longer recovery time. Acute illnesses, such as influenza or the common cold, tend to make elderly individuals sicker and can even be fatal because of declines in reserve capacity and weakened immune defenses. Yet chronic illnesses—which have a slow onset, long duration, and a tendency to worsen over time—pose the greatest threat to older adults' health. Chronic conditions become more common with age, accounting for about half of all disability among older adults in the United States (Merck Institute of Aging/Gerontological Society of America [MIAH/GSA], 2002).

As shown in Figure 17.7, the most common chronic conditions in later life include nonfatal conditions such as arthritis and potentially fatal conditions such as heart disease and cancer. Roughly 80 percent of older adults in the United States have at least one chronic condition (He et al., 2005). Members of ethnic minority groups often experience poorer health in old age. For example, compared with elderly Caucasians, elderly Hispanic Americans and African Americans have higher rates of diabetes, hypertension, strokes, and heart attacks (Cooper et al., 2000).

The likelihood of having *multiple* chronic conditions increases with age. The percent of adults who have three or more chronic conditions rises from just over 7 percent among people in their mid-40s and mid-50s to 28 percent among people in their mid-60s to mid-70s, and 37 percent among people age 75 and older (National Center for Health Statistics, 2007). Multiple chronic conditions often exacerbate each other (Jaur & Stoddard, 1999; Kaplan, Haan, & Wallace, 1999). For example, diabetes increases the risk of heart disease and reduces the likelihood of survival after a heart attack or stroke (Wallace & Lemke, 1991). Similarly, the pain and stiffness caused by arthritis may discourage physical exercise, which can worsen a coexisting condition such as diabetes.

Fortunately, chronic conditions usually do not take a substantial toll on older adults' daily functioning until relatively advanced old age, as shown in Figure 17.8. The kind of activity limitation matters,

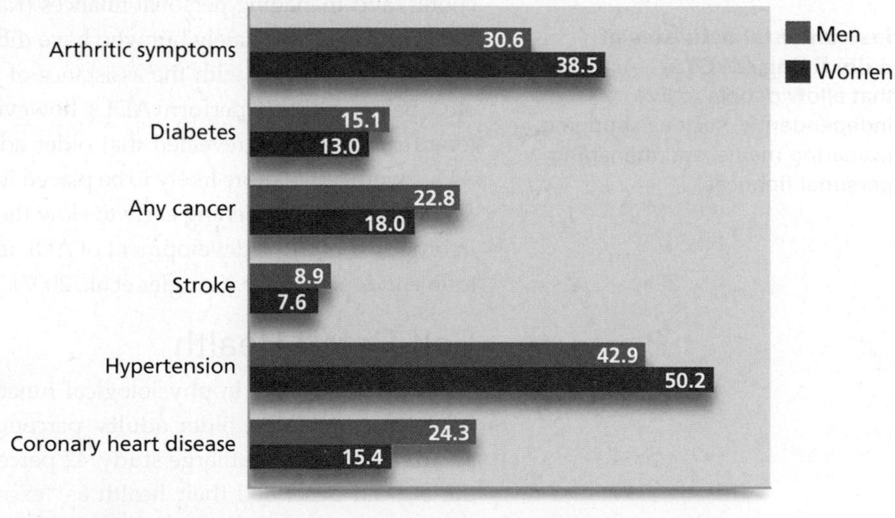

FIGURE 17.7

Common Chronic Conditions in Later Adulthood

Note: This figure shows the percent of men and women age 65 and older in the civilian noninstitutional population who have particular chronic conditions.

Source: National Center for Health Statistics. (2004). National Health Interview Survey, 1997–2000: Prevalence of selected chronic conditions by age, sex, race, and Hispanic origin: United States," Data Warehouse on Trends in Health and Aging, NHIC01c, National Center for Health Statistics, http://www.cdc.gov/nchs/agingact.htm

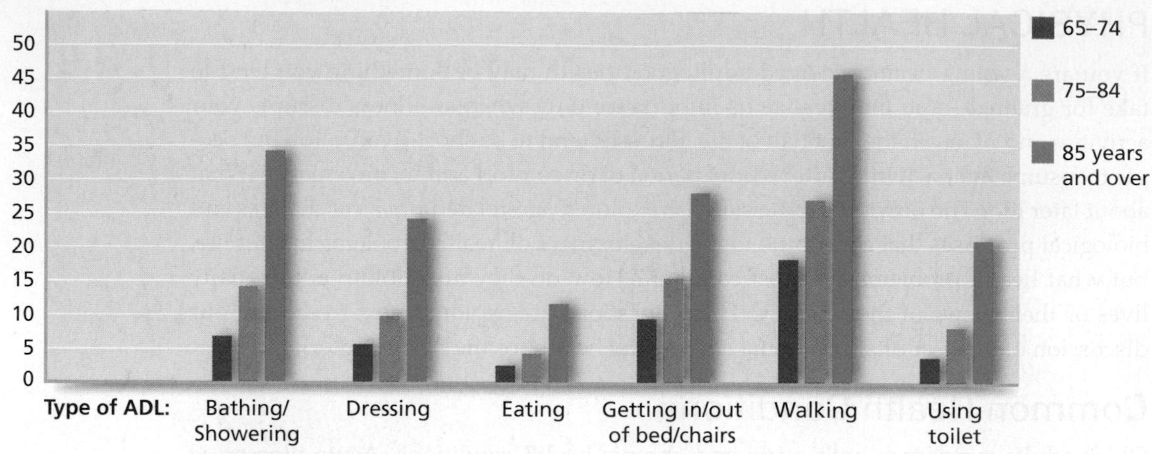

FIGURE 17.8

Percent of People with Limitations in Self-Care Activities (Activities of Daily Living) by Age

Source: American Administration on Aging. (2008a). *Profile of older Americans: 2008.* U.S. Department of Health and Human Services. Washington, DC: U.S. Government.

though, because some limitations make it difficult for an older person to live independently. Researchers usually assess two kinds of activities when they evaluate an older person's ability to carry out everyday tasks of living. **Activities of daily living (ADLs)** refer to basic self-care activities, such as eating, bathing, toileting, dressing, and being able to get in and out of a bed or chair. **Instrumental activities of daily living (IADLs)** refer to more complex daily activities, such as shopping, preparing meals, doing household chores, and managing personal finances (Katz, 1983; Nagi, 1965). Older people who can perform ADLs adequately but who have difficulty with some IADLs may be able to continue living at home with the assistance of others (to shop, help with household tasks, etc.). Being unable to perform ADLs, however, is more problematic. A recent review of 77 longitudinal studies revealed that older adults who had difficulty with three or more ADLs were much more likely to be placed in nursing homes (Gaugler, Duval, Anderson, & Kane, 2007). Intervening early to slow the progression of chronic disease is important in order to delay the development of ADL impairment and preserve older adults' ability to live independently (Gaugler et al., 2007).

activities of daily living (ADLs) Basic self-care activities, such as eating, bathing, toileting, dressing, and being able to get in and out of a bed or chair.

instrumental activities of daily living (IADLs) Activities that allow people to live independently, such as shopping, preparing meals, and managing personal finances.

Self-Rated Health

Despite the declines in physiological functioning and increases in chronic illness that occur as people age, older adults' perception of their health tends to be remarkably positive. In one recent large study, 42 percent of the young-old and even 25 percent of the old-old described their health as "excellent" or "very good" (NIA, 2007b). Older adults may view their health favorably in part because they tend to compare their health to that of other people their age rather than to their own health at a younger age (Robinson-Whelen & Kiecolt-Glaser, 1997). Most older adults do not identify themselves as "old," and they tend to regard their life circumstances, including their own health, as better than those of same-aged peers (National Council on Aging, 2002; Smith, Shelley, & Dennerstein, 1994). Not all older people, of course, rate their health favorably. In advanced old age, as rates of chronic illness increase, the number of people describing their health as poor increases (NIA, 2007b). Elderly Hispanics and African Americans also tend to rate their health less favorably than elderly Caucasians (NIA, 2007b).

Compared to men, women generally rate their health less favorably and report more restrictions of activity and more days of bed rest when they feel ill. This is because women have more, if less lethal, chronic conditions (Austad, 2006; Verbrugge, 2001). This gender difference in self-rated health exists across the lifespan, leading Verbrugge (1989) to conclude that women feel sicker for more of their lives than men do. Although women tend to live longer than men, one price for greater longevity is more disability (Stuck et al., 1999).

Mortality

Mortality rates rise over the course of later adulthood due to the degenerative processes and declines in reserve capacity discussed earlier. In the United States, the leading causes of death among adults ages 65 and older are heart disease, cancer, stroke, chronic obstructive pulmonary disease, pneumonia and influenza, and diabetes (Himes, 2001). Two of these conditions—heart disease and cancer—account for more than half of all deaths among older adults.

The leading causes of death among older adults differ relatively little across demographic groups, but life expectancies are significantly shorter for socially disadvantaged groups, such as some ethnic minority groups and people living in poverty. For example, African Americans have life expectancies that are roughly 5 to 7 years shorter than those of Caucasians (Himes, 2001). In the United States, the poor have life expectancies nearly 20 years shorter than those of the non-poor, even when they have comparable health-risk profiles (such as comparable blood pressure, cholesterol, and body mass index) (Crimmins, Kim, & Seeman, 2009).

Life expectancy also differs for men and women. Throughout the world, women tend to live longer than men (Austad, 2006). In the United States, women live an average of 5 years longer than men (Kung, Hoyert, Xu, & Murphy, 2007). The exact reasons for this sex difference are not clear, but both biological and lifestyle factors (e.g., lower rates of risky behavior among women) are likely to play a role (Austad, 2006; Verbrugge, 1989).

Quantity Versus Quality of Life

As we take stock of physical health and functioning in later life, a crucial issue to consider is whether increased life expectancy has brought about gains in the quantity of life without gains in the quality of life. Some critics worry that living longer means that people will be ill for a greater portion of their lives. Ideally, the amount of time during which older adults suffer from chronic illness could be shortened in the future.

Is the **compression of morbidity** in later life—a shortening of the duration of illness and disability—a realistic goal? Some scientists think so. In their view, the key is to *postpone* the onset of chronic illness to a time in life that approaches the average age of death. If people do not develop a serious illness like cancer until shortly before they die, then the period of illness and suffering would be *compressed* into fewer years (Fries & Crapo, 1981; Rowe, 1997; see Figure 17.9). Scientists who argue that the compression of morbidity is possible believe that the best strategy for postponing chronic illness is to help people modify behavioral risk factors, such as smoking, lack of exercise, obesity, and stress (Fries, 2002; Rowe, 1997). In their view, seeking ways to postpone the onset of chronic disease is a more practical goal for an aging society than trying to find cures for all chronic diseases (Fries & Crapo, 1981).

compression of morbidity A shortening of the duration of morbidity (illness and disability) that results from postponing the onset of chronic illness to a time in life that approaches the average age of death.

But can people modify their health behaviors enough to postpone disease onset and compress the period of disability in later life? The evidence is encouraging. The number of older adults reporting activity limitations due to chronic illness has declined in recent decades, as rates of smoking declined—especially among men (Manton et al., 2006; Waidmann & Liu, 2000). The onset of disability in later life also began to be

Prototypic lingering chronic illness

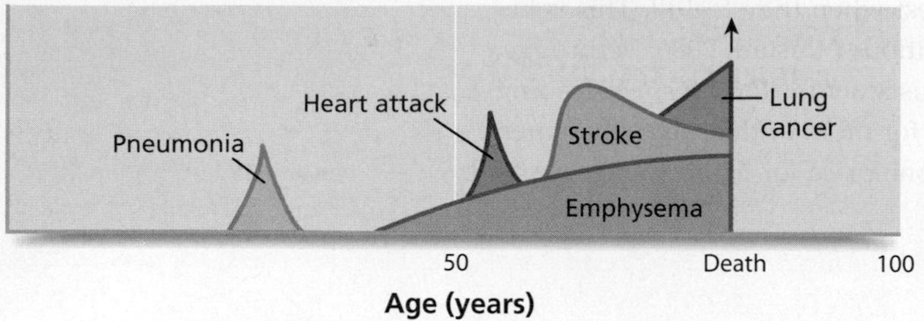

Effects of the postponement of chronic disease

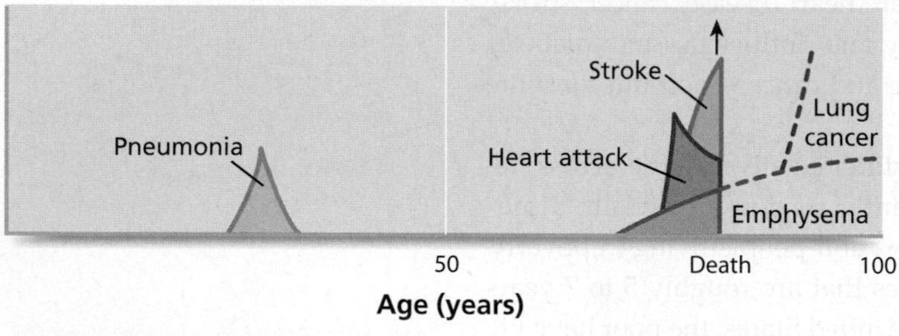

FIGURE 17.9

Compression of Morbidity

Hypothetical life histories for two older adults who experienced the same health problems and who died at the same age (about age 80). One person experienced the onset of chronic health problems much later in life and suffered from a much briefer period of pain and disability (as shown in the bottom panel) than the other person (as shown in the top panel).

Source: Fries, J. F., & Crapo, L. M. (1981). *Vitality and aging.* San Francisco: Freeman, p. 92.

postponed by 7 to 8 years in the 1990s among people with better health behaviors (Fries, 2002, 2003). These are hopeful signs that compressing morbidity into a smaller portion of the lifespan is feasible.

Yet other trends threaten to undo these health gains. Rates of smoking have increased among women in recent years, which may cause future cohorts of elderly women to experience higher rates of lung cancer and heart disease (NAAS, 1999). Soaring rates of childhood and adult obesity may increase the risk of chronic illness and disability—shortening life expectancy—among future cohorts of older adults (Olshansky et al., 2005). Such trends lead some scientists to worry that Americans may not be able to make the lifestyle changes needed to compress morbidity in later life. In fact, they predict an expansion, rather than a compression, of disability in later life in the future (Verbrugge, 1990).

You may begin to see the relevance of the debate about how much life expectancy may increase in the future. If life expectancy increases substantially without a compression of morbidity, then only years of illness, rather than years of health, will have been added. Everyone agrees that the goal for an aging society is to foster quality of life and not merely quantity of life. The crucial question is what mix of preventive health behaviors, medical interventions, and strategies for controlling environmental health threats will best achieve that goal.

As you have seen, a great deal happens to our bodies, our physical functioning, and our health as we age. Some of the changes are relatively small and easily managed; other changes—especially in advanced old age—are more consequential. Many parallels will surface in the exploration of cognitive development in later life that follows. (For a summary of this section, see "Interim Summary 17.4: Physical Health.")

COGNITIVE DEVELOPMENT

We use our memory and other cognitive capacities every day, in virtually everything we do—from remembering new people we have met and things on our "to do" list to managing everyday activities like driving a car or completing tasks at work. Effective cognitive functioning is crucial to older adults' ability to remain productive, to live independently, and to enjoy their lives (Hertzog, Kramer, Wilson, & Lindenberger, 2008). After living 70 to 80 years or more, how well do people still learn and remember things? If changes in cognitive functioning occur in later adulthood, how do they affect older adults' daily lives and, importantly, how do normal changes differ from pathological changes caused by disease? Our discussion focuses on memory, a key aspect of cognitive functioning. The final section of the chapter explores options for preserving and enhancing cognitive functioning in later life and considers whether life experience helps older adults preserve cognitive strengths, such as wisdom.

INTERIM SUMMARY 17.4

Physical Health	
Common Health Conditions	■ Acute illnesses (which have a rapid onset and short duration) often require more bed rest and longer recovery time in later adulthood. Chronic illnesses (which have a slow onset, long duration, and tend to worsen over time) pose the greatest threat to older adults' health. ■ Limitations in **activities of daily living (ADLs**, basic self-care activities, such as eating and bathing) and **instrumental activities of daily living (IADLs**, more complex activities, such as shopping and managing finances) increase in advanced old age. Older people who can perform ADLs but who have difficulty with IADLs may be able to continue living at home with the assistance of others. Being unable to perform ADLs increases the risk of nursing-home placement.
Self-Rated Health	■ Older adults' perceptions of their health tend to be positive. ■ Women generally rate their health less favorably than men and report more restrictions of activity and more days of bed rest when they feel ill because women have more chronic (though less lethal) health conditions.
Mortality	■ Mortality rates rise over the course of later adulthood as a result of the degenerative processes and declines in reserve capacity. ■ The leading causes of death among older adults differ relatively little across demographic groups, but life expectancies are shorter for socially disadvantaged groups. ■ In the United States, women live an average of 5 years longer than men.
Quantity versus Quality of Life	■ Some critics worry that living longer means that people will be ill for a greater portion of their lives. ■ Some scientists argue that a **compression of morbidity** in later life—a shortening of the duration of illness and disability—is a realistic goal. The key to attaining this goal, in their view, is to *postpone* the onset of chronic illness.

Normal Changes in Memory

You may have had the experience of forgetting someone's name at a party or making a mental shopping list on your way to the grocery store but then forgetting to buy some of the items. Apart from feeling embarrassed or inconvenienced, you probably did not give such memory lapses much thought. In later adulthood, memory lapses become more frequent and often take on a different meaning.

Memory Systems As discussed in earlier chapters, a useful framework for understanding how memory changes in later life is to think of memory as involving three systems, each of which performs different functions as we seek to acquire, manipulate, and retain information (Atkinson & Shiffrin, 1968). The first of these systems, **sensory memory**, receives information from our senses and holds it just long enough to be perceived. Sensory memory lasts 1 to 2 seconds and then fades, unless the information is attended to and passed on to working memory. When you

sensory memory A system of memory that registers information from our senses just long enough (usually 1 to 2 seconds) for it to be perceived; the information then fades unless it is attended to and passed to working memory.

call directory assistance and are given a phone number, the information registers in your sensory memory but it will fade unless you try to retain it, perhaps by repeating it to yourself.

When you repeat information to retain it, as with repeating the phone number you just heard, you are using your **working memory**. Working memory holds information long enough—usually 15 to 25 seconds—to be used or manipulated. We can hold about seven items of information in working memory (Miller, 1956). (It is no coincidence that local telephone numbers contain seven digits!)

working memory A short-term memory system that holds information long enough (about 15 to 25 seconds) so that it can be used or manipulated.

long-term memory A memory system with vast capacity that can store information for very long periods of time.

Long-term memory can store information for long periods, ranging from hours to years. The capacity of long-term memory—how much information can be stored in the brain—is virtually unlimited (Brady, Konkle, Alvarez, & Oliva, 2008). Of course, storing information in long-term memory is not the same as getting it out of storage when you need it. This is the frustration you experience when you have memorized material for an exam but are unable to retrieve it during the exam. Memory, then, depends not only on receiving information but also on our ability to encode (or store) and retrieve information.

Age-Related Changes in Memory How does aging affect memory? Researchers often investigate this question by presenting people of different ages with visual or auditory stimuli (digits, letters, symbols, sounds, etc.) to see how long it takes to memorize the information and how long it can be retained. To test *sensory memory*, a research participant might be shown a letter for just a split second, followed by another letter, and then asked to state the letter shown first. Such tests reveal little decline with age in sensory memory. Once older adults detect a stimulus, they retain it in sensory memory for about as long as younger people. Older adults with vision or hearing impairments, however, may need more time to detect sensory input (Baltes & Lindenberger, 1997; Lindenberger & Baltes, 1994). Because such sensory deficits are common in later life, they may be partly responsible for deficits in sensory memory that previously have been attributed to aging (Schneider & Pichora-Fuller, 2000; Wingfield, Tun, & McCoy, 2005).

Working memory might be tested by reading a series of digits aloud (e.g., 731652) and asking the research participant to repeat the digits. Very simple tests of working memory like this also reveal relatively few differences between older and younger adults (Luo & Craik, 2008; Maylor, 2005). The working memory task becomes more challenging if the list of items to be repeated becomes longer (e.g., 40162893) or if the participant has to manipulate the items in some way—for example, by repeating them in reverse order (e.g., 39826104). Challenging tests of working memory are more difficult for people of all age groups, but especially for older adults. In general, the more complex or demanding the cognitive task, the more poorly older adults perform compared to younger people (Luo & Craik, 2008; Park, 2000).

Long-term memory is often tested by presenting research participants with material to be memorized—for example, a series of unrelated words (duck, dish, storm, pencil, etc.). The number of times the list must be presented in order for the research participant to memorize it provides an estimate of the ability to *encode* information in long-term memory. On such tests, older adults do not perform as well as younger adults (Craik, 2006). One reason may be that older adults are less likely to use strategies that aid encoding (Naveh-Benjamin, 2000). You can try an exercise to understand this point: Look at the objects shown in Figure 17.10 for 2 minutes, and don't write anything down while you do this. Then close the book and write down as many objects as you can remember.

After completing this task, think about how you approached it. Perhaps you used a strategy to help you remember more items. For example, in looking at Figure 17.10, you might have made up a story that involved the objects shown (e.g., A *cat* named

FIGURE 17.10

How Many of These Objects Can You Remember?

Clarence was carrying *scissors* toward a *dog* who was chewing a *baseball mitt*. The dog then spotted a *football* and dashed toward it, tripping over an *apple*. . . .). The story itself does not matter, of course—it is simply a strategy to help transfer information into memory. Older adults make less spontaneous use of such strategies compared to younger age groups, which partly accounts for their poorer performance on memory tests that involve encoding (Naveh-Benjamin, 2000).

What about *retrieval*? Retrieval is tested by assessing how much people can remember from previously learned material. Tests of **recall** involve asking people to produce from memory the information they were asked to learn (e.g., "What words were in the list you memorized?"), whereas tests of **recognition** involve asking people to indicate whether a particular item was included in the information learned (e.g., "Was *bucket* in the list of words you memorized?"). Recall is more difficult than recognition (one reason why many students like essay exams less than multiple-choice exams!). Consistent with the general trend for age differences to be greater on more challenging cognitive tasks, the difference between older adults' and younger adults' performance is greater for tests of recall than for tests of recognition (Craik, 2006; Luo & Craik, 2008).

recall Process of retrieving previously learned information from memory without cues.

recognition Process of identifying previously learned information from among several items presented.

Not all long-term memories are the same or show the same rate of decline with age, however. Three different kinds of long-term memory that researchers often distinguish are episodic, semantic, and procedural memory (Tulving, 1985). **Episodic memory** involves learning and retaining new information (such as lists of words or numbers) or remembering details from one's daily life (e.g., where one parked the car) or past experiences (e.g., what happened on one's first day of college). This type

episodic memory Memory for new information (e.g., words or numbers) or details from one's life (e.g., where one parked the car or details from a recent vacation).

semantic memory Memory for facts and general knowledge that one has learned (e.g., vocabulary, historical facts, cultural customs, etc.).

procedural memory Memory for skills and procedures (e.g., how to ride a bicycle) one has learned.

of long-term memory shows the greatest decline with age (Craik, 2000). In contrast, **semantic memory** refers to the ability to remember the general knowledge one has acquired (e.g., vocabulary, historical facts, cultural customs, etc.). Semantic memory, like crystallized intelligence (discussed in Chapter 15), is relatively well preserved into later adulthood (Craik, 2000, 2006). **Procedural memory**, the ability to remember how to do things (such as how to ride a bicycle or hum a song), is also well preserved into later life (Craik, 2006; Luo & Craik, 2008).

Explanations for Age-Related Changes in Memory Why do age-related changes in memory occur? Many researchers believe that particular kinds of deficits affect older adults' cognitive functioning, including their memory (Dennis & Cabeza, 2008). Their explanations most often cite five deficits:

1. According to the *speed-deficit explanation*, the speed of cognitive processing declines in later life (Salthouse, 1996). If people think more slowly as they age, then some of the material they are trying to retain in working memory may decay before they can use it or transfer it to long-term memory. When processing speed is taken into account statistically, the differences between older and younger adults' memory performance is smaller (Salthouse, 1996).

2. The *processing-resources-deficit explanation* suggests that an age-related decline in attentional resources (e.g., being able to attend to two tasks simultaneously or to shift from one task to another) leads older adults to perform worse on challenging cognitive tasks (Craik, 2006; Craik & Byrd, 1982).

3. The *sensory-deficit explanation*, touched on earlier, suggests that older adults who have a sensory deficit (e.g., vision or hearing impairment) must devote extra effort to recognizing sensory input, which leaves fewer resources for encoding information in memory.

4. The *inhibition-deficit explanation* suggests that older adults have more difficulty than younger adults inhibiting irrelevant information from working memory, and this mental "clutter" leads to worse performance on memory tests (Hasher & Zacks, 1988; Zacks, Hasher, & Li, 2000).

5. Finally, the *recollection-deficit explanation* suggests that older adults are less likely than younger people to use encoding and retrieval strategies that create associations between items to be learned (Chalfonte & Johnson, 1996; Naveh-Benjamin, 2000). Such associations aid memory retrieval, as you saw in the demonstration in Figure 17.10 (creating associations between unrelated pictures makes it easier to recall them). When trained in the use of such strategies, older adults' performance on recall tasks is closer to that of younger adults (e.g., Luo, Hendricks, & Craik, 2007).

Each of these explanations has scientific support, and given the complexity of adult cognition, it is likely that each accounts for some of the differences between older and younger adults' memory functioning.

Yet age differences in memory functioning may not be due solely to deficits that emerge in later life. Contextual factors may play a role, too. In particular, internalized stereotypes about aging can impair memory performance (Hess, 2005; O'Brien & Hummert, 2006), just as negative stereotypes about minority groups can undermine their academic performance (see Chapter 13). In experimental studies, exposing participants to negative age stereotypes—either explicitly (e.g., by having them read about age-related declines in memory) or implicitly (e.g., by briefly flashing words such as *confused, forgets, dementia,* and *decrepit*)—leads to worse memory performance by older adults but does not affect the memory performance of younger adults (Hess, Auman, Colcombe, & Rahhal, 2003; Levy, 1996). Evoking negative age stereotypes may erode older adults' confidence and arouse anxiety as they seek to complete the memory tasks. A hopeful finding from this research is that evoking *positive* views of aging—for example, by presenting words associated with wisdom such as *learned, insightful,* and *sage*—enhances older adults' memory performance (Levy, 1996).

Impact of Age-Related Changes in Memory The changes in memory discussed so far are considered to be *normal* changes that occur with age, unlike *pathological* (disease-related) change, which is discussed next. Normal memory changes that occur with age generally do not disrupt older adults' lives (Park & Reuter-Lorenz, 2009). One reason is that our memory systems tend to have much greater capacity than is needed for survival, so that even with age-related declines, ample capacity remains to function effectively in daily life (Verhaeghen, Marcoen, & Goossens, 1993). Another reason is that much of what we do in the course of our daily lives requires us to draw upon accumulated knowledge rather than to learn and remember new knowledge, and both semantic and procedural memory hold up well in later life (Park, 2000; Salthouse, 2004).

Older adults also find ways to compensate for normal changes in their memory (Park, 2000; Salthouse, 2004). The famous neuropsychologist Donald Hebb observed his own memory beginning to decline as he grew older, and he wrote about the strategies he used to compensate for the decline. He made lists, used Post-It notes and other memory cues (e.g., putting an umbrella by the door rather than trying to remember to take it to work the next day), and developed daily routines so that some tasks become habitual (e.g., taking medication at the same time each day; Hebb, 1978). Most older adults adapt relatively easily to normal memory changes, but some find such changes to be quite distressing, especially if they view such changes as signs of Alzheimer's disease, one of the most feared diseases of later life (Harris Interactive, 2006).

dementia A chronic brain disorder characterized by irreversible cognitive decline severe enough to impair self-care and daily activities.

delirium An acute brain disorder characterized by cognitive impairment that can be reversed if it is treated.

Alzheimer's disease Most common form of dementia in later life, characterized by cognitive, behavioral, and motor deficits that gradually worsen over time.

Pathological Changes in Memory

You may know an older person whose memory seems to be seriously impaired. If so, he or she may have **dementia**, a chronic brain disorder characterized by irreversible cognitive decline severe enough to impair self-care and daily activities (Gatz, 2007; NIA, 2008). Many types of dementia exist. The following discussion explores the two most common forms of dementia in later life—Alzheimer's disease and vascular dementia—along with **delirium**, an acute brain disorder characterized by cognitive impairment that can be reversed if it is treated.

Alzheimer's Disease **Alzheimer's disease** is the most common form of dementia in later life, accounting for about 70 percent of cases of dementia (Albert, 2008). Although Alzheimer's disease can affect people in their 40s and 50s, it much more often affects people over age 60. In fact, rates of Alzheimer's disease rise markedly with age, with fewer than 10 percent of the young-old but as many as 50 percent of the old-old having at least mild symptoms of Alzheimer's disease (Hebert, Scherr, Bienias, Bennett, & Evans, 2003; NIA, 2009b) (see Figure 17.11). Approximately 5.1 million adults in the United States currently suffer from Alzheimer's disease (NIA, 2008), but this figure is expected to mushroom as the population continues to age (Hebert et al., 2003). Scientists estimate that 100 million people throughout the world may suffer from Alzheimer's disease by 2050 (Brookmeyer, Johnson, Ziegler-Graham, & Arrighi, 2007).

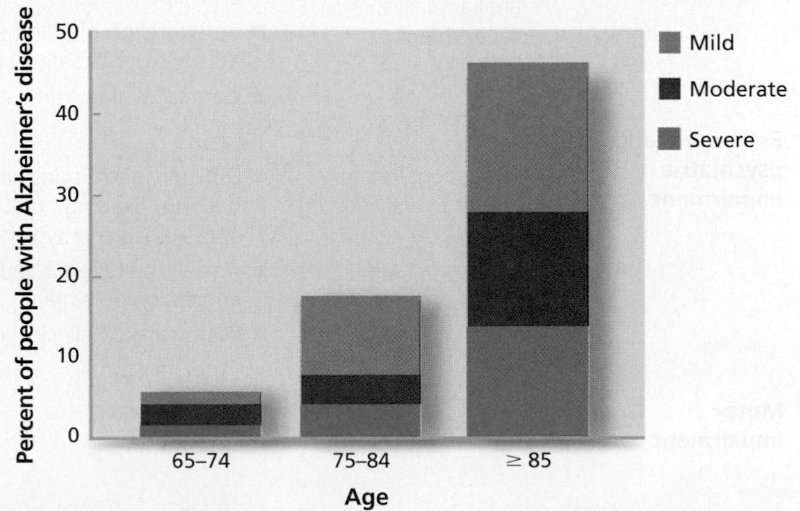

FIGURE 17.11

Mild, Moderate, and Severe Symptoms of Alzheimer's Disease Increase Markedly with Age

Source: Hebert, L.E., Scherr, P.A., Bienias, J. L., Bennet, D. A., & Evans, D. A. (2003) Alzheimer disease in the U.S. population: Prevalence estimates using the 2000 census. *Archive of Neurology, 60*(8), 1119–1122.

Alzheimer's disease develops gradually, and although its course varies across people, *cognitive* deficits usually appear first, followed by *behavioral* deficits, and then eventually by *motor* deficits (Albert, 2008; NIA, 2009b; see Table 17.1). The first signs of the disease nearly always involve memory loss. People may have difficulty remembering where they put things or whether they have paid the bills. They may have trouble organizing their thoughts clearly or expressing themselves as they forget words or names. Signs of impaired judgment (reflected in inappropriate decisions or behavior) and disorientation (uncertainty about where one is or what time of day it is) often appear as well. Depression is common at this stage, as people begin to grasp that they have Alzheimer's disease (NIA, 2009c).

As the disease progresses over time, cognitive deficits (memory loss, language problems, confusion, disorientation) increase, and behavioral deficits begin to emerge (see Table 17.1, middle stage). People begin to have problems performing basic self-care activities (e.g., bathing, dressing, preparing meals), and concerns for their safety can develop as they begin to wander at night or forget to turn off the stove. During this middle stage, people often become fearful or suspicious of others and, as a result, become anxious, agitated, or even aggressive. As the disease progresses, these cognitive and behavioral deficits worsen and motor deficits appear (NIA, 2009c; see Table 17.1, late stage). People need assistance with all self-care tasks, and they may no longer

TABLE 17.1 Symptoms of Alzheimer's Disease in Early, Middle, and Late Stages

	EARLY	MIDDLE	LATE
Cognitive impairment (affecting memory, language, thinking, judgment, and orientation)	*Appears:* ■ Loss of recent memory ■ Trouble finding words ■ Difficulty organizing thoughts and actions ■ Poor judgment ■ Loses way going to familiar places; misplaces things	*Worsens:* ■ Difficulty remembering new information, recognizing familiar people, and recalling past events ■ Difficulty communicating; reduced or repetitive speech ■ Difficulty comprehending information and experiences ■ Deterioration of judgment, inappropriate behavior or safety concerns possible ■ Confusion about time and place	*Becomes severe:* ■ Severe loss of memory; inability to recognize self or family members ■ Loss of ability to understand speech or speak intelligibly ■ Inability to think clearly or comprehend information ■ Severe impairment of judgment ■ Severe confusion about time and place
Behavioral and psychiatric impairment	*Appears:* ■ Depression, loss of interest in activities ■ Withdrawal ■ Frustration, anger possible	*Worsens:* ■ Difficulty performing self-care (e.g., bathing, dressing), lack of concern for appearance and hygiene possible ■ Anxiety, agitation, sleep disruption, aggression possible ■ Paranoia and hallucinations possible	*Becomes severe:* ■ Assistance needed with all self-care tasks ■ Signs of distress possible (e.g., moaning, screaming, discomfort when touched) ■ Weight loss ■ Sleep disturbance
Motor impairment			*Appears* ■ Loss of control over body movements (e.g., walking, standing, swallowing) ■ Loss of control over bodily functions (e.g., bladder and bowel functions)

Source: Adapted from National Institute on Aging (2009c). *Understanding stages and symptoms of Alzheimer's disease.* Retrieved October 28, 2009 from http://www.nia.nih.gov/Alzheimers/Publications/adfact.htm; and Reisberg, B., Borenstein, J., Salob, S. P., Ferris, S. H., Franssen, E., & Georgotas, A. (1987). Behavioral symptoms in Alzheimer's disease: phenomenology and treatment. *Journal of Clinical Psychiatry, 48* (suppl 5), 9–15.

remember how to walk or stand. Control over bodily functions (such as bladder and bowel functions) can be lost at this stage of the disease.

This progression of symptoms unfolds over a period of about 10 years, on average (Albert, 2008), although the disease often has been developing for many years before being diagnosed (Marx, 2005; Tierney, Yao, Kiss, & McDowell, 2005). Former President Ronald Reagan is believed to have begun showing signs of cognitive impairment during his second term in office before being diagnosed with Alzheimer's disease in 1994 (Venneri, Forbes-McKay, & Shanks, 2005). If people do not die of another disease first, Alzheimer's disease ultimately causes their death.

Abnormalities in the brains of people with Alzheimer's disease may be responsible for their impaired functioning (see Figure 17.12). **Amyloid plaques**—abnormal deposits of protein—form in the brain, causing inflammation, destroying neurons and synapses, and reducing levels of neurotransmitters (NIA, 2009b). **Neurofibrillary tangles**—tangled fibers that form in the neurons—interfere with connections between the neurons. These abnormalities initially affect regions of the brain that are crucial for memory, such as the hippocampus. Over time, they spread to more areas of the brain, eventually affecting the temporal, parietal, and frontal lobes. This explains why symptoms of the disease expand to affect many domains of functioning over time (Albert, 2008). The motor cortex is affected last, which is why the ability to perform motor tasks typically does not deteriorate until late in the course of the disease (Albert, 2008).

amyloid plaques Abnormal deposits of protein that form in the brains of people with Alzheimer's disease, causing inflammation, destroying neurons and synapses, and reducing levels of neurotransmitters.

neurofibrillary tangles Tangled fibers that form in the neurons and interfere with connections between the neurons.

Scientists are still investigating what causes these brain abnormalities, and it is likely that multiple factors are involved (NIA, 2009b). Age itself is a risk factor for developing Alzheimer's disease, as noted earlier. Women have a greater risk than men, primarily because women live longer than men. Heredity plays a role as well. People with a primary relative (such as a parent) who developed Alzheimer's disease are 2 to 4 times more likely to develop the disease themselves (Gatz, 2007). A mutation of the gene **apolipoprotein (APOE)** is found in 50 to 60 percent of people with Alzheimer's disease, compared to 20 to 25 percent of healthy older adults (Salmon, 2000). This genetic risk magnifies other risk factors. For example, a head injury early in life increases the risk of developing Alzheimer's disease later in life, particularly among people who

apolipoprotein (APOE) A gene present in 50 to 60 percent of people with Alzheimer's disease (compared to 20 to 25 percent of healthy older adults).

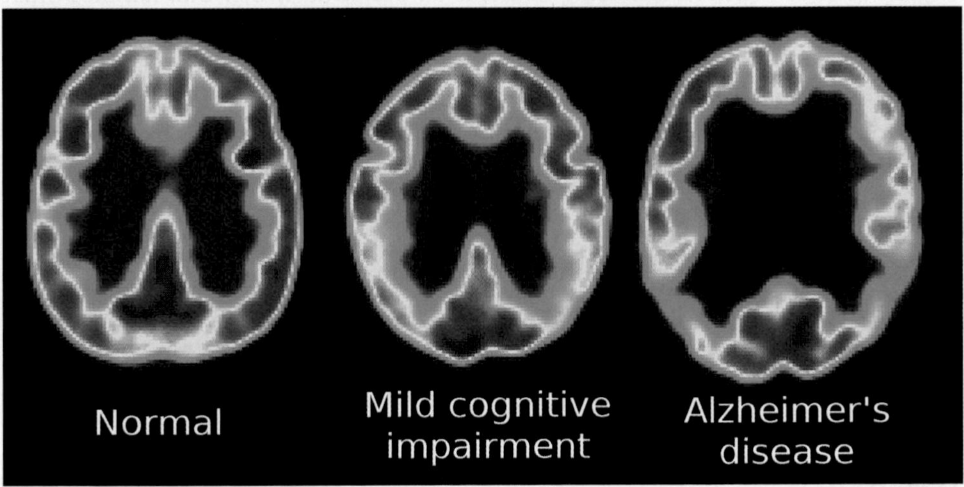

Suzanne Baker, PhD; Susan Landau, PhD; Bill Jagust, MD

FIGURE 17.12

Brain Scans of People with Normal Cognitive Functioning versus Mild Cognitive Impairment versus Alzheimer's Disease

PET (Positron emission tomography) scans reveal fewer areas of high brain activity (shown in red and yellow) and more areas of low brain activity (shown in blue) in the brains of people with mild cognitive impairment and Alzheimer's disease as compared with a normal brain.

have the APOE gene mutation (Jellinger 2004)—a clear example of the sort of gene-environment interaction we discussed in Chapter 2. There is little one can do about some of these risk factors, but other risk factors can be modified. For example, exercising (especially aerobic exercise), refraining from smoking, preventing or controlling high blood pressure and high cholesterol (especially "bad cholesterol," or low-density lipoprotein), engaging in cognitively simulating activity, and being socially engaged with others are under our control and can reduce the risk of Alzheimer's disease (Haan & Wallace, 2004; Hertzog, Kramer, Wilson, & Lindenberger, 2008).

Alzheimer's disease has no cure, unfortunately. Drug treatments are being investigated, but most currently offer only modest, short-term benefits for cognitive functioning. Medications can help to alleviate symptoms of depression and anxiety, but they do not slow the rate of cognitive decline (Albert, 2008). As scientists continue to search for effective treatments for Alzheimer's disease, the best strategy in the interim is to try to prevent or postpone the disease (Marx, 2005; Post, 1999). If the disease could be delayed by even 5 years, the number of cases in the United States could be reduced by half (Brookmeyer, Gray, & Kawas, 1998; Fratiglioni & Wang, 2007). The theme of preventing cognitive decline is revisited in the last section of the chapter.

Alzheimer's disease affects not only the person with the disease but also family members. The progression of cognitive, behavioral, and motor deficits can be devastating, as family members witness the steady, heartbreaking loss of a loved one's personality and independence. The impact on family members is physical as well as emotional, as they take up the tasks involved in providing day-to-day care of the ill relative (Pinquart & Soreson, 2003, 2007). Caregiving can become a full-time job and a source of chronic stress, putting family caregivers at risk of depression and health problems of their own (Alspaugh, Stephens, Townsend, Zarit, & Greene, 1999; Schulz, O'Brien, Bookwala, & Fleissner, 1995; Vitaliano, Scanlan, & Zhang, 2003). Yet caregiving also offers psychological rewards. Care providers can experience feelings of usefulness and increased closeness to the care recipient, and the care recipient can experience the feeling of being loved and cared for (Pinquart & Sorensen, 2003; Walker, Martin, & Jones, 1992).

As Alzheimer's disease progresses, many caregivers eventually find it impossible to care for a loved one with the disease at home. Placing an impaired parent or spouse in an institution, such as a nursing home, is an option to which U.S. families often reluctantly turn after they have exhausted all other options (Merrill, 1997). Research clearly indicates that nursing home placement is a last resort in most cases, contrary to stereotypes that unfairly portray U.S. families as uncaring toward the elderly and quick to turn to institutional care (Shanas, 1979). Nursing home care is expensive, unfortunately, averaging over $75,000 annually in the United States (Houser, 2007), and Medicare and most private insurance programs provide only very limited coverage for long-term care. Finding ways to make long-term care more affordable is a challenge confronting all societies experiencing populating aging.

vascular dementia (sometimes called multi-infarct dementia) A type of dementia caused by a series of strokes that disrupt blood flow to the brain, depriving the brain of oxygen and causing brain tissue to die; accounts for about 10 to 20 percent of dementias in later life.

Vascular Dementia **Vascular dementia** (sometimes referred to as multi-infarct dementia) accounts for about 10 to 20 percent of all dementias in later life (Gatz, 2007; NIA, 2003). It is caused by a series of strokes that disrupt blood flow to the brain, depriving the brain of oxygen and causing brain tissue to die (the term "infarct" refers to this loss of tissue). The symptoms of vascular dementia resemble those of Alzheimer's disease in many ways, but they tend to develop abruptly (rather than gradually) because strokes can occur suddenly (Gatz, 2007; NIA, 2003). The biggest risk factor for vascular dementia is untreated hypertension, although other risk factors include high cholesterol, heart disease, and diabetes (NIA, 2003). More men than women develop vascular dementia because men have more heart disease (NIA, 2003). The brain damage caused by vascular dementia, like the damage caused by Alzheimer's disease, is irreversible. If the damage is substantial, family members face many of the same challenges that arise in the context of Alzheimer's disease.

Delirium Not all brain disorders in later life are irreversible. As noted earlier, delirium is an acute, rather than a chronic, state of cognitive impairment that develops rapidly over a short period of time (Foreman et al., 1996). It can be caused by medication side effects or interactions, vitamin deficiencies, alcohol intoxication, disease (e.g., a tumor caused by cancer), injury (e.g., a blow to the head), surgical complications, or even a sudden environmental change (such as emergency hospitalization or the sudden death of a loved one; Smyer & Qualls, 1999). If the underlying cause (or causes) can be identified and addressed, cognitive functioning can often recover relatively quickly.

Distinguishing Between Chronic and Acute Brain Disorders It is crucial for medical practitioners who work with the elderly to be able to distinguish between chronic and acute brain disorders, because the acute disorders can be reversed, if treated. This diagnostic task is not easy, however, because the symptoms of chronic and acute brain disorders overlap considerably. In addition, depression (discussed in the next chapter) can also cause problems with memory and concentration (Alexopoulos et al., 2002). Unfortunately, there are no simple tests, such as a blood test, that allow a physician to easily pinpoint the cause of cognitive impairment in an older person.

Alzheimer's disease can be confirmed definitively only through a brain autopsy after death. Before then, it is typically diagnosed by exclusion—by carefully evaluating the symptom history and conducting a medical exam and psychological tests to evaluate whether potentially reversible conditions could be causing the cognitive impairment. If those conditions are ruled out, the problem is assumed to be Alzheimer's disease. The danger is that a potentially reversible cause—such as a vitamin deficiency or recent medication change—could go undetected, and untreated. In fact, general-practice physicians are believed to misdiagnose as many as half of all cases of dementia in older adults (Boise, Camicioli, Morgan, Rose, & Congleton, 1999).

Brain imaging techniques (such as magnetic resonance imaging, or MRI) have begun to improve diagnostic accuracy in recent years, but they are not readily available everywhere. If an older relative exhibits cognitive impairment, it is important for family members to provide as much information as possible about the relative's medical history, medications, diet, alcohol or other substance use, possible injuries, and any recent life changes. It may also be useful to consider obtaining a second opinion if Alzheimer's disease is suspected. (For a summary of this section, see "Interim Summary 17.5: Cognitive Development.")

ENHANCING COGNITIVE FUNCTIONING IN LATER LIFE

Some degree of cognitive decline may be a nearly universal experience in later life, but new research shows that there are things we can do to influence when and how much decline occurs. If cognitive decline can be slowed or postponed until very late in life, its negative impact on older adults' lives will be greatly reduced. You may recognize this idea as an example of the compression of morbidity: Just as it may be possible to compress the period of physical illness in later life, it may be possible to compress the period of cognitive decline in later life.

Intense research interest is currently focused on how cognitive functioning can be enhanced in later life (Elias & Wagster, 2007; Fratiglioni & Wang, 2007; Hertzog et al., 2008; Mayr, 2008). Two key questions lie at the heart of this research. First, what lifestyle factors help to preserve cognitive functioning in later life? Second, to what extent can declines in cognitive functioning be reversed? As you'll see, the answers that have begun to emerge are encouraging. You'll also see that cognitive development in later adulthood does not inevitably entail decline. Some areas of cognitive strength, such as wisdom, may be well preserved in later life.

INTERIM SUMMARY **17.5**

Cognitive Development	
Normal Changes in Memory	■ Many changes in memory are *normal* changes that occur gradually with age and generally do not disrupt older adults' lives. ■ Simple tests of **sensory memory** and **working memory** reveal relatively few differences between older and younger adults. However, in challenging tests of working memory and **long-term memory**, older adults perform less well. ■ Five different kinds of deficits may affect older adults' cognitive functioning: (1) *speed deficits*, (2) *processing-resources deficits*, (3) *sensory deficits,* (4) *inhibition deficits,* and (5) *recollection deficits.* ■ Contextual factors, such as negative age stereotypes, can also affect older adults' memory performance.
Pathological Changes in Memory	■ *Pathological* (disease-related) changes in memory are not considered a normal part of aging. ■ **Dementia** is a chronic brain disorder characterized by irreversible cognitive decline severe enough to impair self-care and daily activities. ■ **Alzheimer's disease** is the most common form of dementia in later life. *Cognitive* deficits usually appear first, followed by *behavioral* deficits and then by *motor* deficits. Abnormalities (**amyloid plaques** and **neurofibrillary tangles**) in the brains of people with Alzheimer's may be responsible for their impaired functioning. ■ **Vascular dementia** is caused by a series of strokes that disrupt blood flow to the brain. The biggest risk factor for vascular dementia is untreated hypertension. ■ **Delirium** is an *acute* state of cognitive impairment that develops rapidly. If the underlying cause can be addressed, cognitive functioning can often recover. ■ It is crucial for medical practitioners to be able to distinguish between chronic and acute brain disorders, because the acute disorders can be reversed if treated.

Lifestyle Factors

Lifestyle factors do appear to play a role in preserving cognitive functioning (Albert, 2008; Fratiglioni & Wang, 2007; Hendrie et al., 2006; Hertzog et al., 2008), and four factors are known to be especially important:

- Stimulating cognitive activity
- Physical activity, especially aerobic exercise
- Reducing cardiovascular risk factors
- Social engagement

Stimulating cognitive activity—reading newspapers and books, doing crossword puzzles, and engaging in other cognitively challenging leisure or work activities—has been linked to better cognitive functioning in many studies (Fratiglioni & Wang, 2007; Hertzog et al., 2008; Stine-Morrow, Parisi, Morrow, Greene, & Park, 2007). For example, in a study of over 4,000 older adults, those who engaged more often in stimulating cognitive activities showed less cognitive decline 6 years later, even after adjusting for health and other factors that could have influenced their cognitive functioning (Wilson et al., 2003). In another study, older adults who engaged in more cognitively stimulating activities were 33 percent less likely to develop Alzheimer's disease; importantly, all of the participants began the study free of dementia (Wilson et al., 2002). Engaging in stimulating cognitive activity earlier in life also benefits cognitive functioning later in life. Both education and complex work help to build up a larger cognitive reserve (Fratiglioni & Wang, 2007; Stern, 2006). Among identical twins (who have the same genetic makeup), the twin with greater education is less likely to develop Alzheimer's disease (Gatz, Prescott, & Pedersen, 2006).

Engaging in stimulating cognitive activity may help to preserve cognitive functioning in later life.

Physical exercise, especially aerobic exercise, contributes to greater brain health and better cognitive performance (Raz & Rodrigue, 2006). In a fitness intervention, sedentary older adults who participated in aerobic exercise (a walking program) for 6 months showed significant increases in brain volume, compared to older adults who participated in non-aerobic exercise (a toning-and-stretching program) (Colcombe et al., 2006). Regular physical exercise substantially reduced the risk of developing Alzheimer's disease, as well, in another large study of older adults (Larson et al., 2006).

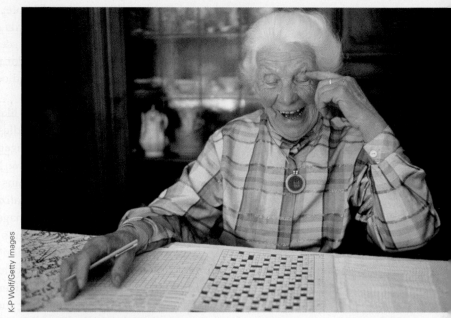

Reducing cardiovascular risk factors—high blood pressure, high cholesterol, obesity, smoking—not only preserves physical health but also slows the development of brain abnormalities in later life, such as amyloid plaques and neurofibrillary tangles (Cotman, Berchtold, & Christie, 2007; Raz, Rodrigue, Kennedy, & Acker, 2007). These brain abnormalities are involved in Alzheimer's disease, so slowing their growth reduces the risk of Alzheimer's (Haan & Wallace, 2004; Hamer & Chida, 2008; Marx, 2005).

Social engagement—interacting with friends and family members and being involved in social activities—is also associated with better cognitive functioning and a decreased risk of Alzheimer's disease in later life (Fratiglioni, Paillard-Borg, & Winblad, 2004; Kramer, Bherer, Colcombe, Dong, & Greenough, 2004; Marx, 2005). Scientists do not yet know why social engagement helps to preserve cognition in later life, but it may involve cognitive stimulation in its own right and it also helps to reduce stress (thereby improving cardiovascular health).

Cognitive Interventions

The research discussed above suggests that healthy and engaged lifestyles may help to slow or postpone cognitive declines in later life. But can cognitive declines that have occurred be reversed? Although it may not be possible to reverse the severe cognitive declines caused by dementia, perhaps normal, age-related cognitive declines can be reversed. Evidence that the brains of healthy older adults exhibit considerable plasticity provides a reason for optimism that their cognitive abilities are also malleable. This possibility has been investigated in studies of cognitive interventions designed to improve older adults' cognitive functioning.

Early intervention studies involved giving older adults several sessions of training in specific cognitive abilities (Hertzog et al., 2008). For example, in conjunction with the Seattle Longitudinal Study, older adults whose intelligence had either remained stable or declined received five 1-hour training sessions in specific cognitive skills that tapped fluid intelligence (see Chapter 15, Schaie & Willis, 1986). By the end of the training program, roughly two-thirds of the participants showed gains in their performance. The greatest gains were seen among those whose intelligence scores had declined prior to the intervention. For many of these individuals, the size of the gains nearly matched the declines that had occurred over more than a decade (Schaie, 2005; Willis, Jay, Diehl, & Marsiske, 1992).

The gains in intervention studies like these often were substantial and durable, lasting for up to 14 years in some studies (Ball et al., 2002; Schaie, 1996; Willis & Nesselroade, 1990). When the gains began to taper off, they could be maintained with periodic "booster" sessions (Willis & Nesselroade, 1990). A key problem with these interventions, though, is that the gains typically were limited to the specific cognitive abilities trained; they did not generalize to other abilities (Hertzog et al., 2008). Older people who learned how to use imagery to remember lists more effectively, for example, did not improve on other kinds of memory or information processing tasks.

A new generation of intervention studies is seeking to overcome that limitation by providing training designed to improve more basic cognitive processes and information-processing efficiency (Hertzog et al., 2008). In one recent study, older adults were immersed in interesting and progressively more stimulating and demanding memory tasks (Mahncke et al., 2006). Participants completed these tasks using computers in their own homes 1 hour per day, 5 days per week, for 8 to 10 weeks. Rather than simply teaching older people a specific memory technique, this intervention was designed to improve how information actually flows through the systems of memory. The participants showed gains in memory not only on the specific tasks that were the focus of training but, importantly, on other kinds of memory tasks that had not been part of the training. New intervention strategies like this hold great promise for achieving broader gains in older adults' cognitive functioning that can generalize to multiple cognitive abilities and to their everyday lives (Hertzog et al., 2008).

Studies of lifestyle factors and cognitive interventions are identifying valuable strategies for preserving brain health and cognitive vitality in later life. Actions can be taken even in old age to enhance cognitive functioning. As the popular saying "Use it or lose it" implies, the key to not "losing it" may be keeping one's mind active and one's body fit.

You can see that experiences over the course of a lifetime influence the extent to which cognitive declines occur. Could life experiences play a role helping to develop cognitive *strengths* in later life? Let's conclude by examining a cognitive strength that is often attributed to the elderly: wisdom.

Wisdom

Do you know someone whom you consider to be especially wise? What characteristics make that person wise in your view? How did he or she come to be wise? Researchers have wrestled with exactly such questions, and it will not surprise you that many different definitions of **wisdom** exist (Brugman, 2006). A widely accepted definition describes wisdom as a form of expert knowledge or judgment about difficult life problems that has five key characteristics (Ardelt, 2004; Baltes, Staudinger, Maercker, & Smith, 1995; Kramer, 2003; Staudinger, Dorner, & Mickler, 2005):

wisdom A form of expert knowledge or judgment about difficult life problems.

- Great breadth and depth of knowledge about life and human nature
- Effective use of this knowledge to make decisions and solve problems
- Understanding of a problem in the context of another person's unique life circumstances
- Concern with human values and the welfare of others
- Comfort with uncertainty and the lack of a perfect solution to many problems

A key issue for developmental researchers is how wisdom develops. If it emerges from life experience, then people who have had more life experience should be wiser. This is why wisdom is often assumed to develop in later life. Perhaps there is a reason why many U.S. Senators and four Supreme Court Justices are in their 70s and older! But are older adults especially likely to be wise, or can people of any age be wise? This question has been examined by asking people of different ages how they would approach challenging life problems, and then scoring their answers for the components of wisdom listed above (e.g., Smith & Baltes, 1990; Staudinger, Smith, & Baltes, 1996). For example, in one study, participants ages 25 to 81 were presented with hypothetical life problems and were asked how they thought each problem should be handled. Here is a sample problem from this study (Smith & Baltes, 1990, p. 497). How would you suggest handling it?

> Joyce, a 60-year-old widow, recently completed a degree in business management and opened her own business. She has been looking forward to this new challenge. She has just heard that her son has been left with two small children to care for. Joyce is considering the following options: she could give up her business and live with her son, or she could plan to arrange for financial assistance for her son to cover child-care costs.

In this study, the average wisdom scores did not differ across age groups (Smith & Baltes, 1990). Other research, too, has failed to find age differences in average wisdom scores (Baltes & Staudinger, 2000; Brugman, 2006; Staudinger, 1999). Yet in another study, the *wisest* group of participants—those whose wisdom scores were in the top 20 percent—contained more older adults than middle-aged or younger adults (Baltes et al., 1995; Staudinger, 1999). It seems, then, that adults of all ages have the capacity to develop wisdom, but those who show the highest levels of wisdom tend to be older adults (Staudinger et al., 1992). (For a summary of this section, see "Interim Summary 17.6: Enhancing Cognitive Functioning in Later Life.")

INTERIM SUMMARY 17.6

Enhancing Cognitive Functioning in Later Life	
Lifestyle Factors	■ Four lifestyle factors are especially important for preserving cognitive functioning: stimulating cognitive activity, physical exercise, reducing cardiovascular risk factors, and social engagement. ■ Healthy and engaged lifestyles may help to prevent or postpone cognitive declines.
Cognitive Interventions	■ Evidence that the brains of healthy older adults exhibit considerable plasticity provides a reason for optimism that cognitive abilities are malleable. This possibility has been investigated in studies of cognitive interventions designed to improve older adults' cognitive functioning. ■ Cognitive training programs produce gains in cognitive functioning. Interventions designed to improve cognitive processing and the efficiency of information processing show broad gains that generalize to many cognitive abilities and to older adults' everyday lives.
Wisdom	■ **Wisdom** is defined as a form of expert knowledge or judgment about difficult life problems. ■ Adults of all ages have the capacity to develop wisdom, but those who show the highest levels of wisdom tend to be older adults.

SUMMING UP AND LOOKING AHEAD

We have seen that later adulthood, a life period that has become commonplace only fairly recently in human history, is characterized by considerable developmental variability, although declines in some aspects of physical and cognitive functioning appear to be inevitable. The declines reflect the effects of biological damage that accumulates over time and begins to overwhelm the body's own capacities for maintenance and self-repair. How this damage affects older adults' health and cognitive functioning depends to a large extent on their biological and cognitive reserves, which are determined by their genes and by lifestyle and environmental factors. Despite the challenges posed by physical and cognitive declines, many older adults are remarkably resilient and adaptable. They find ways to compensate for declines, maintaining generally positive views of their health and experiencing relatively modest limitations of their daily activities until advanced old age. The aging brain is adaptive, too, exhibiting compensatory changes that help to preserve cognitive functioning when declines in brain efficiency occur.

We will see further evidence of older adults' adaptive capacities as we examine social and emotional development in later adulthood in the next chapter. As our exploration of later life continues, you'll see that a balanced picture of old age requires us to acknowledge not only the losses and declines that are inevitable but also the strengths and resilience that come with age.

HERE'S WHAT YOU SHOULD KNOW

Did You Get It?

After reading this chapter, you should understand the following:

- The main theories of the causes of aging
- How genes and longevity are related
- Physical changes that take place in late adulthood
- Health conditions that affect older adults and how older adults rate their own health
- The life expectancy for U.S. adults and what affects life expectancy
- Normal changes in memory that take place in late adulthood
- Pathological changes in memory that may take place in late adulthood
- Factors and interventions that can enhance cognitive functioning in later life
- The meaning of wisdom

Important Terms and Concepts

activities of daily living (ADLs) (p. 554)
ageism (p. 535)
Alzheimer's disease (p. 561)
amyloid plaques (p. 563)
apolipoprotein (APOE) (p. 563)
arteriosclerosis (p. 548)
autoimmune diseases (p. 550)
bodily control systems (p. 548)
caloric restriction (p. 540)
cataracts (p. 545)
centenarian (p. 538)
compensation (p. 543)
compression of morbidity (p. 555)
delirium (p. 561)
dementia (p. 561)
episodic memory (p. 559)
evolutionary theories of aging (p. 539)
frailty (p. 544)
free radicals (p. 540)
Hayflick limit (p. 541)
hypertension (p. 548)
immune system (p. 549)
inflammation (p. 550)
instrumental activities of daily living (IADLs) (p. 554)
life expectancy (p. 536)
long-term memory (p. 558)
loss-based selection (p. 551)
macular degeneration (p. 546)
maximum lifespan (p. 538)
neurofibrillary tangles (p. 563)
old-old (p. 535)
plasticity (p. 543)
population aging (p. 537)
procedural memory (p. 560)
programmed theories of aging (p. 548)
random damage theories of aging (p. 539)
reaction time (p. 549)
recall (p. 559)
recognition (p. 559)
reserve capacity (p. 542)
semantic memory (p. 560)
sensory memory (p. 557)
supercentenarian (p. 538)
t cells (p. 550)
telomeres (p. 541)
urinary incontinence (p. 548)
vascular dementia (p. 564)
wisdom (p. 568)
working memory (p. 558)
young-old (p. 535)

CHAPTER 18

Socioemotional Development in Later Adulthood

ImageState/Alamy

Perhaps our exploration of later adulthood has piqued your interest in what your own old age may be like. You have many clues by now about physical and cognitive changes that might lie ahead, as well as ideas about what you can do to help preserve your health. But what will your life as an older person be like? What goals will be important to you when you are 70 or 80 or possibly much older? Will some of the people in your life now still be part of your social world? Do you expect to retire from work at some point? If so, how will you support yourself? Do you imagine that your old age will be a happy time? How will you deal with the challenges of later life? We explore such questions in this chapter as we examine socioemotional development in later adulthood. You may be surprised by some of the answers scientists are discovering.

We begin by considering whether socioemotional development in later life unfolds in accordance with particular developmental tasks or timetables. We also consider how the three basic processes of developmental regulation that we have discussed in earlier chapters (selection, optimization, and compensation) help older adults shape the course of their development. We then delve into older adults' experiences in three major life domains: intimate partnerships and friendships, family relationships, and retirement. Finally, we explore how experiences in these domains may affect older adults' personalities, emotional well-being, and self-concepts.

DEVELOPMENTAL TASKS, TIMETABLES, AND PROCESSES IN LATER ADULTHOOD

Throughout our exploration of adulthood, you have seen that each period can be characterized by distinctive life *tasks* or goals, a sense of the optimal *timing* for completing these tasks, and particular developmental *processes* that may be especially relevant as people seek to direct the course of their lives. In young adulthood, time seems expansive and efforts are directed toward trying out and ultimately settling into new roles and relationships. In middle adulthood, time left to live begins to be perceived as limited, and efforts often focus on preserving gains that have been achieved in various life domains and evaluating which life goals are still attainable. Do these aspects of development change in later adulthood? We explore that question next.

Developmental Tasks

The major developmental tasks of each life period are determined by biological, social, and personal forces (Havighurst, 1952). However, these three forces may not be equally influential in each life period. Social norms, for example, create expectations for young adults to become financially independent, find full-time work, and establish intimate relationships and families. Consider for a minute social norms that create expectations for older adults to pursue particular tasks. Can you think of examples? If you can't, you're not alone. Sociologist Irving Rosow (1967) once described older adulthood as a "roleless role" in the sense that few social norms specify the goals and tasks that older people should strive to achieve.

The developmental tasks of later life are determined less by social norms and more by biological and personal forces. At a biological level, the inescapable fact of physical decline creates challenges and demands to which older people must adapt. At a personal level, the increasing awareness that time left to live is limited may prompt a reassessment of what is important and a focus on spending one's time meaningfully. For these reasons, some theorists believe that the key developmental tasks of later adulthood involve adapting to physical declines and finding meaning and value in one's life as the end of life approaches (Erikson, 1963; Sheldon & Kasser, 2001).

This idea is prominent in Erikson's (1963, 1982) views of the key psychosocial challenge of later life. As you learned earlier, Erikson believed that each life period is characterized by a unique psychosocial crisis, a struggle between two opposing tendencies that must be resolved for optimal psychological health and development. Erikson regarded the key psychosocial crisis of later life as that of **integrity vs. despair**. Given the declines and losses that accumulate in later life, older adults could easily succumb to despair. The challenge in this life stage is to maintain a sense of dignity and integrity by accepting one's past and current life, including the declines and losses experienced as well as mistakes made along the way (Erikson, 1982). Accepting one's life as it has unfolded helps people feel a sense of completion and makes it easier for them to face the prospect of death. Older adults who are discontent with their life and bitter about lost opportunities or mistakes, in contrast, are vulnerable to despair.

integrity vs. despair The key psychosocial crisis of later life, according to Erikson, in which older adults reflect on their life and accept how it unfolded in order to have a sense of completion as the end of life approaches. Older adults who feel bitter about lost opportunities or mistakes made during the course of their life, in contrast, are vulnerable to despair.

Is there evidence that achieving a sense of integrity about one's life is an especially important goal in later adulthood? Some research suggests that the answer is yes, as illustrated by findings from a study in which people aged 17 to 82 were asked to describe the personal goals they were pursuing in their daily lives (Sheldon & Kasser, 2001). Participants' descriptions of their goals were coded for themes reflecting identity, intimacy, generativity, and integrity. For example, seeking spiritual meaning was considered to reflect a desire to achieve a sense of integrity. Compared to younger participants, the older participants more often described personal goals that reflected generativity and integrity. In addition, the older adults whose goals reflected these themes had greater psychological well-being, consistent with Erikson's view that striving to resolve the key psychosocial challenge for one's life stage benefits psychological health.

Reflecting on one's life is one way older adults can try to resolve the struggle between integrity and despair, according to Erikson (1963, 1982). This idea prompted much interest in **life review** in later adulthood, the process by which people assess their lives, recalling and evaluating events from the past (Butler, 1974; Staudinger, 2001). Researchers have found that older adults do spend time reviewing their lives and that the process can be beneficial (Birren & Schroots, 2004; Bohlmeijer, Roemer, Cuijpers, & Smit, 2007; Cappeliez & O'Rourke, 2006). Life review can help older adults gain a better understanding of themselves and their past actions. It can also help them acquire new insights into the reasons for others' behavior, perhaps yielding new ideas about how to resolve a long-standing conflict, such as estrangement from an adult child, while there is still time to do so. Life review can also facilitate social interaction through sharing memories with others, and it may enhance memory functioning (Bluck, Alea, Habermas, & Rubin, 2005).

life review The process by which people assess their lives, recalling and evaluating events from the past.

People do review and reflect on their lives earlier in adulthood (though rarely in childhood), but life review serves different functions at different ages (Staudinger, 2001). Life review helps young adults solidify their identities and consider how to handle life problems, it helps middle-aged adults balance life goals and commitments, and it helps older adults accept and find meaning in their lives (Cappeliez & O'Rourke, 2006; Staudinger, 2001). There is no guarantee, of course, that life review will have a positive outcome. Some older adults become angry or depressed as they relive past disappointments and losses (Staudinger, 2001). Yet Erikson (1982) and others (Butler, 1974; Garland & Garland, 2001) believe that elderly individuals whose life review leads them to feel that their lives have had meaning are better prepared to face the approaching end of life.

Developmental Timetables

In young and middle adulthood, people often have a sense of a personal or societal timetable for accomplishing important life goals. In middle adulthood, people become aware that the time to achieve life goals is finite, sometimes prompting them to revise their goals and plans. By later adulthood, people often have achieved many of their life goals and have relinquished others that were unattainable. As a result, the developmental tasks of later adulthood are less likely to involve efforts to achieve key life goals within a particular time frame and more likely to involve efforts to engage in emotionally meaningful activities and to derive a sense of integrity about one's life (Charles & Carstensen, 2010; Erikson, 1982).

The sense of time passing, however, is quite salient in later adulthood. It is what drives efforts to review and gain closure about one's life before it ends. As you'll see later in this chapter, this growing awareness that time is limited has a powerful influence on older adults' preference for particular kinds of social interaction (Carstensen, Fung, & Charles, 2003).

Despite experiencing age-related declines in manual dexterity and speed, pianist Arthur Rubinstein continued giving concerts into his 80s by using selection, optimization, and compensation.

Processes of Developmental Regulation

Faced with declining physical capacities and shortened time horizons, do older adults seek to manage their lives using different strategies than they used earlier in life? As you have learned, *selection* is an especially important process of developmental regulation in young adulthood, as people decide which life goals to pursue, and *optimization* becomes important in middle adulthood as people strive to maintain existing achievements and to prevent losses. In later adulthood, *compensation* becomes important, as declining capacities and resources require older adults to find new ways to achieve goals.

In fact, *all three strategies* of developmental regulation are needed in later life (Baltes & Baltes, 1990; Baltes, Lindenberger, & Staudinger, 1998; Heckhausen, 1999). For example, famous concert pianist Arthur Rubinstein used all three processes to continue giving concerts successfully into his early 80s, despite age-related declines in manual dexterity and speed. How? He chose to play a smaller number of pieces (selection), practiced those pieces more often (optimization), and slowed the speed of his playing just before the fast movements in a piece (compensation), giving the audience the impression of speed in the fast movements (Baltes & Baltes, 1990). This combination of strategies served Rubinstein well and, as you read on, you'll see that older adults use these three strategies in a variety of life domains. You'll also see that using these strategies is adaptive because it helps to preserve older adults' well-being. An important life domain in which these developmental processes can be seen at work in later adulthood is close relationships, which we discuss next. (For a summary of this section, see "Interim Summary 18.1: Developmental Tasks, Timetables, and Processes in Later Adulthood.")

INTERIM SUMMARY 18.1

Developmental Tasks, Timetables, and Processes in Later Adulthood	
Developmental Tasks	■ Some theorists argue that the key developmental tasks of later adulthood involve adapting to physical declines and finding meaning in one's life as the end of life approaches. ■ Erikson regarded the key crisis of later life as that of **integrity vs. despair**. ■ Erikson believed that reflecting on one's life is an important means by which older adults seek to resolve the struggle between integrity and despair. This idea has led researchers to study **life review**, the process by which people assess their lives by recalling the past.
Developmental Timetables	■ The developmental tasks of later adulthood are less likely to involve efforts to achieve life goals within a particular time frame and more likely to involve efforts to engage in emotionally meaningful activities and to derive feelings of integrity about life experiences. ■ The sense that time left to live is finite is salient in later adulthood, and it drives efforts to review and gain a sense of closure about one's life before it ends.
Processes of Developmental Regulation	■ Using all three strategies of developmental regulation (*selection*, *optimization*, and *compensation*) helps to preserve older adults' well-being.

SOCIAL NETWORK INVOLVEMENT

Close relationships enhance physical and emotional health across the lifespan, and they may be especially important in later adulthood as people experience physical declines and other life changes (Antonucci, Birditt, & Akiyama, 2009; Rook, 2000). Yet as people age, they tend to have fewer people in their social networks and spend less time interacting with others (Carstensen, 1993; Carstensen & Charles, 2010). This decline in social network involvement in later life has been well documented over the past 50 to 60 years. It was surprising when first reported because many researchers expected older adults' social activity to balloon to fill the void left by retirement (Larson, 1978). Why does social network involvement decline in later life, and what does this decline mean for older adults' well-being? This puzzle has been addressed by several different theories.

Disengagement Theory

Disengagement theory offered the earliest explanation for declining social network involvement in later life (Cumming & Henry, 1961). Echoing Erikson (1982), disengagement theorists argued that a major task of later adulthood is to come to grips with the approaching end of life. In their view, older people need to accomplish this task by disengaging from their social roles and relationships in order to turn inward and reflect on their lives. Such disengagement was seen as normal and adaptive for older adults. It was also seen as advantageous for society: by vacating their social roles, older adults would open up opportunities for younger people, helping to insure continuity of the social system. According to disengagement theorists, then, a voluntary process of turning inward and disengaging from social roles and relationships in later life is mutually beneficial to older adults and society (Cumming & Henry, 1961).

disengagement theory A theory that proposes that declines in social network involvement in later life reflect older adults' voluntary disengagement from social roles and relationships in order to turn inward and reflect on their lives; this process is believed to be mutually beneficial to older adults and society.

Activity Theory

Disengagement theory evoked a storm of protest when it was first published. It was at odds with the value Americans tend to place on being active, and it also portrayed withdrawn or disengaged older adults as content, a portrait that researchers feared would undermine public efforts to improve conditions for the elderly (Carstensen, 1993). **Activity theory** (Maddox, 1963, 1964) was published as a rebuttal to disengagement theory. According to activity theory, a decline in social activity is *not* a normal or adaptive aspect of aging. Rather, it reflects society's rejection of or distancing from the elderly, driven by ageist attitudes. Activity theorists believe that maintaining patterns of social activity established in young and middle adulthood is crucial to preserving well-being in later life. Age-related declines in social activity, in their view, are involuntary and maladaptive (Maddox, 1963, 1964).

activity theory A theory that proposes that declines in social network involvement in later life reflect societal rejection of or distancing from the elderly, rather than a normal process of turning inward; social activity is regarded as important for well-being, and age-related declines in social activity, are viewed as involuntary and maladaptive.

Socioemotional Selectivity Theory

Both disengagement theory and activity theory have been criticized for overlooking the possibility that older adults may remain engaged in some social relationships even as they disengage from others. This selective engagement may reflect a shift in the kinds of social interaction that people desire in later life, an idea at the heart of **socioemotional selectivity theory** (Carstensen, 1993; Carstensen, Fung, & Charles, 2003). According to this theory, social network involvement declines with age because motivations for social interaction change as people grow older. Young adults are motivated to interact with a broad range of people as a means of expanding their knowledge of the world, their culture, and themselves as they plan their future. By later life, people already have acquired a great deal of information and have fewer future goals. As a result, acquiring information becomes a less important motivation for interacting with others, and other motivations become more important.

socioemotional selectivity theory A theory that proposes that declines in social network involvement in later life reflect changes in older adults' motivations for social interaction; as time begins to be perceived as limited, older adults prefer to interact with their closest, most emotionally rewarding social network members.

What social motivations gain importance in later life? Because older adults perceive time to be limited, they value goals that can be achieved in the short term, especially goals that contribute to a sense of meaning and emotional well-being. This preference, according to socioemotional selectivity theory, leads older adults to prefer to interact with their closest, most emotionally rewarding social network members (Carstensen et al., 2003). They tend to prune from their social networks those individuals with whom interaction is less rewarding, while maintaining contact with their closest friends and family members (Lang & Carstensen, 1994). The declines in social network size that occur with age involve mostly peripheral social ties (such as casual friends and acquaintances) rather than close social ties. As you can see in Figure 18.1, this pattern is the same for both Caucasian and African American older adults.

Research testing socioemotional selectivity theory has provided support for the idea that shrinking time horizons lead people to prefer to interact selectively with emotionally rewarding friends and family members. For example, young adults who have experienced a life-threatening illness or other threat that makes the prospect of their own mortality salient, such as the 9/11 terrorist attacks, have a heightened awareness that their life can end abruptly, and they exhibit preferences for social interaction that are remarkably similar to those of older adults (Carstensen & Fredrickson, 1998; Fung & Carstensen, 2006). As age or life experiences change our time horizons, our social goals and preferences change, too, and we gravitate to the people who are most important to us.

Yet not all declines in social network involvement in later life result from older adults being more selective. Instead, some result from the illness or death of loved ones (Rook, 2000). As you read on, you'll see that older adults' social lives are shaped by their preferences regarding the people with whom they most want to spend their

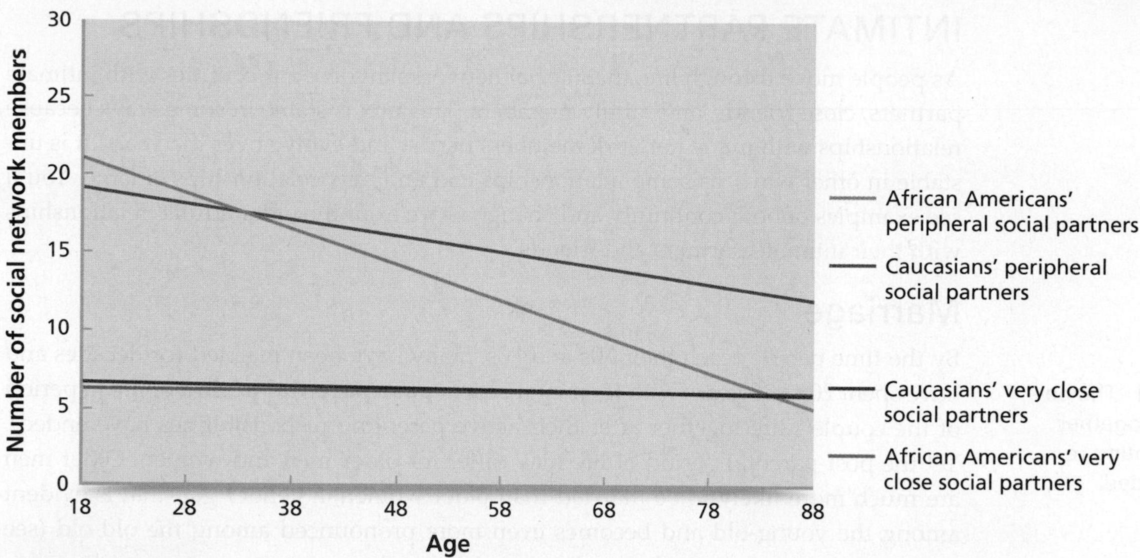

FIGURE 18.1

Social Network Composition by Age and Ethnicity.

Peripheral social network members (such as casual friends and acquaintances), but not very close social network members decline with age for both Caucasians and African Americans.
Source: Adapted from Fung, H. H., Carstensen, L. L., & Lang, F. R. (2001). Age-related patterns in social networks among European Americans and African Americans: Implications for socioemotional selectivity across the life span. *The International Journal of Aging and Human Development, 52*(3), 185–206.

time (selection), their efforts to maintain and enhance these relationships (optimization), and their ability to adjust their social needs or form new relationships when key relationships are lost (compensation). (For a summary of this section, see "Interim Summary 18.2: Social Network Involvement.")

INTERIM SUMMARY 18.2

Social Network Involvement

Disengagement Theory	■ Some researchers believe that close relationships may be especially important in later life, yet as people age they tend to experience a decline in social network involvement. ■ According to **disengagement theory,** a voluntary process of turning inward and disengaging from social roles and relationships in later life is mutually beneficial to older adults and society.
Activity Theory	■ According to **activity theory**, decline in social activity is *not* a normal or adaptive aspect of aging. Rather, it reflects societal rejection of the elderly. Age-related declines in social activity, according to this perspective, are involuntary and maladaptive.
Socioemotional Selectivity Theory	■ According to **socioemotional selectivity theory**, age-related declines in social network involvement occur because motivations for social interaction change as people age. As time begins to be perceived as limited, older adults prefer to interact with their closest, most emotionally rewarding social network members.

INTIMATE PARTNERSHIPS AND FRIENDSHIPS

As people move through life, their social networks involve a mix of ties with intimate partners, close friends, and family members. This mix is stable in some ways because relationships with many network members persist and evolve over the years. It is unstable in other ways, as some relationships end and new relationships emerge. You'll see examples of both continuity and change as we examine older adults' relationships with their intimate partners and friends.

Marriage

post-parental period The period of a couple's life together after their active parenting responsibilities have ended.

By the time people reach their 70s and 80s, many have been married for decades and have spent 20 to 30 years with their spouse in a **post-parental period** of life (a period of the couple's life together after their active parenting responsibilities have ended). Yet the post-parental period of life may differ for older men and women. Older men are much more likely to be married than older women, a gender gap that is evident among the young-old and becomes even more pronounced among the old-old (see Figure 18.2). Women have longer life expectancies than men, on average, and women also often marry men who are older than themselves. As a result, women tend to outlive their husbands. Older men are also more likely than older women to remarry after divorce or widowhood.

What are long-term marriages like? You learned in Chapter 16 that marital satisfaction tends to decline over time, with the decline tapering off in later adulthood (Van Laningham, Johnson, & Amato, 2001). Older married couples have been found to interact in ways that help to preserve marital quality. In observational studies, when middle-aged and older couples discuss a current marital disagreement, the older spouses exhibit less anger, disgust, and hostility and show more affection and humor toward each other (Levenson, Carstensen, & Gottman, 1994). This difference is not due simply to differences in the seriousness of the conflicts discussed by middle-aged and older couples. Instead, older couples seem to be more motivated to protect their marital relationship from conflict and feelings of ill will (Carstensen, Graff, Levenson, &

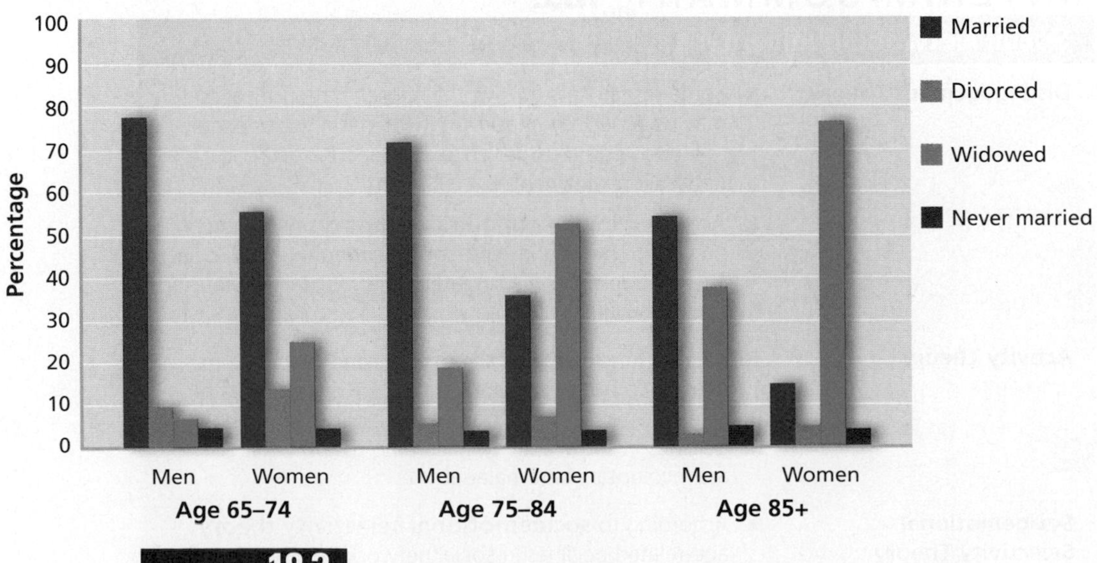

FIGURE 18.2

Older U.S. Adults' Marital Status by Age and Gender, 2008

Source: National Census Age Data for 2008, Table 10. Retrieved April 2, 2010 from http://www.census.gov/population/www/socdemo/age/older_2008.html

Gottman, 1996). They appear to be especially adept at keeping disagreements from becoming corrosive.

Other studies of marital interaction have found that older adults are more likely to view their spouse's behavior favorably and are less likely to blame their spouse for conflicts or disagreements (Blanchard-Fields & Beatty, 2005; Story et al., 2007). In other kinds of social relationships, too, older adults appear to be more likely than younger age groups to make conciliatory responses to upsetting interactions, such as forgiving others and trying to find solutions that benefit everyone (Birditt and Fingerman, 2005; Cheng & Yim, 2008; Sorkin & Rook, 2006). Such constructive ways of dealing with misunderstandings and disagreements may reflect an increase in later adulthood in the motivation to preserve important social relationships (Carstensen et al., 1995; Lang, 2001).

As we discussed earlier, people become increasingly aware with age that time left to live—and to be with the spouse—is limited (Carstensen et al., 2003). This awareness may kindle renewed appreciation for the marriage, making disagreements seem less significant and increasing the desire to foster positive interactions (Henry et al., 2007; Story et al., 2007). As you'll learn later in this chapter, older adults are more skilled at managing their emotions than are younger people, which also may help them preserve good will in their marriages. Intriguing evidence for this idea emerged in a study of over 5,000 adults in which older adults reported fewer marital disagreements than younger and middle-aged adults (Hatch & Bulcroft, 2004). Importantly, this study revealed that the older adults had fewer marital disagreements regardless of how long they had been married. It seems that older adults' greater motivation to maintain harmony in their marriages and their greater emotional control, rather than simply more years of living together and learning how to get along, may explain why later-life marriages are generally characterized by less discord.

The pledge included in many marriage vows to love one's spouse "in sickness and in health" is put to the test in later life, as caregiving for an ill spouse can be physically and emotionally challenging.

Yet older marriages do face challenges. Retirement, while often a welcome event, requires many older couples to adjust their household roles and expectations about spending time together (van Solinge & Henkens, 2005). Most older couples eventually develop mutually satisfying rhythms and routines for the retirement phase of their marriage, but the process takes time and can put strains on the relationship. A decline in the health of one (or both) spouses is another common, and significant, challenge in later life. If the ill spouse needs daily care, the other spouse often assumes the role of caregiver. Because women tend to have less lethal chronic conditions than men and often marry men who are older than themselves, women are more likely than men to care for an ill or disabled spouse in later life (Blieszner, 2006).

Caring for a chronically ill spouse is emotionally and physically demanding, although not all spouses feel burdened by the role (Beach, Schulz, Yee, & Jackson, 2000). Those whose marriages are strong before the spouse becomes ill tend to experience less emotional distress and role overload (Williamson & Schulz, 1990). Being able to turn to adult children, friends, or others for social support also helps caregivers deal with the challenges of caring for a spouse.

Divorce

Divorce is less common in later adulthood than in young or middle adulthood, although rates of divorce among older adults have risen in recent decades. The proportion of older marriages ending in divorce roughly doubled—from 5 to 11 percent—

between 1980 and 2008 (American Administration on Aging [AAA], 2009). Divorce in later adulthood is expected to become more common as younger age groups, who are more accustomed to divorce and who view it less negatively, reach old age (Cooney & Dunne, 2004).

Long-term marriages that end in divorce may be especially distressing because the former spouses had invested so much time in their life together (Uhlenberg, Cooney, & Boyd, 1990; Wang & Amato, 2000). The end of a marriage after so many years sometimes takes spouses by surprise, and even the spouse who initiated the divorce may be taken aback by lingering feelings of attachment to the former spouse (Berscheid, 1983). It takes time for former spouses to adjust emotionally and socially to their new marital status and to changes in their housing and finances. Divorce can take a financial toll, too, and this toll is typically greater for women than for men (McDonald & Robb, 2004; Uhlenberg et al., 1990). As a result, divorced women are much more likely to find themselves in precarious financial circumstances in old age, although researchers expect this financial disadvantage to be reduced in the future because of women's increased participation in the workforce (Cooney & Duune, 2004).

Divorce can also affect the social support older adults receive from their family members. Adult children whose parents divorced, regardless of when the divorce occurred, report less sense of obligation to their parents than children whose parents remain married (Silverstein & Bengtston, 1997). Older divorced fathers are especially likely to have limited contact with their adult children (Cooney & Uhlenberg, 1990; de Graaf & Fokkema, 2007; Kalmijn, 2007; Shapiro, 2003). Given that adult children are a key source of support in later life, particularly for older adults who lack a spouse, older divorced fathers may be at a disadvantage when needs for support arise.

Widowhood

If divorce is still a relatively rare experience in later adulthood, widowhood, sadly, is not. Of the roughly 900,000 people who are widowed each year in the United States, nearly 75 percent are over age 65 (Carr, Wortman, & Neese, 2006). Older women are more likely to be widowed than older men, and, for both men and women, the likelihood of being widowed increases markedly as they reach their mid-70s and mid-80s (see Figure 18.2).

How are older adults affected by the loss of a spouse? The answer is complex because the impact of a spouse's death varies across people and over time (Bonanno et al., 2002). To know how people are affected by the death of a spouse, it is important to study representative samples—not just widowed individuals who are in therapy or self-help groups. It is also important to have information about the widowed individuals' psychological health before the death of the spouse to know whether they were already distressed or became distressed only after the spouse's death (Carr, 2006).

Very few studies meet these requirements, but one—the Changing Lives of Older Couples (CLOC) study—is providing comprehensive information about older adults' adjustment to widowhood because it is tracking the psychological health of a large, representative sample of older adults from before to after the loss of the spouse (Carr, Nesse, & Wortman, 2006). A key finding from the CLOC study is that widowed individuals differed considerably in the intensity and duration of emotional distress they experienced over time. The researchers identified five different patterns of adjustment to widowhood over an 18-month period (Bonanno et al., 2002), as shown in Figure 18.3.

You can see in Figure 18.3 that a marked and persistent rise in depression following the death of a spouse in later life is not the norm. Moreover, researchers have found that the absence of depression is not inevitably a sign of poor adjustment, as was once widely believed (Lee et al., 2007; Wolff & Wortman, 2006). Instead, many older adults adapt to the loss of a loved one without experiencing long-term distress. In addition,

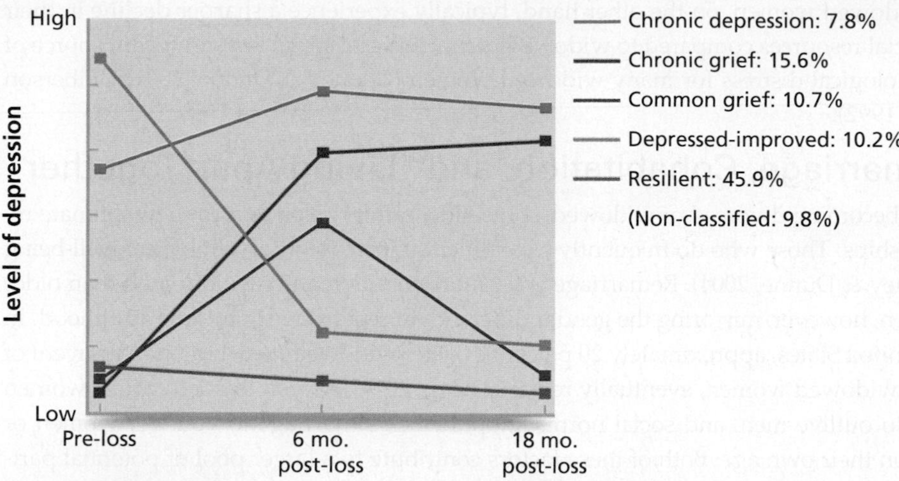

FIGURE 18.3

Five Patterns of Adjustment to Widowhood from Preloss to 18 Months Postloss

Note: In the largest group, the resilient group, depression was low before and after the spouse's death. Other groups included those who were depressed before and after the loss of the spouse (the chronic depression group), those who became depressed after the loss of the spouse and remained depressed over time (the chronic grief group), and those who were depressed before the loss of the spouse but improved afterward (the depressed-improved group). The common grief group, in which depression increased initially but them decreased over time, was relatively small, even though it is widely assumed to reflect the typical course of adjustment to widowhood.

Source: Adapted from Bonanno, G. A., Wortman, C. B., Lehman, D. R., Tweed, R. G., Haring, M., Sonnega, J., Carr, D., & Nesse, R. M. (2002). Resilience to loss and chronic grief: A prospective study from preloss to 18-months postloss. *Journal of Personality and Social Psychology, 83*, 1150–1164.

even though some older individuals do show marked declines in psychological health after the death of a spouse (if the death was unanticipated, for example), others show gains (if the spouse's death ended a protracted illness or an unhappy marriage; Bonanno et al., 2004). An important lesson from the CLOC study is that we should not judge the responses of widowed individuals who seem to show too little or too much emotional distress because people adjust to widowhood in many different ways (Bonanno et al., 2004; Carr et al., 2006).

The death of a spouse may affect older men and women differently. Older widowers are more likely to be depressed, to have worse health behavior, poorer health, and a greater risk of mortality (Lee et al., 2007). One reason may be that the death of the spouse leaves a greater void in men's lives. Compared to women, men tend to have smaller social networks and rely on their spouses more as their primary source of emotional support and companionship (Antonucci & Akiyama, 1995; Lee et al. 1998). Another reason may be that men tend to take care of their health less well than women. Wives often monitor their husbands' health behavior, ensure that nutritional needs are met, and arrange for annual check-ups and visits to doctors (O'Bryant & Hansson, 1995). With the wife's death, older widowers may be less likely to care for themselves and to seek medical care when needed. Widowed men also appear to adapt less well than widowed women to managing a household alone (Umberson, Wortman, & Kessler, 1992). The death of a spouse, therefore, leaves men with more unmet emotional, social, and practical needs.

Widowed women, on the other hand, typically experience a sharper decline in their financial resources compared to widowed men. Financial strain is a significant source of psychological distress for many widowed women (Cooney & Dunne, 2001; Umberson et al., 1992).

Remarriage, Cohabitation, and "Living Apart Together"

After becoming divorced or widowed, some older adults go on to form new intimate relationships. Those who do frequently experience an increase in psychological well-being (Cooney & Dunne, 2004). Remarriage is far more common among older men than older women, however, mirroring the gender difference in remarriage in middle adulthood. In the United States, approximately 20 percent of older widowed men, but only 2 percent of older widowed women, eventually remarry (Carr, 2004). As you learned earlier, women tend to outlive men, and social norms support men's marriage to younger women or women their own age. Both of these factors contribute to a larger pool of potential partners for men. In addition, some older widowed women are hesitant to remarry, voicing concerns that remarriage might reduce their independence or put them in the position of having to care for an ill spouse again at some point in the future (Calasanti & Kiecolt, 2007; Dykstra, 1995). Such women often meet their needs for emotional support and companionship through interactions with their adult children and friends (Bliezner, 2006).

Cohabitation is a new, and increasingly common, trend among older adults (Brown, Lee, & Bulanda, 2006). Roughly 10,000 people over age 60 were cohabiting in 1960, but this figure rose to 500,000 by 2000 (Brown et al., 2006). Cohabitation in later life may become even more common in the future as the current generations of young and middle-aged adults, for whom cohabitation is commonplace, reach old age (Bumpass & Lu, 2000). Cohabitation provides opportunities for intimacy, companionship, and support. For some older adults, it is an appealing alternative to marriage because it avoids tensions with adult children over inheritance issues or perceived disloyalty to the former spouse (Brown et al., 2006; Carr, 2004).

Some older adults prefer to have a relationship with an intimate partner without living together. They maintain their own separate residences, while sharing a household intermittently (e.g., for a few days per week, de Jong Gierveld, 2004). This option has come to be called *living apart together.* It meets the needs of older adults who desire a committed relationship but who also want to maintain some of the independence and freedom from obligations they have come to enjoy after living alone for a period of time (de Jong Gierveld, 2004).

Long-Term Gay and Lesbian Partnerships

Older gay men and lesbians—who number 1 to 3 million in the United States (Cahill & South, 2002)—often have long-term partnerships (Blando, 2001). In one recent study, roughly half of the 416 older lesbian, gay, and bisexual adults studied had a current partner, and the couples had been together for 15 years on average (Grossman, D'Augelli, & Hershberger, 2000). Research on the partnerships of older gay men and lesbians is scarce, but it indicates that these partnerships have much in common with successful heterosexual marriages, including strong bonds of intimacy, support, and companionship (DeVries, 2007; Grossman et al., 2000). One difference is that the greater gender-role flexibility of gay and lesbian relationships may help to ease the partners' adjustment to retirement, a transition that often requires household roles to be revised (Blando, 2001). Sources of stress in the long-term relationships of gay men and lesbians often arise from limited family support systems, negative societal attitudes, and institutional discrimination (Barker, Herdt, & de Vries, 2006).

Older gay men and lesbians are somewhat more likely than their heterosexual counterparts to live alone without a life partner, but this does not mean that they suffer from loneliness (Blando, 2001). Gay men and lesbians tend to have friendship networks that are as strong, or stronger, than those of heterosexuals, and their friends are key sources of social support and life satisfaction (DeVries, 2007; Grossman et al., 2000). Some researchers have noted, though, that intimate partners and family members typically are the first line of defense when older adults need sustained care and assistance during periods of illness or disability. Questions exist, then, about whether friends can substitute for partners and family members in providing such care to older adults who may lack an intimate partner or adult children (Barker et al., 2006; Rook & Zettel, 2005; Shippy, Cantor, & Brennan, 2004). Still, it is important to bear in mind that gay men and lesbians provided a great deal of care to ill friends and loved ones when the HIV/AIDS epidemic erupted in the 1980s. So, perhaps they will do the same when their elderly friends and loved ones need sustained care (Barker et al., 2006).

Queerstock, Inc./Alamy

Many older gay men and lesbians have long-term partnerships that provide intimacy, support, and companionship.

Friendships

As you have seen in earlier chapters, friendships are important throughout the lifespan, and people who have friends are happier and healthier. Friends may be particularly important as sources of support and companionship for people who lack a primary partner, such as widowed, divorced, and never-married individuals (Connidis & Davies, 1992).

Some telling clues of the importance of friendships in later life come from studies of age differences in loneliness. Which age group—young adults, middle-aged adults, or older adults—do you think has the highest rate of loneliness? Knowing that rates of widowhood are high among the elderly, you might think that the elderly are lonelier than other age groups. The image of older adults as lonely and isolated is common in society (Peplau, Bikson, Rook, & Goodchilds, 1982; Pinquart & Sorenson, 2001). Yet reports of loneliness are highest among young adults and lowest among older adults (Peplau et al., 1982; Revenson & Johnson, 1984) (see Figure 18.4). Contacts with friends and neighbors play an important role in preventing feelings of loneliness in later life (Pinquart & Soreson, 2001).

Rates of loneliness do increase sharply among the oldest-old, however, due to declining health, sensory impairments, and the deaths of their spouses and friends (Dykstra, van Tilburg, & Gierveld, 2005; Pinquart & Sorenson, 2001; Schnittker, 2007). Sadly, the loss of friends, like the loss of a spouse, is a common experience in later life. For example, in one longitudinal study, 59 percent of men and 42 percent of women aged 85 and older reported that a close friend had died in the past year (Johnson & Troll, 1994).

Still, older people can be quite resilient in such circumstances, and some of the elderly individuals in this study adapted to the loss of friends by changing their subjective criteria for friendship. For example, they included in their subjective circle of friends people with whom their relationships were (by their own account) relatively superficial and unlikely to become more intimate, such as casual acquaintances, home health aides, and other service providers (Johnson & Troll, 1984). Having intimate discussions was not required to consider someone a friend, as hinted by an elderly participant who commented, "With my new friend, I don't talk about my thoughts—I just talk about what I do." Some of the elderly participants in this study maintained their desire to have friendships but altered their aspirations for the kind of relationships that would meet this need (an example of compensation).

Yet in advanced old age, even such adjustments of aspirations may not be sufficient to ward off feelings of loneliness (Pinquart & Sorenson, 2001). This is a recurring theme

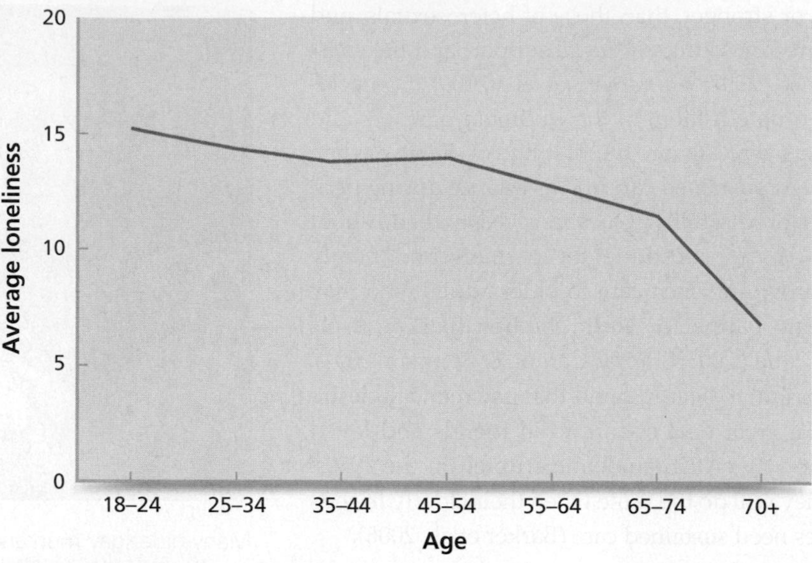

FIGURE 18.4

Loneliness Among Different Age Groups

Source: From *Loneliness: A sourcebook of current theory* by L.A. Peplau & D. Perlman. Copyright © 1982 by John Wiley & Sons, Inc. Reproduced with permission of John Wiley & Sons, Inc.

in later life: Older adults' adaptive capacities function very well to help preserve their well-being in the face of many physical declines and social losses, yet there is a point at which such declines and losses may overwhelm their adaptive capacities (Baltes & Smith, 2003). We return to this theme later when we discuss current conceptions of successful aging. (For a summary of this section, see "Interim Summary 18.3: Intimate Partnerships and Friendships.")

INTERIM SUMMARY 18.3

Intimate Partnerships and Friendships

Marriage	■ By the time people reach their 70s and 80s, many have been married for decades and have spent 20 to 30 years with their spouse in a **post-parental period** of life. ■ Older men are more likely than older women to be married because older women often outlive their husbands and older men are more likely to remarry after divorce or widowhood. ■ Declines in marital satisfaction tend to taper off in later adulthood because older couples appear to be especially skilled at preserving good will in their relationships. However, older marriages do face challenges, including adjusting to retirement and declines in health.
Divorce	■ Divorce is less common in later adulthood, although rates of divorce among older adults are rising. ■ Adjusting to a divorce in later adulthood may be more difficult because of the greater length of time that the former spouses spent together. ■ Divorced women are more likely to have fewer financial resources in old age. Divorce can also affect the social support older adults receive from their children.

(continued)

INTERIM SUMMARY 18.3 *(continued)*

Intimate Partnerships and Friendships	
Widowhood	■ Older women are more likely to be widowed than older men, and for both men and women, the likelihood of being widowed increases markedly as they reach their mid-70s and mid-80s. ■ Widowed individuals differ considerably in the intensity and duration of distress they experience after the death of a spouse.
Remarriage, Cohabitation, and "Living Apart Together"	■ Remarriage is more common among older men than among older women due in part to social norms that support men's marriage to younger women. ■ Cohabitation in later life is becoming more common and provides opportunities for intimacy, companionship, and support. While young adults tend to see cohabitation as a prelude to marriage, older adults regard it as an alternative to marriage.
Long-Term Gay and Lesbian Partnerships	■ Many older gay men and lesbians have long-term partnerships, although they are less likely than their heterosexual counterparts to have a life partner. Living without a life partner does not mean that they suffer from loneliness, however, because they have strong friendship networks.
Friendships	■ Friendships are particularly important as sources of support and companionship for those who lack a primary partner, such as widowed, divorced, and never-married older adults. ■ Rates of loneliness generally decline with age but increase sharply among the oldest-old, due to declining health, sensory impairments, and the death of their spouse and friends.

FAMILY RELATIONSHIPS

The family is a key context for development and an important source of support (and sometimes also conflict) throughout life. Family ties remain vitally important in later adulthood, particularly as social networks become smaller and physical declines and relationship losses begin to mount. Older adults' family ties provide comfort, companionship, and aid, as well as a sense of continuity with the past and connection to the future (Mancini & Sandifer, 1995). Older adults, in turn, can be an important source of support and stability for younger generations within the family.

As we explore family relationships in later adulthood, it is important to realize that these relationships are being shaped in many ways by the changes in health and longevity and in patterns of marriage and family formation that you learned about in earlier chapters:

- As life expectancy has increased and birthrates have declined, the **beanpole family** has emerged as a common family structure (Bengtson, 2001). This family structure is tall and thin, like a beanpole, because it includes multiple family generations (e.g., grandparents, middle-aged parents, young adults, grandchildren, great-grandchildren), but it has relatively few people in each generation (Bengtson, Rosenthal, & Burton, 1990).

beanpole family A family structure that is common today and has a tall, thin shape because it includes multiple family generations but has relatively few people in each generation.

Jose Luis Pelaez Inc./Getty Images

The beanpole family—with multiple generations but few members in each generation—has become a common family structure.

- The particular "beans" on the beanpole are more diverse than ever, reflecting the growing diversity of marital and family configurations (more cohabitation, divorce, single-parent families, blended families, gay and lesbian families, childless couples, and never-married individuals) (Antonucci, Jackson, & Biggs, 2007).
- Gains in life expectancy mean that family relationships now tend to last much longer—often by decades—than was true in earlier eras.
- Families today tend to have more older members, and these older members also tend to be in better health than in the past. Yet physical declines and relationship losses (such as the death of a spouse) increase in advanced old age, creating needs for support. As a result, many families will be called upon at some point to assist with the care of older relatives, and they are likely to do so for longer periods of time than in the past and with fewer siblings or other family members to share the caregiving responsibilities.

As you read on, you might think about how these trends are likely to affect the nature of older adults' relationships with their family members, including their adult children, grandchildren and great-grandchildren, and siblings. How will your own family age?

Relationships with Adult Children

It was once widely believed that older people in contemporary U.S. society were alienated from their families. This view, termed the *alienation myth* by gerontologist Ethel Shanas (1979), was rooted in the belief that, compared with their counterparts today, older adults in earlier eras were more likely to live with their children and grandchildren in multigenerational households (Nydegger, 1983). In fact, though, only relatively recently have gains in life expectancy allowed large numbers of older adults to live long enough to have grandchildren and great-grandchildren (Bengtson, 2001). Studies of the amount of interaction between adult children and their elderly parents also challenges this myth. Nearly 90 percent of older adults in the United States have one or more living children, and 70 to 80 percent of them report seeing their adult child(ren) once a week or more (Lin & Rogerson, 1995; NIA, 2007). Even when the two generations do not live near enough to see each other in person very often, they maintain frequent contact by telephone, e-mail, or letters (Lin & Rogerson, 1995). In addition, evidence indicates that older adults strongly prefer to live near, but not with, their adult children (Himes, 2001; Shanas, 1979). This preference for **intimacy at a distance** reflects older adults' desire to enjoy regular contact with their adult children while maintaining their independence.

intimacy at a distance Older adults' preference to live near, but not with, their adult children in order to enjoy regular contact with their adult children while maintaining their independence.

Despite such evidence, the stereotype of family abandonment of the elderly often persists. It is expressed, for example, in doubts about the quality of contact between older adults and their adult children. One source of these lingering doubts is the worry that adult children may see their elderly parents largely out of feelings of obligation, making their interactions perfunctory or shallow and, therefore, unsatisfying. This idea, too, has proven to be more myth than fact. The majority of older adults describe their relationships with their adult children as close and personally rewarding (Blieszner, 2006). Adult children likewise report feelings of closeness and strong bonds of affection toward their aging parents (Bengtson, 2001).

Adult daughters and their elderly mothers tend to be especially close, although elderly mothers often judge the relationship to be closer than do their daughters (Fingerman, 2000, 2001). This difference between the two generations in the perceived closeness or importance of the relationship is an example of what researchers call the **generational stake** (sometimes called the developmental stake) (Bengtston & Kuypers, 1971; Giarrusso, Feng, & Bengtson, 2005). The generational stake refers to the idea that older adults have a greater investment, or stake, in their relationships with younger family members because they wish to maintain a sense of generational continuity (Bengtston & Kuypers, 1971). Consistent with the idea of a generational stake, older adults often report more positive feelings toward their adult children and grandchildren than these younger generations report toward them (Bengtson, 2001; Giarrusso et al., 2005).

generational stake The idea that older adults have a greater investment, or stake, in their relationships with younger family members than do the younger family members because the older adults wish to maintain a sense of generational continuity. Also called *developmental stake.*

Frequency of contact and feelings of closeness are two important barometers of the quality of older adults' relationships with their adult children. Another barometer is the extent to which care, practical assistance, and financial aid are exchanged in the relationship. Which way do these resources flow: from adult children to their elderly parents, from elderly parents to their adult children, or in both directions? If your hunch is that older adults receive more resources than they provide, you are expressing a widely held view. However, the evidence shows that elderly parents generally provide more assistance to their adult children than they receive (Bengtson, 2001; Silverstein, Gans, & Yang, 2006), particularly when their adult children have limited education or lack other resources (McIlvane, Ajrouch, & Antonucci, 2007).

The flow of assistance between generations does tend to shift over time, however, as elderly parents experience physical declines. Older adults who have difficulties with activities of daily living (ADLs) such as eating, bathing, or dressing often receive more aid from their adult children than they provide (Silverstein et al., 2006; see Figure 18.5). How much aid flows from either generation depends not only on need but also

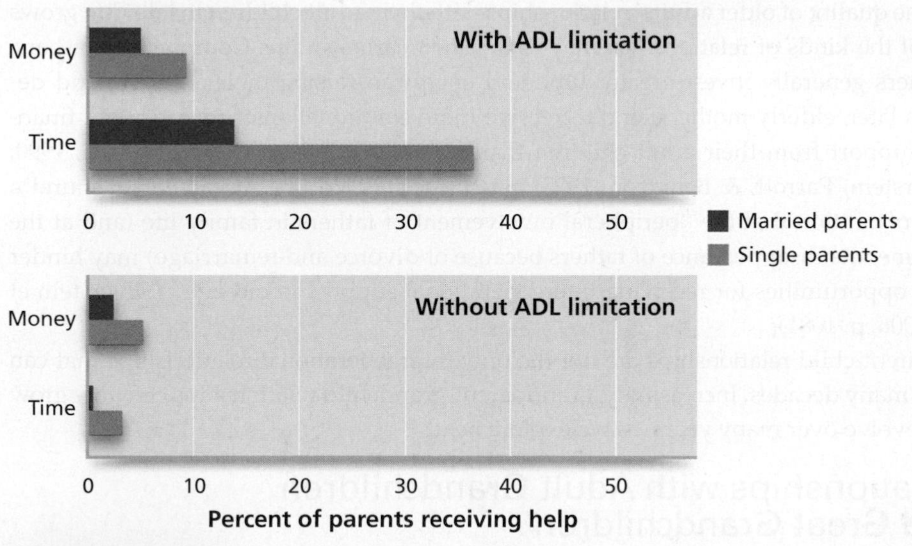

FIGURE 18.5

Provision of Aid by Adult Children to Married and Single Elderly Parents without vs. with Activities of Daily Living (ADL) Limitations

Source: National Institute on Aging (NIA). (2007). *Growing Older in America: The Health & Retirement Study.* Retrieved March 20, 2010 from http://www.nia.nih.gov/ResearchInformation/ExtramuralPrograms/BehavioralAndSocialResearch/HRS.htm.

on the ability of each generation to provide aid. For example, older adults who are married and have more financial resources generally provide more help to younger family members (McIlvane, Ajrouch, & Antonucci, 2007).

filial responsibility The norm that adult children have a duty to support their aging parents.

Norms partly determine how much aid flows between generations. The norm of **filial responsibility,** which says that adult children have a duty to support their aging parents (Cicirelli, 1990), is strong in the United States and other cultures (Lee, Peek, & Coward, 1998; Lowenstein & Daatland, 2006). Filial responsibility is assessed by asking people how much responsibility adult children have, regardless of the sacrifices involved, to provide their elderly parents with companionship, emotional support, practical assistance, help with personal and health care needs, and financial and housing assistance (Silverstein et al., 2006). Adult children who believe more strongly in the norm of filial responsibility provide more support to their aging parents when the need arises (Ikkink, van Tilburg, & Knipscheer, 1999; Silverstein et al., 2006). Compared to adult sons, adult daughters generally provide more support to their aging parents, reflecting a stronger link between daughters' sense of filial responsibility and their willingness to provide support (Silverstein et al., 2006).

Even though the norm of filial responsibility is strong in the United States, so too is the norm of independence, and family tensions can arise when older and younger family members have different expectations for how much support the older generation should receive (Costanzo & Hoy, 2007; Pillemer et al., 2007). Such misunderstandings may be especially common in immigrant families (Treas & Mazumdar, 2002). Elderly immigrants to the United States often have high expectations for family interaction and support, consistent with cultural traditions that encourage strong family ties. Younger, more acculturated family members, in contrast, are more likely to embrace the American value of independence and the desire to pursue busy, independent lives. Disappointed hopes for family involvement can contribute to loneliness and depression among elderly immigrants, especially if language barriers or lack of transportation increase their isolation (Treas & Mazumdar, 2002). Balancing needs for closeness and support with needs for independence in multigenerational families can be challenging, particularly when these needs differ across generations (Pillemer et al., 2007).

The quality of older adults' relationships with their adult children in later life grows out of the kinds of relationships they established earlier in life. Compared to fathers, mothers generally invest greater time and energy in raising their children, and decades later, elderly mothers tend to receive more emotional, instrumental, and financial support from their adult children than do elderly fathers (Rossi & Rossi, 1990; Silverstein, Parrott, & Bengtson, 1995). Such findings led one researcher to sound a note of caution that the "peripheral involvement of fathers in family life (and at the extreme, the disappearance of fathers because of divorce and remarriage) may hinder their opportunities for receiving intergenerational support in old age" (Silverstein et al., 2006, p. 1081).

Parent-child relationships are not the only intergenerational relationships that can span many decades. Increasingly, grandparent-grandchild relationships can now grow and evolve over many years, as we explore next.

Relationships with Adult Grandchildren and Great Grandchildren

Many people become grandparents in midlife, but not so long ago it was uncommon for them to see their grandchildren become adults. Gains in life expectancy, however, have changed things. Today, by the time people reach their 70s and 80s, their grandchildren often have entered adulthood and have begun to establish their own families. Grandparents tend to have less frequent contact with their grandchildren as they grow up and juggle their own family and work roles, but their relationships with their grandchildren often remain affectionate and mutually rewarding (Roberto & Stroes, 1992;

Relationships between grandparents and their grandchildren generally involve less frequent contact as the grandchildren become adults, but the relationships often remain affectionate, mutually rewarding, and supportive.

Sheehan & Petrovic, 2008). Grandparents often express a special interest in their grandchildren and great pride in their grandchildren's accomplishments, which fosters feelings of closeness with the grandchildren (Sheehan & Petrovic, 2008). Adult grandchildren, in turn, often credit their grandparents with being influential in their lives and, in particular, helping to shape their values, beliefs, and identities (Roberto & Skoglund, 1996). Some grandparents and their adult grandchildren describe their relationships as friendships, characterized by trust, sharing of personal confidences, and a desire to spend time together that is based on choice rather than feelings of obligation (Kemp, 2005).

Grandparent-adult grandchild relationships vary, of course, and some are closer than others (Kemp, 2004; Szinovacz, 1998). For example, grandparent-grandchild relationships that were affectionate when the child was young tend to be more affectionate and supportive later in life. Adult grandchildren also tend to be closer to their grandmothers than their grandfathers, and closer to biological grandparents than step-grandparents (Sheehan & Petrovic, 2008).

Relationships between grandparents and their adult grandchildren often serve as a safety-net for both generations (Kemp, 2005). Each generation tends to regard the other as a source of support that can be tapped in an emergency (Sheehan & Petrovic, 2008). A good example of this safety-net function is evidence that emotionally close relationships with grandparents help to protect late-adolescent and young-adult children living in troubled households from becoming depressed (Ruiz & Silverstein, 2007).

By the time older adults have great-grandchildren, advanced age and declining health tend to limit their involvement in the lives of the youngest family generation. Nonetheless, the existence of great-grandchildren in the family helps older adults derive a sense of satisfaction from the family's continuation into the future, and provides tangible affirmation of their own longevity (Doka & Mertz, 1988). Older adults contribute to the sense of family continuity by passing on to their grandchildren and great-grandchildren information about the family's origins, history, and traditions (Kopera-Frye & Wiscott, 2000).

Relationships with Siblings

Family ties in later adulthood include ties within generations as well as between generations. Sibling relationships appear to be the most important within-generation family relationships in later life. The metaphor of an hourglass is sometimes used to describe sibling ties over the lifespan: there is a great deal of interaction between siblings in childhood and adolescence (the wide base of the hourglass), less contact in young and middle adulthood (the narrow neck of the hourglass), and increased contact and interaction in later adulthood (the wide top of the hourglass). Major changes in siblings' lives, such as becoming divorced or widowed, can draw them closer together, as they exchange increased emotional and practical support (Connidis, 1992). Not all changes in sibling relationships in response to such life events are positive, however. Life events that appear to signal a loss of interest in the relationship by one of the siblings (such as getting married) can decrease, rather than increase, sibling closeness and interaction (Bedford, 1996). On balance, though, the changes in siblings' relationships in later life are more often positive than negative (Cicirelli, 1995).

Sibling ties can boost well-being in later life. Relationships with sisters tend to be particularly close in later life and, for both older men and older women, having a close relationship with a sister is linked to greater emotional health (Cicirelli, 1995).

Relationships Gone Awry: Elder Abuse

Relationships with family members are rewarding for the majority of older adults. These relationships are more troubled for some older adults, however, and they sometimes include abuse. **Elder abuse** is mistreatment that causes harm or distress to an older person in the context of a relationship in which trust should be expected (World Health Organization, n.d.). Elder abuse can take many forms, not all of which are readily visible (Acierno, Hernandez-Tejada, Muzzy, & Steve, 2009; Gorbien & Eisenstein, 2005).

elder abuse Mistreatment that causes harm or distress to an older person in the context of a relationship in which trust should be expected.

Emotional abuse, financial exploitation (improper use of an older person's money or assets), and neglect are the most common forms of elder abuse in the United States, with an estimated 2 to 11 percent of older adults experiencing some form of abuse annually (Acierno et al., 2009; Laumann, Leitsch, & Waite, 2008). Elder abuse often occurs in the home, and about two-thirds of the perpetrators are family members (Acierno et al., 2009). Professional caregivers in nursing homes or other institutional settings can be abusers, too. Older adults who are abused by the people they rely on for care are often reluctant to report their mistreatment. As a result, the true extent of elder abuse may be greater than official estimates suggest.

The causes of elder abuse are complex. Abusers often have a history of mental illness and alcohol misuse, and they are frequently dependent on the abused older person, using abuse as a way to gain money or other resources (Gorbien & Eisenstein, 2005; Lachs & Pillemer, 2004). Older adults with dementia are much more likely to be abused, especially if they engage in aggressive behaviors that may provoke retaliation by caregivers (Cooney, Howard, & Lawlor, 2006; Dyer, Pavlik, Murphy, & Hyman, 2000; Lachs & Pillemer, 2004). Social isolation increases the risk of abuse because others are less likely to witness or intervene to stop the abuse (Lachs & Pillemer, 2004). Some clinicians believe that elder abuse grows out of a history of prior violence in the relationship between the abuser and victim, but this idea has not yet been studied extensively (Lachs & Pillemer, 2004).

If an older person is suspected of being abused, an adult protective services agency can be contacted or, if the situation seems urgent, the police can be called. Most states have adult protective services agencies that will investigate reports of elder abuse. It is important for the mistreatment to be reported so the problem can be addressed, even as research continues into ways to prevent elder abuse from occurring. (For a summary of this section, see "Interim Summary 18.4: Family Relationships.")

INTERIM SUMMARY 18.4

Family Relationships	
	■ Family ties remain important in later adulthood, particularly as social networks become smaller and physical declines and relationship losses mount.
Relationships with Adult Children	■ Most older adults prefer to live near, but not with, their adult children (**intimacy at a distance**) in order to retain their independence. ■ Most older adults interact with their adult children frequently and feel close to them, two important barometers of the quality of these relationships. ■ The **generational stake** refers to the idea that older adults are more invested than younger family members in their relationships with the younger generation. ■ Adult children who more strongly endorse the norm of **filial responsibility** tend to provide more support to their aging parents. ■ The quality of older adults' relationships with their adult children earlier in life plays a role in the quality of their relationships later in life.
Relationships with Adult Grandchildren and Great Grandchildren	■ Grandparents tend to have less frequent contact with their grandchildren as they grow up, but their relationships often remain affectionate, mutually rewarding, and supportive. ■ Relationships between grandparents and their adult grandchildren often serve as a source of support that either side can tap in an emergency.
Relationships with Siblings	■ Sibling relationships between older adults are affected by major events in the life of either sibling, such as a divorce or widowhood, which may bring siblings closer together. ■ Relationships between sisters tend to be closest.
Relationships Gone Awry: Elder Abuse	■ **Elder abuse** is mistreatment that causes harm or distress to an older person in the context of a relationship in which trust should be expected.

WORK AND RETIREMENT

Assuming a full-time adult work role is a major transition in young adulthood, and exiting this role is a major transition in later adulthood. **Retirement** refers to exiting one's primary career occupation and ending employment within the formal workforce (Atchley, 1976; Moen, 2003). In the United States, retirement typically occurs when people choose to exit the workforce voluntarily, although the decision to retire is sometimes involuntary, for example, when poor health or an employer's policies force a person to retire. We explore how this transition typically occurs and how it affects older adults' psychological and financial well-being.

retirement Exiting one's primary career occupation and ending employment within the formal workforce.

Let's begin by thinking about retirement in a historical context. If you were to ask several of your friends to guess when people typically retired a century ago, you probably would get several different age estimates. All of their answers would be incorrect, however, because people rarely retired in the past (Marshall & Taylor, 2005). Just as later adulthood is a relatively new life stage, retirement is a relatively new

Dan Saelinger/Getty Images

Most older workers look forward to retiring if their retirement is voluntary and if they have sufficient financial resources to live on.

phenomenon (Costa, 1998). Only recently have large numbers of people lived long enough to retire. In addition, few government programs existed in the past to provide income support for people who left the workforce. That changed in the United States in the 1930s during the Great Depression. During this period, unemployment rates soared to 25 percent, businesses failed and banks collapsed, and many people lost their life savings and other assets. To meet the needs of unemployed older workers and, some believe, to ease older workers out of the workforce in order to create job openings for younger workers (Graebner, 1980), the Old Age Survivors and Disability Insurance (OASDI) Act was passed in 1935. This act established the Social Security program, which guaranteed a monthly income for retired people and for disabled workers and their families. What initially began as a small program of insurance for unemployed older adults and disabled individuals has since grown into a huge program of income maintenance. Today, Social Security is the largest single expenditure in the federal budget.

The notion that people could exit the workforce voluntarily and yet receive financial support was once viewed with great skepticism. Over time, attitudes toward retirement gradually became more positive, and many people now assume that they will spend a sizable chunk of their lives—20 to 30 years or more—retired. In fact, most older adults look forward to retirement and, until recently, the trend has been toward early retirement (Guillemard & Rein, 1993; Mermin, Johnson, & Murphy, 2007). The number of men age 65 and older in the workforce, for example, dropped from nearly 50 percent in 1950 to only 16 percent in 1990 (Mermin et al., 2007).

phased retirement Process by which workers gradually reduce their work hours in the transition from full-time employment to full-time retirement.

Attitudes Toward Retirement

As noted above, most older workers currently report favorable views of retirement, particularly if their current jobs are physically demanding or stressful (Smyer & Pitt-Catsouphes, 2007). Yet many older workers would prefer not to leave the workforce entirely (Moen, 2007). Retirement does not need to be an all-or-nothing experience, and, in recent years, older workers increasingly have indicated that they would like to keep working past the traditional retirement age of 65 (Mermin, Johnson, & Murphy, 2007; Sheaks, 2007). Figure 18.6 shows the work preferences of older workers from a recent large survey in the United States. As you can see, few older workers (only 6 percent) want to keep working full-time, but many would like to work part-time, or to cycle in and out of periods of work rather than to stop working altogether (Moen, 2005, 2007; Sheaks, 2007). Such data reflect a growing preference for **phased retirement**, in which workers gradually reduce their work hours in the transition from full-time employment to full-time retirement (Sheaks, 2007).

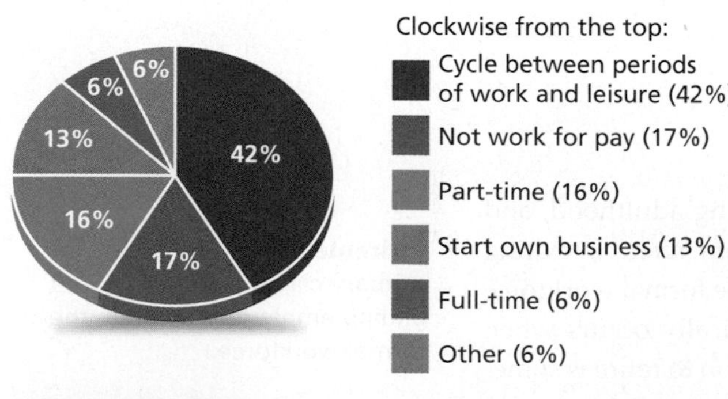

FIGURE 18.6

Work Preferences of Older Workers

Source: Sheaks, C. (2007). The state of phased retirement: Facts, figures, and policies. *Generations, 31*(1), 57-62. Data from Harris Interactive and Dychtwald, K. 2005. The Merrill Lynch New Retirement Survey. Perspective from the Baby Boom Generation. Survey Report. Retrieved August 2, 2006 from http://askmerrill.ml.com/pdf/RetirementSurveyReport.pdf.

Why do older workers, including many Baby Boomers who are nearing retirement age, indicate that they would prefer to remain in the workforce with flexible working arrangements? Three key factors seem to be responsible:

1. Older workers today tend to have better health and to work in less physically demanding jobs than was true in the past, enabling them to work until later ages (Mermin et al., 2007).

2. Many older adults enjoy work and want to remain active and productive, particularly if they could have reduced work schedules to allow them time to be involved with family members and friends, community activities, and engaging forms of leisure (AARP, 2005; Mermin et al., 2007; Moen, 2007; Sheaks, 2007).
3. Needs for income and continued health insurance also motivate some older adults to continue working during retirement (AARP, 2005).

Older adults who leave their full-time positions with the hope of obtaining satisfying part-time employment often face disappointment. They are likely to find primarily low-skill, low-paid work, such as jobs in fast-food chains or retail settings (Sweet, 2007). Many researchers have urged the development of more diverse and flexible options for work and retirement to better accommodate the needs of an aging workforce (Moen, 2007; Riley & Riley, 1994). In the interim, the decision to retire needs to be made carefully precisely because it usually involves a stark choice between full-time employment and full-time leisure.

mandatory retirement Policies that specify a particular age by which people must retire, regardless of their preferences or work performance.

defined-benefit plan A type of pension plan that guarantees an employee a defined amount of income during retirement; this type of plan has become rare in recent years.

defined-contribution plan A type of pension plan in which an employer contributes a specific, or defined, amount of money, to an account established for an employee, with the employee usually having the option to decide how to invest the money in the account (e.g., in a savings account or the stock market); this type of plan has become more common in recent years.

The Decision to Retire

Multiple factors influence the decision to retire, including workers' personal circumstances, their job characteristics, and broader social policies. Workers in poor health often need to retire earlier than those in good health (Smyer & Pitt-Catsouphes, 2007). Workers in good health, on the other hand, may defer retirement until they are confident they will have enough money to live on. Lower-income workers often have no choice but to keep working well into their later years because they would not be able to make ends meet otherwise. The decision to retire can also be affected by the spouse's retirement plans, because spouses often try to coordinate their plans so that they retire at the same time (Smith & Moen, 2004).

Job characteristics also enter into workers' retirement decisions. Older workers who have physically demanding jobs, such as those that involve heavy lifting, often opt to retire sooner. Similarly, workers with highly stressful jobs, such as those with many time pressures, may decide to leave the workforce as soon as it becomes financially feasible.

Social policies can influence the timing of retirement, as well. **Mandatory retirement** policies once were widespread in the United States. They required workers to retire when they reached a specific age, such as 65, regardless of their preferences or work performance. Legislation passed in the United States in the 1980s banned mandatory retirement in all but a few occupations, such as police officer, firefighter, and airline pilot (Atchley & Barusch, 2004). In other countries, including some European countries, mandatory retirement at age 65 or 70 is still common (van Solinge & Henkens, 2008).

Even though mandatory retirement has been largely outlawed in the United States, other social policies continue to influence the timing of retirement. The age of eligibility for full Social Security benefits was recently increased (from age 65 to age 67 for workers born after 1959), which may lead many workers to remain in the workforce longer than they would have before this policy change. Employer-provided pension plans also are shifting from defined-benefit plans to defined-contribution plans (Merman et al., 2007; Sheaks, 2007). **Defined-benefit plans** guarantee an employee a defined amount of income during retirement. **Defined-contribution plans**, in contrast, guarantee a defined contribution to an account established for the employee, with the employee deciding how to invest the money in the account (e.g., in a savings account or the stock market). How much money defined-contribution plans will generate depends on the employee's investment decisions and the overall economic climate. The economic downturn of 2008 wreaked havoc with many workers' retirement plans, as the value of their retirement nest eggs shriveled with the falling stock market (see Figure 18.7).

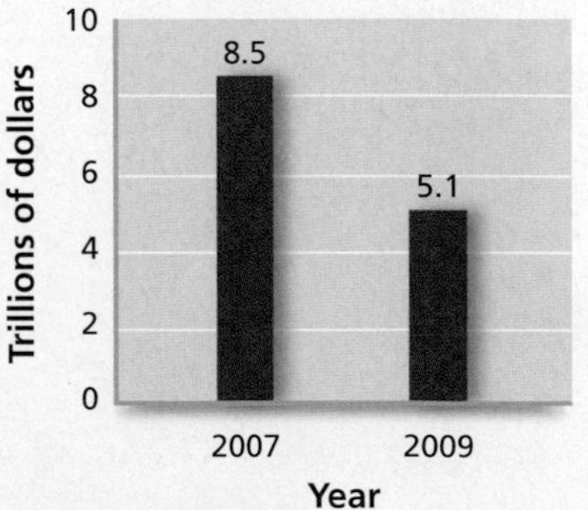

FIGURE 18.7

Decline in Overall Value of U.S. Workers' Retirement Accounts from 2007 to 2009

Note: Estimates are for Sept., 2007 to March, 2009, in inflation-adjusted dollars.

Source: Soto, M. (2009) How is the financial crisis affecting retirement savings? Fact sheet on retirement policy. Urban Institute.

Moreover, as many as 50 percent of U.S. workers have no employer-provided pension plan, a figure that is even higher among low-income workers (Mackenzie & Wu, 2008). Workers who lack employer-provided pensions must depend on Social Security and personal savings as their main sources of income during their retirement. Financial resources affect not only workers' decisions about when to retire but also how they adjust to retirement, as you'll see next.

Adjustment to Retirement

Retirement is one of the major life transitions of adulthood, so it is not surprising that a great deal of research has focused on how people adjust to retirement (Kim & Moen, 2001). A key theme from this research is that retirement is not a single event but rather a process (Kim & Moen, 2001; Pinquart & Schindler, 2007; Schlossberg, 2004). Initial reactions to retirement may differ from later reactions as this process unfolds over time. Some researchers believe that retirees experience an initial "honeymoon" period, characterized by euphoria as they explore leisure activities and enjoy their new freedom from the daily demands of work. This honeymoon period is sometimes followed by a period of *disenchantment*, as the day-to-day reality of retirement begins to sink in. Disenchantment eventually gives way to a period of *reorientation*, as retirees adapt to the social and economic realities of retirement and find new sources of meaning and stimulation in their lives (Atchley & Barusch, 2004; Reitzes & Mutran, 2004). This is only one possible pattern of adjustment, however.

Patterns of adjustment also depend on the context in which retirement occurs (Kim & Moen, 2001; van Solinge & Henkens, 2008). Having better health, more education, greater financial resources, a satisfying marital relationship, and close friendships all reliably predict greater psychological well-being during retirement (Kim & Moen, 2001; Pinquart & Schindler, 2007; Reitzes & Mutran, 2004). In addition, perceiving oneself to have had control over the decision to retire increases satisfaction with retirement and psychological well-being (Gallo, Bradley, Siegel, & Kasl, 2000; van Solinge & Henkens, 2007). Older workers who lose their jobs due to company mergers or downsizing may see little prospect for satisfactory re-employment and feel forced to retire (van Solinge & Henkens, 2008).

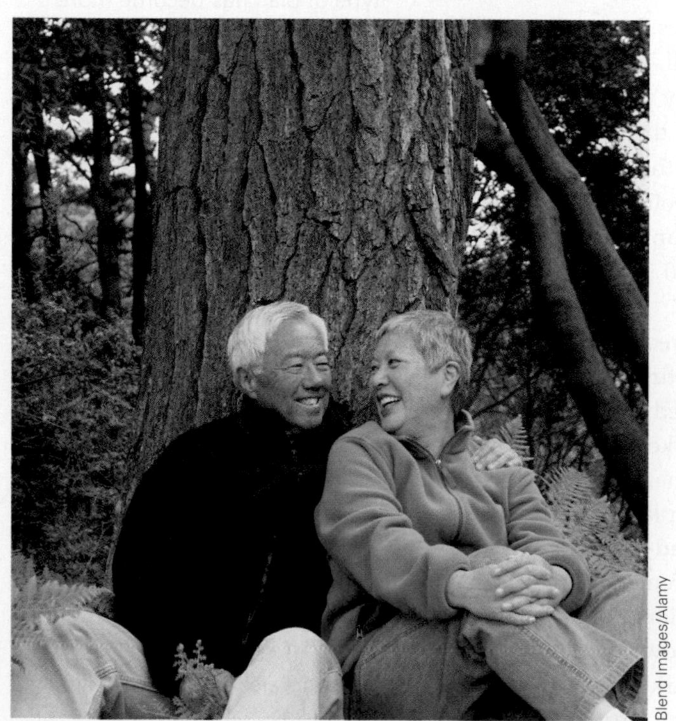
Blend Images/Alamy

Older adults adjust well to retirement if they have good health, more education, greater financial resources, a satisfying marriage, and close friendships.

The retirement transition affects not only retirees but also the people who are close to them, particularly their spouses. When both spouses have been in the workforce, synchronized retirement appears to benefit their adjustment (Smith & Moen, 2004). Satisfaction with retirement and marital quality often dip when one spouse continues working and the other retires, particularly when it is the wife who continues working (Moen, Kim, & Hofmeister, 2001; Szinovacz & Davey, 2005). Retirement experts urge people to plan not only for their financial needs in retirement but also for their social needs. The latter include thinking about how one's marriage may be affected as well as how to spend one's time (Moen, Huang, Plassmann, & Dentinger, 2006; Schlossberg, 2004).

Developing a Post-Retirement Lifestyle

Adjusting to retirement involves more than adjusting to the loss of the work role and the loss of relationships with co-workers; it also involves developing a satisfactory post-retirement lifestyle (Havighurst, Munnichs, Neugarten, & Thomae, 1969; Schlossberg, 2004). Post-retirement lifestyles may involve a mix of household chores, leisure activities, involvement in religious or political activities, and involvement in community service. Many older adults view retirement not just as a time to relax and to enjoy new freedom but also as a time when they can make contributions to their communities (Moen, 2007; Sander & Putnam, 2006).

Volunteer Work Volunteer service is one way that some retirees seek to make such contributions. About 25 percent of Americans age 65 and older are involved in some form of volunteer work (Morrow-Howell, 2007). This is a somewhat lower rate of volunteering than among middle-aged adults, but older adults commit more hours to volunteering once they become involved (Morrow-Howell, 2007). Volunteering can boost emotional well-being, foster social interaction, and contribute to a sense of purpose and meaning. Perhaps it is not surprising, then, that many studies have found that older adults who participate in volunteer work have better physical and psychological health and even live longer (Morrow-Howell, Hinterlong, Rozario, & Tang, 2003; Musick, Herzog, & House, 1999).

Religious Involvement Many elderly retirees find a sense of meaning and purpose in their lives through religious involvement. Older adults with mobility limitations who cannot attend religious services can express their faith or spirituality privately, through prayer or meditation (Ingersoll-Dayton et al., 2002). Religious involvement has been linked in many studies to better psychological and physical health, as well as greater longevity (Idler, 2006; Krause, 2006a). What accounts for these benefits? Religious institutions provide social support and philosophies for dealing with life stress, and they discourage substance use and other health-damaging behavior (Krause, 2006b; Pargament, van Haitsma, & Ensing, 1995). Religious faith also may help elderly individuals to prepare for the approaching end of life, a key element of the last psychosocial crisis of adulthood—the struggle between integrity and despair (Erikson, 1963, 1982).

aging in place Continuing to live in one's existing residence as one ages, modifying it over time in response to changes in one's health and functioning (e.g., by installing assistive devices.).

Residential Relocation or Aging in Place? A common image of life after retirement is that of older couples selling their homes and moving to a Sunbelt state, such as Florida or Arizona, to spend their golden years. However, the elderly are actually *less* likely than other age groups to change their residence and, when they do move, the vast majority remain in the same state (AAA, 2009). Some older adults do relocate to warmer climates, but many prefer the option of **aging in place**—an option that involves continuing to live in their current residence, modifying it in response to changes in their health and functioning (e.g., installing grab bars, ramps, and other assistive devices).

About two-thirds of older adults own their own homes free and clear, and they often are attached to their home and community (AAA, 2009). Strong ties to neighbors and friends in the community provide another reason why many older adults prefer not to relocate. When older adults do move, it is often to be closer to their adult children as their health declines and their need for assistance increases (Longino, Jackson, Zimmerman, & Bradsher, 1991). One component of the alienation myth (Shanas, 1979), discussed earlier, is the idea that U.S. families are quick to abandon their elderly relatives to institutional care such as nursing homes. As discussed in Chapter 17, U.S. families provide a tremendous amount of care to elderly relatives, with nursing homes typically serving as a last resort only after all other options have been exhausted (Merrill, 1997). In fact, only 4 percent of adults over age 65 reside in nursing homes, although this figure rises to about 15 percent among the very old (AAA, 2009). (For a summary of this section, see "Interim Summary 18.5: Work and Retirement.")

Installing ramps or other assistive devices in their homes as their health needs change allows some older adults to age in place.

INTERIM SUMMARY 18.5

Work and Retirement	
Attitudes Toward Retirement	■ Most workers have favorable views of retirement but would prefer a **phased retirement**, in which they gradually reduce their work hours, rather than leave the workforce entirely. ■ Older workers may not want to retire entirely because they tend to be healthier than was true in the past, they enjoy work and want to remain productive, and some need the additional income.
The Decision to Retire	■ The decision to retire is influenced by (1) personal circumstances, such as health, financial resources, and a spouse's retirement; (2) job characteristics, such as whether a job is physically demanding; and (3) social factors (such as certain **mandatory requirement** policies, age of eligibility for Social Security benefits, and pension plans).
Adjustment to Retirement	■ Retirement is a process, rather than an event, and the process may involve an initial *"honeymoon"* period, a period of *disenchantment*, and a period of *reorientation*. ■ How well a person adjusts to retirement depends on factors such as their health, education level, financial resources, marital relationship, friendships, and the perception of being in control of the retirement. ■ The transition to retirement also affects the people close to the retirees, particularly their spouses. Synchronizing the timing of their retirements appears to benefit spouses.
Developing a Post-Retirement Lifestyle	■ A post-retirement lifestyle may involve a mix of household chores, leisure activities, religious or political activities, and volunteering and community service. ■ Although some retirees relocate to warmer places, most prefer to remain living where they have lived (**aging in place**).

THE EVOLVING PERSON IN LATER ADULTHOOD

Over the course of seven to eight decades or longer, people experience an extraordinary number of life changes and challenges. In later adulthood, positive changes that can bring new satisfactions and a sense of renewal include seeing one's family thrive and expand as new generations are added, spending more time with a spouse or partner, and having the freedom to pursue leisure activities with friends. Yet as time marches on, unwelcome life changes are unavoidable, such as witnessing one's own body age and chronic conditions develop, losing close friends and loved ones, relinquishing the work role, and, for some, confronting financial uncertainty or hardship. How might older adults' interior lives be affected by the ups and downs of growing older? We explore this question next, focusing first on personality development and then on self-concept and emotional health in later life.

Personality Development

Two key aspects of our personalities, as discussed in Chapters 14 and 16, are our traits (the structure of personality) and our self-regulatory capacities (the dynamics of personality) (Hooker & McAdams, 2005; Staudinger & Kunzmann, 2005). These two aspects of personality are related to each other, moreover, because personality traits can influence self-regulatory capacities, or how people manage their emotions and cope with life stress.

Personality Traits Given all that transpires in people's lives in the decades that span adulthood, it might be reasonable to expect that personality traits change substantially by later life. Is that true?

You learned earlier that personality traits show a good deal of stability as people move through young and middle adulthood, even though modest changes are common (e.g., gains in psychosocial maturity and emotional adjustment). You may be surprised to learn that many personality traits remain stable through later adulthood, too. Some personality traits do show small changes, however. Of the Big Five personality factors discussed in Chapter 15, extraversion and openness decrease somewhat in later life (Allemand, Zimprich, & Hertzog, 2007; McCrae et al., 1999). These decreases may reflect older adults' preference for familiar, rather than novel, activities and social relationships as they realize that their time is limited and come to prioritize emotionally meaningful goals (Carstensen et al., 2003; Smith, 2006). Older people who have health problems or problems with vision or hearing may find it harder to interact with others or to explore new environments and activities, which could also help to account for modest decreases in extraversion and openness in later life.

Personality traits play an important role in happiness, health, and even longevity (Lucas, 2008; Wilson, Mendes de Leon, Bienias, Evans, & Bennett, 2004). Extraverted people are happier and more satisfied with their lives. Neurotic people are less happy and less satisfied with their lives (Lucas, 2008; Mroczek & Spiro, 2005). But how these personality traits affect emotional well-being may change with age. A good example is evidence showing that the link between neuroticism and unhappiness becomes stronger as people age (Mroczek, Spiro, Griffin, & Neupert, 2006). Why would this be so? Neurotic individuals react strongly to stressful situations and perceive many events in their lives to be stressful (Bolger & Zuckerman, 1995). Over time, their stress-response systems are activated again and again, triggering negative emotions repeatedly. As neurotic individuals grow older, this over-activation of their stress-response system produces heightened sensitivity to stressors, making them quick to react negatively even to minor stressors (Kendler, Thornton, & Gardner, 2001; Wilson, Evans, Bienias, Mendes de Leon, Schneider, et al., 2003). Repeated activation of the stress-response system, unfortunately, can damage bodily systems, contributing to heart disease and other chronic illnesses (Mroczek et al., 2006; see Chapter 15). This may help to explain why neuroticism has been found to increase the risk of mortality in later life (Wilson et al., 2004).

Fortunately, the vast majority of older adults are low, not high, in neuroticism. Moreover, among people who are low in neuroticism, evidence suggests that the elderly may be especially adept at managing their emotions and coping with life stress (Mroczek et al., 2006). A great deal of evidence is beginning to accumulate that suggests that self-regulatory capacities improve with age, as we discuss next (Carstensen, Mikels, & Mather, 2006).

Self-Regulatory Capacities Being able to manage one's emotions and to cope with life stress are two key aspects of self-regulatory capacities, and these capacities appear to improve in later life. Compared to younger age groups, older adults generally experience fewer negative emotions and either more or comparable positive emotions (see Figure 18.8) (Carstensen & Mikels, 2005; Carstensen et al., 2006). Older adults tend to ruminate less about emotionally upsetting events, experience less anger, and report better control over the feelings of anger that they do experience (Blanchard-Fields & Coats, 2008; Consedine & Magai, 2006; Gross et al., 1997). Older adults' ability to prevent or quell anger may help to explain why they are good at resolving conflicts and

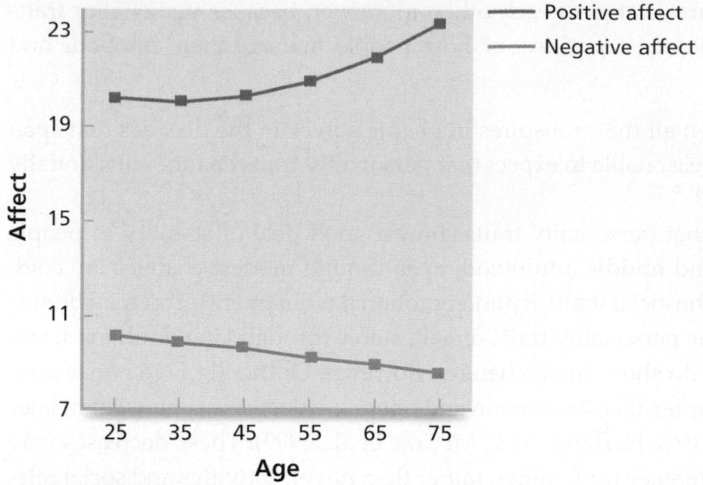

FIGURE 18.8

Age and Affect in Adulthood

Positive affect increases and negative affect decreases with age, supporting the idea that older adults have better emotion regulation skills than younger people.

Source: Mroczek, D. (2001). Age and emotion in adulthood. From *Current Directions in Psychological Science, 10*(3), 87–90. Copyright © 2001. Reprinted with permission of Blackwell/Wiley through Rightslink.

maintaining good will in their close relationships (Blanchard-Fields & Coats, 2008). In general, emotional control and emotional stability appear to increase in later life (Carstensen, Pasupathi, Mayr, & Nesselroade, 2000; Gross, Carstensen, Pasupathi, Tsai, Skorpen, & Hsu, 1997; Lawton, Kleban, Rajagopal, & Dean, 1992).

Older adults' emotion regulation capacities are definitely put to the test in advanced old age, however, as physical declines and social losses mount. In fact, positive affect declines somewhat and negative affect increases among the oldest-old (Smith, Fleeson, Geiselmann, Settersten, & Kunzmann, 1999). Older adults' emotion regulation capabilities may not spare them completely from the negative effects of mounting, chronic stressors, but in ordinary circumstances, their emotional functioning matches or exceeds that of younger people (Charles & Carstensen, 2009).

Gains in emotion regulation in later life provide a striking contrast with evidence of *declines* in physical and cognitive capacities in later life (Charles & Carstensen, 2010). How should we think about this paradox? What contributes to gains in emotion regulation even as declines in physical and cognitive functioning mount? One explanation is that a lifetime of learning how to avoid or handle upsetting situations helps older adults acquire skill in regulating their emotions (Williams et al., 2006). Another explanation can be derived from socioemotional selectivity theory (Carstensen, Fung, & Charles, 2003). Older adults' awareness that their time is limited leads them to prefer to interact selectively with their most gratifying social network members (typically close friends and family members). Gratifying social interaction, in turn, boosts positive mood and helps to dampen negative mood. In addition, because older adults place a high priority on emotional goals, they focus more on emotionally relevant information and memories, particularly those that are positive in nature (Kryla-Lighthall & Mather, 2009; Mather & Carstensen, 2005). In laboratory studies, older people have been found to pay more attention to emotional than neutral material, and they remember the emotional material better. This is especially true for positive, rather than negative, material (Kryla-Lighthall & Mather, 2009; Mather & Carstensen, 2005).

Researchers have used functional magnetic resonance imaging (fMRI) to monitor brain activity while people are asked to view and, later, recall material with varying emotional content. This work has documented greater activation of the amygdala (a key area of the brain involved in processing emotional information) when emotional images are viewed, compared to neutral images. Importantly, older adults, but not younger adults, show greater amygdala activation when the emotional material viewed is positive in nature (Mather et al., 2004). Some researchers believe that older adults' preference for emotionally meaningful (especially positive) information and experiences may actually contribute to brain plasticity that enhances their emotional functioning (Williams et al., 2006).

Being able to manage emotional distress and to draw upon the accumulated experiences of a lifetime plays a critical role in how well people cope with stressful life events. **Coping** refers to individuals' cognitive or behavioral efforts to reduce stress (Lazarus & Folkman, 1984). People can cope with a stressful situation in many different ways, but researchers often distinguish between **problem-focused coping** (externally directed responses aimed at remedying the stressful situation itself) and **emotion-focused coping** (internally directed responses aimed at reducing the negative emotions generated by the stressful event) (Folkman & Moskowitz, 2004; Lazarus & Folkman, 1984). For example, a person who copes with the loss of a job by developing new job skills or seeking job leads from social network members would be engaging in problem-focused coping. A person who copes by trying not to think about the job loss or by reminding himself about other areas of his or her life that are going well would be engaging in emotion-focused coping.

coping Individuals' cognitive or behavioral efforts to reduce stress.

problem-focused coping Externally directed responses aimed at improving a stressful situation.

emotion-focused coping Internally directed responses aimed at reducing the negative emotions generated by a stressful event.

Which kind of coping is likely to be more beneficial in the long run? If you believe that tackling problems directly is the most beneficial coping strategy, your instincts are consistent with the findings of a good deal of research. Many (though not all) studies have found that problem-focused coping predicts better adjustment over time (Aldwin & Revenson, 1987; Folkman & Moskowitz, 2004; Penley, Tomaka, & Wiebe, 2002). Moreover, some forms of emotion-focused coping—such as avoidance or using alcohol to escape negative feelings—predict worse, rather than better, adjustment (Penley et al., 2002; Smith, Patterson, & Grant, 1990).

Yet it would be overly simplistic to conclude that problem-focused coping is always most effective (Aldwin, 2007; Folkman & Moskowitz, 2004). When people experience stressors that cannot be changed—such as chronic illness or the death of a loved one—emotion-focused coping may be more effective (Stanton, Danoff-Burg, Cameron, & Ellis, 1994). Older adults often experience chronic stressors for which practical solutions may simply be lacking. It is not surprising, then, that emotion-focused coping is both more common and more adaptive in later life (Folkman, Lazarus, Pimley, & Novacek, 1987).

Yet even though older adults may make greater use of emotion-focused coping, they remain capable of problem-focused coping. When they face problems that can be resolved through constructive action, they are as likely as younger age groups to engage in problem-focused coping (Aldwin, 2007;Yancura & Aldwin, 2008). In general, older adults tend to have broader and more flexible coping repertoires because they can readily shift from problem-focused coping to emotion-focused coping when the situation calls for it (Blanchard-Fields, 2007; Blanchard-Fields, Mienaltowski, & Seay, 2007).

Laboratory studies confirm that older adults are flexible copers. In such studies people are typically presented with scenarios that describe different kinds of stressful events, and they are asked to indicate how they would deal with the stressors. Researchers then record the types of coping responses generated and rate their effectiveness. This work shows that older adults tend to use versatile strategies that include emotion-focused as well as problem-focused coping. Younger adults, in contrast, tend to favor problem-focused coping across all types of stressors (Blanchard-Fields, Mienaltowski, Seay, 2007). Being able to adjust one's coping responses to the demands of different kinds of stressful situations is a hallmark of effective coping (Blanchard-Fields, Jahnke, & Camp, 1995). So it is not surprising that expert judges rate older adults' flexible coping strategies as more effective than those of younger people (Blanchard-Fields & Coats, 2008).

Emotional Health and Self-Evaluation

Perhaps you can begin to see how older adults' self-regulatory capacities might play a role in both their emotional health and their self-evaluation. We explore those connections next.

Emotional Health Given the physical and social losses that accumulate in later life, we might expect older adults to be less satisfied with their lives and more depressed than people in younger age groups (Blazer, 2010). Yet we have already seen that older adults experience more positive emotion and comparable or less negative emotion than younger people, at least until advanced old age (Carstensen & Mikels, 2005; Carstensen et al., 2006). Life satisfaction is generally as high or higher in later life than in earlier periods (Diener & Suh, 1998; Mroczek & Spiro, 2005). Even centenarians (people who live to be 100 or older) report relatively high life satisfaction. In one study, 59 percent of centenarians rated their current lives as good or very good, a figure that rose to 84 percent when they were asked to rate their lifetimes as a whole (Samuelsson et al., 1997).

Such findings paint a positive portrait of emotional health in later life. But what about depression? Is this form of emotional distress more common among older adults than among younger age groups, as stereotypes of the elderly often suggest (Fiske, Wetherell, & Gatz, 2009)? **Depression** is a condition in which people experience depressed mood and a loss of interest in their usual activities for 2 weeks or longer, along with other symptoms that may include feelings of worthlessness, difficulty concentrating or making decisions, fatigue, psychomotor agitation or retardation, sleep problems, weight changes, and suicidal thoughts (see Chapter 12; American Psychiatric Association, 2000; Blazer, 2003). When more symptoms are present, the condition is considered to be *major depression;* when fewer symptoms are present, the condition is considered to be *minor depression* (American Psychiatric Association, 2000; Blazer, 2003). Given the physical and social losses that accompany aging, are older adults especially vulnerable to depression?

depression A condition in which people experience the following symptoms for 2 weeks or longer: depressed mood and a loss of interest in their usual activities, along with other symptoms (e.g., feelings of worthlessness, difficulty concentrating or making decisions, fatigue, psychomotor agitation or retardation, sleep problems, weight changes, and suicidal thoughts).

Rates of major depression among the elderly, contrary to popular impressions, are generally low, ranging from 1 to 5 percent (Fiske et al., 2009; Zarit, 2009). Minor depression is more common, affecting as many as 15 percent of the elderly (Fiske et al., 2009). Some variations by ethnicity have been reported, with elderly Hispanics having somewhat higher rates of depression than elderly Caucasians and African Americans (Blazer, 2003). Other factors that increase the risk of being depressed in later life include being female, having low socioeconomic status, and having physical or cognitive impairments (Blazer, 2003; Djernes, 2006; Fiske et al., 2009). Importantly, when researchers adjust for these factors, they find either no age differences in rates of depression or lower rates of depression among the elderly than among younger age groups (Blazer & Hybels, 2005; Fiske et al., 2009; Jorm, 2000). In fact, rates of mental disorder are generally lower in later adulthood than in young and middle adulthood (Jorm, 2000; Jorm et al., 2005; Zarit, 2009) (see Figure 18.9).

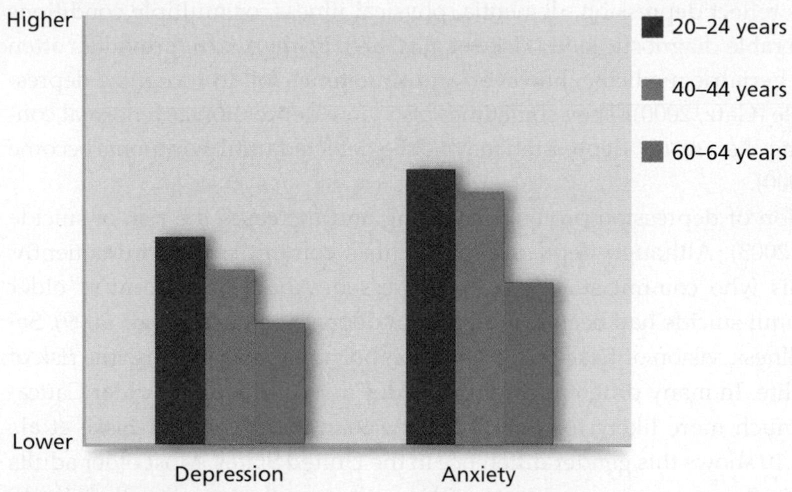

FIGURE 18.9

Age Differences in Rates of Depression and Anxiety

Source: Adapted from Jorm, A. F., Windsor, T. D., Dear, K. B. G., Anstey, K. J., Christensen, H., & Rodgers, B. (2005). Age group differences in psychological distress: The role of psychosocial risk factors that vary with age. *Psychological Medicine, 35*(9), 1253–1263.

Why are depression and other forms of emotional distress less common among older adults? One possibility is that depression decreases longevity, so that by later adulthood, those most prone to depression are no longer alive. Psychological processes may play a role, too. Some stressful life events that can lead to depression, such as the death of a spouse, are more predictable, or on time, in later life than in young or middle adulthood (Blazer, 2010; Blazer & Hybels, 2005). It is generally easier to adjust to events that occur on time, rather than unexpectedly, or off time. Older adults' strong emotion regulation skills and versatile coping repertoires may also help to reduce the negative impact of stressful life events they experience. Similarly, older adults' ability to maintain good will in their close relationships makes them less likely to experience interpersonal conflicts and disagreements that could contribute to depression (Sorkin & Rook, 2006). Finally, religious involvement increases in later life and helps older adults, especially those with physical disabilities, fend off depression (Blazer, 2003; Gatz & Fiske, 2003).

Even though rates of depression may be lower among the elderly than among younger age groups, the seriousness of depression as a mental health problem in later life should not be minimized. Depression is a leading cause of emotional suffering among older adults (Blazer, 2003; Blazer & Hybels, 2005; Gatz, 2000). In addition, although rates of depression are low among the elderly overall, they are high among older adults in hospitals and long-term care settings, such as nursing homes (Blazer, 2010; Cole & Dendukuri, 2003; Fiske et al., 2009).

Researchers also caution that the depression may be underestimated as a problem in later life because it often goes undetected. Compared to younger age groups, older adults report less dysphoria, guilt, self blame, apathy, fatigue, disturbed sleep, and psychomotor retardation (Fisk et al., 2009; Nguyen & Zonderman, 2006). Complaints about memory problems and difficulty concentrating are often reported by depressed older adults, as are complaints about bodily aches and pains. Determining whether such symptoms reflect depression, dementia, physical illness, or multiple conditions requires considerable diagnostic skill (Fiske et al., 2009). Primary care providers often lack training in geriatric medicine, however, and sometimes fail to recognize depression older people (Gatz, 2000). They sometimes also view depression as a normal consequence of aging. As a result, depression may not be detected until symptoms become severe (Gatz, 2000).

Underdetection of depression prolongs suffering and increases the risk of suicide (Gatz & Fiske, 2003). Although depressed individuals commit suicide infrequently, most individuals who commit suicide were depressed. About 85 percent of older adults who commit suicide had been suffering from depression (Fiske et al., 2009). Serious physical illness, vision or hearing loss, and alcohol abuse also increase the risk of suicide in later life. In many different countries, older men (particularly older Caucasian men) are much more likely to commit suicide than older women (Fiske et al., 2009). Figure 18.10 shows this gender difference in the United States. Most older adults who commit suicide saw a primary care provider in the month preceding their death (Gatz, 2000). This underscores the importance of training health care providers in the mental and physical health needs of older adults.

Fortunately, if depression is detected, effective treatments are available—typically antidepressant medication or psychotherapy (Gatz & Fiske, 2003; Thompson, Coon, Gallagher-Thompson, Sommer, & Koin, 2001). Aerobic exercise is also being investigated as a promising alternative or complementary treatment option (Fiske et al., 2009).

Self-Evaluation So far, you have seen that older adults appear to withstand many of the declines and losses associated with aging remarkably well in terms of their emotional health. What about their self-evaluation? We might expect age-related declines and losses, coupled with widespread ageism and negative stereotypes of the elderly, to undermine older adults' feelings of self-worth (Sneed & Whitbourne, 2005). Yet some researchers predict that self-acceptance remains high in later life (Sneed & Whitbourne, 2005). They reason that older adults tend to focus on positive information and memories, which should help to insulate them from negative thoughts about the self (Labouvie-Vief, 2003).

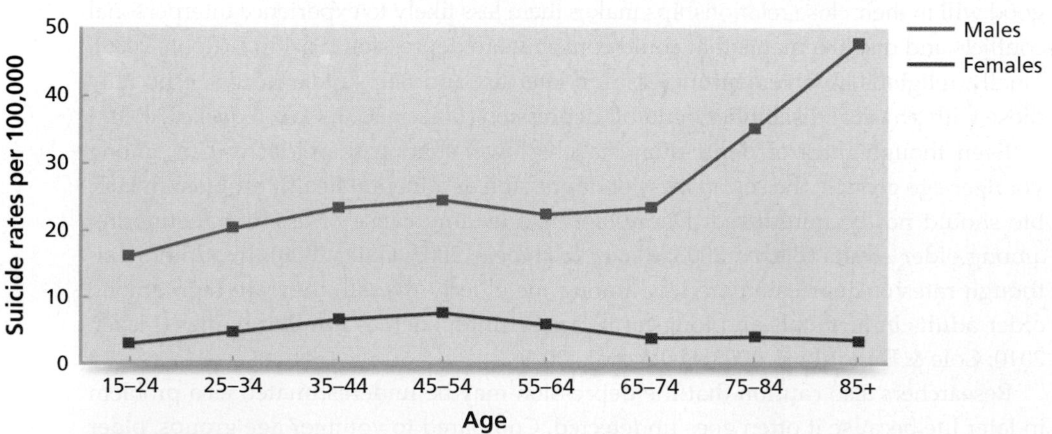

FIGURE 18.10

Suicide Rates by Age and Gender

Source: Yin, S. (2006). Elderly white men afflicted by high suicide rates. *Population Reference Bureau*. Retrieved April 7, 2010 from http://www.prb.org/Articles/2006/ElderlyWhiteMenAfflictedbyHighSuicideRates.aspx

In addition, a shift appears to occur with age from an outer- to an inner-defined self (Labouvie-Vief & Devoe, 1991). Unlike adolescents and young adults, whose feelings of self-worth hinge to a great extent on social approval and group acceptance, older adults rely less on others for external validation and are more self-accepting. Older adults also tend to experience a smaller gap between their ideal selves (who they hope to become in the future) and their actual selves (who they are at present) (Ryff, 1991). This is because older adults have less idealized expectations for the future and are more accepting of their current selves. Later life, according to Carol Ryff (1991, p. 294), is a time when "the ideal self better fits the real self, warts and all, with whom one has become an accustomed traveler."

Yet not all research supports the idea that self-acceptance is high in later life. In a large study of people aged 9 to 90, levels of self-esteem were high in childhood, declined in adolescence, rose during young and middle adulthood, and then declined in later adulthood (Robins, Trzesniewski, Tracy, Gosling, & Potter, 2002). This finding seems to contradict the idea of greater self-acceptance in later life, but does it? Some researchers believe that the decline in self-esteem in later life reflects a shift toward greater modesty, humility, and a more balanced view of the self (Robins et al., 2002; Robins & Trzesniewski, 2005).

The elderly maintain an underlying sense of their own worth, but they are more willing to acknowledge their faults and limitations and have less need to embellish their self-presentation to others (Robins & Trzesniewski, 2005). Consistent with this view, *narcissism*, a tendency toward excessive love and admiration of oneself—declined with age in a large study (Foster, Campbell, & Twenge, 2003). The decline in self-esteem in later life, therefore, may reflect a shift toward a more modest, and perhaps more balanced, view of the self (Robins et al., 2002). Such a shift would be consistent with Erikson's (1963, 1982) view of later adulthood as a time when people reflect on their lives, acknowledging and striving to accept their successes and failures and their strengths and limitations as individuals. (For a summary of this section, see "Interim Summary 18.6: The Evolving Person in Later Adulthood.")

INTERIM SUMMARY **18.6**

The Evolving Person in Later Adulthood

Personality Development	■ Many personality traits remain stable in later adulthood, although some (such as extraversion and openness) do show small changes. ■ Self-regulatory capacities—emotional control and emotional stability—appear to be well-preserved and even enhanced in later life. ■ **Emotion-focused coping** (rather than **problem-focused coping**) becomes more common, and more adaptive, in later life. In general, older adults exhibit greater coping flexibility in terms of coping styles.
Emotional Health and Self-Evaluation	■ Older adults report experiencing more positive emotion and less negative emotion than younger age groups, and life satisfaction tends to be as high or higher in later life than in earlier periods. ■ Depression rates among the elderly are generally low; they are higher among women, those of lower socioeconomic status, and those with physical or cognitive impairments. ■ Most older adults also have a positive sense of self, in part because they are more accepting of themselves.

SUMMING UP AND LOOKING AHEAD

Over the course of a lifetime, people generally develop expanded capacities to interact with the world around them in order to pursue their hopes and dreams, to confront challenges, and to move forward after experiencing setbacks and losses, adapting even to declines in their own bodily functioning. In later adulthood, and especially in advanced old age, physical and social losses often mount in ways that put adaptive capacities to the test. Yet, as you have seen, emotional health generally remains strong in later life, even as physical health declines. With age, people become more adept at adapting to the realities of their aging bodies and changing life circumstances by becoming more selective about their life goals, striving to optimize their abilities to attain their goals, and being flexible about their goals and willing to compensate for declining abilities.

These processes of developmental regulation operate throughout life, but they come together in later adulthood to provide the foundation for *successful aging* (Baltes & Baltes, 1990; Baltes, 1997). Successful aging does not mean that one can grow old without experiencing declines and losses (Rowe & Kahn, 1998). Instead, it means that one can grow old with a more favorable balance of gains to losses and with the capacity to preserve well-being and dignity and to remain engaged with life despite inevitable declines (Baltes, 1997; Baltes & Baltes, 1990; Erikson, 1982; Rowe & Kahn, 1998).

Even though the human body is not designed to last forever (Olshansky, Carnes, & Butler, 2003), human psychological capacities for adaptation appear to remain robust until the very end of life (Jopp & Rott, 2006). The end of life is something that each of us will experience at some point—a passage that concludes the remarkable journey of a human lifetime. We explore this final stage of the journey next.

HERE'S WHAT YOU SHOULD KNOW

Did You Get It?

After reading this chapter, you should understand the following:

- The developmental tasks and timetables of late adulthood
- How the three processes of developmental regulation affect older adults
- How social network involvement changes with age and how different theories explain this change
- The key roles friendships and intimate partnerships play in later adulthood and how older adults preserve goodwill in their close relationships
- How relationships with adult children, grandchildren, and siblings affect older adults
- How older adults make the decision to retire, and then cope with and adjust to retirement
- How personality develops in late adulthood
- Older adults' emotional health and sense of self

Important Terms and Concepts

activity theory (p. 576)
aging in place (p. 595)
beanpole family (p. 585)
coping (p. 599)
defined-benefit plans (p. 599)
defined-contribution plans (p. 599)
depression (p. 600)
disengagement theory (p. 575)
elder abuse (p. 590)
emotion-focused coping (p. 599)
filial responsibility (p. 588)
generational stake (p. 587)
integrity vs. despair (p. 573)
intimacy at a distance (p. 586)
life review (p. 573)
mandatory retirement (p. 593)
phased retirement (p. 592)
post-parental period (p. 578)
problem-focused coping (p. 599)
retirement (p. 591)
socioemotional selectivity theory (p. 576)

Death and Dying

Image Source/Getty Images

An estimated 2,415,000 people died in the United States in 2008 (Tejada-Vera & Sutton, 2009.). Based on this figure, approximately 6,715 Americans will die today. For some, death will come suddenly and unexpectedly, perhaps as the result of a fatal accident or massive heart attack. For others, it will mark the end of a long struggle with a terminal illness. Some people will die at home; many will die in a hospital or nursing home. Death comes in many forms, but one thing is certain—none of us can escape it. Death is the inevitable conclusion of the journey that begins with birth, and it has an important place in our efforts to understand lifespan development in its entirety. In this chapter, we explore how death is defined, how the rights and needs of dying individuals are viewed, what the experience of dying is like, and how dying individuals are cared for. We also examine how family members and friends left behind come to terms with the death of a loved one.

HISTORICAL AND CULTURAL CONTEXTS OF DEATH AND DYING

Before we turn to these topics, we wish to highlight a theme we have emphasized throughout this book: Human development is shaped by the historical and cultural contexts in which it unfolds. This theme applies to death and dying as well, and it sets the stage for our discussion.

Mortality rates were once very high, particularly among children, but as you learned in Chapter 17, they began to decline markedly in economically developed countries in the 20th century. Declining childhood mortality rates reflected a shift from acute, infectious diseases to chronic, degenerative diseases as the leading causes of death. Chronic diseases most often affect the elderly, and, as a result, death rates in developed countries today are the highest among the elderly (see Figure EP.1). In the United States, about 75 percent of deaths occur among people age 65 and older (Kersting, 2004).

The fact that people now tend to die from chronic diseases also means that the process of dying tends to be considerably longer than it was when people tended to die from infectious diseases (Seale, 2000). In the past, dying individuals were most often cared for at home by family members. Today, in developed countries, dying individuals are most often cared for by medical professionals in institutional settings, such as hospitals or nursing homes (Gruneir et al., 2007; Seale, 2000). All of these differences mean that death is much less common and familiar than in the past. Death in contemporary societies tends to be a more remote experience, one removed from everyday life (Kastenbaum, 2007). Another important historical change is that medical advances now make it possible to keep people alive using life-support technologies (Seale, 2000). These historical changes have had a profound impact on definitions of death, on planning for end-of-life health care, and on the process of dying.

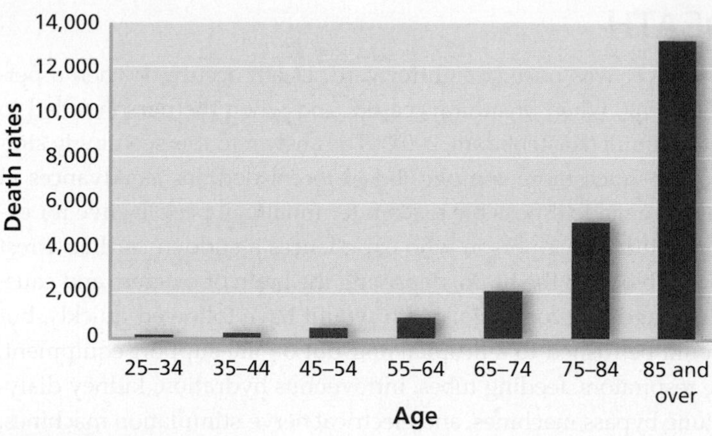

FIGURE EP.1

Death Rates by Age in the United States, 2006

Note: Death rates are per 100,000 in each age group.

Source: CDC, Death Rates by 10-Year Age Groups: United States, 2006. Retrieved March 20, 2010 from http://www.cdc.gov/nchs/data/dvs/MortFinal2006_Worktable23r.pdf

We explore death and dying in this chapter primarily from the perspective of modern, developed—and largely Western—societies. It is important to recognize, however, that death and dying are experienced very differently in other societies. In many less-developed countries, mortality rates among children and adults alike remain high, options for the care of the dying are limited, and life-sustaining treatments and technologies are scarce. Exposure to death in such societies is a more common aspect of everyday life.

Cultural beliefs about death and dying also vary considerably (Kalish, 1985). In societies in which life is both hard and short, and in which the risks of disease and suffering are high, death is less likely to be feared and is sometimes viewed as an entry to a better life. In other societies, death is viewed as a punishment, leading people to fear and dread death. In many societies, death is viewed as a loss—the loss of opportunities to experience the world and carry out one's plans, the loss of relationships with loved ones, and, fundamentally, the loss of one's self (Kalish, 1985). As we explore death and dying, it is important to bear in mind that many cultures view the final chapter of life through lenses that are very different from ours. These historical and cultural contexts affect many aspects of death, including the most basic issue of how we define death. (For a summary of this section, see "Interim Summary EP.1: Historical and Cultural Contexts of Death and Dying.")

INTERIM SUMMARY **EP.1**

Historical and Cultural Contexts of Death and Dying

- The leading causes of death have changed in developed countries, so that death now most often results from chronic, degenerative diseases rather than infectious diseases and most often occurs among the elderly rather than children.
- In the past, death was a more familiar event, often took less time, and happened in the home instead of in institutional settings as it now often does in developed countries.
- The experience of death and dying varies around the world. In many less-developed countries, mortality rates among children and adults remain high, infectious diseases are rampant, options for the care of the dying are limited, and life-sustaining treatments and technologies are scarce. Views about death also vary across cultures.

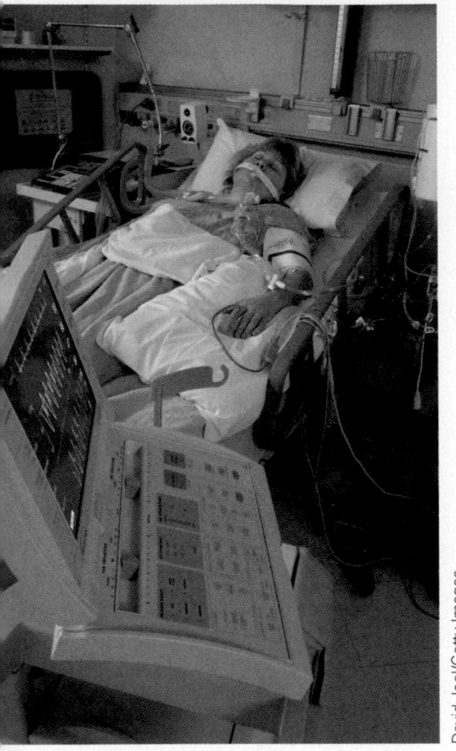
David Joel/Getty Images

Modern life-support technologies make it possible to keep terminally ill individuals alive for extended periods of time, sometimes in a persistent vegetative state.

persistent vegetative state A condition in which higher cortical functioning (responsible for thinking and feeling) has ceased, while brain stem functioning (responsible for the heart beating and for breathing) continues.

brain death Death that is considered to have occurred when all signs of brain activity, as measured by brain waves, have ceased for a specified period of time.

DEFINING DEATH

What is death? The answer was once straightforward. Death occurred when a person's heart stopped beating, when breathing ceased, and when the person failed to react to environmental stimuli (Kastenbaum, 2007). The answer to this seemingly simple question has become much more complicated in recent decades as advances in medical technologies have made it possible to keep terminally ill people alive for extended periods of time. Imagine a person who experiences a sudden cardiac arrest that disrupts the flow of blood to the brain, depriving the brain of oxygen, and causing extensive brain damage. Not long ago, death would have followed quickly, but today the person would be rushed to a hospital and put on life-support equipment, which could include respirators, feeding tubes, intravenous hydration, kidney dialysis machines, heart-lung bypass machines, and electrical nerve-stimulation machines. If the brain damage caused by the cardiac arrest leaves the person unable to move, think, speak, or feel, is the person still living?

This question was at the center of a widely publicized controversy several years ago that concerned the fate of a young woman, Terri Schiavo, who had a sudden cardiac arrest in 1990 that caused irreversible brain damage. It left her in a persistent vegetative state, kept alive only with life-sustaining technology (Wolfson, 2003). A **persistent vegetative state** refers to a condition in which higher cortical functioning (responsible for thinking and feeling) has ceased, while brain stem functioning (responsible for the heart beating and for breathing) continues. Years passed without signs of improvement, but Terri's parents considered her to be living, and they clung to the hope of recovery. Terri's husband, Michael, in contrast, eventually gave up hope of recovery and reached the conclusion that Terri had no quality of life without the ability to think or experience the world around her. He stated that she had once commented that she would never want to be kept alive on life support if something happened to her. In 1998, Michael asked to have Terri's feeding tube removed and hydration discontinued so that she could die. Her parents objected to this request, and legal battles ensued for the next seven years. The courts ultimately ruled in favor of Terri's husband. In 2005, 15 years after her cardiac arrest, her feeding tube was removed, and she died 13 days later. This tragic case raised strong feelings both for and against keeping Terri alive. What would you have decided if you had been Terri's spouse or parent?

Today most experts agree that brain functioning must be considered in the determination of death. **Brain death** occurs when all signs of brain activity, as measured by brain waves, have ceased for a specified period of time. Some medical experts believe, however, that the cessation of *all* brain activity should not be required to determine when a death has occurred. As noted above, irreversible brain damage sometimes causes higher brain functions (the ability to think, feel, and respond to stimuli) to cease even though lower brain functions (for example, breathing and respiration) continue. Because the person has no possibility of leading anything resembling a normal life in such circumstances, some experts believe that the person should be determined to have died (Truog & Fackler, 1992). (For a summary of this section, see "Interim Summary EP.2: Defining Death.")

INTERIM SUMMARY **EP.2**

Defining Death

- Advances in medical technologies now make it possible to keep terminally ill people alive for extended periods of time, making defining death a complex task.
- Most experts agree that brain functioning must be considered in the determination of death. **Brain death** occurs when all signs of brain activity have ceased for a specified period of time.

CHOICES AND DECISIONS AT THE END OF LIFE

Cases like Terry Schiavo's illustrate that defining death has become a complex task. They have also increased public awareness of the fact that decisions about the medical care one receives at the end of life are not always under one's control. If a person becomes incapacitated, others will make such decisions unless the person previously prepared a formal document (discussed later) specifying treatment preferences. Cases like Terri Schiavo's have also called attention to the quality of life as an important consideration when treatment options for terminally ill people are weighed and when the rights of terminally ill people to end their lives are evaluated. As you'll see, choices and decisions at the end of life raise complex medical, legal, and ethical issues.

Determining Medical Care at the End of Life: Advanced Directives

One way that people can have some control over the kind of medical care they will receive at the end of life is to prepare an **advance directive**. This is a legal document that specifies the life-sustaining medical treatments people wish to receive should they become terminally ill and unable to communicate their preferences. Two common forms of advance directives are a *living will* and a *durable power of attorney for health care*.

advance directive A legal document that specifies the life-sustaining medical treatments people wish to receive if they become terminally ill and unable to communicate their preferences.

In a **living will**, people provide directions about specific life-sustaining treatments they do or do not want to receive if they become incurably ill and their death is imminent. For example, a person might indicate that she would not want to have a feeding tube installed for the sole purpose of being kept alive if she developed a terminal condition and was expected to die very soon. On the other hand, she might indicate that she does want to receive medication to provide maximum pain relief, even if the medication hastens her death. Figure EP.2 provides an example of a living will.

living will A type of advance directive in which people provide directions about the specific life-sustaining treatments they do or do not want to receive if they become incurably ill and their death is imminent.

A second type of advance directive is a **durable power of attorney for health care**, which authorizes a specific person to make health care decisions on the terminally ill person's behalf. The person authorized to make health care decisions is called a **health care proxy**. For example, people often designate a spouse or an adult child as their proxy (Ditto et al., 2001). A potential advantage of a durable power of attorney for health care is its flexibility. It does not require all possible medical conditions and treatment preferences to be anticipated in advance. Instead, the health care proxy can talk with medical personnel when the need arises about the best course of action at that time. Such flexibility could be important because people's preferences regarding the medical treatments they wish to receive or to forgo are somewhat unstable (Ditto et al., 2003). A man initially might anticipate that he would not want to be given antibiotics in the final stage of a terminal illness just to be kept alive for a bit longer. Yet, some years later, his feelings might change, and he might regard this treatment option as acceptable. His living will would need to be updated regularly to reflect his changing preferences. A durable power of attorney for health care, in contrast, would not need to be updated so long as the health care proxy knew of the man's most current preferences.

durable power of attorney for health care A type of advance directive that authorizes a specific person (a health care proxy) to make a health care decision on the terminally ill person's behalf if the terminally ill person is unable to communicate his or her preferences.

health care proxy A person legally designated to make health care decisions on behalf of a terminally ill individual who is incapable of making his or health care preferences known. Sometimes called a *health care surrogate*.

That is the catch, however: health care proxies often do not accurately comprehend other people's preferences (Ditto et al., 2001; Moorman, Hauser, & Carr, 2009). In laboratory studies in which people have been asked to discuss their end-of-life treatment preferences with a family member, the family member's accuracy in reporting those preferences has been found to be low even immediately after the discussion (Ditto et al., 2001). Further research is needed to identify the timing and kinds of discussions that will improve family members' accuracy in understanding the treatment preferences of a loved one.

The purpose of advance directives is to avoid having health care decisions made in a vacuum, without clear knowledge of what the terminally ill person would have wanted. Yet several challenges exist in ensuring that advance directives serve this

Living Will Declaration

I, ______________, being of sound mind, willfully and voluntarily make this declaration to be followed if I become incompetent. This declaration reflects my firm and settled commitment to refuse life-sustaining treatment under the circumstances indicated below.

I direct my attending physician to withhold or withdraw life-sustaining treatment that serves only to prolong the process of my dying, if I should be in a terminal condition or in a state of permanent unconsciousness.

I direct that treatment be limited to measures to keep me comfortable and to relieve pain, including any pain that might occur by withholding or withdrawing life-sustaining treatment.

In addition, if I am in the condition described above, I feel especially strong about the following forms of treatment:

I ( ) do ( ) do not want cardiac resuscitation.

I ( ) do ( ) do not want mechanical respiration.

I ( ) do ( ) do not want tube feeding or any other artificial or invasive form of nutrition (food) or hydration (water).

I ( ) do ( ) do not want blood or blood products.

I ( ) do ( ) do not want any form of surgery or invasive diagnostic tests.

I ( ) do ( ) do not want kidney dialysis.

I ( ) do ( ) do not want antibiotics.

I realize that if I do not specifically indicate my preference regarding any of the forms of treatment listed above, I may receive that form of treatment.

Other instructions:

I ( ) do ( ) do not want to make an anatomical gift of all or part of my body, subject to the following limitations, if any:

I made this declaration on the ______________ day of (month, year)

Declarant's signature: ______________

Declarant's address: ______________

The declarant or the person on behalf of and at the direction of the declarant knowingly and voluntarily signed this writing by signature or mark in my presence.

Witness's signature: ______________

Witness's address: ______________

Witness's signature: ______________

Witness's address: ______________

FIGURE **EP.2**

A Sample Living Will.

A living will indicates medical treatments that a person does or does not wish to receive in the event of a terminal illness.

Source: Commonwealth of Pennsylvania—Act 169 of 2006.

purpose. First, many people do not have advanced directives in place. Nearly 95 percent of Americans have heard of a living will, but only 25 to 40 percent actually have a living will or durable power of attorney for health care (Eiser & Weiss, 2001; Harris Interactive, 2007; Pew Research Center, 2006). These figures are even lower for many ethnic minority groups and only slightly higher among seriously ill individuals (Ditto, 2006; Searight & Gafford, 2005).

Why do so few people take the steps to prepare an advance directive? The reasons can include the mistaken beliefs that advance directives are expensive and complicated and that they necessarily involve directions to "pull the plug" (Span, 2009). In fact, forms to complete living wills are widely available on the Internet, and they offer a full range of treatment preferences to be specified, from taking all reasonable actions to preserve the person's life to withholding particular kinds of treatments (Span, 2009). Some Americans do not prepare advance directives simply because they do not want to think about death, even though they can experience a catastrophic accident or develop an incurable illness at any age (Harris Interactive, 2007; Span, 2009).

Even when people have prepared advanced directives, additional steps need to be taken to ensure that the advanced directives are effective when the time comes. People need to review and update their advance directives periodically and talk with their health care proxies to make sure that any changes in their treatment preferences are known. It is also important for people to communicate the treatment preferences specified in their advanced directives to their physicians and other health care providers. Otherwise, patients' preferences may go unheeded. Physicians typically pursue aggressive treatment options unless instructed to do otherwise because their professional training directs them to try to prolong life and because they want to avoid being sued. However, family members experience considerable distress when a terminally ill loved one receives overly aggressive treatment against his or her wishes before dying (Lynn et al., 1997).

If the physician knows that a patient wants to forego life-sustaining treatments, the physician can write a **Do Not Resuscitate (DNR) order** in the patient's chart. A DNR order is an instruction from the physician to all medical personnel that no attempt should be made to resuscitate the patient if he or she experiences a cardiac or respiratory arrest. For example, a patient suffering from terminal kidney failure might have a DNR order written in her chart stating that no resuscitation should be attempted if she stops breathing or her heart stops beating. Yet here, too, challenges exist in insuring that the patients' wishes are actually implemented. In one study, fewer than half of patients who preferred not to be resuscitated in the event of a cardiac or respiratory arrest actually had DNR orders entered into their medical charts (Knaus et al., 1995).

Do Not Resuscitate (DNR) order An order from a physician to all medical personnel that no attempt should be made to resuscitate the patient if he or she experiences a cardiac or respiratory arrest.

Determining the Timing of Death: The Right to Die

People sometimes want to determine not only the kind of medical care they receive at the end of life but also the timing of their death. The desire to hasten the end of life most often arises when a terminally ill patient's pain and suffering cannot be alleviated with medication or when the patient is in a persistent vegetative state, being kept alive only with life-support equipment. Patients or their designated health care proxies may conclude that the patient's quality of life is so low in such circumstances that it would be preferable to die rather than to continue living. **Euthanasia** refers to the intentional act of ending a terminally ill person's life to spare the person from further suffering (Kastenbaum, 2007). The term "euthanasia" is Greek, where its original meaning was "good or easy death" (Reich, 1978).

euthanasia The intentional act of ending a terminally ill person's life to spare the person from further suffering.

Euthanasia can take several different forms. **Passive euthanasia** refers to withholding medical treatment that would prolong life. For example, with the consent of the patient or health care proxy, a physician might remove a feeding tube or turn off a respirator that has been keeping the patient alive. A physician also might administer a very large dose of morphine or other medication to control the patient's pain, even

passive euthanasia Withholding or discontinuing medical treatment that would prolong a terminally ill individual's life, for example, removing a feeding tube or respirator that has been keeping the patient alive.

though such medication often suppresses breathing and hastens death. Passive euthanasia is legal in a number of countries. Even where it is illegal, it is widely practiced and generally accepted when doctors and patients (or their health care proxies) jointly reach the decision that the patient's condition is hopeless and that ending the patient's suffering is the highest priority. (Advanced directives essentially are the patient's prior authorization for the physician to perform passive euthanasia in certain circumstances.)

active euthanasia Actions that deliberately induce death in a terminally ill individual (for example, giving the individual a lethal injection).

Active euthanasia refers to actions that deliberately induce death. For example, a physician might give a terminally ill patient a lethal injection. Some experts question the distinction between passive and active euthanasia, arguing that any steps taken that end a person's life are, in some sense, active (Garrard & Wilkinson, 2005; Gesang, 2008). In their view, no meaningful difference exists between removing a feeding tube and giving a lethal injection (Orentlicher, 1996). Active euthanasia is illegal in most countries, including the United States. It is legal, however, in a few countries, such as the Netherlands and Belgium. The Netherlands had tolerated the practice of active euthanasia (by not prosecuting physicians) for 20 to 30 years before legalizing it in 2002. Today, active euthanasia is legal in the Netherlands for patients experiencing protracted, severe suffering that cannot be alleviated with medical treatments. Patients must discuss their request for euthanasia with their primary physician multiple times, and another physician must independently confirm that the patient's suffering is unbearable and cannot be managed medically.

An example illustrates how the decision to pursue euthanasia might be negotiated by patients and their physicians (Daley, 2000):

> When surgery showed that Dr. Henk Laane's 77-year-old patient, a woman who had been in his care for more than a decade, was riddled with cancer, she immediately asked him to help her die. At first, Dr. Laane said no. There was no unbearable suffering yet, he argued. There were still some good times ahead. But when several months had passed and she was in the grip of chronic diarrhea and nausea, so much so that not an hour went by uninterrupted, Dr. Laane finally agreed to help.
>
> She wanted to die on her birthday and gathered her family around her at home. She had traditional Dutch bon voyage cakes ready for the doctor and his nurse and she asked that they eat the cakes first. Then, with everyone gathered at her bedside, Dr. Laane gave her an injection.
>
> "It is never easy to help someone die," said Dr. Laane, a month later. "You take it with you."

Approximately 3 percent of deaths in the Netherlands involve active euthanasia or physician-assisted dying (van der Mass et al., 1996). When the law legalizing euthanasia was passed, concerns were voiced that it could lead to a "slippery slope," in which the practice of euthanasia could be extended to groups for which it was never intended, such as physically or mentally disabled individuals. Researchers who have examined the available data have found little evidence of this, however (Battin, van der Heide, Ganzini, van der Wal, & Onwuteaka-Philipsen, 2007; van Delden, 1999). Dutch physicians do not approve all requests for euthanasia and, in fact, appear to practice active euthanasia only as a last resort. Yet some critics charge that active euthanasia has been extended inappropriately to people suffering from psychological, rather than physical, illness and to people suffering from chronic, but not terminal, illness (Jochemsen & Keown, 1999).

physician-assisted dying The practice of physicians helping terminally ill patients bring about their own death by prescribing a lethal dose of medication or toxic gas that the patients self-administer; similar to active euthanasia except that the patient, rather than someone else, performs the action that causes death. Sometimes called *physician-assisted suicide*.

Another form of euthanasia is **physician-assisted dying**. This refers to the practice of physicians helping terminally ill patients bring about their own death by prescribing a lethal dose of medication or toxic gas that the patients self-administer. It is similar to active euthanasia except that the patient, rather than someone else, performs the action that causes death. This form of euthanasia is sometimes called *physician-assisted suicide*, but some experts prefer the term *physician-assisted dying* because, unlike healthy people who commit suicide, terminally ill people are not forsaking life and would prefer to live if effective treatments were available. Physician-assisted dying is legal in several European countries—including Belgium, Germany, the Netherlands, and Switzerland—but it is largely illegal elsewhere. Two exceptions in the United States are Oregon, which passed the Death with Dignity Act in 1991, and Washington, which passed similar legislation in 2008. Because the Oregon law has been in effect longer, let's examine what lessons can be drawn from experiences with that law.

The Oregon law allows mentally competent patients who have been advised by their doctors that they have 6 months or less to live to request a lethal prescription of a drug. The law builds in several safeguards to ensure that the request is serious and entirely voluntary and that other alternatives have been considered. The patient is required to make two requests to his or her physician 15 days apart; one of the requests must be witnessed by two other people to ensure it was voluntary; the physician must inform the patient of alternatives; and two physicians must independently confirm that the patient has only 6 months to live, is mentally competent, and is not depressed (Oregon Department of Human Services, n.d.).

The Oregon law has withstood several legal challenges since it was passed, and by 2008, 401 terminally ill patients had received a physician's assistance to end their own lives (Oregon Department of Human Services, 2009a). Physicians do not routinely approve the requests they receive for physician-assisted dying, however. In a 2-year study conducted shortly after the law went into effect, physicians were found to have approved only one-sixth of the requests they received (Ganzini et al., 2000). In addition, approximately half of the patients whose requests were approved changed their minds before receiving the lethal drug. Patients who received more help with management of their pain and emotional needs were especially likely to have changed their mind about their request for physician-assisted dying.

Other patients do follow through on their requests, however, and go on to end their own lives with a physician's assistance. The reasons why such patients want to end their lives often reflect the specific concerns they are experiencing (Ganzini, Goy, & Dobscha, 2008; Sullivan, Hedberg, & Fleming, 2000). The concerns of terminally ill patients who later experienced a physician-assisted death in Oregon are shown in Table EP.1. Paramount to these patients were concerns about the loss of autonomy and dignity, poor quality of life, and the loss of control of bodily functions.

TABLE **EP.1** End-of-Life Concerns of Terminally Ill Individuals Who Experienced a Physician-Assisted Death

END-OF-LIFE CONCERNS	PERCENT
Losing autonomy	89.9
Less able to engage in activities making life enjoyable	87.4
Loss of dignity	83.8
Losing control of body functions	58.7
Burden on family, friends/caregivers	38.3
Inadequate pain control or concern about it	23.9
Financial implications of treatment	2.8

Note: Figures shown are based on 401 terminally ill individuals who experienced a physician-assisted death under the Death with Dignity Act in Oregon from 1998 to 2008.

Source: Oregon Department of Human Services (2009b, March). Table 1: Characteristics and end-of-life care of 401 DWDA patients who died after ingesting a lethal dose of medication, by year, Oregon, 1998–2008. Retrieved April 2, 2010 from http://www.oregon.gov/DHS/ph/pas/docs/yr11-tbl-1.pdf

The Oregon law legalizing physician-assisted dying continues to be studied, but the research conducted so far has revealed little evidence of abuse (Hedberg, Hopkins, Leman, & Kohn, 2009). Like physicians in the Netherlands, physicians in Oregon appear to be reluctant to use this option. The safeguards incorporated in the Death with Dignity Act in Oregon appear to be working well, and terminally ill patients derive comfort from knowing that the option of physician-assisted dying is available to them if they need it at some point (Cerminara & Perez, 2000; Hedberg, Hopkins, & Kohn, 2003; Orentlicher, 2000).

New concerns about the possibility of a "slippery slope" with physician-assisted suicide were stirred in 2009, however, by a highly publicized case in Switzerland (Asthana, 2009). The case involved the joint physician-assisted deaths of a famous British conductor, 85-year old Edward Downes, and his 74-year old wife, Joan, who was terminally ill with cancer and was expected to die within a few months. After 54 years of marriage, Edward felt that he could not face the prospect of living without his wife. People close to the couple described them as deeply devoted to each other and very much in love, and together, they made the decision to die at the same time. The couple traveled from London (where physician-assisted dying is illegal) to Switzerland, and with their adult children present, swallowed lethal doses of a drug prescribed by a Swiss physician. The couple died within minutes, holding hands.

This case made international headlines because Edward was not terminally ill, although he did suffer from health problems, including blindness and hearing loss. Critics felt that it was wrong for the husband to have been helped by a physician to end his life when he did not meet the standard criteria. But the couple's children defended their parents' decision. The couple's daughter said of her father, "He didn't have a terminal illness, but without my mother his life would have been unbearable—he would have been utterly miserable." She added that her parents' death was "calm and dignified—as they wanted. . . . I will always know that they had a peaceful death—together." In support of the couple's decision, some experts argue that either mental *or* physical suffering should be a legitimate basis for requesting physician-assisted suicide. What is your opinion—was the physician justified in helping this couple to die together?

Perhaps you can understand why euthanasia is such a controversial topic, with strong views voiced for and against it. Those who support euthanasia argue that terminally ill patients have the right to make their own decisions about whether they wish to continue living when terminal illness has diminished the quality of their life (Quill & Battin, 2004). Proponents also argue that euthanasia is the most compassionate option for terminally ill patients who are suffering severe pain and that physicians have an obligation to help end terminally ill patients' suffering, even if doing so hastens the patient's death (Ardelt, 2003). Opponents of euthanasia, in contrast, argue that taking a life is morally wrong under any circumstance and that physicians have an obligation to preserve life, not to end it. Strong opposition also stems from the concern that safeguards may be inadequate to prevent euthanasia from being involuntary. Opponents worry, for example, that disadvantaged groups, such as the very poor or the elderly might be tempted to end their lives to contain health care costs, or those with mental or physical disabilities could be pressured into requesting physician-assisted dying (Ardelt, 2003; George, Finlay, Jeffrey, 2005). Opponents of euthanasia also point out that terminally ill patients could be misdiagnosed, or that effective treatments could become available at some point (Lynn et al., 1997). Finally, opponents of euthanasia point out that people who are terminally ill frequently suffer from depression, and treatment of their depression might make them more inclined to want to continue living (O'Mahony et al., 2005).

Debates about the morality and legality of euthanasia are likely to continue, although public support is growing for at least some forms of euthanasia, such as passive euthanasia for terminally ill individuals who are suffering from severe and persistent pain (Dickens, Boyle, & Ganzini, 2008; Quill & Battin, 2004). In a recent survey of 1,500 Americans, 70 percent felt that there are circumstances in which patients should have the right to die. Support for withdrawing medical treatment (passive euthanasia) was much greater than support for physician-assisted dying (Pew Research Center, 2006). Even as public support for euthanasia is increasing, some experts predict that requests for euthanasia will become less common as the care of dying individuals improves. We explore the care of dying individuals later, but we first discuss the experience of dying because it is important to understand the needs of dying individuals before we can consider what kind of care is best. (For a summary of this section, see "Interim Summary EP.3: Choices and Decisions at the End of Life.")

INTERIM SUMMARY **EP.3**

Choices and Decisions at the End of Life

Determining Medical Care at the End of Life: Advanced Directives	■ An **advance directive** is a legal document that specifies the life-sustaining medical treatments people wish to receive should they become terminally ill and unable to communicate their preferences. ■ A common type of advance directive, a **living will**, provides directions about specific life-sustaining treatments people do or do not want to receive if they become incurably ill and their death is imminent. ■ Another common type of advance directive, a **durable power of attorney for health care**, authorizes a specific person (a **health care proxy**) to make a health care decision on the terminally ill person's behalf.
Determining the Timing of Death: The Right to Die	■ **Euthanasia** (**passive** or **active**) refers to the intentional act of ending a terminally ill person's life to spare the person from further suffering. ■ **Physician-assisted dying** refers to the practice of physicians helping terminally ill patients bring about their own death by prescribing a lethal dose of medication or toxic gas that the patients self-administer. ■ Euthanasia is a controversial topic, with strong views voiced for and against it.

THE EXPERIENCE OF DYING

As we noted earlier, for some people, the process of dying occurs suddenly, in response to a catastrophic injury or health event (such as a heart attack or massive stroke). For these individuals, death may come so quickly that they have little awareness that they are dying and little time to process the experience. For other individuals, the process of dying unfolds over a longer period of time, from days or weeks to many months.

What is the experience of dying like for terminally ill individuals who know that their death is expected to occur in the near future? Not so long ago, little was known about the subjective experience of dying because the topic of death was taboo. Health care providers and family members often did not feel it was appropriate to talk to dying individuals about their feelings and concerns. It was fairly common even for physicians to conceal terminal diagnoses from patients, based on the belief that the information would be needlessly upsetting (Oken, 1961; Surbone, 2006).

Changes in the way health care providers and others interact with dying patients did not really come about until after the 1960s, following the publication of a groundbreaking book, *On Death and Dying*, by Elizabeth Kubler-Ross (1969). Dr. Kubler-Ross worked as a psychiatrist at a large hospital in Chicago in the 1960s, and she became convinced that the emotional needs of dying patients were being neglected. Over the objections of her fellow physicians, she began conducting interviews with terminally ill patients. To the surprise of her colleagues, the patients were grateful for the opportunity to talk about what they were experiencing, and most knew they were dying even when their terminal prognosis had been hidden from them. Based on more than 200 interviews, Kubler-Ross observed that dying patients tend to experience a sequence of different emotional reactions as they struggle to come to grips with their impending death. She believed that people experience five **stages of dying**:

stages of dying Five different kinds of emotional reactions that Elizabeth Kubler-Ross believed dying individuals experience as they struggle to come to grips with their impending death; the stages she identified are denial, anger, bargaining, depression, and acceptance.

- *Denial*—"Not me." In the denial stage, people react to the diagnosis of a terminal condition with shock and disbelief, leading some to question the accuracy of the diagnosis or to seek an alternative diagnosis from another physician.
- *Anger*—"It's not fair." When efforts to deny the terminal condition fail, people experience anger, feeling that it is unfair to be dying while others get to continue living. During this anger stage, people may express hostility or even resentment toward their family members, friends, and health care providers.
- *Bargaining*—"If you just give me more time, I promise to . . ." In the bargaining stage, patients understand that they are dying, but they try to extend the time they have to live by striking a deal with God. For example, they may promise to be better parents, to do charity work, or to attend religious services more faithfully if death can be postponed. Kubler-Ross (1969) described a woman who pleaded with God to let her live long enough to attend her oldest son's wedding. The woman left the hospital on the day of the wedding looking radiant. Kubler-Ross commented, "Nobody would have believed her real condition. I wondered what her reaction would be when the time was out for which she had bargained. I will never forget the moment she returned to the hospital. She looked tired and somewhat exhausted and before I could say hello, said 'Now, don't forget, I have another son.'" (p. 83).
- *Depression*—When the hope of bargaining for more time passes, dying people experience a fourth stage, depression. In this stage, the inevitability of impending death leads to deep feelings of loss and sadness.
- *Acceptance*—"I'm ready." Eventually, depression gives way to the fifth stage, acceptance. In this stage, the person is willing to face the reality of death and no longer struggles against it. Dying people are often quite weak at this point, and they may withdraw from all but their closest family members, friends, and caregivers. Kubler-Ross described the acceptance stage as similar to a final period of rest just before death comes.

Getty Images

According to Kubler-Ross, in the fifth stage of dying—acceptance—terminally ill people are willing to face the reality of death and no longer struggle against it.

Do dying people experience these five stages of emotional reactions in the sequence proposed by Kubler-Ross? She cautioned that not *all* dying people experience each of these stages or progress through the stages in exactly the same sequence. Her theory has sometimes been misinterpreted, though, to mean that terminally ill individuals *should* experience the exact sequence of emotional reactions outlined in her book. Health care providers, counselors, and family members have sometimes tried to push dying individuals through the sequence of stages in Kubler-Ross's theory, or, worse, have been judgmental of the way dying persons were coping if their reactions did not conform to the theory (Corr, 1993). Although Kubler-Ross did feel that dying people often experience these emotions in the order identified in her theory, she did not view the sequence as inevitable or inherently superior to other ways of experiencing the dying process. Her goal was not to prescribe how dying people *should* cope with their dying but, instead, to describe common aspects of the experience and, above all, to encourage health care professionals and family members to talk openly with dying people about their thoughts, feelings, and needs.

Critics have noted that not everyone reacts with shock and disbelief to a terminal diagnosis. Kubler-Ross conducted many of her interviews with young and middle-aged individuals, and such reactions are less likely to occur among older people (Retsinas, 1988). Older people are more likely to think about the inevitability of death as they see friends and loved ones die and as they experience physical declines and health problems that make their own mortality salient. Critics also note that dying people often cycle in and out of different emotional reactions, such as denial and anger, or may experience a mix of different emotions at the same time (Copp, 1998). Some terminally ill individuals, moreover, never reach the stage of acceptance, dying instead with great anxiety or depression. Other critics have noted that dying people may experience emotional reactions not included in Kubler-Ross's theory, such as hope, spiritual renewal, altruistic feelings, or yearnings for increased closeness with others (Groopman, 2005; Kastenbaum, 2007).

How people experience the process of dying is also influenced by the duration and symptoms of their illness, their personalities, their social support, and their beliefs about what happens after death (Carver & Scheier, 2002; Hayslip & Peveto, 2005; Stroebe, Stroebe, & Hansson, 1993). Highly religious individuals, for example, appear to be buffered somewhat from the emotional distress associated with dying, due to their beliefs in the existence of a stage of life after death (Wink & Scott, 2005).

Although Kubler-Ross was not able to take into account all of these sources of variability in the experience of dying, an enduring legacy of her pioneering work is that it stimulated a radical shift in the past 40 years in our understanding of how best to meet the emotional and physical needs of dying people. Terminal diagnoses are much less likely to be withheld from patients, and patients have more opportunities to make their needs and concerns known to others. As death has emerged from the shadows—no longer a taboo topic—traditional models of caring for dying persons have begun to be replaced or supplemented by new models of care. (For a summary of this section, see "Interim Summary EP.4: The Experience of Dying.")

INTERIM SUMMARY **EP.4**

The Experience of Dying

- Elizabeth Kubler-Ross believed that many people experience five **stages of dying**: denial, anger, bargaining, depression, and acceptance. Not all people experience these stages, some experience them in a different order, and some experiences other stages as well.
- How people experience dying is influenced by the duration and symptoms of their illness, their personalities, their social support, and their beliefs about what happens after death.

CARING FOR DYING PERSONS

Most people who die in the United States do so in a hospital or nursing home. Although surveys indicate that Americans overwhelmingly prefer to die at home, only about 25 percent will do so, with another 50 percent dying in hospitals and 25 percent dying in nursing homes (Gruneir et al., 2007; Plonk & Arnold, 2005). What kind of care is best for dying individuals? Answering this question requires an understanding of the unique needs and concerns of the dying and their family members (Emanuel, Bennett, & Richardson, 2007). Dying individuals need to have opportunities to talk openly about their concerns and the range of emotions they may be feeling without fear of being judged or dismissed by others (Chochinov, 2006). They need help managing pain and other physical discomfort (e.g., fatigue, difficulty breathing, nausea), and some need help with depression or anxiety. They also need companionship and social support because the process of dying can make a person feel lonely and isolated (Rokach, Matalon, Safarov, & Bercovitch, 2007). Dying individuals often want to avoid burdening their family members with their care, and they want to leave their personal affairs—such as their finances, insurance arrangements for their family, arrangements for the care of pets, plans for the disposition of their property—in good order (Munn et al., 2008).

The family members of dying individuals also have needs that should be considered. Family members need support for the emotional distress and caregiving burdens they experience during the patient's illness and, later, the feelings of grief they experience after the patient has died (Kehl, 2006). Family members are very upset when they see loved ones suffer from persistent pain, which makes pain management an important goal for patients and family members alike.

If the needs of dying patients and their family members are met, they are more likely to consider the death, when it comes, to be a "good death." This concept of a good death (sometimes referred to as a decent or appropriate death) arose in the 1960s and 1970s when euthanasia first began to be discussed and debated (Kehl, 2006). (Recall that the Greek meaning of the term *euthanasia* is "good or easy death.") The concept of the **good death** was later expanded to refer to a process of dying that makes patients as comfortable as possible, treats patients with dignity, provides social support for patients and their family members, and helps patients achieve closure and prepare for death (Kehl, 2006; Munn et al., 2008). Today, ideas about what constitutes a good death help guide practitioners who work with dying individuals and also help researchers evaluate the quality of care for dying individuals (Kehl, 2006).

good death A process of dying that makes patients as comfortable as possible, treats patients with dignity, provides social support for patients and their family members, and helps patients achieve closure and prepare for death.

Care of the Dying in Hospitals

Hospitals generally are not well suited to meeting the needs of dying individuals and their family members (Plonk & Arnold, 2005). Hospitals tend to be large, impersonal environments organized to function as efficiently as possible in delivering medical treatments to save lives. Even though hospital staff may be compassionate, they seldom have adequate time to spend with dying patients, listening to their concerns and providing comfort. In addition, hospital staff may need to maintain some emotional distance from terminally ill patients to limit the distress they would otherwise experience with each death. For these reasons, dying patients who receive traditional hospital care frequently have significant unmet needs (Plonk & Arnold, 2005). Family members often report that the patient's pain is not adequately managed, that hospital staff provide little emotional support and do not treat the patient with respect, that physician's contact with the patient is too limited, and that communication with the hospital staff is problematic (Plonk & Arnold, 2005).

Care of the Dying in Hospice Programs

Recognition of the limitations of hospital care has led to the development of new approaches to care for people with life-threatening or terminal illnesses. **Palliative care** refers to care designed to improve the quality of life for patients with a *life-threatening* (but *not necessarily terminal*) illness by providing relief from physical discomfort along with emotional support for patients and their family members during and after treatment (Haley, Larson, Kasl-Godley, Neimeyer, & Kwilosz, 2003; World Health Organization [WHO], n.d.). Palliative care can be administered at any point after a patient has been diagnosed with a life-threatening illness (National Hospice and Palliative Care Organization, n.d.); patients receiving palliative care may continue to receive treatments aimed at curing the illness.

palliative care Care designed to improve the quality of life for patients with *life-threatening* (but *not necessarily terminal*) illnesses by providing relief from physical discomfort and emotional support for patients and their family members during and after treatment.

Hospice care is a special type of palliative care for patients with a terminal illness who have less than 6 months to live; patients receiving hospice care forego curative treatments (Haley et al., 2003). Hospice care includes a range of services provided by an interdisciplinary team of nurses, doctors, social workers, counselors, and others who work together to:

- manage the dying person's pain and other discomfort;
- show respect for the patient's needs, concerns, and personal priorities;
- provide support for the patient and his or her family; and
- help the patient prepare for impending death (Chochinov, 2006; Haley et al., 2003).

hospice care A special type of palliative care for terminally ill patients who have less than 6 months to live and who are no longer receiving curative treatments; involves a range of services that can include managing the dying person's pain and other discomfort, showing respect for the patient's needs and concerns, providing support for the patient and his or her family, and helping the patient prepare for impending death.

Hospice care can be provided on an inpatient basis in a hospice facility or on an outpatient basis in a home environment (National Hospice and Palliative Care Organization, n.d.). Home-based hospice programs have become much more common in recent years. Some of the services available through hospice programs include nursing care, physician services to manage pain and other symptoms, homemaking services, counseling, and bereavement services for family members. Which services patients receive depends on their medical status and personal preferences.

Hospice programs emphasize the importance of providing care to family members as well as patients (Saunders, 2000). Family members receive support and guidance in their efforts to care for the dying person, especially if the person is being cared for at home. They also receive emotional support through the patient's terminal illness and beyond, through the period of bereavement after the patient has died (Haley et al., 2003).

Hospice care first emerged in the 1960s, when Cicely Saunders, a British social worker who was working in hospitals in London, recognized that many terminally ill patients had significant unmet needs for comfort and emotional support. Her efforts led to the founding of the first hospice in 1967, St. Christopher's Hospice (Chochinov, 2006). This model of care has grown rapidly in the intervening years, extending to many different countries. Hospice care first became available in the United States in 1974 and expanded considerably after it was funded by Medicare in 1983.

Today, approximately 20 percent of Americans die in hospice care, although you'll see later that hospice care is not equally accessible to all who might need it (Krakauer, Crenner & Fox, 2002; Plonk & Arnold, 2005). In the United States, patients receive hospice care, on average, for 22 days (Plonk & Arnold, 2005). About one-third of patients die within a week of enrolling in hospice care; few (only about 7 percent) live more than 6 months after enrolling (Plonk & Arnold, 2005). Common conditions for which people receive hospice care include cancer, AIDS, congestive heart failure, and progressive neurological disorders (Haley et al., 2003). The majority of hospice patients are elderly, although hospice programs for children and young adults are becoming more widely available (Martinson, 1993).

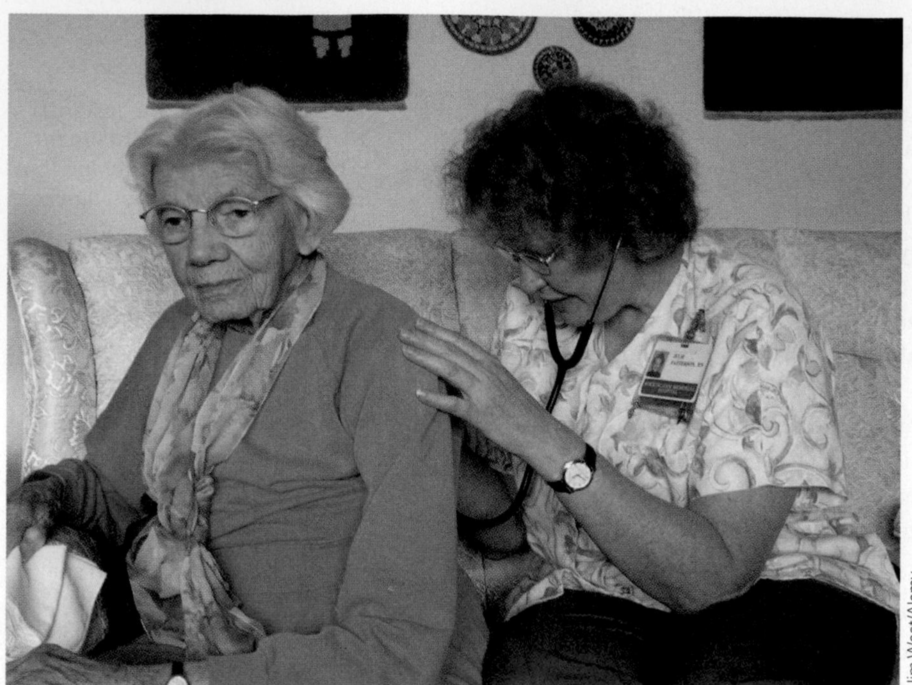

Hospice care can help meet the physical and psychological needs of dying individuals.

As you can see, the mission of hospice care is fundamentally different from that of hospital care—it emphasizes *comfort* rather than *cure* at the end of life (Chochinov, 2006; Haley et al., 2003). How effective is hospice care compared to hospital care? Studies that formally compare hospice care and traditional forms of care are relatively scarce. But existing studies suggest that hospice care does provide distinct benefits. Terminally ill patients appear to be more satisfied with hospice care than with traditional hospital care (Addington-Hall & O'Callaghan, 2009; Follwell et al., 2009). Family members whose loved ones received hospice care report greater satisfaction with the loved one's quality of life during the last stage of the terminal illness, and the family members also adjust better psychologically after the loved one dies (Bradley et al., 2004). Hospice care tends to be more beneficial to patients and their families if it is initiated relatively early in the terminal phase of the patient's illness. Some dying individuals, unfortunately, receive hospice care too close to the time of their death to benefit (Teno et al., 2007).

Other dying individuals face barriers to adequate care at the end of life. Members of ethnic minority groups, in particular, receive poorer quality of care at the end of life, mirroring the poorer quality of medical care they receive over the course of their lives (Krakaueret al., 2002). In a large study of end-of-life care in five major medical centers, significantly fewer resources were used to care for gravely ill African Americans (Borum, Lynn, & Zhong, 2000). Older minority patients are less likely to receive pain medication for conditions such as cancer, and many pharmacies in non-white neighborhoods lack sufficient supplies of pain medication to meet the needs of patients with severe pain (Krakauer et al., 2002). The rate of hospice care is 40 percent lower among African Americans than among Caucasians (Greiner, Perera, & Ahluwalia, 2003). Additionally, as noted earlier, members of ethnic minority groups are less likely to have advance directives in place, which may compromise the care they receive at the end of life (Krakauer et al., 2002). Addressing barriers to high-quality end-of-life care for ethnic minority groups is an important priority.

Delivering end-of-life care in ways that are responsive to cultural values and preferences is also important. The models of care for the dying that we have discussed may not be suitable in all cultures. In some cultures, for example, talking to dying people about their experiences would be considered highly inappropriate (Long, 2004). Similarly, some groups, such as Korean Americans and Mexican Americans, favor disclosing a patient's condition only to the family, and not to the patient—a preference opposite to that generally favored by Caucasians (Krakauer et al., 2002). Health care providers and others who do not understand such cultural variations could inadvertently make the process of dying more, rather than less, distressing (Krakauer et al., 2002). The United States is becoming more culturally diverse, and culturally sensitive care will be more important than ever to help terminally ill patients and their family members navigate life's final passage (Greiner et al., 2003; Krakauer et al., 2002; Searight & Gafford, 2005). (For a summary of this section, see "Interim Summary EP.5: Caring for Dying Persons.")

INTERIM SUMMARY EP.5

Caring for Dying Persons	
	■ Dying people often need to talk about their concerns and emotions; need help managing physical pain, discomfort, depression, and anxiety; need social support; and often want to avoid burdening their family members with their care. ■ If the needs of dying patients and their family members are met, they are more likely to consider the death to be a **good death**.
Care of the Dying in Hospitals	■ Hospitals are not usually well suited to meeting the needs of dying people and their families.
Care of the Dying in Hospice Programs	■ **Palliative care** refers to care designed to improve the quality of life for patients with a *life-threatening* (but *not necessarily terminal*) illness. ■ **Hospice care** is a special type of palliative care for patients with a terminal illness who have less than 6 months to live. These programs provide care to family members as well as patients. ■ Members of ethnic minority groups receive poorer quality care at the end of life, mirroring the poorer-quality medical care they receive over the course of their lives. ■ Models of care for the dying in Western countries may not be suitable in all cultures.

LOSING A LOVED ONE

Death ends the suffering of a dying person, but not those left behind. Surviving family members and friends may experience intense anguish after a loved one dies. In earlier chapters we discussed the impact of losing a parent or spouse. Here we extend that discussion to take a closer look at how people are affected by **bereavement**, or the objective loss of a loved one.

bereavement The objective experience of having lost a loved one.

In the period immediately following the loss of a loved one, people often experience sorrow, intense yeaning for the loved one, anxiety, guilt, or other painful emotions (Bonanno et al., 2004). Some may experience shock or numbness (Parkes, 1972, 1998; Zisook & Shuchter, 1993). The painful emotional responses to the loss of a loved one are referred to as **grief**. Grief can vary over time and from one person to the next. For many bereaved individuals, initial feelings of grief gradually subside and become more manageable (Bonanno et al., 2004). They learn to live with the loss, even if they never truly get over it (Kastenbaum, 2007). As much as 20 years after the death of their spouse, surviving spouses report that they still think about their former spouses every week or two (Carnelley, Wortman, Bolger, & Burke, 2006). Yet within a few years of the spouse's death, many bereaved individuals are no more emotionally distressed than nonbereaved individuals (Bonanno et al., 2004; Stroebe, Stroebe, & Schut, 2001; Zisook & Shuchter, 1993; See Figure 18.3 in Chapter 18).

grief The painful emotional responses to the loss of a loved one.

Overcoming grief can be more difficult, however, for people who experience an unexpected loss, such as the death of a child. Parents expect to outlive their children, and a child's death profoundly upsets their sense of the natural order and robs them of the future they had envisioned for their child (Rubin & Malkinson, 2001). Grief may be more intense and more long-lasting when people must cope with the death of a loved one that is unexpected and untimely (Bonanno et al., 2004). This is a reminder that off-time events often present greater adjustment challenges.

Mourning practices in many cultures, like these preparations for a *puja* ceremony in India, assist bereaved individuals with the grieving process and the transition to a new identity, show respect for the deceased person, and reaffirm social bonds in the community.

dual process model of coping with bereavement A theoretical model that specifies that bereaved individuals need to cope not only with their feelings of sorrow but also with the changed realities of their daily lives; the latter might involve assuming responsibilities previously performed by the deceased loved one and adjusting to a new identity (such as the identity of widow or widower).

mourning The manner in which a person expresses grief, often shaped by cultural practices.

Adjusting to the death of a loved requires bereaved individuals to focus on two key tasks, according to the **dual process model of coping with bereavement** (Stroebe & Schut, 1999): coping with their feelings of loss and coping with the changed realities of their daily lives. A widower, for example, needs to cope not only with his feelings of sorrow but also with day-to-day tasks that his wife once performed, from household tasks to organizing gatherings with friends and relatives. He may also need to adjust his identity to the new reality that he can no longer enact the role of husband (Lofland, 1982). Bereaved individuals who are able to engage in both kinds of coping are likely to adjust more successfully over time (Stroebe & Schut, 1999).

Mourning refers to the manner in which a person expresses grief, and it is often shaped by cultural practices (Lobar, Youngblut, Brooten, & Themes, 2006; Stroebe, Stroebe, & Hansson, 1993). Wearing black clothing, lighting special candles, establishing an altar in remembrance of the deceased person, and visiting the deceased individual's grave are common practices. Funerals, memorial services, and other mourning practices in many cultures are designed to acknowledge and help guide the bereaved individual's grieving process, facilitate the individual's transition to a new identity (e.g., from husband to widower), show respect for the deceased individual, and reaffirm social bonds in the community (Lobar et al., 2006; Osterweis, Solomon, & Morris, 1984).

Helping the Bereaved

Friends and family members can help bereaved individuals through the process of grief and mourning by being willing to discuss their feelings and listen to their concerns (Stylianos & Vachon, 1993). People often find such discussions to be uncomfortable and, as a result, they inadvertently discourage bereaved individuals from talking about their feelings, or their discomfort can lead them to offer clumsy advice (Lehman, Ellard, & Wortman, 1986). It can be more helpful just to show an interest in the bereaved person's experiences and listen sympathetically without feeling the need to offer advice (Parkes, 1998; Stylianos & Vachon, 1993).

Bereaved children may have special needs. Young children have some understanding of death, and by age 9 or 10 most children realize that death is a permanent state and that a dead person no longer has thoughts or feelings (Kenyon, 2001). Compared to adults, though, children generally have much less experience with loss and less well-developed coping abilities. Children who lose a parent or other loved one may experience not only tearfulness and feelings of sadness but also feelings of guilt or responsibility for the death and anxiety about who will care for them (Worden, 1996). Some bereaved children may develop sleeping problems, stomachaches, or other physical symptoms, or may become especially dependent on other family members. Adults can help children cope with bereavement by (Kastenbaum, 2007; Worden, 1996):

- being honest with them (acknowledging the reality of the death rather than referring to the deceased person as sleeping or having gone away);
- encouraging them to express their feelings (by talking or through drawings or play);

- recognizing that grief may be expressed in a variety of ways (helping them deal with feelings and worries that may be causing physical symptoms or unusual behavior);
- providing reassurance and comfort (letting them know others will continue to love and care for them; assuring them that they were not responsible for the death); and
- giving them an age-appropriate book to read about coping with loss.

The deaths of loved ones and one's own dying are inevitable aspects of the human experience. They may stir deep feelings of sadness and test our coping resources to the limit. Yet the bereaved and the dying often discover strengths in themselves, find meaning in the lives that were lived, and embrace opportunities to affirm their relationships with those who live on (Bonanno, 2004; Emanuel, Bennett, & Richardson, 2007; Parkes, 1998). Even in the midst of sorrow and loss, the remarkable human capacity for growth can be seen. (For a summary of this section, see "Interim Summary EP.6: Losing a Loved One.")

INTERIM SUMMARY **EP.6**

Losing a Loved One

	■ People are affected by **bereavement**, or the objective loss of a loved one, in different ways, although feelings of **grief** are common.
	■ According to the **dual process model of coping with bereavement**, adjusting to the death of a loved requires two tasks: coping with feelings of loss and coping with the changed realities of one's daily life.
	■ **Mourning** refers to the manner in which a person expresses grief, and it is often shaped by cultural practices.
Helping the Bereaved	■ Helping bereaved individuals often involves sympathetic listening, honesty, and reassurance and comfort.

SUMMING UP AND FINAL THOUGHTS

Death is an inevitable and universal aspect of human development, although how we regard death, how we treat the dying, and, ultimately, how we experience the dying process ourselves are shaped by the historical and cultural contexts in which we lead our lives. Changes in the leading causes of death and advances in medicine in developed countries have lengthened the dying process and created challenges in understanding when that process ends—culminating in death. These changes have sparked medical, legal, and ethical debates that will continue into the future about our right to determine the health care we receive at the end of life and perhaps even the timing of our deaths. As public awareness of questions about death and dying has grown, so too has recognition of the value of learning about the subjective experience of dying. Discussing the experience of dying is no longer taboo, and strides in understanding the unique needs of dying individuals have paved the way for the development of new approaches to caring for the dying. How bereaved individuals adapt to the death of a loved one, and how we can help rather than hinder their adjustment to the loss, are also coming to be understood.

We recognize that death can be an uncomfortable topic to consider, yet it can also be a great educator. Dying people who know that their time is limited often say that this knowledge spurs them to find a deeper sense of meaning and purpose in life—savoring their time with family members and other loved ones, and finding something to appreciate each day. Randy Pausch, a professor of computer science at Carnegie-Mellon who was diagnosed with terminal pancreatic cancer at age 46, captured worldwide interest when he gave a "Last Lecture" about his experience to a packed auditorium in 2007. Professors are sometimes asked to imagine that they have one last lecture to give in order to find out what they regard as the most important information to relay to their students. For Randy Pausch, imagination was not necessary because this truly would be his last lecture. The themes from his lecture were later compiled in a book, and one of them was gratitude—not for his disease, but for the sense of purpose it lent to the final chapter of his life:

> Many cancer patients say their illness gives them a new and deeper appreciation of life. Some even say they are grateful for their disease. I have no such gratitude for my cancer, although I'm certainly grateful for having advance notice of my death. In addition to allowing me to prepare my family for the future . . . it allowed me to leave the field under my own power. (Pausch & Zaslow, 2008, pp. 204–205)

Seeing terminally ill individuals extract meaning at the end of life, even while they often must grapple with the emotional and physical pain of the dying process, can be deeply moving. It can lead the people around them to reflect on their own life priorities and to reevaluate how they are living their own lives, with the certain knowledge that their lives, too, will end one day. This is the sense in which thinking about death can be instructive. Perhaps we can all be guided to make the best use of our time as we journey through life, knowing that the journey does ultimately end.

HERE'S WHAT YOU SHOULD KNOW

Did You Get It?

After reading this chapter, you should understand the following:

- The importance of historical and cultural contexts of death and dying
- The meaning of brain death
- What advanced directives may include
- The difference between passive and active euthanasia
- The meaning of physician-assisted dying
- The arguments made for and against euthanasia
- Kubler-Ross's five stages of dying, and what influences a person's progression through these stages
- What dying people need from those around them
- What constitutes a "good death"
- What hospice care offers to dying patients and their families
- How bereavement, grief, and mourning differ
- The different ways grief can be expressed and what key tasks bereaved individuals must address, according to the dual process model of coping with bereavement
- How bereaved individuals can be helped to cope with their loss

Important Terms and Concepts

active euthanasia (p. 612)
advance directive (p. 609)
bereavement (p. 621)
brain death (p. 608)
Do Not Resuscitate (DNR) order (p. 611)
dual process model of coping with bereavement (p. 622)
durable power of attorney for health care (p. 609)
euthanasia (p. 611)
good death (p. 618)
grief (p. 621)
health care proxy (p. 609)
hospice care (p. 619)
living will (p. 609)
mourning (p. 622)
palliative care (p. 619)
passive euthanasia (p. 611)
persistent vegetative state (p. 608)
physician-assisted dying (p. 612)
stages of dying (p. 616)

Part VIII Review

CHAPTER 17
Physical and Cognitive Development in Later Adulthood

- **Life expectancy** has increased markedly in economically developed societies, as a result of declines in mortality among infants and children and, more recently, progress in treating chronic diseases.
- Many theories address why people age, including **programmed theories of aging, evolutionary theories of aging**, and **random damage theories of aging**. Changes in appearance and body build and declines in mobility and body system functioning occur in late adulthood, but **reserve capacity** limits the adverse effects of such changes. Some age-related physical declines can also be slowed or even reversed, illustrating plasticity.
- Chronic health problems become more common in later life, yet many older adults evaluate their health favorably.
- Many changes in memory are *normal* changes that occur gradually with age. *Pathological* (disease-related) changes in memory that are not a normal part of aging can cause serious impairment. **Dementia** (including **Alzheimer's disease** and **vascular dementia**) and **delirium** are disorders that cause severe memory loss.
- Four lifestyle factors are especially important for preserving cognitive functioning: stimulating cognitive activity, physical exercise, reducing cardiovascular risk factors, and social engagement. Adults of all ages have the capacity to develop **wisdom**, but those who show the highest levels of wisdom tend to be older adults.

CHAPTER 18
Socioemotional Development in Later Adulthood

- The developmental tasks of later adulthood are less likely to involve efforts to achieve new goals and more likely to involve efforts to engage in emotionally meaningful activities and to develop a sense of integrity about one's life. The awareness that time left to live is finite drives efforts to review and gain closure about one's life before it ends. Using all three strategies of developmental regulation helps to preserve older adults' well-being.
- Close relationships are very important in later life, yet as people age, they tend to experience a decline in social network involvement. This decline reflects **socioemotional selectivity**.
- Older adults tend to be skilled at maintaining harmony in their marriages, although many people do become widowed in later life.
- Family ties remain important in later adulthood, particularly as social networks become smaller and physical declines and relationship losses mount.
- Adjustment to **retirement** depends on factors such as health, education level, finances, marital relationship, friendships, and the perception of being in control of the retirement.
- Many personality traits remain stable in later adulthood, although some (such as extraversion and openness) do show changes. In general, older adults exhibit greater coping flexibility in terms of coping styles. Older adults also experience more positive emotion and less negative emotion than younger age groups, and life satisfaction tends to be as high or higher in later life than in earlier periods.

EPILOGUE
Death and Dying

- In developed countries, death most often results from chronic, degenerative diseases, and the availability of life-support technologies can make defining death challenging.
- Most experts agree that brain functioning must be considered in the determination of death. **Brain death** occurs when all signs of brain activity have ceased for a specified period of time.
- An **advance directive** is a legal document that specifies the life-sustaining treatments people wish to receive should they become ill and unable to communicate their preferences. Two types of advance directive are a **living will** and a **durable power of attorney for health care**. Practices designed to end a terminally ill person's suffering include **euthanasia** or **physician-assisted dying**, although much controversy surrounds these practices.
- Elizabeth Kubler-Ross believed that terminally ill people experience five **stages of dying**: denial, anger, bargaining, depression, and acceptance.
- If the needs of dying patients and their family members are met, they are more likely to consider the death to be a **good death. Palliative care** refers to care designed to improve the quality of life for patients with a *life-threatening* illness. **Hospice care** is a special type of palliative care for patients with a *terminal* illness who have less than 6 months to live.
- According to the **dual process model of coping with bereavement**, adjusting to the death of a loved requires coping with feelings of loss and coping with the changed realities of one's daily life.

References

Abbeduto, L., Pavetto, M., Kesin, E., Weissman, M. D., Karadottir, S., O'Brien, A., & Cawthon, S. (2001). The linguistic and cognitive profile of Down syndrome: Evidence from a comparison with fragile X syndrome. *Down Syndrome Research and Practice, 7*(1), 9–15.

Abraham, J. D., & Hansson, R. O. (1995). Successful aging at work: An applied study of selection, optimization, and compensation through impression management. *Journal of Gerontology: Psychological Sciences, 50*, P94–P103.

Abrahamson, A., Baker, L. A., & Caspi, A. (2002). Rebellious teens? Genetic and environmental influences on the social attitudes of adolescents. *Journal of Personality and Social Psychology, 83*, 1392–1408.

Achenbach, T., & Edelbrock, C. (1987). *The manual for the Youth Self-Report and Profile.* Burlington, VT: University of Vermont.

Acierno, R. M., Hernandez-Tejada, M., Muzzy, W., & Steve, K. (2009). *Final report to the National Institute of Justice: National Elder Mistreatment Study.* Retrieved November 10, 2009 from http://www.ncjrs.gov/pdffiles1/nij/grants/226456.pdf

Acker, M., & Davis, M. H. (1992). Intimacy, passion and commitment in adult romantic relationships: A test of the triangular theory of love. *Journal of Social and Personal Relationships, 9*(1), 21–50.

Acquino, W. S. (1996). The returning adult child and parental experience at midlife. In C. D. Ryff & M. M. Seltzer (Eds.), *The parental experience in midlife.* Chicago, IL: University of Chicago Press.

Adams, G., Gullotta, T., & Montemayor, R. (Eds.). (1992). *Adolescent identity formation.* Newbury Park, CA: Sage.

Addington-Hall, J. M., & O'Callaghan, A. C. (2009). A comparison of the quality of care provided to cancer patients in the UK in the last three months of life in in-patient hospices compared with hospitals, from the perspective of bereaved relatives: Results from a survey using the VOICES questionnaire. *Palliative Medicine, 23*(3), 190–197.

Adolph, K. E., & Berger, S. E. (2005). Physical and motor development. In M. H. Bornstein & M. E. Lamb (Eds.), *Developmental science: An advanced textbook* (5th ed., pp. 223–281). Mahwah, NJ: Erlbaum.

Adolph, K. E., & Berger, S. E. (2006). Motor development. In W. Damon & R. Lerner (Series Eds.) & D. Kuhn & R. S. Siegler (Vol. Eds.), *Handbook of child psychology: Vol. 2. Cognition, perception, and language* (6th ed., pp. 161–213). Hoboken, NJ: Wiley.

Agras, W. S., Schneider, J., Arnow, B., Raeburn, S., & Telch, C. (1989). Cognitive-behavioral and response-prevention treatments for bulimia nervosa. *Journal of Consulting and Clinical Psychology, 57*, 215–221.

Ahnert, L., Gunnar, M. R., Lamb, M. E., & Barthel, M. (2004). Transition to child care: Associations with infant-mother attachment, infant negative emotion, and cortisol elevations. *Child Development, 75*, 639–650.

Ainsworth, M. S., Blehar, M. C., Waters, E., & Wall, S. (1978). *Patterns of attachment: A psychological study of the strange situation.* Oxford, England: Erlbaum.

Ainsworth-Darnell, J., & Downey, D. (1998). Assessing the oppositional culture explanation for racial/ethnic differences in school performance. *American Sociological Review, 63*, 536–553.

Aksan, N., & Kochanska, G. (2005). Conscience in childhood: Old questions, new answers. *Developmental Psychology, 41*, 506–516.

Akushevich, I., Kravchenko, J. S., & Manton, K. G. (2007, May 15). Health-based population forecasting: Effects of smoking on mortality and fertility. *Risk Analysis, 27*, 467–482. doi: 10.1111/j.1539-6924.2007.00898.x

Albaladejo, P., Bouaziz, H., & Benhamou, D. (1998). Epidural analgesics: How can safety and efficacy be improved? *CNS Drugs, 10*, 91–104.

Albert, M. A. (2008). Neuropsychology of the development of Alzheimer's disease. In F. I. M. Craik & T. A. Salthouse (Eds.). *Handbook of aging and cognition* (2nd ed., pp. 97–132). New York: Psychology Press.

Aldwin, C. M. (2007). *Stress, coping, and development: An integrative perspective* (2nd ed.). New York: Guilford Press.

Aldwin, C. M., & Levenson, M. R. (2001). Stress, coping, and health at mid-life: A developmental perspective. In M. E. Lachman (Ed.), *Handbook of midlife development* (pp. 188–214). New York: Wiley.

Aldwin, C. M., & Revenson, T. A. (1987). Does coping help? A reexamination of the relation between coping and mental health. *Journal of Personality and Social Psychology, 53*(2), 337–348.

Alexander, G. M. (2003). An evolutionary perspective of sex-typed toy preferences: Pink, blue, and the brain. *Archives of Sexual Behavior, 32*, 7–14.

Alexander, K. L., Entwisle, D. R., & Kabbani, N. S. (2001). The dropout process in life course perspective: Early risk factors at home and school. *Teachers College Record, 103*, 760–822.

Alexander, K. L., Entwisle, D. R., & Olson. L. S. (2007). Lasting consequences of the summer learning gap. *American Sociological Review, 72*(2), 167–180.

Alexopoulos, G. S., Buckwalter, K., Olin, J., Martinez, R., Wainscott, C., & Krishnan, K. R. R. (2002). Comorbidity of late life depression: An opportunity for research on mechanisms and treatment. *Biological Psychiatry, 52*(6), 543–558.

Allemand, M., Zimprich, D., & Hertzog, C. (2007). Cross-sectional age differences and longitudinal age changes of personality in middle adulthood and old age. *Journal of Personality, 75*(2), 323–358.

Allen, J. P., Porter, M. R., McFarland, F. C., Marsh, P., & McElhaney, K. B. (2005). The two faces of adolescents' success with peers: Adolescent popularity, social adaptation, and deviant behavior. *Child Development, 76*, 747–760.

Allen, R., & Mirabell, J. (1990, May). *Shorter subjective sleep of high school students from early compared to late starting schools.* Paper presented at the second meeting of the Society for Research on Biological Rhythms, Jacksonville, FL.

Alley, D., Ferrucci, L., Barbagallo, M., Studenski, S., & Harris, T. (2008). A research agenda: The changing relationship between body weight and health in aging. *Journal of Gerontology A: Biological Sciences and Medical Sciences, 63*(11), 1257–1259.

Alspaugh, M. E. L., Stephens, M. A. P., Townsend, A. L., Zarit, S. H., & Greene, R. (1999). Longitudinal patterns of risk of depression in dementia caregivers: Objective and subjective primary stress as predictors. *Psychology and Aging, 14*(1), 34–43.

Alter, A. L., Aronson, J., Darley, J. M., Rodriguez, C., & Ruble, D. N. (2010). Rising to the threat: Reducing stereotype threat by reframing the threat as a challenge. *Journal of Experimental Social Psychology, 46*(1), 166–171.

Altman, I., & Taylor, D. A. (1973). *Social penetration: The development of interpersonal relationships*. New York: Holt, Rinehart, & Winston.

Alwin, D. F., McCammon, R. J., & Hofer, S. M. (2006). Studying the Baby Boom cohorts within a demographic and developmental context: Conceptual and methodological issues. In S. K. Whitbourne & S. L. Willis (Eds.), *The Baby Boomers grow up: Contemporary perspectives on midlife* (pp. 45–71). Mahwah, NJ: Lawrence Erlbaum.

Amato, P. R. (1996). Explaining the intergenerational transmission of divorce. *Journal of Marriage and the Family, 58*(3), 628–640.

Amato, P. R. (2000). The consequences of divorce for adults and children. *Journal of Marriage and Family, 62*(4), 1269–1287.

Amato, P. R. (2001). Children and divorce in the 1990s: An update of the Amato and Keith (1991) meta-analysis. *Journal of Family Psychology, 15*, 355–370.

Amato, P. R., & DeBoer, D. D. (2001). The transmission of marital instability across generations: Relationship skills or commitment to marriage? *Journal of Marriage and Family, 63*(4), 1038–1051.

Ambady, N., Paik, S. K., Steele, J., Owen-Smith, A., & Mitchell, J. P. (2004). Deflecting negative self-relevant stereotype activation: The effects of individuation. *Journal of Experimental Social Psychology, 40*(3), 401–408.

American Administration on Aging. (2008a). *Profile of older Americans: 2008*. Retrieved October 24, 2009 from http://www.aoa.gov/AoARoot/Aging_Statistics/Profile/2008/3.aspx

American Administration on Aging (2008b). Projected future growth of the older population. Older population as a percentage of the total population. Retrieved October 24, 2009 from http://www.aoa.gov/AoARoot/Aging_Statistics/future_growth/future_growth.aspx

American Administration on Aging (2008c). Census data and population estimates: National population estimates. Retrieved October 24, 2009 from http://www.aoa.gov/AoARoot/Aging_Statistics/Census_Population/Index.aspx.

American Administration on Aging (AAA). (2009). *A profile of older Americans: 2008*. U. S. Department of Health and Human Services. Washington, DC: U. S. Government Printing Office. Retrieved February 17, 2010 from http://www.aoa.gov/AoAroot/Aging_Statistics/Profile/2009/docs/2009profile_508.pdf

American Association of Retired Persons. (AARP). (2001). *In the middle: A report on multicultural boomers coping with family and aging issues*. Washington, DC: Author.

American Association of Retired Persons. (AARP). (2002). *The grandparent study 2002 report*. Washington, DC: Author.

American Association of Retired Persons. (AARP). (2003a). *Lean on me: Support and minority outreach for grandparents raising grandchildren*. Washington, DC: Author.

American Association of Retired Persons. (AARP). (2003b). Boomers discover age bias. *AARP Bulletin Today*. Retrieved February 11, 2009, from http://www.aarp.org/makeadifference/advocacy/articles/boomers.html

American Association of Retired Persons (AARP). (2005). *Attitudes of individuals 50 and older toward phased retirement*. Washington, DC: Author. Retrieved February 17, 2010 http://assets.aarp.org/rgcenter/post-import/phased_ret.pdf

American Heart Association. (2009). *Heart disease and stroke statistics 2009 update: A report from the American Heart Association Statistics Committee and Stroke Statistics Subcommittee. Circulation, 119*(3), e21-e181. Retrieved December 8, 2009 from http://circ.ahajournals.org/cgi/reprint/CIRCULATIONAHA.108.191261

American Heart Association. (n.d.) *Heart, how it works*. Retrieved February 14, 2010 from http://www.americanheart.org/presenter.jhtml?identifier=4642

American Psychiatric Association. (1994). *Diagnostic and statistical manual of the American Psychiatric Association (DSM-IV)*. Washington, DC: Author.

American Psychiatric Association. (2000). *Diagnostic and statistical manual of mental disorders* (Revised 4th ed.). Washington, DC: Author.

American Psychological Association (1998). *Older adults' health and age-related changes: Reality versus myth*. Retrieved May 20, 2008 from http://www.apa.org/pi/aging/resources/guides/older-adults.pdf

American Psychological Association. (2005). *Sexual orientation and homosexuality*. Proceedings of the American Psychological Association, Incorporated, for the legislative year 2004. Minutes of the meeting of the Council of Representatives July 28 & 30, 2004, Honolulu, HI.

American Psychological Society. (2005). In appreciation: Urie Bronfenbrenner. *APS Observer*, p. 28.

American Society of Reproductive Medicine. *Frequently asked questions about infertility*. Retrieved January 31, 2008, from http://www.asrm.org/Patients/faqs.html#Q2

Ames, E. (1990). Spitz revised: A trip to Romanian "orphanages." *Canadian Psychological Association Developmental Psychology Section Newsletter, 9*, 8–11.

Anda, R. F., Felitti, V. J., & Bremner, J. D. (2006) The enduring effects of abuse and related adverse experiences in childhood: A convergence of evidence from neurobiology and epidemiology. *European Archives of Psychiatry and Clinical Neuroscience, 256*, 174–182.

Anderson, D. R., Huston, A. C., Schmitt, K. L., Linebarger, D. L., & Wright, J. C. (2001). Early childhood television viewing and adolescent behavior. *Monographs of the Society for Research in Child Development, 66*, vii–147.

Anderson, S. W., Aksan, N., Kochanska, G., Damasio, H., Wisnowski, J., & Afifi, A. (2007). The earliest expression of focal damage to human prefrontal cortex. *Cortex, 6*, 767–816.

Andersson, T., & Magnusson, D. (1990). Biological maturation in adolescence and the development of drinking habits and alcohol abuse among young males: A prospective longitudinal study. *Journal of Youth and Adolescence, 19*, 33–42.

Aneshensel, C., Becerra, R., Fielder, E., & Schuler, R. (1990). Onset of fertility-related events during adolescence: A prospective comparison of Mexican American and non-Hispanic white females. *American Journal of Public Health, 80*, 959–963.

Angold, A., Costello, E. J., & Worthman, C. (1998). Puberty and depression: The roles of age, pubertal status, and pubertal timing. *Psychological Medicine, 28*, 51–61.

Annett, M. (2002). *Handedness and brain asymmetry: The right shift theory*. Hove, UK: Psychology Press.

Anstey, K. J., Wood, J., Lord, S., & Walker, J. G. (2005). Cognitive, sensory and physical factors enabling driving safety in older adults. *Clinical Psychology Review, 25*(1), 45–65.

Antonucci, T. C., & Akiyama, H. (1995). Convoys of social relations: Family and friendships within a life span context. In R. Blieszner & V. H. Bedford (Eds.), *Handbook of aging and the family* (pp. 355–371). Westport, CT, Greenwood Press.

Antonucci, T. C., Akiyama, H., & Merline, A. (2001). Dynamics of social relationships in midlife. In M. E. Lachman (Ed.), *Handbook of midlife development* (pp. 188–214). New York: Wiley.

Antonucci, T. C., Birditt, K. S., & Akiyama, H. (2009). Convoys of social relations: An interdisciplinary approach. In V. Bengtson, D. Gans, N. Putney, & M. Silverstein (Eds.), *Handbook of theories of aging* (2nd ed., pp. 247–260). New York: Springer.

Antonucci, T. C., Jackson, J. S., & Biggs, S. (2007). Intergenerational relations: Theory, research, and policy. *Journal of Social Issues, 63(4)*, 679–693.

Apgar, V. (1953). A proposal for a new method of evaluation of the newborn infant. *Current Researches in Anesthesia & Analgesia, 32*, 260–267.

Appel, J. M. (2009, July 16). *Next: Assisted suicide for healthy people.* The Huffington Post. Retrieved July 21, 2009 from http://www.huffingtonpost.com/jacob-m-appel/assisted-suicide-for-heal_b_236664.html

Ardelt, M. (2003). Physician-assisted death. In C. D. Bryant (Ed.), *Handbook of death and dying* (pp. 424–434). Thousand Oaks, CA: Sage.

Ardelt, M. (2004). Wisdom as expert knowledge system: A critical review of a contemporary operationalization of an ancient concept. *Human Development, 47*(5), 257–285.

Ardelt, M., & Day, L. (2002). Parents, siblings, and peers: Close social relationships and adolescent deviance. *Journal of Early Adolescence, 22*, 310–349.

Arendt, R. E., Short, E. J., Singer, L. T., Minnes, S., Hewitt, J., Flynn, S., et al. (2004). Children prenatally exposed to cocaine: Developmental outcomes and environmental risks at seven years of age. *Developmental and Behavioral Pediatrics, 25*, 83–90.

Ariès, P. (1962). *Centuries of childhood.* New York: Random House.

Arnett, J. J. (2000). Emerging adulthood: A theory of development from the late teens through the twenties. *American Psychologist, 55*(5), 469–480.

Arnett, J. J. (2001). Conceptions of the transition to adulthood: Perspectives from adolescence through midlife. *Journal of Adult Development, 8*(2), 133–143.

Arnett, J. J. (2006). Emerging adulthood: Understanding the new way of coming of age. In J. J. Arnett & J. L. Tanner (Eds.), *Emerging adulthood: Coming of age in the 21st century* (pp. 279–299). Washington, DC: American Psychological Association.

Aron, A., Dutton, D. G., Aron, E. N., & Iverson, A. (1989). Experiences of falling in love. *Journal of Social and Personal Relationships, 6*(3), 243–257.

Aron, A., Norman, C. C., Aron, E. N., McKenna, C., & Heyman, R. E. (2000). Couples' shared participation in novel and arousing activities and experienced relationship quality. *Journal of Personality and Social Psychology, 78*(2), 273–284.

Arterberry, M. E., & Bornstein, M. H. (2001). Three-month-old infants' categorization of animals and vehicles based on static and dynamic attributes. *Journal of Experimental Child Psychology, 80*, 333–346.

Arterberry, M. E., & Bornstein, M. H. (2002). Infant perceptual and conceptual categorization: The roles of static and dynamic stimulus attributes. *Cognition: International Journal of Cognitive Science, 86*, 1–24.

Ary, D., Duncan, T., Biglan, A., Metzler, C., Noell, J., & Smolkowski, K. (1999). Development of adolescent problem behavior. *Journal of Abnormal Child Psychology, 27*, 141–150.

Aslin, R. N. (2007). What's in a look? *Developmental Science, 10*, 48–53.

Asthana, A. (2009, July 19). I watched as my parents faced their dignified, peaceful death—together. *The Guardian*. Retrieved July 21, 2009 from http://www.guardian.co.uk/society/2009/jul/19/dignitas-assisted-suicide-edward-downes

Astington, J. W. (1993). *The child's discovery of the mind.* Cambridge, MA: Harvard University Press.

Astley, S. J., & Clarren, S. K. (1996). A case definition and photographic screening tool for the facial phenotype of fetal alcohol syndrome. *Journal of Pediatrics, 129*, 33–41.

Atchley, R. C. (1976). *The sociology of retirement*. New York: Wiley.

Atchley, R. C., & Barusch, A. S. (2004). *Social forces and aging*. Belmont, CA: Wadsworth/Thomson.

Atkinson, R. C. & Shiffrin, R. M. (1968). Human memory: A proposed system and its control processes. In K. W. Spence & J. T. Spence (Eds.), *The psychology of learning and motivation* (Vol. 2, pp. 89–195). London: Academic Press.

Augustine, St. (1961). *Confessions*. New York: Penguin Books.

Austad, S. N. (2006). Why women live longer than men: Sex differences in longevity. *Gender Medicine, 3*(2), 79–92.

Avenevoli, S., & Steinberg, L. (2001). The continuity of depression across the adolescent transition. In H. Reese & R. Kail (Eds.), *Advances in child development and behavior* (vol. 28, pp. 139–173). New York: Academic Press.

Avis, N. E. (1999). Women's health at midlife. In S. L. Willis & J. D. Reid (Eds.), *Life in the middle: Psychological and social development in middle age* (pp. 105–146). San Diego: Academic Press.

Avril, T. (2008, April 28). Philadelphia researchers bring sight to the blind. *The Philadelphia Inquirer*. Retrieved June 2, 2008 from http://www.philly.com/inquirer/health_science/daily/20080428_Phila__researchers_bring_sight_to_the_blind.html

Aw, D., Silva, A. B., & Palmer, D. B. (2007). Immunosenescence: Emerging challenges for an ageing population. *Immunology, 120*(4), 435–446.

Axinn, W. G., & Thornton, A. (1992). The relationship between cohabitation and divorce: Selectivity or causal influence? *Demography, 29*(3), 357–374.

Axinn, W. G., & Thornton, A. (2000). The transformation in the meaning of marriage. In L. Waite (Eds.), *The ties that bind: Perspectives on marriage and cohabitation* (pp. 147–165). New York: Adline de Gruyter.

Ayis, S., Ebrahim, S., Williams, S., Juni, P., & Dieppe, P. (2007). Determinants of reduced walking speed in people with musculoskeletal pain. *Journal of Rheumatology, 34*(9), 1905–1912.

Azar, B. (2006). Wild findings on animal sleep. *Monitor on Psychology, 37*, 54–55.

Azar, S. T. (2002). Parenting and child maltreatment. In M. H. Bornstein (Ed.), *Handbook of parenting: Vol. 4. Applied parenting* (2nd ed., pp. 361–388). Mahwah, NJ: Erlbaum.

Bachman, J. G., O'Malley, P. M., Schulenberg, J. E., Johnston, L. D., Bryant, A. L, & Merline, A. C. (2002). *The decline of substance use in young adulthood: Changes in social activities, roles, and beliefs*. Mahwah, NJ: Lawrence Erlbaum Associates.

Bachman, J. G., Wadsworth, K. N., O'Malley, P. M., Johnston, L. D., & Schulenberg, J. E. (1997). *Smoking, drinking, and drug use in young adulthood: The impacts of new freedoms and new responsibilities.* Mahwah, NJ: Lawrence Erlbaum Associates.

Bada, H. S., Das, A., Bauer, C. R., Shankaran, S., Lester, B., LaGasse, L., et al. (2007). Impact of prenatal cocaine exposure on child behavior problems through school age. *Pediatrics, 119,* 348–359.

Badger, S., Nelson, L. J., & Barry, C. M. (2006). Perceptions of the transition to adulthood among Chinese and American emerging adults. *International Journal of Behavioral Development, 30*(1), 84–93.

Bagwell, C. L., Coie, J. D., Terry, R. A., & Lochman, J. E. (2000). Peer clique participation and social status in preadolescence. *Merrill-Palmer Quarterly, 46,* 280–305.

Bailey, D. B., Bruer, J. T., Symons, F. J., & Lichtman, J. W. (2001). *Critical thinking about critical periods: A series from the National Center for Early Development and Learning.* Baltimore, MD: Brookes Publishing.

Baillargeon, R. (2004). Infants' physical world. *Current Directions in Psychological Science, 13,* 89–94.

Baldwin, D. A., & Markman, E. M. (1989). Establishing word-object relations: A first step. *Child Development, 60,* 381–398.

Balen, A. H., & Rutherford, A. J. (2007). Management of infertility. *British Medical Journal, 335,* 608–611.

Ball, K., Berch, D. B, Helmers, K. F., Jobe, J. B., Leveck, M. D., Marsiske, M., et al. (2002). Effects of cognitive training interventions with older adults: A randomized controlled trial. *Journal of the American Medical Association, 288*(18), 2271–2281.

Ball, K., Edwards, J. D., & Ross, L. A. (2007). The impact of speed of processing training on cognitive and everyday functions. *Journal of Gerontology B: Psychological Sciences and Social Sciences, 62*(Special Issue 1), 19–31.

Baltes, P. B. (1987). Theoretical propositions of lifespan developmental psychology: On the dynamics between growth and decline. *Developmental Psychology, 23,* 611–626.

Baltes, P. B. (1997). On the incomplete architecture of human ontogeny: Selection, optimization, and compensation as foundation of developmental theory. *American Psychologist, 52*(4), 366–380.

Baltes, P. B., & Baltes, M. M. (1990). Psychological perspectives on successful aging: The model of selective optimization with compensation. In P. B. Baltes & M. M. Baltes (Eds.), *Successful aging: Perspectives from the behavioral sciences* (pp. 1–34). New York: Cambridge University Press.

Baltes, P. B., & Baltes, M. M. (1990). *Successful aging: Perspectives from the behavioral sciences.* Cambridge, UK: Cambridge University Press.

Baltes, P. B., & Lindenberger, U. (1997). Emergence of a powerful connection between sensory and cognitive functions across the adult life span: A new window to the study of cognitive aging? *Psychology and Aging, 12,* 12–21.

Baltes, P. B., & Smith, J. (2003). New frontiers in the future of aging: From successful aging of the young old to the dilemmas of the fourth age. *Gerontology, 49*(2), 123–135.

Baltes, P. B., & Staudinger, U. M. (2000). Wisdom. A metaheuristic (pragmatic) to orchestrate mind and virtue toward excellence. *American Psychologist, 55*(1), 122–136.

Baltes, P. B., Lindenberger, U., & Staudinger, U. M. (2006). Lifespan theory in developmental psychology. In W. Damon & R. M. Lerner (Eds.). *Handbook of child psychology: Vol. 1. Theoretical models of human development.* (pp. 569–664). New York: Wiley.

Baltes, P. B., Staudinger, U. M., & Lindenberger, U. (1999). Lifespan psychology: Theory and application to intellectual functioning. *Annual Review of Psychology, 50,* 471–507.

Baltes, P. B., Staudinger, U. M., Maercker, A., & Smith, J. (1995). People nominated as wise: A comparative study of wisdom-related knowledge. *Psychology and Aging, 10,* 155–155.

Bandura, A. (1997). *Self-efficacy: The exercise of control.* New York: W. H. Freeman.

Bandura, A., & Walters, R. (1959). *Adolescent aggression.* New York: Ronald Press.

Bank, L., Burraston, B., & Snyder, J. (2004). Sibling conflict and ineffective parenting as predictors of adolescent boys' antisocial behavior and peer difficulties: Additive and interactional effects. *Journal of Research on Adolescence, 14,* 99–125.

Bankston, C. L., III, & Caldas, S. (1998). Family structure, schoolmates, and racial inequalities in school achievement. *Journal of Marriage and the Family, 60,* 715–723.

Barber, B. (1996). Parental psychological control: Revisiting a neglected construct. *Child Development, 67,* 3296–3319.

Barber, B. L., Eccles, J. S., & Stone, M. R. (2001). Whatever happened to the jock, the brain, and the princess? Young adult pathways linked to adolescent activity involvement and social identity. *Journal of Adolescent Research, 16,* 429–455.

Barber, J. S. (2001). Ideational influences on the transition to parenthood: Attitudes toward childbearing and competing alternatives. *Social Psychology Quarterly, 64*(2), 101–127.

Bargh, J. A., & McKenna, K. Y. A. (2004). The internet and social life. *Annual Review of Psychology, 55,* 573–590.

Barker, J. C., Herdt, G., & de Vries, B. (2006). Social support in the lives of lesbians and gay men at midlife and later. *Sexuality Research and Social Policy, 3*(2), 1–23.

Barna, J., & Legerstee, M. (2005). Nine- and twelve-month-old infants relate emotions to people's actions. *Cognition and Emotion, 19,* 53–67.

Barnard, K. E., & Solchany, J. E. (2002). Mothering. In M. H. Bornstein (Ed.), *Handbook of parenting: Vol. 3. Status and social conditions of parenting* (2nd ed., pp. 3–26). Mahwah, NJ: Erlbaum.

Barnett, R. C. (1999). A new work-life model for the twenty-first century. *The Annals of the American Academy of Political and Social Science, 562*(1), 143–158.

Barnett, R. C. (2004). Women and work: Where are we, where did we come from, and where are we going? *Journal of Social Issues, 60*(4), 667–674.

Baron-Cohen, S. (2004). *The essential difference: Male and female brains.* New York: Basic Books.

Barr, R. (2006). Developing social understanding in a social context. In K. McCartney & D. Phillips (Eds.), *Blackwell handbook of early childhood development* (pp. 188–207). Malden, MA: Blackwell.

Barr, R. G., Hopkins, B., & Green, J. A. (2000). *Crying as a sign, a symptom, and a signal: Clinical emotional and developmental aspects of infant and toddler crying* (Vol. 152). New York: Cambridge University Press.

Barr, R., & Hayne, H. (2000). Age-related changes in imitation: Implications for memory development. In C. Rovee-Collier (Ed.), *Progress in infancy research* (pp. 21–67). Mahwah, NJ: Erlbaum.

Barrett-Connor, E., & Grady, D. (1998). Hormone replacement therapy, heart disease, and other considerations. *Annual Review of Public Health, 19,* 55–72.

Barrett-Connor, E., Grady, D., & Stefanick, M. L. (2005). The rise and fall of menopausal hormone therapy. *Annual Review of Public Health, 26,* 115–140.

Barrett-Connor, E., Siris, E. S., Wehren, L. E., Miller, P. D., Abbott, T. A., Berger, M. L., et al. (2005). Osteoporosis and fracture risk in women of different ethnic groups. *Journal of Bone and Mineral Research, 20*(2), 185–194.

Bar-Tal, D., Raviv, A., & Leiser, T. (1980). The development of altruistic behavior: Empirical evidence. *Developmental Psychology, 16,* 516–524.

Barth, J., & Bastiani, A. (1997). A longitudinal study of emotion regulation and preschool children's social behavior. *Merrill-Palmer Quarterly, 43,* 107–128.

Bartholomew, K., & Horowitz, L. M. (1991). Attachment styles among young adults: A test of a four-category model. *Journal of Personality and Social Psychology, 61*(2), 226–244.

Batalova, J. A., & Cohen, P. N. (2002). Premarital cohabitation and housework: Couples in cross-national perspective. *Journal of Marriage and Family, 64*(3), 743–755.

Bates, E., & Carnevale, G. F. (1993). New directions in research on language development. *Developmental Review, 13,* 436–470.

Bates, E., Devescovi, A., & Wulfeck, B. (2001). Psycholinguistics: A cross-language perspective. *Annual Review of Psychology, 52,* 369–396.

Bates, J. E. & Pettit, G. S. (2007). Temperament, parenting, and socialization. In J. Grusec & P. D. Hastings (Eds.) *Handbook of socialization: Theory and research.* (pp. 153–177). New York: The Guilford Press.

Bates, J. E., Pettit, G. S., & Dodge, K. A. (1995). Family and child factors in stability and change in children's aggressiveness in elementary school. In J. McCord (Ed.), *Coercion and punishment in long-term perspectives* (pp. 124–138). New York: Cambridge University Press.

Bates, J. E., Pettit, G. S., Dodge, K. A., & Ridge, B. (1998). Interaction of temperamental resistance to control and restrictive parenting in the development of externalizing behavior. *Developmental Psychology, 34,* 982–995.

Batshaw, M. L., & Conlon, C. J. (1997). Substance abuse: A preventable threat to development. In M. L. Batshaw (Ed.), *Children with disabilities* (4th ed., pp. 143–162). Baltimore: Brookes.

Battin, M. P., van der Heide, A., Ganzini, L., van der Wal, G., & Onwuteaka-Philipsen, B. D. (2007). Legal physician-assisted dying in Oregon and the Netherlands: Evidence concerning the impact on patients in "vulnerable" groups. *British Medical Journal, 33*(10), 591–597.

Bauer, P. J. (2006). Event memory. In W. Damon & R. M. Lerner (Series Eds.) & D. Kuhn & R. S. Siegler (Vol. Eds.), *Handbook of child psychology: Vol. 2. Cognition, perception, and language* (6th ed., pp. 373–425). Hoboken, NJ: Wiley.

Baum, S., & Ma, J. (2007). *Education pays: The benefits of higher education for individuals and society*. New York: The College Board. Retrieved Februray 2, 2008 from http://professionals.collegeboard.com/data-reports-research/trends/education-pays-2007.

Baumeister, R. F., & Bratslavsky, E. (1999). Passion, intimacy, and time: Passionate love as a function of change in intimacy. *Personality and Social Psychology Review, 3*(1), 49–67.

Baumeister, R. F., & Leary, M. R. (1995). The need to belong: Desire for interpersonal attachments as a fundamental human motivation. *Psychological Bulletin, 117*(3), 497–529.

Baumrind, D. (1967). Child care practices anteceding three patterns of preschool behavior. *Genetic Psychology Monographs,* 76, 43–88.

Baumrind, D. (1971). Current patterns of parental authority. *Developmental Psychology Monographs, 4,* 1–103.

Bayley, N. (1949). Consistency and variability in the growth of intelligence from birth to eighteen years. *Journal of Genetic Psychology, 75,* 165–196.

Beach, S. R., Schulz, R., Yee, J. L., & Jackson, S. (2000). Negative and positive health effects of caring for a disabled spouse: Longitudinal findings from the caregiver health effects study. *Psychology and Aging, 15*(2), 259–271.

Bearman, P. S., & Moody, J. (2004). Suicide and friendships among American adolescents. *American Journal of Public Health, 94,* 89–95.

Bechara, A. (2005). Decision making, impulse control and loss of willpower to resist drugs: A neurocognitive perspective. *Nature Neuroscience, 8,* 1458–1463.

Beckett, C., Maughan, B., Rutter, M., Castle, J., Colvert, E., Groothues, C., et al. (2006). Do the effects of early severe depriviation on cognition persist into early adolescence? Findings from the English and Romanian Adoptees Study. *Child Development, 77,* 696–711.

Bedford, V. H. (1996). Sibling relationships in middle and old age. In R. Blieszner, & V. H. Bedford (Eds.), *Aging and the family: Theory and research* (pp. 201–222). Westport, CT: Praeger.

Behrens, K. Y., Hesse, E., & Main, M. (2007). Mothers' attachment status as determined by the Adult Attachment Interview predicts their 6-year-olds' reunion responses: A study conducted in Japan. *Developmental Psychology, 43,* 1553–1567.

Beighle, A., Morgan, C. F., Le Masurier, G., & Pangrazi, R. P. (2006). Children's physical activity during recess and outside of school. *Journal of School Health, 76,* 516–520.

Bellah, R. N., Madsen, R., Sullivan,W. M., Swidler, A., & Tipton, S. M. (1985). *Habits of the heart: Individualism and commitment in American life.* Berkeley, CA: University of California Press.

Belle, D. (1999). *The after-school lives of children: Alone and with others while parents work.* Mahwah, NJ: Erlbaum.

Belsky, J., & Fearon, R. M. P. (2004). Exploring marriage-parenting typologies and their contextual antecedents and developmental sequelae. *Development and Psychopathology, 16,* 501–523.

Belsky, J., & Jaffee, S. (2006). The multiple determinants of parenting. In D. Cicchetti & D. Cohen (Eds.), *Developmental psychopathology: Vol. 3. Risk, disorder and adaptation* (2nd ed., pp. 38–85). Hoboken, NJ: Wiley.

Belsky, J., & Kelly, J. (1994). *The transition to parenthood: How a first child changes a marriage.* New York: Delacorte Press.

Belsky, J., & Pensky, E. (1988). Marital change across the transition to parenthood. *Marriage and Family Review, 12,* 133–156.

Belsky, J., & Rovine, M. (1990). Patterns of marital change across the transition to parenthood: Pregnancy to three years postpartum. *Journal of Marriage and the Family, 52*(1), 5–19.

Belsky, J., Hsieh, K.-H., & Crnic, K. (1998). Mothering, fathering, and infant negativity as antecedents of boys' externalizing problems and inhibition at age 3 years: Differential susceptibility to rearing experience? *Development and Psychopathology, 10,* 301–319.

Belsky, J., Vandell, D. L., Burchinal, M., Clarke-Stewart, K. A., McCartney, K., Owen, M. T., & The NICHD Early Child Care Research Network. (2007). Are there long-term effects of early child care? *Child Development, 78,* 681–701.

Bendersky, M., Gambini, G., Lastella, A., Bennett, D. S., Lewis, M. (2003). Inhibitory motor control at five years as a function of prenatal cocaine exposure. *Developmental and Behavioral Pediatrics, 24,* 345–351.

Benedict, H. (1979). Early lexical development: Comprehension and production. *Journal of Child Language, 6,* 183–200.

Benenson, J. F., & Christakos, A. (2003). A greater fragility of female's versus male's closest same sex friendships. *Child Development, 74,* 1123–1129.

Benenson, J. F., & Christakos, A. (2003). The greater fragility of females' versus males' closest same-sex friendships. *Child Development, 74,* 1123–1129.

Bengtson, V. L. (2001). Beyond the nuclear family: The increasing importance of multigenerational bonds. *Journal of Marriage and the Family, 63*(1), 1–16.

Bengtson, V. L., & Kuypers, J. A.(1971). Generational difference and the developmental stake. *Aging and Human Development, 2*(1), 249–260.

Bengtson, V. L., Rosenthal, C., & Burton, L. (1990). Families and aging: Diversity and heterogeneity. In R. H. Binstock & L. George (Eds.), *Handbook of aging and the social sciences* (3rd ed., pp. 263–287). New York: Academic Press.

Berardo, D. H. (1982). Divorce and remarriage at middle age and beyond. *Annals of the American Academy of Political and Social Science, 464,* 132–139.

Berenbaum, S. A., & Synder, E. (1995). Early hormonal influences on childhood sex-typed activity and playmate preferences: Implications for the development of sexual orientation. *Developmental Psychology, 31,* 31–42.

Bergeman, C. S. (1997). *Aging: Genetic and environmental influences.* Thousand Oaks, CA: Sage.

Bergman, R. N., Kim, S. P., Hsu, I. R., Catalano, K. J., Chiu, J. D., Kabir, M et al. (2007). Abdominal obesity: Role in the pathophysiology of metabolic disease and cardiovascular risk. *The American Journal of Medicine, 20* (2, Supplement 1) S3–S8.

Berkman, L. F., & Syme, L. S. (1979). Social networks, host resistance, and mortality: A nine-year follow-up study of Alameda County residents. *American Journal of Epidemiology, 109*(2), 186–204.

Berkman, L. F., Glass, T., Brissette, I., & Seeman, T. E. (2000). From social integration to health: Durkheim in the new millenium. *Social Science and Medicine, 51*(6), 843–857.

Berman B. D., Winkleby M., Chesterman E., & Boyce W. T. (1992). After-school child care and self-esteem in school-age children. *Pediatrics, 89,* 654–659.

Berman, R. (Ed.). (2004). *Language development across childhood and adolescence.* Amsterdam: John Benjamins.

Bernbaum, J. C., & Batshaw, M. L. (1997). Born too soon, born too small. In M. L. Batshaw (Ed.), *Children with disabilities* (4th ed., pp. 115–139). Baltimore: Brookes.

Berndt, T. (1979). Developmental changes in conformity to peers and parents. *Developmental Psychology, 15,* 608–616.

Berndt, T. (1982). The features and effects of friendship in early adolescence. *Child Development, 53,* 1447–1460.

Berndt, T. (2004). Children's friendships: Shifts over a half-century in perspectives on the development and their effects. *Merrill-Palmer Quarterly, 50,* 206–223.

Berndt, T., & Perry, T. (1990). Distinctive features and effects of early adolescent friendships. In R. Montemayor, G. Adams, & T. Gullota (Eds.), *Advances in adolescence research* (vol. 2, pp. 269–287). Beverly Hills, CA: Sage.

Berscheid, E. (1983). Emotion. In H. H. Kelley, E. Berscheid, A. Christensen, J. H. Harvey, T. L. Huston, G. Levinger, E. McClintock, L. A. Peplau, & D. R. Peterson. *Close relationships* (pp. 110–168). New York: Freeman.

Berscheid, E., & Ammazzalorso, H. (2004). Emotional experience in close relationships. In M. B. Brewer & M. Hewstone (Eds.), *Emotion and motivation* (pp. 47–69). Malden, MA: Blackwell.

Berscheid, E., & Reis, H. T. (1998). Attraction and close relationships. In D. T. Gilbert, S. T. Fiske, & G. Lindzey (Eds.), *The handbook of social psychology* (Vol. 2, pp. 193–281). New York: McGraw-Hill.

Bertelli, R., Joanni, E., & Martlew, M. (1998). Relationship between children's counting ability and their ability to reason about number. *European Journal of Psychology of Education, 13*(3), 371–384.

Bertenthal, B. I., & Campos, J. J. (1990). A systems approach to the organizing effects of self-produced locomotion during infancy. In C. Rovee-Collier (Ed.), *Advances in infancy research* (Vol. 6, pp. 1–60). Norwood, NJ: Albex.

Bertrand, J., Floyd, R. L., & Weber, M. K. (2004). *Fetal alcohol syndrome: Guidelines for referral and diagnosis.* Atlanta, GA: U.S. Department of Health and Human Services, CDC. Retrieved August 13, 2008, from http://www.cdc.gov/ncbddd/fas/documents/FAS_guidelines_accessible.pdf

Beyers, W., Goossens, L., Vasant, I., & Moors, E. (2003). A structural model of autonomy in middle and late adolescence; Connectedness, separation, detachment, and agency. *Journal of Youth and Adolescence, 32,* 351–365.

Bhardwaj, R. D., Curtis, M. A., Spalding, K. L., Buchholz, B. A., Fink, D., Bjork-Eriksson, T. et al. (2006). Neocortical neurogenesis in humans is restricted to development. *Proceedings of the National Academy of Sciences, 103,* 12564–12568.

Biemiller, A., & Slonim, N. (2001). Estimating root word vocabulary growth in normative and advantaged populations: Evidence for a common sequence of vocabulary acquisition. *Journal of Educational Psychology, 93,* 498–520.

Bierman, K. L. (2004). *Peer rejection: Developmental processes and intervention strategies.* New York: Guilford Press.

Bierman, K., & Wargo, J. (1995). Predicting the longitudinal course associated with aggressive rejected, aggressive non-rejected), and rejected nonaggressive) status. *Development and Psychopathology, 7,* 669–682.

Bigelow, B. J. (1977). Children's friendship expectations: A cognitive developmental study. *Child Development, 48,* 246–253.

Bills, D., Helms, L., & Ozcan, M. (1995). The impact of student employment on teachers' attitudes and behaviors toward working students. *Youth and Society, 27,* 169–193.

Binet, A., & Simon, T. (1908). Le développement de l'intelligence chez les enfants. *Annee Psychologique, 14*(14) 1–94.

Binstock, G., & Thornton, A. (2003). Separations, reconciliations, and living apart in cohabiting and marital unions. *Journal of Marriage and Family, 65*(2), 432.

Birditt, K. S., & Fingerman, K. L. (2005). Do we get better at picking our battles? Age group differences in descriptions of behavioral reactions to interpersonal tensions. *Journals of Gerontology Series B: Psychological Sciences and Social Sciences, 60*(3), 121–128.

Birney, D. P., Citron-Pousty, J. H., Lutz, D. J., & Sternberg, R. J. (2005). The development of cognitive and intellectual abilities. In M. H. Bornstein & M. E. Lamb (Eds.), *Developmental science: An advanced textbook* (pp. 327–358). Mahwah, NJ: Erlbaum.

Birren, J.,E. & Schroots, J. J. F. (2006). Autobiographical memory and the narrative self over the life span. In J. Birren & K. W. Schaie (Eds.), *Handbook of the psychology of aging* (pp. 477–498). San Diego, CA: Academic Press.

Bishop, J., Bishop, M., Gelbwasser, L., Green, S., & Zuckerman, A. (2003). Why do we harass nerds and freaks? Towards a theory of student culture and norms. In D. Ravitch (Ed.), *Brookings papers on education policy* (pp. 141–199). Washington, DC: Brookings Institution Press.

Bjorkland, D. F., Miller, P. H., Coyle, T. R., & Slawinski, J. L. (1997). Instructing children to use memory strategies: Evidence of utilization deficiencies in memory training. *Developmental Review, 17*, 411–442.

Bjorklund, D., & Pellegrini, A. (2001). *The origins of human nature: Evolutionary developmental psychology.* Washington: American Psychological Association.

Black, B., & Logan, A. (1995). Links between communication patterns in mother-child, father-child, and child-peer interactions and children's social status. *Child Development, 66*, 255–271.

Black, M. M, & Matula, K. (1999). *Essentials of Bayley Scales of Infant Development II Assessment*. New York: John Wiley.

Black, S. J., & Weiss, M. R. (1992). The relationship among perceived coaching behaviors, perceptions of ability, and motivation in competitive age-group swimmers. *Journal of Sport and Exercise Psychology, 14*, 309–325.

Blaga, O. M., Shaddy, D. J., Anderson, C. J., Kannass, K. N., Little, T. D., & Colombo, J. (2009). Structure and continuity of intellectual development in early childhood. *Intelligence, 37*, 106–113.

Blair, C., Gamson, D., Thorne, S., & Baker, D. (2005). Rising mean IQ: Changing cognitive demand of mathematics education for young children, population exposure to formal schooling, and the neurobiology of the prefrontal cortex. *Intelligence, 33*(1), 93–106.

Blake, J., Osborne, P., Cabral, M., & Gluck, P. (2003). The development of communicative gestures in Japanese infants. *First Language, 23*, 3–20.

Blakemore, J. E. O., Berenbaum, S. A., & Liben, L. S. (2008). *Gender development.* New York: Taylor & Francis Group, Psychology Press.

Blanchard-Fields, F. (1986). Reasoning on social dilemmas varying in emotional saliency. *Psychology and Aging, 1*, 325–333.

Blanchard-Fields, F. (2007). Everyday problem solving and emotion: An adult developmental perspective. *Current Directions in Psychological Science, 16*(1), 26–31.

Blanchard-Fields, F., & Beatty, C. (2005). Age differences in blame attributions: The role of relationship outcome ambiguity and personal identification. *Journal of Gerontology B: Psychological Sciences and Social Sciences, 60*(1), P19–P26.

Blanchard-Fields, F., & Coats, A. H. (2008). The experience of anger and sadness in everyday problems impacts age differences in emotion regulation. *Developmental Psychology, 44*(6), 1547–1556.

Blanchard-Fields, F., Jahnke, H. C., & Camp, C. (1995). Age differences in problem-solving style: The role of emotional salience. *Psychology and Aging, 10*(2), 173–180.

Blanchard-Fields, F., Mienaltowski, A., & Seay, R. B. (2007). Age differences in everyday problem-solving effectiveness: Older adults select more effective strategies for interpersonal problems. *Journal of Gerontology B: Psychological and Social Sciences, 62*(1), P61–P64.

Blando, J. A. (2001). Twice hidden: Older gay and lesbian couples, friends, and intimacy. *Generations, 25*(2), 87–89.

Blatchford, P., Baines, E., & Pellegrini, A. (2003). The social context of school playground games: Sex and ethnic differences and changes over time after entry to junior high. *British Journal of Developmental Psychology, 21*, 579–599.

Blazer, D. G. (2003). Depression in late life: Review and commentary. *Journal of Gerontology: Medical Sciences, 58*(3), M249–M265.

Blazer, D. G. (2010). Protection from late life depression. *International Psychogeriatrics, 22*, 171–173.

Blazer, D. G., & Hybels, C. F. (2005). Origins of depression in later life. *Psychological Medicine, 35*(9), 1–12.

Blieszner, R. (2006). A lifetime of caring: Dimensions and dynamics in late-life close relationships. *Personal Relationships, 13*(1), 1–18.

Blom-Hoffman, J., George, J. B. E., & Franko, D. L. (2006). Childhood overweight. In G. G. Bear & K. M. Minke (Eds.), *Children's needs III: Development, prevention, and intervention* (pp. 989–1000). Bethesda, MD: National Association of School Psychologists.

Bloom, B., Dey, A. N., & Freeman, G. (2006). Summary health statistics for U.S. children: National Health Interview Survey, 2005. *Vital and Health Statistics*, Series 10, No. 231 (DHHS Publication No. 2007-1559). Hyattsville, MD: U.S. Government Printing Office.

Bloom, K., Russell, A., & Wassenberg, K. (1987). Turntaking affects the quality of infant vocalizations. *Journal of Child Language, 14*, 211–227.

Bloom, L. (1970). *Language development: Form and function in emerging grammars.* Cambridge, MA: MIT Press.

Bloom, L. (1976). An integrative perspective on language development. *Papers and Reports on Child Language Development, 12*, 1–22.

Bloom, L. (1998). Language acquisition in its developmental context. In W. Damon (Series Ed.) & D. Kuhn & R. S. Siegler (Vol. Eds.), *Handbook of child psychology: Vol. 2. Cognition, perception, and language* (5th ed., pp. 309–370). New York: Wiley.

Blossfeld, I., Collins, A., Kiely, M., & Delahunty, C. (2006). Texture preferences of 12-month-old infants and the role of early experience. *Food Quality and Preference, 18*, 396–404.

Bluck, S., Alea, N., Habermas, T., & Rubin, D. (2005). A tale of three functions: The self–reported uses of autobiographical memory. *Social Cognition, 23*(1), 91–117.

Bogartz, R. S., Shinskey, J. L., & Schilling, T. H. (2000). Object permanence in five-and-a-half-month-old infants? *Infancy, 1*, 403–428

Bohlmeijer, E., Roemer, M., Cuijpers, P., & Smit, F. (2007). The effects of life-review on psychological well-being in older adults: A meta-analysis. *Aging and Mental Health, 11*(3), 291–300.

Boise, L., Camicioli, R., Morgan, D. L., Rose, J. H., & Congleton, L. (1999). Diagnosing dementia: Perspectives of primary care physicians. *Gerontologist, 39*(4), 457–464.

Bolger, N. & Zuckerman, A. (1995). A framework for studying personality in the stress process. *Journal of Personality and Social Psychology, 69*(5), 890–902.

Bolzani Dinehart, L. H., Messinger, D. S., Acosta, S. I., Cassel, T., Ambadar, Z., & Cohn, J. (2005). Adult perceptions of positive and negative infant emotional expressions. *Infancy, 8*, 279–303.

Bonanno, G. A.(2004). Loss, trauma, and human resilience: Have we underestimated the human capacity to thrive after extremely aversive events? *American Psychologist, 59*(1), 20–28.

Bonanno, G. A., Wortman, C. B., & Nesse, R. M. (2004). Prospective patterns of resilience and maladjustment during widowhood. *Psychology and Aging, 19*(2), 260–271.

Bonanno, G. A., Wortman, C. B., Lehman, D. R., Tweed, R. G., Haring, M., Sonnega, J., Carr, D., & Nesse, R. M. (2002). Resilience to loss and chronic grief: A prospective study from preloss to 18-months postloss. *Journal of Personality and Social Psychology, 83*(5), 1150–1164.

Bond, J. T., Thompson, C., Galinsky, E., & Protas, D. (2003). *Highlights of the 2002 national study of the changing workforce (No. 3).* New York: Families and Work Institute.

Bonhomme, J., Stephens, T., & Braithwaite, R. (2006). African-American males in the United States prison system: Impact on family and community. *The Journal of Men's Health & Gender, 3*(3), 223–226.

Bookwala, J., & Fekete, E. (2009). The role of psychological resources in the affective well-being of never-married adults. *Journal of Social and Personal Relationships, 26*(4), 411–428.

Bornstein, M. H. (1984). A descriptive taxonomy of psychological categories used by infants. In C. Sophian (Ed.), *Origins of cognitive skills* (pp. 313–338). Hillsdale, NJ: Erlbaum.

Bornstein, M. H. (1989). *Maternal responsiveness: Characteristics and consequences*. San Francisco, CA: Jossey-Bass.

Bornstein, M. H. (1989). Sensitive periods in development: Structural characteristics and causal interpretations. *Psychological Bulletin, 105,* 179–197.

Bornstein, M. H. (1991). *Cultural approaches to parenting*. Hillsdale, NJ: Erlbaum.

Bornstein, M. H. (1995). Form and function: Implications for studies of culture and human development. *Culture and Psychology, 1,* 123–137.

Bornstein, M. H. (2000). Infancy: Emotions and temperament. In A. E. Kazdin (Ed.), *The encyclopedia of psychology* (Vol. 2, pp. 278–284). New York: American Psychological Association and Oxford University Press.

Bornstein, M. H. (2000). Infant into conversant: Language and nonlanguage processes in developing early communication. In N. Budwig, I. C. Uzgiris, & J. V. Wertsch (Eds.), *Communication: An arena of development* (pp. 109–129). Stamford, CT: Ablex.

Bornstein, M. H. (2002). Parenting infants. In M. H. Bornstein (Ed.), *Handbook of parenting: Vol. 1. Children and parenting* (2nd ed., pp. 3–43). Mahwah, NJ: Erlbaum.

Bornstein, M. H. (2003). Sensitive periods. In J. R. Miller, R. M. Lerner, L. B. Schiamberg, & P. M. Anderson (Eds.), *Human ecology: An encyclopedia of children, families, communities, and environments* (Vol. 2, pp. 635–636). Santa Barbara, CA: ABC-CLIO.

Bornstein, M. H. (2006). Hue categorization and color naming: Physics to sensation to perception. In N. J. Pitchford & C. P. Biggam (Eds.), *Progress in colour studies Volume II. Psychological aspects* (pp. 35–68). Amsterdam/Philadelphia: John Benjamins.

Bornstein, M. H. (2006.) Some metatheoretical issues in culture, parenting, and developmental science. In Q. Jing, M. R. Rosenzweig, G. d'Ydewalle, H. Zhang, H. C. Chen, & K. Zhang (Eds.), *Progress in psychological science around the world: Vol. 2. Social and applied issues* (pp. 245–260). Hove, England: Psychology Press.

Bornstein, M. H. (2007). Hue categorization and color naming: Cognition to language to culture. In R. E. MacLaury, G. V. Paramei, & D. Dedrick (Eds.), *Anthropology of color: Interdisciplinary multilevel modeling* (pp. 3–27). Amsterdam/Philadelphia: John Benjamins.

Bornstein, M. H. (2007). On the significance of social relationships in the development of children's earliest symbolic play: An ecological perspective. In A. Göncü & S. Gaskins (Eds.), *Play and development: Evolutionary, sociocultural, and functional perspectives* (pp. 101–129). Mahwah, NJ: Erlbaum.

Bornstein, M. H. (2010). Parents' reports about their children's lives. In A. Ben-Arieh, J. Cashmore, G. Goodman, J. Kampmann, & G. Melton (Eds.), *Handbook of Child Research*. Thousand Oaks, CA: Sage.

Bornstein, M. H., & Arterberry, M. E. (2003). Recognition, discrimination and categorization of smiling by 5-month-old infants. *Developmental Science, 6,* 585–599.

Bornstein, M. H., & Bradley, R. H. (2003). *Socioeconomic status, parenting, and child development*. Mahwah, NJ: Erlbaum.

Bornstein, M. H., & Colombo, J. (2010). Infant cognitive functioning and child mental development. In S. Pauen & M. H. Bornstein (Eds.), *Early childhood development and later achievement*. New York: Cambridge University Press.

Bornstein, M. H., & Cote, L. R., with Maital, S., Painter, K., Park, S.-Y., Pascual, L., Pêcheux, M.-G., Ruel, J., Venuti, P., & Vyt, A. (2004). Cross-linguistic analysis of vocabulary in young children: Spanish, Dutch, French, Hebrew, Italian, Korean, and American English. *Child Development, 75,* 1115–1139.

Bornstein, M. H., & Hahn, C.-S. (2007.) Infant childcare settings and the development of gender-specific adaptive behaviors. *Early Child Development and Care, 177,* 15–41.

Bornstein, M. H., & Lamb, M. E. (in press). *Development in Infancy: An Introduction* (5th ed.). New York: Taylor & Francis.

Bornstein, M. H., & Putnick, D. L. (2007). Chronological age, cognitions, and practices in European American mothers: A multivariate study of parenting. *Developmental Psychology, 43,* 850–864.

Bornstein, M. H., & Ruddy, M. G. (1984). Infant attention and maternal stimulation: Prediction of cognitive and linguistic development in singletons and twins. *Attention and performance X: Control of language processes* (pp. 433–445). Hillsdale, NJ: Erlbaum.

Bornstein, M. H., Arterberry, M. E., & Mash, C. (2004). Long-term memory for an emotional interpersonal interaction occurring at 5 months of age. *Infancy, 6,* 407–416.

Bornstein, M. H., Arterberry, M. E., & Mash, C. (2005). Perceptual development. In M. H. Bornstein & M. E. Lamb (Eds.), *Developmental science: An advanced textbook* (5th ed., pp. 283–325). Mahwah, NJ: Erlbaum.

Bornstein, M. H., Arterberry, M., & Mash, C. (2010). Perceptual development. In M. H. Bornstein & M. E. Lamb (Eds.), *Developmental science: An advanced textbook* (6th ed., pp. 283–325). Mahwah, NJ: Erlbaum.

Bornstein, M. H., DiPietro, J. A., Hahn, C.-H., Painter, K. M., Haynes, O. M., & Costigan, K. A. (2002). Prenatal cardiac function and postnatal cognitive development: An exploratory study. *Infancy, 3,* 475–494.

Bornstein, M. H., Gaughran, J. M., & Segui, I. (1991). Multi-method assessment of infant temperament: Mother questionnaire and mother and observer reports evaluated and compared at five months using the Infant Temperament Measure. *International Journal of Behavioral Development, 14,* 131–151.

Bornstein, M. H., Hahn, C.-S., & Haynes, O. M. (2004). Specific and general language performance across early childhood: Stability and gender considerations. *First Language, 24,* 267–304.

Bornstein, M. H., Hahn, C.-S., Gist, N. F., & Haynes, O. M. (2006.) Long-term cumulative effects of childcare on children's mental development and socioemotional adjustment in a non-risk sample: The moderating effects of gender. *Early Child Development and Care, 176,* 129–156.

Bornstein, M. H., Haynes, O. M., Legler, J. M., O'Reilly, A. W., & Painter, K. M. (1997). Symbolic play in childhood: Interpersonal and environmental context and stability. *Infant Behavior & Development, 20,* 197–207.

Bornstein, M. H., Haynes, O. M., Painter, K. M., & Genevro, J. L. (2000.) Child language with mother and with stranger at home and in the laboratory: A methodological study. *Journal of Child Language, 27,* 407–420.

Bornstein, M. H., Putnick, D. L., Suwalsky, J. T. D., & Gini, M. (2006). Maternal chronological age, prenatal and perinatal history, social support, and parenting of infants. *Child Development, 77,* 875–892.

Bornstein, M. H., Tamis-LeMonda, C. S., & Haynes, O. M. (1999). First words in the second year: Continuity, stability, and models of concurrent and predictive correspondence in vocabulary and verbal responsiveness across age and context. *Infant Behavior and Development, 22,* 65–85.

Bornstein, M. H., Tamis-LeMonda, C. S., Pêcheux, M.-G., & Rahn, C. W. (1991). Mother and infant activity and interaction in France and in the United States: A comparative study. *International Journal of Behavioral Development, 14,* 21–43.

Bornstein, M. H., Tamis-LeMonda, C. S., Tal, J., Ludemann, P., Toda, S., Rahn, C. W., et al. (1992). Maternal responsiveness to infants in three societies: The United States, France, and Japan. *Child Development, 63,* 808–821.

Bornstein, M. H., Venuti, P., & Hahn, C.-S. (2002). Mother-child play in Italy: Regional variation, individual stability, and mutual dyadic influence. *Parenting: Science and Practice, 2,* 273–301.

Bortz, W. M. II. (2002). A conceptual framework of frailty: A review. *Journal of Gerontology A: Biological Sciences and Medical Sciences, 57*(5), M283–288.

Borum, M. L., Lynn, J., & Zhong, Z. (2000). The effects of patient race on outcomes in seriously ill patients in SUPPORT: An overview of economic impact, medical intervention, and end-of-life decisions. *Journal of the American Geriatrics Society, 48*(5), 194–198.

Bosman, E. A., & Charness, N. (1996). Age-related differences in skilled performance and skill acquisition. In F. Blanchard-Fields & T. M. Hess (Eds.), *Perspectives on cognitive change in adulthood and aging* (pp. 428–453). New York: McGraw-Hill.

Botchan, A., Hauser, R., Gamzu, R., Yogev, L., Paz, G., & Yavetz, H. (2001). Results of 6139 artificial insemination cycles with donor spermatozoa. *Human Reproduction, 16*(11), 2298–2304.

Bowlby, J. (1969). *Attachment and loss.* London: Hogarth.

Bowlby, J. (1982). *Attachment and loss: Vol. 1. Attachment* (2nd ed.). New York: Basic Books. (Original work published in 1969)

Bowlby, J. (1988). *A secure base: Clinical applications of attachment theory.* London: Routledge.

Boyce, W. T. (2006). Symphonic causation and the origins of childhood psychopathology. In D. Cicchetti & D. Cohen (Eds.), *Developmental psychopathology: Vol. 2. Developmental neuroscience* (pp. 797–817). New York: Wiley.

Boyle, P., Robertson, C., Mazzetta, C., Keech, M., Hobbs, F. D. R., Fourcade, R., et al. (2003). The prevalence of lower urinary tract symptoms in men and women in four centres. The UrEpik study. *British Journal of Urology International, 92*(4), 409–414.

Boysson-Bardies, B., Sagart, L., & Durand C. (1984). Discernible differences in the babbling of infants according to target language. *Journal of Child Language, 11,* 1–15.

Bradbury, T. N., & Karney, B. R. (2004). Understanding and altering the longitudinal course of marriage. *Journal of Marriage and Family, 66*(4), 862–879.

Bradley, E. H., Prigerson, H., Carlson, M. D. A., Cherlin, E., Johnson-Hurzeler, R., & Kasl, S. V. (2004). Depression among surviving caregivers: Does length of hospice enrollment matter? *American Journal of Psychiatry, 161*(12), 2257–2263.

Bradley, R. H. (2002). Environment and parenting. In M. H. Bornstein (Ed.), *Handbook of parenting: Vol. 2. Biology and ecology of parenting* (2nd ed., pp. 281–314). Mahwah, NJ: Erlbaum.

Bradley, R. H., & Corwyn, R. F. (2002). Socioeconomic status and child development. *Annual Review of Psychology, 53,* 371–399.

Bradley, R. H., Corwyn, R. F., Burchinal, M., Pipes McAdoo, H., & Garcia Coll, C. (2001a). The home environments of children in the United States Part II: Relations with behavioral development through age thirteen. *Child Development, 72,* 1868–1886.

Bradley, R. H., Corwyn, R. F., Burchinal, M., Pipes McAdoo, H., & Garcia Coll, C. (2001b). The home environments of children in the United States Part I: Variations by age, ethnicity, and poverty status. *Child Development, 72,* 1844–1867.

Bradley, R. H., Nader, P., O'Brien, M., Houts, R., Belsky, J., Crosnoe, R., and NICHD Early Child Care Research Network. (2008). Adiposity and internalizing problems: Infancy to middle childhood. In H. D. Davies & H. E. Fitzgerald (Set Eds.) & H. E. Fitzgerald & V. Mousouli (Vol. Eds.), *Obesity in childhood and adolescence: Vol. 2. Understanding development and prevention* (pp. 73–91). Westport, CT: Praeger.

Brady, T. F., Konkle, T., Alvarez, G. A., & Oliva, A. (2008). Visual long-term memory has a massive storage capacity for object details. *Proceedings of the National Academy of Sciences, 105*(38), 14325–14329.

Brainerd, C. J. & Reyna, V. F. (2005). *The science of false memory.* New York: Oxford University Press.

Brainerd, C. J. (1996). Piaget: A centennial celebration. *Psychological Science, 7,* 191–225.

Brainerd, C. J., & Reyna, V. F. (2004). Fuzzy-trace theory and memory development. *Developmental Review, 24,* 396–439.

Brainerd, C. J., Forrest, T. J., Karibian, D., & Reyna, V. F. (2006). Development of the false-memory illusion. *Developmental Psychology, 42,* 962–979.

Bramlett, M. D., & Mosher, W. D. (2002). Cohabitation, marriage, divorce, and remarriage in the United States. *Vital Health Statistic (Series 23, No. 22),* 1–32.

Branche, C. M., Dellinger, A. M., Sleet, D. A., Gilchrist, J., & Olson, S. J. (2004). Unintentional injuries: The burden, risks, and preventative strategies to address diversity. In I. L. Livingston (Ed.), *Praeger handbook of Black American health: Policies and issues behind disparities in health* (2nd ed., pp. 317–327). Westport, CT: Praeger.

Brandstadter, J., & Rothermund, K. (2003). Intentionality and time in human development and aging: Compensation and goal adjustment in changing developmental contexts. In U. Staudinger & U. Lindenberger (Eds.), *Understanding human development: Dialogues with lifespan psychology* (pp. 105–124). Boston, MA: Kluwer.

Brandtstädter, J. (2006). Action perspectives on human development. In W. Damon & R. Lerner (Series Eds.) & R. Lerner (Vol. Ed.), *Handbook of child psychology: Vol. 1. Theoretical models of human development* (6th ed., pp. 519–568). Hoboken, NJ: Wiley.

Bray, I., Gunnell, D., & Smith, G. D. (2006). Advanced paternal age: How old is too old? *Journal of Epidemiology and Community Health, 60,* 851–853.

Brazelton, T. B., & Nugent, J. K. (1995). *Neonatal behavioral assessment scale* (3rd ed.). London: MacKeith Press.

Brehm, S. S., Miller, R. S., Perlman, D., & Campbell, S. M. (2002). *Intimate relationships* (3rd ed.). New York: McGraw Hill.

Bremner, J. G. (2001). Cognitive development: Knowledge of the physical world. In J. G. Bremner & A. Fogel (Eds.), *Blackwell handbook of infant development* (pp. 99–138). Malden, MA: Blackwell.

Brennan, K. A., Clark, C. L., & Shaver, P. R. (1998). Self-report measurement of adult attachment: An integrative overview. In J. A. Simpson & W. S. Rholes (Eds.), *Attachment theory and close relationships* (pp. 46–76). New York: Guilford.

Breslau, N., Paneth, N. S., & Lucia, V. C. (2004). The lingering academic deficits of low birth weight children. *Pediatrics, 114*, 1035–1040.

Bretherton, I., & Munholland, C. (1999). Internal working models in attachment relationships: A construct revisited. In J. Cassidy & P. Shaver (Eds.), *Handbook of attachment* (pp. 89–111). New York: Guilford Press.

Brewer, M. B., & Caporael, L. R. (1990). Selfish genes vs. selfish people: Sociology as origin myth. *Motivation and Emotion, 14*(4), 237–243.

Brewster, K. (1994). Race differences in sexual activity among adolescent women: The role of neighborhood characteristics. *American Sociological Review, 59*, 408–424.

Bridge J., Iyengar, S., Salary, C., Barbe, R., Birmaher, B., Pincus, H., et al. (2007). Clinical response and risk for reported suicidal ideation and suicide attempts in pediatric antidepressant treatment: A meta-analysis of randomized controlled trials. *JAMA, 297*, 1683–1696.

Briggs, G. G., Freeman, R. K., & Yaffe, S. J. (1994). *A reference guide to fetal and neonatal risk: Drugs in pregnancy and lactation* (4th ed.). Baltimore: Williams & Wilkins.

Brim, O. G. (1992). *Ambition: How we manage success and failure throughout our lives*. New York: Basic Books.

Brim, O. G., Ryff, C. D. & Kessler, R. C. (Eds.) (2004). *How healthy are we?: A national study of well-being at midlife*. Chicago: University of Chicago Press.

Brisch, K. H. (2002). *Treating attachment disorders*. New York: Guilford Press.

Brody, E. M. (1985). Parent care as a normative family stress. *The Gerontologist, 25*(1), 19–29.

Brody, G. H. (1998). Sibling relationship quality: Its causes and consequences. *Annual Review of Psychology, 49*, 1–24.

Brody, G. H., Conger, R. Gibbons, F. X., Ge, X., Murry, V. M., Gerrard, M., et al. (2001). The influence of neighborhood disadvantage, collective socialization, and parenting on African American children's affiliation with deviant peers. *Child Development, 72*, 1231–1246.

Brody, G., Ge, X., Yeong, K., McBride, M., Simons, R., Gibbons, F., et al. (2003). Neighborhood disadvantage moderates associations of parenting and older sibling problem attitudes and behavior with conduct disorders in African American children. *Journal of Consulting and Clinical Psychology, 71*, 211–222.

Brody, G., Stoneman, Z., & McCoy, J. (1994). Forecasting sibling relationships in early adolescence from child temperaments and family processes in middle childhood. *Child Development, 65*, 771–784.

Broidy, L. M., Nagin, D. S., Tremblay, R. E., Brame, B. Dodge, K. A., Fergusson, D., et al. (2003). Developmental trajectories of childhood disruptive behaviors and adolescent delinquency: A six-site, cross-national study. *Developmental Psychology, 39*, 222–245.

Bronfenbrenner, U. (1979). *The ecology of human development*. Cambridge, MA: Harvard University Press.

Bronfenbrenner, U., & Morris, P. (1998). The ecology of developmental processes. In W. Damon & R. Lerner (Eds.), *Handbook of child psychology* (5th ed., Vol. 1, pp. 992–1028). New York: Wiley

Bronfenbrenner, U., & Morris, P. (2006). The bioecological model of human development. In W. Damon & R. Lerner (Series Eds.) & R. Lerner (Vol. Ed.), *Handbook of child psychology: Vol. 1. Theoretical models of human development* (6th ed., pp. 793–828). New York: Wiley.

Brookmeyer, R., Gray, S., & Kawas, C. (1998). Projections of Alzheimer's disease in the United States and the public health impact of delaying disease onset. *American Journal of Public Health, 88*(9), 1337–1342.

Brookmeyer, R., Johnson, E., Ziegler-Graham, K., & Arrighi, H. (2007). Forecasting the global burden of Alzheimer's disease. *Alzheimer's and Dementia, 3*(3), 186–191.

Brooks-Gunn, J., Graber, J., & Paikoff, R. (1994). Studying links between hormones and negative affect: Models and measures. *Journal of Research on Adolescence, 4*, 469–486.

Brown, B. (1990). Peer groups. In S. Feldman & G. Elliott (Eds.), *At the threshold: The developing adolescent* (pp. 171–196). Cambridge, MA: Harvard University Press.

Brown, B. (2009). Adolescents' relationships with peers. In R. Lerner & L. Steinberg (Eds.), *Handbook of adolescent psychology* (3rd ed.). New York: Wiley.

Brown, B., & Lohr, M. J. (1987). Peer group affiliation and adolescent self-esteem: An integration of ego-identity and symbolic interaction theories. *Journal of Personality and Social Psychology, 52*, 47–55.

Brown, B., Clasen, D., & Eicher, S. (1986). Perceptions of peer pressure, peer conformity dispositions, and self-reported behavior among adolescents. *Developmental Psychology, 22*, 521–530.

Brown, B., Freeman, H., Huang, B., & Mounts, N. (1992, March). *"Crowd hopping": Incidence, correlates and consequences of change in crowd affiliation during adolescence.* Paper presented at the biennial meetings of the Society for Research on Adolescence, Washington.

Brown, B., Mory, M., & Kinney, D. (1994). Casting crowds in a relational perspective: Caricature, channel, and context. In R. Montemayor, G. Adams, & T. Gullotta (Eds.), *Advances in adolescent development: Vol. 5. Personal relationships during adolescence* (pp. 123–167). Newbury Park, CA: Sage.

Brown, B., Mounts, N., Lamborn, S., & Steinberg, L. (1993). Parenting practices and peer group affiliation in adolescence. *Child Development, 64*, 467–482.

Brown, P. L. (2006, December 2). Supporting boys or girls when the line isn't clear. *New York Times*, pp. A1, A11.

Brown, R. (1973). *A first language*. Cambridge, MA: Harvard University Press.

Brown, S. A., Hutchinson, R., Morrisette, J., Boerwinkle, E., Davis, C. E., & Gotto, A. M., Jr. et al. (1993). Plasma lipid, lipoprotein cholesterol and apoprotein distributions in selected U.S. communities. *Arterioscorosis and Thrombosis, 13*(8), 1139–1158.

Brown, S. L., Lee, G. R., & Bulanda, J. R. (2006). Cohabitation among older adults: A national portrait. *Journal of Gerontology: Social Sciences, 61*(2), 71–79.

Brownell, C. (1990). Peer social skills in toddlers: Competencies and constraints illustrated by same age vs. mixed age interaction. *Child Development, 61*, 838–848.

Brownell, C. A., Ramani, G. B., & Zerwas, S. (2006). Becoming a social partner with peers: Cooperation and social understanding in one- and two-year-olds. *Child Development, 77*, 803–821.

Bruce, C., Desimone, R., & Gross, C. G. (1981). Visual properties of neurons in a polysensory area in superior temporal sulcus of the macaque. *Journal of Neurophysiology, 46*, 369–384.

Brugman, G. M. (2006). Wisdom and aging. In J. E. Birren & K. W. Schaie (Eds.), *Handbook of the psychology of aging* (6th ed., pp. 445–476). Burlington, MA: Elsevier Academic Press.

Bruner, J., Jolly, A. & Silva, K. (1976) *Play: Its role in evolution and development*. Harmondsworth: Penguin.

Brunson, K. L., Kramár, E., Lin, B., Chen, Y., Colgin, L. L., Yanagihara, T. K., Lynch, G., & Baram, T. Z. (2005). Mechanisms of late-onset cognitive decline after early-life stress. *Journal of Neuroscience, 25*, 9328–9338.

Bruvold, W. (1993). A meta-analysis of adolescent smoking prevention programs. *American Journal of Public Health, 83*, 872–880.

Bryan, E. (2003). The impact of multiple preterm births on the family. *British Journal of Obstetrics and Gynaecology, 110*(Suppl 20), 24–28.

Bugental, D. B. (2000). Acquisition of the algorithms of social life: A domain-based approach. *Psychological Bulletin, 126*(2), 187–219.

Bugental, D. B., & Hehman, J. A. (2007). Ageism: A review of research and policy implications. *Social Issues and Policy Review, 1*(1), 173–216.

Bugental, D., & Grusec, J. (2006). Socialization processes. In W. Damon & R. Lerner (Series Eds.) & N. Eisenberg (Vol. Ed.), *Handbook of child psychology: Vol. 3. Social, emotional, and personality development* (6th ed., pp. 366–428). New York: Wiley.

Bugg, J. M., Zook, N. A., DeLosh, E. L., Davalos, D. B., & Davis, H. P. (2006). Age differences in fluid intelligence: Contributions of general slowing and frontal decline. *Brain and Cognition, 62*(1), 9–16.

Buhrmester, D., & Furman, W. (1990). Perceptions of sibling relationships during middle childhood and adolescence. *Child Development, 61*, 1387–1396.

Bullock, B., & Dishion, T. J. (2002). Sibling collusion and problem behavior in early adolescence: Toward a process model for family mutuality. *Journal of Abnormal Child Psychology, 30*, 143–153.

Bumpass, L. L., & Aquilino, W. S. (1995). *A social map of midlife: Family and work over the middle life course*. Vero Beach, FL: MacArthur Foundation Research Network on Successful Midlife Development.

Bumpass, L. & Lu, H-H (2000). Trends in cohabitation and implications for children's family contexts in the United States. *Population Studies, 54*, 29–41.

Bumpass, L., Raley, R. K., & Sweet, J. A. (1995). The changing character of stepfamilies: Implications of cohabitation and nonmarital childbearing. *Demography, 32*(3), 425–436.

Burchinal, M. R., Roberts, J. E., Hooper, S., & Zeisel, S. A. (2000). Cumulative risk and early cognitive development: A comparison of statistical risk models. *Developmental Psychology, 36*, 793–807.

Burchinal, M., Roberts, J. E., Zeisel, S. A., Hennon, E. A., & Hooper, S. (2006). Risk and resiliency: Protective factors in early elementary school years. *Parenting: Science and Practice, 6*, 79–113.

Bureau of Labor Statistics (2009), *Occupational outlook handbook, 2010–11 edition*. Chart 6. Retrieved January 7, 2010 from http://www.bls.gov/oco/oco2003.htm#occupation

Bureau of Labor Statistics (2009). *College enrollment and work activity of 2008 high school graduates*. Retrieved February 5, 2010 from http://www.bls.gov/news.release/hsgec.nr0.htm.

Bureau of Labor Statistics. (2009, December.). *Employment status of the civilian noninstitutionalized population by age, sex, and race*. Retrieved December 13, 2009 from http://www.bls.gov/cps/cpsaat3.pdf

Burgeson, C. R., Wechsler, H., Brener, N. D., Young, J. C., & Spain, C. G. (2001). Physical education and activity: Results from the School Health Policies and Programs Study 2000. *Journal of School Health, 71*, 279–293.

Busnel, M. C., Granier-Deferre, C., & Lecanuet, J. P. (1992). Fetal audition. In G. Turkewitz (Ed.), Developmental psychobiology. *Annals of the New York Academy of Sciences* (Vol. 662, pp. 118–134). New York: The New York Academic of Sciences.

Buss, D. M. (1989). Sex differences in human mate preferences: Evolutionary hypotheses tested in 37 cultures. *Behavioral and Brain Sciences, 12*, 1–14.

Buss, D. M., & Kenrick, D. T. (1998). Evolutionary social psychology. In D. T. Gilbert, Bussey, K., & Bandura, A. (1999). Social cognitive theory of gender development and differentiation. *Psychological Review, 106*, 676–713.

Butler, K. (2006, July 4). The grim neurology of teenage drinking. *The New York Times*, p. D1 and ff.

Butler, R. (2001). Ageism. In G. L. Maddox (Ed.), *The encyclopedia of aging* (3rd ed., Vol. 1, pp. 38–39). New York: Springer.

Butler, R. N. (1974). Successful aging and the role of the life review. *Journal of the American Geriatrics Society, 22*(12), 529–535.

Butterfield, S. A., Lehnhard, R. A., & Coladarci, T. (2002). Age, sex, and body mass index in performance of selected locomotor and fitness tasks by children in grades K–2. *Perceptual and Motor Skills, 94*(1), 80–86.

Butterworth, G. (2001). Joint visual attention in infancy. In J. G. Bremner, & A. Fogel (Eds.), *Blackwell handbook of infant development* (pp. 213–240). Malden, MA: Blackwell.

Byrne, D. (1971). *The attraction paradigm*. New York: Academic Press.

Bytheway, B. (2005). Ageism and age categorization. *Journal of Social Issues, 61*(2), 361–374.

Cabeza, R., Grady, C. L., Nyberg, L., McIntosh, A. R., Tulving, E., Kapur, S., et al. (1997). Age-related differences in neural activity during memory encoding and retrieval: A positron emission tomography study. *Journal of Neuroscience, 17*(1), 391–400.

Cacioppo, J. T., & Bernston, G. G. (2007) The brain, homeostasis and health: Balancing demands of the internal and external milieu. In H. S. Friedman & R. C. Silver (Eds.), *Foundations of health psychology* (pp. 73–91). New York: Oxford University Press.

Cacioppo, J. T., Hawkley, L. C., Crawford, L. E., Ernst, J. M., Burleson, M. H., Kowalewski, R. B., Malarkey, W. B., Van Cauter, E., & Berntson, G. G. (2002). Loneliness and health: Potential mechanisms. *Psychosomatic Medicine, 64*, 407–417.

Cahill, L. (2005, April 25). His brain, her brain. *Scientific American, 292*, 40–47.

Cahill, S., & South, K. (2002). Policy issues affecting lesbian, gay, bisexual, and transgender people in retirement. *Generations, 26*(2), 49–54.

Cairns, R. B., Cairns, B. D., & Neckerman, H. J. (1989). Growth and aggression: I. Childhood to early adolescence. *Developmental Psychology, 25*, 320–330.

Calasanti, T., & Kiecolt, K. J. (2007). Diversity among late-life couples. *Generations, 31*(3), 10–17.

Calof, O. M., Singh, A. B., Lee, M. L., Kenny, A. M., Urban, R. J., Tenover, J., et al. (2005). Adverse events associated with testosterone replacement in middle-aged and older men: A meta-analysis of randomized, placebo-controlled trials. *Journal of Gerontology: Medical Sciences, 60*(11), M1451–M1457.

Campbell, A., Shirley, L., & Candy, J. (2004). A longitudinal study of gender-related cognition and behavior. *Developmental Science, 7*, 1–9.

Campbell, F. A., & Ramey, C. T. (1995). Cognitive and school outcomes for high risk African-American students at middle adolescence: Positive effects of early intervention. *American Educational Research Journal, 32*, 743–772.

Campbell, F. A., Pungello, E. P., Miller-Johnson, S., Burchinal, M., & Ramey, C. T. (2001). The development of cognitive and academic abilities: Growth curves from an early childhood educational experiment. *Developmental Psychology, 37*, 231–242.

Campbell, F. A., Ramey, C. T., Pungello, E. P., Sparling, J., & Miller-Johnson, S. (2002). Early childhood education: Young adult outcomes from the Abecedarian project. *Applied Developmental Science, 6*, 42–57.

Campbell, S. B., Spieker, S., Burchinal, M., Poe, M. D., & The NICHD Early Child Care Research Network. (2006). Trajectories of aggression from toddlerhood to age 9 predict academic and social functioning through age 12. *Journal of Child Psychology and Psychiatry, 47*, 791–800.

Campisi, J. (1997). Aging and cancer: The double-edged sword of replicative senescence. *Journal of the American Geriatrics Society, 45*(4), 482–488.

Campisi, J. (2005). Aging, tumor suppression and cancer: High wire-act! *Mechanisms of Ageing and Development, 126*(1), 51–58.

Campos, J. J., & Stenberg, C. (1981). Perception, appraisal, and emotion: The onset of social referencing. In M. E. Lamb & L. R. Sherrod (Eds.), *Infant social cognition: Empirical and theoretical considerations* (pp. 273–314). Hillsdale, NJ: Erlbaum.

Camras, L. A., Perlman, S. B., Wismer Fries, A. B., & Pollak, S. D. (2006). Post-institutionalized Chinese and Eastern European Children: Heterogeneity in the development of emotion understanding. *International Journal of Behavioural Development, 30*, 193–199.

Cannon, W. B. (1932). *The wisdom of the body.* New York: Norton.

Cantor, M. H. (1979). Neighbors and friends: An overlooked resource in the informal support system. *Research on Aging, 1*(4), 434–463.

Cappeliez, P., & O'Rourke, N. (2006). Empirical validation of a model of reminiscence and health in later life. *Journal of Gerontology B: Psychological and Social Sciences, 61*(4), P237–P244.

Caravale, B., Tozzi, C., Albino, G., & Vicari, S. (2005). Cognitive development in low risk preterm infants at 3–4 years of life. *Archives of Disease in Childhood: Fetal Neonatal Edition, 90*, F474–F479.

Carey, S. (1978). The child as word learner. In M. Halle, J. Bresnan, & G. A. Miller (Eds.), *Linguistic theory and psychological reality* (pp. 264–293). Cambridge, MA: MIT Press.

Carey, S., & Bartlett, E. (1978). Acquiring a single new word. *Proceedings of the Stanford Child Language Conference, 15*, 17–29. (Republished in *Papers and Reports on Child Language Development, 15*, 17–29.)

Carnelley, K. B., Wortman, C. B., Bolger, N., & Burke, C. T. (2006). The time course of grief reactions to spousal loss: Evidence from a national probability sample. *Journal of Personality and Social Psychology, 91*(3), 476–492.

Carr, D. (2004). The desire to date and remarry among older widows and widowers. *Journal of Marriage and Family, 66*(4), 1051–1068.

Carr, D. (2006). Methodological issues in studying late life bereavement. In D. Carr, R. M. Neese, & C. B. Wortman (Eds.) (Eds.) (2006). *Spousal bereavement in late life* (pp. 19–48). New York: Springer Publishing Company.

Carr, D., Nesse, R., & Wortman, C. B. (Eds.) (2006). *Spousal bereavement in late life.* New York: Springer Publishing Company.

Carr, M., Borkowski, J., & Maxwell, S. (1991). Motivational components of underachievement. *Developmental Psychology, 27*, 108–118.

Carrére, S., Buehlman, K. T., Gottman, J. M., Coan, J. A., & Ruckstuhl, L. (2000). Predicting marital stability and divorce in newlywed couples. *Journal of Family Psychology, 14*(1), 42–58.

Carskadon, M., & Acebo, C. (2002). Regulation of sleepiness in adolescence: Update, insights, and speculation. *Sleep, 25*, 606–616.

Carskadon, M., Acebo, C., Richardson, G., Tate, B., & Seifer, R. (1997). Long nights protocol: Access to circadian parameters in adolescents. *Journal of Biological Rhythms, 12*, 278–289.

Carstensen, L. L. (1992). Social and emotional patterns in adulthood: Support for socioemotional selectivity theory. *Psychology and Aging, 7*(3), 331–338.

Carstensen, L. L. (1993). Motivation for social contact across the life span: A theory of socioemotional selectivity. *Nebraska Symposium on Motivation, 40*, 209–254.

Carstensen, L. L., & Charles, S. T. (2003). Human aging: Why is even good news taken as bad. In L. G. Aspinwall & U. M. Staudinger (Eds.), *A psychology of human strengths: Perspectives on an emerging field* (pp. 75–86). Washington, DC: American Psychological Association.

Carstensen, L. L., & Fredrickson, B. L. (1998). Socioemotional selectivity in healthy older people and younger people living with the Human Immunodeficiency Virus: The centrality of when the future is constrained. *Health Psychology, 17*(6), 494–503.

Carstensen, L. L., & Mikels, J. A. (2005). At the intersection of emotion and cognition. *Current Directions in Psychological Science, 14*(3), 117–121.

Carstensen, L. L., Fung, H. H., & Charles, S. T. (2003). Socioemotional selectivity theory and the regulation of emotion in the second half of life. *Motivation and Emotion, 27*(2), 103–123.

Carstensen, L. L., Gottman, J. M., & Levenson, R. W. (1995). Emotional behavior in long-term marriage. *Psychology and Aging, 10*, 140–149.

Carstensen, L. L., Graff, J., Levenson, R. W., & Gottman, J. M. (1996). Affect in intimate relationships: The developmental course of marriage. In C. Magai & S. H. MacFadden (Eds.), *Handbook of emotion, adult development, and aging* (pp. 227–247). San Diego, CA: Academic Press.

Carstensen, L. L., Isaacowitz, D. M., & Charles, S. T. (1999). Taking time seriously: A theory of socioemotional selectivity. *American Psychologist, 54*(3), 165–181.

Carstensen, L. L., Mikels, J. A., Mather, M. (2006). Aging and the intersection of cognition, motivation and emotion. In J. E. Birren & K. W. Schaie (Eds.), *Handbook of the psychology of aging* (pp. 343–362). San Diego, CA: Academic Press.

Carstensen, L. L., Pasupathi, M., Mayr, U., & Nesselroade, J. (2000). Emotional experience in everyday life across the adult life span. *Journal of Personality and Social Psychology, 79*(4), 644–655.

Carver, C. S., & Scheier, M. F. (2002). Coping processes and adjustment to chronic illness In A. J. Christensen & M. H. Antoni (Eds.), *Chronic physical disorders: Behavioral medicine's perspective* (pp. 47–68). Oxford, England: Blackwell.

Carver, P. R., & Iruka, I. U. (2006). *After-school programs and activities: 2005* (NCES 2006–076). Washington, DC: U.S. Department of Education, National Center for Education Statistics.

Case-Smith, J. (2005). *Occupational therapy for children* (5th ed.). St. Louis, MO: Mosby.

Casey, B. J., Giedd, J. N., & Thomas, K. M. (2000). Structural and functional brain development and its relation to cognitive development. *Biological Psychology, 54*, 241–247.

Casey, B. J., Tottenham, N., Liston, C., & Durston, S. (2005). Imaging the developing brain: What have we learned about cognitive development? *Trends in Cognitive Science, 9, 104*–110.

Casper, L. M., & Bianchi, S. M. (2002). *Continuity and change in the American family*. Thousand Oaks, CA: Sage.

Caspi, A. (2000). The child is father of the man: Personality continuities from childhood to adulthood. *Journal of Personality and Social Psychology, 78*, 158–172.

Caspi, A., Harrington, H., Milne, B., Amell, J. W., Theodore, R. F., & Moffitt, T. E. (2003). Children's behavioral styles at age 3 are linked to their adult personality traits at age 26. *Journal of Personality, 71*, 495–513.

Caspi, A., Roberts, B. W., & Shiner, R. (2005). Personality development. *Annual Review of Psychology, 56*, 453–484.

Caspi, A., Sugden, K., Moffitt, T., Taylor, A., Craig, I., Harrington, H., et al. (2003). Influence of life stress on depression: Moderation by a polymorphism in the 5-HTT gene. *Science, 301*, 386–389.

Castelli, D. (2005). Academic achievement and physical fitness in third-, fourth-, and fifth-grade students. *Research Quarterly for Exercise and Sport, 76*(1), A–15.

Castelli, D. M., Hillman, C. H., Buck, S., Erwin, H. E. (2007). Physical fitness and academic achievement in 3rd and 5th grade students. *Journal of Sport and Exercise Psychology, 29*, 239–252.

Caughlin, J. P., & Huston, T. L. (2006). The affective structure of marriage. In A. L. Vangelisti & D. Perlman (Eds.), *The Cambridge handbook of personal relationships* (pp. 131–155). New York: Cambridge University Press.

Caviness, V. S., & Grant, P. E. (2006). Our unborn children at risk? *Proceedings for the National Academy of Sciences, 103*, 12661–12662.

Ceci, S. J., & Roazzi, A. (1994). The effects of context on cognition: Postcards from Brazil. In R. J. Sternberg & R. K. Wagnes (Eds.), *Mind in context: Interactionist perspectives on human intelligence* (pp. 74–101). New York: Cambridge University Press.

Ceci, S. J., Ross, D. F., & Toglia, M. P. (1987). Suggestibility in children's memory: Psychologal implications. *Journal of Experimental Psychology: General, 116*, 38–49.

Cecil, K. M., Brubaker, C. J., Adler, C. M., Dietrich, K. N., & Altaye, M. (2008). Decreased brain volume in adults with childhood lead exposure. *PLoS Med*icine, 5(5): e112 DOI: 10.1371/journal.pmed.0050112.

Centers for Disease Control and Prevention. (2004). *NCHS data on teenage pregnancy.* Washington: Author.

Centers for Disease Control and Prevention. (2004). *Sexual violence prevention: Beginning the dialogue.* Atlanta, GA: U.S. Department of Health and Human Services. Retrieved November 14, 2007 from http://www.cdc.gov/violenceprevention/pdf/SVPrevention-a.pdf.

Centers for Disease Control and Prevention. (2005). Swimming and recreational water safety. In *Health information for international travel 2005–2006.* Atlanta: U.S. Department of Health and Human Services, Public Health Service.

Centers for Disease Control and Prevention. (2006). *Death rates by 10-year age groups: United States.* Retrieved November 18, 2009 from http://www.cdc.gov/nchs/data/dvs/MortFinal2006_Worktable23r.pdf

Centers for Disease Control. (2006). Fatalities and injuries from falls among older adults: United States, 1993–2003 and 2001–2005. *Morbidity and Mortality Weekly Report, 55*(45), 1221–1224. Retrieved August 24, 2008 from http://www.cdc.gov/mmwr/preview/mmwrhtml/mm5545a1.htm

Centers for Disease Control and Prevention. (2006). Youth Risk Behavior Surveillance—United States, 2005. *Morbidity & Mortality Weekly Report, 55*(SS-5), 1–108.

Centers for Disease Control. (2006, April 12). *Why is preconception care a public health concern?* Retrieved August 18, 2008, from http://www.cdc.gov/ncbddd/preconception/whypreconception.htm

Centers for Disease Control. (2006, September 12). *Table 4. Estimated numbers of diagnoses of AIDS in children ,13 years of age, by year of diagnosis and exposure category, 1998–2002—United States.* Retrieved April 2, 2010 from http://www.cdc.gov/hiv/topics/surveillance/resources/reports/2002report/table4.htm

Centers for Disease Control and Prevention. (2006a). *Physical activity and the health of young people.* Atlanta, GA: U.S. Department of Health and Human Services.

Centers for Disease Control and Prevention. (2006b). *The natural history of drug use from adolescence to the mid-thirties in a general population sample.* Atlanta, GA: U.S. Department of Health and Human Services.

Centers for Disease Control and Prevention. (2007). Child passenger safety: Fact sheet. Retrieved (May 8, 2007) from: http://www.cdc.gov/ncipc/factsheets/childpas.htm

Centers for Disease Control and Prevention. (2008a). *Prevalence of overweight, obesity and extreme obesity among adults: United States, trends 1960–62 through 2005–2006.* Retrieved February 3, 2010 from http://www.cdc.gov/nchs/data/hestat/overweight/overweight_adult.pdf

Centers for Disease Control and Prevention. (2008b). *HIV/AIDS among youth.* Retrieved December 31, 2009 from http://www.cdc.gov/hiv/resources/factsheets/youth.htm

Centers for Disease Control and Prevention. (2009). *Health effects of cigarette smoking.* Retrieved February 3, 2010 from http://www.cdc.gov/tobacco/data_statistics/fact_sheets/health_effects/effects_cig_smoking/

Centers for Disease Control. (2008, June 3). *Safe motherhood.* Retrieved August 13, 2008, from http://www.cdc.gov/reproductivehealth/

Centers for Disease Control. (2009). *Falls among older adults: An overview.* Retrieved December 31, 2009 from http://www.cdc.gov/HomeandRecreationalSafety/falls/adultfalls.html

Cerella, J. (1990). Aging and information-processing rate. In J. E. Birren & K. W. Schaie (Eds.), *Handbook of the psychology of aging* (3rd ed., pp. 201–233). New York: Academic Press.

Cerminara, K. L., & Perez, A. (2000). Therapeutic death: A look at Oregon's law. *Psychology Public Policy and Law, 6*(2), 503–525.

Chalfonte, B. L., & Johnson, M. K. (1996). Feature memory and binding in young and older adults. *Memory and Cognition, 24,* 403–416.

Chall, J. (1970). *Learning to read: The great debate.* New York: Wiley.

Champagne F., Francis D., Mar, A., & Meaney, M. (2003). Variations in maternal care in the rat as a mediating influence for the effects of environment on development. *Physiology and Behavior, 79,* 359–371.

Chan, D. (1997). Depressive symptoms and perceived competence among Chinese secondary school students in Hong Kong. *Journal of Youth and Adolescence, 26,* 303–319.

Chandra, A., Martinez, G. M., Mosher, W., D., Abma, J. C., & Jones, J. (2005). Fertility, family planning and reproductive health of U. S. women: Data from the 2002 National Survey of Family Growth. National Center for Health Statistics. *Vital Health Statistics, 23* (25). Retrieved January 28, 2010 from http://www.cdc.gov/nchs/data/series/sr_23/sr23_025.pdf

Chao, R., & Tseng, V. (2002). Parenting of Asians. In M. H. Bornstein (Ed.), *Handbook of parenting: Vol. 4. Social conditions and applied parenting* (pp. 59–93). Mahwah, NJ: Erlbaum.

Chapman, I. (2007). The anorexia of aging. *Clinics in Geriatric Medicine, 23,* 735–756.

Chapman, R. S. (1997). Language development in children and adolescents with Down syndrome. *Mental Retardation and Developmental Disabilities Research Reviews, 3,* 307–312.

Charles, S. T., & Carstensen, L. L. (2010) Social and emotional aging. *Annual Review of Psychology, 61,* 383–409.

Charness, N., Czaja, S. J., & Sharit, J. (2007). Age and technology for work. In K. S. Shultz & G. A. Adams (Eds.), *Aging and work in the 21st century* (pp. 225–249). Mahwah, NJ: Erlbaum.

Chase, W. G., & Simon, H. A. (1973). Perception in chess. *Cognitive Psychology, 4,* 55–81.

Chassin, L., Hussong, A., Barrera, M., Jr., Molina, B., Trim, R., & Ritter, J. (2009). Adolescent substance use. In R. Lerner & L. Steinberg (Eds.), *Handbook of adolescent psychology* (3rd ed.) New York: Wiley.

Chaves, A. P., Diemer, M. A., Blustein, D. L., Gallagher, L. A., DeVoy, J. E., Casares, M. T., & Perry, J. C. (2004). Conceptions of work: The view from urban youth. *Journal of Counseling Psychology, 51*(3), 275–286.

Chen, C., & Stevenson, H. (1995). Motivation and mathematics achievement: A comparative study of Asian-American, Caucasian-American, and East Asian high school students. *Child Development, 66,* 1215–1234.

Chen, K., & Kandel, D. B. (1995). The natural history of drug use from adolescence to the mid-thirties in a general population sample. *American Journal of Public Health, 85*(1), 41–47.

Chen, X, Liu, W., Li, B., Gen, G., Chen, H., & Wang, L. (2000). Maternal authoritative and authoritarian attitudes and mother-child interactions and relationships in urban China. *International Journal of Behavioral Development, 24,* 119–126.

Chen, X. French, D. C., & Schneider, B. H. (2006) Culture and peer relationships. In X. Chen, D. R. French, & B. H. Schneider (Eds.), *Peer relationships in cultural context* (pp. 3–20). New York: Cambridge University Press.

Chen, X., Chang, L., & He, Y. (2003). The peer group as a context: Mediating and moderating effects on the relation between academic achievement and social functioning in Chinese children. *Child Development, 74,* 710–727.

Chen, X., Rubin, K., & Li, Z. (1995). Social functioning and adjustment in Chinese children: A longitudinal study. *Developmental Psychology, 31,* 531–539.

Chen, X., Wu, H., Chen, H., Wang, L. & Cen, G. (2001). Parenting practices and aggressive behavior in Chinese children. *Parenting, 1,* 159–184.

Cheng, M. H., Wang, S. J., Wang, P. H., & Fuh, J. L. (2005). Attitudes toward menopause among middle-aged women: A community survey in an island of Taiwan. *Maturitas, 52*(3–4), 348–355.

Cheng, S., & Yim, Y. (2008). Age differences in forgiveness: The role of future time perspective. *Psychology and Aging, 23*(3), 676–680.

Cherkas, L., Aviv, A., Valdes, A., Hunkin, J., Gardner, J., Surdulescu, G., et al. (2006). The effects of social status on biological aging as measured by white-blood-cell telomere length. *Aging Cell, 5*(5), 361–365.

Cherlin, A. J. (1992). *Marriage, divorce, remarriage.* Cambridge, MA: Harvard University Press.

Cherlin, A. J., & Furstenberg, F. F. (1986). *The new American grandparent.* New York: Basic Books.

Cherlin, A. J., & Furstenberg, F. F. (1994). Stepfamilies in the United States: A reconsideration. *Annual Review of Sociology, 20,* 359–381.

Chervenak, F. A., & McCullough, L. B. (1998). Ethical dimensions of ultrasound screening for fetal anomalies. *Annals of the New York Academy of Sciences, 847,* 185.

Chess, S., & Thomas, A. (1996). *Temperament: Theory and practice.* Philadelphia, PA: Brunner/Mazel.

Chi, M. T. & Koeske, R. D. (1983). Network representation of a child's dinosaur knowledge. *Developmental Psychology, 19*(1), 29–39

Chinn, S., Jarvis, D., Melotti, R., Luczynska, C., Ackermann-Liebrich, U., Antó, J. M., et al. (2005). Smoking cessation, lung function, and weight gain: A follow-up study. *Lancet, 365,* 1629–1635.

Chiriboga, D. (1997). Crisis, challenge, and stability in the middle years. In M. E. Lachman & J. B. James (Eds.), *Multiple paths of midlife development* (pp. 293–322). Chicago, IL: University of Chicago Press.

Chisholm, L., & Hurrelmann, K. (1995). Adolescence in modern Europe. Pluralized transition patterns and their implications for personal and social risks. *Journal of Adolescence, 18*(2), 129–158.

Chochinov, H. M. (2006). Dying, dignity, and new horizons in palliative end-of-life care 1. *CA: A Cancer Journal for Clinicians, 56*(2), 84–103.

Choi, C. Q. (2007), Five New Year's resolutions you owe yourself. *Scientific American 17,* 82–85.

Chomsky, N. (1965). *Aspects of the theory of syntax.* Oxford, England: M.I.T. Press.

Christie-Mizell, C. A., Steelman, L. C. & Stewart, J. (2003). Seeing their surroundings: The effects of neighborhood setting and race on maternal distress, *Social Science Research, 32,* 402–428.

Christopher, F. (1995). Adolescent pregnancy prevention. *Family Relations, 44,* 384–391.

Chu, S. Y., Barker, L. E., & Smith, P. J. (2004). Racial/ethnic disparities in preschool immunizations: United States, 1996–2001. *American Journal of Public Health, 94,* 973–977.

CIA. (2009). *The world factbook. Country comparison: Life expectancy at birth.* Retrieved August 7, 2008 from https://www.cia.gov/library/publications/the-world-factbook/rankorder/2102rank.html

Ciaramelli, E., Muccioli, M., Ladavas, E., & di Pellegrino, G. (2007). Selective deficit in personal moral judgment following damage to ventromedial prefrontal cortex. *Social Cognitive and Affective Neuroscience, 2*(2), 84–92.

Cicchetti, D., & Manly, J. T. (2001). Operationalizing child maltreatment: Developmental processes and outcomes. *Development and Psychopathology, 13,* 755–757.

Cicirelli, V. G. (1990). Family support in relation to health problems of the elderly. In T. H. Brubaker (Ed.), *Family relationships in later life* (pp. 212–228). Newbury Park, CA: Sage.

Cicirelli, V. G. (1995). *Sibling relationships across the life span.* New York: Springer.

Cillessen, A. H. N., Bukowski, W. M., & Haselager, G. T. (2000). Stability of dimensions and types of sociometric status. *New Directions for Child and Adolescent Development: Recent Advances in the Measurement of Acceptance and Rejection in the Peer System, 88,* 75–93.

Clark, E. V. (1998). Morphology in language acquisition. In A. Spencer & A. M. Zwicky (Eds.), *The handbook of morphology* (pp. 374–389). Oxford: Blackwell.

Clarke-Stewart, A., & Allhusen, V. D. (2005). *What we know about child care.* Cambridge, MA: Harvard University Press.

Clarke-Stewart, A., & Brentano, C. (2006). *Divorce: Causes and consequences.* New Haven, CT: Yale University Press.

Clarke-Stewart, K. A. (1998). Historical shifts and underlying themes in ideas about rearing young children in the United States: Where have we been? Where are we going? *Early Development & Parenting, 7,* 101–117.

Clarke-Stewart, K. A., & Allhusen, V. D. (2002). Nonparental caregiving. In M. H. Bornstein (Ed.), *Handbook of parenting: Vol. 3. Status and social conditions of parenting* (2nd ed., pp. 215–252). Mahwah, NJ: Erlbaum.

Clark-Plaskie, M., & Lachman, M. E. (1999). The sense of control in midlife In S. L. Willis & J. D. Reid (Eds), *Life in the middle: Psychological and social development in middle age* (pp. 181–208). San Diego, CA: Academic Press.

Clasen, D., & Brown, B. (1985). The multidimensionality of peer pressure in adolescence. *Journal of Youth and Adolescence, 14,* 451–468.

Claxton, L. J., Keen, R., & McCarty, M. E. (2003). Evidence of motor planning in infant reaching behavior. *Psychological Science, 14,* 354–356.

Clay, R. A. (2006). Battling the self-blame of infertility. *Monitor on Psychology, 37*(4), 44.

Cleary, P. D., Zaborski, L. B., & Ayanian, J. A. (2004). Sex differences in health over the course of midlife. In O. G. Brim, C. D. Ryff, & R. C. Kessler (Eds.), *How healthy are we?: A national study of well-being at midlife* (pp. 37–63). Chicago, IL: University of Chicago Press.

Cohen, P., Kasen, S., Chen, H., Hartmark, C., & Gordon, K. (2003). Variations in patterns of developmental transitions in the emerging adulthood period. *Developmental Psychology, 39*(4), 657–669.

Cohen, S. (2004). Social relationships and health. *American Psychologist, 59*(8), 676–684.

Cohen, S., & Wills, T. A. (1985). Stress, social support, and the buffering hypothesis. *Psychological Bulletin, 98*(2), 310–357.

Cohen, S., Frank, E., Doyle, W. J., Skoner, D. P., Rabin, B. S., & Gwaltney, J. M., Jr. (1998). Types of stressors that increase susceptibility to the common cold in healthy adults. *Health Psychology, 17*(3), 214–223.

Cohen, Y. (1964). *The transition from childhood to adolescence.* Chicago: Aldine.

Cohn, J. F., & Tronick, E. Z. (1983). Three-month-old infants' reaction to simulated maternal depression. *Child Development, 54,* 185–193.

Coie, J., Dodge, K. A., & Coppotelli, H. (1982). Dimensions and types of social status: A cross-age perspective. *Developmental Psychology, 18,* 557–570.

Coie, J., Terry, R., Lenox, K., Lochman, J., & Hyman, C. (1995). Childhood peer rejection and aggression as predictors of stable patterns of adolescent disorder. *Development and Psychopathology, 7,* 697–713.

Colby, A., Kohlberg, L., Gibbs, J., & Lieberman, M. (1983). A longitudinal study of moral judgment. *Monographs of the Society for Research in Child Development, 48*(1–2), 1–124.

Colcombe, S. J., Erickson, K. I., Scalf, P. E., Kim, J. S., Prakash, R., McAuley, E., et al. (2006). Aerobic exercise training increases brain volume in aging humans. *Journal of Gerontology A: Biological Sciences and Medical Sciences, 61*(11), 1166–1170.

Cole, A., & Kerns, K. A. (2001). Perceptions of sibling qualities and activities of early adolescents. *Journal of Early Adolescence, 21,* 204–226.

Cole, D. A., Maxwell, S. E., Martin, J. M., Peeke, L. G., Seroczynski, A. D., Tram, J. M., et al. (2001). The development of multiple domains of child and adolescent self-concept: A cohort sequential longitudinal design. *Child Development, 72,* 1723–1746.

Cole, D., & Jordan, A. (1995). Competence and memory: Integrating psychosocial and cognitive correlates of child depression. *Child Development, 66,* 459–473.

Cole, M., & Dendukuri, N. (2003). Risk factors for depression among elderly community subjects: A systematic review and meta-analysis. *American Journal of Psychiatry, 160*(6), 1147–1156.

Cole, P., Zahn-Waxler, C., & Smith, D. (1994). Expressive control during a disappointment: Variations related to preschoolers' behavior problems. *Developmental Psychology, 30,* 835–846.

Coleman, J., Campbell, E., Hobson, C., McPartland, J., Mood, A., Weinfeld, F., & York, R. (1966). *Equality of educational opportunity.* Washington, DC: U.S. Government Printing Office.

Coleman, L. (1999). Comparing contraceptive use surveys of young people in the United Kingdom. *Archives of Sexual Behavior, 28,* 255–264.

Coleman, M., Ganong, L., & Leon, K. (2006). Divorce and postdivorce relationships. In A. L. Vangelisti & D. Perlman (Eds.), *The Cambridge handbook of personal relationships* (pp. 157–173). Cambridge: Cambridge University Press.

Coles, L. A. (2004). Aging: The reality. Demography of human supercentenarians. *Journal of Gerontology A: Biological Sciences and Medical Sciences, 59,* B579–586.

Coley, R., & Chase-Lansdale, P. L. (1998). Adolescent pregnancy and parenthood: Recent evidence and future directions. *American Psychologist, 53,* 152–166.

Collins, A., & Madsen, S. D. (2006). Personal relationships in adolescence and early adulthood. In A. L. Vangelisti & D. Perlman (Eds.), *The Cambridge handbook of personal relationships* (pp. 191–209). Cambridge: Cambridge University Press.

Collins, W. A. (2003). More than a myth: The developmental significance of romantic relationships during adolescence. *Journal of Research on Adolescents, 13,* 1–24.

Collins, W. A., & Steinberg, L. (2006). Adolescent development in interpersonal context. In W. Damon & R. Lerner (Series Eds.) & N. Eisenberg (Vol. Ed.), *Handbook of child psychology: Vol. 3. Social, emotional, and personality development* (6th ed., pp. 1003–1067). New York: Wiley.

Collins, W. A., Maccoby, E. E., Steinberg, L., Hetherington, E. M., & Bornstein, M. H. (2000). Contemporary research on parenting: The case for nature and nurture. *American Psychologist, 55,* 218–232.

Colman, I, Ploubidis, G. B., Wadsworth, M. E. J., Jones, P. B., & Croudace, T. J. (2008). A longitudinal typology of symptoms of depression and anxiety over the life course. *Biological Psychiatry, 62,* 1265–1271.

Committee on Prospering in the Global Economy. (2007). *Rising above the gathering storm: Energizing and employing America for a brighter economic future.* Washington, DC: National Academies Press.

Commons, M. L., Armon, C., Kohlberg, L., Richards, F. A., Grotzer, T. A., & Sinnott, J. D. (Eds.). (1990). *Adult development: Volume 2: Models and methods in the study of adolescent and adult thought.* New York: Praeger.

Compas, B., Ey, S., & Grant, K. (1993). Taxonomy, assessment, and diagnosis of depression during adolescence. *Psychological Bulletin, 114,* 323–344.

Compas, B., Oppedisano, G., Connor, J., Gerhardt, C., Hinden, B., Achenbach, T., & Hammen, C. (1997). Gender differences in depressive symptoms in adolescence: Comparison of national samples of clinically referred and nonreferred youths. *Journal of Consulting and Clinical Psychology, 65,* 617–626.

Comstock, G., & Scharrer, E. (2006). Media and popular culture. In K. A. Renninger & I. E. Sigel (Eds.), *Handbook of child psychology: Vol. 4. Child psychology in practice* (pp. 817– 863). Hoboken, NJ: Wiley.

Conde-Agudelo, A., Rosas-Bermúdez, A., & Kafury-Goeta, A. C. (2006). Birth spacing and risk of adverse perinatal outcomes a meta-analysis. *JAMA, 295,* 1809–1823.

Conger, K., Conger, R., & Scaramella, L. (1997). Parents, siblings, psychological control, and adolescent adjustment. *Journal of Adolescent Research, 12,* 113–138.

Conger, R. D., & Donnellan, M. B. (2007). An interactionist perspective on the socioeconomic context of human development. *Annual Review of Psychology, 58,* 175–179.

Connell, J., Halpern-Felsher, B., Clifford, E., Crichlow, W., & Usinger, P. (1995). Hanging in there: Behavioral, psychological, and contextual factors affecting whether African American adolescents stay in high school. *Journal of Adolescent Research, 10,* 41–63.

Connidis, I. A. (1992). Life transitions and the adult sibling tie: A qualitative study. *Journal of Marriage and the Family, 54*(4), 972–982.

Connolly, J. (in press). Romantic relationships and intimacy in adolescence. In R. Lerner & L. Steinberg (Eds.) *Handbook of Adolescent Psychology.* New York: Wiley.

Connolly, J., & Johnson, A. (1993, March). *The psychosocial context of romantic relationships in adolescence.* Paper presented at the biennial meetings of the Society for Research in Child Development, New Orleans.

Connor, C. M., Morrison, F. J., & Katch, L. E. (2004). Beyond the reading wars: Exploring the effect of child-instruction interactions on growth in early reading. *Scientific Studies of Reading, 8,* 305–336.

Consedine, N. S., & Magai, C. (2006). Emotional development and adulthood: A developmental functionalist review and critique. In C. M. Hoare (Ed.), *Handbook of adult development and learning* (pp. 123–139). Oxford: Oxford University Press.

Cook, T, D., Church, M. B., Ajanaku, S., Shadish, W. R., Jr., Kim J. R., & Cohen, R. (1996). The development of occupational aspirations and expectations among inner-city boys. *Child Development, 67*(6), 3368–3385.

Cooley, C. H. (1902). *Human nature and the social order.* New York: Charles Scribner & Sons.

Cooney, C., Howard, R., & Lawlor, B. (2006). Abuse of vulnerable people with dementia by their carers: Can we identify those most at risk? *International Journal of Geriatric Psychiatry, 21,* 564–571.

Cooney, T. M., & Uhlenberg, P. (1990). The role of divorce in men's relations with their adult children after mid-life. *Journal of Marriage and the Family, 52*(3), 677–688.

Cooney, T. M., Schaie, K. W., & Willis, S. L. (1988). The relationship between prior functioning on cognitive and personality dimensions and subject attrition in longitudinal research. *Journal of Gerontology B: Psychological Sciences and Social Sciences, 43*(1), P12–17.

Coontz, S. (2007). The origins of modern divorce. *Family Process, 46*(1), 7–16.

Cooper, H. (2004). Is the school calendar dated? In G. Borman & M. Boulay (Eds.), *Summer learning: Research, policies, and programs* (pp. 3–23). Mahwah, NJ: Erlbaum.

Cooper, M. L., Agocha, V. B., & Powers, A. M. (1999). Motivations for condom use: Do pregnancy prevention goals undermine disease prevention among heterosexual young adults? *Health Psychology, 18*(5), 464–474.

Cooper, R., Cutler, J., Desvigne-Nickens, P., Fortmann, S. P., Friedman, L., Havlik, R., et al. (2000). Trends and disparities in coronary heart disease, stroke, and other cardiovascular diseases in the United States: Findings of the National Conference on Cardiovascular Disease Prevention. *Circulation, 102,* 3137–3147.

Coopersmith, S. A. (1967). *The antecedents of self-esteem.* San Francisco: Freeman.

Copp, G. (1998). A review of current theories of death and dying. *Journal of Advanced Nursing, 28*(2), 382–390.

Corbin, C. B., & Pangrazi, R. P. (1998). *Physical activity for children: A statement of guidelines.* Reston, VA: National Association for Sport and Physical Education.

Corr, C. A. (1993). Coping with dying: Lessons that we should and should not learn from the work of Elisabeth Kubler-Ross. *Death Studies, 17*(1), 69–83.

Corsaro, W. A. (2006). Qualitative research on children's peer relations in cultural context. In X. Chen, D. R. French, & B. H. Schneider (Eds.), *Peer relationships in cultural context* (pp. 96–119). New York: Cambridge University Press.

Costa Jr, P. T., & McCrae, R. R. (1980). Still stable after all these years: Personality as a key to some issues in adulthood and old age In P. B. Baltes & O. G. Brim (Eds.), *Life-span development and behavior* (Vol. 3, pp. 65–102). New York: Academic Press.

Costa, D. (1998). *The evolution of retirement: an American economic history, 1880–1990.* Chicago, IL: University of Chicago Press.

Costa, P. T., Jr., & McCrae, R. R. (1988). Personality in adulthood: A six-year longitudinal study of self-reports and spouse ratings on the NEO Personality Inventory. *Journal of Personality and Social Psychology, 54*(5), 853–863.

Costa, P. T., Jr., & McCrae, R. R. (1994). Set like plaster? Evidence for the stability of adult personality. In T. F. Heatherton & J. L. Weinberger (Eds.), *Can personality change?* (pp. 21–40). Washington DC: American Psychological Association.

Costa, P. T., Jr., & McRae, R. R. (2006). Age changes in personality and origins: Comment on Roberts, Walton, and Viechtbauer (2006). *Psychological Bulletin, 132*(1), 26–28.

Costanzo, P. R., & Hoy, M. B. (2007). Intergenerational relations: Themes, prospects, and possibilities. *Journal of Social Issues, 63*(4), 885–902.

Cote, L. R., & Bornstein, M. H. (2005). Child and mother play in cultures of origin, acculturating cultures, and cultures of destination. *International Journal of Behavioral Development, 29,* 479–488.

Cotman, C. W., Berchtold, N. C., & Christie, L. A. (2007). Exercise builds brain health: Key roles of growth factor cascades and inflammation. *Trends in Neurosciences, 30*(9), 464–472.

Couperus, J. W., & Nelson, C. A. (2006). Early brain development and plasticity. In K. McCartney & D. Phillips (Eds.), *Blackwell handbook of early childhood development* (pp. 85–105). Malden, MA: Blackwell.

Cousins, S. O. (2000). "My heart couldn't take it": Older women's beliefs about exercise benefits and risks. *Journal of Gerontology B: Psychological Sciences and Social Sciences, 55*(5), P283–P294.

Cowan, C. P., & Cowan, P. A. (1992). *When parents become partners.* New York: Wiley.

Cox, M. J., & Paley, B. (2003). Understanding families as systems. *Current Directions in Psychological Science*, 12(5), 193–196.

Coylewright, M., Reckelhoff, J. F., & Ouyang, P. (2008). Menopause and hypertension: An age-old debate. *Hypertension, 51*(4), 952–959.

Crago, M. B. (1992). Communicative interaction and second language acquisition: An Inuit Example. *TESOL Quarterly, 26,* 487–505.

Craik, F. I. M. (2000). Age-related changes in human memory. In D. C. Park & N. Schwarz (Eds.), *Cognitive aging: A primer* (pp. 75–92). Philadelphia: Psychology Press.

Craik, F. I. M. (2006). Age-related changes in human memory: Practical consequences. Memory and society: Psychological perspectives. In L. G. Nilsson & N. Ohta (Eds). *Memory and society: Psychological perspectives* (pp. 181–197). New York: Psychology Press.

Craik, F. I. M., & Byrd, M. (1982). Aging and cognitive deficits: The role of attentional resources. In F. I. M. C. S. E. Trehub (Ed.), *Aging and cognitive processes* (pp. 191–211). New York: Plenum Press.

Crews, J. E., & Campbell, V. A. (2004). Vision impairment and hearing loss among community-dwelling older Americans: implications for health and functioning. *American Journal of Public Health, 94*(5), 823–829.

Crick, N. R., & Grotpeter, J. K. (1995). Relational aggression, gender, and social-psychological adjustment. *Child Development*, 66, 710–722.

Crick, N. R., Casas, J. F., & Nelson, D. A. (2002). Toward a more comprehensive understanding of peer maltreatment: Studies of relational victimization. *Current Directions in Psychological Science, 11,* 98–101.

Crick, N. R., Casas, J. J., & Mosher, M. (1997) Relational and overt aggression in preschool. *Developmental Psychology, 33,* 579–588.

Crick, N. R., Ostrov, J. M., & Werner, N. E. (2006). A longitudinal study of relational aggression, physical aggression, and children's social-psychological adjustment. *Journal of Abnormal Child Psychology, 34,* 131–142.

Crimmins, E. M., Kim, J. K., & Seeman, T. E. (2009). Poverty and biological risk: The earlier"aging" of the poor. *Journal of Gerontology A: Biological Sciences and Medical Sciences A, 64A*(2), 286–292.

Cristofalo, V., Tresini, M., Francis, M., & Volker, C. (1999). Biological theories of senescence. In V. L. Bengtson & K. W. Schaie (Eds.), *Handbook of theories of aging* (pp. 98–112). New York: Springer.

Cromie, W. J. (1997, March 20). Midlife crisis disappears. *Harvard University Gazette.* Retrieved December 16, 2009 from http://ww.hno.harvard.edu/gazette/1997/03.20/MidlifeCrisisDi.html

Crosnoe, R., & Needham, B. (2004). Holism, contextual variability, and the study of friendships in adolescent development. *Child Development, 75,* 264–279.

Cross, W. (1978). The Thomas and Cook models of psychological nigrescence: A literature review. *Journal of Black Psychology, 4,* 13–31.

Crouter, A. C., Bumpus, M. F., Maguire, M. C., & McHale, S. M. (1999). Linking parents' work pressure and adolescents' well-being: Insights into dynamics in dual-earner families. *Developmental Psychology, 35*(6), 1453–1461.

Csikszentmihalyi, M., Rathunde, K., & Whalen, S. (1993). *Talented teenagers.* New York: Cambridge University Press.

Cuéllar, I., Arnold, B., & Gonzalez, G. (1995). Cognitive referents of acculturation: Assessment of cultural constructs in Latinos. *Journal of Community Psychology, 23,* 339–356.

Cumming, E., & Henry, W. E. (1961). *Growing old: The process of disengagement*. New York: Basic Books.

Cumming, R. G., Salkeld, G., Thomas, M., & Szonyi, G. (2000). Prospective study of the impact of fear of falling on activities of daily living, SF-36 scores, and nursing home admission. *Journal of Gerontology: A Biological Sciences and Medical Sciences, 55*(5), M299–305.

Cummings, E. M. & Davies, P. (1994). *Children and marital conflict: The impact of family dispute and resolution*. New York: Guilford.

Cummings, E. M., & Cummings, J. S. (2002). Parenting and attachment. In M. H. Bornstein (Ed.), *Handbook of parenting: Vol. 5. Practical parenting* (2nd ed., pp. 35–58). Mahwah, NJ: Erlbaum.

Cunningham, M., Bhattacharyya, S., & Benes, F. (2002), Amygdalo-cortical sprouting continues into early adulthood: Implications for the development of normal and abnormal function during adolescence. *Journal of Comparative Neurology, 453,* 116–30.

Cunningham, W., & Owens, W. A. (1983). The Iowa state study of the adult development of intellectual abilities. In K. W. Schaie (Ed.), *Longitudinal studies of adult psychological development* (pp. 379–406). New York: Guilford Press.

Cutler, N. E., Whitelaw, N. A., & Beattie, B. L. (2002). *American perceptions of aging in the 21st century*. Washington, D.C.: National Council on the Aging. Retrieved Feb 15, 2010 from http://www.healthyagingprograms.org/resources/MRA%20Chartbook%20Complete.pdf

Cyranowski, J., & Frank, E. (2000). Adolescent onset of the gender difference in lifetime rates of major depression. *Archives of General Psychiatry, 57,* 21–27.

Daley, S. (2000, June 20). The Dutch seek to legalize long-tolerated euthanasia. *New York Times*. Retrieved July 9, 2009 from http://www.nytimes.com/2000/06/20/world/the-dutch-seek-to-legalize-long-tolerated-euthanasia.html

Damasio, A. (1994). Descartes' error: Emotion, reason, and the human brain. New York: Putnam.

Darabi, K., & Ortiz, V. (1987). Childbearing among young Latino women in the United States. *American Journal of Public Health, 77*, 25–28.

Darling-Hammond, L. (2008). Creating excellent and equitable schools. *Educational Leadership, 65*(8), 14–21.

Darwin, C. (1872/1975). *The Expression of the emotions in man and animals*. Chicago: University of Chicago Press.

Darwin, C. (2003). *The origin of species*. New York: Signet Classics. (Original work published 1872)

Davidoff, M. J., Dias, T., Damus, K., Russell, R., Bettegowda, V. R., Dolan, S., Schwarz, R. H., Green, N. S. & Petrini, J. (2006). Changes in the gestational age distribution among U.S. Singleton births: Impact on rates of late preterm birth, 1992 to 2002. *Seminars in Perinatology, 30*, 8–15.

Davies, P. T., & Windle, M. (2000). Middle adolescents' dating pathways and psychosocial adjustment. *Merrill-Palmer Quarterly, 46*, 90–118.

Davis, D., Shaver, P. R., & Vernon, M. L. (2003). Physiological, emotional, and behavioral reactions to breaking up: The roles of gender, age, emotional involvement, and attachment. *Personality and Social Psychology Bulletin, 29*(7), 871–884.

Davis, E. P., Snidman, N., Wadhwa, P. D., Glynn, L. M., Schetter, C. D., & Sandman, C. A. (2004). Prenatal maternal anxiety and depression predict negative behavioral reactivity in infancy. *Infancy, 6*, 319–331.

Davison, J., & Marrinan, S. (2007). Falls. *Reviews in Clinical Gerontology, 17*(02), 93–107.

Davison, K. K., & Birch, L. L. (2001). Weight status, parent reaction, and self-concept in five-year-old girls. *Pediatrics, 107*, 46–53.

Dawson, T. L. (2002). New tools, new insights: Kohlberg's moral judgment stages revisited. *International Journal of Behavioral Development, 26*(2), 154–166.

de Graaf, P. M., & Kalmijn, M. (2003). Alternative Routes in the Remarriage Market. *Social Forces, 81*(4), 1459–1498.

de Graaf, P., & Fokkema, T. (2007). Contacts between divorced and non-divorced parents and their adult children in the Netherlands: An investment perspective. *European Sociological Review, 23*(2), 263.

de Haan, M. (2008). Neurocognitive mechanisms for the development of face processing. In C. A. Nelson & M. Luciana (Eds.), *Handbook of developmental cognitive neuroscience* (2nd ed., pp. 509–520). Cambridge, MA: MIT Press.

de Jong Gierveld, J. (2004). Remarriage, unmarried cohabitation, living apart together: Partner relationships following bereavement or divorce. *Journal of Marriage and Family, 66*(1), 236–243.

de St. Aubin, E., & McAdams. D. P. (1995). The relations of generative concern and generative actions to personality traits, satisfaction/happiness with life, and ego development. *Journal of Adult Development*, 2(2), 99–112.

De Wolff, M., & van Ijzendoorn, M. H. (1997). Sensitivity and attachment: A meta-analysis on parental antecedents of infant attachment. *Child Development, 68*, 571–591.

Dearing, E. (2004). The developmental implications of restrictive and supportive parenting across neighborhoods and ethnicities: Exceptions are the rule. *Applied Developmental Psychology, 25*, 555–575.

Dearing, E., Berry, D., & Zaslow, M. (2006). Poverty during early childhood. In K. McCartney & D. Phillips (Eds.), *Blackwell handbook of early childhood development* (pp. 399–423). Malden, MA: Blackwell.

Dearing, E., Kreider, H., Simpkins, S., & Weiss, H. B. (2006). Family involvement in school and low-income children's literacy: Longitudinal associations between and with families. *Journal of Educational Psychology, 98*, 653–664.

Deater-Deckard, K., & Plomin, R. (1999). An adoption study of etiology of teacher and parent reports of externalizing behavior problems in middle childhood. *Child Development, 70*, 144–154.

Décarie, T. G., & Ricard, M. (1996). Revisiting Piaget revisited or the vulnerability of Piaget's infancy theory in the 1990s. In G. G. Noam & K. W. Fischer (Eds.), *Development and vulnerability in close relationships* (pp. 113–132). Hillsdale, NJ: Erlbaum.

DeCasper, A. J., Lecanuet, J. P., Busnel, M. C., Granier-Deferre, C., & Maugeais, R. (1994). Fetal reactions to recurrent maternal speech. *Infant Behavior and Development, 17*, 159–164.

Deci, E., & Ryan, R. (1985). *Intrinsic motivation and self-determination in human behavior.* New York: Plenum.

DeLoache, J. S. (1995). Early understanding and use of symbols: The model model. *Current Directions in Psychological Science, 4*, 109–113.

DeLoache, J. S., Cassidy, D. J., Brown, A. L. (1985). Precursors of Mnemonic Strategies in Very Young Children's Memory. *Child Development, 56*, 125–137.

DeLongis, A., Folkman, S., & Lazarus, R. S. (1988). The impact of daily stress on health and mood: Psychological and social resources as mediators. *Journal of Personality and Social Psychology, 54*(3), 486–495.

Demetriou, A., Christou, C., Spanoudis, G., & Platsidou, M. (2002). The development of mental processing: Efficiency, working memory, and thinking. *Monographs of the Society for Research in Child Development, 67*(1, Serial No. 268).

DeNavas-Walt, C., Proctor, B. D., & Smith, J. C. (2009). *Income, poverty, and health insurance coverage in the United States: 2008*. U. S. Census Bureau, Current Population Reports, P60-236. Washington, DC: U.S. Government Printing Office. Retrieved December 13, 2009 from: http://www.census.gov/prod/2009pubs/p60-236.pdf

Denham, S., Mason, T., Caverly, S., Schmidt, M., Hackney, R., Caswell, C., & DeMulder, E. (2001). Preschoolers at play: Co-socialisers of emotional and social competence. *International Journal of Behavioral Development, 25*, 290–301.

Denham, S., McKinley, M., Couchould, E., & Holt, R. (1990). Emotional and behavioral predictors of preschool peer ratings. *Child Development, 61*, 1145–1152.

Dennerstein, L., Dudley, E., & Guthrie, J. (2002). Empty nest or revolving door? A prospective study of women's quality of life in midlife during the phase of children leaving and re-entering the home. *Psychological Medicine, 32*(3), 545–550.

Denney, N. W. & Palmer, A. M. (1981). Adult age differences on traditional and practical problem-solving measures. *Journal of Gerontology, 36* (3), 323–328.

Denney, N. W., & Pearce, K. A. (1989). A developmental study of practical problem solving in adults. *Psychology and Aging*, 4(4), 438–442.

Dennis, N., & Cabeza, R. (2008). Neuroimaging of healthy cognitive aging. In F. I. M. Craik & T. A. Salthouse (Eds.). *The Handbook of aging and cognition* (2nd ed., pp. 1–54). New York: Psychology Press.

Dennis, T., Bendersky, M., Ramsay, D., & Lewis, M. (2006). Reactivity and regulation in children prenatally exposed to cocaine. *Developmental Psychology, 42*, 688–697.

DePaulo, B. M., & Morris, W. L. (2005). Singles in society and in science. *Psychological Inquiry, 16*(2–3), 57–83.

Desai, M., Pratt, L. A., Lentzner, H., & Robinson, K. N. (2001). Trends in vision and hearing among older Americans. National Center for Health Statistics. *Aging Trends, 2*, 1–8.

Dettling, A. C., Gunnar, M. R., & Donzella, B. (1999). Cortisol levels of young children in full-day child care centers: Relations with age and temperament. *Psychoneuroendocrinology, 24*, 519–536.

Dettling, A. C., Parker, S. W., Lane, S. K., Sebanc, A. M., & Gunnar, M. R. (2000). Quality of care and temperament determine whether cortisol levels rise over the day for children in full-day child care. *Psychoneuroendocrinology, 25*, 819–836.

Deutsch, D., Henthorn, T., & Dolson, M. (2004). Speech patterns heard early in life influence later perception of the tritone paradox. *Music Perception, 21*, 357–372.

Deutsch, D., Henthorn, T., Marvin, E., & Xu H-S. (2006). Absolute pitch among American and Chinese conservatory students: Prevalence differences, and evidence for a speech-related critical period. *Journal of the Acoustical Society of America, 119*, 719–722.

deVries, B. (2007). LGBT couples in later life: A study in diversity. *Generations, 31*, 18–23.

Dewhurst, S. A., & Robinson, C. A. (2004). False memories in children: Evidence for a shift from phonological to semantic associations. *Psychological Science, 15*, 782–786.

Deykin, E. Y., Jacobson, S., Klerman, G., & Solomon, M. (1966). The empty nest: Psychosocial aspects of conflict between depressed women and their grown children. *American Journal of Psychiatry, 122*(12), 422–426.

Diamond, A. (2005). Attention-deficit disorder (attention-deficit/hyperactivity disorder without hyperactivity): A neurobiologically and behaviorally distinct disorder from attention-deficit/hyperactivity disorder (with hyperactivity). *Development and Psychopathology, 17*, 807–825.

Diamond, L. M. (2004). Emerging perspectives on distinctions between romantic love and sexual desire. *Current Directions in Psychological Science, 13*(3), 116–119.

Diamond, L. M., & Savin-Williams, R. C. (2000). Explaining diversity in the development of same-sex sexuality among young women. *Journal of Social Issues, 56*(2), 297–313.

Dick, D. M., Rose, R. J., Pulkkinen, L., & Kaprio, J. (2001). Measuring puberty and understanding its impact: A longitudinal study of adolescent twins. *Journal of Youth and Adolescence, 30*, 385–400.

Dick, D. M., Rose, R. J., Viken, R. J., & Kaprio, J. (2000). Pubertal timing and substance use: Associations between and within families across late adolescence. *Developmental Psychology, 36*, 180–189.

Dickens, B. M., Boyle, J. M., & Ganzini, L. (2008). Euthanasia and assisted suicide. In P. A. Singer & A. M. Viens (Eds.), *The Cambridge textbook of bioethics* (pp. 72–77). Cambridge, England: Cambridge University Press.

Dickens, W. T. & Flynn, J. R. (2001). Heritability estimates versus large environmental effects: The IQ paradox resolved. *Psychological Review, 108*(2), 346–369.

Dickstein, S., & Parke, R. D. (1988). Social referencing in infancy: A glance at fathers and marriage. *Child Development, 59*, 506–511.

Dielman, T. (1994). School-based research on the prevention of adolescent alcohol use and misuse: Methodological issues and advances. *Journal of Research on Adolescence, 4*, 271–293.

Diener, E. , & Seligman, M. E. P. (2004). Beyond money: Toward an economy of well-being. *Psychological Science in the Public Interest, 5*(1), 1–31.

Diener, E., & Suh, E. M. (1998). Subjective well-being and age: An international analysis. *Annual Review Of Gerontology And Geriatrics, 17*, 304–324.

Dietrich, A. (2004). The cognitive neuroscience of creativity. *Psychonomic Bulletin and Review, 11*(6), 1011–1026

Dingfelder, S. (2006). To sleep, perchance to twitch. *Monitor on Psychology, 37*, 51–60.

DiPietro, J. A., Bornstein, M. H., Costigan, K. A., Pressman, E. K., Hahn, C.-S., Painter, K. M. et al. (2002). What does fetal movement predict about behavior during the first two years of life? *Developmental Psychobiology, 40*, 358–371.

DiPietro, J. A., Bornstein, M. H., Hahn, C. S., Costigan, K., & Achy-Brou, A. (2007). Fetal heart rate and variability: Stability and prediction to developmental outcomes in early childhood. *Child Development, 78*, 1788–1798.

DiPietro, J. A., Novak, M. F. S. X., Costigan, K. A., Atella, L. D., & Reusing, S. P. (2006). Maternal psychological distress during pregnancy in relation to child development at age two. *Child Development, 77*, 573–587.

Dishion, T. J., Capaldi, D. M., & Yoerger, K. (1999). Middle childhood antecedents to progressions in male adolescent substance use: An ecological analysis of risk and protection. *Journal of Adolescent Research, 14*, 175–205.

Dishion, T. J., Poulin, F., & Burraston, B. (2001). Peer group dynamics associated with iatrogenic effect in group interventions with high-risk young adolescents. *New Directions for Child and Adolescent Development, 91*, 79–92.

Dishion, T., Patterson, G., Stoolmiller, M., & Skinner, M. (1991). Family, school, and behavioral antecedents to early adolescent involvement with antisocial peers. *Developmental Psychology, 27*, 172–180.

Ditto, P. H. (2006). Self-determination, substituted judgment and the psychology of advance medical decision making. In D. Blevins & J. L. Werth (Eds.), *Psychosocial issues near the end of life: A resource for professional care providers* (pp. 89–109). Washington, DC: American Psychological Association Press.

Ditto, P. H., Danks, J. H., Smucker, W. D., Bookwala, J., Coppola, K. M., Dresser, R.,et al. (2001). Advance directives as acts of communication: A randomized controlled trial. *Archives of Internal Medicine, 161*(3), 421–430.

Ditto, P. H., Smucker, W. D., Danks, J. H., Jacobson, J. A., Houts, R. M., Fagerlin, Aet al. (2003). The stability of older adults' preferences for life-sustaining medical treatment. *Health Psychology, 22*(6), 605–615.

Djernes, J. (2006). Prevalence and predictors of depression in populations of elderly: A review. *Acta Psychiatrica Scandinavica, 113*(5), 372–387.

Dodge, K. A., Coie, J., & Lynam, D. (2006). Aggression and antisocial behavior in youth. In W. Damon & R. M. Lerner (Series Eds.) & N. Eisenberg (Vol. Ed.), *Handbook of child psychology: Vol. 3. Social, emotional, and personality development* (6th ed., pp. 719–788). Hoboken, NJ: Wiley.

Dodge, K. A., McClaskey, C. L., & Feldman, E. (1985). A situational approach to the assessment of social competence in children. *Journal of Consulting and Clinical Psychology, 53*, 344–353.

Dodge, K. A., Pettit, G., & Bates, J. (1994). Socialization mediators of the relation between socioeconomic status and child conduct problems. *Child Development, 65*, 649–665.

Doka, K., & Mertz, M. (1988). The meaning and significance of great-grandparenthood. *Gerontologist, 28*(2), 192–197.

Donaldson, D. L., & Owens J. A. (2006). Sleep and sleep problems. In G. G. Bear & K. M. Minke (Eds.), *Children's needs III: Development, prevention, and intervention* (3rd ed., pp. 1025–1039). Bethesda, MD: National Association of School Psychologists, 2006.

Dong, X. Q., Simon, M., Mendes de Leon, C., Fulmer, T., Beck, T., Hebert, L., et al. (2009). Elder self-neglect and abuse and mortality risk in a community-dwelling population. *JAMA, 302*(5), 517–526.

Donnellan, M., & Lucas, R. (2008). Age differences in the big five across the life span: Evidence from two national samples. *Psychology and Aging, 23*(3), 558–566.

Dooley, D., Catalano, R., & Rook, K. S. (1988). Personal and aggregate unemployment and psychological symptoms. *Journal of Social Issues, 44*(4), 107–123.

Doran, M. F., Pond, G. R., Crowson, C. S., O'Fallon, W. M., & Gabriel, S. E. (2002). Trends in incidence and mortality in rheumatoid arthritis in Rochester, Minnesota, over a forty-year period. *Arthritis & Rheumatism, 46*(3), 625–631.

Dorn, L. D., Nottelmann, E. D., Susman, E. J., Inoff-Germain, G., Cutler, G. B., Jr., & Chrousos, G. P. (1999). Variability in hormone concentrations and self-reported menstrual histories in young adolescents: Menarche as an integral part of a developmental process. *Journal of Youth and Adolescence, 28*, 283–304.

Doss, B. D., Rhoades, G. K., Stanley, S. M., & Markman, H. J. (2009). The effect of the transition to parenthood on relationship quality: An 8-year prospective study. *Journal of Personality and Social Psychology, 96*(3), 601–619.

Douvan, E., & Adelson, J. (1966). *The adolescent experience.* New York: Wiley.

Downer, J. T., & Pianta, R. C. (2006). Academic and cognitive functioning in first grade: Associations with earlier home and child care predictors and with concurrent home and classroom experiences. *School Psychology Review, 35*, 11–30.

Doyle, P., Maconochie, N., Davies, G., Maconochie, I., Pelerin, M., Prior, S., & Lewis, S. (2004). Miscarriage, stillbirth and congenital malformation in the offspring of UK veterans of the first Gulf war: Perinatal and early-life influences on disease. *International Journal of Epidemiology, 33*, 74–86.

Doyle, R. (2006, March). By the numbers: The honeymoon is over. *Scientific American, 294*, 34.

Dromi, E. (1987). *Early lexical development.* New York: Cambridge University Press.

Dromi, E. (2001). Babbling and early words. In N. J. Salkind & L. H. Margolis (Eds.), *Child development: Volume 1 of the Macmillan psychology reference series.* New York: Macmillan References.

Dubbert, P. M. (2002). Physical activity and exercise: Recent advances and current challenges. *Journal of Consulting and Clinical Psychology, 70*(3), 526–536.

DuBois, D. L., Burk-Braxton, C., Swenson, L. P., Tevendale, H. D., & Hardesty, J. L. (2002). Race and gender influences on adjustment in early adolescence: Investigation of an integrative model. *Child Development, 73*, 1573–1592.

Duncan, O. D., Featherman, D. L., & Duncan, B. (1972). *Socioeconomic background and achievement.* New York: Seminar Press.

Duncan, P., Ritter, P., Dornbusch, S., Gross, R., & Carlsmith, J. (1985). The effects of pubertal timing on body image, school behavior, and deviance. *Journal of Youth and Adolescence, 14*, 227–236.

Dunn, J. (1991). Understanding others: Evidence from naturalistic studies of children. In A. Whiten (Ed.), *Natural theories of mind: Evolution, development, and simulation of everyday mindreading* (pp. 51–61). Cambridge, MA: Blackwell.

Dunn, J. (2000). Mind-reading, emotion understanding, and relationships. *International Journal of Behavioral Development, 24*, 142–144.

Dunn, J. (2002). Sibling relationships. In P. K. Smith & C. H. Hart (Eds.), *Blackwell handbook of childhood social development* (pp. 223–237). Malden, MA: Blackwell.

Dunn, J., & Kendrick, C. (1982). The speech of two-and three-year-olds to infant siblings. *Journal of Child Language, 9*, 579–595.

Dunn, J., Brown, J., Slomkowski, C., Telsa, & Youngblade, L. (1991). Young children's understanding of other people's feelings and beliefs: Individual differences and their antecedents. *Child Development, 62*, 1352–1366.

Dupre, M. E., & Meadows, S. O. (2007). Disaggregating the effects of marital trajectories on health. *Journal of Family Issues, 28*(5), 623–652.

Dush, C. M. K., & Amato, P. R. (2005). Consequences of relationship status and quality for subjective well-being. *Journal of Social and Personal Relationships, 22*(5), 607–627.

Dush, C. M. K., Cohan, C. L., & Amato, P. R. (2003). The relationship between cohabitation and marital quality and stability: Change across cohorts? *Journal of Marriage and the Family, 65*(3), 539–549.

Dweck, C., & Licht, B. (1980). Learned helplessness and intellectual achievement. In J. Garber & M. Seligman (Eds.), *Human helplessness* (pp. 197–222). New York: Academic Press.

Dweck, C., & Wortman, C. (1980). Achievement, test anxiety, and learned helplessness: Adaptive and maladaptive cognitions. In H. Krohne & L. Laux (Eds.), *Achievement, stress, and anxiety* (pp. 93–125). Washington, DC: Hemisphere.

Dyer, C. B., Pavlik, V. N., Murphy, K. P., Hyman, D. J. (2000). The high prevalence of depression and dementia in elder abuse or neglect. *Journal of the American Geriatrics Society, 48*(2), 205–208.

Dykstra, P. A. (1995). Loneliness among the never and formerly married: The importance of supportive friendships and a desire for independence. *Journals of Gerontology Series B: Psychological Sciences and Social Sciences, 50*(5), 321–329.

Dykstra, P., van Tilburg, T., & Gierveld, J. (2005). Changes in older adult loneliness: Results from a seven-year longitudinal study. *Research on Aging, 27*(6), 725.

East, P. (2009). Adolescents' relationships with siblings. In R. Lerner & L. Steinberg (Eds.) *Handbook of Adolescent Psychology.* New York: Wiley.

East, P. L. & Rook, K. S. (1992). Compensatory patterns of support among children's peer relationships: Test using school friends, nonschool friends, and siblings. *Developmental Psychology, 28*, 163–172.

East, P. L., & Jacobson, L. J. (2001). The younger siblings of teenage mothers: A follow-up of their pregnancy risk. *Developmental Psychology, 37*, 254–264.

East, P., & Blaustein, E. (1995, March). *Perceived timing of life-course transitions: Race differences in early adolescent girls' sexual, marriage, and childbearing expectations.* Paper presented at the biennial meetings of the Society for Research in Child Development.

East, P., & Rook, K. (1992). Compensatory patterns of support among children's peer relationships: A test using school friends, nonschool friends, and siblings. *Developmental Psychology, 28*, 163–172.

East, W. B., & Hensley, L. D. (1985). The effects of selected sociocultural factors upon the overhand-throwing performance of prepubescent children. In J. E. Clark & J. H. Humphrey (Eds.), *Motor development* (pp. 115–127). Princeton, NJ: Princeton Book Company.

Easterlin, R. A. (1987). *Birth and fortune: The impact of numbers on personal welfare*. New York: Basic Books.

Eaton, M. J., & Dembo, M. H. (1997). Differences in the motivational beliefs of Asian American and non-Asian students. *Journal of Educational Psychology, 89*, 433–440.

Eaton, W. O., & Enns, L. R. (1986). Sex differences in human motor activity level. *Psychological Bulletin, 100,* 19–28.

Eccles, J., & Roeser, R. (2009). Schools, academic motivation, and stage-environment fit. In R. Lerner & L. Steinberg (Eds.), *Handbook of adolescent psychology* (3rd ed.) New York: Wiley.

Eccles, J., Wigfield, A., Harold, R. D., & Blumenfeld, P. (1993). Age and gender differences in children's self- and task perceptions during elementary school. *Child Development, 64,* 830–847.

Eckel, R. H., Grundy, S. M., & Zimmet, P. Z. (2005). The metabolic syndrome. *Lancet, 365,* 1415–1428.

Eder, D. (1985). The cycle of popularity: Interpersonal relations among female adolescents. *Sociology of Education, 58,* 154–165.

Edwards, R., Manstead, A., & MacDonald, C. J. (1984). The relationship between children's sociometric status and ability to recognize facial expressions and emotion. *European Journal of Social Psychology, 14,* 235–238.

Eggebeen, D. J. & Sturgeon, S. (2006) Demography of the Baby Boomers. In S. K. Whitbourne & S. L. Willis (Eds.), *The Baby Boomers grow up: Contemporary perspectives on midlife* (pp. 3–21). Mahwah, NJ: Lawrence Erlbaum.

Ehrenberg, R. G., Brewer, D. J., Gamoran, A., & Willms, J. D. (2001). Class size and student achievement. *Psychological Science in the Public Interest, 2,* 1–30.

Eisenberg, N., & Fabes, R. (1998). Prosocial development. In W. Damon (Ed.) & N. Eisenberg (Vol. Ed.), *Handbook of child psychology: Vol. 3. Social, emotional, and personality development* (5th ed., pp. 701–778). New York: Wiley.

Eisenberg, N., & Morris, A. S. (2004). Moral cognitions and prosocial responding. In R. M. Lerner & L. Steinberg (Eds.), *Handbook of adolescent psychology* (2nd ed), pp. 646–718). New York: Wiley.

Eisenberg, N., Cumberland, A., Spinrad, T. L., Fabes, R. A., Shepard, S. A., Reiser, M., et al. (2001). The relations of regulation and emotionality to children's externalizing and internalizing problem behavior. *Development and Psychopathology, 72,* 1112–1134.

Eisenberg, N., Fabes, R. A., & Spinrad, T. L. (2006). Prosocial development. In W. Damon & R. M. Lerner (Series Eds.) & N. Eisenberg (Vol. Ed.), *Handbook of child psychology: Vol. 3. Social, emotional, and personality development* (6th ed., pp. 646–718). Hoboken, NJ: Wiley.

Eisenberg, N., Fabes, R., Nyman, M. Bernweig, J., & Pinuelas, A. (1994). The relations of emotionality and regulation to young children's anger-related reactions. *Child Development, 62,* 1393–1408.

Eisenberg-Berg, N. (1979). The development of children's prosocial moral judgment. *Developmental Psychology, 15,* 518–534.

Eiser, A. R., & Weiss, M. D. (2001). The underachieving advance directive: Recommendations for increasing advance directive completion. *The American Journal of Bioethics, 1*(4), W10.

Ekman, P. (1984). Expression and the nature of emotion. In K. R. Scherer & P. Ekman (Eds.), *Approaches to emotion* (pp. 319–343). Hillsdale, NJ: Erlbaum.

Ekman, P. (Ed.). (2006). *Darwin and facial expression: A century of research in review*. New York: Malor Books.

Ekwo, E. E., & Moawad, A. (2000). Maternal age and preterm births in a black population. *Paediatric and Perinatal Epidemiology, 14,* 145–151.

Elder, G. H., Johnson, M. K., & Crosnoe, R. (2003). The emergence and development of life course theory. In J. T. Mortimer & M. J. Shanahan (Eds.), *Handbook of the life course* (pp. 3–19). New York: Springer.

Elder, G., Jr., & Shanahan, M. (2006). The life course and human development. In W. Damon & R. Lerner (Series Eds.) & R. Lerner (Vol. Ed.), *Handbook of child psychology: Vol. 1. Theoretical models of human development* (6th ed., pp. 665–716). New York: Wiley.

Elias, J. W. & Wagster, M. V. (2007). Developing context and background underlying cognitive intervention/training studies in older populations. *Journal of Gerontology B: Psychological Sciences and Social Sciences, 62*(Suppl. Special Issue 1), 5–10.

Elkind, D. (1967). Egocentrism in adolescence. *Child Development, 38,* 1025–1034.

Elkind, D. (2001). *The hurried child: Growing up too fast too soon.* Cambridge, MA: Perseus Publishing.

Elkins, I., McGue, M., & Iacono, W. (1997). Genetic and environmental influences on parent-son relationships: Evidence for increasing genetic influence during adolescence. *Developmental Psychology, 33,* 351–363.

Ellickson, P., Bell, R., & McGuigan, K. (1993). Preventing adolescent drug use: Long-term results of a junior high program. *American Journal of Public Health, 83,* 856–861.

Emanuel, L., Bennett, K., & Richardson, V. E. (2007). The dying role. *Journal of Palliative Medicine, 10*(1), 159–168.

Emmerich, W., & Shepard, K. (1982). Development of sex-differentiated preferences during late childhood and adolescence. *Developmental Psychology, 18,* 406–417.

Ennett, S. T., Bauman, K. E., Hussong, A., Faris, R., Foshee, V. A., Cai, L., & DuRant, R. (2006). The peer context of adolescent substance use: Findings from social network analysis. *Journal of Research on Adolescence, 16,* 159–186.

Ennett, S. T., Tobler, N. S., Ringwalt, C. L., & Flewelling, R. L. (1994). How effective is drug abuse resistance education? A meta-analysis of Project DARE outcome evaluations. *American Journal of Public Health, 84,* 1394–1401.

Enright, R., Levy, V., Harris, D., & Lapsley, D. (1987). Do economic conditions influence how theorists view adolescents? *Journal of Youth and Adolescence, 16,* 541–560.

Entwisle, D., & Hayduk, L. (1988). Lasting effects of elementary school. *Sociology of Education, 61,* 147–159.

Epel, E. S. (2009). Telomeres in a life-span perspective: A new" psychobiomarker." *Current Directions in Psychological Science, 18*(1), 6–10.

Epstein, J. (1983). The influence of friends on achievement and affective outcomes. In J. Epstein & N. Karweit (Eds.), *Friends in school* (pp. 177–200). New York: Academic Press.

Erickson, S. J., Robinson, T., Haydel, K., & Killen, J. D. (2000). Are overweight children unhappy? Body mass index, depressive symptoms, and overweight concerns in elementary school children. *Archives of Pediatrics & Adolescent Medicine, 154,* 931–935.

Ericsson, K. A., & Ward, P. (2007). Capturing the naturally occurring superior performance of experts in the laboratory. *Current Directions in Psychological Science, 16*(6), 346–350.

Erikson, E. H. (1959). Identity and the life cycle. *Psychological Issues, 1,* 1–171.

Erikson, E. H. (1963). *Childhood and society.* New York: Norton.

Erikson, E. H. (1982). *The life cycle completed.* New York: Norton.

Erikson, E. H. (1968). *Identity, youth and crisis.* New York: Norton.

Erikson, E. H., Erikson, J. M., & Kivnick, H. Q. (1986). *Vital involvement in old age.* New York: Norton.

Erler, S. F., & Garstecki, D. C. (2002). Hearing loss-and hearing aid-related stigma: perceptions of women with age-normal hearing. *American Journal of Audiology, 11*(2), 83–91.

Erting, C., Thumann-Prezioso, C., & Sonnenstrahl-Benedict, B. (2000). Bilingualism in deaf families: Fingerspelling in early childhood. In P. E. Spencer, C. J. Erting, & M. Marschark (Eds.). *The deaf child in the family and at school* (pp. 41–54). Mahwah, NJ: Erlbaum.

Eskenazi, B., Marks, A. R., Bradman, A., Fenster, L,. Johnson, C., Barr, D. B., & Jewell, N. P. (2006). In utero exposure to dichlorodiphenyltrichloroethane (DDT) and dichlorodiphenyldichloroethylene (DDE) and neurodevelopment among young Mexican American children. *Pediatrics, 118,* 223–241.

Esposito G., Venuti P., Maestro S., & Muratori, F. (2009). Movement in infants with Autism Spectrum Disorder: The analysis of lying. *Brain and Development, 31,*131–138.

Esposito, G., & Venuti, P. (2008). How is crying perceived in children with Autistic Spectrum Disorder? *Research in Autism Spectrum Disorders, 2,* 371–84.

Everett, S. A., Warren, C. W., Santelli, J. S., Kann, L., Collins, J. L., & Kolbe, L. J. (2000). Use of birth control pills, condoms, and withdrawal among U.S. high school students. *Journal of Adolescent Health, 27,* 112–118.

Everett, S. A., Warren, C. W., Sharp, D., Kann, L., Husten, C. G., & Crossett, L. S. (1999). Initiation of cigarette smoking and subsequent smoking behavior among US high school students. *Preventive Medicine, 29*(5), 327–333.

Ewing, M. E., & Seefeldt, V. (2002). Patterns of participation in American agency-sponsored youth sports. In F. L. Smoll & R. E. Smith (Eds.), *Children and youth in sport: A biopsychosocial perspective* (pp. 39–59). Iowa: Kendall/Hunt Publishing Company.

Fabes, R., A., Hanish, L. D., & Martin, C. L. (2007). The next 50 years: Considering gender as a context for understanding young children's peer relationships. In G. Ladd (Ed.), *Appraising the human developmental sciences: Essays in honor of Merrill-Palmer Quarterly* (pp. 186–199). Detroit, MI: Wayne State University Press.

Fabes, R., Eisenberg, N., Nyman, M., & Michaelieu, Q. (1991). Young children's appraisals of others' spontaneous emotional reactions. *Developmental Psychology, 27,* 858–866.

Fagot, B. I., & Leinbach, M. D. (1989). The young child's gender schema: Environmental input, internal organization. *Child Development, 60,* 663–672.

Faith, M. S., Scanlon, K. S., Birch, L. L., Francis, L. A., & Sherry, B. (2004). Parent-child feeding strategies and their relationships to child eating and weight status. *Obesity Research, 12,* 1711–1722.

Farrell, M. P., & Rosenberg, S. D. (1981). *Men at midlife.* Boston, MA Auburn House.

Farrington, D. (2009). Conduct disorder, aggression, and delinquency. In R. Lerner & L. Steinberg (Eds.), *Handbook of adolescent psychology* (2nd ed. New York: Wiley.

Fasick, F. (1994). On the "invention" of adolescence. *Journal of Early Adolescence, 14,* 6–23.

Fauth, R. C., Leventhal, T., & Brooks-Gunn, J. (2007). Welcome to the neighborhood? Long-term impacts of moving to low-poverty neighborhoods on poor children's and adolescents' outcomes. *Journal of Research on Adolescence, 17,* 249–284.

Federal Interagency Forum on Child and Family Statistics. (2007). *America's children: Key national indicators of well-being 2007.* Washington, DC: U.S. Government Printing Office.

Feeney, J. A., Hohaus, L., Noller, P., & Alexander, R. P. (2001). *Becoming parents: Exploring the bonds between mothers, fathers, and their infants.* Cambridge: Cambridge University Press.

Fein, G. G. (1996). Infants in group care: Patterns of despair and detachment. *Early Childhood Research Quarterly, 10,* 261–275.

Fein, G. G., Gariboldi, A., & Boni, R. (1993). The adjustment of infants and toddlers to group care: The first 6 months. *Early Childhood Research Quarterly, 8,* 1–14.

Feiring, C. (1993, March). *Developing concepts of romance from 15 to 18 years.* Paper presented at the biennial meetings of the Society for Research in Child Development, New Orleans.

Feiring, C. (1999). Gender identity and the development of romantic relationships in adolescence. In W. Furman, B. Brown, & C. Feiring (Eds.), *Contemporary perspectives on adolescent romantic relationships* (pp. 211–232). New York: Cambridge University Press.

Feldman, H. A., Longcope, C., Derby, C. A., Johannes, C. B., Araujo, A. B., Coviello, A. D., et al., (2002). Age trends in the level of serum testosterone and other hormones in middle aged men: Longitudinal results from the Massachusetts Male Aging Study. *Journal of Clinical Endocrinology and Metabolism, 87*(2), 589–598.

Feldman, S., & Gehring, T. (1988). Changing perceptions of family cohesion and power across adolescence. *Child Development, 59,* 1034–1045.

Felitti, V. J., Anda, R. F., Nordenberg, D., Williamson, D. F., Spitz, A. M., Edwards, V., Koss, M. P., & Marks, J. S.(1998). Relationship of childhood abuse and household dysfunction to many of the leading causes of death in adults: The Adverse Childhood Experiences (ACE) Study. *American Journal of Preventive Medicine, 14,* 245–258.

Fenichel, E., Lurie-Hurvitz, E., & Griffin, A. (1999). Seizing the moment to build momentum for quality infant/toddler child care. *Zero to Three Bulletin, 19,* 3–17.

Fenson, L., Dale, P. S., Reznick, J. S., Thal, D., Bates, E., & Hartung, J. (1993). *User's guide and technical manual for the MacArthur Communicative Development Inventories.* San Diego, CA: Singular Press.

Ferraro, K. F., Thorpe, R. J., Jr., & Wilkinson, J. A. (2003). The life course of severe obesity: Does childhood overweight matter? *Journal of Gerontology B: Psychological and Social Sciences, 58*(2), S110–S119.

Festinger, L., Schachter, S., & Back, K. (1950). *Social pressures in informal groups: A study of a housing project.* New York: Harper.

Field, T. (1998). Maternal depression effects on infants and early interventions. *Preventive Medicine: An International Journal Devoted to Practice and Theory, 27,* 200–203.

Field, T. M. (2007). Massage therapy effects. In A. Monat, R. S. Lazarus, & G. Reevy (Eds.), *The Praeger handbook on stress and coping* (Vol. 2, pp. 451–473). Westport, CT: Praeger Publishers/Greenwood Publishing Group.

Field, T. M., Woodson, R., Greenberg, R., & Cohen, D. (1982). Discrimination and imitation of facial expressions by neonates. *Science, 218,* 179–181.

Field, T., Diego, M., Hernandez-Reif, M., Vera, Y., Gil, K., & Schanberg, S. (2004). Prenatal predictors of maternal and newborn EEG. *Infant Behavior & Development, 27,* 533–536.

Finch, C. (2007). *The biology of human longevity: Inflammation, nutrition, and aging in the evolution of lifespans.* San Diego, CA: Academic Press.

Finch, C., & Kirkwood, T. (2000). *Chance, development, and aging.* New York: Oxford University Press.

Fincham, F. D., Stanley, S. M., & Beach, S. R. H. (2007). Transformative processes in marriage: An analysis of emerging trends. *Journal of Marriage and Family, 69*(2), 275–292.

Fine, G., Mortimer, J., & Roberts, D. (1990). Leisure, work, and the mass media. In S. Feldman & G. Elliott (Eds.), *At the threshold: The developing adolescent* (pp. 225–252). Cambridge, MA: Harvard University Press.

Fingerman, K. L. (2000). "We had a nice little chat": Age and generational differences in mothers' and daughters' descriptions of enjoyable visits. *Journal of Gerontology B: Psychological and Social Science, 55*(2), P95–P106.

Fingerman, K. L. (2001). *Aging mothers and their adult daughters: A study in mixed emotions.* New York: Springer.

Finkel, T., & Holbrook, N. J. (2000). Oxidants, oxidative stress and the biology of ageing. *Nature, 408,* 239–247.

Finn, J. D., & Achilles, C. M. (1999). Tennessee's class size study: Findings, implications, and misconceptions. *Educational Evaluation and Policy Analysis, 21,* 97–109.

Fisch, H., Hyun, G., Golden, R., Hensle, T. W., Olsson, C. A., & Liberson, G. L. (2003). The influence of paternal age on down syndrome. *Journal of Urology, 169,* 2275–2278.

Fischer, K. W. (2008). Dynamic cycles of cognitive and brain development: Measuring growth in mind, brain, and education. In A. M. Battro, K. W. Fischer, & P. J. Léna (Eds.), *The educated brain* (pp. 127–150). Cambridge, UK: Cambridge University Press.

Fischer, K. W., & Pruyne, E. (2003). Reflective thinking in adulthood: Emergence, development, and variation. In J. Demick & C. Andreoletti (Eds.), *Handbook of adult development* (pp. 169–198). New York: Kluwer Academic/Plenum Publishers.

Fisher, B. S., Cullen, F. T., & Turner, M. (2001). Being pursued: Stalking victimization in a national study of college women. *Criminology & Public Policy, 1*(2), 257–308.

Fisher, C., Wallace, S. A., & Fenton, R. E. (2000). Discrimination distress during adolescence. *Journal of Youth and Adolescence, 29,* 679–695.

Fisher, J. O., Rolls, B. J., & Birch, L. L. (2003). Children's bite size and intake of an entrée are greater with large portions than with age-appropriate or self-selected portions. *American Journal of Clinical Nutrition, 77,* 1164–1170.

Fisher, M., Golden, N., Katzman, D., Kriepe, R., Rees, J., Schebendach, J., et al. (1995). Eating disorders in adolescents: A background paper. *Journal of Adolescent Health, 16,* 420–437.

Fiske, A., Wetherell, J., & Gatz, M. (2009). Depression in older adults. *Annual Review of Clinical Psychology, 5,* 363–389.

Fivush, R. (2001). Owning experience: Developing subjective perspectives in autobiographical narratives. In C. Moore & K. Lemmon (Eds.), *The self in time* (pp. 35–52). Mahwah, NJ: Erlbaum.

Fivush, R., Brotman, M. A., Buckner, J. P., & Goodman, S. H. (2000). Gender differences in parent-child emotion narratives. *Sex Roles, 42,* 233–253.

Fivush, R., Hudson, J. A., & Nelson, K. (1984). Children's long term memory for a novel event: An exploratory study. *Merrill-Palmer Quarterly, 30,* 303–316.

Flavell, J. (1963). *The developmental psychology of Jean Piaget.* Princeton, NJ: Van Nostrand Reinhold.

Flavell, J. H., Flavell, E. R., & Green, F. L. (1983). Development of the appearance-reality distinction. *Cognitive Psychology, 15,* 95–120.

Fleeson, W. (2004). The quality of American life at the end of the century. In O. G. Brim, C. D. Ryff, & R. C. Kessler (Eds.), *How healthy are we?: A national study of well-being at midlife* (pp. 252–272). Chicago: University of Chicago Press.

Flora, D. B., & Chassin, L. (2005). Changes in drug use during young adulthood: The effects of parent alcoholism and transition into marriage. *Psychology of Addictive Behaviors, 19*(4), 352–362.

Flynn, B., Worden, J., Secker-Walker, R., Pirie, P., Badger, G., Carpenter, J., & Geller, B. (1994). Mass media and school interventions for cogarette smoking prevention: Effects 2 years after completion. *American Journal of Public Health, 84,* 1148–1150.

Flynn, J. R. (1987). Massive IQ gains in 14 nations: What IQ tests really measure. *Psychological Bulletin, 101*(2), 171–191.

Fogler, J. (2007, April 30). *Mother-to-child HIV transmission: A thing of the past?* [PowerPoint slides]. Retrieved from http://www.cdc.gov/hiv/topics/perinatal/resources/meetings/2007/pdf/Fogler_MTCT.pdf

Folkman, S., & Moskowitz, J. (2004). Coping: Pitfalls and promise. *Annual Review of Psychology, 55*(1), 745–774.

Folkman, S., Lazarus, R., Pimley, S., & Novacek, J. (1987). Age differences in stress and coping processes. *Psychology and Aging, 2*(2), 171–184.

Follwell, M., Burman, D., Le, L., Wakimoto, K., Seccareccia, D., Bryson, J., et al. (2009). Phase II study of an outpatient palliative care intervention in patients with metastatic cancer. *Journal of Clinical Oncology, 27*(2), 206–213.

Fontana, L., & Klein, S. (2007). Aging, adiposity, and calorie restriction. *Journal of the American Medical Association, 297*(9), 986–994.

Food and Drug Administration (2008, February). *Early communication about an ongoing safety review: Botox and Botox cosmetic (Botulinum toxin Type A) and Myobloc (Botulinum toxin Type B).* Retrieved May 13, 2008 from http://www.fda.gov/cder/drug/early_comm/botulinium_toxins.htm

Forbes, E. E. & Dahl, R. E. (2005). Neural systems of positive affect: Relevance to understanding child and adolescent depression? *Development and Psychopathology, 17,* 827–850.

Foreman, M. D., Fletcher, K., Mion, L. C., & Simon, L. (1996). Assessing cognitive function The complexities of assessment of an individual's cognitive status are important in making an accurate and comprehensive evaluation. *Geriatric Nursing, 17*(5), 228–232.

Foster, J. D., Campbell, K. W., & Twenge, J. M. (2003). Individual differences in narcissism: Inflated self-views across the lifespan and around the world. *Journal of Research in Personality, 37*(6), 469–486.

Foster-Cohen, S., Edgin, J. O., Champion, P. R. & Woodward, L. J. (2007). Early delayed language development in very preterm infants: Evidence from the MacArthur Bates CDI. *Journal of Child Language, 34,* 655–675.

Fouad, N. A. (2007). Work and vocational psychology: Theory, research, and applications. *Annual Review of Psychology, 58,* 543–564.

Fox, N. A., Henderson, H. A., Rubin, K. H., Calkins, S. D., & Schmidt, L. A. (2001). Continuity and discontinuity of behavioral inhibition and exuberance: Psychophysiological and behavioral influences across the first four years of life. *Child Development, 72,* 1–21.

Fozard, J., & Gordon-Salant, S. (2001). Changes in vision and hearing with aging. In J. E. Birren & K. W. Schaie (Eds.), *Handbook of the psychology of aging.* (5th ed., pp. 241–266). San Diego, CA: Academic Press.

Fraley, R. C., & Shaver, P. R. (1998). Airport separations: A naturalistic study of adult attachment dynamics in separating couples. *Journal of Personality and Social Psychology, 75,* 1198–1212.

Fraley, R. C., & Shaver, P. R. (2000). Adult romantic attachment: Theoretical developments, emerging controversies, and unanswered questions. *Review of General Psychology, 4*(2), 132–154.

Franklin, C., Grant, D., Corcoran, J., Miller, P., & Bultman, L. (1997). Effectiveness of prevention programs for adolescent pregnancy: A meta-analysis. *Journal of Marriage and the Family, 59,* 551–567.

Fratiglioni, L., & Wang, H. X. (2007). Brain reserve hypothesis in dementia. *Journal of Alzheimer's Disease, 12*(1), 11–22.

Fratiglioni, L., Paillard-Borg, S., & Winblad, B. (2004). An active and socially integrated lifestyle in late life might protect against dementia. *Lancet Neurology, 3*(6), 343–353.

Fredriksen, K., Rhodes, J., Reddy, R., & Way. N. (2004). Sleepless in Chicago: Tracking the effects of adolescent sleep loss during the middle school years. *Child Development, 75,* 84–95.

Freeman, E. E., Muñoz, B., Turano, K. A. & West, S. K. (2006). Measures of visual function and their association with driving modification in older adults. *Investigative ophthalmology & visual science, 47*(2), 514–520.

Freeman, M. A. (1978). *Life among the Qallunaat.* Edmonton, Canada: Hurtig Publishers.

French, S. E., Seidman, E., Allen, L., & Aber, J. L. (2006). The development of ethnic identity during adolescence. *Developmental Psychology, 42,* 1–10.

French, S., Story, M., Downes, B., Resnick, M., & Blum, R. (1995). Frequent dieting among adolescents: Psychosocial and health behavior correlates. *American Journal of Public Health, 85,* 695–701.

Freud, S. (1910). The origin and development of psychoanalysis. *American Journal of Psychology, 21,* 181–218.

Freud, S. (1916/1917). *Introductory lectures on psychoanalysis.* London: Hogarth Press.

Freud, S. (1949). *An outline of psychoanalysis.* Oxford: W. W. Norton.

Freud, S. (1966). *Psychopathology of everyday life* (J. Strachey, Trans.). London: Ernest Benn. (Original work published in 1901).

Freund, A. M., & Baltes, P. (2002). Life-management strategies of selection, optimization, and compensation: Measurement by self-report and construct validity. *Journal of Personality and Social Psychology, 82*(4), 642–662.

Fried, L. P., Ferrucci, L., Darer, J., Williamson, J. D., & Anderson, G. (2004). Untangling the concepts of disability, frailty, and comorbidity: Implications for improved targeting and care. *Journal of Gerontology A: Biological Sciences and Medical Sciences, 59*(3), M255–263.

Fried, L. P., Tangen, C. M., Walston, J., Newman, A. B., Hirsch, C., Gottdiener, J., et al. (2001). Frailty in older adults: Evidence for a phenotype. *Journal of Gerontology A: Biological Sciences and Medical Sciences, 56*(3), M146–156.

Friedman, D. S., Wilson, M. R., Liebmann, J. M., Fechtner, R. D., & Weinreb, R. N. (2004). An evidence-based assessment of risk factors for the progression of ocular hypertension and glaucoma. *American Journal of Ophthalmology, 138*(3, Suppl. 1), 19–31.

Friedman, H. S. (2007). Personality, disease, and self-healing. In H. S. Friedman & R. C. Silver (Eds.), *Foundations of health psychology* (pp. 172–199). New York: Oxford University Press.

Friedman, M., & Rosenman, R. H. (1959). Association of specific overt behavior patterns with blood and cardiovascular findings: Blood cholesterol level, blood clotting time, incidence of arcus senilis and clinical coronary artery disease. *Journal of the American Medical Association, 169*(12), 1286–1296.

Friedman, T. L. (2007). *The world is flat: A brief history of the twenty-first century (Further updated and expanded).* New York: Farrar, Straus and Giroux.

Fries, A. B. W., Shirtcliff, E. A., & Pollak, S. D. (2008). Neuroendocrine dysregulation following early social deprivation in children. *Developmental Psychobiology, 50,* 588–599.

Fries, J. F. (1980). Aging, natural death, and the compression of morbidity. *New England Journal of Medicine, 303*(32), 130–135.

Fries, J. F. (2002). Reducing disability in old age. *Journal of the American Medical Association, 288,* 3164–3165.

Fries, J. F. (2003). Measuring and monitoring success in compressing morbidity. *Annals of Internal Medicine, 139*(5; Part 2), 455–459.

Fries, J. F., & Crapo, L. M. (1981). *Vitality and aging.* San Francisco, CA: Freeman.

Frisch, R. (1983). Fatness, puberty, and fertility: The effects of nutrition and physical training on menarche and ovulation. In J. Brooks-Gunn & A. Petersen (Eds.), *Girls at puberty* (pp. 29–49). New York: Plenum.

Frost, J., & Forrest, J. (1995). Understanding the impact of effective teenage pregnancy prevention programs. *Family Planning Perspectives, 27,* 188–195.

Fryer, S. L., McGee, C. L., Matt, G. E., Riley, E. P., & Mattson, S. N. (2007). Evaluation of psychopathological conditions in children with heavy prenatal alcohol exposure. *Pediatrics, 119,* 733–741.

Fuligni, A. (1994, February). *Academic achievement and motivation among Asian-American and European-American early adolescents.* Paper presented at the biennial meetings of the Society for Research on Adolescence, San Diego.

Fuligni, A. (1997). The academic achievement of adolescents from immigrant families: The roles of family background, attitudes, and behavior. *Child Development, 68,* 351–363.

Fuligni, A. J., & Witkow, M. (2004). The postsecondary educational progress of youth from immigrant families. *Journal of Research on Adolescence, 14,* 159–183.

Fuligni, A., & Eccles, J. (1993). Perceived parent-child relationships and early adolescents' orientation toward peers. *Developmental Psychology, 29,* 622–632.

Fuligni, A., Tseng, V., & Lam, M. (1999). Attitudes toward family obligations among American adolescents from Asian, Latin American, and European backgrounds. *Child Development, 70,* 1030–1044.

Fuller, B., Wright, J., Gesicki, K., & Kange, E. (2007). Gauging growth: How to judge No Child Left Behind? *Educational Researcher, 36,* 268–278.

Fung, H. H., & Carstensen, L. L. (2006). Goals change when life's fragility is primed: Lessons learned from older adults, the September 11 attacks and SARS. *Social Cognition, 24*(3), 248–278.

Fung, H. H., Carstensen, L. L., & Lang, F. R. (2001). Age-related patterns in social networks among European Americans and African Americans: Implications for socioemotional selectivity across the life span. *International Journal of Aging and Human Development, 52*(3), 185–206.

Furman, W., & Buhrmester, D. (1985). Children's perceptions of the personal relationships in their social networks. *Developmental Psychology, 21,* 1016–1024.

Furman, W., & Lanthier, R. (2002). Parenting siblings. In M. H. Bornstein (Ed.), *Handbook of parenting: Vol. 1. Children and parenting* (2nd ed., pp. 165–188). Mahwah, NJ: Erlbaum.

Furstenberg, F. F., Jr. (1990). Divorce and the American family. *Annual Review of Sociology, 16,* 379–403.

Gable, S. & Lutz, S., (2000). Household, parent, and child contributions to childhood obesity. *Family Relations 49, 293–300.*

Galambos, N. L., Barker, E. T., & Krahn, H. J. (2006). Depression, self-esteem, and anger in emerging adulthood: Seven-year trajectories. *Developmental Psychology, 42,* 350–365.

Galen, B. R., & Underwood, M. K. (1997). A developmental investigation of social aggression among children. *Developmental Psychology, 33,* 589–600.

Gallay, M., Baudouin, J., Durand., K, Lemoine, C., & Lécuyer, R. (2006). Qualitative differences in the exploration of upright and upside-down faces in four month old infants: An eye-movement study. *Child Development, 77,* 984–996.

Gallo, W. T., Bradley, E. H., Siegel, M., & Kasl, S. V. (2000). Health effects of involuntary job loss among older workers findings from the Health and Retirement Survey. *Journals of Gerontology: Social Sciences, 55*(3), S131–S140.

Galton, F. (1907). *Inquiries into human faculty and its development.* London: J. M. Dent & New York: E. R. Dutton. Retrieved September 3 , 2008, from http://www.galton.org/books/human-faculty/

Ganley, J. P., & Roberts, J. (1983). Eye conditions and related need for medical care among persons 1–74 years of age, United States, 1971–72. *Vital and Health Statistics,* Series 11, No. 228 (DHHS Publication No. 83-1678). Washington, DC: U.S. Government Printing Office.

Ganzini, L., Goy, E. R., & Dobscha, S. K. (2008). Why Oregon patients request assisted death: Family members' views. *Journal of General Internal Medicine, 23*(2), 154–157.

Ganzini, L., Nelson, H. D., Schmidt, T. A., Kraemer, D. F., Delorit, M. A., & Lee, M. A. (2000). Physicians' experiences with the Oregon death with dignity act. *New England Journal of Medicine, 342*(8), 557–563.

Garcia Coll, C., Lamberty, G., Jenkins, R., McAdoo, H., Crnic, K., Wasik, B., & Vazquez Garcia, H. (1996). An integrative model for the study of developmental competencies in minority children. *Child Development, 67,* 1891–1914.

Gardner, H. (1980). *Artful scribbles: The significance of children's drawings.* New York: Basic Books.

Gardner, H. (1999). *Intelligence reframed: Multiple intelligences for the 21st century.* New York: Basic Books.

Garland, J., & Garland, C. (2001). *Life review in health and social care: A practitioner's guide.* Philadelphia, PA: Brunner-Routledge.

Garmel, S. H., & D'Alton, M. E. (1994). Diagnostic ultrasound in pregnancy: an overview. *Seminars in Perinatology, 18,* 117–132.

Garner, D. (1998, March 23). The Spock touch. *Salon.* Retrieved March 11, 2008, from http://www.salon.com/mwt/feature/1998/03/23feature.html

Garner, P. W. (1996). The relations of emotional role taking, affective/moral attributions, and emotional display rule knowledge to low-income school-age children's social competence. *Journal of Applied Developmental Psychology, 17,* 19–36.

Garrard, E., & Wilkinson, S. (2005). Passive euthanasia. *British Medical Journal, 31*(2), 64–68.

Gartstein, M. A., Kinsht, I. A., & Slobodskaya, H. R. (2003). Cross-cultural differences in temperament in the first year of life: United States of America (US) and Russia. *International Journal of Behavioral Development, 27,* 316–328.

Garvey, C. (1990). *Play.* Cambridge, MA: Harvard University Press.

Garza, C., & de Onis, M. (2007). New 21st century international growth standards for infants and young children. *Journal of Nutrition, 137,* 142–143.

Gass, M., & Dawson-Hughes, B. (2006). Preventing osteoporosis-related fractures: An overview. *The American Journal of Medicine, 119*(4, Supplement 1), 3–11.

Gates, G. J., & Badgett, M. V. L., Macomber, J. E., & Chambers, K. (2007, March). *Adoption and foster care by gay and lesbian parents in the United States.* Los Angeles: The Williams Institute, UCLA School of Law, and Washington, DC: The Urban Institute. Retrieved September 3, 2008, from http://www.law.ucla.edu/williamsinstitute/publications/FinalAdoptionReport.pdf

Gatz, M. (2000). Variations onf depression in later life. In S. Qualls & N. Abeles (Eds.), *Psychology and the aging revolution* (pp. 239–254). Washington, DC: American Psychological Association.

Gatz, M. (2007). Genetics, dementia, and the elderly. *Current Directions in Psychological Science, 16*(3), 123–127.

Gatz, M., & Fiske, A. (2003). Aging women and depression. *Professional Psychology Research and Practice, 34*(1), 3–9.

Gatz, M., Prescott, C. A., & Pedersen, N. L. (2006). Lifestyle risk and delaying factors. *Alzheimer Disease and Associated Disorders, 20 (Supplement 2),* S84–S88.

Gaugler, J. E, Duval, S., Anderson, K. A, & Kane, R. L. (2007). Predicting nursing home admission in the US: A meta-analysis. *BMC Geriatrics, 7,* 13.

Gauvain, M. (2001). *The social context of cognitive development.* New York: The Guilford Press.

Gayraud, F. & Kern, S. (2007). Influence of preterm birth on early lexical and grammatical acquisition. *First Language, 27,* 159–173.

Gazzaniga, M., Bogen, J., & Sperry, R. (1962). Some functional effects of sectioning the cerebral commisures in man. *Proceedings of the National Academy of Sciences, 48,* 1765–1769.

Ge, X., Kim, I. J., Brody, G. H., Conger, R. D., Simons, R. L., Gibbons, F. X., et al. (2003). It's about timing and change: Pubertal transition effects on symptoms of major depression among African American youths. *Developmental Psychology, 39,* 430–439.

Geary, D. C. (2006). Development of mathematical understanding. In W. Damon & R. M. Lerner (Series Eds.) & D. Kuhn & R. S. Siegler (Vol. Eds.), *Handbook of child psychology: Vol. 2. Cognition, perception, and language* (6th ed., pp. 777–810). Hoboken, NJ: Wiley.

Gelman, R. (2000). The epigenesis of mathematical thinking. *Journal of Applied Developmental Psychology, 21, 27–37.*

Gelman, S. A. & Kalish, C. (2006). Conceptual development. In W. Damon & R. M. Lerner (Series Eds.) & D. Kuhn & R. S. Siegler (Vol. Eds.), *Handbook of child psychology: Vol. 2. Cognition, perception, and language* (6th ed., pp. 687–733). Hoboken, NJ: Wiley.

Gelman, S. A. (2006). Early conceptual development. In K. McCartney & D. Phillips (Eds.), *Blackwell handbook of early childhood development.* (pp. 149–166) Malden, MA: Blackwell.

Gelman, S., Taylor, M. G., & Nguyen, S. P. (2004). Mother-child conversations about gender. *Monographs of the Society for Research in Child Development, 69,* vii–127.

George, L. K. (2001). The social psychology of health. In R. H. Binstock & L. K. George (Eds.), *Handbook of aging and the social sciences* (pp. 217–237). San Diego, CA: Academic Press.

George, R. J. D, Finlay, I. G., & Jeffrey, D. (2005). Legalised euthanasia will violate the rights of vulnerable patients. *British Medical Journal,* 331, 684–685.

Geronimus, A., Bound, J., Waidmann, T., Hillemeier, M., & Burns, P. (1996). Excess mortality among blacks and whites in the United States. *The New England Journal of Medicine, 335*(21), 1552–1558.

Gerrard, M., Gibbons, F. X., & Bushman, B. J. (1996). Relation between perceived vulnerability to HIV and precautionary sexual behavior. *Psychological Bulletin, 119*(3), 390–409.

Gershoff, E. T. (2002). Parental corporal punishment and associated child behaviors and experiences: A meta-analytic and theoretical review. *Psychological Bulletin, 128,* 539–579.

Gesang, B. (2008). Passive and active euthanasia: What is the difference? *Medicine, Health Care and Philosophy, 11*(2), 175–180.

Geschwind, N., & Galaburda, A. (1987). *Cerebral lateralization.* Cambridge, MA: MIT Press.

Gesell, A., & Thompson, H. (1938). *The psychology of early growth including norms of infant behavior and a method of genetic analysis.* New York: Appleton-Century Crofts.

Ghimire, D. J., Axinn, W. G., Yabiku, S. T., & Thornton, A. (2006). Social change, premarital nonfamily experience, and spouse choice in an arranged marriage society. *American Journal of Sociology, 111*(4), 1181–1218.

Giarrusso, R., Feng, D., & Bengtson, V. L. (2005). The intergenerational stake over 20 years. *Annual Review of Gerontology and Geriatrics, 24,* 55–76.

Gibbs, J. C., Basinger, K. S., Grime, R. L., & Snarey, J. R. (2007). Moral judgment development across cultures: Revisiting Kohlberg's universality claims. *Developmental Review, 27*(4), 443–500.

Gibson, E. J., & Walk, R. D. (1960). The "visual cliff." *Scientific American, 202,* 64–71.

Giedd, J. N., Blumenthal, J., Jeffries, N. O., Castellanos, F. X., Liu, H., Zijdenbos, A., et al. (1999). Brain development during childhood and adolescence: A longitudinal MRI study. *Nature Neuroscience, 2,* 861–863.

Gifford-Smith, M. E., & Rabiner, D. L. (2004). Social information processing and children's social adjustment. In J. Kupersmidt & K. A. Dodge (Eds.), *Children's peer relations: From development to interventions* (pp. 69–84). Washington, DC: American Psychological Association.

Gil, A., Vega, W., & Dimas, J. (1994). Acculturative stress and personal adjustment among Hispanic adolescent boys. *Journal of Community Psychology, 22,* 43–54.

Gillick, M. (2001). Pinning down frailty. *Journal of Gerontology A: Biological Sciences and Medical Sciences, 56*(3), M134–135.

Gilligan, C. (1982). *In a different voice: Psychological theory and women's development.* Cambridge, MA: Harvard University Press.

Giltay, E. J., Kamphuis, M. H., Kalmijn, S., Zitman, F. G., & Kromhout, D. (2006). Dispositional optimism in the risk of cardiovascular death: The Zutphen Elderly Study. *Archives of Internal Medicine, 166*(4), 431–436.

Gingras, J. L., Mitchell, E. A., & Grattan, K. E. (2005). Fetal homologue of infant crying. *Archives of Disease in Childhood—Fetal and Neonatal Edition, 90,* 415–418.

Ginsberg, D. (1986). Friendship and postdivorce adjustment. In J. M. Gottman & J. G. Parker (Eds.), *Conversations of friends* (pp. 346–376). Cambridge: Cambridge University Press.

Ginsberg, T. B, Pomerantz, S. C., & Kramer-Feeley, V. (2005). Sexuality in older adults: Behaviours and preferences. *Age and Ageing, 34*(5), 475–480.

Ginsburg, G., & Bronstein, P. (1993). Family factors related to children's intrinsic/extrinsic motivational orientation and academic performance. *Child Development, 64,* 1461–1474.

Ginsburg, H. (1989). *Children's arithmetic: How they learn it and how you teach it.* Austin TX: Pro-Ed.

Ginsburg, H. P., Cannon, J., Eisenband, J., & Pappas, S. (2006). Mathematical thinking and learning. In K. McCartney & D. Phillips (Eds.), *Blackwell handbook on early childhood development* (pp. 208–229). Malden, MA: Blackwell.

Ginsburg, H., & Baroody, A. J. (2003). *The test of early mathematics ability* (3rd ed.). Austin TX: Pro Ed.

Gislen, A., Dacke, M., Kroger, R. H. H., Abrahamsson, M., Nilsson, D. E., & Warrant, E. J. (2003). Superior underwater vision in a human population of sea gypsies. *Current Biology, 13,* 833–836.

Glenn, N. D. (1998). The course of marital success and failure in five American 10-year marriage cohorts. *Journal of Marriage and Family, 60*(3), 569–576.

Glynn, L. M., Wadhwa, P. D., Dunkel-Schetter, C., Chicz-Demet, A., & Sandman, C. A. (2001). When stress happens matters: effects of earthquake timing on stress responsivity in pregnancy. *American Journal of Obstetrics and Gynecology, 184,* 637–642.

Gogate, L. J., Bahrick, L. E., & Watson, J. D. (2000). A study of multimodal motherese: The role of temporal synchrony between verbal labels and gestures. *Child Development, 71,* 878–894.

Gogtay, N., Giedd, J. N., Lusk, L., Hayashi, K., Greenstein, D., Vaituzis, C. et al. (2004, May 25). Dynamic mapping of human cortical development during childhood through early adulthood. *Proceedings of the National Academy of Sciences, 101,* 8174–8179.

Golan, N. (1986). *The perilous bridge: Helping clients through midlife transitions.* New York: Free Press.

Goldberg, S., & DiVitto, B. (2002). Parenting children born preterm. In M. H. Bornstein (Ed.), *Handbook of parenting* (Vol. 2, pp. 329–354). Mahwah, NJ: Erlbaum.

Goldfield, B. A. (1985/1986). Referential and expressive language: A study of two mother-child dyads. *First Language, 6,* 119–131.

Goldin-Meadow, S. (2006). How children learn language: A focus on resilience. In K. McCartney & D. Phillips (Eds.), *Blackwell handbook on early childhood development* (pp. 252–273). Malden, MA: Blackwell.

Goldin-Meadow, S. (2006). Nonverbal communication: The hand's role in talking and thinking. In W. Damon & R. Lerner (Series Eds.) & D. Kuhn & R. S. Siegler (Vol. Eds.), *Handbook of child psychology: Vol. 2. Cognition, perception, and language* (6th ed., pp. 336–369). Hoboken, NJ: Wiley.

Goldscheider, F., & Kaufman, G. (2006). Willingness to stepparent: Attitudes about partners who already have children. *Journal of Family Issues, 27*(10), 1415–1436.

Goldscheider, F., Goldscheider, C., St. Clair, P., & Hodges, J. (1999). Changes in returning home in the United States, 1925–1985. *Social Forces, 78*(2), 695–720.

Goldsmith, H. H., & Lemery, K. S. (2000). Linking temperamental fearfulness and anxiety symptoms: A behavior-genetic perspective. *Biological Psychiatry, 48,* 1199–1209.

Goldsmith, H. H., Lemery, K. S., Aksan, N., & Buss, K. A. (2000). Temperamental substrates of personality. In V. J. Molfese & D. L. Molfese (Eds.), *Temperament and personality development across the life span* (pp. 1–32). Mahwah, NJ: Erlbaum.

Goldstein, B. (1976). *Introduction to human sexuality.* Belmont, CA: Star.

Goldstein, J. R. (1999). The leveling of divorce in the United States. *Demography, 36*(3), 409–414.

Golomb, C. (2004). *The child's creation of a pictorial world* (2nd ed.). Mahwah, NJ: Erlbaum.

Golombok, S. (2002). Parenting and contemporary reproductive technologies. In M. H. Bornstein (Ed.), *Handbook of parenting: Vol. 3. Status and social conditions of parenting* (2nd ed., pp. 339–360). Mahwah, NJ: Erlbaum.

Göncü, A., & Gaskins, S. (Eds.), *Play and development: Evolutionary, sociocultural, and functional perspectives.* Mahwah, NJ: Erlbaum.

Goodpaster, B. H., Park, S. W., Harris, T. B., Kritchevsky, S. B., Nevitt, M., Schwartz, A. V., et al. (2006). The loss of skeletal muscle strength, mass, and quality in older adults: The Health, Aging and Body Composition Study. *Journal of Gerontology A: Biological Sciences and Medical Sciences, 61*(10), 1059–1064.

Goossens, L., Seiffge-Krenke, I., & Marcoen, A. (1992, March). *The many faces of adolescent egocentrism: Two European replications.* Paper presented at the biennial meetings of the Society for Research on Adolescence, Washington, DC.

Goran, M. I., Ball, G. D. C., & Cruz, M. L. (2003). Obesity and risk of type 2 diabetes and cardiovascular disease in children and adolescents. *Journal of Clinical Endocrinology and Metabolism, 88*(4), 417–427.

Gorbien, M. J., & Eisenstein, A. R. (2005). Elder abuse and neglect: an overview. *Clinics in geriatric medicine, 21*(2), 279–292.

Gormley, Jr., W. T., Gayer, T., Phillips, D., & Dawson, B. (2005). The effects of universal Pre-K on cognitive development. *Developmental Psychology, 41,* 872–884.

Gott, M., & Hinchliff, S. (2003). How important is sex in later life? The views of older people. *Social Science and Medicine, 56*(8), 1617–1628.

Gottfredson, D. (1985). Youth employment, crime, and schooling: A longitudinal study of a national sample. *Developmental Psychology, 21,* 419–432.

Gottfredson, L. S. (1996). Gottfredson's theory of circumscription and compromise. In D. Brown & L. Brooks (Eds.), *Career choice and development* (pp. 179–232). San Francisco: Jossey-Brass.

Gottfried, A. E., Fleming, J S., & Gottfried, A. W. (1998). Role of cognitively stimulating home environment in children's academic intrinsic motivation: A longitudinal study. *Child Development, 69,* 1448–1460.

Gottlieb, G., Wahlstein, D., & Lickliter, R. (2006). The significance of biology for human development: A developmental psychobiological systems view. In W. Damon & R. Lerner (Series Eds.) & R. Lerner (Vol. Ed.), *Handbook of child psychology: Vol. 1. Theoretical models of human development* (6th ed., pp. 210–257). New York: Wiley.

Gottman, J. M. (1983). How children become friends. *Monographs of the Society for Research in Child Development, 48*(3), pp. 1–86.

Gottman, J. M. (1994). *What predicts divorce? The relationship between marital processes and marital outcomes.* Hillsdale, NJ: Lawrence Erlbaum.

Gottman, J. M., & Parker, J. G. (1986). *Conversations of friends: Speculations on affective development.* New York: Cambridge University Press.

Gottman, J. M., Katz, L. F., & Hoover, C. (1997). *Meta-emotion.* Hillsdale, NJ: Erlbaum.

Gottman, J., & Silver, N. (1999). *The seven principles for making marriage work.* New York: Three Rivers Press.

Goubet, N., Rattaz, C., Pierrat, V., Allemann, E., Bullinger, A., & Lequien, P. (2002). Olfactory familiarization and discrimination in preterm and full-term newborns. *Infancy, 3,* 53–76.

Goubet, N., Rattaz, C., Pierrat, V., Bullinger, A., & Lequien, P. (2003). Olfactory experience mediates response to pain in preterm newborns. *Developmental Psychobiology, 42,* 171–180.

Gould, M., Wallenstein, S., & Kleinman, M. (1990). Time-space clustering of teenage suicide. *American Journal of Epidemiology, 131,* 71–78.

Gould, R. L, (1972). The phases of adult life: A study in developmental psychology. *American Journal of Psychiatry, 129*(5), 521–531.

Gould, S. (1977). *Ontogeny and phylogeny.* Cambridge, MA: Belknap Press of Harvard University Press.

Goyer, A. (2006, February). *Intergenerational relationships: Grandparents raising grandchildren.* Perspective written for AARP Foundation Grandparent Information Center. Washington, DC: American Association of Retired Persons (AARP). Retrieved February 11, 2009, from http://www.aarpinternational.org/Resourcelibrary/resourcelibrary_show.htm?doc_id5545720

Goyette, K., & Xie, Y. (1999). Educational expectations of Asian American youths: Determinants and ethnic differences. *Sociology of Education, 72,* 22–36.

Graber, J. (2009). Internalizing problems during adolescence. In R. Lerner & L. Steinberg (Eds.), *Handbook of adolescent psychology* (3rd ed.) New York: Wiley.

Graber, J. A., Brooks-Gunn, J., & Warren, M. P. (2006). Pubertal effects on adjustment in girls: Moving from demonstrating effects to identifying pathways. *Journal of Youth and Adolescence, 35,* 391–401.

Grady, C. L., Bernstein, L. J., Beig, S., & Siegenthaler, A. L. (2002). The effects of encoding task on age-related differences in the functional neuroanatomy of face memory. *Psychology and Aging, 17*(1), 7–23.

Grady, C. L., McIntosh, A. R., Horwitz, B., Maisog, J. M., Ungerleider, L. G., Mentis, M. J., et al. (1995). Age-related reductions in human recognition memory due to impaired encoding. *Science, 269,* 218–221.

Graebner, W. (1980). *A history of retirement: The meaning and function of an American institution, 1885–1978*: New Haven, CT: Yale University Press.

Granic, I., Hollenstein, T., Dishion, T. K., & Patterson, G. R. (2003). Longitudinal analysis of flexibility and reorganization in early adolescence: A dynamic systems study of family interactions. *Developmental Psychology, 39,* 606–617.

Gredilla, R., & Barja, G. (2005). Minireview: The role of oxidative stress in relation to caloric restriction and longevity. *Endocrinology, 146*(9), 3713–3717.

Green, J., & Statham, H. (1996). Psychosocial aspects of prenatal screening and diagnosis. In T. Marteau & M. Richards (Eds.), *The troubled helix: Social and psychological implications of the new human genetics* (pp. 140–163). New York: Cambridge University Press.

Greenberger, E., & Steinberg, L. (1986). *When teenagers work: The psychological and social costs of adolescent employment.* New York: Basic Books.

Greenberger, E., Chen, C., Tally, S., & Dong, Q. (2000). Family, peer, and individual correlates of depressive symptomatology among U.S. and Chinese adolescents. *Journal of Consulting and Clinical Psychology, 68,* 209–219.

Greenberger, E., Steinberg, L., & Vaux, A. (1981). Adolescents who work: Health and behavioral consequences of job stress. *Developmental Psychology, 17,* 691–703.

Greene, J. D., Sommerville,R. B., Nystrom, L. E., Darley, J. M., & Cohen, J. D. (2001). An fMRI investigation of emotional engagement in moral judgment. *Science, 293,* 2105–2108.

Greene, J., & Haidt, J. (2002). How (and where) does moral judgment work? *Trends in Cognitive Sciences, 6*(12), 517–523.

Greene, S. M., Anderson, E. R., Doyle, E. A., & Riedelbach, H. (2006). Divorce. In G. Bear & K. M. Minke (Eds.), *Children's needs: Vol. 3. Development, prevention, and intervention* (pp. 745–757). Bethesda, MD: National Association of School Psychologists.

Greenfield, E. A., & Marks, N. F. (2006). Linked lives: Adult children's problems and their parents' psychological and relational well-being. *Journal of Marriage and Family, 68*(2), 442–454.

Greenfield, P. M., Suzuki, L. K., & Rothstein-Fisch, C. (2006). Cultural pathways through human development. In W. Damon & R. Lerner (Eds.), *Handbook of child psychology. Vol 4: Child psychology in practice* (6th ed., pp. 655–699). Hoboken, NJ: Wiley.

Greenough, W. T., Black, J. E., & Wallace, C. S. (1987). Experience and brain development. *Child Development, 58,* 539–559.

Greenstein, T. N. (1996). Husbands' participation in domestic labor: Interactive effects of wives' and husbands' gender. *Journal of Marriage and the Family, 58*(3), 585–595.

Greenwood, P. M. (2007). Functional plasticity in cognitive aging: Review and hypothesis. *Neuropsychology, 21*(6), 657–673.

Greiner, K. A., Perera, S., & Ahluwalia, J. S. (2003). Hospice usage by minorities in the last year of life: Results from the National Mortality Followback Survey. *Journal of the American Geriatrics Society, 51*(7), 970–978.

Grigsby, D. G. & Shashidhar, H. R. (2006). Malnutrition. Retrieved April 2, 2010 from at http://www.emedicine.com/PED/topic1360.htm.

Grisso, T., Steinberg, L., Woolard, J., Cauffman, E., Scott, E., Graham, S., et al. (2003). Juveniles' competence to stand trial: A comparison of adolescents' and adults' capacities as trial defendants. *Law and Human Behavior, 27,* 333–363.

Groome, L. J., Swiber, M. J., Holland, S. B., Bentz, L. S., Atterbury, J. L., & Trimm, R. F. (1999). Spontaneouls motor activity in the perinatal infant before and after birth: Stability in individual differences. *Developmental Psychobiology, 35,* 15–24.

Groopman, J. (2005). *The anatomy of hope: How people prevail in the face of illness*: New York: Random House.

Gros-Louis, J., West, M. J., Goldstein, M. H., & King, A. P. (2006). Mothers provide differential feedback to infants' prelinguistic sounds. *International Journal of Behavioral Development, 30,* 509–516.

Gross, J. J., Carstensen, L. L., Pasupathi, M., Tsai, J., Skorpen, C. G., & Hsu, A. Y. C. (1997). Emotion and aging: Experience, expression, and control. *Psychology and Aging, 12*(4), 590–599.

Grossman, A. H., D'Augelli, A. R., & Hershberger, S. L. (2000). Social support networks of lesbian, gay, and bisexual adults 60 years of age and older. *Journal of Gerontology B: Psychological and Social Sciences, 55*(3), P171–179.

Grossman, D. C. (2000). The history of injury prevention programs and the epidemiology of child and adolescent injuries. *Future of Children, 10,* 23–52.

Grotevant, H. (1997). Adolescent development in family contexts. In W. Damon & R. Lerner (Series Eds.) & N. Eisenberg (Ed.), *Handbook of child psychology: Vol. 3. Social, emotional, and personality development* (5th ed., pp. 1097–1149). New York: Wiley.

Grover, R. L., & Nangle, D. W. (2003). Adolescent perceptions of problematic heterosocial situations: A focus group study. *Journal of Youth and Adolescence, 32,* 129–139.

Gruber, J., & Zinman, J. (2001). Youth smoking in the United States. In J. Gruber (Ed.). *Risky behavior among youths: An economic analysis* (pp. 69–120). Chicago: University of Chicago Press.

Grumbach, M. M., Hughes, I. A., & Conte, F. A. (2002). Disorders of sex differentiation. In P. R. Larsen, H. M. Kronenberg, S. Melmed, & K. S. Polonsky (Eds.), *Williams textbook of endocrinology* (10th ed., pp. 842–1002). Philadelphia: Saunders.

Grunbaum, J., Lowry, R., Kann, L., & Pateman, B. (2000). Prevalence of health risk behaviors among Asian American/Pacific Islander high school students. *Journal of Adolescent Health, 27,* 322–330.

Grundy, S. M. (2008). Metabolic syndrome pandemic. *Arteriosclerosis, Thrombosis, and Vascular Biology. 28,* 629–636.

Gruneir, A., Mor, V., Weitzen, S., Truchil, R., Teno, J., & Roy, J. (2007). Where people die: A multilevel approach to understanding influences on site of death in America. *Medical Care Research and Review, 64*(4), 351–378.

Grusec, J. E., Davidov, M., & Lundell, L. (2002). Prosocial and helping behavior. In P. K. Smith & C. H. Hart (Eds.), *Blackwell handbook of childhood social development* (pp. 457–474). Malden, MA: Blackwell.

Grych, J. H., & Fincham, F. D. (2001), *Interparental conflict and child development: Theory, research, and applications.* Cambridge, England: Cambridge University Press.

Guillemard, AM., & Rein, M. (1993). Comparative patterns of retirement: Recent trends in developed societies. *Annual Review of Sociology, 19,* 469–503.

Gunnar, M. R. (2006). Social regulation of stress in early child development. In K. McCartney & D. Phillips (Eds.), *Blackwell handbook of early childhood development* (pp. 106–125). Malden, MA: Blackwell.

Gunnar, M. R., (2000). Early adversity and the development of stress reactivity and regulation. In C. A. Nelson (Ed.), *The Minnesota Symposia on Child Psychology, Vol. 31, The effects of adversity on neurobehavioral development* (pp. 163–200). Mahwah NJ: Lawrence Erlbaum.

Gunnar, M. R., Fisher, P. A., & the Early Experience, Stress, and Prevention Network. (2006). Bringing basic research on early experience and stress neurobiology to bear on preventive interventions for neglected and maltreated children. *Development and Psychopathology, 18,* 651–677.

Gunnar, M. R., Van Dulmen, M. H. M., and the International Adoption Project Team. (2007). Behavior problems in post-institutionalized internationally adopted children. *Development and Psychopathology, 19,* 129–148.

Gupta, S., Agrawal, A., Agrawal, S., Su, H., & Gollapudi, S. (2006). A paradox of immunodeficiency and inflammation in human aging: Lessons learned from apoptosis. *Immunity & Ageing, 3*(1), 5.

Guralnik, J. M., & Simonsick, E. M. (1993). Physical disability in older Americans. *Journal of Gerontology, 48*(Special Issue), 3–10.

Guralnik, J. M., Simonsick, E. M., Ferrucci, L., Glynn, R. J., Berkman, L. F., Blazer, D. G., Scherr, P. A., & Wallace, R. B. (1994). A short physical performance battery assessing lower extremity function: Association with self-reported disability and prediction of mortality and nursing home admission. *Journal of Gerontology: Medical Sciences, 49*(2), M85–94.

Gutman, L. M., Sameroff, A. J., & Eccles, J. S. (2002). The academic achievement of African American students during early adolescence: An examination of multiple risk, promotive, and protective factors. *American Journal of Community Psychology, 30,* 367–400.

Haan, M. N., & Wallace, R. (2004). Can dementia be prevented? Brain aging in a population-based context. *Annual Review of Public Health, 25,* 1–24.

Hacker, D. (1994). An existential view of adolescence. *Journal of Early Adolescence, 14,* 300–327.

Hafetz, E. (1976). Parameters of sexual maturity in man. In E. Hafetz (Ed.), *Perspectives in human reproduction. Vol. 3. Sexual maturity: Physiological and clinical parameters.* Ann Arbor, MI: Ann Arbor Science Publishers.

Hagestad, G. O., & Neugarten, B. L. (1985). Age and the life course. In R. H. Binstock & E. Shanas (Eds.), *Handbook of aging and the social sciences* (Vol. 2, pp. 35–61). New York: Van Nostrand Reinhold.

Haidt, J. (2001). The emotional dog and its rational tail: A social intuitionist approach to moral judgment. *Psychological Review, 108*(4), 814–834.

Haidt, J. (2007). The new synthesis in moral psychology. *Science, 316,* 998–1002.

Halberstadt, A. G. (1986). Family socialization of emotional expression and nonverbal communication styles and skills. *Journal of Personality and Social Psychology, 51,* 827–836.

Halberstadt, A. G., & Eaton, K. L. (2003). A meta-analysis of family expressiveness and children's emotion expressiveness and understanding. *Marriage & Family Review, 34,* 35–62.

Haley, W. E., Larson, D. G., Kasl-Godley, J., Neimeyer, R. A., & Kwilosz, D. M. (2003). Roles for psychologists in end-of-life care: Emerging models of practice. *Professional Psychology Research and Practice, 34*(6), 626–633.

Halford, G. S. & Andrews, G. (2006). Reasoning and problem solving. In W. Damon & R. M. Lerner (Series Eds.) & D. Kuhn & R. S. Siegler (Vol. Eds.), *Handbook of child psychology: Vol. 2. Cognition, perception, and language* (6th ed., pp. 557–608). Hoboken, NJ: Wiley.

Halford, G. S. (2004). Information-processing models of cognitive development. In U. Goswami (Ed.). *Blackwell handbook of cognitive development* (pp. 555–574). Malden, MA: Blackwell Publishing.

Halgunseth, L. C., Ispa, J. M., & Rudy, D. (2006). Parental control in Latino families: An integrated review of the literature. *Child Development, 77,* 1282–1297.

Hall, D. T., & Mivris, P. H. (1996). The new protean career: Psychological success in the path with a heart. In D. T Hall (Ed.), *The career is dead— long live the career* (pp.15–45). San Francisco: Jossey-Bass.

Hall, H., Song, R., Rhodes, P., Prejean, J., An, Q., Lee, L. M., et al. (2008). Estimation of HIV incidence in the United States. *Journal of the American Medical Association, 300*(5), 520–529.

Halle, T. G. (2003). Emotional development and well-being. In M. H. Bornstein, L. Davidson, C. L. M. Keyes, & K. A. Moore (Eds.), *Well-being: Positive development across the life course* (pp. 125–138). Mahwah, NJ: Erlbaum.

Halpern, C., Joyner, K., Udry, J., & Suchindran, C. (2000). Smart teens don't have sex (or kiss much either). *Journal of Adolescent Health, 26,* 213–225.

Halpern, C., Udry, J., & Suchindran, C. (1996, March). *Monthly measures of salivary testosterone predict sexual activity in adolescent males.* Paper presented at the biennial meetings of the Society for Research on Adolescence, Boston.

Halpern, D. F. (2000). *Sex differences in cognitive abilities.* Mahwah, NJ: Erlbaum.

Halpern, D. F. (2005). Psychology at the intersection of work and family. *American Psychologist, 60*(5), 397–409.

Halpern, D. F., Benbow, C. P. Geary, D. C., Gur, R. C., Hyde, J. S., & Gernsbacher, M. A. (2007). The science of sex differences in science and mathematics. *Psychological Science in the Public Interest, 8*(1), 1–51.

Hamdoun, A., & Epel, D. (2007). Embryo stability and vulnerability in an always changing world. *Proceedings for the National Academy of Sciences, 104,* 1745–1750.

Hamer, M., & Chida, Y. (2008). Physical activity and risk of neurodegenerative disease: A systematic review of prospective evidence. *Psychological Medicine, 39*(1), 3–11.

Hamerman, D. (1999). Toward an understanding of frailty. *Annals of Internal Medicine, 130*(11), 945–950.

Hamill, S. B., & Goldberg, W. A. (1997). Between adolescence and aging grandparents: Midlife concerns of adults in the "sandwich generation." *Journal of Adult Development, 4*(3), 135–147.

Hamilton, S. F., & Hamilton, M. A. (2006). School, work, and emerging adulthood. In J. J. Arnett & J. L. Tanner (Eds.), *Emerging adults in America: Coming of age in the 21st century* (pp. 257–277). Washington, DC: American Psychological Association.

Hamm, J. V. (2000). Do birds of a feather flock together? Individual, contextual, and relationship bases for African American, Asian American, and European American adolescents' selection of similar friends. *Developmental Psychology, 36,* 209–219.

Hamm, J. V., & Coleman, H. K. (2001). African American and White adolescents' strategies for managing cultural diversity in predominantly White high schools. *Journal of Youth and Adolescence, 30,* 281–303.

Hammen, C. (1999). The emergence of an interpersonal approach to depression. In T. Joiner & J. C. Coyne (Eds.), *The interactional nature of depression: Advances in interpersonal approaches* (pp. 21–35). Washington, DC: American Psychological Association.

Hammen, C. (2005). Stress and depression. *Annual Review of Clinical Psycholgy, 1,* 293–319.

Han, G. H. (1996). Tradition and modernity in the culture of aging in Korea. *Korean Journal of Population and Development, 25*(1), 41–57.

Handelsman, D. J., & Liu, P. Y. (2005). Andropause: Invention, prevention, rejuvenation. *Trends in Endocrinology and Metabolism, 16*(2), 39–45.

Hanlon, H. W., Thatcher, R. W., & Cline, M. J. (1999). Gender differences in the development of EEG coherence in normal children. *Developmental Neuropsychology, 16,* 479–506.

Hansson, R. O., DeKoekkoek, P. D., Neece, W. M., & Patterson, D. W. (1997). Successful aging at work: Annual review, 1992–1996: The older worker and transitions to retirement. *Journal of Vocational Behavior, 51,* 202–233.

Hardy, S. A. (2006). Identity, reasoning, and emotion: An empirical comparison of three sources of moral motivation. *Motivation and Emotion, 30*(3), 207–215.

Hardy-Brown, K., & Plomin, R. (1985). Infant communicative development: Evidence from adoptive and biological families for genetic and environmental influences on rate differences. *Developmental Psychology, 21,* 378–385.

Hardy-Brown, K., Plomin, R., & DeFries, J. C. (1981). Genetic and environmental influences on the rate of communicative development in the first year of life. *Developmental Psychology, 17,* 704–717.

Harkness, S., & Super, C. M. (2006). Themes and variations: Parental ethnotheories in Western cultures. In K. H. Rubin & O. B. Chung (Eds.), *Parenting beliefs, behaviors, and parent-child relations: A cross-cultural perspective* (pp. 61–79). New York, NY: Psychology Press.

Harley, C. B., Futcher, A. B., & Greider, C. W. (1990). Telomeres shorten during aging of human fibroblasts. *Nature, 345,* 458–460.

Harlow, H. F. (1958). The nature of love. *American Psychologist, 13,* 673–685.

Harman, D. (2009). Origin and evolution of the free radical theory of aging; A brief personal history, 1954–2009. *Biogerontology, 10,* 773–781.

Harman, K., & Ruyak, P. (2005). Working through the pain: A controlled study of the impact of persistent pain on performing a computer task. *Clinical Journal of Pain, 21*(3), 216–222.

Harnad, S. R. (1987). *Categorical perception: The groundwork of cognition.* New York: Cambridge University Press.

Harris Interactive (2006, May 11). *MetLife Foundation Alzheimer's survey: What Americans think.* Retrieved August 20, 2008, from https://metwebforms.metlife.com/WPSAssets/20538296421147208330V1FAlzheimersSurvey.pdf

Harris Interactive (2007). *Majority of American adults remain without wills.* Retrieved July 13, 2009 from http://www.harrisinteractive.com/news/newsletters/clientnews/2007_Lawyers.pdf

Harris Interactive. (2005, May 6). Many U.S. employees have negative attitudes to their jobs, employers and top managers. *The Harris Poll® #38.* Retrieved February 11, 2009, from http://www.harrisinteractive.com/harris_poll/index.asp?PID=568

Harris, J. R. (1995). Where is the child's environment? A group socialization theory of development. *Psychological Review, 102,* 458–489.

Harris, J. R. (1998). *The nurture assumption.* New York: The Free Press.

Harris, P. L. (2000). Understanding emotion. In M. Lewis & J. Haviland (Eds.) *Handbook of emotion* (2nd ed., pp. 281–292). New York: Guilford Press.

Hart, B., & Risley, T. R. (1995). *Meaningful differences in the everyday experience of young American children.* Baltimore: Paul H. Brookes.

Hart, D., Southerland, N., & Atkins, R. (2003). Community service and adult development. In J. Demick & C. Andreolette (Eds.), *Handbook of adult development* (pp. 585–597). New York: Plenum.

Harter, S. (1998). The development of self-representations. In W. Damon & R. Lerner (Series Eds.) & N. Eisenberg (Vol. Ed.), *Handbook of child psychology: Vol. 3. Social, emotional, and personality development* (5th ed., pp. 53–617). New York: Wiley.

Harter, S. (1999). *The construction of the self.* New York: Guilford Press.

Harter, S. (2006) The self. In W. Damon & R. M. Lerner (Series Eds.) & N. Eisenberg (Vol. Ed.). *Handbook of child psychology: Vol. 3. Social, emotional, and personality development* (pp. 505–570). Hoboken, NJ: Wiley.

Hartup, W. (1983). Peer relations. In E. M. Hetherington (Ed.), *Handbook of child psychology: Vol. 4. Socialization, personality, and social development* (pp. 103–196). New York: Wiley.

Hartup, W. W. (1989). Social relationships and their developmental significance. *American Psychologist, 44,* 120–126.

Hartup, W. W. (1992). Friendships and their developmental significance. In H. McGurk (Ed.) *Childhood social development: Contemporary perspectives* (pp. 175–206). New York: Psychology Press.

Hartup, W. W., & Abecassis, M. (2002). Friends and enemies. In P. K. Smith & C. H. Hart (Eds.). *Blackwell handbook of childhood social development* (pp. 285–306). Malden MA: Blackwell.

Hartup, W. W., & Stevens, N. (1999). Friendships and adaptation across the life span. *Current Directions in Psychological Science, 8*(3), 76–79.

Harvey, W. B., & Anderson, E. L. (2005). *Minorities in higher education: Twenty-first annual status report 2003–2004.* Washington, DC: American Council on Education.

Haselager, G. J. T., Cillissen, H. N., van Lieshout, C. F. M., Riksen-Walraven, J. M. A., & Hartup, W. W. (2002). Heterogeneity among peer rejected boys across middle childhood: Developmental pathways of social behavior. *Child Development, 73,* 446–456.

Hasher, L., & Zacks, R. T. (1988). Working memory, comprehension, and aging: A review and a new view. In G. H. Bower (Ed.), *The psychology of learning and motivation: Advances in research and theory* (Vol. 22, pp. 193–225). San Diego, CA: Academic Press.

Hatch, L. R., & Bulcroft, K. (2004). Does long-term marriage bring less frequent disagreements? Five explanatory frameworks. *Journal of Family Issues, 25*(4), 465–495.

Hatfield, E. (1988). Passionate and companionate love. In R. J. Sternberg & M. Barnes (Eds.), *The psychology of love* (pp. 191–217). New Haven, CT: Yale Univ. Press.

Havighurst, R. J. (1952). *Developmental tasks and education.* New York: McKay.

Havighurst, R. J. (1953). *Human development and education.* New York: Longmans, Green, & Co.

Havighurst, R., Munnichs, J., Neugarten, B., & Thomae, H. (1969). *Adjustment to retirement, A cross-national study:* The Netherlands: Van Gorcum, Assen.

Hawkins, D. N., & Booth, A. (2005). Unhappily ever after: Effects of long-term, low-quality marriages on well-being. *Social Forces, 84*(1), 451–471.

Hay, D. F., & Nash, A. (2002). Social development in different family arrangements. In P. K. Smith & C. H. Hart (Eds.), *Blackwell handbook of childhood social development* (pp. 238–261). Malden, MA: Blackwell.

Hay, D. F., Nash, A., & Pedersen, J. (1983). Interactions between 6-month-olds. *Child Development, 54,* 105–113.

Hayflick, L. (1965). The limited in vitro lifetime diploid cell strains. *Experimental Cell Research, 37*, 614–636.

Hayflick, L. (1994). *How and why we age*. New York: Ballantine Books.

Hayflick, L. (1998). How and why we age. *Experimental Gerontology, 33*(7–8), 639–653.

Hayflick, L. (2004). The not-so-close relationship between biological aging and age-associated pathologies in humans. *Journal of Gerontology A: Biological and Medical Sciences, 59*(6), B547–550.

Hayflick, L. (2007). Biological aging is no longer an unsolved problem. *Annals of the New York Academy of Sciences, 1100*, 1–13.

Haynes, S. G., Feinleib, M., & Kannel, W. B. (1980). The relationship of psychosocial factors to coronary heart disease in the Framingham study: III. Eight-year incidence of coronary heart disease. *American Journal of Epidemiology, 111*(1), 37–58.

Haynie, D. L. (2003). Contexts of risk? Explaining the link between girls' pubertal development and their delinquency involvement. *Social Forces, 82*, 355–397.

Hayslip, B. Jr., & Peveto, C. A. (2005). *Cultural changes in attitudes toward death, dying, and bereavement*. New York: Springer.

Hayward, C., Gotlib, I., Schraedley, P., & Litt, I. (1999). Ethnic differences in the association between pubertal status and symptoms of depression in adolescent girls. *Journal of Adolescent Health, 25*, 143–149.

Hazan, C., & Shaver, P. R. (1987). Romantic love conceptualized as an attachment process. *Journal of Personality and Social Psychology, 52*(3), 511–524.

Hazzard, W. R. (2001). Aging, health, longevity, and the promise of biomedical research: the perspective of a gerontologist and geriatrician. In E. J. Masoro & S. N. Austad (Eds.), *Handbook of the biology of aging* (5th ed., pp. 445–456.). San Diego, CA: Academic Press.

He, W., Sengupta, M., Velkoff, V. A., & DeBarros, K. A. (2005). *65+ in the United States: 2005*. U.S. Census Bureau, Current Population Reports, P23–P209. Washington, DC: U.S. Government Printing Office.

Heath, J. M., & Stuart, M. R. (2002). Prescribing exercise for frail elders. *Journal of the American Board of Family Medicine, 15*(3), 218–228.

Hebb, D. O. (1978, November). Watching myself grow old. *Psychology Today*, 15–23.

Hebert, L. E., Scherr, P. A., Bienias, J. L., Bennett, D. A., & Evans, D. A. (2003). Alzheimer disease in the U.S.: Population prevalence estimates using the 2000 Census. *Archives of Neurology, 60*, 1119–1122.

Heckhausen, J. (1997). Developmental regulation across adulthood: Primary and secondary control of age-related challenges. *Developmental Psychology, 33*(1), 176–187.

Heckhausen, J. (1999). *Developmental regulation in adulthood: Age-normative and sociostructural constraints as adaptive challenges*. New York: Cambridge University Press.

Heckhausen, J. (2001). Adaptation and resilience in midlife. In M. E. Lachman (Ed.), *Handbook of midlife development* (pp. 345–394). New York: Wiley.

Heckhausen, J., & Schulz, R. (1995). A life-span theory of control. *Psychological Review, 102*(2), 284–303.

Heckhausen, J., Dixon, R. A., & Baltes, P. B. (1989). Gains and losses in development throughout adulthood as perceived by different adult age groups. *Developmental Psychology, 25*(1), 109–121

Heckhausen, J., Wrosch, C., & Fleeson, W. (2001). Developmental regulation before and after a developmental deadline: The sample case of "biological clock" for child-bearing. *Psychology and Aging, 16*(3), 400–413.

Heckhausen, J., Wrosch, C., & Schulz, R. (2010). A motivational theory of life-span development. *Psychological Review, 117*(1), 32–60.

Hedberg, K., Hopkins, D., & Kohn, M. (2003). Five years of legal physician-assisted suicide in Oregon. *The New England Journal of Medicine, 348*(10), 961–964.

Hedberg, K., Hopkins, D., Leman, R., & Kohn, M. (2009). The 10-year experience of Oregon's Death with Dignity Act: 1998–2007. *The Journal of Clinical Ethics, 20*(2), 124–132.

Hedges, L., & Nowell, A. (1999). Changes in the black-white gap in achievement test scores. *Sociology of Education, 72*, 111–135.

Heine, S. J. (2008). *Cultural psychology*. New York: Norton.

Heinicke, C. M. (2002). The transition to parenting. In M. H. Bornstein (Ed.), *Handbook of parenting* (2nd ed., Vol. 3, pp. 363–388). Mahwah, NJ: Erlbaum.

Heinz, W. R. (2002). Self-socialization and post-traditional society. In R. A. Settersten, Jr. & T. J. Owens (Eds.), *New frontiers in socialization* (pp. 41–64). New York: Elsevier.

Held, R., & Hein, A. (1963). Movement-produced stimulation in the development of visually guided behavior. *Journal of Comparative and Physiological Psychology, 56*, 872–876.

Helson, R., & Kwan, V. S. Y. (2000). Personality development in adulthood: The broad picture and processes in one longitudinal sample. In S. Hampson (Ed.), *Advances in personality psychology* (Vol. 1, pp. 77–106). London: Routledge.

Helson, R., & Wink, P. (1992). Personality change in women from the early 40s to the early 50s. *Psychology and aging, 7*(1), 46–55.

Helson, R., Kwan, V. S. Y., John, O. P., & Jones, C. (2002). The growing evidence for personality change in adulthood: Findings from research with personality inventories. *Journal of Research in Personality, 36*(4), 287–306.

Helson, R., Mitchell, V., & Moane, G. (1984). Personality and patterns of adherence and nonadherence to the social clock. *Journal of Personality and Social Psychology, 46*(5), 1079–1096.

Helson, R., Soto, C. J., & Cate, R. A. (2006). From young adulthood through the middle ages. In D. K. Mroczek & T. D. Little (Eds.), *Handbook of personality development* (pp. 337–352). Mahwah, NJ: Erlbaum.

Hendrie, H. C., Albert, M. S., Butters, M. A., Gao, S., Knopman, D. S., Launer, L. J., et al. (2006). The NIH cognitive and emotional health project report of the critical evaluation study committee. *Alzheimer's and Dementia, 2*(1), 12–32.

Henning, A., Striano, T., & Lieven, E. V. M. (2005). Maternal speech to infants at 1 and 3 months of age. *Infant Behavior & Development, 28*, 519–536.

Henry, N. J. M., Berg, C. A., Smith, T. W., & Florsheim, P. (2007). Positive and negative characteristics of marital interaction and their association with marital satisfaction in middle-aged and older couples. *Psychology and Aging, 22*, 428–441.

Herdt, G., & McClintock, M. (2000). The magical age of 10. *Archives of Sexual Behavior, 29*, 587–606.

Herek, G. M., & Garnets, L. D. (2007). Sexual orientation and mental health. *Annual Review of Clinical Psychology, 3*, 355–375.

Hermans, H. J. M., & Oles, P. K. (1999). Midlife crisis in men: Affective organization of personal meanings. *Human Relations, 52*(11), 1403–1426.

Heron, M. (2007). Deaths: Leading causes for 2004. *National Vital Statistics Report, 56*(5), 1–95.

Hertzog, C., Kramer, A. F., Wilson, R. S., & Lindenberger, U. (2008). Enrichment effects on adult cognitive development: Can the functional capacity of older adults be preserved and enhanced. *Psychological Science in the Public Interest, 9*(1), 1–65.

Hess, T. M. (2005). Memory and aging in context. *Psychological Bulletin, 131*(3), 383–406.

Hess, T. M., Auman, C., Colcombe, S. J., & Rahhal, T. A.(2003). The impact of stereotype threat on age differences in memory performance. *Journal of Gerontology B: Psychological Sciences and Social Sciences, 58*(1), P3–31.

Hetherington, E. M., Cox, M., & Cox, R. (1982). Effects of divorce on parents and children. In M. E. Lamb (Ed.), *Nontraditional families: Parenting and child development* (pp. 233–288). Hillsdale, NJ: Erlbaum.

Hetherington, E. M., Henderson, S., & Reiss, D. (1999). Adolescent siblings in stepfamilies: Family functioning and adolescent adjustment. *Monographs of the Society for Research in Child Development, 64,* Serial No. 259.

Hetherington, M. M. (1998). Taste and appetite regulation in the elderly. *Proceedings of the Nutrition Society, 57*(04), 625–631.

Hetherington, M., & Clingempeel, W. G. (1992). Coping with marital transitions: A family systems perspective. *Monographs of the Society for Research in Child Development,* 57(2–3, Serial No. 227).

Hewlett, B. S. (2008). Fathers and infants among Aka pygmies. In R. A. LeVine & R. S. New (Eds.). *Anthropology and child development: A cross-cultural reader* (pp. 84–99). Malden, MA: Blackwell Publishing.

Hiedemann, B., Suhomlinova, O., & O'Rand, A. M. (1998). Economic independence, economic status, and empty nest in midlife marital disruption. *Journal of Marriage and Family, 60*(1), 219–231.

Hijazi, R. A., & Cunningham, G. R. (2005). Andropause: Is androgen replacement therapy indicated for the aging male? *Annual Review of Medicine, 56,* 117–137.

Hill, N. E., Castellino, D. R., Lansford, J. E., Nowlin, P., Dodge, K. A., Bates, J. E., & Pettit, G. S. (2004). Parent academic involvement as related to school behavior, achievement, and aspirations: Demographic variations across adolescence. *Child Development, 75,* 1491–1509.

Hilsman, R., & Garber, J. (1995). A test of the cognitive diathesis-stress model of depression in children: Academic stressors, attributional style, perceived competence, and control. *Journal of Personality and Social Psychology, 69,* 370–380.

Himes, C. L. (2001). Elderly Americans. *Population Bulletin, 56,* 3–42

Hinde, R., Titmus, G., Easton, D., & Tamplin, A. (1985). Incidence of "friendship" and behavior toward Strong Associates versus Nonassociates in preschoolers. *Child Development, 56,* 234–245.

Hines, M., & Kaufman, F. R. (1994). Androgen and the development of human sex-typical behavior: Rough-and-tumble play and sex of preferred playmates in children with congenital adrenal hyperplasia (CAH). *Child Development, 65,* 1042–1053.

Hingson, R., Heeren, T, & Winter, M. (2006). Age at drinking onset and alcohol dependence: Age at onset, duration, and severity. *Archives of Pediatric and Adolescent Medicine,* 160, 739–746.

Hirschberger, G., Srivastava, S., Marsh, P., Cowan, C., & Cowan, P. (2009). Attachment, marital satisfaction, and divorce during the first fifteen years of parenthood. *Personal Relationships, 16*(3), 401–420.

Hirshberg, L. M., & Svejda, M. (1990). When infants look to their parents: I. Infants' social referencing of mothers compared to fathers. *Child Development, 61,* 1175–1186

Hirsh-Pasek, K., & Golinkoff, R. M. (2003). *Einstein never used flash cards.* Emmaus, PA: Rodale.

Hoek, H. W., Brown, A. S., & Susser, E. S. (1999). The Dutch famine studies: Prenatal nutritional deficiency and schizophrenia. In E. S. Susser, A. S. Brown, & J. M. Gorman (Eds.), *Prenatal exposures in schizophrenia* (pp. 135–161). Washington, DC: American Psychiatric Association.

Hoff, E. (2006). How social contexts support and shape language development. *Developmental Review, 26,* 55–88.

Hoff, E. (2006). Language experience and language milestones during early childhood. In K. McCartney & D. Phillips (Ed.), *Blackwell handbook on early childhood development.* (pp. 233–251) Malden, MA: Blackwell.

Hofferth, S. L., & Curtin, S. C. (2005). Leisure time activities in middle childhood. In K. A. Moore & L. H. Lippman (Eds.), *What do children need to flourish?: Conceptualizing and measuring indicators of positive development* (pp. 95–110). New York: Springer.

Hofferth, S. L., & Sandberg, J. F. (2001). How American children spend their time. *Journal of Marriage and the Family, 63,* 295–308.

Hoff-Ginsburg, E. (1998). The relation of birth order and socioeconomic status to children's language experience and language development. *Applied Psycholinguistics, 19,* 603–630.

Hoffman, L. W., & Manis, J. D. (1979). The value of children in the United States: A new approach to the study of fertility. *Journal of Marriage and the Family, 41*(3), 583–596.

Hoffman, M. (2008). Empathy and prosocial behaviour. In M. Lewis, J. Haviland-Jones, & L. Feldman-Barrett (Eds.), *Handbook of emotions (3rd ed.)* (pp. 440–455). New York: Guildford Press.

Hogan, D., Sun, R., & Cornwell, G. (2000). Sexual and fertility behaviors of American females aged 15–19 years: 1985, 1990, and 1995. *American Journal of Public Health, 90,* 1421–1425.

Holland, J. L. (1997). *Making vocational choices: A theory of vocational personalities and work environments (3rd ed.).* Odessa, FL: Psychological Assessment Resources.

Hollist, C. S., & Miller, R. B. (2005). Perceptions of attachment style and marital quality in midlife marriage. *Family Relations, 54,* 46–57.

Holloway, S. (1988). Concepts of ability and effort in Japan and the United States. *Review of Educational Research, 58,* 327–345.

Holmbeck, G. N. (2002). A developmental perspective on adolescent health and illness: An introduction to the special issues. *Journal of Pediatric Psychology,* 27(5), 409–416.

Holmen, T., Barrett-Connor, E., Holmen, J., & Bjerner, L. (2000). Health problems in teenage daily smokers versus nonsmokers, Norway, 1995–1997. *American Journal of Epidemiology, 151,* 148–155.

Holtmaat, A., Wilbrecht, L., Knott, G. W., Welker, E., & Svoboda, K. (2006). Experience-dependent and cell-type-specific spine growth in the neocortex. *Nature, 441,* 979–983.

Homel, R. & Burns, A. (1989). Environmental quality and the well-being of children. *Social Indicators Research, 21,* 133–158.

Honig, A. S. (2002). Choosing child care for young children. In M. H. Bornstein (Ed.), *Handbook of parenting: Vol. 5. Practical parenting* (2nd ed., pp. 375–405). Mahwah, NJ: Erlbaum.

Hooker, K., & McAdams, D. P. (2003). Personality reconsidered: A new agenda for aging research. *Journal of Gerontology B: Psychological Sciences and Social Sciences, 58*(6), P296–304.

Hooper, C. J., Luciana, M., Conklin, H. M., & Yarger, R. S. (2004). Adolescents' performance on the Iowa gambling task: Implications for the development of decision making and ventromedial prefrontal cortex. *Developmental Psychology, 40,* 1148–1158.

Hoover-Dempsey, K., & Sandler, H. (1995). Parental involvement in children's education: Why does it make a difference? *Teachers College Record, 97,* 310–331.

Hopkins, B., & Johnson, S. P. (Eds.). (2005). *Prenatal development of postnatal functions (Advances in infancy research).* New York: Praeger.

Hopkins, B., & Westra, T. (1988). Maternal handling and motor development: An intracultural study. *Genetic, Social, and General Psychology, 31,* 384–390.

Hopkins, B., & Westra, T. (1990). Motor development, maternal expectation, and the role of handling. *Infant Behavior and Development, 13,* 117–122.

Hoppa, R. D., & Garlie, T. N. (1998). Secular changes in the growth of Toronto children during the last century. *Annals of Human Biology, 25,* 553–561.

Horn, J. L. (1970). Organization of data on life-span development of human abilities. In L. R. Goulet & P. B. Baltes (Eds.), *Lifespan developmental psychology: Theory and research* (Vol. 1, pp. 211–256). New York: Academic Press.

Horn, J. L., & Cattell, R. B. (1966). Refinement and test of the theory of fluid and crystallized general intelligences. *Journal of Educational Psychology, 57*(5), 253–270.

Hornik, R., Risenhoover, N., & Gunnar, M. (1987). The effects of maternal positive, neutral, and negative affective communications on infant responses to new toys. *Child Development, 58,* 937–944.

Horowitz, L., & Vitkus, J. (1986). The interpersonal basis of psychiatric symptoms. *Clinical Psychology Review, 6,* 443–469.

Horton, S., Baker, J., & Schorer, J. (2008). Expertise and aging: maintaining skills through the lifespan. *European Review of Aging and Physical Activity, 5*(2), 89–96.

Houser, A. N. (2007). *Nursing homes.* Washington, DC: AARP Public Policy Institute.

Howe, M. J. A. (2002). *Genius explained.* New York: Cambridge University Press.

Howe, M. L., & Lewis, M. D. (2005). The importance of dynamic systems approaches for understanding development. *Developmental Review, 25,* 247–251.

Howes, C. (1984). Sharing fantasy: Social pretend play in toddlers. *Child Development, 56,* 1253–1258.

Howes, C. (1992). *The collaborative construction of pretend.* Albany: State University of New York Press.

Howes, C., & Matheson, C. C. (1992). Sequences in the development of competent play with peers: Social and social pretend play. *Developmental Psychology, 28,* 961–974.

Howes, C., Hamilton, C. E., & Phillipsen, L. C. (1998). Stability and continuity of child-caregiver and child-peer relationships. *Child Development, 69,* 418–426.

Hsu, V. C., & Rovee-Collier, C. (2006). Memory reactivation in the second year of life. *Infant Behavior & Development, 29,* 91–107.

Huang, A., Moore, E., Boyko, E., Scholes, D., Lin, F., Vittinghoff, E., et al. (2010). Vaginal symptoms in postmenopausal women: Self-reported severity, natural history, and risk factors. *Menopause. 17*(1),121–126.

Hubel, D. (1981). Evolution of ideas on the primary visual cortex, 1955–1978: A biased historical account. Retrieved December 17, 2007 from http://nobelprize.org/nobel_prizes/medicine/laureates/1981/hubel-lecture.html

Huesmann, L. R., & Taylor, L. D. (2006). Media effects in middle childhood. In A. C. Huston & M. N. Ripke (Eds.), *Developmental contexts in middle childhood: Bridges to adolescence and adulthood* (pp. 303–326). New York: Cambridge University Press.

Huesmann, L. R., Moise-Titus, J., Podolsky, C., and Eron, L. D. (2003). Longitudinal relations between children's exposure to TV violence and their aggressive and violent behavior in young adulthood: 1977–1992. *Developmental Psychology, 39,* 201–221.

Huh, N. Y. (2008, April 18). Happiest Americans are the oldest. *Associated Press.* Retrieved April 6, 2010 from http://www.msnbc.msn.com/id/24201693/

Hulley, S., & Grady, D. (2004). The WHI estrogen-alone trial: Do things look any better? *Journal of the American Medical Association, 291*(14), 1769–1771.

Hulley, S., Grady, D., Bush, T., Furberg, C., Herrington, D., Riggs, B., et al. (1998). Randomized trial of estrogen plus progestin for secondary prevention of coronary heart disease in postmenopausal women. *Journal of the American Medical Association, 280*(7), 605–613.

Hunnius, S., & Geuze, R. H. (2004). Developmental changes in visual scanning of dynamic faces and abstract stimuli in infants: A longitudinal study. *Infancy, 6,* 231–255.

Hunter, G. R., McCarthy, J. P., & Bamman, M. M. (2004). Effects of resistance training on older adults. *Sports Medicine, 34*(5), 329–348.

Huston, A. C., Wright, J. C., Marquis, J., & Green, S. B. (1999). How young children spend their time: Television and other activities. *Developmental Psychology, 35,* 921–925.

Huston, T. L., & Melz, H. (2004). The case for (promoting) marriage: The devil is in the details. *Journal of Marriage and Family, 66*(4), 943–958.

Huston, T. L., Caughlin, J. P., Houts, R. M., Smith, S. E., & George, L. J. (2001). The connubial crucible: Newlywed years as predictors of marital delight, distress, and divorce. *Journal of Personality and Social Psychology, 80*(2), 237–252.

Huston, T. L., Niehuis, S., & Smith, S. E. (2001). The early marital roots of conjugal distress and divorce. *Current Directions in Psychological Science, 10*(4), 116–119.

Huttenlocher, J., Vasilyeva, M., Cymerman, E., & Levine, S. (2002). Language input and child syntax. *Cognitive Psychology, 45,* 337–374.

Huttenlocher, P. R. (2002). *Neural plasticity: The effects of environment on the development of the cerebral cortex.* Cambridge, MA: Harvard University Press.

Hyde, J. S. (2005). The gender similarity hypothesis. *American Psychologist, 60,* 581–592.

Hyde, J. S., Fennema, E., & Lamon, S. J. (1990). Gender differences in mathematics performance: A meta-analysis. *Psychological Bulletin, 107,* 139–155.

Hyde, J. S., Fennema, E., Ryan, M., Frost, L. A., & Hopp, C. (1990). Gender comparisons of mathematics attitudes and affect: A meta-analysis. *Psychology of Women Quarterly, 14*(3), 299–324.

Hymel, S., Vaillancourt, T., McDougall, P., & Renshaw, P. (2002). Peer acceptance and rejection in childhood. In P. K. Smith & C. H. Hart (Eds.), *Blackwell handbook of childhood social development* (pp. 265–284). Malden, MA: Blackwell.

Idler, E. (2006). Religion and aging. In R. H. Binstock & L. K. George (Eds.), *Handbook of aging and the social sciences* (6th ed., pp. 277–302). New York: Elsevier.

Ikkink, K. K., van Tilburg, T., & Knipscheer, K. C. P. M. (1999). Perceived instrumental support exchanges in relationships between elderly parents and their adult children: Normative and structural explanations. *Journal of Marriage and the Family, 61*(4), 831–844.

Impett, E. A., Strachman, A., Finkel, E. J., & Gable, S. L. (2008). Maintaining sexual desire in intimate relationships: The importance of approach goals. *Journal of Personality and Social Psychology, 94*(5), 808–823.

Impett, I. A., & Peplau, L. A. (2006). "His" and "her" relationships? A review of the empirical evidence. In A. L. Vangelisti & D. Perlman (Eds.), *The Cambridge handbook of personal relationships* (pp. 273–291). Cambridge: Cambridge University Press.

Ingersoll, E. W., & Thoman, E. B. (1999). Sleep/wake states of preterm infants: Stability, developmental change, diurnal variation, and relation with caregiving activity. *Child Development, 70,* 1–10.

Ingersoll-Dayton, B., Krause, N., & Morgan, D. (2002). Religious trajectories and transitions over the life course. *The International Journal of Aging and Human Development, 55*(1), 51–70.

Inhelder, B., & Piaget, J. (1964). *The early growth of logic: Classification and seriation.* London: Routledge & Kegan Paul.

Inlow, J. K., & Restifo, L. L. (2004). Molecular and comparative genetics of mental retardation. *Genetics, 166,* 835–881.

Institute of Medicine. (2006). *Food marketing to children and youth: Threat or opportunity?* Washington: National Academies Press.

Institute of Medicine. (2006). *Preterm birth: Causes, consequences, and prevention.* Washington DC: Institute of Medicine. http://www.iom.edu/CMS/3740/25471/35813.aspx

International Human Genome Sequencing Consortium. (2001). Initial sequencing and analysis of the human genome. *Nature, 409,* 860–921.

Irwin, C., Jr. (1986). Biopsychosocial correlates of risk-taking behavior during adolescence: Can the physician intervene? *Journal of Adolescent Health Care, 7,* 82–96.

Izard, C. E. (1979). *The Maximally Discriminative Facial Movement Coding System (MAX).* Newark: University of Delaware, Instructional Resources Center.

Izard, C. E., & Dougherty, L. M. (1982). Two complementary systems for measuring facial expressions in infants and children. In C. E. Izard (Ed.), *Measuring emotions in infants and children* (pp. 97–126). New York: Cambridge University Press.

Izard, C. E., & Malatesta, C. 2. (1987). Perspectives on emotional development: I. Differential emotions theory of early emotional development. In J. D. Osofsky (Ed.), *Handbook of infant development* (2nd ed., pp. 494–554). New York: Wiley-Interscience.

Izard, C. E., Fantauzzo, C. A., Castle, J. M., Haynes, O. M., Rayias, M. F., & Putnam, P. H. (1995). The ontogeny and significance of infants' facial expressions in the first 9 months of life. *Developmental Psychology, 31,* 997–1013.

Jackson, J. S., & Knight, K. M. (2006). Race and self regulatory health behaviors: The role of the stress response and the HPA axis in physical and mental health disparities. In L. L. Carstensen & K. W. Schaie (Eds.), *Social structure, aging and self regulation in the elderly* (pp. 189–207). New York: Springer.

Jackson, J. S., Knight, K. M., & Rafferty, K. M. (2009). Race and unhealthy behaviors: Chronic stress, the HPA axis, and physical and mental health disparities over the life course. *American Journal of Public Health, 99*(12), 1–7.

Jackson, L. A., von Eye, A., Biocca, F. A., et al. (2006). Does home Internet use influence the academic performance of low-income children? Findings from the HomeNetToo project. Special Section on Children, Adolescents, and the Internet, *Developmental Psychology 42,* 429–435.

Jacobi, C., Hayward, C., de Zwaan, M., Kraemer, H. C., & Agras, W. S. (2004). Coming to terms with risk factors for eating disorders: Application of risk terminology and suggestions for a general taxonomy. *Psychological Bulletin, 130,* 19–65.

Jacobs, J. E., Lanza, S., Osgood, D., Eccles, J. S., & Wigfield, A. (2002). Changes in children's self-competence and values: Gender and domain differences across grades one through twelve. *Child Development, 73,* 509–527.

Jacoby, S. (2005). *Sex in America.* American Association of Retired Persons. Retrieved May 1, 2008 from http://www.aarpmagazine.org/lifestyle/relationships/sex_in_america.html

Jacques, E. (1965). Death and the mid-life crisis. *International Journal of Psychoanalysis, 46,* 502–514.

Jaffee, S., & Hyde, J. S. (2000). Gender differences in moral orientation: A meta-analysis. *Psychological Bulletin, 126*(5), 703–725.

Jager, R. D., Mieler, W. F., & Miller, J. W. (2008). Age-related macular degeneration. *New England Journal of Medicine, 358*(24), 2606–2617.

Jakobson, R. (1968). *Child language, aphasia, and phonological universals.* Oxford, England: Mouton.

James, J., Thomas, P., Cavan, D., & Kerr, D. (2004). Preventing childhood obesity by reducing consumption of carbonated drinks: Cluster randomized controlled trial. *British Medical Journal, 328*(7450).

James, W. (1924). *Some problems of philosophy.* New York: Longmans, Green and Co.

Jarvinen, D., & Nicholls, J. (1996). Adolescents' social goals, beliefs about the causes of social success, and satisfaction in peer relations. *Developmental Psychology, 32,* 435–441.

Jasnow, M., & Feldstein, S. (1986). Adult-like temporal characteristics of mother-infant vocal interactions. *Child Development, 57,* 754–761.

Jaur, L., & Stoddard, S. (1999). *Chartbook on women and disability in the U.S.* Washington, DC: National Institute on Disability and Rehabilitation Research.

Jensen, L. A. (2008). Through two lenses: A cultural–developmental approach to moral psychology. *Developmental Review, 28*(3), 289–315.

Jochemsen, H., & Keown, J. (1999). Voluntary euthanasia under control? Further empirical evidence from The Netherlands. *Journal of Medical Ethics, 25*(1),16–21.

Jodl, K. M., Michael, A., Malanchuk, O., Eccles, J. S., & Sameroff, A. (2001). Parents' roles in shaping early adolescents' occupational aspirations. *Child Development, 72,* 1247–1265.

John, O. P., & Srivastava, S. (1999). The Big-Five trait taxonomy: History, measurement, and theoretical perspectives. In L. A. Pervin & O. P. John (Eds.), *Handbook of personality: Theory and research* (2nd ed., pp. 102–139). New York: Guilford.

Johnson, C. L., & Troll, L. (1994). Constraints and facilitators to friendships in late late life. *Gerontologist, 34*(1), 79–87.

Johnson, M. H. (2010). Developmental neuroscience, psychophysiology, and genetics. In M. H. Bornstein & M. E. Lamb (Eds.), *Developmental science: An advanced textbook* (6th ed, pp. 187–222). New York: Taylor & Francis.

Johnson, M. K. (2001). Change in job values during the transition to adulthood. *Work and Occupations, 28*(3), 315–345.

Johnson, M. K. (2002). Social origins, adolescent experiences, and work value trajectories during the transition to adulthood. *Social Forces, 80*(4), 1307–1340.

Johnson, R. W., Mermin, G. B. T., & Resseger, M. (2007). *Employment at older ages and the changing nature of work.* AARP Public Policy Institute Issue Paper 2007-20. Washington, DC: American Association of Retired Persons (AARP). Retrieved April 21, 2008 from http://www.aarp.org/research/work/employment/2007_20_work.html

Johnson, W., Emde, R. N., Pannabecker, B., Stenberg, C., & Davis, M. (1982). Maternal perception of infant emotion from birth through 18 months. *Infant Behavior & Development, 5,* 313–322.

Johnson, W., Bouchard, T. J., McGue, M., Segal, N. L., Tellegen, A., & Keyes, M. (2007). Genetic and environmental influences on the Verbal-Perceptual-Image Rotation (VPR) model of the structure of mental abilities in the Minnesota study of twins reared apart. *Intelligence, 35,* 542–562.

Jones, G., Steketee, R. W., Black, R. E., Bhutta, Z. A., Morris, S. S., & the Bellagio Child Survival Study Group. (2003, July 5). How many child deaths can we prevent this year? *Lancet, 362,* 65–71.

Jones, H. E. (2006). Drug addiction during pregnancy: Advances in maternal treatment and understanding child outcomes. *Current Directions in Psychological Science, 15,* 126–130.

Jones, K. L., Robinson, L. K., Bakhireva, L. N., Marintcheva, G., Storojev, V., Strahova, A., et al. (2006). Accuracy of the diagnosis of physical features of fetal alcohol syndrome by pediatricians after specialized training. *Pediatrics, 118,* 1734–1738.

Jones, K. M., Whitbourne, S. K., & Skultety, K. M. (2006). Identity processes and the transition to midlife among Baby Boomers. In S. K. Whitbourne & S. L. Willis (Eds.), *The Baby Boomers grow up: Contemporary perspectives on midlife* (pp. 149–164). Mahwah, NJ: Lawrence Erlbaum.

Jopp, D., & Rott, C. (2006). Adaptation in very old age: Exploring the role of resources, beliefs, and attitudes for centenarians' happiness. *Psychology and Aging, 21*(2), 266–280.

Jordan, K. E., & Brannon, E. M. (2006). The multisensory representation of number in infancy. *Proceedings of the National Academy of Sciences, 103,* 3486–3489.

Jordan, W. J., & Nettles, S. M. (2000). How students invest their time outside of school: Effects on school-related outcomes. *Social Psychology of Education, 3,* 217–243.

Jordan, W., Lara, J., & McPartland, J. (1996). Exploring the causes of early dropout among race-ethnic and gender groups. *Youth and Society, 28,* 62–94.

Jorm, A. F. (2000). Does old age reduce the risk of anxiety and depression? A review of epidemiological studies across the adult life span. *Psychological Medicine, 30*(1), 11–22.

Jorm, A. F., Windsor, T. D., Dear, K. B. G., Anstey, K. J., Christensen, H., & Rodgers, B. (2005). Age group differences in psychological distress: The role of psychosocial risk factors that vary with age. *Psychological Medicine, 35*(9), 1253–1263.

Josephson, W. L., (1987). Television violence and children's aggression: Testing the priming, social script, and disinhibition predictions. *Journal of Personality and Social Psychology 535,* pp. 882–890.

Joyner, K., & Udry, J. R. (2000). You don't bring me anything but down: Adolescent romance and depression. *Journal of Health and Social Behavior, 41,* 369–391.

Judge, B. & Billick, S. B. (2004). Suicidality in adolescence: Review and legal considerations. *Behavioral Sciences & the Law, 22,* 681–695.

Juvonen, J., & Murdock, T. (1995). Grade-level differences in the social value of effort: Implications for self-presentation tactics of early adolescents. *Child Development, 66,* 1694–1705.

Kagan, J. (2006). Biology, culture, and temperamental biases. In W. Damon & R. Lerner (Series Eds.) & D. Kuhn & R. S. Siegler (Vol. Eds.), *Handbook of child psychology: Vol. 2. Cognition, perception, and language* (6th ed., pp. 167–225). Hoboken, NJ: Wiley.

Kagan, S., & Knight, G. (1979). Cooperation-competition and self-esteem: A case of cultural relativism. *Journal of Cross-Cultural Psychology, 10,* 457–467.

Kail, R. (2003). Information processing and memory. In M. Bornstein, L. Davidson, C. L. M. Keyes, K. A. Moore, & the Center for Child Well-Being (Eds.), *Well-being: Positive development across the life course* (pp. 269–279). Mahwah, NJ: Erlbaum.

Kail, R. V., & Ferrer, E. (2007). Processing speed in childhood and adolescence: Longitudinal models for examining developmental change. *Child Development, 78,* 1760–1770.

Kalichman, S. C., & Cain, D. (2005). Perceptions of local HIV/AIDS prevalence and risks for HIV/AIDS and other sexually transmitted infections: Preliminary study of intuitive epidemiology. *Annals of Behavioral Medicine, 29*(2), 100–105.

Kalish, C. W. (1996). Preschoolers' understanding of germs as invisible mechanisms. *Cognitive Development, 11,* 83–106.

Kalish, R. A. (1985). The social context of death and dying. In R. H. Binstock & E. Shanas (Eds.), *Handbook of aging and the social sciences* (2nd Ed., pp. 149–170). New York: Van Nostrand Reinhold.

Kalmijn, M. (2007). Gender differences in the effects of divorce, widowhood and remarriage on intergenerational support: Does marriage protect fathers? *Social Forces, 85*(3), 1079–1104.

Kamarck, T. W., Schwartz, J. E., Shiffman, S., Muldoon, M. F., Sutton-Tyrrell, K., & Janicki, D. L. (2005). Psychosocial stress and cardiovascular risk: What is the role of daily experience? *Journal of Personality, 73*(6), 1749–1774.

Kampfe, C. M., & Smith, S. M. (1998). Intrapersonal aspects of hearing loss in persons who are older. *The Journal of Rehabilitation, 64*(2), 24–28.

Kandel, D., Johnson, J., Bird, H., & Canino, G. (1997). Psychiatric disorders associated with substance use among children and adolescents: Findings from the Methods for the Epidemiology of Child and Adolescent Mental Disorders (MECA) Study. *Journal of Abnormal Child Psychology, 25,* 121–132.

Kandel, E. C. (2007). *In search of memory: The emergence of a new science of mind.* New York: W. W. Norton.

Kanemura, H., Aihara, M., Aoki, S., Araki, T., & Nakazawa, S. (2003). Development of the prefrontal lobe in infants and children: A three-dimensional magnetic resonance volumetric study. *Brain & Development, 25,* 195–199.

Kannus, P., Sievänen, H., Palvanen, M., Järvinen, T., & Parkkari, J. (2005). Prevention of falls and consequent injuries in elderly people. *The Lancet, 366*(9500), 1885–1893.

Kao, G., & Tienda, M. (1998). Educational aspirations of minority youth. *American Journal of Education, 106,* 349–384.

Kaplan, G. A., Haan, M. N., & Wallace, B. R. (1999). Understanding changing risk factor associations with increasing age in adults. *Annual Review of Public Health, 20,* 89–108.

Kaplan, H., & Dove, H. (1987). Infant development among the Ache of eastern Paraguay. *Developmental Psychology, 23,* 190–198.

Karney, B. R., & Bradbury, T. N. (1995). The longitudinal course of marital quality and stability: A review of theory, methods, and research. *Psychological Bulletin, 118*(1), 3–34.

Karney, B. R., & Bradbury, T. N. (2005). Contextual influences on marriage: Implications for policy and intervention. *Current Directions in Psychological Science, 14*(4), 171–174.

Karon, J. M., Fleming, P. L., Steketee, R. W., & DeCock, K. M. (2001). HIV in the United States at the turn of the century: An epidemic in transition. *American Journal of Public Health, 91*(7), 1060–1068.

Karzon, R. G. (1985). Discrimination of polysyllabic sequences by one- to four-month old infants. *Journal of Experimental Child Psychology, 39,* 326–342.

Kastenbaum, R. J. (2007). *Death, society, and the human experience* (9th ed., paperback). Boston, MA: Allyn & Bacon.

Katchadourian, H. (1990). Sexuality. In S. Feldman & G. Elliott (Eds.), *At the threshold: The developing adolescent* (pp. 330–351). Cambridge, MA: Harvard University Press.

Katz, L. F., & Gottman, J. M. (1993). Patterns of marital conflict predict children's internalizing and externalizing behaviors. *Developmental Psychology, 29,* 940–950.

Katz, L. F., Kramer, L., & Gottman, J. M. (1992). Conflict and emotions in marital, sibling, and peer relationships. In C. U. Shantz & W. W. Hartup (Eds.), *Conflict in child and adolescent development* (pp. 122–149). Cambridge: Cambridge University Press.

Katz, S. (1983). Assessing self-maintenance: Activities of daily living, mobility and instrumental activities of daily living. *Journal of the American Geriatrics Society,* 3(12)1, 721–727.

Kavšek, M. (2004). Predicting later IQ from infant visual habituation and dishabituation: A meta-analysis. *Applied Developmental Psychology, 25,* 369–393.

Kawasaki, C., Nugent, J. K., Miyashita, H., Miyahara, H., & Brazelton, T. B. (1994). The cultural organization of infants' sleep. *Children's Environments, 13,* 135–141.

Keating, D. (2004). Cognitive and brain development. In R. Lerner & L. Steinberg (Eds.), *Handbook of adolescent psychology* (2nd ed., pp. 45–84). New York: Wiley.

Kedesdy, J., & Budd, K. S. (1998). *Childhood feeding disorders.* Baltimore, MD: Paul Brookes.

Keegan, R. T. (1996). Creativity from childhood to adulthood: A difference of degree and not of kind. *New Directions for Child and Adolescent Development, 72,* 57–76.

Keen, C. L., Bendich, A., & Willhite, C. C. (1993). Maternal nutrition and pregnancy outcome. *Annals of the New York Academy of Sciences, 678,* 1–372.

Keen, R., Carrico, R. L., Sylvia, M. R., & Berthier, N. E. (2003). How infants use perceptual information to guide action. *Developmental Science, 6,* 221–231.

Keenan, K., & Shaw, D. S. (1997). Developmental and social influences on young girls' early problem behavior. *Psychological Bulletin, 121,* 95–113.

Kehl, K. A. (2006). Moving toward peace: An analysis of the concept of a good death. *American Journal of Hospice and Palliative Medicine, 23*(4), 277–286.

Keil, F. C. (2006). Cognitive science and cognitive development. In W. Damon & R. Lerner (Series Eds.) & D. Kuhn & R. S. Siegler (Vol. Eds.), *Handbook of child psychology: Vol. 2. Cognition, perception, and language* (6th ed., pp. 609–635). Hoboken, NJ: Wiley.

Kelemen, D. (2004). Are children "intuitive theists"? Reasoning about purpose and design in nature. *Psychological Science, 15,* 295–301.

Kellman, P. J., & Arterberry, M. E. (2006). Infant visual perception. In W. Damon & R. Lerner (Series Eds.) & D. Kuhn & R. Siegler (Vol. Eds.), *Handbook of child psychology: Vol. 2. Cognition, perception, and language* (6th ed., pp. 109–160). Hoboken, NJ: Wiley.

Kellogg, R. (1969). *Analyzing children's art.* Palo Alto, CA: National Press Books.

Kelly, J. A., & Kalichman, S. C. (2002). Behavioral research in HIV/AIDS primary and secondary prevention: Recent advances and future directions. *Journal of Consulting and Clinical Psychology, 70*(3), 626–639.

Kelly, S. J., Day, N., & Streissguth, A. P. (2000). Effects of prenatal alcohol exposure on social behavior in humans and other species. *Neurotoxicology and Teratology, 22,* 143–149.

Kemp, C. (2005). Dimensions of grandparent-adult grandchild relationships: From family ties to intergenerational friendships. *Canadian Journal on Aging, 24*(2), 161–178.

Kemp, J. S., Unger, B., Wilkins, D., Psara, R. M., Ledbetter, T. L., Graham, M. C., & Thach, B. T. (2000). Unsafe sleep practices and an analysis of bedsharing among infants dying suddenly and unexpectedly: Results of a four-year, population-based, death-scene investigation study of sudden infant death syndrome and related deaths. *Pediatrics, 106,* e41– 48.

Kempermann, G., Kuhn, H. G., & Gage, F. H. (1997). More hippocampal neurons in adult mice living in an enriched environment. *Nature, 386,* 493–495.

Kendler, K. S., Thornton, L. M., & Gardner, C. O. (2001). Genetic risk, number of previous depressive episodes, and stressful life events in predicting onset of major depression. *American Journal of Psychiatry,* 158, 582–586.

Kenney-Benson, G. A., Pomerantz, E. M., Ryan, A. M., & Patrick H. (2006). Sex differences in math performance: The role of children's approach to schoolwork. *Developmental Psychology, 42,* 11–26.

Kenyon, B. L. (2001). Current research in children's conceptions of death: A critical review. *OMEGA—Journal of Death and Dying, 43*(1), 69–91.

Kerckhoff, A. C. (2003). From student to worker. In J. T. Mortimer & M. J. Shanahan (Eds.), *Handbook of the life course* (p. 251–267). New York: Springer.

Kerckhoff, A. C., & Davis, K. E. (1962). Value consensus and need complementarity in mate selection. *American Sociological Review, 27*(3), 295–303.

Kerig, P. K. (1993). Assessing the links between interpersonal conflict and child adjustment: The conflicts and problem-solving scale. *Journal of Family Psychology, 4,* 454–473.

Kerns, K. A., Cole, A., & Andrews, P. B. (1998). Attachment security, parent peer management practices, and peer relationship in preschoolers. *Merrill-Palmer Quarterly, 44,* 504–522.

Kersting, K. (2004, November). Improving the end of life for older adults. *American Psychological Association Monitor on Psychology, 35* (10). Retrieved July 6, 2009 from http://www.apa.org/monitor/nov04/improve.aspx

Kestenbaum, R., Farber, E. A., & Sroufe, L A. (1989). Individual differences in empathy among preschoolers: relation to attachment history. *New Directions in Child Development, 44,* 51–64.

Keyes, C. L., & Ryff, C. D. (1998). Generativity in adult lives: Social structural contours and quality of life consequences. In D. P. McAdams & E. de St. Aubin (Eds.), *Generativity and adult development* (pp. 227–263). Washington, DC: American Psychological Association.

Keyes, C. L., & Ryff, C. D. (1999). Psychological well-being in midlife. In S. L. Willis & J. D. Reid (Eds), *Life in the middle: Psychological and social development in middle age* (pp. 161–180). San Diego, CA: Academic Press.

Khaleque, A., & Rohner, R. P. (2002). Perceived parental acceptance-rejection and psychological adjustment: A meta-analysis of cross-cultural and intracultural studies. *Journal of Marriage and Family, 64,* 54–64.

Khashan, A. S., Abel, K. M., McNamee, R., Pedersen, M. G., Webb, R. T., Baker, P. N. Kenny, L. C., & Mortensen, P. B. (2008). Higher risk of offspring schizophrenia following antenatal maternal exposure to severe adverse life events. *Archives of General Psychiatry, 65,*146–152.

Kidd, S. A. (2004). "The walls were closing in, and we were trapped": A qualitative analysis of street youth suicide. *Youth and Society, 36,* 30–55.

Kiecolt-Glaser, J. K., McGuire, L., Robles, T. F., & Glaser, R. (2002). Psychoneuroimmunology: Psychological influences on immune function and health. *Journal of Consulting and Clinical Psychology, 70*(3), 537–547.

Killian, K. (1994). Fearing fat: A literature review of family systems understandings and treatments of anorexia and bulimia. Family Relations, 43, 311–318.

Kilpatrick, J., Swafford, J., & Findell, B. (2001). *Adding it up: Helping children learn mathematics.* Washington, DC: National Academy Press.

Kim, J. E., & Moen, P. (2001). Is retirement good or bad for subjective well-being? *Current Directions in Psychological Science, 10*(3), 83–86.

Kim, S. (2009, Mar. 30). *Uncertainty, angst roll on for U.S. auto workers.* Reuters. Retrieved January 7, 2010 from http://www.reuters.com/assets/print?aid=USTRE52U01U20090331/

King, D. E., Mainous, A. G., & Geesey. M. E. (2007). Turning back the clock: Adopting a healthy lifestyle in middle age. *The American Journal of Medicine, 120*(7), 598–603.

King, P. M., & Mayhew, M. J. (2002). Moral judgment development in higher education: Insights from the Defining Issues Test. *Journal of Moral Education, 31*(3), 247–270.

Kingsberg, S. A. (2002). The[UU1] impact of aging on sexual function in women and their partners. *Archives of Sexual Behavior, 31*(5), 431–437.

Kinsella, K. (2000). Demographic dimensions of global aging. *Journal of Family Issues, 21*(5), 541–558.

Kinsella, K., & Velkoff, V. A. (2001). *An aging world: 2001.* U. S. Census Bureau, Series P95/01-1. Washington, CD: U. S. Government Printing Office.

Kirby, D., Korpi, M., Barth, R., & Cagampang, H. (1997). The impact of the Postponing Sexual Involvement curriculum among youths in California. *Family Planning Perspectives, 29,* 100–108.

Kirkpatrick, L. A., & Hazan, C. (1994). Attachment styles and close relationships: A four-year prospective study. *Personal Relationships, 1*(2), 123–142.

Kirkwood, T. B. L. (2008). A systematic look at an old problem. *Nature, 451,* 644–647.

Kitamura, C., Thanavishuth, C., Burnham, D., & Luksaneeyanawin, S. (2002). Universality and specificity in infant-directed speech: Pitch modifications as a function of infant age and sex in a tonal and non-tonal language. *Infant Behavior & Development, 24,* 372–392.

Kitayama, S. (2001). Culture and emotion. In N. J. Smelser & P. B. Baltes (Eds.), *International encyclopedia of social and behavioral sciences* (pp. 3134–3139). Oxford, UK: Elsevier.

Kitchener, K. S., & King, P. M. (1981). Reflective judgment: Concepts of justification and their relationship to age and education. *Journal of Applied Developmental Psychology,* 2(2), 89–116.

Kitchener, K. S., King, P. M., & DeLuca, S. (2006). Development of reflective judgment in adulthood. In C. Hoare (Ed.), *Handbook of adult development and learning* (pp. 73–98). New York: Oxford University Press.

Klaczynski, P., & Narasimham, G. (1998). Development of scientific reasoning biases: Cognitive versus ego-protective explanations. *Developmental Psychology, 34,* 175–187.

Klein, B. E., Klein, R., Lee, K. E., & Cruickshanks, K. J. (1998). Performance-based and self-assessed measures of visual function as related to history of falls, hip fractures, and measured gait time: The Beaver Dam Eye Study. *Ophthalmology, 105*(1), 160–164.

Kleinfield, N. R. (2006, January 9). Bad blood: Diabetes and its awful toll quietly emerge as a crisis. *The New York Times.*

Klibanoff, R. S, Levine, S. C., Huttenlocher, J., Vasilyeva, M., & Hedges, L. V. (2006). Preschool children's mathematical knowledge: The effect of teacher "math talk." *Developmental Psychology, 42,* 59–69.

Kling, K. C., Hyde, J. S., Showers, C. J., & Buswell, B. N. (1999). Gender differences in self-esteem: A meta-analysis. *Psychological Bulletin, 125,* 470–500.

Klinger, E. (1977). *Meaning and void: Inner experiences and the incentives in people's lives.* Minneapolis: University of Minnesota Press.

Klinnert, M. D., Emde, R. N., Butterfield, P., & Campos, J. J. (1986). Social referencing: The infant's use of emotional signals from a friendly adult with mother present. *Developmental Psychology, 22,* 427–432.

Knafo, A., & Plomin, R. (2006). Prosocial behavior from early to middle childhood: Genetic and environmental influences on Stability and change. *Developmental Psychology, 42,* 771–786.

Knaus, W. A., Harrell, F. E., Lynn, J., Goldman, L., Phillips, R. S., Connors, A. F., et al. (1995). The SUPPORT prognostic model: objective estimates of survival for seriously ill hospitalized adults. *Annals of Internal Medicine, 122*(3), 191–203.

Knecht, S., Dräger, B., Deppe, M., Bobe, L., Lohmann, H., Flöel, A. et al. (2000). Handedness and hemispheric language dominance in healthy humans. *Brain, 123,* 2512–2518.

Knight, G. P., & Kagan, S. (1977). Acculturation of prosocial and competitive behaviors among second and third generation Mexican American children. *Journal of Cross-Cultural Psychology, 8,* 275–284.

Knight, G. P., Kagan, S., & Buriel, R. (1981). Confounding effects of individualism in children's cooperation-competition social motive measures. *Motivation and Emotion, 5,* 167–178.

Kobak, R. R., & Sceery, A. (1988). Attachment in late adolescence: Working models, affect regulation, and representations of self and others. *Child Development, 59,* 135–146.

Kochanska, G. (1995). Children's temperament, mothers' discipline, and security of attachment: Multiple pathways to emerging internalization. *Child Development, 66,* 597–615.

Kochanska, G., & Aksan, N. (2007). Conscience in childhood: Past, present, and future. In G. W. Ladd (Ed.), *Appraising the human development sciences: Essays in honor of Merrill-Palmer Quarterly* (pp. 238–249). Detroit: Wayne State Press.

Kochanska, G., & Knaack, A. (2003). Effortful control as a personality characteristic of young children: Antecedents, correlates, and consequences. *Journal of Personality, 71,* 1087–1112.

Kochanska, G., Coy, K. C., & Murray, K. T. (2001). The development of self-regulation in the first four years of life. *Child Development, 72,* 1091–1111.

Koerner, K., & Jacobson, N. S. (1994). Emotion and behavior couple therapy. In S. M. Johnson & L. S. Greenberg (Eds.), *The heart of the matter: Perspective on emotion in marital therapy* (pp. 207–226). New York: Brunner/Mazel.

Kohlberg, L. (1969). Stage and sequence: The cognitive-developmental approach to socialization. In D. A. Goslin (Ed.), *Handbook of socialization theory and research* (pp. 347–480). Chicago, IL: Rand McNally.

Kohlberg, L. (1973). The claim to moral adequacy of a highest stage of moral judgment. *Journal of Philosophy, 70,* 630–646.

Kohlberg, L. (1976). Moral stages and moralization: The cognitive developmental approach. In T. Lickona (Ed.), *Moral development and behavior: Theory, research, and social issues* (pp. 31–53.) New York: Holt, Rinehart & Winston.

Kohlberg, L. (1986). A current statement on some theoretical issues. In S. Modgil & C. Modgil (Eds.), *Lawrence Kohlberg: Consensus and controversy* (pp. 485–546). Philadelphia: The Falmer Press.

Kohn, M. L., & Schooler, C. (1982). Job conditions and personality: A longitudinal assessment of their reciprocal effects. *American Journal of Sociology, 87*(6), 1257–1286.

Koivula, I., Sten, M., & Makela, P. (1999). Prognosis after community-acquired pneumonia in the elderly: A population-based 12-year follow-up study. *Archives of Internal Medicine,* 159, 1550–1555.

Kolata, G. (1997, April 24). A record and big questions as woman gives birth at 63. *New York Times,* A1, A25.

Kopera-Frye, K., & Arendt, R. (1999). An alternative path to exceptionality: Prenatal effects of teratogenic substances on developmental processes. In V. L. Schwean & D. H. Saklofske (Eds.), *Handbook of psychosocial characteristics of exceptional children* (pp. 347–376). New York: Kluwer Academic/Plenum.

Kopera-Frye, K., & Wiscott, R. (2000). Intergenerational continuity: Transmission of beliefs and culture. In B. Hayslip Jr. & R. S. Goldberg-Glen (Eds)., *Grandparents raising grandchildren: Theoretical, empirical, and clinical perspectives* (pp. 65–84). New York: Spring.

Kopitzke, E., & Wilson, J. F. (2000, June). *ART and quality of life: Physical and emotional distress.* 16th annual meeting of the European Society for Human Reproduction and Embryology, Bologna, Italy.

Koropeckyj-Cox, T. (2002). Beyond parental status: Psychological well-being in middle and old age. *Journal of Marriage and Family, 64*(4), 957–971.

Kossek, E. E., & Distelberg, B. (2009). Work and family employment policy for a transformed labor force: Current trends and themes. In A. C. Crouter & A. Booth (Eds.), *Work life policies* (pp. 3–49). Washington, D.C.: Urban Institute Press.

Kostovic, I., Judas, M., & Petanjek, Z. (2008). Structural development of the human prefrontal cortex. In C. A. Nelson & M. Luciana (Eds.), *The handbook of developmental cognitive neuroscience* (2nd ed., pp. 213–236). Cambridge, MA: MIT Press.

Kotlowitz, A. (1991). *There are no children here.* New York: Nan A. Talese.

Kposowa, A. J. (2001). Unemployment and suicide: A cohort analysis of social factors predicting suicide in the U. S. National Longitudinal Mortality Study. *Psychological Medicine, 31,* 127–138.

Krain, A. L., & Castellanos, F. X. (2006). Brain development and ADHD. *Clinical Psychology Review, 26,* 433–444.

Krakauer, E. L., Crenner, C., & Fox, K. (2002). Barriers to optimum end-of-life care for minority patients. *Journal of the American Geriatrics Society, 50*(1), 182–190.

Kramer, A. F., Bherer, L., Colcombe, S. J., Dong, W., & Greenough, W. T. (2004). Environmental influences on cognitive and brain plasticity during aging. *Journal of Gerontology A: Biological Sciences and Medical Sciences, 59*(9), M940–957.

Kramer, D. A. (2003). The ontogeny of wisdom in its variations. In J. Demick & C. Andreoletti (Eds.), *Handbook of adult development* (pp. 131–151). New York: Plenum Press.

Kramer, L., & Kowal, A. K. (2005). Sibling relationship quality from birth to adolescence: The enduring contributions of friends. *Journal of Family Psychology, 19,* 503–511.

Krause, N. (2006). Aging. In H. R. Ebaugh (Ed), *Handbook of religion and social institutions* (pp. 139–160). New York: Springer.

Krebs, D. L., & Denton, K. (2005). Toward a more pragmatic approach to morality: A critical evaluation of Kohlberg's model. *Psychological Review, 112*(3), 629–649.

Krieder, R. M. (2003). *Adopted children and stepchildren: 2000.* U.S. Bureau of the Census. Retrieved January 7, 2010 from http://www.census.gov/prod/2003pubs/censr-6.pdf

Kroger, J. (1993). The role of historical context in the identity formation process of late adolescence. *Youth and Society, 24,* 363–376.

Krogh, D. (2005). *Biology: A guide to the natural world* (3rd ed.). Upper Saddle River, NJ: Pearson Education.

Krojgaard, P. (2003). Object individuation in 10-month-old infants: Manipulating the amount of introduction. *British Journal of Developmental Psychology, 21,* 447–463.

Krueger, R. F., Johnson, W., & Kling, K. C. (2006). Behavior genetics and personality development. In D. K. Mroczek & T. D. Little (Eds.), *Handbook of personality development* (pp. 81–108). Mahwah, NJ: Erlbaum.

Krug, E. G., Dahlberg, L. L., Mercy, J. A., Zwi, A. B., & Lozano, R. (2002). *World report on violence and health.* Geneva: World Health Organization. Retrieved June 28, 2007 from http://whqlibdoc.who.int/hq/2002/9241545615.pdf

Kryla-Lighthall, N., & Mather, M. (2009). The role of cognitive control in older adults' emotional well-being. In V. Bengtson, D. Gans, N. Putney, & M. Silverstein (Eds.), *Handbook of theories of aging* (2nd ed., pp. 323–344). New York: Springer.

Kubler-Ross, E. (1969). *On death and dying.* New York: Macmillan.

Kubzansky, L. D., Sparrow, D., Vokonas, P., & Kawachi, I. (2001). Is the glass half empty or half full? A prospective study of optimism and coronary heart disease in the Normative Aging Study. *Psychosomatic Medicine,* 63(6), 910–916.

Kuchuk, A., Vibbert, M., & Bornstein, M. H. (1986). The perception of smiling and its experiential correlates in 3-month-old infants. *Child Development, 57,* 1054–1061.

Kuczmarski, R. J., Ogden, C. L., Grummer-Strawn, L. M., Flegal, K. M., Guo, S. S., Wei, R., et al. (2000). *CDC growth charts: United States. Advance Data.* Retrieved September 2, 2008, from http://www.cdc.gov/nchs/data/ad/ad314.pdf

Kuhn, D. (2006) Do cognitive changes accompany developments in the adolescent brain? *Perspectives on Psychological Science, 1*(1), 59–67.

Kuhn, D. (2009). Cognitive and brain development. In R. Lerner & L. Steinberg (Eds.), *Handbook of adolescent psychology* (3rd ed.) New York: Wiley.

Kuhn, D., Langer, J., Kohlberg, L., & Haan, N. (1977). The development of formal operations in logical and moral judgment. *Genetic Psychology Monographs, 95,* 97–188.

Kuhn, D., Schauble, L., & Garcia-Mila, M. (1992). Cross domain development of scientific reasoning. *Cognition and Instruction, 9,* 285–327.

Kumar, J., Muntner, P., Kaskel, K. J., Hailpern, S. M., & Melamed, M. L., (2009). Prevalence and associations of 25-Hydroxyvitamin D deficiency in U.S. children: NHANES 2001–2004. Retrieved August 3, 2009 from http://pediatrics.aappublications.org/cgi/content/full/124/3/e362

Kung, H. C., Hoyert, D. L., Xu, J., & Murphy, S. L. (2007). *Deaths: Preliminary data for 2005.* Centers for Disease Control: National Center for Health Statistics, Division of Vital Statistics. *Health E-Stats,* Sept 2007.

Kurdek, L. A. (1999). The nature and predictors of the trajectory of change in marital quality for husbands and wives over the first 10 years of marriage. *Developmental Psychology, 35*(5), 1283–1296.

Kurdek, L. A. (2004). Are gay and lesbian cohabiting couples really different from heterosexual married couples? *Journal of Marriage and Family, 66*(4), 880–901.

Kurdek, L. A. (2005). What do we know about gay and lesbian couples? *Current Directions in Psychological Science, 14*(5), 251–254.

Kurdek, L., & Sinclair, R. (1988). Relation of eighth graders' family structure, gender, and family environment with academic performance and school behavior. *Journal of Educational Psychology, 80,* 90–94.

Kwak, K., Putnick, D. L., & Bornstein, M. H. (2008). Child and mother play in South Korea: A longitudinal study across the second year of life. *Psychologia: An International Journal of Psychology in the Orient, 51,* 14–27.

Labouvie-Vief, G. (1980). Beyond formal operations: Uses and limits of pure logic in life-span development. *Human Development, 23*(3), 141–161.

Labouvie-Vief, G. (1997). Cognitive-emotional integration in adulthood. In K. W. Schaie & M. P. Lawton (Eds.), *Annual review of gerontology and geriatrics* (Vol. 17, pp. 206–237).

Labouvie-Vief, G. (2003). Dynamic integration: affect, cognition, and the self in adulthood. *Current Directions in Psychological Science, 12*(6), 201–206.

Labouvie-Vief, G. (2006). Emerging structures of adult thought. In J. J. Arnett & J. L. Tanner (Eds.), *Emerging adulthood: Coming of age in the 21st century* (pp. 59–84). Washington, DC: American Psychological Association.

Labouvie-Vief, G., & DeVoe, M. (1991). Emotional regulation in adulthood and later life: A developmental view. *Annual review of gerontology and geriatrics, 11,* 172–194.

Labouvie-Vief, G., & Gonzales, M. M. (2004). Dynamic integration: Affect optimization and differentiation in development. In D. D. Yun; & R. J. Sternberg (Eds.), *Motivation, emotion, and cognition: Integrative perspectives on intellectual functioning and development* (pp. 237–232). Mahwah, NJ: Lawrence Erlbaum.

Lachman, M. E. (2004). Development in midlife. *Annual Review of Psychology, 55,* 305–331.

Lachs, M. S., & Pillemer, K. (2004). Elder abuse. *The Lancet, 364*(9441), 1263–1272.

Lacourse, R., Nagin, D., & Tremblay, R. E. (2003). Developmental trajectories of boys' delinquent group membership and facilitation of violent behaviors during adolescence. *Development and Psychopathology, 15,* 183–197.

Ladd, G. W., & Kochenderfer, B. (1996). Friendship quality as predictor of young children's early school adjustment. *Child Development, 67,* 1103–1118.

Ladd, G. W., & Pettit, G. D. (2002). Parents and children's peer relationships. In M. H. Bornstein (Ed.), *Handbook of parenting: Vol. 5. Practical parenting* (2nd ed., pp. 269–309). Mahwah, NJ: Erlbaum.

Ladd, G. W., & Price, J. M. (1987). Predicting children's social and school adjustment following the transition from preschool to kindergarten. *Child Development, 58,* 1168–1189.

Ladd, G. W., Price, J. M., & Hart, C. H. (1988). Predicting preschoolers' peer status from their playground behaviors. *Child Development, 59,* 986–992.

Lagattuta, K., Wellman, H., & Flavell, J (1997). Preschoolers' understanding of the link between thinking and feeling: Cognitive cueing and emotional change. *Child Development, 68,* 1081–1104.

Lahey, J. N. (2005). *Do older workers face discrimination?* Issues in Brief No. 33. Chestnut Hill, MA: Boston College Center for Retirement Research.

Laible, D. (2004). Mother-child discourse in two contexts: Links with child temperament, attachment security, and socioemotional competence. *Developmental Psychology, 40,* 979–992.

Lamb, M. E., & Ahnert, L. (2006). Nonparental child care: context, concepts, correlates, and consequences. In W. Damon & R. M. Lerner (Series Eds.) & K. A. Renninger & I. E. Sigel (Vol. Eds.), *Handbook of child psychology: Vol. 4. Child psychology in practice* (6th ed., pp. 950–1016). New York: Wiley.

Lampl, M., & Emde, R. N. (1983). Episodic growth in infancy: A preliminary report on length, head circumference, and behavior. In K. W. Fischer (Ed.), *Levels and transitions in children's development,* (pp.21–36). San Francisco: Jossey–Bass.

Landale, N. S., & Oropesa, R. S. (2007). Hispanic families: Stability and change. *Annual Review of Psychology, 33,* 381–405.

Landry, D., Kaeser, L., & Richards, C. (1999). Abstinence promotion and the provision of information about contraception in public school district sexuality education policies. *Family Planning Perspectives, 31,* 280–286.

Landry, D., Singh, S., & Darroch, J. E. (2000). Sexuality education in fifth and sixth grades in U.S. public schools, 1999. *Family Planning Perspectives, 32,* 212–219.

Lang, F. R. (2001). Regulation of social relationships in later adulthood. *Journal of Gerontology B: Psychological Sciences and Social Sciences, 56*(6), P321–326.

Lang, F. R., & Carstensen, L. L. (1994). Close emotional relationships in late life: Further support for proactive aging in the social domain. *Psychology and Aging, 9,* 315–324.

Lang, S., Waller, P., & Shope, J. (1996). Adolescent driving: Characteristics associated with single-vehicle and injury crashes. *Journal of Safety Research, 27,* 241–257.

Lansford, J. E., Chang, L., Dodge, K. A., Malone, P. S., Oburu, P., Palmérus, K., et al. (2005). Physical discipline and children's adjustment: Cultural normativeness as a moderator. *Child Development, 76,* 1234–1246.

Lansford, J. E., Criss, M. M., Pettit, G. S., Dodge, K. A., & Bastes, J. E. (2003). Friendship quality, peer group affiliation, and peer antisocial behavior as moderators of the link between negative parenting and adolescent externalizing behavior. *Journal of Research on Adolescence, 13,* 161–184.

Lansford, J. E., Miller-Johnson, S., Berlin, L. J., Dodge, K. A., Bates, J. E., & Pettit, G. S. (2007). Early physical abuse and later violent delinquency: A prospective longitudinal study. *Child Maltreatment, 12,* 233–245.

Lanz, M., Scabini, E., Vermulst, A. A., & Gerris, J. M. (2001). Congruence on child rearing in families with early adolescent and middle adolescent children. *International Journal of Behavioral Development, 25*(2), 133–139.

Lareau, A. (2003) *Unequal childhoods: Class, race, and family life.* Berkeley, CA: University of California Press.

Larson, E. B., Wang, L., Bowen, J. D., McCormick, W. C., Teri, L., Crane, P., et al. (2006). Exercise is associated with reduced risk for incident dementia among persons 65 years of age and older. *Annals of Internal Medicine, 144*(2), 73–81.

Larson, R. (1978). Thirty years of research on the subjective well-being of older Americans. *Journal of Gerontology, 33*(1), 109–125.

Larson, R. W. (2000). Toward a psychology of positive youth development. *American Psychologist, 55,* 170–183.

Larson, R. W., & Almeida, D. M. (1999). Emotional transmission in daily lives of families: A new paradigm for studying family process. *Journal of Marriage and the Family, 61*(1), 5–20.

Larson, R., & Richards, M. (1994). *Divergent realities: The emotional lives of mothers, fathers, and adolescents.* New York: Basic Books.

Larson, R., Clore, G., & Wood, G. (1999). The emotions of romantic relationships: Do they wreak havoc on adolescents? In W. Furman, B. Brown, & C. Feiring (Eds.), *Contemporary perspectives on adolescent romantic relationships* (pp. 19–49). New York: Cambridge University Press.

Laub, J., & Sampson, R. (1995). The long-term effect of punitive discipline. In J. McCord (Ed.), *Coercion and punishment in long-term perspectives* (pp. 247–258). New York: Cambridge University Press.

Laumann, E. O., Leitsch, S. A., & Waite, L. J. (2008). Elder mistreatment in the United States: Prevalence estimates from a nationally representative study. *Journal of Gerontology: Social Sciences, 63*(4), S248–S254.

Laumann, E. O., Paik, A., & Rosen, R. C. (1999). Sexual dysfunction in the United States: Prevalence and predictors. *Journal of the American Medical Association, 281*(13), 537–544.

Lauritsen, J. (1994). Explaining race and gender differences in adolescent sexual behavior. *Social Forces, 72,* 859–884.

Laursen, B. & Hartup, W. (1989). The dynamics of preschool children's conflicts. *Merrill-Palmer Quarterly, 35,* 281–297.

Laursen, B., & Jensen-Campbell, L. (1999). The nature and functions of social exchange in adolescent romantic relationships. In W. Furman, B. Brown, & C. Feiring (Eds.), *Contemporary perspectives on adolescent romantic relationships* (pp. 50–74). New York: Cambridge University Press.

Laursen, B., Coy, K. C., & Collins, W. A. (1998). Reconsidering changes in parent-child conflict across adolescence: A meta-analysis. *Child Development, 69,* 817–832.

Lawler, R. W. (1985). *Computer experience and cognitive development: A child's learning in a computer culture.* New York: Wiley.

Lawrence, E., Rothman, A. D., Cobb, R. J., Rothman, M. T., & Bradbury, T. N. (2008). Marital satisfaction across the transition to parenthood. *Journal of Family Psychology, 22*(1), 41–50.

Lawton, M., Kleban, M., Rajagopal, D., & Dean, J. (1992). Dimensions of affective experience in three age groups. *Psychology and Aging, 7*(2), 171–184.

Lazarus, R. S., & Folkman, S. (1984). *Stress, appraisal, and coping.* New York: Springer.

Leaper, C. (2002). Parenting girls and boys. In M. H. Bornstein (Ed.), *Handbook of parenting: Vol. 1. Children and parenting* (2nd ed., pp. 189–225). Mahwah, NJ: Erlbaum.

Leavitt, D. H., Tonniges, T. F., & Rogers, M. F. (2003). Good nutrition: The imperative for positive development. In M. H. Bornstein, L. Davidson, C. L. M. Keyes, & K. A. Moore (Eds.), *Well-being: Positive development across the life course* (pp. 35–49). Mahwah, NJ: Erlbaum.

Lecanuet, J. P., Fiferm W. P., Krasnegor, N. A., & Smotherman, W. P. (1995). *Fetal development: A psychobiological perspective.* Hillsdale, NJ: Erlbaum.

Lederberg, A. R., Chapin, S. L., Rosenblatt, V., & Vandell, D. L. (1986). Ethnic, gender, and age preferences among deaf and hearing preschool peers. *Child Development, 57,* 375–386.

Lee, G. R., & DeMaris, A. (2007). Widowhood, gender, and depression: A longitudinal analysis. *Research on Aging, 29*(1), 56–72.

Lee, G. R., Peek, C. W., & Coward, R. (1998). Race differences in filial responsibility expectations among older parents. *Journal of Marriage and the Family, 60*(2), 404–412.

Lee, H. K., & Tucker, J (October 27, 2009). Richmond High student gang-raped outside dance. San Francisco Chronicle. Retrieved February 3, 2010 from http://www.sfgate.com/cgi-bin/article.cgi?f5/c/a/2009/10/26/BAG11AAR56.DTL&tsp=1

Lee, R. (2003). The demographic transition: Three centuries of fundamental change. *Journal of Economic Perspectives, 17*(4), 167–190.

Lefkowitz, E. S., & Gillen, M. M. (2006). "Sex is just a normal part of life": Sexuality in emerging adulthood. In J. J. Arnett & J. L. Tanner (Eds.), *Emerging adulthood: Coming of age in the 21st century* (pp. 279–299). Washington, DC: American Psychological Association.

Legerstee, M., & Varghese, J. (2001). The role of maternal affect mirroring on social expectancies in three-month-old infants. *Child Development, 72,* 1301–1313.

Lehman, D. R., Ellard, J. H., & Wortman, C. B. (1986). Social support for the bereaved: Recipients' and providers' perspectives on what is helpful. *Journal of Consulting and Clinical Psychology, 54*(4), 438–446.

Lehn, H., Derks, E. M., Hudziak, J. J., Heutink, P., Van Beijsterveldt, T. C. E. M., & Boomsma, D. I. (2007). Attention problems and attention-deficit/hyperactivity disorder in discordant and concordant monozygotic twins: Evidence of environmental mediators. *Journal of the American Academy of Child and Adolescent Psychiatry, 46*(1), 83–91.

Leiberman, L. D., Gray, H., Wier, M., Fiorentino, R., & Maloney, P. (2000). Long-term outcomes of an abstinence-based, small-group pregnancy prevention program in New York city schools. *Family Planning Perspectives, 32,* 237–245.

Lemerise, E. A., & Dodge, K. A. (2000). The development of anger and hostile interactions. In M. Lewis & J. M. Haviland-Jones (Eds.), *Handbook of emotions* (pp. 594–606). New York: Guilford Press.

Lempers, J., & Clark-Lempers, D. (1992). Young, middle, and late adolescents' comparisons of the functional importance of five significant relationships. *Journal of Youth and Adolescence, 21,* 53–96.

Lenroot, R. K., & Giedd, J. N. (2006). Brain development in children and adolescents: Insights from anatomical magnetic resonance imaging. *Neuroscience and Biobehavioral Reviews, 30,* 718–729.

Leon, P., Chedraui, P., Hidalgo, L., & Ortiz, F. (2007). Perceptions and attitudes toward the menopause among middle aged women from Guayaquil, Ecuador. *Maturitas, 57*(3), 233–238.

Leong, F., & Serafica, F. (2001). Cross-cultural perspective on Super's career development theory: Career maturity and cultural accommodation. In F. Leong & A. Barak (Eds.), *Contemporary models in vocational psychology: A volume in honor of Samuel H. Osipow* (pp. 167–205). Mahwah, NJ: Erlbaum.

Leopold, W. F. (1949). *Speech development of a bilingual child.* Evanston, IL: Northwestern University Press.

Lerner, R. (2006). Developmental science, developmental systems, and contemporary theories of human development. In W. Damon & R. Lerner (Series Eds.) & R. Lerner (Vol. Ed.), *Handbook of child psychology: Vol. 1. Theoretical models of human development* (6th ed., pp. 1–17). New York: Wiley.

Lerner, R. M., Fisher, C. B., & Gianinno, L. (2006). Editorial: Constancy and change in the development of applied developmental science. *Applied Developmental Science, 10,* 172–173.

Lerner, R. M., Freund, A. M., DeStefanis, I., & Habermas, T. (2001). Understanding developmental regulation in adolescence: The use of the selection, optimization, and compensation model. *Human Development, 44*(1), 29–50.

Lerner, R. M., Theokas, C., & Bobek, D. L. (2005). Concepts and theories of human development: Contemporary dimensions. In M. H. Bornstein & M. E. Lamb (Eds.), *Developmental science: An advanced textbook* (pp. 3–44). Mahwah, NJ: Erlbaum.

Leu, D. J., Zawilinski, L., Castek, J., Banerjee, M., Housand, B., Liu, Y., and O'Neil. M (2007). What is new about the new literacies of online reading comprehension? In L. Rush, J. Eakle, & A. Berger, (Eds.). *Secondary school literacy: What research reveals for classroom practices.* (pp. 37–68). Urbana, IL: National Council of Teachers of English.

Levenson, R. W., Carstensen, L. L., & Gottman, J. M. (1994). The influence of age and gender on affect, physiology, and their interrelations: A study of long-term marriages. *Journal of Personality and Social Psychology, 67*(1), 56–68.

Leventhal, E. A., & Prohaska, T. R. (1986). Age, symptom interpretation, and health behavior. *Journal of the American Geriatrics Society, 34*(3), 185–191.

Leventhal, H., & Keeshan, P. (1993). Promoting healthy alternatives to substance abuse. In S. Millstein, A. Petersen, & E. Nightingale (Eds.), *Promoting the health of adolescents: New directions for the twenty-first century* (pp. 260–284). New York: Oxford University Press.

Leventhal, T., & Brooks-Gunn, J. (2000). The neighborhoods they live in: The effects of neighborhood residence on child and adolescent outcomes. *Psychological Bulletin, 126,* 309–337.

Leventhal, T., & Brooks-Gunn, J. (2003). Moving to opportunity: An experimental study of neighborhood effects on mental health. *American Journal of Public Health, 93,* 1576–1582.

Levi, S., & Chervenak, F. A. (1998). Preface. *Annals of the New York Academy of Sciences, 847,* 1.

Levin, E., & Rubin, K. H. (1983). Getting others to do what you wanted them to do: The development of requestive strategies. In K. Nelson (Ed.), *Child language* (vol. 4, pp. 157–186). Hillsdale NJ: Erlbaum.

Levine, S. (2003). Stress: An historical perspective. In T. Steckler, N. Kalin, & J. M. M. Read (Eds.), *Handbook on stress, immunology and behavior* (pp. 3–23). Amsterdam: Elsevier.

Levinson, D. J. (1977). The mid-life transition: A period in adult psychosocial development. *Psychiatry, 40*(2), 99–112.

Levinson, D. J., Darrow, C. N., Klein, E. B., Levinson, M. H., & McKee, B. (1978). *The seasons of a man's life.* New York: Knopf.

Levy, B. (1996). Improving memory in old age through implicit self-stereotyping. *Journal of Personality and Social Psychology, 71*(6), 1092–1107.

Levy, K. N., Blatt, S. J., & Shaver, P. R. (1998). Attachment styles and parental representations. *Journal of Personality and Social Psychology, 74*(2), 407–419.

Lewandowsky, S., & Thomas, J. L. (2009). Expertise: Acquisition, limitations, and control. *Reviews of Human Factors and Ergonomics, 5*(1), 140–165.

Lewinsohn, P. M., Joiner, T. E., Jr., & Rohde, P. (2001). Evaluation of cognitive diathesis-stress models in predicting major depressive disorder in adolescents. *Journal of Abnormal Psychology, 110,* 203–215.

Lewinsohn, P. M., Pettit, J. W., Joiner, T. E., Jr., & Seeley, J. R. (2003). The symptomatic expression of major depressive disorder in adolescents and young adults. *Journal of Abnormal Psychology, 112,* 244–252.

Lewinsohn, P. M., Rohde, P., & Seeley, J. (1994). Psychosocial risk factors for future adolescent suicide attempts. *Journal of Consulting and Clinical Psychology, 62,* 297–305.

Lewinsohn, P. M., Rohde, P., Seeley, J. R., Klein, D. N., & Gotlib, I. H. (2003). Psychosocial functioning of young adults who have experienced and recovered from major depressive disorder during adolescence. *Journal of Abnormal Psychology, 112,* 353–363.

Lewis, M. (2000). Self-conscious emotions: Embarrassment, pride, shame, and guilt. In M. Lewis J. Haviland (Eds.), *Handbook of emotions* (2nd ed., pp. 623–636). New York: Guilford Press.

Lewis, M. D. (2000). Emotional self-organization at three time scales. In M. D. Lewis & I. Granic (Eds.), *Emotion, development, and self-organization: Dynamic systems approaches to emotional development* (pp. 37–69). New York: Cambridge University Press.

Lewis, M., & Ramsay, D. (2002). Cortisol response to embarrassment and shame. *Child Development, 73,* 1034–1045.

Lewis, M., Sullivan, M. W., Stanger, C., & Weiss, M. (1989). Self development and self-conscious emotions. *Child Development, 60,* 146–156.

Lewis, Marc D. (2005). Self-organizing individual differences in brain development. *Developmental Review, 25,* 252–277.

Licastro, F., Candore, G., Lio, D., Porcellini, E., Colonna-Romano, G., Franceschi, C., & Caruso, C. (2005). Innate immunity and inflammation in ageing: A key for understanding age-related diseases. *Immunity & Ageing, 2,* 8.

Lichtenberger, E. O. (2005). General measures of cognition for the preschool child. *Mental Retardation and Developmental Disabilities Research Reviews, 11,* 197–208.

Lin, G., & Rogerson, P. A. (1995). Elderly parents and the geographic availability of their adult children. *Research on Aging, 17*(3), 303–331

Lindenberger, U., & Baltes, P. B. (1994). Sensory functioning and intelligence in old age: A strong connection. *Psychology and Aging, 9*(3), 339–355.

Lindsey, E. W., Mize, J., & Pettit, G. (1997). Mutuality in parent-child play: Consequences for children's competence. *Journal of Social and Personal Relationships, 14,* 523–538.

Lippa, R. A. (2007). The preferred traits of mates in a cross national study of heterosexual and homosexual men and women: An examination of biological and cultural influences. *Archives of Sexual Behavior, 36*(2), 193–208.

Little, M., & Steinberg, L. (2006). Psychosocial predictors of adolescent drug dealing in the inner-city: Potential roles of opportunity, conventional commitments, and maturity. *Journal of Research on Crime and Delinquency, 4,* 1–30.

Livingstone, M., & Hubel, D. (1988). Segregation of form, color, movement, and depth: Anatomy, physiology, and perception. *Science, 240,* 740–749.

Lobar, S. L., Youngblut, J. A. M., Brooten, D., & Themes, P. (2006). Cross-cultural beliefs, ceremonies, and rituals surrounding death of a loved one. *Pediatric Nursing, 32*(1):44–50.

Locke, A. (2001). Preverbal communication. In J. G. Bremner, & A. Fogel (Eds.), *Blackwell handbook of infant development* (pp. 379–403). Malden, MA: Blackwell.

Locke, J. (1690). *An essay concerning human understanding.* London: Eliz. Holt.

Loeber, R., Farrington, D. P., Stouthamer-Loeber, M., & van Kammen, W. B. (1998). *Antisocial behavior and mental health problems.* Mahwah, NJ: Erlbaum.

Lofland, L. H. (1982). Loss and human connection: An exploration into the nature of the human bond. In W. Ickes & E. S. Knowles (Eds.), *Personality, roles, and social behavior* (pp. 219–242). New York: Springer.

Long, S. O. (2004). Cultural scripts for a good death in Japan and the United States: Similarities and differences. *Social Science and Medicine, 58,* 913–928.

Longino Jr., C. F., Jackson, D. J., Zimmerman, R. S., & Bradsher, J. E. (1991). The second move: Health and geographic mobility. *Journal of Gerontology: Social Sciences, 46*(4), S218–S224.

Longino, C. F., & Erler, J. R. (1996). Who are the grandparents at century's end? *Generations, 20*(1), 13–16.

Loomis, L. S., & Booth, A. (1995). Multigenerational caregiving and well-being: The myth of the beleaguered sandwich generation. *Journal of Family Issues,16*(2), 131–148.

Lord, H., & Mahoney, J. L. (2007). Neighborhood crime and self-care: Risks for aggression and lower academic performance. *Developmental Psychology, 43,* 1321–1333.

Lourenco, O. (1996). In defense of Piaget's theory: A reply to 10 common criticisms. *Psychological Review, 103,* 143–164.

Love, J. M., Tarullo, L. B., Raikes, H., & Chazan-Cohen, R. (2006). Head Start: What do we know about its effectiveness? What do we need to know? In K. McCartney & D. Phillips (Eds.), *Blackwell handbook of early childhood development* (pp. 550–576). Malden, MA: Blackwell.

Lovgren, S. (2005, February). U.S. racking up huge "sleep debt." *National Geographic News.* Retrieved April 16, 2008 from http://news.nationalgeographic.com/news/2005/02/0224_050224_sleep.html

Low, S., Ang, L. W., Goh, K. S., & Chew, S. K. (2008). A systematic review of the effectiveness of Tai Chi on fall reduction among the elderly. *Archives of Gerontology and Geriatrics, 48*(3), 325–331.

Lowe, J., Handmaker, N., & Aragon, C. (2006). Impact of mother interactive style on infant affect among babies exposed to alcohol in utero. *Infant Mental Health Journal, 27,* 371–382.

Lowenstein, A., & Daatland, S. (2006). Filial norms and family support in a comparative cross-national context: Evidence from the OASIS study. *Ageing and Society, 26*(02), 203–223.

Lucas, R. (2008). Personality and subjective well-being. In M. Eid & R. J. Larsen (Eds.), *The Science of Subjective Well-Being* (pp. 171–194). New York: Guilford.

Luciana, M., Conklin, H. M., Hooper, C. J. & Yarger, R. S. (2005). The development of nonverbal working memory and executive control processes in adolescents. *Child Development, 76,* 697.

Luna, B., Thulborn, K. R., Munoz, D. P., Merriam, E. P., Garver, K. E., Minshew, N. J., et al. (2001). Maturation of widely distributed brain function subserves cognitive development. *Neuroimage, 13,* 786–793.

Luo, L., & Craik, F. I. M. (2008). Aging and memory: A cognitive approach. *Canadian Journal of Psychiatry, 53*(6), 346–353.

Luo, L., Hendriks, T., & Craik, F. I. M. (2007). Age differences in recollection: Three patterns of enhanced encoding. *Psychology and Aging, 22*(2), 269–280.

Lustig, R. H. (1998). Sex hormonal modulation of neural development in vitro: Implications for brain sex differentiation. In L. Ellis & L. Ebertz (Eds.), *Males, females, and behavior: Toward biological understanding* (pp. 13–25). Westport, CT: Praeger Publishers/Greenwood Publishing Group.

Luthar, S. S., & Becker, B. E. (2002). Privileged but pressured? A study of affluent youth. *Child Development, 73,* 1593–1610.

Lynn, J. M, Teno, J., Phillips, R. S., Wu, A., Desbiens, N., Harrold, J., et al. (1997). Perceptions by family members of the dying experience of older and seriously ill patients. *Annals of Internal Medicine, 126*(2), 97–106.

Lytton, H., & Romney, D. M. (1991). Parents' differential socialization of boys and girls: A meta-analysis. *Psychological Bulletin, 109,* 267–296.

Mac Iver, D., Stipek, D., & Daniels, D. (1991). Explaining within-semester changes in student effort in junior high school and senior high school courses. *Journal of Educational Psychology, 83,* 201–211.

Maccoby, E. (1990). Gender and relationships: A developmental account. *American Psychologist, 45,* 513–520.

Maccoby, E. (2003). *The two sexes: Growing up apart, coming together.* Cambridge, MA: Harvard University Press.

Maccoby, E. E., & Martin, J. A. (1983). Socialization in the context of the family: Parent-child interaction. In E. M. Hetherington (Ed.), *Handbook of child psychology: Vol. 4. Socialization, personality and social development* (4th ed., pp. 1–101). New York: Wiley.

MacDorman, M. F., Callaghan, W. M., Mathews, T. J., Hoyert, D. L., & Kochanek, K. D. (2007, May). *Trends in preterm-related infant mortality by race and ethnicity: United States, 1999–2004.* Retrieved from http://www.cdc.gov/nchs/products/pubs/pubd/hestats/infantmort99-04/infantmort99-04.htm#ref01

MacDorman, M. F., Declercq, E., Menacker, F., & Malloy, M. H. (2006). Infant and neonatal mortality for primary cesarean and vaginal births to women with "no indicated risk," United States, 1998–2001 birth cohorts. *Birth, 33,* 175–182.

Mace, N. L. & Rabins, P. V. (2006). *The 36-hour day: A family guide to caring for people with Alzheimer's disease, other dementias, and memory loss in later life* (4th ed.). Baltimore, MA: Johns Hopkins Press.

Macintyre, C., & McVitty, K. (Eds.). (2004). *Movement and learning in the early years: Supporting dyspraxia (DCD) and other difficulties.* London: Paul Chapman.

Mack, K. (December 15, 2009). Stigma of "snitching" creates of code of silence that hampers Chicago cops. *Chicago Tribune.* Retrieved January 15, 2009 from http://archives.chicagotribune.com/2009/dec/15/news/chi-snitching-dec15

Mackenzie, S., & Wu, K. B. (2008). The coverage of employer-provided pensions: Partial and uncertain. Washington, DC: American Association of Retired Persons Pubic Policy Institute.

MacWhinney, B. (2005). Language development. In M. H. Bornstein & M. E. Lamb (Eds.), *Developmental science: An advanced textbook* (pp. 359–387). Mahwah, NJ: Erlbaum.

MacWhinney, B., & Bornstein, M. H. (2003). Language and literacy. In M. H. Bornstein, L. Davidson, C. L. M. Keyes, & K. A. Moore (Eds.), *Well-being: Positive development across the life course* (pp. 331–339). Mahwah, NJ: Erlbaum.

Madden, D. J. (2001). Speed and timing of behavioral processes. In J. E. Birren & K. W. Schaie (Eds.), *Handbook of the psychology of aging* (5th ed., pp. 288–312). San Diego, CA: Academic Press.

Maddox, G. L. (1963). Activity and morale: A longitudinal study of selected elderly subjects. *Social Forces, 42*(2), 195–204.

Maddox, G. L. (1964). Disengagement theory: A critical evaluation. *Gerontologist, 4*,(2, Part 1), 80–82.

Maggs, J. L., & Schulenberg, J. E. (2004). Trajectories of alcohol use during the transition to adulthood. *Alcohol Research and Health, 28*(4), 195–210.

Magkos, F., Manios, Y., Christakis, G., & Kafatos, A. G., (2005). Secular trends in cardiovascular risk factors among school-aged boys from Crete, Greece, 1982–2002. *European Journal of Clinical Nutrition, 59*, 1–7.

Magnusson, D., & Stattin, H. (2006). The person in context: A holistic-interactionistic approach. In W. Damon & R. Lerner (Series Eds.) & R. Lerner (Vol. Ed.), *Handbook of child psychology: Vol. 1. Theoretical models of human development* (6th ed., pp. 400–464). New York: Wiley.

Magnusson, D., Stattin, H., & Allen, V. (1986). Differential maturation among girls and its relation to social adjustment in a longitudinal perspective. In P. Baltes, D. Featherman, & R. Lerner (Eds.), *Life span development and behavior*, (vol. 7, pp. 135–172). Hillsdale, NJ: Erlbaum.

Maguire, A. M., Simonelli, F., Pierce, E. A., Puch, E. N., Jr., Mingozzi, F., Bennicelli, J.,et al. (2008). Safety and efficacy of gene transfer for Leber's congenital amaurosis. *New England Journal of Medicine, 358*(21), 2240–2248.

Mahncke, H. W., Connor, B. B., Appelman, J., Ahsanuddin, O. N., Hardy, J. L, Wood, R. A., et al. (2006). Memory enhancement in healthy older adults using a brain plasticity-based training program: A randomized, controlled study. *Proceedings of the National Academy of Sciences, 103*(33), 12523–12428.

Mahoney, J. L., & Zigler, E. F. (2006). Translating science to policy under the No Child Left Behind Act of 2001: Lessons from the national evaluation of the 21st-Century Community Learning Centers. *Journal of Applied Developmental Psychology, 27*, 282–294.

Mahoney, J. L., Lord, H., & Carryl, E. (2005). Afterschool program participation and the development of child obesity and peer acceptance. *Applied Developmental Science, 9*(4), 202–215.

Mahoney, J. L., Lord, H., & Carryl, E. (2005). An ecological analysis of after-school program participation and the development of academic performance and motivational attributes for disadvantaged children. *Child Development, 76*, 811–825.

Main, M., & Cassidy, J. (1988). Categories of response to reunion with the parent at age 6: Predictable from infant attachment classifications and stable over a 1-month period. *Developmental Psychology, 24*, 415–426.

Main, M., & Solomon, J. (1990). Procedures for identifying infants as disorganized/disoriented during the Ainsworth Strange Situation. In M. T. Greenberg, D. Cicchetti, & E. M. Cummings (Eds.), *Attachment in the preschool years: Theory, research, and intervention* (pp. 121–160). Chicago: University of Chicago Press.

Main, M., Kaplan, N., & Cassidy, J. (1985). Security in infancy, childhood, and adulthood: A move to the level of representation. *Monographs of the Society for Research in Child Development, 50*, 66–104.

Maital, S. L., Dromi, E., Sagi, A., & Bornstein, M. H. (2000). The Hebrew Communicative Development Inventory: Language specific properties and cross-linguistic generalizations. *Journal of Child Language, 27*, 43–67.

Mancini, J., & Sandifer, D. (1995). Family dynamics and the leisure experiences of older adults: Theoretical viewpoints. In R. Blieszner, & V. H. Bedford (Eds.), *Handbook of aging and the family* (pp. 133–147). Westport, CT: Greenwood Press.

Mandel, M. (May 24, 2009). Lack of tears taken for guilt. *Toronto Sun*. Retrieved February 5, 2010 from http://www.torontosun.com/news/columnists/michele_mandel/2009/05/24/9551116-sun.html

Mandler, G. (1975). *Mind and emotion*. New York: Wiley.

Mandler, G. (1997). *Human nature explored*. New York: Oxford University Press.

Manlove, J. (1998). The influence of high school dropout and school disengagement on the risk of school-age pregnancy. *Journal of Research on Adolescence, 8*, 187–220.

Manning, W. D., Longmore, M. A., & Giordano, P. C. (2007). The changing institution of marriage: Adolescents' expectations to cohabit and to marry. *Journal of Marriage and the Family, 69*(3), 559–575.

Manning, W., & Landale, N. (1996). Racial and ethnic differences in the role of cohabitation in premarital childbearing. *Journal of Marriage and the Family, 58*, 63–77.

Manning, W., Longmore, M. A., & Giordano, P. C. (2000). The relationship context of contraceptive use at first intercourse. *Family Planning Perspectives, 32*, 104–110.

Mannino, D. M., Homa, D. M., Akinbami, L. J., Moorman, J. E., Gwynn, C., & Redd, S. C. (2002). Surveillance for asthma—United States, 1980–1999. *MMWR Surveillance Summaries, 51*(No. SS01), 1–13.

Manton, K. G., Gu, X. L., & Lamb, V. (2006). Change in chronic disability from 1982 to 2004/2005 as measured by long-term changes in function and health in the U.S. elderly population. *Proceedings of the National Academy of Sciences, 103*(48), 18374–18379.

Marcell, T. J. (2003). Sarcopenia: Causes, consequences, and preventions. *Journal of Gerontology A: Biological Sciences and Medical Sciences, 58*(10), M911–916.

March of Dimes, Pregnancy & Newborn Health Education Center. (2008). *Your first tests.* Retrieved from http://www.marchofdimes.com/pnhec/159_519.asp

March of Dimes. (2008). *Professionals and researchers, quick reference: Smoking during pregnancy* [Fact sheet]. Retrieved from http://www.marchofdimes.com/professionals/14332_1171.asp

Marchman, V. A. , & Fernald, A. (2008). Speed of word recognition and vocabulary knowledge in infancy predict cognitive and language outcomes in later childhood. *Developmental Science, 11*(3), F9–F16.

Marcia, J. (1966). Development and validation of ego identity status. *Journal of Personality and Social Psychology, 3*, 551–558.

Mares, M. L. & Woodard, E. (2005). Positive effects of television on children's social interactions: A meta-analysis. *Media Psychology, 7*, 301–322.

Markman, E. M. (1999). Multiple approaches to the study of word learning in children. *Japanese Psychological Research, 41*, 79–81.

Markovits, H., & Valchon, R. (1989). Reasoning with contrary-to-fact propositions. *Journal of Experimental Child Psychology, 47*, 398–412.

Markovits, H., Venet, M., Janveau-Brennan, G., Malfait, N., Pion, N., & Vadeboncoeur, I. (1996). Reasoning in young children: Fantasy and information retrieval. *Child Development, 67,* 2857–2872.

Marks, N. F. (1998). Does it hurt to care? Caregiving, work-family conflict, and midlife well-being. *Journal of Marriage and Family, 60*(4), 951–966.

Marks, N. F., & Lambert, J. D. (1998). Marital status continuity and change among young and midlife adults: Longitudinal effects on psychological well-being. *Journal of Family Issues, 19*(6), 652–686.

Marmot, M., & Fuhrer, R. (2004). Socioeconomic position and health across midlife. In O. G. Brim, C. D. Ryff, & R. C. Kessler (Eds.), *How healthy are we?: A national study of well-being at midlife* (pp. 64–89). Chicago, IL: University of Chicago Press.

Marsh, H., & Yeung, A. (1997). Coursework selection: Relations to academic self-concept and achievement. *American Educational Research Journal, 34,* 691–720.

Marshall, B. L. (2007). Climacteric redux? (Re)medicalizing the male menopause. *Men and Masculinities, 9*(4), 519–529.

Marshall, J. D., & Bouffard, M. (1997). The effects of quality daily physical education on movement competency in obese versus nonobese children. *Adapted Physical Activity Quarterly, 14*(3), 222–237.

Marshall, N. L., Coll, C. G., Marx, F., Mccartney, K., Keefe, N., & Ruh, J. (1997). After-school time and children's behavioral adjustment. *Merrill-Palmer Quarterly, 43,* 497–514.

Marshall, V. W., & Taylor, P. (2005). Restructuring the lifecourse: Work and retirement. *The Cambridge handbook of age and ageing* (pp. 572–582). Cambridge, England: Cambridge University Press.

Marshall, W. (1978). Puberty. In F. Falkner & J. Tanner (Eds.), *Human growth: Vol. 2. Postnatal growth* (pp. 141–181). New York: Plenum.

Martin, A., Ruchkin, V., Caminis, A., Vermeiren, R., Henrich, C. C., & Schwab-Stone, M. (2005). Early to bed: A study of adaptation among sexually active urban adolescent girls younger than age sixteen. *Journal of the American Academy of Child & Adolescent Psychiatry, 44,* 358–367.

Martin, C. L., & Fabes, R. A. (2001). The stability and consequences of young children's same-sex peer interactions. *Developmental Psychology, 37,* 431–446.

Martin, C. L., Ruble, D. N., & Szkrybalo, J. (2002). Cognitive theories of early gender development. *Psychological Bulletin, 128,* 903–933.

Martin, S. P., & Parashar, S. (2006). Women's changing attitudes toward divorce, 1974–2002: Evidence for an educational crossover. *Journal of Marriage and Family, 68*(1), 29–40.

Martinez, M. (2010). *Learning and cognition: The design of the mind.* Upper Saddle River, NJ: Merrill.

Martinez, R., & Dukes, R. (1997). The effects of ethnic identity, ethnicity, and gender on adolescent well-being. *Journal of Youth and Adolescence, 26,* 503–516.

Martinson, I. M. (1993). Hospice care for children: Past, present, and future. *Journal of Pediatric Oncology Nursing, 10*(3), 93–98.

Marx, J. (2005). Preventing Alzheimer's: A lifelong commitment? *Science, 309,* 864–866.

Mash, C., Arterberry, M., & Bornstein, M. H. (2007). Mechanisms of visual object recognition in infancy: 5-month-olds generalize beyond the interpolation of familiar views. *Infancy, 12,* 31–43.

Masoro, E. J. (2005). Overview of caloric restriction and ageing. *Mechanisms of ageing and development, 126*(9), 913–922.

Mather, M., & Carstensen, L. (2005). Aging and motivated cognition: The positivity effect in attention and memory. *Trends in Cognitive Sciences, 9*(10), 496–502.

Mather, M., Canli, T., English, T., Whitfield, S., Wais, P., Ochsner, K., et al. (2004). Amygdala responses to emotionally valenced stimuli in older and younger adults. *Psychological Science, 15*(4), 259–263.

Matsuba, M. K., & Walker, L. J. (2004). Extraordinary moral commitment: Young adults involved in social organizations. *Journal of Personality, 72*(2), 413–436.

Matthews, T. J., & Hamilton, B. E. (2009). Delayed childbearing: More women are having their first child later in life. *NCHS Data Brief,* 21. Hyattsville, MD: National Center for Health Statistics. Retrieved January 14, 2010 from http://www.cdc.gov/nchs/data/databriefs/db21.pdf

Maume, D. J. (2004). Is the glass ceiling a unique form of inequality? Evidence from a random-effects model of managerial attainment. *Work and Occupations, 31*(2), 250–274.

May, J. C., Delgado, M. R., Dahl, R., Fiez, J. A., Stenger, V. A., Ryan, N., & Carter, C. S. (2004). Event-related fMRI of reward related brain activity in children and adolescents. *Biological Psychiatry, 55*(4), 359–366.

Mayes, L. C., & Truman, S. D. (2002). Substance abuse and parenting. In M. H. Bornstein (Ed.), *Handbook of parenting: Vol. 4. Applied parenting* (2nd ed., pp. 329–359). Mahwah, NJ: Erlbaum.

Mayes, L. C., Bornstein, M. H., Chawarska, K., Haynes, O. M., & Granger, R. H. (1996). Impaired regulation of arousal in 3-month-old infants exposed prenatally to cocaine and other drugs. *Development and Psychopathology, 8,* 29–42.

Mayes, L. C., Cicchetti, D., Acharyya, S., & Zhang, H. (2003). Developmental trajectories of cocaine-and-other-drug-exposed and non-cocaine-exposed children. *Developmental and Behavioral Pediatrics, 24,* 323–335.

Mayes, L. C., Feldman, R., Granger, R. H., Haynes, O. M., Bornstein, M. H., & Schottenfeld, R. (1997). The effects of polydrug use with and without cocaine on mother-infant interaction at 3 and 6 months. *Infant Behavior and Development, 20,* 489–502.

Mayes, L. C., Granger, R. H., Frank, M. A., Schottenfeld, R., & Bornstein, M. H. (1993). Neurobehavioral profiles of neonates exposed to cocaine prenatally. *Pediatrics, 91,* 778–783.

Maylor, E. A. (2005). Age-related changes in memory. In M. L. Johnson, V. L. Bengtson, P. G. Coleman, & T. B. L. Kirkwood (Eds.), *The Cambridge Handbook of Age and Ageing* (pp, 200–208). Cambridge, UK: Cambridge University Press.

Mayo Clinic (2008, April). *Testosterone therapy: Can it help older men feel young again?* Retrieved from May 1, 2008 http://www.mayoclinic.com/health/testosterone-therapy/MC00030#

Mayo Clinic. (2006). Growing pains. Retrieved October 2, 2008 from: http://www.mayoclinic.com/health/growing-pains/DS00888

Mayr, U. (2008). Introduction to the special section on cognitive plasticity in the aging mind. *Psychology and Aging, 23*(4), 681–684.

McAdams. D. P. (2001). Generativity in midlife. In M. E. Lachman (Ed.), *Handbook of midlife development* (pp. 395–446). New York: Wiley.

McAdams. D. P., & de St. Aubin, E. (1992). A theory of generativity and its assessment through self-report, behavioral acts, and narrative themes in autobiography. *Journal of Personality and Social Psychology, 62*, 1003–1015.

McCabe, K. M., Hough, R., Wood, P. A., & Yeh, M. (2001). Childhood and adolescent onset conduct disorder: A test of the developmental taxonomy. *Journal of Abnormal Child Psychology, 29*, 305–316.

McCall, R. B., Appelbaum, M., & Hogarty, P. S. (1973). Developmental changes in mental performance. *Monographs of the Society for Research in Child Development, 38*(3, Serial No. 150).

McClelland, D., Atkinson, J., Clark, R., & Lowell, E. (1953). *The achievement motive*. New York: Appleton-Century-Crofts.

McClintock, M. (1980). Major gaps in menstrual cycle research: Behavioral and physiological controls in a biological context. In P. Komenich, M. McSweeney, J. Noack, & N. Elder (Eds.), *The menstrual cycle* (vol. 2, pp. 7–23). New York: Springer.

McCrae, R. R. & John, O. P. (1992). An introduction to the five-factor model and its applications. *Journal of Personality, 60*, 175–215.

McCrae, R. R. (2002). NEO-PI-R data from 36 cultures: Further intercultural comparisons. In R. R. McCrae & J. Allik (Eds.), *The five-factor model of personality across cultures* (pp. 105–125). New York: Kluwer Academic/Plenum.

McCrae, R. R., & Costa, P. T., Jr. (2003). *Personality in adulthood: A five-factor theory perspective*. New York: Guilford.

McCrae, R. R., Costa, P. T., Jr., de Lima, M. P., Simões, A., Ostendorf, F., Angleitner, A., et al. (1999). Age differences in personality across the adult life span: Parallels in five cultures. *Developmental Psychology, 35*(2), 466–477.

McCrae, R. R., Costa, P. T., Martin, T. A., Oryol, V. E., Rukavishnikov, A. A., Senin, I. G., et al. (2004). Consensual validation of personality traits across cultures. *Journal of Research in Personality, 38*(2), 179–201.

McDonald, L., & Robb, A. (2004). The economic legacy of divorce and separation for women in old age. *Canadian Journal on Aging, 23*(1, Supplement), S83–S97.

McElwain, N., Cox, M., Burchinal, M., & Macfie, J. (2003). Differentiating among insecure mother-infant attachment classifications: A focus on child-friend interaction and exploration during solitary play at 36 months. *Attachment & Human Development, 5*, 136–164.

McEwen, B. S. (2006). Protective and damaging effects of stress mediators: Central role of the brain. *Dialogues in Clinical Neuroscience, 8*(4), 367–381.

McEwen, B. S., & Stellar, E.(1993). Stress and the individual: Mechanisms leading to disease. *Archives of Internal Medicine, 153*(18), 2093–2101.

McGhee, P. E., & Frueh, T. (1980). Television viewing and the learning of sex-role stereotypes. *Sex Roles, 6*, 179–188

McGrew, W. (2004). *The cultured chimpanzee.* New York: Cambridge University Press.

McHale, J., Khazan, I., Rotman, T., DeCourcey, W., & McConnell, M. (2002). Co-parenting in diverse family systems. In M. H. Bornstein (Ed.), *Handbook of parenting Vol. 3 Status and social conditions of parenting* (2nd ed., pp. 75–107). Mahwah, NJ: Erlbaum.

McHale, S. M, Crouter, A. C., & Tucker, C. J. (2001). Free time activities in middle childhood Links with adjustment in early adolescence. *Child Development, 72*, 1764–1778.

McHale, S. M., Shanahan, L., Updegraff, K. A., Crouter, A. C., & Booth, A. (2004). Developmental and individual differences in girls' sex-typed activities. *Child Development, 75*, 1575–1593.

McIlvane, J. M., Ajrouch, K. J., & Antonucci, T. C. (2007). Generational structure and social resources in mid-life: Influences on health and well-being. *Journal of Social Issues, 63*(4), 759–773.

McKenna, J., Mosko, S., Richard, C., Drummond, S., Hunt, L., Cetel, M. B., & Arpaia, J. (1994). Experimental studies of infant-parent co-sleeping: Mutual physiological and behavioral influences and their relevance to SIDS (sudden infant death syndrome). *Early Human Development, 38*, 187–201.

McLaughlin, C. S., Chen, C., Greenberger, E., & Beiermeir, C. (1997). Family, peer, and individual correlates of sexual behavior among Caucasian and Asian American late adolescents. *Journal of Research on Adolescence, 7*(1), 33–53.

McLoyd, V. C. (1990). The impact of economic hardship on Black families and children: Psychological distress, parenting, and socioemotional development. *Child Development, 61*, 311–346.

McLoyd, V. C., Aikens, N. L., & Burton, L. M. (2006). Childhood poverty, policy, and practice. In K. A. Renninger & I. E. Sigel (Ed.), W. Damon (Series Ed.), *Handbook of child psychology: Vol. 4. Child psychology in practice* (6th ed., pp. 700–775). Hoboken, NJ: Wiley.

McMaster, J., Pitts, M., & Poyah, G. (1997). The menopausal experiences of women in a developing country: "There is a time for everything: to be a teenager, a mother and a granny". *Women and health, 26*(4), 1–13.

McNaught, W., & Barth, M. C. (1992). Are older workers good buys? A case study of Days Inns of America. *Sloan Management Review, 33*(3), 53–63.

McNelles, L. R., & Connolly, J. A. (1999). Intimacy between adolescent friends: Age and gender differences in intimate affect and intimate behaviors. *Journal of Research on Adolescence, 9*, 143–159

McQuaid, E. L., Mitchell, D. K., & Esteban, C. A. (2006). Allergies and asthma. In G. G. Bear & K. M. Minke (Eds.), *Children's needs III: Development, prevention, and intervention* (pp. 909–924). Bethesda, MD: National Association of School Psychologists.

Meade, M. L., Nokes, T. J., & Morrow, D. G. (2009). Expertise promotes facilitation on a collaborative memory task. *Memory, 17*(1), 39–48.

Meaney, M. (2001). Maternal care, gene expression, and the transmission of individual differences in stress reactivity across generations. *Annual Review of Neuroscience, 24*, 1161–1192.

Meeus, W., Iedema, J., Helsen, M., & Vollebergh, W. (1999). Patterns of adolescent identity development: Review of literature and longitudinal analysis. *Developmental Review, 19*, 419–461.

Mei, Z., Grummer-Strawn, L. M., Thompson, D., & Dietz, W. H. (2004). Shifts in percentiles of growth during early childhood: Analysis of longitudinal data from the California Child Health and Development Study. *Pediatrics, 113*, 617–627.

Meisels, S. J., & Atkins-Burnett, S. (2006). Evaluating early childhood assessments: A differential analysis. In K. McCartney & D. Phillips (Eds.), *Blackwell handbook of early childhood development* (pp. 533–549). Malden, MA: Blackwell.

Meissner, H. C., Strebel, P. M., & Orenstein, W. A. (2004). Measles vaccines and the potential for worldwide eradication of measles. *Pediatrics, 114*, 1065–1069.

Melby, M. K., Lock, M., & Kaufert, P. (2005). Culture and symptom reporting at menopause. *Human Reproduction Update, 11*(5), 495–512.

Meltzoff, A. N. (1988). Infant imitation and memory: Nine-month-olds in immediate and deferred tests. *Child Development, 59,* 217–225.

Meltzoff, A. N. (1993). Molyneux's babies: Cross-modal perception, imitation, and the mind of the preverbal infant. In N. Eilan, R. McCarthy, & B. Brewer (Eds.), *Spatial representation: Problems in philosophy and psychology* (pp. 219–235). Oxford, UK: Blackwell.

Meltzoff, A. N., & Moore, M. K. (1999). Persons and representation: Why infant imitation is important for theories of human development. In J. Nadel & G. Butterworth (Eds.), *Imitation in infancy* (pp. 9–35). New York: Cambridge University Press.

Mendelsohn, M. E., & Karas, R. H. (1999). The protective effects of estrogen on the cardiovascular system. *New England Journal of Medicine, 340*(23), 1801–1811.

Ment, L. R., Vohr, B., Allan, W., Katz, K. H., Schneider, K. C., Westerveld, M., et al. (2003). Change in cognitive function over time in very low-birth-weight infants. *Journal of the American Medical Association, 289,* 705–711.

Merck Institute of Aging and Health, & Gerontological Society of America. (2002). *The state of aging and health in America.* Washington, DC: Gerontological Society of America.

Mermin, G., Johnson, R., & Murphy, D. (2007). Why do boomers plan to work longer? *Journal of Gerontology: Social Sciences, 62*(5), S286–S294.

Merrill, D. M. (1997). *Caring for elderly parents: Juggling work, family and caregiving in middle and working class families.* Westport, CT: Auburn House.

Merrill, S. S., & Verbrugge, L. M. (1999). Health and disease in midlife. In S. L. Willis & J. D. Reid (Eds.), *Life in the middle: Psychological and social development in middle age* (pp. 77–103). San Diego, CA: Academic Press.

Mervis, C. B., Pani, J. R., & Pani, A. M. (2003). Transaction of child cognitive-linguistic abilities and adult input in the acquisition of lexical categories at the basic and subordinate levels. In D. H. Rakison & L. M. Oakes (Eds.), *Early category and concept development: Making sense of the blooming, buzzing confusion* (pp. 242–274). New York: Oxford University Press.

Mesquita, B., & Karasawa, M. (2004). Self conscious emotions as dynamic cultural processes. *Psychological Inquiry, 15,* 161–166.

Mewes, A. U. J., Hüppi, P. S., Als, H., Rybicki, F. J., Inder, T. E., McAnulty, G. B., Mulkern, R. V., Robertson, R. L., Rivkin, M. J. & Warfield, S. K. (2006). Regional brain development in serial Magnetic Resonance Imaging of low-risk preterm infants. *Pediatrics, 118,* 23–33.

Meyer, I. H. (2003). Prejudice, social stress, and mental health in lesbian, gay, and bisexual populations: Conceptual issues and research evidence. *Psychological Bulletin, 129*(5), 674–697.

Michael, R., Laumann, E., & Kolata, G. (1994). *Sex in America.* New York: Warner Books.

Mickelson, K. D., Kessler, R. C., & Shaver, P. R. (1997). Adult attachment in a nationally representative sample. *Journal of Personality and Social Psychology, 73*(3), 1092–1106.

Mickelson, R. (1990). The attitude-achievement paradox among black adolescents. *Sociology of Education, 63,* 44–61.

Midgley, C., Berman, E., & Hicks, L. (1995). Differences between elementary and middle school teachers and students: A goal theory approach. *Journal of Early Adolescence, 15,* 90–113.

Mihalic, S., & Elliot, D. (1997). Short- and long-term consequences of adolescent work. *Youth and Society, 28,* 464–498.

Mikulincer, M., & Shaver, P. R., (2007a). *Attachment in adulthood: Structure, dynamics, and change.* New York: Guilford Press.

Mikulincer, M., & Shaver, P. R., (2007b). Boosting attachment security to promote mental health, prosocial values, and intergroup tolerance. *Psychological Inquiry, 18*(3), 139–156.

Mikulincer, M., Florian, V., Cowan, P. A., & Cowan, C. P. (2002). Attachment security in couple relationships: A systemic model and its implications for family dynamics. *Family Process, 41*(3), 405–434.

Miles, S. B., & Stipek, D. (2006). Contemporaneous and longitudinal associations between social behavior and literacy achievement in a sample of low-income elementary school children. *Child Development, 77,* 103–117.

Miljkovitch, R., Pierrehumbert, B., Bretherton, I., & Halfon, O. (2004). Associations between parental and child attachment representations. *Attachment & Human Development, 6,* 305–325.

Millar, S. (1975). Visual experience or translation rules? Drawing the human figure by blind and sighted children. *Perception, 4,* 363–371.

Miller, B. C., Fan, X., Christensen, M., Grotevant, H. D., & van Dulmen, M. (2000). Comparisons of adopted and non-adopted adolescents in a large, nationally representative sample. *Child Development, 71,* 1458–1473.

Miller, B., & Moore, K. (1990). Adolescent sexual behavior, pregnancy, and parenting: Research through the 1980s. *Journal of Marriage and the Family, 52,* 1025–1044.

Miller, G. A. (1956). The magical number seven, plus or minus two: Some limits on our capacity for processing information. *Psychological Review, 63,* 81–97.

Miller, G. E., & Blackwell, E. (2006) Turning up the heat: Inflammation as a mechanism linking chronic stress, depression, and heart disease. *Current Directions in Psychological Science, 15,* 269–272.

Miller, G. E., & Wrosch, C. (2007). You've gotta know when to fold 'em: Goal disengagement and systemic inflammation in adolescence. *Psychological Science, 18*(9), 773–777.

Miller, K. A., & Kohn, M. L. (1983). The reciprocal effects of job conditions and the intellectuality of leisure-time activities. In M. L. Kohn & C. Schooler (Eds), *Work and personality: An inquiry into the impact of social stratification* (pp. 217–241). Norwood, NJ: Ablex.

Miller, P. H., & Seier, W. L. (1994). Strategy utilization deficiencies in children: When, where, and why? In H. W. Reese (Ed.), *Advances in child development and behavior* (Vol. 25, pp. 107–156). New York: Academic Press.

Miller, P., Wiley, A. R., Fung, H., & Liang, C-H. (1997). Personal storytelling as a medium of socialization in Chinese and American families. *Child Development, 68,* 557–568.

Miller, R. A. (1996). The aging immune system: Primer and prospectus. *Science, 273,* 70–74.

Mills, D. L., Prat, C., Zangl, R., Stager, C. L., Neville, H. J., Werker, J. F. (2004). Language experience and the organization of brain activity to phonetically similar words: ERP evidence from 14- and 20-month-olds. *Journal of Cognitive Neuroscience, 16,* 1452–1464.

Minassian, V. A., Drutz, H. P., & Al-Badr, A. (2003). Urinary incontinence as a worldwide problem. *International Journal of Gynecology and Obstetrics, 82*(3), 327–338.

Mindell, J. Owens, J. A., & Carskadon, M. A.(1999). Developmental features of sleep. *Child & Adolescent Psychiatric Clinics of North America, 8,* 695–725.

Minturn, L., & Lambert, W. W. (1964). *Mothers of six cultures: Antecedents of child rearing.* New York: Wiley.

Misra, M., Pacaud, D., Petryk, A., Collett-Solberg, P. F., Kappy, M. on behalf of the Drug and Therapeutics Committee of the Lawson Wilkins Pediatric Endocrine Society. (2008). Vitamin D deficiency in children and its management: Review of current knowledge and recommendations. *Pediatrics, 122,* 398–417.

Mitchell, B. A. (2006). *The boomerang age: Transitions to adulthood in families.* New Brunswick, NJ: Aldine-Transaction.

Mitchell, E. (Ed.). (1985). *Anorexia nervosa and bulimia: Diagnosis and treatment.* Minneapolis: University of Minnesota Press.

Mitka, M. (2004). Improvement seen in US immunization rates. *Journal of the American Medical Association. 292,* 1167.

Modell, J., & Goodman, M. (1990). Historical perspectives. In S. Feldman & G. Elliott (Eds.), *At the threshold: The developing adolescent* (pp. 93–122). Cambridge, MA: Harvard University Press.

Moen, P. (2003). Midcourse: Navigating retirement and a new life stage. In J. T. Mortimer & M. J. Shanahan (Eds.), *Handbook of the life course* (pp. 269–291). New York: Springer.

Moen, P. (2005). Beyond the career mystique: "Time in," "time out," and "second acts." *Sociological Forum, 20(2),* 189–208.

Moen, P. (2007). Not so big jobs and retirements: What workers (and retirees) really want. *Generations, 31*(1), 31–36.

Moen, P., Huang, Q., Plassmann, V., & Dentinger, E. (2006). Deciding the future: Do dual-earner couples plan together for retirement? *American Behavioral Scientist, 49*(10), 1422–1443.

Moen, P., Kim, J. E., & Hofmeister, H. (2001). Couples' work/retirement transitions, gender, and marital quality. *Social Psychology Quarterly, 64*(1), 55–71.

Moffitt, T. (1993). Adolescence-limited and life-course persistent antisocial behavior: A developmental taxonomy. *Psychological Review, 100,* 674–701.

Moffitt, T. (2006). Life-course persistent versus adolescence-limited antisocial behavior. In D. Cicchetti & D. Cohen (Eds.), *Developmental psychopathology* (2nd ed., pp. 570–598). New York: Wiley.

Moffitt, T. E., Caspi, A., Harrington, H., & Milne, B. J. (2002). Males on the life-course-persistent and adolescence-limited antisocial pathways: Follow-up at age 26 years. *Development and Psychopathology, 14,* 179–207.

Molfese, D. L., & Molfese, V. J. (1994). Short-term and long-term developmental outcomes: The use of behavioral and electrophysiological measures in early infancy as predictors. In G. Dawson and K. W. Fischer (Eds.), *Human behavior and the developing brain* (pp. 493–517). New York: Guilford.

Mondschein, E. R., Adolph, K. E., & Tamis-LeMonda, C. S. (2000). Gender bias in mothers' expectations about infant crawling. *Journal of Experimental Child Psychology, 77,* 304–316.

Monitoring the Future. (2005). The Monitoring the Future Study, University of Michigan (available at www.monitoringthefuture.org).

Monroe, S. M., Rohde, P., Seeley, J. R., & Lewinsohn, P. M. (1999). Life events and depression in adolescence: Relationship loss as a prospective risk factor for first onset of major depressive disorder. *Journal of Abnormal Psychology, 108,* 606–614.

Monset-Couchard, M., de Bethmann, O., & Kastler, B. (2002). Mid-and long-term outcome of 166 premature infants weighing less than 1,000 g at birth, all small for gestational age. *Biology of the Neonate, 81,* 244–254.

Montepare, J., & Lachman, M. E. (1989). "You're only as old as you feel": Self-perceptions of age, fears of aging, and life satisfaction from adolescence to old age. *Psychology and Aging, 4*(1), 73–78.

Montgomery, M. (1996). "The fruit that hangs highest": Courtship and chaperonage in New York high society, 1880–1920. *Journal of Family History, 21,* 172–191.

Moon, R. Y., Kotch, L., & Aird, L. (2006). State child care regulations regarding infant sleep environment since the Healthy Child Care America-Back to Sleep campaign. *Pediatrics, 118*(1), 73–83.

Moore, G. A., Cohn, J. F., & Campbell, S. B. (2001). Infant affective responses to mother's still face at 6 months differentially predict externalizing and internalizing behaviors at 18 months. *Developmental Psychology, 37,* 706–714.

Moore, K. L. (1998). *The developing human: Clinically oriented embryology* (6th ed.). Philadelphia: Saunders.

Moore, K. L., & Persaud, T. V. N. (1993). The branchial or pharyngeal apparatus. In K. L. Moore & T. V. N. Persaud, Eds., *The developing human: Clinically oriented embryology* (5th ed., pp. 192–198). Philadelphia: Saunders.

Moore, K. L., & Persaud, T. V. N. (2003). *Before we are born: Essentials of embryology and birth defects* (6th ed.). Philadelphia: Saunders.

Moorman, S. M., Hauser, R. M., & Carr, D. (2009). Do older adults know their spouses' end-of-life treatment preferences? *Research on Aging, 31*(4), 463–491.

Moorrees, C. F. A. (1959). *The dentition of the growing child: A longitudinal study of dental development between 3 and 18.* Cambridge, MA: Harvard University Press.

Moos, R. (1978). A typology of junior high and high school classrooms. *American Educational Research Journal, 15,* 53–66.

Morata, T. C. (2007). Young people: Their noise and music exposures and the risk of hearing loss. *International Journal of Audiology, 46*(3), 111–112.

Mor-Barak, M. E. (1995). The meaning of work for older adults seeking employment: The generativity factor. *International Journal of Aging and Human Development, 41*(4), 325–344.

Morcom, A. M, Good, C. D., Frackowiak, R. S. J., & Rugg, M. D. (2003). Age effects on the neural correlates of successful memory encoding. *Brain, 126*(1), 213.

Morgan, H. J., & Shaver, P. R. (1999). Attachment processes and commitment to romantic relationships. In J. M. Adams & W. H. Jones (Eds.), *Handbook of interpersonal commitment and relationship stability* (pp. 109–124). New York: Kluwer Academic/Plenum.

Morley, J. E. (2002). A fall is a major event in the life of an older person. *Journal of Gerontology: Medical Sciences, 57*(8), M492–495.

Morris, B., & Sloutsky, V. (2001). Children's solutions of logical versus empirical problems: What's missing and what develops? *Cognitive Development, 16,* 907–928.

Morrison, F. J., & Connor, C. M. (2002). Understanding schooling effects on early literacy: A working research strategy. *Journal of School Psychology, 40,* 493–500.

Morrow-Howell, N. (2007). A longer worklife: The new road to volunteering. *Generations, 31*(1), 63–67.

Morrow-Howell, N., Hinterlong, J., Rozario, P., & Tang, F. (2003). Effects of volunteering on the well-being of older adults. *Journal of Gerontology: Social Sciences, 58*(3), S137–S145.

Mortimer, J. (2003). *Working and growing up in America.* Cambridge, MA: Harvard University Press.

Mortimer, J. T., & Lorence, J. (1979). Work experience and occupational value socialization: A longitudinal study. *American Journal of Sociology, 84*(6), 1361–1385.

Mortimer, J., & Johnson, M. (1998). New perspectives on adolescent work and the transition to adulthood. In R. Jessor & M. Chase (Eds.), *New perspectives on adolescent risk behavior* (pp. 425–496). New York: Cambridge University Press.

Moss, M. A., & Moss, S. Z. (1983). The impact of parental death on middle aged children. *OMEGA—Journal of Death and Dying, 14*(1), 65–75.

Mroczek, D. K., & Spiro III, A. (2005). Change in life satisfaction during adulthood: Findings from the Veterans Affairs Normative Aging Study. *Journal of Personality and Social Psychology, 88*(1), 189–202.

Mroczek, D. K., & Spiro, A., III. (2003). Modeling intraindividual change in personality traits: Findings from the Normative Aging Study. *Journal of Gerontology: Psychological Sciences, 58*(3), P135–P165.

Mroczek, D., Spiro III, A., Griffin, P. W., & Neupert, S. D. (2006). Social influences on adult personality, self-regulation, and health. In K. W. Schaie & L. L. Carstensen (Eds.), *Social structures, aging, and self-regulation in the elderly* (pp. 69–83). New York: Springer.

Mueller, E. (1972). The maintenance of verbal exchanges between young children. *Child Development, 43,* 930–938.

Mueller, E., & Vandell, D. L. (1979) Infant-infant interaction. In J. Osofsky (Ed.), *Handbook of infant development* (pp. 591–622). New York: Wiley.

Mulligan, G. M., Brimhall, D., & West, J. (2005). Child care and early education arrangements of infants, toddlers, and preschoolers: 2001 (NCES 2006–039). U.S. Department of Education, National Center for Education Statistics. Washington, DC: U.S. Government Printing Office.

Munakata, Y. (2006). Information processing approaches to development. In W. Damon & R. M. Lerner (Series Eds.) & D. Kuhn & R. S. Siegler (Vol. Eds.), *Handbook of child psychology: Vol. 2. Cognition, perception, and language* (6th ed., pp. 426–463). Hoboken, NJ: Wiley.

Mundy, P. & Sigman, M. (2006). Joint attention, social competence and developmental psychopathology. In D. Cicchetti & D. Cohen (Eds.), *Developmental psychopathology: Volume one: Theory and methods.* (pp. 296–332). Hoboken, NJ: Wiley.

Munn, J. C., Dobbs, D., Meier, A., Williams, C. S., Biola, H., & Zimmerman, S. (2008). The end-of-life experience in long-term care: Five themes identified from focus groups with residents, family members, and staff. *The Gerontologist, 48*(4), 485–494.

Munn, P., & Dunn, J. (1989). Temperament and the developing relationship between siblings. *International Journal of Behavioral Development, 12,* 433–451.

Muotri, A. R., & Gage, F. H. (2006). Generation of neuronal variability and complexity. *Nature, 441,* 1087–1093.

Murphy, C., Schubert, C. R., Cruickshanks, K. J., Klein, B. E. K., Klein, R., & Nondahl, D. M. (2002). Prevalence of olfactory impairment in older adults. *Journal of the American Medical Association, 288*(18), 2307–2312.

Muscarella, F., & Cunningham, M. R. (1996). The evolutionary significance and social perception of male pattern baldness and facial hair. *Ethology and Sociobiology, 17*(2), 99–117.

Musick, M., Herzog, A., & House, J. (1999). Volunteering and mortality among older adults: Findings from a national sample. *Journals of Gerontology: Social Sciences, 54*(3), 173–180.

Mustanski, B. S., Viken, R. J., Kaprio, J., Pulkkinen, L., & Rose, R. J. (2004). Genetic and environmental influences on pubertal development: Longitudinal data from Finnish twins at ages 11 and 14. *Developmental Psychology, 40,* 1188–1198.

Myers, J. E., & Perrin, N. (1993). Grandparents affected by parental divorce: A population at risk? *Journal of Counseling and Development, 72*(1), 62–66.

Nader, P. R., O'Brien, M., Houts, R., Bradley, R., Belsky, J., Crosnoe, R., Friedman, S., Mei, Z., Susman, E., & the NICHD Early Child Care Research Network. (2006). Identifying risk for obesity in early childhood. *Pediatrics, 118,* 594–601.

Nagi, S. (1965). Some conceptual issues in disability and rehabilitation. In M. Sussman (Ed.), *Sociology and rehabilitation* (pp. 100–113). Washington, DC: American Sociological Association.

Nagin, D. S., & Tremblay, R. E. (2005). Developmental trajectory groups: Fact or useful statistical fiction? *Criminology, 43,* 873–904.

Nagin, D., & Tremblay, R. (1999). Trajectories of boys' physical aggression, opposition, and hyperactivity on the path to physically violent and nonviolent juvenile delinquency. *Child Development, 70,* 1181–1196.

Nagin, D., & Tremblay, R. (2005). What has been learned from group-based trajectory modeling?: Examples from physical aggression and other problem behaviors. *Annals of the American Academy of Political and Social Science,* 602, 82–117.

Nagin, D., Farrington, D., & Moffitt, T. (1995). Life-course trajectories of different types of offenders. *Criminology, 33,* 111–139.

Naimi, T. S., Brewer, R. D., Mokdad, A., Denny, C., Serdula, M. K., & Marks, J. S. (2003). Binge drinking among US adults. *Journal of the American Medical Association, 289*(1), 70–75.

Namaguchi, K. M., & Milkie, M. A. (2003). Costs and rewards of children: The effects of becoming a parent on adults' lives. *Journal of Marriage and Family, 65*(2), 356–374.

National Academy on an Aging Society. (1999). *Chronic conditions: A challenge for the 21st Century.* Retrieved July 18, 2002 from http://www.agingsociety.org/agingsociety/pdf/chronic.pdf

National Cancer Institute. (2008, Feb. 14) *Human Papillomaviruses and cancer: Questions and answers.* Washington, DC: National Institutes of Health. Retrieved January 18, 2010 from http://www.cancer.gov/cancertopics/factsheet/Risk/HPV

National Center for Education Statistics. (2003). *Trends in international mathematics and science study.* Retrieved September 3, 2008, from http://nces.ed.gov/timss/results03.asp.

National Center for Education Statistics. (2006). *After-school programs and activities: 2005.* Report NCES 2006: 076. Retrieved September 3, 2008, from http://nces.ed.gov/pubs2006/afterschool/index.asp

National Center for Education Statistics. (2007). *The condition of education.* Retrieved September 3, 2008, from http://nces.ed.gov/pubsearch/pubsinfo.asp?pubid=2007064

National Center for Education Statistics. (2008). Digest of Education Statistics U.S. Department of Education. Retrieved from http://nces.ed.gov/PUBSEARCH/pubsinfo.asp?pubid=2008022

National Center for Health Statistics. (2000a). 2 to 20 years: Boys stature-for-age and weight-for-age percentiles. Available at http://www.cdc.gov/growthcharts

National Center for Health Statistics. (2000b). 2 to 20 years: Girls stature-for-age and weight-for-age percentiles. Available at http://www.cdc.gov/growthcharts

National Center for Health Statistics. (2007). *Health, U.S., 2007 with Chartbook on Trends in the Health of Americans*. Retrieved October 20, 2008 from http://www.cdc.gov/nchs/data/hus/hus07.pdf

National Center for Health Statistics. (2007). *Prevalence of overweight among children and adolescents: United States, 2003–2004*. Hyattsville, MD: Author. Retrieved March 22, 2007, from http://www.cdc.gov/nchs/products/pubs/pubd/hestats/overweight/overwght_child_03.htm

National Center for Health Statistics, (2009). *Health, United States, 2008*. Hyattsville, MD: National Center for Health Statistics. Retreived November 30, 2009 from http://www.cdc.gov/nchs/data/hus/hus08.pdf

National Council on Aging. (2002). *American perceptions of aging in the 21st century: The NCOA's continuing study of the myths and realities of aging*. Retrieved February 15, 2010 from http://www.healthyagingprograms.org/resources/MRA%20Chartbook%20Complete.pdf.

National Diabetes Education Program. (2006). *Overview of diabetes in children and adolescents: A fact sheet from the National Diabetes Education Program*. Washington, DC: U.S. Department of Health and Human Services. Retrieved September 2, 2008, from www.ndep.nih.gov/diabetes/youth

National Eye Institute (2009). *Facts about cataract*. Retrieved March 15, 2010 from http://www.nei.nih.gov/health/cataract/cataract_facts.asp#4d

National Hospice and Palliative Care Organization (n.d.) *How can palliative care help?* Retrieved July 6, 2009 from http://www.caringinfo.org/LivingWithAnIllness/PalliativeCare.htm

National Institute of Allergy and Infectious Diseases. (December 2004). The common cold. Retrieved August 28, 2006 from http://www.niad.nih.gov/factsheets/cold.htm

National Institute of Child Health and Human Development. (2000). *Report of the National Reading Panel. Teaching children to read: An evidence-based assessment of the scientific research literature on reading and its implications for reading instruction* (NIH Publication No. 00-4769). Washington, DC: U.S. Government Printing Office.

National Institute on Aging. (1996). *In search of the secrets of aging* (2nd ed.). Bethesda, MD: U.S. Government Printing Office.

National Institute on Aging (2003). *Multi-infarct dementia fact sheet*. Retrieved March 9, 2005 from Alzheimer's Disease Education and Referral Center (a service of the National Institute on Aging), http://www.alzheimers.org/pubs/mid.htm

National Institute on Aging. (2005). *Aging hearts and arteries*. Retrieved March 15, 2010 from http://www.nia.nih.gov/NR/rdonlyres/0BBF820F-27D0-48EA-9820-736B7E9F08BB/0/HAFinal_0601.pdf

National Institute on Aging. (2006). *Aging under the microscope: A biological quest*. U.S. Department Of Health and Human Services: National Institutes of Health. Retrieved July 12, 2007 from http://www.nia.nih.gov/NR/rdonlyres/0161ED5A-4D01-4649-8B90-EAAA2A3624E6/0/Aging_Under_the_Microscope2006.pdf

National Institute on Aging. (2006). *Aging under the microscope: A biological quest*. Retrieved July 12, 2007 from http://www.nia.nih.gov/NR/rdonlyres/0161ED5A-4D01-4649-8B90-EAAA2A3624E6/0/Aging_Under_the_Microscope2006.pdf

National Institute on Aging. (2007). *Growing Older in America: The Health & Retirement Study*. Retrieved June 19, 2007 from http://www.nia.nih.gov/ResearchInformation/ExtramuralPrograms/BehavioralAndSocialResearch/HRS.htm

National Institute on Aging. (2007a). *Age page: Aging and your eyes*. Retrieved June 21, 2008 from http://www.nia.nih.gov/NR/rdonlyres/033E4E9E-221A-4A2C-8BC6-8A1D41F7D45C/12957/EyepartsAP71709FINALfortheWeb.pdf

National Institute on Aging. (2007b). *Growing older in America: The Health and Retirement Study*. Retrieved October 27, 2008 from http://www.nia.nih.gov/ResearchInformation/ExtramuralPrograms/BehavioralAndSocialResearch/HRS.htm

National Institute on Aging. (2008). *Fact sheet on Alzheimer's disease*. Retrieved August 20, 2008 from http://www.nia.nih.gov/Alzheimers/Publications/adfact.htm.

National Institute on Aging (2009a). *Hearing loss*. Retrieved December 30, 2009 from http://www.nia.nih.gov/HealthInformation/Publications/hearing.htm

National Institute on Aging. (2009b). *Can Alzheimer's disease be prevented?* Retrieved March 16, 2010 from http://www.nia.nih.gov/NR/rdonlyres/63B5A29C-F943-4DB7-91B4-0296772973F3/0/PreventAlzBkletBLU_042909.pdf

National Institute on Aging (2009c). *Understanding stages and symptoms of Alzheimer's disease*. Retrieved October 28, 2009 from http://www.nia.nih.gov/Alzheimers/Publications/stages.htm

National Institute on Aging (2009, November). *Menopause*. Retrieved February 16, 2010 from http://www.nia.nih.gov/HealthInformation/Publications/menopause.htm

National Institutes of Health. (2005). *NIH state-of-the-science conference statement on management of menopause-related symptoms*. NIH Consensus and State-of-the-Science Statements, 22 (1). Retrieved June 21, 2008 from https://vpn.nacs.uci.edu/+CSCO+ch756767633A2F2F706261667261668662E6176752E746269+893610053@119152640@1260333289@F5D30FDD7D85CA1CDE16CB906A55B1C5102F7AA0+/2005/2005MenopausalSymptomsSOS025PDF.pdf

National Osteoporosis Foundation (2007). *Bone tool kit*. Washington, DC: National Osteoporosis Foundation. Retrieved April 29, 2008 from http://www.nof.org/awareness2/index.htm#bonetoolkit

National Research Council. (1998). *Preventing reading difficulties in young children*. Washington, DC. National Academy Press.

National Research Council. (1998). *Protecting youth at work*. Washington, DC: National Academy Press.

National Research Council. (2004). *Children's health, the nation's wealth: Assessing and improving child health*. Washington, DC: National Academies Press.

National SAFE KIDS Campaign. (2006). Childhood injury fact sheet. Washington, DC.

Naveh-Benjamin, M. (2000). Adult age differences in memory performance: Tests of an associative deficit hypothesis. *Journal of Experimental Psychology: Learning, Memory, and Cognition*, 26(5), 1170–1187.

Neemann, J., Hubbard, J., & Masten, A. (1995). The changing importance of romantic relationship involvement to competence from late childhood to late adolescence. *Development and Psychopathology, 7*, 727–750.

Neff, L. A., & Karney, B. R. (2004). How does context affect intimate relationships? Linking external stress and cognitive processes within marriage. *Personality and Social Psychology Bulletin, 30*(2), 134–148.

Neff, L. A., & Karney, B. R. (2007). Stress crossover in newlywed marriage: A longitudinal and dyadic perspective. *Journal of Marriage and Family, 69*(3), 594–607.

Neisser, U., Boodoo, G., Bouchard, T. J. Jr., Wade, B. A., Brody, N., Ceci, S., Halpern, D. F., Loehlin, J. C., Perloff, R., Sternberg, R. J., & Urbina, S. (1996). Intelligence: Knowns and unknowns. *American Psychologist, 51,* 77–101.

Nelson, C. A., Thomas, K., & deHaan, M. (2006). Neural bases of cognitive development. In W. Damon & R. Lerner (Series Eds.) & D. Kuhn & R. S. Siegler (Vol. Eds.), *Handbook of child psychology: Vol. 2. Cognition, perception, and language* (6th ed.). (3–57) Hoboken, NJ: Wiley.

Nelson, C., Bloom, F., Cameron, J., Amaral, D., Dahl, R., & Pine, D. (2002). An integrative, multidisciplinary approach to the study of brain-behavior relations in the context of typical and atypical development. *Development and Psychopathology, 14,* 499–520.

Nelson, D. V. (2007). *AARP bulletin poll on workers, 50+: Executive summary.* Washington, DC: American Association of Retired Persons (AARP).

Nelson, E. A., & Dannefer, D. (1992). Aged heterogeneity: Fact or fiction? The fate of diversity in gerontological research. *The Gerontologist, 32*(1), 17–23.

Nelson, E., Leibenluft E., McClure E., & Pine D. (2005) The social re-orientation of adolescence: A neuroscience perspective on the process and its relation to psychopathology. *Psychological Medicine, 35,* 163–174.

Nelson, K. (1993). Events, narratives, memory: What develops. In C. A. Nelson (Ed.), *Minnesota Symposium on Child Psychology: Vol. 26. Memory and affect* (pp. 1–24). Hillsdale, NJ: Erlbaum.

Nelson, K. (2006). *Young minds in social worlds: Experience, meaning and memory.* Cambridge, MA: Harvard University Press.

Nelson, K., & Fivush, R. (2004). The emergence of autobiographical memory: A social cultural developmental theory. *Psychological Review, 111,* 485–511.

Nelson, T. D. (2002). (Ed.) *Ageism: Stereotyping and prejudice against older adults.* Cambridge, MA: MIT Press.

Nettles, S. M., Caughy, M. O., & O'Campo, P. J. (2008). School adjustment in the early grades: Toward an integrated model of neighborhood, parental, and child processes. *Review of Educational Research, 78,* 3–32.

Neugarten, B. L, Moore, J. W., & Lowe, J. C. (1965). Age norms, age constraints, and adult socialization. *American Journal of Sociology, 70*(6), 710–717.

Neugarten, B. L. (1974). Age groups in American society and the rise of the young-old. *The Annals of the American Academy of Political and Social Science, 415*(1), 187–198.

Neugarten, B. L. (1979). Time, age, and the life cycle. *American Journal of Psychiatry, 136,* 887–894.

Neugarten, B. L., & Datan, N. (1974). The middle years. In S. Arieti (Ed.), *The foundations of psychiatry* (pp. 592–608). New York: Basic Books.

Neugarten, B. L., & Neugarten, D. A. (1987). The changing meanings of age. *Psychology Today, 21,* 29–33.

Neumark, D. (2009). The Age Discrimination in Employment Act and the challenge of population aging. *Research on Aging, 31*(1), 41–68.

Neville, H. J., & Lawson, D. (1987). Attention to central and peripheral visual space in a movement detection task. III. Separate effects of auditory deprivation and acquisition of a visual language. *Brain Research, 405,* 284–294.

Newcomb, A. F., & Bagwell, C. (1995). Children's friendship relations: A meta-analytic review. *Psychological Bulletin, 117,* 306–347.

Newcomb, A. F., Bukowski, W. M., & Pattee, L. (1993). Children's peer relations: A meta-analytic review of popular, rejected, neglected, controversial, and average sociometric status. *Psychological Bulletin, 113,* 99–128.

Newcomb, M., & Bentler, P. (1989). Substance use and abuse among children and teenagers. *American Psychologist, 44,* 242–248.

Newman, C. G. (1985). Teratogen update: Clinical aspects of thalidomide embryopathy—a continuing preoccupation. *Teratology, 32*(1), 133–144.

Newman, D. L. (2005). Ego development and ethnic identity formation in rural American Indian adolescents. *Child Development, 76,* 734–746.

Ng, T. W. H., & Feldman, D. C. (2008). The relationship of age to ten dimensions of job performance. *Journal of Applied Psychology, 93*(2), 392–422.

Nguyen, H. T., & Zonderman, A. B. (2006). Relationship between age and aspects of depression: consistency and reliability across two longitudinal studies. *Psychology and Aging, 21*(1), 119–126.

Nguyen, H.-H. D., & Ryan, A. M. (2008). Does stereotype threat affect test performance of minorities and women? A meta-analysis of experimental evidence. *Journal of Applied Psychology, 93*(6), 1314–1334.

NICHD Early Child Care Research Network. (1996). Characteristics of infant child care: Factors contributing to positive caregiving. *Early Childhood Research Quarterly, 11*(3), 269–306.

NICHD Early Child Care Research Network. (1997). The effects of infant child care on infant-mother attachment security: Results of the NICHD Study of Early Child Care. *Child Development, 68,* 860–879.

NICHD Early Child Care Research Network. (1999). Child outcomes when child care center classes meet recommended standards for quality. *American Journal of Public Health, 89,* 1072–1077.

NICHD Early Child Care Research Network. (2000a). Characteristics and quality of child care for toddlers and preschoolers. *Applied Developmental Science, 4*(3), 116–135.

NICHD Early Child Care Research Network. (2000b). The relation of child care to cognitive and language development. *Child Development, 71,* 960–980.

NICHD Early Child Care Research Network. (2001). A new guide for evaluating child care quality. *Zero to Three, 21*(5), 40–47.

NICHD Early Child Care Research Network. (2001). Child care and children's peer interaction at 24 and 36 months: The NICHD Study of Early Child Care. *Child Development, 72,* 1478–1500.

NICHD Early Child Care Research Network. (2002). Early child care and children's development prior to school entry: Results from the NICHD Study of Early Child Care. *American Educational Research Journal, 39*(1), 133–164.

NICHD Early Child Care Research Network. (2003). Frequency and intensity of activity of third-grade children in physical education. *Archives of Pediatrics & Adolescent Medicine, 157,* 185–190.

NICHD Early Child Care Research Network. (2003a). Child care and common communicable illnesses in children aged 37 to 54 months. *Archives of Pediatrics and Adolescent Medicine, 157*(2), 196–200.

NICHD Early Child Care Research Network. (2003b). Do children's attention processes mediate the link between family predictors and school readiness? *Developmental Psychology, 39,* 581–593.

NICHD Early Child Care Research Network. (2004). Trajectories of physical aggression from toddlerhood to middle childhood. *Monographs of the Society for Research in Child Development, 69,* Whole No. 4, Serial 611–621.

NICHD Early Child Care Research Network. (2004a). Are child developmental outcomes related to before- and after-school care arrangements? Results from the NICHD Study of Early Child Care. *Child Development, 75,* 280–295.

NICHD Early Child Care Research Network. (2004b). Trajectories of physical aggression from toddlerhood to middle childhood: Predictors, correlates and outcomes. *Monograph of the Society for Research in Child Development, 69* (4, Serial No. 278).

NICHD Early Child Care Research Network. (2005). Early child care and children's development in the primary Grades: Results from the NICHD Study of Early Child care. *American Educational Research Journal, 42,* 537–570.

NICHD Early Child Care Research Network. (2005a). *Child care and child development: Results for the NICHD Study of Early Child Care and Youth Development.* New York: Guilford Press.

NICHD Early Child Care Research Network. (2005a). Pathways to reading: The role of oral language in the transition to reading. *Developmental Psychology, 41,* 428–442.

NICHD Early Child Care Research Network. (2005b). Early child care and children's development in the primary grades: Follow–up results from the NICHD Study of Early Child Care. *American Educational Research Journal, 43,* 537–570.

NICHD Early Child Care Research Network. (2005c). Pathways to reading: The role of oral language in the transition to reading. *Developmental Psychology, 41,* 428–441.

NICHD Early Child Care Research Network. (2006). Child-care effect sizes for the NICHD study of early child care and youth development. *American Psychologist, 61,* 99–116.

NICHD Early Child Care Research Network. (2008). Mothers' and fathers' support for child autonomy and early school achievement. *Developmental Psychology, 44,* 895–907.

NICHD Early Child Care Research Network. (2008). Social competence with peers in third grade: Associations with earlier peer experiences in child care. *Social Development 17,* 419–453.

Nichols, S. L., & Berliner, D. C. (2007). *Collateral damage: How high-stakes testing corrupts America's schools.* Cambridge MA: Harvard University Press.

Nolen-Hoeksema, S., Girgus, J., & Seligman, M. (1992). Predictors and consequences of childhood depressive symptoms: A 5–year longitudinal study. *Journal of Abnormal Psychology, 101,* 405–422.

Nowakowski, Richard S. (2006). Stable neuron numbers from cradle to grave. *Proceedings of the National Academy of Sciences, 103,* 12219–12220.

Nunes, T., Schliemann, A-L., & Carraher, D. (1993). *Street mathematics and school mathematics.* New York: Cambridge University Press.

Nurmi, J. E. (1992). Age differences in adult life goals, concerns, and their temporal extension: a life core's approach to future-oriented motivation. *International Journal of Behavioral Development, 15,* 487–508.

Nurmi, J. E., Pulliainen, H., & Salmela-Aro, K. (1992). Age differences in adults' control beliefs related to life goals and concerns. *Psychology and aging, 7*(2), 194–196.

Nyce, S. A. (2007). The aging workforce: Is demography destiny? *Generations, 31*(1), 9–15.

Nydegger, C. N. (1983). Family ties of the aged in the cross-cultural perspective. *The Gerontologist, 23,* 26–32.

O'Brien, L. T., & Hummert, M. L. (2006). Memory performance of late middle–aged adults: Contrasting self–stereotyping and stereotype threat accounts of assimilation to age stereotypes. *Social Cognition, 24*(3), 338–358.

O'Brien, M., & Huston, A. C. (1985a). Activity level and sex-stereotyped toy choice in toddler boys and girls. *Journal of Genetic Psychology, 146,* 527–533.

O'Brien, M., & Huston, A. C. (1985b). Development of sex-typed play behavior in toddlers. *Developmental Psychology, 21,* 866–871.

O'Brien, M., Nader, P. R., Houts, R. M., Bradley, R., Friedman, S. L., Belsky, J., Susman, E., & NICHD Early Child Care Research Network. (2007). The ecology of childhood overweight: A 12-year longitudinal analysis. *International Journal of Obesity, 31*(9), 1469–1478.

O'Bryant, S. & Hansson, R. (1995). Widowhood. In R. Blieszner, & V. H. Bedford (Eds.), *Handbook of aging and the family* (pp. 440–458). Westport, CT: Greenwood Press.

O'Connor, T. G., Rutter, M., & the English and Romanian Adoptees (ERA) Study Team. (2000). Attachment disorder behavior following early severe deprivation: Extension and longitudinal follow-up. *Journal of the American Academy of Child and Adolescent Psychiatry, 39,* 703–712.

O'Connor, T. G., Rutter, M., Beckett, C., Kreppner, J. M., & Keaveney, L. and the English and Romanian Adoptees Study Team (2000). The effects of global severe privation on cognitive competence: Extension and Longitudinal Follow-up. *Child Development, 71,* 376–390.

O'Donnell, A. B., Araujo, A. B., & McKinlay, J. B. (2004). The health of normally aging men: the Massachusetts Male Aging Study (1987–2004). *Experimental Gerontology, 39*(7), 975–984.

O'Mahony, S., Goulet, J., Kornblith, A., Abbatiello, G., Clarke, B., Kless-Siegel, S., et al. (2005). Desire for hastened death, cancer pain and depression: Report of a longitudinal observational study. *Journal of Pain and Symptom Management, 29*(5), 446–457.

O'Malley, J. (2006, July 31). Love, in translation: Lao couple found ears and voice in daughter. *Anchorage Daily News.*

O'Malley, P., & Johnston, L. (1999). Drinking and driving among US high school seniors, 1984–1997. *American Journal of Public Health, 89,* 678–684.

O'Neil, R., Parke, R. D., & McDowell, D. J. (2001). Objective and subjective features of children's neighborhoods: Relations to parental regulatory strategies and children's social competence. *Journal of Applied Developmental Psychology, 22,* 135–155.

Oakley, D., & Bogue, E. (1995). Quality of condom use as reported by female clients of a family planning clinic. *American Journal of Public Health, 85,* 1526–1530.

Oeppen, J., & Vaupel, J. W. (2002). Broken limits to life expectancy. *Science, 296,* 1029–1031.

Ogburn, W. F., & Nimkoff, M. F. (1955). *Technology and the changing family.* Boston: Houghton Mifflin.

Ogden, C. L., Carroll, M. D., Curtin, L. R., McDowell, M. A., Tabak, C. J., & Flegal, K. M. (2006). Prevalence of overweight and obesity in the United States, 1999–2004. *Journal of the American Medical Association, 295,* 1549–1555.

Ogden, C. L., Yanovski, S. Z., Carroll, M. D., & Flegal, K. M. (2007). The epidemiology of obesity. *Gastroenterology, 132,* 2087–2103.

Oken, D. (1961). What to tell cancer patients: A study of medical attitudes. *Journal of the American Medical Association, 175*(13), 1120–1128.

Oller, D. K. (2000). *The emergence of the speech capacity*. Mahwah, NJ: Erlbaum.

Olney, R. S., Moore, C. A., Khoury, M. J., Erickson, J. D., Edmonds, L. D, & Botto, L. D. (1995). Chorionic villus sampling and amniocentesis: Recommendations for prenatal counseling. *Morbidity and Mortality Weekly Report, 44*, 1–12.

Olshansky, S. J., Carnes, B. A., & Butler, R. I. (2003). If humans were built to last. *Scientific American*(Special edition)*13*, 94–100.

Olshansky, S. J., Hayflick, L., & Carnes, B. A. (2002). Position statement on human aging. *Journal of Gerontology A: Biological and Medical Sciences, 57*(8), B292–297.

Olshansky, S. J., Passaro, D. J., Hershow, R. C., Layden, J., Carnes, B. A., Brody, J., et al. (2005). A potential decline in life expectancy in the United States in the 21st century. *New England Journal of Medicine, 352*(11), 1138–1145.

Olson, E. A., & Luciana, M. (2008) The development of prefrontal cortex functions in adolescence. In C. A. Nelson & M. Luciana (Eds.), *Handbook of developmental cognitive neuroscience* (2nd ed., pp. 575–590). Cambridge, MA: MIT Press.

Olweus, D. (1993). *Bullying at school: What we know and what we can do.* Cambridge, MA: Blackwell.

Oncale, R. M., & King, B. M. (2001). Comparison of men's and women's attempts to dissuade sexual partners from the couple using condoms. *Archives of Sexual Behavior, 30*(4), 379–391.

Onder, G., Penninx, B. W., Ferrucci, L., Fried, L. P., Guralnik, J. M., & Pahor, M. (2005). Measures of physical performance and risk for progressive and catastrophic disability: Results from the Women's Health and Aging Study. *Journal of Gerontology A: Biological Sciences and Medical Sciences, 60*(1), M74–79.

Oneill, C., Jamison, J., McCulloch, D., & Smith, D. (2001). Age-related macular degeneration: Cost-of-illness issues. *Drugs and Aging, 18*(4), 233–241.

Oppenheim, D., Sagi, A., & Lamb, M. E. (1988). Infant-adult attachments on the kibbutz and their relation to socioemotional development 4 years later. *Developmental Psychology, 24*, 427–433.

Orbuch, T. L., House, J. S., Mero, R. P., & Webster, P. S. (1996). Marital quality over the life course. *Social Psychology Quarterly, 59(2)*, 162–171.

Oregon Department of Human Services (2009a, March). *2008 Summary of Oregon's Death with Dignity Act*. Retrieved November 24, 2009 from http://www.oregon.gov/DHS/ph/pas/docs/year11.pdf

Oregon Department of Human Services (2009b, March). Table 1: Characteristics and end-of-life care of 401 DWDA patients who died after ingesting a lethal dose of medication, by year, Oregon, 1998–2008. Retrieved November 24, 2009 from http://www.oregon.gov/DHS/ph/pas/docs/yr11-tbl-1.pdf

Oregon Department of Human Services (n.d.). *Death with Dignitiy Act Requirements.* Retrieved November 24, 2009 from http://www.oregon.gov/DHS/ph/pas/docs/Requirements.pdf

Orellana, M. F., Reynolds, J., Dorner, L., & Meza, M. (2003). In other words: Translating or "para-phrasing" as a family literacy practice in immigrant households. *The Reading Research Quarterly, 38*, 12–34.

Orentlicher, D. (1996). The legalization of physician-assisted suicide. *New England Journal of Medicine, 335*, 663–667.

Orentlicher, D. (2000). The implementation of Oregon's Death with Dignity Act: Reassuring, but more data are needed. *Psychology Public Policy and Law, 6*(2), 489–502.

Orlando, M., Tucker, J. S., Ellickson, P., & Klein, D. (2004). Developmental trajectories of cigarette smoking and their correlates from early adolescence to young adulthood. *Journal of Consulting and Clinical Psychology, 72*, 400–410.

Oster, H. (2005). The repertoire of infant facial expressions: An ontogenetic perspective. In J. Nadel & D. Muir (Eds), *Emotional development* (pp. 261–292). New York: Oxford University Press.

Osterweis, M., Solomon, F., & Morris, G. (1984). *Bereavement: Reactions, consequences, and care.* Washington, DC: National Academies Press.

Otero, G. A. Pliego-Rivero, F. B. Fernandez, T. & Ricardo, J. (2003). EEG development in children with sociocultural disadvantages: A follow-up study. *Clinical Neurophysiology, 114*, 1918–1925.

Ouslander, J. G. (1997). Aging and the lower urinary tract. *The American Journal of the Medical Sciences, 314*(4), 214–218.

Overton, W. (2006). Developmental psychology: Philosophy, concepts, methodology. In W. Damon & R. Lerner (Series Eds.) & R. Lerner (Vol. Ed.), *Handbook of child psychology: Vol. 1. Theoretical models of human development* (6th ed., pp. 18–88). New York: Wiley.

Pakaslahti, L., Karjalainen, A., & Keltikangas-Jarvinen, L. (2002). Relationships between adolescent prosocial problem-solving strategies, prosocial behavior, and social acceptance. *International Journal of Behavioral Development, 26*, 137–144.

Papoušek, H., & Papoušek, M. (1978). Interdisciplinary parallels in studies of early human behavior: From physical to cognitive needs, from attachment to dyadic education. *International Journal of Behavioral Development, 1*, 37–49.

Papoušek, H., & Papoušek, M. (2002). Intuitive parenting. In M. H. Bornstein (Ed.), *Handbook of parenting: Vol. 2. Biology and ecology of parenting* (2nd ed., pp. 183–203). Mahwah, NJ: Erlbaum.

Papoušek, M. (1996). Origins of reciprocity and mutuality in prelinguistic parent-infant "dialogues." In I. Markova, C. F. Graumann, & K. Foppa (Eds.), *Mutualities in dialogue* (pp. 58–81). New York: Cambridge University Press.

Papoušek, M., Papoušek, H., & Bornstein, M. H. (1985). The naturalistic vocal environment of young infants: On the significance of homogeneity and variability in parental speech. In T. M. Field & N. A. Fox (Eds.), *Social perception in infants* (pp. 269–297). Norwood, NJ: Ablex.

Paquette, J. A., & Underwood, M. K. (1999). Gender differences in young adolescents' experiences of peer victimization: Social and physical aggression. *Merrill-Palmer Quarterly, 45*, 242–266.

Pargament, K. I., van Haitsma, K. S., & Ensing, D. S. (1995). Religion and coping. In M. A. Kimble, S. H. McFadden, J. W. Ellor, & J. J. Seeber (Eds.), *Aging, spirituality, and religion: A handbook* (pp. 9–29). Minneapolis, MN: Fortress Press.

Park, D. C. (2000). The basic mechanisms accounting for age-related decline in cognitive function. In D. C. Park & N. Schwarz (Eds.), *Cognitive aging: A primer* (pp. 3–21). Philadelphia, PA: Psychology Press.

Park, D. C., & Reuter-Lorenz, P. A. (2009). The adaptive brain: Aging and neurocognitive scaffolding. *Annual Review of Psychology, 60*, 173–196.

Park, J. J., Tang, Y., Lopez, I., & Ishiyama, A. (2001). Age-related change in the number of neurons in the human vestibular ganglion. *The Journal of Comparative Neurology, 431*(4), 437–443.

Park, M. J., Mulye, T. P., Adams, S. H., Brindis, C. D, & Irwin, C. E. (2006). The health status of young adults in the United States. *Journal of Adolescent Health, 39*(3), 305–317.

Parke, R. D. (2002). Fathers and families. In M. H. Bornstein (Ed.), *Handbook of parenting: Vol. 3. Being and becoming a parent* (2nd ed., pp. 27–73). Mahwah, NJ: Erlbaum.

Parke, R. D., & Buriel, R. (2006). Socialization in the family: Ethnic and ecological perspectives. In N. Eisenberg (Vol. Ed.), *Handbook of child psychology: Vol. 3. Social, emotional, and personality development* (pp. 429–504). Hoboken, NJ: Wiley.

Parke, R. D., Simpkins, S. D., McDowell, D. J., Kim, M., Killian, C., Dennis, J., et al. (2002). Relative contributions of families and peers to children's social development. In P. K. Smith & C. H. Hart (Eds.), *Blackwell handbook of child development* (pp. 156–177). Oxford: Blackwell.

Parker, J. G., Low, C. M., Walker, A. R., & Gamm, B. K. (2005). Friendship jealousy in young adolescents: Individual differences and links to sex, self-esteem, aggression, and social adjustment. *Developmental Psychology, 41*, 235–250.

Parker, S. W., Nelson, C. A., Zeanah, C. H., Smyke, A. T., Koga, S. F., Nelson, C. A., et al. (2005). The impact of early institutional rearing on the ability to discriminate facial expressions of emotion: An event-related potential study. *Child Development, 76*, 54–72.

Parkes, C. M. (1972). *Bereavement: Studies in grief in adult life.* London: Tavistock.

Parkes, C. M. (1998). The dying adult. *British Medical Journal, 316*, 1313–1315.

Parkhurst, J., & Asher, S. (1992). Peer rejection in middle school: Subgroup differences in behavior, loneliness, and interpersonal concerns. *Developmental Psychology, 28*, 231–241.

Parmar, P., & Rohner, R. P. (2008). Relations among spouse acceptance, remembered parental acceptance in childhood, and psychological adjustment among married adults in India. *Cross-Cultural Research: The Journal of Comparative Social Science, 42*, 57–66.

Parsons, T., & Bales, R. (1956). *Family, socialization and interaction process.* London: Routledge & Kegan Paul.

Parten, M. B. (1932). Social participation among pre-school children. *The Journal of Abnormal and Social Psychology, 27*(3), 243–269.

Pascalis, O., de Schonen, S., Morton, J., Fabre-Grenet, M., & Deruelle, C. (1995). Mother's face recognition by neonates: A replication and an extension. *Infant Behavior and Development, 18*, 79–85.

Pascarella, E. T., & Terenzini, P. (1979). Student-faculty informal contact and college persistence: A further investigation. *Journal of Educational Research, 72*(4), 214–218.

Pascerella, E. T., & Terenzini, P. T. (2005). *How college affects students: A third decade of research* (Vol. 2). San Francisco, CA: Jossey-Bass.

Paschall, M. J., Flewelling, R. L., & Russell, T. (2004). Why is work intensity associated with heavy alcohol use among adolescents? *Journal of Adolescent Health, 34*, 79–87.

Passuth, P. M., Maines, D. R., & Neugarten, B. (1984, April). *Age norms and age constraints Twenty years later*. Paper presented at the annual meeting of the Midwest Sociological Society, Chicago, IL.

Pastereski, V. L., Geffner, M. E., Brain, C. Hindmarsh, P., Brook, C., & Hines, M. (2005). Prenatal hormones and postnatal socialization by parents as determinants of male-typical toy play in girls with congenital adrenal hyperplasia. *Child Development, 76*, 264–278.

Paternoster, R., Bushway, S., Brame, R. & Apel, R. (2003). The effect of teenage employment on delinquency and problem behaviors. *Social Forces, 82*, 297–335.

Patterson, C. J. (2006). Children of lesbian and gay parents. *Current Directions in Psychological Science, 15*, 241–244.

Patterson, G. R. (1986). *Development of antisocial and prosocial behavior*. New York: Academic Press.

Patterson, G. R., Capaldi, D., & Bank, L. (1991). An early starter model for predicting delinquency. In D. J. Pepler & K. H. Rubin (Eds.), *The development and treatment of childhood aggression* (pp. 139–168). Hillsdale, NJ: Erlbaum.

Paus, T., Zijdenbos, A., Worsley, K., Collins, D. L., Blumenthal, J., Giedd, J. N., et al. (1999). Structural maturation of neural pathways in children and adolescents: in vivo study. *Science, 283*, 1908–1911.

Pausch, R., & Zaslow, J. (2008). *The last lecture*. New York: Hyperion.

Pawelec, G., Barnett, Y., Forsey, R., Frasca, D., Globerson, A., McLeod, J., et al. (2002). T cells and aging, January 2002 update. *Frontiers in Biosciences, 7*, d1056–d1183.

Penley, J., Tomaka, J., & Wiebe, J. (2002). The association of coping to physical and psychological health outcomes: A meta-analytic review. *Journal of Behavioral Medicine, 25*(6), 551–603.

Peplau, L. A. (2001). Rethinking women's sexual orientation: An interdisciplinary, relationship-focused approach. *Personal Relationships, 8*, 1–19.

Peplau, L. A. (2003). Human sexuality: How do men and women differ? *Current Directions in Psychological Research, 12*(2), 37–40.

Peplau, L. A., & Beals, K. P. (2001). Lesbians, gay men and bisexuals in relationships. In J. Worell (Ed.), *Encyclopedia of women and gender* (pp. 657–666). San Diego, CA: Academic Press.

Peplau, L. A., & Fingerhut, A. W. (2007). The close relationships of lesbians and gay men. *Annual Review of Psychology, 58*, 405–424.

Peplau, L. A., & Garnets, L. D. (2000). A new paradigm for understanding women's sexuality and sexual orientation. *Journal of Social Issues, 56*(2), 330–350.

Peplau, L. A., Bikson, T. K., Rook, K. S., & Goodchilds, J. (1982). Being old and living alone. In L. A. Peplau & D. Perlman (Eds.), *Loneliness: A sourcebook of current theory, research and therapy* (pp. 327–347). New York: Wiley.

Pereira, A. C., Huddletson, D. E., Brickman, A. M., Sosunov, A. A., Hen, R., McKhann, G. M., et al. (2007). An *in vivo* correlate of exercise-induced neurogenesis in the adult denate gyrus. *Proceedings of the National Academy of Sciences, 104*, 5638–5643.

Perera, F. P., Li, Z., Whyatt, R., Hoepner, L., Wang, S., Camann, D., & Rauh, V. (2009). Prenatal airborne polycyclic aromatic hydrocarbon exposure and child IQ at age 5 years. *Pediatrics, 124*, pp. e195–e202.

Perera, F. P., Rauh, V., Whyatt, R. M., Tsai, W. Y., Tang, D., Diaz, D., et al. (2006). Effect of prenatal exposure to airborne polycyclic aromatic hydrocarbons on neurodevelopment in the first 3 years of life among inner-city children. *Environmental Health Perspectives, 114*, 1287–1292.

Perera, F., Li, T. Y., & Zhou, Z. J. (2008). Benefits of reducing prenatal exposure to coal burning pollutants to children's neurodevelopment in China. *Environmental Health Perspectives, 116*, 1396 –1400.

Perrig-Chiello, P., & Höpflinger, F. (2005). Aging parents and their middle-aged children: Demographic and psychosocial challenges. *European Journal of Ageing, 2*(3), 183–191.

Perry, C., Williams, C., Veblen-Mortenson, S., Toomey, T., Komro, K., Anstine, P., et al. (1996). Project Northland: Outcomes of a communitywide alcohol use prevention program during early adolescence. *American Journal of Public Health, 86*, 956–965.

Perry, D. G., Perry, L., & Kennedy, E. (1992). Conflict and the development of antisocial behavior. In C. Shantz & W. W. Hartup (Eds.), *Conflict in child and adolescent development* (pp. 301–329). New York: Cambridge University Press.

Perry, W. G. (1970). *Forms of ethical and intellectual development in the college years*. New York: Holt, Rinehart, & Winston.

Perry, W. G. (1981). Cognitive and ethical growth: The making of meaning. In A. Chickering & Associates (Eds.), *The modern American college: Responding to the new realities of diverse students and a changing society* (pp. 76–116). San Francisco: Jossey-Bass.

Perry, W. G. (1999). *Forms of ethical and intellectual development in the college years* (paperback edition). San Francisco: Jossey-Bass.

Peterson, M. J., Giuliani, C., Morey, M. C., Pieper, C., F. Evenson, K. R., Mercer, V., et al. (2009). Physical activity as a preventative factor for frailty: The Health, Aging, and Body Composition Study. *Journal of Gerontology A: Biological and Medical Sciences, 64A*(1), 61–68.

Peterson, R. R. (1996). A re-evaluation of the economic consequences of divorce. *American Sociological Review, 61(3)*, 528–536.

Petitto, L. A., Holowka, S., Sergio, L. E., & Ostry, D. (2001). Language rhythms in baby hand movements. *Nature, 413*, 35–36.

Petitto, L. A., Zatorre, R. J., Gauna, K. Nikeiski, E. J., Dostie, d., & Evands, A. C. (2000). Speech-like cerebral activity in profoundly deaf people processing signed languages: Implications for the neural basis of human language. *Proceedings of the National Academy of Sciences, 97*, 13961–13966.

Petraitis, J., Flay, B., & Miller, T. (1995). Reviewing theories of adolescent substance use: Organizing pieces in the puzzle. *Psychological Bulletin, 117*, 67–86.

Petrill, S. A., Hewitt, J. K., Cherny, S. S., Lipton, P. A., Plomin, R., Corley, R., & DeFries, J. C. (2004). Genetic and environmental contributions to general cognitive ability through the first 16 years of life. *Developmental Psychology, 40*, 805–812.

Petrill, S., Kovas, Y., Hart, S. A., Thompson, L. A., & Plomin, R. (2009). The genetic and environmental etiology of high math performance in 10-year-olds. *Behavioral Genetics, 39*, 371–379.

Pettine, A., & Rosén, L. A. (1998). Self-care and deviance in elementary school-age children. *Journal of Clinical Psychology, 54*, 629–643.

Pettit, G. S., Laird, R. D., Bates, J. E., & Dodge, K. A. (1997). Patterns of after-school care in middle childhood: Risk factors and developmental outcomes. *Merrill-Palmer Quarterly, 43*, 515–538.

Pettit, G. S., Laird, R. D., Dodge, K. A., Bates, J. E., & Criss, M. M. (2001). Antecedents and behavior-problem outcomes of parental monitoring and psychological control in early adolescence. *Child Development, 72*, 583–598.

Pew Research Center (2006). Strong public support for right to die: More Americans discussing—and planning—end-of-life treatment Retrieved July 13, 2009 from http://people-press.org/reports/pdf/266.pdf

Pew Research Center (2009). *College enrollment hits all-time high.* Retrieved February 5, 2010 from http://pewsocialtrends.org/assets/pdf/college-enrollment.pdf.

Phillips, K. W., Liljenquist, K. A., & Neale, M. A. (2009). Is the pain worth the gain? The advantages and liabilities of agreeing with socially distinct newcomers. *Personality and Social Psychology Bulletin, 35*(3), 336–350.

Phillipsen, L. C. (1999). Associations between age, gender, and group acceptance and three components of friendship quality. *Journal of Early Adolescence, 19*, 438–464.

Phinney, J., & Alipuria, L. (1987). *Ethnic identity in older adolescents from four ethnic groups.* Paper presented at the biennial meetings of the Society for Research in Child Development, Baltimore.

Phinney, J., Devich-Navarro, M., DuPont, S., Estrada, A., & Onwughala, M. (1994, February). *Bicultural identity orientations of African American and Mexican American adolescents.* Paper presented at the biennial meetings of the Society for Research on Adolescence, San Diego.

Phinney, J., DuPont, S., Espinosa, Revill, J., & Sanders, K. (1994). Ethnic identity and American identification among ethnic minority adolescents. In F. van de Vijver (Ed.), *Proceedings of 1992 conference of the international association for cross-cultural psychology.* Tilburg, The Netherlands: Tilburg University Press.

Piaget, J. (1923/1955). *The language and thought of the child.* New York: Meridian Books.

Piaget, J. (1932). *The moral judgment of the child.* New York: Free Press.

Piaget, J. (1952). *The origins of intelligence in children.* New York: International Universities Press. (Original work published 1936).

Piaget, J. (1954). *The construction of reality in the child* (M. Cook, Trans.). New York: Ballantine. (Original work published 1937).

Piaget, J. (1955). *The child's conception of the world.* London: Routledge & Kegan Paul. (Originally published in 1929)

Piaget, J. (1955). *The language and thought of the child.* New York: Meridian Books. (Originally published in 1923)

Piaget, J. (1962). *Play, dreams, and imitation in childhood.* New York: W. W. Norton & Co. (Originally published in 1951).

Piaget, J. (1964). Development and learning. In T. Ripple & V. Rockcastle (Eds.), *Piaget rediscovered* (pp. 7–20). Ithaca, NY: Cornell University Press.

Piaget, J. (1965). *The child's conception of number.* New York: The Norton Library. (Originally published in 1941).

Piaget, J. (1970). Piaget's theory. In P. H. Mussen (Ed.), *Carmichael's manual of child psychology* (Vol. 1, pp. 703–732). New York: Wiley.

Piaget, J. (1970). *The science of education and the psychology of the child.* New York: Orion Press.

Piaget, J. (1972). *To understand is to invent: The future of education.* New York: Grossman Publishers. (Originally published in 1948)

Piaget, J. (1973). *The psychology of intelligence.* Totowa, NJ: Littlefield, Adams & Co. (Originally published in 1947 in France)

Piaget, J. (1980). Intellectual evolution from adolescence to adulthood. In R. E. Muuss (Ed.), *Adolescent behavior and society: A book of readings* (3rd ed.). New York: Random House.

Piaget, J. (1983). Piaget's theory. In P. Mussen (Ed.), *Handbook of child psychology* (Vol. 1, 4th ed.). New York: Wiley.

Piaget, J., & Inhelder, B. (1967). *The psychology of the child.* New York: Basic Books.

Piazza, J. R., & Charles, S. T. (2006). Mental health among the Baby Boomers. http://books.google.com/books?hl=en&lr=&id=qXhaRyN0F-wC&oi=fnd&pg=PA111&dq=Jennifer+Piazza+%26+Charles,+2006&ots=8UoOiKGg1L&sig=o5r1B8eN8bFc-vXO5qLjgdpTUts. In S. K. Whitbourne & S. L. Willis (Eds.), *The Baby Boomers grow up: Contemporary perspectives on midlife* (pp. 111–146). Mahwah, NJ: Lawrence Erlbaum.

Pierce, K. M., Bolt, D. M., & Vandell, D. L. (in press). Specific features of after-school program quality: Differential associations with children's functioning in middle childhood. *American Journal of Community Psychology*.

Pillay, A. L. (1988). Midlife depression and the 'empty nest' syndrome in Indian women. *Psychological Reports, 63*(2), 591–594.

Pillemer, K., & Suitor, J. J. (1991). "Will I ever escape my child's problems?" Effects of adult children's problems on elderly parents *Journal of Marriage and Family, 53*(3), 585–594.

Pillemer, K., Suitor, J. J., Mock, S. E., Sabir, M., Pardo, T. B., & Sechrist, J. (2007). Capturing the complexity of intergenerational relations: Exploring ambivalence within later-life families. *Journal of Social Issues, 63*(4), 775–791.

Pillow, B. H., & Henrichon, A. J. (1996). There's more to the picture than meets the eye: Young children's difficulty understanding biased interpretation. *Child Development, 67*, 803–819.

Pine, D., Cohen, P., Gurley, D., Brook, J., & Ma,Y. (1998). The risk for early-adulthood anxiety and depressive disorders in adolescents with anxiety and depressive disorders. *Archives of General Psychiatry, 55*, 56–64.

Pinker, C. (2008, January 13). The moral instinct. *The New York Times Magazine*.

Pinquart, M. (2003). Loneliness in married, widowed, divorced, and never-married older adults. *Journal of Social and Personal Relationships, 20*(1), 31–53.

Pinquart, M., & Schindler, I. (2007). Changes of life satisfaction in the transition to retirement: A latent-class approach. *Psychology and Aging, 22*(3), 442–455.

Pinquart, M., & Sorensen, S. (2001). Influences on loneliness in older adults: A meta-analysis. *Basic and Applied Social Psychology, 23*(4), 245–266.

Pinquart, M., & Sorensen, S. (2003). Associations of stressors and uplifts of caregiving with caregiver burden and depressive mood: a meta-analysis. *Journal of Gerontology B: Psychological Sciences and Social Sciences, 58*(2), P112–P129.

Pinquart, M., & Sorensen, S. (2007). Correlates of physical health of informal caregivers: a meta-analysis. *Journal of Gerontology B: Psychological Sciences and Social Sciences, 62*(2), P126–P137.

Pintrich, P., Roeser, R., & De Groot, E. (1994). Classroom and individual differences in early adolescents' motivation and self-regulated learning. *Journal of Early Adolescence, 14*, 139–161.

Pipp-Siegel, S., Robinson, J. L., Bridges, D., & Bartholomew, S. (1997). Sources of individual differences in infant social cognition: Cognitive and affective aspects of self and other. In R. J. Sternberg & E. L. Grigorenko (Eds.), *Intelligence, heredity, and environment* (pp. 505–528). New York: Cambridge University Press.

Piquero, A. R., & Chung, H. L. (2001). On the relationship between gender, early onset, and the seriousness of offending. *Journal of Criminal Justice, 29*, 189–206.

Pistelli, F., Bottai, M., Carrozzi, L., Di Pede, F., Baldacci, S., Maio, S., et al. (2008). Changes in obesity status and lung function decline in a general population sample. *Respiratory Medicine, 102*(5), 674–680.

Pleis, J. R., & Lethbridge-Çejku, M. (2006). Summary health statistics for U.S. adults: National Health Interview Survey, 2005. *Vital HealthStatistics, Series 10, 232*, 1–153.

Plomin, R. (2004). *Nature and nurture: An introduction to human behavioral genetics.* London: Wadsworth.

Plomin, R. (2007). Genetics and developmental psychology. In G. W. Ladd (Ed.), *Appraising the human developmental sciences: Essays in honor of Merrill-Palmer Quarterly* (pp. 250–261). Detroit: Wayne State University Press.

Plomin, R., & Daniels, D. (1987). Why are children in the same family so different from one another? *Behavioral and Brain Sciences, 10*, 1–60.

Plomin, R., DeFries, J. C., & Loeblin, J. C. (1977). Genotype–environment interaction and correlation in the analysis of human behaviour. *Psychological Bulletin, 85*, 309–322.

Plomin, R., DeFries, J. C., McClearn, G. E., & McGuffin, P. (2001). *Behavioral genetics* (4th ed.). New York: Worth.

Plonk, W. M., & Arnold, R. M. (2005). Terminal care: The last weeks of life. *Journal of Palliative Medicine, 8*(5), 1042–1054.

Polacek, G. N. L., Hicks, J. A., & Oswalt, S. B. (2007). 20 years later and still at risk: College students' knowledge, attitudes, and behaviors about HIV/AIDS. *Journal of Hispanic Higher Education, 6*(1), 73–88.

Pollak, S. D. (2005). Early adversity and mechanisms of plasticity: Integrating affective neuroscience with developmental approaches to psychopathology. *Development and Psychopathology, 17*, 735–752.

Pollak, S. D., & Kistler, D. J. (2002). Early experience is associated with the development of categorical representations for facial expressions of emotion. *Proceedings of the National Academy of Sciences, USA, 99*, 9072–9076.

Pollak, S. D., Klorman, R., Brumaghim, J., & Cicchetti, D. (2001). P3b reflects maltreated children's reactions to facial displays of emotion. *Psychophysiology, 38*, 267–274.

Pollak, S. D., Vardi, S., Bechner, A. M. B., & Curtin, J. J. (2005). Physically abused children's regulation of attention in response to hostility. *Child Development, 76*, 968–977.

Polygenis, D., Wharton, S., Malmberg, C., Sherman, N., Kennedy, D., Koren, G., et al. (1998). Moderate alcohol consumption during pregnancy and the incidence of fetal malformations a meta-analysis. *Neurotoxicology and Teratology, 20*, 61–67.

Pong, S. (1998). The school compositional effect of single parenthood on 10th-grade achievement. *Sociology of Education, 71*, 23–42.

Porter, R. H., & Winberg, J. (1999). Unique salience of maternal breast odors for newborn infants. *Neuroscience and Biobehavioral Reviews, 23*, 439–449.

Porter, R. H., Makin, J. W., Davis, L. B., & Christensen, K. M. (1992). Breast-fed infants respond to olfactory cues from their own mother and unfamiliar lactating females. *Infant Behavior & Development, 15*, 85–93.

Posner, J. K., & Vandell, D. L. (1999). After-school activities and the development of low-income urban children: A longitudinal study. *Developmental Psychology, 35*, 868–879.

Post, S. G. (1999). Future scenarios for the prevention and delay of Alzheimer disease onset in high-risk groups: An ethical perspective. *American Journal of Preventive Medicine, 16*(2), 105–110.

Prader, A., Tanner, J. M., & von Harnack, G. A. (1963). Catch-up growth following illness or starvation. *Journal of Pediatrics, 62*, 646–659.

Prentice, A. (2006). The emerging epidemic of obesity in developing countries. *International Journal of Epidemiology, 35*(1), 93–99.

Pressley, M., & Hilden, K. (2006). Cognitive strategies. In W. Damon & R. M. Lerner (Series Eds.) & D. Kuhn & R. S. Siegler (Vol. Eds.), *Handbook of child psychology: Vol. 2. Cognition, perception, and language* (6th ed., pp. 511–556). Hoboken, NJ: Wiley.

Pressman, S. D., & Cohen, S. (2005). Does positive affect influence health? *Psychological Bulletin, 131*(6), 925–971.

Prinstein, M. J., & Aikins, J. W. (2004). Cognitive moderators of the longitudinal association between peer rejection and adolescent depressive symptoms. *Journal of Abnormal Child Psychology, 32*, 147–158.

Prinstein, M. J., & La Greca, A. M. (2002). Peer crowd affiliation and internalizing distress in childhood and adolescence: A longitudinal follow-back study. *Journal of Research on Adolescence, 12*, 325–351.

Pruchno, R., & Rosenbaum, J. (2003). Social relationships and adulthood in old age. In R. M. Lerner, M. A., Easterbrooks, & J. Mistry (Eds.), *Handbook of Psychology. Vol. 6* (pp. 487–509). Hoboken, NJ: Wiley.

Pruden, S. M., Hirsh-Pasek, K., Golinkoff, R. M., & Hennon, E. A. (2006). The birth of words: Ten-month-olds learn words through perceptual salience. *Child Development, 77*, 266–280.

Pudrovska, T. (2008). Psychological implications of motherhood and fatherhood in midlife: Evidence from sibling models. *Journal of Marriage and Family, 70*(1), 168–181.

Putnam, S. P., Sanson, A. V., & Rothbart, M. K. (2002). Child temperament and parenting. In M. H. Bornstein (Ed.), *Handbook of parenting: Vol. 1. Children and parenting* (2nd ed., pp. 255–277). Mahwah, NJ: Erlbaum.

Putney, N. M., & Bengston, V. L. (2001). Families, intergenerational relationships, and kin keeping in midlife. In M. E. Lachman (Ed.), *Handbook of midlife development* (pp. 528–570). New York: Wiley.

Qaseem, A., Snow, V., Denberg, T. D., Casey D. E., Jr., Forciea, M. A., Owens, D. K., et al. (2009). Hormonal testing and pharmacologic treatment of erectile dysfunction: A clinical practice guideline from the American College of Physicians. *Annals of Internal Medicine, 151*(9), I–44.

Quadrel, M., Fischhoff, B., & Davis, W. (1993). Adolescent (in)vulnerability. *American Psychologist, 48*, 102–116.

Quill, T. E., & Battin, M. P. (Eds.). (2004). *Physician-assisted dying: The case for palliative care and patient choice*. Baltimore, MD: Johns Hopkins University Press.

Raffaelli, M. (1997). Young adolescents' conflicts with siblings and friends. *Journal of Youth and Adolescence, 26*, 539–558.

Raffaelli, M., & Larson, R. (1987). Sibling interactions in late childhood and early adolescence. Paper presented at the biennial meetings of the Society for Research in Child Development, Baltimore.

Raine, A., Loeber, R., Stouthamer-Loeber, M., Moffitt, T. E., Caspi, A., & Lynam, D. (2005). Neurocognitive impairments in boys on the life-course persistent antisocial path. *Journal of Abnormal Psychology, 114*, 38–49.

Rajah, M. N., & D'Esposito, M. (2005). Region-specific changes in prefrontal function with age: A review of PET and fMRI studies on working and episodic memory. *Brain, 128*(9), 1964–1983.

Rakison, D. H., & Oakes, L. M. (2003). Issues in the early development of concepts and categories. In D. H. Rakison & L. M. Oakes (Eds.), *Early category and concept development: Making sense of the blooming, buzzing confusion* (pp. 3–23). Oxford, England: University Press.

Raley, R. K., & Bumpass, L. (2003). The topography of the divorce plateau: Levels and trends in union stability in the United States after 1980. *Demographic Research, 8*(8), 245–259.

Ramey, C. T., & Ramey, S. L. (2004). Early learning and school readiness. *Merrill-Palmer Quarterly, 50*, 471–491.

Ramey, C. T., Campbell, F. A., & Blair, C. (1998). The Abecedarian Project: Long-term effectiveness of educational day care beginning at birth. In J. Crane (Ed.), *Social programs that work* (pp. 163–183). New York: Russell Sage.

Randel, B., Stevenson, H. W., & Witruk, E. (2000). Attitudes, beliefs, and mathematics achievement of German and Japanese high school students. *International Journal of Behavioral Development, 24*, 190–198.

Ranzjin, R., Carson, E., Winefield, A. H., & Price, D. (2006). On the scrap-heap at 45: The human impact of mature-aged unemployment. *Journal of Occupational and Organizational Psychology, 79*(3), 467–479.

Rao, N., & Stewart, S. M. (1999). Cultural influences on sharer and recipient behavior: Sharing in Chinese and Indian preschool children. *Journal of Cross-Cultural Psychology, 30*, 219–241.

Rattan, S. I. S. (2007). The science of healthy aging: Genes, milieu, and chance. *Annals of the New York Academy of Sciences, 1114*(1), 1–10.

Rauh, H., Ziegenhain, U., Müller, B., & Wijnroks, L. (2000). Stability and change in infant-mother attachment in the second year of life: Relations to parenting quality and varying degrees of day-care experience. In P. M. Crittenden & A. H. Claussen (Eds.), *The organization of attachment relationships: Maturation, culture, and context* (pp. 251–276). New York: Cambridge University Press.

Raz, N. (2000). Aging of the brain and its impact on cognitive performance: Integration of structural and functional findings. In F. I. M. Craik & T. A. Salthouse (Eds.), *The Handbook of aging and cognition* (2nd ed, pp. 1–90). Mahwah, NJ: Lawrence Erlbaum.

Raz, N., & Rodrigue, K. M. (2006). Differential aging of the brain: Patterns, cognitive correlates and modifiers. *Neuroscience and Biobehavioral Reviews, 30*(6), 730–748.

Raz, N., Rodrigue, K. M., Kennedy, K. M., & Acker, J. D. (2007). Vascular health and longitudinal changes in brain and cognition in middle-aged and older adults. *Neuropsychology, 21*(2), 149–157.

Reed, E., Amaro, H., Matsumoto, A., & Kaysen, D. (2009). The relation between interpersonal violence and substance use among a sample of university students: Examination of the role of victim and perpetrator substance use. *Addictive Behaviors, 34*(3), 316–318.

Regan, P. C., & Berscheid, E. (1996). Beliefs about the states, goals, and objects of sexual desire. *Journal of Sex and Marital Therapy, 22*(2), 110–120.

Reich, K., Oser, F., & Valentin, P. (1994). Knowing why I now know better: Children's and youth's explanations of their worldview changes. *Journal of Research on Adolescence, 4*, 151–173.

Reich, W. T. (1978). *Encyclopedia of bioethics* (Vol. 1). New York: Free Press.

Reichenberg, A., Gross, R., Weiser, M., Bresnahan, M., Silverman, J., Harlap, S. et al. (2006). Advancing paternal age and autism. *Archives of General Psychiatry, 63,* 1026–1032.

Reime, B., Schücking, B. A., & Wenzlaff, P. (2008). Reproductive outcomes in adolescebnts who had a previous birth or an induced abortion compared to adolescents' first pregnancies. *BMC Pregnancy and Childbirth, 8,* 4.

Reimer, M. (1996). "Sinking into the ground": The development and consequences of shame in adolescence. *Developmental Review, 16,* 321–363.

Reitzes, D. C., & Mutran, E. J. (2004). Grandparent identity, intergenerational family identity, and well-being. *The Journal of Gerontology: Social Sciences, 59*(4), S213–S219.

Reitzes, D., & Mutran, E. (2004). The transition to retirement: Stages and factors that influence retirement adjustment. *The International Journal of Aging and Human Development, 59*(1), 63–84.

Renzulli, J. S. (1986). The three-ring conception of giftedness: A developmental model for creative productivity. In R. J. Sternberg & J. E. Davidson (Eds.), *Conceptions of giftedness* (pp. 53–92). New York: Cambridge University Press.

Retsinas, J. (1988). A theoretical reassessment of the applicability of Kübler-Ross's stages of dying. *Death Studies, 12*(3), 207–216.

Reuter-Lorenz, P. A., & Lustig, C. (2005). Brain aging: Reorganizing discoveries about the aging mind. *Current Opinion in Neurobiology, 15*(2), 245–251.

Reuter-Lorenz, P. A., Jonides, J., Smith, E. E., Hartley, A., Miller, A., Marshuetz, C., et al. (2000). Age differences in the frontal lateralization of verbal and spatial working memory revealed by PET. *Journal of Cognitive Neuroscience, 12*(1), 174–187.

Revenson, T. A., & Johnson, J. L. (1984). Social and demographic correlates of loneliness in late life. *American Journal of Community Psychology, 12*(1), 71–85.

Reyna, V. F., & Farley, F. (2006). Risk and rationality in adolescent decision making: Implications for theory, practice, and public policy. *Psychological Science in the Public Interest, 7*(1), 1–44

Reynolds, A. (2003). The added value of continuing early intervention into the primary grades. In A. J. Reynolds, M. C. Wang, & H. J. Walberg (Eds.), *Early childhood programs for a new century* (pp. 163–196). Washington, DC: CWLA Press.

Reynolds, A. J., Temple, J. A., Robertson, D. L., & Mann, E. A. (2001). Long-term effects of an early childhood intervention on educational achievement and juvenile arrest: A 15-year follow-up of low-income children in public schools. *Journal of the American Medical Association, 285,* 2339–2346.

Reynolds, G. D. & Richards, J. E. (2005). Familiarization, attention, and recognition memory in infancy: An event-related potential and cortical source localization study. *Developmental Psychology, 41,* 598–615.

Reynolds, J., Stewart, M., MacDonald, R., & Sischo, L. (2006). Have adolescents become too ambitious? High school seniors' educational and occupational plans, 1976 to 2000. *Social Problems, 53*(2), 186–206.

Rhodes, S. R. (1983). Age-related differences in work attitudes and behavior: A review and conceptual analysis. *Psychological Bulletin, 93*(2), 328–367.

Rhodes, T., Girman C. J., Savin, R. C., Kaufman, K. D., Guo, S., Lilly, F. R., Siervogel, R. M., & Chumlea, W. C. (1998). Prevalence of male pattern hair loss in 18–49 year old men. *Dermatologic Surgery, 24,* 1330–1332.

Rich, L. M., & Kim, S.-B. (2002). Employment and the sexual and reproductive behavior of female adolescents. *Perspectives on Sexual and Reproductive Health, 34*(3), 127–134.

Richard, J. F., Normandeau, J., Brun, V., & Maillet, M. (2004). Attracting and maintaining infant attention during habituation: Further evidence of the importance of stimulus complexity. *Infant and Child Development, 13,* 277–286.

Richards, M. H., & Larson, R. (1989). The life space and socialization of the self: Sex Differences in the Young Adolescent. *Journal of Youth and Adolescence, 18,* 617–626.

Richards, M., & Larson, R. (1993). Pubertal development and the daily subjective states of young adolescents. *Journal of Research on Adolescence, 3,* 145–169.

Rickford, J. R., & Rickford, R. J. (2000). *Spoken soul: The story of Black English.* Hoboken, NJ: Wiley.

Ridgeway, D., Waters, E., & Kuczaj, S. A. (1985). Acquisition of emotional-descriptive language: Receptive and productive norms for ages 18 months to 6 years. *Developmental Psychology, 21,* 901–908.

Ridley, M. (2003). *Nature via nurture: Genes, experience, and what makes us human.* HarperCollins.

Riediger, M., Freund, A. M., & Baltes, P. B. (2005). Managing life through personal goals: Intergoal facilitation and intensity of goal pursuit in younger and older adulthood. *Journal of Gerontology B: Psychological Sciences and Social Sciences, 60B (2),* P84–91.

Riediger, M., Lindenberger, U., Li, S-C., Baltes, P. B., & Ebner, N. C. (2004). Research Project 4: Selection, optimization, and compensation (SOC): Regulation of goals and preferences in lifespan development. In the Annual Report 2004, Center for Lifespan Psychology, Max Plank Institute. Retrieved from http://www.baltes-paul.de/SOC.html; http://www.baltes-paul.de/LIP_annual_report_2004.pdf

Riegel, K. F. (1973). Dialectic operations: The final period of cognitive development. *Human Development, 16*(5), 346–370.

Rigby, K. (2002). Bullying in childhood. In P. K. Smith & C. H. Hart (Eds.), *Blackwell handbook of childhood social development* (pp. 549–568). Malden, MA: Blackwell.

Riley, M. W., & Riley, J. W., Jr. (1994). Structural lag: Past and future. In M. W. Riley, R. L. Kahn, & A. Foner (Eds.) *Age and structural lag: Society's failure to provide meaningful opportunities in work, family, and leisure.* New York: Wiley.

Rimm-Kaufman, S. E., Pianta, R. C., & Cox, M. J. (2000). Teachers' judgments of success in the transition to kindergarten. *Early Childhood Research Quarterly, 15,* 147–166.

Ritter, K. (1978). The development of knowledge of an external retrieval cue strategy. *Child Development, 49,* 1227–1230.

Rivkees, Scott A. (2004). Developing circadian rhythmicity in infants. *Pediatrics, 112,* 373–381.

Rizzo, T. A. (1989). *Friendship development among children in school.* Norwood, NJ: Ablex.

Rizzolatti, G., et al. (1996). Premotor cortex and the recognition of motor actions. *Cognitive Brain Research, 3,* 131–141.

Roberto, K. A, & Stroes, J. (1992). Grandchildren and grandparents: Roles, influences, and relationships. *The International Journal of Aging and Human Development, 34*(3), 227–239.

Roberto, K. A., & Skoglund, R. R. (1996). Interactions with grandparents and great-grandparents: A comparison of activities, influences, and relationships. *International Journal of Aging And Human Development, 43*(2), 107–117.

Roberts B. W., & Caspi, A. (2003). The cumulative continuity model of personality development: Striking a balance between continuity and change in personality traits across the life course. In U. M. Staudinger, U. Lindenberger (Eds). *Understanding human development: Lifespan psychology in exchange with other disciplines* (pp. 183–214). Dordrecht, the Netherlands: Kluwer Academic.

Roberts, B. W., & DelVecchio, W. F. (2000). The rank-order consistency of personality traits from childhood to old age: A quantitative review of longitudinal studies. *Psychological Bulletin, 126*(1), 3–25.

Roberts, B. W., & Wood, D. (2006). Personality development in the context of the Neo-Socioanalytic Model of personality. In D. Mroczek, & T. Little (Eds.), *Handbook of personality development* (pp. 11–39). Mahwah, NJ: Erlbaum.

Roberts, B. W., O'Donnell, M., & Robins, R. W. (2004). Goal and personality development in the emerging adulthood. *Journal of Personality and Social Psychology, 87*, 541–550.

Roberts, B. W., Walton, K. E., & Viechtbauer, W. (2006). Patterns of mean-level change in personality traits across the life course: A meta-analysis of longitudinal studies. *Psychological Bulletin, 132*(1), 1–25.

Roberts, B., W., Caspi, A., & Moffit, T. E. (2003). Work experiences and personality development in young adulthood. *Journal of Personality and Social Psychology, 84*, 582–593.

Roberts, D. F., & Foehr, U. G. (2004). *Kids and media in America.* New York: Cambridge University Press.

Roberts, D. F., & Foehr, U. G. (2008). Trends in the media use. *The Future of Children, 18*, 1–37.

Roberts, D., Henriksen, L., & Foehr, U. (2004). Adolescents and media. In R. Lerner & L. Steinberg (Eds.), *Handbook of adolescent psychology* (2nd ed., pp. 487–521). New York: Wiley.

Roberts, J. E., Burchinal, M. R., Jackson, S. C., Hooper, S. R., Roush, J., Mundy, M., Neebe, E., & Zeisel, S. A. (2000). Otitis media in early childhood in relation to preschool language and school readiness skills among African American children. *Pediatrics, 106(4)*, 1–11.

Roberts, R., Phinney, J., Masse, L., Chen, Y., Roberts, C., & Romero, A. (1999). The structure of ethnic identity of young adolescents from diverse ethnocultural groups. *Journal of Early Adolescence, 19*, 301–322.

Robertson, S. S., & Bacher, L. F. (1995). Oscillation and chaos in fetal motor activity. *Fetal Development: A Psychobiological Perspective, 10*, 20.

Robine, J. M., & Vaupel, J. W. (2002). Emergence of supercentenarians in low-mortality countries. *North American Actuarial Journal, 6*(3), 54–63.

Robins, R., & Trzesniewski, K. (2005). Self-esteem development across the lifespan. *Current Directions in Psychological Science, 14*(3), 158–162.

Robins, R., Trzesniewski, K., Tracy, J., Gosling, S., & Potter, J. (2002). Global self-esteem across the life span. *Psychology and Aging, 17*(3), 423–434.

Robinson, G. E., & Wisner, K. L. (1993). Fetal anomalies. In D. E. Stewart & N. L. Statland (Eds.), *Psychological aspects of women's health care: The interface between psychiatry and obstetrics and gynecology* (pp. 37–54). Washington, DC: American Psychiatric Association.

Robinson, N., Garber, J., & Hilsman, R. (1995). Cognitions and stress: Direct and moderating effects on depressive versus externalizing symptoms during the junior high school transition. *Journal of Abnormal Psychology, 104*, 453–463.

Robinson, T. N. (1999). Reducing children's television viewing to prevent obesity: A randomized controlled trial. *Journal of the American Medical Association, 282*, 1561–1567.

Robinson-Whelen, S., & Kiecolt-Glaser, J. (1997). The importance of social versus temporal comparison appraisals among older adults. *Journal of Applied Social Psychology, 27*(11), 959–966.

Robles, T. F., Glaser, R., & Kiecolt-Glaser, J. K. (2005). Out of balance. A new look at chronic stress, depression, and immunity. *Current Directions in Psychological Science, 14*(2), 111–115.

Robson, S. M., & Hansson, R. O. (2007). Strategic self-development for successful aging at work. *International Journal of Aging and Human Development, 64*(4), 331–339.

Rochat, P. (1997). Early development of the ecological self. In C. Dent-Read & P. Zukow-Goldring (Eds.), *Evolving explanations of development* (pp. 91–121). Washington, DC: American Psychological Association.

Roebuck, T. M., Mattson, S. N., & Riley, E. P. (1999). Behavioral and psychosocial profiles of alcohol-exposed children. *Alcoholism: Clinical and Experimental Research, 23*, 1070–1076.

Rogoff, B. (2003). *The cultural nature of human development.* New York: Oxford University Press.

Rohner, R. P. (2004). The parental "acceptance-rejection syndrome": Universal correlates of perceived rejection. *American Psychologist, 59*, 830–840.

Roisman, G. I., & Fraley, C. R. (2006). The limits of genetic influence: A behavior-genetic analysis of infant-caregiver relationship quality and temperament. *Child Development, 77*, 1656–1667.

Rokach, A. M. I.,, Matalon, R., Safarov, A., & Bercovitch, M. (2007). The loneliness experience of the dying and of those who care for them. *Palliative and Supportive Care, 5*(2), 153–159.

Rook, K. S. (1984). Promoting social bonding: Strategies for helping the lonely and socially isolated. *American Psychologist, 39*, 1389–1407.

Rook, K. S. (1987). Social support versus companionship: Effects on life stress, loneliness, and evaluations by others. *Journal of Personality and Social Psychology, 52*(6), 1132–1147.

Rook, K. S. (2000). The evolution of social relationships in later adulthood. In S. Qualls & N. Abeles (Eds.), *Psychology and the aging revolution* (pp. 173–191). Washington, DC: American Psychological Association.

Rook, K. S., & Peplau, L. A. (1982). Perspectives on helping the lonely. In L. A. Peplau & D. Perlman (Eds.), *Loneliness: A sourcebook of current theory, research and therapy* (pp. 351–378). New York: Wiley.

Rook, K. S., & Zettel, L. A. (2005). The purported benefits of marriage viewed through the lens of physical health. *Psychological Inquiry, 16*, 116–121.

Rook, K. S., Catalano, R., & Dooley, D. (1989). The timing of major life events: Effects of departing from the social clock. *American Journal of Community Psychology, 17*, 233–258.

Rook, K. S., Charles, S. T., & Heckhausen, J. H. (2006). Aging and health. In H. Friedman & R. C. Silver (Eds.), *Foundations of health psychology* (pp. 234–262). New York: Oxford University Press.

Roschelle, J. M., Pea, R. D., Hoadley, C. M., Gordon, D. N., & Means, B. M. (2000). Changing how and what children learn in school with computer-based technologies. *Children and Computer Technology, 10*, 76–101.

Roseboom, T., de Rooij, S., & Painter, R. (2006). The Dutch famine and its long-term consequences for adult health. *Early Human Development, 82*, 485–491.

Rosen, A. C., Prull, M. W., O'Hara, R., Race, E. A., Desmond, J. E., Glover, G. H., et al. (2002). Variable effects of aging on frontal lobe contributions to memory. *NeuroReport, 13*(18), 2425–2428.

Rosen, B., & D'Andrade, R. (1959). The psychosocial origins of achievement motivation. *Sociometry, 22,* 185–218.

Rosenthal, C. J., Martin-Matthews, A., & Matthews, S. H. (1996). Caught in the middle? Occupancy in multiple roles and help to parents in a national probability sample of Canadian adults. *Journal of Gerontology B: Psychological Sciences and Social Sciences, 51*(6), S274–283.

Rossi, A. S. (2004). The menopausal transition and aging processes. In O. G. Brim, C. D. Ryff, & R. C. Kessler (Eds.), *How healthy are we?: A national study of well-being at midlife* (pp. 153–201). Chicago, IL: University of Chicago Press.

Rossi, A. S., Rossi, P. H. (1990). *Of human bonding: Parent-child relations across the life course.* Hawthorne, NY: Aldine.

Rostad, A., Nyberg, P., & Sivberg, B. (2008). Predicting development deficiences at the age of four based on data from the first seven months of life. *Infant Mental Health Journal, 29,* 588–608.

Rosvold, H. E., Mirsky, A. F., Saranson, I., Bransome, E. D., & Beck, L. H. (1956). A continuous performance test of brain damage. *Journal of Consulting Psychology, 20,* 343–350.

Rothbart, M. K. (2005). Early temperament and psychosocial development. In R. E. Tremblay, R. G. Barr, & R. deV. Peters (Eds.), *Encyclopedia on early childhood development* [online], Montreal, Quebec: Centre of Excellence for Early Childhood Development.

Rothbart, M. K., & Bates, J. E. (2006). Temperament. In W. Damon & R. M. Lerner (Series Eds.) & N. Eisenberg (Vol. Ed.), *Handbook of child psychology: Vol. 3. Social, emotional, and personality development* (6th ed., pp. 99–166). Hoboken NJ: Wiley.

Rothbart, M. K., Posner, M. I., & Kieras, J. (2006). Temperament, attention, and the development of self-regulation. In K. McCartney & D. Phillips (Eds.), *Blackwell handbook of early childhood development* (pp. 338–357). Malden, MA: Blackwell.

Rotheram-Borus, M. (1990). Adolescents' reference group choices, self-esteem, and adjustment. *Journal of Personality and Social Psychology, 59,* 1075–1081.

Rousseau, J. (1911). *Emile* (B. Foxley, trans.). London: Dent. (Original work published 1762.)

Rovee-Collier, C., & Barr, R. (2001). Infant learning and memory. In J. G. Bremner & A. Fogel (Eds.), *Blackwell handbook of infant development* (pp. 139–168). Malden, MA: Blackwell.

Rowe, J. W., & Kahn, R. L. (1998). *Successful aging.* New York: Pantheon.

Rowe, D., Rodgers, J., Meseck-Bushey S., & St. John, C. (1989). Sexual behavior and nonsexual deviance: A sibling study of their relationship. *Developmental Psychology, 25,* 61–69.

Rowe, J. W. (1997). The new gerontology. *Science, 278,* 367.

Rowe, J. W., & Kahn, R. L. (1998). *Successful aging.* New York: Pantheon.

Rozin, P., Bauer, R., & Catanese, D. (2003). Food and life, pleasure and worry, among American college students: Gender differences and regional similarities. *Journal of Personality and Social Psychology, 85,* 132–141.

Rozow, I. (1967). *Social integration of the aged.* New York: Free Press.

Rubin, K. H., Bukowski, W. M., & Parker, J. G. (2006). Peer interactions, relationships, and groups. In W. Damon & R. M. Lerner (Series Eds.), & N. Eisenberg (Vol. Ed.), *Handbook of child psychology: Vol. 3. Social, emotional, and personality development* (6th ed., pp. 571–645). Hoboken, NJ: Wiley.

Rubin, K. H., Burgess, K. B., & Coplan, R. J. (2002). Social withdrawal and shyness. In P. K. Smith & C. H. Hart (Eds.), *Blackwell handbook of childhood social development* (pp. 330–352). Malden, MA: Blackwell Publishers.

Rubin, K. H., Burgess, K. B., Dwyer, K. M., & Hastings, P. D. (2003). Predicting preschoolers' externalizing behaviors from toddler temperament, conflict, and maternal negativity. *Developmental Psychology, 39,* 164–176.

Rubin, S. S., & Malkinson, R. (2001). Parental response to child loss across the life cycle: Clinical and research perspectives. In M. S. Stroebe, R. O. Hansson, & W. Stroebe (Eds.), *Handbook of bereavement research: Consequences, coping, and care* (pp. 219–240). Washington, DC: American Psychological Association.

Rubin, Z. (1973). *Liking and loving.* New York: Holt, Rinehart, & Winston.

Ruble, D. N., & Martin, C. L. (1998). Gender development. In W. Damon (Series Ed.) & N. Eisenberg (Vol. Ed.), *Handbook of child psychology: Vol. 3. Personality and social development* (5th ed., pp. 933–1016). New York: Wiley.

Ruble, D. N., Martin, C. L., & Berenbaum, S. A. (2006). Gender development. In W. Damon & R. Lerner (Series Eds.) & D. Kuhn & R. S. Siegler (Vol. Eds.), *Handbook of child psychology: Vol. 2. Cognition, perception, and language* (6th ed., pp. 858–932). Hoboken, NJ: Wiley.

Rudman, L. A., Ashmore, R. D., & Gary, M. L. (2001). " Unlearning" automatic biases: The malleability of implicit prejudice and stereotypes. *Journal of Personality and Social Psychology, 81*(5), 856–868.

Rudolph, K., & Hammen, C. (1999). Age and gender as determinants of stress exposure, generation, & reactions in youngsters: A transactional perspective. *Child Development, 70,* 660–677.

Rueter, M. A., & Kwon, H. (2005). Developmental trends in adolescent suicidal ideation. *Journal of Research on Adolescence, 15,* 205–222.

Rueter, M., & Conger, R. (1995a). Interaction style, problem-solving behavior, and family problem-solving effectiveness. *Child Development, 66,* 98–115.

Rueter, M., & Conger, R. (1995b). Antecedents of parent-adolescent disagreements. *Journal of Marriage and the Family, 57,* 435–448.

Ruff, H. A. (1982). Infants' exploration of objects. *Infant Behavior and Development, 5,* 207.

Ruff, H. A. (1985). Detection of information specifying the motion of objects by 3- and 5-month-old infants. *Developmental Psychology, 21,* 295–305.

Ruff, H. A., & Capozzoli, M. C. (2003). Development of attention and distractibility in the first four years of life. *Developmental Psychology, 39,* 877–890.

Ruiz, S. A., & Silverstein, M. (2007). Relationships with grandparents and the emotional well-being of late adolescent and young adult grandchildren. *Journal of Social Issues, 63*(4), 793–808.

Rumberger, R. (1995). Dropping out of middle school: A Multilevel analysis of students and schools. *American Educational Research Journal, 32,* 583–625.

Rumberger, R., & Larson, K. (1998). Student mobility and the increased risk of high school dropout. *American Journal of Education, 107,* 1–35.

Russell, A., Mize, J., & Bissaker, K. (2002). Parent-child relationships. In P. K. Smith & C. H. Hart (Eds.), *Blackwell handbook of childhood social development* (pp. 205–222). Malden, MA: Blackwell.

Rutstein, R. M., Conlon, C. J., & Batshaw, M. L. (1998). HIV and AIDS: From mother to child. In M. L. Batshaw (Ed.), *Children with disabilities* (4th ed., pp. 163–181). Baltimore, MD: Brookes Publishing.

Rutter, M. (1983). School effects on pupil progress: Research findings and policy implications. *Child Development, 54,* 1–29.

Rutter, M. (2006). *Genes and behaviour: Nature-nurture interplay explained.* London: Blackwell.

Rutter, M., & Garmezy, N. (1983). Developmental psychopathology. In E. M. Hetherington (Ed.), *Handbook of child psychology: Vol. 4. Socialization, personality, and social development* (pp. 775–911). New York: Wiley.

Ryalls, B. O., Gull, R. E., & Ryalls, K. R. (2000). Infant imitation of peer and adult models: Evidence for a peer model advantage. *Merrill-Palmer-Quarterly, 46,* 188–202.

Ryff, C. (1991). Possible selves in adulthood and old age: A tale of shifting horizons. *Psychology and Aging, 6*(2), 286–295.

Ryff, C. D. (1989). Happiness is everything, or is it? Explorations on the meaning of psychological well-being. *Journal of Personality and Social Psychology, 57,* 1069–1081.

Ryu, M. (2009). *Minorities in higher education. Twenty-third status report. 2009 supplement.* Washington, DC: American Council on Education. Retrieved January 6, 2010 from http://www.acenet.edu/AM/Template.cfm?Section=CAREE&Template=/CM/ContentDisplay.cfm&ContentID=34214

S. T. Fiske, & G. Lindzey (Eds.), *The handbook of social psychology:* (4th ed., Vol. 2, pp. 982–1026). New York: McGraw-Hill.

Saarni, C. (2000). Emotional competence: A developmental perspective. In R. Bar-On & J. D. A. Parker (Eds.), *The handbook of emotional intelligence: Theory, development, assessment, and application at home, school, and in the workplace* (pp. 68–91). San Francisco: Jossey-Bass.

Saarni, C., Campos, J. J., Camras, L. A., & Witherington, D. (2006). Emotional development: Action, communication, and understanding. In W. Damon & R. Lerner (Series Eds.) & D. Kuhn & R. S. Siegler (Vol. Eds.), *Handbook of child psychology: Vol. 2. Cognition, perception, and language* (6th ed., pp. 226–299). Hoboken, NJ: Wiley.

Saarni, C., Mumme, D. L., & Campos, J. J. (1998). Emotional development: Action, communication, and understanding. In W. Damon & N. Eisenberg (Eds.), *Handbook of child psychology: Vol 3. Social, emotional, and personality development* (5th ed., pp. 237–309). Hoboken, NJ: Wiley.

Sabatini, M., Ebert, P., Lewis, D., Levitt, P., Cameron, J., & Mirnics, K. (2007). Amygdala gene expression correlates of social behavior in monkeys experiencing maternal separation. *Journal of Neuroscience, 27,* 3295–3304.

Saffran, J. R., Werker, J. F., & Werner, L. A. (2006). The infant's auditory world: Hearing, speech, and the beginnings of language. In W. Damon & R. Lerner (Series Eds.) & D. Kuhn & R. Siegler (Vol. Eds.), *Handbook of child psychology: Vol. 2. Cognition, Perception, and language* (6th ed., pp. 58–108). Hoboken, NJ: Wiley.

Saffrey, C., & Ehrenberg, M. (2007). When thinking hurts: Attachment, rumination, and postrelationship adjustment. *Personal Relationships, 14,* 351–368.

Safron, J., Sy, S., & Schulenberg, J. (2003). Wishing to work: New perspectives on how adolescents' part-time work intensity is linked to educational disengagement, substance use, and other problem behaviours. *International Journal of Behavioral Development, 27,* 301–315.

Sagi, A. (1981). Mothers' and non-mothers' identification of infant cries. *Infant Behavior & Development, 4,* 37–40.

Sagi, A., Koren-Karie, N., Gini, M., Ziv, Y., & Joels, T. (2002). Shedding further light on the effects of various types and quality of early child care on infant-mother attachment relationship: The Haifa Study of Early Child Care. *Child Development, 73,* 1166–1186.

Saigal, S. (2000). Follow-up of very low birthweight babies to adolescence. *Seminars in Neonatology, 5,* 107–118.

Saigal, S., Hoult, L., Streiner, D., Stoskopf, B., & Rosenbaum, P. (2000). School difficulties at adolescence in a regional cohort of children who were extremely low birth weight. *Pediatrics, 105,* 325–331.

Sakai, K. L. (2005). Language acquisition and brain development. *Science, 310,* 815–819.

Sale, E., Sambrano, S., Springer, J. F., Peña, C., Pan, W., & Kasim, R. (2005). Family protection and prevention of alcohol use among Hispanic youth at high risk. *American Journal of Community Psychology, 36,* 195–205.

Salmon, D. P. (2000). Disorders of memory in Alzheimer's disease. In L. S. Cermak (Ed.), *Handbook of neuropsychology: Vol 2. Memory and its disorders* (2nd ed., pp. 155–195). Amsterdam: Elsevier.

Salovey, P., & Mayer, J. D. (1990). Emotional intelligence. Imagination, *Cognition, and Personality, 9,* 185–211.

Saltaris, C., Serbin, L. A., Stack, D. M., Karp, J. A., Schwartzman, A. E., & Ledingham, J. E. (2004). Nurturing cognitive competence in preschoolers: A longitudinal study of intergenerational continuity and risk. *International Journal of Behavioral Development, 28,* 105–115.

Salthouse, T. A. (1984). Effects of age and skill in typing. *Journal of Experimental Psychology: General, 113*(3), 345–371.

Salthouse, T. A. (1996). The processing-speed theory of adult age differences in cognition. *Psychological Review, 103*(3), 403–428.

Salthouse, T. A. (2004). What and when of cognitive aging. *Current Directions in Psychological Science, 13*(4), 140–144.

Saluter, A. F., & Lugala, T. A. (1998). *Marital status and living arrangements: March 1996* (Current Populations Reports, Series P20–496). Washington, D.C.: U.S. Bureau of the Census.

Samuelsson, S., Alfredson, B., Hagberg, B., Samuelsson, G., Nordbeck, B., Brun, A., et al. (1997). The Swedish Centenarian Study: A multidisciplinary study of five consecutive cohorts at the age of 100. *International Journal of Aging and Human Development, 45*(3), 223–253.

Samuelsson, S., Finnström, O. Flodmark, O., Gäddlin, P.-O., Leijon, I., & Wadsby, M. (2006). A longitudinal study of reading skills among very-low-birthweight children: Is there a catch-up? *Journal of Pediatric Psychology, 31,* 967–977.

Sander, T. H., & Putnam, R. (2006). Social capital and civic engagement of individuals over age fifty in the United States. In L. Wilson & S. Simson (Eds.), *Civic engagement and the baby boomer generation: Research, policy and practice perspectives* (pp. 21–41). New York: Haworth Press.

Sandstrom, M. J., & Coie, J. D. (1999). A developmental perspective on peer rejection: Mechanisms of stability and change. *Child Development, 70,* 955–966.

Sansavini, A., Guarini, A., Alessandroni, R., Faldella, G., Giovanelli, G. & Salvioli, G. (2006). Early relations between lexical and grammatical development in very immature Italian preterms. *Journal of Child Language, 33,* 199–216.

Santelli, J. S., Lindberg, L., Abma, J., McNeely, C., & Resnick, M. (2000). Adolescent sexual behavior: Estimates and trends from four nationally representative surveys. *Family Planning Perspectives, 32,* 156–165.

Santelli, J., Warren, C., Lowry, R., Sogolow, E., Collins, J., Kann, L., et al. (1997). The use of condoms with other contraceptive methods among young men and women. *Family Planning Perspectives, 29,* 261–267.

Saunders, C. (2000). The evolution of palliative care. *Patient Education and Counseling, 41*(1), 7–13.

Savickas, M. L. (2001). Toward a comprehensive theory of career development: Dispositions, concerns, and narratives. In F. T. L. Leong & A. Barak (Eds.), *Contemporary models in vocational psychology: A volume in honor of Samuel H. Osipow* (pp. 295–320). Mahwah, NJ: Erlbaum.

Savin-Williams, R., & Diamond, L. (2004). Sex. In R. Lermer & L. Steinberg (Eds.), *Handbook of adolescent psychology* (pp. 189–231). New York: Wiley.

Saw, S-M, Chua, W-H, Hong, C-Y, Wu, H-M, Chan, W-Y, Chia, K-S, et al. (2002). Nearwork in early-onset myopia. *Investigative Ophthalmology and Visual Science, 43,* 332–339.

Saxe, G. B. (1991). *Culture and cognitive development: Studies in mathematical understanding.* Hillsdale, NJ: Erlbaum.

Scarr, S., & McCartney, K. (1983). How people make their own environments: A theory of genotype-environment effects. *Child Development, 54,* 424–435.

Scarr, S., & Weinberg, R. (1983). The Minnesota adoption studies: Genetic differences and malleability. *Child Development, 54,* 260–267.

Scarr, S., Weinberg, R., & Levine, A. (1986). *Understanding development.* San Diego: Harcourt.

Schacter, D. L., & Tulving, E. (1994). What are the memory systems of 1994? In D. L. Schacter, & E. Tulving (Eds.), *Memory systems 1994* (pp. 1–38). Cambridge, MA: MIT Press.

Schafer, G., & Plunkett, K. (1998). Rapid word learning by fifteen-month-olds under tightly controlled conditions. *Child Development, 6,* 309–320.

Schlagmuller, M., & Schneider, W. (2002). The development of organizational strategies in children: Evidence from a microgenetic longitudinal study. *Journal of Experimental Child Psychology, 81,* 298–319.

Schaie, K. W. (1958). Rigidity-flexibility and intelligence: A cross-sectional study of the adult life span from 20 to 70 years. Psychological Monographs, 72(9, Whole No. 462).

Schaie, K. W. (1994). The course of adult intellectual development. *American Psychologist, 49*(4), 304–313.

Schaie, K. W. (1996). *Intellectual development in adulthood: The Seattle Longitudinal Study.* New York: Cambridge University Press.

Schaie, K. W. (2005). *Developmental influences on adult intelligence: The Seattle Longitudinal Study.* New York: Oxford University Press.

Schaie, K. W., & Willis, S. L. (1986). Can decline in adult intellectual functioning be reversed? *Developmental Psychology, 22*(2), 223–232.

Schama, K. F., Howell, L. L., & Byrd, L. D. (1998). Prenatal exposure to cocaine. In S. T. Higgins & J. L. Katz (Eds.), *Cocaine abuse, behavior, pharmacology, and clinical applications* (pp. 159–179). New York: Academic Press.

Scharf, M., Shulman, S., & Avigad-Spitz, L. (2005). Sibling relationships in emerging adulthood and in adolescence. *Journal of Adolescent Research, 20,* 64–90.

Schellenbach, C., Whitman, T., & Borkowski, J. (1992). Toward an integrative model of adolescent parenting. *Human Development, 35,* 81–99.

Scher, A., Epstein, R., & Tirosh, E. (2004). Stability and changes in sleep regulation: A longitudinal study from 3 months to 3 years. *International Journal of Behavioral Development, 28,* 268–274.

Scherling, D. (1994). Prenatal cocaine exposure and childhood psychopathology: a developmental analysis. *American Journal of Orthopsychiatry, 64,* 9–19.

Schieber, F. (2006). Vision and aging. In J. E. Birren & K. W. Schaie (Eds.), *Handbook of the psychology of aging* (pp. 129–161). San Diego, CA: Academic Press.

Schiffman, S. S. (1997). Taste and smell losses in normal aging and disease. *Journal of the American Medical Association, 278*(16), 1357–1362.

Schiller, J. S., & Bernadel, L. (2004). Summary health statistics for the U.S. population: National Health Interview Survey, 2002. *Vital and Health Statistics, 10*(220). Hyattsville, MD: National Center for Health Statistics.

Schlegel, A., & Barry, H. (1991). *Adolescence: An anthropological inquiry.* New York: Free Press.

Schlossberg, N. K. (2004). *Retire smart, retire happy: Finding your true path in life.* Washington, DC: American Psychological Association.

Schmader, T., Johns, M., & Forbes, C. (2008). An integrated process model of stereotype threat effects on performance. *Psychological Review, 115*(2), 336–356.

Schmidt, M. E. & Vandewater, E. W. (2008). Electronic media and learning and achievement. *The Future of Children, 18,* 63–86.

Schneider, B. A., & Pichora-Fuller, M. K. (2000). Implications of perceptual deterioration for cognitive aging research. In F. I. M. Craik & T. A. Salthouse (Eds.). *The handbook of aging and cognition* (2nd ed., pp. 155–219). Mahwah, NJ: Lawrence Erlbaum.

Schneider, B. H. (2000). *Friends and enemies: Peer relations in childhood.* London: Oxford University Press.

Schneider, B. H., Atkinson, L., & Tardif, C. (2001). Child parent attachment and children's peer relations: A quantitative review. *Developmental Psychology, 37,* 86–100.

Schneider, B., & Stevenson, D. (1999). *The ambitious generation: American's teenagers, motivated but directionless.* New Haven, CT: Yale University Press.

Schneider, W. (2004). Memory development in children. In U. Goswami (Ed.), *Blackwell handbook of cognitive development* (pp. 236–256). Malden, MA: Blackwell Publishing.

Schneider, W., Gruber, H., Gold, A., & Opwis, K. (1993). Chess expertise and memory for chess positions in children and adults. *Journal of Experimental Child Psychology, 56,* 328–349.

Schnittker, J. (2007). Look (closely) at all the lonely people: Age and the social psychology of social support. *Journal of Aging and Health, 19*(4), 659–682.

Schochet, T., Kelley, A., & Landry, C. (2004). Differential behavioral effects of nicotine exposure in adolescent and adult rats. *Psychopharmacology, 175,* 265–273.

Schochet, T., Kelley, A., & Landry, C. (2005). Differential expression of arc mRNA and other plasticity-related genes induced by nicotine in adolescent rat forebrain. *Neuroscience, 135,* 285–297.

Schoenborn, C. A., Adams, P. F., & Barnes, P. M. *Body weight status of adults: United States, 1997–1998. Advanced data from vital and health statistics; no. 330.* Hyattsville, MD: National Center for Health Statistics.

Schooler, C. (1984). Psychological effects of complex environments during the life span: A review and theory. *Intelligence, 8*(4), 259–281.

Schooler, C., Mulatu, M. S., & Oates, G. (1999). The continuing effects of substantively complex work on the intellectual functioning of older workers, *Psychology and Aging, 14*(3), 483–506.

Schooler, C., Mulatu, M. S., & Oates, G. (2004). Occupational self-direction, intellectual functioning, and self-directed orientation in older workers: Findings and implications for individuals and societies. *American Journal of Sociology, 110*(1), 161–197.

Schretlen, D., Pearlson, G. D., Anthony, J. C., Aylward, E. H., Augustine, A. M., Davis, A., et al. (2000). Elucidating the contributions of processing speed, executive ability and frontal lob volume to normal age-related differences in fluid intelligence. *Journal of the International Neuropsychological Society, 6*(1), 52–61.

Schroeder, D. B., Martorell, R., Rivera, J. A., Ruel, M. T., & Habicht, J. (1995). Age differences in the impact of nutritional supplementation on growth. *Journal of Nutrition, 125,* 1051S–1059S.

Schuetze, P., & Eiden, R. D. (2005). The association between maternal smoking and secondhand exposure and autonomic functioning at 2–4 weeks of age. *Infant Behavior & Development, 29,* 32–43.

Schulenberg, J. E., Bryant, A. L., & Schulenberg, J. E. (2004). Taking hold of some kind of life: How developmental tasks relate to trajectories of well-being during the transition to adulthood. *Development and Psychopathology, 16*(4), 1119–1140

Schulenberg, J. E., O'Malley, P. M., Bachman, J. G., & Johnston, L. D. (2005). Early adult transitions and their relation to well-being and substance use. In R. A. Settersten, F. F. Furstenberg, & R. G. Rumbaut, (Eds.), *On the frontier of adulthood: Theory, research, and public policy* (pp. 417–453). Chicago, IL: University of Chicago Press.

Schultz, R. R., & Curnow, C. (1988). Peak performance and age among superathletes: Track and field, swimming, baseball, tennis, and golf. *Journal of Gerontology B: Psychological and Social Sciences, 43*(5), P113–P120.

Schulz, R., O'Brien, A. T., Bookwala, J., & Fleissner, K. (1995). Psychiatric and physical morbidity effects of dementia caregiving: Prevalence, correlates, and causes. *Gerontologist, 35*(6), 771–791.

Schwartz , A. N. (1977). *Survival handbook for children of aging parents.* New York: Follett.

Schwartz, C. E., Wright, C. I., Shin, L. M., Kagan, J., & Rauch, S. L. (2003). Inhibited and uninhibited infants "grown up": Adult amygdalar response to novelty. *Science, 300,* 1952–1953.

Schwartz, D., Farver, J. M., Chang, L., & Lee-Shin, Y. (2002). Victimization in South Korean children's peer groups. *Journal of Abnormal Child Psychology, 30,* 113–125.

Schweinhart, L. J., Barnes, H. V., & Weikart, D. P. (1993). *Significant benefits: The Perry Preschool Study Through Age 27.* Ypsilanti, MI: High/Scope Press.

Schweinhart, L. J., Montie, J., Xiang, Z., Barnett, W. S., Belfield, C. R., & Nores, M. (2005). Lifetime effects: The High/Scope Perry Preschool study through age 40. *Monographs of the High/Scope Educational Research Foundation, 14.* Ypsilanti, MI: High/Scope Press.

Schwimmer, J. B., Burwinkle, T. M., & Varni, J. W. (2003). Health-related quality of life of severely obese children and adolescents. *Journal of the American Medical Association, 289,* 1813–1819.

Seale, C. (2000). Changing patterns of death and dying. *Social Science & Medicine, 51*(6), 917–930.

Searight, H. R., & Gafford, J. (2005). Cultural diversity at the end of life: Issues and guidelines for family physicians. *American Family Physician, 71*(3), 515–522.

Seeman, T. E., Singer, B. H., Rowe, J. W., Horwitz, R. I., & McEwen. B. S. (1997). Price of adaptation—allostatic load and its health consequences: MacArthur studies of successful aging. *Archives of Internal Medicine, 157*(19), 2259–2268.

Segal, N. L., McGuire, S. A., Havlena, J., Gill, P., & Hershberger, S. L. (2007). Intellectual similarity of virtual twin pairs: Developmental trends. *Personality and Individual Differences, 42,* 1209–1219.

Segalowitz, S. J., & Davies, P. L. (2004). Charting the maturation of the frontal lobe: An electrophysiological strategy. *Brain and Cognition, 55,* 116–133.

Selfhout, M., Denissen, J., Branje, S., & Meeus, W. (2009). In the eye of the beholder: Perceived, actual, and peer-rated similarity in personality, communication, and friendship intensity during the acquaintanceship process. *Journal of Personality and Social Psychology, 96*(6), 1152–1165.

Sellers, R. M., Copeland-Linder, N., Martin, P. P., & Lewis, R. L. (2006). Racial identity matters: The relationship between racial discrimination and psychological functioning in African American Adolescents. *Journal of Research on Adolescence, 16,* 187–216.

Seltzer, J. A. (2004). Cohabitation in the United States and Britain: Demography, kinship and the future. *Journal of Marriage and Family, 66*(4), 921–928.

Selye, H. (1983). The stress concept: Past, present, and future. In C. L. Cooper (Ed.), *Stress research: Issues for the 80s.* New York: Wiley.

Serbin, L. A., Poulin-Dubois, D., & Eichstedt, J. A. (2002). Infant's response to gender inconsistent events. *Journal of Infancy, 3,* 531–542.

Sethi, S., & Nolen-Hoeksema, S. (1997). Gender differences in internal and external focusing among adolescents. *Sex Roles, 37,* 687–700.

Settersten, R. A. (2003). Age structuring and the rhythm of the life course. In J. T. Mortimer & M. J. Shanahan (Eds.), *Handbook of the life course* (pp. 81–98). New York: Springer.

Settersten, R. A., & Hagestad, G. O. (1996a). What's the latest? Cultural age deadlines for family transitions. *The Gerontologist, 36,* 178–188.

Settersten, R. A., & Hagestad, G. O. (1996b). What's the latest? Cultural age deadlines for educational and work transitions. *The Gerontologist, 36,* 602–613.

Shackelford, T. K., Schmitt, D. P., & Buss, D. M. (2005). Universal dimensions of human mate preferences. *Personality and Individual Differences, 39,* 447–458.

Shanas, E. (1979). Social myth as hypothesis: The case of the family relations of old people. *Gerontologist, 19*(1), 3–9.

Shanas, E. (1979). The family as a social support system in old age. *The Gerontologist, 19*(2), 169–174.

Shapiro, A. (2003). Later-life divorce and parent-adult child contact and proximity: A longitudinal analysis. *Journal of Family Issues, 24*(2), 264–285.

Shapiro, A. F., Gottman, J. M., & Carrère, S. (2000). The baby and the marriage: Identifying factors that buffer against decline in marital satisfaction after the first baby arrives. *Journal of Family Psychology, 14*(1), 59–70.

Sharkey, P. (2009). *Neighborhoods and the black-white mobility gap.* Economic Mobility Project. Washington, DC: The Pew Charitable Trusts.

Sharma, G., & Goodwin, J. (2006). Effect of aging on respiratory system physiology and immunology. *Clinical Interventions in Aging, 1*(3), 253–260.

Sharpee, T. O., Sugihara, H., Kurgansky, A. V., Rebrik, S. P., Stryker, M. P., & Miller, K. D. (2006). Adaptive filtering enhances information transmission in visual cortex. *Nature, 439,* 936–942.

Shatz, M., & Gelman, R. (1973). The development of communication skills: Modifications in the speech of young children as a function of listener. *Monographs of the Society for Research in Child Development, 38*(5), 1–38.

Shaver P. R., & Mikulincer, M. (2002). Attachment-related psychodynamics. *Attachment and Human Development, 4,* 133–161.

Shaver, P. R., & Mikulincer, M. (2006). Attachment theory, individual psychodynamics, and relationship functioning. In A. L. Vangelisti & D. Perlman (Eds.), *The Cambridge handbook of personal relationships* (pp. 252–271). Cambridge: Cambridge University Press.

Shaw, B. A., Krause, N., Chatters, L. M., Connell, C. M., & Ingersoll-Dayton, B. (2004). Emotional support from parents early in life, aging, and health. *Psychology and Aging, 19,* 4–12.

Shaw, M., & White, D. (1965). The relationship between child-parent identification and academic underachievement. *Journal of Clinical Psychology, 21,* 10–13.

Shaw, P., Eckstrand, K., Sharp, W., Blumenthal, J., Lerch, J. P., Greenstein, D., et al. (2007). Attention-deficit/hyperactivity disorder is characterized by a delay in cortical maturation. *Proceedings of the National Academy of Sciences, 104,* 19649–19654.

Shaw, P., Greenstein, D., Lerch, J., Clasen, L., Lenroot, R., Gogtay, N., Evans, A., Rapoport, J., & Giedd, J. (2006). Intellectual ability and cortical development in children and adolescents. *Nature, 440,* 676–679.

Sheaks, C. (2007). The state of phased retirement: Facts, figures, and policies. *Generations, 31*(1), 57–62.

Sheehan, N. W., & Petrovic, K. (2008). Grandparents and their adult grandchildren: Recurring themes from the literature. *Marriage & Family Review, 44*(1), 99–124.

Sheehy, G. (Ed.). (1976). *Passages: Predictable crises of adult life.* New York: Dutton.

Sheffield, E. G., & Hudson, J. A. (2006). You must remember this: Effects of video and photograph reminders on 18-month-olds' event memory. *Journal of Cognition and Development, 7,* 73–93.

Sheldon, K., & Kasser, T. (2001). Getting older, getting better? Personal strivings and psychological maturity across the life span. *Developmental Psychology, 37*(4), 491–501.

Shevell, T., Malone, F. D., Vidaver, J., Porter, T. F., Luthy, D. A., Comstock, C. H., et al. (2005). Assisted reproductive technology and pregnancy outcome. *Obstetrics and Gynecology, 106,* 1039–1045.

Shippy, R., Cantor, M., & Brennan, M. (2004). Social networks of aging gay men. *The Journal of Men's Studies, 13*(1), 107–120.

Shumow, L., & Miller, J. D. (2001). Parents' at-home and at-school academic involvement with youth adolescents. *Journal of Early Adolescence, 21,* 68–91.

Shumow, L., Vandell, D. L., & Posner, J. (1998). Perceptions of danger: A psychological mediator of neighborhood demographic characteristics. *American Journal of Orthopsychiatry, 68,* 468–478.

Shumow, L., Vandell, D. L., & Posner, J. (1999). Risk and resilience in the urban neighborhood: Predictors of academic performance among low-income elementary school children. *Merrill-Palmer Quarterly, 45,* 309–331.

Shweder, R. A., Much, N. C., Mahapatra, M., & Park, L. (1997). The "big three" of morality (autonomy, community, and divinity) and the " big three" explanations of suffering. In A. M. Brandt & P. Rozin (Eds.), *Morality and health* (pp. 119–169). New York: Routledge.

Shweder, R., Goodnow, J., Hatano, G., LeVine, R., Markus, H., & Miller, P. (2006). The cultural psychology of development: One mind, many mentalities. In W. Damon & R. Lerner (Series Eds.) & R. Lerner (Vol. Ed.), *Handbook of child psychology: Vol. 1. Theoretical models of human development* (6th ed., pp. 716–782). New York: Wiley.

Siegel, J., Aneshensel, C., Taub, B., Cantwell, D., & Driscoll, A. (1998). Adolescent depressed mood in a multiethnic sample. *Journal of Youth and Adolescence, 27,* 413–427.

Siegler, R. S. (1995). How does change occur? A microgenetic study of number conservation. *Cognitive Psychology, 25,* 225–273.

Siegler, R. S. (1996). *Emerging minds: The process of change in children's thinking.* New York: Oxford University Press.

Siegler, R. S. (2002). Variability and infant development. *Infant Behavior & Development, 25,* 550–557.

Siegler, R. S. (2006). Microgenetic analyses of learning. In W. Damon & R. M. Lerner (Series Eds.) & D. Kuhn & R. S. Siegler (Eds.), *Handbook of child psychology: Vol. 2. Cognition, perception, and language* (6th ed., pp. 464–510). Hoboken, NJ: Wiley.

Siegler, R. S. (2007). Cognitive variability. *Developmental Science, 10,* 104–109.

Siegler, R. S., & Stern, E. (1998). A microgenetic analysis of conscious and unconscious strategy discoveries. *Journal of Experimental Psychology: General, 127,* 377–397.

Siegler, R. S., & Svetina, M. (2006). What leads children to adopt new strategies? A microgenetic/cross-sectional study of class inclusion. *Child Development, 77,* 997–1015.

Silverberg, S. B., & Steinberg, L. (1990). Psychological well-being of parents with early adolescent children. *Developmental Psychology, 26(40,* 658–666.

Silverberg, S. B., Marczak, M. S., & Gondoli, D. M. (1996). Maternal depressive symptoms and achievement-related outcomes among adolescent daughters: Variations by family structure. *Journal of Early Adolescence, 16*(1), 90–109.

Silverberg, S., & Samuel, A. G. (2004). The effect of age of second language acquisition on the representation and processing of second language words. *Journal of Memory and Language,* 51, 381–398.

Silverstein, M., & Bengtson, V. (1997). Intergenerational solidarity and the structure of adult child-parent relationships in American families. *American Journal of Sociology, 103*(2), 429–460.

Silverstein, M., Parrott, T. M., & Bengtson, V. L. (1995). Factors that predispose middle-aged sons and daughters to provide social support to older parents. *Journal of Marriage and the Family, 57,* 465–475.

Silverstein, M., Gans, D., & Yang, F. M. (2006). Intergenerational support to aging parents: The role of norms and needs. *Journal of Family Issues, 27*(8), 1068–1084.

Simmons, R., & Blyth, D. (1987). *Moving into adolescence.* New York: Aldine de Gruyter.

Simmons, R., Blyth, D., & McKinney, K. (1983). The social and psychological effects of puberty on white females. In J. Brooks-Gunn & A. Petersen (Eds.), *Girls at puberty* (pp. 229–272). New York: Plenum.

Simmons, R., Rosenberg, F., & Rosenberg, M. (1973). Disturbance in the self-image at adolescence. *American Sociological Review, 38,* 553–568.

Simonton, D. K. (1989). This swan-song phenomenon: Last-works effects for 172 classical composers. *Psychology and Aging,* 4(1), 42–47.

Simonton, D. K. (1991). *Creative productivity through the adult years. Generations, 15*(2), pp. 13–16.

Simonton, D. K. (2000). Creativity: Cognitive, personal, developmental, and social aspects. *American Psychologist, 55*(1), 151–158.

Singer, L. T., Arendt, R., Fagan, J., Minnes, S., Salvator, A., Bolek, T., & Becker, M. (1999). Neonatal visual information processing in cocaine-exposed and non-exposed infants. *Infant Behavior & Development, 22*, 1–15.

Singer, L. T., Eisengart, L. J., Minnes, S., Noland, J., Jey, A., Lane, C., & Min, M. O. (2005). Prenatal cocaine exposure and infant cognition. *Infant Behavior & Development, 28*, 431–444.

Singh, A. (2005). Medical therapy of glaucoma. *Ophthalmology Clinics of North America, 18*(3), 397–408.

Singh, S., & Darroch, J. (1999). Trends in sexual activity among adolescent American women: 1982–1995. *Family Planning Perspectives, 31*, 212–219.

Sinnott, J. D. (1984). Postformal reasoning: The relativistic stage. In M. Commons, F. Richards, & C. Armon (Eds.), *Beyond formal operations* (pp. 298–325). New York: Praeger.

Sinnott, J. D. (2002). Postformal thought and adult development: Living in balance. In J. Demick & C. Andreoletti (Eds.), *Adult development* (pp. 221–238). New York: Plenum Press.

Sirois, S., & Mareschal, D. (2002). Models of habituation in infancy. *Trends in Cognitive Sciences, 6*, 293–298.

Siroky, M. B. (2004). The aging bladder. *Reviews in Urology, 6*(Supplement 1), S3–S7.

Skeels, H. M. (1966). Adult status of children with contrasting early life experiences. *Monographs of the Society for Research in Child Development, 31* (3, Serial No. 105).

Skenkin, S. D., Starr, J. M., & Deary, I. J. (2004). Birth weight and cognitive ability in childhood: systematic review. *Psychological Bulletin, 130*, 989–1013.

Skinner, B. F. (1953). *Science and human behavior.* New York: Free Press.

Skinner, B. F. (1957). *Verbal behavior.* East Norwalk, CT: Appleton-Century-Crofts.

Skinner, E. A., & Zimmer-Gembeck, M. J. (2006). The development of coping. *Annual Review of Psychology, 58*, 119–144.

Slomkowski, C., Rende, R., Conger, K. J., Simons, R. L., & Conger, R. D. (2001). Sisters, brothers, and delinquency: Evaluating social influence during early and middle adolescence. Child Development, *72*, 271–283.

Smith, A. M. A., Shelley, J. M., & Dennerstein, L. (1994). Self-rated health: Biological continuum or social discontinuity? *Social Science and Medicine, 39*(1), 77–83.

Smith, D. B., & Moen, P. (2004). Retirement satisfaction for retirees and their spouses: Do gender and the retirement decision-making process matter? *Journal of Family Issues, 25*(2), 262.

Smith, J., & Baltes, P. B. (1990). Wisdom-related knowledge: Age/cohort differences in response to life-planning problems. *Developmental Psychology, 26*(3), 494–505.

Smith, J., Fleeson, W., Geiselmann, B., Settersten Jr., R., & Kunzmann, U. (1999). Sources of well-being in very old age. In P. B. Baltes & K. U. Mayer (Eds.), *The Berlin Aging Study: Aging from 70 to 100* (pp. 450–471). New York: Cambridge University Press.

Smith, L. W., Patterson, T. L., & Grant, I. (1990). Avoidant coping predicts psychological disturbance in the elderly. *Journal of Nervous and Mental Disease, 178*, 525–530.

Smith, R. E., Smoll, F. L., Curtis, B. (1978). Coaching behaviors in Little League Baseball. In F. L. Smoll & R. E. Smith (Eds.), *Psychological perspectives in youth sports* (pp. 173–201). Hoboken, NJ: Wiley.

Smith, T. W. (2006). Personality as risk and resilience in physical health. *Current Directions in Psychological Science, 15*(5), 227–231.

Smith, T. W., & MacKenzie, J. (2006). Personality and risk of physical illness. *Annual Review of Clinical Psychology, 2*, 435–467.

Smith, T. W., Uchino, B. N., Berg, C. A., Florsheim, P., Pearce, G., Hawkins, M., et al. (2007). Hostile personality traits and coronary artery calcification in middle-aged and older married couples: Different effects for self-reports versus spouse ratings. *Psychosomatic Medicine, 69*(5), 441–448.

Smock, P. J. (2000). Cohabitation in the United States: An appraisal of research themes, findings, and implications. *Annual Review of Sociology*, 26: 1–20.

Smoll, F. L., & Smith, R. E. (2002). Coaching behavior research and intervention in youth sports. In F. L. Smoll & R. E. Smith (Eds.), *Children and youth in sport: A biopsychosocial perspective* (pp. 211–233). Iowa: Kendall/Hunt Publishing Company.

Smyer, M. A., & Pitt-Catsouphes, M. (2007). The meanings of work for older workers. *Generations, 31*(1), 23–30.

Smyer, M. A., & Qualls, S. H. (1999). *Aging and mental health.* Malden, MA: Blackwell Publishers.

Snarey, J. (1985). Cross-cultural universality of social-moral development: A critical review of Kohlbergian research. *Psychological Bulletin, 97*(2), 202–232.

Sneed, J., & Whitbourne, S. (2005). Models of the aging self. *Journal of Social Issues, 61*(2), 375–388.

Snow, C. E. (2006). What counts as literacy in early childhood? In K. McCartney & D. Phillips (Eds.), *Blackwell handbook on early childhood development* (pp. 274–294). Malden, MA: Blackwell.

Snow, C. E., & Kang, J. Y. (2006). Becoming bilingual, biliterate, and bicultural. In K. A. Renninger & I. E. Sigel (Eds.), *Handbook of child psychology. Vol. 4: Child psychology research in practice* (pp. 75–102). Hoboken NJ: Wiley.

Snow, C. E., Burns, M. S., & Griffin, P. (1998). *Preventing reading difficulties in young children.* Washington DC: National Academy Press.

Snowling, M. J. (2004). Reading development and dyslexia. In U. Goswami (Ed.), *Blackwell handbook of childhood cognitive development* (pp. 394–411). Malden, MA: Blackwell Publishing.

Snyder, J., Bank, L., & Burraston, B. (2005). The consequences of antisocial behavior in older male siblings for younger brothers and sisters. *Journal of Family Psychology, 19*, 643–653.

Society for Research in Child Development. (1993). *Ethical Standards for Research with Children.* Ann Arbor: Author.

Sokol, R. J., Delaney-Black, V., & Nordstrom, B. (2003). Fetal alcohol spectrum disorder. *The Journal of the American Medical Association, 290*, 2996–2999.

Soons, J. P. M., & Liefbroer, A. C. (2008). Together is better? Effects of relationship status and resources on young adults' well-being. *Journal of Social and Personal Relationships, 25*(4), 603–624.

Sorkhabi, N. (2005). Applicability of Baumrind's parent typology to collective cultures: Analysis of cultural explanations of parent socialization effects. *International Journal of Behavioral Development, 29*, 552–563.

Sorkin, D. H., & Rook, K. S. (2006). Dealing with negative social exchanges in later life: Coping responses, goals, and effectiveness. *Psychology and Aging, 21*, 715–725.

Sousa, D. A. (2006). *How the brain learns* (3rd ed.). Thousand Oaks, CA: Corwin Press.

Sowell, E. R., Trauner, D. A., Gamst, A., & Jernigan, T. L. (2002). Development of cortical and subcortical brain structures in childhood and adolescence: A structural MRI study. *Developmental Medicine and Child Neurology, 44,* 4–16.

Span, P. (2009, April 20). Why do we avoid advance directives? *New York Times*. Retrieved July 9, 2009 from http://newoldage.blogs.nytimes.com/2009/04/20/why-do-we-avoid-advance-directives/

Spanier, G. B., Lewis, R. A., & Cole, C. L. (1975). Marital adjustment over the family lifecycle: The issue of curvilinearity. *Journal of Marriage and Family, 37*(2), 263–275.

Spelke, E., & Newport, E. (1998). Nativism, empiricism, and the development of knowledge. In W. Damon & R. Lerner (Series Eds.) & R. Lerner (Vol. Ed.), *Handbook of child psychology: Vol. 1: Theoretical models of human development* (5th ed., pp. 275–340). New York: Wiley.

Spencer, M. (2005). Crafting identities and accessing opportunities post-Brown. *American Psychologist, 60,* 821–830.

Spencer, M., & Dornbusch, S. (1990). Challenges in studying minority youth. In S. Feldman & G. Elliott (Eds.), *At the threshold: The developing adolescent* (pp. 123–146). Cambridge, MA: Harvard University Press.

Spencer, M., & Markstrom-Adams, C. (1990). Identity processes among racial and ethnic minority children in America. *Child Development, 61,* 290–310.

Spillman, B. C., & Black, K. J. (2005). *Staying the course: Trends in family caregiving*. AARP Public Policy Institute Issue Paper 2005-17. Washington, DC: American Association of Retired Persons (AARP).

Spillman, B. C., & Pezzin, L. E. (2000). Potential and active family caregivers: Changing networks and the "sandwich generation." *Milbank Quarterly, 78*(3), 347–374.

Spira, E. G., Bracken, S. S., & Fischel, J. E. (2005). Predicting improvement after first-grade reading difficulties: The effects of oral language, emergent literacy, and behavior skills. *Developmental Psychology, 41,* 225–234.

Spitz, R. (1945). Hospitalism: An inquiry into the genesis of psychiatric conditions in early childhood. *Psychoanalytic Study of the Child, 1,* 53–74.

Spock, B. (1946). *The common sense book of baby and child care*. New York: Duell, Sloan and Pearce.

Sprecher, S. (1989). The importance to males and females of physical attractiveness, earning potential, and expressiveness in initial attraction. *Sex Roles, 21*(9), 591–607.

Sprecher, S., & Regan, P. C. (1998). Passionate and companionate love in courting and young married couples. *Sociological Inquiry, 68*(2), 163–185.

Sprecher, S., Sullivan, Q., & Hatfield, E. (1994). Mate selection preferences: Gender differences examined in a national sample. *Journal of Personality and Social Psychology, 66*(6), 1074–1080.

Sprung, J., Flick, R. P., Wilder, R. T., Katusic, S. K., Pike, T. L., Dingli, M., et al. (2009). Anesthesia for Cesarean delivery and learning disabilities in a population-based birth cohort. *Anesthesiology, 111,* 302–310.

Srivastava, S., John, O. P., Gosling, S. D., & Potter, J. (2003). Development of personality in early and middle adulthood: Set like plaster or persistent change? *Journal of Personality and Social Psychology, 84*(5), 1041–1053.

Sroufe, L. A., Egeland, B., Carlson, E. A., & Collins, W. A. (2005). *The development of the person: The Minnesota study of risk and adaptation from birth to adulthood*. New York: Guilford Publications.

St. James-Roberts, I. (2007). Infant crying and sleeping: Helping parents to prevent and manage problems. *Sleep Medicine Clinics, 2,* 363–375.

Stack, D. M. (2001). The salience of touch and physical contact during infancy: Unraveling some of the mysteries of the somesthetic sense. In J. G. Bremner, & A. Fogel (Eds.), *Blackwell handbook of infant development* (pp. 351–378). Malden, MA: Blackwell.

Staff, J., Messersmith, E., & Schulenberg. (2009). Work and leisure in adolescence. In R. Lerner & L. Steinberg (Eds.), *Handbook of adolescent psychology* (3rd ed.) New York: Wiley.

Stams, G. J., Juffer, F., & van Ijzendoorn, M. H. (2002). Maternal sensitivity, infant attachment, and temperament in early childhood predict adjustment in middle childhood: The case of adopted children and their biologically unrelated parents. *Developmental Psychology, 38,* 806–821.

Stanton, A. L., Lobel, M., Sears, S., & DeLuca, R. S. (2002). Psychosocial aspects of selected issues in women's reproductive health: Current status and future directions. *Journal of Consulting and Clinical Psychology, 70*(3), 751–770.

Stanton, A., Danoff-Burg, S., Cameron, C., & Ellis, A. (1994). Coping through emotional approach: Problems of conceptualization and confounding. *Journal of Personality and Social Psychology, 66*(2), 350–362.

Stanton-Salazar, R., & Dornbusch, S. (1995). Social capital and the reproduction of inequality: Information networks among Mexican-origin high school students. *Sociology of Education, 68,* 116–135.

Starkey, P., & Gelman, R. (1982). The development of addition and subtraction abilities prior to formal schooling in arithmetic. In T. P. Carpenter, J. M. Moser, & T. A. Romberg (Eds.), *Addition and subtraction: A cognitive perspective* (pp. 99–116). Hillsdale, NJ: Erlbaum.

Staudinger, U. (2001). Life reflection: A social-cognitive analysis of life review. *Review of general psychology, 5*(2), 148–160.

Staudinger, U. M. (1999). Older and wiser? Integrating results on the relationship between age and wisdom-related performance. *International Journal of Behavioral Development, 23*(3), 641–664.

Staudinger, U. M., & Bluck, S. (2001). A view on midlife development from life-span theory. In M. E. Lachman (Ed.), *Handbook of midlife development* (pp. 3–39). New York: Wiley.

Staudinger, U. M., Dörner, J., & Mickler, C. (2005). Wisdom and personality. In R. J. Sternberg & J. Jordan (Eds.), *A handbook of wisdom: Psychological perspectives* (pp. 191–219). New York: Cambridge University Press.

Staudinger, U. M., Freund, A. M., Linden, M., & Maas, I. (1999). Self, personality, and life management: Psychological resilience and vulnerability. In P. B. Baltes & K. U. Mayer (Eds.). *The Berlin Aging Study: Aging from 70 to 100* (pp. 302–328). New York: Cambridge University Press.

Staudinger, U. M., Smith, J., & Baltes, P. B. (1992). Wisdom-related knowledge in a life-review task: Age differences and role of professional specialization. *Psychology and Aging, 7*(2), 271–281.

Staudinger, U., & Kunzmann, U. (2005). Positive adult personality development: Adjustment and/or growth? *European Psychologist, 10*(4), 320.

Stearn, W. B. (1995). Youth sports contexts: Coaches' perceptions and implications for intervention. *Journal of Applied Sport Psychology, 7,* 23–37.

Steele, C. M., & Aronson, J. (1995). Stereotype threat and the intellectual test performance of African Americans. *Journal of Personality and Social Psychology, 69*(5), 797–811.

Steele, C., Spencer, S. J., & Aronson, J. (2002). Contending with group image: The psychology of stereotype and social identity threat. *Advances in experimental social psychology, 34*, 379–440.

Stein, Z. (1975). *Famine and human development: The dutch hunger winter of 1944–1945.* New York: Oxford University Press.

Steinberg, L. (1990). Autonomy, conflict, and harmony in the family relationship. In S. S. Feldman & G. R. Elliott (Eds.), *At the threshold: The developing adolescent* (pp. 54–89). Cambridge, MA: Harvard University Press.

Steinberg, L. (1996). *Beyond the classroom: Why school reform has failed and what parents need to do.* New York: Simon & Schuster.

Steinberg, L. (2005). Cognitive and affective development in adolescence. *Trends in Cognitive Sciences, 9*(2), 69–74.

Steinberg, L. (2007). Risk-taking in adolescence: New perspectives from brain and behavioral science. *Current Directions in Psychological Science, 16*, 55–59.

Steinberg, L. (2008). *Adolescence* (8th ed.). New York: McGraw-Hill.

Steinberg, L., & Cauffman, E. (1995). The impact of employment on adolescent development. In R. Vasta (Ed.), *Annals of Child Development, Vol. 11.* (pp. 131–166). London: Jessica Kingsley Publishers.

Steinberg, L., & Dornbusch, S. (1991). Negative correlates of part-time work in adolescence: Replication and elaboration. *Developmental Psychology, 17*, 304–313.

Steinberg, L., & Monahan, K. (2007). Age differences in resistance to peer influence. *Developmental Psychology, 43*, 1531–1543.

Steinberg, L., & Silverberg, S. (1986). The vicissitudes of autonomy in early adolescence. *Child Development, 57*, 841–851.

Steinberg, L., & Steinberg, W. (1994). *Crossing paths: How your child's adolescence triggers your own crisis.* New York: Simon & Schuster.

Steinberg, L., Dahl, R., Keating, D., Kupfer, D., Masten, A., & Pine, D. (2006). Psychopathology in adolescence: Integrating affective neuroscience with the study of context. In D. Cicchetti & D. Cohen (Eds.), *Developmental psychopathology: Vol. 2. Developmental neuroscience* (pp. 710–741). New York: Wiley.

Steinberg, L., Dornbusch, S., & Brown, B. (1992). Ethnic differences in adolescent achievement: An ecological perspective. *American Psychologist, 47*, 723–729.

Steinberg, L., Fegley, S., & Dornbusch, S. (1993). Negative impact of part-time work on adolescent adjustment: Evidence from a longitudinal study. *Developmental Psychology, 29*, 171–180.

Steinberg, L., Greenberger, E., Garduque, L., Ruggiero, M., & Vaux, A. (1982). Effects of working on adolescent development. *Developmental Psychology, 18*, 385–395.

Steiner, J. E. (1979). Human facial expressions in response to taste and smell stimulation. In H. Reese and L. Lipsitt (Eds.), *Advances in child development and behavior* (Vol. 13). New York: Academic Press.

Stern, Y. (2006). Cognitive reserve and Alzheimer disease. *Alzheimer Disease and Associated Disorders, 20*(3, Suppl. 2), S69–S74.

Sternberg, R. J. (1986). A triangular theory of love. *Psychological Review, 93*(2), 119–135.

Sternberg, R. J. (1988). *The triarchic mind: A theory of human intelligence.* New York: Viking.

Sternberg, R. J. (1988). Triangulating love. In R. J. Sternberg & M. Barnes (Eds.), *The psychology of love* (pp. 119–138). New Haven, CT: Yale University Press.

Sternberg, R. J. (1999) The theory of successful intelligence. *Review of General Psychology, 3*, 292–316.

Sternberg, R. J. (2004). Individual differences in cognitive development. In U. Goswami (Ed.), *Blackwell handbook of childhood cognitive development* (pp. 600–619). Malden, MA: Blackwell Publishing.

Sternberg, R. J., & Lubart, T. I. (1999). The concept of creativity: Prospects and paradigms. In R. J. Sternberg (Ed.), *Handbook of creativity* (pp. 3–15). New York: Cambridge University Press.

Sterns, H. L., & Huyck, H. (2001). The role of work in midlife. In M. E. Lachman (Ed.), *Handbook of midlife development* (pp. 447–486). New York: Wiley.

Stetsenko, A., Little, T. D., Gordeeva, T., Grasshof, J., & Oettingen, G. (2000). Gender effects in children's beliefs about school performance: A cross-cultural study. *Child Development, 71*, 517–527.

Stevenson, H., & Stigler, J. (1992). *The learning gap: Why our schools are failing and what we can learn from Japanese and Chinese education.* New York: Simon & Schuster.

Stewart, A., & Ostrove, J. M. (1998). Women's personality in middle age: Gender, history, and midcourse corrections. *American Psychologist, 53*(11), 1185–1194.

Stewart, S. M., & McBride-Chang, C. (2000). Influences on children's sharing in a multicultural setting. *Journal of Cross-Cultural Psychology, 31*, 333–348.

Stice, E., Presnell, K., & Bearman, S. (2001). Relation of early menarche to depression, eating disorders, substance abuse, and comorbid psychopathology among adolescent girls. *Developmental Psychology, 37*, 608–619.

Stilson, S. R., & Harding, C. G. (1997). Early social context as it relates to symbolic play: a longitudinal investigation. *Merrill-Palmer Quarterly, 43*, 682–693.

Stine-Morrow, E. A. L., Parisi, J. M, Morrow, D. G., Greene, J., & Park, D. C. (2007). An engagement model of cognitive optimization through adulthood. *Journal of Gerontology B: Psychological Sciences and Social Sciences, 62*(Special Issue), P62–P69.

Stipek, D. (1995). The development of pride and shame in toddlers. In J. Tangney & K. Fischer (Eds.), *Self conscious emotions: The psychology of shame, guilt, embarrassment, and pride* (pp. 237–252). New York: Guilford.

Stocker, C. M., Burwell, R. A., & Briggs, M. L. (2002). Sibling conflict in middle childhood predicts children's adjustment in early adolescence. *Journal of Family Psychology, 16*, 50–57.

Stoller, E. P. (1993). Interpretations of symptoms by older people: A health diary study of illness behavior. *Journal of Aging and Health, 5*(1), 58–81.

Stoolmiller, M., Kim, H. K., & Capaldi, D. M. (2005). The course of depressive symptoms in men from early adolescence to young adulthood: Identifying latent trajectories and early predictors. *Journal of Abnormal Psychology, 114*, 331–345.

Story, T. N., Berg, C. A., Smith, T. W., Beveridge, R., Henry, N. J. M., & Pearce, G. (2007). Age, marital satisfaction, and optimism as predictor of positive sentiment override in middle-aged and older married couples. *Psychology and Aging, 22*, 719–727.

Stovall, K. C., & Dozier, M. (2000). The development of attachment in new relationships: Single subject analyses for ten foster infants. *Development and Psychopathology, 12*, 133–156.

Straus, S. (2008). A 16-week tai chi programme prevented falls in healthy older adults. *British Medical Journal, 13*(2), 54–54.

Strayer, F. F., & Strayer, J. (1976). An ethological analysis of agonism and dominance relations among preschool children. *Child Development, 47*, 980–989.

Streissguth, A. P., Bookstein, F. L., Barr, H. M., Sampson, P. D., O'Malley, K., & Young, J. K. (2004). Risk factors for adverse life outcomes in fetal alcohol syndrome and fetal alcohol effects. *Developmental and Behavioral Pediatrics, 25,* 228–238.

Strid, K., Tjus, T., Smith, L., Meltzoff, A. N., & Heimann, M. (2006). Infant recall memory and communication predicts later cognitive development. *Infant Behavior & Development, 29,* 545–553.

Stroebe, M. S., & Schut, H. (1999). The dual process model of coping with bereavement: Rationale and description. *Death Studies, 23*(3), 197–224.

Stroebe, M. S., Stroebe, W., & Hansson, R. O. (1993). Bereavement theory and research: An introduction to the Handbook. In M. S. Stroebe, W. Stroebe, & R. O. Hansson (Eds.), *Handbook of bereavement: Theory, research, and intervention* (pp. 3–19). Cambridge, England: Cambridge Univ. Press.

Stroebe, M. S., Stroebe, W., & Schut, H. (2001). Gender differences in adjustment to bereavement: An empirical and theoretical review. *Review of General Psychology, 5*(1), 62–83.

Stryker, S., & Statham, A. (1985). Symbolic interaction role theory. In G. Lindzey & E. Aronson (Eds.), *Handbook of Social Psychology* (pp. 311–378). Hillsdale, NJ: Erlbaum.

Stuck, A. E., Walthert, J. M., Nikolaus, T., Buela, C. J., Hohmann, C., & Beck, J. C. (1999). Risk factors for functional status decline in community-living elderly people: A systematic literature review. *Social Science and Medicine, 48*(4), 445–469.

Sturmhöfel, S., & Swartzwelder, H. (2004). Alcohol's effects on the adolescent brain: what can be learned from animal models. *Alcohol Research and Health, 28,* 213–221.

Stylianos, S. K., & Vachon, M. L. S. (1993). The role of social support in bereavement. In M. S. Stroebe, W. Stroebe, & R. O. Hansson (Eds.), *Handbook of bereavement: Theory, research, and intervention* (pp. 397–410). Cambridge, England: Cambridge Univ. Press.

Suárez-Orozco, C., & Suárez-Orozco, M. (2001). *Children of immigration.* Cambridge: Harvard University Press.

Sugarman, A. (2001). *Peer influences on adolescent girls' eating behavior and attitudes: A grounded theory approach.* Unpublished doctoral dissertation, Temple University.

Sugita, Y. (2008). Face perception in monkeys reared with no exposure to faces. *Proceedings of the National Academy of Sciences, 105,* 394–398.

Sui-Chu, E., & Willms, J. (1996). *Effects of parental involvement on eighth-grade achievement. Sociology of Education, 69,* 126–141.

Suizzo, M.-A., & Bornstein, M. H. (2006). French and European American child-mother play: Culture and gender considerations. *International Journal of Behavioral Development, 30,* 498–508.

Sullivan, A. D., Hedberg, K., & Fleming, D. W. (2000). Legalized physician-assisted suicide in Oregon-the second year. *New England Journal of Medicine, 342*(8), 598–604.

Sullivan, S. E. (1999). The changing nature of careers: A review and research agenda. *Journal of Management, 25*(3), 457–484.

Sun, Y., & Li, Y. (2001). Marital disruptions, parental investment, and children's academic achievement: A longitudinal analysis. *Journal of Family Issues, 22,* 27–62.

Sun, Y., & Li, Y. (2002). Children's well-being during parents' marital disruption process: A pooled time-series analysis. *Journal of Marriage and the Family, 64,* 472–488.

Sundin, O., Öhman, A., Palm, T. & Ström, G. (1995) Cardiovascular reactivity, Type A behavior, and coronary heart disease: Comparisons between myocardial infarction patients and controls during laboratory-induced stress. *Psychophysiology, 32*(1), 28–35.

Sunstein, C. R. (2005). Moral heuristics. *Behavioral and Brain Sciences, 28*(4), 531–573.

Super, D. E. (1957). *Psychology of careers.* New York: Harper.

Super, D. E. (1984). Career and life development. In D. Brown & L. Brooks (Eds.), *Career choice and development* (pp. 192–234). San Francisco, CA: Jossey Bass.

Super, D. E. (1992). Toward a comprehensive theory of career development. In D. H. Montross & C. J. Shrinkman (Ed.), *Career development: Theory and practice* (pp. 35–64). Springfield, IL: Charles Thomas.

Super, D. E., Savickas, M. L., & Super, C. M. (1996). The life-span, life-space approach to careers. In D. Brown & L. Brooks (Eds.), *Career choice and development* (pp. 121–178). San Francisco, CA: Jossey-Bass.

Sur, M., & Rubenstein, J. L. R. (2005). Patterning and plasticity of the cerebral cortex. *Science, 310,* 805–810.

Surbone, A. (2006). Telling the truth to patients with cancer: What is the truth? *Lancet Oncology, 7*(11), 944–950.

Susman, E. (1997). Modeling developmental complexity in adolescence: Hormones and behavior in context. *Journal of Research on Adolescence, 7,* 283–306.

Susman, E., & Dorn, L. (2009). Puberty: Its role in development. In R. Lerner & L. Steinberg (Eds.), *Handbook of adolescent psychology* (3rd ed.) New York: Wiley.

Suzman, R. M., Willis, D. P., & Manton, K. G. (Eds.). (1992). *The oldest old.* New York: Oxford University Press.

Swail, W. S., Redd, K. E., & Perna, L. W. (2003). Retaining minority students in higher education: A framework for success. *ASHE-ERIC Higher Education Report, 30*(2), 1–187.

Sweet, S. (2007). The older worker, job insecurity, and the new economy. *Generations, 31*(1), 45–49.

Swody, C. A., & Powell, G. N. (2007). Determinants of employee participation in organizations' family-friendly programs: A multi-level approach. *Journal of Business and Psychology, 22*(2), 111–122.

Szinovacz, M. E. (Ed.), (1998). *Handbook of grandparenthood.* Westport, CT : Greenwood.

Szinovacz, M., & Davey, A. (2005). Retirement and marital decision making: Effects on retirement satisfaction. *Journal of Marriage and Family, 67*(2), 387–398.

Tagney, J. P., Stuewig, J., & Mashek, D. J. (2007). Moral emotions and moral behavior. *Annual Review of Psychology, 58,* 345–372.

Talan, J. (2007, February 5). Low-level toxicants can harm brain. *Newsday.* Retrieved February 6, 2007, from http://www.newsday.com/news/health/ny-hslead0206,0,3014503.story?coll=ny-lea

Tamis-Lemonda, C. S., & Bornstein, M. H. (1990). Language, play, and attention at one year. *Infant Behavior & Development, 13,* 85–98.

Tamis-LeMonda, C. S., & Bornstein, M. H. (1991). Individual variation, correspondence, stability, and change in mother and toddler play. *Infant Behavior & Development, 14,* 143–162.

Tamis-LeMonda, C. S., & Bornstein, M. H. (2002). Maternal responsiveness and early language acquisition. In R. V. Kail & H. W. Reese (Eds.), *Advances in child development and behavior* (Vol. 29, pp. 89–127). New York: Academic Press.

Tan, R. S., & Culberson, J. W. (2003). An integrative review on current evidence of testosterone replacement therapy for the andropause. *Maturitas, 45*(1), 15–27.

Tannen, D. (1994). *Gender and discourse.* New York: Oxford University Press.

Tanner, J. (1972). Sequence, tempo, and individual variation in growth and development of boys and girls aged twelve to sixteen. In J. Kagan & R. Coles (Eds.), *Twelve to sixteen: Early adolescence* (pp. 1–23). New York: Norton.

Tanner, J. L. (2006). Recentering during emerging adulthood. In J. J. Arnett & J. L. Tanner (Eds.), *Emerging adulthood: Coming of age in the 21st century* (pp. 21–55). Washington, DC: American Psychological Association.

Tanner, J. M. (1990). *Foetus into man* (2nd ed.). Cambridge: Harvard University Press.

Tasbihsazan, R., Nettelbeck, T., & Kirby, N. (2003). Predictive validity of the Fagan Test of Infant Intelligence. *British Journal of Developmental Psychology, 21*, 585–597.

Tasker, F. (2005). Lesbian mothers, gay fathers, and their children: A review. *Journal of Developmental & Behavioral Pediatrics, 26*(3), 224–240.

Taylor, J. L., Kennedy, Q., Noda, A., & Yesavage, J. A. (2007). Pilot age and expertise predict flight simulator performance: A 3-year longitudinal study. *Neurology, 68*(9), 648–654.

Taylor, P., & Walker, A. (1998). Employers and older workers: Attitudes and employment practices. *Ageing and Society, 18*, 641–658.

Taylor, R., Casten, R., Flickinger, S., Roberts, D., & Fulmore, C. (1994). Explaining the school performance of African-American adolescents. *Journal of Research on Adolescence, 4*, 21–44.

Teachman, J. D., Tedrow, L. M., & Crowder, K. D. (2000). The changing demography of America's families. *Journal of Marriage and Family, 62*(4), 1234–1246.

Tedla, F. M., & Friedman, E. A. (2008). The trend toward geriatric nephrology. *Primary Care: Clinics in Office Practice, 35*(3), 515–530.

Tejada-Vera, B., & Sutton, P. D. (2009). Births, marriages, divorces, and deaths: provisional data for 2008. *National Vital Statistics Reports, 57*(19), 1–6. Retrieved January 7, 2010 from http://www.cdc.gov/nchs/fastats/deaths.htm

Teno, J. M., Shu, J. E., Casarett, D., Spence, C., Rhodes, R., & Connor, S. (2007). Timing of referral to hospice and quality of care: Length of stay and bereaved family members' perceptions of the timing of hospice referral. *Journal of Pain and Symptom Management, 34*(2), 120–125.

Terman, L. M. (1916). *The measurement of intelligence.* Boston: Houghton Mifflin.

Terry, R., & Coie, J. D. (1991). A comparison of methods for defining sociometric status among children. *Developmental Psychology, 27*, 867–880.

Thelen, E., & Smith, L. B. (2006). Dynamic systems theories. In W. Damon & R. Lerner (Series Eds.) & R. Lerner (Vol. Ed.), *Handbook of child psychology: Vol. 1. Theoretical models of human development* (6th ed., pp. 258–312). Hoboken, NJ: Wiley.

Thomas, A., Chess, S., & Birch, H. G. (1970). The origin of personality. *Scientific American, 223*, 102–109.

Thomas, J. R., & French, K. E. (1985). Gender differences across age in motor performance: A meta-analysis. *Psychological Bulletin, 98*(2), 260–282.

Thompson, L., Coon, D., Gallagher-Thompson, D., Sommer, B., & Koin, D. (2001). Comparison of desipramine and cognitive/behavioral therapy in the treatment of elderly outpatients with mild-to-moderate depression. *American Journal of Geriatric Psychiatry, 9*(3), 225–240.

Thompson, P., Giedd, J., Woods, R., MacDonald, D., Evans, A., & Toga, A. (2000). Growth patterns in the developing brain detected using continuum mechanical tensor maps. *Nature, 404*, 190–193.

Thompson, R. A. (2006). The development of the person: Social understanding, relationships, conscience, and self. In W. Damon & R. M. Lerner (Series Eds.) & N. Eisenberg (Vol. Ed.), *Handbook of child psychology: Vol. 3. Social, emotional, and personality development* (6th ed., pp. 24–98). Hoboken, NJ: Wiley.

Thompson, R. A., & Goodvin, R. (2005). The individual child: Temperament, emotion, self, and personality. In M. H. Bornstein & M. E. Lamb (Eds.), *Developmental science: An advanced textbook* (pp. 391–428). Mahwah, NJ: Erlbaum.

Thornton, W. J. L., & Dumke, H. A. (2005). Age differences in everyday problem-solving and decision-making effectiveness: A meta-analytic review. *Psychology and Aging, 20*(1), 85–99.

Tierney, M. C., Yao, C., Kiss, A., & McDowell, I. (2005). Neuropsychological tests accurately predict incident Alzheimer disease after 5 and 10 years. *Neurology, 64*(11), 1853–1859.

Tiezzi, L., Lipshutz, J., Wrobleski, N., Vaughan, R., & McCarthy, J. (1997). Pregnancy prevention among urban adolescents younger than 15: Results of the 'In Your Face' program. *Family Planning Perspectives, 29*, 173–176, 197.

Tizard, B., & Hodges, J. (1978). The effect of institutional rearing on the development of 8-year-old children. *Journal of Child Psychology, Psychiatry, and Allied Disciplines, 19*, 99–118.

Tizard, B., & Rees, J. (1975). The effect of early institutional rearing on the behavior problems and affectional relationships of four-year-old children. *Journal of Child Psychology, Psychiatry, and Allied Disciplines, 27*, 61–73.

Tjaden, P., & Thoennes, N. (2006). *Extent, nature, and consequences of rape victimization: Findings from the National Violence Against Women Survey.* Washington, DC: National Institute of Justice.

Tomasello, M. (2006). Acquiring linguistic constructions. In W. Damon & R. M. Lerner (Series Eds.) & D. Kuhn & R. S. Siegler (Vol. Eds.), *Handbook of child psychology: Vol. 2. Cognition, perception, and language* (6th ed., pp. 255–298). Hoboken, NJ: Wiley.

Toth, S. L. Cicchetti, D., Macfie, J., Maughan, A., & Vanmeenen, K. (2000). Narrative representations of caregivers and self in male preschoolers. *Attachment and Human Development, 2*, 271–305.

Towfighi, A., Saver, J. L., Engelhardt, R., & Ovbiagele, B. (2007). A midlife stroke surge among women in the United States. *Neurology, 69*(2), 1898–1904.

Travison, T. G., Araujo, A. B., Kupelian, V., O'Donnell, A. B., & McKinlay, J. B. (2007). The relative contributions of aging, health, and lifestyle factors to serum testosterone decline in men. *Journal of Clinical Endocrinology & Metabolism, 92*(2), 549–555.

Treas, J., & Mazumdar, S. (2002). Older people in America's immigrant families: Dilemmas of dependence, integration, and isolation. *Journal of Aging Studies, 16*(3), 243–258.

Trehub, S. E., Trainor, L. J., & Unyk, A. M. (1993). Music and speech processing in the first year of life. *Advances in Child Development and Behavior, 24*, 1–35.

Troen, B. R. (2003). The biology of aging. *Mount Sinai Journal of Medicine, 70*(1), 3–22.

Trommsdorff, G. (2006). Development of emotions as organized by culture. *International Society for the Study of Behavioural Development Newsletter, 49*, 1–4.

True, M. M., Pisani, L., & Oumar, F. (2001). Infant-mother attachment among the Dogon of Mali. *Child Development, 72*, 1451–1466.

Truog, R. D., & Fackler, J. C. (1992). Rethinking brain death. *Critical Care Medicine, 20*(12), 1705–1713.

Trzesniewski, K. H., Robins, R. W., Roberts, B. W., & Caspi, A. (2003). Personality and self-esteem development across the lifespan. In P. Costa & I. C. Siegler (Eds.), *Recent advances in psychology and aging* (pp. 163–185). Amsterdam: Elsevier.

Tsao, F., Liu, H., & Kuhl, P. K. (2004). Speech perception in infancy predicts language development in the second year of life: A longitudinal study. *Child Development, 75,* 1067–1084.

Tucker, C. J., McHale, S. M., & Crouter, A. C. (2001). Conditions of sibling support in adolescence. *Journal of Family Psychology, 15,* 254–271.

Tucker, C. J., McHale, S. M., & Crouter, A. C. (2003). Dimensions of mothers' and fathers' differential treatment of siblings: Links with adolescents' sex-typed personal qualities. *Family Relations, 52,* 82–89.

Tulving, E. (1985). How many memory systems are there? *American Psychologist, 40*(4), 385–398.

Turati, C., Cassia, V. M., Simion, F., & Leo, I. (2006). Newborns' face recognition: Role of inner and outer facial features. *Child Development, 77,* 297–311.

Turiel, E. (2006). The development of morality. In N. Eisenberg (Vol. Ed.), *Handbook of child psychology: Vol. 3. Social, emotional, and personality development* (pp. 789–857). Hoboken, NJ: Wiley.

Turk, D. C., & Okifuji, A. (2002). Psychological factors in chronic pain: evolution and revolution. *Journal of Consulting and Clinical Psychology, 70*(3), 678–690.

Turkheimer, E. (1998). Heritability and biological explanation. *Psychological Review, 105,* 782–791.

Turnheim, K. (2003). When drug therapy gets old: Pharmacokinetics and pharmacodynamics in the elderly. *Experimental Gerontology, 38*(8), 843–853.

Twenge, J. M., Campbell, W. K., & Foster, C. A. (2003). Parenthood and marital satisfaction: A meta-analytic review. *Journal of Marriage and the Family, 65*(3), 574–583.

U.S. Bureau of the Census. (2004, March). Children and the households they live in: 2000. Retrieved October 7, 2008 from http://www.census.gov/population/www/socdemo/hh-fam.html

U.S. Bureau of the Census. (2006). *Current population survey.* Washington, DC: Author.

U.S. Bureau of the Census. (2006, September 21). *Table MS-2. Estimated Median Age at First Marriage, by Sex: 1890 to the Present.* Retrieved January 13, 2010 from www.census.gov/population/socdemo/hh-fam/ms2.pdf

U.S. Bureau of the Census. (2008). *Educational attainment data set: 2006–2008 American Community Survey 3-year estimates.* Retrieved January 18, 2010 from http://factfinder.census.gov/servlet/STTable?_bm=y&-geo_id=01000US&-qr_name=ACS_2008_3YR_G00_S1501&-ds_name=ACS_2008_3YR_G00_

U.S. Bureau of the Census. (2009). *Table AD-1. Young Adults Living At Home: 1960 to Present.* Retrieved February 14, 2010 from http://www.census.gov/population/www/socdemo/hh-fam.html#ht

U.S. Bureau of the Census. (2009). *Table MS-2. Estimated median age at first marriage, by sex: 1890 to the present.* Retrieved February 14, 2010 from http://www.census.gov/population/socdemo/hh-fam/ms2.xls

U.S. Centers for Disease Control and Prevention. (2007). Prevalence of autism spectrum disorders — Autism and developmental disabilities monitoring network, six sites, United States, 2000. http://www.cdc.gov/mmwr/preview/mmwrhtml/ss5601a1.htm

U.S. Department of Agriculture. (2006, March). *WIC: The special supplemental nutrition program for women, infants and children* [Fact sheet]. Retrieved from http://www.fns.usda.gov/wic/factsheets.htm

U.S. Department of Health and Human Services. (2005, February 21). *U.S. Surgeon General releases advisory on alcohol use in pregnancy.* Retrieved August 13, 2008, from http://www.surgeongeneral.gov/pressreleases/sg02222005.html

Uchino, B. N. (2006). Social support and health: A review of physiological processes potentially underlying links to disease outcomes. *Journal of Behavioral Medicine, 29*(4), 377–387.

Uhlenberg, P., Cooney, T., & Boyd, R. (1990). Divorce for women after midlife. *Journal of Gerontology: Social Sciences, 45*(1), S3–S11.

Umaña-Taylor, A. J. (2004). Ethnic identity and self-esteem: Examining the role of social context. *Journal of Adolescence, 27,* 139–146.

Umberson, D. (1996). Demographic position and stressful midlife events: Effects on the quality of parent-child relationships. In C. D. Ryff & M. M. Seltzer (Eds.), *The parental experience in midlife* (pp. 493–531). Chicago, IL: University of Chicago Press.

Umberson, D. (2003). *Death of a parent: Transition to a new adult identity.* Cambridge, England: Cambridge University Press.

Umberson, D., Williams, K., Powers, D. A., Chen, M. D., & Campbell, A. M. (2005). As good as it gets?A life course perspective on marital quality *Social Forces, 84*(1), 493–511.

Umberson, D., Wortman, C. B., & Kessler, R. C. (1992). Widowhood and depression: Explaining long-term gender differences in vulnerability. *Journal of Health and Social Behavior, 33*(1), 10–24.

Underwood, M. (2003). *Social aggression among girls.* New York: Guilford Press.

Underwood, M. K. (2002). Sticks and stones and social exclusion: Aggression among girls and boys. In P. K. Smith & C. H. Hart (Eds.), *Blackwell handbook of childhood social development* (pp. 533–548). Malden, MA: Blackwell.

Underwood, M. K., Beron, K. & Gentsch, J. J. (2007). *Girls' and boys' aggression in middle childhood and adolescence: Forms, contexts, and social processes.* Paper presented at the biennial meeting of the Society for Research in Child Development, Boston, MA.

UNICEF. (1999). *The progress of nations, 1999.* New York: Author.

UNICEF. (2006). *Report on the Third Global Partners Forum on Children Affected by HIV and AIDS: Universal access to prevention, treatment, and care.* New York: Author.

UNICEF. (2007). *The state of the world's children 2008.* New York: Author.

UNICEF and the World Health Organization. (2008). State of the World's Children http://www.unicef.org.nz/speaking-out/publications-multimedia/publications/sowc/index.html (downloaded July 27, 2008)

United Nations. (2009). *World population ageing.* Retrieved March 16, 2010 from http://www.un.org/esa/population/publications/WPA2009/WPA2009_WorkingPaper.pdf.

Upchurch, D., Levy-Storms, L., Sucoff, C., & Aneshensel, C. (1998). Gender and ethnic differences in the timing of first sexual intercourse. *Family Planning Perspectives, 30,* 121–127.

Updegraff, K., McHale, S. M., & Crouter, A. C. (2000). Adolescents' sex-typed friendship experiences: Does having a sister versus and brother matter? *Child Development, 71,* 1597–1610.

Ursin, H., & Eriksen, H. R. (2004). The cognitive activation theory of stress. *Psychoneuroendocrinology, 29*(5), 567–592.

Valdes, G. (1996). Con respecto: *Bridging the distances between culturally diverse families and schools: An ethnographic portrait.* New York: Teachers College Press.

Vallance, J. K., Murray, T. C., Johnson, S. T., & Elavsky, S. (2010). Quality of life and psychosocial health in postmenopausal women achieving public health guidelines for physical activity. *Menopause, 17*(1), 64–71.

Valsiner, J. (2006). Developmental epistemology and implications for methodology. In W. Damon & R. Lerner (Series Eds.) & R. Lerner (Vol. Ed.), *Handbook of child psychology: Vol. 1. Theoretical models of human development* (6th ed., pp. 166–209). New York: Wiley.

Van Cauter, E., Leproult, R., & Plat, L. (2000). Age-related changes in slow wave sleep and REM sleep and relationship with growth hormone and cortisol levels in healthy men. *Journal of the American Medical Association, 284*(7), 861–868.

Van de Walle, G. A., Carey, S., & Pervor, M. (2000). Bases for object individuation in infancy: Evidence from manual search. *Journal of Cognition and Development, 1*, 249–280.

van de Weijer-Bergsma, E., Wijnroks, L., & Jongmans, M. J. (2008). Attention development in infants and preschool children born preterm: A review. *Infant Behavior & Development, 31*, 333–351.

Van Delden, J. J. (1999). Slippery slopes in flat countries—a response. *Journal of Medical Ethics, 25*(1), 22–24.

van den Boom, D. C. (1991). The influence of infant irritability on the development of the mother-infant relationship in the first 6 months of life. In J. K. Nugent, B. M. Lester & T. B. Brazelton (Eds.), *The cultural context of infancy: Vol. 2. Multicultural and interdisciplinary approaches to parent-infant relations* (pp. 63–89). Westport, CT: Ablex.

van den Boom, D. C. (2001). First attachments: Theory and research. In J. G. Bremner, & A. Fogel (Eds.), *Blackwell handbook of infant development* (pp. 296–325). Malden, MA: Blackwell.

Van der Maas, P. J., van der Wal, G., Haverkate, I., De Graaff, C. L. M., Kester, J. G. C., Onwuteaka-Philipsen, B. D., et al. (1996). Euthanasia, physician-assisted suicide, and other medical practices involving the end of life in the Netherlands, 1990–1995. *The New England Journal of Medicine, 335*(22), 1699–1705.

Van Geert, P. & Steenbeek, H. (2005). Explaining after by before: Basic aspects of a dynamic systems approach to the study of development. *Developmental Review, 25*, 408–442.

van IJzendoorn, M. (2005). Attachment at an early age (0–5) and its impact on children's development. In R. E. Tremblay, R. G. Barr, & R. deV Peters (Eds.), *Encyclopedia on early childhood development* [online], Montreal, Quebec: Centre of Excellence for Early Childhood Development.

van IJzendoorn, M. H. (1997). Attachment, emergent morality, and aggression: Toward a developmental socioemotional model of antisocial behaviour. *Child Development, 68*, 571–591.

van IJzendoorn, M. H., Bakermans-Kranenburg, M. J., & Sagi-Schwartz, A. (2006). Attachment across diverse sociocultural contexts: The limits of universality. In K. H. Rubin & O. B. Chung (Eds.), *Parenting beliefs, behaviors, and parent-child relations: A cross-cultural perspective* (pp. 107–142). New York: Psychology Press.

van IJzendoorn, M., & Bakermans-Kranenburg, M. (2006). DRD4 7-repeat polymorphism moderates the association between maternal unresolved loss or trauma and infant disorganization. *Attachment & Human Development, 8*, 291–307.

van IJzendoorn, M., & Juffer, F. (2005) Adoption is a successful natural intervention enhancing adopted children's IQ and school performance. *Current Directions in Psychological Science, 14*, 326–330.

Van Laningham, J., Johnson, D. R., & Amato, P. (2001). Marital happiness, marital duration, and the U-shaped curve: Evidence from a five-wave panel study. *Social Forces, 78*(4), 1313–1341.

van Solinge, H., & Henkens, K. (2005). Couples' adjustment to retirement: A multi-actor panel study. *Journal of Gerontology Series: Social Sciences, 60*(1), S11–S20.

van Solinge, H., & Henkens, K. (2007). Involuntary retirement: The role of restrictive circumstances, timing, and social embeddedness. *Journal of Gerontology: Social Sciences, 62*(5), S295.

van Solinge, H., & Henkens, K. (2008). Adjustment to and satisfaction with retirement: Two of a kind? *Psychology and Aging, 23*(2), 422–434.

Vandell, D. L. (2000). Parents, peer groups, and other socializing influences. *Developmental Psychology, 36*, 699–710.

Vandell, D. L. (2007). Early child care: The known and the unknown. In G. Ladd (Ed.), *Appraising the human development sciences: Essays in honor of Merrill-Palmer Quarterly* (pp. 300–328). Detroit, MI: Wayne State University Press.

Vandell, D. L., & Bailey, M. D. (1992). Conflicts between siblings. In C. Shantz & W. W. Hartup (Eds.), *Conflict in child and adolescent development* (pp. 242–269). Cambridge: Cambridge University Press.

Vandell, D. L., & Ramanan, J. (1991). Children of the National Longitudinal Survey of Youth: Choices in after-school care and child development. *Developmental Psychology, 27*, 637–643.

Vandell, D. L., & Wolfe, B. (2000) Child care quality: Does it matter and does it need to be improved? Report prepared for the United States Department of Health and Human Services, Office for Planning and Evaluation. http://www.wcer.wisc.edu/childcare/publication.html#pdf.

Vandell, D. L., Pierce, K. M., & Dadisman, K. (2005). Out-of-school settings as a developmental context for children and youth. In R. V. Kail (Ed.), *Advances in child development and behavior* (Vol. 33, pp. 43–77). New York: Academic.

Vanhatalo, A. M., Ekblad, H., Kero, P., & Erkkola, R. (1994). Incidence of bronchopulmonary dysplasia during an 11-year period in infants weighing less than 1500 g at birth. *Annales Chirurgiae et Gynaecologiae. Supplementum, 208*, 113–116.

Varan, A., Rohner, R. P., & Eryuksel, G. (2008). Intimate partner acceptance, parental acceptance in childhood, and psychological adjustment among Turkish adults in ongoing attachment relationships. *Cross-Cultural Research: The Journal of Comparative Social Science, 42*, 46–56.

Vaughn, B. E., Egeland, B. R., Sroufe, L. A., & Waters, E. (1979). Individual differences in infant-mother attachment at twelve and eighteen months: Stability and change in families under stress. *Child Development, 50*, 971–975.

Vaughn, B. E., Kopp, C. B., & Krakow, J. B. (1984). The emergence and consolidation of self-control from eighteen to thirty months of age: Normative trends and individual differences. *Child Development, 55*, 990–1004.

Vaupel, J. W., Carey, J. R., Christensen, K., Johnson, T. E., Yashin, A. I., Holm, N. V., et al. (1998). Biodemographic trajectories of longevity. *Science, 280*, 855–860.

Vega, W., Khoury, E., Zimmerman, R., Gil, A., & Warheit, G. (1995). Cultural conflicts and problem behaviors of Latino adolescents in home and school environments. *Journal of Community Psychology, 23,* 167–179.

Venneri, A., Forbes-Mckay, K. E., & Shanks, M. F. (2005). Impoverishment of spontaneous language and the prediction of Alzheimer's disease. *Brain, 128*(4), E27–E28.

Venter, J., Adams, M., Myers, E., Li, P., Mural, R., Sutton, G., et al. (2001). The sequence of the human genome. *Science, 291,* 1304–1351.

Venuti, P., Giusti, Z., Gini, M., & Bornstein, M. H. (2008). La disponibilità emotiva madre-gemelli in bambini italiani nel secondo anno di vita [Emotional availability in mothers and twins in the second year of life]. *Psicologia Clinica dello Sviluppo, 12,* 41–67.

Verbrugge, L. M. (1989). The twain meet: Empirical explanations of sex differences in health and mortality. *Journal of Health and Social Behavior, 30,* 282–304.

Verbrugge, L. M. (1990). The iceberg of disability. In S. M. Stahl (Eds.), *The legacy of longevity* (pp. 55–75). Newbury Park, CA: Sage Publications.

Verbrugge, L. M. (2001). Sex differences in health. In G. L. Maddox, R. C. Atchley, J. G. Evans, C. E. Finch, R. A. Kane, M. D. Mezey, et al. (Eds.), *Encyclopedia of aging: A comprehensive multidisciplinary resource in gerontology and geriatrics* (3rd ed., pp. 850–854). New York: Springer.

Verhaeghen, P., Marcoen, A., & Goossens, L. (1993). Facts and fiction about memory aging: A quantitative integration of research findings. *Journal of Gerontology: Psychological Sciences, 48*(4), P157–P171.

Vitaliano, P. P., Scanlan, J. M., & Zhang, J. (2003). Is caregiving hazardous to one's physical health? A meta-analysis. *Psychological Bulletin, 129*(6), 946–972.

Vitaro, F., Brendgen, M., & Barker, E. D. (2006). Subtypes of aggressive behaviors: A developmental perspective. *International Journal of Behavioral Development, 30,* 12–19.

Voelkl, K. (1997). Identification with school. *American Journal of Education, 105,* 294–318.

Volkow, N. D., Gur, R. C., Wang, G. J., Fowler, J. S., Moberg, P. J., Ding, Y. S., et al. (1998). Association between decline in brain dopamine activity with age and cognitive and motor impairment in healthy individuals. *American Journal of Psychiatry, 155,* 344–349.

Volkow, N., & Li, T.-K. (2005). The neuroscience of addiction. *Nature Neuroscience, 8,* 1429–1430.

Volling, B. L. (2003). Sibling relationships. In M. H. Bornstein, L. Davidson, C. L. M. Keyes, & K. A. Moore (Eds.), *Well-being: Positive development across the life course* (pp. 205–220). Mahwah, NJ: Erlbaum.

Von Hofsten, C. (2007). Action in development. *Developmental Science, 10,* 54–60.

Vukman, K. B. (2005). Developmental differences in metacognition and their connections with cognitive development in adulthood, *Journal of Adult Development, 12*(4), 211–221.

Vygotsky, L. S. (1978). *Mind in society: The development of higher psychological processes.* Cambridge, MA: Harvard University Press.

Vygotsky, L. S. (1986). *Thought and language.* Cambridge, MA: MIT Press.

Wachs, T. D. (1987). Specificity of environmental action as manifest in environmental correlates of infant's mastery motivation. *Developmental Psychology, 23,* 782–790.

Wachs, T. D., & Gandour, M. J. (1983). Temperament, environment, and six-month cognitive-intellectual development: A test of the organismic specificity hypothesis. *International Journal of Behavioral Development, 6*(2), 135–152.

Waddington, C. H. (1940). *Organisers and genes.* Cambridge: Cambridge University Press.

Wagner, S. H., & Walters, J. (1982). A longitudinal analysis of early number concepts: From numbers to number. In G. E. Forman (Ed.), *Action and thought: From sensorimotor schemes to symbolic operations* (pp. 137–161). New York: Academic Press.

Waidmann, T. A., & Liu, K. (2000). Disability trends among elderly persons and implications for the future. *Journal of Gerontology B: Psychological Sciences and Social Sciences, 55*(5), S298–S307.

Wainwright, J., Russell, S. T., & Patterson, C. J. (2004). Psychosocial adjustment, school outcomes, and romantic relationships of adolescents with same-sex parents. *Child Development, 75*(6), 1886–1898.

Walden, T., & Knieps, L. (1996). Reading and responding to social signals. In. M. Lewis & M. W. Sullivan (Eds.), *Emotional development in atypical children* (pp. 29–42). Hillsdale, NJ: Erlbaum.

Walden, T., Lemerise, E., & Smith, M. C. (1999). Friendship and popularity in preschool classrooms. *Early Education and Development, 10,* 351–371.

Waldstein, S. R. (1995). Hypertension and neuropsychological function: A lifespan perspective. *Experimental Aging Research, 21*(4), 321–352.

Walker, A. J., Martin, S. S. K., & Jones, L. L. (1992). The benefits and costs of caregiving and care receiving for daughters and mothers. *Journal of Gerontology: Social Sciences, 47*(3), S130–S139.

Walker, E. F., Sabuwalla, Z., & Huot, R. (2004). Pubertal neuromaturation, stress sensitivity, and psychopathology. *Development and Psychopathology, 16,* 807–824.

Wallace, R. B., & Lemke, J. H. (1991). The compression of comorbidity. *Journal of Aging and Health, 3*(2), 237–246.

Wallen, K. (2005). Hormonal influences on sexually differentiated behaviors in nonhuman primates. *Frontiers in Neuroendocrinology, 26,* 7–26.

Wallhagen, M. I. (2010). The stigma of hearing loss. *Gerontologist, 50*(1), 66–75.

Wallis, C. (2008, February 25). How to make great teachers. *Time Magazine,* pp. 28–34.

Wallis, C., & Steptoe, S. (2006, December 18). How to bring our schools out of the 20th century. *Time Magazine.*

Walton, G. M., & Cohen, G. L. (2003). Stereotype lift. *Journal of Experimental Social Psychology, 39,* 456–467.

Walton, G. M., & Cohen, G. L. (2007). A question of belonging: Race, social fit, and achievement. *Journal of Personality and Social Psychology, 92*(1), 82–96.

Wang, H., & Amato, P. (2000). Predictors of divorce adjustment: Stressors, resources, and definitions. *Journal of Marriage and Family, 62*(3), 655–668.

Wang, Q. (2006). Developing emotion knowledge in cultural contexts. *International Journal of Behavioral Development, 30*(Suppl. 1), 8–12.

Wang, Q., & Fivush, R. (2005). Mother-child conversations of emotionally salient events: Exploring the functions of emotional reminiscing in European American and Chinese families. *Social Development, 14,* 473–495.

Wang, Y., & Marcotte, D. E. (2007). Golden years? The labor market effects of caring for grandchildren. *Journal of Marriage and Family, 69*(5), 1283–1296.

Ward, R. A., & Spitze, G. D. (2004). Marital implications of parent-adult child: residents: A longitudinal view. *Journal of Gerontology: Social Sciences, 59*(1), S2–S8.

Wargo, E. (2007). Understanding the have-knots: The role of stress and just about everything. *Association for Psychological Science Observer, 20*, 18–23.

Warren, C., Santelli, J., Everett, S., Kann, L., Collins, J., Cassell, C., et al. (1998). Sexual Behavior Among U.S. High School Students, 1990–1995. *Family Planning Perspectives, 30*, 170–172, 200.

Warren, J. (2002). Reconsidering the relationship between student employment and academic outcomes: A new theory and better data. *Youth and Society, 33*, 366–393.

Warschauer, M. (2003). *Technology and social inclusion: Rethinking the digital divide*. Cambridge, MA: MIT Press.

Wassenberg, R., Hurks, P. P. M., Feron, F. J. M., Hendriksen, J. G. M., Meijs, C. J. C., Vles, J. S. H. & Jolles, J., 2007. Age-related improvement in complex language comprehension: Results of a cross-sectional study with 361 children aged 5 to 15. *Journal of Clinical and Experimental Neuropsychology, 29*, 1–14.

Watamura, S. E., Donzella, B., Alwin, J., & Gunnar, M. R. (2003). Morning-to-afternoon increases in cortisol concentrations for infants and toddlers at child care: Age differences and behavioral correlates. *Child Development, 74*, 1006–1020.

Waters, E. (1978). The reliability and stability of individual differences in infant-mother attachment. *Child Development, 49*, 483–494.

Waters, E., Hay, D., & Richters, J. (1986). Infant-parent attachment and the origins of prosocial and antisocial behavior. In D. Olweus, J. Block, & M. Radke-Yarrow (Eds.), *Development of antisocial and prosocial behavior: Research, theories, and issues* (pp. 97–125). New York: Academic Press.

Watson, J. B. (1930). *Behaviorism* (rev. ed.). Chicago: University of Chicago Press.

Watson, J., & Rayner, R. (1920). Conditioned emotional reactions. *Journal of Experimental Psychology, 3*, 1–14.

Watson, K. (1924). *Behaviorism*. New York: People's Institute Publishing Company.

Watts, C., & Zimmerman, C. (2002). Violence against women: global scope and magnitude. *The Lancet, 359*, 1232–1237.

Waxman, S. R., & Lidz, J. L. (2006). Early word learning. In W. Damon & R. M. Lerner (Series Eds.) & D. Kuhn & R. S. Siegler (Vol. Eds.), *Handbook of child psychology: Vol. 2. Cognition, perception, and language* (6th ed., pp. 299–335). Hoboken, NJ: Wiley.

Way, N. & Greene, M. L. (2006). Trajectories of perceived friendship quality during adolescence: The patterns and contextual predictors. *Journal of Research on Adolescence, 16*, 293–320.

Weaver, I., Cervoni, N., Champagne, F., D'Alessio, A., Sharma, S., Seckl, J., et al. (2004). Epigenetic programming by maternal behavior. *Nature Neuroscience, 7*, 847–854.

Webb, S. J., Monk, C. S., & Nelson, C. A. (2001). Mechanisms of postnatal neurobiological development: Implications for human development. *Developmental Neuropsychology, 19*, 147–171.

Wechsler, D. (1991). *Manual for the Wechsler Intelligence Scales for Children (WISC III)* (3rd ed.). San Antonio, TX: Psychological Corp.

Weight Control Information Network (2008, November). *Weight and waist measurement tools for adults*. National Institute of Diabetes and Digestive and Kidney Diseases. Retrieved February 16, 2010 from http://win.niddk.nih.gov/publications/tools.htm#circumf.

Weindruch, R., & Sohal, R. S. (1997). Caloric intake and aging. *New England Journal of Medicine, 337*(14), 986–994.

Weiner, D. K., Rudy, T. E., Morrow, L., Slaboda, J., & Lieber, S. (2006). The relationship between pain, neuropsychological performance, and physical function in community-dwelling older adults with chronic low back pain. *Pain Medicine, 7*(1), 60–70.

Weinfield, N. S., Sroufe, L. A., & Egeland, B. (2000). Attachment from infancy to early adulthood in a high risk sample: Continuity, discontinuity, and their correlates. *Child Development, 71*, 695–702.

Weinstein, B. E. (1994). Age-related hearing loss: How to screen for it, and when to intervene. *Geriatrics, 49*(8), 40–45.

Weinstock, H., Berman, S., & Cates, W., Jr. (2004). Sexually transmitted diseases among American youth: Incidence and prevalence estimates, 2000. *Perspectives on Sexual and Reproductive Health, 36*(1), 6–10.

Weir, L. A., Etelson, D., & Brand, D. A. (2006). Parents' perceptions of neighborhood safety and children's physical activity, *Preventive Medicine, 43*, 212–217.

Weir, R. H. (1962). *Language in the crib*. The Hague: Mouton.

Weisner, T. S., & Gallimore, R. (1977). My brother's keeper: Child and sibling caretaking. *Current Anthropology, 18*, 169–190.

Weiss, R. S. (1973). *Loneliness*. Cambridge, MA: MIT Press.

Weizman, Z. O., & Snow, C. E. (2001). Lexical input as related to children's vocabulary acquisition: Effects of sophisticated exposure and support for meaning. *Developmental Psychology, 37*, 265–279.

Wellman, H. M. (2002). Understanding the psychological world: Developing a theory of mind. In C. Goswami (Ed.), *Blackwell handbook of childhood cognitive development* (pp. 167–187). Malden, MA: Blackwell.

Wentzel, K. (2002). Are effective teachers like good parents? Teaching styles and student adjustment in early adolescence. *Child Development, 73*, 287–301.

Werner, E. (1971). *The children of Kauai: A longitudinal study from the prenatal period to age ten*. Honolulu, HI: University of Hawaii Press.

Wethington, E. (2000). Expecting stress: Americans and the "midlife crisis". *Motivation and Emotion, 24*(2), 85–103.

Weyer, M., & Sandler, I. N. (1998). Stress and coping as predictors of children's divorce-related ruminations. *Journal of Clinical Child Psychology, 27*, 78–86.

Whalen, C. K. (2000). Attention-deficit/hyperactivity disorder. In A. E. Kazdin (Ed.), *Encyclopedia of psychology: Vol. 1* (pp. 299–303). New York: Oxford University Press/American Psychological Association.

Whitbourne, S. K. (2001). The physical aging process in midlife. In M. E. Lachman (Ed.), *Handbook of midlife development* (pp. 109–155). New York: Wiley.

Whitbourne, S. K. (2002). *The aging individual: Physical and psychological perspectives* (2nd ed.). New York: Springer.

Whitbourne, S. K., & Willis, S. L. (2006). Preface. In S. K. Whitbourne & S. L. Willis (Eds.), *The Baby Boomers grow up: Contemporary perspectives on midlife* (pp. vii–ix). Mahwah, NJ: Lawrence Erlbaum.

White, B. L., Castle, R., & Held, R. (1964). Observations on the development of visually directed reaching. *Child Development, 35*, 349–364.

White, L., & Edwards, J. N. (1990). Emptying the nest and parental well-being: An analysis of national panel data. *American Sociological Review, 55*, 235–242.

Whiteman, S. D., McHale, S. M., & Crouter, A. C. (2007). Longitudinal changes in marital relationships: The role of offspring's pubertal development. *Journal of Marriage and Family, 69*(4), 1005–1020.

Whiting, B. B., & Whiting, J. W. M. (1975). *Children of six cultures: a psycho-cultural analysis.* Cambridge, MA: Harvard University Press

Wichstrøm, L. (1999). The emergence of gender difference in depressed mood during adolescence: The role of intensified gender socialization. *Developmental Psychology, 35,* 232–245.

Wiebe, S. A., Cheatham, C. L., Lukowski, A. F., Haight, J. C., Muehleck, A. J., & Bauer, P. J. (2006). Infants' ERP response to novel and familiar stimuli change over time: implications for novelty detection and memory. *Infancy, 9,* 21–44.

Wiesel, T. N., & Hubel, D. H. (1974). Ordered arrangement of orientation columns in monkeys lacking visual experience. *Journal of Comparative Neurology, 158,* 307–318.

Wiesner, M., & Ittel, A. (2002). Relations of pubertal timing and depressive symptoms to substance use in early adolescence. *Journal of Early Adolescence, 22,* 5–23.

Wight, R. G., Sepúlveda, J. E., & Aneshensel, C. S. (2004). Depressive symptoms: How do adolescents compare with adults? *Journal of Adolescent Health, 34,* 314–323.

Willcox, D. C., Willcox, B. J., Todoriki, H., Curb, J. D., & Suzuki, M. (2006). Caloric restriction and human longevity: What can we learn from the Okinawans? *Biogerontology, 7*(3), 173–177.

Willford, J. A., Leech, S. L., & Day, N. L. (2006). Moderate prenatal alcohol exposure and cognitive status of children at age 10. *Alcoholism: Clinical and Experimental Research, 30,* 1051–1059.

Williams, J. H. G., Whiten, A., Suddendorf, T., & Perrett, D. I. (2001). Imitation, mirror neurons and autism. *Neuroscience and Biobehavioral Reviews, 25,* 287–295.

Williams, K., & Dunne-Bryant, A. (2006). Divorce and adult psychological well-being: Clarifying the role of gender and child age. *Journal of Marriage and Family, 68*(5), 1178–1196.

Williams, K., & Umberson, D. (2004). Marital status, marital transitions, and health: A gendered life course perspective. *Journal of Health and Social Behavior, 45*(1), 81–98.

Williams, L. M., Brown, K. J., Palmer, D., Liddell, B. J., Kemp, A. H., Olivieri, G., Peduto, A., & Gordon, E. (2006). The mellow years?: Neural basis of improving emotional stability over age. *Journal of Neuroscience, 26*(24), 6422–6430.

Williams, P. G., Holman, G. N., & Greenley, R. N. (2002). Adolescent health psychology. *Journal of Consulting and Clinical Psychology, 70*(3), 828–842.

Williams, R. B., Barefoot, J. C., & Schneiderman, N. (2003). Psychosocial risk factors for cardiovascular disease: more than one culprit at work. *Journal of the American Medical Association, 290*(16), 2190–2192.

Williams, W. M. (1998). Are we raising smarter children today? School- and home-related influences on IQ. In U. Neisser (Ed.), *The rising curve: Long-term gains in IQ and related measures* (pp. 125–154). Washington, DC: American Psychological Association.

Williamson, G., & Schulz, R. (1990). Relationship orientation, quality of prior relationship, and distress among caregivers of Alzheimer's patients. *Psychology and Aging, 5*(4), 502–509.

Willis, S. L., & Nesselroade, C. S. (1990). Long-term effects of fluid ability training in old-old age. *Developmental Psychology, 26*(6), 905–910.

Willis, S. L., & Schaie, K. W. (2006). Cognitive functioning in the Baby Boomers: Longitudinal and cohort effects. In S. K. Whitbourne & S. L. Willis (Eds.), *The Baby Boomers grow up: Contemporary perspectives on midlife* (pp. 205–234). Mahwah, NJ: Lawrence Erlbaum.

Willis, S. L., Jay, G. M., Diehl, M., & Marsiske, M. (1992). Longitudinal change and prediction of everyday task competence in the elderly. *Research on Aging, 14*(1), 68–91.

Wilson B. J. (2008). Media and children's aggression, fear, and altruism. *The Future of Children, 18,* 87–118.

Wilson, P., & Wilson, J. (1992). Environmental influences on adolescent educational aspirations: A logistic transform model. *Youth and Society, 24,* 52–70.

Wilson, R. S. (1978). Synchronies in menatal development: An epigenetic perspective. *Science, 202,* 939–938.

Wilson, R. S., Evans, D. A., Bienias, J. L., Mendes de Leon, C. F., Schneider, J. A., & Bennett, D. A. (2003). Proneness to psychological distress is associated with risk of Alzheimer's disease. *Neurology, 61,* 1479–1485.

Wilson, R. S., Mendes de Leon, C. F., Bienias, J. L, Evans, D. A., & Bennett, D. A. (2004). Personality and mortality in old age. *Journal of Gerontology: Psychological Sciences, 59*(3), 110–116.

Wilson, R. S., Mendes de Leon, C., Barnes, L. L., Schneider, J. A., Bienias, J. L., Evans, D. A., et al. (2002). Participation in cognitively stimulating activities and risk of incident alzheimer disease. *Journal of the American Medical Association, 287,* 742–748.

Wilton, M., Craig, W., & Pepler, D. (2000). Emotion regulation and display is classroom victims of bullying: Characteristic expressions of affect, coping styles, and relevant contextual factors. *Social Development, 9,* 226–245.

Wingfield, A., Tun, P. A., & McCoy, S. L. (2005). Hearing loss in older adulthood: What it is and how it interacts with cognitive performance. *Current Directions in Psychological Science, 14*(3), 144–148.

Wink, P., & Scott, J. (2005). Does religiousness buffer against the fear of death and dying in late adulthood? Findings from a longitudinal study. *Journal of Gerontology B: Psychological Sciences and Social Sciences, 60*(4), P207–214.

Winn, R. L., & Newton, N. (1982). Sexuality in aging: A study of 106 cultures. *Archives of Sexual Behavior, 11*(4), 283–298.

Wintemute, G., Kraus, J., Teret, S., & Wright, M. (1987). Drowning in childhood and adolescence: A population-based study. *American Journal of Public Health, 77,* 830–832.

Winterbottom, M. (1958). The relation of need for achievement to learning experiences in independence and mastery. In J. Atkinson (Ed.), *Motives in fantasy, action, and society* (pp. 453–478). Princeton, NJ: Van Nostrand.

Wirt, J., Choy, S., Rooney, P., Provasnik, S., Sen, A., & Tobin, R. (2004). *The condition of education 2004.* Washington, DC: National Center for Education Statistics.

Wismer Fries, A. B., & Pollak, S. (2004). Emotion understanding in postinstitutionalized Eastern European Children. *Development and Psychopathology, 16,* 355–369.

Wojslawowicz, J. C., Rubin, K. H., Burgess, K. B., Booth-LaForce, C., & Rose-Krasnor, L. R. (2006). Behavioral characteristics associated with stable and fluid best friendship patterns in middle childhood. *Merrill-Palmer Quarterly, 52,* 671–693.

Wolf, D., & Perry, M. (1988). From endpoints to repertoires: New conclusions about drawing development. *Journal of Aesthetic Education, 22,* 17–35.

Wolf, S. A., & Heath, S. B. (1992). *The braid of literature: Children's world of reading.* Cambridge MA: Harvard University Press.

Wolff, K., & Wortman, C. (2006). Psychological consequences of spousal loss among older adults. In D. Carr, R. M. Neese, & C. B. Wortman (Eds.), *Spousal bereavement in late life* (pp. 81–115). New York: Springer.

Wolfson, J. (2003, December). *A report to Governor Jeb Bush and the Sixth Judicial Circuit in the matter of Theresa Marie Schiavo.* Retrieved July 9, 2009 from http://abstractappeal.com/schiavo/WolfsonReport.pdf

Woodward, A. L., Markman, E. M., & Fitzsimmons, C. M. (1994). Rapid word learning in 13-and 18-month-olds. *Developmental Psychology, 30,* 553–566.

Woodward, L. J., Mogridge, N., Wells, S. W. & Inder, T. E. (2004). Can neurobehavioral examination predict the presence of cerebral injury in the very low birth weight infant? *Journal of Developmental and. Behavioral Pediatrics, 25,* 326–334.

Worden, J. W. (1996). *Children and grief: When a parent dies.* New York: Guilford.

World Bank (2006). Repositioning Nutrition as Central to Development. http://siteresources.worldbank.org/NUTRITION/Resources/281846–1131636806329/NutritionStrategy.pdf (retrieved October 14, 2006).

World Health Organization (2010). *Obesity and overweight.* Retrieved February 3, 2010 from http://www.who.int/dietphysicalactivity/publications/facts/obesity/en/

World Health Organization. (2008, August). *Priority interventions: HIV/AIDS prevention, treatment and care in the health sector.* Retrieved from http://www.who.int/hiv/pub/priority_interventions_web.pdf

World Health Organization. (n.d.). *WHO Definition of Palliative Care.* Retrieved July 13, 2009 from http://www.who.int/cancer/palliative/definition/en/

World Health Organization. *Elder abuse.* Retrieved November 10, 2009 from http://www.who.int/ageing/projects/elder_abuse/en/index.html

Wright, J. P., Dietrich, K. N., Ris, M. D., Hornung, R. W., & Wessel, S. D. (2008). Association of prenatal and childhood blood lead concentrations with criminal arrests in early adulthood. *PLoS Medicine, 5*(5): e101 DOI: 10.1371/journal.pmed.0050101

Wright, J., Cullen, F., & Williams, N. (1997). Working while in school and delinquent involvement: Implications for social policy. *Crime and Delinquency, 43,* 203–221.

Wrobel, G. M., Hendrickson, Z., & Grotevant, H. D. (2006). Adoption. In G. Bear & K. M. Minke (Eds.), *Children's needs: Vol. 3. Development, prevention, and intervention* (pp. 675–688). Bethesda, MD: National Association of School Psychologists.

Wrosch, C., & Freund, A. M. (2001). Self-regulation of normative and non-normative developmental challenges. *Human Development, 44*(5), 264–283.

Wrosch, C., & Heckhausen, J. (1999). Control processes before and after passing a developmental deadline: Activation and deactivation of intimate relationship goals. *Journal of Personality and Social Psychology, 77*(2), 415–427.

Wrosch, C., Scheier, M. F., & Carver, C. S., & Schulz, R. (2003). The importance of goal disengagement in adaptive self-regulation: When giving up is beneficial. *Self and Identity, 2*(1), 1–20.

Wu, L. L., Bumpass, L. L., & Musik, K. (2001). Historical and life course trajectories of nonmarital childbearing. In L. L. Wu & B. Wolfe (Eds.), *Out of wedlock: Causes and consequences of nonmarital fertility* (pp. 3–48). New York: Russell Sage.

Wu, L., & Anthony, J. (1999). Tobacco smoking and depressed mood in late childhood and early adolescence. *American Journal of Public Health, 89,* 1837–1840.

Wu, L., Schlenger, W. E., & Galvin, D. M. (2003). The relationship between employment and substance use among students aged 12 to 17. *Journal of Adolescent Health, 32,* 5–15.

Wysocki, C. J., & Gilbert, A. N. (1989). National Geographic smell survey: Effects of age are heterogenous. *Annals of the New York Academy of Sciences, 561,* 12–28.

Xu, F. (2003). The development of object individuation in infancy. In H. Hayne (Ed.), *Progress in infancy research* (pp. 159–192). Mahwah, NJ: Erlbaum.

Xue, Y., Leventhal, T., Brooks-Gunn, J., & Earls, F. (2005). Neighborhood of residence and mental health problems of 5- to 11-year-olds. *Archives of General Psychiatry, 62,* 554–563.

Yan, L. L., Liu, K., Matthews, K. A., Daviglus, M. L., Freeman Ferguson, T., & Kiefe, C. I. (2003). Psychosocial factors and risk of hypertension: The Coronary Artery Risk Development in Young Adults (CARDIA) Study. *Journal of the American Medical Association, 290*(16), 2138–2148.

Yancura, L. A., & Aldwin, C. M. (2008). Coping and health in older adults. *Current Psychiatry Reports, 10*(1), 10–15.

Yasui, M., Dorham, C. L., & Dishion, T. J. (2004). Ethnic identity and psychological adjustment: A validity analysis for European American and African American adolescents. *Journal of Adolescent Research, 19,* 807–825.

Yeh, H., & Lempers, J. D. (2004). Perceived sibling relationships and adolescent development. *Journal of Youth and Adolescence, 33,* 133–147.

Yehuda, R., Mulherin Engel, S. R., Seckl, J., Marcus, S. M., & Berkowitz, G. S. (2005). Transgenerational effects of posttraumatic stress disorder in babies of mothers exposed to the World Trade Center attacks during pregnancy. *Journal of Clinical Endocrinology & Metabolism, 20,* 1–15.

Yin, D., & Chen, K. (2005). The essential mechanisms of aging: Irreparable damage accumulation of biochemical side-reactions. *Experimental Gerontology, 40*(6), 455–465.

Yin, S. (2006). Elderly white men afflicted by high suicide rates. *Population Reference Bureau.* Retrieved April 7, 2010 from http://www.prb.org/Articles/2006/ElderlyWhiteMenAfflictedbyHighSuicideRates.aspx

Youngblade, L. M., & Dunn, J. (1995). Individual differences in young children's pretend play with mother and sibling: Links to relationships and understanding of other people's feelings and beliefs. *Child Development, 66,* 1472–1492.

Younge, S. N., Salem, D., & Bybee, D. (2008). Risk revisited: The perception of HIV risk in a community sample of low-income African American women. *Journal of Black Psychology, 35*(1), 49–74.

Yu, B. P. (1996). Aging and oxidative stress: Modulation by dietary restriction. *Free Radical Biology and Medicine, 21*(5), 651–668.

Zacks, R. T., Hasher, L., & Li, Z. H. (2000). Human memory. In F. I. M. Craik & T. A. Salthouse (Eds.). *The Handbook of aging and cognition* (2nd ed, pp. 293–357). Mahwah, NJ: Lawrence Erlbaum.

Zahn-Waxler, C., & Radke-Yarrow, M. (1990). The origins of empathic concern. *Motivation and Emotion, 14,* 107–129.

Zamboanga, B. L., Olthuis, J. V., Horton, N. J., McCollum, E. C., Lee, J. J., & Shaw, R. (2009). Where's the house party? Hazardous drinking behaviors and related risk factors. *Journal of Psychology: Interdisciplinary and Applied, 143*(3), 228–244.

Zangl, R., & Mills, D. L. (2007). Increased brain activity to infant-directed speech in 6-and 13-month-old infants. *Infancy, 11,* 31–62.

Zarit, S. H. (2009). A good old age: Theories of mental health and aging. In V. L. Bengtson, M. Silverstein, N. M. Putney, & D. Gans (Eds.). (2008). *Handbook of Theories of Aging* (pp. 675–691). New York: Springer.

Zaskind, P. S., & Gingras, J. L. (2006). Maternal cigarette-smoking during pregnancy disrupts rhythms in fetal heart rate. *Journal of Pediatric Psychology, 31,* 5–14.

Zaslavsky, C. (1973). *Africa counts: Number and pattern in African culture.* Boston, MA: Prindle, Weber & Schmidt, Inc.

Zeanah, C. H., Smyke, A. T., Koga, S. F., & Carlson, E. (2005). Attachment in institutionalized and community children in Romania. *Child Development, 76,* 1015–1028.

Zeiss, A. M., & Kasl-Godley, J. (2001). Sexuality in older adults' relationships. *Generations, 25*(2), 18–25.

Zeleznik, J. (2003). Normative aging of the respiratory system. *Clinics in Geriatric Medicine, 19*(1), 1–18.

Zhen-Wang, B. & Cheng-Ye, J. (2005). Secular growth changes in body height and weight in children and adolescents in Shandong, China between 1939 and 2000. *Annals of Human Biology, 32,* 650–665.

Zhou, Q., Eisenberg, N., Wang, Y., & Reiser, M. (2004). Chinese children's effortful control and dispositional anger/frustration: Relations to parenting styles and children's social functioning. *Developmental Psychology, 40,* 352–366.

Zigler E, (1998). School should begin at age 3 years for American children. *Journal of Developmental and Behavioral Pediatrics, 19*(1), 38–40.

Zisook, S., & Shuchter, S. R. (1993). Major depression associated with widowhood. *American Journal of Geriatric Psychiatry, 1*(4), 316–326.

Zito, J. M., Safer, D. J., DosReis, S., Gardner, J. F., Soeken, K., Boles, M., et al. (2002). Rising prevalence of antidepressants among U.S. youths. *Pediatrics, 109,* 721–727.

Zook, N. A., & Davalos, D. B. (2006). Can fluid and general intelligence be differentiated in an older population? *Behavioral and Brain Sciences, 29*(2), 143–145.

Zucker, K. J. (2004). Gender identity disorder in children and adolescents. *Annual Review of Clinical Psychology, 1,* 467–492.

Zuckerman, B., Stevens, G. D., Inkelas, M., & Halfon, N. (2004). Prevalence and correlates of high-quality basic pediatric preventive care. *Pediatrics, 114,* 1522–1529.

Name Index

C

G

H

I

L

M

N

O

P

Q

R

S

T

X

Y

Z

Subject Index/Glossary

Bold entries indicate definitions in the margin glossary. Entries followed by "f" indicate figures. Entries followed by "t" indicate tables.

Extension problem, 145–146
Externalizing problems *Psychosocial problems that are manifested in outward symptoms, such as aggression or noncompliance,* **237**
adolescence and, 392
Extrinsic motivation *Motivation based on the rewards one will receive for successful performance,* **359**

F

Facial expressions, 153
False memory *A memory that is a distortion of an actual experience, or a confabulation of an imagined one,* **276**
False-belief task, 205–206
Familism *Placing a high value on the interests of the family rather than the individual,* **55**
Family and families
adolescents relationships with, 380–382
blended, 40, 310–311
dual-earner, 462–463
elder abuse and, 590
grandparent's role in, 516–517
household structures, 308–310
influences of, 52
in later life, 585–586
launching of, 454–547
marital relationships in, 313
multigenerational, 308–309
parent-child relationships in, 312–313
postmodern, 308
school involvement by, 293
sibling relationships in, 313–314
stories of, 229
structures of, 175
Family relatedness studies *A method for estimating heritability by comparing the similarity of children who vary in their genetic relatedness (e.g., siblings, half-siblings, and stepsiblings),* **40**
Fast-mapping *A phenomenon that refers to how easily children pick up words they have heard only a few times,* **146**
onset age of, 213
Fathers, infants' interaction with, 174–175
Fearful-avoidant individuals, 447
Fertility drugs *Hormone-based agents that enhance ovarian activity,* **66**
Fertilization *Insemination of an ovum by a sperm,* **65**
Fetal alcohol effects *Deformities that are the result of significant (but not chronic) prenatal exposure to alcohol,* **80**
Fetal alcohol syndrome *A pattern of disabilities found in babies and children of mothers who consumed alcohol during pregnancy,* **80**
Fetus
behavior of, 68–69
development of, 68–71
maternal characteristics and, 77–78
outside risks to, 78–83
prenatal testing of, 75–76
ultrasound image of, 71*f*
Filial responsibility *The norm that adult children have a duty to support their aging parents,* **588**
Fine motor skills *Abilities required to control the smaller movements of the hands and fingers, such as picking up small objects and trying one's shoes,* **192**
in early childhood, 193–195
environmental factors influencing, 193–195
in middle childhood, 267–269
milestones, 194*t*
Fluid intelligence *The ability to solve novel problems, recognize patterns, and draw inferences in ways that do not require prior knowledge or experience (also referred to as the mechanics of intelligence),* **491**
Flynn effect *Gains in intelligence observed across successive cohorts in the 20th Century,* **494**
Formal codes, 283
Formal operational stage *In Piaget's theory, the stage of cognitive development that emerges approximately at age 11, during which individuals develop the ability to apply logical reasoning to abstract phenomena,* **15**
Forms, 111–113
Founder effect, 74
Fragile X syndrome *A condition in which children have a change in a single gene on the X chromosome; one of the most common genetic causes of mental retardation,* **281**
Frailty *A state of increased vulnerability to stressors that results from diminished reserve capacity and impaired functioning of multiple bodily systems,* **544**
Fraternal twins *Twins born when two separate eggs are fertilized, who are therefore no more alike genetically than other brothers and sisters,* **39**
Free radicals *Unstable oxygen molecules produced during metabolism that can penetrate or collide with other molecules, causing damage to cells,* **540**
Friendships
in adolescence, 387–388
in later adulthood, 583–585
in middle childhood, 314–316, 511
in young adulthood, 448–449
Frontal cortex *The brain's command central responsible for thinking, planning, initiative, impulse control, and creativity,* **99**
Frontal lobes *Sometimes called the "executive" of the brain, the frontal lobes are responsible for planning and organizing new actions, problem solving, and regulating emotions, as well as focusing attention,* **191**; *Part of the brain located in front of the parietal lobe and above the temporal lobe that is involved in recognizing future consequences, overriding unacceptable social responses, and remembering emotional experiences,* **262**

G

Gametes *Reproductive cells, sperm in males and ova (eggs) in females,* **47**
IVF use of, 66–67
Gender constancy *The concept that gender is permanent and immutable,* **231**
Gender development
behavioral differences, 231–235
identity in, 230–231
Gender differentiation. *See also* Men; Women
aggressive behavior, 245, 306–307
depression rates, 397
friendships, 316, 387–388
mathematical abilities, 287
in middle childhood, 299–302
organized activities, 320–321
physical attractiveness, 446
in play, 231
prenatal initiation of, 70
process of, 64
puberty onset, 336–338
sexual attitudes, 417
sexual maturation, 334
socialization and, 71
socioemotional development, 177–179
sources of, 232–235
widowhood effects, 581
Gender identity *A person's sense of self as male or female,* **230**
Gender identity disorders of childhood (GIDC), 231
Gender schema *A mental network of beliefs and expectations about males versus females,* **234**
gender differences in, 301
Gender socialization *Social norms conveyed to children that concern characteristics associated with being male or female,* **234**
Gene expression *The process through which genes influence the production of specific proteins, which in turn influences the phenotype,* **57**
environmental influences on, 49*f*, 57–58
Gene-environment interaction *The process through which genotypes produce different phenotypes in different contexts,* **59**
Gene-gene interaction, 47
Generational stake *The idea that older adults have a greater investment, or stake, in their relationships with younger family members than do the younger family members because they older adults wish to maintain a sense of generational continuity. Also called developmental stake,* **587**
Generativity *The desire to contribute to one's family, community, and society by nurturing and guiding the next generation,* **502**
assessing, 503*t*
life satisfaction and, 504
Generic memory *A script or general outline of how familiar activities occur based on experience,* **210**
scripts in, 211–212
Genes. *Segments of DNA occupying a specific place on a chromosome,* **46**
abnormalities of, 73–74
context interplay with, 56–61
environmental influences, 49–50, 60–61
5-HTT, 49
function of, 43
human traits and, 43–46
longevity and, 541–542
recessive, 73–74
regulator, 49
structure of, 46
Genetic counseling *A profession designed to help couples understand how heredity might affect their child,* **74**
Genetic determinism *The idea that human qualities are genetically determined and cannot be changed by nature or education,* **38**
Genetic disorders, 73–74
Genotypes *The underlying genetic makeup of an individual organism (contrast with genotype),* **46**
additive heredity and, 47–48
phenotype conversion process, 59
uniqueness of, 47
Gestation *The period from conception to birth that lasts about 280 days, counting from the mother's last menstrual period,* **64**
Gestures, 142–143
Giftedness *Indicated by extraordinary creativity or performance in music, sports, or art, as well as traditional academic subjects,* **280**
Gist memory *A generalized, rather than specific, memory of common occurrences,* **276**

K